# Out of Many

# Out of Many

*Fifth Edition*

## A History of the American People

TEACHING AND LEARNING CLASSROOM EDITION

COMBINED VOLUME

**John Mack Faragher**
YALE UNIVERSITY

**Mari Jo Buhle**
BROWN UNIVERSITY

**Daniel Czitrom**
MOUNT HOLYOKE COLLEGE

**Susan H. Armitage**
WASHINGTON STATE UNIVERSITY

PEARSON
Prentice
Hall

Upper Saddle River, New Jersey 07458

**Library of Congress Cataloging-in-Publication Data**

Out of many: a history of the American people / John Mack Faragher ... [et al.]. — Brief
  TLC 5th ed.
     p. cm.
  Includes bibliographical references and index.
  ISBN 0-13-601565-4 (combined volume) — ISBN 0-13-601567-0 (v. 1) — ISBN  0-13-601566-2 (v. 2)
  1.  United States–History–Textbooks.   I. Faragher, John Mack, 1945–
  E178.1.O935 2008
  973—dc22                                                                       2008001076

> # To Our Students,
> # Our Sisters,
> # And Our Brothers

**AVP, Publisher:** Charlyce Jones Owen
**Executive Marketing Manager:** Sue Westmoreland
**Editorial Assistant:** Maureen Diana
**Marketing Assistant:** Sarah Aswell
**Operations Specialist:** Maura Zaldivar
**Media Editor:** Mayda Bosco
**Creative Design Director:** Maria Lange
**Interior Design:** Ilze Lemesis
**Cover Design:** Blair Brown
**AV Project Manager:** Mirella Signoretto

**Project Manager:** Denise Brown
**Full-Service Production and Composition:** Fiorella Mari/Prepare
**Director, Image Resource Center:** Melinda Patelli
**Manager, Rights and Permissions:** Zina Arabia
**Manager, Visual Research:** Beth Brenzel
**Manager, Cover Visual Research and Permissions:** Karen Sanatar
**Image Permission Coordinator:** Michelina Viscusi
**Printer/Binder:** Quebecor
**Cover Printer:** Phoenix Color

Credits and acknowledgments borrowed from other sources and reproduced, with permission, in this textbook appear on appropriate page within text (or on pages C1–C4).

Pearson Education LTD.
Pearson Education Australia PTY, Limited
Pearson Education Singapore, Pte. Ltd
Pearson Education North Asia Ltd

Pearson Education, Canada, Ltd
Pearson Educación de Mexico, S.A. de C.V.
Pearson Education–Japan
Pearson Education Malaysia, Pte. Ltd

PEARSON
Prentice
Hall

10   9   8   7   6   5   4   3   2   1

ISBN-10:            0-13-601565-4
ISBN-13:      978-0-13-601565-9

**1**

**2**

**3**

## Seeing History

## Interpreting the Past

# 4

## Seeing History

# 5

## Seeing History

# 6

## FROM EMPIRE TO INDEPENDENCE, 1750–1776    126

# 7

## THE AMERICAN REVOLUTION, 1776–1786    154

# 8

### Seeing History

# 9

### Seeing History

# 10

## THE SOUTH AND SLAVERY, 1790s–1850s  238

### Seeing History

# 11

## THE GROWTH OF DEMOCRACY, 1824–1840  266

### Seeing History

# 14

## THE TERRITORIAL EXPANSION OF THE UNITED STATES, 1830s–1850s  350

Seeing History

# 15

## THE COMING CRISIS, THE 1850s  378

Seeing History

# 16

## THE CIVIL WAR, 1861–1865  404

# 17

## RECONSTRUCTION, 1863–1877  432

# 18

## CONQUEST AND SURVIVAL, 1860–1900  464

## 19

## PRODUCTION AND CONSUMPTION IN THE GILDED AGE, 1865–1900  498

### Seeing History

## 20

## DEMOCRACY AND EMPIRE, 1870–1900  524

### Seeing History

### Interpreting the Past

# 21

## URBAN AMERICA AND THE PROGRESSIVE ERA, 1900–1917   556

### Seeing History

# 22

## A GLOBAL POWER, 1901–1920   590

### Seeing History

# 29

## WAR ABROAD, WAR AT HOME, 1965–1974   822

### Seeing History

# 30

## THE CONSERVATIVE ASCENDANCY, 1974–1991   854

### Seeing History

# 31

## THE UNITED STATES IN A GLOBAL AGE, 1992–2008 884

### Seeing History

**The 9/11 Attacks 899**

### Interpreting the Past

**The Threat of War to Democratic Institutions 910**

# MAPS

*Denotes Interactive Map Exploration*

SPECIAL FEATURES

# CHARTS, GRAPHS & TABLES

# SEEING HISTORY

# INTERPRETING THE PAST

# AMERICAN COMMUNITIES

# OVERVIEW TABLES

*Out of Many: A History of the American People*, fifth edition, offers a distinctive and timely approach to American history, highlighting the experiences of diverse communities of Americans in the unfolding story of our country. The stories of these communities offer a way of examining the complex historical forces shaping people's lives at various moments in our past. The debates and conflicts surrounding the most momentous issues in our national life—independence, emerging democracy, slavery, westward settlement, imperial expansion, economic depression, war, technological change—were largely worked out in the context of local communities. Through communities we focus on the persistent tensions between everyday life and those larger decisions and events that continually reshape the circumstances of local life.

Each chapter opens with a description of a representative community. Some of these portraits feature American communities struggling with one another: African slaves and English masters on the rice plantations of colonial Georgia, or *Tejanos* and Americans during the Texas war of independence. Other chapters feature portraits of communities facing social change: the feminists of Seneca Falls, New York, in 1848, or the African Americans of Montgomery, Alabama, in 1955. As the story unfolds we find communities growing to include ever larger groups of Americans: the soldiers from every colony who forged the Continental Army into a patriotic national force at Valley Forge during the American Revolution, or the moviegoers who aspired to a collective dream of material prosperity and upward mobility during the 1920s.

*Out of Many* is also the only American history text with a truly continental perspective. With community vignettes from New England to the South, the Midwest to the far West, we encourage students to appreciate the great expanse of our nation. For example, a vignette of seventeenth-century Santa Fé, New Mexico, illustrates the founding of the first European settlements in the New World. We present territorial expansion into the American West from the viewpoint of the Mandan villagers of the upper Missouri River of North Dakota. A continental perspective drives home to students that American history has never been the preserve of any particular region.

*Out of Many* includes extensive coverage of our diverse heritage. Our country is appropriately known as "a nation of immigrants," and the history of immigration to America, from the seventeenth to the twenty-first centuries, is fully integrated into the text. There is sustained and close attention to our place in the world, with special emphasis on our relations with the nations of the Western Hemisphere, especially our near neighbors, Canada and Mexico.

In these ways *Out of Many* breaks new ground, but without compromising its coverage of the traditional turning points that we believe are critically important to an understanding of the American past. *Out of Many* also looks back in a new and comprehensive way—t... vantage point of the beginning of a new century a... end of the Cold War—at the salient events of the last ... years and their impact on American communities. The community focus of *Out of Many* weaves the stories of the people and the nation into a single compelling narrative.

*Out of Many*, fifth edition, is completely updated with the most recent scholarship on the history of America and the United States. All the chapters have been extensively reviewed, revised, and rewritten. The final chapter details the tumultuous events of the new century, including a completely new section on the "war on terror," and concluding with the national election of 2004. Throughout the book the text and graphics are presented in a stunning new design. Moreover, this edition incorporates two important new features designed to bring history vividly alive for students: *Interpreting the Past*, featuring primary sources on a controversial provocative historical issue and *Seeing History*, carefully chosen images that show how visual sources can illuminate their understanding of American history.

## SPECIAL FEATURES

With each edition of *Out of Many, Teaching and Learning Classroom Edition*, we have sought to strengthen its unique integration of the best of traditional American history with its innovative community-based focus and strong continental perspective and engage students through special features that encourage their exploration of the questions that historians seek to answer about the past. This new version is no exception. A wealth of special features and pedagogical aids reinforces our narrative and motivates students desire to understand and appreciate America's history. The special walkthrough on pages xxiii–xlii highlights these features.

## COMMUNITY AND DIVERSITY

This special introductory essay begins students' journey into the narrative history that unfolds in *Out of Many*. The essay acquaints students with the major themes of the book and provides them with a framework for understanding American History. (pp. xliii–xlv)

## SUPPLEMENTARY MATERIAL

*Out of Many* is supported by an extensive supplements package for instructors and students that gives flexibility to the process of teaching and learning. A full description of the supplements available with the text is provided on page xlii.

## ACKNOWLEDGMENTS

In the years it has taken to bring *Out of Many* from idea to reality and to improve it in successive editions, we have often been reminded that although writing histo-

PREFACE

ry sometimes feels like isolated work, it actually involves a collective effort.We want to thank the dozens of people whose efforts have made the publication of this book possible.

We wish to thank our many friends at Prentice Hall for their efforts in creating the fifth edition of *Out of Many*: Yolanda de Rooy, President; Charlyce Jones Owen, Publisher; Jeannine Cilotta and James Miller, Development Editors; Rochelle Diogenes, Editor-in-Chief, Development Sue Westmoreland, Executive Marketing Manager; Brandy Dawson, Director of Marketing; Mayda Bosco, Media Editor; Denise Brown, Production Liaison; Mary Carnis, Managing Editor; Blair Brown, Cover Designer; Fiorella Mari, Production Editor; and Donna Mulder, Copyeditor. We also thank John Reisbord for his editorial contributions to the fifth edition.

Although we share joint responsibility for the entire book, the chapters were individually authored: John Mack Faragher wrote chapters 1–8; Susan Armitage wrote chapters 9–16; Mari Jo Buhle wrote chapters 18–20, 25–26, 29; and Daniel Czitrom wrote chapters 17, 21–24, 27–28. (For this edition Buhle and Czitrom co-authored Chapters 30–31.)

Each of us depended on a great deal of support and assistance with the research and writing that went into this book.We want to thank: Kathryn Abbott, Nan Boyd, Krista Comer, Jennifer Cote, Crista DeLuzio, Keith Edgerton, Carol Frost, Jesse Hoffnung Garskof, Pailin Gaither, Jane Gerhard, Todd Gernes, Mark Krasovic, Melani McAlister, Cristi, Rebecca McKenna, and Mitchell, J. C. Mutchler, Keith Peterson, Alan Pinkham, Tricia Rose, Gina Rourke, Jessica Shubow, Gordon P. Utz Jr., Maura Young, Teresa Bill, Gill Frank, and Naoko Shibusawa.

Our families and close friends have been supportive and ever so patient over the many years we have devoted to this project.But we want especially to thank Paul Buhle, Meryl Fingrutd, Bob Greene, and Michele Hoffnung.

**John Mack Faragher**  John Mack Faragher is Arthur Unobskey Professor of American History and director of the Howard R. Lamar Center for the Study of Frontiers and Borders at Yale University. Born in Arizona and raised in southern California, he received his B.A. at the University of California, Riverside, and his Ph.D. at Yale University. He is the author of *Women and Men on the Overland Trail* (1979), *Sugar Creek: Life on the Illinois Prairie* (1986), *Daniel Boone: The Life and Legend of an American Pioneer* (1992), *The American West: A New Interpretive History* (2000), and *A Great and Noble Scheme: The Tragic Story of the Expulsion of the French Acadians from their American Homeland* (2005).

**Daniel Czitrom**  Daniel Czitrom is Professor of History at Mount Holyoke College. Born and raised in New York City, he received his B.A. from the State University of New York at Binghamton and his M.A. and Ph.D. from the University of Wisconsin, Madison. He is the author of *Media and the American Mind: From Morse to McLuhan* (1982), which won the First Books Award of the American Historical Association and has been translated into Spanish and Chinese. He is co-author of *Rediscovering Jacob Riis: Exposure Journalism and Photography in Turn of the Century New York* (2007). He has served as a historical consultant and featured on-camera commentator for several documentary film projects, including the PBS productions *New York: A Documentary Film; American Photography: A Century of Images;* and *The Great Transatlantic Cable*. He currently serves on the Executive Board of the Organization of American Historians.

**Mari Jo Buhle**  Mari Jo Buhle is William R. Kenan Jr. University Professor and Professor of American Civilization and History at Brown University, specializing in American women's history. She received her B.A. from the University of Illinois, Urbana–Champaign, and her Ph.D. from the University of Wisconsin, Madison. She is the author of *Women and American Socialism, 1870–1920* (1981) and *Feminism and Its Discontents: A Century of Struggle with Psychoanalysis* (1998). She is also coeditor of *Encyclopedia of the American Left*, second edition (1998). Professor Buhle held a fellowship (1991–1996) from the John D. and Catherine T. MacArthur Foundation.

**Susan H. Armitage**  Susan H. Armitage is Claudius O. and Mary R. Johnson Distinguished Professor of History at Washington State University. She earned her Ph.D. from the London School of Economics and Political Science. Among her many publications on western women's history are three coedited books, *The Women's West* (1987), *So Much To Be Done: Women on the Mining and Ranching Frontier* (1991), and *Writing the Range: Race, Class, and Culture in the Women's West* (1997). She currently serves as an editor of a series of books on women and American history for the University of Illinois Press.

# Out of Many

**Dear Reader,**

*Out of Many* grew out of our years of experience teaching the American history survey course. When we were young professors, the old narrative of strict political history was in the process of being supplemented with a new narrative of social history. But the two remained mostly unconnected. New textbooks sequestered these two narratives in separate chapters. Isn't there a way, we wondered, to write a new, unified narrative of American history, in which political and social history might be combined? This was the inspiration behind *Out of Many*, one of the most successful American history textbooks of this generation. Organized around the theme of American communities, the text offers a single, engaging narrative of American social, economic, and political history.

We began working on this book twenty years ago. It has been a long and rewarding journey. We are proud to have been the first American history college text to put the diversity of America's peoples at the center of our historical experience. Our narrative weaves the distinct experiences and voices of northerners, southerners, and westerners, of African Americans, Latinos, and immigrants, of women and men, throughout each chapter. Coming ourselves from different backgrounds and from different regions of the country, we developed a continental approach to the American past, demonstrating how each region has been closely linked to the broader currents of global development. It is our hope that *Out of Many* will best help students understand the history that has produced the increasingly complex America of the twenty-first century.

# *O*ut *of* Many, you experience America's history...

*Out of Many* provides truly integrated coverage of American social and political history. The authors weave the everyday stories of individuals and communities and the major events of the nation's political history into a single compelling narrative that both enlightens and inspires students. This integrated approach to history offers students the best possible insight into the American experience.

*Here individuals of all nations are melted into a new race of men, whose labours and posterity will one day cause great changes in the world.*
—Hector St. John Crevecœur

Congress voting on the issue of independence.

# 8
## THE NEW NATION
1786–1800

**WHAT WERE** the tensions and conflicts between local and national authorities in the decades after the American Revolution?

GENERAL GEORGE WASHINGTON

**HOW DID** Americans differ in their views of the new Constitution, and how were those differences reflected in the struggle to achieve ratification?

**WHAT WERE** the essential structures of national government under the Constitution?

**HOW DID** American political parties first begin?

**WHAT WERE** the first stirrings of an authentic American national culture?

The TLC Edition of *Out of Many* offers **an engaging visual presentation** to pique—and retain—student interest. The text is packed with **stunning visuals** including chapter openers that highlight key events in the chapter. **Chapter opening questions** provide an overview and guide to the important concepts students need to learn.

The TLC Edition of *Out of Many* includes **a variety of pedagogical tools** to help students organize and reinforce their learning.

## AMERICAN COMMUNITIES
### Expansion Touches Mandan Villages on the Upper Missouri

IN MID-OCTOBER 1804, NEWS ARRIVED AT THE MANDAN VILLAGES, prominently situated on bluffs overlooking the upper Missouri River, that an American military party led by Meriwether Lewis and William Clark was coming up the river. The principal chiefs, hoping for expanded trade and support against their enemies the Sioux, welcomed these first American visitors. As the expedition's three boats and forty-three men approached the village, Clark wrote, "great numbers on both sides flocked down to the bank to view us." That evening, the Mandans welcomed the Americans with an enthusiastic dance and gifts of food.

Lewis and Clark had been sent by President Thomas Jefferson to survey the Louisiana Purchase and to find an overland route to the Pacific Ocean. They were also instructed to inform the Indians that they now owed loyalty—and trade—to the American government. Meeting with the village chiefs, the Americans off...
economi...

...ies, the party reached the Pacific Ocean at the mouth of the Columbia River, where they spent the winter. Overdue and feared lost, they returned in triumph to St. Louis in September 1806. Before long the Americans had established Fort Clark at the Mandan villages, giving American traders a base for challenging British dominance of the western fur trade. The permanent American presence brought increased contact, and with it much more disease. In 1837, a terrible smallpox epidemic carried away the vast majority of the Mandans, reducing the population to fewer than 150. Four Bears, a Mandan chief who had been a child at the time of the Lewis and Clark visit, spoke these last words to the remnants of his people:

"I have loved the whites," he declared. "I have lived with them ever since I was a boy." But in return for the kindness of the Mandans, the Americans had brought this plague. "I do not fear death, my friends," he said, "but to die with my face rotten, that even the wolves will shrink with horror at seeing me, and ...ay to themselves, that is Four Bears, the friend of the whites. ...have deceived me," he pronounced with his last breath. ...I always considered as brothers turned ou...

*Out of Many* is among the first texts to focus on the many ethnic and multicultural communities that have played a vital role in the evolution of the United States. Each chapter begins with an *American Community* feature that shows how the events discussed in the chapter affected a particular community. These snapshots of life add up to a well-rounded understanding of the American story.

## Creating Celebrity

A common definition for "celebrity" is one who is famous for being famous. Although politics, the arts, science, and the military have produced famous people for centuries, the celebrity is a twentieth-century phenomenon, one closely linked to the emergence of modern forms of mass media. In the 1920s Hollywood's "star system," along with tabloid newspapers and the new profession of public relations, created the modern celebrity. Film producers were at first wary of identifying screen actors by name, but they soon discovered that promoting popular leading actors would boost the box office for their movies. The use of "close-ups" in movies and the fact that screen images were literally larger than life distinguished the images of film actors from, say, stage performers or opera singers.

**WHAT VISUAL** themes strike you as most powerful in the accompanying images? How do they compare to celebrity images of today? Why do you think male stars such as Valentino and Fairbanks were so often portrayed as exotic foreigners?

Fans identified with their favorites in contradictory ways. Stars like Charlie Chaplin and Mary Pickford were like royalty. Audiences were also curious about the stars' private lives. Film studios took advantage of this curiosity by carefully controlling the public image . . . . . . . releases, planted stories in newspapers, and ca . . . . . . . . arances. By the 1920s film stars were essenti . . . . . . . . . . . uiring enormous capital investment. ∎

*Seeing History*

New *Seeing History* features offer in-depth analysis of an image or series of images from a particular historical period. These visually engaging features help students to understand how various individuals and events have been depicted throughout American history and underscore the important role images and illustrations play in understanding and interpreting the past.

**New** to the Fifth Edition, *Interpreting the Past* features provide documents and images on a key event or topic to help students see how historians understand and interpret the past. A critical thinking question provides students with the opportunity to analyze how these historical records illuminate this event or topic.

## Realities of Freedom

The Freedmen's Bureau established in 1865 by Congress provided freedmen with clothing, temporary shelter, food, and series of freedmen's schools across the South. Southern response was to fall into the use of terror to deter blacks from becoming economically independent using the agencies of groups like the Ku Klux Klan. Sharecropping, tenant farming, and peonage were insidious economic arrangements that placed whites and blacks in a form of economic slavery to large land holders in the South of the post-Civil War era.

**FOLLOWING EMANCIPATION,** what economic and social opportunities existed for African Americans in the United States? How did these opportunities change the lives of freedmen after the official end to slavery?

The story of African Americans after the end of slavery is complex and varied. Some blacks attempted to seek out better places to establish their new lives while others remained in the security of the only home they had known as slaves. ∎

### AN ACT TO ESTABLISH A BUREAU FOR THE RELIEF OF FREEDMEN AND REFUGEES, 1865

**BE IT** enacted, That there is hereby established in the War Department, to continue during the present war of rebellion, and for one year thereafter, a bureau of refugees, freedmen, and abandoned lands, to which shall be committed, as hereinafter provided, the supervision and management of all abandoned lands, and the control of all subjects relating to refugees and freedmen from rebel states, or from any district of country within the territory embraced in the operations of the army, under such rules and regulations as may be prescribed by the head of the bureau and approved by the President. The said bureau shall be under the management and control of a commissioner to be appointed by the President, by and with the advice and consent of the Senate . . . ∎

African-American family working together in the cotton fields.

### WHEN WE WORKED ON SHARES, WE COULDN'T MAKE NOTHING

**AFTER SLAVERY** we had to get in before night too. If you didn't, Ku Klux would drive you in. They would come and raid you anyway. . . . When he got you good and scared he would drive on away. They would whip you if they would catch you out in the night time . . .

I've forgot who it is that that told us that we was free. Somebody come and told us we're free now. I done forgot who it was.

After freedom, we worked on shares a while. Then we rented. When we worked on shares, we couldn't make nothing, just overalls and something to eat. Half went to the other man and you would destroy your half if you weren't careful. A man that didn't know how to count would always lose. He might lose anyhow. They didn't give no itemized statement. No, you just had to take their word. They never give you no details. They just say you owe so much. No matter how good account you kept, you had to go by their account and now, Brother, I'm tellin' you the truth about this. It's been that way for a long time. You had to take the white man's word on note, and everything. Anything you

Share croppers and their families were evicted from the plantation they were working after being convicted of engaging in a conspiracy to retain their homes. This picture was taken just after the evictions before the families were moved into a tent colony.

wanted, you could git if you were a good hand. You could git anything you wanted as long as you worked. If you didn't make no money, that's all right; they would advance you more. But you better not leave him, you better not try to leave and get caught. They'd keep you in debt. . . . Anything that kept you a slave because he was always right and you were always wrong. . . .

### SHARE CROPPER CONTRACT, 1882

To every one applying to rent land upon shares, the following conditions must be read, and agreed to.

To every 30 or 35 acres, I agree to furnish the team, plow, and farming implements, except cotton planters, and I do not agree to furnish a cart to every cropper. The croppers are to have half of the cotton, corn and fodder (and peas and pumpkins and potatoes if any are planted . . .

Croppers are to have no part or interest in the cotton seed raised from the crop planted and worked by them. No vine crops of any description, that is, no watermelons, muskmelons, . . . squashes or anything of that kind, except peas and pumpkins, and potatoes, are to be planted in the cotton or corn. All must work under my direction. All plantation work to be done by the croppers. . . .

For every mule or horse furnished by me there must be 1000 good sized rails . . . hauled, and the fence repaired as far as they will go, the fence to be torn down and put up from the bottom if I so direct. All croppers to haul rails and work on fence whenever I may order. Rails to be split when I may see . . .

Each cropper must keep in good repair all bridges in his crop or over ditches that he has to clean out and when a bridge needs repairing that is outside of all their crops, then any one that I call on must repair it . . .

No cropper to work off the plantation when there is any work to be done on the land he has rented, or when his work is needed by me or other croppers. Trees to be cut down on Orchard, House field & Evanson fences, leaving such as I may designate. . . . ∎

*Interpreting the Past*

# $O$ut of Many, you experience America's history...

*Out of Many's* Teaching and Learning Classroom (TLC) Edition offers an engaging visual design and numerous tools that help students learn and review the material.

---

864   CHAPTER 30   THE CONSERVATIVE ASCENDANCY, 1974–1991

**QUICK REVIEW**

**Hostages**
- November 4, 1979: Iranian fundamentalists seized U.S. embassy in Tehran.
- Fifty-two Americans held hostage for 444 days.
- Crisis doomed the Carter presidency.

leaving eight Americans dead, their burned corpses displayed by the enraged Iranians. Short of an all-out
death, Carter had used

The political and
secretary of state in six
the president. The price
he had proclaimed cen
violated his own huma
mark on American fore

## THE NEW RIG

**WHAT EXPLAINS** the rise of the New Right in the 1980s?

**myhistorylab**
Review Summary

The failures in U
played a large
resentment."

**NEOCONSERVATIS**
By the mid-1970s, a new
scape: neoconservatism
been liberal Democrats
tling social movement
Deal–style liberalism ar
to repeal affirmative a
enacted during the Joh
was, however, foreign po
neoconservatives called

Neoconservatives
dation for the rightwar
donors, they established
shaping discussions. T
neoconservatives and p

**QUICK REVIEW**

**The Conservative Critique**
- Free markets work better than government programs.
- Government intervention does more harm than good.
- Government assistance saps the initiative of the poor.

**THE RELIGIOUS R**
Evangelical Protestants,
the backbone of the n
neoconservative positio
they provided the politi

**Critical thinking questions** from the chapter opener are repeated in the margins at each major section of the chapter to promote critical reading. **Quick reviews** help students review selected topics as they go through the chapter.

**WHAT MAJOR** groups made up the Southern Republicans?

**myhistorylab**
Review Summary

**Union League**   Republican party organizations in Northern cities that became an important organizing device among freedmen in Southern cities after 1865.

**Carpetbaggers**   Northern transplants to the South, many of whom were Union soldiers who stayed in the South after the war.

A **running glossary** provides definitions for key terms and concepts, which are then listed at the end of the chapter for review.

ican political activ
out the South.

Begun during the wa
club, the Union League now be
Union League chapters brought togethe
Freedmen's Bureau agents to demand the vote and p
tion against African Americans. It brought out African American voters, inst
freedmen in the rights and duties of citizenship, and promoted Republican candidates. Not surprisingly, newly enfranchised freedmen voted Republican and formed the core of the Republican Party in the South. For most ordinary African Americans, politics was inseparable from economic issues, especially the land question. Grassroots political organizations frequently intervened in local disputes with planters over the terms of labor contracts. African American political groups closely followed the congressional debates over Reconstruction policy and agitated for land confiscation and distribution. Perhaps most important, politics was the only arena where black and white Southerners might engage each other on an equal basis.

## SOUTHERN POLITICS AND SOCIETY

By the summer of 1868, when the South had returned to the Union, the majority of Republicans believed the task of Reconstruction to be finished. Ultimately, they put their faith in a political solution to the problems facing the vanquished South. Most Republican congressmen were moderates, conceiving Reconstruction in limited terms. They rejected radical calls for confiscation and redistribution of land, as well as permanent military rule of the South. The Reconstruction Acts of 1867 and 1868 laid out the requirements for the readmission of southern states, along with the procedures for forming and electing new governments.

Yet over the next decade, the political structure created in the southern states proved too restricted and fragile to sustain itself. To most southern whites, the active participation of African Americans in politics seemed extremely dangerous. Federal troops were needed to protect Republican governments and their supporters from violent opposition. Congressional action to monitor southern elections and protect black voting rights became routine. Despite initial successes, southern Republicanism proved an unstable coalition of often conflicting elements, unable to sustain effective power for very long. By 1877, Democrats had regained political control of all the former Confederate states.

### SOUTHERN REPUBLICANS

Three major groups composed the fledgling Republican coalition in the postwar South. African American voters made up a large majority of southern Republicans throughout the Reconstruction era. Yet African Americans outnumbered whites in only three southern states; Republicans would have to attract white support to win elections and sustain power.

A second group consisted of white Northerners, derisively called "**carpetbaggers**" by native white Southerners. Most were veterans of the Union army who stayed in the South after the war. Others included Freedmen's Bureau agents and businessmen who had invested capital in cotton plantations and other enterprises. Although they made up a tiny percentage of the population, carpetbaggers played

# ...through an engaging learner-centered format.

## OVERVIEW | Currents of Progressivism

| | Key Figures | Issues |
|---|---|---|
| **Local Communities** | Jane Addams, Lillian Wald, Florence Kelley, Frederic C. Howe, Samuel Jones | • Improving health, education, welfare in urban immigrant neighborhoods<br>• Child labor, eight-hour day<br>• Celebrating immigrant cultures<br>• Reforming urban politics<br>• Municipal ownership/regulation of utilities |
| **State** | Robert M. La Follette, Hiram Johnson, Al Smith | • Limiting power of railroads, other corporations<br>• Improving civil service<br>• Direct democracy<br>• Applying academic scholarship to human needs |
| **National** | James K. Vardaman, Hoke Smith, Theodore Roosevelt, Woodrow Wilson | • Disfranchisement of African Americans<br>• Trust-busting<br>• Conservation and western development<br>• National regulation of corporate and financial excesses<br>• Reform of national banking |
| **Intellectual/Cultural** | Jacob Riis, Lincoln Steffens, Ida Tarbell, Upton Sinclair, S. S. McClure | • Muckraking |
| | John Dewey, Louis Brandeis, Edwin A. Ross | • Education reform<br>• Sociological jurisprudence<br>• Empowering "ethical elite" |

**myhistorylab**

**Overview:** *Currents of Progressivism*

She offered Henry Street as a meeting place to the National Negro Conference in 1909, out of which emerged the National Association for the Advancement of Colored People.

Social reformer Florence Kelley helped direct the support of the settl— behind groundbreaking state and federal lab—

**Overview tables** help students review key points of complex topics and issues. References to the **Myhistorylab** website and the **Primary Source CDROM** are included in the margins throughout the chapters to alert students to documents, activities, and additional content related to topics in the chapters.

**Map Explorations** are selected maps that can be explored interactively on the Web and MyHistoryLab. **Critical thinking questions** help to strengthen map analysis skills and geographic literacy.

depressed Northeast to boost the region's population (see Map 30.2).

The Sunbelt witnessed a dramatic turnaround in demographic and economic trends. Southern cities reversed the century-long trend of out-migration among African Americans. The Southwest and West changed yet more dramatically. California became the nation's most populous state; Texas moved to third, behind New York. Former farms and deserts were turned almost overnight into huge metropolitan areas ringed by new automobile-dependent suburbs. Phoenix grew from 664,000 in 1960 to 1,509,000 in 1980, Las Vegas from 127,000 to 463,000.

Much Sunbelt wealth tended to be temporary or sharply cyclical, producing a boom-and-bust economy. Income was also distributed unevenly. Older Hispanic populations made only modest gains, while recent Mexican immigrants and Indian peoples suffered from a combination of low wages and poor public services. The Sunbelt states directed their tax and federal dollars to strengthening police forces, building roads or sanitation systems for the expanding suburbs, and creating budget surpluses.

The "Snowbelt" (or "Rustbelt") states, longtime centers of voting strength for the Democratic Party, meanwhile suffered severe population losses accompanying the sharp decline of industry.

New York City offered a spectacular example of decline. A fiscal crisis in 1975 forced Democratic Mayor Abraham Beame to choose between wage freezes for public employees and devastating cuts and layoffs. Eventually, with the municipal government teetering on the brink of bankruptcy, he chose both. In respon— —backs in mass transit and the deteriorati— —r of the middle class fled.

**MAP EXPLORATION**

To explore an interactive version of this map, go to http://www.prenhall.com/faraghertlc/map30.2

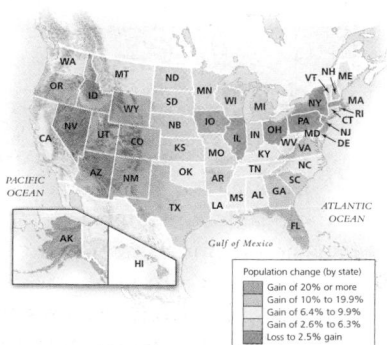

Population change (by state)
- Gain of 20% or more
- Gain of 10% to 19.9%
- Gain of 6.4% to 9.9%
- Gain of 2.6% to 6.3%
- Loss to 2.5% gain

**MAP 30.2**
**Population Shifts, 1970–80** Industrial decline in the Northeast coincided with an economic boom in the Sunbelt, encouraging millions of Americans to head for warmer climates and better jobs.

HOW WERE the changes in population between 1970 and 1980 reflected in the American economy?

# *O*ut *of* Many, you experience America's history…

Every new copy of *Out of Many* includes the *Primary Source: Documents in U.S. History* CD-ROM. This versatile resource offers 400 primary source documents—in accessible PDF format—and over 350 images and maps. It also provides a number of features that help students work with documents, including headnotes, focus questions, highlighting and note-taking tools, and a glossary of terms for certain documents.

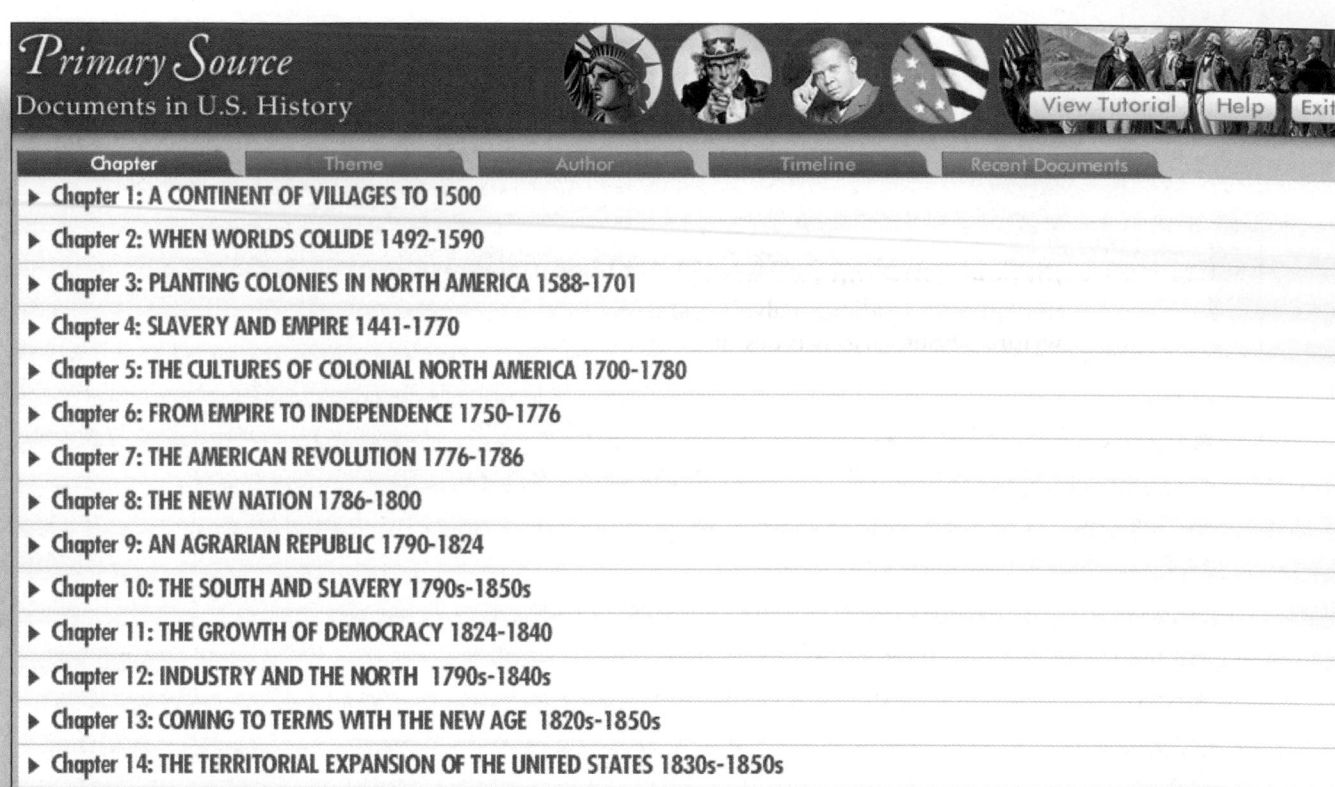

An **easy navigation function** allows students to search for documents by chapter, theme, author, or timeline.

# ...through a collection of primary sources bound into the text.

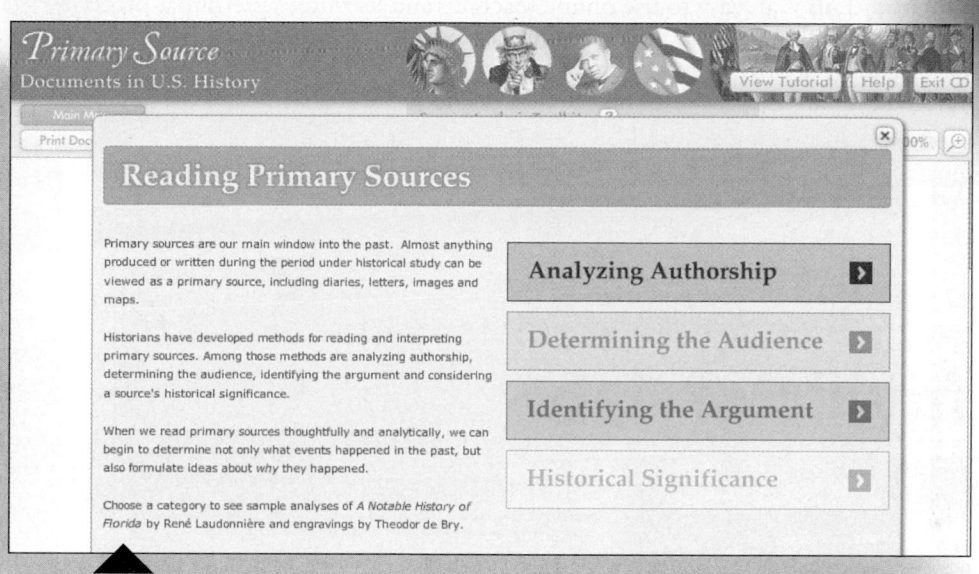

**Reading Primary Sources**

Primary sources are our main window into the past. Almost anything produced or written during the period under historical study can be viewed as a primary source, including diaries, letters, images and maps.

Historians have developed methods for reading and interpreting primary sources. Among those methods are analyzing authorship, determining the audience, identifying the argument and considering a source's historical significance.

When we read primary sources thoughtfully and analytically, we can begin to determine not only what events happened in the past, but also formulate ideas about *why* they happened.

Choose a category to see sample analyses of *A Notable History of Florida* by René Laudonnière and engravings by Theodor de Bry.

**Analyzing Authorship**

**Determining the Audience**

**Identifying the Argument**

**Historical Significance**

An **interactive tutorial** offers strategies for reading, analyzing, and writing about various types of documents.

**Primary Source**
Documents in U.S. History

Main Menu | Print Document | Glossary Terms | Focus Questions | Source Analysis Toolkit

Identifying the Argument
Analyzing Authorship
Determining the Audience
Identifying the Argument
Historical Significance
Add/Remove Categories...

Save/Print Notes | 100%

THOMAS JE... DISON

Paris, January 30th, 1787.

Dear Sir,

My last to you was of the 16th of December; since which, I have received yours of November 25 and December 4, which afforded me, as your letters always do, a treat on matters public...

*Identifying the Argument Note*

...may apprehend too much from these instances of irregularity. They may conclude too hastily that nature has formed man insusceptible of any other government than that of force, a conclusion not founded in truth or experience.

Societies exist under three forms, sufficiently distinguishable: (1) without ...

An accessible *Source Analysis Toolkit* helps students easily utilize reading, analyzing, and writing tools.

# Out of Many, you experience America's history...

**MyHistoryLab** is an easy to use online teaching and learning system that provides helpful tools to both students and instructors. In addition to numerous instructor and student resources, it includes a complete e-book version of *Out of Many*, making an interactive online text available to students.

## For students

**MyHistoryLab** is packed with **readings that expand upon the material** found in the text. These include over 300 primary source documents with questions for analysis as well as classic works such as Thomas Paine's *Common Sense*.

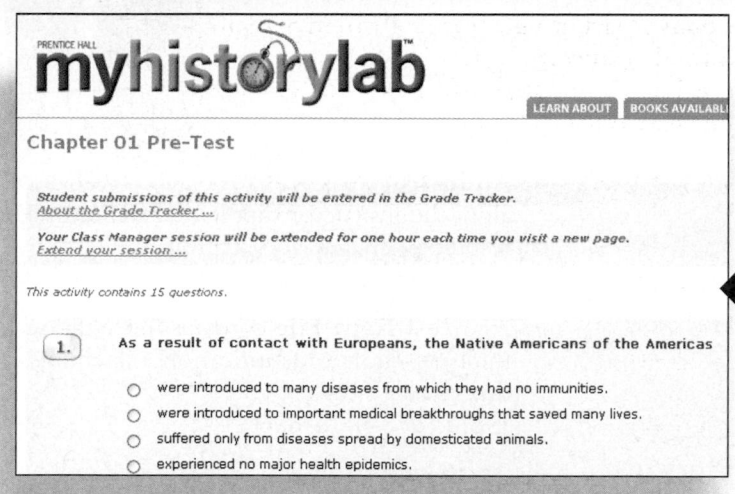

**MyHistoryLab** offers students various **review and assessment tools** in one convenient online platform. Self-study quizzes with targeted feedback help students assess their progress. A study guide, PowerPoint™ presentations, and key terms flashcards help students master the material in preparation for exams.

**MyHistoryLab interactive activities and exercises** let students explore materials from the text in an engaging fashion. MyHistoryLab brings U.S. history to life via *Exploring America* interactive learning activities, map explorations, animation, and audio and video clips.

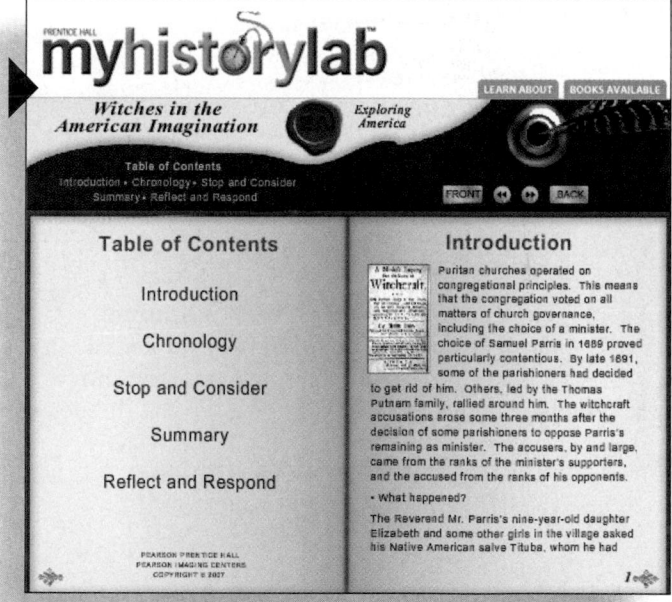

## For instructors

**MyHistoryLab** is a one-stop collection of instructional material for teaching from *Out of Many*, including the instructor's manual, the test item file, images, maps, charts, and graphs from the text, video and audio clips, and PowerPoint™ lecture presentations. In addition, MyHistoryLab provides instructor access to all student resources.

*For more information, contact your local Pearson sales representative or visit www.myhistorylab.com and click Prentice Hall.*

# Out of Many, you experience America's history...
## ...with tools for instructors and students.

Prentice Hall is proud to offer a number of supplementary resources that help students and instructors get the most from *Out of Many*.

## For students

- A robust **Study Guide** provides practice tests, essay questions, chronologies, an expanded map skills section, and *Interpreting the Past* activities for each chapter.
  For **Volume I**: 978-0-13-602836-9
  For **Volume II**: 978-0-13-602835-2

- A full-color **Atlas of United States History** offers maps and charts depicting crucial times and events in U.S. History. An index lists historically important places, areas, events, and geographical features.
  978-0-13-603349-3

- **VangoNotes** downloadable audio study guides are ideal for both concept review and exam preparation. The content includes *Big Ideas* overviews, practice tests, audio flashcards of key terms, and *Rapid Review* quick drill sessions.
  **www.vangonotes.com**

- The print version of **Primary Source: Documents in U.S. History** presents a collection of more than 300 primary source documents that directly relate to the themes and content of the text.
  For **Volumes I**: 978-0-13-605198-5
  For **Volume II**: 978-0-13-605199-2

## For instructors

- The **Instructor's Resource Manual** contains everything instructors need for developing and preparing lecture presentations, including chapter outlines and overviews, lecture topics, discussion questions, and information about audio–visual resources. It also includes a new section on teaching American history.
  ISBN: 978-0-13-606049-9

- An **Instructor's Resource CD-ROM** includes all of the instructor supplements, multimedia resources, images, and art from the text.
  ISBN: 978-0-13-606052-9

- The **Test Item File** contains more than 3,000 multiple-choice, identification, matching, and essay questions.
  ISBN: 978-0-13-606051-2

- **Test Generator**—a computerized test management program available for Windows and Macintosh environments—allows instructors to design their own exams by selecting items from the Test Item File. Instructors may download the Test Gen from the Pearson Instructor Resource Center.
  **www.prenhall.com/irc**

- The **Transparencies Set** offers over 150 full-color transparency acetates of all the maps, charts, and graphs in the text for easy classroom presentation.
  978-0-13-602839-0

- A customized **Retrieving the American Past reader** may be created to accompany *Out of Many*. Instructors can select from a database of 300 primary source documents on key topics in American history to create a reader ideally suited to their course.
  **http://www.pearsoncustom.com/database/rtap.html**

- The two-volume **American Stories: Biographies in United States History, Third Edition** presents sixty-two biographies of key figures in American history with introductions, pre-reading questions, suggested readings, and a special prologue about the role of biography in the study of American history.
  For **Volumes I**: 978-0-13-182654-0
  For **Volume II**: 978-0-13-182653-3

- The Prentice Hall **Package a Penguin program** provides instructors an opportunity to receive significant discounts on Penguin American history titles when ordered with *Out of Many*.

One of the most characteristic features of our country is its astounding variety. The American people include the descendants of native Indians, colonial Europeans of British, French, and Spanish background, Africans, and migrants from virtually every country and continent. Indeed, at the beginning of the new century the United States is absorbing a flood of immigrants from Latin America and Asia that rivals the great tide of people from eastern and southern Europe one hundred years before. The struggle to meld a single nation out of our many far-flung communities is what much of American history is all about. That is the story told in this book.

Every human society is made up of communities. A community is a set of relationships linking men, women, and their families to a coherent social whole that is more than the sum of its parts. In a community people develop the capacity for unified action. In a community people learn, often through trial and error, how to transform and adapt to their environment. The sentiment that binds the members of a community together is the mother of group consciousness and ethnic identity. In the making of history, communities are far more important than even the greatest of leaders, for the community is the institution most capable of passing a distinctive historical tradition to future generations.

Communities bind people together in multiple ways. They can be as small as local neighborhoods, in which people maintain face-to-face relations, or as large as the nation itself. This book examines American history from the perspective of community life—an ever-widening frame that has included larger and larger groups of Americans.

Networks of kinship and friendship, and connections across generations and among families, establish the bonds essential to community life. Shared feelings about values and history establish the basis for common identity. In communities, people find the power to act collectively in their own interest. But American communities frequently took shape as a result of serious conflicts among groups, and within communities there was often significant fighting among competing groups or classes. Thus the term *community*, as we use it here, includes conflict and discord as well as harmony and agreement.

For decades Americans have complained about the "loss of community." But community has not disappeared—it has been continuously reinvented. Until the late eighteenth century, community was defined

Harvey Dinnerstein, *Underground, Together* 1996, oil on canvas, 90" × 107".

Photograph courtesy of Gerold Wunderlich & Co., New York, NY.

primarily by space and local geography. But in the nineteenth century communities were reshaped by new and powerful historical forces such as the marketplace, industrialization, the corporation, mass immigration, mass media, and the growth of the nation-state. In the twentieth century, Americans struggled to balance commitments to multiple communities. These were defined not simply by local spatial arrangements, but by categories as varied as race and ethnicity, occupation, political affiliation, and consumer preference. The "American Communities" vignettes that open each chapter reflect these transformations.

The title for our book was suggested by the Latin phrase selected by John Adams, Benjamin Franklin, and Thomas Jefferson for the Great Seal of the United States: *E Pluribus Unum*—"Out of Many Comes Unity." These men understood that unity could not be imposed by a powerful central authority but had to develop out of mutual respect among Americans of different backgrounds. The revolutionary leadership expressed the hope that such respect could grow on the basis of a remarkable proposition: "We hold these truths to be self-evident, that all men are created equal; that they are endowed by their Creator with certain unalienable rights; that among these are life, liberty, and the pursuit of happiness." The na-

tional government of the United States would preserve local and state authority but would guarantee individual rights. The nation would be strengthened by guarantees of difference.

"Out of Many" comes strength. That is the promise of America and the premise of this book. The underlying dialectic of American history, we believe, is that as a people we must locate our national unity in the celebration of the differences that exist among us; these differences can be our strength, as long as we affirm the promise of the Declaration. Protecting the "right to be different," in other words, is absolutely fundamental to the continued existence of democracy, and that right is best protected by the existence of strong and vital communities. We are bound together as a nation by the ideal of local and cultural differences protected by our common commitment to the values of the American Revolution.

Our history demonstrates that the promise has always been problematic. Centrifugal forces have been powerful in the American past, and at times the country seemed about to fracture into its component parts. Our transformation from a collection of groups and regions into a nation was marked by painful and often violent struggles.

Our most influential leaders have also sometimes suffered a crisis of faith in the American project of "liberty

Thomas Satterwhite Noble, *Last Sale of Slaves on the Courthouse Steps*, 1860, oil on canvas, Missouri Historical Society.

and justice for all." Thomas Jefferson not only believed in the inferiority of African Americans but feared that immigrants from outside the Anglo-American tradition might "warp and bias" the development of the nation "and render it a heterogeneous, incoherent, distracted mass." We have not always lived up to the American promise and there is a dark side to our history. It took the bloodiest war in American history to secure the human rights of African Americans, and the struggle for full equality for all our citizens has yet to be won.

The process by which diverse communities have come to share a set of common American values is one of the most fundamental aspects of our history. It did not occur, however, because of compulsory Americanization programs, but because of free public education, popular participation in democratic politics, and the impact of popular culture. Contemporary America does have a common culture: We share a commitment to freedom of thought and expression, we join in the aspirations to own our own homes and send our children to college, we laugh at the same television programs or video clips on You Tube.

To a degree that too few Americans appreciate, this common culture resulted from a complicated process of mutual discovery that took place when different ethnic and regional groups encountered one another.

The American educator John Dewey recognized this diversity early in the last century. "The genuine American, the typical American, is himself a hyphenated character," he declared, "international and interracial in his make-up." It was up to all Americans, Dewey argued, "is to see to it that the hyphen connects instead of separates." We, the authors of *Out of Many*, endorse Dewey's perspective. "Creation comes from the impact of diversity," the American philosopher Horace Kallen wrote about the same time. We also endorse Kallen's vision of the American promise: "A democracy of nationalities, cooperating voluntarily and autonomously through common institutions, . . . a multiplicity in a unity, an orchestration of mankind." And now, let the music begin.

# Out of Many

**Native Americans build** thatch houses beside a massive pyramid in "Community Life at Cahokia" by Michael Hampshire.

# 1

# A CONTINENT OF VILLAGES

## TO 1500

**WHAT EVENTS** led to the migration of Asian peoples into North America?

**IN WHAT** ways did native communities adapt to the distinct regions of North America?

**WHAT WERE** the consequences of the development of farming for native communities?

**WHAT IMPORTANT** differences were there between Indian societies in the Southwest, South, and Northeast on the eve of colonization?

# AMERICAN COMMUNITIES
## Cahokia: Thirteenth-Century Life on the Mississippi

AS THE SUN ROSE OVER THE RICH FLOODPLAIN, THE PEOPLE OF THE riverbank city set about their daily tasks. Some went to shops where they manufactured tools, crafted pottery, worked metal, or fashioned ornamental jewelry—goods destined to be exchanged in the far corners of the continent. Others left their densely populated neighborhoods for the outlying countryside, where in the summer heat they worked the seemingly endless fields that fed the city. From almost any point people could see the great temple that rose from the city center—the place where priests in splendid costumes acted out public rituals.

The Indian residents of this thirteenth-century city lived and worked on the east banks of the Mississippi River, across from present-day St. Louis, a place known today as **Cahokia**. In the thirteenth century, Cahokia was an urban cluster of twenty or thirty thousand people. Its farm fields were abundant with corn, beans, and squash. The temple, a huge earthwork pyramid, covered fifteen acres at its base and rose as high as a ten-story building. On top were the sacred quarters of priests and chiefs.

By the fourteenth century Cahokia had been abandoned, but its great central temple mound and dozens of smaller ones in the surrounding area, as well as hundreds of other large mounds throughout the Mississippi Valley, remained to puzzle the colonists and settlers who came in the eighteenth and nineteenth centuries.

The Europeans and Americans who explored and excavated those mounds were convinced they were the ruins of a vanished civilization, not the work of Indians. They were wrong. The ancestors of contemporary Native Americans constructed massive earthworks in the Mississippi Valley. The vast urban complex of Cahokia, which at its height stretched six miles along the Mississippi River, flourished from the tenth to the fourteenth centuries. Its residents were not nomadic hunters but farmers, participants in a complex agricultural culture archaeologists term "Mississippian." Hundreds of acres of crops fed the people of Cahokia, the largest urban community north of the Aztec civilization of central Mexico. Mississippian farmers constructed ingenious raised plots of land on which they heaped compost in wide ridges for improved

drainage and protection against unseasonable frosts. To their square houses of wood and mud they attached pens in which they kept flocks of domesticated turkeys and small herds of young deer, slaughtered for meat, feathers, and hide. Cahokia stood at the center of a long-distance trading system that linked it to other Indian communities over a vast area. Copper came from Lake Superior, mica from the southern Appalachians, conch shells from the Atlantic coast. Cahokia's specialized artisans were renowned for the manufacture of high-quality flint hoes, which were exported throughout the Mississippi Valley.

Archaeological evidence suggests that Cahokia was a city-state supported by tribute and taxation. Like the awe-inspiring public works of other early urban societies in other parts of the world, most notably the pyramids of ancient Egypt and the acropolis of Athens, the great temple mound of Cahokia was intended to showcase the city's wealth and power. The mounds and other colossal public works at Cahokia were the monuments of a society ruled by a class of elite leaders. From their residences atop the mound, priests and chiefs looked down on their subjects both literally and figuratively.

The 1848 Smithsonian report on Cahokia reflected the stereotypical American view that all Indian people were hunters. It is a view that persists. But the long history of North America before European colonization reveals that the native inhabitants developed a great variety of societies. Beginning as migrant hunting and gathering bands, they found ways to fine-tune their subsistence strategies to fit environmental possibilities and limitations. Communities in the highlands of Mexico invented systems of farming that spread to all the regions where cultivation was possible. Not only the Aztecs of Mexico and the Mayans of Central America but also communities in the Southwest and the Mississippi Valley constructed densely settled urban civilizations. North America before colonization was, as historian Howard R. Lamar phrases it, "a continent of villages," a land spread with thousands of communities. The wonders and mystery of the lost city of Cahokia are but one aspect of the little-understood history of the Indians of the Americas.

Cahokia

**Cahokia**   One of the largest urban centers created by Mississippian peoples, containing 30,000 residents in 1250.

# THE FIRST AMERICAN SETTLERS

"Why do you call us Indians?" a Massachusetts native complained to Puritan missionary John Eliot in 1646. Christopher Columbus, who mistook the Taino people of the Caribbean for the people of the East Indies, called them "**Indios**." Within a short time this Spanish word had passed into English as "Indians" and was commonly used to refer to all the native peoples of the Americas. Today anthropologists sometimes employ the term "Amerindians," and others use "Native Americans." But in the United States most of the descendants of the original inhabitants refer to themselves as "Indian people."

## WHO ARE THE INDIAN PEOPLE?

At the time of their first contacts with Europeans at the beginning of the sixteenth century, the inhabitants of the Western Hemisphere represented over 2,000 separate cultures, spoke several hundred different languages, and made their livings in scores of different environments. No single physical type characterized all the peoples of the Americas. Indeed, it was only when Europeans had compared Indian peoples with natives of other continents, such as Africans, that they seemed similar enough to be classified as a group.

Once Europeans realized that the Americas were in fact a "New World," rather than part of the Asian continent, a debate began over how people might have moved there from Europe and Asia, where (according to the Judeo-Christian Bible) God had created the first man and woman. In 1590, the Spanish Jesuit missionary Joseph de Acosta reasoned that because Old World animals were present in the Americas, they must have crossed by a land bridge that could have been used by humans as well.

## MIGRATION FROM ASIA

Acosta was the first to propose the Asian migration hypothesis that is widely accepted today. Analysis of the genetic drift of Siberian and American Indian populations suggests that migrants to North America began leaving Asia approximately 30,000 years ago (see Map 1.1).

The migration was possible because during the last Ice Age, from 70,000 to 10,000 years ago, huge glaciers locked up massive volumes of water, and sea levels were as much as 300 feet lower than they are today. Asia and North America, now separated by the Bering Straits, were joined by a huge subcontinent of ice-free, treeless grassland, which geologists have named **Beringia**.

**A forensic artist** reconstructed this bust from the skull of "Kennewick Man," whose skeletal remains were discovered along the Columbia River in 1996. Scientific testing suggested that the remains were more than nine thousand years old.

**MAP 1.1**
**Migration Routes from Asia to America**    During the Ice Age, Asia and North America were joined where the Bering Straits are today, forming a migration route for hunting peoples. These migrants began making their way to the heartland of the continent as much as 30,000 years ago.

WHAT GEOGRAPHICAL features shaped the dispersal of Asian migrants throughout the Americas?

**Athapascan**    A people that began to settle the forests in the northwestern area of North America around 5000 BCE.

Access to lands to the south, however, was blocked by huge ice sheets covering much of what is today Canada. How did the migrants get through those 2,000 miles of deep ice? The standard hypothesis is that with the warming of the climate and the end of the Ice Age, about 13,000 BCE (Before the Common Era), glacial melting created an ice-free corridor—an original "Pan-American Highway"—along the eastern front range of the Rocky Mountains. Using this thoroughfare, the hunters of big game reached the Great Plains as early as 11,000 BCE.

Recently, however, new archaeological finds along the Pacific coast of North and South America have complicated this hypothesis. Radiocarbon analysis of remains discovered at several newly excavated human sites suggested dates of 12,000 BCE or earlier. A number of archaeologists believe that the people who founded these settlements moved south in boats along a coastal route—an ancient "Pacific Coast Highway."

There were two later migrations into North America. About 5000 BCE the **Athapascan** people moved across Beringia and began to settle the forests in the northwestern area of the continent. Eventually groups of Athapascan speakers, the ancestors of the Navajos and Apaches, migrated across the Great Plains to the Southwest. A third and final migration began about 3000 BCE, long after Beringia had disappeared under rising seas, when a maritime hunting people crossed the Bering Straits in small boats.

## THE CLOVIS CULTURE: THE FIRST ENVIRONMENTAL ADAPTATION

The tools found at the earliest North American archaeological sites, crude stone or bone choppers and scrapers, are similar to artifacts from the same period found in Europe or Asia. About 11,000 years ago, however, ancient Americans developed a much more sophisticated style of making fluted blades and lance points, a tradition named "Clovis," after the location of the initial discovery near Clovis, New Mexico, in 1926. In the years since, archaeologists have unearthed Clovis stone tools at sites throughout the continent all dating within 1,000 or 2,000 years of one another, suggesting that the Clovis technology spread quickly throughout the continent.

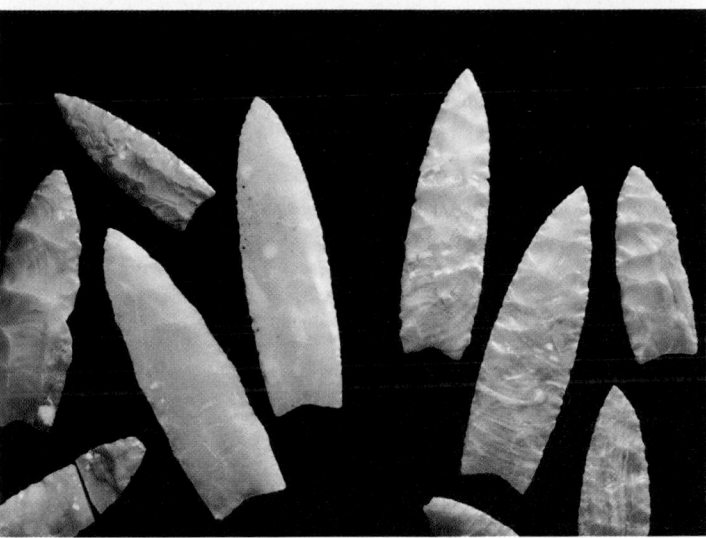

**These Clovis points** are typical of thousands that archaeologists have found at sites all over the continent, dating from a period about 12,000 years ago. When inserted in a spear shaft, these three- to six-inch fluted points made effective weapons for hunting mammoth and other big game. The ancient craftsmen who made these points often took advantage of the unique qualities of the stone they were working to enhance their aesthetic beauty.

The global warming trend that ended the Ice Age dramatically altered the North American climate. About 15,000 years ago the giant continental glaciers began to melt and the northern latitudes were colonized by plants, animals, and humans. Meltwater created the lake and river systems of today and raised the level of the surrounding seas.

## NEW WAYS OF LIVING ON THE LAND

These huge transformations produced new patterns of wind, rainfall, and temperature, reshaping the ecology of the entire continent and gradually producing the distinct North American regions of today (see Map 1.2). The great integrating force of a single continental climate faded, and with its passing the continental Clovis culture fragmented into a number of different regional patterns.

The retreat of the glaciers led to new ways of finding food: hunting in the Arctic, foraging in the arid deserts, fishing along the coasts, hunting and gathering in the forests. These developments took place roughly 10,000 to 2,500 years ago, during what archaeologists call the Archaic period (corresponding to the Mesolithic period in the archaeological chronology of Eurasia).

**Hunting Traditions** One of the most important effects of this massive climatic shift was the stress it placed on the big-game animals best suited to an Ice Age environment. The archaeological record documents the extinction of thirty-two classes of large New World mammals. Changing climatic conditions lowered the reproduction and survival rates of these large mammals, forcing hunting bands to intensify their hunting.

As the other large-mammal populations declined, hunters on the Great Plains concentrated on the herds of American bison (known more familiarly as buffalo). To hunt these animals, people needed a new weapon. In archaeological sites dating from about 10,000 years ago, a new style of tool is found mingled with animal remains. This technology, named "Folsom" (for the site of the first major find near Folsom, New Mexico) was a refinement of Clovis that featured more delicate but deadlier spear points. Hunters probably hurled the lances to which these points were attached with wooden spear-throwers, attaining far greater momentum than possible using their arms alone.

These archaeological finds suggest the growing complexity of early Indian communities. Hunters frequently stampeded herds of bison into canyon traps or over cliffs. Such tasks required a sophisticated division of labor among dozens of men and women and the cooperation of a number of communities. Taking food in such great quantities also suggests a knowledge of basic preservation techniques.

# MAP EXPLORATION

To explore an interactive version of this map, go to **http://www.prenhall.com/faraghertlc/map1.2**

**MAP 1.2**

**Native North American Culture Areas and Trade Networks, ca. 1400 CE**   By considering the ways in which Indian peoples developed distinct cultures and adapted to their environments, anthropologists developed the concept of "culture areas." Just as regions shaped the lifeways and history of Indian peoples, after the coming of the Europeans they nurtured the development of regional American cultures. And by determining the origin of artifacts found at ancient sites, historians have devised a conjectural map of Indian trade networks. Among large regional centers and smaller local ones, trade connected Indian peoples of many different communities and regions.

HOW DID the environment influence the relationship between trade and culture?

**Desert Culture**  In the Great Basin, the warming trend created a desert where once there had been enormous inland seas. Here Indian people developed what anthropologists call "**Desert culture**," a way of life based on the pursuit of small game and the intensified foraging of plant foods. Small communities of desert foragers migrated seasonally within a small range.

Archaeologists today find the artifacts of desert foragers in the caves and rock shelters in which they lived. In addition to stone tools, there are objects of wood, hide, and fiber, wonderfully preserved for thousands of years in the dry climate. Desert culture persisted into the nineteenth century among modern Shoshone and Ute communities.

The innovative practices of Desert culture gradually spread from the Great Basin to the Great Plains and the Southwest, where foraging for plant foods began to supplement hunting. About 6,000 years ago, these techniques were carried to California, where, in the natural abundance of the valleys and coasts, communities developed economies capable of supporting some of the densest populations and the first permanently settled villages in North America. Another dynamic center developed along the coast of the Pacific Northwest, where Indian communities developed a way of life based on the abundance of fish and sea mammals. Densely populated and permanently settled communities developed there as well.

**Forest Efficiency**  There were similar trends east of the Mississippi. In the centuries prior to colonization and settlement by Europeans, the whole of eastern North America was a vast forest. Communities of native people achieved a comfortable and secure life by developing a sophisticated knowledge of the rich and diverse available resources, a principle anthropologists term "**forest efficiency**."

**When, in 1927,** archaeologists at Folsom, New Mexico, uncovered this dramatic example of a projectile point embedded in the ribs of a long-extinct species of bison, it was the first proof that Indians had been in North America for many thousands of years.
Courtesy of the Denver Museum of Nature and Science.

**Desert culture**  A way of life based on hunting small game and the foraging of plant foods.

**Forest Efficiency**  Creation of a comfortable life through the development of a sophisticated knowledge of available resources.

Archaeological sites in the East suggest that during the late **Archaic period**, community populations grew and settlements became increasingly permanent, providing convincing evidence of the practicality of forest efficiency.

# THE DEVELOPMENT OF FARMING

A t the end of the Stone Age, communities in different regions of the world independently created systems of farming, each based on a unique staple crop: rice in Southeast Asia, wheat in the Middle East, potatoes in the Andean highlands of South America, and maize (what Americans call "corn") in Mexico. The dynamic center of this development in North America was in the highlands of Mexico, from which the new technology spread north and east.

## ORIGINS IN MEXICO

Archaeological evidence suggests that plant cultivation in the highlands of central Mexico began about 5,000 years ago. Ancient Mexicans developed crops that responded well to human care and produced larger quantities of food in a limited space than did plants growing in the wild. Maize was particularly productive.

As farming became increasingly important, it radically reshaped social life. Where a foraging society might require 100 square miles to support 100 people, a farming society required only a single square mile. Farming provided not only the incentive for larger families (more workers for the fields) but also the means to feed them. People became less mobile, built more substantial residences near their crops, and developed more effective means of storage. Villages grew into towns and eventually into large, densely settled communities like Cahokia. Autumn harvests had to be stored during winter months, and the storage and distribution of food had to be managed. The division of labor increased with the appearance of specialists like toolmakers, craft workers, administrators, priests, and rulers.

By 1000 BCE urban communities governed by permanent bureaucracies had begun to form in **Mesoamerica**, the region stretching from central Mexico to Central America. By the beginning of the first millennium CE (Common Era), highly productive farming was supporting complex urban civilizations in the Valley of Mexico (the location of present-day Mexico City), the Yucatan Peninsula, and other parts of Mesoamerica. Like many of the ancient civilizations of Asia and the Mediterranean, these Mesoamerican civilizations were characterized by the concentration of wealth and power in the hands of an elite class of priests and rulers, the construction of impressive temples and other public structures, and the development of systems of mathematics and astronomy and several forms of hieroglyphic writing. These civilizations also engaged in warfare between states and practiced ritual human sacrifice.

The great city of Teotihuacan in the Valley of Mexico, which emerged about 100 BCE, had a population of as many as 200,000 at the height of its power around 500 CE. Teotihuacan's elite class of religious and political leaders controlled an elaborate state-sponsored trading system that stretched from

**Mesoamerican maize cultivation**, as illustrated by an Aztec artist for the *Florentine Codex*, a book prepared a few years after the Spanish conquest. The peoples of Mesoamerica developed a greater variety of cultivated crops than those found in any other region in the world, and their agricultural productivity helped sustain one of the world's great civilizations.

Image #1739-3, courtesy the Library, American Museum of Natural History.

**Archaic period**   The period roughly 10,000 to 2,500 years ago marked by the retreat of glaciers.

**Mesoamerica**   The region stretching from central Mexico to Central America.

present-day Arizona to Central America and may have included coastal shipping connections with the civilizations of Peru.

Teotihuacan began to decline in the sixth century, and by the eighth century it was mostly abandoned. A new empire, that of the Toltecs, dominated central Mexico from the tenth to the twelfth centuries. By the fourteenth century a people known as the **Aztecs**, migrants from the north, had settled in the Valley of Mexico and begun a dramatic expansion into a formidable imperial power (see Chapter 2).

The Mayan peoples of the Yucatan Peninsula developed a group of competing city-states that flourished from about 300 BCE until 900 CE. Their achievements included advanced writing and calendar systems and a sophisticated knowledge of mathematics.

## INCREASING SOCIAL COMPLEXITY

In a few areas, farming truly did result in a revolutionary change in Indian communities, producing urban civilizations like those in Mesoamerica or on the banks of the Mississippi at Cahokia. It is likely that among the first social transformations was the development of significantly more elaborate systems of kinship. Greater population density prompted families to group themselves into clans, and separate clans gradually became responsible for different social, political, or ritual functions. Clans may have been an important mechanism for binding together the people of several communities into larger social units based on ethnic, linguistic, and territorial unity. These "tribes" were headed by leaders or chiefs from honored clans, often advised by councils of elders.

Chiefs' primary functions were the supervision of the economy, the collection and storage of the harvest, and the distribution of food to the clans. Differences in wealth, though small by the standards of modern societies, might develop between the families of a farming tribe. These inequalities were kept in check by redistribution according to principles of sharing similar to those operating in foraging communities. Nowhere in North America did Indian cultures develop a concept of the private ownership of land or other resources, which were usually considered the common resource of the people and were worked collectively.

Indian communities practiced a rather strict division of labor according to gender. In foraging communities, hunting was generally men's work, while the gathering of food and the maintenance of home-base camps were the responsibility of women. The development of farming may have challenged that pattern. Where hunting remained an important activity, women took responsibility for the growing of crops. But in areas like Mexico, where communities were almost totally dependent on cultivated crops for their survival, both men and women worked the fields.

In most North American Indian farming communities, women and men belonged to separate social groupings, each with its own rituals and lore. Membership in these gender societies was one of the most important elements of a person's identity. Marriage ties, on the other hand, were relatively weak, and in most Indian communities divorce was a simple matter: the couple separated without a great deal of ceremony, and the children almost always remained with the mother.

Farming communities were far more complex than foraging communities, but they were also less stable. Growing populations demanded increasingly large surpluses of food, and this need often led to social conflict and warfare. Moreover, farming systems were especially vulnerable to changes in climate, such as drought, as well as to crises of their own making, such as soil depletion or erosion.

**The creation of** man and woman depicted on a pot (dated about 1000 CE) from the ancient villages of the Mimbres River of southwestern New Mexico, the area of Mogollon culture. Mimbres pottery is renowned for its spirited artistry. Such artifacts were usually intended as grave goods to honor the dead.

Mimbres black on white bowl, with painted representations of man and woman under a blanket. Grant County, New Mexico. Diam. 26.7 cm. Courtesy National Museum of the American Indian, Smithsonian Institution, 24/3198.

## QUICK REVIEW

**Indian Agrarian Society**

◆ Families grouped themselves in clans which, in turn, were grouped in tribes.

◆ Chiefs supervised economic activities.

◆ No concept of private ownership of land.

◆ Strict division of labor according to gender.

**Aztecs**   A warrior people who dominated the Valley of Mexico from 1100–1521.

## THE RESISTED REVOLUTION

Some scholars describe the transition to farming as a revolution. Their argument is that farming offered such obvious advantages that communities rushed to adopt it. But there is very little evidence to support the notion that farming was a clearly superior way of life. Anthropologists have demonstrated that farmers work considerably longer and harder than do foragers. Moreover, farmers depend on a relatively narrow selection of plants and animals for food and are vulnerable to famine. Foragers experience periods of want, but they have a much higher probability of securing food under stressful conditions. Finally, compared to foragers, farmers experienced degenerative conditions of the spine (probably the result of hard labor), a threefold increase in iron-deficiency anemia, and twice the amount of tooth decay and loss.

Moreover, ignorance of cultivation was never the reason communities failed to take up farming. All foraging cultures understand a great deal about plant reproduction. When gathering wild rice, the Menominee Indians of the northern forests of Wisconsin purposely allowed some of it to fall back into the water to ensure a crop for the next season. Paiutes of the Great Basin systematically irrigated stands of their favorite wild food sources. Cultures in different regions assessed the relative advantages and disadvantages of adopting farming. In California and the Pacific Northwest, acorn gathering or salmon fishing made the cultivation of food crops seem a waste of time. In the Great Basin, there were attempts to farm but without much success. Before the invention of modern irrigation systems, which require sophisticated engineering, only the Archaic Desert culture could prevail in this harsh environment.

# FARMING IN EARLY NORTH AMERICA

Maize farming spread north from Mexico into the area now part of the United States in the first millenuim BCE. Over time maize was adapted to a range of climates and its cultivation spread to all the temperate regions.

## FARMERS OF THE SOUTHWEST

Farming communities began to emerge in the arid Southwest during the first millennium BCE. Among the first to develop a settled farming way of life was a culture known to archaeologists as Mogollon. These people farmed maize, beans, squash, and constructed ingenious food storage pits in permanent village sites along what is today the southern Arizona–New Mexico border.

During the same centuries, a culture known as Hohokam ("those who are gone," in the language of the modern tribes of the region) flourished in the region along the floodplain of the Salt and Gila Rivers in southern Arizona. The Hohokam, who lived in farming villages, built and maintained the first irrigation system in America north of Mexico, channeling river water through five hundred miles of canals to water desert fields of maize, beans, squash, tobacco, and cotton.

## THE ANASAZIS

The best-known ancient farming culture of the Southwest is the Anasazi, which developed around the first century CE in the Four Corners area, where the states of Arizona, New Mexico, Utah, and Colorado meet on the great plateau of the Colorado River. Around 750 CE, possibly in response to population pressure and an

WHAT WERE the consequences of the development of farming for native communities?

myhistorylab
Review Summary

**Cliff Palace, at** Mesa Verde National Park in southwest Colorado, was created 900 years ago when the Anasazis left the mesa tops and moved into more secure and inaccessible cliff dwellings. Facing southwest, the building gained heat from the rays of the low afternoon sun in winter, and overhanging rock protected the structure from rain, snow, and the hot midday summer sun. The numerous round kivas, each covered with a flat roof originally, suggest that Cliff Palace may have had a ceremonial importance.

increasingly dry climate, the residents of communities there began shifting from pit-house villages to densely populated, multistoried apartment complexes that the Spanish invaders called "pueblos." These farmers grew high-yield varieties of maize in terraced fields irrigated by canals flowing from mountain catchment basins. To supplement this vegetable diet, they hunted animals for their meat, using the bow and arrow that first appeared in the region in the sixth century.

The Anasazis faced a major challenge in the thirteenth and fourteenth centuries. The arid climate became even drier, and growing populations had to redouble their efforts to improve food production, building increasingly complex irrigation canals, dams, and terraced fields. A devastating drought resulted in repeated crop failures and eventual famine. The ecological crisis was heightened by the arrival in the fourteenth century of Athapascan migrants, ancestors of the Navajos and the Apaches. Athapascans raided Anasazi farming communities, taking food, goods, and possibly slaves. Gradually Anasazi communities abandoned the Four Corners area altogether, most resettling along the Rio Grande, joining with local residents to form the Pueblo communities that were living there when the Spanish arrived.

## FARMERS OF THE EASTERN WOODLANDS

Archaeologists date the beginning of the farming culture of eastern North America, known as Woodland culture, from the first appearances of pottery in the region about 3,000 years ago. Woodland culture was based on a sophisticated way of life that combined gathering and hunting with the cultivation of a few local crops. Woodland people began cultivating maize during the first millennium CE, but even before that they had begun to adopt an increasingly settled existence and a more complex social organization, evidenced by complex earthen constructions.

Mound building was also a characteristic activity of the peoples living in the Ohio Valley during this period. The people of a culture known as Adena lived in semipermanent villages and constructed large burial mounds during the first millennium BCE. They were succeeded by a culture called Hopewell, which honored the dead with even larger and more elaborate burial mounds.

**The Great Serpent** Mound in southern Ohio, the shape of an uncoiling snake more than 1,300 feet long, is the largest effigy earthwork in the world. Monumental public works like these suggest the high degree of social organization of the Mississippian people.

**This bottle in** the shape of a nursing mother (dated about 1300 BCE) was found at a Mississippian site. Historians can only speculate about the thoughts and feelings of the Mississippians, but such works of art are testimonials to the universal human emotion of maternal affection.

"Nursing Mother Effigy Bottle." From the Whelpley Collection at the St. Louis Science Center. Photograph © 1985 the Detroit Institute of Arts.

## MISSISSIPPIAN SOCIETY

The Hopewell culture collapsed in the fifth century CE, perhaps as a result of an ecological crisis brought on by shifting climate patterns. Over the next several centuries, however, a number of important technological innovations were introduced in the East. The bow and arrow, developed first on the Great Plains, appeared east of the Mississippi in about the seventh century, greatly increasing the efficiency of hunting. At about the same time maize farming spread widely through the East. Indian farmers developed a new variety (known today as Northern Flint) that matured in a short enough time to make it suitable for cultivation in temperate northern latitudes. A shift from digging sticks to flint hoes also took place about this time, further increasing the productive potential of maize farming.

On the basis of these innovations, a powerful new culture known as Mississippian arose in the seventh or eighth century CE. The peoples of Mississippian culture were master maize farmers living in permanent community sites along the floodplains of the Mississippi Valley. Cahokia was the largest and most spectacular, with its monumental temple mounds, its residential neighborhoods, and its surrounding farmlands. But there were dozens of other urban communities, each with thousands of residents. Archaeologists have excavated sites on the Arkansas River near Spiro, Oklahoma; on the Black Warrior River at Moundville, Alabama; at Hiawassee Island on the Tennessee River; and along the Etowah and Okmulgee Rivers in Georgia. The Great Serpent Mound, the largest effigy earthwork in the world, was constructed by Mississippian peoples in southern Ohio.

## THE POLITICS OF WARFARE AND VIOLENCE

These centers, linked by the vast river transportation system of the Mississippi River and its many tributaries, became the earliest city-states north of Mexico, hierarchical chiefdoms that extended political control over the farmers of the surrounding countryside (see Map 1.3 for an illustration of

# MAP EXPLORATION

To explore an interactive version of this map, go to **http://www.prenhall.com/faraghertlc/map1.3**

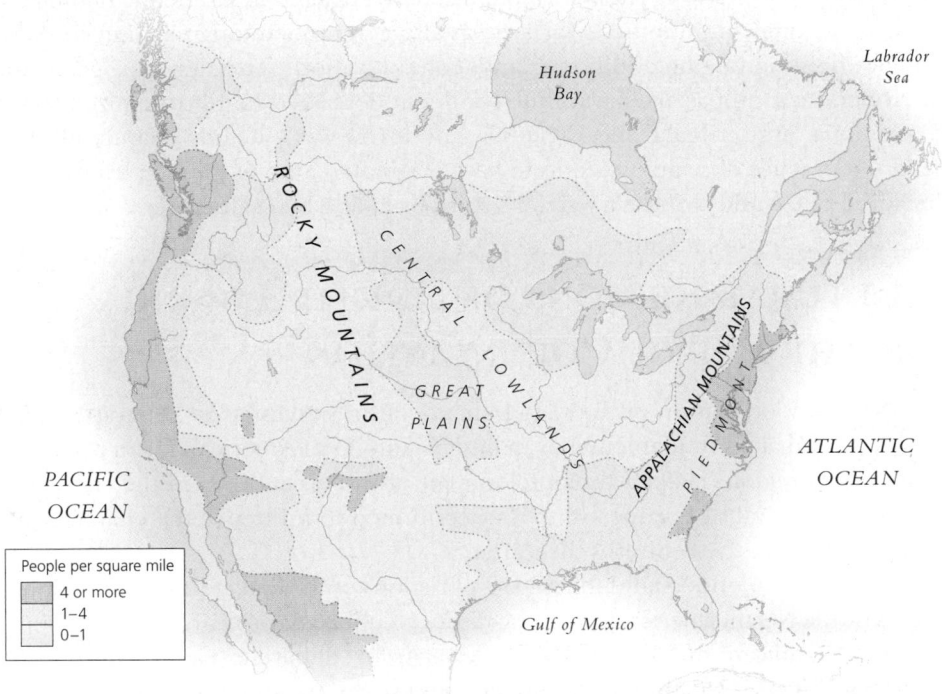

**MAP 1.3**

**Population Density of Indian Societies in the Fifteenth Century**    Based on what is called the "carrying capacity" of different subsistence strategies—the population density they could support—historical demographers have mapped the hypothetical population density of Indian societies in the fifteenth century, before the era of European colonization. Populations were densest in farming societies or in coastal areas with marine resources and sparsest in extreme environments like the Great Basin.

WHY WERE some regions more populated than others?

trade networks). With continued population growth, these cities engaged in vigorous and probably violent competition for the limited space along the rivers. It may have been the need for more orderly ways of allocating territories that stimulated the evolution of political hierarchies. The tasks of preventing local conflict, storing large food surpluses, and redistributing foodstuffs from farmers to artisans and elites required a leadership class with the power to command. Mound building and the use of tribute labor in the construction of other public works testified to the power of chiefs, who lived in sumptuous quarters atop the mounds.

Mississippian culture reached its height between the eleventh and thirteenth centuries CE, the same period in which the Anasazi culture constructed its desert cities. Both groups adapted to their own environment the technology that was spreading northward from Mexico. Both developed impressive artistic traditions, and their feats of engineering reflect the beginnings of science and technology. They were complex societies characterized by urbanism, social stratification, craft specialization, and regional trade—except for the absence of a writing system, all the traits of European civilization.

Warfare among Indian peoples certainly predated the colonial era. Organized violence was probably rare among hunting bands, which could seldom manage more than a small raid against an enemy. Certain hunting peoples, though, such as the southward-moving Athapascans, must have engaged in systematic raiding of settled farming communities. Warfare was also common among farming confederacies fighting to gain additional lands for cultivation. The first Europeans to arrive in the southeastern part of the continent described highly organized combat among large tribal armies. The bow and arrow was a deadly weapon of war, and the practice of scalping seems to have originated among warring tribes, who believed one could capture a warrior's spirit by taking his scalp lock.

# CULTURAL REGIONS OF NORTH AMERICA ON THE EVE OF COLONIZATION

An appreciation of the ways human cultures adapted to geography and climate is fundamental to an understanding of American history, for just as regions shaped the development of Indian cultures in the centuries before the arrival of Europeans, so they continued to influence the character of American life in the centuries thereafter.

In order to understand the impact of regions on Indian cultures, anthropologists divide North America into several distinct "culture areas" within which groups shared a significant number of cultural traits: Arctic, Subarctic, Great Basin, Great Plains, California, Northwest, Plateau, Southwest, South, and Northeast.

## THE POPULATION OF INDIAN AMERICA

Determining the size of early human population is a tricky business, and estimates vary greatly, but there seems to be general agreement among historical demographers that the population of the North American continent (excluding Mesoamerica) numbered between 5 and 10 million at the time of the first European voyages of discovery. Millions more lived in the complex societies of Mexico and Central America (estimates run from 5 to 25 million). The population of the Western Hemisphere as a whole may have numbered 50 million or more, the same order of magnitude as Europe's population at the time.

Demographers may disagree about numbers but agree that population varied tremendously by cultural region. The largest populations of the continent were concentrated in the farming regions of the Southwest, South, and Northeast. These were the areas in which European explorers, conquerors, and colonists concentrated their first efforts, and they deserve more detailed examination (see Map 1.4).

## THE SOUTHWEST

The single overwhelming fact of life in the Southwest is aridity. Summer rains average only ten to twenty inches annually, and on much of the dry desert cultivation is impossible. A number of rivers, however, flow out of the pine-covered mountain plateaus, making possible irrigation farming along their courses.

On the eve of European colonization, Indian farmers in the Southwest had been cultivating their fields for nearly 3,000 years. In the floodplain of the Gila and Salt Rivers lived the Pimas and Tohono O'Odhams, descendants of the ancient Hohokam culture, and along the Colorado River, even on the floor of the Grand

---

**WHAT IMPORTANT** differences were there between Indian societies in the Southwest, South, and Northeast on the eve of colonization?

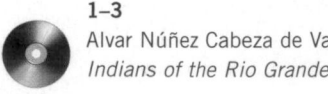
**Review Summary**

---

**1–3**
Alvar Núñez Cabeza de Vaca,
*Indians of the Rio Grande*

# An Early European Image
# of Native Americans

From the very beginning of Europeans' contact with native American peoples, they depicted Indians as savages rather than as peoples with complex cultures. This woodcut by German artist Johann Froschauer was included in a 1505 German edition of Amerigo Vespucci's account of his voyage to the New World in 1499 and is among the very first images of Native Americans published. The image is a complete fantasy, lacking any ethnographic authenticity. Indians gather for a feast on the beach. The caption in the original publication read, in part: "The people are naked, handsome, brown, well-shaped in body. ... No one has anything, but all things are in common. And the men have as wives those who please them, be they mothers, sisters, or friends; therein they make no distinction. They also fight with each other; and they eat each other, even those who are slain, and hang the flesh of them in the smoke." A cannibalized body is being devoured. A couple is kissing. Women display their breasts. The image sent a powerful message: that some of the strongest taboos of Europeans—nakedness, sexual promiscuity, and cannibalism—were practiced by the people of the New World. It is an unrelentingly negative picture. The arrival of European vessels in the background of the image suggests that all this was about to change. Images like these continued to dominate the depiction of Indians for the next four hundred years, and were used as justifications for conquest. ■

**HOW ARE** European stereotypes of savage people conveyed visually in this image?

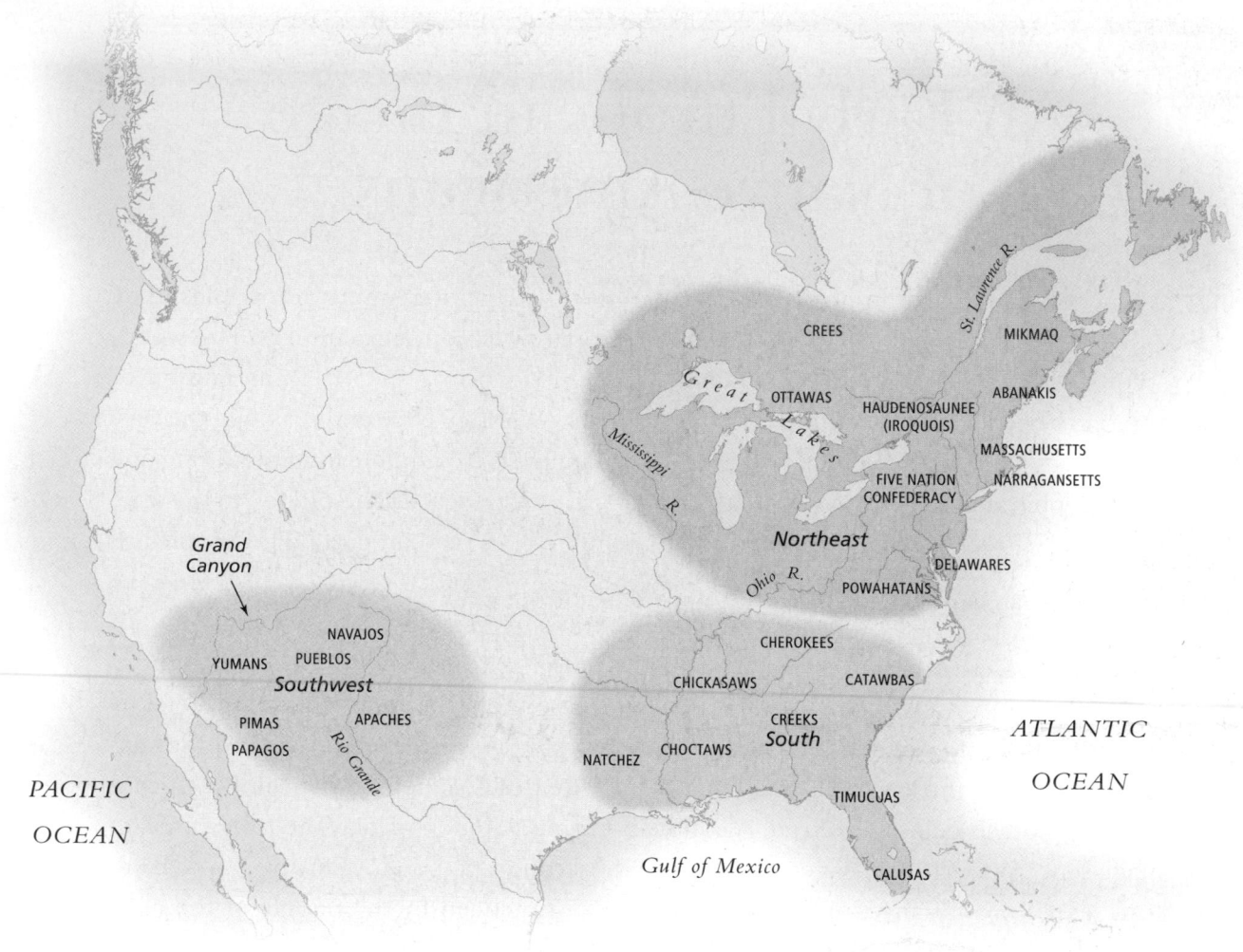

**MAP 1.4**

**Indian Groups in the Areas of First Contact**   The Southwest was populated by desert farmers like the Pimas, Tohono O'Odhams, Yumans, and Pueblos, as well as by nomadic hunters and raiders like the Apaches and Navajos. On the eve of colonization, the Indian societies of the South shared many traits of the complex Mississippian farming culture. The Indians of the Northeast were mostly village peoples.

HOW DID the lack of rain shape the lives of the Indians of the Southwest?

Canyon, the Yuman peoples worked small irrigated fields. In their oasis communities, desert farmers cultivated corn, beans, squash, sunflowers, and cotton, which they traded throughout the Southwest. Often described as individualists, desert farmers lived in dispersed settlements that the Spanish called **rancherias**, their dwellings separated by as much as a mile. That way, say the Pimas, people avoid getting on each other's nerves. Rancherias were governed by councils of adult men whose decisions required unanimous consent, although a headman was chosen to manage the irrigation works.

East of the Grand Canyon lived the Pueblo peoples. Although speaking several languages, the Pueblos had a great deal in common, most notably their commitment to communal village life. A strict communal code of behavior that regulated personal conduct was enforced by a maze of matrilineal clans and secret religious societies; unique combinations of these clans and societies formed the governing systems of different Pueblo villages. Seasonal public ceremonies in the

**Rancherias**   Dispersed settlements of Indian farmers in the Southwest.

**"The New Queen** Being Taken to the King," engraved by Theodor de Bry in the sixteenth century from a drawing by Jacques le Moyne, an early French colonist of Florida. The communities of Florida were hierarchical, with classes and hereditary chiefs, some of whom were women. Here, le Moyne depicted a "queen" being carried on an ornamental litter by men of rank.

Neg. No. 324281, Photographed by Rota, Engraving by de Bry. American Museum of Natural History Library.

village squares included singing and chanting, dancing, colorful impersonations of the ancestral spirits called *kachinas*, and the comic antics of clowns who mocked in slapstick style those who did not conform to the communal ideal.

The Pueblos inhabit the oldest continuously occupied towns in the United States. The village of Oraibi, Arizona, dates from the twelfth century, when the Hopis ("peaceful ones") founded it in the isolated central mesas of the Colorado Plateau. Using dry-farming methods and drought-resistant plants, the Hopis produced rich harvests of corn and squash amid shifting sand dunes. On a mesa top about fifty miles southwest of present-day Albuquerque, New Mexico, Anasazi immigrants from Mesa Verde built Acoma, the "sky city," in the late thirteenth century. The Pueblo peoples established approximately seventy other villages over the next two centuries; fifty of these were still in existence in the seventeenth century when the Spanish founded Santa Fé, and two dozen survive today, including the large Indian towns of Laguna, Isleta, Santo Domingo, Jémez, San Felipe, and Taos.

The Athapascans, more recent immigrants to the Southwest, also lived in the arid deserts and mountains. They hunted and foraged, traded meat and medicinal herbs with farmers, and often raided and plundered these same villages and rancherias. One group of Athapascans, the Apaches, continued to maintain

## QUICK REVIEW

**The South**

- ◆ Mild, moist climate ideal for farming.
- ◆ Indian peoples of the South farmed, fished, and hunted.
- ◆ Peoples of the South shared agricultural festivals.

# OVERVIEW | Origins of Some Indian Tribal Names

| | |
|---|---|
| **Cherokee** | A corruption of the Choctaw *chiluk-ki*, meaning "cave people," an allusion to the many caves in the Cherokee homeland in the highlands of present-day Georgia. The Cherokees called themselves *Ani-Yun-Wiya*, or "real people." |
| **Cheyenne** | From the Sioux *Sha-hiyena*, "people of strange speech." The Cheyennes of the Northern Plains called themselves *Dzi-tsistas*, meaning "our people." |
| **Hopi** | A shortening of the name the Hopis of northern Arizona use for themselves, *Hópitu*, which means "peaceful ones." |
| **Mohawk** | From the Algonquian *Mohawaúuck*, meaning "man-eaters." The Mohawks of the upper Hudson Valley in New York called themselves *Kaniengehaga*, "people of the place of the flint." |
| **Pawnee** | From the Pawnee term *paríki*, which describes a distinctive style of dressing the hair with paint and fat to make it stand erect like a horn. The Pawnees, whose homeland was the Platte River valley in present-day Nebraska, called themselves *Chahiksichahiks*, "men of men." |

**Overview:** *Origins of Some Indian Tribal Names*

their nomadic ways. But another group, known as the Navajos, gradually adopted the farming and handicraft skills of their Pueblo neighbors.

## THE SOUTH

The South enjoys a mild, moist climate with short winters and long summers, ideal for farming. From the Atlantic and Gulf Coasts, a broad fertile plain extends inland to the Piedmont, a plateau separating the coastal plains from the Appalachian Mountains. The upper courses of the waterways originating in the Appalachian highlands offered ample rich bottom land for farming. The extensive forests, mostly of yellow pine, offered abundant animal resources. In the sixteenth century, large populations of Indian peoples farmed this rich land, fishing or hunting local fauna to supplement their diets. They lived in communities ranging from villages of twenty or so dwellings to large towns of a thousand or more inhabitants (see Map 1.4).

Mississippian cultural patterns continued among many of the peoples of the South. Along the waterways, many farming towns were organized into chiefdoms. Because most of these groups were decimated by disease in the first years of colonization, they are poorly documented. Archaeologists have excavated sites on the east bank of the Mississippi, in what is now Arkansas, inhabited by the Caddo people. The evidence suggests that in the fifteenth century they lived in complex ranked communities, built monumental temple mounds, and counted a population of more than 200,000. There is historical evidence about the Natchez, who survived into the eighteenth century before being defeated and dispersed in a war with the French. They too lived on the Mississippi, on the opposite bank from the Caddos, where they farmed the rich floodplains. The Natchez were also a ranked society, with a small group of nobility ruling over the majority. Persistent territorial conflict with other confederacies elevated warriors to an honored status. Public torture and human sacrifice of enemies were common.

These chiefdoms were rather unstable. Under the pressure of climate change, population growth, and warfare, many were weakened and others collapsed. As a result, thousands of people left behind the grand mounds and earthworks and migrated to the woodlands and hill country, where they took up hunting and foraging, returning to the tried and true methods of "forest efficiency." They formed communities and banded together in confederacies, which were less centralized and more egalitarian than the Mississippian chiefdoms and would prove considerably more resilient to conquest.

Among the most prominent of these new ethnic groups were a people in present-day Mississippi and Alabama who came to be known as the Choctaws. Another group in western Tennessee became known as the Chickasaws, and another people in Georgia later became known as the Creeks. On the mountain plateaus lived the Cherokees, the single largest confederacy, which included more than sixty towns. For these groups, farming was somewhat less important, hunting somewhat more so. There were no ruling classes or kings, and leaders included women as well as men. Women controlled household and village life and were influential in the matrilineal clans that linked communities together. Councils of elderly men governed the confederacies but were joined by clan matrons for annual meetings at the central council house.

## THE NORTHEAST

The Northeast, the colder sector of the eastern woodlands, has a varied geography of coastal plains and mountain highlands, great rivers, lakes, and valleys. In the first millennium CE, farming became the main support of the Indian economy in those places where the growing season was long enough to bring a crop of corn to maturity. In such areas of the Northeast, along the coasts and in the river valleys, Indian populations were large and dense (see Map 1.4).

The Iroquois of present-day Ontario and upstate New York have lived in the Northeast for at least 4,500 years and were among the first northeastern peoples to adopt cultivation.

Population growth and the resulting intensification of farming in Iroquoia stimulated the development of chiefdoms there as it did elsewhere. By the eleventh century, several centers of population, each in a separate watershed, had coalesced from east to west across upstate New York. These were the five Iroquois chiefdoms or nations: the Mohawks, Oneidas, Onondagas, Cayugas, and Senecas. Oral histories collected from Iroquois speakers during the nineteenth century remember this as an era of persistent violence, possibly the consequence of conflicts over territory.

To control this violence, the five nations established a confederacy. The Iroquois called their confederacy Haudenosaunee, meaning "people of the longhouse." Each nation, they said, occupied a separate hearth but acknowledged a common mother. As in the longhouse, women played important roles in the confederacy, choosing male leaders who would represent their lineages and chiefdom on the Iroquois council. The confederacy suppressed violence among its members but did not hesitate to encourage war against neighboring Iroquoian speakers, such as the Hurons or the Eries, who constructed defensive confederacies of their own at about the same time.

The other major language group of the Northeast was Algonquian, whose speakers divided among at least fifty distinct cultures. The Algonquian peoples

**This deerskin cape,** embroidered with shells by an Indian craftsman, is thought to be the chief's mantle that Powhatan, leader of a confederacy of Algonquian villages in the Chesapeake region, gave to an English captain as part of an exchange of presents in 1608. The animal effigies are suggestive of the complex of religious beliefs centering on the relationship of hunters to their prey.

Ashmolean Museum, Oxford, England, U.K.

### QUICK REVIEW

**The Northeast**
- Varied geography of plains, mountains, rivers, lakes, and valleys.
- The Iroquois have lived in the region for 4,500 years.
- Population growth and intensification of farming led to the development of chiefdoms.

 **1-10**
Thomas Harriot, *The Algonquian Peoples of the Atlantic Coast*

## CHRONOLOGY

| | | | |
|---|---|---|---|
| 30,000 BCE | First humans populate Beringia | 1000 BCE | First urban communities in Mexico |
| 13,000 BCE | Global warming trend begins | 200 BCE–400 CE | Hopewell culture flourishes |
| 12,500 BCE | Monte Verde site in southern Chile flourishes | 650 | Bow and arrow, flint hoes, and Northern Flint corn in the Northeast |
| 10,000 BCE | Clovis technology | 775–1150 | Hohokam culture flourishes |
| 9000 BCE | Extinction of big-game animals | 1000 | Tobacco in use throughout North America |
| 8000 BCE | Beginning of the Archaic period | | |
| 7000 BCE | First cultivation of plants in the Mexican highlands | 1142 | Founding of Haudenosaunee Confederacy |
| 5000 BCE | Athapascan migration to America begins | 1150 | Founding of Hopi village of Oraibi, oldest continuously occupied town in the United States |
| 4000 BCE | First settled communities along the Pacific coast | 1200 | High point of Mississippian and Anasazi cultures |
| 3000 BCE | Inuit, Yupik, and Aleut migrations begin | 1276 | Severe drought begins in the Southwest |
| 1500–1000 BCE | Maize and other Mexican crops introduced into the Southwest | 1300 | Arrival of Athapascans in the Southwest |

north of the Great Lakes and in northern New England were hunters and foragers, organized into bands with loose ethnic affiliations. Several of these peoples, including the Míkmaq, Crees, Montagnais, and Ojibwas (also known as the Chippewas), were the first to become involved in the fur trade with European newcomers. Among the Algonquians of the Atlantic coast from present-day Massachusetts south to Virginia, as well as among those in the Ohio Valley, farming led to the development of settlements as densely populated as those of the Iroquois.

In contrast to the Iroquois, most Algonquian peoples were patrilineal. In general, they lived in less extensive dwellings and in smaller villages, often without palisade fortifications. Although Algonquian communities were relatively autonomous, they began to form confederacies during the fifteenth and sixteenth

**The Hiawatha wampum** belt of the Haudenosaunee or Iroquois Five Nation Confederacy is exquisitely constructed of nearly seven thousand purple and white drilled shell beads, woven together with buckskin thongs and hemp thread. It is a ceremonial artifact, a symbol of the unity of the five Iroquois nations. With the central tree or heart pointed up, the first two squares on the right represent the Mohawk and Oneida, the tree stands for the Onondaga, where the council met, and the third and fourth squares for the Cayuga and Seneca nations. The belt itself dates from the early eighteenth century, but the design is thought to have originated with the Confederacy itself, in the twelfth century CE.

centuries. Among these groupings were those of the Massachusetts, Narragansetts, and Pequots of New England; the peoples of the Delaware Valley and Chesapeake Bay on the mid-Atlantic coast; and the Shawnees, Miamis, Kickapoos, and Potawatomis of the Ohio Valley.

## CONCLUSION

Over the thousands of years that elapsed between the initial settlement of North America and the arrival of Europeans at the end of the fifteenth century, Indian peoples developed dozens of distinctive cultures, each fine-tuned to the geographic and climatic possibilities and limitations of their environments. In the northern forests, they hunted game and perfected the art of processing furs and hides. Along the coasts and rivers they harvested the abundant runs of fish and learned to navigate the waters with sleek and graceful boats. In the arid Southwest, they mastered irrigation farming and made the deserts bloom, while in the humid Southeast, they mastered the large-scale production of crops that sustained large cities with sophisticated political systems. The ruins of the ancient city of Cahokia provide dramatic evidence that North America was not the "virgin" continent Europeans proclaimed it to be. Indians had transformed the natural world, making it into a human landscape.

## REVIEW QUESTIONS

1. List the evidence for the hypothesis that the Americas were settled by migrants from Asia.

2. Discuss the impact of environmental change and human hunting on the big-game populations of North America.

3. Review the principal regions of the North American continent and the human adaptations that made social life possible in each of them.

4. Define the concept of "forest efficiency." How does it help to illuminate the major development of the Archaic period?

5. Why did the development of farming lead to increasing social complexity? Discuss the reasons why organized political activity began in farming societies.

6. What were the hunting and agrarian traditions? In what ways did the religious beliefs of Indian peoples reflect their environmental adaptations?

7. What factors led to the organization of the Iroquois Five Nation Confederacy?

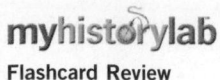
Flashcard Review

## KEY TERMS

**Archaic period** (p. 8)   **Desert culture** (p. 7)
**Athapascan** (p. 4)   **Forest Efficiency** (p. 7)
**Aztecs** (p. 9)   **Indios** (p. 3)
**Beringia** (p. 3)   **Mesoamerica** (p. 8)
**Cahokia** (p. 2)   **Rancherias** (p. 16)

## RECOMMENDED READING

Colin G. Calloway, *One Vast Winter Count: The Native American West Before Lewis and Clark* (2003). A masterful synthesis that emphasizes the continuities between the precolonial and colonial history of North America.

Sally Kitt Chappell, *Cahokia: Mirror of the Cosmos* (2002). An engaging, comprehensive, and thoughtful account of America's most impressive ancient monument.

Tom D. Dillehay, *The Settling of the Americas: A New Prehistory* (2000). A summary of the most recent archaeological findings, suggesting a much earlier migration to the Americas. For the newest discoveries, see recent issues and websites of *National Geographic* and *Scientific American.*

Patricia Galloway, *Choctaw Genesis, 1500–1700* (1995). A path-breaking work that uses both archaeological and written evidence to tie together the precolonial and colonial periods of a tribal people of the South.

Alvin M. Josephy Jr., ed., *America in 1492* (1992). Important essays by leading scholars of the North American Indian experience. Includes beautiful illustrations and maps as well as an excellent bibliography.

Alice Beck Kehoe, *America Before the European Invasions* (2002). A major new synthesis of the history of North America in the centuries before 1492.

Charles C. Mann, *1491: New Revelations of the Americas Before Columbus* (2005). A popular and engaging journalistic account of the increasing recognition among historians "that the Western Hemisphere played a role in the human story just as interesting and important as that of the Eastern Hemisphere."

Stephen Plog, *Ancient Peoples of the American Southwest* (1998). Covers the shift to agriculture with a focus on both the costs and the benefits. An accessible text with wonderful photographs.

Robert Silverberg, *Mound Builders of Ancient America: The Archaeology of a Myth* (1968). A history of opinion and theory about the mound builders.

William C. Sturtevant, general editor, *Handbook of North American Indians*, 20 vols. proposed (1978– ). The most comprehensive collection of the best current scholarship. When completed the series will include a volume for each of the culture regions of North America, plus volumes on origins, Indian-white relations, languages, and art; a biographical dictionary; and a general index.

David Hurst Thomas, *Skull Wars: Kennewick Man, Archaeology, and the Battle for Native American Identity* (2000). A page-turner that details the controversy over the discovery of "Kennewick Man" and changing ideas about ancient North American history.

Russell Thornton, *American Indian Holocaust and Survival: A Population History since 1492* (1987). The best introduction to the historical demography of North America. Provides a judicious review of all the evidence in a field of considerable controversy.

For study resources for this chapter, go to **www.myhistorylab.com** and choose *Out of Many, Teaching and Learning Classroom Edition.* You will find a wealth of study and review material for this chapter, including pretests and posttests, customized study plan, key-term review flash cards, interactive map and document activities, and documents for analysis.

*Our lord and king it is true that the strange people have come to the shores of the great sea . . .*
—Miguel Leon-Portilla

**The French, under** the command of Jean Ribault, discover the River of May (St Johns River) in Florida on 1 May 1562: colored engraving, 1591, by Theodor de Bry after a now lost drawing by Jacques Le Moyne de Morgues. The Granger Collection.

# 2

# WHEN WORLDS COLLIDE
## 1492–1590

## HOW DID social change in Europe contribute to European expansion overseas?

## WHAT FACTORS contributed to the defeat of the Aztecs and Incas by European forces?

## WHAT IMPORTANT differences were there between Spanish, English, and French patterns of colonization?

1492    1590

# AMERICAN COMMUNITIES
## The English at Roanoke

IN LATE AUGUST 1590 GOVERNOR JOHN WHITE RETURNED TO Roanoke Island, the first English community established in America. He had left three years before, sailing home to appeal for additional support. He was extremely anxious about the fate of the colonists, including his daughter, son-in-law, and grand-daughter Virginia Dare, the first English child born in the New World. Rowing ashore, he found the colonists' houses "taken down," their possessions "spoiled and scattered about." Looking around for some sign of hope, White noticed a word carved on a nearby tree trunk: "CROATOAN," the name of a friendly Indian village some fifty miles south. White had left instructions that in the event of trouble the colonists were to leave the sign of a cross, and not finding one he reassured himself that his people awaited him at Croatoan. He returned to his vessel, anxious to rescue them.

In 1584 Sir Walter Raleigh sponsored a small group of adventurers who first landed on the island the Indians called Roanoke. The men found the coastal region densely popu-lated by a "very handsome and goodly people" and were "entertained with all love and kindness" by a local chief named Wingina. To Wingina, the English were potential allies in his struggle to extend authority over more vil-lages, and he granted the men permission to plan a large English settlement. He even sent two of his leading men, Manteo and Wanchese, back to England to help pre-pare the enterprise.

When the Englishmen returned in 1585, the two Indians offered Wingina con-flicting reports. Manteo argued that English technology made these men powerful allies. But Wanchese told of the disturbing inequalities he had seen among the English and warned his chief of the potential bru-tality of these men. He rightly suspected their intentions, for Raleigh's plans were based on the expectation of exploiting the Indians. Raleigh hoped for profits from a lucrative trade in furs, a flourishing plantation agriculture, or the possibility of gold and silver mines. In each case the Indians were to supply the labor.

After building a rough fort on the island, the English requested supplies from Wingina. With the harvest in the stor-age pits, fish running in the streams, and fat game in the woods, the chief did the hospitable thing. But as fall turned to winter and the stores diminished, he grew weary of their persistent

demands. In the spring Wingina ran out of patience. Before the Indians could act, however, the Englishmen caught wind of the rising hostility and in a surprise attack in May 1586 they killed several leaders, including Wingina. Leaving his head on a stake, they fled back to England.

John White and Thomas Harriot, who had spent their time exploring the physical and human world of the coast and recording their findings in notes and sketches, were appalled by the turn of events. White proposed a new plan for a colony of genuine settlers, families who would attempt to live in harmony with the natives.

In 1587, with Raleigh's financial support, John White returned to Virginia as governor of a new colony of 117 men, women, and children. They were supposed to land on Chesa-peake Bay after checking on the situation at Roanoke. But the captain, eager to get on with the profitable activity of plundering Spanish shipping, insisted on dropping the colonists there. White found himself among Indians who had already been com-pletely alienated. Within a month, one of the colonists had been shot full of arrows. White's counterattack only increased the Indians' resolve to expel the intruders. The colonists begged White to sail home in their only seaworthy vessel to ask Raleigh for additional support. He left reluctantly, never to return.

Blinded by their desire for immediate rewards, the colonists wasted the opportu-nity presented by the natives' initial wel-come. But the Roanoke story also says something about the importance of commu-nity in the first attempts at colonization. Bits of evidence suggest that the so-called lost colonists lived out the rest of their lives as residents of Indian villages. Virginia Dare and other English children may have been adopted by Indian families, grown up and taken Indian spouses, in the process creating the first mixed community of English and Indi-ans in North America.

European colonists came to the Americas for a variety of reasons, but high on their list of priorities were plunder and profit. The invasion of America often included terrible violence, as well as frequent possibilities for accommodation and coopera-tion between natives and newcomers. The invasion also intro-duced mortal epidemic diseases that devastated native communities. The encounter of communities at Roanoke was, in numerous ways, a template for New World colonization.

Roanoke

# THE EXPANSION OF EUROPE

The connection between Europe and America established by Columbus' 1492 voyage had earthshaking consequences. Within a generation, the exchanges of peoples, crops, animals, and germs had transformed the world. The key to understanding these remarkable events is the transformation of Europe during the several centuries preceding the voyage of Columbus.

## WESTERN EUROPE BEFORE COLUMBUS

Western Europe was an agricultural society: Most Europeans lived in family households clustered in farming villages. Farming and raising livestock had been practiced in Europe for thousands of years, but during the late Middle Ages there were great advances in technology. Water mills, iron plows, improved devices for harnessing ox and horse power, and systems of crop rotation greatly increased productivity. From the eleventh to the fourteenth centuries the quantity of land under cultivation in western Europe more than doubled. During the same period the population nearly tripled.

Europe was divided into hundreds of small territories, each ruled by a family of lords that held a monopoly of wealth and power. Lords commanded labor service from peasants and tribute in the form of crops. They were the main beneficiaries of medieval economic expansion, accumulating great estates and building imposing castles.

Western Europe was officially Christian, united under the authority of the Roman Catholic Church, whose complex organization spanned thousands of local communities with a hierarchy that extended from parish priests to the pope in Rome. The Catholic Church was one of the most powerful landowners in Europe. It insisted on its dogmas and actively persecuted heretics, nonbelievers, and devotees of older "pagan" religions. The Church provided legitimacy for the relationship of lord and peasant, counseling the poor and downtrodden to place their hopes in heavenly rewards.

For the great majority of Europeans, living conditions were harsh. Most rural people survived on bread and porridge, supplemented with seasonal vegetables and an occasional piece of meat or fish. Infectious diseases abounded and famines periodically ravaged the countryside. In the fourteenth century, for example, a series of crop failures resulted in widespread starvation and death. This episode prepared the way for the so-called Black Death, a widespread epidemic of bubonic plague that swept in from Asia and wiped out a third of Europe's population between 1347 and 1353.

Strengthened by the technological developments of the Middle Ages, Europe's agricultural economy quickly recovered. By 1500 the population had rebounded to its former high of 65 million.

## THE MERCHANT CLASS AND THE RENAISSANCE

The economic growth of the late Middle Ages was accompanied by the expansion of commerce. Commercial expansion stimulated the growth of markets and towns. The heart of this dynamic European commercialism lay in the city-states of Italy.

During the late Middle Ages, the cities of Venice, Genoa, and Pisa launched armed commercial fleets that seized control of Mediterranean trade. The merchants of these cities became the principal outfitters of the Crusades, a series of great military expeditions promoted by the Catholic Church to recover Palestine from

HOW DID social change in Europe contribute to European expansion overseas?

**Review Summary**

## IMAGE KEY
for pages 24–25

a. An illustration of a banana blossom.
b. The French, under the command of Jean Ribault, discover St Johns River in Florida on May 1, 1562.
c. Pyramid of Kukulcan at Chichen Itza.
d. Peter Minuet purchases Manhattan island from the local Native Americans.
e. Aztec Indians, with smallpox contracted from the Spaniards, ministered to by a medicine man.
f. John White finding no trace of the colony of Roanoke on his return to Virginia in 1590.

**QUICK REVIEW**

**European Society**
◆ European states were hierarchical.
◆ Most Europeans were peasant farmers.
◆ European society was patriarchal.

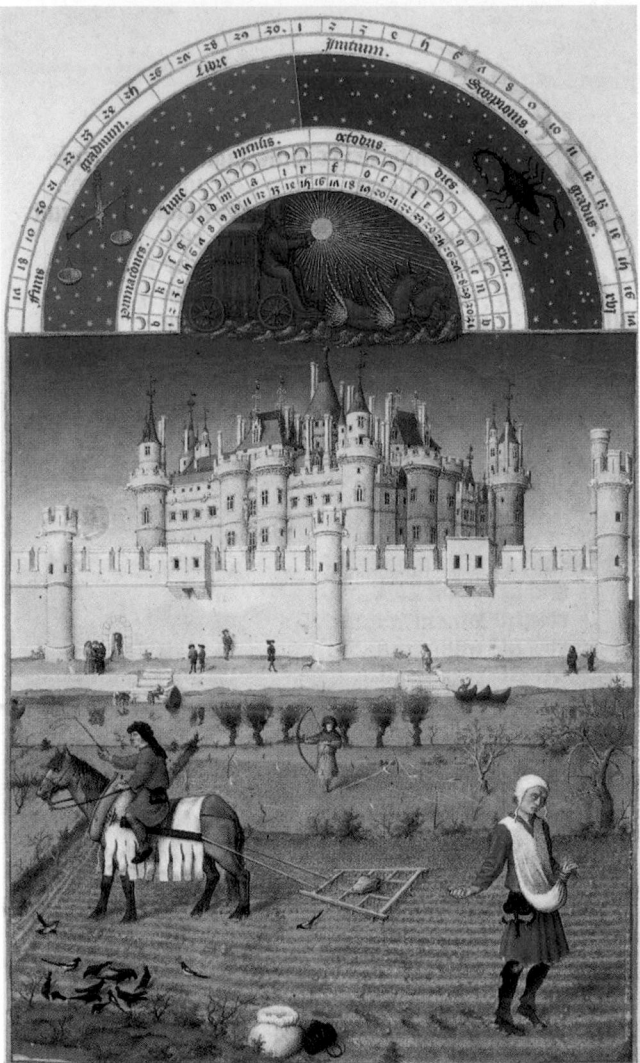

**A French peasant** labors in the field before a spectacular castle in a page taken from the illuminated manuscript *Tres Riches Heures*, made in the fifteenth century for the duc de Berry. In 1580 the essayist Montaigne talked with several American Indians at the French court who "noticed among us some men gorged to the full with things of every sort while their other halves were beggars at their doors, emaciated with hunger and poverty" and "found it strange that these poverty-stricken halves should suffer such injustice, and that they did not take the others by the throat or set fire to their houses."

the Muslims. With the conquest of Jerusalem at the end of the eleventh century, the silk and spice trades of Asia were delivered into the hands of Italian merchants. Asian civilization also supplied a number of technical innovations that further propelled European economic growth.

Contact with Muslim civilization provided access to important ancient texts, long lost in Europe but preserved in the great libraries of Alexandria (Egypt) and Baghdad (Iraq). The revived interest in classical antiquity triggered a period of intellectual and artistic flowering from the fourteenth to sixteenth centuries that later generations called the **Renaissance**.

The Renaissance celebrated human possibility. "The nature of all other beings is limited," wrote the Italian intellectual Pico della Mirandola in 1486; "but you, constrained by no limits, in accordance with your own free will, shall ordain for yourself the limits of your nature." This human-centered perspective was part of what became known as humanism, in which human life on earth took precedence over the afterlife of the soul. This outlook was a critical component of the inquisitive and acquisitive spirit that motivated the exploration of the Americas.

## THE NEW MONARCHIES

The Renaissance began amid the ruins of the plague. Famine and disease led to violence, as groups battled for their share of a shrinking economy. A series of peasant rebellions culminated in the great English Peasants' Revolt of 1381. Warfare among the nobility weakened and greatly reduced the power of the landed classes, and the Catholic Church was seriously destabilized by an internal struggle between French and Italian factions.

It was during this period of social and political chaos that the monarchs of western Europe began to replace the lords as the new centers of power. They built their legitimacy by promising internal order as they unified their realms (see Map 2.1). In many cases, the new monarchs found support among the increasingly wealthy merchants, who in return sought lucrative royal contracts and trading monopolies. This alliance between commerce and political power was another important development that prepared the way for European expansion.

## THE PORTUGUESE VOYAGES

Portugal, a narrow land along the western coast of the Iberian Peninsula with a long tradition of seafaring, became the first of the new Renaissance kingdoms to send out explorers on voyages to distant lands. Lisbon, the principal port on the sea route between the Mediterranean and northwestern Europe, was a bustling, cosmopolitan city with large enclaves of Italian merchants. By 1385 the local merchant community had grown powerful enough to place João I, their favorite, on the throne. João had ambitious plans to establish a Portuguese trading empire.

A central figure in this development was the king's son, Prince Henry, known to later generations as "the Navigator." Prince Henry established an academy of

**Renaissance**   The intellectual and artistic flowering in Europe during the fourteenth, fifteenth, and sixteenth centuries sparked by a revival of interest in classical antiquity.

# ⚲ MAP EXPLORATION

To explore an interactive version of this map, go to **http://www.prenhall.com/faraghertlc/map2.1**

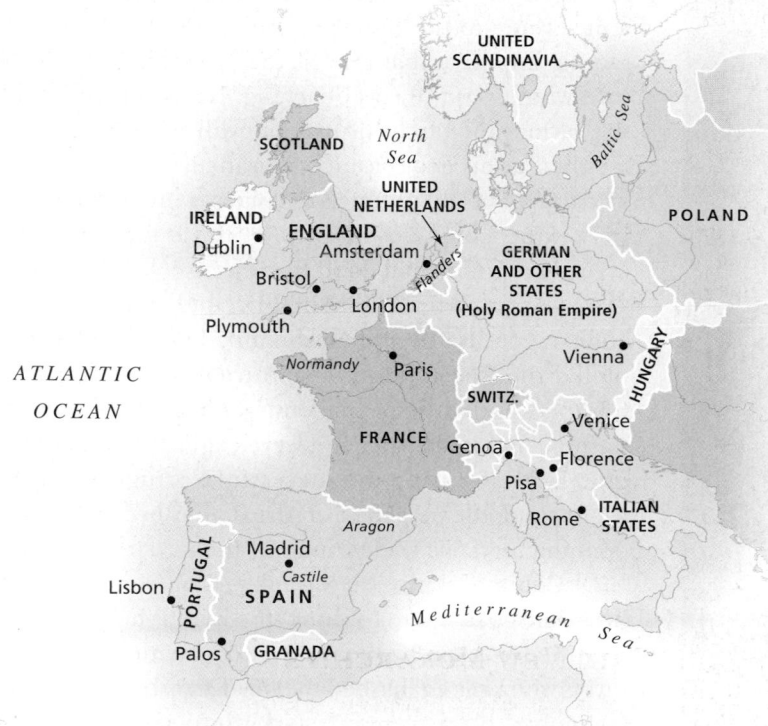

**MAP 2.1**

**Western Europe in the Fifteenth Century**   By the middle of the century, the monarchs of western Europe had begun to build royal bureaucracies and standing armies and navies. These states sponsored the voyages that inaugurated the era of European colonization.

WHY WERE some European states better positioned for colonizing than others?

eminent geographers, instrument makers, shipbuilders, and seamen at his institute on the southwestern tip of Portugal at Sagres Point. By the mid-fifteenth century, as a result of their efforts, most educated Europeans knew the earth was round. Studying the seafaring traditions of Asia and the Muslim world, the learned men of Sagres Point incorporated them into the design of a new ship called the *caravel,* faster and better-handling than any ship previously known in Europe. They promoted the use of Arab instruments for astronomical calculation. With such innovations, Europeans became the masters of the world's seas, a supremacy that would continue until the twentieth century.

The Portuguese explored the Atlantic coast of northwestern Africa for direct access to the lucrative gold and slave trades of that continent. The Portuguese eventually built strategic trading forts along the coasts of Africa, India, Indonesia, and China, the first and longest-lasting outposts of European world colonization, and gained control of much of the Asian spice trade. Most important for the history of the Americas, the Portuguese established the Atlantic slave trade. (For a full discussion of slavery, see Chapter 4.)

## QUICK REVIEW

**Portuguese Explorations**

- Prince Henry the Navigator played a key role in sponsoring exploration.
- Technological innovations made longer sea voyages possible.
- The Portuguese explored the Atlantic coast of Africa seeking direct access to gold and slaves.

**The astrolabe, an** instrument used for determining the precise position of heavenly bodies, was introduced into early modern Europe by the Arabs. This is one of the earliest examples, an intricately engraved brass astrolabe produced by a master craftsman in Syria in the thirteenth century.

© National Maritime Museum Picture Library, London, England. Neg. #E5555-3.

**1–2**

Christopher Columbus, *Letter to Ferdinand and Isabella of Spain* (1494)

**Reconquista** The long struggle (ending in 1492) during which Spanish Christians reconquered the Iberian peninsula from Muslim occupiers.

## COLUMBUS REACHES THE AMERICAS

In 1476, Christopher Columbus, a young Genoan sailor, joined his brother in Lisbon, where he became a seafaring merchant for Italian traders. He developed the simple idea of opening a new route to the Indies by sailing west across the Atlantic Ocean, known at that time as the "Western Sea." Such a venture would require royal backing, but when he approached the various monarchs of Europe with his idea, their advisers laughed at his geographic ignorance, pointing out that his calculation of the distance to Asia was much too short. They were right, Columbus was wrong. But it turned out to be an error of monumental good fortune.

Columbus finally sold his plan to the monarchs of Castile and Aragon, Isabel and Ferdinand. These two had just completed the **Reconquista**, a centuries-long struggle between Catholics and Muslims that ended Muslim rule in Spain. The Catholic monarchs of Spain were eager for new lands to conquer, and observing the successful Portuguese push to the south along the west coast of Africa, they became interested in opening lucrative trade routes of their own to the Indies.

Columbus' mission was more than commercial. One of his prime goals was to "occupy" the islands he found, establishing title for Spain by the right of occupancy. Like the adventurers who later established the first English colony at Roanoke, Columbus' objectives were starkly imperial.

Columbus' three vessels reached the Bahamas in October 1492. But Columbus believed he was in the Indies, somewhere near the Asian mainland. He explored the northern island coasts of Cuba and Hispaniola before heading home, fortuitously catching the westerly winds that blow from the American coast toward Europe north of the tropics.

Leading Columbus' triumphal procession to the royal court were half a dozen Taíno Indians, taken by force from their homes, and dressed for the occasion in bright feathers with ornaments of gold. "Should your majesties command it," Columbus told the monarchs, "all the inhabitants could be made slaves." Moreover, he reported, "there are many spices and great mines of gold and of other metals." In fact, none of the Eastern spices familiar to Europeans grew in the Caribbean and there were only small quantities of alluvial gold in the riverbeds of the islands. But the sight of the gold ornaments worn by the Taínos infected Columbus with gold fever. He reported that he had left a small force behind in a rough fort on the northern coast of Hispaniola to explore for gold—the first European foothold in the Americas.

The enthusiastic monarchs financed a return convoy of seventeen vessels and 1,500 men that sailed in late 1493 to begin the systematic colonization of the islands. But returning to Hispaniola, Columbus found his fort in ruins and his men all killed by the Taínos. Columbus directed his men to attack and destroy the nearby Taíno villages, enslaving the inhabitants and demanding tribute in gold.

Columbus' voyages were a disaster for the Taínos. The combined effects of warfare, famine, and demoralization resulted in the collapse of their society. By the 1520s they had been effectively eliminated as a people. As the native population fell, the colony plunged into depression. As early as 1500 the Spanish monarchs had grown so dissatisfied that they ordered Columbus arrested and sent back to Spain in irons.

**Columbus bids farewell** to the monarchs Isabel and Ferdinand at the port of Palos in August 1492, illustrated in a copperplate engraving published in 1594 by Theodore de Bry of Frankfort. While armed men are ferried out to the vessels, three accountants in a room directly above the monarchs count out the gold to fund the journey.

Columbus made two additional voyages to the Caribbean, both characterized by the same obsessive searching for gold and violent raiding for slaves. He died in Spain in 1506, still convinced he had opened a new way to Asia. This belief persisted among many Europeans well into the sixteenth century.

# THE SPANISH IN THE AMERICAS

The Spanish had created a huge and wealthy empire in the Americas. In theory, all law and policy for the empire came from Spain; in practice, the isolation of the settlements led to a good deal of local autonomy. The Spanish created a caste system, in which a small minority of settlers and their offspring controlled the lives and labor of millions of Indian and African workers. But it was also a society in which colonists, Indians, and Africans mixed to form a new people.

## THE INVASION OF AMERICA

The first stages of the Spanish invasion of America included frightful violence. Columbus and his successors established an institution known as the *encomienda*, in which Indians were compelled to labor in the service of Spanish lords. Faced with labor shortages, slavers raided the Bahamas and soon depopulated them of native people. The depletion of gold on Hispaniola led to the invasion of the islands of Puerto Rico and Jamaica in 1508, then Cuba in 1511. Meanwhile, rumors of wealthy native societies to the west led to scores of probing expeditions (see Map 2.2). The Spanish invasion of Central America began in 1511, and two years later Vasco Núñez de Balboa crossed the Isthmus of Panama to the Pacific Ocean. In 1517, Spaniards landed on the coast of Mexico, and within a year they made contact with the Aztec empire.

**WHAT FACTORS** contributed to the defeat of the Aztecs and Incas by European forces?

**myhistorylab**
Review Summary

**myhistorylab**
Exploring America: *Exploitation of the Americas*

## ✳ MAP EXPLORATION

To explore an interactive version of this map, go to **http://www.prenhall.com/faraghertlc/map2.2**

**MAP 2.2**

**The Invasion of America**    In the sixteenth century, the Spanish first invaded the Caribbean and used it to stage their successive wars of conquest in North and South America. In the seventeenth century, the French, English, and Dutch invaded the Atlantic coast. The Russians, sailing across the northern Pacific, mounted the last of the colonial invasions in the eighteenth century.

WHAT IMPORTANT differences were there among the Spanish, French, and English approaches to conquest and settlement of the Americas?

**1–12**

*An Aztec Remembers the Conquest of Mexico a Quarter Century Afterwards* (1550)

Hernán Cortés, a veteran of the conquest of Cuba, landed on the Mexican coast in 1519 with armed troops. Within two years he overthrew the Aztec empire, a spectacular military accomplishment that has no parallel in the annals of conquest. Cortés skillfully exploited the resentment of the many peoples who lived under Aztec domination, forging Spanish–Indian alliances that became a model for the subsequent European colonization of the Americas. The Aztecs were militarily powerful. They succeeded in driving the Spaniards from Tenochtitlán, then put up a bitter and prolonged defense when Cortés returned with tens of thousands of Indian allies to besiege the capital. In the meantime, however, the Aztecs suffered a devastating epidemic of smallpox that killed thousands and undermined their ability to resist. In the aftermath of conquest, the Spanish plundered Aztec society, providing the Catholic monarchs with wealth beyond their wildest imagining.

### THE DESTRUCTION OF THE INDIES

The Indian peoples of the Americas resisted Spanish conquest with determination, but most proved a poor match for mounted warriors with steel swords. The record of the conquest includes many brave Indian leaders and thousands of martyrs.

This map of Tenochtitlán, published in 1524 and attributed to the celebrated engraver Albrecht Dürer, shows the city before its destruction, with the principal Aztec temples in the main square, causeways connecting the city to the mainland, and an acqueduct supplying fresh water. The information on this map must have come from Aztec sources, as did much of the intelligence Cortés relied on for the Spanish conquest.

Some Europeans protested the horrors of the conquest. In 1511 the Catholic priest Antonio de Montesinos condemned the violence in a sermon delivered to colonists on Hispaniola. In the congregation was Bartolomé de las Casas, a man who had participated in the plunder of Cuba. Renouncing his own wealth, las Casas entered the priesthood and dedicated his life to the protection of the Indians. Long before the world recognized the concept of universal human rights, las Casas was proclaiming that "the entire human race is one," earning him a reputation as one of the towering moral figures in the early history of the Americas.

In his brilliant history of the conquest, *The Destruction of the Indies* (1542), las Casas blamed the Spanish for cruelties resulting in millions of Indian deaths—in effect he accused them of genocide. Translated into several languages and widely circulated throughout Europe, las Casas's book was cynically used by other European colonial powers to condemn Spain, thereby covering up their own dismal colonial practices.

**1–13**
Bartolomé de Las Casas, *The Devastation of the Indies* (1565)

## THE VIRGIN SOIL EPIDEMICS

Las Casas was incorrect, however, in attributing most of these Indian deaths to warfare. The primary cause of the drastic reduction in native populations was epidemic disease—influenza, plague, smallpox, measles, typhus. Although preconquest America was by no means disease free, there were no diseases of epidemic potential. Indian peoples lacked the antibodies necessary to protect them from

**This drawing of** victims of the smallpox epidemic that struck the Aztec capital of Tenochtitlán in 1520 is taken from the *Florentine Codex*, a postconquest history written and illustrated by Aztec scribes. "There came amongst us a great sickness, a general plague," reads the account, "killing vast numbers of people. It covered many all over with sores: on the face, on the head, on the chest, everywhere. . . . The sores were so terrible that the victims could not lie face down, nor on their backs, nor move from one side to the other. And when they tried to move even a little, they cried out in agony."

European germs and viruses. Such devastating outbreaks of disease, striking for the first time against a completely unprotected population, are known as "virgin soil epidemics." Smallpox made its first appearance in America in 1518, exploding in an epidemic so virulent that, in the words of an early Spanish historian, "it left Hispaniola, Puerto Rico, Jamaica, and Cuba desolated of Indians." The epidemic hit Mexico in 1520, destroying the Aztecs and preparing the way for their conquest, then spreading along the Indian trade network. In 1524 it strategically weakened the Inca civilization of the Andes eight years before their empire was conquered by Francisco Pizarro. Disease was the secret weapon of the Spanish, and it helps explain their extraordinary success in the conquest.

Warfare, famine, lower birthrates, and epidemic disease knocked the native population of the Americas into a downward spiral that was not reversed until the twentieth century (see Figure 2.1). By that time native population had fallen by more than 90 percent. It was the greatest demographic disaster in world history.

## QUICK REVIEW

**Causes of Indian Population Decline**

- Disease
- Warfare
- Famine
- Declining birthrates

**Figure 2.1**
**North America's Indian and Colonial Populations in the Seventeenth and Eighteenth Centuries**
The primary factor in the decimation of native peoples was epidemic disease, brought to the New World from the Old. In the eighteenth century, the colonial population overtook North America's Indian populations.

Historical Statistics of the United States (Washington, DC: Government Printing Office, 1976), 8, 1168; Russell Thornton, *American Indian Holocaust and Survival* (Norman: University of Oklahoma Press, 1987), 32.

# THE COLUMBIAN EXCHANGE

1–19
Jose de Acosta, *The Columbian Exchange* (1590)

The passage of diseases between the Old and New Worlds was one part of the large-scale exchange of people, animals, plants, and goods—what the historian Alfred Crosby terms "the Columbian Exchange"—that marks the beginning of the modern era of world history (see Map 2.3). The most obvious exchange was the vast influx into Europe of the precious metals plundered from the Aztec and Incan empires of the New World. Most of this golden booty was melted down, destroying forever thousands of priceless native artifacts. Silver from mines the Spanish discovered and operated with Indian labor in Mexico and Peru tripled the amount of silver coin circulating in Europe between 1500 and 1550, then tripled it again before 1600. The result of so much new coin in circulation was runaway inflation, which stimulated commerce and raised profits but lowered the standard of living for most people.

Of even greater long-term importance were the New World crops brought to Europe. Maize (Indian corn), the staff of life for most native North Americans, became a staple crop in Mediterranean countries, the dominant feed for livestock elsewhere in Europe, and the primary provision for the slave ships of Africa. Potatoes provided the margin between famine and subsistence for the peasant peoples of northern Europe and Ireland.

**MAP 2.3**

**The Columbian Exchange**    Europeans voyaging between Europe, Africa, Asia, and the Americas in the fifteenth and sixteenth centuries began a vast intercontinental movement of plants, animals, and diseases that shaped the course of modern history.

THE COLUMBIAN EXCHANGE marked the beginning of the modern era of world history. What developments and events contributed to this? What were its advantages and disadvantages?

Although the Spanish failed to locate valuable spices such as black pepper or cloves in the New World, new tropical crops more than compensated. Tobacco, first introduced to Europe about 1550 as a cure for disease, was soon in wide use as a stimulant. American vanilla and chocolate both became highly valued. American cotton proved far superior to Asian varieties for the production of cheap textiles. Each of these native plants—along with tropical transplants from the Old World to America, with sugar, rice, and coffee being the most important—supplied the basis for important new industries and markets that altered the course of world history.

Columbus introduced domesticated animals into Hispaniola and Cuba, and livestock were later transported to Mexico. The movement of Spanish settlement northward through Mexico was greatly aided by an advancing wave of livestock, for grazing animals did serious damage to native fields and forests. Horses, used by Spanish stockmen to tend their cattle, also spread northward. In the seventeenth century, horses reached the Great Plains of North America, where they eventually transformed the lives of the nomadic hunting Indians (see Chapter 5).

## THE SPANISH IN NORTH AMERICA

Ponce de León, governor of Puerto Rico, was the first Spanish conquistador to attempt to extend the Spanish conquest to North America (see Map 2.4). In search of slaves, he made his first landing on the mainland coast, which he named Florida, in 1513. Warriors from the powerful Indian chiefdoms there beat back this and several other attempts at invasion, and in 1521 succeeded in killing Ponce. Seven years later, another Spanish attempt to colonize Florida, under the command of Pánfilo de Narváez, also ended in disaster. Most of Narváez's men were lost in a shipwreck, but a small group of them survived. One of these castaways, Alvar Núñez Cabeza de Vaca, published an account of his adventures in which he repeated rumors of a North American empire known as Cíbola, with golden cities "larger than the city of Mexico."

**1–3**
Alvar Núñez Cabeza de Vaca,
*Indians of the Rio Grande*
(1528-1536)

Cabeza de Vaca's report inspired two great Spanish expeditions into North America. The first was mounted in Cuba by Hernán de Soto, a veteran of the conquest of Peru. Landing in Florida in 1539 with over 700 men, de Soto pushed hundreds of miles through the heavily populated South, commandeering food and slaves from the Mississippian towns in his path. But de Soto failed to locate another Aztec empire. Moving westward, his expedition was twice mauled by powerful native armies and reduced by half. When he reached the Mississippi, he was met by a great flotilla of 200 vessels said to have come down river from a great city to the west. The Spaniards crossed the river and pushed westward through present-day Arkansas, but failing to find the great city, returned to the Mississippi. There de Soto fell sick and died. Some 300 dispirited survivors eventually made it back to Mexico on rafts. The native peoples of the South had successfully turned back Spanish invasion. But de Soto had introduced epidemic disease, which over the next several years drastically depopulated and undermined the Mississippian chiefdoms of the South.

In the same year of 1539, Spanish officials in Mexico launched a second attempt to conquer North America, this one aimed at the Southwest. Francisco Vásquez de Coronado led 300 mounted men and infantry and 800 Indian porters north along well-marked Indian trading paths, passing through the settlements of Piman Indians near the present border of the United States and Mexico and finally reaching the Pueblo villages along the Rio Grande. Coronado sent out expeditions in all directions in search of the legendary golden cities of Cíbola. He led his army as far north as the Great Plains, where they observed great herds of "shaggy cows"

**MAP 2.4**

**European Exploration, 1492–1591**  By the mid-sixteenth century, Europeans had explored most of the Atlantic coast of North America and penetrated into the interior in the disastrous expeditions of de Soto and Coronado.

WHAT WERE the reasons behind the different experiences of the French, Spanish, and English explorations?

(buffalo) and made contact with nomadic hunting peoples, but returned without gold. For the next fifty years Spain would lose all interest in the Southwest.

## THE SPANISH NEW WORLD EMPIRE

A century after Columbus, some 250,000 European immigrants, most of them Spaniards, had settled in the Americas. Another 125,000 Africans had been forcibly resettled as slaves on the Spanish plantations of the Caribbean, as well as on the Portuguese plantations of Brazil.

Spanish women came to America as early as Columbus' second expedition, but over the course of the sixteenth century they made up only about 10 percent of the immigrants. Most male colonists married or cohabited with Indian or African women. Indians died by the thousands in the conquest, but Indian genes were passed on in mixed-ancestry people who quickly became the majority population in the mainland Spanish American empire.

Populated by Indians, Africans, Spanish colonists, and their hybrid descendants, the New World colonies of Spain made up one of the largest and most powerful empires in world history. In theory the empire operated as a highly centralized and bureaucratic system. But the Council of the Indies, the advisers of the Spanish king who made all the laws and regulations for the empire, was located far away in Spain. What looked in the abstract like a centrally administered empire was in fact a fragmented collection of colonial regions that tolerated a great deal of local decision making.

# NORTHERN EXPLORATIONS AND ENCOUNTERS

When the Spanish empire was at the height of its power in the sixteenth century, the merchants and monarchs of other European seafaring states began looking across the Atlantic for opportunities of their own (see Map 2.4). France was first to sponsor expeditions to the New World in the early sixteenth century. The French first attempted to plant settlements on the coasts of Brazil and Florida, but Spanish opposition forced them to concentrate on the North Atlantic. England did not develop its own plans to colonize North America until the second half of the sixteenth century.

## TRADE NOT CONQUEST: FISH AND FURS

Long before France and England made attempts to found colonies, however, European fishermen were exploiting the coastal North American waters of the North Atlantic. The first European voyages of exploration in the North Atlantic used the talents of these experienced European sailors and fishermen. Giovanni Caboto (or John Cabot) reached Labrador in 1497, but the English did little to follow up on his voyage. In 1524, Giovanni da Verrazano, sailing for the French, explored the North American coast. Encouraged by his report, the French crown commissioned experienced captain Jacques Cartier to locate a "Northwest Passage" to the Indies. In a series of voyages undertaken in 1534, 1535, and 1541, Cartier failed to locate such a passage but became the first European to explore the St. Lawrence River, which led to the Great Lakes, and provided easy access to the Ohio and Mississippi rivers. Cartier's exploration established France's imperial claim to the lands of Canada and provided the French with an incomparable geographic advantage over other colonial powers.

**WHAT IMPORTANT** differences were there between Spanish, English, and French patterns of colonization?

myhistorylab
Review Summary

The French and other northern Europeans thus discovered the Indian people of the northern woodlands, and the Indians in turn discovered them. Contacts here were quite different than those of the tropics, based on commerce rather than conquest. The natives immediately appreciated the usefulness of textiles, glass, copper, and ironware. For his part, Cartier was interested in the fur coats of the Indians.

The fur trade would continue to play an important role in the Atlantic economy for the next three centuries. The trade also had familiar negative consequences. European epidemic disease soon followed in the wake of the traders, and violent warfare broke out between tribes over access to hunting grounds. Moreover, as European-manufactured goods, such as metal knives, kettles, and firearms, became essential to their way of life, Indians grew dependent upon European suppliers.

By the end of the sixteenth century over a thousand European ships were trading for furs each year along the northern Atlantic coast. The village of Tadoussac on the St. Lawrence, where a wide bay offered Europeans safe anchorage, became the customary place for a late summer trading fair. Within a few years the French would attempt to monopolize the northern trade by planting colonies along the coast and on the St. Lawrence. The first French colonies in North America, however, were planted farther south by a group of French Protestant religious dissenters known as the **Huguenots**.

## THE PROTESTANT REFORMATION AND THE FIRST FRENCH COLONIES

The **Protestant Reformation**—the religious revolt against the Roman Catholic Church—began in 1517 when German priest Martin Luther publicized his differences with Rome. Luther declared that eternal salvation was a gift from God and not related to works or service to the Catholic Church. One of Luther's most prominent converts was Jean Chauvin (known to English speakers as John Calvin), a young theology student in Paris. In 1533, as the persecution of **Protestants** intensified, Calvin fled France, eventually taking up residence in Geneva, Switzerland, where civic leaders had renounced the Catholic Church and expelled the city's bishop. Working with those leaders, Calvin established a Protestant theocracy in Geneva. His systematic writings and teachings concerning theology, liturgy, ritual, and church government proved highly influential among Protestants. His followers in France, known as Huguenots, largely came from the urban middle class but also included a portion of the nobility, those opposed to the central authority of the Catholic monarch. In 1560 the French crown successfully defeated a plot among powerful Huguenots to seize royal power, inaugurating nearly forty years of violent religious conflict in France.

The first French colonies developed as attempts to establish a religious refuge in the New World for Huguenots. In 1562 French naval officer Jean Ribault and a group of 150 Huguenots from Normandy landed on Parris Island, near present-day Beaufort, South Carolina, and began construction of a fort and crude mud huts. In 1564, Ribault and his followers established a second Huguenot colony, Fort Caroline, on the St. Johns River of Florida, south of present-day Jacksonville.

The Spanish were alarmed by these moves. They had shown little interest themselves in colonizing Florida but worried about protecting their convoys, riding home to Spain on the offshore Gulf Stream, loaded with gold and silver. Not only was Fort Caroline manned by Frenchmen but also by Protestants—mortal enemies of the Catholic monarchs of Spain. In 1565 King Philip II of Spain sent Don Pedro Menéndez de Avilés, captain general of the Indies, to

**1–4**
Jacques Cartier, *First Contact with the Indians* (1534)

---

### QUICK REVIEW

**The Fur Trade**
◆ Fur traders were critical to New France's success.
◆ New France ruled by royal appointees.
◆ *Coureurs de bois*: independent fur traders living among the Indians.

---

**Huguenots**  French Protestant religious dissenters who planted the first French colonies in North America.

**Protestant Reformation**  Martin Luther's challenge to the Catholic Church, initiated in 1517, calling for a return to what he understood to be the purer practices and beliefs of the early church.

**Protestants**  All European supporters of religious reform under Charles V's Holy Roman Empire.

**This watercolor of** Jacques Le Moyne, painted in 1564, depicts the friendly relations between the Timucuas of coastal Florida and the colonists of the short-lived French colony of Fort Caroline. The Timucuas hoped that the French would help defend them against the Spanish, who plundered the coast in pursuit of Indian slaves.

Jacques Le Moyne, "Rene de Loudonniere and Chief Athore," 1564. Gouache and metallic pigments on vellum. Print Collection, The New York Public Library, New York. The New York Public Library/Art Resource, NY.

1–8
Pedro Menéndez de Avilés,
*The Founding of St. Augustine*
(1565)

crush the Huguenots, which he did. To prevent further French incursions the Spanish built massive Castillo San Marcos (still standing) and established a garrison at St. Augustine, which has the distinction of being the oldest continuously occupied European city in North America.

## SOCIAL CHANGE IN SIXTEENTH-CENTURY ENGLAND

The English movement across the Atlantic, like the French, was tied to social change at home. Perhaps most important were changes in the economy. As prices for goods rose steeply—the result of New World inflation—English landlords, their rents fixed by custom, sought ways to increase their incomes. Seeking profits in the woolen trade, many converted the common pasturage used by tenants into grazing land for sheep, dislocating large numbers of farmers.

Sixteenth-century England also became deeply involved in the Protestant Reformation. At first King Henry VIII of England (reigned 1509–47) supported the Catholic Church and opposed the Protestants. But when the pope refused to grant Henry an annulment of his marriage to Catherine of Aragon, daughter of Ferdinand and Isabel of Spain, the king took up the cause of reform. In 1534, he declared himself head of a separate Church of England. He later took over the English estates of the Catholic Church and utilized their revenues in the construction of a powerful English state system, including a standing army and navy. Working through Parliament, Henry carefully enlisted the support of the merchants and landed gentry for his program. By 1547, when Henry died, he had forged a solid alliance between the English monarchy and the wealthy merchant class.

# A Watercolor from the First Algonquian–English Encounter

Some of the first accurate images of the native inhabitants of North America were produced by the artist John White during his stay in 1685 at the first English colony in North America, at Roanoke Island on North Carolina's Outer Banks.

**IN WHAT** ways does this image document John White's powers of observation?

Two years later White would become governor of the famous "Lost Colony." This image of an Indian mother and daughter illustrates the care White brought to the task of recording as fully as possible the Indians' way of life. The woman wears an apron-skirt of fringed deerskin, its borders edged with white beads, and a woven beadwork necklace. The body decorations on her face and upper arms are tattooed. One of her arms rests in a sling, an unusual posture, something quite unique to this culture. In the other hand she holds an empty gourd container for carrying water. The little girl holds an English wooden doll, a gift from White, and it seems to greatly please her. In the written account that accompanied White's images, Thomas Harriot wrote that all the Indian girls "are greatly delighted with puppetts and babes which were brought out of England" as gifts of exchange. Historic images bear close observation, for it is often small details like this one that are most revealing. ■

Henry was succeeded by his young and sickly son Edward VI (reigned 1547–53), who soon died. Next in succession was Edward's Catholic half-sister Mary (reigned 1553–58), who persecuted and martyred hundreds of English Protestants and married Philip II of Spain, self-declared defender of the Catholic faith. With Mary's premature death, however, her Protestant half-sister Elizabeth I (reigned 1558–1603) reversed course, tolerating a variety of perspectives within the English church. Spain's monarch, Mary's widower, head of the most powerful empire in the world, vowed to overthrow Elizabeth.

Fearing Spanish subversion on the neighboring Catholic island of Ireland, Elizabeth urged enterprising supporters such as Walter Raleigh and his half-brother Humphrey Gilbert to subdue the Irish Catholics and settle homeless English families on their land. During the 1560s, Raleigh, Humphrey, and many other commanders invaded the island and viciously attacked the Irish, forcing them to retreat beyond a frontier line of English settlement along the coast. The English considered the Irish an inferior race, and the notion that civilized people could not mix with such "savages" was an assumption English colonists would carry with them to the Americas.

## EARLY ENGLISH EFFORTS IN THE AMERICAS

England's first ventures in the New World were made against the backdrop of its conflict with Spain. In 1562, John Hawkins violated Spanish regulations by transporting a load of African slaves to the Caribbean, bringing back valuable tropical goods. (For a full discussion of the slave trade, see Chapter 4.) The Spanish attacked Hawkins on another of his voyages in 1567, an event English privateers such as Francis Drake used as an excuse for launching a series of devastating and lucrative raids against Spanish New World ports and fleets.

A consensus soon developed among Elizabeth's closest advisers that the time had come to enter the competition for American colonies, and Elizabeth autho-

**The Armada Portrait** of Elizabeth I, painted by an unknown artist in 1648. The queen places her hand on the globe, symbolizing the rising seapower of England. Through the open windows, we see the battle against the Spanish Armada in 1588 and the destruction of the Spanish ships in a providential storm, interpreted by the queen as an act of divine intervention.

"Elizabeth I", Armada portrait, c. 1588 (oil on panel) by English School (C16th) Private Collection/The Bridgeman Art Library, London/New York.

## CHRONOLOGY

| | |
|---|---|
| **1000** | Norse settlement at L'Anse aux Meadows |
| **1347–53** | Black Death in Europe |
| **1381** | English Peasants' Revolt |
| **1488** | Bartolomeu Días sails around the African continent |
| **1492** | Christopher Columbus first arrives in the Caribbean |
| **1494** | Treaty of Tordesillas |
| **1497** | John Cabot explores Newfoundland |
| **1500** | High point of the Renaissance |
| **1508** | Spanish invade Puerto Rico |
| **1513** | Juan Ponce de León lands in Florida |
| **1514** | Bartolomé de las Casas begins preaching against the conquest |
| **1516** | Smallpox introduced to the New World |
| **1517** | Martin Luther breaks with the Roman Catholic Church |
| **1519** | Hernán Cortés lands in Mexico |
| **1534** | Jacques Cartier first explores the St. Lawrence River |
| **1539–40** | Hernán de Soto and Francisco Vásquez de Coronado expeditions |
| **1550** | Tobacco introduced to Europe |
| **1552** | Bartolomé de las Casas's *Destruction of the Indies* published |
| **1558** | Elizabeth I of England begins her reign |
| **1562** | Huguenot colony planted along the mid-Atlantic coast |
| **1565** | St. Augustine founded |
| **1583** | Humphrey Gilbert attempts to plant a colony in Newfoundland |
| **1584–87** | Walter Raleigh's colony on Roanoke Island |
| **1588** | English defeat the Spanish Armada |
| **1590** | John White returns to find Roanoke colony abandoned |

rized several private attempts at exploration and colonization. In the late 1570s, Martin Frobisher conducted three voyages of exploration in the North Atlantic. Next Gilbert and Raleigh, fresh from the Irish wars, planned the first true colonizing ventures. In 1583 Gilbert sailed with a flotilla of ships from Plymouth and landed at St. John's Bay, Newfoundland. He encountered fishermen from several other nations but nevertheless claimed the territory for his queen. But Gilbert's ship was lost on the return voyage.

Following his brother's death, Raleigh moved to establish a colony to the south, in the more hospitable climate of the mid-Atlantic coast. The Roanoke enterprise of 1584–87 seemed far more promising than Gilbert's, but it too failed. In contrast to the French, who concentrated on commerce, the English attempted to dominate and conquer the natives, drawing on their Irish experience.

Philip II was outraged at the English incursions into territory reserved by the pope for Catholics. He committed himself to smashing England. In 1588, he sent a fleet of 130 ships carrying 30,000 men to invade the British Isles. Countered by captains such as Drake and Hawkins, who commanded smaller and more maneuverable ships, and frustrated by an ill-timed storm that the English chose to interpret as an act of divine intervention, the Spanish Armada foundered. The Spanish monopoly of the New World had been broken in the English Channel.

# CONCLUSION

The era of European colonization in the Americas opened with Columbus' voyage in 1492. The subsequent Spanish invasion of America had catastrophic consequences for the Indian peoples of the Caribbean, Mesoamerica, and beyond. Wars of conquest and dispossession, and especially the introduction of epidemic disease, took an enormous toll in human life. Civilizations collapsed and whole cultures disappeared. Amidst this destruction, the Spanish succeeded in constructing the world's most powerful empire through the use of forced labor. Enormous wealth flowed across the Atlantic to Spain.

Inspired by the Spanish success, the French and the English sought to plant colonies on the coast of North America in the second half of the century, but neither succeeded in establishing lasting communities. Meanwhile, a very different kind of colonial encounter, one based on commerce rather than conquest, was taking place along the coasts of northeastern North America. Early in the next century the French would turn this development to their advantage.

The English would move in a different direction. The colony of Roanoke in the land the English called Virginia failed because of the imperial assumptions and the brutal behavior of the first colonists toward the native residents. The experience might have suggested the importance and necessity of "discreet dealing" with native peoples. But instead the English would put their Irish experience to use, pioneering an altogether new kind of American colonialism.

# REVIEW QUESTIONS

1. Discuss the roles played by the rising merchant class, the new monarchies, Renaissance humanism, and the Reformation in the development of European colonialism.

2. Define a "frontier of inclusion." In what ways does this description apply to the Spanish empire in the Americas?

3. Make a list of the major exchanges that took place between the Old World and the New World in the centuries following the European invasion of America. Discuss some of the effects these exchanges had on the course of modern history.

4. In what ways did colonial contact in the Northeast differ from contacts in the Caribbean and Mexico?

5. In what ways might the English experience in Ireland have shaped expectations about American colonization?

**Flashcard Review**

# KEY TERMS

**Huguenots** (p. 39)                           **Reconquista** (p. 30)
**Protestant Reformation** (p. 39)    **Renaissance** (p. 28)
**Protestants** (p. 39)

# RECOMMENDED READING

David Noble Cook, *Born to Die: Disease and New World Conquest, 1492–1650* (1998). A synthetic history of the impact of disease, including Indian and European views.

Alfred W. Crosby Jr., *The Columbian Exchange: Biological and Cultural Consequences of 1492* (1972). Pathbreaking account of the intersection of the biospheres of the Old and New Worlds.

Kathleen Deagan and José María Cruxent, *Columbus's Outpost Among the Taínos: Spain and America at La Isabela, 1493–1498* (2002). An archaeological and historical account of the first European outpost in the New World.

Richard Flint, *Great Cruelties Have Been Reported: The 1544 Investigation of the Coronado Expedition* (2001). Testimony regarding the treatment of Indians and subsequent human rights debates in Spain.

Lewis Hanke, *The Spanish Struggle for Justice in the Conquest of America* (1949). The classic account of las Casas's attempts to rectify the wrongs committed by the Spanish against the Indians.

Charles M. Hudson, *Knights of Spain, Warriors of the Sun: Hernando de Soto and the South's Ancient Chiefdoms* (1997). A very readable history of the de Soto expedition, told from the viewpoint of the Indians.

Henry Kamen, *Spain's Road to Empire: The Making of a World Power, 1492–1763* (2002). A fascinating account arguing that it was not Spain that made the empire but rather the empire that made Spain.

John T. McGrath, *The French in Early Florida: In the Eye of the Hurricane* (2000). A meticulously researched history of the French Huguenot colony in Florida.

Samuel Eliot Morison, *The European Discovery of America: The Northern Voyages, A.D. 500–1600* (1971) and *The Southern Voyages, A.D. 1492–1616* (1974). The most detailed treatment of all the important European explorations of the Americas.

Karen Vieira Powers, *Women in the Crucible of Conquest: The Gendered Genesis of Spanish American Society, 1500–1600* (2005). This new interpretation of the conquest demonstrates the ways native women adapted to the new order imposed upon them.

Matthew Restall, *Seven Myths of the Spanish Conquest* (2003). A concise and refreshing new perspective on Spain's intrusion into the New World.

David Beers Quinn, *Set Fair for Roanoke: Voyages and Colonies, 1584–1606* (1985). The story of Roanoke—the Indian village, the English settlement, and the Lost Colony.

Carl Ortwin Sauer, *Sixteenth Century North America: The Land and the People as Seen by the Europeans* (1971). A classic source for the explorations of the continent, providing abundant descriptions of the Indians.

Hugh Thomas, *Conquest: Montezuma, Cortés, and the Fall of Old Mexico* (1993). A fascinating account, written by a master of historical style, that incorporates the Aztec view as well as the words of the conquerors.

Gustavo Verdesio, *Forgotten Conquests: Rereading New World History from the Margins* (2001). An argument that the old master historical narrative represents only one of many possible histories and a suggestion for finding the colonial subjects who did not produce documents.

myhistorylab™

Where it's a good time to connect to the past!

For study resources for this chapter, go to **www.myhistorylab.com** and choose *Out of Many, Teaching and Learning Classroom Edition.* You will find a wealth of study and review material for this chapter, including pretests and posttests, customized study plan, key-term review flash cards, interactive map and document activities, and documents for analysis.

*These seventeen ships . . . made a long, a troublesome, and costly voyage . . . with contrary winds after they set sail, and so scattered with mist and tempests that few of them arrived together . . .*
—Thomas Dudley, March 28, 1631

New Mexico. Pueblos de Taos.

# 3

# PLANTING COLONIES IN NORTH AMERICA
## 1588–1701

**HOW DID** conditions in New Spain and New France differ from Virginia and New England?

**HOW DID** tobacco change the nature of English colonization in Virginia?

**WHAT WERE** the social and political values of Puritanism and how did religious dissent shape the history of the New England colonies?

**WHAT ROLE** did the crown play in the founding of English colonies after 1660?

**WHAT LED** to violent conflict between Indians and colonists?

# AMERICAN COMMUNITIES
## Communities and Diversity in Seventeenth-Century Santa Fé

IT WAS A HOT AUGUST DAY IN 1680 WHEN THE FRANTIC MESSENGERS rode into the small mission outpost of El Paso with the news that the Pueblo Indians to the north had risen in revolt. The corpses of more than 400 Spanish colonists lay bleeding in the dust. Two thousand survivors huddled inside the Palace of Governors in Santa Fé, surrounded by 3,000 angry warriors. The Pueblo leaders had sent two crosses into the palace—white for surrender, red for death. Which would the colonists choose?

Spanish colonists had been in New Mexico for a century. Franciscan priests from Mexico came first, in the 1580s, followed by a military expedition in search of precious metals. In 1609, colonial authorities founded La Villa Real de la Santa Fé de San Francisco soon known simply as Santa Fé. The Pueblos were to be converted to Christianity, subjected to the authority of the king of Spain, and forced to labor for the Hispanic colonists. The Pueblos at first resisted, but in the face of Spanish armed might, they were forced to give in.

Colonization took a tremendous toll on them. Epidemic disease, striking in successive waves, claimed thousands of lives. Taxes, tribute, and labor service left Pueblo storehouses empty, and starving times came much more frequently. Nomadic Apache neighbors, mounted on stolen Spanish horses, raided their villages with increasing frequency. From 1610 to 1680 the Pueblo population plummeted by two-thirds to fewer than 20,000 people.

A devastating drought in the 1670s seemed a sign of final and complete collapse. Over the decades thousands of Pueblos had accepted Christianity, but in the face of disaster there was a revival of their traditional religious rituals. Outraged Franciscan missionaries invaded the underground *kivas*, destroyed sacred Indian artifacts, and publicly humiliated holy men. In 1675 the Spanish governor rounded up religious leaders from many villages, publicly executed three of them, and whipped the others. One of those men, Popé of San Juan Pueblo, vowed to overthrow the regime. During the next several years he and other rebel leaders organized a conspiracy among more than twenty Pueblo communities.

In response to the Pueblo demand of surrender, the besieged colonists were defiant, sending back the red cross. Three days later, with supplies running out, they counterattacked, winning just enough time to allow for the evacuation of the capital. Harassed by the Pueblos, they made their way south to El Paso, "the poor women and children on foot and unshod,"

Santa Fé

in the words of one account, and "of such a hue that they looked like dead people." The Pueblos ransacked the missions, desecrating the holy furnishings and leaving the mutilated bodies of priests lying upon the altars. They transformed the governor's chapel into a traditional *kiva*, his palace into a communal dwelling.

Santa Fé became the capital of a Pueblo confederacy led by Popé. He forced Christian Indians "to plunge into the rivers" to wash away the taint of baptism and ordered the destruction of everything Spanish. Getting rid of Jesus was one thing, but the rest was harder. Horses and sheep, fruit trees and wheat, new tools and new crafts—these things the Pueblos found useful. They also found that they missed the support of the Spanish in their struggle against the Apaches. With chaos mounting, Popé was deposed in 1690.

In 1692, a Spanish force under Governor Diego de Vargas returned to New Mexico in an attempt to reestablish the colonial regime. Some communities welcomed him while others resisted. In 1696 there was another attempt at revolt, but Vargas crushed it with overwhelming force. The Spanish succeeded in their reconquest, but they seemed to have learned something in the process. They began to practice greater restraint, which enabled the Pueblos to accept their authority. As long as Pueblos dutifully observed Catholic rituals in the missionary chapels, missionaries looked the other way when the people also resorted to their *kivas* and their old faith. Royal officials promised the inviolability of Pueblo title to their lands, and Pueblos in turn swore loyalty to the Spanish monarch. Pueblos turned out for service on colonial lands, while colonists abandoned the system of forced labor. New Mexico remained a colony under the authority of the Spanish. But in the aftermath of the Pueblo Revolt, the governing principle was accommodation.

Thus did the Spanish in New Mexico and elsewhere seek to include native peoples as subjects of the king and communicants of the Church. Because the French developed a commercial empire, they too came to rely on a policy of native inclusion. In New England, Virginia, and Carolina, however, where English settlers developed agricultural colonies, the policy was one of exclusion. Indians were pushed to the periphery. These differences help explain the very different histories of the three principal colonial empires in North America.

# The Spanish, the French, and the Dutch in North America

At the beginning of the seventeenth century the Spanish controlled the only colonial outposts on the North American mainland, a series of forts along the Florida coast to protect the Gulf Stream sea-lanes used by the convoys carrying wealth from their New World colonies to Spain. During the first two decades of the new century, however, the Spanish, French, Dutch, and English were all drawn into planting far more substantial colonies in North America.

## New Mexico

After the 1539 expedition of Francisco Vásquez de Coronado failed to turn up vast Indian empires to conquer in the northern Mexican deserts, Spanish interest in the Southwest faded. The densely settled farming communities of the Pueblos did offer a harvest of converts for Christianity, however, and by the 1580s Franciscan missionaries were at work there. Soon rumors drifted back to Mexico City of rich mines along the Rio Grande. In 1598, Juan de Oñate financed an expedition made up of Indians and *mestizos* (people of mixed Indian and European ancestry) with the purpose of mining both gold and souls.

Moving north into the upper Rio Grande Valley, Oñate encountered varying degrees of resistance. He lay siege at Acoma, set high atop a great outcropping of desert rock. Indian warriors killed dozens of Spaniards with their arrows, and women and children bombarded them with stones. But in the end, the attackers succeeded in climbing the rock walls and laying waste to the town, killing 800 men, women, and children. All surviving warriors had one of their feet severed, and more than 500 people were enslaved. In 1606 Spanish authorities in Mexico recalled Oñate for his failure to locate the fabled gold mines. The Church, however, convinced the Spanish monarchy to subsidize New Mexico as a special missionary colony. In 1609, a new governor founded the capital of Santa Fé, and from this base the Franciscan missionaries penetrated all the surrounding Indian villages (see Map 3.1).

**HOW DID** conditions in New Spain and New France differ from Virginia and New England?

myhistorylab
**Review Summary**

**1–6**
Don Juan de Oñate, *Spanish Exploration in the Southwest* (1599)

## IMAGE KEY
for pages 46–47

a. Several sugarcane stems. Sugar was an important New World crop.
b. New Mexico. Pueblos de Taos.
c. Beavers were a plentiful source of clothing and income for their pelts.
d. Matoaka, or Pocahontas (c. 1595–1617), the daughter of Native American Chief Powhatan, after her conversion to Christianity and marriage to settler John Rolfe under the new name Rebecca.
e. A tattered historical beaver hat from 1620.
f. New Amsterdam traders bargaining with each other.
g. An illustration of a tobacco plant.
h. John Winthrop (1588–1649), governor of the Massachusetts Bay Colony.
i. Ships sail into the port of New Amsterdam (New York).
j. Colonists square off against Indians in a detail of a 17th century map of new England.

**Acoma Pueblo, the** "sky city," was founded in the thirteenth century and is one of the oldest continuously inhabited sites in the United States. In 1598, Juan de Oñate attacked and laid waste to the pueblo, killing some 800 inhabitants and enslaving another 500.

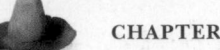

2–2
Samuel de Champlain, *Journal of Samuel de Champlain* (1609)

**MAP 3.1**

**New Mexico in the Seventeenth Century**   By the end of the seventeenth century, New Mexico numbered 3,000 colonial settlers in several towns, surrounded by an estimated 50,000 Pueblo Indians living in some fifty farming villages.

WHAT ROLE did church officials play in the government of New Mexico?

**Coureurs de bois**   French for "woods runner," an independent fur trader in New France.

The colonial economy of New Mexico, based on small-scale agriculture and sheep raising, was never very prosperous. Very few newcomers came from Mexico. Population growth was almost entirely the result of marriages between colonial men and Indian women. By 1700 this northernmost outpost of the Spanish empire in America contained some 3,000 *mestizos* in a few towns along the Rio Grande, surrounded by an estimated 50,000 Pueblos in some fifty villages. New Mexico was a "frontier of inclusion."

## NEW FRANCE

In the early seventeenth century the French devised a strategy to monopolize the northern fur trade. In 1608 Samuel de Champlain, acting as the agent of a royal monopoly, founded the settlement of Quebec on the St. Lawrence River at a site where he could intercept the traffic in furs. He forged an alliance with the Huron Indians, who controlled access to the rich fur grounds of the Great Lakes, and in 1609 and 1610 joined them in making war on their traditional enemies, the Five Nation Iroquois Confederacy. Champlain sent agents and traders to live among native peoples, where they learned native languages and customs, and directed the flow of furs to Quebec.

Thousands of Frenchmen went to New France as *engagés* ("hired men") in the fur trade or the fishery, but nine out of ten returned to France when the term of their service ended. The French might have populated their American empire with thousands of willing Huguenot religious dissenters, but the state resolved that New France would be exclusively Catholic. As a result, the population grew very slowly, reaching a total of only 15,000 colonists by 1700.

Rather than facing the Atlantic, the communities of Canada tended to look westward toward the continental interior. It was typical for the sons of habitants to take to the woods, working as independent traders or **coureurs de bois**, paid agents of the fur companies. Most eventually returned to their home communities, but others married Indian women and raised mixed-ancestry families in distant Indian villages. French traders were living on the Great Lakes as early as the 1620s, and both missionaries and traders were exploring the upper Mississippi River by the 1670s. In 1681–82, fur-trade commandant Robert Sieur de La Salle navigated the mighty river to its mouth on the Gulf of Mexico and claimed its entire watershed for France (see Map 3.2).

Thus, the French, like the Spanish, established a frontier of inclusion in North America. But in other ways the two colonial systems were quite different. The Spanish program was the conquest of native peoples and their exploitation as a labor force in mining, farming, or livestock raising. The French, on the other hand, lacking sufficient manpower to bully, dispossess, or enslave native peoples, sought to build an empire

This drawing by Samuel de Champlain shows how Huron men funneled deer into enclosures, where they could be trapped and easily killed.

**3–3**
James Marquette, *Early French Explorations of the Mississippi River* (1673)

through alliance and commerce with independent Indian nations. There were also important differences between Spanish and French missionary efforts. Unlike Franciscans in seventeenth-century Santa Fé, who insisted that natives must accept European cultural norms as part of their conversion, Jesuit missionaries in New France learned native languages and attempted to understand native customs, in an effort to introduce Christianity as a part of the existing Indian way of life.

## NEW NETHERLAND

The United Provinces of the Netherlands, commonly known as Holland, was only a fraction of the size of France, but in the sixteenth century it became the center of Europe's economic transformation. Amsterdam became the site of the world's first stock exchange and investment banks. Dutch investors built the largest commercial fleet in Europe and captured the lucrative Baltic and North Sea trade in fish, lumber, iron, and grain. It was said that the North Sea was Holland's "America."

Soon, however, the Dutch were establishing trading outposts in America itself. Early in the seventeenth century the United Netherlands organized two great monopolies, the Dutch East India Company and the Dutch West India Company, combining naval military might and commercial strength in campaigns to seize the maritime trade of Asia and the Atlantic. The Dutch first established themselves in North America with the explorations of Henry Hudson in 1609, and within a few years had founded settlements on the Hudson River at the head of oceangoing navigation, a place they called Fort Orange (today's Albany), and at New Amsterdam on Manhattan Island, which guards the entrance to the river. In the 1640s the Dutch also succeeded in overwhelming a small colony of Swedes planted by a Swedish company on the lower Delaware River in 1637, incorporating that region as well into their sphere of influence (see Map 3.2).

**MAP 3.2**
**New France in the Seventeenth Century**   By the late seventeenth century, French settlements were spread from the town of Port Royal in Acadia to the post and mission at Sault Ste. Marie on the Great Lakes.

HOW DID French settlements differ from their English counterparts?

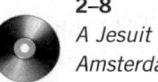
**2–8**
*A Jesuit Priest Describes New Amsterdam* (1642)

**HOW DID** tobacco change the nature of English colonization in Virginia?

**myhistorylab**

Review Summary

**myhistorylab**

Exploring America: *Jamestown*

**Beaver Wars** Series of bloody conflicts, occurring between 1640s and 1680s, during which the Iroquois fought the French for control of the fur trade in the east and the Great Lakes region.

**Virginia Company** A group of London investors who sent ships to Chesapeake Bay in 1607.

**Powhatan Confederacy** A village of communities of the Chesapeake united under Chief Wahunsonacook, who was called King Powhatan by the colonists.

Seeking to match French success in the fur trade, the Dutch West India Company negotiated a commercial alliance with the Five Nation Iroquois Confederacy. Access to Dutch products, including metal tools and firearms, greatly augmented the power of the Iroquois, and they soon launched a campaign to make themselves into the strategic middlemen of the fur trade. Beginning in the 1640s the Iroquois conducted a series of military expeditions against their northern, western, and southern neighbors, known as the **Beaver Wars**. They attacked and dispersed the Hurons, who had long controlled the flow of furs from the Great Lakes to their French allies.

# THE CHESAPEAKE: VIRGINIA AND MARYLAND

England first attempted to plant colonies in North America during the 1580s in Newfoundland and at Roanoke Island in present-day North Carolina (see Chapter 2). Both attempts were dramatic failures. England's war with Spain (1588–1604) suspended further efforts, but thereafter the English once again turned to the Americas.

## JAMESTOWN AND THE POWHATAN CONFEDERACY

In 1607, a group of London investors known as the **Virginia Company** sent a small convoy of vessels to Chesapeake Bay, where a hundred men built a fort they named Jamestown in honor of King James I (reigned 1603–1625). It was destined to become the first permanent English settlement in North America.

The Chesapeake was already home to an estimated 14,000 Indian inhabitants. The village communities of the Chesapeake were united in a politically sophisticated union known as the **Powhatan Confederacy**, led by a powerful chief named Wahunsonacook, whom the Jamestown colonists called "King Powhatan." Powhatan's feelings about Europeans were mixed. He knew they could mean trou-

**This illustration, taken** from Samuel de Champlain's 1613 account of the founding of New France, depicts him joining the Huron attack on the Iroquois in 1609. The French and their Huron allies controlled access to the great fur grounds of the West. The Iroquois then formed an alliance of their own with the Dutch, who had founded a trading colony on the Hudson River. The palm trees in the background of this drawing suggest that it was not executed by an eyewitness, but rather by an illustrator more familiar with South American scenes.

# John Smith's Cartoon History of His Adventures in Virginia

This elaborate illustration, executed by English engraver Robert Vaughan, accompanied John Smith's 1624 account of his years at the English settlement of Jamestown, from 1606 to 1609. It constitutes an early kind of cartoon history. Smith knew how to spin a tale, and these illustrations depict some of the most important turns in his story. A map of "Ould Virginia" (bottom center) is surrounded by vignettes depicting Smith's adventures, including his seizure by the Powhatans (top left), his capture of notable leaders (top right and bottom left), and his rescue from execution by Pocahontas (bottom right). The images told a story of conflict and violence. Much more was to come. One interesting detail is the immense size of the chiefs compared to Smith. The costume, hairstyles, and body decorations of the Indians were taken directly from the images produced by English artist and colonial governor John White. ■

**WHAT MESSAGE** do you think Smith and Vaughan were trying to send with this complex illustration?

John Smith, *The General History of Virginia* (1624) from Beinecke Rare Book and Manuscript Library, Yale University.

ble. In 1571, Spanish missionaries had attempted to plant a colony on the Chesapeake shore, but after they interfered with the practice of native religion they were violently expelled. Still, Powhatan was eager to forge an alliance with these people from across the sea to obtain access to supplies of metal tools and weapons. He allowed the English colonists to build their outpost at Jamestown.

The Jamestown colonists had come to find gold and a passage to the Indies, and failing at both they spent their time gambling and drinking. They survived only because of Powhatan's help. But as more colonists arrived from England and demands for food multiplied, Powhatan had second thoughts. He now realized, he declared to Smith, that the English had come "not for trade, but to invade my people and possess my country." During the terrible winter of 1609–10 more than 400 colonists starved and a number resorted to cannibalism. Of the 500 colonists at Jamestown in the fall, only 60 remained alive by the spring.

Determined to prevail, the Virginia Company sent out a large additional force of men, women, and livestock, committing itself to a protracted war against native men, women, and children. The grim fighting persisted until 1613, when the English captured one of Powhatan's favorite daughters, Matoaka, a girl of about fifteen whom the colonists knew by her nickname, Pocahontas. Eager for the return of his child, and worn down by violence and disease, the next year Powhatan accepted a treaty of peace. The peace was sealed by the marriage of Pocahontas, who converted to Christianity, to John Rolfe, one of the leading colonists. For a brief moment it seemed the English too might move in the direction of a society of inclusion.

In 1617 Rolfe traveled with his wife and son to England, where they were greeted as a new American noble line. But Pocahontas fell ill and died there. Crushed by the news, Powhatan abdicated in favor of his brother Opechancanough before dying of despair. Economic and social developments, however, were already pushing Virginia in the direction of a frontier of exclusion.

## TOBACCO, EXPANSION, AND WARFARE

Tobacco had been introduced to the English by Francis Drake in the 1580s, and by the 1610s a craze for smoking had created strong demand for the product. Pocahontas's husband John Rolfe developed a mild hybrid variety, and soon the first commercial shipments of cured Virginia leaf reached England. Tobacco provided the Virginia Company with the first returns on its investment.

Questions of land and labor would dominate the history of colonial Virginia. Tobacco cultivation required a great deal of hand labor, and it quickly exhausted the soil. The Virginia Company instituted a program of "headright grants," awards of large plantations to wealthy colonists who agreed to transport workers from England at their own cost. Because thousands of English families were being thrown off the land (see Chapter 2), many were attracted to Virginia. Thus, English colonization took a different turn from the Spanish, who mostly sent male colonists. Moreover, the English concentration on plantation agriculture contrasted with the French emphasis on trade. With little need to incorporate Indians into the colony as workers or marriage partners, the English pushed natives out. Virginia became a "frontier of exclusion."

Pressed for additional lands on which to grow tobacco, Chief Opechancanough decided on an assault that would expel the English for good. He encouraged a cultural revival under the guidance of a native shaman named Nemattanew, who instructed his followers to reject the English and their ways. This was the first of many Indian resistance movements led jointly by strong political and religious figures. Opechancanough's uprising, which began on Good Friday, March 22, 1622, completely surprised the English, claiming the lives of 347 colonists, nearly a third of Virginia's colonial population. Yet the colony managed to hang on. The attack stretched into a ten-year war of attrition with horrors committed by both sides.

A TOBACCO PLANTATION

In this eighteenth-century engraving used to promote the sale of tobacco, slaves pack tobacco leaves into "hogsheads" for shipment to England, overseen by a Virginia planter and his clerk. Note the incorporation of the Indian motif.

The Powhatans finally sued for peace in 1632. In the meantime, however, the war had bankrupted the Virginia Company. In 1624 England converted Virginia into a royal colony with civil authorities appointed by the crown, although property-owning colonists continued to elect representatives to the colony's **House of Burgesses**, created in 1619 in an attempt to encourage immigration.

In 1644 Opechancanough organized a final desperate revolt in which more than 500 colonists were killed. But the next year the Virginians crushed the Powhatans, capturing and executing their leader. A formal treaty granted the Indians a number of small reserved territories. By 1670 the Indian population had fallen to just 2,000, overwhelmed by the 40,000 English colonists.

## MARYLAND

In 1632, King Charles I (reigned 1625–49) granted 10 million acres at the northern end of Chesapeake Bay to the Calvert family, important Catholic supporters of the English monarchy. The Calverts named their colony Maryland. Two features distinguished Maryland from Virginia. First, it was a "proprietary" colony in which the Calvert family held the sole power to appoint civil officers and was sole owner of all the land. Second, the Calvert family encouraged settlement by Catholics, a persecuted minority in seventeenth-century England. In fact, Maryland became the only English colony in North America with a substantial Catholic minority.

Yet Maryland quickly became much like neighboring Virginia. The tobacco plantation economy created pressures for labor and land. In 1640, the colony adopted the system of headright grants previously developed in Virginia, and settlements of independent planters quickly spread out on both sides of Chesapeake Bay.

## COMMUNITY LIFE IN THE CHESAPEAKE

At least three-quarters of the English migrants to the Chesapeake came as **indentured servants**. In exchange for the cost of their transportation to the New World, men and women contracted to labor for a master for a fixed term. Most were young, unskilled males, who served for two to seven years, but some were skilled craftsmen, unmarried women, or even orphan children. African slaves were first

**House of Burgesses**   The legislature of colonial Virginia. First organized in 1619, it was the first institution of representative government in the English colonies.

**Indentured Servants**   Individuals who contracted to serve a master for a period of four to seven years in return for payment of the servant's passage to America.

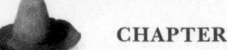

introduced to the Chesapeake in 1619, but slaves were more expensive than servants, and as late as 1680 they made up less than 7 percent of the population. In the hard-driving economy of the Chesapeake, however, masters treated servants as cruelly as they treated slaves.

Many indentured servants who survived their terms and were able to raise the price of passage quickly returned to England. Those who remained became eligible for "freedom dues"—clothing, tools, a gun, or a spinning wheel to help them get started on their own. They often headed west in the hope of cutting a farm from the forest.

Because most emigrants were men, whether free or indentured, free unmarried women often married as soon as they arrived in the Chesapeake, and widows remarried quickly, sometimes within days. Their scarcity provided women with certain advantages. Shrewd widows bargained for a remarriage agreement that gave them a larger share of the estate than what was set by common law. So notable was the concentration of wealth in the hands of these widows that one historian has suggested early Virginia was a "matriarchy." But because of high mortality rates, family size was smaller and kinship bonds—one of the most important components of community—were weaker than in England.

Prosperous planters, investing everything in tobacco production, lived in rough wooden dwellings. On the western edge of the settlements, freed servants lived with their families in shacks, huts, even caves. Colonists spread across the countryside in search of new tobacco lands, creating dispersed settlements with hardly any towns. Before 1650 there were few community institutions such as schools and churches.

Nevertheless, the Chesapeake was a growing region. By the end of the seventeenth century the combined population of the Maryland and Virginia colonies was nearly 90,000. In contrast to the colonists of New France, who were developing a distinctive identity because of their connections with native peoples, the English residents of the Chesapeake maintained close emotional ties to the mother country.

# THE NEW ENGLAND COLONIES

Both in climate and in geography, the northern coast of North America was far different from the Chesapeake. "Merchantable commodities" such as tobacco could not be produced there, and thus it was far less favored for investment and settlement. Instead, the region became a haven for Protestant dissenters from England, who gave the colonies of the north a distinctive character of their own (see Map 3.3).

## PURITANISM

Most English men and women continued to practice a Christianity little different from traditional Catholicism. But the English followers of John Calvin, known as **Puritans** because they wished to purify and reform the English church from within, grew increasingly influential during the last years of Elizabeth's reign at the end of the sixteenth century. The Calvinist emphasis on enterprise meant that **Puritanism** appealed to merchants, entrepreneurs, and commercial farmers, those most responsible for the rapid economic and social transformation of England. Yet the Puritans were also the most vocal critics of the disruptive effects of that change, condemning the decline of the traditional rural community and the growing number of "idle and masterless men" produced by the enclosure of common

---

### QUICK REVIEW

**The Pilgrims**

- Plymouth Colony founded in 1620.
- Puritans wanted reform of the Church of England.
- Pilgrims were separatists who believed the Church of England could not be reformed.

**WHAT WERE** the social and political values of Puritanism and how did religious dissent shape the history of the New England colonies?

**myhistorylab**
**Review Summary**

**Puritans** Individuals who believed that Queen Elizabeth's reforms of the Church of England had not gone far enough in improving the church. Puritans led the settlement of Massachusetts Bay Colony.

**Puritanism** Movement to purify and reform the English Church.

lands. They argued for reviving communities by placing reformed Christian congregations at their core to monitor the behavior of individuals.

James I abandoned Queen Elizabeth's policy of religious tolerance. His persecution of the Puritans, however, merely stiffened their resolve and turned them toward open political opposition. James's son and successor, Charles I (reigned 1625–49), was heavily criticized by the increasingly vocal Puritan minority for marrying a French Roman Catholic princess and supporting "High Church" policies, emphasizing the authority of the clerical hierarchy and traditional forms of worship. In 1629, determined to rule without these troublesome opponents, Charles dismissed Parliament and launched a campaign of repression against the Puritans. This political turmoil provided the context for the migration of thousands of English Protestants to New England.

## PLYMOUTH COLONY

The first English colony in New England was founded by a group of religious dissenters known to later generations as the **Pilgrims**. At the time they were called **Separatists** because they believed the English church was so corrupt they had to establish independent congregations. One group moved to Holland in 1609, but fearful that tolerant and secular Dutch society was seducing their children, they decided on emigration to North America. Backed by the Virginia Company of London and led by tradesman William Bradford, 102 people sailed from England on the *Mayflower* in September 1620.

The little group, mostly families but including a substantial number of single men hired by the investors, arrived in Massachusetts Bay at the site of the former Indian village of Pawtuxet, which the English renamed Plymouth. Soon the hired men began to grumble about being excluded from decision making, and to reassure them Bradford drafted an agreement by which all the male members of the expedition did "covenant and combine together into a civil body politic." The **Mayflower Compact** was the first document of self-government in North America.

Weakened by scurvy and malnutrition, nearly half the colonists perished over the first winter. Like the earlier settlers of Roanoke and Jamestown, however, they were rescued by Indians. Massasoit, the *sachem* or chief of the Pokanokets, offered the newcomers food and advice in return for an alliance against his enemies, the Narragansets. It was the familiar pattern of Indians attempting to incorporate European colonists into their own world.

The Pilgrims supported themselves by farming, but like all colonies Plymouth needed a source of revenue, in their case in order to pay off their English investors. The foundation of their commercial economy was the cod fishery in the rich coastal banks of the Atlantic. With this revenue the Pilgrims were able to establish a self-sufficient community.

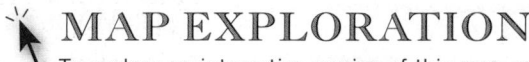

## MAP EXPLORATION

To explore an interactive version of this map, go to
**http://www.prenhall.com/faraghertlc/map3.3**

**MAP 3.3**

**European Colonies of the Atlantic Coast, 1607–39**   Virginia, on Chesapeake Bay, was the first English colony in North America, but by the mid-seventeenth century, Virginia was joined by settlements of Scandinavians on the Delaware River and Dutch on the Hudson River, as well as English religious dissenters in New England.

HOW MANY European nations had established colonies on the Atlantic coast by the middle of the seventeenth century?

**Pilgrims**   Settlers of Plymouth Colony, who viewed themselves as spiritual wanderers.

**Separatists**   Members of an offshoot branch of Puritanism. Separatists believed that the Church of England was too corrupt to be reformed and hence were convinced they must "separate" from it to save their souls.

**Mayflower Compact**   The first document of self-government in North America.

**2–5**

John Winthrop, *A Modell of Christian Charity* (1630)

**Massachusetts Bay Company**   A group of wealthy Puritans who were granted a royal charter in 1629 to settle in Massachusetts Bay.

## THE MASSACHUSETTS BAY COLONY

In England, the political climate of the late 1620s convinced growing numbers of influential Puritans that the only way to protect their congregations was by emigration. In 1629 a royal charter was granted to a group of wealthy Puritans who called their enterprise the **Massachusetts Bay Company**, and an advance force of 200 settlers left for the fishing settlement of Naumkeag on Massachusetts Bay, which they renamed Salem.

The colonists hoped to establish what John Winthrop, their leader and first governor, called "a city on a hill," a New England model of reform for old England. In this they differed from the Pilgrims, who never considered returning. Between 1629 and 1643 some 20,000 individuals relocated to Massachusetts, establishing the port town of Boston and ringing it with towns. By the 1640s their settlements had spread seventy-five miles west to the Connecticut River Valley.

Taking advantage of a loophole in their charter, in 1629 Puritan leaders transferred company operations from England to Massachusetts, and within a few years had transformed the company into a civil government. The original charter established a General Court composed of a governor and his deputy, a board of magistrates (or advisers), and the members of the corporation, known as freemen. In 1632, Governor Winthrop and his advisers declared that all the male heads of households in Massachusetts, who were also church members, were freemen. Two years later, the freemen secured their right to select delegates to represent the towns in drafting the laws of the colony. These delegates and the magistrates later became the colony's two legislative houses. Thus, the procedures of a joint-stock company provided the origins for democratic suffrage and the bicameral division of legislative authority in America.

## DISSENT AND NEW COMMUNITIES

Doctrinal disagreements among the Puritans often led to the establishment of new colonies. In 1636 Thomas Hooker, minister of the congregation at Cambridge, after objecting to the Massachusetts policy of restricting male suffrage to church members, led his followers west to the Connecticut River, where they founded the town of Hartford. The same year Roger Williams, the minister at Salem, was banished from Massachusetts for advocating religious tolerance. With a group of his followers, Williams emigrated to the country surrounding Narraganset Bay.

In 1637 religious controversy produced another schism. Anne Hutchinson, the brilliant and outspoken wife of a Puritan merchant, criticized a number of Boston ministers. Their concentration on good works, she argued, led people to believe they could earn their way to heaven. Hutchinson was called before the General Court, and in an extraordinary hearing was reprimanded, excommunicated, and banished. She and a group of followers relocated to the Williams colony on Narraganset Bay.

To protect the dissenters in his settlement from Puritan interference, Williams won royal charters in 1644 and 1663 establishing the independent colony of Rhode Island, with guarantees of self-government and complete religious liberty.

**Governor John Winthrop**, ca. 1640, a portrait by an unknown artist. Winthrop was first elected governor of Massachusetts Bay Colony in 1629, then was voted out of office and reelected a total of twelve times.

## INDIANS AND PURITANS

The Indian communities of southern New England discovered soon after the arrival of the Pilgrims and the Puritans that these colonists were quite different from the French and Dutch traders who had preceded them. Although the fur trade was an important part of the economy of Plymouth and Massachusetts, the principal concern of the colonists was the acquisition of Indian land for their growing settlements.

Like the Jamestown colonists, most Puritans believed they had the right to take what they considered "unused" lands, that is, lands not used in the English way. Potential conflicts among settlers over title, however, made it necessary to obtain original deeds from Indians, and the English used a variety of tactics to pressure leaders into signing "quitclaims," relinquishing all claim to specified properties. Meanwhile epidemic disease continued to devastate Indian villages. Disorganized and demoralized, many coastal native communities not only gave up their lands but also placed themselves under the protection of the English. By the late 1630s only a few tribes in southern New England retained the power to challenge Puritan expansion. The Pequots, who lived along the shores of Long Island Sound near the mouth of the Connecticut River, were one of the most powerful. Allies of the Dutch, the Pequots controlled the production of wampum, woven belts of seashells used as a medium of exchange in the Indian trade. In 1637, Puritan leaders pressured the Pequots' traditional enemies, the Narragansets of present-day Rhode Island, to join them in waging war on the Pequots. Narragansett warriors and English troops attacked the main Pequot village, burning the houses and killing most of their slumbering residents.

## THE ECONOMY: NEW ENGLAND MERCHANTS

In England, the dispute between King Charles I and the Puritans in Parliament escalated into armed conflict in 1642. Several years of revolutionary confrontation finally led to Charles's arrest, his execution in 1649, and the creation of an English Commonwealth, headed by the Puritan military leader Oliver Cromwell. Because the Puritans were on the victorious side in the English civil war, they no longer had the same incentive to migrate to New England. A number of colonists returned to England.

New England's economy had depended on the sale of supplies and land to arriving immigrants, but this market collapsed as the migration tailed off. Puritan merchants turned to the flourishing fishery, shipping cod (in addition to lumber and farm products) to the West Indies, where they bartered for sugar, molasses and rum. By midcentury New England had constructed a commercial fleet of more than 300 vessels, and by the end of the century Boston had become the third largest English commercial center in the Atlantic (after London and Bristol). The development of a diversified economy provided New England with important long-term strength and offered a striking contrast with the specialized fur-trade economy of New France.

## COMMUNITY AND FAMILY IN NEW ENGLAND

Pilgrims and Puritans stressed the importance of well-ordered communities. Settlers typically clustered their dwellings in a central village, near the meetinghouse that served as both church and civic center. Clustered settlements and strong communities distinguished New England from the dispersed and weak communities of the Chesapeake.

**2–7**
*The Trial of Anne Hutchinson*
(1638)

---

**QUICK REVIEW**

---

**Early Dissenters**

◆ Thomas Hooker: Objected to restrictions on male suffrage.

◆ Anne Hutchinson: Voiced theological disagreements with Boston ministers.

◆ Roger Williams: Advocated religious toleration.

**2–6**
John Mason, *The Taking of the Fort at Mystic* (1637)

**The first map** printed in the English colonies, this view of New England was published in Boston in 1677. With north oriented to the right, it looks west from Massachusetts Bay, the two vertical black lines indicating the approximate boundaries of the Commonwealth of Massachusetts. The territory west of Rhode Island is noted as an Indian stronghold, the homelands of the Narraganset, Pequot, and Nipmuck peoples.

The ideal Puritan family was also well ordered. Parents often participated in the choice of mates for their offspring, and children typically married in the order of their births, younger children waiting until arrangements had been made for their elder siblings. Another source of New England's strength was the impressive Puritan education system. In 1647 the Massachusetts General Court required that towns with 50 families or more support a public school; those with 100 families were to establish a grammar school instructing students in Latin, knowledge of which was required for admission to Harvard College, founded in 1636. The Puritan colony of Connecticut enacted similar requirements. By the mid-seventeenth century, New England men boasted the highest rates of literacy in North America and much of Europe. Because girls were excluded from grammar schools, however, women's literacy remained relatively low.

The Puritans were not "puritanical" in the modern sense of the word. Although they treated adultery as a capital crime, they celebrated sexual expression within marriage. Courting couples were encouraged to engage in "petting," and married couples were expected to enjoy sexual relations.

## THE POSITION OF WOMEN

Families were supposed to operate as "little commonwealths," with everyone working cooperatively. The domestic economy required the combined efforts of husband and wife. Men were generally responsible for fieldwork, women for the work of the household, garden, henhouse, and dairy.

Still, the cultural ideal was the subordination of women to men. Married women could not make contracts, own property, vote, or hold office. A typical woman, marrying in her early twenties and surviving through her forties, could expect to bear eight children and devote herself to husband and family. Aside from abstinence, there was no form of birth control. Wives who failed to have

**Exploring America:** *Witches in the American Imagination*

children, or widows who were economically independent, aroused significant suspicion among their neighbors.

## THE SALEM WITCH TRIALS

The cultural mistrust of women came to the surface most notably in periodic witchcraft scares. During the seventeenth century, according to one historian, 342 New England women were accused by their neighbors of witchcraft. The majority of the accused were unmarried, or childless, or widowed, or had reputations in their communities for assertiveness and independence. In the vast majority of cases, the charges were dismissed by authorities as baseless. In the infamous 1692 case of Salem, Massachusetts, however, the whole community was thrown into a panic of accusations when a group of girls claimed that they had been bewitched by a number of old women. Before the colonial governor finally called a halt to the persecutions in 1693, twenty people had been tried, condemned, and executed.

The Salem witchcraft scare may have reflected social tensions that found their outlet through an attack on people perceived as outsiders. Salem was a booming commercial port, but while some residents were prospering, others were not. Most of the victims came from the commercial eastern end of town, the majority of their accusers from the economically stagnant western side. Most of the accused also came from Anglican, Quaker, or Baptist families. Finally, a majority of the victims were old women, suspect because they lived alone, without the guidance of men. The Salem witchcraft crisis exposed the dark side of Puritan thinking about women.

## THE PROPRIETARY COLONIES

Oliver Cromwell died in 1658 and two years later Parliament, anxious for stability, restored the Stuart monarchy, placing on the throne Charles II (reigned 1660–85), eldest son of the deposed king. Charles took an active interest in North America, establishing several new proprietary colonies on the model of Maryland (see Map 3.4).

### THE CAROLINAS

Charles II issued the first of his charters in 1663, establishing a new colony called Carolina, which stretched along the Atlantic coast from Virginia south to the northern limits of Spanish Florida. Virginians had already begun moving into the vicinity of Albermarle Sound in the northern part of this territory, and in 1664 the Carolina proprietors appointed a governor and created a popularly elected assembly. By 1700 North Carolina, as it became known, included 11,000 small farmers and large tobacco planters.

Settlement farther south began in 1670 with the founding of coastal Charles Town (renamed Charleston in

WHAT ROLE did the crown play in the founding of English colonies after 1660?

**myhistorylab**
**Review Summary**

## MAP EXPLORATION

To explore an interactive version of this map, go to
**http://www.prenhall.com/faraghertlc/map3.4**

**MAP 3.4**

**The Proprietary Colonies**   After the restoration of the Stuart monarchy in 1660, King Charles II of England created the new proprietary colonies of Carolina, New York, Pennsylvania, and New Jersey. New Hampshire was set off as a royal colony in 1680, and in 1704, the lower counties of Pennsylvania became the colony of Delaware.

EXAMINE THE processes underlying the founding of the Proprietary Colonies. How had the political landscape changed since 1639?

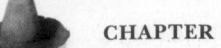

**The earliest known** view of New Amsterdam, published in 1651. Indian traders are shown arriving with their goods in a dugout canoe of distinctive design known to have been produced by the native people of Long Island Sound. Twenty-five years after its founding, the Dutch settlement still occupies only the lower tip of Manhattan Island.

Fort New Amsterdam, New York, 1651. Engraving. Collection of The New-York Historical Society, 77354d.

FORT NEW AMSTERDAM (NEW YORK), 1651.

1783). Most South Carolina settlers came from the sugar colony of Barbados, a Caribbean colony founded by the English in 1627. They lent a distinctly West Indian character to the colony. By 1700 South Carolina's population was more than 6,000, including some 3,000 enslaved Africans. (For a complete discussion of slavery see Chapter 4.)

## NEW YORK AND NEW JERSEY

Charles also coveted the lucrative Dutch colony of New Netherland. In 1651, Parliament passed a Trade and Navigation Act that barred Dutch vessels from English colonial possessions. This led to an inconclusive naval war between the two nations from 1652 to 1654. Ten years later the two powers clashed once again, this time along the West African coast, leading to a second Anglo-Dutch war. In September 1664 a small English fleet sailed into Manhattan harbor and forced the surrender of New Amsterdam without firing a shot. When the war ended with an inconclusive peace in 1667, the English were left in possession. Holland briefly regained control during a third and final conflict from 1672 to 1674, but the English won the war and won possession of the colony in the peace negotiations. This final war bankrupted the Dutch West India Company and marked the ascension of the English to dominance in the Atlantic, although Holland remained supreme in the Baltic and the East Indies.

Charles II issued a proprietary charter granting the former Dutch colony to his brother James, the Duke of York, renaming it New York in his honor. Ethnically and linguistically diversified, and accommodating a wide range of religious sects, New York society was the most heterogeneous in North America. In 1665, the communities of the Delaware Valley were split off as the **proprietary colony** of New Jersey.

**Proprietary colony** A colony created when the English monarch granted a huge tract of land to an individual or group of individuals, who became "lords proprietor."

**Quakers** Members of the Society of Friends, a radical religious group that arose in the mid-seventeenth century. Quakers rejected formal theology, focusing instead on the Holy Spirit that dwelt within them.

## THE FOUNDING OF PENNSYLVANIA

In 1676, the proprietary rights to the western portion of New Jersey were sold to a group of English religious dissenters, including William Penn. A member of the Society of Friends (known popularly as the **Quakers**), Penn intended to

**The Delawares presented** William Penn with this wampum belt after the Shackamaxon Treaty of 1682. In friendship, a Quaker in distinctive hat clasps the hand of an Indian. The diagonal stripes on either side of the figures represent the "open paths" between the English and the Delawares. Wampum belts like this one, made from strings of white and purple shell beads, were used to commemorate treaties throughout the colonial period, and were the most widely accepted form of money in the northeastern colonies during the seventeenth century.

make the colony a haven for religious toleration and pacifism. In 1681, to settle a large debt he owed William Penn's father, King Charles issued to his son a proprietary grant to a huge territory west of the Delaware River.

Penn wanted this colony to be a "holy experiment." In his first **Frame of Government**, drafted in 1682, he included guarantees of religious freedom, civil liberties, and elected representation. He also attempted to deal fairly with the native peoples, refusing to permit colonization to begin until settlement rights were negotiated and lands purchased. Although relations between Pennsylvania and Indian peoples later soured, during Penn's lifetime his reputation for fair dealing led a number of native groups to resettle in the Quaker colony.

During the first two decades of Pennsylvania's settlement, nearly 20,000 settlers spread agricultural communities from the banks of the Delaware to the fertile interior valleys. In 1704 Penn approved the creation of a separate colony called Delaware for the governance of the counties near the mouth of the river formerly controlled first by the Swedes and then the Dutch.

# CONFLICT AND WAR

Pennsylvania's ability to maintain peaceful relations with the Indians proved the great exception. The last quarter of the seventeenth century became a time of great violence throughout the colonial regions of the continent, mostly because of the expansion of European settlement (see Map 3.5). Much of this warfare was between colonists and Indians, but intertribal warfare and intercolonial rivalry greatly contributed to the violence.

## KING PHILIP'S WAR

In New England, nearly forty years of peace followed the **Pequot War** of 1637. Natives and colonists lived in close, if tense, contact. Some two thousand native converts eventually relocated to Christian communities known as "praying towns." But there remained several independent tribes, including the Pokanokets, the

---

**3–6**
William Penn, *Charter of Privileges* (1701)

**QUICK REVIEW**

**Pennsylvania**

◆ Territory west of the Delaware River granted to William Penn in 1681.

◆ Penn supervised the establishment of Philadelphia in 1682.

◆ Penn, a Quaker, saw the colony as a "holy experiment."

**WHAT LED** to violent conflict between Indians and colonists?

myhistorylab
**Review Summary**

**Frame of Government**   William Penn's constitution for Pennsylvania which included a provision allowing for religious freedom.

**Pequot War**   Conflict between English settlers and Pequot Indians over control of land and trade in eastern Connecticut.

**MAP 3.5**
**Spread of Settlement: British Colonies, 1650–1700**    The spread of settlement in the English colonies in the late seventeenth century created the conditions for a number of violent conflicts, including King Philip's War, Bacon's Rebellion, and King William's War

WHAT FACTORS were behind the spread of British settlement in the second half of the seventeenth century?

**3–4**
Edward Randolph, *King Philip's War* (1685)

**King Philip's War**    Conflict in New England (1675–1676) between Wampanoags, Narragansetts, and other Indian peoples against English settlers; sparked by English encroachments on native lands.

**Covenant Chain**    An alliance between the Iroquois Confederacy and the colony of New York which sought to establish Iroquois dominance over all other tribes.

Narragansets, and the Abenakis of northern New England. The extraordinary expansion of the colonial population, and the increasing hunger for land, created inexorable pressures for expansion into their territories.

The Pokanokets, whose homeland lay between Rhode Island and Plymouth, were led by the sachem Metacom, whom the English called King Philip. Metacom had been raised among English colonists and educated in their schools. He operated on the assumption that his people had a future in the English colonial world but was gradually forced to conclude that the colonists had no room for the Pokanokets. In 1671 the colonial authorities of Plymouth pressured Metacom into granting them sovereign authority over his homeland. This humiliation convinced him that he had to break the half-century alliance with Plymouth and take up armed resistance. The Puritan colonies, meanwhile, prepared for a war of conquest.

What became known as **King Philip's War** came in the spring of 1675, and at first things went well for the Indians. They forced the abandonment of English settlements on the Connecticut River and torched towns less than twenty miles from Boston. By the beginning of 1676, however, their campaign was collapsing. A combined colonial army defeated a large Indian force in a battle known as the Great Swamp Fight in Narraganset country. Metacom led his men and fled west to the border with New York where he appealed for support from the Iroquois. But instead of helping, the Iroquois attacked forcing Metacom back to Pokanoket territory, where colonists annihilated his army in August 1676. Metacom was quartered, his severed head mounted on a pike at Plymouth.

In attacking the Pequots, the Iroquois were motivated by interests of their own. Extending the role they had played in the Dutch trading system, they now cast themselves as powerful intermediaries between other tribes and the English. In a series of negotiations conducted at Albany in 1677, the Iroquois Confederacy and the colony of New York created an alliance known as the **Covenant Chain**. It envisioned Iroquois dominance over all other tribes, thus putting New York in an economically and politically dominant position among the other colonies.

An estimated 4,000 natives and 2,000 colonists died during the war, and dozens of native and colonial towns lay in ruins. Fearing attack from Indians close at hand, colonists also destroyed most of the Indian praying towns, killing many of the Christian residents. Calculated in the number of lives lost, King Philip's War was the most destructive Indian–colonist conflict in early American history.

## BACON'S REBELLION AND SOUTHERN CONFLICTS

While King Philip's War raged in New England, another English–Indian confrontation took shape in the Chesapeake and mutated into civil war. The basic cause of the conflict was the old problem of land and labor. By the 1670s Indian communities residing on the frontier of the colony were under assault by colonists in search of new tobacco lands. The insatiable hunger came not only from established planters with lands reaching exhaustion but also from former servants who had served out their indentures. Governor William Berkeley, in office since the 1640s, ruled in alliance with the big planters, who feared landless freemen even more than they did Indians. In 1670 the Burgesses had enacted legislation restricting the suffrage to property owners; nevertheless every man still had to pay taxes. Smoldering class antagonism thus added to the volatile mix. When in 1675 the governor declined to send the militia against the Indians, colonists under the leadership of wealthy backcountry planter Nathaniel Bacon embarked on unauthorized raids resulting in the indiscriminate murder of many natives, including those allied with the colony. Bacon became a hero to former servants, and although Berkeley fumed, he ordered the first elections in many years in an attempt to appease the people.

But Berkeley's move backfired when Bacon went further, demanding the death or removal of all Indians from the colony as well as an end to the rule of aristocratic "grandees" and "parasites." Berkeley fled across the Chesapeake, Bacon seized control, and his volunteer force burned Jamestown to the ground. Soon thereafter, however, the rebel leader came down with dysentery. He died and the rebellion collapsed. Berkeley returned, reestablished control, and ordered the execution of Bacon's lieutenants.

This brief but violent clash signaled a developing conflict between backcountry districts and more established coastal regions where the "Indian problem" had long since been settled. Backcountry men in the Albermarle region of North Carolina staged a similar revolt in 1677, an episode known as **Culpeper's Rebellion**. They overthrew the established government and held power for two years before the proprietors reestablished authority. These rebellions revealed the power of class antagonism. But they also suggested that the Indians could play the role of convenient scapegoats.

3–2
Nathaniel Bacon's Challenge to William Berkeley and the Governor's Response

**Culpeper's Rebellion** The overthrow of the established government in the Albermarle region of North Carolina by backcountry men in 1677.

Colonial officials in South Carolina seemed to be paying attention. They encouraged Indians allied with the colony—Yamasees, Creeks, Cherokees, and Chickasaws—to wage war on tribes affiliated with rival colonial powers, including the mission Indians of Spanish Florida, the Choctaw allies of the French, and the Tuscaroras, trading partners of the Virginians. In addition to opening new lands for settlement, the brutal fighting resulted in the capture of many thousands of Indians who were sold into slavery. These wars continued into the first quarter of the eighteenth century.

## THE GLORIOUS REVOLUTION IN AMERICA

Dynastic change in England was another factor in the violence in North America. After Charles II died in 1685, his brother and successor, James II (reigned 1685–88), began a concerted effort to strengthen royal control over the colonies. The king's ministers believed colonial assemblies had grown too powerful and independent and were determined to rein them in. The New York assembly, considered particularly troublesome, was abolished and all power placed in the hands of the colony's royal governor. In the other colonies governors challenged the authority of assemblies. The king annulled the charter governments of New England, New York, and New Jersey and combined them into a single supercolony known as the Dominion of New England. Edmund Andros, appointed royal governor, imposed Anglican forms of worship in Puritan areas and overthrew long-standing traditions of local autonomy.

James ruled England in the same imperious style. He was a practicing Catholic, and his appointment of Catholics to high positions of state added to rising discontent and protest. The last straw was the birth of a royal son in 1688. Fearing the establishment of a Catholic dynasty, Parliamentary leaders deposed James and replaced him with his Protestant daughter Mary, who was married to William of Orange, hereditary head of state of the Netherlands. When the army refused to prevent William and Mary from landing in England, James fled to France. The relatively nonviolent "Glorious Revolution," as it came to be known, included a Bill of Rights, issued by the new monarchs at the insistence of Parliament, in which they promised to respect traditional civil liberties, to summon and consult with Parliament annually, and to enforce and administer its legislation. These were significant concessions with profound implications for the future of English politics. In essence, England had become a "constitutional monarchy."

In North America, news of the Glorious Revolution sparked a series of colonial rebellions against the authorities set in place by King James. In the spring of 1689, Governor Andros was attacked by a Boston mob. He escaped their wrath but was arrested and deported. The Boston uprising inspired another in New York led by merchant Jacob Leisler that included many prominent Dutch residents. They seized control of the city and called for the formation of a new legislature. In Maryland, rumors of a Catholic plot led to the overthrow of the proprietary rule of the Calvert family by an insurgent group calling itself the Protestant Association.

The new regime in London carefully measured its response to these uprisings. When Jacob Leisler attempted to prevent the landing of the king's troops in New York, he was arrested, tried, and executed. But William and Mary also consented to the breakup of the Dominion of New England and the termination of proprietary rule in Maryland. All the affected colonies quickly revived their assemblies and returned to their tradition of self-government. The monarchs strengthened royal authority, however, by decreeing that henceforth Massachusetts, New York, and Maryland would be royal colonies.

## CHRONOLOGY

| | |
|---|---|
| 1598 | Juan de Oñate leads Spanish into New Mexico |
| 1607 | English found Jamestown |
| 1608 | French found Quebec |
| 1609 | Spanish found Santa Fé |
| 1620 | Pilgrim emigration |
| 1622 | Indian uprising in Virginia |
| 1625 | Jesuit missionaries arrive in New France |
| 1629 | Puritans begin settlement of Massachusetts Bay |
| 1637 | Pequot War |
| 1649 | Charles I executed |
| 1660 | Stuart monarchy restored, Charles II becomes king |

| | |
|---|---|
| 1675 | King Philip's War |
| | Bacon's Rebellion |
| 1680 | Pueblo Revolt |
| 1681–82 | Robert Sieur de La Salle explores the Misissippi |
| 1688 | The Glorious Revolution |
| 1689 | King William's War |
| 1696 | Spanish reconquest of the Pueblos completed |
| 1701 | English impose royal governments on all colonies but Massachusetts, Connecticut, and Pennsylvania |

### KING WILLIAM'S WAR

The year 1689 also marked the beginning of nearly seventy-five years of armed conflict between English and French forces for control of the North American interior. The competition in the colonies was part of a larger conflict between England and France over the European balance of power. Armed conflict in what is known as the War of the Grand Alliance began in Europe in 1688 and spread to the colonies, where it was known as **King William's War** (for the new king of England). The inconclusive war ended in 1697 with an equally inconclusive peace. War between England and France would resume only five years later.

The persistent violence of the last quarter of the seventeenth century greatly concerned English authorities, who began to fear the loss of their North American possessions by outside attack or internal disorder. In 1701 the English Board of Trade converted the remaining charter and proprietary colonies into royal ones. Eventually William Penn succeeded in regaining private control of Pennsylvania, and Rhode Island and Connecticut won reinstatement of their charter governments. But the most lasting result of this quarter-century of turmoil was the tightening of English control over its North American colonies.

**King William's War** The first of a series of colonial struggles between England and France, these conflicts occur principally on the frontiers of northern New England and New York between 1689 and 1697.

## CONCLUSION

At the beginning of the seventeenth century, the European presence north of Mexico was extremely limited: Spanish bases in Florida, a few Franciscan missions among the Pueblos, and fishermen along the North Atlantic coast. By 1700 the human landscape of the Southwest, the South, and the Northeast had been transformed. More than a quarter million migrants from the Old World had come to North America, the great majority of them to the English colonies. Indian societies had been disrupted, depopulated, and in some cases destroyed. The violence that flared during the last quarter of the seventeenth century was a measure of the cost of empire. Indian people resisted colonial rule in New Mexico, New England, and the Chesapeake.

Like King Philip's War and Bacon's Rebellion, the Pueblo Revolt was an episode of great violence and destruction. Yet it resulted in a long period of accommodation between the Pueblos and the Spanish colonists. The English colonists, however, took a different lesson from the violent conflicts in their colonies. They renewed their commitment to establishing communities of exclusion with ominous implications for the future of relations between colonists and natives.

## REVIEW QUESTIONS

1. Using examples drawn from this chapter, discuss the differences between colonizing "frontiers of inclusion" and "exclusion."

2. What factors turned England's Chesapeake colony of Virginia from stark failure to brilliant success?

3. Discuss the role of religious dissent in the founding of the first New England colonies and in stimulating the creation of others.

4. Compare and contrast William Penn's policy with respect to Indian tribes with the policies of other English settlers, in the Chesapeake and New England, and with the policies of the Spanish, the French, and the Dutch.

5. What were the principal causes of colonial violence and warfare of the late seventeenth century?

## KEY TERMS

Flashcard Review

Beaver Wars (p. 52)
*Coureurs de bois* (p. 50)
Covenant Chain (p. 64)
Culpeper's Rebellion (p. 65)
Frame of Government (p. 63)
House of Burgesses (p. 55)
Indentured Servants (p. 55)
King Philip's War (p. 64)
King William's War (p. 67)
Massachusetts Bay Company (p. 58)

Mayflower Compact (p. 57)
Pequot War (p. 63)
Pilgrims (p. 57)
Powhatan Confederacy (p. 52)
Proprietary colony (p. 62)
Puritans (p. 56)
Puritanism (p. 56)
Quakers (p. 62)
Separatists (p. 57)
Virginia Company (p. 52)

## RECOMMENDED READING

James Axtell, *The European and the Indian: Essays in the Ethnohistory of Colonial America* (1981). A readable introduction to the dynamics of mutual discovery between natives and colonizers.

Leslie Choquette, *Frenchmen into Peasants: Modernity and Tradition in the Peopling of French Canada* (1997). A history of French immigrants to North America, based on a comprehensive database of hundreds of individuals. The most detailed study of French colonization.

James Horn, *A Land as God Made It: Jamestown and the Birth of America* (2005). Near the 400th anniversary of Jamestown's founding, a new history that includes important archaeological evidence.

Andrew L. Knaut, *The Pueblo Revolt of 1680* (1995). The most complete and sophisticated account of the revolt.

Edmund S. Morgan, *American Slavery, American Freedom* (1975). A classic interpretation of early Virginia, arguing that early American ideas of freedom for some were based on the reality of slavery for many.

Diana Newton, *Papists, Protestants, and Puritans, 1559–1714* (1998). The best survey of religious change during the Protestant Reformation with a focus on the turmoil in England.

Daniel K. Richter, *Facing East from Indian Country: A Native History of Early America* (2001). Colonial history from the point of view of the Indians. Includes remarkable biographical chapters on Pocahontas and Metacom.

Nicholas A. Robins, *Native Insurgencies and the Genocidal Impulse in the Americas* (2005). A comparative study of several native insurgencies on the Spanish frontier, prominently featuring the Pueblo Revolt.

Helen C. Rountree, *Pocahontas, Powhatan, Opechancanough: Three Indian Lives Changed by Jamestown* (2005). The leading authority on the Indians of eastern Virginia tells the story of colonization from the native perspective.

Susan Sleeper-Smith, *Native Women and French Men: Rethinking Cultural Encounter in the Western Great Lakes* (2001). A study of Indian women who married French traders and became cultural intermediaries.

David J. Weber, *The Spanish Frontier in North America* (1992). A powerful overview that includes comprehensive histories of New Mexico and Florida.

For study resources for this chapter, go to **www.myhistorylab.com** and choose *Out of Many, Teaching and Learning Classroom Edition.* You will find a wealth of study and review material for this chapter, including pretests and posttests, customized study plan, key-term review flash cards, interactive map and document activities, and documents for analysis.

# Democratic Roots in New England Soil

The Puritans of New England were less than democratic in both beliefs and goals. Contrary to popular myth, they did not migrate to the New World to establish religious freedom. They were seeking to establish a religious utopia to serve as what Governor John Winthrop called a "light upon a hill" for the world to emulate. They forbid the establishment of other religious doctrine, especially the Quakers and Roman Catholic faith. In Puritan communities nonconformist behavior was looked upon with deep suspicion, especially if it was religious in nature.

**WHY COULD** New England society move from a firm condemnation of democracy to embracing the basic ideals that would lead to the Declaration of Independence and the Constitution of 1787?

However, the Puritans unknowingly planted the seeds for the very democracy that they viewed as an abomination of the purity of God's social order. In the Mayflower Compact, Puritan separatists agreed to a governmental covenant that allowed for majority rule and later established the idea of the town meeting. The charter of the Massachusetts Bay Colony provided for the elections of governors, colonial legislatures, and a General Court. Puritan customs forbid church ministers from serving in public office, an early version of separation of Church and State. Most important of all, the Puritans required that all church members be able to read and interpret the Bible. This emphasis upon the individual and his right to interpret the Bible, within certain doctrinal limits, without the intercession of a priest or minister would lead to political consequences.

A hundred years later, the political seeds they planted would bear democratic fruit.■

▲The Signing of the *Mayflower Compact* a painting by E. Percy Moran shows the historic ceremonial signing on November 21, 1620 below the deck of the Mayflower.

## MAYFLOWER COMPACT, 1620

**IN THE NAME OF GOD, AMEN**. We, whose names are underwritten, the Loyal Subjects of our dread Sovereign Lord King James, by the Grace of God, of Great Britain, France, and Ireland, King, Defender of the Faith, &c. Having undertaken for the Glory of God, and Advancement of the Christian Faith, and the Honour of our King and Country, a Voyage to plant the first Colony in the northern Parts of Virginia; Do by these Presents, solemnly and mutually, in the Presence of God and one another, covenant and combine ourselves together into a civil Body Politick, for our better Ordering and Preservation, and Furtherance of the Ends aforesaid: And by Virtue hereof do enact, constitute, and frame, such just and equal Laws, Ordinances, Acts, Constitutions, and Officers, from time to time, as shall be thought most meet and convenient for the general Good of the Colony; unto which we promise all due Submission and Obedience. IN WITNESS whereof we have hereunto subscribed our names at Cape-Cod the eleventh of November, in the Reign of our Sovereign Lord King James, of England, France, and Ireland, the eighteenth, and of Scotland the fifty-fourth, Anno Domini; 1620.■

## JOHN WINTHROP, *ON LIBERTY* (1645)

**THERE IS** a twofold liberty, natural (I mean as our nature is now corrupt) and civil or federal. The first is common to man with beasts and other creatures. By this, man, as he stands in relation to man simply, hath liberty to do what he lists; it is a liberty to evil as well as to good. This liberty is incompatible and inconsistent with authority and cannot endure the least restraint of the most just authority. The exercise and maintaining of this liberty makes men grow more evil and in time to be worse than brute beasts: omnes sumus licentia deteriores. This is that great enemy of truth and peace, that wild beast, which all of the ordinances of God are bent against, to restrain and subdue it. The other kind of liberty I call civil or federal; it may also be termed moral, in reference to the covenant between God and man, in the moral law, and the politic covenants and constitutions amongst men themselves. This liberty is the proper end and object of authority and cannot subsist without it; and it is a liberty to that only which is good, just, and honest. This liberty you are to stand for, with the hazard (not only of your goods, but) of your lives, if need be. Whatsoever crosseth this is not authority but a distemper thereof.... If you will be satisfied to enjoy such civil and lawful liberties, such as Christ allows you, then will you quietly and cheerfully submit unto that authority which is set over you, in all the administrations of it, for your good.■

## FUNDAMENTAL ORDERS OF CONNECTICUT (1639)

It is Ordered, sentenced, and decreed, that there shall be yearly two General Assemblies or Courts, the one the second Thursday in April, the other the second Thursday in September following; the first shall be called the Court of Election, wherein shall be yearly chosen from time to time, so many Magistrates and other public Officers as shall be found requisite: Whereof one to be chosen Governor for the year ensuing and until another be chosen, and no other Magistrate to be chosen for more than one year: provided always there be six chosen besides the Governor, which being chosen and sworn according to an Oath recorded for that purpose, shall have the power to administer justice according to the Laws here established....

It is Ordered, sentenced, and decreed, that the election of the aforesaid Magistrates shall be in this manner: every person present and qualified for choice shall bring in (to the person deputed to receive them) one single paper with the name of him written in it whom he desires to have Governor, and that he that hath the greatest number of papers shall be Governor for that year. And the rest of the Magistrates or public officers to be chosen in this manner: the Secretary for the time being shall first read the names of all that are to be put to choice and then shall severally nominate them distinctly, and every one that would have the person nominated to be chosen shall bring in one single paper written upon, and he that would not have him chosen shall bring in a blank; and every one that hath more written papers than blanks shall be a Magistrate for that year....

It is Ordered, sentenced, and decreed, that no person be chosen Governor above once in two years, and that the Governor be always a member of some approved Congregation....■

## FUNDAMENTAL AGREEMENT, OR ORIGINAL CONSTITUTION OF THE COLONY OF NEW HAVEN (1639)

Query II. WHEREAS there was a covenant solemnly made by the whole assembly of free planters of this plantation, the first day of extraordinary humiliation, which we had after we came together, that as in matters that concern the gathering and ordering of a church, so likewise in all public officers which concern civil order, as choice of magistrates and officers, making and repealing laws, dividing allotments of inheritance, and all things of like nature, we would all of us be ordered by those rules which the scripture holds forth to US; this covenant was called a plantation covenant, to distinguish it from a church covenant. which could not at that time be made a church not being then gathered, but was deferred till a church might be gathered, according to GOD. It was demanded whether all the free planters do hold themselves bound by that covenant, in all businesses of that nature which are expressed in the covenant, to submit themselves to be ordered by the rules held forth in the scripture....■

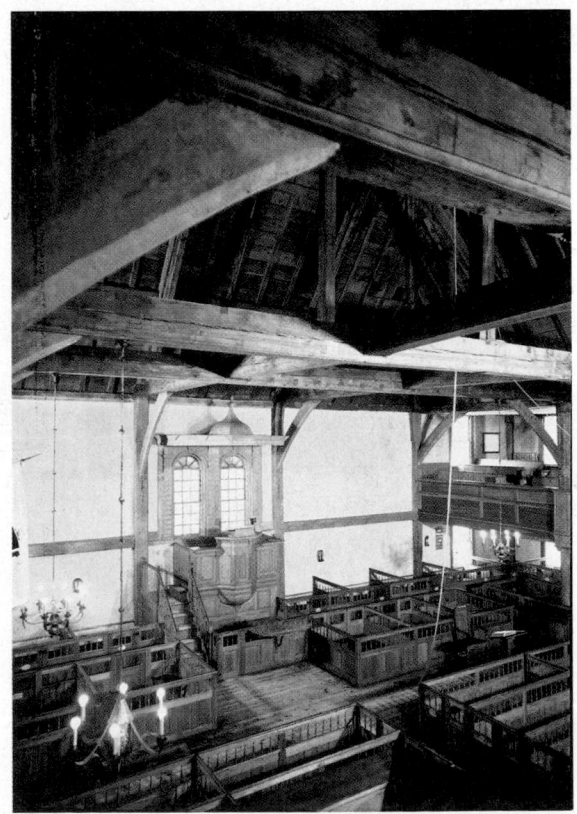

The wooden Old Ship Meeting House in Hingham, Massachusetts hosted the annual town meeting where Puritans voted and openly debated town policy.

Interpreting the Past

*The first object that saluted my eyes when
I arrived on the coast was the sea, and a
slave ship, which was then riding at
anchor, and waiting for its cargo.*

—*from* The Interesting Life of Olaudah Equiano

**Slaves on the** deck of the captured ship "Wildfire."

# 4

# SLAVERY AND EMPIRE
## 1441–1770

**HOW DID** the modern system of slavery develop?

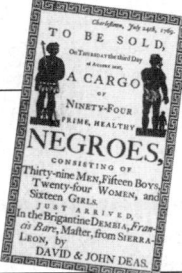

**WHAT IS** the history of the slave trade and the Middle Passage?

**HOW DID** slavery in the North differ from slavery in the South?

**HOW DID** African slaves attempt to preserve African culture in America?

**HOW DID** slavery fuel the economic development of Europe in the seventeenth and eighteenth centuries?

**HOW DID** slavery shape southern colonial society?

# AMERICAN COMMUNITIES
## Rebellion in Stono, South Carolina

ON SUNDAY MORNING, SEPTEMBER 9, 1739, WHILE MOST PLANTER families were attending church, a group of twenty slaves gathered on the banks of the Stono River, twenty miles south of Charles Town, South Carolina. Led by an Angolan known in some accounts as Jemmy, in others as Cato, the slaves made their way to Hutchinson's general store in the hamlet of Stono Bridge. They killed the two storekeepers, ransacked the place, and arming themselves with firearms and ammunition, set off on the road headed southwest for Florida, where the Spanish governor had issued a proclamation promising freedom for all runaway British slaves. They made no attempt to hide themselves but marched boldly to the beat of drummers and shouts of "Liberty!" The commotion drew the attention of curious slaves from the numerous rice plantations scattered across the swampy countryside, and dozens joined the marchers, women and children as well as men. They plundered and burned the homes of planters and pursued and killed every white person they encountered along the way, with the exception of an innkeeper, who was spared when several rebels spoke up in his defense, saying he had been kind to his slaves.

Word of the rebellion quickly spread throughout the planter community, and soon a heavily armed and mounted posse was hot on the rebels' trail. Late in the afternoon, near the crossing of the Edisto River, the posse overtook them. The rebel band, grown to nearly a hundred strong, had halted in a field where, in the words of the report, they "set to dancing, singing, and beating drums to draw more Negroes to them." Bottles of rum were passed and there was a good deal of drinking. Quietly the planters surrounded the field, then opened fire. Most of the slaves scattered, although according to the report the group of original conspirators "behaved boldly," forming themselves into a body and returning several volleys with the stolen firearms. But they were outmanned and outgunned, and at least two dozen slaves were killed. According to another account, the posse "cutt off their heads and set them up at every mile post" along the road leading back to Charles Town. Over the next few weeks the remaining fugitives were tracked down and killed by Indian allies of the South Carolina colony. A total of forty-five or fifty African Americans died. Thus ended the Stono Rebellion, the most violent slave uprising of the colonial period.

That slaves would rise up with the odds so stacked against them was a sign of their desperation. Most of these men and women were West Africans who had endured the shock of enslavement. On the rice plantations of low-country South Carolina, they suffered from overwork, poor diet, minimal clothing, and inadequate housing. Colonial laws permitted masters to discipline and punish harshly and indiscriminately. Slaves were whipped, confined in irons, mutilated, sold away, even murdered.

That slaves would rise up was also a sign of their community. The Stono Rebellion required the kind of careful organization possible only with the social trust and confidence built by community ties. Plantation slaves married, raised children, and constructed kinship networks. They passed on African names and traditions and created new ones. Many of the slaves of coastal South Carolina came from the central African rice coast, from Angola or the Kingdom of the Kongo, where men not only knew about the cultivation of rice but also shared a military tradition and knew how to handle firearms.

Community is also what enables a people to remember their history, to pass tales down the generations. In the 1930s, nearly two hundred years after the uprising at Stono, George Cato, great-great-grandson of the leader of the Stono Rebellion, had stories to tell. "As it come down to me, I thinks de first Cato take a darin' chance on losin' his life, not so much for his own benefit as it was to help others." He and the other rebels died in their attempt to free themselves, and not only did slavery continue, but also it grew even harsher and more oppressive as planters sought to stamp out the merest possibility of revolt. Yet the slaves' cry of "Liberty!" had not been in vain. Although in the twentieth century most white Americans had never heard of the Stono Rebellion, stories of the rebels' bravery and daring continued to inspire the local African American community. "I sho' does come from dat old stock who had de misfortune to be slaves," said Cato, who had been born into slavery himself. But the rebels "decided to be men," he declared, "and I's right proud of it."

Stono, SC

# THE BEGINNINGS OF AFRICAN SLAVERY

Household slaves had been a part of the Mediterranean world since ancient times. In the fifteenth century, merchants did a booming business in the sale of captive Slavs—the word "slave" derives from "Slav"—as well as Muslims and Africans. Many Europeans were disturbed, however, by the moral implications of enslaving other Europeans, and in the early fifteenth century the pope excommunicated a number of merchants engaged in selling Christians. But the same penalty did not apply to selling Africans and Muslims.

One of the goals of Portuguese expansion in the fifteenth century was to gain access to the lucrative West African trade in gold, ivory, textiles, and slaves previously dominated by the Moors of northern Africa. The first African slaves to arrive in Lisbon had been kidnapped by a Portuguese captain in 1441. But European traders found it more efficient to leave the dirty work of taking captives to Africans who were willing to exchange slaves for European commodities. By the mid-fifteenth century, the Portuguese were shipping a thousand or more slaves each year from Africa. Most of them were sent to labor on the sugar plantations on the Portuguese island colony of Madeira, off the coast of northern Africa.

## SUGAR AND SLAVERY

Sugar and slaves had gone together since Italian merchants of the fourteenth century set up the first modern sugar plantations on islands in the Mediterranean. Columbus introduced sugar to Hispaniola on his second voyage, and plantations were soon in operation there. Because the Indian population had been devastated by warfare and disease, colonists imported African slaves as laborers. Meanwhile, the Portuguese, aided by Dutch financiers, created a center of sugar production in their Brazilian colony that became a model for the efficient and brutal exploitation of African labor.

**HOW DID** the modern system of slavery develop?

**myhistorylab**
Review Summary

## IMAGE KEY
for pages 72–73

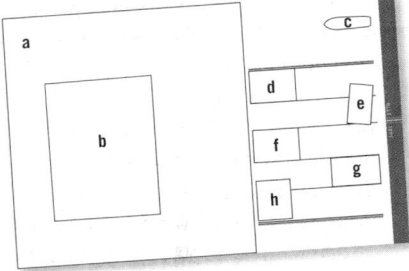

a. White Hills map by John Foster, 1677, woodcut. America's first map.
b. Slaves on the deck of the captured ship "Wildfire."
c. Model of the slave ship *Brookes*, showing plan view of slave positions.
d. William Clark's *Ten Views Found in the Island of Antigua* shows slaves working on a plantation.
e. "To be sold, a cargo of ninety-four prime, healthy Negroes."
f. The London Coffee House near the docks of Philadelphia was the site of many slave auctions in the mid-eighteenth century.
g. The Old Plantation, showing slaves at work.
h. Goods from the American colonies being unloaded from eighteenth-century ships on London's Old Custom House Quay.

**This image of** Mansa Musa (1312–37), the ruler of the Muslim kingdom of Mali in West Africa, is taken from the *Catalan Atlas*, a magnificent map presented to the king of France in 1381 by his cousin, the king of Aragon. In the words of the Catalan inscription, Musa was "the richest, the most noble lord in all this region on account of the abundance of gold that is gathered in his land." He holds what was thought to be the world's largest gold nugget. Under Musa's reign, Timbuktu became a capital of world renown.

Skilled at finance and commerce, the Dutch greatly expanded the European market for sugar, converting it from a luxury item for the rich to a staple for ordinary people. Once the demand for sugar and its profitability had been demonstrated, England and France began seeking West Indian sugar colonies of their own. They began by seizing islands of the Lesser Antilles, constructing plantations, and importing slaves. By the 1640s, English Barbados and French Martinique had become highly profitable sugar colonies. In 1655 the English seized the island of Jamaica from the Spanish, and by 1670 the French had established effective control over the western portion of Hispaniola, which they renamed Saint Domingue (present-day Haiti) when they acquired it by treaty. By then, Caribbean sugar and slavery had become the centerpiece of the European colonial system.

## WEST AFRICANS

The men and women whose labor made these tropical colonies so profitable came from the long-established societies and local communities of West Africa. In the sixteenth century more than a hundred different peoples lived along the coast of West Africa, from Cape Verde south to Angola. Farming sustained large populations and thriving networks of commerce. There were a number of lesser states and kingdoms along the coast, and it was with these that the Portuguese first bargained for Africans who could be sold as slaves.

Varieties of household slavery were common in West African societies, although slaves there were often treated more as members of the family than as mere possessions. They were allowed to marry, and their children were born free. When African merchants sold the first slaves to the Portuguese, they may have thought that European slavery would be similar.

**African slaves operate** a sugar mill on the Spanish island colony of Hispaniola, illustated in a copperplate engraving published by Theodore de Bry in 1595. Columbus introduced sugar on his second voyage and plantations were soon in operation. Because the native population was devastated by warfare and disease, colonists imported African slaves as laborers.

# THE AFRICAN SLAVE TRADE

The movement of Africans across the Atlantic to the Americas was the largest forced migration in world history (see Map 4.1). Africans made up the largest group of people to come to the Americas before the nineteenth century, outnumbering European immigrants by a ratio of six to one. The Atlantic slave trade, which began with the Portuguese in the fifteenth century and did not end in the United States until 1807 (and continued elsewhere in the Americas until the 1870s), is a brutal chapter in the making of America.

**WHAT IS** the history of the slave trade and the Middle Passage?

## myhistorylab
**Review Summary**

 **MAP EXPLORATION**

To explore an interactive version of this map, go to **http://www.prenhall.com/faraghertlc/map4.1**

NORTH AMERICA

ATLANTIC OCEAN

EUROPE

ASIA

Azores

Madeira

Canary Islands

Cape Blanco
Cape Verde

*Sahara Desert*

AFRICA

• Timbuktu
GUINEA    BORNU

SPANISH SOUTH AMERICA

West Indies

Senegambia

Windward Coast

Gold Coast

*Bight of Benin*

*Bight of Biafra*

West Central Africa

CONGO

BRAZIL

SOUTH AMERICA

ANGOLA    MOZAMBIQUE

PACIFIC OCEAN

| | |
|---|---|
| to British North America | 522,400 |
| to French Americas | 1,045,000 |
| to Spanish Americas | 1,115,000 |
| to Portuguese Brazil | 1,428,000 |
| to British Caribbean | 1,500,000 |

**MAP 4.1**

**The African Slave Trade**   The enslaved men, women, and children transported to the Americas came from West Africa, the majority from the lower Niger River (called the Slave Coast) and the region of the Congo and Angola.

HOW AND why were the people of Africa enslaved and brought to America?

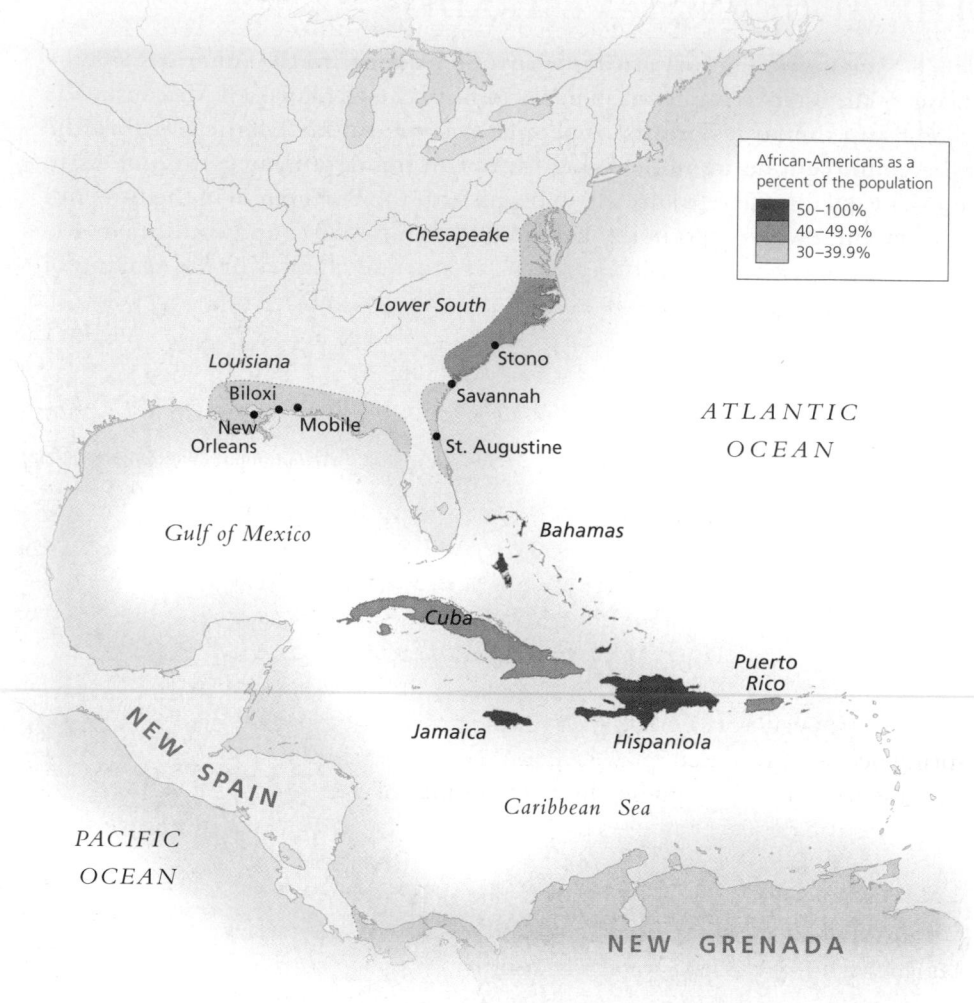

**MAP 4.2**
**Slave Colonies of the Seventeenth and Eighteenth Centuries**   By the eighteenth century, the system of slavery had created societies with large African populations throughout the Caribbean and along the southern coast of North America.

HOW DID the sugar boom contribute to the importation of large numbers of Africans to the Americas?

## A GLOBAL ENTERPRISE

Scholars estimate that 10 to 12 million Africans arrived in the Americas during the four-century history of the trade. Seventy-six percent arrived from 1701 to 1810, the peak period of colonial demand for labor, when tens of thousands were shipped from Africa each year. Of this vast multitude, about half were delivered to Dutch, French, or British sugar plantations in the Caribbean, a third to Portuguese Brazil, and a tenth to Spanish America (see Map 4.2). A much smaller proportion, about one in twenty, a total of approximately 600,000 individuals, were transported to the British colonies of North America. With the exception of the 1750s, when the British colonies were engulfed by the **Seven Years' War**, the slave trade continued to rise in importance in the decades before the Revolution (see Figure 4.1).

### QUICK REVIEW

**Demography of Slavery**

- 10 to 12 million Africans brought to the Americas over the course of four hundred years.
- Almost twice as many men as women were enslaved.
- Most Africans captured and transported to the Americas were between the ages of fifteen and thirty.

**Seven Years' War**   War fought in Europe, North America, and India between 1756 and 1753, pitting France and its allies against Great Britain and its allies.

All the nations of Western Europe participated in the slave trade. Dutch slavers began challenging Portuguese control of the trade at the end of the sixteenth century, and during the sugar boom of the seventeenth century Holland was the most prominent slave-trading nation. The English entered the trade at the same time. As a result, the number of slaves shipped to North America skyrocketed. The Dutch and Portuguese, however, continued to play important roles, alongside slave traders from France, Sweden, and several German duchies.

The European presence in Africa generally was confined to coastal outposts. As the volume of slave trading expanded, the forts of trading companies gave way to the smaller coastal posts of independent traders who set up operations with the cooperation of local headmen or chiefs. This informal manner of trading offered opportunities for small operators, such as the slave traders of New England. Many great American fortunes were built from profits in the slave trade.

The slave trade was a collaboration between European or American and African traders. Dependent on the favor of local rulers, many colonial slave traders lived permanently in coastal forts and married African women, reinforcing their commercial ties with family relations. In many areas their mixed-ancestry offspring became prominent players in the slave trade. Continuing the practice of the Portuguese, the grim business of slave raiding was left to the Africans themselves.

## THE SHOCK OF ENSLAVEMENT

Most Africans were enslaved through warfare. Sometimes large armies launched massive attacks, burning whole towns and taking hundreds of prisoners. More common were smaller raids in which a group of armed men attacked at nightfall, seized everyone within reach, then escaped with their captives. Enslavement was an unparalleled shock. Venture Smith, an African born in Guinea in 1729, was eight years old when he was captured. After many years in North American slavery, he still vividly recalled the attack on his village, the torture and murder of his father, and the long march of his people to the coast.

On the coast, European traders and African raiders assembled their captives. Prisoners waited in dark dungeons or in open pens called "barracoons." To lessen the possibility of collective resistance, traders split up families and ethnic groups. Captains carefully inspected each man and woman, and those selected for transport were branded on the back or buttocks with the mark of the buyer. Olaudah Equiano remembered that he and his fellow captives became convinced that they "had got into a world of bad spirits" and were about to be eaten by cannibals.

## THE MIDDLE PASSAGE

In the eighteenth century, English sailors christened the voyage of slave vessels across the Atlantic as the "**Middle Passage**," the middle part of a trading triangle from England to Africa, to America, and back to England. From coastal forts and barracoons, crews rowed small groups of slaves out to the waiting transports and packed them into shelves below deck only six feet long by two and a half feet high. People were forced to sleep "spoon fashion," and the tossing of the ship knocked them about so violently that the skin over their elbows sometimes was worn to the bone from scraping on the planks.

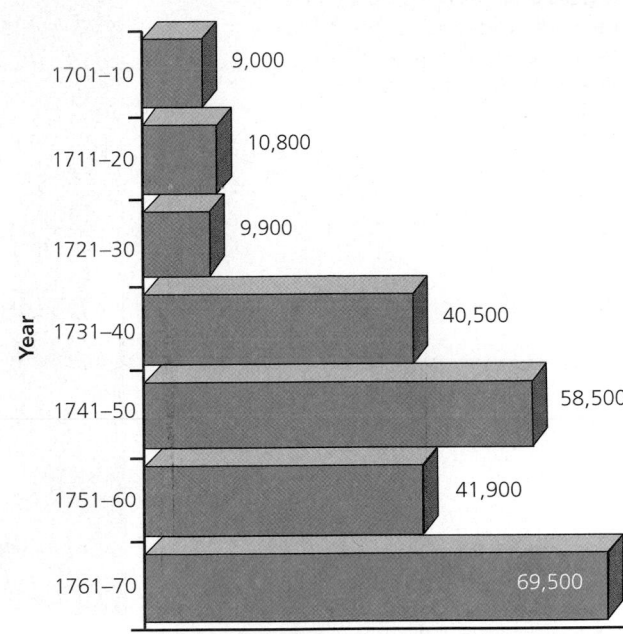

**Figure 4.1 Estimated Number of Africans Imported to British North America, 1701–70**
These official British statistics include only slaves imported legally and, consequently, undercount the total number who arrived on American shores. But the trend over time is clear. With the exception of the 1750s, when the British colonies were engulfed by the Seven Years' War, the slave trade continued to rise in importance in the decades before the Revolution.
R. C. Simmons, *The American Colonies: From Settlement to Independence* (London: Longman, 1976), 186.

**Middle Passage** The voyage between West Africa and the New World slave colonies.

**A group of** slaves being led from the interior to the West African coast by two traders, from Rene Geoffroy de Villeneuve, *l' Afrique* (1814).

**Portrait of Olaudah** Equiano, by an unknown English artist, ca. 1780. Captured in Nigeria in 1756 when he was eleven years old, Equiano was transported to America and was eventually purchased by an English sea captain. After ten years as a slave, he succeeded in buying his own freedom and dedicated himself to the antislavery cause. His book, *The Interesting Narrative of the Life of Olaudah Equiano* (1789), was published in numerous editions, translated into several languages, and became the prototype for dozens of other slave narratives in the nineteenth century.

Royal Albert Memorial Museum, Exeter, Devon, UK/Bridgeman Art Library.

Their holds filled with human cargo, the transports headed up the African coast to Cape Verde where they caught the trade winds blowing toward America. A favorable voyage from Senegambia to Barbados might be accomplished in as little as three weeks, but a ship from Guinea or Angola, becalmed in the doldrums or driven back by storms, might take as much as three months.

Most voyages were marked by a daily routine. In the morning the crew opened the hatch and brought the captives on deck, attaching their leg irons to a great chain running the length of the bulwarks. After a breakfast of beans the crew commanded men and women to jump up and down, a bizarre session of exercise known as "dancing the slave." A day spent chained on deck was concluded by a second bland meal and then the stowing away. Down in the hold, the groans of the dying, the shrieks of women and children, and the suffocating heat and stench were, in the words of Olaudah Equiano, "a scene of horror almost inconceivable"

Among the worst of the horrors was the absence of adequate sanitation. Crews were supposed to swab the holds daily, but so sickening was the task that it was rarely performed, and Africans were left to wallow in their own wastes. According to Atlantic sailors, they could "smell a slaver five miles down wind." Many captives sickened and died in these conditions. Others contracted dysentery, known as the "flux." Frequent shipboard epidemics of smallpox, measles, and yellow fever added to the misery. The dying continued even as the ships anchored at their destinations. Historians estimate that one in every six Africans perished during the Middle Passage.

The unwilling voyagers offered plenty of resistance. As long as ships were still within sight of the African coast, hope remained alive and the danger of revolt was great. Once on the open sea, however, the captives' resistance took more desperate form. Equiano witnessed several Africans jump overboard and drown, "and I believe many more would very soon have done the same if they had not been prevented by the ship's crew."

**Slaves below deck** on a Spanish slaver, a sketch made when the vessel was captured by a British warship in the early nineteenth century. Slaves were "stowed so close, that they were not allowed above a foot and a half for each in breadth," wrote one observer. The close quarters and unsanitary conditions created a stench so bad that Atlantic sailors said you could "smell a slaver five miles down wind."

As the vessels approached their destination, crews prepared the human cargo for market. All but the most rebellious were freed from their chains and allowed to wash themselves and move about the deck. Buyers painstakingly examined the Africans, who once again suffered the indignity of probing eyes and poking fingers. In ports such as Charles Town in South Carolina, sales were generally made by auction or by a cruel method known as the scramble: with prices fixed in advance the Africans were driven into a corral, and on cue the buyers would rush in among them, grabbing their pick. The noise, clamor, and eagerness of the buyers, Equiano remembered, renewed all their apprehensions. "In this manner, without scruple, are relations and friends separated, most of them never to see each other again."

## POLITICAL AND ECONOMIC EFFECTS ON AFRICA

Africa began the sixteenth century with genuine independence. But as surely as Europe and America grew stronger as a result of the transport of Africans, so Africa grew weaker by their loss. For every individual taken captive, at least another died in the chronic slave raiding. Death and destruction spread deep into the African interior. Coastal slave-trading kingdoms drew slaves from central Africa. Many of the new states became little more than machines for supplying captives to European traders, and a "gun-slave cycle" pushed them into a destructive arms race with each other. Soldiers captured in these wars were themselves enslaved.

More serious still was the long-term stagnation of the West African economy. Labor was drawn away from productive activities while imported consumer goods stifled local manufacturing. African traders were expert at driving a hard bargain for slaves, but even when they appeared to get the best of the exchange, the ultimate advantage lay with the

**Africans herded from** a slave ship to a corral where they were to be sold by the cruel method known as "the scramble," buyers rushing in and grabbing their pick. This image was featured in an antislavery narrative published in 1796.

Europeans, who received wealth-producing workers in return for mere consumer goods. This political, economic, and cultural demoralization prepared the way for the European conquest of Africa in the nineteenth century.

# THE DEVELOPMENT OF NORTH AMERICAN SLAVE SOCIETIES

HOW DID slavery in the North differ from slavery in the South?

**myhistorylab**
Review Summary

**2–12**
Robert Beverly, *A Virginian Describes the Difference between Servants and Slaves* (1722)

New World slavery was nearly two centuries old before it became an important system of labor in North America. There were slaves in all the British colonies of the seventeenth century, but as late as 1700 slaves accounted for less than 12 percent of the colonial population. During the eighteenth century, however, slavery expanded greatly, and by 1770 there were 460,000 Africans and African Americans in British North America, making up more than 20 percent of the population (see Figure 4.2).

## SLAVERY COMES TO NORTH AMERICA

The first Africans arrived in Virginia in 1619 when a Dutch slave trader exchanged "20 and odd Negars" for badly needed provisions with planter John Rolfe, the widower of Pocahontas and pioneering Virginia tobacco planter. But because slaves generally cost twice as much as indentured servants yet had the same appallingly short life expectancy, they proved to have little economic benefit for planters. Consequently, seventeenth-century Chesapeake planters employed far more indentured servants than slaves. Servants and the small number of slaves worked together, ate and slept in common quarters, and often developed intimate relationships. The Chesapeake was what one historian has termed a "society with slaves," a society in which slavery was one form of labor among several.

Under these circumstances the status of black Virginians could be ambiguous. Seventeenth-century Virginia records document Africans acquiring farms, servants, and slaves of their own. Many slaves were Christians, and it raised traditional legal and moral doubts about whether co-religionists could be enslaved. Moreover, sexual relations among Africans, Indians, and Europeans produced a sizable group of free people of mixed ancestry known as mulattoes. It was only later that dark skin came automatically to mean slavery, segregation, and the absence of the rights of freemen.

During the last quarter of the seventeenth century, however, the Chesapeake became a "slave society," a place where slavery was the dominant form of labor. Among several developments, perhaps most important was the sharp decline in the number of indentured servants migrating to the Chesapeake. The incentive had been the availability of land after the term of service, but by midcentury most of the arable land had fallen into the hands of the planter elite. Bacon's and Culpeper's rebellions (see Chapter 3) offered examples of the violent potential of the land crisis. They also suggested how much serious trouble servants and former servants could make for planters. After Bacon's Rebellion, English immigrants turned away from the Chesapeake to colonies such as Pennsylvania, where there was more land and, thus, more opportunity.

The British Royal African Company, which began to import slaves directly to North America in the 1670s, was more than happy

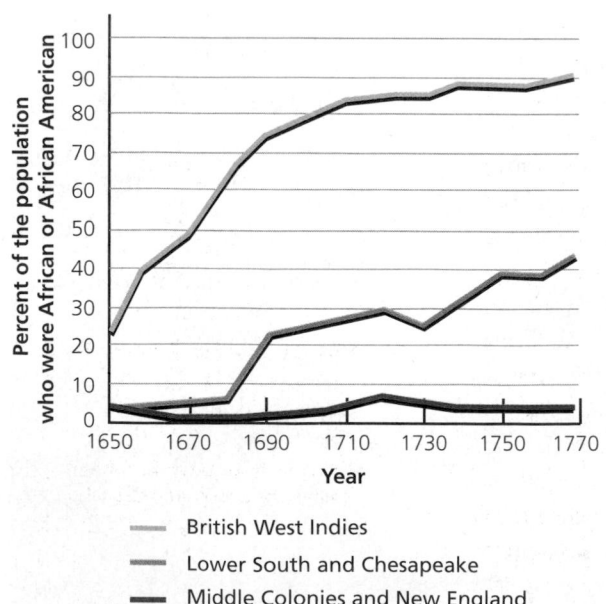

**Figure 4.2 Africans as a Percentage of Total Population of the British Colonies, 1650–1770**
Although the proportion of Africans and African Americans was never as high in the South as in the Caribbean, the ethnic structure of the South diverged radically from that of the North during the eighteenth century.

Robert W. Fogel and Stanley L. Engerman, *Time on the Cross* (Boston: Little, Brown, 1974), 21.

to supply planters' need for labor. Slaves were expensive, but planters expected to keep them in the fields for longer hours, with fewer days off, and hopefully with less risk of an uprising. By 1700 there were 5,000 slaves in Virginia, and more than 22 percent of the Chesapeake population was of African descent.

Slavery had no English legal precedent, no laws or traditions allowing for life-time enslavement or for making that status inheritable. So as the proportions of slaves in the colonial population gradually rose, colonists wrote slavery into law, a process best observed in the case of Virginia. In 1662 the planter assembly declared that henceforth children would be "bond or free only according to the condition of the mother." Five years later they passed a law that Christian baptism could no longer alter conditions of servitude. Thus, two important avenues to freedom were closed. The colony then gave masters the right to administer life-threatening violence, declaring in 1669 that the death of a slave during punishment "shall not be accounted felony." Such rules accumulated piecemeal until 1705, when Virginia gathered them into a comprehensive slave code that became a model for other colonies.

Thus, slavery was institutionalized just as the Atlantic slave trade reached flood tide in the eighteenth century. In the single decade of 1701 to 1710 more Africans were imported into North America than during the entire previous century. The English colonies were primed for an unprecedented growth of plantation slavery.

## THE TOBACCO COLONIES

During the eighteenth century the European demand for tobacco increased more than tenfold, and it was supplied largely by increased production in the Chesapeake region. Tobacco was far and away the single most important commodity produced in eighteenth-century North America, accounting for more than a quarter of the value of all colonial exports.

The expansion of tobacco production could not have taken place without a corresponding growth in the size of the slave labor force. Unlike sugar, tobacco did not require large plantations and could be produced successfully on small farms. But the crop demanded a great deal of hand labor and close attention. As tobacco production expanded, slaveholding became widespread. By 1770 more than a quarter million slaves labored in the colonies of the Upper South (Maryland, Virginia, and North Carolina), and because of the exploding market for tobacco, their numbers expanded at about double the rate of the general population. From 1700 to 1770, an estimated 80,000 Africans were imported into the tobacco region. But natural increase was even more important. In the Caribbean and Brazil, where profits from sugar were extremely high, many planters literally worked their slaves to death, replenishing them with a constant stream of new arrivals from Africa. In the Chesapeake, however, significantly lower profits led tobacco planters to pay more attention to the health of their labor force, establishing work routines that were not as deadly. Moreover, food supplies were more plentiful in North America and slaves better fed, making them more resistant to disease. As a consequence, by the 1730s the slave population of the Chesapeake had become the first in the Western Hemisphere to achieve self-sustained growth. By the 1750s, about 80 percent of Chesapeake slaves were "country-born."

## THE LOWER SOUTH

South Carolina was a slave society from the beginning. The most valuable part of the early Carolina economy was the Indian slave trade. Practicing a strategy of divide and conquer, using Indian tribes to fight one another, Carolinians established a trade in Indian captives during the 1670s. By the early eighteenth century more

**2–3**
William Waller Hening, *The Statutes at Large; Being a Collection of All the Laws of Virginia, from the First Session of the Legislature in the Year 1619*

---

### QUICK REVIEW

**Growth of Slavery**

- Slavery grew rapidly in the South.
- The use of slaves made economic sense on tobacco and rice plantations.
- Northern slaves worked as servants, craftsmen, and day laborers.

**Residence and Slave** Quarters of Mulberry Plantation, by Thomas Coram, ca. 1770. The slave quarters are on the left in this painting of a rice plantation near Charleston, South Carolina. The steep roofs of the slave cabins, an African architectural feature introduced in America by slave builders, kept living quarters cool by allowing the heat to rise and dissipate in the rafters.

Thomas Coram, "View of Mulberry Street, House and Street." Oil on paper, 10 × 17.6 cm. Gibbes Museum of Art/Carolina Art Association. 68.18.01.

than 12,000 mission Indians from Florida had been captured and sold into slavery and thousands more killed or dispersed.

In the early eighteenth century, however, planter preference turned toward African rather than Indian slaves. Rice production had become the most dynamic sector of the South Carolina economy, and their experience in agriculture made West Africans much better rice workers. Another important crop was added to the mix in the 1740s when a young South Carolina woman named Elizabeth Lucas Pinckney successfully adapted West Indian indigo to the low-country climate. The indigo plant, native to India, produced a deep blue dye important in textile manufacture. Rice grew in the lowlands, but indigo could be cultivated on high ground, and with different seasonal growing patterns, planters were able to harmonize their production. Rice and indigo became two of the most valuable commodities exported from the mainland colonies of North America. The boom in these two crops depended on the growth of African slavery. Before the international slave trade to the United States was ended in 1808, at least 100,000 slaves landed in South Carolina.

By the 1740s many of these arriving Africans were being taken to Georgia, a colony created by an act of the English Parliament in 1732. Its leader, James Edward Oglethorpe, hoped to establish a buffer against Spanish invasion from Florida and make the colony a haven for poor British farmers who could sell their products in the markets of South Carolina. Under Oglethorpe's influence, Parliament agreed to prohibit slavery in Georgia. But soon Georgia's coastal regions were being colonized by South Carolina rice planters with their slaves. By the time Oglethorpe and Georgia's trustees opened their colony to slavery in 1752, the Georgia coast had already become an extension of the Carolina low-country slave system.

By 1770 nearly 90,000 African Americans made up about 80 percent of the coastal population of South Carolina and Georgia. The African American communities of the Lower South had achieved self-sustained growth by the middle of the eighteenth century, a generation later than those in the Chesapeake.

## SLAVERY IN THE SPANISH COLONIES

Slavery was basic to the Spanish colonial labor system, yet doubts about the enslavement of Africans were raised by both church and crown. The papacy denounced slavery as a violation of Christian principles. But the institution remained intact, and later in the eighteenth century, when sugar production expanded in Cuba, the slave system there turned as brutal as any in the history of the Americas.

In New Mexico, the Spanish depended on Indian slavery. In the sixteenth century the colonial governor sent Indian slaves to the mines of Mexico. The enslavement of Indians was one of the causes of the **Pueblo Revolt** (see Chapter 3). In the aftermath of the revolt the Spanish became much more cautious in their treatment of the Pueblos, who were officially considered Catholics. But they participated in a robust trade in captured and enslaved "infidel Indians," mostly nomadic people from the Great Plains, employing them as house servants and fieldworkers.

**Pueblo Revolt** Rebellion in 1680 of Pueblo Indians in New Mexico against their Spanish overlords.

## SLAVERY IN FRENCH LOUISIANA

Slavery was also important in Louisiana, the colony founded by the French in the lower Mississippi Valley. In the early eighteenth century, French colonists established settlements and forts at Biloxi and Mobile on the Gulf of Mexico and in 1718 laid out the city of New Orleans on the lower Mississippi River. The French Company of the Indies imported some 6,000 African slaves, and planters invested in tobacco and indigo plantations along the river banks north of the city. This was the country of the Natchez Indians, who greatly resented the French intrusion. In 1729 the Natchez joined forces with rebellious slaves in an armed uprising. The Natchez Rebellion claimed the lives of more than 200 French settlers, 10 percent of the population. An alliance of slaves and Indians was the greatest of all planter fears. The French colonial militia put down the rebellion with brutal force, crushing and dispersing the Natchez people in the process.

Bitter memories of the Natchez Rebellion kept the Louisiana French from committing themselves totally to slavery. In 1750 African slaves amounted to less than a third of the colonial population of 10,000. It was not until the end of the century that the colony of Louisiana became an important North American slave society.

## SLAVERY IN THE NORTH

Slavery was a fundamental, acceptable, thoroughly American institution. None of the northern colonies could be characterized as slave societies, but slavery was an important form of labor in a number of localities. During the eighteenth century

*London Coffee House.*

The London Coffee House, near the docks of Philadelphia, was the center of the city's business and political life in the mid-eighteenth century. Sea captains and merchants congregated here to do business, and as this contemporary print illustrates (in the detail on the far right), it was the site of many slave auctions. Slavery was a vital part of the economy of northern cities.

John F. Watson, "Annals of Philadelphia," being a collection of memoirs, anecdotes, and incidents of Philadelphia. The London Coffee House. The Library Company of Philadelphia.

it grew increasingly significant in the commercial farming regions of southeast Pennsylvania, central New Jersey, and Long Island, areas where slaves made up about 10 percent of rural residents. In Rhode Island—a center of the slave trade—large gangs of slaves were used in cattle and dairy operations, and the proportion of slaves in the population of Narragansett County reached nearly a third.

Slavery was common in all northern port cities, including Boston. Slave ownership was nearly universal among the wealthy and ordinary among craftsmen and professionals. By 1750 slaves along with small populations of free blacks made up 15 to 20 percent of the residents of Boston, New York City, and Philadelphia.

The Quakers of Pennsylvania and New Jersey, many of whom kept slaves, were the first colonists to voice antislavery sentiment. In 1715, John Hepburn of New Jersey published the first North American critique of slavery, but his was a lonely voice. By midcentury, however, there was a significant antislavery movement among the Quakers.

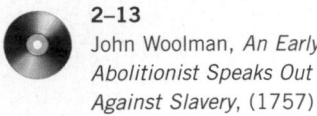

**2–13**
John Woolman, *An Early Abolitionist Speaks Out Against Slavery*, (1757)

**HOW DID** African slaves attempt to preserve African culture in America?

**myhistorylab**
**Review Summary**

# AFRICAN TO AFRICAN AMERICAN

Men and women from dozens of ethnic groups, representing many different languages, religions, and customs, were transported across the Atlantic without any of their cultural possessions. In America they were subjected to the control of masters intent on maximizing their work and minimizing their liberty. Yet African Americans carved out lives of their own with a degree of independence. Their African heritage was not erased; it provided them with a fundamental outlook, the basis for a common identity.

The majority of Africans transported to North America arrived during the eighteenth century. They joined a rapidly growing population of country-born slaves or "creoles" (from the Spanish *criollo* and Portuguese *creole*, meaning "born" or "raised"), a term first used by slaves in Brazil to distinguish their children, born in the New World, from newly arrived Africans. The perspective of creoles was shaped by their having grown up under slavery, and that perspective helped them to determine which elements of African culture they would incorporate into the emerging culture of the African American community. That community was formed out of the relationship between creoles and Africans, and between slaves and their European masters.

## THE DAILY LIFE OF SLAVES

Slaves did the work that made the plantation colonies so profitable. As an agricultural people, Africans, both women and men, were accustomed to the routines of field labor. Most slaves were field hands, and even domestic servants labored in the fields when necessary. Masters provided their workers with rude clothing, sufficient in the summer but nearly always inadequate in the winter.

On small plantations and farms, typical in the tobacco country of the Chesapeake, Africans might work side by side with their owners and, depending on the character of the master, might enjoy a standard of living not too different from that of other family members. The work was more demanding and living conditions far worse on the great rice and indigo plantations of the Lower South, where slaves usually lived separately from the master in their own quarters. But large plantations, with large numbers of slaves, created a concentration of population that made for more resilient African American communities. It was one of the profound ironies of American slavery: life was much harder on the great plantations, but slaves had more opportunity for some autonomy.

## FAMILIES AND COMMUNITIES

The family was the most important institution for the development of community and culture, but **slave codes** did not provide for legal slave marriages: that would have contradicted the master's freedom to dispose of his property as he saw fit. Planters commonly separated families by sale or bequest, dividing husbands from wives and even separating mothers from children. Charles Ball was a mere boy in Virginia when his family was separated by sale. "Oh, master, do not take me from my child!" his mother cried. But her new owner gave her two or three heavy blows on the shoulders with a rawhide whip, "snatched me from her arms, and seizing her by one arm, dragged her back towards the place of sale." Ball never saw her again. Later, after he had grown and married, his master sold him to a rice planter in Georgia. "My heart died away within me," Ball remembered vividly. "I felt incapable of weeping or speaking, and in my despair I laughed loudly." On his journey south he dreamed his wife and children were "beseeching and imploring my master on their knees." He never saw them again.

Despite the odds against them, however, slaves in both the Chesapeake and the Lower South created the families that were essential for the development of African American culture. On large plantations throughout the southern colonies, travelers found Africans living in family households. In the Lower South, where there were greater concentrations of slaves on the great rice plantations, husbands and wives often lived together in the slave quarters. On the smaller plantations of the Upper South, men frequently married women from neighboring farms, and with the permission of both owners visited their families in the evenings or on Sundays.

Emotional ties to particular places, connections between the generations, and relations of kinship and friendship linking neighboring plantations and farms were the foundation stones of African American community life. Kinship was especially important. African American parents encouraged their children to use family terms in addressing unrelated persons: "auntie" or "uncle" became a respectful way of addressing older men and women, "brother" and "sister" affectionate terms for agemates. This may have been one of the first devices enslaved Africans used to humanize the world of slavery.

## AFRICAN AMERICAN CULTURE

The eighteenth century was the formative period in the development of the African American community, for it was then that the high birthrate and the growing numbers of country-born provided the necessary stability for the evolution of culture. During this period, men and women from dozens of African ethnic groups molded themselves into a new people. Distinctive patterns in music and dance, religion, and oral tradition illustrate the resilience of the human spirit under bondage as well as the successful struggle of African Americans to create a spiritually sustaining culture of their own.

Eighteenth-century masters were reluctant to allow their slaves to become Christians, fearing that baptism would open the way to claims of freedom or give Africans dangerous notions of universal brotherhood and equality with masters. Large numbers of African Americans were not converted to Christianity until the **Great Awakening**, which swept across the South just before the American Revolution (see Chapter 5).

**Mum Bett, also** known as Elizabeth Freeman, was born into slavery in a Massachusetts household about 1742. As a young woman she was subjected to the violent abuse of her mistress, who struck her with a hot shovel, leaving an indelible scar. Fleeing her owner, Mum Bett enlisted the aid of antislavery lawyer Thomas Sedgwick, who helped win her freedom in 1772. This miniature was painted by Sedgwick's daughter Susan in 1811.

**2–9**
James Oglethorpe, *The Colonial Records of the State of Georgia* (1739)

### QUICK REVIEW

**Slave Society**
- Traces of African culture remained in slave society.
- Labor consumed most of slave's time.
- Kinship played a key role in solidifying African American communities.

**Slave codes** A series of laws passed mainly in the Southern colonies in the late seventeenth and early eighteenth centuries to defend the status of slaves and codify the denial of basic civil rights to them.

**Great Awakening** Tremendous religious revival in colonial America striking first in the Middle Colonies and New England in the 1740s and then spreading to the southern colonies.

One crucial area of religious practice concerned the rituals of death and burial. African Americans generally believed that the spirits of their dead would return to Africa. The burial ceremony was often held at night to keep it secret from masters, who objected to the continuation of African traditions. The deceased was laid out, and around the body men and women would move counterclockwise in a slow dance step while singing ancestral songs. The pace gradually increased, finally reaching a frenzied but joyful conclusion. As slaves from different backgrounds joined together in the circle, they were beginning the process of cultural unification.

Music and dance may have formed the foundation of African American culture, coming even before a common language. Many Africans were accomplished players of stringed instruments and drums, and their style featured improvisation and rhythmic complexity, elements that would become prominent in African American music. In America, slaves re-created African instruments such as the banjo, and mastered the art of the European violin and guitar.

One of the most important developments of the eighteenth century was the invention of an African American language. An English traveler during the 1770s complained he could not understand Virginia slaves, who spoke "a mixed dialect between the Guinea and English." But such a language made it possible for country-born and "saltwater" Africans to communicate. The two most important dialects were Gullah and Geechee, named after two of the African peoples most prominent in the Carolina and Georgia low country, the Golas and Gizzis of the African Windward Coast. These creole languages were a transitional phenomenon, gradually giving way to distinctive forms of black English, although in certain isolated areas, such as the sea islands of the Carolinas and Georgia, they persisted into the twentieth century.

## THE AFRICANIZATION OF THE SOUTH

The African American community often looked to recently arrived Africans for religious leadership and medical magic. Throughout the South, many whites had as much faith in slave conjurers and herb doctors as the slaves themselves did, and slaves won fame for their healing powers. This was one of many ways in which white and black Southerners came to share a common culture. Acculturation was by no means a one-way street; English men and women in the South were also being Africanized.

Slaves worked in the kitchens of their masters and thus introduced an African style of cooking into colonial diets already transformed by the addition of Indian crops. African American culinary arts are responsible for such southern culinary specialties as barbecue, fried chicken, black-eyed peas, and collard greens. And the liberal African use of red pepper, sesame seeds, and other sharp flavors established the southern preference for highly spiced foods.

Mutual acculturation was also evident in many aspects of material culture. Southern basket weaving used Indian techniques and African designs. Woodcarving often featured African motifs. African architectural designs featuring high, peaked roofs (to drain off the heat) and broad, shady porches gradually became part of a distinctive southern style.

Even more important were less tangible aspects of culture. Slave mothers nursed white children as well as their own. As one English observer wrote, "each child has its [black] Momma, whose gestures and accent it will necessarily copy, for children, we all know, are imitative beings." In this way many Africanisms passed into the English language of the South. Some linguists have argued that the southern "drawl," evident among both black and white speakers, derived from the incorporation of African intonations of words and syllables.

# A Musical Celebration in the Slave Quarters

This anonymous watercolor, discovered in South Carolina, dates from the last quarter of the eighteenth century. It offers a wonderfully detailed depiction of Africans or African Americans gathered together in the slave quarters celebrating with music. This is clearly a community celebration, involving several families. Seated on the right, two men play instruments that suggest continuity with the African heritage. One plucks on something that looks like a banjo, and indeed, the banjo can be traced back to West Africa. "The instrument proper to them," Thomas Jefferson wrote of his slaves, "is the *banjar,* which they brought hither from Africa." The other man plays a drum that resembles the gudugudu, a small wooden kettledrum from Nigeria played with two long thin rawhide sticks. The dancing man with the carved stick may indicate that this is a wedding ceremony that involves jumping the broom, an African custom for newly married couples. One planter's description of a slave dance seems to fit this scene: the men leading the women in "a slow shuffling gait, edging along by some unseen exertion of the feet, from one side to the other—sometimes courtesying down and remaining in that posture while the edging motion from one side to the other continued." The women, he wrote, "always carried a handkerchief held at arm's length, which was waved in a graceful motion to and fro as she moved." The painting is a tribute to the celebration of life amidst adversity. ■

**WHY DO** you think the plantation master is omitted from this painting?

Abby Aldrich Rockefeller Folk Art Museum, Colonial Williamsburg Foundation, VA.

Seeing History

**Fugitive slaves flee** through the swamps in Thomas Moran's *The Slave Hunt* (1862). Many slaves ran away from their masters, and colonial newspapers included notices urging readers to be on the lookout for them. Some fled in groups or collected together in isolated communities called "maroon" colonies, located in inaccessible swamps and woods.

Thomas Moran (American, 1837–1926), Slave Hunt, Dismal Swamp, Virginia, 1862. Gift of Laura A. Clubb, 1947.8.44. © 2007 The Philbrook Museum of Art, Inc., Tulsa, Oklahoma.

## VIOLENCE AND RESISTANCE

Slavery was made possible by the threat and reality of violence. The only way to make slaves work, Virginia planter Robert "King" Carter instructed his overseer, was "to make them stand in fear." Even the most cultured plantation owners thought nothing about floggings of fifty or seventy-five lashes. Some masters were downright sadistic, stabbing, burning, maiming, mutilating, raping, and even castrating their slaves.

Yet African Americans demonstrated a resisting spirit. In their day-to-day existence they often refused to cooperate: they malingered, they mistreated animals and broke tools, they wantonly destroyed the master's property. Flight was another option. An analysis of hundreds of eighteenth-century advertisements for runaways concludes that 80 percent were young men in their twenties, suggesting that most runaways were unattached males.

Runaways sometimes collected together in isolated and hidden communities called "maroons," from the Spanish word *cimarron*, meaning "wild and untamed." Slaves who escaped from South Carolina or Georgia into Spanish Florida created maroon communities among the Creek Indians there. These mixed African and Indian peoples came to call themselves "Seminoles," a name deriving from their pronunciation of "cimarron."

The most direct form of resistance was revolt. The first notable slave uprising of the colonial era occurred in New York City in 1712. Taking an oath of secrecy, twenty-three Africans vowed revenge for what they called the "hard usage" of their masters. They armed themselves, killed nine colonists, and burned several buildings before being surrounded by the militia. Six of the conspirators committed suicide rather than surrender. Thirteen were hanged, another was starved to death in chains, another broken on the wheel, and three more burned at the stake.

A series of small rebellions and rumors of large ones in 1720s' Virginia culminated in the Chesapeake Rebellion of 1730, the largest slave uprising of the colonial period. Several hundred slaves assembled in Norfolk and Princess Anne counties where they chose commanders for their "insurrection." More than three hundred escaped en masse. Hunted down by Indians hired by the colony, their

## QUICK REVIEW

**Resistance to Slavery**

♦ Refusal to cooperate or destruction of property.

♦ Running away and establishing fugitive communities.

♦ Revolting.

community was soon destroyed. Twenty-nine leaders were executed and the rest were returned to their masters.

In the Lower South, where slaves were a majority of the population, there were isolated but violent uprisings in 1704, 1720, and 1730. In 1738 a series of revolts broke out in South Carolina and Georgia. These prepared the way for the **Stono Rebellion** of 1739 (see Introduction), the most violent slave rebellion of the colonial period. In the aftermath of Stono several similar uprisings were quickly crushed by planters. Attributing these revolts to the influence of newly arrived Africans, colonial officials shut down the slave trade through Charles Town for the next ten years.

Wherever masters held slaves, fears of uprisings persisted. But compared with such slave colonies as Jamaica, Guiana, or Brazil, there were relatively few revolts in North America. The conditions favoring revolt (large African majorities, brutal exploitation with correspondingly low survival rates, little acculturation, and geographic isolation) prevailed only in some areas of the Lower South. Indeed, the very success of African Americans in British North America at establishing families, communities, and a culture of their own inevitably made them less likely to take the risks that rebellions required.

## SLAVERY AND THE ECONOMICS OF EMPIRE

The British slave colonies—the sugar plantations of the West Indies, the tobacco plantations of the Chesapeake, and the rice and indigo plantations of the Lower South—accounted for 95 percent of exports from the Americas to Great Britain from 1714 to the eve of the American Revolution. Moreover, there was the prime economic importance of the slave trade itself, which one eighteenth-century economist described as the "foundation" of the British economy, "the mainspring of the machine which sets every wheel in motion." The labor of African slaves was largely responsible for the economic success of the British Empire in the Americas. New World slavery contributed enormously to the growth and development of the Old World economy. During the eighteenth century slavery was the most dynamic force in the Atlantic economy, responsible for the capital formation that made possible the beginnings of the industrial economy.

### SLAVERY: FOUNDATION OF THE BRITISH ECONOMY

Slavery contributed to the economic development of Great Britain in three principal ways. First, it generated enormous profits. Profits derived from the triangular trade in slaves, plantation products, and manufactured goods (see Map 4.3) furnished from 21 to 35 percent of Great Britain's fixed capital formation in the eighteenth century. This capital funded the first modern banks and insurance companies and, through loans and investments, found its way into a wide range of economic activities. Merchant capitalists were prominent investors in the expansion of the merchant marine, the improvement of harbors, and the construction of canals.

Second, slave colonies in the Caribbean supplied 69 percent of the raw cotton for British textile mills, the earliest sector of industrial development. The insatiable demand for cotton would eventually lead to the development of the cotton gin and the rise of cotton plantations in the United States (see Chapter 11).

Third, slavery provided an enormous stimulus to the growth of manufacturing by creating a huge colonial market for exports. From 1700 to 1740, the growth in American and African demand for manufactured goods accounted for nearly 70 percent of the expansion of British exports.

The multiplier effects of these activities are best seen in the growth of English ports such as Liverpool and Bristol. There the African and American trades provided

**Stono Rebellion** One of the largest and most violent slave uprisings during the Colonial Period that occurred in Stono, South Carolina.

**HOW DID** slavery fuel the economic development of Europe in the seventeenth and eighteenth centuries?

**myhistorylab**
Review Summary

### QUICK REVIEW

**British Trade Policy**

- All trade in empire to be conducted in English or colonial ships.
- Channeling of colonial trade through England or another English colony.
- Subsidization of English goods offered for sale in the colonies.
- Colonists prohibited from large-scale manufacture of certain products.

# ➤ MAP EXPLORATION

To explore an interactive version of this map, go to **http://www.prenhall.com/faraghertic/map4.3**

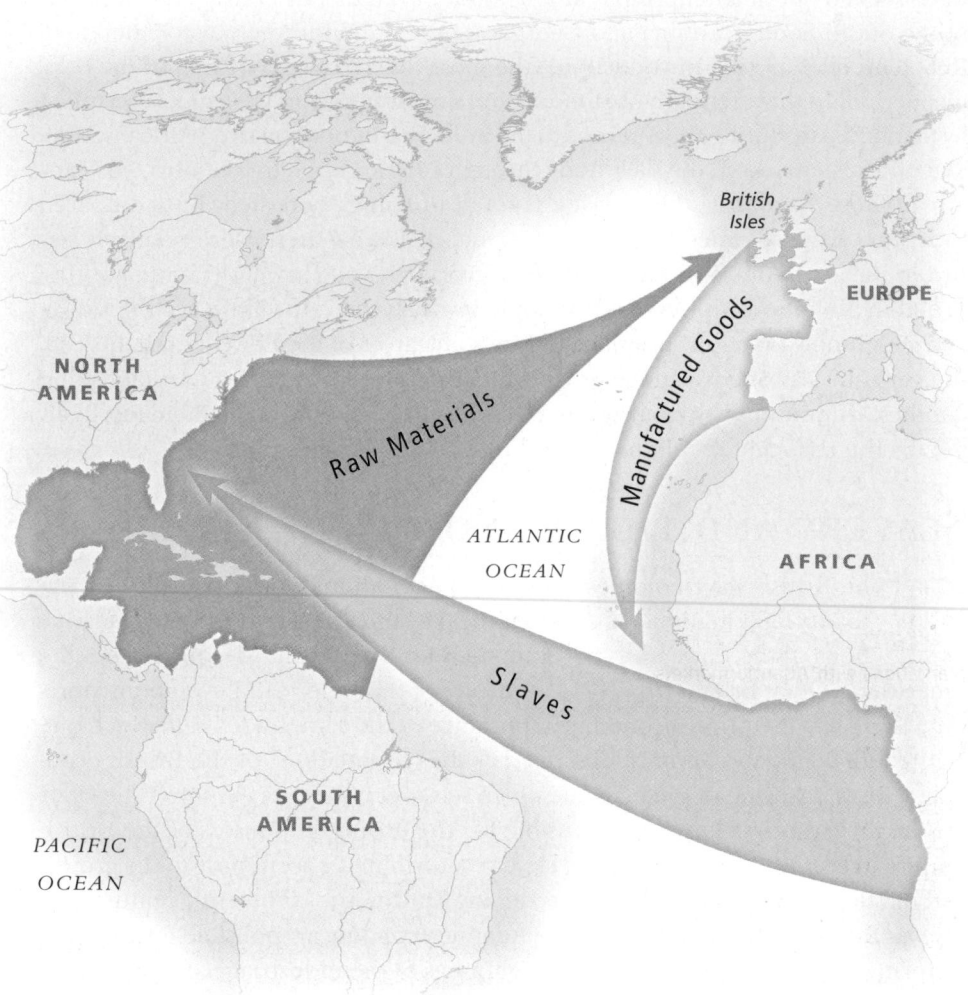

**MAP 4.3**

**Triangular Trade Across the Atlantic**  The pattern of commerce among Europe, Africa, and the Americas became known as the "triangular trade." Sailors called the voyage of slave ships from Africa to America the "Middle Passage" because it formed the crucial middle section of this trading triangle.

HOW WERE Europe, Africa, and America linked together by commerce?

employment for ships' crews, dockmen, construction workers, traders, shopkeepers, lawyers, clerks, factory workers, and officials of all ranks down to the humblest employees of the custom house. It was said of Bristol that "there is not a brick in the city but what is cemented with the blood of a slave." In the countryside surrounding Liverpool and elsewhere, capital acquired through slavery was invested in the new industrial methods of producing cotton textiles, the beginning of the Industrial Revolution.

## THE POLITICS OF MERCANTILISM

Imperial officials argued that colonies existed solely for the benefit of the mother country. What they principally had in mind was the great wealth produced by slavery. To ensure that this wealth benefited their own nation-state, imperialists cre-

**The New England** artist John Greenwood painted this amusing view of New England sea captains in Surinam in 1757. By the early eighteenth century, New England merchant traders like these had become important participants in the traffic in slaves and sugar to and from the West Indies. Northern ports thus became important pivots in the expanding commercial network linking slave plantations with Atlantic markets.

John Greenwood, "Sea Captains Carousing in Surinam," 1758. Oil on bed ticking, 95.9 × 191.1 cm. Saint Louis Art Museum, Museum Purchase.

ated a system of regulations that became known as "**mercantilism**." The essence of mercantilist policy was the political control of the economy by the state. The British monarchy and Parliament established a uniform national monetary system, regulated wages, subsidized agriculture and manufacturing, and protected themselves from foreign competition by erecting tariff barriers. Britain also sought to organize and control colonial trade to the maximum advantage of its own shippers, merchants, manufacturers, and bureaucrats.

The mercantilists viewed the economy as a "zero-sum game," in which total economic gains were equal to total losses. The essence of the competition between states, the mercantilists argued, was the struggle to acquire and hoard the fixed amount of wealth that existed in the world. The nation that accumulated the largest treasure of gold and silver would be the most powerful.

## BRITISH COLONIAL REGULATION

The Spanish monarchy created the Casa de Contratación, the first state trading monopoly, to manage the commerce of its empire in the sixteenth century. It was widely emulated by other powers. The Dutch East Indies Company, the French Company of the Indies, the English East India Company, the Hudson's Bay Company, and the Royal African Company were all state-sponsored trading monopolies.

English manufacturers complained that the nation's trading monopolies too frequently carried foreign (particularly Dutch) products to colonial markets, ignoring English domestic industry. Parliament reacted by passing a series of Navigation Acts between 1651 and 1696, creating the legal and institutional structure of Britain's eighteenth-century colonial system. The acts defined the colonies as both suppliers of raw materials and as markets for English manufactured goods. Merchants from

**Mercantilism** Economic system whereby the government intervenes in the economy for the purpose of increasing national wealth.

other nations were forbidden from doing business in the English colonies, and colonial commodities were required to be transported in English vessels.

The regulations specified a list of "enumerated commodities" that could be shipped to England only. Those included the products of the southern slave colonies (sugar, molasses, rum, tobacco, rice, and indigo), those of the northern Indian trade (furs, pelts, and skins), and those essential for supplying the shipping industry (pine masts, tar, pitch, resin, and turpentine). The bulk of these products was not destined for English consumption but was exported elsewhere at great profit.

England also placed limitations on colonial enterprises that might compete with those at home. A series of enactments—including the Wool Act of 1699, the Hat Act of 1732, and the Iron Act of 1750—forbade the manufacture of those products in the colonies. Moreover, colonial assemblies were forbidden to impose tariffs on English imports as a way to protect colonial industries. Banking was disallowed, local coinage prohibited, and the export of coin from England forbidden.

Robert Walpole, prime minister of the king's government from 1721 to 1742, argued that it made little sense to tamper with such a prosperous system. Walpole pursued a policy later characterized as "salutory neglect." Any colonial rules and regulations deemed contrary to good business practice were simply ignored and not enforced. Between 1700 and 1760 the quantity of goods exported from the colonies to the mother country rose 165 percent, while imports from Britain to North America increased by more than 400 percent. In part because of the lax enforcement, but mostly because the system operated to the profit of colonial merchants, colonists complained very little about the operation of the mercantilist system before the 1760s. It seemed that everyone was getting rich off the labor of slaves.

## WARS FOR EMPIRE

During the 1720s and 1730s, Prime Minister Walpole steered Great Britain away from war with other mercantilist powers. Earlier in the century, a war pitting Great Britain against Spain and France (known as the War of the Spanish Succession in Europe, **Queen Anne's War** in America) had ended in a significant British victory and in the Peace of Utrecht in 1713 Britain gained a good deal. France was forced to cede Acadia, Newfoundland, and Hudson Bay to Great Britain in exchange for guarantees of security for the French-speaking residents of those provinces. Spain was forced to open its American ports to British traders, who were also granted the exclusive right to supply slaves to the Spanish colonies.

For more than fifteen years Walpole prevailed over militant factions in the House of Commons that demanded complete elimination of Spanish competition in the Americas. But in 1739, at their urging, a one-eared sea captain by the name of Robert Jenkins testified about the indignities suffered by British merchant sailors at the hands of Spanish authorities in Caribbean ports. In a dramatic flourish, Jenkins produced a dried and withered ear, which he claimed the Spanish had cut from his head. The public outrage that followed forced Walpole to agree to a war of Caribbean conquest known as the War of Jenkins's Ear. "They now ring the bells," Walpole declared, "but they will soon wring their hands."

Walpole was right. The British underestimated Spanish strength and the troops were ravaged by yellow fever and other diseases. The only success of the war for the British came when the Georgia militia blocked a Spanish invasion from Florida in 1742. The war ended with no territorial gains on either side.

The war with Spain merged into a war with France that began in 1744. Known as **King George's War** in America (the War of the Austrian Succession in Europe), it began with a French invasion of their former colony of Acadia, which the British had renamed Nova Scotia. Indian and Canadian raids again devastated the border

**Queen Anne's War**  American phase (1702–1713) of Europe's War of the Spanish Succession.

**King George's War**  The third Anglo-French war in North America (1744–1748), part of the European conflict known as the War of the Austrian Succession.

# OVERVIEW | The Colonial Wars

| | | |
|---|---|---|
| 1689–97 | **King William's War** | France and England battle on the northern frontiers of New England and New York. |
| 1702–13 | **Queen Anne's War** | England fights France and Spain in the Caribbean and on the northern frontier of New France. Part of the European conflict known as the War of the Spanish Succession. |
| 1739–43 | **War of Jenkins's Ear** | Great Britain versus Spain in the Caribbean and Georgia. Part of the European conflict known as the War of the Austrian Succession. |
| 1744–48 | **King George's War** | Great Britain and France fight in Acadia and Nova Scotia; the second American round of the War of the Austrian Succession. |
| 1754–63 | **French and Indian War** | Last of the great colonial wars pitting Great Britain against France and Spain. Known in Europe as the Seven Years' War. |

towns of New England and New York, and hundreds of British subjects were killed or captured. New England forces attacked and conquered the great French fortress at Louisbourg. But Great Britain fared less well in the European fighting, and the war ended in stalemate with the return of all territory.

myhistorylab

**Overview:** *The Colonial Wars*

## THE COLONIAL ECONOMY

Despite the resumption of warfare, the colonial economy continued to operate to the great benefit of planters, merchants, and white colonists in general. Southern slave owners made healthy profits on the sale of their commodities. They enjoyed a protected market in which competing goods from outside the empire were heavily taxed. Planters found themselves with steadily increasing purchasing power. Pennsylvania, New York, and New England, and increasingly the Chesapeake as well, produced grain, flour, meat, and dairy products. None of these was included in the list of **enumerated goods** and could be sold freely abroad. Most of this trade was carried in New England ships.

The greatest benefits for the port cities of the North came from their commercial relationship to the slave colonies (see Figure 4.3). In addition to entering the slave trade itself, New England merchants began to make inroads into the export trade of the West Indian colonies. It was in the Caribbean that northern merchants most blatantly ignored mercantilist laws. In violation of Spanish, French, and Dutch regulations prohibiting foreign trade, New Englanders traded foodstuffs for sugar in foreign colonies. By 1750, more than sixty distilleries in Massachusetts were exporting more than 2 million gallons of rum, most of it produced from molasses obtained illegally. Because the restrictive rules and regulations enacted by Britain for its colonies were not enforced, the merchants and manufacturers of the port cities of the North prospered.

By the mid-eighteenth century, the Chesapeake and Lower South regions were major exporters of tobacco, rice, and indigo to Europe, and the middle colonies were major exporters of grain. The carrying trade in the products of slave labor made it possible for the northern and middle colonies to earn the income necessary to purchase British imports despite the lack

**Enumerated goods**   Items produced in the colonies and enumerated in acts of Parliament that could be legally shipped from the colony of origin only to specified locations.

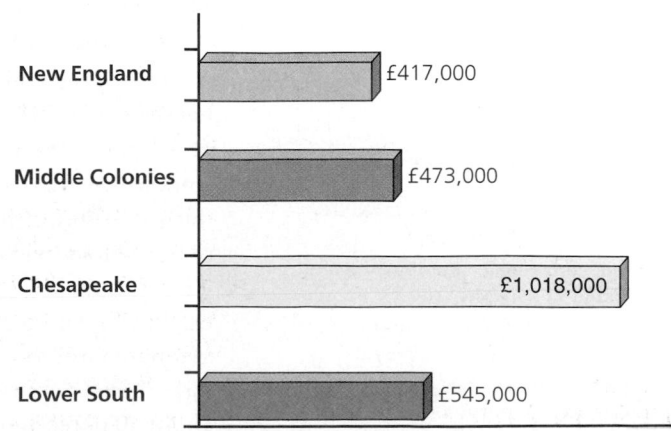

| | |
|---|---|
| New England | £417,000 |
| Middle Colonies | £473,000 |
| Chesapeake | £1,018,000 |
| Lower South | £545,000 |

**Figure 4.3 Value of Colonial Exports by Region, Annual Average, 1768–72**
With tobacco, rice, grain, and indigo, the Chesapeake and Lower South accounted for nearly two-thirds of colonial exports in the late eighteenth century.

James F. Shepherd and Gary M. Walton, *Shipping, Maritime Trade and the Economic Development of Colonial America* (Cambridge: Cambridge University Press, 1972), 211–27.

## QUICK REVIEW

**Colonial Exports**

- Chesapeake colonies: tobacco.
- South Carolina: rice and indigo.
- Middle colonies: wheat.

**HOW DID** slavery shape southern colonial society?

myhistorylab

Review Summary

of valuable products from their own regions. Gradually, the commercial economies of the Northeast and the South were becoming integrated. Like London, Liverpool, and Bristol—though on a smaller scale—the port cities of the North became pivots in the expanding trade network linking slave plantations with Atlantic markets. This trade provided northern merchants with the capital that financed commercial growth and development in their cities and the surrounding countryside. Slavery thus contributed to the growth of a score of northern port cities, forming an indirect but essential part of their economies.

# SLAVERY, PROSPERITY, AND FREEDOM

The prosperity of the eighteenth-century plantation economy thus improved the living conditions for the residents of northern cities as well as for a large segment of the white population of the South, providing them with the opportunity for a kind of freedom unknown in the previous century. The price of this prosperity and freedom, however, was the enslavement and exploitation of millions of Africans and African Americans. Freedom for white men based on the enslavement of black people is one of the most glaring contradictions in American history.

## THE SOCIAL STRUCTURE OF THE SLAVE COLONIES

Slavery produced a highly stratified class society. At the summit of power stood an elite of wealthy planters who held more than half the cultivated land and over 60 percent of the wealth. Although there was no formal colonial aristocracy—no royal recognition of social rank—the landed elite of the slave colonies sought to present itself as one.

The typical wealthy Virginia planter of the eighteenth century lived in a Tidewater county; owned several thousand acres of prime farmland and more than a hundred slaves; resided in a luxurious plantation mansion, built perhaps in the fashionable Georgian style; and had an estate valued at more than £10,000. Elected to the House of Burgesses and forming the group from which the magistrates and counselors of the colony were chosen, these "first families of Virginia" were a self-perpetuating governing class.

A similar elite ruled the Lower South, although wealthy landowners spent little time on their plantations. They lived instead in fashionable Charles Town, where they made up a close-knit group who controlled the colonial government.

A considerable distance separated this elite from typical southern landowners. About half the adult white males were small planters and farmers. But while the gap between rich and middling colonists grew larger during the eighteenth century, the prosperity of the plantation economy created generally favorable conditions for the landowning class as a whole. Slave ownership, for example, became widespread among this group during the eighteenth century. In Virginia at midcentury, 45 percent of heads of household held one to four slaves and even poorer farmers kept one or two.

Despite the prosperity that accompanied slavery, however, a substantial number of white colonists owned no land or slaves at all. Some rented land or worked as tenant farmers, some hired out as overseers or farm workers, and still others were indentured servants. Throughout the plantation region, landless men constituted about 40 percent of the population. A New England visitor found a "much greater disparity between the rich and poor in Virginia" than at home.

## WHITE SKIN PRIVILEGE

But all the white colonists of eighteenth-century North America shared the privileged status of their color. In the early seventeenth century, there had been more diversity in views about race. As slavery became increasingly important, however, Vir-

## QUICK REVIEW

**Southern Social Structure**

- Topped by small elite of wealthy planters.
- About half of all white adult males were small planters and farmers.
- A substantial portion of colonists owned no land or slaves.

myhistorylab

**Exploring America:** *Racism in American History*

ginia officials took considerable care to create legal distinctions between the status of colonists and that of Africans. Beginning in 1670, free Africans were prohibited from owning Christian servants. Ten years later, another law declared that any African, free or slave, who struck a Christian would receive thirty lashes on his bare back. One of the most important measures was designed to suppress intimate interracial contacts between white servants and enslaved Africans. A 1691 act "for prevention of that abominable mixture and spurious issue which hereafter may encrease in this dominion" established severe penalties for interracial sexual relationships. Such penalties were rarely applied to masters who had sexual relations with their slave women. Because by law the children of slave mothers were born into bondage, many plantations included light-skinned slaves who were the masters' kin.

RUN away from the subscriber in *Albemarle*, a Mulatto slave called *Sandy*, about 35 years of age, his stature is rather low, inclining to corpulence, and his complexion light; he is a shoemaker by trade, in which he uses his left hand principally, can do coarse carpenters work, and is something of a horse jockey; he is greatly addicted to drink, and when drunk is insolent and disorderly, in his conversation he swears much, and in his behaviour is artful and knavish. He took with him a white horse, much scarred with traces, of which it is expected he will endeavour to dispose; he also carried his shoemakers tools, and will probably endeavour to get employment that way. Whoever conveys the said slave to me, in *Albemarle*, shall have 40 s. reward, if taken up within the county, 4 l. if elsewhere within the colony, and 10 l. if in any other colony, from
THOMAS  JEFFERSON.

**Thomas Jefferson placed** this advertisement in the *Virginia Gazette* on September 14, 1769. Americans need to seriously consider the historical relationship between the prosperity and freedom of white people and the oppression and exploitation of Africans and African Americans.

Relationships between free whites and enslaved blacks produced a large mixed-ancestry group known as mulattoes. The majority of them were slaves; a minority, the children of European women and African men, were free. According to a Maryland census of 1755, more than 60 percent of the mulattoes of that colony were slaves. But mulattoes also made up three-quarters of the small free African American population. This group, numbering about four thousand in the 1770s, was denied the right to vote, to hold office, or to testify in court—all on the basis of racial background. Denied the status of citizenship enjoyed by even the poorest white men, free blacks were an outcast group who raised the status of white colonials by contrast. Racial distinctions were a constant reminder of the freedom of white colonists and the debasement of all blacks, slave or free.

Racism set up a wall of contempt between colonists and African Americans.

2–11
William H. Browne, *Maryland Addresses the Status of Slaves* (1664)

# CONCLUSION

During the eighteenth century, nearly half a million Africans were kidnapped from their homes, marched to the African coast, and packed into ships for up to three months before arriving in British North America. They provided the labor that made colonialism profitable. Southern planters, northern merchants, and especially British traders and capitalists benefited greatly from the commerce in slave-produced crops, and that prosperity filtered down to affect many of the colonists of British North America. Slavery was fundamental to the operation of the British empire in North America. Mercantilism was a system designed to channel colonial wealth produced by slaves to the nation-state, but as long as profits were high, the British tended to wink at colonists' violations of mercantilist regulations.

African Americans helped to build the greatest accumulation of capital Europe had ever seen, receiving nothing in return but blood, sweat, and tears. It is little wonder that slaves resisted, by malingering, by fleeing, by rising up in rebellion, as did the slaves of the Stono River. Yet that rebellion itself was a sign that despite enormous hardship and suffering, African Americans were forming new communities, rebuilding families, restructuring language, and reforming

## CHRONOLOGY

| | |
|---|---|
| 1441 | African slaves first brought to Portugal |
| 1619 | First Africans brought to Virginia |
| 1655 | English seize Jamaica |
| 1662 | Virginia law makes slavery hereditary |
| 1672 | Royal African Company organized |
| 1691 | Virginia prohibits interracial sexual contact |
| 1698 | Britain opens the slave trade to all its merchants |
| 1699 | Spanish declare Florida a refuge for escaped slaves |
| 1702 | South Carolinians burn St. Augustine |
| 1705 | Virginia Slave Code established |
| 1706 | French and Spanish navies bombard Charles Town |
| 1710 | English capture Port Royal in Acadia |
| 1712 | Slave uprising in New York City |
| 1713 | Peace of Utrecht |
| 1721–48 | Robert Walpole leads British cabinet |
| 1729 | Natchez Rebellion in French Louisiana |
| 1739 | Stono Rebellion in South Carolina |
| 1739–43 | War of Jenkins's Ear |
| 1741 | Africans executed in New York for conspiracy |
| 1744–48 | King George's War |
| 1752 | Georgia officially opened to slavery |
| 1770s | Peak period of the English colonies' slave trade |
| 1808 | Importation of slaves into the United States ends |

culture. African American culture added important components of African knowledge and experience to colonial agriculture, art, music, and cuisine. The African Americans of the English colonies lived better lives than the slaves worked to death on Caribbean sugar plantations but lives of misery compared with the men they were forced to serve.

## REVIEW QUESTIONS

1. Trace the development of the system of slavery and discuss the way it became entrenched in the Americas.

2. Describe the effects of the slave trade both on enslaved Africans and on the economic and political life of Africa.

3. Describe the process of acculturation involved in becoming an African American. In what ways did slaves "Africanize" the South?

4. Explain the connection between the institution of slavery and the building of a commercial empire.

5. In what ways did colonial policy encourage the growth of racism?

## KEY TERMS

**Flashcard Review**

**Enumerated goods** (p. 95)
**Great Awakening** (p. 87)
**King George's War** (p. 94)
**Mercantilism** (p. 93)
**Middle Passage** (p. 79)

**Pueblo Revolt** (p. 85)
**Queen Anne's War** (p. 94)
**Seven Years' War** (p. 78)
**Slave codes** (p. 87)
**Stono Rebellion** (p. 91)

# RECOMMENDED READING

Ira Berlin, *Many Thousands Gone: The First Two Centuries of Slavery in North America* (1998). A history of colonial slavery with attention to the differences between the regions of the Chesapeake, the Lower South, Louisiana, and the North. Emphasizes the distinction between slave societies and societies with slaves.

Andrew Burstein, *Jefferson's Secrets: Death and Desire at Monticello* (2005). An examination of the last decade of Jefferson's life, as he looks back on political struggles, slavery, and personal relationships.

Michael Craton, *Sinews of Empire: A Short History of British Slavery* (1974). An introduction to the British mercantilist system that emphasizes the importance of slavery. Includes a comparison of the mainland colonies with the Caribbean.

Winthrop D. Jordan, *White over Black: American Attitudes Toward the Negro, 1550–1812* (1968). Remains the best and most comprehensive history of racial attitudes. A searching examination of British and American literature, folklore, and history.

Herbert S. Klein, *The Atlantic Slave Trade* (1999). A new and important synthesis of the most recent studies of the slave trade, covering the social and cultural effects of the trade, especially for Africans.

Philip D. Morgan, *Slave Counterpoint: Black Culture in the Eighteenth-Century Chesapeake and Lowcountry* (1998). A comprehensive and detailed examination of cultural forms and ways of life in the two regions that leaves hardly a stone unturned.

Anthony S. Parent Jr., *Foul Means: The Formation of a Slave Society in Virginia, 1660–1740* (2003). A vivid and disturbing portrayal of colonial Virginia's patriarchal and violent character. An analysis of the apparatus of oppression from the planters' seizure of land to the efforts to keep poor whites and slaves apart.

Walter Rodney, *How Europe Underdeveloped Africa* (1974). This highly influential book traces the relationship between Europe and Africa from the fifteenth to the twentieth centuries, and demonstrates how Europe's industrialization became Africa's impoverishment.

Mechal Sobel, *The World They Made Together: Black and White Values in Eighteenth-Century Virginia* (1987). Demonstrates the ways in which both Africans and Europeans shaped the formation of American values, perceptions, and identities.

Lucia Stanton, *Some Free Day: The African-American Families of Monticello* (2001). The stories of six enslaved families who lived and worked for Jefferson at Monticello.

Ian K. Steele, *Warpaths: Invasions of North America* (1994). A new synthesis of the colonial wars from the sixteenth to the eighteenth centuries that places Indians as well as empires at the center of the action.

Henry Wiencek, *Imperfect God: George Washington, His Slaves, and the Creation of America* (2003). The story of Washington as planter and slave master, a man tormented by the contradictions.

*Mr. Lawrence, Be pleased to send me
a geenteel sute of Cloaths made of superfine
broad Cloth handsomely chosen…*
—George Washington, April, 26, 1763

**George Whitefield preaches** an outdoor sermon to a crowd
of worshippers.

# 5

# THE CULTURES OF COLONIAL NORTH AMERICA

## 1700–1780

**HOW DID** Indian America adapt to the new conditions created by colonization?

**HOW DID** the structure of colonial society differ from European social structure?

**TO WHAT** extent did North America participate in the Enlightenment?

1700 1780

# AMERICAN COMMUNITIES
## The Revival of Religion and Community in Northampton

JONATHAN EDWARDS, MINISTER OF THE PURITAN CHURCH IN Northampton, a rural town on the Connecticut River in western Massachusetts, rose before his congregation and began to preach. His words were frightening: "God will crush you under his feet without mercy, He will crush out your blood and make it fly, and it shall be sprinkled on His garments." Such torments would continue for "millions of millions of ages," and there could be no hope of relief from hell's fires. The people needed to "have their hearts touched," Edwards believed, and he was gratified by their response to his sermon.

"Before the sermon was done," one Northampton parishioner later recalled, "there was a great moaning and crying through the whole house—What shall I do to be saved?—I am going to Hell!—Oh what shall I do for Christ?" Religious fervor swept through the community, and church membership increased. A few years later an even greater revival known as the Great Awakening swept through all the colonies and plunged Northampton into turmoil once again. Important underlying issues prepared the ground for these religious revivals. They reflected the tensions that had arisen in the maturing communities of the colonies in which frontier opportunity was giving way to class inequity.

Founded in 1654 on the site of an Algonquin village, Northampton had grown from the original fifty households to more than 200 by the time of the 1734 revival. The last of the community's land had been parceled out to its residents. With the French and their Indian allies barring movement northward, and the colony of New York to the west, there was little opportunity for young men. Few could afford to buy land at the high market prices, so they had to rely on gifts or bequests from their fathers. Meanwhile, a small elite of well-to-do families, known as the "River Gods," controlled a disproportionately large share of local real estate. From their ranks came the majority of the officials of local and county government, as well as the ministers and elders of the Puritan congregations.

By the time Edwards became pastor in 1729, the authority and influence of the church had declined greatly from the heyday of Puritan power in the seventeenth century. In those early days, church and community had been one, but as Northampton's leaders devoted their energies to the pursuit of wealth, the fires of religious enthusiasm dimmed. The Northampton community, Edwards believed, had been divided into "two parties," the rich and the envious.

Many of the town's young people faced a bleak future. The farm household was the most important economic unit, and the tight supply of real estate meant that most couples were forced to postpone marriage until they were in their late twenties. Restless young people of both sexes began to meet together at nightly "frolics," and pastor Edwards issued a warning about the "growth of uncleanness that has been in the land."

This group became Edwards's special constituency. It was the same everywhere throughout the British colonies. Young people in their early twenties played the most important role in the movement to restore religious enthusiasm. Reversing a long-standing tendency for women to be more active in the church, young men predominated among the reborn. Edwards and other revival preachers called for a return to the Calvinist traditions of the Puritan faith, criticizing what they saw as the growing materialism, joining the rising generation in questioning the order of the world into which they had been born.

The revival of religion that shook communities throughout the British colonies in the mid-eighteenth century was one of the first unifying events in American history. Thousands of people experienced conversion, new sects and churches sprang up, and old ones split into opposing factions. In the town of South Hadley, near Northampton, the congregation voted to dismiss their minister, who lacked the emotional fire they desired in a preacher. When he refused to vacate his pulpit they pulled him down, roughed him up, and threw him out the church door. According to one minister: "Multitudes were seriously, soberly, and solemnly out of their wits."

The disaffection of young people with the social and economic conditions of the mid-eighteenth century created the conditions for the Great Awakening, but the revival remained a religious event. The social order in Northampton was challenged, but it remained intact. The "River Gods" had always been uncomfortable with the message Edwards preached, and when the fervor died down, as it inevitably did, they succeeded in voting him out. The turmoil in Northampton subsided, yet the tensions remained.

Northampton, MA

# NORTH AMERICAN REGIONS

American history too often is written as if only the British colonists really mattered. It is an error residents of the British colonies could not afford to make. Most critically, there was Indian America. In the mid-eighteenth century Indian peoples retained their majority in North America (see Table 5.1). From the fringes of colonial societies to the native heart of the continent, thousands of native communities, despite being deeply affected by the spread of colonial cultures, remained firmly in control of their homelands.

Neither could British colonists afford to ignore their colonial competitors. North and west of the English-speaking enclaves along the Atlantic coast, French-speaking communities were clustered along the St. Lawrence and scattered down the Mississippi to the Gulf of Mexico. South and west, isolated Spanish-speaking communities of the northern Spanish borderlands stretched from Florida to Texas and on to California (see Map 5.1).

## INDIAN AMERICA

After two centuries of European colonization, Indian peoples had adapted and changed. They incorporated firearms and metal tools and learned to build their homes of logs. They participated enthusiastically in the fur trade. But in the process they became dependent on European commerce.

**HOW DID** Indian America adapt to the new conditions created by colonization?

myhistorylab
**Review Summary**

## IMAGE KEY
for pages 100–101

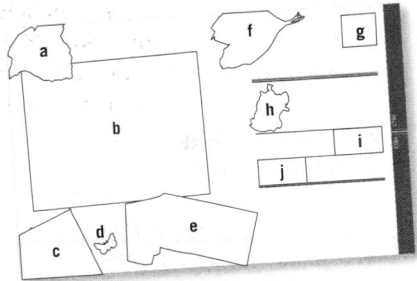

a. A brown patterned neckcloth.
b. George Whitefield preaches an outdoor sermon to a crowd of worshippers.
c. A small pile of muscovado sugar.
d. A mounted moth.
e. A half-loom width of oyster silk damask of the 18<sup>th</sup> century.
f. Dried tobacco leaves.
g. A merchant ship.
h. A Jesuit missionary baptizing an Indian in New France.
i. A hand-colored woodcut of a settler's log cabin in the Blue Ridge Mountains (Appalachians).
j. George Whitefield extends his hands over kneeling worshippers while wearing black ministerial robes in a 1770 painting by John Wallaston.

**MAP 5.1**
**Regions in Eighteenth-Century North America**   By the middle of the eighteenth century, European colonists had established a number of distinctive colonial regions in North America. The northern periphery of New Spain, stretched from Baja California to eastern Texas, then jumped to the settlements on the northern end of the Florida peninsula. New France was like a great crescent, extending from the plantation communities along the Mississippi near New Orleans to the French colonial communities along the St. Lawrence.

WHAT STEPS did Spain take to reinforce and expand its holdings in North America in the eighteenth century?

### TABLE 5.1

## Population of North America in 1750

| Region | Population |
|---|---|
| New France | 70,000 |
| New England | 400,000 |
| New York | 100,000 |
| Pennsylvania | 230,000 |
| Chesapeake | 390,000 |
| Lower South | 100,000 |
| Backcountry | 100,000 |
| Northern New Spain | 20,000 |
| Indian America | 1,500,000 |
| TOTAL | 2,910,000 |

*[handwritten margin notes:]* population decline – old war diseases among Indian communities from Europeans

*[handwritten margin notes:]* growth of pop in British colonies

**myhistorylab**

**Exploring America:** *America and the Horse*

**A portrait of** the Delaware chief Tishcohan by Gustavus Hesselius, painted in 1732. In his purse of chipmunk hide is a clay pipe, a common item of the Indian trade. Tishcohan was one of the Delaware leaders forced by Pennsylvania authorities into signing a fraudulent land deal that reversed that colony's history of fair dealing with Indians over land. He moved west to the Ohio River as settlers poured into his former homeland.

Gustavus Hesselius, "Tishcohan," Native American Portrait, 1735. Courtesy of the Historical Society of Pennsylvania Collection, Atwater Kent Museum of Philadelphia.

Yet Indian peoples continued to assert a proud independence and demonstrated considerable skill in playing off colonial powers one against the other. In 1701 the Iroquois, allies of the British, signed a treaty of neutrality with the French. Exploiting the vulnerabilities of these two powers, the Iroquois Confederacy became a major power broker during the first half of the eighteenth century. In the Lower South native peoples found similar room to maneuver between the competing interests of Britain, France, and Spain.

But native leaders confronted enormous difficulties. In the eastern portion of the continent the preeminent concern was the tremendous growth of the population in the British colonies and especially the movement of settlers westward. In the 1730s and 1740s Pennsylvania abandoned its tradition of fair dealing and perpetrated a series of fraudulent seizures of western lands from the Delawares. It was a disturbing sign of things to come.

Meanwhile, Indian communities continued to suffer from long-term population decline as the result of epidemic Old World diseases. Historical demographers estimate that from a high of 7 to 10 million north of Mexico in 1500, the native population had fallen to around a million by 1800. Population loss did not affect all Indian tribes equally, however. Native peoples with a century or more of colonial contact and interaction had lost 50 percent or more of their numbers, but most Indian societies in the interior had yet to be struck by the epidemics.

Other changes offered opportunity. By the early eighteenth century, Indians on the southern fringe of the Great Plains had acquired horses from Spanish colonists in New Mexico (see Map 5.2). Horses enabled Indian hunters to exploit the buffalo herds much more efficiently. Great numbers of Indian peoples moved onto the plains during the eighteenth century, pulled by this new way of life and pushed by colonial invasions and disruptions radiating southwest from Canada and north from the Spanish borderlands. The invention of nomadic Plains Indian culture was another of the dramatic cultural innovations of the eighteenth century.

## THE SPANISH BORDERLANDS

In the mid-eighteenth century the region now known as the Sunbelt formed the periphery of the largest and most prosperous European colony on the North American continent, the viceroyalty of New Spain, with a population of approximately 1 million Spanish-speaking inhabitants and 2 million Indians. Mexico City, the administrative capital of New Spain, was the most sophisticated city in the Western Hemisphere. New Spain's northern provinces of Florida, Texas, New Mexico, and California, however, were far removed from this sophistication. Officials who oversaw these colonies thought of them as buffer zones, protecting New Spain from the expanding empires of Spain's rivals. Compared to the dynamic changes going on in the English colonies, society in the Spanish borderland was relatively static.

In Florida, the oldest of the European colonies in North America, fierce fighting with the British and their Indian allies had reduced the Spanish presence to little more than the forts of St. Augustine on the Atlantic and Pensacola on the Gulf of Mexico, each surrounded by small colonized territories populated with the families of Spanish troops. In their weakened condition, the Spanish had no choice but to establish cooperative relations with the Creek and Seminole Indians who dominated the region, as well as hundreds of African American runaways who fled to Florida.

Nearly 2,000 miles to the west, New Mexico was similarly isolated from the mainstream of New Spain. In 1750 New Mexico included some 20,000 Pueblo Indians (their numbers greatly reduced by disease) and perhaps 10,000 mestizo colonists. The prosperity of these colonists, who supported themselves with subsistence agriculture, was severely limited by a restrictive colonial economic policy that required them to exchange their wool, pottery, and buffalo hides for imported goods at unfavorable rates. But unlike the population of Florida, that of colonial New Mexico was gradually expanding, as settlers left the original colonial outposts along the upper Rio Grande to follow the valleys and streams leading north and east.

Concerned about the expansion of other colonial empires, the Spanish founded several new northern outposts in the eighteenth century. French activity in the Mississippi Valley prompted authorities to establish a number of military posts or presidios on the fringes of Louisiana and in 1716 to begin the construction of a string of Franciscan missions among the Indian peoples of Texas. By 1750 the settlement of San Antonio had become the center of a developing frontier province known as Tejas (Texas). New colonial outposts were also founded west of New Mexico in what is today southern Arizona. In the 1690s, Jesuit missionaries built missions among the desert Indians of the lower Colorado River and Gila River Valleys and introduced cattle herding.

In 1769, acting on rumors of Russian expansion in the north Pacific (for a discussion of Russian America, see Chapter 9), officials in Mexico City ordered Gaspar de Portolá, governor of what is today Baja California, to establish a Spanish presence along the Pacific coast to the north. With Portolá were Franciscan missionaries

# MAP EXPLORATION
To explore an interactive version of this map, go to
http://www.prenhall.com/faraghertlc/map5.2

**MAP 5.2**
**Growing Use of the Horse by Plains Indians**  In the seventeenth and eighteenth centuries, Spanish settlers introduced horses into their New Mexican colony. The horse offered the Indian peoples of the Great Plains the opportunity to create a distinctive hunting and warrior culture.

HOW DID the spread of the horse transform Indian lifestyles?

**A mounted Soldado** de Cuera (Leather-Coated Soldier), a watercolor by Ramón de Murillo, c. 1803. Thick leather coats offered protection from Indian arrows for the cavalry posted to the northern frontiers of eighteenth-century New Spain.

led by Junípero Serra, president of the missions in Baja. At the harbor of San Diego their company, composed of some 200 men, founded the first mission and presidio in present-day California. Over the next fifty years the number of California settlements grew to include twenty-one missions and a half-dozen presidios and pueblos (towns).

The Spanish plan for California called for converting the natives to Catholicism, subjecting them to the rule of the crown, and putting them to work raising the subsistence necessary for a small civil and military establishment that would hold the province against colonial rivals. The first contacts between Franciscans and natives were not encouraging, but numerous native families were attracted by offerings of food and clothing, by new tools and crafts, and by fascination with the spiritual power of the newcomers. Gradually the Spanish built a flourishing local economy based on irrigated farming and livestock raising.

Indians were not forced to join the missions, but once they did so they were not permitted to leave. The Franciscan missionaries resorted to cruel and sometimes violent means of controlling their Indian subjects, including shackles, solitary confinement, and whipping posts. Resistance developed early. In 1775, the natives at San Diego rose up and killed several priests, and over the years several other missions experienced similar revolts. But Spanish soldiers suppressed the uprisings. Another form of protest was flight. Soldiers hunted the runaways down and brought many back. Aggressive tribes in the hills and deserts, however, often proved even more threatening than the Spanish, so many Indians remained at the missions despite the harsh discipline. Overwork, inadequate nutrition, overcrowding, poor sanitation, and epidemic disease contributed to death rates that exceeded birthrates. During the period of the mission system, the native population of coastal California fell by 74 percent.

Throughout the Spanish borderlands the Catholic Church played a dominant role in community life. The object of colonization, one colonial promoter wrote in 1584, was "enlarging the glorious gospel of Christ, and leading the infinite multitudes of these simple people that are in error into the right and per-

## QUICK REVIEW

**Spanish Colonies**

♦ Mexico City was the capital of New Spain.

♦ Conflict with Indians and the British reduced the Spanish presence in Florida.

♦ New Mexico was isolated from the mainstream of New Spain.

**The Church of** San Xavier del Bac, constructed in the late eighteenth century, is located a few miles south of the city of Tucson, where Jesuit Father Eusebio Kino founded a mission among the Pima Indians in 1700. Known as the White Dove of the Desert, it is acclaimed as the most striking example of Spanish colonial architecture in the United States.

fect way of salvation." Although these were the words of the English imperialist Richard Hakluyt, they could as easily have come from a Jesuit missionary in New France or the Spanish padres Kino or Serra. There was no tradition of religious dissent.

## THE FRENCH CRESCENT

In France, as in Spain, church and state were closely interwoven. During the seventeenth century the chief ministers to the French monarchy, Cardinal Richelieu and his successor Cardinal Mazarin, laid out a fundamentally Catholic imperial policy, and under their guidance colonists constructed a second Catholic empire in North America. In 1674 church and state collaborated in establishing the bishopric of Quebec, which founded local seminaries, oversaw the appointment and review of priests, and laid the foundation of the resolutely Catholic culture of New France. Jesuit missionaries, meanwhile, continued to carry Catholicism deep into the continent.

The French sent few colonists to New France, but by natural increase the population rose from less than 15,000 in 1700 to more than 70,000 by 1750. The French used their trade and alliance network to establish colonies, military posts, and settlements that extended in a great crescent from the mouth of the St. Lawrence River southwest through the Great Lakes, then down the Mississippi River to the Gulf of Mexico (see Map 5.3). The great port and fortress of Louisbourg on Ile Royale (Cape Breton Island) was built to guard the northern approach to New France. The southern approach was protected by French troops at the port of New Orleans in Louisiana. Between these two points, the French laid a thin colonial veneer. By the middle of the century, the French were ascending the Missouri and Arkansas Rivers, placing missionaries and traders in Indian communities on the fringe of the Great Plains.

At the heart of the French empire in North America were the communities of farmers or habitants that stretched along the banks of the St. Lawrence between the provincial capital of Quebec and the fur trade center of Montreal. There were

French – wheat & sugar plantations

**MAP 5.3**

**The French Crescent**   The French empire in North America was based on a series of alliances and trade relations with Indian nations linking a great crescent of colonies, settlements, and outposts that extended from the mouth of the St. Lawrence River to the Gulf of Mexico.

WHAT GEOGRAPHIC rationale might have been behind French decisions to convert native peoples to Catholic Christianity?

also farming communities in the Illinois country, supplying wheat to sugar plantations in Louisiana. By the 1750s, those plantations, extending along the Mississippi from Natchez and Baton Rouge to New Orleans, had become the most profitable French enterprise in North America.

Among the most distinctive French stamps on the North American landscape were the "long lots" stretching back from the rivers, providing each settler a share of good bottomland to farm and frontage on the waterways, the "interstate highway system" of the French Crescent. Long lots were laid out along the Mississippi River in Louisiana and Illinois and at the strategic passages of the Great Lakes. Detroit, the most important of those, was a stockaded town with a military garrison, a small administrative center, several stores, a Catholic church, and 100 households of *métis* (French for mestizo) families. Farmers worked the land along the Detroit River, not far from communities inhabited by several thousand Indians from the Ottawa, Potawatomi, and Huron tribes.

Communities of this sort, combining both European and native American elements, were in the tradition of the inclusive frontier. Detroit had much of the character of a mixed community. Family and kinship were cast in the Indian pattern, yet the people focused their activities on commerce and overwhelmingly identified themselves as Catholics.

## NEW ENGLAND

Just as New Spain and New France had their official church, so too did the inhabitants of New England. Rather than the centralized authority of the Catholic hierarchy, however, communities in New England (except Rhode Island) were governed by Puritan congregations. Adult male church members constituted the freemen of the town, so there was very little distinction between religious and secular authority. At the town meeting the freemen chose their minister, voted on his salary, and elected local men to offices ranging from town clerk to animal warden.

The Puritan tradition was a curious mix of freedom and repression. Although local communities had considerable autonomy, they were tightly bound by the religious restrictions. The Puritans had not come to America to create a society where religion could be freely practiced but in order to establish their own version of the "right and perfect way." Puritan authorities banned and exiled Anglicans, Baptists, Quakers, and other dissidents. Between 1659 and 1661 four Quakers were executed for proselytizing.

Soon after the last of these executions King Charles II, newly placed on the throne, ordered a stop to religious persecution in Massachusetts. Several years later Roger Williams, whose Rhode Island colony had no established religion, made one of the first formal arguments for religious toleration. The new climate of opinion was best expressed by English political philosopher John Locke in "A Letter Concerning Tolerance," written in 1689. Churches were voluntary societies, Locke argued, and could gain genuine converts only through persuasion. The state, he asserted, had no legitimate concern with religious belief. That same year Parliament passed **The Act of Toleration**, granting religious freedom to Protestant dissenters (but not to Catholics). It was at first resisted by New England Puritans, but in 1700, under pressure from English authorities, Massachusetts and Connecticut reluctantly permitted other Protestant denominations to meet openly.

By then New Englanders were less concerned with religious conformity than with the problem of land. As population grew, groups of residents left established towns, "hiving off" to form new congregations and towns elsewhere. By the 1730s, Puritan communities had taken up most of the available land of Massachusetts, Connecticut, and Rhode Island, leaving only a few isolated reservations for small

**The persistence of** French colonial long lots in the pattern of modern landholding is clear in this enhanced satellite photograph of the Mississippi River near New Orleans. Long lots, the characteristic form of property holding in New France, were designed to offer as many settlers as possible a share of good bottomland as well as a frontage on the waterways, which served as the basic transportation network.

**The Act of Toleration**  Act passed in 1661 by King Charles II ordering a stop to religious persecution in Massachusetts.

**This view of** the Philadelphia waterfront, painted about 1720, conveys the impression of a city firmly anchored to maritime commerce. The long narrow canvas was probably intended for display over the mantel of a public room.

Peter Cooper, "The South East Prospect of the City of Philadelphia," ca. 1720. The Library Company of Philadelphia.

communities of Pequots, Narragansets, and Wampanoagas. New England had reached the limit of its land supply.

## THE MIDDLE COLONIES

New York featured one of the most ethnically diverse populations on the continent. At midcentury, society along the lower Hudson River, including the counties in northern New Jersey, was a veritable mosaic of ethnic communities. African Americans, both slave and free, constituted more than 15 percent of the population of the lower Hudson. Puritan, Baptist, Quaker, and Catholic congregations worshiped without legal hindrance, and in New York City, several hundred Jewish families built North America's first synagogue in 1730.

Although New York City grew by leaps and bounds in the eighteenth century, the colony as a whole was less attractive to immigrants than neighboring Pennsylvania. The region along the Delaware River—encompassing not only Pennsylvania but New Jersey, Delaware, and the northern portion of Maryland—grew more dramatically than any other in North America during the eighteenth century. Immigration played the dominant role in achieving the astonishing annual growth rate of nearly 4 percent. With access to some of the best farmland in North America, farmers and merchants were soon exporting abundant produce through the prosperous port at Philadelphia.

The Quakers quickly became a minority, but unlike the Puritans they were generally comfortable with religious and ethnic pluralism. This was a perspective well suited to the ethnically and religiously diverse population of the colony. Most German immigrants were Lutherans or Calvinists, most North Britons were Presbyterians, and there were plenty of Anglicans and Baptists as well.

The institutions of government were another pillar of community organization. Colonial officials appointed justices of the peace who provided judicial authority for the countryside. Property-owning farmers chose their own local officials. Country communities were bound together by kinship bonds as well as economic relations between neighbors. These communities were more loosely bound than those of New England. Because land was sold in individual lots rather than in communal parcels, farmers tended to disperse themselves over the open countryside. Villages gradually developed at crossroads and ferries but with little forethought or planning.

## THE BACKCOUNTRY

By 1750 Pennsylvania's exploding population had pushed beyond the first range of the Appalachian highlands (see Map 5.4). Settlers moved southwest, through western Maryland and down the valley of the Shenandoah River into western Virginia (see Seeing History).

# A Plan of an American New Cleared Farm

P atrick Campbell, a Scottish gentleman traveler, included this plate in the account of his tour of the American backcountry, published in 1793. The illustration provides a composite view of the raw frontier farms he visited, entirely typical of the eighteenth century. Note the way the pioneers hacked out their farms from the forest, leaving stumps standing in the fields. See how they fenced their fields to keep out livestock, which were allowed to forage freely. The engraving illustrates

**HOW DOES** the presence of Indians in this image contradict the popular view of frontier life?

four different types of fencing: plain log (marked 4), worm fence made of split poles (5), post-and-rail (6), and Virginia rail fence of crossed stakes (7). The use of wood from the abundant forest was an essential economic strategy. Campbell was notably free of the prejudice of many British visitors to the frontier, but he could not disguise his scorn of pioneer cabins, which he described as "miserable little hovels covered with bark." He included one of them in the engraving (14), one of the first illustrations of a log cabin to appear in print. Also notable here are the Indian canoes, one poled by a man, the other paddled by two women with what Campbell's note mistakenly labels a "Babose." Campbell made the entire trip with his own hunting dog, seen in the front of the canoe on the left. Note also the wonderful little "Indian dog" (15). ■

Patrick Campbell, *Travels in the Interior Inhabited Parts of North America* (1793).

# MAP EXPLORATION

To explore an interactive version of this map, go to
**http://www.prenhall.com/faraghertlc/map5.4**

Areas settled by 1720
Areas settled by 1760

Lake Superior
Lake Michigan
Lake Huron
Lake Ontario
Lake Erie
St. Lawrence R.
NEW ENGLAND
NEW YORK
APPALACHIAN MOUNTAINS
Missouri R.
Ohio R.
Mississippi R.
UPPER SOUTH
LOWER SOUTH
ATLANTIC OCEAN
Gulf of Mexico

0    300 mi
0    300 km

**MAP 5.4**

**Spread of Settlement: Movement into the Backcountry, 1720–60**

The spread of settlement from 1720 to 1760 shows the movement of population into the backcountry during the midcentury.

HOW DID the movement into the backcountry affect the relations among colonists, Indians, and English authorities?

The movement into the Pennsylvania and Virginia backcountry that began during the 1720s was the first of the great pioneer treks that would take white pioneers into the continental interior. Many, perhaps most, of these pioneers held no legal title to the lands they occupied. They simply hacked out and defended squatter's claims from native proprietors and all other comers. To the Delawares and Shawnees, who had been pushed into the interior, or the Cherokees, who occupied the Appalachian highlands to the south, these settlers presented a new and deadly threat. Rising fears and resentments over this expanding population triggered much eighteenth-century violence.

## THE SOUTH

The Chesapeake and the Lower South were triracial societies, with intermingled communities of white colonists and black slaves, along with substantial Indian communities living on the fringes of colonial settlement. Much of the population growth of the region resulted from the forced migration of enslaved Africans, who by 1750 made up 40 percent of the population. Specializing in rice, tobacco, and other commercial crops, these colonies were overwhelmingly rural. Farms and plantations were dispersed across the countryside, and villages or towns were few.

English authorities established the Church of England as the state religion in the Chesapeake colonies. Residents paid taxes to support the church and were required to attend services. No other churches were allowed into Virginia or Maryland (despite its founding by Catholics) and dissenters were excluded or exiled. Yet the Anglican establishment was internally weak. It maintained neither a colonial bishop nor local institutions for training clergy.

Along the rice coast, the dominant social institution was the large plantation. Transforming the tangle of woods and swamps along the region's rivers into an ordered pattern of dams, dikes, and flooded fields required heavy capital investment. Consequently, only men of means could undertake rice cultivation. By midcentury established rice plantations typically were dominated by a large main house, generally located on a spot of high ground overlooking the fields. Nearby, but a world apart, were the slave quarters, rough wooden cabins lining two sides of a muddy pathway near the outbuildings and barns.

Because tobacco, unlike rice, could be grown profitably in small plots, the Chesapeake included a greater variety of farmers and a correspondingly diverse landscape. The poorest farmers lived in wooden cabins little better than the shacks of the slaves. More prosperous farm families lived with two or three slaves in houses that nevertheless were considerably smaller than the substantial homes of New England.

Compared to the Lower South, where there was almost no community life outside the plantation, the Chesapeake boasted well-developed neighborhoods constructed from kinship networks and economic connections. The most important community institution was the county court, which held both executive and judicial power. The gentleman justices of the county, appointed by the governor, included the heads of the elite planter families. These men in turn selected the grand jury, composed of substantial freeholders. One of the most significant bonding forces in this free white population was a growing sense of racial solidarity in response to the increasing proportion of African slaves dispersed throughout the neighborhoods.

# SOCIAL AND POLITICAL PATTERNS

Despite important similarities among the colonial regions of North America, during the eighteenth century the trajectory of the British colonies began to diverge sharply from that of the French and Spanish. Immigration, economic growth, and provincial political struggles all pushed British colonists in a radically new direction.

### THE PERSISTENCE OF TRADITIONAL CULTURE IN THE NEW WORLD

In each of the regional North American societies, family and kinship, the church, and the local community were the most significant factors in everyday life. Everywhere colonists tended to live much as people had lived in European homeland communities at the time the colonies were settled. The residents of New Mexico, Quebec, and New England continued to be attached to the religious passions of the seventeenth century long after their mother countries had put those religious controversies aside in favor of imperial geopolitics. Nostalgia for Europe helped to fix a conservative colonial attitude toward culture.

These were oral cultures, depending on the transmission of information by the spoken rather than the printed word, on the passage of traditions through oral story and song. North American colonial folk cultures, traditional and suspicious of change, preserved an essentially medieval worldview. The rhythms of life were regulated by the hours of sunlight and the seasons of the year. People rose with the sun and went to bed soon after sundown. The demands of the season determined their working routines. They farmed with simple tools, and drought, flood, or pestilence might quickly sweep away their efforts. Experience told them that the natural world imposed limitations within which men and women had to learn to live.

These were also communal cultures. In Québec, villagers worked side by side to repair the roads. In New Mexico they collectively maintained the irrigation ditches. In New England they gathered in town meetings to decide the dates when common fields were to be plowed, sowed, and harvested. Houses offered little privacy, with families often sleeping together in the same chamber, sitting together on benches rather than in chairs, and taking their supper from a common bowl or trencher. For most North American colonists of the mid-eighteenth century, the community was more important than the individual.

Most colonists continued the traditional European occupation of working the land. The majority of North American farmers grew crops and raised livestock for their own needs or for local barter, and communities were largely self-sufficient. Most farmers attempted to produce small surpluses as well, which they sold to pay their taxes and buy some manufactured goods. But rather than specializing in the production of one or two crops for sale, most farmers diversified production in order to remain as independent of the market as possible. The primary goal was ownership of land and the assurance that children and descendants would be able to settle on lands nearby.

Colonial cities, by contrast, were centers of commerce. Artisans and craftsmen worked at their trades full time, organizing themselves according to the European craft system. A young man who wished to pursue a trade served several

*Instead of focusing on 1 crop, they cultivated a variety*

---

HOW DID the structure of colonial society differ from European social structure?

myhistorylab
Review Summary

**3–15**
Peter Kalm, *A Swedish Visitor Tells about Philadelphia* (1748)

A Potter.

**A spinner and** carpenter from *The Book of Trades*, an eighteenth-century British survey of the crafts practiced in colonial America. In colonial cities, artisans organized themselves into the traditional European craft system with apprentices, journeymen, and masters. There were few opportunities for the employment of women outside the household, but women sometimes earned income by establishing sidelines as midwives or spinners.

years as an apprentice, working in exchange for learning the skills and secrets of the craft. After completing his apprenticeship, the young craftsman sought employment in a shop, often necessitating his migration to some other area, thus becoming a "journeyman." Most craftsmen remained at the journeyman level for the whole of their careers. But by building a good name and carefully saving, a journeyman hoped to become a master craftsman, opening his own shop and employing journeymen and apprentices of his own. As in farming, the ultimate goal was independence.

There were few opportunities for women outside the household. By law, husbands held managerial rights over family property, but widows received support in the form of a one-third lifetime interest, known as "dower," in a deceased husband's real estate (the rest of the estate being divided among the heirs). And in certain occupations, such as printing (which had a tradition of employing women), widows succeeded their husbands in business. As a result, some colonial women played active roles in eighteenth-century journalism.

## QUICK REVIEW

**Key Aspects of Early Colonial Culture**

- Family and kinship.
- Church and religion.
- Local community.

## THE FRONTIER HERITAGE

The colonial societies of eighteenth-century North America also shared a set of assumptions originating in their common frontier heritage. European colonists came from Old World societies in which land was scarce and monopolized by property-owning elites. They settled in a continent where, for the most part, land was abundant and cheap. The widespread and general expectation of property ownership was the most important cultural distinction between North America and Europe.

*[handwritten margin note: very different from Europe]*

This expectation led to rising popular demands in all the colonial regions of the continent that land be taken from the Indian inhabitants and opened to colonial settlement. The majority of colonists—whether British, Spanish, or French—endorsed the violence directed against Indian peoples as an essential aspect of colonial life. This attitude was as true of inclusive as exclusive societies, with the difference that in the former, native peoples were incorporated into colonial society, while in the latter, tribes were pushed from the frontier.

American historians once tied the existence of this "free land" directly to the development of democracy. But the frontier heritage encouraged the popular acceptance of forced labor, a system that was anything but democratic. When asked how to achieve a good living, a woman of eighteenth-century South Carolina offered the following advice: "get a few slaves and beat them well to make them work hard." Labor was the key to prosperity, and it was in short supply throughout the colonies. In a land where free men and women could work for themselves on their own plot of ground, there was little incentive to work for wages. The use of forced labor was one of the few ways a landowner could secure an agricultural workforce.

More than half the immigrants to eighteenth-century British America arrived as indentured servants. Agents paid for the Atlantic crossing of poor immigrants in exchange for several years of service in America. But at the conclusion of their indentures, eighteenth-century servants enjoyed considerably more opportunity than their seventeenth-century counterparts, probably because of the rise in overall prosperity in the British colonies.

## POPULATION GROWTH AND IMMIGRATION

All the colonial regions of North America experienced unprecedented growth in the eighteenth century. "Our people must at least be doubled every twenty years," Benjamin Franklin wrote in a remarkable 1751 essay on population, and he was nearly right. In 1700, there were 290,000 colonists north of Mexico; fifty years later they had grown to approximately 1.3 million, an average annual growth rate of about 3 percent. Preindustrial societies typically grew at rates of less than 1 percent per year.

High fertility and low mortality played important roles. Colonial women typically bore seven or more children during their childbearing years. And blessed with an abundance of food, colonists enjoyed generally good health and relatively low mortality.

But the British colonies grew far more rapidly than those of France or Spain (see Figure 5.1). It was immigration that made the difference. Fearful of depleting their population at home, the Spanish severely limited the migration of their own subjects and absolutely forbade the immigration of foreigners. Dedicated to keeping their colonies exclusively Catholic, the French ignored

### QUICK REVIEW

**Population Growth**

♦ 1700: 290,000 colonists north of Mexico.

♦ 1750: 1.3 million colonists north of Mexico.

♦ High fertility rates fueled population growth.

 **5–1**
Benjamin Franklin, *Observations Concerning the Increase of Mankind, Peopling of Countries, &c.* (1751)

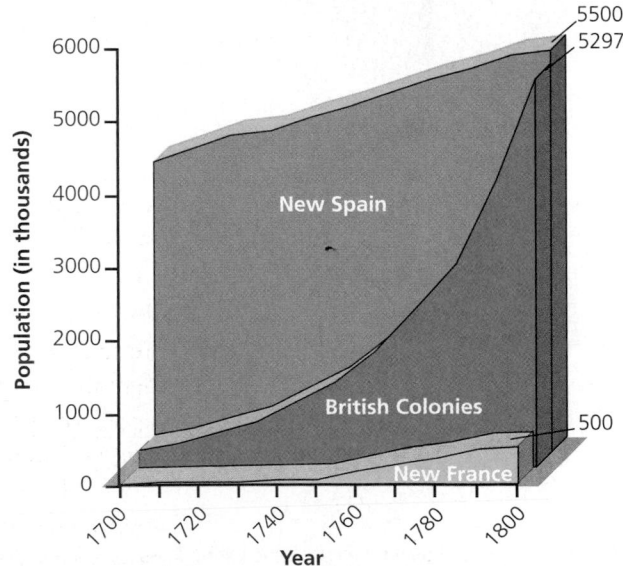

**Figure 5.1 Estimated Total Population of New Spain, New France, and the British North American Colonies, 1700–1780**
Although the populations of all three North American colonial empires grew in the eighteenth century, the explosive growth of the British colonies was unmatched.

*Historical Statistics of the United States* (Washington, DC: Government Printing Office, 1976), 1168.

**Engagés** Catholic immigrants to New France.

**Encomienda** In the Spanish colonies, the grant to a Spanish settler of a certain number of Indian subjects, who would pay him tribute in goods and labor.

**3–7**
William Byrd II, *Diary—An American Gentleman* (1709)

**MAP 5.5**

**Ethnic Groups in Eighteenth-Century British North America** The first federal census, taken in 1790, revealed remarkable ethnic diversity. New England was filled with people from the British Isles, but the rest of the colonies were a patchwork. Most states had at least three different ethnic groups within their borders.

**IN WHAT** areas were Scots and Scots-Irish most heavily concentrated? Why?

the desire of Protestant Huguenots to emigrate, instead sending thousands of Catholic **engagés** to Canada, most of whom returned, discouraged by the climate and the lack of commercial opportunity. But the English dispatched an estimated 400,000 of their own countrymen to populate their North American colonies during the seventeenth and eighteenth centuries. Moreover, the British were the only colonial power to encourage the immigration of foreign nationals.

Trans-Atlantic migration made for colonies characterized by extraordinary ethnic diversity (see Map 5.5 and Figure 5.2). First there were the Africans, the largest group to come to North America in the colonial period, larger even than the English. Forced relocation brought an estimated 600,000 to the colonies before the official end of the slave trade to the United States in 1807. Then there was the massive emigration from the northern British Isles. Squeezed by economic hardship, an estimated 150,000 Highland Scots and Protestant Irish from the Ulster region of northern Ireland (known as the "Scots-Irish") emigrated in the eighteenth century. German speakers were next in importance, at least 125,000 of them settling in the colonies. It is worth noting once again that a majority of these immigrants to British North America came as bonded servants or slaves.

## SOCIAL CLASS

In New France, landowning seigneurs (lords) claimed privileges similar to those enjoyed by their aristocratic counterparts at home; the Spanish system of **encomienda** and the great manors created by the Dutch and continued by the English along the Hudson River also represented attempts to transplant European feudalism to North America. But because settlers in most areas had relatively free access to land, these monopolies proved difficult or impossible to maintain. North American society was not aristocratic in the European fashion, but neither was it without social hierarchy.

In New Spain the official criterion for status was racial purity. *Españoles* (Spaniards), also known as *gente de razon* (literally, "people of reason"), occupied the top rung of the social ladder, with mestizos, mulattoes, and others on descending levels, with Indians and African slaves at the bottom. In the isolated northern borderlands, however, such distinctions tended to blur, with castas (persons of mixed background) enjoying considerably more opportunity. Mestizos who acquired land might suddenly be reclassified as españoles. Even so, Spanish and French colonial societies were cut in the style of the Old World, with its hereditary ranks and titles.

In the British colonies the upper class was made up of large landowners, merchants, and prosperous professionals. Despite the lack of titles, wealthy planters and merchants of the British colonies lived far more extravagantly than the seigneurs of New France or the dons of the Spanish borderlands. What separated the culture of class in the British colonies from that of New France or New Mexico was not so much the material conditions of life as the prevailing attitude toward social rank. In the Catholic cultures, the upper class attempted to obscure its origins, claiming descent from European nobility. But British North America celebrated social mobility. The class system was remarkably open, and the entrance of newly successful planters, commercial farmers, and merchants into the upper ranks was not only possible but also common.

There was also a large and impoverished lower class in the British colonies. Slaves, bound servants, and poor laboring families made up 40 percent or more of the population. For them the standard of living did not rise above bare subsistence. American slaves stood apart from the gains in the standard of living enjoyed by immigrants from Europe. Their lives in America had been degraded beyond measure from the conditions that had prevailed in their native lands.

The feature of the class system most often commented on by eighteenth-century observers was not the character or composition of the lower ranks, but rather the size and strength of the middle class, a rank entirely absent in the colonies of France and Spain. More than half the population of the British colonies, and nearly 70 percent of all white settlers, might have been so classified. Most were landowning farmers of small to moderate means, but the group also included artisans, craftsmen, and small shopkeepers. Households solidly in the center of this broad ranking enjoyed a standard of living higher than that of the great majority of people in England and Europe.

## ECONOMIC GROWTH AND ECONOMIC INEQUALITY

One of the most important differences among North American colonial regions in the eighteenth century was the economic stagnation of New France and New Spain compared with the impressive economic growth of the British colonies. Weighed down by royal bureaucracies and regulations, the communities of the French Crescent and New Spain never evidenced much prosperity. In eighteenth-century British North America, by contrast, per capita production grew at an annual rate of 0.5 percent. As economic growth increased the size of the economic pie, most middle- and upper-class British Americans began to enjoy improved living conditions. Improving standards of living and open access to land encouraged British colonists to see theirs as a society where hard work and savings could translate into prosperity.

At the same time, economic growth produced increasing social inequality. In the commercial cities, for example, prosperity was accompanied by a concentration of assets in the hands of wealthy families. The general standard of living may have been rising, but the rich were getting richer and the poor poorer. The greatest concentrations of wealth occurred in the cities and in regions dominated by commercial farming, whether slave or free, while the greatest economic equality was found in areas of self-sufficient farming.

Another eighteenth-century trend, however, stymied upward economic mobility in the countryside. As population grew and as generations succeeded one another in older settlements, all the available land eventually was taken up. Under the pressure of increased demand, land prices rose beyond the reach of families of modest means. And as a family's land was divided among the heirs of the second and third generations, parcels became ever smaller and more intensively

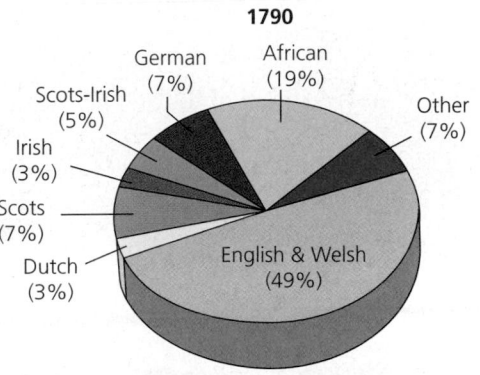

**Figure 5.2  The Ancestry of the British Colonial Population**
The legacy of eighteenth-century immigration to the British colonies was a population of unprecedented ethnic diversity.

Thomas L. Purvis, "The European Ancestry of the United States Population," *William and Mary Quarterly* 61 (1984): 85–101.

---

**QUICK REVIEW**

**Poverty in the Colonies**

♦ Gap between rich and poor widened in the eighteenth century.

♦ Most cities had workhouses or shelters.

♦ Much smaller percentage of population depended on public assistance in the colonies than in England.

**An eighteenth-century** genre painting from New Spain showing various racial *castas*, the result of ethnic mixing.

farmed. Eventually, the soil was exhausted. There were increases in the number of landless poor, as well as the disturbing appearance of what were called the "strolling poor," homeless people who traveled from town to town looking for work or simply a handout.

## COLONIAL POLITICS

The administration of the Spanish and French colonies was highly centralized. Although local communities had informal independence, these highly bureaucratized and centralized governments left little room for the development of vigorous traditions of self-government.

The situation in the British colonies was quite different. During the early eighteenth century the British government of Prime Minister Robert Walpole assumed that a decentralized administration would best accomplish the nation's economic goals. With the exception of Connecticut and Rhode Island, both of which retained their charters and continued to choose their own governors, the colonies were administered by royally appointed governors. But taxation and spending continued to be controlled by elected assemblies. The right to vote was restricted to men with property. Yet the proportion of adult white males who qualified approached 50 percent in the British colonies, considerably higher in New England, considerably lower in some southern jurisdictions.

That did not mean that the colonies were democratic. The basic principle of order in eighteenth-century British culture was the ideal of deference to natural hierarchy. The common metaphor for civil order was the well-ordered family, in which children were strictly governed by their parents, wives by their husbands. Members of subordinate groups, such as women, non-English immigrants, African American slaves, servants, and Indians, were not allowed to vote or hold public office. Moreover, for the most part, the men who did vote nearly always chose wealthy landowners, planters, or merchants to serve as their leaders. Consequently, provincial assemblies were controlled by colonial elites.

Yet over the century there was an important trend toward stronger institutions of representative government. By midcentury most colonial assemblies in British North America had achieved considerable power over provincial affairs, sharing authority with governors. They collected local revenues and allocated funds for government programs, asserted the right to audit the accounts of public officers, and in some cases even acquired the power to approve the appointment of provincial officials. Because the assemblies controlled the finances of government—the "purse strings"—most royal governors were unable to resist this trend.

The royal governors who were most successful at realizing their agendas were those who became adept at playing one provincial faction off against another. All this had the important effect of schooling the colonial elite in the art of politics—not democratic politics, but the politics of patronage, coalition-building, and behind-the-scenes intrigue. This would have important implications for the development of American institutions.

# THE CULTURAL TRANSFORMATION OF BRITISH NORTH AMERICA

Inspired by the sixteenth- and seventeenth-century revolution in scientific thought represented by giants such as Copernicus, Galileo, Descartes, and Newton, intellectuals in Europe and Great Britain became advocates for the power of human reason rather than spiritual revelation or mystical illumination as the sole way of discovering natural law. They sought to establish an authoritative canon of logic, ethics, and aesthetics, as well as political philosophy.

The Catholic Church banned the works of hundreds of rationalist thinkers whose opinions were considered threats to the authority of faith. In New Spain and New France colonial officials worked diligently to suppress such challenging ideas and writings. Cultural censorship in the French and Spanish colonies was effective because literacy was confined to a tiny minority of elite men. In the British colonies, by contrast, literacy was widespread. British colonial officials made little attempt at cultural censorship, and as a result these new ideas sparked a cultural transformation in eighteenth-century British North America.

## THE ENLIGHTENMENT CHALLENGE

The **Enlightenment** is a simple label for a complex movement encompassing many different thinkers with many different ideas. But Enlightenment writers shared some things in common. They were optimistic about the ability of the rational human mind to discover the natural laws that were thought to govern the physical world and human affairs. Coupled with their commitment to reason was their belief in progress.

Such thinking was most attractive to the British colonial elite, families experiencing rising prosperity. This group had good reason to believe in progress. They sent their sons to colonial colleges, the focal point for the dissemination of Enlightenment ideas. The curricula of these colleges, modeled on those of Oxford and Cambridge in England, were designed to train ministers, but gradually each institution changed to curricula influenced by Enlightenment thinking.

The tastes of ordinary readers ran to traditional rather than Enlightenment fare. By the mid-eighteenth century there were more than twenty newspapers in the British colonies. These papers did not employ reporters but instead depended on official government announcements, travelers' and correspondents' reports, and articles reprinted from other sources. Most literate people had access to them, and they were often read aloud in local taverns, making their information available to all within hearing.

The best-selling book of the colonial era, not surprisingly, was the Bible. But in second place was a unique American literary form, the captivity narrative. The genre originated with the appearance of *The Sovereignty and Goodness of God* (1682), Mary Rowlandson's tale of her captivity among Indians during King Philip's War.

Another popular literary genre was the **almanac**, a combination calendar, astrological guide, sourcebook of medical advice, and farming tips that largely reflected the concerns of traditional folk culture.

A mixture of traditional and Enlightenment views characterized the thinking of many colonial intellectuals. Boston minister Cotton Mather offers a good example. A conservative defender of the old order, Mather wrote of the existence of witches and supported the executions during the Salem witchcraft crisis (see Chapter 3). Yet he

---

**TO WHAT** extent did North America participate in the Enlightenment?

**myhistorylab**
**Review Summary**

*[handwritten note: Unlike Europe w/ Catholic church censorship]*

*[handwritten note: Books & newspapers]*

**3–8**
*Manners and Etiquette in the Eighteenth Century* (1748)

**4–1**
*John Peter Zenger and the Responsibility of the Press* (1734)

**3–5**
Cotton Mather, *Memorable Providences, Relating to Witchcrafts and Possessions* (1689)

**Enlightenment** Intellectual movement stressing the importance of reason and the existence of discoverable natural laws.

**Almanac** A combination calendar, astrological guide, and sourcebook of medical advice and farming tips.

was also a member of the Royal Society (Great Britain's national academy of science), a defender of the Copernican sun-centered model of the universe, and an early supporter of inoculation against smallpox.

## A DECLINE IN RELIGIOUS DEVOTION

As Enlightenment thinking gradually gained in popularity, religious commitment seemed to decline. In the South, by the 1730s, only one adult in fifteen was affiliated with a church. The Anglican establishment in the Chesapeake and the Lower South was institutionally feeble, its ministers uninspiring, and many families "unchurched."

Puritan churches in New England also suffered declining membership and falling attendance. By the second decade of the eighteenth century only one in five New Englanders belonged to an established congregation. And among the churched, an increasing number began to question the **Calvinist theology of election**, the belief that salvation was the result of God's sovereign decree, that only a small number of men and women would be the recipients of God's grace. Many turned instead to the view that people had a natural ability to accept God's grace by developing their faith and doing good works. It became a force at Harvard and Yale in the first quarter of the eighteenth century, and soon a generation of ministers with more liberal ideas were taking positions in New England churches. Their ideas appealed to the same men and women attracted to Enlightenment thinking, those experiencing rising prosperity and social improvement. Among ordinary people in the countryside, however, especially among those in communities with narrowing opportunities, there was a good deal of opposition to these unorthodox ideas.

## THE GREAT AWAKENING

The first stirrings of a movement challenging the rationalist approach to religion occurred during the 1730s, most notably in the revival sparked by Rev. Jonathan Edwards in the community of Northampton. Similar revivals soon broke out in other New England communities, as well as among German Lutherans and Scots-Irish Presbyterians in Pennsylvania. Not all the revivalists were Calvinists. Some promoted a theology that emphasized human choice. But the common thread was a complaint of "spiritual coldness," of ministers whose sermons read like rational dissertations. People clamored for preaching that was more emotional.

These local revivals became an intercolonial phenomenon thanks to the preaching of George Whitefield, an evangelical Anglican minister from England, who in 1738 made the first of several tours of the colonies. By all accounts, his preaching had a powerful effect. Even Benjamin Franklin, a religious skeptic, wrote of the "extraordinary influence of his oratory" after attending an outdoor service in Philadelphia where 30,000 people crowded the streets to hear him preach. Whitefield began as Edwards did, chastising his listeners as "half animals and half devils," but he parted company from Edwards by leaving them with the hope that God would be responsive to their desire for salvation. Whitefield avoided sectarian differences. "God help us to forget party names and become Christians in deed and truth," he declared.

This widespread colonial revival of religion, which later generations called the **Great Awakening**, was an American version of the second phase of the Protestant Reformation (see Chapter 2). Religious leaders condemned the lax-

**3–16**
Jonathan Edwards, *A Puritan Preacher Admonishes His Flocks* (1741)

**myhistorylab**

**Exploring America:** *The Great Awakening*

### QUICK REVIEW

**The Great Awakening**

♦ Opposition to rationalist approach to religion grew in the 1730s.

♦ Jonathan Edwards focused his attention on inspiring young people.

♦ Movement spread throughout the colonies.

**Calvinist theology of election**  Belief that salvation was the result of God's sovereign decree and that few people would receive God's grace.

**Great Awakening**  North American religious revival in the middle of the eighteenth century.

ity, decadence, and bureaucracy of established Protestantism and sought to reinvigorate it with renewed piety and purity. People undergoing the economic and social stresses of the age, unsure about their ability to find land, marry, and participate in the promise of a growing economy—like those in Northampton—found relief in religious enthusiasm.

Among Presbyterians, open conflict broke out between the revivalists and the old guard, and in some regions the church hierarchy divided into separate organizations. In New England, where these factions were known as the **New Lights** and the **Old Lights**, the two sides accused each other of heresy. New Lights railed against liberal theology as a "rationalist heresy" and called for a revival of Calvinism. Old Lights condemned emotional enthusiasm as a "lawless heresy," the belief in a personal and direct relationship with God outside the order of the church. Itinerant preachers appeared in the countryside, stirring up trouble. Many congregations split into feuding factions, and ministers found themselves challenged by their newly awakened parishioners. Never had there been such turmoil in New England churches.

The revivals began somewhat later in the South, first developing in the mid-1740s, reaching full impact in the 1760s. They affected not only white Southerners but also for the first time introduced many slaves to Christianity. Baptist churches of the South in the era of the American Revolution included members of both races and featured spontaneous preaching by slaves as well as masters. In the nineteenth century white and black Christians would go their separate ways, but the joint experience of the eighteenth-century Awakening shaped the religious cultures of both groups.

Many other "unchurched" colonists were brought back to Protestantism by revivalism. But a careful examination of statistics suggests that the proportion of church members in the general population did not increase during the middle decades of the century. While the number of churches more than doubled from 1740 to 1780, the colonial population grew even faster, increasing threefold. The greatest impact was on families already associated with congregations. Before the Awakening, attendance at church had been mostly an adult affair, but throughout the colonies the revival of religion had its deepest effects on young people, who flocked to church in greater numbers than ever before. For years the number of people experiencing conversion had been steadily falling but now full membership surged. Church membership previously had been concentrated among women, leading Cotton Mather, for one, to speculate that perhaps women were indeed more godly. But men were particularly affected by the revival of religion, and their attendance and membership rose.

**George Whitefield (who,** contemporaries noted, was cross-eyed) enjoyed a remarkable career as a powerful preacher on both sides of the Atlantic. This portrait shows him preaching indoors to a rapt audience. During his tour of the colonies, Whitefield reportedly had a similar effect on crowds of thousands who gathered outdoors to hear his sermons.

John Wollaston, "George Whitefield" ca. 1770. By courtesy of the National Portrait Gallery, London.

**New Lights**   People who experienced conversion during the revivals of the Great Awakening.

**Old Lights**   Religious faction that condemned emotional enthusiasm as part of the heresy of believing in a personal and direct relationship with God outside the order of the church.

## THE POLITICS OF REVIVALISM

Revivalism appealed most of all to groups that felt bypassed by the economic and cultural development of the British colonies during the first half of the eighteenth century. The New Lights tended to draw their greatest strength from small farmers and less prosperous craftsmen. Many members of the upper class and the comfortable "middling sort" viewed the excesses of revivalism as indications of anarchy, and they became even more committed to rational religion.

Revivalism sometimes had political implications. In Connecticut, for example, Old Lights politicized the religious dispute by passing a series of laws in the General Assembly designed to suppress revivalism. In one town, revivalists refused to pay taxes supporting the established church and were jailed. Judges sympathetic to New Light views were thrown off the bench, and others were denied their elected seats in the assembly. The arrogance of these actions was met with popular outrage: by the 1760s the Connecticut New Lights had organized themselves politically and, in what amounted to a political rebellion, succeeded in turning the Old Lights out of office. New Light politicians would provide the leadership for the American Revolution in Connecticut.

Such direct connections between religion and politics were rare. There can be little doubt, however, that for many people revivalism offered the first opportunity to participate actively in public debate and public action that affected the direction of their lives. Choices about religious styles, ministers, and doctrine were thrown open for public discourse, and ordinary people began to believe that their

**Baptism by Full** Immersion in the Schuylkill River of Pennsylvania, an engraving by Henry Dawkins illustrating events in the history of American Baptists, was published in Philadelphia in 1770. With calls for renewed piety and purity, the Great Awakening reinvigorated American Protestantism. The Baptists preached an egalitarian message, and their congregations in the South often included both white and black Protestants.

Henry Dawkins, "Baptismal Ceremony Beside the Schuylkill." Engraving, 1770. John Carter Brown Library at Brown University.

## CHRONOLOGY

| | | | | |
|---|---|---|---|---|
| **1636** | Harvard College founded | | **1732** | Franklin begins publishing *Poor Richard's Almanac* |
| **1674** | Bishopric of Quebec established | | **1738** | George Whitefield first tours the colonies |
| **1680s** | William Penn begins recruiting settlers from the European continent | | **1740s** | Great Awakening gets under way in the Northeast |
| **1682** | Mary Rowlandson's *The Sovereignty and Goodness of God* | | **1740** | Parliament passes a naturalization law for the colonies |
| **1689** | Toleration Act passed by Parliament | | **1746** | College of New Jersey (Princeton University) founded |
| **1690s** | Beginnings of Jesuit missions in Arizona | | **1760s** | Great Awakening achieves full impact in the South |
| **1693** | College of William and Mary founded | | **1769** | Spanish colonization of California begins |
| **1700s** | Plains Indians begin adoption of the horse | | **1775** | Indian revolt at San Diego |
| **1701** | Yale College founded; Iroquois sign treaty of neutrality with France | | **1781** | Los Angeles founded |
| **1716** | Spanish begin construction of Texas missions | | | |

opinions actually counted for something. Underlying the debate over these issues were insecurities about warfare, economic growth, and the development of colonial society. Revivalism empowered ordinary people to question their leaders, an experience that would prove critical in the political struggles to come.

## CONCLUSION

By the middle of the eighteenth century a number of distinct colonial regions had emerged in North America, all of them with rising populations demanding that more land be seized from the Indians. Some colonies attempted to ensure homogeneity, whereas others embraced diversity. Within the British colonies, New England in particular seemed bound to the past, whereas the middle colonies and the backcountry pointed the way toward pluralism and expansion. These developments placed them in direct competition with the expansionist plans of the French and at odds with Indian peoples committed to the defense of their homelands.

The economic development of the British colonies introduced new social and cultural tensions that led to the Great Awakening, a massive revival of religion that was the first transcolonial event in American history. Beginning in small communities like Northampton, Massachusetts, the revivals affected thousands of people, leading to a renewal of religious passions. Rather than resuscitating old traditions, however, the Awakening seemed to point people toward a more active role in their own political futures. Those transformations added to the differences between the British colonies, on the one hand, and New Spain and the French Crescent on the other.

## REVIEW QUESTIONS

1. What were the principal colonial regions of North America? Discuss their similarities and their differences. Contrast the development of their political systems.

2. Why did the Spanish and the French close their colonies to immigration? Why did the British open their colonies? How do you explain the ethnic homogeneity of New England and the ethnic pluralism of New York and Pennsylvania?

3. What were the principal trends in the history of Indian America in the eighteenth century?

4. Discuss the development of class differences inthe Spanish, French, and British colonies in the eighteenth century.

5. Discuss the effects of the Great Awakening on the subsequent history of the British colonies.

**Flashcard Review**

## KEY TERMS

**The Act of Toleration** (p. 109)
**Almanac** (p. 119)
**Calvinist theology of election** (p. 120)
**Encomienda** (p. 116)
**Engagés** (p. 116)

**Enlightenment** (p. 119)
**Great Awakening** (p. 120)
**New Lights** (p. 121)
**Old Lights** (p. 121)

## RECOMMENDED READING

Jon Butler, *Becoming America: The Revolution Before 1776* (2000). A history that emphasizes the diversity, economic prosperity, participatory politics, and religious pluralism of the eighteenth-century British colonies.

Edward Countryman, *Americans: A Collision of Histories* (1996). An important synthesis that includes the many peoples and cultures of North America.

W. J. Eccles, *The Canadian Frontier, 1534–1760* (1983). An introduction to the history of French America by a leading scholar of colonial Canada.

David Hackett Fischer, *Albion's Seed: Four British Folkways in America* (1990). An engaging history with fascinating details on the regions of New England, Pennsylvania, Virginia, and the backcountry.

Jack P. Greene, *Pursuits of Happiness: The Social Development of Early Modern British Colonies and the Formation of American Culture* (1986). A distillation of a tremendous amount of historical material on community life in British North America.

Frank Lambert, *Inventing the "Great Awakening"* (1999). Argues that the revivialists themselves created the idea of the Great Awakening to further their evangelical work.

Jackson Turner Main, *The Social Structure of Revolutionary America* (1965). A classic study of colonial social structure, with statistics, tables, and enlightening interpretations.

George Marsden, *Jonathan Edwards: A Life* (2005). A new and comprehensive biography that emphasizes Edwards's work as both a pastor and an intellectual.

Martha McCollough, *Three Nations, One Place: A Comparative Ethnohistory of Social Change Among the Comanches and Hasinais During Spain's Colonial Era, 1689–1821* (2004). A detailed study of change and innovation among native peoples of the Great Plains during the eighteenth century.

Lucy Eldersveld Murphy, *A Gathering of Rivers: Indians, Métis, and Mining in the Western Great Lakes, 1737–1832* (2000). Demonstrates the success of Indian communities in adapting to colonialism through the diversification of their economies, intermarriage, and constructing multiethnic communities.

James A. Sandos, *Converting California: Indians and Franciscans in the Missions* (2004). A balanced treatment of missionaries and natives in eighteenth- and nineteenth-century California.

David J. Weber, *The Spanish Frontier in North America* (1992). A magnificent treatment of the entire Spanish borderlands from Florida to California. Includes important chapters on colonial government and social life.

Marianne S. Wokeck, *Trade in Strangers: The Beginning of Mass Migration to North America* (1999). The first important study of immigration in the eighteenth century, arguing that these migrations served as models for European mass migration of the next century.

*My dear Jack, All the Provinces [are]
arming and Training in the same Manner,
for they are all determined to die or be Free . . .*
—Eliza Farmer, June 28, 1775

**Chaplain Jacob Duche'** leading the first prayer
in the First Continental Congress at
Carpenter's Hall, Philadelphia, September
1774.

# 6

# FROM EMPIRE TO INDEPENDENCE

## 1750–1776

**WHAT WERE** the most important weaknesses of the British Empire in North America at the outset of the Seven Years' War?

**WHAT FACTORS** led to the growth of American nationalism in the 1760s?

**HOW DID** political and economic problems in Britain contribute to unrest in the colonies?

**WHAT STEPS** did Britain take to punish Massachusetts for the colonists' acts of resistance?

**WHO MADE** up the second Continental Congress and why was it formed?

# AMERICAN COMMUNITIES
## The First Continental Congress Begins to Shape a National Political Community

THE OPENING MINUTES OF THE FIRST CONTINENTAL CONGRESS, HELD in Philadelphia in September 1774, did not bode well. One of the delegates moved that the session open with prayer, but others objected. "We were so divided in religious sentiments," wrote John Adams, a representative from Massachusetts, "that we could not join in the same act of worship." Was the Congress to be stymied, here at the very beginning, by the things separating them? Putting aside their religious differences, the delegates agreed to a prayer by a local clergyman, who took as his text the Thirty-fifth Psalm: "Plead my cause, O Lord, with them that strive with me; fight against them that fight against me."

This incident highlighted the most important task confronting the First Continental Congress—strengthening their common cause without compromising their local identities. The delegates, noted Adams, were like "ambassadors from a dozen belligerent powers of Europe." They represented distinct colonies with traditions and histories as different as those of separate countries. Moreover, these lawyers, merchants, and planters, leaders in their respective colonies, were strangers to one another.

Britain's North American colonies enjoyed considerable prosperity during the first half of the eighteenth century. But in 1765—in the aftermath of the great war for empire during which Great Britain soundly defeated France and forced the cession of the French North American colonies—the British government began to apply new trade restrictions and levy new taxes, inspiring resistance among the colonists. By the opening session of the First Continental Congress peaceful protest had escalated into violent riot, and in an attempt to force the colonists to acknowledge the power of Parliament to make laws binding them "in all cases whatsoever," the British had proclaimed a series of repressive measures. In this atmosphere of crisis, the colonial assemblies (with the exception of Georgia's) elected delegates for a "Continental Congress" to map out a coordinated response.

Despite their differences, during seven weeks of deliberations, the delegates succeeded in forging an agreement on the principles and policies they would follow in this, the most serious crisis in the history of the British North American colonies. These were the first tentative steps toward the creation of an American national political community. Communities are not simply local but can also be regional, national, even international. In a town or village, feelings of association come from daily, face-to-face contacts, but for larger groups those connections must be deliberately constructed. In their final declaration the delegates pledged to "firmly agree and associate, under the sacred ties of virtue, honor and love of our country." They asked their countrymen to remember "the poorer sort" among them during the time of trouble they knew was coming. They demanded that patriotic Americans "break off all dealings" with those refusing to act, thus drawing a distinction between "insiders" and "outsiders," one of the essential first steps in the construction of community identity.

Patrick Henry, a Virginia delegate strongly committed to American independence, was exuberant by the time the Congress adjourned in late October. "The distinctions between Virginians, Pennsylvanians, New Yorkers, and New Englanders, are no more," he declared. "I am not a Virginian, but an American." He was exaggerating the unity. It remained a work in progress. Local, provincial, and regional differences would continue to clash. But Henry voiced an important truth.

In its attempt to force the colonists to pay a share of the costs of empire through taxation, Great Britain had sparked a revolt of both elite and ordinary colonists. The road to a shared community of interest among British colonists that distinguished them from the mother country had been marked by milestones with legendary names: the Stamp Act, the Boston Massacre, the Tea Party, the Intolerable Acts. The violent events that would follow the First Continental Congress—the first clash at Lexington and Concord, the siege of Boston, the Battle of Bunker Hill—would lead to a second session of the Congress. Reluctantly at first, then enthusiastically, the delegates would move toward independence. The difficult months and years of warfare would sorely test the imagined community of the united colonies, and the differences among them would frequently threaten to abort the nation being born. But the sessions of the First Continental Congress marked the moment when Americans first began the struggle to overcome local differences in pursuit of national goals.

Philadelphia

# THE SEVEN YEARS' WAR IN AMERICA

L eaders of the British colonies made an early attempt at cooperation in 1754, when representatives from New England, New York, Pennsylvania, and Maryland met to consider a joint approach to military challenges from the French and their Indian allies. Even as the delegates met, fighting between French Canadians and Virginians began near the headwaters of the Ohio River in the Appalachian Mountains, the first shots in a great global war for empire pitting Great Britain (and Prussia) against the combined might of France, Spain, and Austria.

## THE ALBANY CONFERENCE OF 1754

The British Board of Trade convened the 1754 meeting in the New York town of Albany on the Hudson River. They wanted the colonies to consider a collective response to the continuing conflict with New France and the Indians of the interior. High on the agenda was the negotiation of a settlement with the leaders of the Iroquois Confederacy, who had grown impatient with colonial land grabbing. But as the negotiations began, behind the scenes real estate developers were bribing minor Iroquois chiefs, affixing their signatures on a "deed" for an enormous tract of land in Pennsylvania, and turning the meeting into a vehicle for the very abuses the British sought to correct. Angered by these manipulations, the official Iroquois delegation walked out of the conference, refusing all offers to join a British alliance.

The **Albany Conference** did adopt a "**Plan of Union**" put forward by Benjamin Franklin, a delegate from Pennsylvania. Franklin, whom the British had appointed Postmaster General of the North American colonies, was especially sensitive to the need for cooperation. His proposal would have placed Indian affairs, western settlement, and other items of mutual interest under the authority of a grand council composed of representatives elected by the colonial assemblies and led by a British-appointed president. All the colonies rejected the Albany Plan of Union, fearful of losing their autonomy. The absence of cooperation among the colonies would prove one of the greatest weaknesses during the subsequent war with the French.

## FRANCE VS. BRITAIN IN AMERICA

There were three violent flash points in the conflict between Great Britain and France for control of North America. First was the northern Atlantic coast, the ragged boundary between New France and New England. To protect the ocean approach to their colonial heartland, the French constructed the port and fortress of Louisbourg on Cape Breton Island. In 1749 the British established a large naval facility at Halifax in Nova Scotia, but worried about the loyalty of the 18,000 French-speaking Acadians of the province.

The second flash point was the border region between New France and New York, extending from Niagara Falls to Lake Champlain, where Canadians and New Yorkers were rivals for the lucrative Indian trade. The French, who found it difficult to compete against superior English goods, resorted instead to military might, garrisoning fortifications on Lake George and at Niagara. In this zone the strategic advantage was held by the Iroquois Confederacy.

Third was the Ohio country, the trans-Appalachian region bisected by the Ohio River. This rich country was a prime target of British land speculators and backcountry settlers, whom the French feared would overrun their isolated outposts and threaten their entire Mississippi trading empire. To reinforce their claim, in 1749 the French sent a heavily armed force down the Ohio River to ward off the British, and in 1752 they attempted to expel all British traders from the region.

WHAT WERE the most important weaknesses of the British Empire in North America at the outset of the Seven Years' War?

**myhistorylab**
Review Summary

## IMAGE KEY
for pages 126–127

a. Green tea and dried tea leaves.
b. Flank and breast feathers.
c. Chaplain Jacob Duche' leading the first prayer in the First Continental Congress at Carpenter's Hall, Philadelphia, September 1774.
d. A "No Stamp Act" teapot.
e. Three Imrie/Risley by Wilson 1750s 77mm diorama figures, Roger Ranger with two soldiers, French and Indian War, on a diorama base.
f. Propaganda of 1765 against the Stamp Act that was emblazoned on teapots.
g. American colonists force feed hot tea to an English tax collector after tar and feathering the agent under a Liberty Tree in colonial Boston.
h. Colored engraving, published by Paul Revere, shows British troops disembarking from a ship in Boston in 1768.
i. The Declaration of Independence.

**Albany Conference**  A 1754 meeting, held in Albany, NY, between the British and leaders of the Iroquois Confederacy.

**Plan of Union**  Plan put forward by Benjamin Franklin in 1754 calling for an intercolonial union to manage defense and Indian affairs. The plan was rejected by participants at the Albany Congress.

French Canadian troops then began in 1753 the construction of a line of forts running south from Lake Erie to the headwaters of the Ohio River. In a direct challenge to the French claims in the West, the British government issued a royal charter for more than 200,000 acres to the Ohio Company, organized by London and Virginia investors.

The Indian peoples of the Ohio country had interests of their own. In addition to native inhabitants, the region had become a refuge for Indian peoples who had fled the Northeast. Most of the Indians of the Ohio country opposed British expansion and were anxious to make the Appalachians into a wall of protection. Meanwhile the Iroquois Confederacy continued the game of playing the British against the French. In the South the Creeks (and to a lesser extent the Cherokees and Choctaws) attempted to carve out a similar balancing role for themselves among the British in the Lower South, the French in Louisiana, and the Spanish in Florida. These Indian confederacies saw it as in their interest to perpetuate the existing colonial stalemate. Their position would be greatly undermined by an overwhelming victory for either side.

## FRONTIER WARFARE

As the delegates to the Albany Conference conducted their business they received news of the first clash with the French. Colonel George Washington, a young militia officer sent by the governor of Virginia to expel the French from the upper Ohio, had been forced to surrender his troops to a French Canadian force. The French now commanded the interior country from Fort Duquesne, at the "Forks of the Ohio," the junction of the Allegheny and Monongahela Rivers.

Taking up the challenge, in 1755 the British launched an effort to strike the French in all three zones. An army of New England militiamen succeeded in capturing two important French forts on the border of Nova Scotia. Elsewhere the British campaigns failed. In northern New York a large colonial force was repulsed by the French. And on July 9, 1755, 1,500 British troops were ambushed and destroyed by a much smaller force of 600 confederated Indian fighters supported by a mere 30 French Canadians. It was the worst military defeat of a British army during the eighteenth century.

Full-scale warfare between Great Britain (supported by Prussia) and France (supported by Spain) began the next year in 1756. It was truly a global war, fought in Europe, Asia, and America, and known to history as the Seven Years' War (or the **French and Indian War** in America) (see Map 6.1). The first two years were a near catastrophe for Great Britain. Indians pounded backcountry settlements, killed thousands of settlers, and raided deep into the coastal colonies, throwing British colonists into panic. French Canadians captured British forts in northern New York. The lack of colonial cooperation greatly hampered the British attempt to mount a counterattack. When British commanders tried to exert direct control over provincial troops, they succeeded only in angering local authorities.

## THE CONQUEST OF CANADA

In 1757 William Pitt, an enthusiastic advocate of British expansion, became prime minister of Great Britain. Believing that the global war could be won in North America, he subsidized Prussian allies to fight the war in Europe, reserving his own forces for naval and colonial operations. Pitt committed himself to the conquest of Canada and the final elimination of French competition in North America. Promising that the war would be fought "at His Majesty's expense," Pitt secured colonial cooperation with a massive infusion of British currency and credit.

**3–9**
*The Storm Arising in the West, George Washington Delivers a Warning to the French* (1753)

**French and Indian War** The last of the Anglo-French colonial wars (1754–1763) and the first in which fighting began in North America. The war ended with France's defeat. Also known as the **Seven Years' War.**

# MAP EXPLORATION
To explore an interactive version of this map, go to **http://www.prenhall.com/faraghertlc/map6.1**

**MAP 6.1**
**The War for Empire in North America, 1754–1763**   The Seven Years' War in America was fought in three principal areas: Nova Scotia and what was then Acadia, the frontier between New France and New York, and the upper Ohio River.

HOW DID the Indian trade affect the war? Which military defeats dealt the worst blows to the French?

The British were also effective at attracting Indian support. In 1758 officials promised the Iroquois and the Ohio Indians that the crown would "agree upon clear and fixed boundaries between our settlements and their hunting grounds, so that each party may know their own and be a mutual protection to each other of their respective possessions."

Thus did Pitt succeed in reversing the course of the war. Regular and provincial forces captured the fortress of Louisbourg in July 1758, setting the stage for the invasion of New France. A month later a force of New Englanders captured the strategic French fort of Oswego on Lake Ontario, thereby preventing the Canadians from resupplying their western posts. Encouraged by British promises,

**The death of** General James Wolfe, at the conclusion of the battle in which the British captured Quebec in 1759, became the subject of American artist Benjamin West's most famous painting, which was exhibited to tremendous acclaim in London in 1770.

Benjamin West (1738–1820), "The Death of General Wolfe," 1770. Oil on canvas, 152.6 × 214.5 cm. Transfer from the Canadian War Memorials, 1921 (Gift of the 2nd Duke of Westminster, Eaton Hall, Cheshire, 1918). National Gallery of Canada, Ottawa, Ontario.

## QUICK REVIEW

**European Territories, 1763**

- Britain: territories in North America from Hudson's Bay to the Caribbean, from the Atlantic to the Mississippi.
- France: territory on the mainland reduced to two small islands.
- Spain: Cuba, the Philippines, Louisiana, and California.

**Treaty of Paris** The formal end to British hostilities against France and Spain in February 1763.

numerous Indian tribes deserted the French, forcing them to abandon Fort Duquesne, which the British occupied and renamed Fort Pitt (today's Pittsburgh) in honor of the prime minister. The last of the French forts in northern New York fell in 1759. In the South, regular and provincial British troops crushed the Cherokees and opened negotiations with the Creeks and Choctaws.

British forces now converged on French Canada. In 1759 colonial and British troops, acting on General James Wolfe's order to "burn and lay waste the country," plundered farms along the St. Lawrence and shelled the city of Quebec. The British army prevailed and Quebec fell. The next year another British force moved up the Hudson and conquered Montreal. Its fall marked the end of the French empire in America.

In the final two years of the war the British swept French ships from the seas, conquered the Spanish colony of Cuba, captured the Spanish Philippines, and achieved dominance in India. In the 1763 **Treaty of Paris**, France lost all its possessions on the North American mainland, ceding to Great Britain all its claims east of the Mississippi, with the exception of New Orleans, which was passed to Spain, along with other French claims to the trans-Mississippi region. In exchange for the return of its Caribbean and Pacific colonies, Spain ceded Florida to Britain. Three centuries of European imperial rivalry in eastern North America ended with complete victory for the British Empire (see Map 6.2).

**MAP 6.2**
**European Claims in North America, 1750 and 1763**   As a result of the British victory in the Seven Years' War, the map of colonial claims in North America was fundamentally transformed.

HOW DID the balance of power in North America change between 1750 and 1763?

## THE STRUGGLE FOR THE WEST

The Ohio Indians were shocked when told of the French cession. "The French had no right to give away [our] country," they responded. They were "never conquered by any nation." A new set of British policies soon shocked them even more. The French and the British had long used gift-giving as a way of gaining favor with Indians. Spanish officials who replaced the French in Louisiana continued that old policy. But in one of his first official acts, General Jeffery Amherst, British military governor of the western region, banned presents to Indian chiefs and tribes, demanding that they learn to live without "charity." Not only were Indians angered by Amherst's reversal of custom, but they were also frustrated by his refusal to supply them with the ammunition they needed for hunting. Many were left destitute.

In this climate, hundreds of Ohio Indians became disciples of an Indian visionary named Neolin ("The Enlightened One"), known to the English as the Delaware Prophet. The core of Neolin's teaching was that Indians had been corrupted by European ways and needed to purify themselves by returning to their traditions and

**3–10**
*The Closing of the Frontier*
(1763)

preparing for a holy war. In the spring of 1763 a confederacy of tribes inspired by Neolin's ideas laid plans for a coordinated attack on British frontier posts. The principal leader of this resistance was the Ottawa chief Pontiac, renowned as an orator and political leader. In May 1763 Pontiac's confederacy simultaneously attacked all British forts in the West, destroying eight but failing to take the key posts of Niagara, Detroit, and Pitt. Pontiac and his followers fought on for another year, but most Indians sued for peace.

They were encouraged by the announcement of the British **Royal Proclamation of 1763**, which declared the trans-Appalachian region to be "Indian Country." Specific authorization from the crown would be required for any purchase of these protected Indian lands. British colonists had expected that the removal of the French threat would allow them to move into the West. They were outraged that the British would award territory to mortal enemies who during the war had slaughtered more than 4,000 settlers.

In fact, the British proved unable and ultimately unwilling to prevent the westward migration that was to be a dynamic part of the colonization of British North America. Within a few years of the war, New Englanders by the thousands were moving into the northern Green Mountain district, known as Vermont. In the middle colonies, New York settlers pushed ever closer to the homeland of the Iroquois, while others settled within the protective radius of Fort Pitt in western Pennsylvania. Hunters, stock herders, and farmers crossed over the first range of the Appalachians in Virginia and North Carolina, planting pioneer communities in what are now the states of West Virginia and Tennessee. In response to demands by settlers and speculators, British authorities were soon pressing the Iroquois and Cherokees for cessions of land in Indian Country. No longer able to play off rival colonial powers, Indians were reduced to a choice between compliance and resistance. Weakened by the recent war, they chose to sign away lands.

The individual colonies were even more aggressive. Locked in a dispute with Pennsylvania about jurisdiction in the Ohio country, in 1773 Virginia governor John Murray, Earl of Dunmore, sent a force to occupy Fort Pitt. In 1774, in an attempt to gain legitimacy for his dispute with Pennsylvania, Dunmore provoked

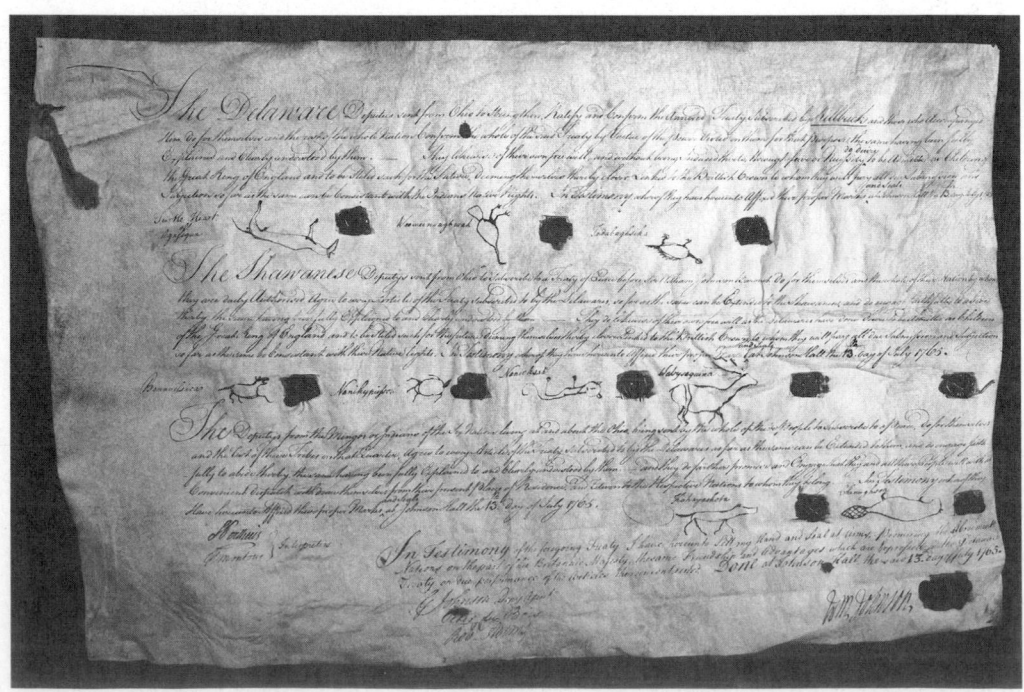

**A treaty between** the Delaware, Shawnee, and Mingo (western Iroquois) Indians and Great Britain, July 13, 1765, at the conclusion of the Indian uprising. The Indian chiefs signed with pictographs symbolizing their clans, each notarized with an official wax seal.

a frontier war with the Shawnees. After dealing them a humiliating defeat, Dunmore forced them to cede the upper Ohio River Valley to Virginia. The continuing struggle for the West would be an important issue in the coming Revolutionary struggle.

# THE EMERGENCE OF AMERICAN NATIONALISM

No colonial power of the mid-eighteenth century could match Britain in projecting imperial power over the face of the globe. During the years following its victory in the Seven Years' War, Britain turned confidently to the reorganization of its North American empire. The new colonial policy plunged British authorities into a new and ultimately more threatening conflict with the colonists, who had begun to develop a sense of a separate identity.

## AN AMERICAN IDENTITY

Despite the anger of frontier settlers over the Proclamation of 1763, the conclusion of the Seven Years' War left most colonists proud of their place in the British Empire. But many people had begun to note important contrasts between themselves and the mother country. The arrival of thousands of British troops raised the problem of where to house them. British commanders demanded they be quartered in private homes. British subjects at home were protected against such demands by an act of Parliament, but that protection had expressly not been extended to the colonies.

Americans who were thrown into contact with regular British troops were shocked by their profanity, lewdness, and violence. They were equally shocked by the swift and terrible punishment inflicted by aristocratic officers to keep those men in line. A Massachusetts militiaman wrote of witnessing the punishment of two soldiers sentenced to eight hundred lashes apiece. Men who had witnessed such scenes found it easy to believe in the threat of British "slavery."

Colonial forces, by contrast, were composed of volunteer companies. Militia officers were moderate in the administration of punishment, knowing they had to maintain the enthusiasm of their troops. Discipline thus fell considerably below the standards to which British officers were accustomed. Many Americans believed the British ignored the important role they had played in the Seven Years' War. The mutual scorn and suspicion were sometimes expressed in name-calling. Regular soldiers derisively called New Englanders "Yankees," while colonists heckled the red-coated British as "lobsters." During the war many colonists began to view themselves as distinct from the British.

The Seven Years' War also strengthened a sense of intercolonial identity among the colonists. Farm boys who never before had ventured outside the communities of their birth fought in distant regions with men like themselves from other colonies. Such experiences reinforced a developing nationalist perspective and sense of national community. From 1735 to 1775, while trade with Great Britain doubled, commerce among the colonies quadrupled. People and ideas moved along with goods. The first stagecoach lines linking seaboard cities began operation in the 1750s. Spurred by Postmaster Benjamin Franklin, many colonies built or improved post roads for transporting the mails.

## THE PRESS, POLITICS, AND REPUBLICANISM

One of the most important means of intercolonial communication was the weekly newspaper. Newspapers became a lively means of public discourse, and by 1760 more than twenty weekly papers were being published in the British colonies.

**WHAT FACTORS** led to the growth of American nationalism in the 1760s?

myhistorylab
Review Summary

**A protest against** the Stamp Act from newspaper editor William Bradford, publisher of *The Pennsylvania Journal and Weekly Advertiser*. Bradford decorated his masthead with skull and crossbones, reproduced a satiric version of "the fatal Stamp," also with skull and crossbones, and included the note, "The TIMES are Dreadful, Dismal, Doleful, Dolorous, and Dollar-less." The text below is an open letter from Bradford to his readers.

**Republicanism** A complex, changing body of ideas, values, and assumptions that influenced American political behavior during the eighteenth and nineteenth centuries.

**Sugar Act** Law passed in 1764 to raise revenue in the American colonies. It lowered the duty from 6 pence to 3 pence per gallon on foreign molasses imported into the colonies and increased the restrictions on colonial commerce.

The papers carried an increasing amount of colonial news. From the 1730s to the 1770s intercolonial coverage in the colonial press increased sixfold. Editors began to look at events from what they called a "continental" perspective. The trend accelerated during the Seven Years' War, when communities demanded news of the distant places where their men were fighting. The war promoted a new spirit of nationalism and a wider notion of community. Editors began using the term "American" to denote the common identity of British colonists. It was an early sign of the political community the delegates began to construct at the First Continental Congress.

Colonial editors frequently reprinted writings by British authors, poems by Alexander Pope, satiric essays by Jonathan Swift, and political philosophy by John Locke. They frequently reprinted essays by British republicans, who warned of the growing threat to liberty posed by the unchecked exercise of government power. Some essayists suggested that a conspiracy existed among European monarchs, aristocrats, and Catholics to quash liberty and reinstitute tyranny. These ideas came to define a political consensus in the British colonies, a point of view called "**republicanism**."

Republicanism asserted that state power, by its very nature, was antithetical to liberty and, consequently, must be limited. The authority of rulers should be conditional rather than absolute, and the people had the inherent right to draw up their own form of government and to withdraw their support if it did not fulfill their expectations. The best guarantee of good government was the broad distribution of power to the people, who could not only select their own leaders but also vote them out of office. Republican government depended on the virtue of the people, on their willingness to make the stability and justice of the political community their first priority. But that kind of virtue was possible only for an "independent" population that controlled its own affairs.

This was a political theory that fit well with the circumstances of American life, with its wide base of property ownership, its tradition of representative assemblies, and its history of struggle with royal authority. Contrast the assumptions of republicans with those of British monarchists, who argued that the good society was one in which a strong state, controlled by a hereditary elite, kept a vicious and unruly people in line.

## THE SUGAR AND STAMP ACTS

The emerging sense of American political identity was soon tested by British measures designed to raise revenues in the colonies. To quell Indian uprisings and stifle discontent among the French and Spanish populations of Quebec and Florida, the British kept 10,000 regular troops stationed in North America at the conclusion of the war. The cost of maintaining this force added to the enormous debt run up during the fighting. In 1764 Prime Minister George Grenville decided to obtain the needed revenue from America, and Parliament passed a measure known as the **Sugar Act**, which placed a tariff on sugar imported into the colonies.

Anticipating that American importers would attempt to avoid the duty by smuggling, Parliament broadened the jurisdiction of the vice-admiralty court at

Halifax, which had jurisdiction over customs cases. Courts of vice-admiralty were hated and feared because they neither provided for trial by jury nor acted on the presumption of innocence. Both merchants and artisans viewed the Sugar Act as a threat to their livelihoods, and there were public protests in many port towns. Boston was especially vocal. The town meeting proposed a boycott of certain English imports, and the tactic of nonimportation soon spread to other port towns.

James Otis, a brilliant Massachusetts lawyer, became one of the first Americans to give voice to these protests, striking a number of themes that were repeated many times over the next fifteen years. Every man, Otis declared in rhetoric lifted directly from the Great Awakening, "was an independent sovereign, subject to no law but the law written on his heart and revealed to him by his Maker." No government, he argued in the tradition of the radical **Whigs**, could rightfully deprive a man of the right "to his life, his liberty, and his property." His most memorable phrase would echo for the next decade: "Taxation without representation is tyranny."

## THE STAMP ACT CRISIS

Wasn't it only fair, Prime Minister Grenville responded, that the colonists help pay the costs of the empire? And what better way to do so than by taxation? Although colonial assemblies had raised taxes during the war, colonial tax rates remained significantly lower than rates in the mother country. Ignoring American protests, in early 1765 Grenville pushed through a considerably more sweeping revenue measure known as the **Stamp Act**. This legislation required the purchase of specially embossed paper for all newspapers, legal documents, licenses, insurance policies, ship's papers, even dice and playing cards. It affected nearly every colonial resident in one way or another.

The American reaction to the Stamp Act during the summer and autumn of 1765 created a crisis of unprecedented proportions. The stamped paper had to be purchased with hard money, and it came during a period of economic stagnation. Many colonists complained of being "miserably burdened and oppressed with taxes." But constitutional objections had more importance over the long term. Although colonial male property owners elected their own assemblies, they could not vote in British elections and had no representatives in Parliament. The British government argued that colonists were still subject to the acts of Parliament because of what they termed "**virtual representation**." As one British conservative put it, the colonists were "represented in Parliament in the same manner as those inhabitants of Britain are who have not voices in elections," such as women, children, and servants.

Americans did not take well to the comparison. Just such constitutional issues were emphasized in the Virginia Stamp Act Resolutions, written by Patrick Henry, a passionate young backcountry lawyer and member of the House of Burgesses. Although his colleagues rejected the most radical of Henry's resolutions, all of them were reprinted in the colonial press. By the end of 1765 the assemblies of eight other colonies had approved similar measures denouncing the Stamp Act and proclaiming their support of "no taxation without representation."

The most violent protests took place in Boston. The city's elite had prospered over the previous decade, but conditions for workers and the poor had worsened. Unemployment, inflation, and high taxes greatly increased the level of poverty during the depression following the Seven Years' War. Ordinary Bostonians were resentful. Their discontent was channeled by Samuel Adams, the son of a brewer, who became a powerful local politician. Adams was a leader of the anti-British alliance spanning Boston's social classes. In the late summer of 1765 he and his associates organized a protest of Boston workingmen.

**5–2**
James Otis, *The Rights of the British Colonies Asserted and Proved* (1763)

**myhistorylab**

**Exploring America:** *The Stamp Act*

**4–3**
Benjamin Franklin, *Testimony Against the Stamp Act* (1766)

**4–4**
John Dickinson, *Letters from a Farmer in Pennsylvania* (1767)

**Whigs** The name used by advocates of colonial resistance to British measures during the 1760s and 1770s.

**Stamp Act** Law passed by Parliament in 1765 to raise revenue in America by requiring taxed, stamped paper for legal documents, publications, and playing cards.

**Virtual representation** The notion that parliamentary members represented the interests of the nation as a whole, not those of the particular district that elected them.

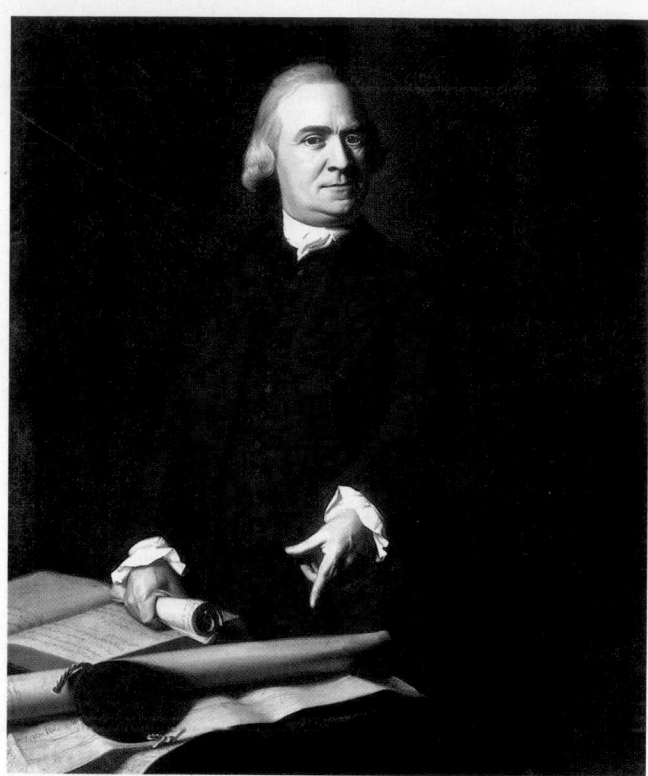

**Samuel Adams, a** second cousin of John Adams, was a leader of the Boston radicals and an organizer of the Sons of Liberty. The artist of this portrait, John Singleton Copley, was known for setting his subjects in the midst of everyday objects; here he portrays Adams in a middle-class suit with the charter guaranteeing the liberties of Boston's freemen.

John Singleton Copley (1738–1815), "Samuel Adams," ca. 1772. Oil on canvas, 49 1/2 × 39 1/2 in. (125.7 cm × 100.3 cm). Deposited by the City of Boston, 30.76c. Courtesy, Museum of Fine Arts, Boston. Reproduced with permission. © 2000 Museum of Fine Arts, Boston. All Rights Reserved.

HOW DID political and economic problems in Britiain contribute to unrest in the colonies?

**myhistorylab**

**Review Summary**

**Sons of Liberty**   Secret organizations in the colonies formed to oppose the Stamp Act.

**Nonimportation movement**   A tactical means of putting economic pressure on Britain by refusing to buy its exports to the colonies.

**Declaratory Act**   Law passed in 1776 to accompany repeal of the Stamp Act that stated that Parliament had the authority to legislate for the colonies "in all cases whatsoever."

On August 14 a large crowd assembled near Boston Common, and in an old elm, known as the "Liberty Tree," strung up effigies of several British officials, including Boston's stamp distributor, Andrew Oliver. The restless crowd then invaded and vandalized Oliver's office as well as his home. Soon thereafter, Oliver resigned his commission. Several days later another mob broke into the mansion of Thomas Hutchinson, lieutenant governor of the colony. During the fall and winter, urban crowds protested in port towns from Halifax in the north to Savannah in the south (see Map 6.3). Growing alarmed at the rising potential for violence, merchants, lawyers, and respectable craftsmen seized control of the resistance movement. Calling themselves the **Sons of Liberty**, these leaders encouraged more moderate forms of protest, such as circulating petitions and publishing pamphlets. Always they emphasized limited political goals. There were few repetitions of mob attacks, but by the end of 1765 almost all the stamp distributors had resigned or fled, making it impossible for Britain to enforce the Stamp Act. Pressured by British merchants, worried over the effects of the growing **nonimportation movement** among the colonists, in March 1766 Parliament repealed the Stamp Act and reduced the duties under the Sugar Act. This news was greeted with celebrations throughout the American colonies.

Overlooked in the mood of optimism, however, was the fact that repeal was coupled with what was termed a "**Declaratory Act**," in which Parliament affirmed its full authority to make laws binding the colonies "in all cases whatsoever." The Declaratory Act signaled that the conflict between the mother country and the colonies had not been resolved but merely postponed.

# "SAVE YOUR MONEY AND SAVE YOUR COUNTRY"

Colonial resistance to the Stamp Act was stronger in urban than in rural communities, stronger among merchants, craftsmen, and planters than among farmers and frontiersmen. When Parliament next moved to impose its will, as it had promised to do in the Declaratory Act, the American opposition again adopted the tactic of nonimportation. But this time resistance spread from the cities and towns into the countryside. As the editor of the *Boston Gazette* phrased the issue, "Save your money and you save your country." It became the slogan of the movement.

## THE TOWNSHEND REVENUE ACTS

The foremost problem facing the new British government in the mid-1760s was the national debt. Britain suffered massive unemployment, riots over high prices, and tax protests. Fearing opposition at home more than the protest in the colonies, in June 1767 Charles Townshend, Chancellor of the Exchequer, proposed a new series of **Revenue Acts** placing tariffs on the importation of commodities such as lead, glass, paint, paper, and tea into the colonies.

The most influential colonial response came in a series of articles by wealthy Philadelphia lawyer John Dickinson, which were reprinted in nearly every colonial newspaper. Posing as a humble farmer, Dickinson argued that Parliament had no constitutional authority to tax goods in order to raise revenue in America. Other Americans warned that the Revenue Acts were part of a British conspiracy to suppress American liberties. Their fears were reinforced by stringent enforcement.

In response some colonists argued for violent resistance. But it was Dickinson's essays that had the greatest effect on the public debate, not only because of their convincing arguments but also because of their mild and reasonable tone. "Let us behave like dutiful children," Dickinson urged, "who have received unmerited blows from a beloved parent." No sentiment for independence yet existed in the British colonies.

## AN EARLY POLITICAL BOYCOTT

In October 1767 the Boston town meeting revived the tactic of nonimportation, drawing up a long list of British products to boycott. Over the next few months other port cities, including Providence, Newport, and New York, set up nonimportation campaigns of their own. Artisans took to the streets in towns and cities throughout the colonies to force merchants to stop importing British goods. Coercion was very much a part of the movement, and occasionally there was violence.

Protestors formed "nonimportation associations," pledging to curtail luxuries and stimulate local industry. These aims had great appeal in small towns and rural districts, which previously had been uninvolved in the anti-British struggle. In 1768 and 1769 colonial newspapers paid a great deal of attention to women's support for the boycott. "The industry and frugality of American ladies," wrote the editor of the *Boston Evening Post*, "are contributing to bring about the political salvation of a whole continent."

Nonimportation was greatly strengthened in May 1769 when the Virginia House of Burgesses enacted the first provincial legislation banning the importation of goods enumerated in the Townshend Acts. Over the next few months all the colonies but New Hampshire enacted similar legislation. Because of these efforts, the value of colonial imports from Britain declined by 41 percent.

## THE MASSACHUSETTS CIRCULAR LETTER

Boston and Massachusetts were at the center of the agitation over the Townshend Revenue Acts. In February 1768 the Massachusetts House of Representatives approved a letter addressed to the speakers of the other colonial assemblies. The letter denounced the Revenue Acts, attacked the British plan to make royal officials independent of colonial assemblies, and urged the colonies to find a way to "harmonize with each other." Massachusetts governor Francis Bernard condemned the document for stirring up rebellion and dissolved the legislature. In Britain, Lord Hillsborough, secretary of state for the colonies, ordered each royal governor in America to dissolve his colony's assembly if it should endorse the letter. Before this

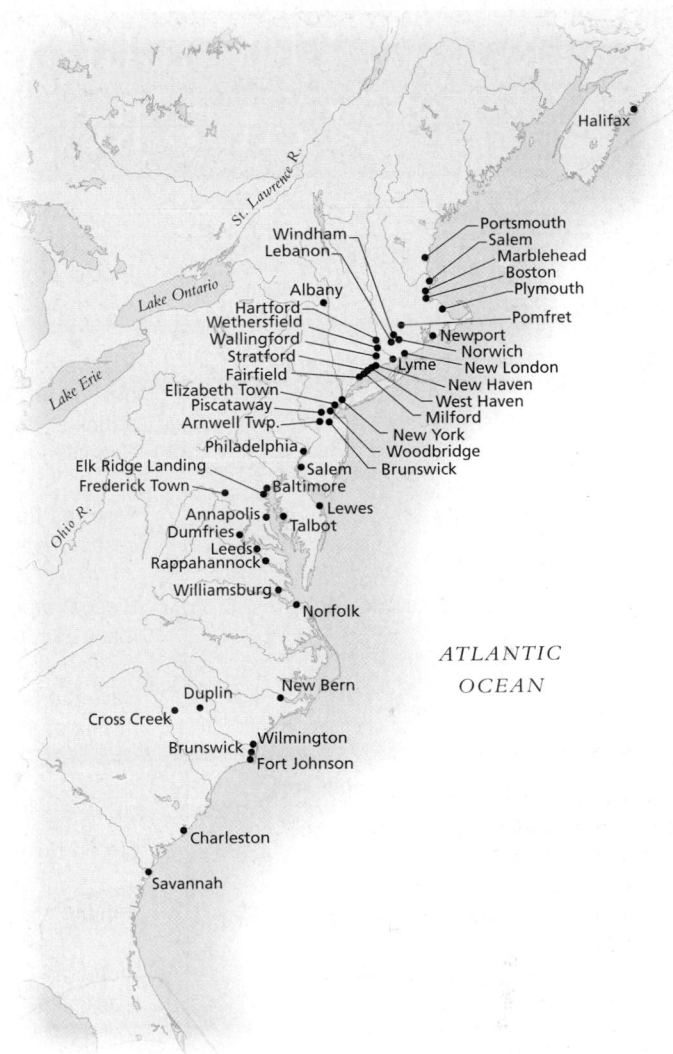

**MAP 6.3**

**Demonstrations Against the Stamp Act, 1765** Popular demonstrations against the Stamp Act forced the resignation of British tax officials.

WHAT GROUPS in British North America were most opposed to the Stamp Act?

**Townshend Revenue Acts** Act of Parliament, passed in 1767, imposing duties on colonial tea, lead, paint, paper, and glass.

## QUICK REVIEW

**Resistance**

◆ Response to the Sugar Act divided.

◆ 1764: New York and Boston merchants launch nonimportation movement.

◆ Response to Stamp Act overwhelming and intense.

# OVERVIEW | Eleven British Measures that Led to Revolution

| Year | Legislation | |
|------|-------------|---|
| 1764 | Sugar Act | Placed prohibitive duty on imported sugar; provided for greater regulation of American shipping to suppress smuggling |
| 1765 | Stamp Act | Required the purchase of specially embossed paper for newspapers, legal documents, licenses, insurance policies, ships' papers, and playing cards; struck at printers, lawyers, tavern owners, and other influential colonists. Repealed in 1766 |
| 1766 | Declaratory Act | Asserted the authority of Parliament to make laws binding the colonies "in all cases whatsoever" |
| 1767 | Townshend Revenue Acts | Placed import duties, collectible before goods entered colonial markets, on many commodities including lead, glass, paper, and tea. Repealed in 1770 |
| 1773 | Tea Act | Gave the British East India Company a monopoly on all tea imports to America, hitting at American merchants |
| 1774 | Coercive or Intolerable Acts | |
| | Boston Port Bill | Closed Boston Harbor |
| | Massachusetts Government Act | Annulled the Massachusetts colonial charter |
| | Administration of Justice Act | Protected British officials from colonial courts by sending them home for trial if arrested |
| | Quartering Act | Legalized the housing of British troops in private homes |
| | Quebec Act | Created a highly centralized government for Canada |

**myhistorylab**

**Overview:** *Eleven British Measures that Led to Revolution*

**4–6**
*The Boston "Massacre" or Victims of Circumstance (1770)*

demand reached America, the assemblies of New Hampshire, New Jersey, and Connecticut had commended Massachusetts. Virginia, moreover, had issued a circular letter encouraging a "hearty union" among the colonies and urging common action against the British measures that "have an immediate tendency to enslave us."

Throughout this crisis there were rumors and threats of mob rule in Boston. Fearful of insurrection, on October 1, 1768, the British occupied Boston with infantry and artillery regiments. This action added greatly to the growing tensions.

## THE BOSTON MASSACRE

British troops stationed in the colonies were the object of scorn and hostility over the next two years. There were regular conflicts between soldiers and radicals in New York City, often focusing on protests organized by the Sons of Liberty. In Boston Sam Adams played up each and every rumor of soldiers harassing women, picking fights with men, or simply taunting residents with versions of "Yankee Doodle." There were a number of violent confrontations.

A persistent source of conflict was the competition between troops and townsmen over jobs. Soldiers were permitted to work when they were off-duty, thus competing with poor day laborers. In early March 1770 a British soldier walked into a Boston rope-walk in search of a job. "You can clean my shit-house," the owner told him. The soldier returned later with his friends and a small riot resulted. Over the next few days sporadic fighting between soldiers and townsmen continued. Finally, on the evening of March 5, 1770, a crowd at the Customs House began taunting a guard, calling him a "damned rascally scoundrel lobster" and worse. A captain and a company of seven soldiers went to his rescue, only to be pelted with snowballs and stones. Suddenly someone shouted "Fire!" and the frightened soldiers shot indiscriminately into the crowd. Five men fell dead and six more were wounded, two dying later. The soldiers escaped to their barracks, but a mob numbering in the hundreds rampaged through the streets demanding vengeance.

What became known as "the **Boston Massacre**" was soon infamous throughout the colonies. For many colonists the incident was a disturbing reminder of the extent to which relations with the mother country had deteriorated. During the next two years many people found themselves pulling back from the brink.

The growth of American resistance was slowed as well by the news that Parliament had repealed most of the Revenue Acts on March 5—the same day as the Boston Massacre. In the climate of apprehension and confusion, there were few celebrations of the repeal, and the non-importation associations almost immediately collapsed. The parliamentary retreat on the question of duties, like the earlier repeal of the Stamp Act, was accompanied by a face-saving measure—retention of the tax on tea.

**In Paul Revere's** version of the Boston Massacre, issued three weeks after the incident, the British fire an organized volley into a defenseless crowd. Revere's print—which he plagiarized from another Boston engraver—may have been inaccurate, but it was enormously effective propaganda. It hung in so many Patriot homes that the judge hearing the murder trial of these British soldiers warned the jury not to be swayed by "the prints exhibited in our houses."

# FROM RESISTANCE TO REBELLION

There was a lull in the American controversy during the early 1770s, but the situation turned violent once more in 1773, when Parliament again infuriated the Americans. This time it was an ill-advised tax on tea, and it propelled the colonists onto a swift track from resistance to outright rebellion.

## COMMITTEES OF CORRESPONDENCE

In June 1772, Governor Hutchinson of Massachusetts inaugurated another controversy by announcing that henceforth his salary and those of other royally appointed officials would be paid by the crown. In effect this made the executive and judiciary branches of the colony's government independent of control by elected representatives. In October, the Boston town meeting appointed a committee of correspondence to communicate with other communities regarding this challenge.

**WHAT STEPS** did Britain take to punish Massachusetts for the colonists' acts of resistance?

**myhistorylab**
**Review Summary**

**Boston Massacre**   After months of increasing friction between townspeople and the British troops stationed in the city, on March 5, 1770, British troops fired on American civilians in Boston.

In March 1773 the Virginia House of Burgesses appointed a standing committee of correspondence. The Virginia committee served as a model for the other colonies, and within a year all but Pennsylvania (where conservatives were in control of the legislature) had created committees of their own. The committees of correspondence became the principal channel for sharing information, shaping public opinion, and building cooperation among the colonies before the opening meeting of the First Continental Congress in 1774.

The information most damaging to British influence came from the radicals in Boston. In June 1773 the Boston committee circulated a set of confidential letters from Governor Hutchinson to the ministry in Britain. The letters revealed Hutchinson's call for "an abridgement of what are called English liberties" in the colonies. "I wish to see some further restraint of liberty," he had written, "rather than the connection with the parent state should be broken." This statement seemed to be the "smoking gun" of the conspiracy theory, and it created a torrent of anger against the British and their officials in the colonies.

## THE BOSTON TEA PARTY

**4–7**
John Andrews, *Letter Regarding the Boston Tea Party* (1773)

**4–12**
Jonathan Boucher, *An Anglican Preacher Denounces the American Rebels* (1775)

It was in this context that the colonists received the news that Parliament had passed the **Tea Act**. Colonists were major consumers of tea, typically drinking from five to ten cups a day. But because of the Townshend duties the market for tea had collapsed. The British East India Company, the sole agent of British power in India, was on the brink of bankruptcy. Parliament would not allow it to fail and devised a scheme to offer tea to Americans at prices that would tempt even the most patriotic drinker. The radicals argued that this was merely a device to make palatable the payment of unconstitutional taxes and further evidence of the British effort to seduce and corrupt the colonists.

In October 1773 a mass meeting in Philadelphia denounced anyone importing the tea as "an enemy of his country." A group calling itself "the Committee for Tarring and Feathering" published a poster, plastered all over the city, asking if the captains of ships carrying the tea might like "ten gallons of liquid tar decanted on your pate—with the feathers of a dozen wild geese laid over that to enliven your appearance." The Philadelphia consignees resigned in terror. Similar protests in New York City forced resignations there as well. The town meeting in Boston soon passed resolutions patterned on those of Philadelphia.

The first of three tea ships arrived in Boston Harbor late in November. Mass meetings in Old South Church, including many country people drawn to the scene of the crisis, resolved to keep the tea from being unloaded. On the evening of December 16, 1773, a disciplined group of fifty or sixty men, including farmers, artisans, merchants, professionals, and apprentices, marched to the wharf. Dressed as Indians and cheered on by Boston's citizens, they boarded the ships and dumped into the harbor some forty-five tons of tea, valued at £18,000. Boston's was the first tea party, and other incidents of property destruction soon followed. But it was the initial action in Boston that infuriated the British. The government became convinced that something had to be done about the rebellious colony of Massachusetts. Strong measures were required, King George III (reigned 1760–1820) wrote to Lord North, for "we are now to dispute whether we have, or have not, any authority in that country."

## THE INTOLERABLE ACTS

**Tea Act** Act of Parliament that permitted the East India Company to sell through agents in America without paying the duty customarily collected in Britain, thus reducing the retail price.

**Boston Tea Party** Incident that occurred on December 16, 1773, in which Bostonians, disguised as Indians, destroyed £18,000 worth of tea belonging to the British East India Company in order to prevent payment of the duty on it.

**Coercive Acts** Legislation passed by Parliament in 1774; included the Boston Port Act, the Massachusetts Government Act, the Administration of Justice Act, and the Quartering Act of 1774.

**Intolerable Acts** American term for the Coercive Acts and the Quebec Act.

During the spring of 1774 an angry Parliament passed a series of acts—officially called the **Coercive Acts** but known by Americans as the **Intolerable Acts**—calculated to punish the colony of Massachusetts and strengthen the British

# The Bostonians Paying the Excise-Man, or Tarring and Feathering

Political cartoons played an important role in the public controversy leading to the American Revolution. This print, published in London in 1774 and sold on the streets for a few pennies, depicts the violent attack of a Boston mob on customs commissioner John Malcolm several weeks after the "Tea Party." Malcolm, an ardent Loyalist, had been the frequent target of protests. That night a mob dragged Malcolm from his house and covered him with tar and feathers, a ritual of public humiliation. Hot tar produced painful blistering of the skin, and the effort to remove it made the condition worse. The feathers made the victim into an object of ridicule. Hauled to the Liberty Tree in Boston Common, Malcolm was threatened with hanging if he did not apologize and renounce his commission. When he did he was allowed to return home. The pro-Loyalist print includes a number of telling details. Malcolm is attacked by a group that includes a leather-aproned artisan. A broadside announcing the Stamp Act is posted upside down on the Liberty Tree. A hangman's noose dangles from a branch. The Boston Tea Party takes place in the background. In the foreground is a tar bucket and a pole topped by a "liberty cap," a symbol of freedom adopted by American protesters (and later an icon of the French Revolution). These details were intended to mock the Americans. But when the print found its way to North America it was embraced by Patriots and became an enduring American favorite. In the nineteenth century it was reprinted as a celebration of the righteous violence of the Revolution. ■

> **HOW COULD** this image, intended to ridicule and shame the American patriots, have been embraced and celebrated by them?

Philip Dawe, "The BOSTONIANS Paying the EXCISE-MAN, or TARRING & FEATHERING" (1774).

# MAP EXPLORATION
To explore an interactive version of this map, go to
**http://www.prenhall.com/faraghertlc/map6.4**

**MAP 6.4**
**The Quebec Act of 1774**   With the Quebec Act, Britain created a centralized colonial government for Canada.

HOW DID the boundaries set by the Quebec Act of 1774 contribute to rising tensions between the colonists and imperial authorities?

## QUICK REVIEW

**The Intolerable Acts**

- Boston Port Bill.
- Massachusetts Government Act.
- Administration of Justice Act.
- Quartering Act.
- Quebec Act.

**Quartering Act**   Acts of Parliament requiring colonial legislatures to provide supplies and quarters for the troops stationed in America.

**Quebec Act**   Law passed by Parliament in 1774 that provided an appointed government for Canada, enlarged the boundaries of Quebec, and confirmed the privileges of the Catholic Church.

hand. The Boston Port Bill prohibited the loading or unloading of ships in any part of Boston Harbor until the town fully compensated the East India Company and the customs service for the destroyed tea. The Massachusetts Government Act annulled the colonial charter. Town meetings, an important institution of the resistance movement, were prohibited from convening more than once a year except with the approval of the governor, who was placed in control of their agendas. With these acts, the British terminated the long history of self-rule by communities in the colony of Massachusetts.

Additional measures affected the other colonies and encouraged them to see themselves in league with suffering Massachusetts. The Administration of Justice Act protected British officials from colonial courts, thereby encouraging them to pursue the work of suppression. Those accused of committing capital crimes while putting down riots or collecting revenue were now to be sent to England for trial. The **Quartering Act** legalized the housing of troops at public expense not only in taverns and abandoned buildings but also in occupied dwellings and private homes.

Finally, in the **Quebec Act**, the British authorized a permanent government for the territory taken from France during the Seven Years' War: a strictly antirepublican government with an appointed council (see Map 6.4). To the American colonists it seemed a frightening preview of what imperial authorities had in store for them, and it confirmed the contention of the committees of correspondence that there was a British plot to destroy American liberty.

## THE FIRST CONTINENTAL CONGRESS

It was amid this crisis that town meetings and colonial assemblies alike chose representatives for the **First Continental Congress**. The delegates who arrived in Philadelphia in September 1774 included the most important leaders of the American cause. Cousins Samuel and John Adams from Massachusetts were joined by Patrick Henry and George Washington of Virginia and Christopher Gadsden of South Carolina. Many of the delegates were conservatives, including John Dickinson and Joseph Galloway of Philadelphia, and John Jay and James Duane from New York. With the exception of Gadsden, a hothead who proposed an attack on British forces in Boston, the delegates wished to avoid war and favored a policy of economic coercion.

After one of their first debates, the delegates passed a Declaration and Resolves, in which they asserted that all the colonists sprang from a common tradition and enjoyed rights guaranteed "by the immutable laws of nature, the principles of the English constitution, and the several charters or compacts" of their provinces. Thirteen acts of Parliament, passed since 1763, were declared in violation of these rights. Until these acts were repealed, the delegates pledged, they would impose a set of sanctions against the British. These would include not only the nonimportation and nonconsumption of British goods but also a prohibition on the export of colonial commodities to Britain or its other colonies.

To enforce these sanctions, the Continental Congress urged that "a committee be chosen in every county, city, and town, by those who are qualified to vote for representatives in the legislature, whose business it shall be attentively to observe the conduct of all persons." Known as the committees of observation and safety, these groups took over the functions of local government throughout the colonies. By dissolving the colonial legislatures, royal governors had unwittingly aided the work of these committees. Throughout most of the colonies the committees formed a bridge between the old colonial administrations and the revolutionary governments organized over the next few years. Committees began to link localities together in the cause of a wider American community.

## LEXINGTON AND CONCORD

On September 1, 1774, General Thomas Gage sent troops to seize stores of gunpowder and arms from several storehouses on the outskirts of Boston. In response, the Massachusetts House of Representatives, calling itself the Provincial Congress, created a committee of safety empowered to call up the militia. On October 15 the committee authorized the creation of special units, to be known as "minutemen," who stood ready to be called at a moment's notice. The armed militia of the towns and communities surrounding Boston faced the British army, quartered in the city. The stalemate continued throughout the fall and winter.

British monarch George III believed the time for war had come. "The New England Governments are in a State of Rebellion," he wrote privately, "blows must decide whether they are to be subject to this Country or independent." In Virginia, at almost the same moment, Patrick Henry predicted that hostilities soon would begin. Three weeks later, on April 14, 1775, General Gage received instructions to immediately strike against the Massachusetts militia.

On the evening of April 18, Gage ordered 700 troops to Concord, some miles outside Boston, to take possession of the armory there. Learning of the operation, the Boston committee dispatched two men, Paul Revere and William Dawes, to alert the militia of the countryside. By the time the British forces had reached Lexington, midway to their destination, some seventy armed minutemen had assembled on the green in the center of town, but they were disorganized and confused. In the fact of what appeared overwhelming force, the Americans began to withdraw with their arms. No order to fire was given, but suddenly shots rang out. Eight Americans were killed, ten wounded.

The British marched on to Concord where they burned a small quantity of supplies and cut down a liberty pole. Meanwhile, news of the skirmish at Lexington had spread throughout the country, and the militia companies from communities from miles around converged on the town. At Concord bridge they encountered the enemy and opened fire. Three soldiers were killed, the first British casualties. Seeing that their men were greatly outnumbered by Massachusetts militia, British officers immediately ordered a return to Boston, but at many points along the way they were subjected to withering fire

**First Continental Congress**   Meeting of delegates from most of the colonies held in 1774 in response to the Coercive Acts.

**Ignoring the Olive** Branch Petition from the Continental Congress, on August 23, 1775, King George III issued this Proclamation, declaring that the colonies stood in open rebellion to his authority and were subject to severe penalty, as was any British subject who failed to report the knowledge of rebellion or conspiracy. This document literally transformed loyal subjects into traitorous rebels.

(see Map 6.5). The engagement forecast what would be a central problem for the British: they would be forced to fight an armed population defending their own communities against outsiders.

# DECIDING FOR INDEPENDENCE

"We send you momentous intelligence," read the letter reporting the violence received by the committee of correspondence in Charleston, South Carolina, on May 8, 1775. Throughout the colonies community militia companies mobilized for war. At Boston, thousands of militiamen besieged the city, leaving the British no escape but by sea. The siege would last for nearly a year. Meanwhile, delegates from twelve colonies converged again on Philadelphia.

## THE SECOND CONTINENTAL CONGRESS

The Second Continental Congress, which opened on May 10, 1775, included representatives from twelve of the British colonies on the mainland of North America. Few conservatives or Loyalists were among them. Georgia, unrepresented at the First Continental Congress, remained absent at the opening of the Second. But in 1775 the political balance in Georgia shifted in favor of the radicals, and by the end of the summer the colony had delegates in Philadelphia.

On May 15 the representatives resolved to put the colonies in a state of defense but were divided on how best to do it. They lacked the power and the funds to raise and supply an army. John Adams made the winning proposal that they simply designate as a Continental Army the militia forces besieging Boston. In order to emphasize their national aspirations, they decided to select a man from the South to command these New England forces. On June 15 Jefferson and Adams nominated George Washington to be commander-in-chief, and he was elected by acclaim. Washington served without salary. On June 22, in a highly significant move, the Congress voted to finance the army with an issue of $2 million in bills of credit, backed by the good faith of the "Confederated Colonies." Thus began the long and complicated process of financing the Revolution.

During the early summer of 1775 the Congress began to move cautiously toward independence. Few would admit, even to themselves, that this was their goal. Before the Second Continental Congress adjourned at the beginning of August, the delegates appointed commissioners to negotiate with the Indian nations in an attempt to keep them out of the conflict.

## CANADA AND THE SPANISH BORDERLANDS

How did the rest of North America react to the coming conflict? The Continental Congress made contact with leaders of all the British colonies. In one of their first acts, delegates called on "the oppressed inhabitants of Canada" to join in the struggle for "common liberty." When the Canadians failed to respond positively and immediately, the Congress reversed itself and voted to authorize a military expedition against Quebec to eliminate any possibility of a British invasion from that quarter, thus killing any chance of the Canadians joining the anti-British cause. This set a course toward the development of the separate nations of the United States and Canada.

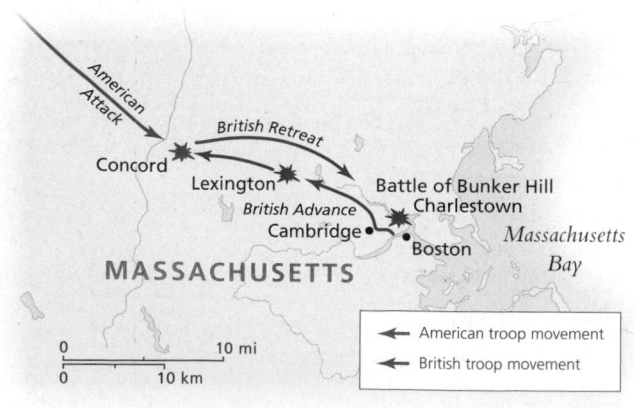

**MAP 6.5**
**The First Engagements of the Revolution**   The first military engagements of the American Revolution took place in the spring of 1775 in the countryside surrounding Boston.

**British soldiers fire** upon Massachusetts militia at Lexington, the first of four hand-colored engravings included in Amos Doolittle's *View of the Battle of Lexington and Concord* (1775). It is the only contemporary pictorial record of the events of April 19, 1775, from an America point of view. Doolittle, a Connecticut silversmith, traveled to the site of the conflict in the weeks afterward, and his engravings are based on first-hand observation. Important buildings, individuals, or groups of people are keyed to a legend that explains what is happening. Doolittle intended his prints to be informative in the same sense as a photograph in a modern newspaper.

In the British island colonies, there was at first considerable sympathy for the American struggle. The island colonies, however, would remain aloof from the imperial crisis, largely because the colonists there were dependent on a British military presence to guard against slave revolts. Things at first seemed more promising in Nova Scotia (not then a part of Canada), where many New Englanders had relocated after the expulsion of the Acadians. The British naval stronghold at Halifax, however, secured the province for the empire. Large contingents of British troops also kept Florida (which Britain had divided into two colonies, East and West Florida) solidly in the empire.

In Cuba, some 3,000 exiled Spanish Floridians, who had fled there in 1763 rather than live under British rule, now clamored for Spain to take advantage of the situation and retake their homeland. Many of them were active supporters of American independence.

In 1775 Spain publicly declared itself neutral but secretly searched for an opportunity to support the Americans. One presented itself in the late spring of 1776 when a contingent of Americans arrived in Spanish New Orleans via the Mississippi River bearing a proposal from patriot forces in Virginia. Would the Spanish be willing to quietly sell guns, ammunition, and other provisions to the Americans in New Orleans and allow them to be shipped by way of the Mississippi and Ohio Rivers? If the Spanish could be cooperative, the Americans might agree to a Spanish "protectorate" of the Floridas. The Spanish government eventually approved the plan, turning Havana and New Orleans into important supply centers for the Americans.

*[margin handwritten note: Spanish allied w/ the Americans]*

## FIGHTING IN THE NORTH AND SOUTH

Violent conflict took place between British forces and American rebels in both the northern and southern colonies in 1775 and early 1776. On the evening of May 10, 1775, a small force of armed New Englanders jointly commanded by Ethan Allen of Vermont and Benedict Arnold of Connecticut surprised the

**5–6**
*Petition of "A Grate Number of Blackes of the Province" to Governor Thomas Gage and the Members of the Massachusetts General Court (1774)*

British garrison at Fort Ticonderoga on Lake Champlain. With great effort, the Americans hauled the fort's cannon overland to be used in the siege of Boston.

At Boston, the British reinforced Gage's forces, and by the middle of June had approximately 6,500 soldiers in the city. They were beseiged by more than 10,000 New England militia. Fearing a move by Gage to occupy the heights south of town, the Americans made a countermove, occupying the Charlestown peninsula on the north. Gage decided on a frontal assault to dislodge them. In bloody fighting at Breed's and Bunker Hill, the British overran the Americans, killing 140 men, but not before suffering over a thousand casualties of their own, including 226 dead. The fierce patriotic reaction in England to this enormous loss ended any possibility of a last-minute reconciliation. In August 1775 King George issued a royal proclamation declaring the colonists in "open and avowed rebellion."

In June Congress assembled an expeditionary force against Canada. One thousand Americans moved north up the Hudson River corridor, and in November General Richard Montgomery forced the capitulation of Montreal. In the meantime Colonel Benedict Arnold set out from Massachusetts with another American army and, after a torturous march through the forests and mountains of Maine, joined Montgomery outside the walls of Quebec. But the American assault failed to take the city. Although Arnold held his position, the American siege was broken the following spring by British reinforcements. By the summer of 1776 the Americans had been forced back from Canada.

Elsewhere there were successes. In the South local militia rose against the Loyalist forces of Virginia's Governor Dunmore, who alienated the planter class by promising freedom to any slave who would fight with the British. After Dunmore was decisively defeated, he retreated to British naval vessels and shelled the city of Norfolk, nearly obliterating it. The next month the North Carolina rebel militia crushed a Loyalist force at the Battle of Moore's Creek Bridge near Wilmington, ending British plans for an invasion there. The British elected to attack Charleston, but an American force turned back the assault. It would be more than two years before the British would try to invade the South again. At Boston, Washington installed the captured British artillery on the heights south of town, placing the city and harbor within cannon range. The British had little choice but to evacuate. In March 1776 they sailed out of Boston Harbor heading northeast to Halifax, accompanied by at least a thousand American Loyalists.

## No Turning Back

Hopes of reconciliation died with the mounting casualties. The Second Continental Congress, which was rapidly assuming the role of a general government for all the colonies (increasingly called states), reconvened in Philadelphia in September 1775, where the delegates received the royal proclamation that they were in open rebellion. Although the Congress continued to disclaim any intention of denying the sovereignty of the king, it now moved to organize an American navy. It declared British vessels open to capture and authorized privateering. The Congress took further steps toward independence when it authorized contacts with foreign powers through its agents in Europe. In the spring of 1776 France joined Spain in approving the shipping of supplies to the rebellious provinces. The Continental Congress then declared colonial ports open to the trade of all nations but Britain.

But the emotional ties to Great Britain proved difficult to break. Help arrived in January 1776 in the form of *Common Sense* written by Thomas Paine,

**The Connecticut artist** John Trumbull painted *The Battle of Bunker Hill* in 1785, the first of a series that earned him the informal title of "the Painter of the Revolution." Trumbull was careful to research the details of his paintings but composed them in the grand style of historical romance. In the early nineteenth century, he repainted this work and three other Revolutionary scenes for the rotunda of the Capitol in Washington, DC.

a radical Englishman recently arrived in Philadelphia. For years Americans had defended their actions by wrapping themselves in the mantle of British tradition. But Paine argued that the British system rested on "the base remains of two ancient tyrannies," aristocracy and monarchy, neither of which was appropriate for America. *Common Sense* was the single most important piece of writing during the Revolutionary era. It reshaped popular thinking and put independence squarely on the agenda.

In April, the North Carolina convention, operating as the revolutionary substitute for the old colonial assembly, became the first to empower its delegates to the Continental Congress to vote for independence. News that the British were recruiting a force of German mercenaries to use against the Americans provided an additional push toward what now began to seem inevitable. In May the Congress voted to recommend that the individual states move as quickly as possible toward the adoption of state constitutions. In the preamble to this statement John Adams wrote that "the exercise of every kind of authority under the said crown should be totally suppressed." This sent a strong signal that the delegates were on the verge of approving a momentous declaration.

## THE DECLARATION OF INDEPENDENCE

On June 7, 1776, Richard Henry Lee of Virginia offered the first motion for independence. After some debate, a vote was postponed until July, but a committee composed of John Adams, Thomas Jefferson, Benjamin Franklin, Roger Sherman of Connecticut, and Robert Livingston of New York was asked to prepare

5–8
Thomas Jefferson, *"Original Rough Draught" of the Declaration of Independence* (1776)

5–11
*The Declaration of Independence* (1776)

**The Manner in** Which the American Colonies Declared Themselves INDEPENDENT of the King of ENGLAND, a 1783 English print. Understanding that the coming struggle would require the steady support of ordinary people, in the Declaration of Independence, the upper-class men of the Continental Congress asserted the right of popular revolution and the great principle of human equality.

5–9

*Abigail Adams and John Adams, Letters on the Rights of Women in an Independent Republic* (1776)

a draft declaration of American independence. The committee assigned the writing to Jefferson.

The intervening time allowed the delegates to debate and receive instructions from their state conventions. By the end of the month all the states but New York had authorized a vote for independence. When the question came up for debate again on July 1, a large majority supported independence. The final vote, taken on July 2, was twelve in favor of independence, none against, with New York abstaining. The delegates then turned to the declaration itself and made a number of changes in Jefferson's draft, striking out, for example, a long passage condemning slavery. In this and a number of other ways the final version was more cautious than the draft, but it was still a stirring document.

The central section of the Declaration reiterated the "long train of abuses and usurpations" on the part of George III that had led the Americans to their drastic course. But it was the first section that expressed the highest ideals of the delegates:

We hold these truths to be self-evident, that all men are created equal, that they are endowed by their creator with certain unalienable rights, that among these are life, liberty, and the pursuit of happiness. That to secure these rights, governments are instituted among men, deriving their just powers from the consent of the governed. That whenever any form of government becomes destructive of these ends, it is the right of the people to alter or to abolish it, and to institute a new government, laying its foundation on such principles, and organizing its powers in such form, as to them shall seem most likely to effect their safety and happiness.

There was very little debate in the Continental Congress about this extraordinary statement. The unanimity was the result of the widespread influence of Enlightenment and republican thought. Notably, there was no recourse to biblical authority. The delegates, mostly men of wealth and position, realized that the coming struggle for independence would require the steady support of ordinary people, and thus they asserted this great principle of equality and the right of revolution. The idea of equality would inspire the poor as well as the wealthy, women as well as men, blacks as well as whites.

By voting for independence, the delegates were not only proclaiming a belief in their newly conceived national community, but they were also committing treason against their king and empire. They would be condemned as traitors, hunted as criminals, and might stand on the scaffold in payment for their sentiments. On July 4, 1776, the Declaration of Independence was adopted without dissent.

## CHRONOLOGY

| | |
|---|---|
| **1713** | France cedes Acadia to Britain |
| **1745** | New Englanders capture Louisbourg |
| **1749** | French send an expeditionary force down the Ohio River |
| **1753** | French begin building forts from Lake Erie to the Ohio |
| **1754** | Albany Conference |
| **1755** | British General Edward Braddock defeated by a combined force of French and Indians |
| | Britain expels Acadians from Nova Scotia |
| **1756** | Seven Years' War begins in Europe |
| **1757** | William Pitt becomes prime minister |
| **1758** | Louisbourg captured by the British for the second time |
| **1759** | British capture Quebec |
| **1763** | Treaty of Paris |
| | Pontiac's uprising |
| | Proclamation of 1763 creates "Indian Country" |
| | Paxton Boys massacre |

| | |
|---|---|
| **1764** | Sugar Act |
| **1765** | Stamp Act and Stamp Act Congress |
| **1766** | Declaratory Act |
| **1767** | Townshend Revenue Acts |
| **1768** | Treaties of Hard Labor and Fort Stanwix |
| **1770** | Boston Massacre |
| **1772** | First Committee of Correspondence organized in Boston |
| **1773** | Tea Act |
| | Boston Tea Party |
| **1774** | Intolerable Acts |
| | First Continental Congress |
| | Dunmore's War |
| **1775** | Fighting begins at Lexington and Concord |
| | Second Continental Congress |
| **1776** | Americans invade Canada |
| | Thomas Paine's *Common Sense* |
| | Declaration of Independence |

## CONCLUSION

Great Britain emerged from the Seven Years' War as the dominant power in North America. Yet despite its attempts at strict regulation and determination of the course of events in its colonies, it faced consistent resistance. The British underestimated the political consensus that existed among the colonists about the importance of republican government. They also underestimated the ability of the colonists to inform one another, to work together, to build the bonds of national community cutting across boundaries of ethnicity, region, and economic condition. Through newspapers, pamphlets, committees of correspondence, community organizations, and group protest, the colonists discovered the concerns they shared, and in so doing fostered a new American identity. Without that identity it would have been difficult for them to consent to the treasonous act of declaring independence, especially when the independence they sought was from an international power that dominated much of the globe.

## REVIEW QUESTIONS

1.  How did overwhelming British success in the Seven Years' War lead to an imperial crisis in British North America?

2.  Outline the changes in British policy toward the colonies from 1750 to 1776.

3.  Trace the developing sense of an American national community over this same period.

4.  What were the principal events leading to the beginning of armed conflict at Lexington and Concord?

5.  How were the ideals of American republicanism expressed in the Declaration of Independence?

**myhistorylab**

**Flashcard Review**

## KEY TERMS

**Albany Conference** (p. 129)

**Boston Massacre** (p. 141)

**Boston Tea Party** (p. 142)

**Coercive Acts** (p. 142)

**Declaratory Act** (p. 138)

**First Continental Congress** (p. 145)

**French and Indian War** (p. 130)

**Intolerable Acts** (p. 142)

**Nonimportation movement** (p. 138)

**Plan of Union** (p. 129)

**Quartering Act** (p. 144)

**Quebec Act** (p. 144)

**Republicanism** (p. 136)

**Royal Proclamation of 1763** (p. 134)

**Sons of Liberty** (p. 138)

**Stamp Act** (p. 137)

**Sugar Act** (p. 136)

**Tea Act** (p. 142)

**Townshend Revenue Acts** (p. 139)

**Treaty of Paris** (p. 132)

**Virtual representation** (p. 137)

**Whigs** (p. 137)

## RECOMMENDED READING

Benedict Anderson, *Imagined Communities: Reflections on the Origin and Spread of Nationalism*, rev. ed. (1991). An argument that the essential first act of national consciousness is the effort to create a community that encompasses more than just local individuals and groups.

Fred Anderson, *The Crucible of War: The Seven Years' War and the Fate of Empire in British North America, 1754–1766* (2000). A new and powerful history of the war, arguing that it created a "hollow British empire."

Bernard Bailyn, *The Ideological Origins of the American Revolution* (1967). This classic argument emphasizes the role of ideas in the advent of the Revolution. Includes an analysis of American views of the imperial crisis.

Gregory Evans Dowd, *War Under Heaven: Pontiac, the Indian Nations, and the British Empire* (2002). Artfully crafted and gracefully written, this book restores Pontiac as a preeminent figure in the uprisings that bore his name.

Eric Foner, *Tom Paine and Revolutionary America* (1976). Combines a biography of Paine with a community study of the Revolution in Philadelphia and Pennsylvania.

Pauline Maier, *American Scripture: Making the Declaration of Independence* (1997). The deep background of this foundation of American democracy.

Richard L. Merritt, *Symbols of American Community, 1735–1775* (1966). A study of colonial newspapers that provides evidence for a rising sense of national community. The French and Indian War emerges as the key period for the growth of nationalist sentiment.

Gary B. Nash, *The Unknown American Revolution: The Unruly Birth of Democracy and the Struggle to Create America* (2005). A noted social historian focuses on the revolution's lesser-known freedom fighters.

Ray Raphael, *First American Revolution: Before Lexington and Concord* (2002). A vivid account of the turbulent days in Massachusetts from the time the province received word of the Massachusetts Government Act in August 1774 until the fighting broke out at Lexington and Concord the following April.

For study resources for this chapter, go to **www.myhistorylab.com** and choose *Out of Many, Teaching and Learning Classroom Edition.* You will find a wealth of study and review material for this chapter, including pretests and posttests, customized study plan, key-term review flash cards, interactive map and document activities, and documents for analysis.

*These are the times that try men's souls. . .*
—Thomas Paine

NC
NJ
V                    NY
M
P        NE
UNITE OR DIE

Article 10.

**The surrender of** Lord Cornwallis at Yorktown on October 19, 1781, led to the British decision to withdraw from the war. Cornwallis, who claimed to be ill, absented himself from the ceremony and is not in the picture. Washington, who is astride the horse under the American flag, designated General Benjamin Lincoln (on the white horse in the center) as the one to accept the submission of a subordinate British officer. John Trumbull, who painted The Battle of Bunker Hill and some three hundred other scenes from the Revolutionary War, finished this painting while he was in London about fifteen years after the events depicted. A large copy of the work now hangs in the rotunda of the United States Capitol in Washington, D.C. Source: Surrender of Lord Cornwallis at Yorktown, by John Trumbull (American, 1756-1843). Oil on canvas, 20 7/8 × 30 5/8 in.

# 7

# THE AMERICAN REVOLUTION
## 1776–1786

**WHAT STRATEGIES** and tactics did American forces employ in the war for independence?

**WHAT CONCERNS** were reflected in the terms of the Articles of Confederation?

**HOW DID** political debate in America change in the years after 1774?

# AMERICAN COMMUNITIES
## A National Community Evolves at Valley Forge

A DRUM ROLL ANNOUNCED THE DAWN OF A COLD JANUARY MORNING IN 1778. Along a two-mile line of rude log cabins, doors slowly opened and the ragged men of the Continental Army stepped out onto the frozen ground of Valley Forge. The reek of unwashed bodies and foul straw filled the air. "No bread, no soldier!" The chant began as a barely audible murmur, then was picked up by men all along the line. "No bread, no soldier! No bread, no soldier!" At last the chanting grew so loud it could be heard at General Washington's headquarters, a mile away. The 11,000 men of the American army were surviving on little more than "firecake," a mixture of flour and water baked hard before the fire. Two thousand men were without shoes; others were without blankets and had to sit up all night about the fires to keep from freezing. Washington fired off an appeal to the Continental Congress for supplies. "Three or four days of bad weather," he wrote, "would prove our destruction."

The hard winter at Valley Forge became a national symbol of endurance. After suffering a series of shattering defeats at the hands of a British force nearly twice their number, the soldiers of the Continental Army straggled into winter headquarters in this valley, some twenty miles northwest of Philadelphia, only to find themselves at the mercy of indifferent local suppliers. Congress refused to pay the exorbitant rates demanded by contractors for food and clothing. Local farmers preferred to deal with the British, who paid in pounds sterling rather than depreciated Continental currency.

The 11,000 men of the Continental Army were divided into sixteen brigades composed of regiments from the individual states. Many were drawn from the ranks of the poor and disadvantaged. They included landless tenant farmers, indentured servants, and nearly a thousand African Americans, both slave and free. A majority of the men came from rural districts or small towns. Some 2,500 men died that winter. The women encamped at Valley Forge—an estimated 700 wives, lovers, laundresses, cooks, and prostitutes—were kept busy nursing the sick and burying the dead. "What then is to become of this army?" Washington worried in December.

Yet the army that marched out of Valley Forge five months later was considerably stronger for its experience there. The men of the Continental Army spent the late winter and spring drilling under the strict discipline of Friedrich Wilhelm Augustus von Steuben, a Prussian officer who came to America to volunteer for the American cause. But most important were the bonds forged among the men. In their small cabins they "shared with each other their hardships, dangers, and sufferings," wrote Private Joseph Plumb Martin, "sympathized with each other in trouble and sickness, assisted in bearing each other's burdens, [and] endeavored to conceal each other's faults." In short, he concluded, the men fashioned "a band of brotherhood" among themselves. On May Day they celebrated the end of winter and the coming of spring by raising maypoles before the cabins of each state regiment. Led by a sergeant decked out as King Tammany, the great Delaware chief of American folklore, and accompanied by thirteen honor guards representing each of the states, the men paraded through the rough streets of camp, pausing at each maypole to dance together. It was a ritual of their new sense of national community.

To some American Patriots—as the supporters of the Revolution called themselves—the European-style Continental Army betrayed the revolutionary ideals of the citizen-soldier and the autonomy of local communities. Washington argued strongly, however, that the Revolution could not be won without a national army insulated from politics and able to withstand shifts in the popular mood. Moreover, during the critical period of the nation's founding, the Continental Army acted as a popular democratic force, counterbalancing the conservatism of the new republic's elite leadership. The national spirit built at places like Valley Forge sustained the fighting men through years of war and provided momentum for the long process of forging a national political system out of the persistent localism of American politics. The soldiers of the Continental Army were among the first of their countrymen to think of themselves as Americans.

Valley Forge

The Revolutionary years were characterized by warfare not only between armed American and British forces but also between Patriots and Loyalists, settlers and Indians, masters and slaves. Jealous of their autonomy, the individual colonies shaped a weak central government that just barely managed to keep them unified. Battered and bruised by British armies, the Continental Army pulled off an unexpected and remarkable victory against a large British force in upper New York State that led to financial support from Holland and a military alliance with France that in the end proved to be a decisive element in winning American independence. The glue that held Americans together during this long struggle was the sense of national community that emerged in places like Valley Forge during the winter of 1777.

# THE WAR FOR INDEPENDENCE

At the beginning of the Revolution, the British had the world's best-equipped and most disciplined army, as well as a navy that was unopposed in American waters. But this overwhelming force encouraged them to greatly underestimate the American capacity to fight. The British also misperceived the sources of the conflict. Seeing the rebellion as the work of a small group of disgruntled conspirators, they defined their objective as defeating this Patriot opposition. They believed that in the wake of a military victory they could easily reassert political control. But the geography of eastern North America offered no single vital center whose conquest would end the war. When the British succeeded in defeating the **Patriots** in one area, resistance would spring up in another. The key factor in the outcome of the war for independence was popular support for the American cause.

## THE PATRIOT FORCES

Most American men of fighting age had to face the call to arms. From a population of approximately 350,000 eligible men, more than 200,000 saw action. More than 100,000 served in the **Continental Army** under Washington's command, the rest in militia companies.

These militias—armed bodies of men drawn from local communities— proved important in the defense of their own areas, for they had homes as well as local reputations to protect. But the Revolution was not won by citizen-soldiers who traded plows for guns or backcountry riflemen who picked off Redcoats from behind trees. Because men preferred to serve with their neighbors in local companies rather than subject themselves to the discipline of the regular service, the states failed to meet their quotas for regiments in the Continental Army. Indeed, in the face of battle, militia companies demonstrated appalling rates of desertion.

The final victory resulted primarily from the steady struggle of the Continental Army. The American Revolution had little in common with modern national liberation movements in which armed populations engage in guerrilla warfare. Washington and his officers wanted a force that could directly engage the British, and from the beginning of the war, he argued that victory could be won only with a full commitment to

**Jean Baptiste Antoine** de Verger, a French officer serving with the Continental Army, made these watercolors of American soldiers during the Revolution. Some 200,000 men saw action, including at least 5,000 African Americans; more than half of these troops served with the Continental Army.

**WHAT STRATEGIES** and tactics did American forces employ in the war for independence?

**myhistorylab**
**Review Summary**

## IMAGE KEY
for pages 154–155

a. An 18th-century powder horn decorated with a map.
b. An engraving printed by Benjamin Franklin in 1754 urging the colonies to unite.
c. The 1783 Treaty of Paris that ended the American Revolution and recognized the independence of the United States.
d. A drum belonging to William Diamond (Lexington Historical Society) and a fife said to have been played at the Lexington fight early in the morning of April 19, 1775.
e. A painting by a French army officer showing the diversity of American soldiers.
f. Benjamin West's painting of the American commissioners who negotiated the Peace of Paris.
g. Mather Brown's sensitive portrait of Thomas Jefferson is the earliest known likeness of him.
h. The *Surrender of Lord Cornwallis at Yorktown* on October 19, 1781, a painting by John Trumbull.

**Patriots** British colonists who favored independence from Britain.

**Continental Army** The regular or professional army authorized by the Second Continental Congress and commanded by General George Washington during the Revolutionary War.

a truly national army. His views conflicted with popular fears of a standing army. Would they not be defeating their own purpose, many wondered, by adopting the corrupt institutions of their British enemies? Led by such views, Congress initially refused to invoke a draft or mandate army enlistments exceeding one year.

The failings of the militias in the early battles of the war, however, sobered Congress, and it responded with greatly enlarged state quotas for the army and terms of service that extended for the duration. To spur enlistment, Congress offered bounties, regular wages, and promises of free land after victory. By the spring of 1777, Washington's army had grown to nearly 9,000 men.

The New England militia companies that made up the original core of the Continental Army included small numbers of African Americans. But in late 1775, under pressure from Southern delegates, the Continental Congress barred blacks from the army. After an appeal from Washington, African Americans already serving were allowed to remain, but new enlistments were forbidden. The northern states continued to recruit African Americans. As the war spread to the South, slaves responded enthusiastically to a British promise of liberty for those who would fight for the crown. Thousands of slaves enlisted. In response, Maryland, Virginia, and North Carolina grudgingly allowed free persons of color and even slaves into their armed forces. By war's end, at least 5,000 African Americans had served in Patriot militias or the Continental Army, and in the Upper South some slaves won their freedom through military service. In the Lower South, however, where the numerical superiority of slaves inspired fears of rebellion among whites, there was no similar movement.

The Continental Army played an important political role during the war. At a time when Americans identified most strongly with their local communities or their states, the Continental Army evolved into a powerful force for nationalist sentiment. Over 100,000 men from every state served in the Continental Army, contributing mightily to the unity of purpose—the formation of a national political community—that was essential to the process of nation making.

## The Toll of War

The best estimate is that 25,324 American men died in the fighting, approximately 6,800 from wounds suffered in battle, most of the rest from the effects of disease. But since these numbers include only the major battles, the total death toll must have been considerably higher. The Continental Army experienced the heaviest casualty rates, losses in some regiments approaching 40 percent. Indeed, the casualty rate overall was higher than in any other American conflict except the Civil War. In New England and the mid-Atlantic states the war claimed few civilian lives, for it was confined largely to direct engagements between armies. In the South and backcountry, however, where Patriot and Loyalist militias waged violent and often vicious campaigns, there were many noncombatant casualties. There are no overall statistics for Loyalist casualties, but British forces suffered at least 10,000 killed or wounded in the major battles of the war.

## The Loyalists

Not all Americans were Patriots. Many were confused by the conflict and waited for a clear turn in the tide of the struggle before

**A Patriot mob** torments Loyalists in this print published during the Revolution. One favorite punishment was the "grand Tory ride," in which a crowd hauled the victim through the streets astride a fence rail. In another, men were stripped to "buff and breeches" and their naked flesh coated liberally with heated tar and feathers.

The TORY'S Day of JUDGMENT.

declaring their allegiance. Between a fifth and a third of the population, somewhere between a half a million and a million people, remained loyal to the British crown. They called themselves **Loyalists** but were known to Patriots as **Tories**, the popular name for the conservative party in England, traditionally supporters of the king's authority over that of Parliament.

A large proportion of the Loyalists were relatively recent migrants to the colonies, born in England, Scotland, or Ireland. Others, such as royal office-holders or Anglican clergymen, were dependent on the British government for their salaries. Many Loyalists were men of conservative temperament, fearful of political or social upheaval. The Loyalists included ethnic minorities who had been persecuted by the dominant majority, such as the Highland Scots of the Carolinas and western New York, or southern tenant farmers who had Patriot landlords. Loyalists were particularly strong in some colonies. They were nearly a majority in New York and were so numerous in Pennsylvania that an officer of the Continental Army described that colony as "the enemy's country." In Georgia, Loyalists made up such a large majority that the colony would probably have abandoned the revolutionary movement had the British not surrendered at Yorktown in 1781.

Patriots passed state treason acts that prohibited speaking or writing against the Revolution. They also punished Loyalists by issuing bills of attainder, a legal process (later made illegal by the United States **Constitution**) by means of which Loyalists were deprived of civil rights and property. In some areas, notably New York, South Carolina, Massachusetts, and Pennsylvania, Loyalists faced mob violence.

The British strategy for suppressing the Revolution depended on mobilizing the Loyalists, as many as 50,000 of whom took up arms for Great Britain. Many joined Loyalist militias or engaged in irregular warfare, especially in the Lower South.

As many as 80,000 Loyalists fled the country during and after the Revolution. Although the British government compensated many Loyalists for their losses when their property was confiscated by the states and sold at auction, most were unhappy exiles. "I earnestly wish to spend the remainder of my days in America," William Pepperell, formerly of Maine, wrote from London in 1778. "I love the country. I love the people." Despite their disagreement with the Patriots on essential political questions, they remained Americans, and they mourned the loss of their country.

## WOMEN AND THE WAR

As men marched off to war, thousands of women assumed the management of farms and businesses. Abigail Adams ran the Adams family's farm at Quincy for years, reporting on operations in frequent letters to her husband John, letters that included commentary on the American struggle for independence and the political structure of the new republic. Some women participated even more directly in Patriot politics. Mercy Otis Warren, sister of the Massachusetts leader James Otis, turned her home into a center of Patriot political activity and published a series of satires supporting the American cause and scorning the Loyalists. Thousands of women volunteered to support the war effort by working as seamstresses, nurses, even spies.

**Loyalists** British colonists who opposed independence from Britain.

**Tories** A derisive term applied to Loyalists in America who supported the king and Parliament just before and during the American Revolution.

**Constitution** The written document providing for a new central government of the United States.

**John Singleton Copley's** portrait of Mercy Otis Warren captured her at the age of thirty-six, in 1765. During the Revolution, her home in Boston was a center of Patriot political activity.

John Singleton Copley (American, 1738–1815), "Mrs. James Warren (Mercy Otis)," ca.1763. Oil on canvas. 49 5/8 × 39 1/2 in. (126 × 100.3 cm). Bequest of Winslow Warren. Courtesy, Museum of Fine Arts, Boston (31.212). Reproduced with permission. © 2000 Museum of Fine Arts, Boston. All Rights Reserved.

Thousands of women also traveled with the armies of both sides. Some camp followers were prostitutes, but most were wives, nurses, cooks, and laundresses. These women not only shared the hardships of the soldiers, but also they were on the battlefields bringing water, food, and supplies to the front lines under withering cannon and musket fire and nursing the wounded and dying. The Continental Congress and state legislatures awarded pensions to numerous women wounded in battle. According to one estimate, several hundred women dressed themselves as men and enlisted.

## THE CAMPAIGN FOR NEW YORK AND NEW JERSEY

During the winter of 1775–76, the British developed a strategic plan for the war. From his base at Halifax, Sir William Howe would take his army to New York City, which the British navy would protect. From there Howe was to drive north along the Hudson, while another British army marched south from Canada. The two armies would converge at Albany, cutting New England off from the rest of the colonies, then turn eastward. Washington, in command of Patriot forces at Boston, shifted his forces southward toward New York in the spring of 1776.

In early July, as Congress adopted the Declaration of Independence, the British began their operation by landing 32,000 troops on Staten Island. The Patriots set up fortified positions across the harbor in Brooklyn. In late August the British attacked, inflicting heavy casualties. The Battle of Long Island ended in disaster for the Patriots, and they were forced to withdraw across the East River to Manhattan.

The British then offered Congress an opportunity to negotiate, and on September 6, Benjamin Franklin, John Adams, and Edward Rutledge sat down on Staten Island with General Howe and his brother, Admiral Richard Howe. But the meeting broke up when the Howes demanded repeal of the Declaration of Independence, setting the stage for another round of fighting. By November, the Americans were fleeing south across New Jersey in a frantic attempt to avoid the British under General Charles Cornwallis (see Map 7.1).

With morale desperately low, whole militia companies deserted. American resistance seemed to be collapsing, and Washington was pessimistic. "Our Troops will not do their duty," he wrote painfully to Congress as he crossed the Delaware River into Pennsylvania. But rather than fall back farther, which would surely have meant the dissolution of his entire force, he decided to risk a counterattack. On Christmas night 1776, Washington led 2,400 troops back across the Delaware, and the next morning defeated the Hessian forces in a surprise attack on their headquarters at Trenton, New Jersey. The Americans inflicted further heavy losses on the British at Princeton, then drove them all the way back to the environs of New York City.

These victories had little strategic importance, but they salvaged American morale. As Washington settled into winter headquarters at Morristown, he realized he had to pursue a defensive strategy, avoiding direct confrontations with the British while checking their advances and hurting them wherever possible. The most important thing would be the survival of the Continental Army.

**MAP 7.1**
**Campaign for New York and New Jersey, 1775–77**

HOW DID American victories at Trenton and Princeton help turn the tide of the war?

## THE NORTHERN CAMPAIGNS OF 1777

The fighting with American forces prevented Howe from moving north up the Hudson River, and the British advance southward from Canada was stalled by American resistance at Lake Champlain. In 1777, however, the British decided to replay their strategy. From Canada they dispatched General John Burgoyne with nearly 8,000 British and allied German troops. Howe was to move his force from New York, first taking the city of Philadelphia, the seat of the Continental Congress, and then moving north to meet Burgoyne (see Map 7.2).

Fort Ticonderoga fell to Burgoyne on July 6, but by August the general found himself bogged down and harassed by Patriot militias in the rough country south of Lake George. After several defeats in September at the hands of an American army commanded by General Horatio Gates, Burgoyne retreated to Saratoga. There he was surrounded by a considerably larger force of Americans, and on October 19 he surrendered his army. It would be the biggest British defeat until Yorktown, decisive because it forced the nations of Europe to recognize that the Americans had a fighting chance to win their Revolution.

The Americans were less successful against Howe. A force of 15,000 British troops left New York in July and landed a month later at the northern end of Chesapeake Bay. In September, at Brandywine Creek outside Philadelphia, the British outflanked the Americans, inflicting heavy casualties and forcing a retreat. Ten days later they routed the Americans a second time. This cleared the way for the British occupation of Philadelphia.

After this campaign, the Continentals headed into winter quarters at Valley Forge, the bitterness of their defeats muted somewhat by news of Burgoyne's surrender at Saratoga. The British had possession of Philadelphia, the most important city in North America, but it would prove of little strategic value to them. The Continental Congress continued to function, so the unified effort suffered little disruption. At the end of two years of fighting, despite numerous military victories, the British strategy for suppressing the Revolution had been a failure.

## A GLOBAL CONFLICT

During these two years of fighting, the Americans were sustained by loans from France and Spain, traditional enemies of Great Britain. Both saw an opportunity to win back North American territories lost as a result of the Seven Years' War. Seeking more support, the Continental Congress sent a diplomatic delegation to Paris headed by Benjamin Franklin.

**MAP 7.2**
**Northern Campaigns, 1777–78**

WHAT WAS the significance of the Battle of Saratoga?

The American victory at Saratoga, and the fear that Great Britain might enter into negotiations with the revolutionaries, persuaded the French to recognize American independence in December 1777. Neither country was to conclude peace with the British "without the formal consent of the other." The treaty was to take effect "should war break out" between France and Great Britain. The alliance was sealed when fighting between the two traditional enemies began in June. Americans also found much support in the Netherlands. Although officially allied with Great Britain, the Dutch maintained a position of neutrality and opened secret negotiations with the Americans for a treaty of trade and friendship. Clandestine trade through the Dutch island of St. Eustatius in the Caribbean helped sustain the Patriot cause. In 1779 the British shelled the Dutch colony and the next year declared war on the Netherlands. The Dutch became the second European nation to recognize the United States and its financiers became the most important source of loans for the new nation.

Spain had entered the war in 1779. As early as 1775 Spanish officials in New Orleans were providing substantial ammunition and provisions for American forts in the West, including supplies of beef from herds of cattle driven to New Orleans by vaqueros (cowboys) from Texas. The viceroy of New Spain levied a special tax to pay for these supplies, and borderland colonists in Sonora, Texas, New Mexico, and California contributed their share. But unlike France and the Netherlands, the Spanish refused to establish a formal alliance with the United States.

Thus, the Spanish pursued an independent strategy against the British, seizing the weakly defended Mississippi River towns of Natchez and Baton Rouge in 1779, and winning the important Gulf ports of Mobile in 1780 and Pensacola in 1781. The victory at Pensacola was achieved with the help of several companies of Florida exiles, many of them African Americans.

With France and Spain now in the war, the British rethought their military strategy. Considering their West Indies sugar colonies at risk, they shipped 5,000 troops from New York to the Caribbean, where they succeeded in beating back a French attack. Fearing the arrival of the French fleet along the North American coast, the new British commander in America, General Henry Clinton, evacuated Philadelphia in June 1778. Washington's Continentals, fresh out of Valley Forge, went in hot pursuit. In the Battle of Monmouth, fought in stifling New Jersey heat on June 28, the British blunted the American drive and succeeded in making an orderly retreat to New York City. After a failed American-French joint campaign against the British at Newport, Rhode Island, Washington decided on a defensive strategy. Although the Americans enjoyed several small successes in the Northeast over the next two years, the war there went into a stalemate.

## INDIAN PEOPLES AND THE REVOLUTION IN THE WEST

At the beginning of the conflict, both sides looked for Indian support. Most important was the stance of the Iroquois Confederacy, long one of the most potent political forces in colonial North America. A delegation from Congress told the Iroquois that the conflict was a "family quarrel" and urged them to keep out of it. British agents, on the other hand, pressed the Iroquois to unite against the Americans. Many Indian leaders were reluctant to get involved: "We are unwilling to join on either side of such a contest," declared one Oneida chief. "Let us Indians be all of one mind, and live with one another, and you white people settle your own disputes between yourselves."

## QUICK REVIEW

**French Alliance**

♦ Congress negotiates alliance with France against the British.

♦ France guarantees northern parts of the country to the U.S.

♦ Warfare between France and Britain breaks out.

**Joseph Brant, the** brilliant chief of the Mohawks who sided with Great Britain during the Revolution, in a 1786 painting by the American artist Gilbert Stuart. After the Treaty of Paris, Brant led a large faction of Iroquois people north into British Canada, where they established a separate Iroquois Confederacy.

Ultimately, however, the British proved persuasive. It became clear to Indians that a Patriot victory would mean the extension of American settlements into their homelands. Native peoples fought in the Revolution for some of the same reasons Patriots did—for political independence, cultural integrity, and the protection of their land and property—but Indian fears of American expansion led them to oppose the Patriot rhetoric of natural rights and the equality of all men. Almost all the tribes that engaged in the fighting did so on the side of the British.

In the summer of 1776 a large number of Cherokees, led by the warrior chief Dragging Canoe (Tsiyu-Gunsini), attacked dozens of American settlements. It required hard fighting before Patriot militia companies managed to drive the Cherokees into the mountains. Although the Cherokees eventually made an official peace, sporadic violence between Patriots and Indians continued along the southern frontier.

Among the Iroquois of New York, the Mohawk leader Joseph Brant (Thayendanegea) succeeded in bringing most Iroquois warriors into the British camp, although he was opposed by the chiefs of the Oneidas and Tuscaroras, who supported the Patriots. In 1777 and 1778, Iroquois and Loyalist forces raided the northern frontiers of New York and Pennsylvania. In retaliation an American army invaded the Iroquois homelands in 1779. Supported by Oneida and Tuscarora warriors, the Americans destroyed dozens of western villages and thousands of acres of crops. For the first time since the birth of their confederacy centuries before, the Iroquois were fighting each other (see Map 7.3).

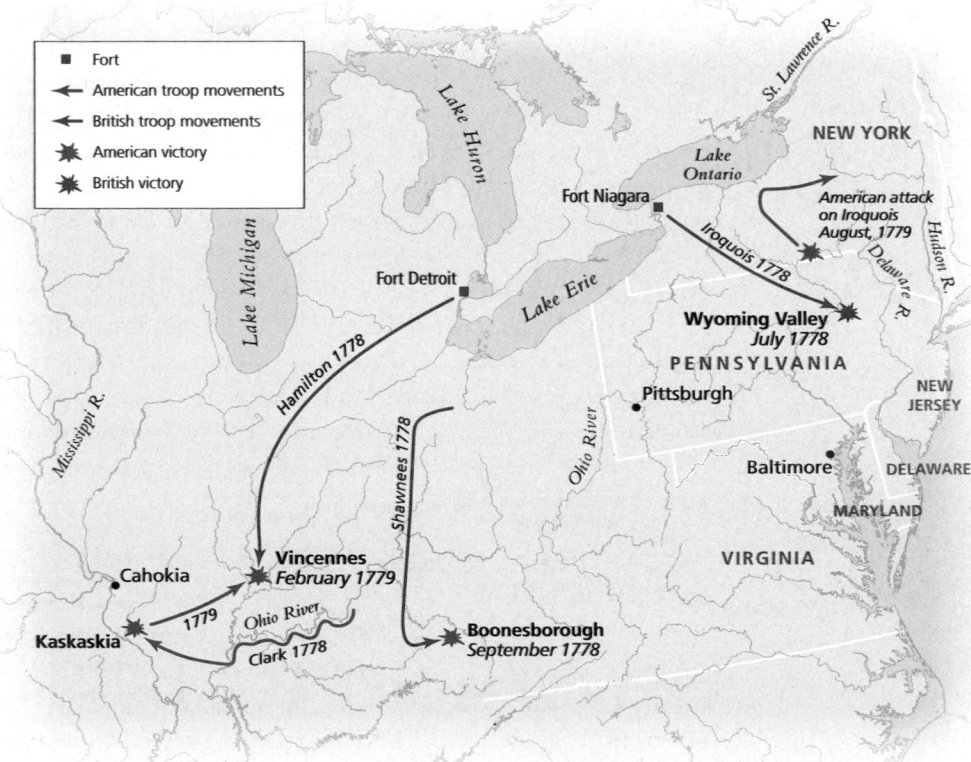

**MAP 7.3**
**Fighting in the West, 1778–79**

WHAT ROLE did Indian peoples play in the fighting in the West?

*Indians sided w/ british 4 independence & so American colonies wouldn't take more of their land*

Across the mountains, the **Ohio Indians** formed an effective alliance under the British at Detroit, and in 1777 and 1778 they sent warriors south against pioneer communities in western Virginia and Kentucky that had been founded in defiance of the Proclamation of 1763. Virginian George Rogers Clark countered by organizing an expedition of Kentucky militia against the old French settlements in the Illinois country, which were controlled by the British. They succeeded in taking the British post at Kaskaskia in the summer of 1778, and in early 1779, in a daring winter raid on Vincennes, they captured Colonel Henry Hamilton, British commander in the West.

But Clark lacked the strength to attack the strategic British garrison at Detroit. Coordinating his Iroquois forces with those in Ohio, Brant mounted a new set of offensives that cast a shadow over Clark's successes. The war in the West would not end with the conclusion of hostilities in the East. With barely a pause, the fighting in the trans-Appalachian West between Americans and Indians would continue for another two decades.

## THE WAR IN THE SOUTH

The most important fighting of the Revolution took place in the South (see Map 7.4). General Clinton regained the initiative for Britain in December 1778 by sending a force from New York against Georgia, the weakest of the colonies. The British

**MAP 7.4**
**Fighting in the South, 1778–81**

**WHAT ROLE** did African American slaves play in the fighting in the South?

**In 1845 Artist** William Ranney depicted a famous moment during the Battle of Cowpens that took place in January 1781. Lieutenant Colonel William Washington, leader of the Patriot cavalry and a relative of George Washington, was attacked by a squadron of British dragoons. As Washington was about to be cut down, he was saved by his servant William Ball, who fired a pistol that wounded the attacker. Nothing more is known about Ball, but he was one of a number of African Americans who fought on the Patriot side in the battle.

William Ranney, "The Battle of Cowpens." Oil on canvas. Photo by Sam Holland. Courtesy South Carolina State House.

crushed the Patriot militia at Savannah and began to organize the Loyalists in an effort to reclaim the colony. Encouraged by their success in Georgia, the British decided to apply the lessons learned there throughout the South. This involved a fundamental change from a strategy of military conquest to one of pacification. Territory would be retaken step by step, then handed over to Loyalists who would reassert the crown's authority.

In October 1779 Clinton evacuated Rhode Island, the last British stronghold in New England, and proceeded with 8,000 troops for a campaign against Charleston. Outflanking the American defenders, he forced the surrender of more than 5,000 troops in May. It was the most significant American defeat of the war. Patriot resistance collapsed in the Lower South, and American fortunes were suddenly at their lowest ebb since the beginning of the war.

The southern campaign was marked by vicious fighting between partisan militias of Patriots and Loyalists. The violence peaked in September 1780 with Cornwallis's invasion of North Carolina, where the Patriots were stronger and better organized. There the British found their southern strategy untenable: plundering towns and farms in order to feed the army in the interior had the effect of producing angry support for the Patriots.

Into 1781 the Continentals and Patriot militias waged what General Greene called a fugitive war of hit and run against the British. Finally in the summer of 1781, deciding he would not be able to hold the Carolinas as long as Virginia remained a base of support and supply for the Americans, Cornwallis led his army north. After marauding through the Virginia countryside, he reached the Chesapeake where he expected reinforcements from New York. The British withdrawal from North Carolina allowed Greene to reestablish Patriot control of the Lower South.

5–10
William Dobein James, *The Rise of Partisan Warfare in the South* (1778)

## THE YORKTOWN SURRENDER

While the British raged through the South, the stalemate continued in the Northeast. In the summer of 1780, taking advantage of the British evacuation of Rhode Island, the French landed 5,000 troops at Newport under the command of General Jean Baptiste Donatien de Vimeur, comte de Rochambeau. But it was not until the spring of 1781 that Rochambeau risked joining his force to Washington's Continentals north of New York City. In August Washington learned that the French Caribbean fleet was headed for the Chesapeake. If he and Rochambeau could move their troops south, they might lock up Cornwallis in his camp at Yorktown. Leaving a small force behind as a decoy, they marched their 16,000 men overland to the Virginia shore in little more than a month.

The maneuver was a complete success. The French and Americans surrounded and besieged the British encampment. French and American heavy artillery hammered the British unmercifully until the middle of October. After the failure of a planned retreat across the York River, Cornwallis opened negotiations for the surrender of his army. Two days later, on October 19, 1781, between lines of victorious American and French soldiers, the British troops came out from their trenches to surrender (see Seeing History). Everyone was aware that it was an event of incalculable importance, but few guessed it was the end of the war. The British still controlled New York.

In London a month later Lord North received the news "as he would have taken a ball in the breast," the colonial secretary reported. "Oh God!" North moaned, "it is all over!" The American Revolution had turned into war with France and Spain, and British fortunes were at low ebb in India, the West Indies, Florida, and the Mediterranean. The cost of the war was enormous, and there was little support for it among either the British public or the members of Parliament. George III wished to press on, but North submitted his resignation, and in March 1782 the king was forced to offer the office of prime minister to Charles Watson-Wentworth, Lord Rockingham, who long had favored granting the Americans their independence.

# THE UNITED STATES IN CONGRESS ASSEMBLED

The motion for independence, offered to the Continental Congress by Richard Henry Lee on June 7, 1776, called for a confederation of the states. The Articles of Confederation, the first written constitution of the United States, created a national government of sharply limited powers. This arrangement reflected the concerns of people fighting to free themselves from a coercive central government. But the weak Confederation government had a difficult time forging the unity and assembling the resources necessary to fight the war and win the peace.

## THE ARTICLES OF CONFEDERATION

The debate over confederation that took place in the Continental Congress during 1776 made it clear that delegates favoring a loose union of autonomous states outnumbered those who wanted a strong central government. A consensus finally emerged in 1777, and the "**Articles of Confederation**" were formally adopted by the Continental Congress in November and sent to the states for ratification. The Articles created a national assembly, called the Congress, in which each state had a single vote. Delegates, selected annually in a manner determined by the individual state legislatures, could serve no more than three years out of six. A presiding president, elected annually by Congress, was eligible to hold office no more than

**QUICK REVIEW**

**Yorktown**

- American and French forces surround British encampment.
- British General Cornwallis forced to surrender his army.
- Defeat forced the British to accept American independence.

*British surrendered*

**WHAT CONCERNS** were reflected in the terms of the Articles of Confederation?

**myhistorylab**
Review Summary

**Articles of Confederation** Written document setting up the loose confederation of states that comprised the first national government of the United States.

# The Surrender of Lord Cornwallis

American artist John Trumbull displayed a preliminary version of *Surrender of Lord Cornwallis* in 1797 along with three other history paintings of the Revolution, including his depiction of the signing of the Declaration of Independence, the surrender of General Burgoyne at Saratoga, and the resignation of General Washington from his military commission at the war's conclusion. Young Trumbull had been an officer in the Continental Army and served for a time as Washington's aide-de-camp, but he had not been at Yorktown. By that time he was in London studying with the American expatriate artist Benjamin West. This painting was done in the heroic style of nationalist art popular at the time in Great Britain and Europe. Trumbull was at pains to get the details right. He visited Yorktown to sketch the landscape and traveled across the United States and France to capture the likenesses of the senior American and French officers, including Washington and Rochambeau, shown lining the two sides, colors flying, as the British troops file by. But Trumbull was criticized by the public for getting one detail appallingly wrong. He depicted Cornwallis on horseback in the center, when in fact the British commander was not present at the ceremony but was sulking in his tent. Trumbull corrected his error by changing the color of the central figure's uniform from red to blue, thereby turning Cornwallis into General Benjamin Lincoln, who is seen reaching for the sword in the possession of the British second-in-command, General Charles O'Hara. In 1817 the Senate commissioned Trumbull to repaint his Revolutionary scenes for placement in the Rotunda of the Capitol. ■

**IN WHAT** ways does Trumbull create a heroic painting by the arrangement of his subjects?

one year out of three. Votes would be decided by a simple majority of the states, except for major questions, which would require the agreement of nine states.

Congress was granted national authority in the conduct of foreign affairs, matters of war and peace, and maintenance of the armed forces. It could raise loans, issue bills of credit, establish a coinage, and regulate trade with Indian peoples, and it was to be the final authority in jurisdictional disputes between states. It was charged with establishing a national postal system as well as a common standard of weights and measures. Lacking the power to tax citizens directly, however, the national government was to apportion its financial burdens among the states according to the extent of their surveyed land. The Articles explicitly guaranteed the sovereignty of the individual states, reserving to them all powers not expressly delegated to Congress. Ratification or amendment required the agreement of all thirteen states. The Articles of Confederation thus created a national government of specific yet sharply circumscribed powers.

The legislatures of twelve states soon voted in favor of the Articles, but final ratification was held up for more than three years by the state of Maryland. Representing the interests of states without claims to lands west of the Appalachians, Maryland demanded that states cede to Congress their western claims, the new nation's most valuable resource, for "the good of the whole" (see Map 7.5). It was 1781 before Virginia, the state with the largest western claims, broke the logjam by agreeing to the cession. Maryland then ratified the Articles of Confederation, and in March they took effect.

## QUICK REVIEW

**Powers of the Central Government under the Articles of Confederation**

- No national judiciary.
- No separate executive branch.
- Congress sole national authority.
- No Congressional authority to raise troops or impose taxes.

*Maryland didn't vote in favor of articles*

**MAP 7.5**

**State Claims to Western Lands** The ratification of the Articles of Confederation in 1781 awaited settlement of the western claims of eight states. Vermont, claimed by New Hampshire and New York, was not made a state until 1791, after disputes were settled the previous year. The territory north of the Ohio River was claimed in whole or in part by Virginia, New York, Connecticut, and Massachusetts. All of them had ceded their claims by 1786, except for Connecticut, which had claimed an area just south of Lake Erie, known as the Western Reserve; Connecticut ceded this land in 1800. The territory south of the Ohio was claimed by Virginia, North Carolina, South Carolina, and Georgia; in 1802, the latter became the last state to cede its claims.

WHAT WAS the reason for the delay in ratifying the Articles of Confederation?

## FINANCING THE WAR

Lacking the authority to levy direct taxes, Congress financed the Revolution through grants and loans from friendly foreign powers and by issuing paper currency. The total foreign subsidy by the end of the war approached $9 million, but this was not enough to back the circulating Continental currency that Congress authorized, the face value of which amounted to $200 million. In an attempt to retire this currency, Congress called on the states to raise taxes, payable in Continental dollars. But most of the states were unwilling to do this. In fact, most had resorted to printing currency of their own, estimated at a face value of another $200 million by war's end. The result of this expansion in the money supply was the rapid depreciation of Continental currency. By the time Robert Morris, one of the wealthiest merchants in the country, became secretary of finance in May 1781, Continental currency had ceased to circulate. In the jargon of the day, things of no value were "not worth a Continental." Yet the paper currency had funded a revolution.

Morris was able to turn things around. He persuaded Congress to charter a "Bank of North America" located in Philadelphia, the first private commercial bank in the United States. Into its vaults he deposited large quantities of gold and silver coin and bills of exchange obtained through loans from Holland and France. He then issued new paper currency backed by this treasure. Once he established confidence in the bank, Morris was able to supply the Continental Army through private contracts. He also began making interest payments on the debt, which in 1783 was estimated at $30 million.

## NEGOTIATING INDEPENDENCE

Peace talks between the United States and Great Britain opened in July 1782, when Benjamin Franklin sat down with the British emissary in Paris, Congress had issued its first set of war aims in 1779. The fundamental demand was recognition of American independence and withdrawal of British forces. American negotiators were instructed to press for the largest territorial limits possible, as well as guarantees of American rights to fish North Atlantic waters. As for its French ally, Congress instructed the commissioners to be guided by friendly advice, but also by "knowledge of our interests, and by your own discretion, in which we repose the fullest confidence." The French were not happy with this, and partly as a result of French pressure, in June 1781 Congress issued a new set of instructions. The commissioners were to settle merely for a grant of independence and withdrawal of troops and to be subject to the guidance and control of the French in the negotiations.

Ben Franklin, John Jay, and John Adams, the peace commissioners in Paris, were well aware of French attempts to manipulate the outcome of negotiations and place limits on American power. In violation of both Congressional instructions and treaty obligations to France, they signed a preliminary treaty with Britain in November 1782 without consulting the French. In the treaty, Britain acknowledged the United States as "free, sovereign & independent" and agreed to withdraw its troops from all forts within American territory "with all convenient speed." The American commissioners pressed the British for Canada but settled for western territorial boundaries extending to the Mississippi (see Map 7.6) with unencumbered navigation of the river.

Eighteen Pence.
To counterfeit is *Death.*

*Burlington in* NEW-JERSEY,
Printed by Isaac Collins, 1776.

**The Continental Congress** printed currency to finance the Revolution. Because of widespread counterfeiting, engravers attempted to incorporate complex designs, like the unique vein structure in the leaf on this eighteen-pence note. In case that wasn't enough, the engraver of this note also included the warning: "To counterfeit is Death."

### QUICK REVIEW

**Peace of Paris**

- ◆ Signed September 3, 1783.
- ◆ United States got virtually everything it sought at peace talks.
- ◆ Treaty addressed important economic issues, but said nothing about slavery.

# ✴ MAP EXPLORATION

To explore an interactive version of this map, go to **http://www.prenhall.com/faraghertlc/map7.6**

ARCTIC
OCEAN

*Bering
Sea*

**RUSSIAN**

NORTHWEST TERRITORIES

*Labrador
Sea*

*Gulf of
Alaska*

*Hudson
Bay*

BRITISH NORTH AMERICA

New
Brunswick

*Newfoundland*

Prince Edward Island
Cape Breton Island
Nova Scotia

**SPANISH
LOUISIANA**

**UNITED
STATES**

*ATLANTIC
OCEAN*

*PACIFIC
OCEAN*

*California*

*Texas*

**SPANISH
NORTH
AMERICA**

**SPANISH
FLORIDA**

*Bahamas*
**(British)**

*Gulf of
Mexico*

*Hispaniola*
**(Spanish)**

*Puerto Rico*
**(Spanish)**

*Lesser Antilles*
**(French)**

**NEW
SPAIN**

*Cuba*
**(Spanish)**

*Jamaica*
**(British)**

*Lesser Antilles*
**(British)**

*Belize*
**(British)**

*St. Dominique*
**(French)**

*Caribbean Sea*

Disputed areas:

| | |
|---|---|
| | Russia, Spain, and Britain |
| | United States and Britain |
| | United States and Spain |

*PACIFIC  OCEAN*

**MAP 7.6**
**North America After the Treaty of Paris, 1783**    The map of European and American claims to North America was radically altered by the results of the American Revolution.

HOW DID the Treaty of Paris alter the balance of power in North America?

The British guaranteed Americans "the right to take fish" in the waters of the North Atlantic. Britain received American promises that Congress would erect "no lawful impediments" to the recovery of debts, end the confiscation of Loyalist property, and attempt to persuade the states to fairly compensate Loyalist exiles. All in all, it was an astounding coup for the Americans.

The preliminary treaty confronted France with an accomplished fact. When French diplomats criticized the American commissioners, they responded by hinting that resistance to the treaty provisions could result in a British–American alliance. Thereupon France quickly made an agreement of its own with the British.

Spain did not participate in the negotiations with the Americans. But having waged a successful campaign against the British on the Mississippi and the Gulf Coast, its government issued a claim of sovereignty over much of the trans-Appalachian territory granted to the United States by Great Britain. Spain arranged a separate peace with Great Britain, in which it won the return of Florida. The final Treaty of Paris—actually a series of separate agreements among the United States, Great Britain, France, and Spain—was signed at Versailles on September 3, 1783.

**American artist Benjamin** West never completed his painting of the "American Commissioners of the Preliminary Peace Negotiations with Great Britain, 1783–1785," but he left this "cartoon" or study. It features portraits of (left to right) John Jay, John Adams, Henry Laurens, Benjamin Franklin, and William Temple Franklin, who served as secretary for his grandfather. West intended to include the British commissioners, but the death of one and the uncooperative attitude of the other aborted the project.

Benjamin West, 1783 "American Commissioners of Preliminary Negotiations". Courtesy, Winterthur Museum.

## THE CRISIS OF DEMOBILIZATION

In 1778 Continental officers had won from Congress a promise of life pensions at half pay in exchange for enlistment for the duration of the war. By 1783, however, Congress had still not made any specific provisions for officers' pensions. With peace at hand, the officers began to fear that the army would be disbanded before the problem was resolved, and they would lose whatever power they had to pressure Congress. In January 1783, a group of prominent senior officers petitioned Congress, demanding that pensions be converted to a bonus equal to five years of full pay. "Any further experiments on their patience," they warned, "may have fatal effects." Despite the barely veiled threat of military intervention, Congress rejected their petition.

With the backing of congressional nationalists, a group of army officers associated with General Horatio Gates circulated a letter arguing for direct military intervention and calling an extraordinary meeting of the officer corps at Newburgh. But General Washington, on whom the officers counted for support, criticized the meeting as "disorderly" and called an official meeting of his own. There was enormous tension as the officers assembled on March 15, 1783. Washington strode into the room and mounted the platform. Turning his back in disdain on Gates, he delivered an address from memory condemning the circular letter. After he left, the officers adopted resolutions rejecting intervention, and a week later, on Washington's urging, Congress converted the promised pensions to bonuses.

Washington's role in this crisis was one of his greatest contributions to the nation. At stake was nothing less than the possibility of a military coup at the very moment of victory. The American Revolution was the first of many successful colonial revolutions, and in hindsight it is clear that postindependence military rule was a common outcome in many of them. In December 1783 Washington resigned his commission as general of the army despite calls for him to remain. There is little doubt he could have assumed the role of an American dictator. Instead, by his actions and example, the principle of military subordination to civil authority was firmly established.

As for the common soldiers, they wanted simply to be discharged. In May 1783, Congress voted the soldiers three months' pay as a bonus and instructed Washington to begin dismissing them. By the beginning of 1784, the Continental Army had shrunk to no more than a few hundred men.

6–3
George Washington, *The Newburgh Address* (1783)

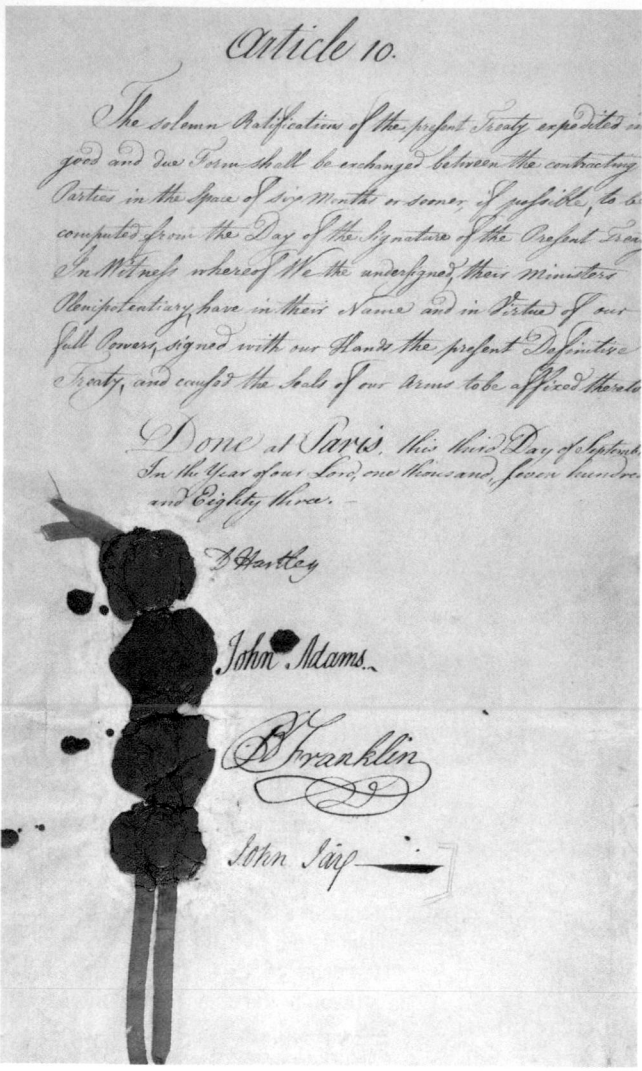

**The last page** of the Treaty of Paris, signed in Paris on September 3, 1783, by David Hartley for Great Britain, and for the United States by John Adams, Benjamin Franklin, and John Jay.

**5–12**
*Congress Decides What to Do with the Western Lands* (1785)

**Land Ordinance of 1785**  Act passed by Congress under the Articles of Confederation that created the grid system of surveys by which all subsequent public land was made available for sale.

**Northwest Ordinance of 1787** Legislation that prohibited slavery in the Northwest Territories and provided the model for the incorporation of future territories into the union as co-equal states.

## THE PROBLEM OF THE WEST

Even during the Revolution thousands of Americans migrated westward, and after the war settlers poured over the mountains and down the Ohio River. Thousands of Americans pressed against the Indian country north of the Ohio River, and destructive violence continued along the frontier. British troops continued to occupy posts in the Great Lakes region and encouraged Indian attacks on vulnerable settlements. Spain refused to accept the territorial settlement of the Treaty of Paris and closed the port of New Orleans to Americans, effectively blockading the Mississippi River. Westerners who saw that route as their primary access to markets were outraged.

John Jay, appointed secretary for foreign affairs by the Confederation Congress in 1784, attempted to negotiate with the British for their complete withdrawal but was told that was not possible until all outstanding debts from before the war were settled. Jay also negotiated with the Spanish for guarantees of territorial sovereignty and commercial relations, but they insisted that the Americans relinquish free navigation of the Mississippi. Congress would approve no treaty under those conditions, and some frustrated Westerners considered leaving the Confederation. In the West, local community interest continued to override the fragile development of national community sentiment.

In 1784, Congress took up the problem of extending national authority over the West. Legislation was drafted, principally by Thomas Jefferson, providing "Government for the Western Territory." The legislation proposed a remarkably republican colonial policy. The western public domain would be divided into states, fully the equals of the original thirteen, with Congressional guarantees of self-government and republican institutions. Once the population of a territory numbered 20,000, the residents could call a convention and establish a constitution and government of their own choosing. And once the population grew to equal that of the smallest of the original thirteen states, the territory could petition for statehood, provided it agreed to remain forever a member of the Confederation. Congress accepted these proposals but rejected by a vote of seven to six Jefferson's clause forever prohibiting slavery in the West.

Passed the following year, the **Land Ordinance of 1785** provided for the survey and sale of western lands. The settlement of Kentucky had been characterized by a chaos of overlapping surveys and land claims, a problem the Land Ordinance was designed to solve by creating an ordered system of survey, dividing the land into townships composed of thirty-six sections of one square mile (640 acres) each. Jefferson argued that land ought to be given away to actual settlers. But, eager to establish a revenue base for the government, Congress provided for the auction of public lands for not less than one dollar per acre.

In the treaties of Fort Stanwix in 1784 and Fort McIntosh in 1785, congressional commissioners forced the Iroquois and a number of Ohio tribes, respectively, to cede portions of their territory in what is now eastern Ohio. These treaties were not the result of negotiation but intimidation. The commissioners dictated the terms by seizing hostages and forcing compliance. Surveyors were immediately sent west to divide up the land. The first surveyed lands did not come onto the market until the fall of 1788, and in the meantime Congress, desperate for revenue, sold a tract of more than 1.5

# MAP EXPLORATION

To explore an interactive version of this map, go to **http://www.prenhall.com/faraghertlc/map7.7**

**MAP 7.7**

**The Northwest Territory and the Land Survey System of the United States**   The Land Ordinance of 1785 created an ordered system of survey, dividing the land into townships and sections.

IN WHAT ways did the Northwest Ordinance affect the admission of new states into the Union? What were the consequences for western lands?

million acres to the Ohio Company, a new consortium of land speculators, for a million dollars. Thousands of Westerners chose not to wait for the official opening of the public lands north of the Ohio River but simply settled illegally by making squatters' claims. In 1785 Congress raised troops and evicted many of them, but once the troops departed the squatters returned. The persistence of this problem convinced many congressmen to revise Jefferson's democratic territorial plan.

In the **Northwest Ordinance of 1787,** Congress established a system of government for the territory north of the Ohio (see Map 7.7). Three to five states were to be carved from the giant

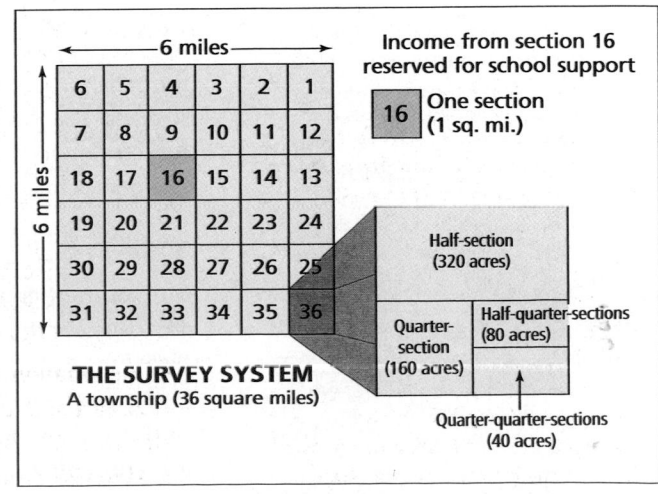

THE SURVEY SYSTEM
A township (36 square miles)

Northwest Territory. Slavery was prohibited. But the initial guarantee of self-government in Jefferson's plan was replaced by a congressionally appointed governor and court of judges. Once the free white male population of the territory had grown to 5,000, these citizens would be permitted to choose an assembly, but the governor had the power of absolute veto on all territorial legislation. National interest would be imposed on the local western communities.

The creation of the land system of the United States was the major achievement of the Confederation government. But there were other important accomplishments. Under the Articles of Confederation, Congress led the country through the Revolution and its commissioners negotiated the terms of a comprehensive peace treaty. And by organizing the departments of war, foreign affairs, finance, and the post office, the Confederation government created the beginnings of a national bureaucracy.

# REVOLUTIONARY POLITICS IN THE STATES

HOW DID political debate in America change in the years after 1774?

**myhistorylab**
Review Summary

Despite the accomplishments of the Confederation, most Americans were focused on the governments of their own states. The national government was distant and had relatively little effect on people's lives. Social and political identity was located in local communities and states rather than the American nation. People spoke of "these United States," emphasizing the plural. The states were the setting for the most important political struggles of the Confederation period.

## A NEW DEMOCRATIC IDEOLOGY

The political mobilization that took place in 1774 and 1775 greatly broadened political participation. Mass meetings in which ordinary people expressed their opinions, voted, and gained political experience were common not only in the cities but in small towns and rural communities as well. During these years a greater proportion of the population began to participate in elections. Compared with the colonial assemblies, the new state legislatures included more men from rural and western districts—farmers and artisans as well as lawyers, merchants, and large landowners.

This transformation was accompanied by a dramatic shift in the content of political debate. During the colonial period, when only the upper classes were truly engaged in the political process, the principal argument followed the lines of the traditional Tory and Whig divide in Great Britain. The Tory position, taken by colonial officials, was that colonial governments were simply convenient instruments of royal prerogative, serving at the king's pleasure. The Whig position, adopted by colonial elites who sought to preserve and increase their own power, emphasized the need for a government balancing the power of a governor with an upper house and an assembly. As a result of the Revolution, the Tory position lost all legitimacy and the Whig position was challenged by farmers, artisans, and ordinary people armed with a new and radical democratic ideology. The spectrum of politics shifted to the left.

## THE FIRST STATE CONSTITUTIONS

One of the first post-Revolution debates focused on an appropriate governmental structure for the new states. The thinking of democrats was indicated by the title of a New England pamphlet of 1776: *The People the Best Governors*. Power, this anonymous author argued, should be vested in a single, popularly elected assembly. The people, in the words of this pamphlet, "best know their wants and necessities, and therefore are best able to govern themselves." The ideal form of government, according to

QUICK REVIEW

**The New Politics**

♦ Ordinary people gained political experience during the Revolution.

♦ New state legislatures included more men from rural and western districts.

♦ Political spectrum shifted left.

democrats, was the community or town meeting, in which the people set their own tax rates, created a militia, controlled their own schools and churches, and regulated the local economy. State government was necessary only for coordination among communities.

Conservative Americans took up the Whig argument of the need for balanced government. The "unthinking many," wrote a conservative pamphleteer, should be checked by a strong executive and an upper house. Both of these would be insulated from popular control by property qualifications and long terms in office. The greatest danger, according to conservatives, was the possibility of majority tyranny, which might lead to the violation of property rights and dictatorship.

Fourteen states—the original thirteen plus Vermont, an independent republic from 1777 until 1791—adopted constitutions between 1776 and 1780. Each of those political charters was shaped by the debate between radicals and conservatives, democrats and Whigs, and reflected a particular political alignment. Pennsylvania was the first state to adopt a radically democratic constitution, with a unicameral assembly elected annually by all free male taxpayers. North Carolina, Georgia, and Vermont followed the Pennsylvania model. Indeed, Vermont went even further and became the first state to adopt universal manhood suffrage. At the other extreme, South Carolina and Maryland created a conservative set of institutions designed to keep citizens and rulers as far apart as possible. The other states adopted constitutional systems somewhere in the middle.

## DECLARATIONS OF RIGHTS

One of the most important innovations of the state constitutions were the guarantees of rights patterned on the Virginia "Declaration of Rights" of June 1776. Written by George Mason—a wealthy planter, democrat, and brilliant political philosopher—the Virginia declaration set a distinct tone in its very first article: "That all men are by nature equally free and independent, and have certain inherent rights, namely, the enjoyment of life and liberty, with the means of acquiring and possessing property and pursuing and obtaining happiness and safety." The fifteen articles of the Virginia Declaration declared, among other things, that sovereignty resided in the people, that government was the servant of the people, and that the people had the "right to reform, alter, or abolish" that government. There were guarantees of due process and trial by jury in criminal prosecutions, as well as prohibitions against excessive bail and "cruel and unusual punishment." Freedom of the press was guaranteed as "one of the great bulwarks of liberty," and the people were assured of "the free exercise of religion, according to the dictates of conscience."

Eight state constitutions included a general declaration of rights similar to the first article of the Virginia declaration; others incorporated specific guarantees. A number of states proclaimed the right of the people to engage in free speech and free assembly, to instruct their representatives, and to petition for the redress of grievances—rights either inadvertently or deliberately omitted from Virginia's declaration. These declarations were important precedents for the **Bill of Rights**, the first ten amendments to the federal Constitution of 1789. Indeed, George Mason of Virginia would be the leader of the democrats who insisted that the Constitution stipulate such rights.

## THE SPIRIT OF REFORM

The political upheaval of the Revolution raised the possibility of other reforms in American society. The New Jersey constitution of 1776 granted the vote to "all inhabitants of this colony, of full age, who are worth fifty pounds . . . and have resided within the county . . . for twelve months," thus enfranchising women as well

**5–13**
*Territorial Governments are Established by Congress* (1787)

**6–1**
*Constitution of Pennsylvania* (1776)

**6–2**
John Adams, *A Declaration of the Rights of the Inhabitants of the Commonwealth of Massachusetts* (1780)

**Bill of Rights** A written summary of inalienable rights and liberties.

**By giving the** vote to "all free inhabitants," the 1776 constitution of New Jersey enfranchised women as well as men who met the property requirements. The number of women voters eventually led to male protests. Wrote one: "What tho' we read, in days of yore, / The woman's occupation / Was to direct the wheel and loom, / Not to direct the nation." In 1807, a new state law explicitly limited the right of franchise to "free white male citizens."

as men. Because married women could own no property in their own names, only single women voted in New Jersey, but large numbers of them participated in elections and spoke out on political issues. There were male protests of this "irregular" situation, and in 1807 the legislature passed a law explicitly limiting the right to vote to "free white male citizens."

The New Jersey controversy was something of an anomaly, yet women's participation in the Revolution wrought subtle but important changes. In the aftermath of the Revolution, there was evidence of increasing sympathy in the courts for women's property rights and fairer treatment of women's petitions for divorce. And the postwar years witnessed an increase in opportunities for women seeking an education. From a strictly legal and political point of view, the Revolution may have done little to change women's role in society, but it did seem to help change expectations.

The most steadfast reformer of the day was Thomas Jefferson, who after completing work on the Declaration of Independence returned to Virginia to take a seat in its House of Delegates. In 1776 he introduced a bill in the Virginia legislature abolishing entail (restriction of inheritance to particular heirs in order that landed property remain undivided) and primogeniture (the inheritance of all the family property by the firstborn son), legal customs long in effect in aristocratic England that Jefferson believed had no place in a republican society. Jefferson's reform of inheritance law passed and had a dramatic effect. By 1798, every state had followed Virginia's lead.

Jefferson's other notable success was his **Bill for Establishing Religious Freedom**. He considered it one of his greatest accomplishments. At the beginning of the Revolution, there were established churches—denominations officially supported and funded by the government—in nine of the thirteen colonies. Many Anglican clergymen harbored Loyalist sympathies, and as part of an anti-Loyalist backlash, New York, Maryland, the Carolinas, and Georgia had little difficulty passing acts that disestablished the Anglican Church. In Virginia, however, many planters viewed Anglicanism as a bulwark against Baptist and Methodist democratic thinkers, resulting in bitter and protracted opposition to Jefferson's bill. It did not pass until 1786.

Jefferson proposed several more reforms of Virginia law, all of which failed to pass. He would have created a system of public education, revised the penal code to restrict capital punishment to the crimes of murder and treason, and established the gradual emancipation of slaves by law. On the whole, Jefferson and the Revolutionary generation were more successful at raising questions than at accomplishing reforms. The problems of penal reform, public education, and slavery remained for later generations of Americans to resolve.

## AFRICAN AMERICANS AND THE REVOLUTION

For most African Americans there was little to celebrate, for the American victory guaranteed the continuation of slavery as an institution. Few people were surprised when thousands of black fighters and their families departed with the Loyalists and the British at the end of the war, settling in the West Indies, Canada, and Africa. Most of

**Bill for Establishing Religious Freedom** A bill authored by Thomas Jefferson establishing religious freedom in Virginia.

these refugees were fugitive slaves rather than committed Loyalists. In Virginia alone, some 30,000 slaves fled during the Revolution.

There was an obvious contradiction in waging a war for liberty while continuing to support the institution of slavery. "How is it," English critic and essayist Samuel Johnson asked pointedly in 1775, "that we hear the loudest yelps for liberty among the drivers of Negroes?" The contradiction was not lost on Washington, who during the Revolution began to agonize over the morality of slavery. He was not alone. Revolutionary idealism, in combination with a shift away from tobacco farming, weakened the commitment of many Chesapeake planters to the slave system. After the Revolution, a sizable number of Virginians granted freedom to their slaves, and there was a small but important movement to encourage gradual emancipation by convincing masters to free their slaves in their wills.

George Washington was one of them, making a will that not only freed several hundred slaves upon his death but also included an elaborate plan for apprenticeship and tenancy for the able-bodied, and lodging and pensions for the aged. Planters in the Lower South, however, heavily dependent as they were on slave labor, resisted the growing calls for an end to slavery. Between 1776 and 1786 all the states but South Carolina and Georgia prohibited or heavily taxed the international slave trade, and this issue became an important point of conflict at the **Constitutional Convention** in 1787 (see Chapter 8).

Perhaps the most important result of this development was the growth of the free African American population. From a few thousand in 1750, their number grew to more than 200,000 by the end of the century. The increase was most notable in the Upper South. Largely excluded from the institutions of white Americans, the African American community now had enough strength to establish schools, churches, and other institutions of its own. At first, this development was opposed by whites. In Williamsburg, Virginia, for instance, the leader of a black congregation was seized and whipped when he attempted to gain recognition from the Baptist Association. But by the 1790s the Williamsburg African Church had grown to over 500 members, and the Baptist Association reluctantly recognized it. The incorporation of the word "African" in the names of churches, schools, and mutual benefit societies reflected the pride African Americans took in their heritage.

In the North, slavery was first abolished in the state constitution of Vermont in 1777, in Massachusetts in 1780, and New Hampshire in 1784. Pennsylvania, Connecticut, and Rhode Island adopted systems of gradual emancipation during these years, freeing the children of slaves at birth. By 1804, every northern state had provided for abolition or gradual emancipation, although as late as 1810, 30,000 African Americans remained enslaved in the North.

During the era of the Revolution, a small group of African American writers rose to prominence. Benjamin Banneker, born free in Maryland, where he received an education, became one of the most accomplished mathematicians and astronomers of late eighteenth-century America. In the 1790s, he published a popular almanac that both white and black Americans consulted. Jupiter Hammon, a New York slave, took up contemporary issues in his poems and essays, one of the most important of which was his "Address to the Negroes of the State of New York," published in 1787. But the most famous African American writer was Phyllis Wheatley, who came to public attention when her *Poems on Various Subjects, Religious and Moral* appeared in London in 1773, while she was still serving as a domestic slave in Boston. Kidnapped in Africa as a young girl and converted to Christianity during the Great Awakening, Wheatley wrote poems combining piety with a concern

**This portrait of** the African American poet Phyllis Wheatley was included in the collection of her work published in London in 1773, when she was only twenty years old. Kidnapped in Africa when a girl, then purchased off the Boston docks, she was more like a daughter than a slave to the Wheatley family. She later married and lived as a free woman of color before her untimely death in 1784.

## QUICK REVIEW

**African Americans and the Revolution**

- Revolutionary principles sparked some to challenge slavery.
- More than 50,000 slaves gained freedom as result of the war.
- By 1800 free black population reached 100,000.

**Constitutional Convention**
Convention of delegates from the colonies that first met to organize resistance to the Intolerable Acts.

## CHRONOLOGY

| | |
|---|---|
| 1775 | Lord Dunmore, royal governor of Virginia, appeals to slaves to support Britain |
| 1776 | July: Declaration of Independence |
| | August: Battle of Long Island initiates retreat of Continental Army |
| | September: British land on Manhattan Island |
| | December: George Washington counterattacks at Trenton |
| 1777 | Slavery abolished in Vermont |
| | September: British General William Howe captures Philadelphia |
| | October: British General John Burgoyne surrenders at Saratoga |
| | November: Continentals settle into winter quarters at Valley Forge |
| | December: France recognizes American independence |
| 1778 | June: France enters the war |
| | June: Battle of Monmouth hastens British retreat to New York |
| | July: George Rogers Clark captures Kaskaskia |
| | December: British capture Savannah |
| 1779 | Spain enters the war |
| 1780 | February: British land at Charleston |
| | July: French land at Newport |
| | September: British General Charles Cornwallis invades North Carolina |
| 1781 | March: Articles of Confederation ratified |
| | May: Robert Morris appointed secretary of finance |
| | October: Cornwallis surrenders at Yorktown |
| 1782 | Peace talks begin |
| 1783 | March: Washington mediates issue of officer pensions |
| | September: Treaty of Paris signed |
| | November: British evacuate New York |
| 1784 | Treaty of Fort Stanwix |
| | Postwar depression begins |
| 1785 | Land Ordinance of 1785 |
| | Treaty of Fort McIntosh |
| 1786 | Jefferson's Bill for Establishing Religious Freedom |

for her people. Writing to the Mohegan Indian minister Samuel Occom in 1774, Wheatley penned a line that not only applied to African Americans but also to all Americans struggling to be free. "In every human breast God has implanted a principle, which we call love of freedom; it is impatient of oppression, and pants for deliverance. The same principle lives in us."

## CONCLUSION

The Revolution was a tumultuous era, marked by violent conflict between Patriots and Loyalists, masters and slaves, settlers and Indian peoples. The advocates of independence emerged successfully, largely because of their ability to pull together and consolidate their identification with the national community. Fearful of the power of central authority, however, Americans created a relatively weak national government. People identified strongly with their local and state communities, and these governments became the site for most of the struggles over political direction that characterized the Revolution and its immediate aftermath. But not all problems, it turned out, could be solved locally. Within a very few years, the nation would sink into a serious economic depression that sorely tested the resources of local communities. By the mid-1780s, many American nationalists were paraphrasing the question Washington had asked at Valley Forge in 1777: "What then is to become of this nation?"

## REVIEW QUESTIONS

1. Assess the relative strengths of the Patriots and the Loyalists in the American Revolution.

2. What roles did Indian peoples and African Americans play in the Revolution?

3. Describe the structure of the Articles of Confederation. What were its strengths and weaknesses?

4. How did the Revolution affect politics within the states?

5. What was the effect of the Revolution on African Americans?

## KEY TERMS

**Articles of Confederation** (p. 166)
**Bill for Establishing Religious Freedom** (p. 176)
**Bill of Rights** (p. 175)
**Constitution** (p. 159)
**Continental Army** (p. 157)

**Constitutional Convention** (p. 177)
**Land Ordinance of 1785** (p. 172)
**Loyalists** (p. 159)
**Northwest Ordinance of 1787** (p. 172)
**Patriots** (p. 157)
**Tories** (p. 159)

myhistorylab
**Flashcard Review**

## RECOMMENDED READING

Carol Berkin, *Revolutionary Mothers: Women in the Struggle for America's Independence* (2005). Uses a topical and biographical approach to introduce to general readers women's experiences during the Revolution.

Merrill Jensen, *The New Nation: A History of the United States during the Confederation, 1781–1789* (1950). Still the standard work on the 1780s.

Max M. Mintz, *Seeds of Empire: The American Revolutionary Conquest of the Iroquois* (1999). The Revolution as a war for the control of Iroquois lands in upstate New York.

John W. Pulis, *Moving On: Black Loyalists in the Afro-Atlantic World* (1999). Essays on their military role and especially on their communities in Canada, Great Britain, and Africa. In each place, they remained second-class citizens.

Charles Royster, *A Revolutionary People at War* (1979). A pathbreaking study of the Continental Army and popular attitudes toward it. Emphasizes the important role played by the officer corps and the enlisted men in the formation of the first nationalist constituency.

Henry Wiencek, *Imperfect God: George Washington, His Slaves, and the Creation of America* (2003). An award-winning study of Washington's changing attitude toward slavery.

myhistorylab™
Where it's a good time to connect to the past!

For study resources for this chapter, go to **www.myhistorylab.com** and choose *Out of Many, Teaching and Learning Classroom Edition.* You will find a wealth of study and review material for this chapter, including pretests and posttests, customized study plan, key-term review flash cards, interactive map and document activities, and documents for analysis.

*Here individuals of all nations
are melted into a new race of men,
whose labours and posterity will one day
cause great changes in the world.*
—Hector St. John Crèvecoeur

**Congress voting on the issue of independence.**

PHILLIS WHEATLEY NEGRO SERVANT to Mr JOHN WHEATLEY of BOSTON

# 8

# THE NEW NATION
## 1786–1800

**WHAT WERE** the tensions and conflicts between local and national authorities in the decades after the American Revolution?

GENERAL GEORGE WASHINGTON.
Reviewing the Western army at Fort Cumberland, the 18th of October 1794

**HOW DID** Americans differ in their views of the new Constitution, and how were those differences reflected in the struggle to achieve ratification?

**WHAT WERE** the essential structures of national government under the Constitution?

**HOW DID** American political parties first begin?

**WHAT WERE** the first stirrings of an authentic American national culture?

1786  1800

# AMERICAN COMMUNITIES

## A Rural Massachusetts Community Rises in Defense of Liberty

SEVERAL HUNDRED FARMERS FROM THE TOWN OF PELHAM AND SCORES of other rural communities in western Massachusetts converged on the courthouse in Northampton, the county seat, before sunrise on Tuesday, August 29, 1786. They arrived in military formation, fifes playing and drums beating, armed with muskets, broadswords, and cudgels, the men's tricorner hats festooned with sprigs of evergreen, symbols of freedom frequently worn by Yankee soldiers during the war for independence, which had concluded only four years before. At least a third of the men and virtually all their officers were veterans. The country was in the midst of an economic depression that had hit farm communities particularly hard. Two-thirds of the men who marched on Northampton had been sued for debt, and many had spent time in debtor's prison. Dozens of rural towns petitioned the state government for relief, but not only did the merchant-dominated legislature reject their pleas, but also it raised the property tax in order to pay off the enormous debt the state had accumulated during the Revolution. The new tax was considerably more oppressive than any levied by the British and was considered even more odious, since the revenue would go to a small group of wealthy eastern Massachusetts creditors, to whom the debt was owed.

The farmers decided to take matters into their own hands. When outsiders threatened a man's property, they argued, the community had the right, indeed the duty, to rise up in defense. During the Revolution, armed men had marched on the courts, shutting down the operation of government, and now they were doing it again. The judges of the Northampton court had no choice but to shut down, and that success led to similar actions in many other Massachusetts counties.

This uprising quickly became known as Shays' Rebellion, named for Daniel Shays, a decorated Revolutionary officer and one of the leaders from the town of Pelham. Although rebellion was most widespread in the state of Massachusetts, similar disorders occurred in the country districts of New Hampshire, Vermont, Pennsylvania, Maryland, and Virginia. Conservatives around the country were thrown into panic.

Washington and other conservative leaders saw Shays' Rebellion as a class conflict pitting poor against rich, debtor against creditor. Yet the residents of Pelham and other rural towns acted in common, without regard to rank or property. Big farmers and small farmers alike marched on the county court. They came from tight-knit communities, bound together by family and kinship. Whether well-to-do or poor, they considered themselves "husbandmen," and they directed their protest against "outsiders," the urban residents of Boston and other coastal towns. "I am a man that gets his living by hard labor," one rebel announced, "and I think that husbandry is as honest a calling as any in the world." The country would be a lot better off, he concluded, "if there were less white shirts and more black frocks."

The crisis in Massachusetts ended when a militia force raised by the "white shirts" in the eastern part of the state, and financed by the great merchants, marched west and crushed the Shaysites in January 1787. Daniel Shays fled the state and never returned. Fifteen of the leaders were tried and sentenced to death. Two were hanged before the remainder were pardoned, and some four thousand other farmers temporarily lost their right to vote, to sit on juries, or to hold office. Yet many of them considered their rebellion a success. The next year Massachusetts voters rejected the old governor and elected a new legislature, which passed a moratorium on debts and cut taxes to only 10 percent of what they had been.

The most important consequence of Shays' Rebellion, however, was its effect on conservative nationalists unhappy with the distribution of power between the states and national governments under the Articles of Confederation. The uprising "wrought prodigious changes in the minds of men respecting the powers of government," noted Henry Knox. "Everybody says they must be strengthened and that unless this shall be effected, there is no security for liberty and property." Popular participation had been a necessity during the Revolution. But now the time had come, he declared, "to clip the wings of a mad democracy."

The economic and political crisis of the 1780s would lead to the Constitutional Convention and a new charter for a national state. It would be enthusiastically supported by many, passionately opposed by many others. Its ratification would bring a new and stronger government to power, headed by the leaders of the Revolution. Before the end of the century, that government would lay the groundwork for the longest-lived democratic republic in the world.

Pelham

**5–14**
Daniel Gray, *Massachusetts Farmers Take Up Arms in Revolt Against Taxes, 1786*

180
150
200
300

# THE CRISIS OF THE 1780S

The depression of the mid-1780s and the political protests it generated were instrumental in the development of strong nationalist sentiment among elite circles. In the aftermath of Shays' Rebellion, these sentiments coalesced into a powerful political movement dedicated to strengthening the national government.

## THE ECONOMIC CRISIS

The economic crisis that produced Shays' Rebellion had its origins in the Revolution. The shortage of goods resulting from the British blockade, the demand for supplies by the army and the militias, and the flood of paper currency issued by the Confederation Congress and the states combined to create the worst inflation in American history (see Figure 8.1). Most of this paper money ended up in the hands of merchants who had paid only a fraction of its face value.

After the war ended, inflation gave way to depression. Political revolution could not alter economic realities: the independent United States continued to be a supplier of raw materials and an importer of manufactured products, and Great Britain remained the country's most important trading partner. In 1784, British merchants began dumping goods in the American market, offering easy terms of credit. But the production of exportable goods had been drastically reduced by the fighting, and thus the trade deficit with Britain for the period 1784–86 rose to approximately £5 million (see Figure 8.2). The deficit acted like a magnet, drawing hard currency from American accounts, leaving the country with little silver or gold coin in circulation. Commercial banks insisted on the repayment of old loans and refused to issue new ones. By the end of 1784, the country had fallen into the grip of economic depression, and within two years, prices had fallen by 25 percent.

The depression struck while the nation was attempting to dig out from the huge mountain of debt incurred during the Revolution. Creditors were owed more than $75 million by national and state governments. Not allowed to raise taxes on its own, the Confederation Congress requisitioned the states for the funds necessary for debt repayment. The states in turn taxed their residents. At a time when there was almost no money in circulation, ordinary Americans feared being crushed by the burden of private debt and public taxes. The economic problem became a political problem.

WHAT WERE the tensions and conflicts between local and national authorities in the decades after the American Revolution?

myhistorylab
Review Summary

**Figure 8.1 Postwar Inflation, 1777–80: The Depreciation of Continental Currency**
The flood of Continental currency issued by Congress, and the shortage of goods resulting from the British blockade, combined to create the worst inflation Americans have ever experienced. Things of no value were said to be "not worth a Continental."

John McCusker, "How Much Is That in Real Money?" *Proceedings of the American Antiquarian Society*, N.S. 102 (1992): 297–359.

 6–6
*Shays' Rebellion: Letters of Generals William Shepard and Benjamin Lincoln to Governor James Bowdoin of Massachusetts (1787)*

**Figure 8.2 The Trade Deficit with Great Britain**
The American trade deficit with Great Britain rose dramatically with the conclusion of the Revolution.

*Historical Statistics of the United States* (Washington, DC: Government Printing Office, 1976), 1176.

## IMAGE KEY
for pages 180–181

a. The Articles of Confederation.
b. Congress voting on the issue of independence.
c. Phyllis Wheatley, an acclaimed African American poet.
d. The first Stars and Stripes, 1777.
e. The Bill of Rights–the first ten amendments to the U.S. Constitution.
f. A 1794 painting of President George Washington reviewing troops at Fort Cumberland.
g. John Adams in a framed painting by John Trumbull.
h. A 1792 cartoon from *Lady's Magazine* shows allegorical figure of "Columbia" receiving a petition for the "Rights of Woman."

**Annapolis Convention**  Conference of state delegates at Annapolis, Maryland, that issued a call in September 1786 for a convention to meet at Philadelphia to consider fundamental changes.

**HOW DID** Americans differ in their views of the new Constitution, and how were those differences reflected in the struggle to achieve ratification?

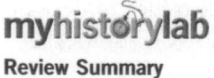

**myhistorylab**
**Review Summary**

### STATE REMEDIES

In the states, radicals called for regulation of the economy. Farmers and debtors pressed their state governments for legal tender laws, which required creditors to accept a state's paper currency at face value (rather than depreciated market value) for all debts public and private. Despite the opposition of creditors, seven states enacted such laws. For the most part, these were modest programs that worked rather well, caused little depreciation, and did not result in the problems creditors feared.

It was the plan of the state of Rhode Island, however, that received most of the attention. A rural political party campaigning under the slogan "To Relieve the Distressed" captured the legislature in 1786 and enacted a radical currency law. The supply of paper money issued in relation to the population was much greater under this program than in any other state. The law declared the currency legal tender for all debts. If creditors refused to accept it, debtors were allowed to satisfy their obligations by depositing the currency with a county judge, who would then advertise the debt as paid.

Some states erected high tariff barriers to curb imports and protect domestic industries. But foreign shippers found it easy to avoid these duties simply by unloading their cargo in states without tariffs and distributing the goods by overland transport. To be effective, commercial regulations had to be national. Local sentiment had to give way to the unity of a national community.

### TOWARD A NEW NATIONAL GOVERNMENT

In 1786 the legislature of Virginia invited all the states to appoint delegates to a convention where they might consider political remedies for the economic crisis. The meeting, held in Annapolis, Maryland, in September was sparsely attended (only twelve delegates from five states), but the men shared their alarm over the rebellion that was simultaneously taking place in Massachusetts, and the possibility of others like it. Convinced of the absolute necessity of strengthening the national government, the **Annapolis Convention** passed a resolution requesting that the Confederation Congress call on all the states to send delegates to a national convention that they might "render the constitution of the federal government adequate to the exigencies of the union." A few weeks later, with some reluctance, the Congress voted to endorse a convention, to be held in Philadelphia in May 1787, "for the sole and express purpose of revising the Articles of Confederation."

Conservatives had in mind more than simply a revision of the Articles, however. They looked forward to a considerably strengthened national government. Believing that the consolidation of power in a strong central government would better serve their interests as merchants, bankers, and planters, the conservatives hid their motives behind the call for revision of the Articles.

## THE NEW CONSTITUTION

In late May 1787, a few weeks after the suppression of Shays' Rebellion, fifty-five men from twelve states (the radical government of Rhode Island refusing to send a delegation) assembled at the Pennsylvania State House in Philadelphia. A number of prominent men were missing. Thomas Jefferson and John Adams were serving as ambassadors in Europe, and Patrick Henry of backcountry Virginia declared that he "smelt a rat." But most of America's best-known leaders were present. There were no ordinary farmers or artisans and, of course, no women, African Americans, or Indians. The Constitution was framed by white men who represented America's social and economic elite.

These men were patriots, however, and committed to republicanism: that government must rest on the consent of the governed, and that the authority of rulers must be conditional on popular support. But they were not democrats. They believed that the country already suffered from too much democracy. They feared that ordinary people, if given ready access to power, would enact policies against the interests of the privileged classes and, thus, the nation as a whole. The specter of Shays' Rebellion hung over the proceedings.

## THE CONSTITUTIONAL CONVENTION

On their first day of work, the delegates agreed to vote by states, as was the procedure of Congress. They chose Washington to chair the meeting. Although the sessions were closed to the public, James Madison, a young, conservative Virginian with a profound knowledge of history and political philosophy, took voluminous daily minutes that provide the best record of the proceedings. Madison and his fellow Virginians had drafted what became known as the **Virginia Plan**. Presented to the convention shortly after it convened, their plan set the agenda for the convention.

The Virginia Plan proposed scrapping the Articles of Confederation in favor of a "consolidated government" with the power to tax and to enforce its laws directly rather than through the states. The Virginia Plan would have reduced the states to little more than administrative institutions, something like counties. There would be a bicameral national legislature with all seats apportioned by population; members of the House of Representatives would be elected by popular vote, but members of the Senate chosen indirectly by state legislators, insulating them from democratic pressure. The Senate would lead, controlling foreign affairs and the appointment of officials. An appointed chief executive and a national judiciary would together form a Council of Revision having the power to veto both national and state legislation.

The main opposition to the Virginia Plan came from the delegates of the small states who feared being swallowed up by the large ones. After two weeks of debate, William Paterson of New Jersey introduced an alternative, a set of "purely federal" principles that became known as the **New Jersey Plan**. This plan also proposed increasing the powers of the central government but retained the single-house Congress of the Confederation government in which the states were equally represented. After much debate and a series of votes that split the convention down the middle, the delegates finally agreed to what has been called the **Great Compromise**. Representation would be proportional to population in the House, with equal representation to each of the states in the Senate. The compromise allowed for the creation of a strong national government while still providing an important role for the states.

Part of this Great Compromise was a second fundamental agreement between North and South. Southern delegates wanted protections for slavery. They wanted provision for the mandatory return of fugitive southern slaves from the free northern states. To boost their power in Congress, they wanted slaves counted for the purpose of determining a state's proportional representation but excluded from

**George Washington presides** over a session of the Constitutional Convention meeting in Philadelphia's State House (now known as Independence Hall) in an engraving of 1799.

 **6–8**
James Madison, *The "Distracting Question" in Philadelphia* (1787)

**Virginia Plan**   Proposal calling for a national legislature in which the states would be represented according to population.

**New Jersey Plan**   Proposal of the New Jersey delegation for a strengthened national government in which all states would have an equal representation in a unicameral legislature.

**Great Compromise**   Plan proposed at the 1787 Constitutional Convention for creating a national bicameral legislature in which all states would be equally represented in the Senate and proportionally represented in the House.

the apportioning of taxes. Northern delegates, who wanted a central government with the power to regulate commerce, agreed to count five slaves as the equivalent of three free men—the so-called "three-fifths rule"—in exchange for southern support for a "commerce clause," providing the federal government with the power to regulate commerce with foreign nations, among the several states, and with Indian tribes. Furthermore, representatives from South Carolina and Georgia demanded protection for the slave trade, and after bitter debate the delegates also agreed to include a provision preventing any federal restriction on the importation of slaves for twenty years.

The word "slave" appeared nowhere in the text. Instead the drafters employed phrases such as "persons held to labor." But these provisions amounted to national guarantees for southern slavery. Although a minority of delegates were opposed to slavery and regretted having to give in on this issue, they agreed with Madison, who wrote that "great as the evil is, a dismemberment of the union would be worse."

There was still much to decide regarding the other branches of government. Madison's Council of Revision was scratched in favor of a strong federal judiciary with the implicit power to declare unconstitutional acts of Congress. There were demands for a powerful chief executive, and Alexander Hamilton made the antirepublican proposal that the executive should be appointed for life, raising fears that the office might prove to be, in the words of Edmund Randolph of Virginia, "the fetus of monarchy." But there was considerable support for a president with veto power to check the legislature. To keep the president independent, the delegates decided he should be elected rather than appointed by the Congress, as was the procedure under the Articles of Confederation. But fearing that ordinary voters would never "be sufficiently informed" to select wisely, they insulated the process from popular choice by creating the electoral college. Voters in the states would not actually vote for president. Rather, each state would select a slate of "electors" equal in number to the state's total representation in the House and Senate. Following the general election, the electors in each state would meet to cast their ballots and elect the president.

The delegates voted their approval on September 17, 1787, and transmitted the document to the Confederation Congress, agreeing that it would become operative after ratification by nine states. A number of congressmen were outraged that the convention had exceeded its charge of simply modifying the Articles, but Congress agreed to issue a call for a special ratifying convention in each of the states.

## RATIFYING THE NEW CONSTITUTION

The supporters of the new Constitution immediately adopted the name Federalists to describe themselves. In this, as in much of the subsequent process of ratification, the Federalists (or nationalists) grabbed the initiative, and their opponents had to content themselves with the negative label Anti-Federalists (see Map 8.1). The critics of the Constitution were by no means a unified group. But most believed it granted far too much power to the central government, weakening the autonomy of local communities and states.

The argument between **Federalists** and **Anti-Federalists** played out in dozens of essays published in the popular press in 1787 and early 1788. It is doubtful, however, whether any of them made much of a difference in the voting to select delegates for the state ratification conventions. The alignment of forces generally followed the lines laid down during the fights over economic issues in the years since the Revolution.

**7–5**
Alexander Hamilton, *Opposing Visions for the New Nation* (1791)

---

**QUICK REVIEW**

**Central Government Under the Constitution**

- More powerful than Congress under the Articles of Confederation.
- Establishment of strong single person executive.
- Establishment of the Supreme Court.
- Expanded economic powers for Congress.

---

**myhistorylab**

**Exploring America:** *Ratifying the Constitution*

**6–17**
*The Constitution of the United States of America* (1789)

**Federalists**  Supporters of the Constitution who favored its ratification.

**Anti-Federalists**  Opponents of the Constitution in the debate over its ratification.

An agrarian-localist versus commercial-cosmopolitan alignment characterized most of the states. The most critical convention took place in Massachusetts in early 1788. Five states—Delaware, Pennsylvania, New Jersey, Georgia, and Connecticut—had already voted to ratify, but the states with the strongest Anti-Federalist movements had yet to convene. If the Constitution lost in Massachusetts, its fate would be in great danger.

At the Massachusetts convention, the opponents of ratification—which included supporters of Shays' Rebellion—enjoyed a small majority. But several important Anti-Federalist leaders, including Governor John Hancock and Revolutionary leader Samuel Adams, were swayed by the enthusiastic support for the Constitution among Boston's townspeople, whose livelihoods were tied to the commercial economy. On February 16, the convention voted narrowly in favor of ratification. To no one's surprise, Rhode Island rejected the Constitution in March, but Maryland and South Carolina approved it in April and May. On June 21, 1788, New Hampshire became the ninth state to ratify. The Constitution was now the law of the land.

New York, Virginia, and North Carolina were left with the decision of whether to join the new Union. Anti-Federalist support was strong in these states. North Carolina voted to reject. (It would reconsider and join the next year, followed by a still reluctant Rhode Island in 1790.) In New York the delegates were moved to vote their support by a threat from New York City to secede from the state and join the Union separately if the state convention failed to ratify. The Virginia convention was almost evenly divided, but promises to amend the Constitution to protect the people from the potential abuses of the federal government persuaded enough delegates to produce a victory for the Constitution. The promise of such a "Bill of Rights" was important in the ratification vote of five of the states.

## MAP EXPLORATION

To explore an interactive version of this map, go to
**http://www.prenhall.com/faraghertlc/map8.1**

**MAP 8.1**

**The Ratification of the Constitution, 1787–90**  The distribution of the vote for the ratification of the Constitution demonstrated its wide support in sections of the country linked to the commercial economy and its disapproval in more remote and backcountry sections. (Note that Maine remained a part of Massachusetts until admitted as a separate state in 1820.)

WHY DID some regions support the Constitution and others did not?

## THE BILL OF RIGHTS

The Constitutional Convention had considered a bill of rights patterned on the declarations of rights included in several state constitutions but then rejected it as superfluous. Anti-Federalist delegates in numerous state ratification conventions, however, had proposed a grab bag of over 200 potential amendments protecting the rights of the people against the power of the central government. In June 1789, James Madison, elected to the first Congress as a representative from Virginia, set about transforming these proposed amendments into a coherent series of proposals. Congress approved twelve and sent them to the states, and ten survived the ratification process to become the **Bill of Rights** in 1791.

The First Amendment prohibited Congress from establishing an official religion and provided for the freedom of assembly. It also ensured freedom of speech, a free press, and the right of petition. The other amendments guaranteed the right to bear arms, to limit the government's power to quarter troops in private homes, and to restrain the government from unreasonable searches or seizures; they guaranteed the traditional legal rights under the common law, including the prohibition of double

**7–1**
*James Madison Defends the Constitution* (1788)

**7–2**
William Maclay, *"For the Independent Gazetteer"* (1790)

Bill of Rights   The first ten amendments to the Constitution.

**A cartoon published** in July 1788, when New York became the eleventh state to ratify the Constitution. After initially voting to reject, North Carolina soon reconsidered, but radical and still reluctant Rhode Island did not join the Union until 1790.

The Federal Edifice "On the Erection of the Eleventh Pillar," caricature from the "Massachusetts Centinal," August 2, 1788. Neg. #33959. Collection of The New York Historical Society.

**WHAT WERE** the essential structures of national government under the Constitution?

myhistorylab
**Review Summary**

**6–4**
Henry Knox, *Letter to George Washington* (1786)

jeopardy, the right not to be compelled to testify against oneself, and due process of law before life, liberty, or property could be taken away. Finally, the unenumerated rights of the people were protected, and the powers not delegated to the federal government were reserved to the states.

The first ten amendments to the Constitution have been a restraining influence on the growth of government power over American citizens. Their provisions have become an admired aspect of the American political tradition throughout the world. The Constitution was authored by the Federalists, but the Bill of Rights is the most important legal legacy of the Anti-Federalists.

# THE FIRST FEDERAL ADMINISTRATION

Ratification of the Constitution was followed in the fall of 1788 by the first federal elections for Congress and the presidency, and in the spring of 1789 the new federal government assumed power. The first years under the new federal Constitution were especially important for the future because they shaped the structure of the American nation-state in ways that would be enormously significant for later generations.

## THE WASHINGTON PRESIDENCY

Although he dressed in plain American broadcloth at his inauguration and claimed to be content with a plain republican title, Washington was anything but a man of the people. By nature reserved and solemn, he chose to ride about town in a grand carriage drawn by six horses and attended by uniformed liverymen. In the tradition of British royalty, he delivered his addresses personally to Congress and received from both houses an official reply. On the other hand, Washington worked hard to adhere to the letter of the Constitution, refusing, for example, to use the veto power except where he thought Congress had acted unconstitutionally and personally seeking the "advice and consent" of the Senate.

Congress quickly moved to establish departments to run the affairs of state, and Washington soon appointed Thomas Jefferson as secretary of state, Alexander Hamilton as secretary of the treasury, Henry Knox as secretary of war (continuing in the position he held under the Confederation government), and

**Two coins from** the first decade of the federal republic illustrate political controversies of the period. The Washington cent was proposed by Treasury Secretary Alexander Hamilton in 1792, in the hope of enhancing popular respect for the new government by having the president's bust impressed on coins in the manner of European kings. But after long debate, Congress defeated the plan, the opponents claiming it smacked of monarchy. The Liberty coin, issued by the Mint of the United States in 1795, when under the authority of Secretary of State Thomas Jefferson, features Liberty wearing a liberty cap and bearing a marked resemblance to the French Revolutionary icon Marianne.

Edmund Randolph as attorney general. The president consulted each of these men regularly and during his first term met with them as a group to discuss matters of policy. By the end of Washington's presidency the secretaries had coalesced in what came to be known as the cabinet, an institution that has survived to the present despite the absence of constitutional authority. Washington understood the importance of national unity, and in his style of leadership, his consultations, and his appointments he sought to achieve a balance of conflicting political perspectives and sectional interests. His intentions would be sorely tested during the eight years of his administration.

## THE FEDERAL JUDICIARY

The most important piece of legislation to emerge from the first session of Congress was the **Judiciary Act of 1789**, implementing the judicial clause of the Constitution, which empowered Congress to set the number of justices on the Supreme Court and create a system of federal courts. The act established a High Court of six justices (increased to nine in 1869) and established circuit and district federal courts. Strong nationalists argued for a powerful federal legal system that would provide a uniform code of civil and criminal justice throughout the country. But the localists in Congress, intent on preserving local community autonomy, successfully fought to retain the various bodies of law that had developed in the states. The act gave federal courts limited original jurisdiction, restricting them mostly to appeals from state courts. But it established the principle of federal **judicial review** of state legislation, despite the silence of the Constitution on this point.

Washington appointed and the Senate confirmed the six Supreme Court justices, including John Jay, who became Chief Justice. During the Court's first decade it heard relatively few cases yet managed to raise considerable political controversy. In *Chisholm* v. *Georgia* (1793) the Court ruled in favor of two South Carolina residents suing the State of Georgia for the recovery of confiscated property, thus supporting the Constitution's grant of federal jurisdiction over disputes "between a state and citizens of another state." Many localists believed the ruling threatened the integrity of the states, and in response, they proposed an Eleventh Amendment to the Constitution, protecting states against suits by citizens of another state. It was ratified in 1798. The Supreme Court nevertheless established itself as the final authority on questions of law when it invalidated a Virginia statute in *Ware* v. *Hylton* (1796) and upheld the constitutionality of an act of Congress in *Hylton* v. *United States* (1796).

**Judiciary Act of 1789** Act of Congress that implemented the judiciary clause of the Constitution by establishing the Supreme Court and a system of lower federal courts.

**Judicial review** A power implied in the Constitution that gives federal courts the right to review and determine the constitutionality of acts passed by Congress and state legislatures.

**Alexander Hamilton (ca.** 1804) by John Trumbull. Although Hamilton's fiscal program was controversial, it restored the financial health of the United States.

## HAMILTON'S FISCAL PROGRAM

Fiscal and economic affairs were important in the new government. Lacking revenue and facing the massive national debt run up during the Revolution, the government took power in a condition of virtual bankruptcy.

Treasury Secretary Hamilton took on the task of reorganizing the nation's finances. In 1790 he submitted a "Report on the Public Credit," recommending the federal "redemption" at full value of the national debt owed to foreign and domestic creditors, as well as the "assumption" of the obligations accumulated by the states during the previous fifteen years. Congress readily agreed to settle the $11 million owed to foreign creditors but balked at the redemption of the domestic debt of $42 million and the assumption of the state debts of another $25 million. Hamilton proposed issuing new interest-bearing government bonds that would be exchanged for the full face value of all the notes, warrants, and securities the government had distributed during the Revolution.

Thousands of veterans had been rewarded for their service with warrants for land or money, but as they waited for Congress to mark out the territory or provide the funding, many had been forced by necessity to sell to speculators at deep discounts. Hamilton's proposal, his colleague James Madison objected, would result in windfall profits for speculators and create a permanent federal debt. Hamilton did not dispute these claims but instead argued that they were good things. The creation of a federal debt by the issue of securities would give the government the ability to finance national projects or provide for national defense in the event of war, and the possession of those securities in the hands of a wealthy class of citizens would offer a guarantee for the government's stability. There was even greater congressional opposition to Hamilton's proposal for the assumption of state debts. Some states (mostly in the South) had already arranged to pay off their debts, whereas others (mostly in the North) had not, so the plan seemed to reward the insolvent and punish the thrifty. Congress remained deadlocked on these issues for six months, until congressmen from Pennsylvania and Virginia arranged a compromise that facilitated the eventual passage of Hamilton's credit program.

Hamilton now proposed a second component of his fiscal program, the establishment of a Bank of the United States. The bank, a public corporation funded by private capital, would serve as the depository of government funds and the fiscal agent of the Treasury. Congress narrowly approved it, but Madison's opposition raised doubts in the president's mind about the constitutionality of the measure, and Washington solicited the opinion of his cabinet. Here for the first time were articulated the classic interpretations of constitutional authority. Jefferson took a "strict constructionist" position, arguing that the powers of the federal government must be limited to those specifically enumerated in the Constitution. This position came closest to the basic agreement of the men who had drafted the document. Hamilton, on the other hand, reasoned that the Constitution "implied" the power to use whatever means were "necessary and proper" to carry out its enumerated powers, the "loose constructionist" position. Persuaded by Hamilton's opinion, Washington signed the bill, and the bank went into operation in 1791.

The final component of Hamilton's fiscal program, out-lined in his famous "Report on Manufactures," was an ambitious plan, involving the use of government securities as investment capital for "infant industries" and high protective tariffs to encourage the development of an industrial economy. Congressmen from farming areas, whose previous objections to Hamilton's preference for the "monied interests" had not prevailed, were finally able to frustrate him on this last proposal. Hamilton's views, they argued, would limit them to roles exactly like those they had played within the British empire and would amount to exchanging British for Boston and New York masters. Of equal importance, the plan failed to inspire the enthusiasm of American capitalists, who continued to be more interested in investments in shipping or in land speculation than in industrial production.

Many of Hamilton's specific proposals for increased tariff protection, however, became part of the revision of duties that took place in 1792. Moreover, his fiscal program as a whole dramatically restored the financial health of the United States.

The Federalist political coalition, forged during the ratification of the Constitution, was sorely strained by these debates over fiscal policy. By the middle of 1792 Jefferson—representing southern agrarians—and Hamilton—speaking for northern capitalists—were locked in a full-scale feud within the administration. Hamilton conducted himself more like a prime minister than a cabinet secretary, greatly offending Jefferson, who considered himself the president's heir apparent. But the dispute went deeper than a mere conflict of personalities. Hamilton stated the difference clearly when he wrote that "one side appears to believe that there is a serious plot to overturn the State governments, and substitute a monarchy to the present republican system," while "the other side firmly believes that there is a serious plot to overturn the general government and elevate the separate powers of the States upon its ruins."

Distressed by these political disputes, Washington considered retiring at the end of his first term, but both factions encouraged him to remain in office to bridge their differences. The factions did contest the vice presidency. In December 1792 Washington was reelected by unanimous vote in the electoral college, but incumbent Vice President John Adams was only narrowly returned to office. It was an indication of things to come.

## AMERICAN FOREIGN POLICY

The conflict between Hamilton and Jefferson grew even more bitter over the issue of American foreign policy. The commanding event of the Atlantic world during the 1790s was the French Revolution, which broke out in 1789. Most Americans enthusiastically welcomed the fall of the French monarchy. But with the inauguration of the Reign of Terror in 1793, which claimed the lives of hundreds of aristocrats and politicians upon the guillotine, American conservatives began to voice their opposition. The execution of King Louis XVI in January 1793 and the outbreak of war between revolutionary France and monarchical Great Britain a few weeks later firmly divided American opinion.

Most at issue was whether the Franco-American alliance of 1778 required the United States to support France in its war with Britain. All of Washington's cabinet agreed on the importance of American neutrality. With France and Britain

**Little Turtle, a** war chief of the Miami tribe of the Ohio Valley, led a large pan-Indian army to victory over the Americans in 1790 and 1791. After his forces were defeated at the Battle of Fallen Timbers in 1794, he became a friend of the United States. This lithograph is a copy of an oil portrait, which no longer survives, by the artist Gilbert Stuart.

Little Turtle, or Mich-i-kin-i-qua, Miami War Chief, Conqueror of Harmar and St. Clair. Lithograph made from a portrait painted in 1797 by Gilbert Stuart. Indiana Historical Society Library (negative no. C2584).

**6–13**
Thomas Jefferson, *The Secretary of State and the Secretary of the Treasury Battle about the Constitution* (1791)

## QUICK REVIEW

**Hamilton's Reports**

- ◆ Plan to address Revolutionary War debt.
- ◆ Proposal to charter a national bank
- ◆ Recommendation for government to promote industry.

prowling for each other's vessels on the high seas, the vast colonial trade of Europe was delivered up to neutral powers, the United States prominent among them. Jefferson believed it highly unlikely that the French would call upon the Americans to honor the 1778 treaty and that the administration should simply wait and see. But Hamilton argued that so great was the danger of American involvement in the war that Washington should immediately declare the treaty "temporarily and provisionally suspended."

These disagreements revealed two contrasting perspectives on the course the United States should chart in international waters. Hamilton and the nationalists believed in the necessity of an accommodation with Great Britain, the most important trading partner of the United States and the world's greatest naval power. Jefferson, Madison, and their supporters, on the other hand, looked for more international independence, less connection with the British, and thus closer relations with Britain's traditional rival, France. They pinned their hopes for the future on American western expansion.

The debate in the United States grew hotter with the arrival in early 1793 of French ambassador Edmond Genêt. Knowing he must act before "Citizen" Genêt (as the ambassador was popularly known) compromised American sovereignty and involved the United States in a war with Britain, Washington issued a proclamation of neutrality on April 22, 1793. In it he assured the world that the United States intended to pursue "a conduct friendly and impartial towards the belligerent powers," while continuing to do business with all sides.

Hamilton's supporters applauded the president, but Jefferson's friends were outraged. Throughout the country, activists sympathetic to France organized Democratic Societies, political clubs modeled after the Sons of Liberty. Society members corresponded with each other, campaigned on behalf of candidates, and lobbied with congressmen.

Citizen Genêt miscalculated, however, alienating even his supporters, when he demanded that Washington call Congress into special session to debate neutrality. Jefferson, previously a confidant of the ambassador, now denounced Genêt as "hot-headed" and "indecent towards the President." But his words came too late to save his reputation with Washington, and at the end of 1793 Jefferson left the administration.

## THE UNITED STATES AND THE INDIAN PEOPLES

One of the most pressing problems of the Washington presidency concerned the West. The American attempt to treat western Indian tribes as conquered peoples after the Revolution had resulted only in further violence and warfare. In the Northwest Ordinance of 1787 (see Chapter 7), the Confederation Congress abandoned that course for a new approach. "The utmost good faith shall always be observed towards the Indians," the ordinance read. "Their lands and property shall never be taken from them without their consent." Yet the ordinance was premised on the survey and sale to American settlers of Indian land north of the Ohio River and the creation of new state governments. The ordinance pointed in wildly contradictory directions.

The new federal government continued to pursue this inconsistent policy. In 1790 Congress passed the **Intercourse Act**, the basic law by which the United States would "regulate trade and intercourse with the Indian tribes." The act declared public treaties between the United States and the Indian nations the only legal means of obtaining Indian land. Treaty making, thus, became the procedure for establishing and maintaining relations with Indian nations. To eliminate the abuses of unscrupulous traders, the act also created a federal licensing

**Intercourse Act**   Passed in 1790, this law regulated trade and intercourse with the Indian tribes and declared public treaties between the United States and Indian nations the only means of obtaining Indian lands.

system, and subsequent legislation authorized the creation of subsidized trading houses, or "factories," where Indians could obtain manufactured goods at reasonable prices. These provisions indicated the best intentions of the Washington administration.

On the other hand, one of the federal government's highest priorities was the acquisition of western Indian land to support a growing population of farmers (see Map 8.2). The federal government, in fact, was unable to control the flood of settlers coming down the Ohio River. In defense of their homelands, villages of Shawnees, Delawares, and other Indian peoples confederated with the Miamis under their war chief Little Turtle. In the fall of 1790 Little Turtle lured federal forces led by General Josiah Harmar into the confederacy's stronghold in Ohio and badly mauled them. In November 1791 the confederation inflicted an even more disastrous defeat on a large American force. More than 900 Americans were killed or wounded, making this the worst defeat of an army by Indians in North American history (see Seeing History).

## SPANISH FLORIDA AND BRITISH CANADA

The position of the United States in the West was made even more precarious by the hostility of Spain and Great Britain, which controlled the adjoining territories. Under the dynamic leadership of King Carlos III and his able ministers, Spain introduced liberal reforms to revitalize the rule-bound bureaucracy of its American empire. As a result the economy of New Spain grew rapidly in the 1780s. Moreover, Spain had reasserted itself in North America, acquiring the French claims to Louisiana before the end of the Seven Years' War, expanding into California, seizing the Gulf Coast during the American Revolution, and regaining Florida from Britain in the Treaty of Paris in 1783. Spain claimed for itself much of the territory that today makes up the states of Tennessee, Alabama, and Mississippi and pursued a policy designed to block the continued expansion of the young republic (see Map 8.3).

Spain's anti-American policy in the West had several facets. Controlling both sides of the lower Mississippi, the Spanish closed the river to American shipping, making it impossible for western American farmers to market their crops through the port of New Orleans. They also sought to create a barrier to American settlement by promoting immigration to Louisiana and Florida. They succeeded in attracting several thousand Acadians, whom the British had deported from Nova Scotia during the Seven Years' War. Reassembling their distinctive communities in the bayou country of Louisiana, these tough emigrants became known as the Cajuns.

But otherwise, the Spanish had little success with immigration and relied mostly on creating a barrier of pro-Spanish Indian nations in the lower Mississippi Valley.

North of the Ohio River, the situation was much the same. Thousands of Loyalists had fled the United States in the aftermath of the Revolution and settled

## MAP EXPLORATION

To explore an interactive version of this map, go to
**http://www.prenhall.com/faraghertlc/map8.2**

| | |
|---|---|
| ☐ | Areas settled by 1770 |
| ■ | Areas settled by 1790 |

**MAP 8.2**

**Spread of Settlement: The Backcountry Expands, 1770–90**   From 1770 to 1790, American settlement moved across the Appalachians for the first time. The Ohio Valley became the focus of bitter warfare between Indians and settlers.

WHY DID tensions between Indians and settlers increase during this period?

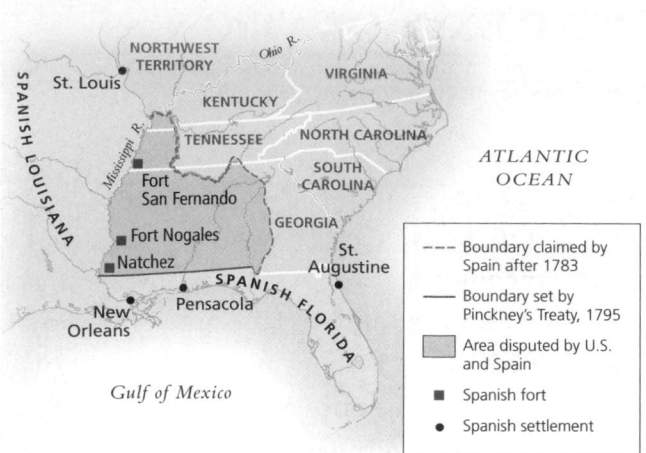

**MAP 8.3**

**Spanish Claims to American Territory, 1783–95** Before 1795, the Spanish claimed the American territory of the Old Southwest and barred Americans from access to the port of New Orleans, effectively closing the Mississippi River. This dispute was settled by Pinckney's Treaty in 1795.

WHAT WERE the terms of Pinckney's Treaty?

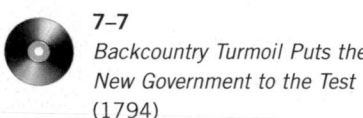

**7–7**
*Backcountry Turmoil Puts the New Government to the Test* (1794)

**Whiskey Rebellion** Armed uprising in 1794 by farmers in western Pennsylvania who attempted to prevent the collection of the excise tax on whiskey.

**Treaty of Greenville** Treaty of 1795 in which Native Americans in the Old Northwest were forced to cede most of the present state of Ohio to the United States.

north of lakes Ontario and Erie. They were understandably hostile to the new republic. In 1791 the British Parliament passed the Canada Act, creating the province of Upper Canada (later renamed Ontario) and granting the Loyalists limited self-government. To protect this province, British troops remained at a number of posts within American territory, such as Detroit, where they supplied arms to the Indian nations, in hopes of creating a buffer to American expansion.

## THE CRISES OF 1794

These conditions laid the groundwork for the gravest crisis of Washington's presidency in 1794. In the West, the inability of the federal government to subdue the Indians, eliminate the British from the northern fur trade, or arrange with the Spanish for unencumbered use of the Mississippi River stirred frontiersmen to loud protest. Secret agents for Great Britain and Spain sought to entice American settlers to quit the Union and join themselves to Canada or Florida. In the Atlantic, Great Britain declared a blockade of France and its colonies in the West Indies, and by early 1794 the Royal Navy had confiscated the cargoes of more than 250 American ships, threatening hundreds of merchants with ruin.

To make matters worse a rebellion broke out among farmers in western Pennsylvania in the summer of 1794. To produce needed revenue, Congress had placed an excise tax on the distillation of whiskey, which many farm families produced from their surpluses of corn. Throughout rural America, farmers protested that the new tax ran counter to the principles of the Revolution. "Internal taxes upon consumption," declared the citizens of Mingo Creek, in western Pennsylvania, are "most dangerous to the civil rights of freemen, and must in the end destroy the liberties of every country in which they are introduced." Protest turned to riot when the Mingo Creek militia attempted to seize the tax collector, and several of their number were killed in the confrontation.

The "**Whiskey Rebellion**" came at a time when Washington considered the nation to be under siege. The combination of Indian attack, international intrigue, and domestic insurrection, he believed, posed the greatest threat to the nation since the Revolution. He called up a federal army of 13,000 men, approximately the same size as the one he had commanded during the Revolution, and ordered the occupation of western Pennsylvania. Authorities arrested twenty people, and a judge convicted two of treason. The protests gradually died down and Washington pardoned the felons, sparing their lives. The president overreacted, for there was no organized insurrection in western Pennsylvania. Nevertheless, his mobilization of federal military power was a dramatic demonstration of his commitment to the preservation of the Union, the protection of the western boundary, and the supremacy of the national over the local community.

Washington's action was reinforced by an impressive American victory against the western Indian confederacy. Following the disastrous defeat inflicted by Little Turtle, the president directed General Anthony Wayne to lead a greatly strengthened American force to secure the Northwest. At the Battle of Fallen Timbers, fought in northern Ohio on August 20, 1794, Wayne crushed the Indians. This American victory set the stage for the **Treaty of Greenville** in 1795, in which the representatives of twelve Indian nations ceded a huge territory encompassing

# The Columbian Tragedy

Broadsides—large sheets printed on one side, suitable for posting—were an important medium of popular communication in the late eighteenth and early nineteenth centuries. This one, lamenting the disastrous defeat of an American expeditionary force at the hands of the Ohio Indian confederacy in 1791, in which more than 900 Americans were killed or wounded was published in Boston and sold throughout New England for the price of six cents. The struggle against the Ohio Indian confederacy was one of the most critical issues during Washington's presidency. Across the top are the names of the officers killed in battle, each accompanied by the icon of a black coffin. On the left is a woodcut of Major-General Richard Butler, the highest-ranking officer to die, and beneath it an Indian warrior alongside a skull and crossbones. On the right is a crude representation of the battleground. As one contemporary critic put it, all the images are "of the commonest description," yet the broadside survives in a number of copies, indicating that it probably sold quite well. The broadside did double duty—as both memorial for the dead and protest against the incompetence of the army's leaders. Most of the broadside is devoted to a mournful ballad that nevertheless concludes that the nation will ultimately prevail because "the *Lord* is on our side." ∎

**WHY WOULD** Americans purchase this broadside and display it in their homes?

"The Columbian Tragedy" (1791), courtesy Beinecke Rare Book and Manuscript Library, Yale University.

In this 1794 painting, President George Washington reviews some 13,000 troops at Fort Cumberland on the Potomac before dispatching them to suppress the Whiskey Rebellion. Washington's mobilization of federal military power dramatically demonstrated the federal commitment to the preservation of the Union and the protection of the western boundary.

Francis Kemmelmeyer, "General George Washington Reviewing the Western Army at Fort Cumberland the 18th of October 1794," after 1794. Oil on paper backed with linen, 18 1/8 × 23 1/8 . Courtesy of Winterthur Museum.

GENERAL GEORGE WASHINGTON.
Reviewing the Western army at Fort Cumberland the 18th of october 1794.

most of present-day Ohio, much of Indiana, and other enclaves in the Northwest, including the town of Detroit and the tiny village of Chicago.

## SETTLING DISPUTES WITH BRITAIN AND SPAIN

The strengthened American position in the West encouraged the British finally to settle their dispute with the United States so that they might concentrate on defeating republican France. Washington dispatched Chief Justice John Jay to London to arrange a settlement with the British, and in November 1794 Jay and his British counterpart signed an agreement providing for British withdrawal from American soil by 1796, for limited American trade with British colonies, and for "most-favored-nation" status (meaning that each nation would enjoy terms of trade equal to the best terms accorded any other nation). The treaty represented a solid gain for the young republic. With only a small army and no navy to speak of, the United States was in no position to wage war.

**Jay's Treaty** enshrined Hamilton's conception of American neutrality. Hamilton's opponents, on the other hand, were enraged at what they considered an accommodation with the British at the expense of the French. Moreover, Southerners were alienated by Jay's failure to negotiate compensation for masters whose slaves had fled to the British during the Revolution. Throughout the country opponents of the treaty organized protests and demonstrations. Chief Justice Jay joked he found his way across country by the light of his burning effigies. Nevertheless, the Senate, dominated by supporters of Hamilton, ratified the agreement in June 1795. In the House, a coalition of Southerners, Westerners, and friends of France attempted to stall the treaty by threatening to withhold the necessary appropriations. They demanded they be allowed to examine the diplomatic correspondence regarding the whole affair, but the president refused, establishing the precedent of "executive privilege" in matters of state.

The deadlock continued until late in the year, when word arrived that the Spanish had abandoned their claims to the territory south of the Ohio River.

**Jay's Treaty** Treaty with Britain negotiated in 1794 in which the United States made major concessions to avert a war over the British seizure of American ships.

Spain had declared war on revolutionary France but quickly suffered a humiliating defeat. Fearing the loss of its American empire, the Spanish found it expedient to come to an agreement with the Americans. In 1795 American envoy Thomas Pinckney negotiated a treaty setting the international boundary at the 31st parallel (the southern boundary of Mississippi and Alabama) and opening the Mississippi to American shipping. This treaty was compatible with the Jeffersonian conception of empire, and congressmen from the South and West were delighted with its terms. Administration supporters, however, demanded that the House agree in the matter of Jay's Treaty before the Senate would approve Pinckney's.

With the ratification of these important treaties, the United States established its sovereignty over the land west of the Appalachians and opened to American commerce a vast market extending from Atlantic ports to the Mississippi Valley. From a political standpoint, however, the events of 1794 and 1795 brought Washington down from his pedestal. Vilified by the opposition press, sick of politics, and longing to return to private life, Washington rejected the idea of a third term.

## WASHINGTON'S FAREWELL ADDRESS

During the last months of his term, Washington published a "Farewell Address" to the nation. In the best-remembered portion of the address, he urged that the United States seek commercial connections with all nations but "have with them as little political connection as possible." Why, he asked, "entangle our peace and prosperity in the toils of European ambition, rivalship, interest, humor, or caprice?" Looking forward, he expressed great concern about the growing acrimony between political factions, which, he argued, "agitates the community with ill-founded jealousies and false alarms, . . . and opens the door to foreign influence and corruption."

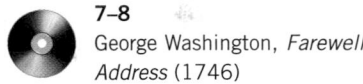

**7–8**
George Washington, *Farewell Address* (1746)

# FEDERALISTS AND DEMOCRATIC REPUBLICANS

The framers of the Constitution envisioned a one-party state in which partisan distinctions would be muted by patriotism and public virtue. "Among the numerous advantages promised by a well constructed Union," Madison had written, is "its tendency to break and control the violence of faction." Not only did he fail to anticipate the rise of political parties or factions, but also he saw them as potentially harmful to the new nation. Yet it was Madison who took the first steps toward organizing the opposition to the policies of the Washington administration, and it was Hamilton, Madison's coauthor of *The Federalist Papers*, who organized administration supporters into a disciplined political faction. Despite the intentions of the framers, in the twelve years between the ratification of the Constitution and the federal election of 1800, political parties became a fundamental part of the American system of government.

**HOW DID** American political parties first begin?

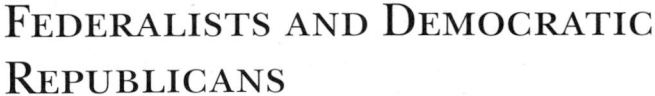

**Review Summary**

## THE RISE OF POLITICAL PARTIES

Evident in the debates and votes of Congress from 1789 to 1795 was a series of shifting coalitions. These coalitions first began to polarize into opposing political factions during the debate over Jay's Treaty in 1795, when agrarians, Westerners, Southerners, and supporters of France came together in opposition. By the time of the election of 1796, the factions had taken names for themselves.

# OVERVIEW | The First American Party System

| | |
|---|---|
| **Federalist Party** | Organized by figures in the Washington administration who were in favor of a strong federal government, friendship with the British, and opposition to the French Revolution; its power base was among merchants, property owners, and urban workers tied to the commercial economy. A minority party after 1800, it was regionally strong only in New England. |
| **Democratic Republican Party** | Arose as the opposition to the Federalists; its adherents were in favor of limiting federal power; they were sympathetic to the French Revolution and hostile to Great Britain; the party drew strength from southern planters and northern farmers and was the majority party after 1800. |

**myhistorylab**

**Overview:** *The First American Party System*

---

### QUICK REVIEW

**Party Politics**

◆ Washington's farewell address denounced partisanship.

◆ Candidates in presidential election of 1796: John Adams (Federalist), Thomas Jefferson (Republican).

◆ Adams won despite Hamilton's interference.

---

**XYZ Affair**   Diplomatic incident in 1798 in which Americans were outraged by the demand of the French for a bribe as a condition for negotiating with American diplomats.

---

Hamilton's supporters continued to claim the mantle of Federalism. But Jefferson's supporters christened themselves Republicans, suggesting by implication that the Federalists were really monarchists at heart. (Historians use the term "Democratic Republicans" to distinguish them from the modern Republican Party, founded in 1854.)

The two political factions played a fitful role in the presidential election of 1796, which pitted Vice President John Adams against Thomas Jefferson. Partisan organization was strongest in the Middle States, where there was a real contest of political forces, weakest in New England and the South, where sectional loyalty prevailed and organized opposition was weaker. The absence of party discipline was demonstrated when the ballots of the presidential electors, cast in their respective state capitals, were counted in the Senate. Adams was victorious, but in accordance with the Constitution the vice presidency went to the candidate with the second-highest total, and that was Jefferson. The new administration was born divided.

## THE ADAMS PRESIDENCY

Adams was put in the difficult situation of facing a political opposition led by his own vice president. On the other hand, Adams benefited from rising tensions between the United States and France. Angered by Jay's Treaty, the French suspended diplomatic relations with the United States at the end of 1796 and inaugurated a tough new policy toward American shipping. Hoping to resolve the crisis, Adams sent an American delegation to France. But in dispatches sent back to the United States, the envoys reported that three agents of the French foreign ministry had demanded a bribe before any negotiations could begin. Skeptical Republicans demanded the release of the dispatches, which Adams agreed to in 1798, substituting the letters X, Y, Z for the names of the French agents. The documents upheld Adams's case and proved a major liability for the Republicans, sparking powerful anti-French sentiment throughout the country. "Millions for defense, but not one cent for tribute!" was the slogan of the day. The **XYZ Affair**, as it became known, sent Adams's popularity soaring.

## THE ALIEN AND SEDITION ACTS

During the spring of 1798 Adams and the Federalists prepared the country for war with France. Congress authorized tripling the size of the army, and Washington came out of retirement to command the force. Fears of a French invasion declined

The presidential election of 1800 was the first to feature campaign advertising. "T. Jefferson, President of the United States of America; John Adams—no more," reads the streamer on this election banner, illustrated with an American eagle and a portrait of Jefferson. This was mild rhetoric in a campaign characterized by wild charges. The Republicans labeled Adams a warmonger and a monarchist, while the Federalists denounced Jefferson as an atheist, Jacobin, and sexual libertine.

after word arrived of a British naval victory over the French at Aboukir Bay in Egypt in August 1798, but what became known as the **"Quasi-War"** between France and the United States continued.

The Democratic Republicans contested the Federalist war measures and began for the first time to act as a genuine opposition party, complete with caucuses, floor leaders, and partisan discipline. They contested the election of Speaker of the House of Representatives, which henceforth became a partisan office. The more effective the Republicans became as an opposition, the more treasonous they appeared in the eyes of the Federalists.

In the summer of 1798 the Federalist majority in Congress, with the acquiescence of President Adams, passed four acts severely limiting both freedom of speech and the freedom of the press and threatening the liberty of foreigners in the United States. The Naturalization Act extended the period of residence required for citizenship from five to fourteen years. The **Alien Act** and the Alien Enemies Act authorized the president to order the imprisonment or deportation of suspected aliens during wartime. Finally, the **Sedition Act** provided heavy fines and imprisonment for anyone convicted of writing, publishing, or speaking anything of "a false, scandalous and malicious" nature against the government or any of its officers.

The Federalists intended these repressive laws as weapons to defeat the Democratic Republicans. They prosecuted dissent by indicting leading opposition newspaper editors and writers, fining and imprisoning at least twenty-five of them. The most vilified was Congressman Matthew Lyon of Vermont, scorned by Federalists as "Ragged Matt the Democrat." In July 1798 Lyon was convicted of publishing libelous statements about President Adams and thrown into prison. Later that year, he conducted a campaign from his jail cell and was reelected to Congress.

## THE REVOLUTION OF 1800

In 1799 the French convinced President Adams that they were willing to settle their dispute with the United States when they released seized American ships and requested negotiations. Adams sensed a public mood running toward peace. But the Hamiltonian wing of the party, always scornful of public sentiment, continued to beat the drums of war. When Federalists in Congress attempted to block

**7–9**
*The Alien and Sedition Acts*
(1798)

**7–10**
*Questions of Constitutionality and the Roots of Nullification*
(1798)

**Quasi-War**   Undeclared naval war of 1797 to 1800 between the United States and France.

**Alien Act**   Act passed by Congress in 1798 that authorized the president to imprison or deport suspected aliens during wartime.

**Sedition Act**   An act passed by Congress in 1798 that provided fines for anyone convicted of writing, publishing, or speaking out against the government or its officers.

**States' rights** Favoring the rights of individual states over rights claimed by the national government.

the negotiations, Adams threatened to resign and turn the government over to Vice President Jefferson.

The presidential campaign of 1800 was the first to be contested by two disciplined political parties. Caucuses of congressmen nominated respective slates: Adams and Charles Cotesworth Pinckney of South Carolina for the Federalists, Jefferson and Aaron Burr of New York for the Republicans. Both tickets thus represented attempts at sectional balance. The Democratic Republicans presented themselves as the party of traditional agrarian purity, of liberty and **states' rights**, of "government rigorously frugal and simple," in the words of Jefferson. The Federalists, divided and embittered, waged a defensive struggle for strong central government and public order and often resorted to negative campaigning. They denounced Jefferson as an atheist, a Jacobin, and the father of mulatto children.

Adams won in New England but elsewhere was overwhelmed (see Map 8.4). Jefferson called it "the Revolution of 1800." Party discipline was so effective, in fact, that it created a constitutional crisis. By casting all their ballots for Jefferson and Burr, Republican electors thoughtlessly produced a tie vote, thus forcing the election into the lame duck House of Representatives controlled by the Federalists. Eventually the Federalists arranged with their opponents to elect Jefferson without any of them having to vote in his favor. Afterward, Congress passed and the states ratified the Twelfth Amendment, creating separate ballots for president and vice president in time for the next presidential election.

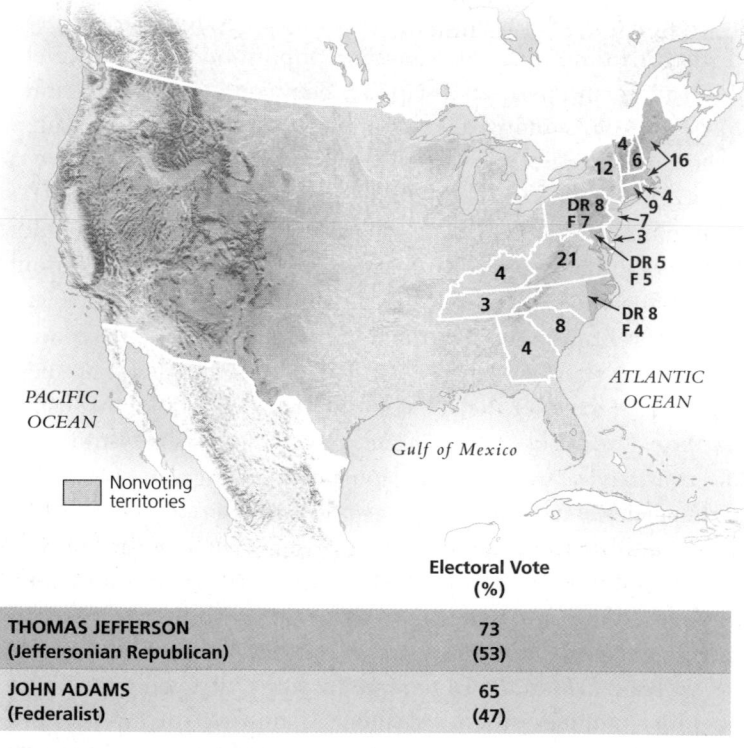

| | Electoral Vote (%) |
|---|---|
| **THOMAS JEFFERSON** (Jeffersonian Republican) | 73 (53) |
| **JOHN ADAMS** (Federalist) | 65 (47) |

**MAP 8.4**

**The Election of 1800** In the presidential election of 1800, Democratic Republican victories in New York and the divided vote in Pennsylvania threw the election to Jefferson. The combination of the South and these crucial Middle States would keep the Democratic Republicans in control of the federal government for the next generation.

WHAT WERE the key issues in the election of 1800?

## DEMOCRATIC POLITICAL CULTURE

Accompanying the rise of partisan politics was a transformation in popular political participation. Consider the custom of celebrating Independence Day. At the beginning of the 1790s, in many communities, the day featured demonstrations of military prowess by veteran officers, followed by banquets for leaders. Relatively few Americans played a direct role. But during the political controversies of the decade, a tradition of popular celebration developed. People took to the streets, set off fireworks, erected liberty poles, and listened to readings of the preamble of the Declaration of Independence, which more than any other document encapsulated and symbolized republican ideology.

There was a corresponding increase in the **suffrage**. In 1789 state regulations limited the franchise to a small percentage of the adult population. Women, African Americans, and Indians could not vote, but neither could a third to a half of all free adult males, who were excluded by tax-paying or property-owning requirements. Moreover, even among the eligible, the turnout was generally low.

The situation changed with the increasing competition between Democratic Republicans and Federalists. Popular pressure resulted in the introduction of universal white manhood suffrage in four states by 1800 and the reduction of property requirements in others. Thus was inaugurated a movement that would sweep the nation over the next quarter century. As a consequence voter turnout increased in all the states. The growth of popular interest in politics was a transformation as important as the peaceful transition from Federalists to Democratic Republicans in national government.

# "THE RISING GLORY OF AMERICA"

In 1771, Philip Freneau and Hugh Henry Brackenridge addressed their graduating class at Princeton on "The Rising Glory of America." Thus far American contributions to learning and the arts had been slim, they admitted, but they were boundlessly optimistic about the potential of their country.

## THE LIBERTY OF THE PRESS

At the beginning of the Revolution in 1775, there were thirty-seven weekly or semi-weekly newspapers in the thirteen colonies, only seven of which were Loyalist in sentiment. By 1789, the number of papers in the United States had grown to ninety-two, including eight dailies; three papers were being published west of the Appalachians. Relative to population, there were more newspapers in the United States than in any other country in the world—a reflection of the remarkably high literacy rate of the American people. During the political controversy of the 1790s, the press became the principal medium of Federalist and Jeffersonian Republican opinion, and papers came to be identified by their politics.

The prosecutions under the Sedition Act, however, threatened to curb the further development of the media, and in their opposition to these measures Democratic Republicans played an important role in establishing the principle of a free press. In *An Essay on Liberty of the Press* (1799), the Virginia lawyer George Hay, later appointed to the federal bench by President Jefferson, wrote that "a man may say everything which his passions suggest." Were this not true, he argued, the First Amendment would have been "the grossest absurdity that was ever conceived by the human mind." In his first inaugural address, Jefferson echoed this early champion of the freedom of expression. "Error of opinion

**Suffrage**   The right to vote in a political election.

**WHAT WERE** the first stirrings of an authentic American national culture?

**myhistorylab**
**Review Summary**

## CHRONOLOGY

1786    Annapolis Convention

1787    Constitutional Convention

1787–88    *The Federalist Papers* published

1788    Constitution ratified

First federal elections

1789    President George Washington inaugurated in New York City

Judiciary Act

French Revolution begins

1790    Agreement on site on the Potomac River for the nation's capital

Indian Intercourse Act

Judith Sargent Murray publishes *On the Equality of the Sexes*

1791    Bill of Rights ratified

Bank of the United States chartered

Alexander Hamilton's "Report on Manufactures"

Ohio Indians defeat General Arthur St. Clair's army

1792    Washington reelected

1793    England and France at war; America reaps trade windfall

Citizen Genêt affair

President Washington proclaims American neutrality in Europe

Supreme Court asserts itself as final authority in *Chisholm* v. *Georgia*

1794    Whiskey Rebellion

Battle of Fallen Timbers

Jay's Treaty with the British concluded

1795    Pinckney's Treaty negotiated with the Spanish

Treaty of Greenville

1796    President Washington's Farewell Address

John Adams elected president

1797–98    French seize American ships

1798    XYZ Affair

"Quasi-War" with France

Alien and Sedition Acts

1800    Convention of 1800

Thomas Jefferson elected president

Mason Locke Weems publishes *Life of Washington*

---

**myhistorylab**

**Exploring America:** *The Partisan Press*

### QUICK REVIEW

**The Press**

- By 1789 the United States had ninety-two newspapers.
- The press played a key role in the politics of the 1790s.
- Prosecutions under the Sedition Act threatened to curb further development of a free press.

may be tolerated," he declared, "where reason is left free to combat it." During Jefferson's presidency the Alien and Sedition Acts, which had justified the suppression of political opinion, were repealed or allowed to expire.

## BOOKS, BOOKS, BOOKS

During the post-Revolutionary years there was an enormous outpouring of American publications. In the cities the number of bookstores grew in response to the demand for reading matter. Perhaps even more significant was the appearance in the countryside of numerous book peddlers who supplied farm households with Bibles, gazettes, almanacs, sermons, and political pamphlets.

Some of the most interesting American books of the postwar years examined the developing American character. The French emigrant Michel-Guillaume Jean de Crevecoeur, in *Letters from an American Farmer* (1782), proposed that the American, a product of many cultures, was a "new man" with ideas new to the world. John Filson, the author of *The Discovery, Settlement, and Present State of Kentucke* (1784), presented the narrative of one such new man, the Kentucky pioneer Daniel Boone. In doing so, he took an important step toward the creation of that most American of literary genres, the western.

But for Americans, the most important "new man" was George Washington. In 1800, an itinerant bookseller, Mason Locke Weems, published a short biography of the first president that became the new nation's first best seller. Weems's *Life of Washington* introduced a series of popular and completely fabricated anecdotes, including the story of young Washington and the cherry tree. The biography was beloved by ordinary Americans of all political persuasions. Decades later, Abraham Lincoln recalled that he had read Weems "away back in my childhood, the earliest days of my being able to read," and had been profoundly impressed by "the struggles for the liberties of the country." Although Washington had in fact become a partisan leader of the Federalists during his second term, Weems presented him as a unifying figure for the political culture of the new nation, and that was the way he would be remembered.

## WOMEN ON THE INTELLECTUAL SCENE

One of the most interesting literary trends of the 1790s was the growing demand for books appealing to women readers. Susanna Haswell Rowson's *Charlotte Temple* (1791), a tale of seduction and abandonment, ran up tremendous sales and remained in print for more than a century. The young republic thus marked the first dramatic appearance of women writers and women readers. Although women's literacy rates continued lower than men's, they rose steadily as girls joined boys in common schools. This increase was one of the most important social legacies of the democratic struggles of the Revolutionary era.

Some writers argued that the new republican order ought to provide new roles for women as well as for men. The first avowed feminist in American history was Judith Sargent Murray. Her essay "On the Equality of the Sexes," written in 1779 and published in 1790, threw down a bold challenge to men. "Yes, ye lordly, ye haughty sex," she wrote, "our souls are by nature equal to yours," and predicted that American women would commence "a new era in female history." Federalists listened to such opinions with horror. "Women of masculine minds," one Boston minister sneered, "have generally masculine manners."

There seemed to be general agreement among all parties, however, that the time had come for women to be better educated. Republican institutions of self-government were widely thought to depend on the wisdom and self-discipline of the American people. Civic virtue, so indispensable for the republic, needed to be taught at home. Thus were women provided the opportunity to be not simply "helpmates" but also people "learned and wise." But they were also expected to be content with a narrow role, not to wish for fuller participation in the American experiment.

**Judith Sargent Murray,** a portrait by John Singleton Copley, completed in 1771. Born into an elite merchant family, she became a wife and mother but also a poet, essayist, playwright, novelist, and historian.

John Singleton Copley (1738–1815), "Portrait of Mrs. John Stevens (Judith Sargent, later Mrs. John Murray)," 1770–72. Oil on canvas, 50 × 40 in. Daniel J. Terra Art Acquisition Endowment Fund, 2000.6. © Terra Foundation for American Art, Chicago/Art Resource, New York.

**6–12**
Molly Wallace, *Valedictory Oration* (1792)

## CONCLUSION

During the last years of the eighteenth century, the United States adopted a new constitution and established a new national government. It repaid the debt run up during the Revolution and made peace with adversaries abroad and Indian peoples at home. Americans began to learn how to channel their disagreements into political struggle. The new government, born in the economic and political crisis that surrounded Shays' Rebellion, had withstood a first decade of stress, but tensions would continue to divide the people. At the beginning of the new century, it remained uncertain whether the new nation would find a way to control and channel the energies of an expanding people.

## REVIEW QUESTIONS

1. Discuss the conflicting ideals of local and national authority in the debate over the Constitution.

2. What were the major crises faced by the Washington and Adams administrations?

3. Describe the roles of Madison and Hamilton in the formation of the first American political parties.

4. What did Jefferson mean when he talked of "the Revolution of 1800"?

5. Discuss the contributions of the Revolutionary generation to the construction of a national culture.

## KEY TERMS

**myhistorylab**

Flashcard Review

| | |
|---|---|
| **Alien Act** (p. 199) | **New Jersey Plan** (p. 185) |
| **Annapolis Convention** (p. 184) | **Quasi-War** (p. 199) |
| **Anti-Federalists** (p. 186) | **Sedition Act** (p. 199) |
| **Bill of Rights** (p. 187) | **States' rights** (p. 200) |
| **Federalists** (p. 186) | **Suffrage** (p. 201) |
| **Great Compromise** (p. 185) | **Treaty of Greenville** (p. 194) |
| **Intercourse Act** (p. 192) | **Virginia Plan** (p. 185) |
| **Jay's Treaty** (p. 196) | **Whiskey Rebellion** (p. 194) |
| **Judicial review** (p. 189) | **XYZ Affair** (p. 198) |
| **Judiciary Act of 1789** (p. 189) | |

## RECOMMENDED READING

Akhil Reed Amar, *The Bill of Rights: Creation and Reconstruction* (1998). A legal analysis arguing that the first ten amendments were meant to protect the majority from the potential tyranny of the federal government.

Robert A. Dahl, *How Democratic Is the American Constitution?* (2003). An eminent political scientist examines the antidemocratic character of the nation's defining political document.

Stanley Elkins and Eric McKitrick, *The Age of Federalism* (1993). A massive and informative account of the politics of the 1790s, from the ratification of the Constitution to the election of Jefferson.

Paul Finkelman, *Slavery and the Founders: Race and Liberty in the Age of Jefferson* (2001). A persuasive historical argument that the Constitution legitimated a "slaveholders' republic."

Joanne B. Freeman, *Affairs of Honor: National Politics in the New Republic* (2001). A major reassessment of political culture in the new republic, stressing the importance of the culture of honor.

Reginald Horsman, *The Frontier in the Formative Years, 1783–1815* (1970). A sensitive survey of developments in the West, emphasizing that the "western question" was one of the most important facing the young republic.

Calvin H. Johnson, *Righteous Anger at the Wicked States: The Meaning of the Founders' Constitution* (2005). An argument that the authors of the Constitution were responding to the turmoil of the "wicked states," particularly their economic and fiscal policies.

Jackson Turner Main, *The Antifederalists: Critics of the Constitution, 1781–1788* (1961). A detailed examination of the localist tradition in early American politics. Includes a discussion of the ratification of the Constitution from the point of view of its opponents.

Simon P. Newman, *Parades and the Politics of the Street: Festive Culture in the Early American Republic* (1997). The participation of ordinary Americans in the political culture of the new republic.

Leonard L. Richards, *Shays' Rebellion: The American Revolution's Final Battle* (2002). A new interpretation that significantly broadens the meaning of the uprising of farmers in western Massachusetts.

James M. Smith, *Freedom's Fetters: The Alien and Sedition Laws and American Civil Liberties* (1966). Remains the best overview of the Federalist threat to liberty, as well as the Jeffersonian Republican counterattack.

Bernard A. Weisberger, *America Afire: Jefferson, Adams, and the Revolutionary Election of 1800* (2000). Shows that the election and the transfer of power were victories for popular self-government and that they set a major precedent for all other elections.

Gordon Wood, *The Creation of the American Republic, 1776–1787* (1969). This general survey provides the best overview of the Constitutional Convention.

Where it's a good time to connect to the past!

For study resources for this chapter, go to **www.myhistorylab.com** and choose *Out of Many, Teaching and Learning Classroom Edition.* You will find a wealth of study and review material for this chapter, including pretests and posttests, customized study plan, key-term review flash cards, interactive map and document activities, and documents for analysis.

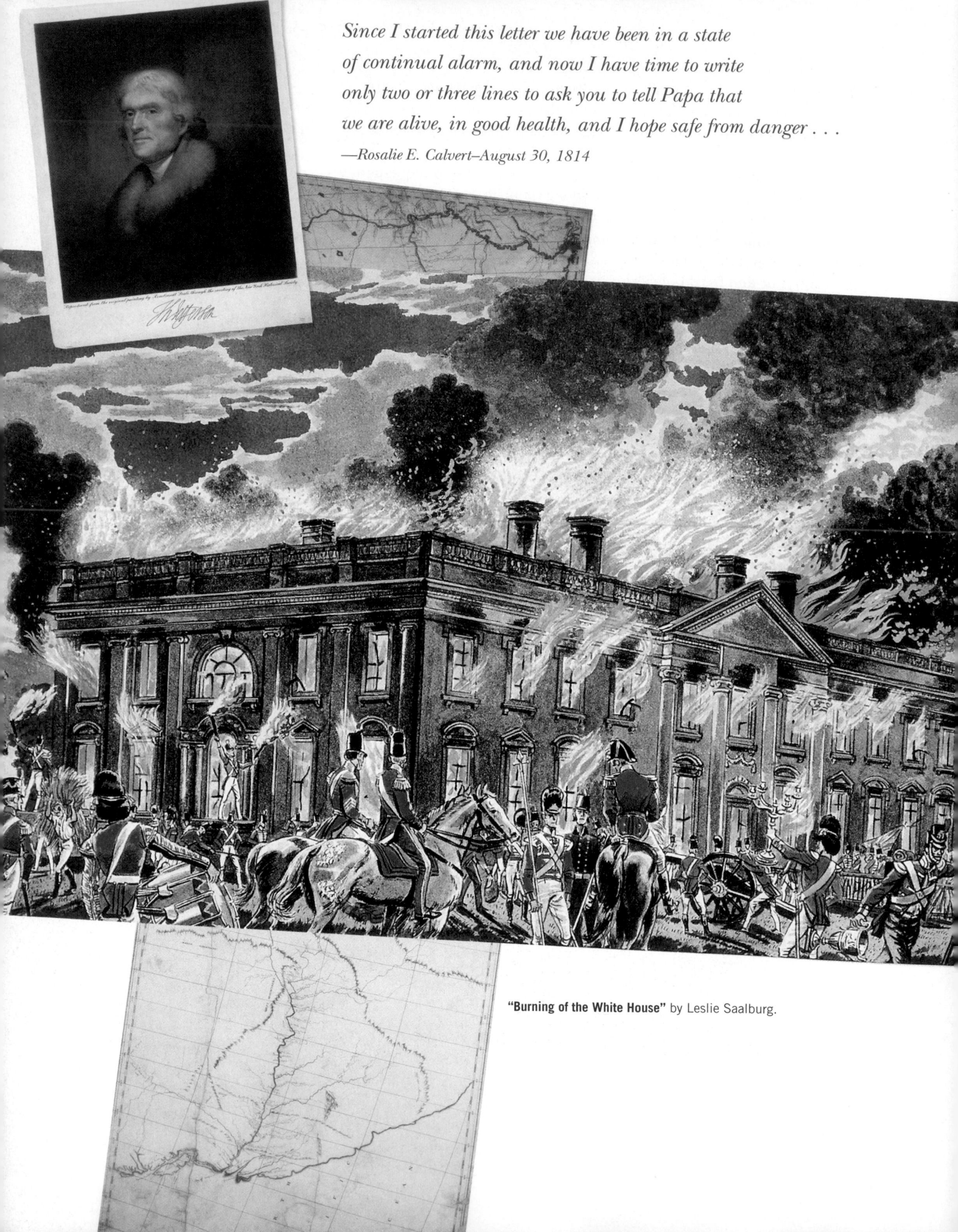

*Since I started this letter we have been in a state of continual alarm, and now I have time to write only two or three lines to ask you to tell Papa that we are alive, in good health, and I hope safe from danger . . .*
—Rosalie E. Calvert–August 30, 1814

**"Burning of the White House"** by Leslie Saalburg.

# 9

# AN EMPIRE FOR LIBERTY
## 1790–1824

**WITH WHAT** powers did the United States share North America in the decades after independence?

**WHAT WERE** the most important strengths of the American economy in the early 1800s?

**WHAT VALUES** were embodied in agrarian republicanism?

**WHAT FACTORS** led to conflict between the United States and Britain in North America?

**WHAT WERE** the consequences of the War of 1812?

**WHAT WERE** the principle provisions of the Missouri Compromise?

# AMERICAN COMMUNITIES

## Expansion Touches Mandan Villages on the Upper Missouri

IN MID-OCTOBER 1804, NEWS ARRIVED AT THE MANDAN VILLAGES, prominently situated on bluffs overlooking the upper Missouri River, that an American military party led by Meriwether Lewis and William Clark was coming up the river. The principal chiefs, hoping for expanded trade and support against their enemies the Sioux, welcomed these first American visitors. As the expedition's three boats and forty-three men approached the village, Clark wrote, "great numbers on both sides flocked down to the bank to view us." That evening, the Mandans welcomed the Americans with an enthusiastic dance and gifts of food.

Lewis and Clark had been sent by President Thomas Jefferson to survey the Louisiana Purchase and to find an overland route to the Pacific Ocean. They were also instructed to inform the Indians that they now owed loyalty—and trade—to the American government. Meeting with the village chiefs, the Americans offered the Mandans a military and economic alliance. His people would like nothing better, responded Chief Black Cat, for the Mandans had fallen on hard times over the past decade. [Some twenty years earlier], "the smallpox destroyed the greater part of the nation," the chief said. "All the nations before this malady [were] afraid of them, [but] after they were reduced, the Sioux and other Indians waged war, and killed a great many."

The Americans spent the winter with the Mandans, joining in their communal life and establishing firm and friendly relations with them. Lewis and Clark spent many hours acquiring important geographic information from the Mandans. The information provided by the Mandans and other Indian peoples to the west was vital to the success of the expedition. Lewis and Clark's "voyage of discovery" depended largely on the willingness of Indian peoples to share their knowledge of the land with the Americans.

In need of interpreters who could help them communicate with other Indian communities on their way, the Americans hired several multilingual Frenchmen who lived with the Mandans. They also acquired the services of Sacajawea, the fifteen-year-old Lemhi wife of one of the Frenchmen, who became the only woman to join the westward journey.

When the party left the Mandan villages in March, Clark wrote, his men were "generally healthy, except venereal complaints which is very common amongst the natives and the men catch it from them." After an arduous journey across the Rock-

ies, the party reached the Pacific Ocean at the mouth of the Columbia River, where they spent the winter. Overdue and feared lost, they returned in triumph to St. Louis in September 1806. Before long the Americans had established Fort Clark at the Mandan villages, giving American traders a base for challenging British dominance of the western fur trade. The permanent American presence brought increased contact, and with it much more disease. In 1837, a terrible smallpox epidemic carried away the vast majority of the Mandans, reducing the population to fewer than 150. Four Bears, a Mandan chief who had been a child at the time of the Lewis and Clark visit, spoke these last words to the remnants of his people:

"I have loved the whites," he declared. "I have lived with them ever since I was a boy." But in return for the kindness of the Mandans, the Americans had brought this plague. "I do not fear death, my friends," he said, "but to die with my face rotten, that even the wolves will shrink with horror at seeing me, and say to themselves, that is Four Bears, the friend of the whites. They have deceived me," he pronounced with his last breath. "Those that I always considered as brothers turned out to be my worst enemies."

In sending Lewis and Clark on their "voyage of discovery" to claim the land and the loyalty of the Mandans and other western Indian communities, President Jefferson was motivated by his vision of an expanding American republic of self-sufficient farmers. During his and succeeding presidencies, expansion became a key element of national policy and pride. Yet, as the experience of the Mandans showed, what Jefferson viewed as enlargement of "the empire for liberty" had a dark side—the destruction, from disease and coerced displacement, of the communities created by America's first peoples.

In the first quarter of the nineteenth century, the young American nation was preoccupied with defining its place on the North American continent and in the larger world of independent nations. At the same time that America found opportunities in world trade and in territorial expansion, it encountered international opposition from Britain and resistance at home from hard-pressed Indian nations. This chapter describes the ways in which, through war and diplomacy, the United States defined and controlled the nation's expanded boundaries, a vital step in building a sense of national identity and community.

Mandan Villages

# NORTH AMERICAN COMMUNITIES FROM COAST TO COAST

In spite of the political turmoil of the 1790s, the young United States entered the new century full of national pride and energy. But the larger issue, America's place in the world, was still uncertain, beginning with its situation on the North American continent (see Map 9.1).

## THE NEW NATION

At first glance, the United States of America in 1800 was little different from the scattered colonies of the pre-Revolution era. Two-thirds of the young nation's people still lived in a long thin line of settlement within fifty miles of the Atlantic coast. Most people lived on farms or in small towns. Because they rarely traveled far from home, peoples' horizons were limited and local.

Although only 3 percent of the nation's population lived in cities, the Atlantic ports continued to dominate the nation economically and politically. In 1800, the nation's most important urban centers were all Atlantic seaports: Charleston (population 20,000), Baltimore (26,000), Philadelphia (70,000), New York (60,000), and Boston (25,000).

Nevertheless, the new nation was already transforming itself: between 1790 and 1800, according to the first and second federal censuses, the American population grew from 3.9 million to 5.3 million. Growth by migration was greatest in the trans-Appalachian West, a region that was already home to approximately 100,000 Indians. To the immediate north was the continuing presence of the British in what is now Canada and the growing Russian presence in Alaska. To the west and south loomed the Spanish empire, while closer still was the nearby racial powder keg in the Caribbean.

## NORTHERN NEIGHBORS: BRITISH NORTH AMERICA AND RUSSIAN AMERICA

Although Britain had lost its war to keep the American colonies, it kept a firm grasp on British North America, which had once been French Canada (see Chapter 6). Legislative assemblies were established in Upper and Lower Canada and in the Maritimes in 1791, but, learning from their American fiasco, Britain kept the legislatures under strong executive control. British North America dominated the continental fur trade and the great succession of waterways—the St. Lawrence River, the Great Lakes, and the rivers beyond—that made it possible. Britain was on friendly terms with many of the native peoples who were part of the trade. This economic grip was a challenge and frustration to many westward-moving Americans. At the same time, the dispersed nature of the Canadian colonies made them, at least in the eyes of some Americans, ripe for conquest.

Russian settlement of what is now Alaska posed another more remote threat to the United States. Alaska was an extension of the Russian conquest of Siberia, which was driven by the fur trade.

The Russians sometimes took furs by force, holding whole villages hostage and brutalizing the native Inuit and Aleut peoples. After the Aleut Revolt of 1766, the Russian authorities promised to end the abuse, but by 1800, the precontact population of 25,000 Aleuts had been greatly reduced. At the same time, sexual relations and intermarriage between fur trappers and Aleut women created a large group of Russian creoles who assumed an increasingly prominent position in the Alaskan fur trade as navigators, explorers, clerks, and traders.

**WITH WHAT** powers did the United States share North America in the decades after independence?

**myhistorylab**
Review Summary

## IMAGE KEY
for pages 206–207

a. Thomas Jefferson (1743–1826), by Rembrandt Peale, c. 1805.
b. "Burning of the White House" by Leslie Saalburg.
c. A map of the Erie Canal.
d. An antique wooden compass used by Lewis and Clark.
e. The clipper ship *Flying Cloud*, which sailed in 1894 from New York to San Francisco in 89 days.
f. A symbol of the Philadelphia Society for Promoting Agriculture.
g. An 1833 portrait of two Sauk Indians by John Wesley Jarvis.
h. The Battle of Lake Erie in the War of 1812.
i. James Monroe and Robert R. Livingstone negotiations with Comte Talleyrand for the Louisiana Purchase.

RUSSIAN AMERICA

Sitka (1802)

RUPERT'S LAND

*Hudson Bay*

BRITISH NORTH AMERICA

OREGON COUNTRY

Fort Ross (Russian 1812)

ALTA CALIFORNIA

Los Angeles (1781)

Tucson (1776)

Santa Fé (1609)

SPANISH LOUISIANA

St. Louis (1763)

Nacogdoches (1791)

San Antonio de Bejar (1718)

New Orleans (1716)

NEW SPAIN

Mexico City

*Gulf of Mexico*

UPPER CANADA

LOWER CANADA

Halifax

VERMONT (1791)

NORTHWEST TERRITORY

Pittsburgh (1704)

Boston

New York

Cincinnati (1788)

Philadelphia

Baltimore

Louisville (1778)

KENTUCKY (1792)

Nashville (1779)

TENNESSEE (1796)

SOUTHWEST TERRITORY

Charleston

SPANISH FLORIDA

*ATLANTIC OCEAN*

*PACIFIC OCEAN*

Cuba (Spanish)

Saint-Domingue / Haiti (French)

Puerto Rico (Spanish)

Jamaica (British)

*West Indies* (British)

Barbados (British)

*Caribbean Sea*

**MAP 9.1**

**North America in 1800** In 1800, the new United States of America shared the North American continent with territories held by the European powers: British Canada, French Louisiana (secretly ceded that year to France by Spain), Spanish Florida, Spanish Mexico, and Russian Alaska, expanding southward along the Pacific Coast. Few people could have imagined that by 1850, the United States would span the continent. But the American settlers who had crossed the Appalachians to the Ohio River Valley were already convinced that opportunity lay in the West.

WHAT MOTIVATED American settlers to move to the West?

The Russian-American Company, chartered by the tsar in 1799, first set up American headquarters at Kodiak. When overhunting caused a scarcity of furs, the Russians moved their headquarters south to Sitka, in what is now the southeastern panhandle of Alaska, only to have their first fortress destroyed in the Tlingit Revolt of 1802. The Russians reestablished Sitka by force in 1804, and over the next generation, established Russian settlements along the Pacific Coast as far south as Fort Ross, which was just north of San Francisco Bay.

**This view shows** Sitka, the center of Russian activities in Alaska, in 1827. Russian architectural styles and building techniques are apparent in the Church of St. Michael the Archangel in the right background, contrasting with the Asian and Indian origins of most of Sitka's inhabitants.

## THE SPANISH EMPIRE

On paper, Spain posed the greatest threat to the United States because it possessed most of North and South America. Mexico City, with a population of 200,000, was by far the largest and most elegant city on the continent. But Spanish control crumbled rapidly in the 1790s. Tensions mounted between the Spanish-born *peninsulares,* high officials and bureaucrats, and the native-born *criollos* of Spanish descent, who chafed at their subordination, especially after the success of the American Revolution. Furthermore, none of New Spain's northern provinces, created to protect the approaches to Mexico's fabulously wealthy silver mines, thrived.

In 1769, in their last effort to protect their rich colony of Mexico, the Spanish established a chain of twenty-one missions in Alta California that stretched north from San Diego (1769) to Sonoma (1823). Despite Spain's desire to seal its territory from commerce with other nations, a brisk but illegal trade in otter skins, hides, and tallow developed between the United States and California.

American traders were making inroads on Spanish-held territory along the Mississippi River as well. New Orleans, acquired by Spain from France at the end of the Seven Years' War in 1763, was becoming a thriving international port. Every year, a greater proportion of products for the New Orleans trade was supplied by Americans living some distance up the Mississippi River. Pinckney's 1795 treaty with Spain guaranteed Americans free navigation of the Mississippi River and the right to deposit goods at the port of New Orleans. Nevertheless, Americans were uncomfortably aware that the city's crucial location at the mouth of the Mississippi meant that whatever foreign nation possessed New Orleans had the power to choke off the flourishing trade in the vast Mississippi Valley river system.

More than 600 miles north was the small trading town of St. Louis, founded by the New Orleans trader Pierre Laclède in 1763. By 1800, the town had fewer than a thousand residents, three-quarters of whom were involved in the Indian trade of the Missouri River. Spanish officials tried to supervise that trade from their offices in the town, but real control rested in the hands of the Laclèdes and other French traders.

## HAITI AND THE CARIBBEAN

The Caribbean posed other challenges. The rich sugar-producing islands, variously colonies of Spain, France, and Britain provided 80 to 90 percent of the European supply of sugar. All the sugar plantations used enslaved Africans as the labor force. Thus, they shared with the slaveholding American South a distinctive Afro–North American society that cut across national boundaries. This world was jolted in 1791 by the revolt of black slaves in Saint-Domingue, France's richest colony. Under the leadership of Toussaint L'Ouverture, the former colony, renamed Haiti, became North America's first independent black nation. Its existence struck fear into the hearts of white slaveowners at the same time that it served as a beacon of hope to the enslaved.

## TRANS-APPALACHIA

Within the United States itself, the region of greatest growth was territory west of the Appalachian Mountains, and it was this area that was most affected by fears of continuing British influence on Indian peoples. By 1800, about 500,000 people (the vast majority from Virginia and North Carolina) had found rich and fertile land along the Ohio River system. Soon there was enough population for statehood. Kentucky (1792) and Tennessee (1796) were the first trans-Appalachian states admitted to the Union.

Migration to the west was generally a family affair, with groups of kin moving together to a new area. One observer wrote of a caravan moving across the mountains: "They had prepared baskets made of fine hickory withe or splints, and fastening two of them together with ropes they put a child in each basket and put it across a pack saddle." Once pioneers had managed to struggle by road over the Appalachians, they gladly took to the rivers, especially the Ohio, to move farther west.

Cincinnati, strategically situated 450 miles downstream from Pittsburgh, was a particularly dramatic example of the rapid community growth and development that characterized the trans-Appalachian region. Founded in 1788, Cincinnati began life as a military fort, defending settlers in the fertile Miami River Valley of Ohio from resistance by Shawnee and Miami Indians. After the Battle of Fallen Timbers broke Indian resistance in 1794, Cincinnati became the point of departure for immigrants arriving by the Ohio River on their way to settle the interior of the Old Northwest: Ohio, Indiana, and Illinois.

Cincinnati merchants were soon shipping farm goods from the fertile Miami Valley down the Ohio–Mississippi River system to New Orleans, 1,500 miles away. River traffic increased yearly, and control of New Orleans became a key concern of western farmers and merchants. If New Orleans refused to accept American goods, Cincinnati merchants and many thousands of trans-Appalachian farmers would be ruined.

**WHAT WERE** the most important strengths of the American economy in the early 1800s?

myhistorylab

**Review Summary**

# A NATIONAL ECONOMY

Concern about New Orleans illustrates the new nation's weak position in international trade. In 1800, the United States was a producer of raw materials. It faced the same challenge that developing nations confront today. At the mercy of fluctuating world commodity prices they cannot control, such countries have great difficulty protecting themselves from economic dominance by stronger, more established nations.

## COTTON AND THE ECONOMY OF THE YOUNG REPUBLIC

In 1800, the United States was predominantly rural and agricultural. Farming families followed centuries-old traditions of working with hand tools and draft animals, producing most of their own food and fiber. Crops were grown for subsistence (home use) rather than for sale. Commodities such as whiskey and hogs (both easy to transport) provided small and irregular cash incomes or items for barter.

The situation was very different in the South, where plantation agriculture based on enslaved workers was wholly commercial and international. Cotton, and the slave labor system that produced it, assumed a commanding place in southern life and in the foreign trade of the United States. The essential contribution of cotton to the nation's economy was the most important social and political reality of the early nineteenth century.

In 1790, however, increasing foreign demand for American goods and services hardly seemed likely. Trade with Britain, still the biggest customer for American raw materials, was considerably less than it had been before the Revolution. Britain and France both excluded Americans from their lucrative West Indian trade and taxed American ships with discriminatory duties. It was difficult to be independent in a world dominated by great powers.

**The cotton gin,** invented in 1793, was a simple device with huge consequences. It transformed the South, condemned millions of African Americans to slavery, and was the single largest source of American economic growth before 1860.

## SHIPPING AND THE ECONOMIC BOOM

Despite these restrictions on American commerce, the strong shipping trade begun during the colonial era and centered in the Atlantic ports became a major asset in the 1790s, when events in Europe provided America with extraordinary opportunities. The French Revolution, which began in 1789, initiated nearly twenty-five years of warfare between Britain and France. All along the Atlantic seaboard, urban centers thrived as American ships carried European goods that could no longer be transported on British ships without danger of French attack (and vice versa). Because America was neutral, its merchants had the legal right to import European goods and promptly reexport them to other European countries. In spite of British and French efforts to prevent the practice (see Chapter 8), reexports amounted to half of the profits in the booming shipping trade (see Figure 9.1). The long series of European wars also allowed enterprising Americans to seize such lucrative international opportunities, such as the China trade.

The active American participation in international trade fostered a strong and diversified shipbuilding industry. All the major Atlantic ports boasted expanding shipbuilding enterprises. Demands for speed increased as well, resulting in what many people have regarded as the flower of American shipbuilding, the clipper ship. The narrow-hulled, many-sailed clipper ships of the 1840s and 1850s set records for ships of their size. In 1854, *Flying Cloud,* built in the Boston shipyards of Donald McKay, sailed from New York to San Francisco—a 16,000-mile trip that usually took 150 to 200 days—in a mere 89 days.

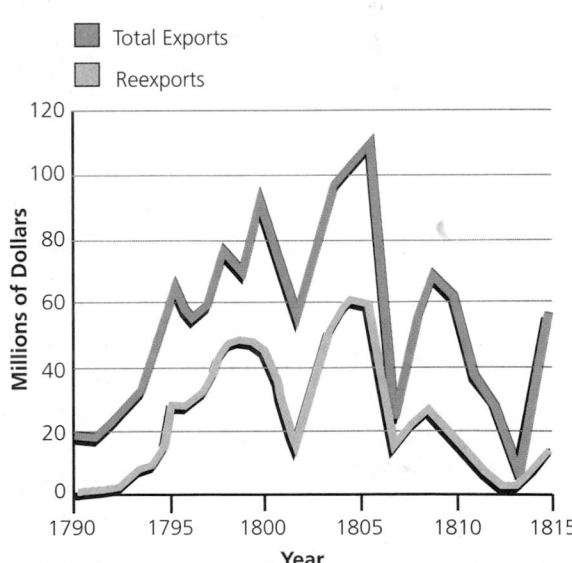

**Figure 9.1 American Export Trade, 1790–1815**
This graph shows how completely the American shipping boom was tied to European events. Exports, half of which were reexports, surged when Britain and France were at war and America could take advantage of its neutral status. Exports slumped in the brief period of European peace from 1803 to 1805 and plunged following the Embargo Act of 1807 and the outbreak of the War of 1812.

WHAT VALUES were embodied in agrarian republicanism?

**myhistorylab**

Review Summary

**8–2**
Thomas Jefferson, *First Inaugural Address* (1801)

**8–7**
Fisher Ames, *The Republican. No. II* (1804)

## QUICK REVIEW

**Growth of American Trade: 1793–1807**

- French Revolution initiated renewed period of warfare between France and Britain.
- American merchants wanted to supply both sides.
- Expansion of trade led to development of shipbuilding industry and growth of coastal cities.

# THE JEFFERSON PRESIDENCY

At noon on March 4, 1801, Thomas Jefferson walked from his modest boardinghouse through the swampy streets of the new federal city of Washington to the unfinished Capitol. George Washington and John Adams had ridden in elaborate carriages to their inaugurals. Jefferson, although accepting a military honor guard, demonstrated by his actions that he rejected the elaborate, quasi-monarchical style of the two Federalist presidents and (to his mind) their autocratic style of government as well.

For all its lack of pretension, Jefferson's inauguration as the third president of the United States was a momentous occasion in American history, for it marked the peaceful transition from one political party, the Federalists, to their hated rivals, the Jeffersonian Republicans. Beginning in an atmosphere of exceptional political bitterness, Jefferson's presidency was to demonstrate that a strongly led party system could shape national policy without leading either to dictatorship or to revolt. Jefferson's own moderation may have been the crucial factor. Setting a tone of conciliation in his inaugural address, he announced, "We are all republicans; we are all federalists" and during his eight years in office he paid close attention to ways to attract moderate Federalists to the Jeffersonian Republican party.

## REPUBLICAN AGRARIANISM

Behind all the events of Jefferson's administration (1801–1809) was a clear set of beliefs that embodied his interpretation of the meaning of republicanism for Americans. Jefferson's years as ambassador to France in the 1780s were particularly important in shaping his political thinking. Recoiling from the extremes of wealth and poverty he saw there, he came to believe that it was impossible for Europe to achieve a just society that could guarantee to most of its members the "life, liberty and . . . pursuit of happiness" of which he had written in the Declaration of Independence. Only America, he believed, provided fertile earth for the true citizenship necessary to a republican form of government. What America had, and Europe lacked, was room to grow.

Jefferson envisaged a nation of small family farms clustered together in rural communities—an agrarian republic. He believed that only a nation of roughly equal yeoman farmers, each secure in his own possessions and not dependent on someone else for his livelihood, would exhibit the concern for the community good that was essential in a republic. Indeed, Jefferson said that "those who labor in the earth are the chosen people of God," and so he viewed himself, though his "farm" was the large slave-owning plantation of Monticello.

Jefferson's vision of an expanding agrarian republic remains to this day one of our most compelling ideas about America's uniqueness and special destiny. But expansionism contained some negative aspects. The lure of the western lands fostered constant mobility and dissatisfaction rather than the stable, settled communities Jefferson envisaged. Expansionism caused environmental damage, in particular soil exhaustion—a consequence of abandoning old lands, rather than conserving them, and moving on to new ones. Expansionism encouraged the spread of plantations based on slave labor in the South (see Chapter 10). Finally, it bred a ruthlessness toward Indian peoples, who were pushed out of the way for white settlement or who, like the Mandans, were devastated by the diseases that accompanied European trade and contact. Jefferson's agrarianism thus bred some of the best and some of the worst traits of the developing nation.

VENERATE THE PLOUGH

**Tall, ungainly, and** diffident in manner, Thomas Jefferson was nonetheless a man of genius: an architect, naturalist, philosopher, and politician. His political philosophy, republican agrarianism, is illustrated by this symbol of the Philadelphia Society for Promoting Agriculture, in which the farmer exemplifies Jefferson's hopes for America. As he said, "those who labor in the earth are the chosen people of God."

## JEFFERSON'S GOVERNMENT

Thomas Jefferson came to office determined to reverse the Federalist policies of the 1790s and to ensure an agrarian "republic of virtue." Accordingly, he proposed a program of "simplicity and frugality," promising to cut all internal taxes, to reduce the size of the army, the navy, and the government staff, and to eliminate the entire national debt inherited from the Federalists. He kept all of these promises, even the last, although the Louisiana Purchase of 1803 cost the Treasury $15 million. This diminishment of government was a key matter of republican principle to Jefferson. If his ideal yeoman farmer was to be a truly self-governing citizen, the federal government must not, Jefferson believed, be either large or powerful.

Perhaps one reason for Jefferson's success was that the federal government he headed was small and unimportant by today's standards. The national government's main service to ordinary people was mail delivery, and already in 1800 there were persistent complaints about the slowness, unreliability, and expense of the Postal Service! Everything else—law and order, education, welfare, road maintenance, economic control—rested with state or local governments. Power and political loyalty were still local, not national.

## AN INDEPENDENT JUDICIARY

Although determined to reverse Federalist fiscal policies, Jefferson was much more moderate concerning Federalist officeholders. He resisted demands by other Jeffersonian Republicans that "the board should be swept" and all

**8–3**
Margaret Bayard Smith,
On *Thomas Jefferson and the Peaceful Transfer of Power from the Federalists to the Jeffersonian Republicans* (1801)

Federalist officeholders replaced with party loyalists. During his term of office, Jefferson allowed 132 Federalists to remain at their posts, while placing Jeffersonian Republicans in 158 other posts. Jefferson's restraint, however, did not extend to the most notorious Federalist appointees, the so-called midnight judges.

In the last days of the Adams administration, the Federalist-dominated Congress passed several acts that created new judgeships and other positions within the federal judiciary. Jeffersonian Republicans feared that the losing Federalist Party was trying to politicize the judiciary by appointing Federalists who would use their positions to strengthen the powers of the federal government, a policy the Jeffersonians opposed. In one of his last acts in office, President Adams appointed Federalists—quickly dubbed the "midnight judges"—to these new positions. William Marbury, whom President Adams had appointed justice of the peace for Washington, DC, and three other appointees sued James Madison, Jefferson's secretary of state, to receive their commissions for their offices. Before the case came to trial, however, Congress, controlled by Jeffersonian Republicans, repealed the acts. This case, *Marbury* v. *Madison*, provoked a landmark decision from the U.S. Supreme Court.

At issue was a fundamental constitutional point: Was the judiciary independent of politics? In his celebrated 1803 decision in ***Marbury* v. *Madison***, Chief Justice John Marshall, himself a strong Federalist and an Adams appointee, managed to find a way to please both parties. Marshall ruled that Marbury was entitled to his commission but that the Supreme Court did not have the power to force the executive branch to give it to him. At first glance, Jefferson's government appeared to have won the battle. But in the long run, Marshall established the principle that only the federal judiciary could "say what the law is," thus unequivocally defending the independence of the judiciary and the principle of judicial review. This was a vital step in realizing the three-way balance of power among the branches of the federal government—executive (president), legislative (Congress), and judiciary (courts)—envisaged in the Constitution. Equally important, during his long tenure in office (1801–35), Chief Justice Marshall consistently led the Supreme Court in a series of decisions that favored the federal government over state governments (see Chapter 12). Under Marshall's direction, the Supreme Court became a powerful nationalizing force, often to the dismay of defenders of states' rights, Jefferson's Republicans among them.

## OPPORTUNITY: THE LOUISIANA PURCHASE

In 1800, the United States was a new and fragile democracy in a world dominated by two contending great powers: Britain and France. In 1799, the young general Napoleon Bonaparte seized control of France and began a career of military conquests. Great Britain promptly went to war against him. If England and France fought in North America, as they had in the Seven Years' War (see Chapter 6), America's national security would be directly threatened. Jefferson, who had once ardently supported the goals of the French Revolution, viewed Napoleon's ambitions with increasing apprehension. He feared a resumption of the political animosity of the 1790s, when Federalists and Jeffersonian Republicans had so bitterly disagreed on policy toward France (see Chapter 8).

As had his predecessors, Napoleon considered North America a potential battleground on which to fight the British. He looked first at the Caribbean, where he planned to reconquer Haiti, the world's first independent black nation, reenslave its people, and use the rich profits from sugar to finance his European wars. As a first step, in 1800, France secretly reacquired the Louisiana Territory, the vast western drainage of the Mississippi and Missouri Rivers, from Spain, which had held the region since 1763.

---

### QUICK REVIEW

***Marbury* v. *Madison* (1803)**

• Case sparked by Jefferson's refusal to recognize Adams's "midnight judges."

• Justice Marshall ruled that the duty of the courts was "to say what the law is."

• Ruling made the Supreme Court a powerful nationalizing force.

---

**myhistorylab**

**Exploring America:** *Continentalism*

---

*Marbury* v. *Madison*    Supreme Court decision of 1803 that created the precedent of judicial review by ruling as unconstitutional part of the Judiciary Act of 1789.

In 1801, when President Jefferson first learned of the French–Spanish secret agreement about Louisiana, he was concerned about the threat to American commerce on the Mississippi River. In fact, in 1802, the Spanish commander at New Orleans (the French had not yet taken formal control) closed the port to American shippers, thus disrupting commerce as far away as Cincinnati. As Jefferson feared, Federalists in Congress clamored for military action to reopen the port.

In the summer of 1802, Jefferson instructed Robert Livingston, the American ambassador to France, to negotiate to buy New Orleans and the surrounding area for $2 million (or up to $10 million, if necessary). The initial bargaining was not promising, but suddenly, in early 1803, Napoleon was ready to sell. His effort to reconquer Haiti failed, defeated by yellow fever and by an army of former slaves led by Toussaint L'Ouverture. Expecting the British to declare war against him again, and in need of money for European military campaigns, Napoleon suddenly offered the entire Louisiana Territory, including the crucial port of New Orleans, to the Americans for $15 million. In an age when it took at least two months for messages to cross the Atlantic, special American envoy James Monroe and Ambassador Livingston could not wait to consult Jefferson. They seized the opportunity: they bought the entire Louisiana Territory from Napoleon in Paris in April 1803. Overnight, the size of the United States more than doubled. It was the largest peaceful acquisition of territory in U.S. history.

At home, Jefferson suffered brief qualms. The Constitution did not authorize the president to purchase territory, and Jefferson had always rigidly insisted on a limited interpretation of executive rights. But he had also long held a sense of destiny about the West and had planned the Lewis and Clark expedition before the Louisiana Purchase was a reality. Jefferson now argued that Louisiana was vital to the nation's republican future. "By enlarging the empire of liberty," Jefferson wrote, "we . . . provide new sources of renovation, should its principles, at any time, degenerate, in those portions of our country which gave them birth." In other words, expansion was essential to liberty. But for African American slaves and Native Americans, the Louisiana Purchase simply increased the scope of their enslavement and destruction. By 1850, four of the six states in the Louisiana Purchase had entered the Union as slave states (see Chapter 10), and Indian Territory, envisaged by Jefferson as a distant refuge for beleaguered eastern Indian peoples, was surrounded by new settlements (see Chapter 15). No matter how noble Jefferson's rhetoric, neither African Americans nor American Indians shared in his "empire of liberty" (see Map 9.2).

**8–4**
Thomas Jefferson,
*Constitutionality of the
Louisiana Purchase* (1803)

## INCORPORATING LOUISIANA

In 1803, when the region that is now the state of Louisiana became American property, it had a racially and ethnically diverse population of 43,000 people, of whom only 6,000 were American. French and French-speaking people were numerically and culturally dominant, especially in the city of New Orleans. The city itself had a population of about 8,000, half white and half black. Two-thirds of the black population were slaves; the remainder were "free persons of color," who under French law enjoyed legal rights equal to those of white people. In New Orleans the French community effectively challenged the initial American plan of rapidly supplanting French culture and institutions with American ones. As a result, with Claiborne's full support, Louisiana adopted a legal code in 1808 that was based on French civil law rather than English common law. This was not a small concession. French law differed from English law in many fundamental respects, such as in family property (communal versus male ownership), in inheritance (forced heirship versus free disposal), and even in contracts, which were much more strictly

# MAP EXPLORATION

To explore an interactive version of this map, go to **http://www.prenhall.com/faraghertlc/map9.2**

RUSSIAN AMERICA

*Hudson Bay*

BRITISH NORTH AMERICA

BLACKFOOT

CHINOOK    *Columbia R.*

Fort Clatsop
(winter quarters
1805–06)

CLATSOP

NEZ PERCÉ

*Missouri R.*

Mandan Villages
(winter quarters
1804–05)

MANDAN

CROW

SHOSHONI

OREGON
COUNTRY

CHEYENNE

SIOUX

VERMONT

MAINE
(part of Mass.)

NEW HAMPSHIRE

MASSACHUSETTS

NEW
YORK

RHODE ISLAND

CONNECTICUT

PENNSYLVANIA    NEW JERSEY

OHIO    DELAWARE

MARYLAND

Fort Ross
(Russian 1812)

*PACIFIC
OCEAN*

SPANISH

TERRITORY

ARAPAHO

PAWNEE

LOUISIANA
PURCHASE
(1803)

OSAGE

INDIANA
TERRITORY

St. Louis

KENTUCKY

VIRGINIA

TENNESSEE

NORTH
CAROLINA

SOUTH
CAROLINA

*ATLANTIC
OCEAN*

Los Angeles

Santa Fé

APACHE

*Mississippi R.*

MISSISSIPPI
TERRITORY

GEORGIA

COMANCHE

*Rio Grande*

Nacogdoches

Natchez

St. Augustine

San Antonio
de Bejar

New Orleans

SPANISH
FLORIDA

*Gulf of Mexico*

Louisiana Purchase

⟵ Route of Lewis and Clark, 1804–06

**MAP 9.2**

**Louisiana Purchase**    The Louisiana Purchase of 1803, the largest peaceful acquisition of territory in U.S. history, more than doubled the size of the nation. The Lewis and Clark expedition (1804–06) was the first to survey and document the natural and human richness of the area. The American sense of expansiveness and continental destiny owes more to the extraordinary opportunity provided by the Louisiana Purchase than to other factors.

HOW DID the terrain of the Lewis and Clark expedition influence the routes of the journey?

regulated in the French system. In 1812, with the required 60,000 free inhabitants, Louisiana was admitted to the Union. New Orleans remained for years a distinctively French city, illustrating the flexibility possible under a federal system.

## TEXAS AND THE STRUGGLE FOR MEXICAN INDEPENDENCE

Spain objected, in vain, to Napoleon's 1803 sale of Louisiana to America. For years, Spain had attempted to seal off its rich colony of Mexico from commerce with other nations. Now, American Louisiana shared a vague and disputed boundary with Mexico's northern province of Texas.

Soon Napoleon brought turmoil to all of Mexico. In 1808, having invaded Spain, he installed his brother Joseph Bonaparte as king, forcing Spain's king, Charles IV, to renounce his throne. For the next six years, as warfare convulsed Spain, the country's long-prized New World empire slipped away. Mexico, divided between royalists loyal to Spain and populists seeking social and economic justice for mestizos and Indians, edged toward independence. Two populist revolts were suppressed by the royalists.

In 1812, a small force, led by Mexican republican Bernardo Gutiérrez but composed mostly of American adventurers, invaded Texas, captured San Antonio, assassinated the provincial governor Manuel Salcedo, and declared Texas independent. A year later, however, the Mexican republicans were defeated by a royalist army, which then killed suspected collaborators and pillaged the province so thoroughly that the local economy was devastated. The Mexican population declined to fewer than 2,000. Under these circumstances, Mexico's difficult path toward independence seemed, at least to some Americans, to offer yet another opportunity for expansion.

# RENEWED IMPERIAL RIVALRY IN NORTH AMERICA

Fresh from the triumph of the Louisiana Purchase, Jefferson scored a major victory over the Federalist Charles Cotesworth Pinckney in the presidential election of 1804. Jefferson's shrewd wooing of moderate Federalists had been so successful that the remaining Federalists dwindled to a highly principled but sectional group, unable to attract voters outside of its home base in New England. Jefferson's Louisiana success was not repeated, however, and few other consequences of the ongoing struggle between Britain and France were so easy to solve.

**WHAT FACTORS** led to conflict between the United States and Britain in North America?

**my**history**lab**
Review Summary

## PROBLEMS WITH NEUTRAL RIGHTS

In his first inaugural address in 1801, Jefferson had announced a foreign policy of "peace, commerce, and honest friendship with all nations, entangling alliances with none." This was a difficult policy to pursue after 1803, when the Napoleonic Wars resumed. By 1805, Napoleon had conquered most of Europe, but Britain, the victor at the great naval battle of Trafalgar, controlled the seas. The United States, trying to profit from trade with both countries, was caught in the middle. Beginning in 1805, the British targeted the American reexport trade between the Caribbean and France by seizing American ships that were bringing French West Indian goods to Europe. Angry Americans viewed these seizures as violations of their rights as shippers of a neutral nation.

An even more contentious issue arose from the substantial desertion rate of British sailors. Many deserters promptly signed up on American ships, where they drew better pay and sometimes obtained false naturalization papers as well. As many as a quarter of the 100,000 seamen on American ships were British. Soon the British were stopping American merchant vessels and removing any man they believed to be British, regardless of his papers. The British refusal to recognize genuine naturalization papers (on the principle "once a British subject, always a British subject") was particularly insulting to the new American sense of nationhood. At least 6,000 innocent American citizens suffered forced impressment into the British navy from 1803 to 1812.

## THE EMBARGO ACT

Fully aware that commerce was essential to the new nation, Jefferson was determined to insist on America's right as a neutral nation to ship goods to Europe. He first tried diplomatic protests, then negotiations, and finally threats, all to no avail. In 1806, Congress passed the Non-Importation Act, hoping that a boycott of British goods, which had worked so well during the Revolutionary War, would be effective once again. It was not. Finally, in desperation, Jefferson imposed the **Embargo Act** in December 1807. This act forbade American ships from sailing to any foreign port, thereby cutting off all exports as well as imports. The intent of the act was to force both Britain and France to recognize neutral rights by depriving them of American-shipped raw materials.

But the results were a disaster for American trade. The commerce of the new nation, which Jefferson himself had done so much to promote, came to a standstill. Exports fell from $108 million in 1807 to $22 million in 1808, and the nation was driven into a deep depression. There was widespread evasion of the embargo. Pointing out that the American navy's weakness was due largely to the deep cuts Jefferson had inflicted on it, the Federalists sprang to life with a campaign of outspoken opposition to Jefferson's policy.

## MADISON AND THE FAILURE OF "PEACEABLE COERCION"

In this troubled atmosphere, Thomas Jefferson despondently ended his second term, acknowledging the failure of what he called "peaceable coercion." He was followed in office by his friend and colleague James Madison of Virginia. Although Madison defeated the Federalist candidate—again Charles Cotesworth Pinckney—Pinckney's share of the votes was three times what it had been in 1804.

Ironically, the Embargo Act had almost no effect on its intended victims. The French used the embargo as a pretext for seizing American ships, claiming they must be British ships in disguise. The British, in the absence of American competition, developed new markets for their goods in South America. In March 1809, Congress admitted failure, and the Embargo Act was repealed. But the struggle to remain neutral in the confrontation between the European giants continued.

## A CONTRADICTORY INDIAN POLICY

The United States faced other conflicts besides those with Britain and France over neutral shipping rights. In the West, the powerful Indian nations of the Ohio Valley were determined to resist the wave of expansion that had carried thousands of white settlers onto their lands.

According to the Indian Intercourse Act of 1790, the United States could not simply seize Indian land; it could only acquire it when the Indians ceded it by treaty. But this policy conflicted with the harsh reality of westward expansion. Commonly, settlers pushed ahead of treaty boundaries. When Indian peoples resisted the invasion of their lands, the pioneers fought back and called for military protection. Defeat of an Indian people led to further land cessions. The result for the Indians was a relentless cycle of invasion, resistance, and defeat.

Thomas Jefferson was deeply concerned with the fate of the western Indian peoples. Convinced that Indians had to give up hunting in favor of the yeoman-farmer lifestyle he so favored for all Americans, Jefferson directed the governors of the Northwest Territories to "promote energetically" his vision for civilizing the Indians, which included Christianizing them and teaching them to read.

After the Louisiana Purchase, Jefferson offered traditionalist Indian groups new lands west of the Mississippi River, where they could live undisturbed by white settlers. But he failed to consider the pace of westward expansion. Less than twenty

**Embargo Act** Act passed by Congress in 1807 prohibiting American ships from leaving for any foreign port.

years later, Missouri, the first trans-Mississippi state, was admitted to the Union. Western Indians like the Mandans, who had seemed so remote, were now threatened by further westward expansion.

In fact, Jefferson's Indian policy, because it did nothing to slow down the ever-accelerating westward expansion, offered little hope to Indian peoples. The alternatives they faced were stark: acculturation, removal, or extinction. Deprived of hunting lands, decimated by disease, increasingly dependent on the white economy for trade goods and annuity payments in exchange for land cessions, many Indian peoples despaired. Nearly every tribe found itself bitterly split between accommodationists and traditionalists. Some, like groups of Cherokees and associated tribes in the South, advocated adapting their traditional agricultural lifestyles and pursuing a pattern of peaceful accommodation. In the Northwest Territory, however, many Indians chose the path of armed resistance.

## INDIAN RESISTANCE

The Shawnees, a seminomadic hunting and farming tribe (the men hunted, the women farmed) of the Ohio Valley, had resisted white settlement in Kentucky and Ohio since the 1750s. Anthony Wayne's decisive defeat of the Indian confederacy led by Little Turtle at Fallen Timbers (1794) and the continuing pressure of American settlement, however, had left the Shawnees divided. One group, led by Black Hoof, accepted acculturation. The rest of the tribe tried to maintain traditional ways. Most broke into small bands and tried to eke out a living by hunting. One group of traditional Shawnees, however, led by the warrior Tecumseh, sought refuge farther west.

**(left) Tecumseh, a** Shawnee military leader, and (right) his brother Tenskwatawa, a religious leader called The Prophet, led a pan-Indian revitalization and resistance movement that posed a serious threat to American westward expansion. Tecumseh traveled widely, attempting to build a military alliance on his brother's spiritual message. He achieved considerable success in the Old Northwest but less in the Old Southwest, where many Indian peoples put their faith in accommodation. Tecumseh's death at the Battle of the Thames (1813) and British abandonment of their Shawnee allies at the end of the War of 1812 brought an end to organized Indian resistance in the Old Northwest.

(right): 1830. Oil on canvas. 29 × 24 in. (73.7 × 60.9 cm) Location: Smithsonian American Art Museum, Washington, DC, U.S.A.

**Pan-Indian military resistance movement**   Movement calling for the political and cultural unification of Indian tribes in the late eighteenth and early nineteenth centuries.

**9–2**
*The Cherokee Treaty of 1817*

But there was no escape from white encroachment. Between 1801 and 1809, William Henry Harrison, governor of Indiana Territory, concluded fifteen treaties with the Delawares, Potawatomis, Miamis, and other tribes. These treaties opened eastern Michigan, southern Indiana, and most of Illinois to white settlement and forced the Indians onto ever-smaller reservations. Many of these treaties were obtained by coercion, bribery, and outright trickery, and most Indians did not accept them.

In 1805, Tecumseh's brother, Tenskwatawa, known as The Prophet, began preaching a message of Indian revitalization: a rejection of all contact with the Americans and a return to traditional practices of hunting and farming. He preached an end to quarreling, violence, and sexual promiscuity and to the accumulation of private property.

Tecumseh succeeded in molding his brother's religious following into a powerful **pan-Indian military resistance movement**. With each new treaty that Harrison concluded, Tecumseh gained new followers among the Northwest Confederation tribes. Significantly, he also had the support of the British, who, after 1807, began sending food and guns to him from Canada, and who promised an alliance with the Indians if war broke out between Britain and America.

Tecumseh's pan-Indian strategy was at first primarily defensive, aimed at preventing further westward expansion. But after the Treaty of Fort Wayne in 1809, in which the United States gained 3 million acres of Delaware and Potawatomi land in Indiana, Tecumseh moved from passive to active resistance. He warned that any surveyors or settlers who ventured into the 3 million acres would risk their lives.

Tecumseh took his message of common land ownership and military resistance to all the Indian peoples of the Northwest Confederacy. He was not uniformly successful, even among the Shawnees. Black Hoof, for example, refused to join. Tecumseh also recruited, with mixed success, among the tribes south of the Ohio River (see Map 9.3).

In November 1811, while Tecumseh was still recruiting among the southern tribes, Harrison marched to the pan-Indian village of Tippecanoe with 1,000 soldiers. The 600 to 700 Indian warriors at the town, urged on by Tenskwatawa, attacked Harrison's forces before dawn on November 7, hoping to surprise them. The attack failed, and in the battle that followed, the Americans inflicted about 150 Indian casualties, while sustaining about as many themselves. Although Harrison claimed victory, the truth was far different. Dispersed from Tippecanoe, Tecumseh's angry followers fell on American settlements in Indiana and southern Michigan, killing many pioneers and forcing the rest to flee to fortified towns. Tecumseh himself entered into a formal alliance with the British. For western settlers, the Indian threat was greater than ever.

**8–9**
Chief Tecumseh, *An "Uncommon Genius" Advocates Indian Unity* (1809)

# THE WAR OF 1812

Many Westerners blamed the British for Tecumseh's attacks on pioneer settlements in the Northwest. British support of western Indians and the long-standing difficulties over neutral shipping rights were the two grievances cited by President Madison when he asked Congress for a declaration of war against Britain on June 1, 1812. Congress obliged him on June 18. But the war had other, more general causes as well.

**WHAT WERE** the consequences of the War of 1812?

**myhistorylab**
**Review Summary**

## THE WAR HAWKS

A rising young generation of political leaders, first elected to Congress in 1810, strongly resented the continuing influence of Britain, the former mother country, on American affairs. Eager to assert independence from England once and for all, these

**MAP 9.3**

**Indian Resistance, 1790–1816**   American westward expansion put relentless pressure on the Indian nations in the trans-Appalachian South and West. The trans-Appalachian region was marked by constant warfare from the time of the earliest settlements in Kentucky in the 1780s to the War of 1812. Tecumseh's Alliance in the Old Northwest (1809–11) and the Creek Rebellion in the Old Southwest (1813–14) were the culminating struggles in Indian resistance to the American invasion of the trans-Appalachian region. Indian resistance was a major reason for the War of 1812.

WHAT HAPPENED to the Indians of the Trans-Appalachian region after 1814?

**8–10**
*Indian Hostilities* (1812)

**War Hawks**    Members of Congress, predominantly from the South and West, who aggressively pushed for a war against Britain after their election in 1810.

**War of 1812**    War fought between the United States and Britain from June 1812 to January 1815 largely over British restrictions on American shipping.

young men saw themselves finishing the job begun by the aging revolutionary generation. They also wanted to occupy Florida to prevent runaway slaves from seeking refuge with the Seminole Indians. Westerners wanted to invade Canada, hoping thereby to end threats from British-backed Indians in the Northwest, such as Tecumseh and his followers. As resentments against England and frustrations over border issues merged, the pressure for war—always a strong force for national unity—mounted.

Unaware that the British, seriously hurt by the American trade embargo, were about to adopt a more conciliatory policy, President James Madison yielded to the **War Hawks**' clamor for action in June 1812, and his declaration of war passed the U.S. Senate by the close vote of 19 to 13, the House by 79 to 49. All the Federalists voted against the war. (The division along party lines continued in the 1812 presidential election, in which Madison garnered 128 electoral votes to 89 for his Federalist opponent, DeWitt Clinton.) The vote was sectional, with New England and the Middle States in opposition and the West and South strongly prowar. Thus, the United States entered the **War of 1812** more deeply divided along sectional lines than during any other foreign war in American history.

As a result of Jefferson's economizing, the American army and navy were small and weak. In contrast, the British, fresh from almost ten years of Napoleonic Wars, were in fighting trim. At sea, the British navy quickly established a strong blockade, harassing coastal shipping along the Atlantic seaboard and attacking coastal settlements at will. In the most humiliating attack, the British burned Washington in the summer of 1814, forcing the president and Congress to flee (see Map 9.4).

## THE CAMPAIGNS AGAINST THE NORTHERN AND SOUTHERN INDIANS

The American goal of expansion fared badly as well. Americans envisaged a quick victory over sparsely populated British Canada that would destroy British support for Tecumseh and his Northwest Indian allies, but instead the British–Indian alliance defeated them (see Seeing History).

One reason for the abortive Canadian invasion, aside from failure to appreciate the strength of the British–Indian forces, was that the New England states actively opposed the war. Massachusetts, Rhode Island, and Connecticut refused to provide militia or supplies, and other New England governors turned a blind eye to the flourishing illegal trade across the U.S.–Canadian border. Another reason was the reaction of Canadians themselves, the majority of whom were former Americans. Ironically, the most decisive effect of the American attacks was the formation of a Canadian sense of national identity and a determination never to be invaded or absorbed by the United States.

In the South, warfare similar to that waged against Tecumseh's pan-Indian resistance movement in the Northwest dramatically affected the southern Indian peoples. The first of the Indian peoples to battle the Americans were the Creeks, a trading nation with a long history of contacts with the Spanish and French. When white settlers began to occupy Indian lands in northwestern Georgia and central Alabama early in the nineteenth century, the Creeks, like the Shawnees in the Northwest, were divided in their response. Although many Creek bands argued for accommodation, a group known as the Red Sticks were determined to fight. During the War of 1812, the Red Sticks, allied with the British and Spanish, fought not only the Americans but also other Indian groups.

**MAP 9.4**

**The War of 1812** On land, the War of 1812 was fought to define the nation's boundaries. In the North, where military action was most intense, American armies attacked British forts in the Great Lakes region with little success, and several invasions of Canada failed. In the South, the Battle of New Orleans made a national hero of Andrew Jackson, but it occurred after the peace treaty had been signed. On the sea, with the exception of Oliver Perry's victory in the Great Lakes, Britain's dominance was so complete and its blockade so effective that British troops were able to invade the Chesapeake and burn the capital of the United States.

WHAT EVENTS and ambitions led to the outbreak of war in 1812?

# "A Scene on the Frontiers as Practiced by the 'Humane' British and their 'Worthy' Allies"

This American cartoon, published during the War of 1812, shows a British officer paying for a scalp from an Indian, while another man is shown in the act of scalping a dead American soldier. The cartoon may have been prompted by an actual event: the offer of bounties for scalps made by British Colonel Proctor at Fort Dearborn (Chicago) in August 1815. In any case, the cartoon evoked horror at Indian barbarity and indignation at the British for using them as pawns in the war. Similar charges had been made against the British and their Indian allies during the American Revolution.

In reality, Indian resistance in the War of 1812 was different from the earlier war. The western Indians were not British pawns. The Shawnee leader Tecumseh and other western Indian groups allied with him claimed that they had been deprived of their lands by fraudulent treaties and stripped of the ability to maintain their traditional culture. Tecumseh began organizing resistance long before the outbreak of war between the United States and Britain. He did accept arms from the British in Canada, and once the war broke out he formally allied with them and became an officer in their army. By allying with the British, the Indians hoped to retain their homelands, but at the peace negotiations the British failed to insist on a buffer state for neutral Indians as they had promised. ■

**THIS CARTOON** inflamed popular fears of Indians that existed long before the War of 1812. Does it contribute anything to our historical understanding of the reasons for western Indian resistance?

A SCENE ON THE FRONTIERS AS PRACTICED BY THE HUMANE BRITISH AND THEIR WORTHY ALLIES!

Arise Columbia's Sons and forward press,
Your Country's wrongs, call loudly for redress,
The savage Indian with his scalping knife,
Or tomahawk may seek to take your life.

By bravery aw'd they'll in a dreadfull fright
Shrink back for refuge to the woods in flight.
Their British leaders then will quickly shake,
And for those wrongs shall restitution make.

In August 1813, the Red Sticks attacked Fort Mims on the Alabama River, killing more than 500 Americans and mixed-race Creeks who had gathered there for safety. Led by Andrew Jackson, troops from the Tennessee and Kentucky militias combined with the Creeks' traditional foes—the Cherokees, Choctaws, and Chickasaws—to exact revenge. Jackson's troops matched the Creeks in ferocity, shooting the Red Sticks "like dogs," one soldier reported.

At the end of the Creek War in 1814, Jackson demanded huge land concessions from the Creeks (including concessions from some Creek bands that had fought on his side): 23 million acres, or more than half the Creek domain. The Treaty of Fort Jackson (1814) confirming these land concessions earned Jackson his Indian name, Sharp Knife. In early 1815 (after the peace treaty had been signed but before news of it arrived in America), Andrew Jackson achieved his best-known victory, an improbable win over veteran British troops in the Battle of New Orleans.

## THE HARTFORD CONVENTION

America's occasional successes failed to diminish the angry opposition of New England Federalists to the War of 1812. That opposition culminated in the Hartford Convention of 1814, where Federalist representatives from the five New England states met to discuss their grievances. At first the air was full of talk of secession from the Union, but soon cooler heads prevailed. The convention did insist, however, that a state had the right "to interpose its authority" to protect its citizens against unconstitutional federal laws. This **nullification** doctrine was not new; Madison and Jefferson had proposed it in the Virginia and Kentucky Resolves opposing the Alien and Sedition Acts in 1798 (see Chapter 8). In any event, the nullification threat from Hartford was ignored, for peace with Britain was announced as delegates from the convention made their way to Washington to deliver their message to Congress. There the convention's grievances were treated not as serious business but as an anticlimactic joke.

**8–12**
*Report and Resolutions of the Hartford Convention* (1814)

## THE TREATY OF GHENT

By 1814, the long Napoleonic Wars in Europe were slowly drawing to a close, and the British decided to end their war with the Americans. The peace treaty, after months of hard negotiation, was signed at Ghent, Belgium, on Christmas Eve in 1814. Like the war itself, the treaty was inconclusive. The major issues of impressment and neutral rights were not mentioned, but the British did agree to evacuate their western posts, and late in the negotiations they abandoned their insistence on a buffer state for neutral Indian peoples in the Northwest.

For all its international inconsequence, the war did have an important effect on national morale. Andrew Jackson's victory at New Orleans allowed Americans to believe that they had defeated the British. It would be more accurate to say that by not losing the war the Americans had ended their own feelings of colonial dependency. Equally important, they convinced the British government to stop thinking of America as its colony.

The only clear losers of the war were the northwestern Indian nations and their southern allies. With the death of Tecumseh at the Battle of the Thames in 1813 and the defeat of the southern Creeks in 1814, the last hope of a united Indian resistance to white expansion perished forever. Britain's abandonment of its Indian allies in the **Treaty of Ghent** sealed their fate. By 1815, American settlers were on their way west again.

**Nullification**  A constitutional doctrine holding that a state has a legal right to declare a national law null and void within its borders.

**Treaty of Ghent**  Treaty signed in December 1814 between the United States and Britain that ended the War of 1812.

**WHAT WERE** the principle provisions of the Missouri Compromise?

**myhistorylab**

Review Summary

# DEFINING THE BOUNDARIES

With the War of 1812 behind them, Americans turned, more seriously than ever before, to the tasks of expansion and national development. The so-called Era of Good Feelings (1817–23) found politicians largely in agreement on a national agenda, and a string of diplomatic achievements forged by John Quincy Adams gave the nation sharper definition. But the limits to expansion also became clear: the Panic of 1819 showed the dangers in economic growth, and the Missouri Crisis laid bare the sectional split that attended westward expansion.

## ANOTHER WESTWARD SURGE

The end of the War of 1812 was followed by a westward surge to the Mississippi River. The extent of the population redistribution was dramatic: in 1790, about 95 percent of the nation's population had lived in states bordering the Atlantic Ocean; by 1820 fully 25 percent of the population lived west of the Appalachians (see Map 9.5).

**MAP 9.5**

**Spread of Settlement: Westward Surge, 1800–1820**    Within a period of twenty years, a quarter of the nation's population had moved west of the Appalachian Mountains. The westward surge was a dynamic source of American optimism.

HOW DID westward movement vary by region between 1800 and 1820?

What accounted for this extraordinary westward surge? There were both push and pull factors. Between 1800 and 1820, the nation's population almost doubled, increasing from 5.3 million to 9.6 million. Overpopulated farmland in all of the seaboard states pushed farmers off the land, while new land pulled them westward. The defeat and removal of Indians in the War of 1812 was another important pull factor.

The most important pull factor, however, was the attractive price of western land. The Land Ordinance of 1785 priced western lands too high for all but speculators and the wealthy (see Chapter 7), but subsequent realities had slowly forced Congress to enact land laws more favorable to the small farmer. The most sustained challenge came from "squatters," who repeatedly took up land before it was officially open for sale and then claimed a "preemption" right of purchase at a lower price that reflected the value of improvements they had made to the land. Congress sought to suppress this illegal settlement and ordered the expulsion of squatters on several occasions but to no avail.

Finally, in the Land Act of 1820, Congress set the price of land at $1.25 an acre, the minimum purchase at eighty acres (in contrast to the 640-acre minimum in 1785), and a down payment of $100 in cash. This was the most liberal land law yet passed in American history, but the cash requirement still favored speculators, who had more cash than most small farmers (see Figure 9.2). Except in southern Ohio and parts of Kentucky and Tennessee, there was very little contact among regional cultures. New Englanders carried their values and lifestyles directly west and settled largely with their own communities; Southerners did the same. One section of northern Ohio along Lake Erie, for example, had been Connecticut's western land claim since the days of its colonial charter. Rather than give up the land when the Northwest Territory was established in 1787, Connecticut held onto the Western Reserve (as it was known) and encouraged its citizens to move there. Group settlement was common. These New Englanders brought to the Western Reserve their religion (Congregational), their love of learning, and their adamant opposition to slavery.

Western migration in the South was very different. On this frontier, the people clearing the land were African American slaves creating plantations not for themselves but for their owners. Even before the war, plantation owners in the Natchez district of Mississippi had made fortunes growing cotton, which they shipped to Britain from New Orleans. After the war, as cotton growing expanded, hopeful slave owners from older parts of the South (Virginia, North and South Carolina, Georgia) flooded into the region, bringing their slaves with them or, increasingly, purchasing new ones supplied by the internal slave trade. More than half of the migrants to the Old Southwest after 1812 were enslaved African Americans. This involuntary migration of slaves tore African American families apart at the same time that white families viewed migration as a chance to replicate the lifestyle and values of older southern states on this new frontier (see Chapter 10).

The western transplantation of distinctive regional cultures explains why, although by 1820 western states accounted for more than a third of all states (eight out of twenty-three), the West did not form a third, unified political region. Although there were common western issues—in particular, the demand for better roads and other transportation routes—communities in the Old Northwest, in general, shared New England political attitudes, whereas those in the Old Southwest shared southern attitudes.

**Figure 9.2 Western Land Sales**
Surges in western land sales reflect surges in westward expansion. Western land sales following the War of 1812 reached an unprecedented 3.5 million acres, but that was small in comparison with what was to come in the 1830s and 1850s. Not all land sales reflected actual settlement, however, and speculation in western lands was rampant. Collapse of the postwar speculative boom contributed to the Panic of 1819, and the abrupt end to the boom of the 1830s led to the Panic of 1837.

Robert Riegel and Robert Athearn, *America Moves West* (New York: Holt Rinehart 1964).

---

**QUICK REVIEW**

**Westward Surge, 1800–1820**

◆ By 1820 25 percent of the population lived west of the Appalachians.

◆ Group settlement was common.

◆ Lure of new land pulled farmers west.

**The hopes of** every westward migrant are exemplified in this series of four illustrations imagining inevitable progress from pioneer cabin to prosperous farm. The illustrations, "The Pioneer Settler and His Progress," appeared in a booster history advertising land in western New York.

## THE ELECTION OF 1816 AND THE ERA OF GOOD FEELINGS

In 1816, James Monroe, the last of the Virginia Dynasty, was easily elected president over his Federalist opponent Rufus King. This was the last election in which Federalists ran a candidate. Monroe had no opponent in 1820 and was reelected nearly unanimously (231 to 1). The triumph of the Jeffersonian Republicans over the Federalists seemed complete.

Monroe's politics reflected changing times. When he visited Boston, as recently as 1815 the heart of a secession-minded Federalist region, he received an enthusiastic welcome, prompting the Federalist *Columbian Centinel* to proclaim an "**Era of Good Feelings.**" The phrase has been applied to Monroe's presidency (1817–25) ever since.

## THE AMERICAN SYSTEM

Monroe sought a government of national unity, and he chose men from North and South, Jeffersonian Republicans and Federalists, for his cabinet. He selected John Quincy Adams, a former Federalist, as his secretary of state, virtually assuring that Adams, like his father, would become president. To balance Adams, Monroe picked John C. Calhoun of South Carolina, a prominent War Hawk, as secretary of war. And Monroe supported the **American System**, a program of national economic development that became identified with westerner Henry Clay, Speaker of the House of Representatives.

In supporting the American System, Monroe was following President Madison, who had proposed the program in his message to Congress in December 1815. Madison and Monroe broke with Jefferson's agrarianism to embrace much of the Federalist program for economic development, including the chartering of a national bank, a tax on imported goods to protect American manufactur-

**Era of Good Feelings** The period from 1817 to 1823 in which the disappearance of the Federalists enabled the Republicans to govern in a spirit of seemingly nonpartisan harmony.

**American System** The program of government subsidies favored by Henry Clay and his followers to promote American economic growth and protect domestic manufacturers from foreign competition.

ers, and a national system of roads and canals. All three of these had first been proposed by Alexander Hamilton in the 1790s (see Chapter 8). At the time, these proposals had met with bitter Jeffersonian Republican opposition. The support that Madison and Monroe gave to Hamilton's ideas following the War of 1812 was a crucial sign of the dynamism of the American commercial economy. Many Republicans now acknowledged that the federal government had a role to play in fostering the economic and commercial conditions in which both yeoman farmer and merchant could succeed.

In 1816, Congress chartered the Second Bank of the United States for twenty years. Because they feared the economic power of rich men, Jeffersonian Republicans had allowed the charter of the original Bank of the United States, founded in 1791, to expire in 1811. The Republican about-face in 1816 was a sign that the strength of commercial interests had grown to rival that of farmers, whose distrust for central banks persisted.

The **Tariff of 1816** was the first substantial protective tariff in American history. In 1815, British manufacturers, who had been excluded for eight years (from the Embargo Act of 1807 to the end of the War of 1812), flooded the U.S. market with their products. American manufacturers complained that the British were dumping goods below cost in order to prevent the growth of American industries. Congress responded with a tariff on imported woolens and cottons, on iron, leather, hats, paper, and sugar. The measure had southern as well as northern support, although in later years, differences over the passage of higher tariffs would become one of the most persistent sources of sectional conflict.

The third item in the American System, funding for roads and canals—internal improvements, as they came to be known—was more controversial. Monroe and Madison both supported genuinely national (that is, interstate) projects such as the National Road from Cumberland, Maryland, to Vandalia, Illinois. Congressmen, however, aware of the urgent need to improve transportation in general, and sensing the political advantages from directing funds to their districts, proposed spending federal money on local projects. Both Madison and Monroe vetoed such local proposals, believing them to be unconstitutional.

The support of Madison and Monroe for measures initially identified with their political opposition was an indicator of their realism. The three aspects of the American System—bank, tariff, roads—were all parts of the basic infrastructure that the American economy needed in order to develop. Briefly, during the Era of Good Feelings, politicians agreed about the need for all three. Later, each would be a source of heated partisan argument.

## The Diplomacy of John Quincy Adams

The diplomatic achievements of the Era of Good Feelings were due almost entirely to the efforts of one man, John Quincy Adams, Monroe's secretary of state. Adams set himself the task of tidying up the borders of the United States. Two accords with Britain—the **Rush-Bagot Treaty of 1817** and the Convention of 1818—fixed the border between the United States and Canada at the 49th parallel and resolved conflicting U.S. and British claims to Oregon with an agreement to occupy it jointly for ten (eventually twenty) years.

Adams's major diplomatic accomplishment was the Adams-Onís or Transcontinental Treaty of 1819, in which he skillfully wrested concessions from the faltering Spanish empire. Adams convinced Spain not only to cede Florida but also to drop all previous claims it had to the Louisiana Territory and Oregon. In return, the United States relinquished claims on Texas and assumed responsibility for the $5 million in claims that U.S. citizens had against Spain.

**9–7**
Henry Clay, *Defense of the American System* (1832)

**Tariff of 1816**   A tax imposed by Congress on imported goods.

**Rush-Bagot Treaty of 1817**   Treaty between the United States and Britain that effectively demilitarized the Great Lakes by sharply limiting the number of ships each power could station on them.

**Monroe Doctrine** Declaration by President James Monroe in 1823 that the Western Hemisphere was to be closed off to further European colonization and that the United States would not interfere in the internal affairs of European nations.

**9–6**

*The Monroe Doctrine and a Reaction* (1823)

Finally, Adams picked his way through the remarkable changes occurring in Latin America, developing the policy that bears his president's name, the **Monroe Doctrine**. The United States was the first country outside Latin America to recognize the independence of Spain's former colonies. When the European powers (France, Austria, Russia, and Prussia) began to talk of a plan to help Spain recover the lost colonies, what was the United States to do? The British, suspicious of the European powers, proposed a British-American declaration against European intervention in the hemisphere. Others might have been flattered by an approach from the British empire, but Adams would have none of it. Showing the national pride that was so characteristic of the era, Adams insisted on an independent American policy. He therefore drafted for the president the hemispheric policy that the United States has followed ever since.

On December 2, 1823, the president presented the Monroe Doctrine to Congress and the world. He called for the end of colonization of the Western Hemisphere by European nations (this was aimed as much at Russia and its Pacific Coast settlements as at other European powers). Intervention by European powers in the affairs of the independent New World nations would be considered by the United States a danger to its own peace and safety. Finally, Monroe pledged that the United States would not interfere in the affairs of European countries or in the affairs of their remaining New World colonies.

All of this was a very loud bark from a very small dog. In 1823, the United States lacked the military and economic force to back up its grand statement. In fact, what kept the European powers out of Latin America was British opposition to European intervention, enforced by the Royal Navy. The Monroe Doctrine was, however, useful in Adams's last diplomatic achievement, the Convention of 1824, in which Russia gave up its claim to the Oregon Territory and accepted 54°40' north latitude as the southern border of Russian America. Thus, Adams had contained another possible threat to American continental expansion (see Map 9.6).

## THE PANIC OF 1819

Across this impressive record of political and economic nation building fell the shadow of the Panic of 1819. A delayed reaction to the end of the War of 1812 and the Napoleonic Wars, the panic forced Americans to come to terms with their economic place in a peaceful world. As British merchant ships resumed trade on routes they had abandoned during the wars, the American shipping boom ended. And as European farm production recovered from the wars, the international demand for American foodstuffs declined and American farmers and shippers suffered.

Domestic economic conditions made matters worse. The western land boom that began in 1815 turned into a speculative frenzy. Land sales, which had totaled 1 million acres in 1815, mushroomed to 3.5 million in 1818. Many settlers bought on credit, aided by small "wildcat" state banks that made loans far beyond their resources. This was not the first—or the last—speculative boom in western lands. But it ended like all the rest—with a sharp contraction of credit, begun on this occasion by the Second Bank of the United States, which in 1819 forced state banks to foreclose on many bad loans. Many small farmers were ruined, and they blamed the faraway Bank of the United States for their troubles. In the 1830s, Andrew Jackson would build a political movement on their resentment.

Urban workers lost their jobs as international trade declined and as manufacturers failed because of competition from British imports. As they lobbied for local relief, many workers became deeply involved in urban politics, where they could express their resentment against the merchants and owners who had laid them off. Thus developed another component of Andrew Jackson's new political coalition.

Legend:
- Adams-Onis Treaty, 1819
- Rush-Bagot Treaty, 1817, with Convention of 1818
- Convention of 1824

RUSSIAN TERRITORY
54°40′

BRITISH NORTH AMERICA

OREGON COUNTRY (US and Great Britain)

49°0′

Missouri R.

UNORGANIZED TERRITORY

Mississippi R.

Fort Ross

SPANISH TERRITORY

Arkansas R.

Red R.

Rio Grande

MICHIGAN TERRITORY

INDIANA
OHIO
Ohio R.
ILLINOIS
St. Louis
MISSOURI TERRITORY
KENTUCKY
ARKANSAS TERRITORY
TENNESSEE
MISSISSIPPI
ALABAMA
GEORGIA
LOUISIANA
New Orleans

VERMONT
MAINE (MASS.)
NEW HAMPSHIRE
MASSACHUSETTS
NEW YORK
RHODE ISLAND
CONNECTICUT
PENNSYLVANIA
NEW JERSEY
DELAWARE
MARYLAND
VIRGINIA
NORTH CAROLINA
SOUTH CAROLINA

FLORIDA TERRITORY

PACIFIC OCEAN

ATLANTIC OCEAN

Gulf of Mexico

**MAP 9.6**
**John Quincy Adams's Border Treaties**   John Quincy Adams, secretary of state in the Monroe administration (1817–25), solidified the nation's boundaries in several treaties with Britain and Spain: the Rush-Bagot Treaty of 1817 and the Conventions of 1818 and 1824 and the Adams-Onís Treaty of 1819.

WHAT AGREEMENTS were reached in the treaties signed by John Quincy Adams to settle U.S. borders?

Another confrontation arose over the tariff. Southern planters, hurt by a decline in the price of cotton, began to actively protest the protective tariff, which kept the price of imported goods high even when cotton prices were low. Manufacturers, hurt by British competition, lobbied for even higher rates, which they achieved in 1824 over southern protests. Southerners then began to express doubts about the fairness of a political system in which they were always outvoted.

The Panic of 1819 was a symbol of this transitional time. It showed how far the country had moved since 1800, from Jefferson's republic of yeoman farmers toward a nation dominated by commerce. And the anger and resentment expressed by the groups harmed by the depression—farmers, urban workers, and southern planters—were portents of the politics of the upcoming Jackson era.

9–5
*Thomas Jefferson Reacts to the "Missouri Question" (1820)*

## THE MISSOURI COMPROMISE

In the Missouri Crisis of 1819–21, the nation confronted the momentous issue that had been buried in the general enthusiasm for expansion: as America moved west, would the largely southern system of slavery expand as well? Until 1819, this question was decided regionally. The Northwest Ordinance of 1787 explicitly banned slavery in the northern section of trans-Appalachia but made no mention of it elsewhere. Because so much of the expansion into the Old Northwest and Southwest was lateral (Northerners stayed in the North, Southerners in the South), there was little conflict over sectional differences. In 1819, however, the sections collided in Missouri, which applied for admission to the Union as a slave state (see Map 9.7).

The northern states, all of which had abolished slavery by 1819, were opposed to the extension of slavery. In addition to the moral issue, the Missouri question raised the political issue of sectional balance. Northern politicians did not want to

**MAP 9.7**

**The Missouri Compromise** Before the Missouri Compromise of 1820, the Ohio River was the dividing line between the free states of the Old Northwest and the slaveholding states of the Old Southwest. The compromise stipulated that Missouri would enter the Union as a slave state (balanced by Maine, a free state), but slavery would be prohibited in the Louisiana Territory north of 36°30' (Missouri's southern boundary). This awkward compromise lasted until 1846, when the Mexican-American War reopened the issue of the expansion of slavery.

HOW DID westward expansion create added pressure to resolve the question of slavery?

## CHRONOLOGY

| | | | | |
|---|---|---|---|---|
| **1800** | Thomas Jefferson elected president | | **1815** | Battle of New Orleans |
| **1802** | Russian-American Company headquarters established at Sitka, Alaska | | **1816** | James Monroe elected president |
| | | | | Congress charters Second Bank of the United States |
| **1803** | Louisiana Purchase | | | Indiana admitted to the Union |
| | *Marbury* v. *Madison* | | **1817** | Mississippi admitted to the Union |
| | Ohio admitted to the Union | | **1818** | Illinois admitted to the Union |
| **1804** | Lewis and Clark expedition leaves St. Louis | | **1819** | Panic of 1819 |
| | Thomas Jefferson reelected president | | | Adams-Onís Treaty |
| **1807** | *Chesapeake–Leopard* incident | | | Alabama admitted to the Union |
| | Embargo Act | | **1819–20** | Missouri Crisis and Compromise |
| **1808** | James Madison elected president | | **1820** | James Monroe reelected president |
| **1809** | Tecumseh forms military alliance among Northwest Confederacy peoples | | | Maine admitted to the Union |
| **1811** | Battle of Tippecanoe | | **1821** | Missouri admitted to the Union as a slave state |
| **1812** | War of 1812 begins | | **1823** | Monroe Doctrine |
| | James Madison reelected president | | | |
| | Louisiana admitted to the Union | | | |
| **1814** | Treaty of Ghent | | | |

admit another slave state. To do so would tip the balance of power in the Senate. For their part, Southerners believed they needed an advantage in the Senate; because of faster population growth in the North, they were already outnumbered (105 to 81) in the House of Representatives. But above all, Southerners did not believe Congress had the power to limit the expansion of slavery. Slavery, in southern eyes, was a question of property and, therefore, a matter for state rather than federal legislation.

In 1819, Representative James Tallmadge Jr. of New York began more than a year of congressional controversy when he demanded that Missouri agree to the gradual end of slavery as the price of entering the Union. At first, the general public paid little attention, but religious reformers (Quakers prominent among them) organized a number of antislavery rallies in northern cities that made politicians take notice. This was the first time that the growing northern reform impulse had intersected with sectional politics. It was also the first time that southern threats of secession were made openly in Congress.

In 1820, Congress achieved compromise over the sectional differences. Henry Clay forged the first of the many agreements that were to earn him the title of "the Great Pacificator" (peacemaker). The **Missouri Compromise** maintained the balance between free and slave states: Maine (which had been part of Massachusetts) was admitted as a free state in 1820 and Missouri as a slave state in the following year. A policy was also enacted with respect to slavery in the rest of the Louisiana Purchase: slavery was prohibited north of 36°30′ north latitude—the southern boundary of Missouri—and permitted south of that line. This meant that the vast majority of the Louisiana Territory would be free. In reality, then, the Missouri Compromise could be only a temporary solution, because it left open the question of how the balance between slave and free states would be maintained.

**Missouri Compromise** Sectional compromise in Congress in 1820 that admitted Missouri to the Union as a slave state and Maine as a free state and prohibited slavery in the northern Louisiana Purchase territory.

# CONCLUSION

In complex ways a developing economy, geographical expansion, and even a minor war helped shape American unity. Local, small, settled, face-to-face communities in both the North and the South began to send their more mobile, expectant members to new occupations in urban centers or west to form new settlements.

The westward population movement dramatically changed the political landscape and Americans' view of themselves. But expansion did not create the "empire for liberty" that Thomas Jefferson had hoped for. While expansion did indeed create economic opportunity, it also displaced and destroyed Indian communities such as the Mandans, the Shawnee, and many others. And it also created an even greater denial of liberty, as we shall see in the next chapter, in a greatly expanded community tied to cotton and to the slave labor that produced it.

# REVIEW QUESTIONS

1. What economic and political problems did the United States face as a new nation in a world dominated by war between Britain and France? How successful were the efforts by the Jefferson, Madison, and Monroe administrations to solve these problems?

2. The anti-European cast of Jefferson's republican agrarianism made it appealing to many Americans who wished to believe in their nation's uniqueness, but how realistic was it?

3. Some Federalists opposed the Louisiana Purchase, warning of the dangers of westward expansion. What are arguments for and against expansion?

4. What contradictions in American Indian policy did the confrontations between Tecumseh's alliance and soldiers and settlers in the Old Northwest reveal? Can you suggest solutions to these contradictions?

5. What did the War of 1812 accomplish?

6. What were the issues that made it impossible for the Era of Good Feelings to last?

**myhistorylab**
Flashcard Review

# KEY TERMS

American System (p. 230)
Embargo Act (p. 220)
Era of Good Feelings (p. 230)
*Marbury* v. *Madison* (p. 216)
Missouri Compromise (p. 235)
Monroe Doctrine (p. 232)
Nullification (p. 227)

Pan-Indian military resistance movement (p. 222)
Rush-Bagot Treaty of 1817 (p. 231)
Tariff of 1816 (p. 231)
Treaty of Ghent (p. 227)
War Hawks (p. 224)
War of 1812 (p. 224)

# RECOMMENDED READING

Catharine Allgor, *Parlor Politics: In Which the Ladies of Washington Help Build a City and a Government* (2000). Describes the vital role that women played in the politics of the new capital city.

Stephen E. Ambrose, *Undaunted Courage: Meriwether Lewis, Thomas Jefferson, and the Opening of the American West* (1996). This heroic version of the expedition is told by a master storyteller. It ought, however, to be supplemented by the Ronda version cited below that pays attention to the Indian side of the story.

Walter Borneman, *1812: The War That Forged a Nation* (2004). A very readable account.

R. David Edmunds, *Tecumseh and the Quest for Indian Leadership* (1984). A sympathetic portrait.

Joseph J. Ellis, *American Sphinx: The Character of Thomas Jefferson* (1998). An engaging exploration of Jefferson's many contradictions.

John Mack Faragher, *Sugar Creek* (1987). The fullest examination of the lives of pioneers in the Old Northwest.

Robert Pierce Forbes, *The Missouri Compromise and Its Aftermath: Slavery and the Meaning of America* (2007). Discusses both contemporary debates over the compromise and its impact.

Jon Kukla, *A Wilderness So Immense: The Louisiana Purchase and the Destiny of America* (2003). A personality-filled account of the negotiations and of various hopes and plans for Louisiana.

Glover Moore, *The Missouri Controversy, 1819–1821* (1953). The standard account.

Peter S. Onuf, *Jefferson's Empire* (2000). A thoughtful study of Jefferson's ideas about republicanism, empire, and nationalism.

James Ronda, *Lewis and Clark among the Indians* (1984). An innovative look at the famous explorers through the eyes of the Indian peoples they encountered.

myhistorylab™
Where it's a good time to connect to the past!

For study resources for this chapter, go to **www.myhistorylab.com** and choose *Out of Many, Teaching and Learning Classroom Edition*. You will find a wealth of study and review material for this chapter, including pretests and posttests, customized study plan, key-term review flash cards, interactive map and document activities, and documents for analysis.

. . . *whatever accidents or misfortunes might attend my flight nothing could be worse than what threatened my stay.*

— *Hannah Crafts*

A slave auction in Virginia. 1861

# 10
# THE SOUTH AND SLAVERY
## 1790s–1850s

**HOW DID** attitudes in the South toward slavery change after the invention of the cotton gin?

**WHAT WAS** life like for the typical slave in the American South?

SLAVE COLLAR
RICHMOND VIRGINIA
SLAVE MARKET

THIS ANTE-BELLUM SLAVE COLLAR HAS AN
OLD TAG ATTACHED FROM AN EARLY
HISTORICAL SOCIETY COLLECTION. A RARE
AND CHOICE RELIC FROM EARLY VIRGINIA

**WHAT ROLE** did religion play in African American slave communities?

**WHAT WERE** the values of yeoman farmers?

**WHO MADE** up the planter elite?

**WHAT PROSLAVERY** arguments were developed in the first half of the nineteenth century?

# AMERICAN COMMUNITIES
## Cotton Communities in the Old Southwest

IN 1834, SAMUEL TOWNES OF SOUTH CAROLINA CAUGHT "ALABAMA Fever." Restive under what seemed to him excessive demands from his large and well-connected family, Samuel rebelled by marrying a woman of whom his family disapproved and moving with her and his slaves to Perry County, Alabama, a newly opened part of the Old Southwest suitable for growing cotton. There he practiced law in the village of Marion, bought a plantation on the banks of the Cahaba River, and acquired ten to fifteen more slaves. Almost all of Samuel's new possessions were bought on credit. Samuel's desire for wealth caused him to drive his slaves very hard. Always convinced that they were malingering, he demanded that his overseer "whip them like the devil" to pick more cotton.

The Panic of 1837 devastated Samuel's ambitions. As the price of cotton fell to 7 cents a pound (from 15 cents in 1836), banks demanded repayment of their generous loans. Samuel sold some slaves, and rented out the labor of others, but he was forced to ask for loans from the family he had been so eager to escape. In 1844 his plantation was sold at auction. Three years later, his health failed, and he and his wife, Joanna, had no choice but to return to South Carolina and the charity of kinfolk.

The rapid westward expansion of cotton cultivation exposed the undeveloped state of community formation among the southern elite. The plantation form of agriculture, which had been the rule in the South since its earliest days, meant that cities were few and community institutions like churches and schools were rare. Slave-owning families depended almost entirely on kinship networks for assistance (and the obligations that Samuel Townes wished to avoid) and for sociability. Families who moved west frequently found themselves lost without their customary family connections. Wider community connections and support lagged behind the pursuit of profits to be made from cotton.

What of the slaves that Samuel brought with him? Once part of a larger Townes family group in South Carolina, the slaves that Samuel owned were separated from their kinfolk permanently and had to adjust to living with a number of newly purchased slaves in Alabama. Most of the new slaves were bought as individuals and were usually still in their teens or even younger. Young male slaves were favored for the backbreaking work of cut-

ting trees and clearing land for cultivation. Sometimes owners worked side by side with their workers at this initial stage. But generally, uniformity and strict discipline were the rule on cotton plantations. Owners eager to clear land rapidly and make quick profits often drove the clearing crews at an unmerciful pace. And, as Samuel Townes had, they attempted to impose strict discipline and a rapid pace on the work gangs that planted, hoed, and harvested cotton. Slaves from other parts of the South, used to more individual and less intense work, hated the cotton regime and most of all hated the overseers who enforced it.

Only long-practiced African American community-building strategies saved these young transported slaves—some called it a "Second Middle Passage"—from complete isolation. Beginning in the earliest days of slavery, Africans from many different tribes built their own communities by using the language of kinship (for example, "brother," "sister," "uncle," "aunt," and "child") to encompass everyone in new imagined families. On one hand, the cultivation of cotton required many workers, thus creating the conditions necessary for large slave communities in the Old Southwest. On the other hand, because the price of cotton was unstable, probably many shared the experience of the Townes slaves, who were sold again when the plantation failed.

Thus, the new land in the Old Southwest that appeared to offer so much opportunity for owners bred tensions caused by forcible sale and migration, by the organization and pace of cotton cultivation, and by the owners' often violent efforts to control their slaves in a new region where community bonds were undeveloped. For planters and slaves alike, migration broke long-standing family ties that were the most common form of community throughout the South. The irony is that African Americans, who were the most cruelly affected, knew better how to build new communities than did their privileged owners.

In the first half of the nineteenth century, world demand for cotton transformed the South, promoting rapid expansion and unprecedented prosperity. But it also tied the South to a slave system that was inherently unstable and violent. Although southern slave owners frequently talked about their plantations as communities and their slaves as family, the slave system was not one community but two with the strengths of the slave community largely invisible to the owners.

Marion, AL

# KING COTTON AND SOUTHERN EXPANSION

Slavery had long dominated southern life. African American slaves grew the great export crops of the colonial period—tobacco, rice, and indigo—on which slave owners' fortunes were made, and their presence shaped southern society and culture (see Chapter 4). Briefly, in the early days of American independence, the slave system waned, only to be revived by the immense profitability of cotton in a newly industrializing world. Cotton became the dominant crop in a rapidly expanding South that more than doubled in size (see Map 10.1). The overwhelming economic success of cotton and of the slave system on which it depended created a distinctive regional culture quite different from that developing in the North.

## COTTON AND EXPANSION INTO THE OLD SOUTHWEST

Short-staple cotton had long been recognized as a crop ideally suited to southern soils and growing conditions. But it had one major drawback: the seeds were so difficult to remove from the lint that it took an entire day to hand-clean a single pound of cotton. The invention in 1793 that made cotton growing profitable was the result of collaboration between a young Northerner named Eli Whitney and Catherine Greene, a South Carolina plantation owner. Whitney built a prototype cotton engine, dubbed "gin" for short, a simple device consisting of a hand-cranked cylinder with teeth that tore the lint away from the seeds. At Greene's suggestion, the teeth were made of wire. With the cotton gin, it was possible to clean more than fifty pounds of cotton a day. Soon large and small planters in the inland regions of Georgia and South Carolina had begun to grow cotton. By 1811, this area was producing 60 million pounds of cotton a year and exporting most of it to England.

Other areas of the South quickly followed South Carolina and Georgia into cotton production. New land was needed because cotton growing rapidly depleted the soil. The profits to be made from cotton growing drew a rush of southern farmers into the so-called black belt—an area stretching through western Georgia, Alabama, and Mississippi that was blessed with exceptionally fertile soil. Following the War of 1812, Southerners were seized by "Alabama Fever." In one of the swiftest migrations in American history, white Southerners and their slaves flooded into western Georgia and the areas that would become Alabama and Mississippi (the Old Southwest). On this frontier, African American pioneers (albeit involuntary ones) cleared the forests, drained the swamps, broke the ground, built houses and barns, and planted the first crops.

Like the simultaneous expansion into the Old Northwest, settlement of the Old Southwest took place at the expense of the region's Indian population (see Chapter 9). Beginning with the defeat of the Creeks at Horseshoe Bend in 1814 and ending with the Cherokee forced migration along the "Trail of Tears" in 1838, the Five Civilized Tribes—the Cherokees, Chickasaws, Choctaws, Creeks, and Seminoles—were forced to give up their lands and move to Indian Territory (see Chapter 11).

Following the "Alabama Fever" of 1816–20, several later surges of southern expansion (1832–38, and again in the mid-1850s) carried cotton planting over the Mississippi River into Louisiana and deep into Texas. In the minds of the mobile, enterprising Southerners who sought their fortunes in the West, cotton profits and expansion went hand in hand. But the expansion of cotton meant the expansion of slavery.

**HOW DID** attitudes in the South toward slavery change after the invention of the cotton gin?

## myhistorylab
Review Summary

## IMAGE KEY
for pages 238–239

a. A chain used to tie gangs of slaves.
b. "The Shadow" plantation of Louisiana.
c. A slave auction in Virginia, 1861.
d. A whip of coiled rope used on slaves.
e. An auction of eight black slaves.
f. Mature cotton bolls on the stem of a plant.
g. Slaves carry sacks of cotton on their heads on a South Carolina plantation field.
h. A slave collar with an attached tag from the slave market in Richmond, Virginia.
i. African American worshippers in a sketch by Joseph Becker.
j. A log cabin in New Braunfels, Texas in a painting by Carl G. von Iwonski.
k. Colonel and Mrs. James A. Whiteside in a James Cameron painting.
l. A proslavery cartoon, 1841.

# MAP EXPLORATION

To explore an interactive version of this map, go to **http://www.prenhall.com/faraghertlc/map10.1**

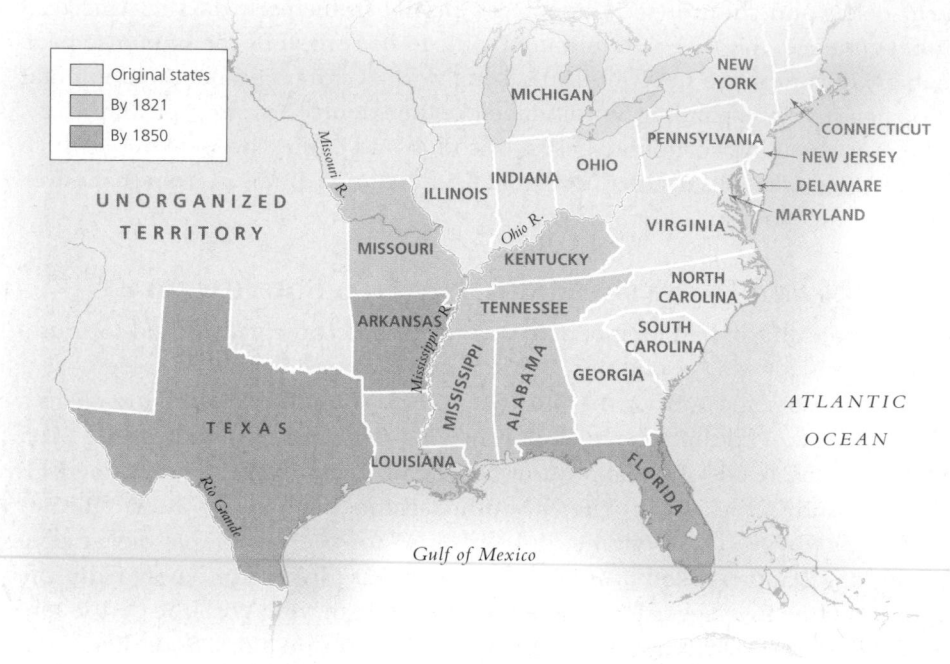

**MAP 10.1**

**The South Expands, 1790–1850**    This map shows the dramatic effect cotton production had on southern expansion. From the original six states of 1790, westward expansion, fueled by the search for new cotton lands, added another six states by 1821 and three more by 1850.

WHY WAS cotton production especially suited to slave labor?

## SLAVERY THE MAINSPRING—AGAIN

The export of cotton from the South was the dynamic force in the developing American economy in the 1790–1840 period. Just as the international slave trade had been the dynamic force in the Atlantic economy of the eighteenth century (see Chapter 4), southern slavery financed northern industrial development in the nineteenth century.

The rapid growth of cotton production was an international phenomenon. The insatiable demand for cotton was a result of the technological and social changes that we know today as the **Industrial Revolution**. Beginning early in the eighteenth century, a series of inventions resulted in the mechanized spinning and weaving of cloth in the world's first factories in the north of England. The ability of these factories to produce unprecedented amounts of cotton cloth revolutionized the world economy. The invention of the cotton gin came at just the right time. British textile manufacturers were eager to buy all the cotton that the South could produce. By the time of the Civil War, cotton accounted for almost 60 percent of American exports.

The connection between southern slavery and northern industry was very direct. Most mercantile services associated with the cotton trade (insurance,

**Industrial Revolution**   Revolution in the means and organization of production.

**This 1855 illustration** of black stevedores loading heavy bales of cotton onto waiting steamboats in New Orleans is an example of the South's dependence on cotton and the slave labor that produced it.

for example) were in northern hands and, significantly, so was shipping. This economic structure was not new. In colonial times, New England ships dominated the African slave trade. Some New England families invested some of their profits in the new technology of textile manufacturing in the 1790s. Other merchants made their money from cotton shipping and brokerage. Thus, as cotton boomed, it provided capital for the new factories of the North (see Chapter 12).

## A Slave Society in a Changing World

In the flush of freedom following the American Revolution, all the northern states abolished slavery or passed laws for gradual emancipation, and a number of slave owners in the Upper South freed their slaves (see Chapter 7). On January 1, 1808, the earliest date permitted by the Constitution, a bill to abolish the importation of slaves became law. Nevertheless, southern legislatures were unwilling to write steps toward emancipation into law, preferring to depend on the charity of individual slave owners.

But attitudes toward slavery rapidly changed in the south following the invention of the cotton gin in 1793 and the realization of the riches to be made from cotton. White Southerners believed that only African slaves could be forced to work day after day, year after year, at the rapid and brutal pace required in the cotton fields of large plantations in the steamy southern summer. As the production of cotton climbed higher every year in response to a seemingly inexhaustible international demand, so too did the demand for slaves and the conviction of Southerners that slavery was an economic necessity.

As had been true since colonial times, the centrality of slavery to the economy and the need to keep slaves under firm control required the South to become a slave society, rather than merely a society with slaves, as had been the case in the North. What this meant was that one particular form of social relationship, that of master and slave (one dominant, the other subordinate), became the model for all relationships, including personal interactions between white husbands and wives as well as interactions in politics and at work.

At a time when the North was experiencing the greatest spurt of urban growth in the nation's history (see Chapter 13), most of the South remained rural: less than 3 percent of Mississippi's population lived in cities of more than 2,500 residents, and only 10 percent of Virginia's did. The agrarian ideal, bolstered by

**QUICK REVIEW**

**The Economics of Slavery**

- Worldwide demand for cotton supported slavery.
- Export of cotton a dynamic part of American economy.
- Northern industry directly connected to slavery.

 **7–6**
Benjamin Banneker, *An African American Calls for an End to Slavery* (1791)

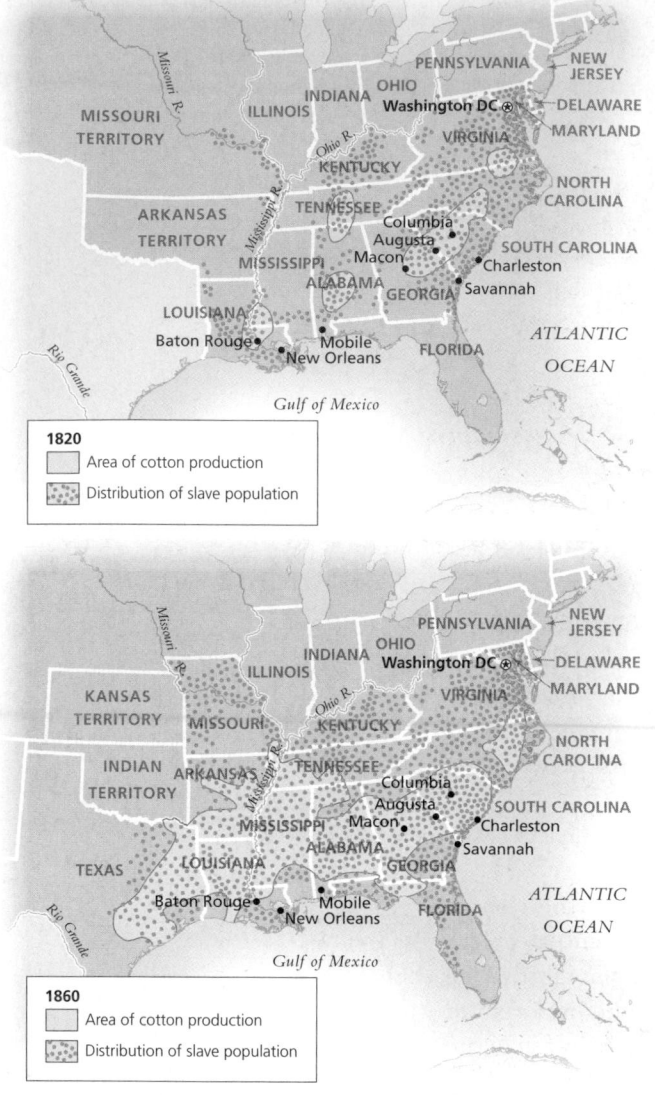

**MAP 10.2**
**Cotton Production and the Slave Population, 1820–60** In the forty years from 1820 to 1860, cotton production grew dramatically in both quantity and extent. Rapid westward expansion meant that by 1860 cotton production was concentrated in the black belt (so called for its rich soils) in the Lower South. As cotton production moved west and south, so did the enslaved African American population that produced it, causing a dramatic rise in the internal slave trade.

Sam Bowers Hilliard, *Atlas of Antebellum Southern Agriculture* (Baton Rouge: Lousiana State University Press, 1984).

WHY WAS the increasing dominance of cotton cultivation in the Lower South accompanied by a growing concentration of slaves in that region?

the cotton boom, encouraged the antiurban and anticommercial sentiments of many white Southerners. The South also lagged behind the North in industrialization and in canals and railroads (see Chapter 12). In 1860, only 15 percent of the nation's factories were located in the South.

Other changes, however, could not be so easily ignored. Nationwide, the slave states were losing their political dominance because their population was not keeping pace with that of the North. Equally alarming, outside the South, antislavery sentiment was growing rapidly. Southerners felt directly threatened by growing abolitionist sentiment in the North and by the 1834 action of the British government eliminating slavery on the sugar plantations of the West Indies. The South felt increasingly hemmed in by northern opposition to the expansion of slavery.

## THE INTERNAL SLAVE TRADE

The cotton boom caused a huge increase in the domestic slave trade. Plantation owners in the Upper South (Delaware, Kentucky, Maryland, Virginia, and Tennessee) sold their slaves to meet the demand for labor in the new and expanding cotton-growing regions of the Old Southwest. Cumulatively, between 1820 and 1860, nearly 50 percent of the slave population of the Upper South took part against their will in southern expansion (see Map 10.2). More slaves—an estimated 1 million—were uprooted by this internal slave trade and enforced migration in the early nineteenth century than were brought to North America during the entire time the international slave trade was legal (see Chapter 4).

Purchased by slave traders from owners in the Upper South, slaves were gathered together in notorious "slave pens" in places like Richmond and Charleston and then moved south by train or boat. Often slaves moved on foot, chained together in groups of fifty or more known as "coffles." Chained slaves in coffles were a common sight on southern roads and one difficult to reconcile with the notion of slavery as a benevolent institution. Arriving at a central market in the Lower South like Natchez, New Orleans, or Mobile, the slaves, after being carefully inspected by potential buyers, were sold at auction to the highest bidder (see Map 10.3).

In New Orleans, in the streets outside large slave pens near the French Quarter, thousands of slaves were displayed and sold each year. Dressed in new clothes provided by the traders and exhorted by the traders to walk, run, and otherwise show their stamina, slaves were presented to buyers. For their part, suspicious buyers, unsure that traders and slaves themselves were truthful, poked, prodded, and frequently stripped male and female slaves to be sure they were as healthy as the traders claimed.

Although popular stereotype portrayed slave traders as unscrupulous outsiders who persuaded kind and reluctant masters to sell their slaves, the historical truth is

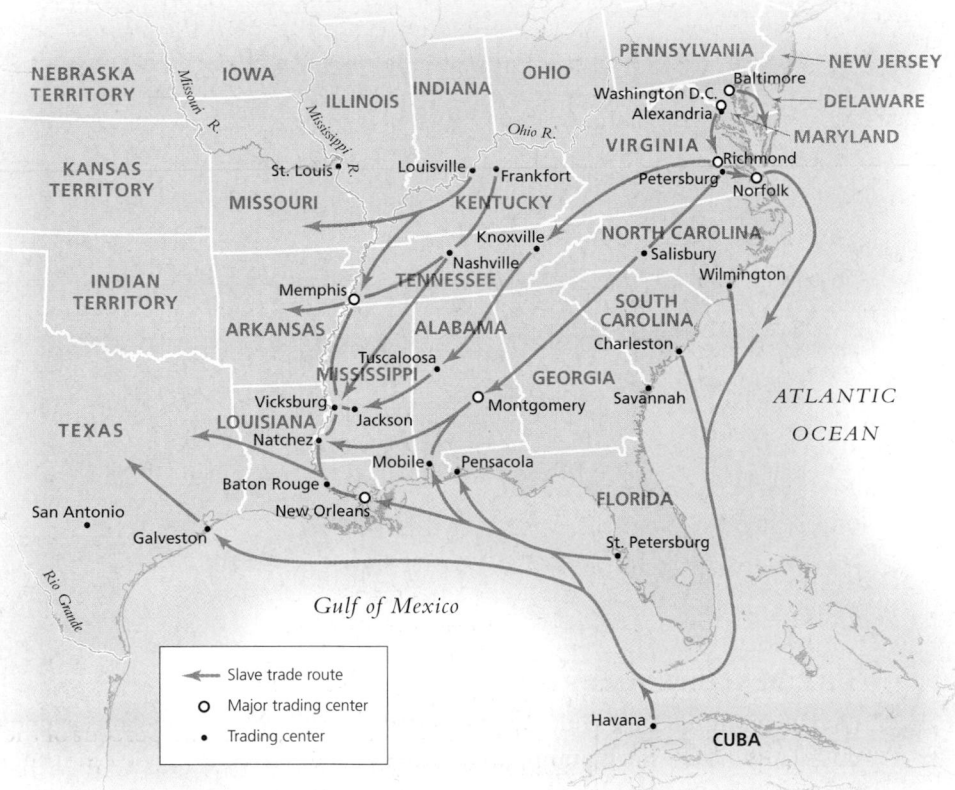

**MAP 10.3**
**Internal Slave Trade, 1820–60**   Between 1820 and 1860, nearly 50 percent of the slave population of the Upper South was sold to labor on the cotton plantations of the Lower South. This map shows the various routes by which they were "sold down the river," shipped by boat or marched south.
*Historical Atlas of the United States* (Washington, DC: National Geographic Society, 1988).

WHAT AGRICULTURAL trends help explain the relative decline of slavery in the Upper South?

much harsher. Traders, far from being shunned by slave-owning society, were often respected community members. Similarly, the sheer scale of the slave trade makes it impossible to believe that slave owners only reluctantly parted with their slaves at times of economic distress. Instead, it is clear that many owners sold slaves and separated slave families not out of necessity but to increase their profits. The sheer size and profitability of the internal slave trade made a mockery of southern claims for the benevolence of the slave system.

# THE AFRICAN AMERICAN COMMUNITY

Surely no group in American history has faced a harder job of community building than the black people of the antebellum South. Living in intimate, daily contact with their oppressors, African Americans nevertheless created an enduring culture of their own, a culture that had far-reaching and lasting influence on all of southern life and American society as a whole (see Chapter 4).

WHAT WAS life like for the typical slave in the American South?

**Review Summary**

**This engraving from** *Harper's Weekly* shows slaves, dressed in new clothing, lined up outside a New Orleans slave pen for inspection by potential buyers before the actual auction began. They were often threatened with punishment if they did not present a good appearance and manner that would fetch a high price.

## THE MATURE AMERICAN SLAVE SYSTEM

On January 1, 1808, the United States ended its participation in the international slave trade. Although a small number of slaves continued to be smuggled in from Africa, the growth of the slave labor force depended primarily on natural increase—that is, through births within the slave population. The slave population, estimated at 700,000 in 1790, grew to more than 4 million in 1860. A distinctive African American slave community, which had first emerged in the eighteenth century (see Chapter 4), expanded dramatically in the early years of the nineteenth century. This community was as much shaped by King Cotton as was the white South.

Cotton growing concentrated slaves on plantations, in contrast to the more dispersed distribution on smaller farms in earlier generations. The size of cotton plantations fostered the growth of slave communities. Over half of all slaves lived on plantations with twenty or more other slaves, and others, on smaller farms, had links with slaves on nearby properties. Urban slaves were able to make and sustain so many secret contacts with other African Americans in cities or towns that slave owners wondered whether slave discipline could be maintained in urban settings. There can be no question that the bonds among African Americans were what sustained them during the years of slavery.

In law, slaves were property, to be bought, sold, rented, worked, and otherwise used (but not abused or killed) as the owner saw fit. But slaves were also human beings, with feelings, needs, and hopes. Even though most white Southerners believed black people to be members of an inferior, childish race, all but the most brutal masters acknowledged the humanity of their slaves. White masters learned to live with the two key institutions of African American community life: the family and the African American church, and in their turn slaves learned, however painfully, to survive slavery.

## THE GROWTH OF THE SLAVE COMMUNITY

Of all the New World slave societies, the one that existed in the American South was the only one that grew by natural increase rather than through the constant importation of captured Africans. This fact alone made the African American community of the South different from the slave societies of Cuba, the Caribbean islands, and Brazil. In order to understand, we must examine the circumstances of survival and growth.

The growth of the African American slave population was not due to better treatment than in other New World slave societies, but to the higher fertility of African American women, who in 1808 (the year the international slave trade ended) had a crude birthrate of 35 to 40, causing a 2.2 percent yearly population growth. This was still below the fertility rate of white women, who had a crude birthrate of 55 and a 2.9 percent annual population growth. But by midcentury, the white rate had dropped to 1.99 percent, while the black rate remained high. African American slave women adopted the white practice of breastfeeding for only one year, and on average gave birth to six or eight children at year-and-a-half intervals. But they also suffered from the contradictory demands of slave owners, who wanted them to work hard while still having children, for every slave baby increased the wealth of the owners.

As a result, because pregnant black women were inadequately nourished, worked too hard, or were too frequently pregnant, mortality rates for slave children under five were twice those for their white counterparts. At the time, owners often accused slave women of smothering their infants by rolling over them when asleep.

Health remained a lifelong issue for slaves. Malaria and infectious diseases such as yellow fever and cholera were endemic in the South. White people as well as black died, as the life expectancy figures for 1850 show: 40 to 43 years for white people and 30 to 33 years for African Americans. Slaves were more at risk because of the circumstances of slave life: poor housing, poor diet, and constant, usually heavy, work. Sickness was chronic: 20 percent or more of the slave labor force on most plantations were sick at any one time.

## FROM CRADLE TO GRAVE

Slavery was a lifelong labor system, and the constant and inescapable issue between master and slave was how much work the slave would—or could—be forced to do. Southern white slave owners claimed that by housing, feeding, and clothing their slaves from infancy to death they were acting more humanely than northern industrialists who employed people only during their working years. But in spite of occasional instances of **manumission**—the freeing of a slave—the child born of a slave was destined to remain a slave.

Children lived with their parents (or with their mother if the father was a slave on another farm or plantation) in housing provided by the owner. Husband and wife cooperated in loving and sheltering their children and teaching them survival skills. From birth to about age seven, slave children played with one another and with white children, observing and learning how to survive. They saw the penalties: black adults, perhaps their own parents, whipped for disobedience; black women, perhaps their own sisters, violated by white men. And they might see one or both parents sold away as punishment or for financial gain. They would also see signs of white benevolence: special treats for children at holidays, appeals to loyalty from the master or mistress, perhaps friendship with a white child.

The children would learn slave ways of getting along: apparent acquiescence to white demands; pilfering; malingering, sabotage, and other methods of slowing the relentless work pace. But many white Southerners genuinely believed that their slaves were both less intelligent and more loyal than they really were. Frederick Douglass, whose fearless leadership of the abolitionist movement made him the most famous African American of his time, wryly noted, "As the master studies to keep the slave ignorant, the slave is cunning enough to make the master think he succeeds."

**Manumission**   The freeing of a slave.

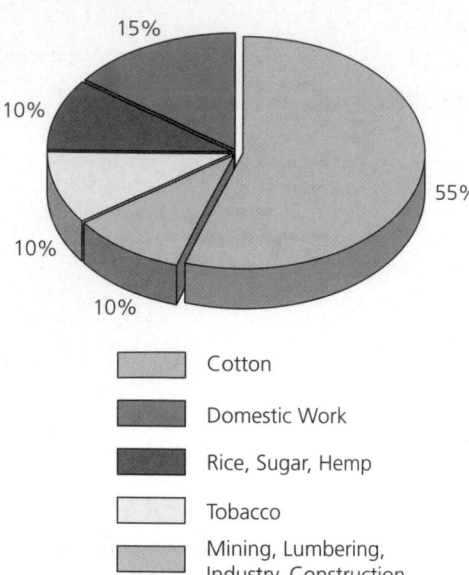

**Figure 10.1 Distribution of Slave Labor, 1850**
In 1850, 55 percent of all slaves worked in cotton, 10 percent in tobacco, and another 10 percent in rice, sugar, and hemp. Ten percent worked in mining, lumbering, industry, and construction, and 15 percent worked as domestic servants. Slave labor was not generally used to grow corn, the staple crop of the yeoman farmer.

**Gang System**  The organization and supervision of slave field hands into working teams on Southern plantations.

Black children had no schooling of any kind: in most of the southern states, it was against the law to teach a slave to read, although indulgent owners often rewarded their "pet" slaves by teaching them in spite of the law. At age twelve, slaves were considered full grown and put to work in the fields or in their designated occupation.

The explosive growth of cotton plantations changed the nature of southern slave labor. In 1850, 55 percent of all slaves were engaged in cotton growing. Another 20 percent labored to produce other crops: tobacco (10 percent), rice, sugar, and hemp. About 15 percent of all slaves were domestic servants, and the remaining 10 percent worked in mining, lumbering, industry, and construction (see Figure 10.1).

## FIELD WORK AND THE GANG SYSTEM

The field workers, 75 percent of all slaves, were most directly affected by the gang labor system employed on cotton plantations (as well as in tobacco and sugar). Cotton was a crop that demanded nearly year-round labor: from planting in April, to constant hoeing and cultivation through June, to a picking season that began in August and lasted until December. Owners divided their slaves into gangs of twenty to twenty-five, a communal labor pattern reminiscent of parts of Africa, but with a crucial difference— these workers were supervised by overseers with whips. On most plantations, the bell sounded an hour before sunup, and slaves were expected to be on their way to the fields as soon as it was light. Work continued till noon, and after an hour or so for lunch and rest, the slaves worked until nearly dark. In the evening, the women prepared dinner at the cabins and everyone snatched a few hours of unsupervised socializing before bedtime.

Work was tedious in the hot and humid southern fields, and the overseer's whip was never far away. Cotton growing was hard work: plowing and planting, chopping weeds with a heavy hoe, and picking the ripe cotton from the stiff and scratchy bolls, at the rate of 150 pounds a day.

Slaves aged fast in this regime. Poor diet and heavy labor undermined health. When they were too old to work, they took on other tasks within the black community, such as caring for young children. Honored by the slave community, the elderly were tolerated by white owners, who continued to feed and clothe them until their deaths. Few actions show the hypocrisy of southern paternalism more clearly than the speed with which white owners evicted their elderly slaves in the 1860s when the end of the slave system was in sight.

## HOUSE SERVANTS

In the eighteenth century, as profits from slavery grew, slave owners diverted an increasing proportion of slave labor from the fields to the house service necessary to sustain their rich lifestyles. By one calculation, fully one-third of the female slaves in Virginia worked as house servants by 1800, but the figures were much lower in the newly opened cotton lands in the West.

At first glance, working in the big house might seem to have been preferable to working in the fields. Physically, it was much less demanding, and house slaves were often better fed and clothed. They also had much more access to information, for white people, accustomed to servants and generally confident of their loyalty, often forgot their presence and spoke among themselves about matters of interest to the slaves: local gossip, changes in laws or attitudes, or policies toward disobedient or rebellious slaves.

For many white people, one of the worst surprises of the Civil War was the eagerness of their house slaves to flee. Considered by their masters the best treated and the most loyal, these slaves were commonly the first to leave or to organize mass desertions.

From the point of view of the slave, the most unpleasant thing about being a house servant (or the single slave of a small owner) was the constant presence of white people. There was no escape from white supervision. Many slaves who were personal maids and children's nurses were required to live in the big house and rarely saw their own families. Cooks and other house servants were exposed to the tempers and whims of all members of the white family, including the children, who prepared themselves for lives of mastery by practicing giving orders to slaves many times their own age. And house servants, more than any others, were forced to act grateful and ingratiating. At the same time, genuine intimacy was possible, especially between black nurses and white children. But these were bonds that the white children were ultimately forced to reject as the price of joining the master class.

## ARTISANS AND SKILLED WORKERS

A small number of slaves were skilled workers: weavers, seamstresses, carpenters, blacksmiths, mechanics. Black people worked as lumberjacks (of the 16,000 lumber workers in the South, almost all were slaves), as miners, as deckhands and stokers on Mississippi riverboats, as stevedores loading cotton on the docks of Charleston, Savannah, and New Orleans, and sometimes as workers in the handful of southern factories. Because slaves were their masters' property, the wages of the slave belonged to the owner, not the slave.

The extent to which slaves made up the laboring class was most apparent in cities. A British visitor to Natchez in 1835 noted slave "mechanics, draymen, hostelers, labourers, hucksters and washwomen and the heterogeneous multitude of every other occupation." In the North, all these jobs were performed by white workers. In part because the South failed to attract as much immigrant labor as the North, southern cities offered both enslaved and free black people opportunities in skilled occupations such as blacksmithing and carpentering that free African Americans in the North were denied.

## SLAVE FAMILIES

As had been true in the eighteenth century, families remained essential to African American culture (see Chapter 4). No southern state recognized slave marriages in law. Most owners, though, not only recognized but also encouraged them, sometimes even performing a kind of wedding ceremony for the couple. Masters encouraged marriage among their slaves, believing it made the men less rebellious, and for economic reasons they were eager for the slave women to have children. Whatever marriages meant to the masters, to slaves they were a haven of love and intimacy in a cruel world and the basis of the African American community. Husbands and wives had a chance, in their own cabins, to live their own lives among loved ones. The relationship between slave husband and wife was different from that of the white husband and wife. The master–slave system dictated that the white marriage be unequal, for the man had to be dominant and the woman dependent and submissive. Slave marriages were more equal, for husband and wife were both powerless within the slave system. Both knew that neither could protect the other from abuse at the hands of white people.

Family meant continuity. Parents made great efforts to teach their children the family history and to surround them with a supportive and protective kinship network. The strength of these ties is shown by the many husbands, wives, children,

8–1
Isaac, *Memoirs of a Monticello Slave* (1847)

QUICK REVIEW

**Slave Families**

- Marriage not legally recognized but encouraged among slaves.
- Parents made great efforts to teach and protect their children.
- The internal slave trade made separation a constant danger.

**Slave quarters built** by slave owners, like these pictured on a South Carolina plantation, provided more than basic shelter. Slave quarters were the center of the African American community life that developed during slavery.

Collection of The New-York Historical Society. Photograph by G.N. Barnard, Bagoe Collection, ca. 1865, negative number 48169.

**WHAT ROLE** did religion play in African American slave communities?

**myhistorylab**

**Review Summary**

**Second Great Awakening** Religious revival among black and white Southerners in the 1790s.

and parents who searched for each other after the Civil War when slavery came to an end.

Given the vast size of the internal slave trade, fear of separation was constant—and real. One in every five slave marriages was broken, and one in every three children sold away from their families. These figures clearly show that slave owners' support for slave marriages was secondary to their desire for profits. The scale of the trade was a strong indication of the economic reality that underlay their protestations of paternalism.

In the face of constant separation, slave communities attempted to act like larger families. Following practices developed early in slavery, children were taught to respect and learn from all the elders, to call all adults of a certain age "aunt" or "uncle," and to call children of their own age "brother" or "sister" (see Chapter 4). Thus, in the absence of their own family, separated children could quickly find a place and a source of comfort in the slave community to which they had been sold.

This emphasis on family and on kinship networks had an even more fundamental purpose. The kinship of the entire community, where old people were respected and young ones cared for, represented a conscious rejection of white paternalism. The slaves' ability, in the most difficult of situations, to structure a community that expressed their values, not those of their masters, was extraordinary. Equally remarkable was the way in which African Americans reshaped Christianity to serve their needs.

# FREEDOM AND RESISTANCE

Whatever their dreams, most slaves knew they would never escape. Freedom was too far away. Almost all successful escapes in the nineteenth century (approximately a thousand a year) were from the Upper South (Delaware, Maryland, Virginia, Kentucky, and Missouri). A slave in the Lower South or the Southwest simply had too far to go to reach freedom. That meant that ways to endure and to resist became all the more important.

## AFRICAN AMERICAN RELIGION

Black Christianity was an enabling religion: it helped slaves to survive, not as passive victims of white tyranny but as active opponents of an oppressive system that they daily protested in small but meaningful ways. In their faith, African Americans expressed a spiritual freedom that white people could not destroy.

African religions managed to survive from the earliest days of slavery in forms that white people considered as "superstition" or "folk belief." In the nineteenth century, these African traditions allowed African Americans to reshape white Christianity into their own distinctive faith that expressed their deep resistance to slavery.

The Great Awakening, which swept the South after the 1760s, introduced many slaves to Christianity, often in mixed congregations with white people (see Chapter 5). The transformation was completed by the **Second Great Awakening**, which took root among black and white Southerners in the 1790s. The number of African American converts, preachers, and lay teachers grew rapidly, and a distinctive form of Christianity took shape. Free African Americans founded their own independent churches and denominations. By the 1830s, free African American ministers like Andrew Marshall of Savannah and many more enslaved black preachers and lay ministers preached, sometimes secretly, to slaves. Their message was one of faith and love, of deliverance, of the coming of the promised land.

African Americans found in Christianity a powerful vehicle to express their longings for freedom and justice. But why did their white masters allow it? Some white people, themselves converted by the revivals, doubtless believed that they should not deny their slaves the same religious experience. But many southern slave owners expected Christianity to make their slaves obedient and peaceful. Forbidding their slaves to hold their own religious gatherings, owners insisted that their slaves attend white church services. On many plantations, slaves attended religious services with their masters every Sunday, sitting quietly in the back of the church or in the balcony, as the minister preached messages justifying slavery and urging obedience. But at night, away from white eyes, they held their own prayer meetings.

In churches and in spontaneous religious expressions, the black community made Christianity its own. Fusing Christian texts with African elements of group activity, such as the circle dance, the call-and-response pattern, and, above all, group singing, black people created a unique community religion full of emotion, enthusiasm, and protest. Nowhere is this spirit more compelling than in the famous spirituals: "Go Down Moses," with its mournful refrain "Let my people go"; the rousing "Didn't My Lord Deliver Daniel . . . and why not every man"; the haunting "Steal Away."

**African cultural patterns** persisted in the preference for night funerals and for solemn pageantry and song, as depicted in British artist John Antrobus's *Plantation Burial,* ca. 1860. Like other African American customs, the community care of the dead contained an implied rebuke to the masters' care of the living slaves.

John Antrobus, "Negro Burial." Oil painting. The Historic New Orleans Collection. #1960.46.

**Harriet Tubman was** 40 years old when this photograph (later hand-tinted) was taken. Already famous for her daring rescues, she gained further fame by serving as a scout, spy, and nurse during the Civil War.

**This drawing shows** the moment, almost two months after the failure of his famous and bloody slave revolt, when Nat Turner was accidentally discovered in the woods near his home plantation. Turner's cool murder of his owner and methodical organization of his revolt deeply frightened many white Southerners.

## OTHER KINDS OF RESISTANCE

The rapid geographical spread of cotton introduced a new source of tension and resistance into the slave–master relationship. White Southerners did everything they could to prevent escapes and rebellions. But despite almost certain recapture, slaves continued to flee and to help others do the same. Escaped slave Harriet Tubman of Maryland, who made twelve rescue missions freeing sixty to seventy slaves in all (later inflated to three hundred as Tubman's rescues became legendary), had extraordinary determination and skill. As a female runaway, she was unusual, too: most escapees were young men, for women often had small children they were unable to take and unwilling to leave behind.

Slaves who knew they could not reach freedom still frequently demonstrated their desire for liberty or their discontent over mistreatment by taking unauthorized leave from their plantation. Hidden in nearby forests or swamps, provided with food smuggled by other slaves from the plantation, the runaway might return home after a week or so, often to rather mild punishment. Although in reality, most slaves could have little hope of gaining freedom, even failed attempts at rebellion shook the foundations of the slave system, and thus temporary flight by any slave was a warning sign of discontent that a wise master did not ignore.

## SLAVE REVOLTS

The ultimate resistance, however, was the slave revolt. Southern history was dotted with stories of former slave conspiracies and rumors of current plots (see Chapter 4). But when in 1831, Nat Turner actually started a rebellion in which a number of white people were killed, southern fears were greatly magnified.

A literate man, Nat Turner was a lay preacher, but he was also a slave. It was Turner's intelligence and strong religious commitment that made him a leader in the slave community. Turner began plotting his revolt after a religious vision in which he saw "white spirits and black spirits engaged in battle." Turner and five other slaves struck on the night of August 20, 1831. Moving from plantation to plantation and killing a total of fifty-five white people, the rebels numbered sixty by the next morning, when they fled from a group of armed white men. More than forty blacks were executed after the revolt, including Turner, who was captured accidentally after he had hidden for two months in the woods.

Conspiracies and actual or rumored slave resistance began in colonial times (see Chapter 4) and never ceased. These plots exposed the truth white Southerners preferred to ignore: only force kept Africans and African Americans enslaved, and because no system of control could ever be total, white Southerners could never be completely safe from the possibility of revolt. Nat Turner brought white Southerners' fears to the surface. After 1831, the possibility of slave insurrection was never far from their minds.

## FREE AFRICAN AMERICANS

Another source of white disquiet was the growing number of free African Americans. By 1860, nearly 250,000 free black people lived in the South. For most, freedom dated from before 1800, when antislavery feeling among slave owners in the Upper South was widespread and cotton cultivation had yet to boom.

Most free black people lived in the countryside of the Upper South, where they worked as tenant farmers or farm laborers. Urban African Americans were much more visible. Life was especially difficult for female-headed families, because only the most menial work—street peddling and laundry work, for example—was available to free black women. The situation for African American males was somewhat better. Although they were discriminated against in employment and in social life, there were opportunities for skilled black craftsmen in trades such as blacksmithing and carpentry. Cities such as Charleston, Savannah, and Natchez were home to flourishing free African American communities that formed their own churches and fraternal orders.

Throughout the South in the 1830s, state legislatures tightened **black codes**—laws concerning free black people. Free African Americans could not carry firearms, could not purchase slaves (unless they were members of their own family), and were liable to the criminal penalties meted out to slaves (that is, whippings and summary judgments without a jury trial). They could not testify against whites, hold office, vote, or serve in the militia. White people increasingly feared the influence free black people might have on slaves, for free African Americans were a living challenge to the slave system. Their very existence disproved the basic southern equations of white equals free, and black equals slave. No one believed more fervently in those equations than the South's largest population group, white people who did not own slaves.

**One of the ways** Charleston attempted to control its African American population was to require all slaves to wear badges showing their occupation. After 1848, free black people also had to wear badges, which were decorated, ironically, with a liberty cap.

 **13–3**
Nat Turner, *Confession* (1831)

## THE WHITE MAJORITY

The pervasive influence of the slave system in the South is reflected in the startling contrast of two facts: two-thirds of all Southerners did not own slaves, yet slave owners dominated the social and political life of the region.

### POOR WHITE PEOPLE

From 30 to 50 percent of all southern white people were landless, a proportion similar to that in the North. But the existence of slavery limited the opportunities for poor white people. Slaves made up the permanent, stable workforce in agriculture and in many skilled trades. Many poor white people led highly transient lives in search of work, such as farm labor at harvest time, which was only temporary. Others were tenant farmers working under share-tenancy arrangements that kept them in debt to the landowner. Although they farmed poorer land with less equipment than landowning farmers, most tenant farmers grew enough food to sustain their families. Like their landowning neighbors, tenant farmers aspired to independence.

Relationships between poor whites and black slaves were complex. White men and women often worked side by side with black slaves in the fields and were socially and sexually intimate with enslaved and free African Americans. White people engaged in clandestine trade to supply slaves with items like liquor that slave

**WHAT WERE** the values of yeoman farmers?

**myhistorylab**
**Review Summary**

**Black codes** Laws passed by states and municipalities denying many rights of citizenship to free black people before the Civil War.

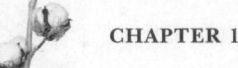

owners prohibited, helped slaves to escape, and even (in an 1835 Mississippi case)
were executed for their participation in planning a slave revolt. At the same time,
the majority of poor white people insisted, sometimes violently, on their racial
superiority over blacks. But the fact was that the difficult lives of poor whites served
to blur the crucial racial distinction between independent whites and supposedly
inferior, dependent black people on which the system of slavery rested.

## SOUTHERN "PLAIN FOLK"

The word "**yeoman**," originally a British term for a farmer who works his own land,
is often applied to independent farmers of the South, most of whom lived on family-sized farms. Southerners themselves referred to them as "plain folk," as opposed
to the gentry who owned slaves. Although yeoman farmers sometimes owned a few
slaves, in general they and their families worked their land by themselves.

Just as elsewhere in the South, family was the mainstay of community. Farm
men and women depended on their relatives and neighbors for assistance in large
farm tasks such as planting, harvesting, and construction. Projects requiring lots
of hands, like logrollings, corn shuckings, and quilting bees, were community
events. Farmers repaid this help and obtained needed goods through complex systems of barter with other members of the community.

Where yeomen and large slave owners lived side by side, as in the Georgia black
belt where cotton was the major crop, slavery again provided a link between the rich
and the "plain folk." Large plantation owners often bought food for their slaves from
small local farmers, ground the latter's corn in the plantation mill, ginned their cotton, and transported and marketed it as well. But although planters and much
smaller yeomen were part of a larger community network, in the black belt the large
slave owners were clearly dominant. Only in their own up-country communities
did yeomen feel truly independent.

**The goal of** yeoman farm families was economic independence. Their mixed farming and grazing
enterprises, supported by kinship and community ties, afforded them a self-sufficiency epitomized
by Carl G. von Iwonski's painting of this rough but comfortable log cabin in New Braunfels, Texas.

The dominance of the large planters was due at least in part to the ambition of many yeomen, especially those with two or three slaves, to expand their holdings and become rich. These farmers, enthusiastic members of the lively democratic politics of the South, supported the leaders they hoped to join.

But for a larger group of yeomen, independence and not wealth was most important. Many southern yeomen lived apart from large slaveholders in the up-country regions where plantation agriculture was unsuitable. The very high value southern yeomen placed on freedom grew directly from their own experience as self-sufficient property-owning farmers in small, family-based communities, and from the absolute, patriarchal control they exercised over their own wives and children. This was a way of life that southern "plain folk" were determined to preserve. It made them resistant to the economic opportunities and challenges that capitalism and industrialization posed for northern farmers, which southern yeomen perceived as encroachments on their freedom.

The irony was that the freedom yeomen so prized rested on slavery. White people could count on slaves to perform the hardest and worst labor, and the degradation of slave life was a daily reminder of the freedom they enjoyed in comparison. Slavery meant that all white people, rich and poor, were equal in the sense that they were all free. The democratization of politics in the early nineteenth century and the enactment of nearly universal white manhood suffrage perpetuated the belief in white skin privilege, even though the gap between rich and poor white people was widening.

## THE MIDDLING RANKS

In the predominantly rural South, cities provided a home for a small commercial middle class of merchants, bankers, factors (agents), and lawyers on whom the agricultural economy depended to sell its produce to a world market. As in the North, small industrial cities, often including textile mills and heavier industry, clustered along the fall line where the rivers dropped down from the highlands to the coastal plains.

The effort of William Gregg of South Carolina to establish the cotton textile industry illustrates some of the problems facing southern entrepreneurs. Gregg, a successful jeweler from Columbia, South Carolina, became convinced that textile factories were a good way to diversify the southern economy and to provide a living for poor whites who could not find work in the slave-dominated employment system. He enthusiastically publicized the findings of his tour of northern textile mills but found a cool reception. His request to the planter-dominated South Carolina legislature for a charter of incorporation for a textile mill passed by only one vote. In 1846, he built a model mill and a company town in Graniteville, South Carolina, that attracted poor white families as employees. Gregg adapted southern paternalism to industry, providing a school and churches and prohibiting alcohol and dancing, yet paying his workers 20 percent less than northern wages. His experience in the competitive textile industry led him to favor the protective tariff, thus putting him at odds with the general attitude in South Carolina that had solidified at the time of the Nullification Crisis (see Chapter 11).

Another noteworthy exception was the Tredegar Iron Works. Many southern planters scorned members of the commercial middle class like William Gregg because they had to please their suppliers and customers and thus lacked, in planters' eyes, true independence. This was an attitude strikingly different from that in the North, where the commercial acumen of the middle class was increasingly valued (see Chapter 12).

WHO MADE up the planter elite?

myhistorylab

**Review Summary**

**Figure 10.2 Slaveholding and Class Structure in the South, 1830**
The great majority of the southern white population were yeoman farmers. In 1830, slave owners made up only 36 percent of the southern white population; owners of more than fifty slaves constituted a tiny 2.5 percent. Yet they and the others who were middling planters dominated politics, retaining the support of yeomen who prized their freedom as white men above class-based politics.

U.S. Bureau of the Census.

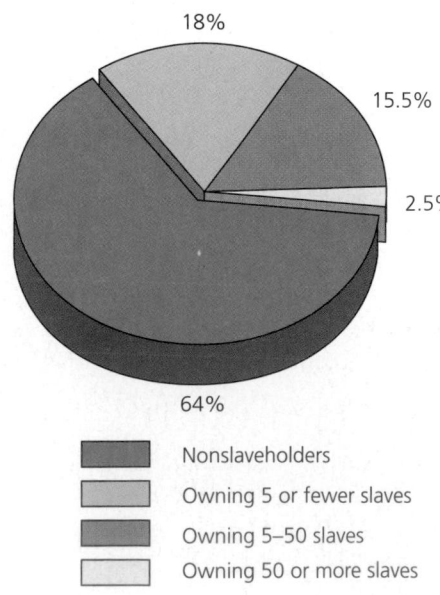

18%

15.5%

2.5%

64%

■ Nonslaveholders
■ Owning 5 or fewer slaves
■ Owning 5–50 slaves
□ Owning 50 or more slaves

# PLANTERS

Remarkably few slave owners fit the popular stereotype of the rich and leisured plantation owner with hundreds of acres of land and hundreds of slaves. Only 36 percent of southern white people owned slaves in 1830, and only 2.5 percent owned fifty slaves or more. Just as yeomen and poor whites were diverse, so, too, were southern slave owners (see Figure 10.2).

## SMALL SLAVE OWNERS

The largest group of slave owners were small yeomen taking the step from subsistence agriculture to commercial production. To do this in the South's agricultural economy, they had to own slaves. But upward mobility was difficult. Owning one or two slaves increased farm production only slightly, and it was hard to accumulate the capital to buy more.

Such a slave owner was economically vulnerable: a poor crop or a downturn in cotton prices could wipe out his gains and force him to sell his slaves. When times improved, he might buy a new slave or two and try again, but getting a secure footing on the bottom rung of the slave-owner ladder was very difficult. The roller-coaster economy of the early nineteenth century did not help matters, and the Panic of 1837 was a serious setback to many small farmers.

For a smaller group of slave owners, the economic struggle was not so hard. Middle-class professional men—lawyers, doctors, and merchants—frequently managed to become large slave owners because they already had capital (the pay from their professions) to invest in land and slaves. Sometimes they received payment for their services, not in money, but in slaves. These owners were the most likely to own skilled slaves—carpenters, blacksmiths, and other artisans—and to rent them out for profit. By steady accumulation, the most successful members of this middle class were able to buy their way into the slave-owning elite and to confirm that position by marrying their sons or daughters into the aristocracy.

## THE PLANTER ELITE

The slave-owning elite, those 2.5 percent who owned fifty slaves or more, enjoyed the prestige, the political leadership, and the lifestyle to which many white Southerners aspired. Almost all great slave owners inherited their wealth. Increasingly after 1820, as universal manhood suffrage spread, planters had to learn how to appeal to the popular vote, but most never acquired "the common touch." The smaller slave owners, not the great planters, formed a clear majority in every southern state legislature.

The eastern seaboard had first given rise to a class of rich planters in the colonial period. In the nineteenth century, these planters ranged from land rich but labor poor Thomas Chaplin of Tombee Plantation who grew sea-island cotton, to rice planter Nathaniel Heyward, who through wealthy marriages and land purchases amassed 45,000 acres of land and over 2,000 slaves.

As Southerners and slave owning spread westward, membership in the elite broadened to include the new wealth of Alabama, Mississippi, Louisiana, and Texas. Natchez, on the Mississippi River, became so wealthy that its rich planters were popularly called "nabobs" (from a Hindi word for Europeans who had amassed fabulous wealth in India).

The extraordinary concentration of wealth in Natchez—in 1850, it was the richest county in the nation—fostered a self-consciously elite lifestyle that derived not from long tradition but from suddenly acquired riches. Fastidious Northerners such as Thomas Taylor, a Pennsylvania Quaker who visited Natchez in 1847, noted: "Many of the chivalric gentry whom I have been permitted to see dashing about here on highbred horses, seem to find their greatest enjoyment in recounting their bear hunts, 'great fights,' and occasional exploits with revolvers and Bowie knives—swearing 'terribly' and sucking mint juleps & cherry cobblers with straws."

## PLANTATION LIFE

The urban life of the Natchez planters was unusual. Many wealthy planters, especially those on new lands in the Old Southwest, lived in isolation on their plantations with their families and slaves. Through family networks, common boarding school experience, political activity, and frequent visiting, the small new planter elite consciously worked to create and maintain a distinctive lifestyle that was modeled on that of the English aristocracy, as Southerners understood it. This entailed a large estate, a spacious, elegant mansion, and lavish hospitality.

But this gracious image was at odds with the economic reality. Large numbers of black slaves had to be forced to work to produce the wealth that supported the planters' gracious lifestyle. Each plantation, like the yeoman farm but on a larger scale, aimed to be self-sufficient, producing not only the cash crop but also most of the food and clothing for both slaves and family. A large plantation was an enterprise that required many hands, many skills, and a lot of management. Large plantation owners might have overseers or black drivers to supervise field work, but frequently they themselves had direct financial control of daily operations.

The planter elite developed a paternalistic ideology to justify their rigorous insistence on the master–slave relationship. According to this ideology, each plantation was a family composed of both black and white. The master, as head of the plantation, was head of the family, and the mistress was his "helpmate." The master was obligated to provide for all of his family, both black and white, and to treat them with humanity. In return, slaves were to work properly and do as they were told, as children would. Most elite slave owners spoke of their position of privilege as a duty and a burden. John C. Calhoun spoke for many slave owners when he described the plantation as "a little community" in which the master directed all operations so that the abilities and needs of every member, black and white, were "perfectly harmonized." Convinced of their own benevolence, slave owners expected not only obedience but also gratitude from all members of their great "families."

## THE PLANTATION MISTRESS

The paternalistic model locked plantation mistresses into positions that bore heavy responsibility but carried no real authority. The difficulties experienced by these privileged women illustrate the way the master–slave relationship of a slave society affected every aspect of the personal life of slave owners.

Plantation mistresses spent most of their lives tending "family" members—including slaves—in illness and in childbirth, and supervising their slaves' performance of such daily tasks as cooking, housecleaning, weaving, and sewing. In addition, the plantation mistress often had to spend hours, even days, of behind-the-scenes preparation for the crowds of guests she was expected to welcome in her role as elegant and gracious hostess.

Despite the reality of the plantation mistress's daily supervision of an often extensive household, she did not rule it: her husband did. The plantation master was the source of authority to whom wife, children, and slaves were expected to look for both rewards and punishments. A wife who challenged her husband or sought

### QUICK REVIEW

**Plantation Mistresses**

- Mistresses ran the household staff.
- Mistresses were responsible for arrangements for visitors.
- Husbands were usually the real authority on the plantation.

more independence from him threatened the entire paternalistic system of control. After all, if she were not dependent and obedient, why should slaves be?

In addition to their strictly defined family roles, many southern women also suffered deeply from their isolation from friends and kin. Sometimes the isolation of life on rural plantations could be overcome by long visits, but women with many small children and extensive responsibilities found it difficult to leave.

Although on every plantation black women served as nursemaids to young white children and as lifelong maids to white women, usually accompanying them when they moved as brides into their own homes, there are few historical examples of genuine sympathy and understanding of black women by white women of the slave-owning class. Few of the latter seemed to understand the sadness, frustration, and despair often experienced by their lifelong maids, who were forced to leave their own husbands and children to serve in their mistresses' new homes.

## COERCION AND VIOLENCE

**13–1**
*State v. Boon* (1801)

There were generous and benevolent masters, but most large slave owners believed that constant discipline and coercion were necessary to make slaves work hard (see Seeing History). Some slave owners used their slaves with great brutality. Owners who killed slaves were occasionally brought to trial (and usually acquitted), but no legal action was taken in the much more frequent cases of excessive punishment, general abuse, and rape. All southern slave owners, not just those who experienced the special tensions of new and isolated plantations in the Old Southwest, were engaged in a constant battle of wills with their slaves that owners frequently resolved by violence.

One of the most common violations of the paternalistic code of behavior (and of southern law) was the sexual abuse of female slaves by their masters. Usually, masters forcibly raped their women slaves at will, and slave women had little hope of defending themselves from these attacks. Sometimes, however, long-term intimate relationships between masters and slaves developed.

**9–12**
Harriet Jacobs, *The Trials of a Slave Girl* (1861)

It was rare for slave owners to publicly acknowledge fathering slave children or to free these children, and black women and their families were helpless to protest their treatment. Equally silenced was the master's wife, who for reasons of modesty as well as her subordinate position was not supposed to notice either her husband's infidelity or his flagrant crossing of the color lines.

An owner could do what he chose on his plantation, and his sons grew up expecting to do likewise. Unchecked power is always dangerous, and it is not surprising that it was sometimes misused. Perhaps the most surprising thing about the southern slave system is how much humanity survived despite the intolerable conditions. For that, most of the credit goes not to white paternalism, but to African Americans and the communities they created under slavery.

## THE DEFENSE OF SLAVERY

**WHAT PROSLAVERY** arguments were developed in the first half of the nineteenth century?

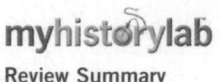

**Review Summary**

“Slavery informs all our modes of life, all our habits of thought, lies at the basis of our social existence, and of our political faith,” announced South Carolina planter William Henry Trescot in 1850, explaining why the South would secede from the Union before giving up slavery. Slavery bound white and black Southerners together in tortuous ways that eventually led, as Trescot had warned, to the Civil War. Population figures tell much of the story of the complex relationship between whites and blacks: of the 12 million people who lived in the South in 1860, 4 million were slaves. These

# "Gordon Under Medical Inspection"

This horrifying image of the badly scarred back of a former slave named Gordon appeared in *Harper's Weekly* in July 1863. He was an escaped slave who entered Union lines in Baton Rouge in March 1863, arriving in the bedraggled condition shown on the left. Under medical examination, he revealed the scars from a whipping three months earlier. As the third picture shows, he promptly joined the Union Army.

**AFTER VIEWING** this image, how seriously would you consider claims that southern slavery was a benign, paternalistic system?

Although abolitionist literature frequently described brutal whippings endured by slaves, few people in the North can have seen such graphic examples before the publication of this article in 1863. Since that time, the picture of Gordon's back has frequently been used to illustrate the violence of the slave system. There is no question that whipping was a frequent punishment in the slaveholding South and that masters, mistresses, and overseers, in fits of temper, whipped harshly. Although we do not know if Gordon's scars were representative, the image makes it impossible to deny the reality of brutality in the slave system. ■

Illustrations from photographs by McPherson and Oliver, in *Harper's Weekly*, July 4, 1863, p. 429.

sheer numbers of African Americans reinforced white people's perpetual fears of black retaliation for the violence exercised by the slave master. Every rumor of slave revolts, real or imagined, kept those fears alive. The basic question was this: What might slaves do if they were not controlled?

## DEVELOPING PROSLAVERY ARGUMENTS

Once the cotton boom began in the 1790s, Southerners increasingly sought to justify slavery. They found justifications for slavery in the Bible and in the histories of Greece and Rome, both slave-owning societies. The strongest defense was a legal one: the Constitution allowed slavery.

The Missouri Crisis of 1819–20 alarmed most Southerners, who were shocked by the evidence of widespread antislavery feeling in the North. South Carolinians viewed **Denmark Vesey's conspiracy**, occurring only two years after the Missouri debate, as an example of the harm that irresponsible northern antislavery talk could cause. In the wake of the Vesey conspiracy, Charlestonians turned their fear and anger outward by attempting to seal off the city from dangerous outside influences. In December 1822, the South Carolina legislature passed a bill requiring that all black seamen be seized and jailed while their ships were in Charleston harbor. Initially most alarmed about free black people from Haiti, Charlestonians soon came to believe that northern free black seamen were spreading antislavery ideas among their slaves.

After **Nat Turner's Revolt** in 1831, Governor John Floyd of Virginia blamed the uprising on "Yankee peddlers and traders" who supposedly told slaves that "all men were born free and equal." Thus, northern antislavery opinion and the fear of slave uprisings were firmly linked in southern minds. This extreme reaction, which Northerners viewed as paranoid, stemmed from the basic nature of a slave society: *anything* that challenged the master–slave relationship was viewed as a basic threat to the entire system.

## AFTER NAT TURNER

In 1831, the South began to close ranks in defense of slavery. Several factors contributed to this regional solidarity. Nat Turner's revolt was important, linked as it was in the minds of many Southerners with antislavery agitation from the North. Militant abolitionist William Lloyd Garrison began publishing the *Liberator*, the newspaper that was to become the leading antislavery organ, in 1831. The British gave notice that they would soon abolish slavery on the sugar plantations of the West Indies, an action that seemed to many Southerners much too close to home. Emancipation for West Indian slaves came in 1834. Finally, 1831 was the year before the Nullification Crisis (see Chapter 11) was resolved. Although the other southern states did not support the hotheaded South Carolinians who called for secession, they did sympathize with the argument that the federal government had no right to interfere with a state's special interest (namely, slavery).

By 1835, every southern legislature had tightened its laws concerning control of slaves. For example, they tried to blunt the effect of abolitionist literature by passing laws forbidding slaves to learn how to read. In only three border states—Kentucky, Tennessee, and Maryland—did slave literacy remain legal. Slaves were forbidden to gather for dances, religious services, or any kind of organized social activity without a white person present. They were forbidden to have whiskey because it might encourage them toward revolt. The penalty for plotting insurrection was death. Other laws made manumission illegal and placed even more restrictions on the lives of free black people. In many areas, slave patrols were augmented and became more vigilant in restricting African American movement and communication between plantations.

**13–4**
Lewis Tappan, *An Abolitionist Defends the* Amistad *Mutineers* (1839)

**14–1**
William Lloyd Garrison, *The Liberator* (1831)

**Denmark Vesey's conspiracy**  The most carefully devised slave revolt in which rebels planned to seize control of Charleston in 1822 and escape to freedom in Haiti, a free black republic, but they were betrayed by other slaves, and seventy-five conspirators were executed.

**Nat Turner's Revolt**  Uprising of slaves in Southampton County, Virginia, in the summer of 1831 led by Nat Turner that resulted in the death of fifty-five white people.

In 1836, Southerners introduced a "gag rule" in Washington to prevent congressional consideration of abolitionist petitions. Attempts were made to stifle all open debate about slavery within the South; dissenters were pressured to remain silent or to leave.

In addition to fueling fears of slave rebellions, the growing abolitionist sentiment of the 1830s raised the worry that southern opportunities for expansion would be cut off. Southern politicians painted melodramatic pictures of a beleaguered white South hemmed in on all sides by "fanatic" antislavery states. At home, Southerners were forced to contemplate what might happen when they had "to let loose among them, freed from the wholesome restraints of patriarchal authority . . . an idle, worthless, profligate set of free negroes" whom they feared would "prowl the . . . streets at night and [haunt] the woods during the day armed with whatever weapons they could lay their hands on."

Finally, southern apologists moved beyond defensiveness to develop proslavery arguments. One of the first to do this was James Henry Hammond, elected a South Carolina congressman in 1834. In 1836, Hammond delivered a major address to Congress in which he denied that slavery was evil. Rather, he claimed, it had produced "the highest toned, the purest, best organization of society that has ever existed on the face of the earth." In 1854, another southern spokesman, George Fitzhugh, asserted that "the negro slaves of the South are the happiest, and, in some sense, the freest people in the world" because all the responsibility for their care was borne by concerned white masters. Fitzhugh contrasted southern paternalism with the heartless individualism that ruled the lives of northern "wage slaves."

## CHANGES IN THE SOUTH

In spite of these defensive and repressive proslavery measures, which made the South seem monolithic in northern eyes, there were some surprising indicators of dissent. One protest occurred in the Virginia state legislature in 1832, when nonslaveholding delegates, alarmed by the Nat Turner rebellion, forced a two-week debate on the merits of gradual abolition. In the final vote, abolition was defeated 73 to 58. Although the subject was never raised again, this debate was a startling indicator of frequently unvoiced doubts about slavery that existed in the South.

But slavery was not a static system. From the 1830s on, financial changes increasingly underlined class differences among southern whites. It was much harder to become a slaveholder: from 1830 to 1860, slave owners declined from 36 to 25 percent of the population. In 1860, the average slaveholder was ten times as wealthy as the average nonslaveholder. A major reason for the shrinking number of slave owners and their increased wealth was the rapidly increasing price of slaves. High prices caused the internal slave trade to flourish: during the 1850s, slave owners from the Upper South sold some 250,000 slaves to the Lower South for handsome profits. By 1850, in the Chesapeake (Virginia, Maryland, and Delaware), where American slavery had its origin, the percentage of slave owners had fallen to 28 percent, while the comparable figures for Louisiana and Mississippi were 45 percent. Such differences in the extent of slaveholding between the Upper and Lower South threatened regional political unity (see Map 10.4).

Another alarming trend was the disintegration of the slave system in southern cities. The number of urban slaves greatly decreased because plantation owners deeply distrusted the effect of cities on the institution of slavery. Urban slaves led much more informed lives than rural ones and were often in daily contact with free blacks and urban poor whites. Many slaves were hired out and a number even hired out their own time, making them nearly indistinguishable from northern

**13–2**
David Walker, *A Black Abolitionist Speaks Out* (1829)

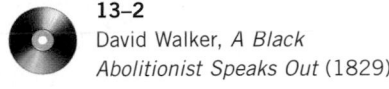

**Exploring America:** *Alexis de Tocqueville*

**MAP 10.4**

**Population Patterns in the South, 1850**   In South Carolina and Mississippi, the enslaved African American population outnumbered the white population; in four other Lower South states, the percentage was above 40 percent. These ratios frightened many white Southerners. White people also feared the free black population, though only three states in the Upper South and Louisiana had free black populations of over 3 percent. Six states had free black populations that were so small (less than 1 percent) as to be statistically insignificant.

WHERE WERE the greatest concentrations of African Americans? How would you explain the patterns the map reveals?

"free labor." Other urban slaves worked in commercial and industrial enterprises in jobs that were nearly indistinguishable from those of whites.

Economic changes adversely affected poor whites and yeomen as well. Increased commercialization of agriculture (other than cotton) led to higher land prices that made it harder for poor whites to buy or rent land. Extensive railroad building in up-country regions during the boom of the 1850s ended the isolation of many yeomen, exposing them for the first time to the temptations and dangers of the market economy. While slave owners grew increasingly worried about threats from the abolitionist and capitalist North, yeomen worried about local threats to their independence from banks, railroads, and activist state governments.

In spite of these signs of tension and dissent, the main lines of the southern argument were drawn in the 1830s and remained fixed thereafter. The defense of slavery stifled debate within the South, prevented a search for alternative labor systems, and narrowed the possibility of cooperation in national politics. In time, it made compromise impossible.

## CHRONOLOGY

| | |
|---|---|
| **1790s** | Second Great Awakening |
| | Black Baptist and African Methodist Episcopal churches founded |
| **1793** | Cotton gin invented |
| **1800** | Gabriel Prosser's revolt discovered in Virginia |
| **1806** | Virginia tightens law on manumission of slaves |
| **1808** | Congress prohibits U.S. participation in the international slave trade |
| **1816–20** | "Alabama Fever": migration to the Old Southwest |
| **1819–20** | Missouri Crisis |
| **1822** | Denmark Vesey's conspiracy in Charleston |
| **1831** | Nat Turner's revolt in Virginia |
| | William Lloyd Garrison begins publishing an antislavery newspaper, the *Liberator* |
| **1832** | Nullification Crisis |
| **1832–38** | "Flush Times": second wave of westward expansion |
| **1832** | Virginia legislature debates and defeats a measure for gradual emancipation |
| **1834** | Britain frees slaves throughout the empire, including in its Caribbean colonies |
| **1835** | Charleston crowd burns abolitionist literature |
| | Tightening of black codes completed by southern legislatures |
| **1836** | Congress passes "gag rule" to prevent discussion of antislavery petitions |
| | James Henry Hammond announces to Congress that slavery is not evil |
| **1846** | William Gregg opens model textile mill at Graniteville, South Carolina |
| **1854** | George Fitzhugh publishes *Sociology for the South*, a defense of slavery |
| **1857** | Hinton Helper publishes *The Impending Crisis*, an attack on slavery |
| **1858** | James Henry Hammond's "King Cotton" speech |

# CONCLUSION

The amazing growth of cotton production after 1793 transformed the South and the nation. Physically, the South expanded explosively westward: in all, seven southern states were admitted to the Union between 1800 and 1845. Cotton production fastened the slave system of labor upon the region. Although the international slave trade was abolished in 1808, the internal slave trade flourished, with devastating effects on African American families. Nationally, the profitable cotton trade fueled economic development and provided much of the original capital for the infant factory system of the North. Cotton production was based on the labor of African American slaves, who built strong communities under extremely difficult circumstances. The cohesion of African American families and the powerful faith of African American Christianity were the key community elements that bred a spirit of endurance and resistance. White Southerners, two-thirds of whom did not own slaves, denied their real dependence on slave labor by claiming equality in white skin privilege, while slave owners boasted of their own paternalism. But the extreme fear generated by a handful of slave revolts and the growing number of free African Americans in many areas gave the lie to white claims of benevolence. In the 1830s, the South defensively closed ranks against real and perceived threats to the slave system. In this sense, the white South was nearly as trapped as the African American slaves they claimed to control. And in its growing concern for the defense of the slave system, the South's role in national politics became more rigid, as we shall see in the next chapter.

## REVIEW QUESTIONS

1. How did cotton production after 1793 transform the social and political history of the South? How did the rest of the nation benefit? In what way was it an "international phenomenon"?

2. What were the two key institutions of the African American slave community? How did they function, and what beliefs did they express?

3. The circumstances of two groups—poor whites and free African Americans—put them outside the dominant southern equations of white equals free and black equals slave. Analyze the difficulty each group encountered in the slave-owning South.

4. Who were the yeoman farmers? What was their interest in slavery?

5. Southern slaveholders claimed that their paternalism justified their ownership of slaves, but paternalism implied obligations as well as privileges. How well do you think slaveholders lived up to their paternalistic obligations?

6. How did slave owners justify slavery? How did their defense change over time?

**myhistorylab**

Flashcard Review

## KEY TERMS

**Black codes** (p. 253)
**Denmark Vesey's conspiracy** (p. 260)
**Gang System** (p. 248)
**Industrial Revolution** (p. 242)

**Manumission** (p. 247)
**Nat Turner's Revolt** (p. 260)
**Second Great Awakening** (p. 250)
**Yeoman** (p. 254)

## RECOMMENDED READING

Ira Berlin, *Generations of Captivity* (2003). A compelling survey of the changing nature of American slavery.

Joan E. Cashin, *A Family Venture: Men and Women on the Southern Frontier* (1991). Explores the effects on slave owners of separation from family networks.

Erskine Clarke, *Dwelling Place: A Plantation Epic* (2005). This story of the intertwined lives of a white Christian slaveowning minister and his slaves on a Georgia plantation shows how he failed to reconcile the enslaved to their condition.

Steven Deyle, *Carry Me Back: The Domestic Slave Trade in American Life* (2005). The effects of the trade on American life.

Eugene Genovese, *Roll, Jordan, Roll: The World the Slaves Made* (1974). The landmark book that redirected the attention of historians from slaves as victims to the slave community as an active participant in paternalism.

Anthony E. Kaye, *Joining Places: Slave Neighborhoods in the Old South* (2007). An innovative study about the ways the informal and unnoticed ways of slaves linked plantations into African American neighborhoods.

Peter Kolchin, *American Slavery 1619–1877* (1993). A well-written, comprehensive survey.

Stephanie McCurry, *Masters of Small Worlds: Yeoman Households, Gender Relations, and the Political Culture of the Antebellum South Carolina Low Country* (1995). A study of yeomen that links their prized political and economic independence with their strong patriarchal control over their own families.

Donald P. McNeilly, *The Old South Frontier: Cotton Plantations and the Formation of Arkansas Society, 1819–1861* (2000). Traces slavery and society in Arkansas from frontier to cotton plantations.

Michael O'Brien, *Conjectures of Order: Intellectual Life and the American South* (2004). An outstanding two-volume study of southern life and thought from 1800 to 1865.

Marie Jenkins Schwartz, *Born in Bondage: Growing Up Enslaved in the Antebellum South* (2001). How slave communities sought to protect their children.

myhistorylab
Where it's a good time to connect to the past!

For study resources for this chapter, go to **www.myhistorylab.com** and choose *Out of Many, Teaching and Learning Classroom Edition*. You will find a wealth of study and review material for this chapter, including pretests and posttests, customized study plan, key-term review flash cards, interactive map and document activities, and documents for analysis.

*I blush for my country when I see such things, and I often tremble with apprehension that our Constitution will not long withstand the current which threatens to overwhelm it . . .*

—Benjamin B. French, September 1828

**Andrew Jackson speaking to a crowd after his election.** Politics in the olden time— General Jackson, President-elect, on his way to Washington.

# 11

# THE GROWTH OF DEMOCRACY
## 1824–1840

**HOW DID** suffrage expand between 1800 and 1840?

**WHAT STEPS** did Andrew Jackson take to strengthen the executive branch of the federal government?

**WHO WERE** Andrew Jackson's most important opponents and what did they support?

**WHAT WERE** the main issues of the campaign of 1840?

**WHAT ROLE** did newspapers and pamphlets play in American popular culture in the first half of the nineteenth century?

# AMERICAN COMMUNITIES
## A Political Community Replaces Deference with Democracy

PHILADELPHIA HAD LONG BEEN A STRONGHOLD OF CRAFT associations for skilled workers. Their organizations, and their parades and celebrations, were recognized parts of the urban community. Groups of master craftsmen marching in community parades with signs such as "By Hammer and Hand All Arts Do Stand" not only demonstrated pride in their craft but also asserted their importance to the community as a whole. Pennsylvania enfranchised all men who were taxpayers in 1776, enabling many of Philadelphia's skilled workers to vote, but they were willing to follow the leadership of the city's political elite. This was the accepted rule of republican government as understood by leaders such as Thomas Jefferson: an independent and virtuous people willingly deferred to wealthy and enlightened leaders who would govern in the public interest. In reality, most states limited the vote to property owners, and so many ordinary men had little choice but to accept the decisions of the wealthy.

By the 1820s, the lives of workers in Philadelphia had changed. As the Market Revolution transformed the economy, many skilled workers lost their independence and became wage earners in factories owned by others. Members of urban workers' associations realized that their own economic interests were different from those of the owners. In other states, where many men gained the vote for the first time in the 1820s, a similar process of identifying common interests at odds with the traditional political elite was also underway. The spread of universal manhood suffrage marked the transition from traditional deferential politics to democracy.

In 1827, the British-born shoemaker William Heighton urged his fellow workers in Philadelphia to band together under "the banner of equal rights" and form their own political party to press for issues of direct concern to workingmen, including the ten-hour day, free public education for their children, the end of imprisonment for debt, and curbing the powers of banks. "Surely we, the working class, who constitute a vast majority of the nation . . . have a right to expect [that] an improvement in our *individual condition* will be the natural result of legislative proceedings."

Heighton saw in the rising tide of universal manhood suffrage the possibility of reaching his overarching aim of "economic democracy." In response to his new vision of majority rule, the Philadelphia Working Men's Party was formed in 1828 and elected a slate of local officials as well as voting for Andrew Jackson for president. Andrew Jackson, who was so untraditional that at first national politicians did not take him seriously as a candidate, perfectly personified the new democratic mood and its animosity toward what was often termed "the monied aristocracy."

Thus, when a committee of the Philadelphia Working Men's Party attacked the banking system in 1829, Andrew Jackson paid attention. Their report decried the control by wealthy men of banks and of the paper money each bank issued (there was no national government-controlled currency until 1862), concluding: "If the present system of banking and paper money be perpetuated, the great body of the working people must give over all hopes of ever acquiring any property." This fear of the threat to democracy from a moneyed aristocracy was common among voters in rural areas of the South and West as well as in urban areas. Jackson not only understood this public resentment, but he also shared it. In 1832 he had Philadelphia's workers and others in mind when, speaking for "the humble members of society—the farmers, mechanics and laborers," he refused to renew the charter of the Bank of the United States and thereby instigated the events that we call the **Bank War**.

The Philadelphia Working Men's Party did not last very long. Too small and too narrowly focused to have wide appeal, it was quickly absorbed into Jackson's Democratic Party, with most of its specific demands unmet. Nevertheless, its brief history is significant for marking the end of traditional ideas about a unitary local political community and the transition to the more diverse and contentious community of competing interests that has characterized American democracy ever since. But it also set some limits. Politicians were quick to note that most Americans were uncomfortable with President Jackson's use of the language of class warfare in his veto message. Henceforth, whatever the competing interests might be, appeal to resentment alone was rarely successful. Rather, politicians sought to create national coalitions of voters with similar interests, creating new and more democratic political communities than had existed before.

Philadelphia

**Bank War**   The political struggle between President Andrew Jackson and the supporters of the Second Bank of the United States.

# THE NEW DEMOCRATIC POLITICS
# IN NORTH AMERICA

The early years of the nineteenth century were a time of extraordinary growth and change, not only for the United States but for all the countries of North America as well. Seen in continental perspective, the American embrace of popular democracy was unusual. Elsewhere, crises over popular rights dominated.

## STRUGGLES OVER POPULAR RIGHTS: MEXICO, THE CARIBBEAN, CANADA

In 1821, after eleven years of revolts (see Chapter 9), Mexico achieved its independence from Spain. Briefly united under the leadership of Colonel Agustin de Iturbide, Mexico declared itself a constitutional monarchy that promised equality for everyone—peninsulares, criollos, mestizos, and Indians alike. But because Spanish colonial rule had left a legacy of deep social divisions, the initial unity was short-lived. Iturbide reigned as Emperor of Mexico for little more than a year before he was overthrown by a military junta and later executed as a traitor. A series of weak presidents repeatedly invoked emergency powers and relied on the army, as they attempted to revive a faltering economy and reconcile the differences between the centralists—the vested interests of clergy, large landowners, and the military—and the federalists, largely criollos and mestizos, who hoped to create a liberal republic modeled on the American one. The unresolved issue of elite versus popular rule continued to undermine the hope for unity, popular rights, and stable government in an independent Mexico.

The independence of Haiti in 1804 (see Chapter 9) set the pattern for events in many other Caribbean islands in subsequent years. Independence destroyed the sugar industry, for freed slaves asserted their popular rights by refusing to perform the killing labor demanded of them on sugar plantations. The British Caribbean islands were racked with revolts, the largest occurring on Barbados in 1816 and on Jamaica in 1831. In response the British Parliament abolished slavery in all British colonies in 1834. As in Haiti, sugar production then plunged. The economic collapse that followed emancipation destroyed the political authority of local white elites, forcing the British government to impose direct rule.

Still a third crisis of popular rights occurred in British North America. In 1837, both Upper and Lower Canada rebelled against the limited representative government that the British government had imposed in the Constitutional Act of 1791. By far the most serious revolt was in predominantly French Lower Canada, where armed uprisings were brutally suppressed by British troops. In 1840, Britain abolished the local government of Lower Canada and joined it to Upper Canada in a union that most French Canadians opposed and in which they were a minority.

In comparison to these experiences, the rapid spread of suffrage in the United States and the growth of a vibrant but stable democratic political culture seemed all the more extraordinary. But after a brilliant start, in the 1850s the United States, like its neighbors, foundered on a basic sectional difference—slavery—that not even political democracy could reconcile (see Chapter 15).

**HOW DID** suffrage expand between 1800 and 1840?

*my*hist*o*rylab
Review Summary

## IMAGE KEY
for pages 266–267

a. A $5 note of the Second Bank of the United States.
b. Andrew Jackson speaking to a crowd after his election.
c. A Cherokee Indian newspaper, *Cherokee Phoenix*.
d. An old, antique Bible bound in leather with a gold cross on the cover.
e. A portrait of Andrew Jackson by Thomas Scully.
f. Political cartoon showing Andrew Jackson destroys the Second Bank of the United States.
g. Americans endured poverty and unemployment by drinking, begging, and rioting in the streets of a city during the 1837 Specie Panic.
h. A banner for William Henry Harrison and John Tyler features political slogans of the Log Cabin campaign above the date of the rally.
i. An 1841 issue of the *Crockett Almanac*.

## THE EXPANSION AND LIMITS OF SUFFRAGE

Before 1800, most of the original thirteen states had limited the vote to property owners or taxpayers, thereby excluding about half of the white male population. Westward expansion changed the nature of American politics by undermining the traditional authority structures in the older states and supporting democracy in the newer states (see Map 11.1).

Most of the new states extended the right to vote to all white males over the age of twenty-one. Vermont led the way in 1791, followed by Kentucky in 1792. Tennessee (1796) and Ohio (1803) entered with low taxpayer qualifica-

**MAP 11.1**

**Population Trends: Westward Expansion, 1830**    Westward population movement, only a trickle in 1800, had become a flood by 1830. Between 1800 and 1830, the U.S. white and African American population more than doubled (from 5.3 million to 12.9 million), but the trans-Appalachian population grew tenfold (from 370,000 to 3.7 million). By 1830, more than a third of the nation's inhabitants lived west of the original thirteen states.

WHO WERE the western settlers and why did they leave the East?

tions that approached universal suffrage. By 1820, most of the older states had followed suit. The War of 1812 was an important impetus to change in many states, for the propertyless men called up for militia service in that war questioned why they were eligible to fight but not to vote. By 1840, more than 90 percent of adult white males in the nation could vote. And they could vote for more officials: governors and (most important) presidential electors were now elected by direct vote, rather than chosen by small groups of state legislators).

Universal white manhood suffrage, of course, was far from true universal suffrage: the right to vote remained barred to most of the nation's free African American males and to women of any race. Only in five New England states (Maine, New Hampshire, Vermont, Massachusetts, and Rhode Island) could free African American men vote before 1865. In the rest of the northern states, the right of free African American men to vote was restricted to only the most affluent property owners. Free African American men were denied the vote in all of the new western states as well. The constitutions of Illinois, Indiana, Michigan, Iowa, Wisconsin, and (later) Oregon—attempted to solve the "problem" of free African Americans by simply denying them entry into the state at all. Of course, all free black men were prohibited from voting in the slave states of the South.

What accounted for this nearly universal denial of voting rights to free black men? Racism accounted for much of it, an attitude that was strengthened by the backlash against the extremely controversial abolitionist movement of the 1830s and 1840s (see Chapter 13). In addition, as party lines hardened, northern Democrats, the party most closely aligned with the slave South, opposed enfranchising African American men who were almost certain to vote for their opponents. Above all, it was a sign of the growing influence that the southern slave system cast over all of American politics.

In contrast, the reason for the denial of suffrage to white women stemmed from the patriarchal belief that men headed households and represented the interests of all household members. Even wealthy single women who lived alone were considered subordinate to male relatives and denied the right to vote. Although unable to vote, women of the upper classes had long played important informal roles in national politics. At the local level as well, women—often the wives of leading citizens—were accustomed to engaging informally in politics through their benevolent groups. These groups, often church related, had since colonial times not only provided charity to the poor but also raised money to support basic community institutions such as schools, churches, and libraries, in effect setting community priorities in the process.

Although the extension of suffrage to all classes of white men seemed to indicate that women had no role in public affairs, in fact women's informal involvement in politics grew along with the increasing pace of political activity. At the same time, however, as "manhood" rather than property became the qualification for voting, men began to ignore women's customary political activity and to regard their participation as inappropriate, an attitude that politically active women increasingly resented.

## THE ELECTION OF 1824

The 1824 election marked a dramatic end to the political truce that James Monroe had established in 1817. Five candidates, all of them members of the Republican Party, ran for president in the elections of 1824: William H. Crawford of Georgia, Secretary of State John Quincy Adams of Massachusetts, Henry Clay of Kentucky, Andrew Jackson of Tennessee, and John C. Calhoun of South Carolina, who withdrew before the election, to run for vice president. Jackson, a

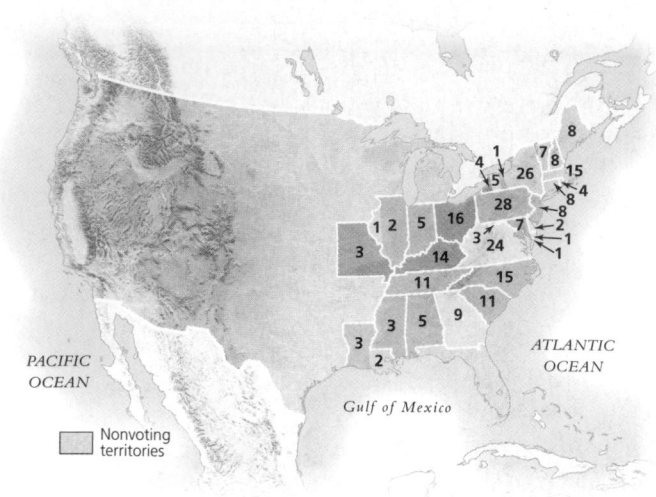

| | Electoral Vote (%) | Popular Vote (%) |
|---|---|---|
| Andrew Jackson | 99 (38) | 153,544 (43) |
| JOHN QUINCY ADAMS | 84 (32) | 108,740 (31) |
| William H. Crawford | 41 (16) | 46,618 (13) |
| Henry Clay | 37 (14) | 47,136 (13) |

**MAP 11.2**

**The Election of 1824** The presidential vote of 1824 was clearly sectional. John Quincy Adams carried his native New England and little else, Henry Clay carried only his own state of Kentucky and two adjoining states, and Crawford's appeal was limited to Virginia and Georgia. Only Andrew Jackson moved beyond the regional support of the Old Southwest to wider appeal and the greatest number of electoral votes. Because no candidate had a majority, however, the election was thrown into the House of Representatives, which chose Adams.

WHAT ROLE did political parties play in the election of 1824?

**10–2**
John Quincy Adams, *A "Corrupt Bargain" or Politics as Usual?* (1824)

latecomer to the race, was at first not taken seriously because his record as a legislator was lackluster and his political views unknown. He was not a member of the elite political group that had made up the governing class since 1790. However, owing to his national reputation as a military leader, Jackson won 43 percent of the popular vote and 99 electoral votes—more than any other candidate. The runner-up, John Quincy Adams, won 31 percent of the popular vote and 84 electoral votes. But neither had an electoral majority, leaving it up to the House of Representatives, as in the election of 1800, to pick the winner.

After some political dealing, Henry Clay threw his support to Adams, and the House elected Adams president. This was customary and proper: the Constitution gave the House the power to decide, and Clay had every right to advise his followers how to vote. But when Adams named Clay his secretary of state, the traditional stepping-stone to the highest office, Jackson's supporters promptly accused them of a "corrupt bargain." Popular opinion, the new element in politics, supported Jackson. John Quincy Adams served four miserable years as president, knowing that Jackson would challenge him, and win, in 1828 (see Map 11.2).

## THE NEW POPULAR DEMOCRATIC CULTURE

Mass campaigns—huge political rallies, parades, and candidates with wide "name recognition," such as military heroes—were the hallmarks of the new popular democratic culture. So were less savory customs, such as the distribution of lavish food and (especially) drink at polling places, which frequently turned elections into rowdy, brawling occasions. The spirit that motivated the new mass politics was democratic pride in participation. And as the election of 1824 showed, along with the spread of universal male suffrage went a change in popular attitudes that spelled the end of the dominance of small political elites. New national parties that superseded sectional interests were beginning to emerge and to succeed, they had to appeal to the interests of a diverse range of voters.

A print revolution helped to democratize politics by spreading word far beyond the nation's cities about the parades, protests, and celebrations that became a basic part of popular democracy. The print revolution had begun in 1826, when a reform organization, the American Tract Society, installed the country's first steam-powered press and rapidly turned out 300,000 Bibles and 6 million religious tracts. The greatest growth, however, was in newspapers that reached a mass audience. The number of newspapers soared from 376 in 1810 to 1,200 in 1835. This rise paralleled the growth of interest in politics, for most newspapers were published by political parties and were openly partisan. Packed with articles that today would be considered libelous and scandalous, newspapers were entertaining and popular reading, and they rapidly became a key part of democratic popular culture.

**This well-known** painting by George Caleb Bingham, *Stump Speaking*, shows a group of men (and boys and dogs) of all social classes brought together by their common interest in politics.

George Caleb Bingham (American 1811–1879), "Stump Speaking," 1853–54. Oil on canvas, 42 1/2 × 58 in. Saint Louis Art Museum, Gift of Bank of America.

The new politics placed great emphasis on participation and party loyalty. One way for ordinary citizens to show their loyalty was to turn out for parades, which derived from processions like those of Philadelphia artisans' associations in earlier times. Political processions were huge affairs, marked by the often spontaneous participation of men carrying badges and party regalia, banners and placards, and portraits of the candidates, accompanied by bands, fireworks, and the shouting and singing of party slogans and songs. The political party provided some of the same satisfactions that popular sports offer today: excitement, entertainment, and a sense of belonging. In effect, political parties functioned as giant national men's clubs. They made politics an immediate and engrossing topic of conversation and argument for men of all walks of life. In this sense, the political party was the political manifestation of a wider social impulse toward community (see Figure 11.1).

## THE ELECTION OF 1828

The election of 1828 was the first to demonstrate the power and effectiveness of the new popular democratic culture and party system. With the help of Martin Van Buren, his campaign manager, Andrew Jackson rode the wave of the new democratic politics to

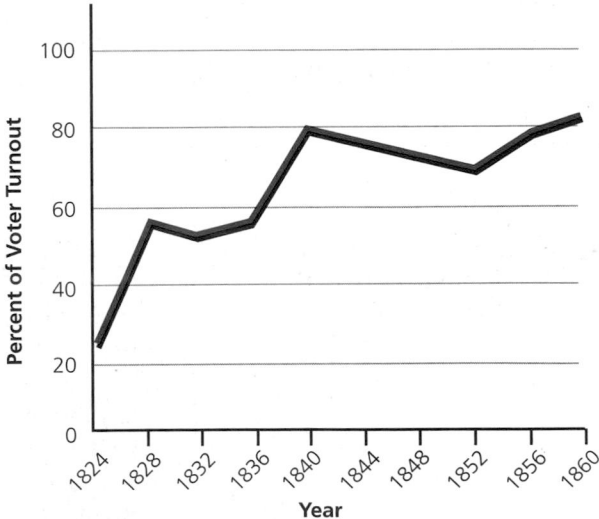

**Figure 11.1 Pre–Civil War Voter Turnout**
The turnout of voters in presidential elections more than doubled from 1824 to 1828, the year Andrew Jackson was first elected. Turnout surged to 80 percent in 1840, the year the Whigs triumphed. The extension of suffrage to all white men, and heated competition between two political parties with nationwide membership, turned presidential election campaigns into events with great popular appeal.

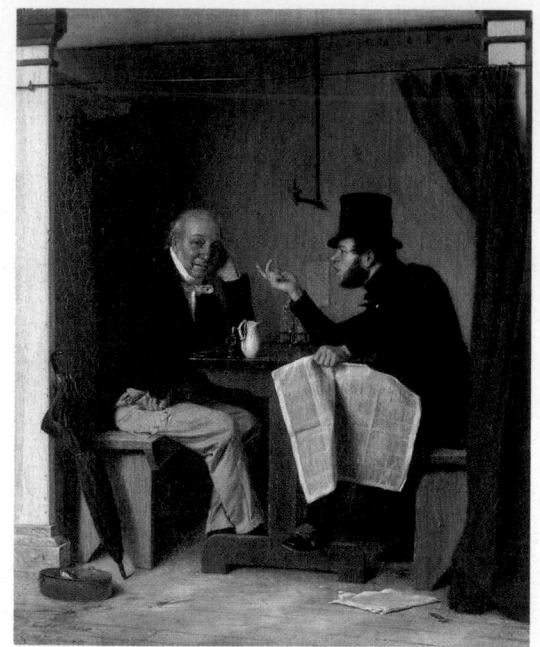

**Politics, abetted by** the publication of inexpensive party newspapers, was a great topic of conversation among men in early nineteenth-century America, as Richard Caton Woodville's 1845 painting *Politics in an Oyster House* suggests.

Richard Caton Woodville, "Politics in an Oyster House," 1848. Oil on canvas. The Walters Art Museum, Baltimore.

the presidency. Voter turnout in 1828 was more than twice that of 1824. Jackson's party, the Democratic Republicans (they soon dropped "Republicans" and became simply the **Democrats**), spoke the language of democracy, and they opposed the special privilege personified for them by President John Quincy Adams and his National Republican (as distinguished from the earlier Jeffersonian Republican) Party. Neither Jackson nor Adams campaigned on his own—that was considered undignified. But the supporters of both candidates campaigned vigorously, freely, and negatively. Jackson's supporters, playing on popular resentment of a wealthy political elite, portrayed the campaign as a contest between "the democracy of the country, on the one hand, and a lordly purse-proud aristocracy on the other." In their turn, Adams's supporters depicted Jackson as an illiterate backwoodsman, a murderer (he had ordered the execution of deserters in the Tennessee militia), and an adulterer (apparently unwittingly, he had married Rachel Robards before her divorce was final).

Jackson won 56 percent of the popular vote (well over 80 percent in much of the South and West) and a decisive electoral majority of 178 votes to Adams's 83. The vote was interpreted as a victory for the common man. But the most important thing about Jackson's victory was the coalition that achieved it. The new democratically based political system worked together to elect him. Popular appeal, which Jackson the military hero certainly possessed, was not enough to ensure victory. To be truly national, a party had to create and maintain a coalition of North, South, and West. The Democrats were the first to do this (see Map 11.3).

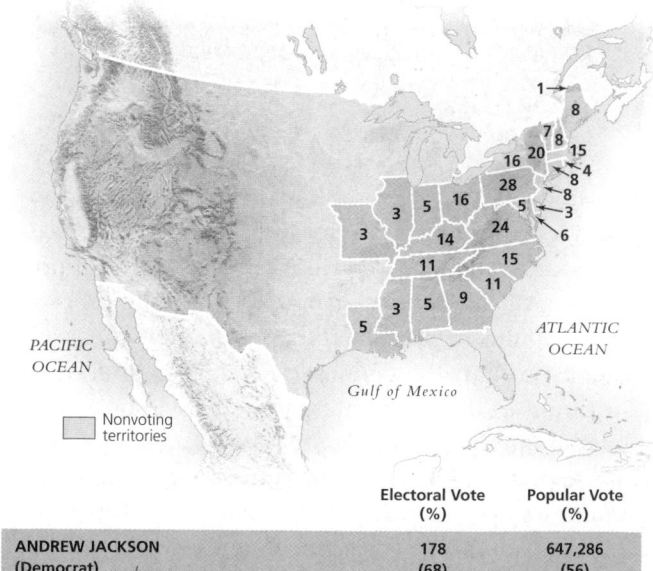

| | Electoral Vote (%) | Popular Vote (%) |
|---|---|---|
| **ANDREW JACKSON** (Democrat) | 178 (68) | 647,286 (56) |
| **John Quincy Adams** (National Republican) | 83 (32) | 508,064 (44) |

**MAP 11.3**

**The Election of 1828**    Andrew Jackson's victory in 1828 was the first success of the new national party system. The coalition of state parties that elected him was national, not regional. Although his support was strongest in the South and West, his ability to carry Pennsylvania and parts of New York demonstrated his national appeal.

**Democrats**    Political party formed in the 1820s under the leadership of Andrew Jackson; favored states' rights and a limited role for the federal government.

TO WHAT extent was Andrew Jackson a "popular" president?

# THE JACKSON PRESIDENCY

Andrew Jackson's election ushered in a new era in American politics, an era that historians have called the "Age of the Common Man." Jackson himself, however, was no common man: he was a military hero, a rich slave owner, and an imperious and decidedly undemocratic personality. "Old Hickory," as Jackson was affectionately called, was tough and unbending, just like hickory itself, one of the hardest of woods. Yet he had a mass appeal to ordinary people, unmatched—and indeed unsought—by earlier presidents. The secret to Jackson's extraordinary appeal lies in the changing nature of American society. Jackson was the first to respond to the ways in which westward expansion and the extension of the suffrage were changing politics at the national as well as the local and state levels.

## A POPULAR PRESIDENT

Jackson was born in 1767 and raised in North Carolina. During the American Revolution, he was captured and beaten by the British, an insult he never forgot. As a young man without wealth or family support, he moved west to the frontier station (fort) at Nashville, Tennessee, in 1788. There he made his career as a lawyer and his considerable wealth as a slave-owning planter. He first became a national hero with his underdog win against the British in the Battle of New Orleans in 1815. In the popular mind, his fierce belligerence came to symbolize pioneer independence. The fact that he had little political experience, which would have made his nomination impossible under the traditional system of politics, was not a hindrance in the new age of popular politics.

On March 4, 1829, Andrew Jackson was inaugurated as president of the United States. Jackson himself was still in mourning for his beloved wife Rachel, whose recent death he attributed to the slanders of the campaign. But everyone else was celebrating. The small community of Washington was crowded with strangers, many of them Westerners and common people who had come especially for Jackson's inauguration. Jackson's brief inaugural address was almost drowned out by the cheering of the crowd, and after the ceremony the new president was mobbed by well-wishers. The same unrestrained enthusiasm was evident at a White House reception, where the crowd was large and disorderly (see Seeing History). This was the exuberance of democracy in action. It marked something new in American politics. Indeed, Jackson's administration was different from all those before it.

## A STRONG EXECUTIVE

The mob scene that accompanied Jackson's inauguration was more than a reflection of the popular enthusiasm for Old Hickory. It also signaled a higher level of controversy in national politics. Jackson's personal style quickly stripped national politics of the polite and gentlemanly aura of cooperation it had acquired during the Era of Good Feelings. Jackson had played rough all his life, and he relished controversy. His administration (1829–37) had plenty of it. Andrew Jackson dominated his administration. Except for Martin Van Buren, whom he appointed secretary of state, he mostly ignored the heads of government departments

WHAT STEPS did Andrew Jackson take to strengthen the executive branch of the federal government?

**myhistorylab**
Review Summary

**10–4**
Andrew Jackson, *The "Commoner" Takes Office* (1828)

**This anti-Jackson** "coffin bill" from the election of 1828 accuses Jackson of murder because he ordered three men executed for desertion during the War of 1812.

who made up his official cabinet. Instead he consulted with an informal group, dubbed the "Kitchen Cabinet," made up of Van Buren and old western friends.

Jackson freely used the tools of his office to strengthen the executive branch of government at the expense of the legislature and judiciary. By using the veto more frequently than all previous presidents combined (twelve vetoes compared with nine by the first six presidents), Jackson forced Congress to constantly consider his opinions. Even more important, Jackson's "negative activism" restricted federal activity (see Chapter 9). Only his strong and popular leadership made this sharp change of direction possible.

## THE NATION'S LEADER VERSUS SECTIONAL SPOKESMEN

Despite his western origins, Jackson was a genuinely national figure. He was more interested in asserting strong national leadership than in promoting sectional compromise. He believed that the president, who symbolized the popular will of the people, ought to dominate the government. As he put it in his first annual message, "the first principle of our system [is that] the majority is to govern." This was new. Voters were much more accustomed to thinking of politics in sectional terms. Jackson faced a Congress full of strong and immensely popular sectional figures. Three stood out: Southerner John C. Calhoun, Northerner Daniel Webster, and Westerner Henry Clay.

Intense, dogmatic, and uncompromising, John C. Calhoun of South Carolina had begun his political career as an ardent nationalist and expansionist in his early days as a War Hawk before the War of 1812. Since the debate over the Missouri Compromise in 1820, however, Calhoun had wholeheartedly identified with southern interests, first and foremost among which was the preservation and expansion of slavery.

Senator Daniel Webster of Massachusetts was the outstanding orator of the age. Large, dark, and stern, Webster delivered his speeches in a deep, booming voice that, listeners said, "shook the world." Webster became the main spokesman for the new northern commercial interests, supporting a high protective tariff, a national bank, and a strong federal government.

In contrast with the other two, Henry Clay of Kentucky, spokesman of the West, was charming, witty, and always eager to forge political compromises. Clay held the powerful position of Speaker of the House of Representatives from 1811 to 1825 and later served several terms in the Senate. Well known for his ability to make a deal—he was known as "the Great Pacificator" (compromiser)—Clay worked to incorporate western desires for cheap and good transportation into national politics. Clay might well have forged a political alliance between the North and the West if not for the policies of President Jackson, his fellow Westerner and greatest rival. Jackson's preeminence thwarted Clay's own ambition to be president.

The prominence and popularity of these three politicians show that sectional interests remained strong even under a president as determined as Jackson to override them and disrupt "politics as usual" by imposing his own personal style. Nothing showed the power of sectional interests more clearly than the unprecedented confrontation provoked by South Carolina in Jackson's first term, the **Nullification Crisis**.

## THE NULLIFICATION CRISIS

The crisis raised the fundamental question concerning national unity in a federal system: What was the correct balance between local interests—the rights of the states—and the powers of the central government? The men who wrote the federal

**Nullification Crisis** Sectional crisis in the early 1830s in which a states' rights party in South Carolina attempted to nullify federal law.

# "President's Levee, or all Creation Going to the White House"

ntil 1829, presidential inaugurations had been small, polite, and ceremonial occasions. Andrew Jackson's popularity, however, brought a horde of well-wishers to Washington for his inaugural. "Thousands and thousands of people, without distinction of rank," reported Washington resident Margaret Bayard Smith, "collected in an immense mass round the Capitol, silent, orderly and tranquil," to watch Jackson's swearing-in. But afterwards, when the crowd followed Jackson to an open house at the White House, says Smith, "what a scene did we witness! . . . a rabble, a mob of boys, negros, women, children, scrambling, fighting, romping. What a pity what a pity." Her consternation was echoed by many respectable people who feared that "the reign of King Mob" had begun.

**DOES IT** matter that the details are not authentic? Why or why not?

This famous illustration of the raucous crowd at the White House reception is by the British caricature artist Robert Cruikshank. It was probably first shown, along with other pictures, in a London printmaker's window display in 1829, with copies sold for two shillings. For the British, amusement came from the fact that American democracy so quickly turned into a rowdy mob, just as the British had always predicted.

Cruikshank was not in Washington at the time of Jackson's inaugural. At best, the details of the illustration are based on accounts provided to him by others or perhaps simply invented. Nevertheless, the illustration captures the mood of the celebrating crowd. ∎

Margaret Bayard Smith, *The First Forty Years of Washington Society* (New York: Charles Scribner's Sons, 1906); Robert Cruikshank, *President's Levee, or all Creation Going to the White House,* illustrated in *The Playfair Papers* (London: Saunders and Otley, 1841).

**Three Great Sectional** Leaders. The years of Jackson's presidency were also notable for the prominence of regional spokesmen, among them John C. Calhoun (left), who spoke for the South and slavery, Henry Clay (center) who spoke for the West, and Daniel Webster (right), who represented northern business. Clay's great personal charm is captured in this 1824 portrait, contrasting with Calhoun's dour expression and Webster's stern image.

(center) Matthew H. Joulett (1788–1827), "Henry Clay," c. 1824. Oil on panel. (attr. to Joulett) © Chicago Historical Society, Chicago, USA.

Constitution in Philadelphia in 1787 had not been able to reach agreement on this question. Because the Constitution deliberately left the federal structure ambiguous, all sectional disagreements automatically became constitutional issues that carried a threat to national unity.

The political issue that came to symbolize the divergent economic interests of North and South was the protective tariff that placed a duty (or surcharge) on imported goods. The first substantial tariff was enacted in 1816 after northern manufacturing interests clamored for protection from the ruthless British competition that followed the War of 1812 (see Chapter 9). As a group, wealthy southern planters were opposed to tariffs, both because duties raised the cost of the luxury goods they imported from Europe and because they feared that American tariffs would cause other countries to retaliate with tariffs against southern cotton. Most southern congressmen, assured that the 1816 tariff was a temporary postwar recovery measure, voted for it. But it was not temporary.

As the North industrialized and new industries demanded protection, tariff bills in 1824 and 1828 raised rates still higher and protected more items. Southerners protested, but they were outvoted in Congress by northern and western representatives. The 1828 tariff imposed especially high tariffs on imported textiles and iron. Southern opponents of the tariff insisted that it was not a truly national measure but rather a sectional one that helped only some groups while harming others. Thus, they claimed, it was unconstitutional because it violated the rights of some of the states.

South Carolina, Calhoun's home state, reacted the most forcefully to the Tariff of 1828. Of the older southern states, South Carolina had been the hardest hit by the opening of the new cotton lands in the Old Southwest, which had drained both population and commerce from the state. To these economic woes were added the first real fears about national attitudes toward slavery. South Carolinians, who had always had close personal ties with slave owners in the Caribbean islands, were shaken by the news that the British Parliament, bowing to popular pressure at home, was planning to emancipate all the slaves in the British West Indies. If Congress had the power to impose tariffs that were harmful to some states, South Carolinians asked, what would prevent it from enacting legislation like Britain's, depriving Southerners of their slaves and, thus, of their livelihood? In this sense, although the Nullification Crisis was about the tariff, it was also about the greatest of all sectional issues, slavery.

The result of these fears was a renewed interest in the doctrine of nullification, a topic that became the subject of widespread discussion in South Carolina. The doctrine upheld the right of a state to declare a federal law null and void and to refuse to enforce it within the state. Calhoun wrote a widely circulated defense of the doctrine, the *Exposition and Protest,* in 1828. Because Calhoun was soon to serve as Andrew Jackson's vice president, he wrote the *Exposition* anonymously. He hoped to use his influence with Jackson, a fellow slave owner, to gain support for nullification, but he was disappointed.

Where Calhoun saw nullification as a safeguard of the rights of the minority, Jackson saw it as a threat to national unity. The president and the vice president were thus in open disagreement on a matter of crucial national importance. The outcome was inevitable: Calhoun lost all influence with Jackson, and two years later, he took the unusual step of resigning the vice presidency. Martin Van Buren was elected to the office for Jackson's second term. Calhoun, his presidential aspirations in ruins, became a senator from South Carolina, and in that capacity, participated in the last act of the nullification drama.

In 1832, the nullification controversy became a full-blown crisis. In passing the Tariff of 1832, Congress (in spite of Jackson's disapproval) retained high taxes on woolens, iron, and hemp, although it reduced duties on other items. South Carolina responded with a special convention and an Ordinance of Nullification, in which it rejected the tariff and refused to collect the taxes it required. The state further issued a call for a volunteer militia and threatened to secede from the Union if Jackson used force against it. Jackson responded vehemently, denouncing the nullifiers and obtaining from Congress a Force Bill authorizing the federal government to collect the tariff in South Carolina at gunpoint if necessary. Intimidated, the other southern states refused to follow South Carolina's lead. More quietly, Jackson also asked Congress to revise the tariff. Henry Clay, the Great Pacificator, swung into action and soon, with Calhoun's support, had crafted the Tariff Act of 1833.

The Nullification Crisis was the most serious threat to national unity that the United States had ever experienced. South Carolinians, by threatening to secede, had forced concessions on a matter they believed to be of vital economic importance. They—and a number of other Southerners—believed that the resolution of the crisis illustrated the success of their uncompromising tactics.

**10–8**
*President Andrew Jackson's Proclamation Regarding Nullification* (1832)

**10–9**
*The Force Bill* (1833)

## CHANGING THE COURSE OF GOVERNMENT

As Martin Van Buren later recalled, Jackson came to the presidency with a clear agenda: "First, the removal of the Indians from the vicinity of the white population and their settlement beyond the Mississippi. Second, to put a stop to the abuses of the Federal government in regard to internal improvements [and] Third, to oppose as well the existing re-incorporation of the existing National Bank." As Jackson enacted his agenda, which he believed expressed the popular will, he changed the course of the federal government as decisively as Jefferson had during his presidency (see Chapter 9). But the opposition that Jackson evoked also revealed the limits of presidential authority in an age of democratic politics.

**WHO WERE** Andrew Jackson's most important opponents and what did they support?

**myhistorylab**
**Review Summary**

## INDIAN REMOVAL

The official policy of the U.S. government from the time of Jefferson's administration was to promote the assimilation of Indian peoples by encouraging them to adopt white ways. To Indian groups that resisted "civilization" or that needed more time to adapt, Jefferson offered the alternative of removal from settled areas in the East to the new Indian Territory west of the Mississippi River. Following this logic, at the end of the War of 1812, the federal government signed removal treaties with a number of Indian nations of the Old Northwest, thereby opening up large tracts of land for white settlement (see Chapter 9). In the Southwest, however, the Five Civilized Tribes—the Cherokees, Chickasaws, Choctaws, Creeks, and Seminoles—remained.

Of these, the Cherokees took the most extensive steps to adopt white ways. Their tribal lands in northwestern Georgia boasted prosperous farms, businesses, grain and lumber mills, and even plantations with black slaves. Intermarriage with whites and African Americans had produced an influential group of mixed-bloods within the Cherokee nation, some of whom were eager to accept white ways. Schooled by Congregationalist, Presbyterian, and Moravian missionaries, the Cherokees were almost totally literate in English.

**10–6**
"*Memorial of the Cherokee Nation*" (1830)

Despite the evidence of the Cherokees' successful adaptation to the dominant white culture, in the 1820s, the legislatures of Georgia, Alabama, and Mississippi, responding to pressures from land-hungry whites, voted to invalidate federal treaties granting special self-governing status to Indian lands. Because the federal government, not the states, bore responsibility for Indian policy, these state actions constituted a sectional challenge to federal authority. In this instance, however, unlike the Nullification Crisis, the resisting states had presidential support. Living up to his reputation as a ruthless Indian fighter, Jackson determined on a federal policy of wholesale removal of the southern Indian tribes.

In 1830, at President Jackson's urging, the U.S. Congress passed the hotly debated **Indian Removal Act**, which appropriated funds for relocation, by force if necessary. When Jackson increased the pressure by sending federal officials to negotiate removal treaties with the southern tribes, most reluctantly signed and prepared to move. The Cherokees, however, fought their removal by using the white man's weapon—the law. At first they seemed to have won: in *Cherokee Nation* v. *Georgia* (1831) and *Worcester* v. *Georgia* (1832), Chief Justice John Marshall ruled that the Cherokees, though not a state or a foreign nation, were a "domestic dependent nation" that could not be forced by the state of Georgia to give up its land against its will. Ignoring the decision, Jackson continued his support for removal.

Although some Seminole bands mounted a successful resistance war in the Florida Everglades, the majority of Seminoles and members of other tribes were much less fortunate: most of the Choctaws moved west in 1830; the last of the Creeks were forcibly moved by the military in 1836, and the Chickasaws a year later. And in 1838, in the last and most infamous removal, resisting Cherokees were driven west to Oklahoma along what came to be known as the "**Trail of Tears.**" A 7,000-man army escorting them watched thousands (perhaps a quarter of the 16,000 Cherokees) die along the way (see Map 11.4).

Indian removal was a deeply divisive national issue. President Jackson's sweeping policy undoubtedly expressed the opinion of most Southerners and Westerners. But northern opinion, led by Protestant missionaries and reform groups, was strongly opposed. Among the groups mobilized in protest were members of female benevolent societies who had a direct interest in the issue, for they had long raised money to support missionary activities aimed at assimilating, not removing, American Indians. Now, they joined together to organize the first national female petition drive. A surprised Congress was deluged by women's petitions against removal,

**Indian Removal Act**   President Andrew Jackson's measure that allowed state officials to override federal protection of Native Americans.

**Trail of Tears**   The forced march in 1838 of the Cherokee Indians from their homelands in Georgia to the Indian Territory in the West.

**MAP 11.4**

**Southern Indian Cessions and Removals, 1830s**   Pressure on the five major southern Indian peoples—the Cherokees, Chickasaws, Choctaws, Creeks, and Seminoles—that began during the War of 1812 culminated with their removal in the 1830s. Some groups from every tribe ceded their southern homelands peacefully and moved to the newly established Indian Territory west of Arkansas and Missouri. Some, like the Seminoles, resisted by force. Others, like the Cherokees, resisted in the courts, but finally lost when President Andrew Jackson refused to enforce a Supreme Court decision in their favor. The Cherokees, the last to move, were forcibly removed by the U.S. Army along the "Trail of Tears" in 1838.

WHAT GROUPS supported the Indian Removal Act?

many with hundreds of signatures (670 from Pittsburgh alone). In the end, the protest failed, but by the barest of margins: the Indian Removal Act passed the House of Representatives by only 3 votes (out of 200).

## INTERNAL IMPROVEMENTS

Because Jackson was a Westerner, his supporters expected him to recognize the nation's urgent need for better transportation and to provide federal funding for internal improvements, especially in the West. Jackson's veto of the Maysville Road Bill of 1830 was, therefore, one of his most unexpected actions. Jackson refused to allow federal funding of a southern spur of the National Road in Kentucky, claiming it should be paid for by the state. Jackson argued that federal funding for extensive and expensive transportation measures was unconstitutional because it infringed on the "reserved powers" the Constitution left to the states.

Internal improvements were a part of Clay's American System (which had been supported by the Monroe and Adams administrations) that envisaged the national government as planner and administrator of a coordinated policy to encourage economic growth and foster the development of a national market. But since 1816, it had proved impossible to propose a nationally funded transportation plan

**QUICK REVIEW**

**Georgia and the Cherokees**

- Georgia stole land of Creek Indians in 1825.
- Georgia moved against Cherokees in 1828, stripping them of all legal rights.
- Stage was set for Indian Removal Act.

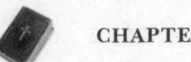

that satisfied everyone. Repeatedly, disappointed claimants for federal funds accused each administration of favoritism and corruption. Jackson ended most of the debate over internal improvements by refusing federal funds for all but the most obviously interstate projects (such as the National Road).

But the country still needed a basic infrastructure of roads, canals, and railroads to tie the national economy together. Without federal funding and planning, the initiative passed to private developers, who turned to individual states. States and towns, especially in newly populated areas of the West, competed in giving land, subsidies, and other forms of encouragement to road, canal, and railroad companies to provide transportation to their particular localities.

## FEDERAL AND STATE SUPPORT FOR PRIVATE ENTERPRISE

At the same time that funding for internal improvements passed to the states, a series of decisions by federal courts asserted broad federal powers over interstate commerce. The effect of these decisions, contradictorily, was to vastly encourage commercial enterprise by limiting the regulatory power of the states at the same time that they were putting up most of the money for the new transportation network. By preventing states from interfering with interstate commerce, the courts encouraged development by assuring entrepreneurs the freedom and security to operate in the risky new national market. Two key decisions were handed down by Chief Justice John Marshall (who had been on the bench since 1801). In *Dartmouth College* v. *Woodward* (1819), the Supreme Court prevented states from interfering in contracts, and in *Gibbons* v. *Ogden* (1824), it enjoined the State of New York from giving a monopoly over a steamboat line to Robert Fulton, inventor of the vessel. Although Fulton's invention was protected by a federal patent, its commercial application was not. A decision handed down by Marshall's successor, Roger Taney, *Charles River Bridge* v. *Warren Bridge* (1837), again supported economic opportunity by denying a monopoly.

At the state level, another crucial commercial protection was the passage of laws concerning incorporation of businesses that had grown too large for individual proprietorship, family ownership, or limited partnership. Businesses that needed to raise large amounts of capital by attracting many investors found the contractual protections provided by incorporation to be essential. The protection investors wanted most was limited liability—the assurance that they would lose no more than what they had invested in a corporation if it were sued or went bankrupt. The net effect of state incorporation laws was to encourage large-scale economic activity and to hasten the commercialization of rural areas, both crucial aspects of the Market Revolution (see Chapter 12).

## THE BANK WAR

In the case of internal improvements, Jackson rejected, on behalf of popular democracy, the notion of coordinated economic planning by the government. His rejection set up the conditions for a speculative frenzy. Precisely the same result occurred in his epic battle with the Second Bank of the United States.

In 1816, Congress had granted a twenty-year charter to the Second Bank of the United States. The Bank was owned by private investors, with the U.S. government holding only one-fifth of the shares. But its most important function was the control it exercised over state banks. Because state banks tended to issue more paper money than they could back with hard currency, the Bank always demanded repayment of its loans to them in hard currency. This policy forced state banks to maintain adequate reserves and restricted speculative activities. In times of recession, the Bank eased the pressure on state banks, demanding only partial payment in coin. Thus, the Bank acted as a currency stabilizer by helping to control the money supply.

**In this political** cartoon, Jackson destroys the Second Bank of the United States by withdrawing government deposits. As the Bank crashes, it crushes the director Nicholas Biddle (depicted as the Devil), wealthy investors (with moneybags), and the newspaper editors (surrounded by paper) who opposed Jackson on this issue.

The concept of a strong national bank controlled by wealthy investors, not the federal government, was supported by the majority of the nation's merchants and businessmen. Nevertheless, the Bank had many opponents. Both western farmers and urban workers had bitter memories of the Panic of 1819, which the Bank had caused (at least in part) by sharply cutting back on available credit. Many ordinary people believed that a system based on paper currency would be manipulated by bankers—the "monied aristocracy"—in selfish and dangerous ways.

Early in his administration, Jackson hastened to tell Nicholas Biddle, the director of the Bank: "I do not dislike your Bank any more than all banks." By 1832, Jackson's opinion had changed, and he and Biddle were locked in a personal conflict that harmed not only the national economy but also the reputations of both men. Biddle, urged on by Henry Clay and Daniel Webster, precipitated the conflict by making early application for rechartering the Bank. Congress approved the application in July 1832. Jackson immediately decided on a stinging veto, announcing to Van Buren, "The bank . . . is trying to kill me, but I will kill it!"

And kill it he did that same July, with one of the strongest veto messages in American history. Denouncing the Bank as unconstitutional, harmful to states' rights, and "dangerous to the liberties of the people," Jackson presented himself as the spokesman for the majority of ordinary people and the enemy of special privilege.

Jackson's veto message was a great popular success, and it set the terms for the presidential election of 1832. Henry Clay, the nominee of the anti-Jackson forces, lost the battle for popular opinion. Democrats successfully painted Clay as the defender of the Bank and of privilege. These were accusations with great popular appeal. Clay's defeat was decisive: he drew only 49 electoral votes to Jackson's 219.

**10–7**
Andrew Jackson, *Veto of the Bank Bill* (1832)

**This figurehead of** Andrew Jackson, carved in 1834 for the navy frigate *Constitution,* captures the unmovable resolve that made Jackson so popular early in his presidency and so reviled during the Bank War.

Museum of the City of New York (M52.11).

**Whigs**   The name used by advocates of colonial resistance to British measures during the 1760s and 1770s.

**Specie Circular**   Proclamation issued by President Andrew Jackson in 1836 stipulating that only gold or silver could be used as payment for public land.

Although the election was a triumph for Jackson, the Bank War continued because Jackson decided to kill the Bank by transferring its $10 million in government deposits to favored state banks ("pet banks," critics called them).

Jackson's refusal to renew the charter of the Second Bank of the United States had lasting economic and political consequences. Economically, it inaugurated the economic policy known as *laissez-faire,* where decision-making power rests with commercial interests, not with government. Politically, it so infuriated Jackson's opponents that they formed a permanent opposition party. It was from the heat of the Bank War that the now characteristic American two-party system emerged.

## WHIGS, VAN BUREN, AND THE PANIC OF 1837

In 1833, as the government withdrew its deposits, Nicholas Biddle, the Bank's director, counterattacked by calling in the Bank's commercial loans, thereby causing a sharp panic and recession in the winter of 1833–34. Merchants, businessmen, and southern planters were all furious—at Jackson. His opponents, only a loose coalition up to this time, coalesced into a formal opposition party that called itself the **Whigs**. Just as Jackson's own calls for popular democracy had appealed to voters in all regions, so his opponents overcame their sectional differences to unite in opposition to his economic policies and arbitrary methods.

Vice President Martin Van Buren, Jackson's designated successor, won the presidential election of 1836 because the Whigs ran four sectional candidates, hoping their combined votes would deny Van Buren a majority and force the election into the House of Representatives.

Meanwhile, the consequences of the Bank War continued. The recession of 1833–34 was followed by a wild speculative boom, caused as much by foreign investors as by the expiration of the Bank. Many new state banks were chartered that were eager to give loans, the price of cotton rose rapidly, and speculation in western lands was feverish. A government surplus of $37 million distributed to the states in 1836 made the inflationary pressures worse. Jackson became alarmed at the widespread use of paper money (which he blamed for the inflation), and in July 1836, he issued the **Specie Circular**, announcing that the government would accept payment for public lands only in hard currency. At the same time, foreign investors, especially British banks, affected by a world recession, called in their American loans. The sharp contraction of credit led to the Panic of 1837 and a six-year recession, the worst the American economy had yet known.

In neither 1837 nor 1819 did the federal government take any action to aid victims of economic recession. No banks were bailed out, no bank depositors were saved by federal insurance, no laid-off workers got unemployment payments. Nor did the government undertake any public works projects or pump money into the economy. All of these steps, today seen as essential to prevent economic collapse and to alleviate human suffering, were unheard of then. Soup kitchens and charities were mobilized in major cities, but only by private, volunteer groups, not by local or state governments. As a result, workers, farmers, and members of the new business middle class suddenly realized that participation in America's booming economy was very dangerous.

Martin Van Buren (quickly nicknamed "Van Ruin") spent a dismal four years in the White House presiding over bank failures, bankruptcies, and massive unemployment. Van Buren, who lacked Jackson's compelling personality, could find no remedies to the depression. His misfortune gave the opposition party, the newly formed Whigs, its opportunity.

# THE SECOND AMERICAN PARTY SYSTEM

The First American Party System, the confrontation between the Federalists and the Jeffersonian Republicans that began in the 1790s, had been widely viewed at the time as an unfortunate factional squabble that threatened the common good of the republic (see Chapter 8). By the 1830s, with the expansion of suffrage, attitudes had changed. The political struggles of the Jackson era, coupled with the dramatic social changes caused by expansion and economic growth, created the basic pattern of American politics: two major parties, each with at least some appeal among voters of all social classes and in all sections of the country. That pattern, which we call the "**Second American Party System**," continues to this day.

## WHIGS AND DEMOCRATS

There were genuine differences between the Whigs and the Democrats, but they were not sectional differences. Instead, the two parties reflected just-emerging class and cultural differences. The Democrats, as they themselves were quick to point out, had inherited Thomas Jefferson's belief in the democratic rights of the small, independent yeoman farmer. They had nationwide appeal, especially in the South and West, the most rural regions. As a result of Jackson's presidency, Democrats came to be identified with independence and a distaste for interference, whether from the government or from economic monopolies such as the Bank of the United States. They favored expansion, Indian removal, and the freedom to do as they chose on the frontier. Most Democratic voters were opposed to the rapid social and economic changes of the 1830s and 1840s.

The Whigs were themselves often the initiators and beneficiaries of economic change and were more receptive to it. They supported Henry Clay's American System: a strong central government, the Bank of the United States, a protective tariff, and internal improvements. Whigs favored government intervention in both economic and social affairs, calling for education and

**WHAT WERE** the main issues of the campaign of 1840?

**myhistorylab**
Review Summary

**8–13**
Davy Crockett, *Advice to Politicians* (1833)

**Second American Party System** The basic pattern of American politics of two parties, each with appeal among voters of all social voters and in all sections of the country.

**This contemporary cartoon** bitterly depicts the terrible effects of the Panic of 1837 on ordinary people—bank failures, unemployment, drunkenness, and destitution—which the artist links to the insistence of the rich on payment in specie (as Jackson had required in the Species Circular of 1836). Over the scene waves the American flag, accompanied by the ironic message, "61st Anniversary of Our Independence."

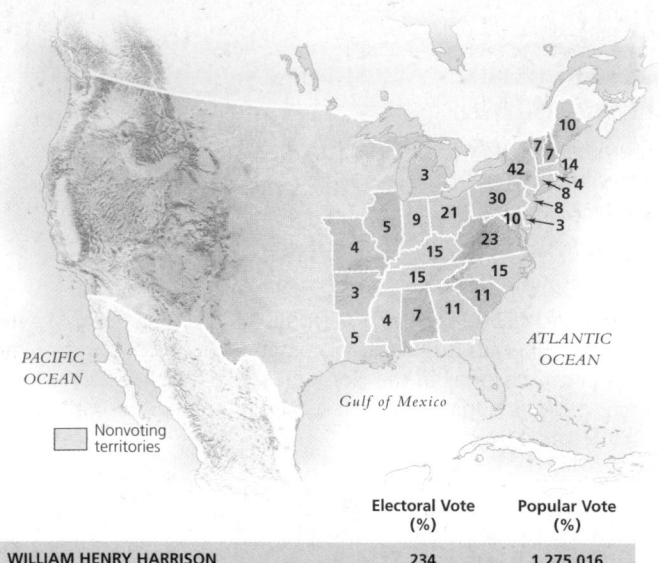

| | Electoral Vote (%) | Popular Vote (%) |
|---|---|---|
| **WILLIAM HENRY HARRISON** (Whig) | 234 (80) | 1,275,016 (53) |
| Martin Van Buren (Democrat) | 60 (20) | 1,129,102 (47) |

**MAP 11.5**
**The Election of 1840**  The Whigs triumphed in the election of 1840 by beating the Democrats at their own game. Whigs could expect to do well in the commercializing areas of New England and the Old Northwest, but their adopted strategy of popular campaigning worked well in the largely rural South and West as well, contributing to Harrison's victory. The Whigs' choice of John Tyler as vice presidential candidate, another strategy designed to appeal to southern voters, backfired when Harrison died and Tyler, who did not share Whig principles, became America's first vice president to succeed to the presidency.

WHAT POLICIES did Tyler promote? Which did he reject?

WHAT ROLE did newspapers and pamphlets play in American popular culture in the first half of the nineteenth century?

**myhistorylab**
**Review Summary**

social reforms, such as temperance, that aimed to improve the ordinary citizen. Many rich men were Whigs, but so were many poorer men who had a democratic faith in the perfectibility of all Americans. The Whigs' greatest strength was in New England and the northern part of the West (the Old Northwest), the areas most affected by commercial agriculture and factory work (see Chapter 13).

### THE CAMPAIGN OF 1840

In 1840, the Whigs set out to beat the Democrats at their own game. Passing over the ever-hopeful Henry Clay, the Whigs nominated a man as much like Andrew Jackson as possible, the aging Indian fighter William Henry Harrison, former governor of the Indiana Territory from 1801 to 1812. The Whigs reached out to ordinary people with torchlight parades, barbecues, songs, coonskin caps, bottomless jugs of hard cider, and claims that Martin Van Buren, Harrison's hapless opponent, was a man of privilege and aristocratic tastes. Nothing could be further from the truth: Van Buren was the son of a tavern keeper.

The Whig campaign tactics, added to the popular anger at Van Buren because of the continuing depression, gave Harrison a sweeping electoral victory (see Map 11.5).

### THE WHIG VICTORY TURNS TO LOSS: THE TYLER PRESIDENCY

Although the Whig victory of 1840 was a milestone in American politics, the triumph of Whig principles was short-lived. William Henry Harrison, who was sixty-eight, died of pneumonia a month after his inauguration. For the first time in American history, the vice president stepped up to the presidency. John Tyler of Virginia, quickly nicknamed "His Accidency," was a former Democrat who had left the party because he disagreed with Jackson's autocratic style. The Whigs had sought him primarily for his sectional appeal and had not inquired too closely into his political opinions, which turned out to be anti-Whig as well as anti-Jackson.

President Tyler vetoed a series of bills embodying all the elements of Henry Clay's American System: tariffs, internal improvements, a new Bank of the United States. In exasperation, congressional Whigs forced Tyler out of the party, and his entire cabinet of Whigs resigned. To replace them, Tyler appointed former Democrats like himself.

## AMERICAN ARTS AND LETTERS

Jackson's presidency was a defining moment in the development of an American identity. His combination of western belligerency and combative individualism was the strongest statement of American distinctiveness since Thomas Jefferson's agrarianism. Did Jackson speak for all of America? The Whigs did not think so. And the definitions of American identity that were beginning to emerge in popular culture and in intellectual circles were more complex than

# OVERVIEW | The Second American Party System

| | |
|---|---|
| **Democrats** | First organized to elect Andrew Jackson to the presidency in 1828. The Democratic Party spoke for Jeffersonian democracy, expansion, and the freedom of the "common man" from interference from government or from financial monopolies like the Bank of the United States. It found its power base in the rural South and West and among some northern urban workers. The Democratic Party was the majority party from 1828 to 1860. |
| **Whigs** | Organized in opposition to Andrew Jackson in the early 1830s. Heir to Federalism, the Whig Party favored a strong role for the national government in the economy (for example, it promoted Henry Clay's American System) and supported active social reform. Its power base lay in the North and Old Northwest among voters who benefited from increased commercialization and among some southern planters and urban merchants. The Whigs won the elections of 1840 and 1848. |

the message coming from the White House. Throughout the nation, however, there was a widespread interest in information and literature of all kinds. The Age of the Common Man would prove to be the period when American writers and painters found the national themes that allowed them to produce the first distinctively American literature and art.

## POPULAR CULTURES AND THE SPREAD OF THE WRITTEN WORD

Newspapers and pamphlets fostered a variety of popular cultures. For western readers, the Crockett almanacs offered a mix of humorous stories and tall tales. In New York City, the immensely popular "penny papers" (so called from their price) that began appearing in 1833 fostered a distinctive urban culture. These papers, with lurid headlines such as "Double Suicide" and "Secret Tryst," fed the same popular appetite for scandal as did other popular publications. Throughout the country, religious literature was still most widely read, but a small middle-class audience existed for literary magazines and, among women especially, for sentimental magazines and novels.

Accompanying all these changes in print communication was an invention that outsped them all: telegraph. The impact of this revolutionary invention, the first to separate the message from the speed at which a human messenger could travel, was immediate. The timeliness of information available to the individual, from important national news to the next train's arrival time, vastly increased. Distant events gained new and exciting immediacy. Everyone's horizon and sense of community were widened.

## CREATING A NATIONAL AMERICAN CULTURE

In the early years of the nineteenth century, eastern seaboard cities actively built the cultural foundation that would nurture American art and literature. Philadelphia's American Philosophical Society, founded by Benjamin Franklin in 1743, boasted a distinguished roster of scientists. Culturally, Boston ran a close second to Philadelphia. Southern cities were much less successful in supporting culture. Charleston had a Literary and Philosophical Society (founded in 1814), but the widely dispersed residences of the southern elite made urban cultural institutions difficult to sustain. Thus, unwittingly, the South ceded cultural leadership to the North.

myhistorylab

*Overview: The Second American Party System*

---

### QUICK REVIEW

**William Henry Harrison of Ohio**

- Untainted by association with Bank of the United States, Masonic Order, or slaveholding.
- Hero of War of 1812.
- Selected John Tyler of Virginia as his running mate.

**The Boston Athenaeum** was one of Boston's leading cultural institutions. The library, shown in this engraving, was probably the finest in the country in the early nineteenth century.

**9–10**
James F. Cooper, *Notions of the Americans* (1840)

**10–11**
Alexis de Tocqueville, *A French Traveler Reports on American Society* (1835)

## QUICK REVIEW

**The Print Revolution**

- 1826: American Tract Society installs first steam-powered press in the United States.
- Greatest growth was in newspapers.
- Newspapers and pamphlets fostered a variety of popular cultures.

The cultural picture was much spottier in the West. A few cities had civic cultural institutions, and some transplanted New Englanders maintained connections with New England culture. A group of pioneers in Ames, Ohio, for example, founded a "coonskin library" composed of books purchased from Boston and paid for in coonskins. But most pioneers were at best uninterested and at worst actively hostile to traditional literary culture. This was neither from lack of literacy nor from a failure to read. Newspaper and religious journals both had large readerships in the West: the *Methodist Christian Advocate,* for example, reached 25,000 people yearly (compared with the *North American Review*'s 3,000 readers). The frontier emphasis on the practical was hard to distinguish from anti-intellectualism.

Thus, in the early part of the nineteenth century, the gap between the intellectual and cultural horizons of a wealthy Bostonian and a frontier farmer in Michigan widened. Part of the unfinished task of building a national society was the creation of a national culture that could fill this gap. For writers and artists, the challenge was to find distinctively American themes.

Of the eastern cities, New York produced the first widely recognized American writers. In 1819, Washington Irving published *The Sketch Book,* thus immortalizing Rip Van Winkle and the Headless Horseman. Within a few years, James Fenimore Cooper's Leatherstocking novels (of which *The Last of the Mohicans,* published in 1826, is the best known) achieved wide success in both America and Europe. Cooper's novels established the experience of westward expansion, of which the conquest of the Indians was a vital part, as a serious and distinctive American literary theme.

It was New England, however, that claimed to be the forge of American cultural independence from Europe. As Ralph Waldo Emerson proclaimed in "The American Scholar," a lecture he delivered in 1837 to the Harvard faculty, "Our day of dependence, our long apprenticeship to the learning of other lands, draws to a close."

## CHRONOLOGY

| | | | | |
|---|---|---|---|---|
| 1819 | *Dartmouth College* v. *Woodward* | | 1834 | Whig Party organized |
| 1821 | Mexican independence from Spain | | | British abolish slavery in their Caribbean colonies |
| 1824 | *Gibbons* v. *Ogden* | | 1836 | Jackson issues Specie Circular |
| | John Quincy Adams elected president by the House of Representatives | | | Martin Van Buren elected president |
| 1826 | First American use of the steam-powered printing press | | 1837 | *Charles River Bridge* v. *Warren Bridge* |
| 1828 | Congress passes "Tariff of Abominations" | | | Revolts against Britain in Upper and Lower Canada |
| | Andrew Jackson elected president | | | Ralph Waldo Emerson first presents "The American Scholar" |
| | John C. Calhoun publishes *Exposition and Protest* anonymously | | | Panic of 1837 |
| 1830 | Jackson vetoes Maysville Road Bill | | 1838 | Cherokee removal along the "Trail of Tears" |
| | Congress passes Indian Removal Act | | 1840 | Whig William Henry Harrison elected president |
| 1832 | Nullification Crisis begins | | | Act of Union merges Upper and Lower Canada |
| | Jackson vetoes renewal of Bank of the United States charter | | 1841 | John Tyler assumes presidency at the death of President Harrison |
| | Jackson reelected president | | | |
| 1833 | General Antonio Lopez de Santa Anna elected president of Mexico | | | |

## ARTISTS AND BUILDERS

Artists were as successful as novelists in finding American themes. Thomas Cole, who came to America from England in 1818, painted American scenes in the style of the British romantic school of landscape painting. Cole founded the Hudson River school of American painting, a style and subject matter frankly nationalistic in tone.

The western painters—realists such as Karl Bodmer and George Catlin as well as the romantics who followed them, like Albert Bierstadt and Thomas Moran—drew on the dramatic western landscape and its peoples. All these painters found much to record and to celebrate in American life.

The haste and transience of American life are nowhere as obvious as in the architectural record of this era, which is sparse. The monumental neoclassical style (complete with columns) that Jefferson had recommended for official buildings in Washington continued to be favored for public buildings elsewhere and by private concerns trying to project an imposing image, such as banks. But in general, Americans were in too much of a hurry to build for the future, and in balloon-frame construction they found the perfect technique for the present. Balloonframe structures—which consist of a basic frame of wooden studs fastened with crosspieces top and bottom—could be put up quickly, cheaply, and without the help of a skilled carpenter. Covering the frame with wooden siding was equally simple, and the resultant dwelling was as strong, although not as well insulated, as a house of solid timber or logs.

**myhistorylab**

**Exploring America:** *American Art*

# CONCLUSION

Andrew Jackson's presidency witnessed the building of a strong national party system based on nearly universal white manhood suffrage. Sectionalism and localism seemed to have been replaced by a more national consciousness that was clearly expressed in the two national political parties, the Whigs and the Democrats. The Second American Party System created new democratic political communities united by common political opinions and often mobilized by common political resentments.

Culturally, American writers and artists began to establish a distinctive American identity in the arts. But as the key battles of the Jackson presidency—the Nullification Crisis, Indian removal, and the Bank War—showed, the forces of sectionalism resisted the strong nationalizing tendencies of the era. Equally clearly, popular political opinion, once aroused, was not always as controllable as politicians may have wished. As the next chapter will show, economic developments in the North were beginning to create a very different society and electorate from that of the slave South or the rural West.

## REVIEW QUESTIONS

1. What reasons might a person of the 1820s and 1830s give for opposing universal white manhood suffrage? Suffrage for free African American men? For women of all races?

2. Opponents believed that Andrew Jackson was unsuited in both political experience and temperament to be president of the United States, yet his presidency is considered one of the most influential in American history. Why?

3. Both the Nullification Crisis and Indian removal raised the constitutional issue of the rights of a minority in a nation governed by majority rule. What rights, in your opinion, does a minority have, and what kinds of laws are necessary to defend those rights?

4. Why was the issue of government support for internal improvements so controversial? What *is* the appropriate role for government in economic development?

5. What were the key differences between Whigs and Democrats? What did each party stand for? Who were their supporters? What were the links between each party's programs and party supporters?

6. What distinctive American themes did the writers, artists, and builders of the 1820s and 1830s express in their works? Are they still considered American themes today?

## KEY TERMS

**myhistorylab**
Flashcard Review

Bank War (p. 268)
Democrats (p. 274)
Indian Removal Act (p. 280)
Nullification Crisis (p. 276)

Second American Party System (p. 285)
Specie Circular (p. 284)
Trail of Tears (p. 280)
Whigs (p. 284)

# RECOMMENDED READING

Anne M. Boylan, *The Origins of Women's Activism: New York and Boston 1797–1840* (2002). How and why the first women's volunteer associations were formed and their political influence.

Bray Hammond, *Banks and Politics in America* (1957). The classic study of the Bank War and its consequences.

Patrick J. Jung, *The Black Hawk War of 1832* (2007). An up-to-date study of one of the last Indian wars in the eastern United States.

Alexander Keyssar, *The Right to Vote: The Contested History of Democracy in the United States* (2000). A survey that examines the reasons for continual limits on the franchise.

Simon Newman, *Parades and the Politics of the Street* (1997). Examines how festive culture became an expression of popular political culture.

Robert Remini, *Andrew Jackson and the Source of American Freedom* (1981). An account of Jackson's White House years by his major biographer.

Alan Taylor, *William Cooper's Town: Power and Persuasion on the Frontier of the Early American Republic* (1995). An engrossing study of the effects of the democratization of politics.

Harry L. Watson, *Liberty and Power: The Politics of Jacksonian America* (1990). An excellent overview of Jacksonian politics.

Sean Wilentz, *The Rise of American Democracy: Jefferson to Lincoln* (2005). A massive new political study that traces the different histories of "city" and "country" democracy.

# Jacksonian Democracy and American Politics

**TO WHAT** degree was the election of 1824 a turning point in American political history? Considering the role of the common man, changes in party operations and campaign tactics, and the growing influence of political patronage, how did the events initiated in that election change American politics between 1824 and 1840?

Historians have referred to the years of Jackson's presidency as the Age of the Common Man and the Rise of Democracy. Perhaps this does carry a little too much elaboration with it, but the time of Andrew Jackson was a period of great ferment and change. The Second Great Awakening was stirring the religious and reform values of American citizens. The rise of the second two party system was creating both conflict and confrontation in American politics. The issues of national tariffs and slavery were beginning to divide the states and the slow movement toward civil war was becoming clearly apparent.

John Adams, Andrew Jackson, and Henry Clay and the election of 1824 comprise a turning point in U.S. politics. With a field of four candidates, the election for president was thrown to the U.S. House of Representatives where Henry Clay was the Speaker of the House and had heavy influence upon the vote of the members of that chamber. After Adams was elected over Jackson, who had the largest share of popular votes, Adams appointed Clay as the Secretary of State, then seen as a stepping stone to the presidency. Jackson's supporters immediately screamed "corrupt bargain" and the campaign of 1828 was underway before Adams was even inaugurated. Jackson's people coalesced into the Democratic party. Adams' followers became the National Republicans, later evolving into the Whigs.■

 Henry Clay

## John Quincy Adams, A "Corrupt Bargain" or Politics as Usual? (1824)

**9TH.** . . . Mr. Clay came at six, and spent the evening with me in a long conversation explanatory of the past and prospective of the future. He said that the time was drawing near when the choice must be made in the House of Representatives of a President from the three candidates presented by the electoral colleges; that he had been much urged and solicited with regard to the part in that transaction that he should take, and had not been five minutes landed at his lodgings before he had been applied to by a friend of Mr. Crawford's, in a manner so gross that it had disgusted him; that some of my friends also, disclaiming, indeed, to have any authority from me, had repeatedly applied to him, directly or indirectly, urging considerations personal to himself as motives to his cause. He had thought it best to reserve for sometime his determination to himself: first, to give a decent time for his own funeral solemnities as a candidate; and, secondly, to prepare and predispose all his friends to a state of neutrality between the three candidates who would be before the House, so that they might be free ultimately to take that course which might be most conducive to the public interest. The time had now come at which he might be explicit in his communication with me, and he had for that purpose asked this confidential interview. He wished me, as far as I might think proper, to satisfy him with regard to some principles of great public importance, but without any personal considerations for himself. In the question to come before the House between General Jackson, Mr. Crawford, and myself, he had no hesitation in saying that his preference would be for me.■

Charles Francis Adams, ed. Memoirs of John Quincy Adams, 12 Volumes (Philadelphia: J. B. Lippincott & Co., 1875)

# PRESIDENTIAL CANDIDATES AND POLITICAL PARTIES, 1788–1840

IN THE slightly more than fifty years covered in this list, some parties flourished and some died. Some parties rose up to replace earlier parties and some changed into a new political alliance with a different name and evolved political goals.

1788    George Washington – No Party Designation
           John Adams – No Party Designation

1792    George Washington – No Party Designation
           John Adams – No Party Designation
           George Clinton – No Party Designation

1796    John Adams – Federalist
           Thomas Jefferson – Democratic-Republican
           Thomas Pinckney – Federalist
           Aaron Burr – Democratic-Republican

1800    Thomas Jefferson – Democratic-Republican
           Aaron Burr – Democratic-Republican
           John Adams – Federalist
           Charles C. Pinckney – Federalist

1804    Thomas Jefferson – Democratic-Republican
           Charles C. Pinckney – Federalist

1808    James Madison – Democratic-Republican
           Charles C. Pinckney – Federalist
           George Clinton – Democratic-Republican

1812    James Madison – Democratic-Republican
           Dewitt Clinton – Federalist

1816    James Monroe – Democratic-Republican
           Rufus King – Federalist

1820    James Monroe – Democratic-Republican
           John Q. Adams – Independent Republican

1824    John Q. Adams – Democratic-Republican
           Andrew Jackson – Democratic-Republican
           William H. Crawford – Democratic-Republican
           Henry Clay – Democratic-Republican

1828    Andrew Jackson – Democratic
           John Q. Adams – National Republican

1832    Andrew Jackson – Democratic
           Henry Clay – National Republican
           William Wirt – Anti-Masonic
           John Floyd – National Republican

1836    Martin Van Buren – Democratic
           William H. Harrison – Whig
           Hugh L. White – Whig
           Daniel Webster – Whig
           W.P. Mangum – Whig

1840    William H. Harrison – Whig
           Martin Van Buren – Democratic. ■

---

## SENATOR WILLIAM MARCY

SENATOR WILLIAM Marcy gave the name "spoils system" to the practice of awarding political office to the supporters of your own party once you had won control of either state or federal government. His famous statement on the floor of the U.S. Senate: "When they are contending for victory, they avow the intention of enjoying it. If they are defeated, they expect to retire from office. If they are successful, they claim as matter of right the advantages of success. They see nothing wrong in the rule that to the victors belong the spoils of the enemy." This principal had been used heavily in the states of New York and Pennsylvania where Marcy engaged brutally in applying the practice. It was not until Jackson's election in 1828 the spoils system was introduced at the federal level. Previous presidents had been circumspect in removing federal office servers from their jobs. Washington had removed only 9 in two terms; Adams had removed 9 in one term. After the Federalists were defeated in 1800 and the Democratic Republicans took office, Jefferson refused to utilize the spoils system and removed only 39 federal office holders in two terms. Madison then dropped only 5 in two terms, Monroe removed only 9 in two terms, and John Q. Adams fired only 2 in one administration. This changed in 1829 when Jackson removed a total of 734 federal office holders in a single year of his first administration. The age of the spoils system had arrived. The Democrats clearly used the spoils system to their advantage. How did the other political parties respond to this concept?

◀ William Learned Marcy (1786–1857). American political leader. Steel engraving, 19th century.

### ANDREW JACKSON, STATE OF THE UNION MESSAGE TO CONGRESS, DECEMBER 8, 1829

…The duties of all public officers are, or at least admit of being made, so plain and simple that men of intelligence may readily qualify themselves for their performance; and I can not but believe that more is lost by the long continuance of men in office than is generally to be gained by their experience. I submit, therefore, to your consideration whether the efficiency of the Government would not be promoted and official industry and integrity better secured by a general extension of the law which limits appointments to four years. ■

*Now if rights are founded on the nature of moral being, then the mere circumstance of sex does not give to man higher rights and responsibilities, than to woman. To suppose that it does, would be to deny the self-evident truth, that the physical constitution is the mere instrument of the moral nature.*

—Angelina Emily Grimké, October 2, 1837

# 12

# INDUSTRY AND THE NORTH

## 1790s–1840s

**WHAT WERE** the effects of the transportation revolution?

**WHAT WAS** the market revolution?

**WHAT IMPACT** did advances in transportation have in the Old Northwest?

**HOW DID** industrialization affect workers in early factories?

**HOW DID** the market revolution change the lives of ordinary people?

**WHAT VALUES** were promoted by the new middle class?

# AMERICAN COMMUNITIES
## Women Factory Workers Form a Community in Lowell, Massachusetts

IN THE 1820s AND 1830s, YOUNG FARM WOMEN FROM ALL OVER NEW England flocked to Lowell to work a twelve-hour day in one of the first cotton textile factories in America. Living six to eight to a room in nearby boardinghouses, the women of Lowell earned an average of $3 a week. Some also attended inexpensive nighttime lectures or classes. Lowell, considered a model factory town, drew worldwide attention. As one admirer of its educated workers said, Lowell was less a factory than a "philanthropic manufacturing college."

The choice of young women as factory workers seemed shockingly unconventional. In the 1820s and 1830s, young unmarried women simply did not live alone; they lived and worked with their parents until they married. In these years of growth and westward expansion, however, America was chronically short of labor, and the Lowell manufacturers were shrewd enough to realize that young farm women were an untapped labor force. To attract respectable young women, Lowell offered supervision both on the job and at home, with strict rules of conduct, compulsory religious services, cultural opportunities such as concerts and lectures, and cash wages.

When they first arrived in Lowell, the young women were often bewildered by the large numbers of townspeople and embarrassed by their own rural clothing and country ways. It was company policy for senior women to train the newcomers, and often sisters or neighbors who had preceded them to the mill helped them adjust to their new surroundings.

Textile mills ran on a rigid work schedule with fines or penalties imposed on latecomers and slackers. Power-driven machinery operated at a sustained, uniform pace throughout every mill; human workers had to learn to do the same. This precise work schedule represented the single largest change from preindustrial work habits, and it was the hardest adjustment for the workers. Moreover, each mill positioned one or two male overseers on every floor to make sure the pace was maintained.

Why did young farm women come to Lowell? Some worked out of need, but most regarded Lowell as an opportunity: an escape from rural isolation and from parental supervision, a chance to buy the latest fashions and learn "city ways," to attend lectures and concerts, to save for a dowry, or to pay for an education. As writer Lucy Larcom, one of the most famous workers, said, the women who came to Lowell sought "an opening into freer life." Working side by side and living with six to twelve other women, some of whom might be relatives or friends from home, the Lowell women built a close, supportive community for themselves.

The owners of Lowell made large profits and also drew praise for their carefully managed community, with its intelligent and independent workforce. But their success was short-lived. In the 1830s, facing competition and poor economic conditions, the owners imposed wage cuts and work speedups that their model workforce did not take lightly. Despite the system of paternalistic control at the mills, the close bonds the women forged gave them the courage and solidarity to "turn out" in spontaneous protests, which were, however, unsuccessful in reversing the wage cuts. By 1850, the "philanthropic manufacturing college" was no more. The original Lowell workforce of New England farm girls had been largely replaced by poor Irish immigrants of both sexes, who earned much less than their predecessors. Now Lowell was simply another mill town.

Lowell

The history of Lowell epitomizes the process by which the North (New England and the Middle Atlantic states) industrialized. A society composed largely of self-sufficient farm families (Jefferson's "yeoman farmers") changed to one of urban wage earners. Industrialization did not occur overnight. Once under way, the market revolution changed how people worked, how they thought, and how they lived: the very basis of community. In the early years of the nineteenth century, northern communities led this transformation, fostering attitudes far different from those prevalent in the agrarian South.

# THE TRANSPORTATION REVOLUTION

Between 1800 and 1840, the United States experienced truly revolutionary improvements in transportation. More than any other development, these improvements encouraged Americans to look beyond their local communities to broader ones and to foster the enterprising commercial spirit for which they became so widely known (see Map 12.1).

## ROADS

In 1800, travel by road was difficult for much of the year. Mud in the spring, dust in the summer, and snow in the winter all made travel by horseback or carriage uncomfortable, slow, and sometimes dangerous. Localities and states tried to improve local roads or contracted with private turnpike companies to build, maintain, and collect tolls on important stretches of road. In general, however, local roads remained poor. The federal government demonstrated its commitment to the improvement of interregional transportation by funding the National Road in 1808, at the time the greatest single federal transportation expense. Stretching from Cumberland, Maryland, to Vandalia, Illinois, the National Road tied the East and the West together, strong evidence of the nation's commitment to both expansion and cohesion, and helped to foster a national community.

**WHAT WERE** the effects of the transportation revolution?

myhistorylab
**Review Summary**

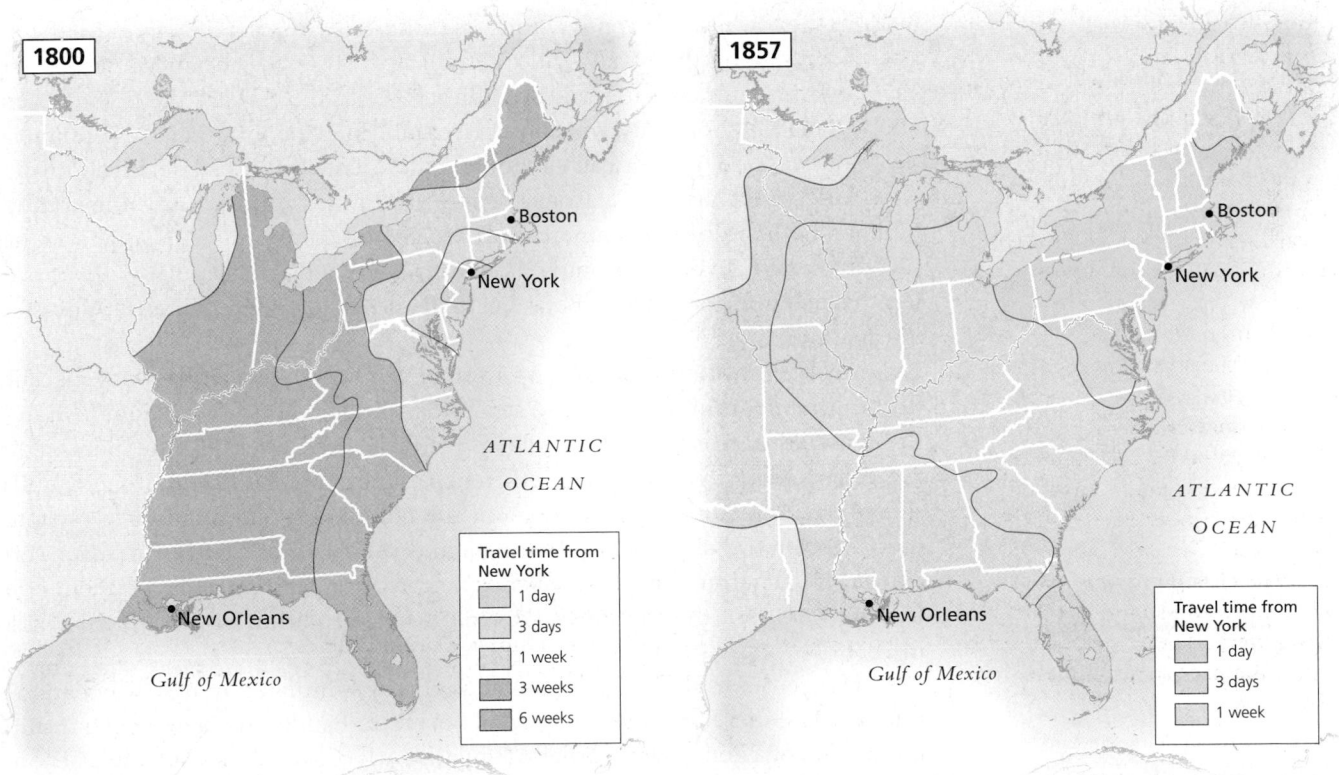

**MAP 12.1**

**Travel Times, 1800 and 1857**   The transportation revolution dramatically reduced travel times and vastly expanded everyone's horizons. Improved roads, canals, and the introduction of steamboats and railroads made it easier for Americans to move and made even those who did not move less isolated. Better transportation linked the developing West to the eastern seaboard and fostered a sense of national identity and pride.

HOW DID the federal government's funding of the National Road affect life in the United States?

## IMAGE KEY

for pages 294–295

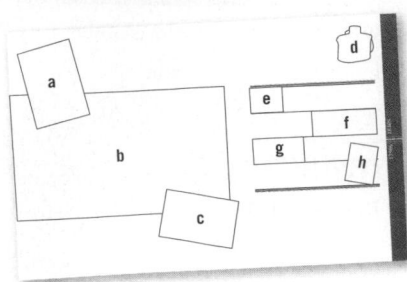

**a.** A magazine from the Lowell, Massachusetts mills.

**b.** The Merrimack textile mills with boarding houses Middlesex Company Woolen Mills, Lowell, Massachusetts.

**c.** Well-dressed nineteenth-century adults enjoy a formal picnic outdoors.

**d.** A metal lunch pail of a nineteenth-century factory worker.

**e.** 1849 Currier and Ives print, *The Express Train.*

**f.** A one dollar banknote from the Manufacturers Bank of Lowell, Massachusetts.

**g.** Cyrus McCormick demonstrating his reaper to farmers.

**h.** A nineteenth-century family portrait.

**9–3**

Jesse Hawley, *The Case for the Erie Canal* (1807)

### QUICK REVIEW

**The Erie Canal**

♦ Link between New York City and the Great Lakes.

♦ Built first by local farmers and then by Irish and imigrant labor.

♦ Completed in 10 years.

## CANALS AND STEAMBOATS

However much they helped the movement of people, the National Road and other roads were unsatisfactory in a commercial sense. Shipments of bulky goods like grain were too slow and expensive by road. Waterborne transportation was much cheaper and still the major commercial link among the Atlantic seaboard states and in the Mississippi–Ohio River system. But before the 1820s, most water routes were north–south or coastal (Boston to Charleston, for example); east–west links were urgently needed. Canals turned out to be the answer.

The Erie Canal—the most famous canal of the era—was the brainchild of New York governor DeWitt Clinton, who envisioned a link between New York City and the Great Lakes through the Hudson River, and a 364-mile-long canal stretching from Albany to Buffalo.

DeWitt Clinton had promised, to general disbelief, that the Erie Canal would be completed in less than ten years, and he made good on his promise. The canal was the wonder of the age. The Erie Canal provided easy passage to and from the interior, both for people and for goods. It drew settlers like a magnet from the East and, increasingly, from overseas: by 1830, some 50,000 people a year were moving west on the canal to the rich farmland of Indiana, Illinois, and territory farther west. Earlier settlers now had a national, indeed an international, market for their produce. Moreover, farm families along the canal began purchasing household goods and cloth, formerly made at home. Indeed, one of the most dramatic illustrations of the canal's impact was a rapid decline in the production of homespun cloth in the towns and counties along its route.

Towns along the canal—Utica, Rochester, Buffalo—became instant cities, each an important commercial center in its own right. Perhaps the greatest beneficiary was New York City, which quickly established a commercial and financial supremacy no other American city could match. The Erie Canal decisively turned New York's merchants away from Europe and toward America's own heartland, building both interstate commerce and a feeling of community. The phenomenal success of the Erie Canal prompted other states to construct similar waterways to tap the rich interior market. Between 1820 and 1840, $200 million was invested in canal building.

An even more important improvement in water transportation, especially in the American interior, was the steamboat. Robert Fulton first demonstrated the commercial feasibility of steamboats in 1807, and they were soon operating in the East. Redesigned with more efficient engines and shallower, broader hulls, steamboats transformed commerce on the country's great inland river system: the Ohio, the Mississippi, the Missouri, and their tributaries. Steamboats were extremely dangerous, however; boiler explosions, fires, and sinkings were common, leading to one of the first public demands for regulation of private enterprise in 1838.

Dangerous as they were, steamboats greatly stimulated trade in the nation's interior. The increased river- and canal-borne trade, like the New England shipping boom of a generation earlier, stimulated urban growth and all kinds of commerce. Cities such as Cincinnati, already notable for its rapid growth, experienced a new economic surge. A frontier outpost in 1790, Cincinnati was by the 1830s a center of steamboat manufacture and machine tool production as well as a central shipping point for food for the southern market.

**This Currier and** Ives print of 1849, *The Express Train*, captures the popular awe at the speed and wonder of the new technology. This "express" probably traveled no more than 30 miles per hour.

## RAILROADS

Remarkable as all these transportation changes were, the most remarkable was still to come. Railroads, new in 1830 (when the Baltimore and Ohio Railroad opened with 13 miles of track), grew to an astounding 31,000 miles by 1860. By that date, New England and the Old Northwest had laid a dense network of rails, and several lines had reached west beyond the Mississippi. The South, the least industrialized section of the nation, had fewer railroads.

Early railroads, like the steamboat, had to overcome many technological and supply problems. For example, locomotives, to generate adequate power, had to be heavy. Heavy locomotives, in turn, required iron rather than wooden rails. The resulting demand forced America's iron industry to modernize. Heavy engines also required a solid gravel roadbed and strong wooden ties. Arranging steady supplies of both and the labor to lay them was a construction challenge on a new scale. Finally, there were problems of standardization: because so many early railroads were short and local, builders used any gauge (track width) that served their purposes. It was not until the 1850s that consolidation of local railroads into larger systems began in earnest. But already it was clear that this newest transportation innovation would have far-reaching social consequences.

## THE EFFECTS OF THE TRANSPORTATION REVOLUTION

The new ease of transportation fueled economic growth by making distant markets accessible. The startling successes of innovations such as canals and railroads attracted large capital investments, including significant amounts from foreign investors ($500 million between 1790 and 1861), which fueled further growth.

Every east–west road, canal, and railroad helped to reorient Americans away from the Atlantic and toward the heartland. This new focus was decisive in the creation of national pride and identity. The transportation revolution fostered an optimistic, risk-taking mentality in the United States that stimulated invention and innovation. More than anything, the transportation revolution allowed people to move with unaccustomed ease. Transportation improvements such as the Erie Canal and the National Road linked Americans in larger communities of interest, beyond the local communities in which they lived. And improved transportation made possible the larger market on which commercialization and industrialization depended (see Map 12.2).

# THE MARKET REVOLUTION

The **market revolution**, the most fundamental change American communities had ever experienced, was the outcome of three interrelated developments: the rapid improvements in transportation just described, commercialization, and industrialization.

## THE ACCUMULATION OF CAPITAL

In the northern states, the business community was composed largely of merchants in the seaboard cities: Boston, Providence, New York City, Philadelphia, and Baltimore. Many had made substantial profits in the international shipping boom period from 1790 to 1807 (as discussed in Chapter 9).

When the early years of the nineteenth century posed difficulties for international trade, some of the nation's wealthiest men turned to local investments. In Providence, Rhode Island, Moses Brown and his son-in-law William Almy began to invest some of the profits the Brown family had reaped from a worldwide trade in iron, candles, rum, and African slaves in the new manufacture of cotton textiles. Cincinnati merchants banded together to finance the building of the first steamboats to operate on the Ohio River.

Much of the capital for the new investments came from banks, both those in seaport cities that had been established for the international trade and those, like the Lynn, Massachusetts, Mechanics Bank, founded in 1814 by a group of Lynn's Quaker merchants, that served local clients. An astonishing amount of capital, however, was raised through family connections. In the late eighteenth century, members of the business communities in the seaboard cities had begun to consolidate their position and property by intermarriage.

Southern cotton provided the capital for continuing development. Because Northerners built the nation's ships, controlled the shipping trade, and provided the nation's banking, insurance, and financial services, the astounding growth in southern cotton exports enriched northern merchants almost as much as southern planters. Southerners complained that their combined financial and shipping costs diverted forty cents of every dollar paid for their cotton to Northerners. Although imperfectly understood at the time, the truth is that the development of northern industry was paid for by southern cotton produced by enslaved African American labor. The surprising wealth that cotton brought to southern planters fostered the market revolution.

Finally, the willingness of American merchants to "think big" and risk their money in the development of a large domestic market was caused in part by American nationalism. Their confidence in a future that did not yet exist was not simply a sober economic calculation but an assertion of pride in the potential of this new and expanding nation.

**WHAT WAS** the market revolution?

**myhistorylab**
Review Summary

**Market revolution** The outcome of three interrelated developments: rapid improvements in transportation, commercialization, and industrialization.

**MAP 12.2**

**Commercial Links: Rivers, Canals, Roads, 1830, and Rail Lines, 1850** By 1830, the United States was tied together by a network of roads, canals, and rivers. This transportation revolution fostered a great burst of commercial activity and economic growth. Transportation improvements accelerated the commercialization of agriculture by getting farmers' products to wider, nonlocal markets. Access to wider markets likewise encouraged new textile and other manufacturers to increase their scale of production. By 1850, another revolutionary mode of transportation, the railroad, had emerged as a vital link to the transportation infrastructure.

HOW DID the transportation revolution of the mid-nineteenth century fuel the American economy?

**Putting-out system** Production of goods in private homes under the supervision of a merchant who "put out" the raw materials, paid a certain sum per finished piece, and sold the completed item to a distant market.

## THE PUTTING-OUT SYSTEM

Initially, the American business community invested not in machinery and factories, but in the "**putting-out system**" of home manufacture, thereby expanding and transforming it. In this significant departure from preindustrial work, people still produced goods at home, but under the direction of a merchant, who "put out" the raw materials to them, paid them a certain sum per finished piece, and sold the completed item to a distant market. A look at the shoe industry in Lynn, Massachusetts, shows how the putting-out system transformed American manufacturing.

Long a major center of the shoe industry, Lynn, in 1800, produced 400,000 pairs of shoes—enough for every fifth person in the country. Skilled craftsmen in Lynn controlled production through the traditional system of apprenticeship. Apprentices lived with the master craftsman and were treated like members of the family. Commonly, apprentices became journeymen craftsmen, working for wages in the shops of master craftsmen until they had enough capital to set up shop for themselves. In Lynn, 200 master artisans and their families, including their journeymen and apprentices, worked together in hundreds of small home workshops called "ten-footers" (from their size, about ten feet square). The artisans and journeymen cut the leather, the artisans' wives and daughters did the binding of the upper parts of the shoe, the men stitched the shoe together, and children and apprentices helped where needed. In the early days, the artisan commonly bartered his shoes for needed products. Sometimes an artisan sold his shoes to a larger retailer in Boston or Salem. Although production of shoes in Lynn increased yearly from 1780 to 1810 as markets widened, shoes continued to be manufactured in traditional ways.

The investment of merchant capital in the shoe business changed everything. In Lynn, a small group of Quaker shopkeepers and merchants, connected by family, religious, and business ties, took the lead in reorganizing the trade. Financed by the bank they founded in 1814, Lynn capitalists like Micajah Pratt built large, two-story central workshops. Pratt employed a few skilled craftsmen to cut leather for shoes, but he put out the rest of the shoemaking to less-skilled workers who were no longer connected by family ties. Putting-out workers were paid on a piecework basis and much less than a master craftsman or a journeyman. This arrangement allowed the capitalist to employ much more labor for the same investment than the traditional artisan workshop. Gradually the putting-out system and central workshops replaced artisans' shops.

The putting-out system moved the control of production from the individual artisan households to the merchant capitalists, who could now control labor costs, production goals, and shoe styles to fit certain markets. For example, the Lynn trade quickly monopolized the market for cheap boots for southern slaves and western farmers, leaving workshops in other cities to produce shoes for wealthier customers. Additionally, and most important from the capitalist's point of view, the owner of the business controlled the workers and could cut back or expand the labor force as economic and marketplace conditions warranted. The unaccustomed severity of economic slumps like the Panics of 1819 and 1837 made this flexibility especially desirable.

**This carved and** painted figure, designed as a whirligig and trade sign, shows a woman at a spinning wheel. Until the transportation revolution made commercial cloth widely available, spinning was one of the most time-consuming tasks that women and young girls did at home.

# Industrialization and Rural Life

George Inness was an American artist of the Hudson River School. Like the better-known Thomas Cole (see Chapter 11), Inness specialized in painting settled and cultivated eastern landscapes. This painting was commissioned by the president of the Delaware Lackawanna and Western Railroad to mark its opening. Inness rose to the challenge of showing both the double tracks (foreground) and the roundhouse (background) in a rural landscape, but the railroad committee was not satisfied, demanding that he show all four company locomotives (three are in the background) and that the letters *D.L.&W* be painted on the side of the locomotive. At first Inness refused on artistic grounds, but being in need of money, he finally agreed. The painting is thus one of the first American examples of a "fine art" advertisement. Even at this early date, there was conflict between the demands of art and those of the advertiser.

**WHAT DOES** the Inness painting insist that you notice about the impact of industrialization on rural life?

The presence of a locomotive, the symbol of the machine age, in this pastoral setting must have been a real shock to the first viewers, who were familiar with pastoral landscapes but uncomfortable with new inventions like the steam locomotive. Contrast this painting to the Currier and Ives print *The Express Train* on p. 299. ■

LeRoy Ireland, *The Works of George Inness; An Illustrated Catalogue Raisonne* (Austin: University of Texas Press, 1965), p. 28.

George Inness, The Lackawanna Valley Painting, 1825. © 1856. Oil on canvas, 86 × 127.5 cm (33 7/8 × 50 3/16 in.) Gift of Mrs. Huttleston Rogers. Board of Trustees, National Gallery of Art, Washington, D.C.

**QUICK REVIEW**

**The Putting-Out System**

◆ Production of goods at home under the supervision of a merchant.

◆ Lynn, Massachusetts used putting-out system to become a center of the shoe industry.

◆ System gave control of production to merchant capitalists.

**WHAT IMPACT** did advances in transportation have in the Old Northwest?

myhistorylab
**Review Summary**

While the central workshop system prevailed in Lynn and in urban centers like New York City, the putting-out system also fostered a more dispersed form of home production. By 1810, there were an estimated 2,500 so-called outwork weavers in New England, operating handlooms in their own homes. Other crafts that rapidly became organized according to the putting-out system were flax and wool spinning, straw braiding, glove making, and the knitting of stockings.

## THE SPREAD OF COMMERCIAL MARKETS

Although the putting-out system meant a loss of independence for artisans such as those in Lynn, Massachusetts, New England farm families liked it. From their point of view, the work could easily be combined with domestic work, and the pay was a new source of income that they could use to purchase mass-produced goods rather than spend the time required to make those things themselves. In this way farm families moved away from the local barter system and into a larger market economy.

Commercialization, or the replacement of barter by a cash economy, did not happen immediately or uniformly throughout the nation. Fixed prices for goods produced by the new principles of specialization and division of labor appeared first along established trade routes. Rural areas in established sections of the country that were remote from trade routes continued in traditional ways (see Seeing History). Strikingly, however, western farming frontiers were commercial from the very start. The existence of a cash market was an important spur to westward expansion.

# THE YANKEE WEST

Every advance in transportation—better roads, canals, steamboats, railroads—made it easier for farmers to get their produce to market. Improvements in agricultural machinery increased the amount of acreage a farmer could cultivate. These two developments, added to the availability of rich, inexpensive land in the heartland, dramatically changed the Old Northwest. The sudden change from subsistence to commercial agriculture in the Old Northwest is a particularly vivid example of the impact of transportation changes and commercialization.

## NEW ROUTES WEST

The impact of the transportation revolution on the Old Northwest was startling. Settlement of the region, ongoing since the 1790s, vastly accelerated. In the decade of the 1830s, three quarters of a million people migrated to the region, and by 1850 the population of the Old Northwest almost quadrupled.

Migrants of New England origin (Yankees) accounted for at least 40 percent of the population, and they brought with them a distinctive culture that stressed community building. New Englanders immediately established schools, churches, and town government in their new locations. Southern migrants, like their counterparts who migrated to the Old Southwest, were much more likely to rely on kinship ties rather than found community institutions, except for churches. Yankees were different from Southerners in another way: they welcomed commercial agriculture.

## COMMERCIAL AGRICULTURE IN THE OLD NORTHWEST

The long period of subsistence farming that had characterized colonial New England and the early Ohio Valley frontier before 1830 was superseded by commercial agriculture stimulated by the transportation revolution.

**Cyrus McCormick is** shown demonstrating his reaper to skeptical farmers. When they saw that the machine cut four times as much wheat a day as a hand held scythe, farmers flocked to buy McCormick's invention. Agricultural practices, little changed for centuries, were revolutionized by machines such as this.

The very need for cash to purchase land involved western settlers in commercial agriculture from the beginning. Farmers, and the towns and cities that grew up to supply them, needed access to markets for their crops. Local residents clamored for the canals and railroads (often financed by state as well as private money) that tied the individual farm into national and international commercial networks. Commercial agriculture in turn encouraged regional specialization. Because in each new western area wheat yields were higher than in earlier ones, farmers in older regions were forced to shift away from wheat to other crops. The constant opening of new farmland encouraged mobility. Prepared to move on when the price was right, they regarded their farmland not as a permanent investment but as a speculation. This too marked a difference from colonial and southern attitudes in which permanent ownership of farms, with enough to land to endow one's sons, had always been the goal.

New tools made western farmers unusually productive. John Deere's steel plow (invented in 1837) and Cyrus McCormick's reaper (patented in 1834) greatly increased potential production. Western farmers rushed to buy the new machines, confident that increased production would rapidly pay for them. In most years, their confidence was justified. But in bad years, farmers found that their new levels of debt could mean failure and foreclosure.

Thus, within a few short years the Old Northwest became the nation's agricultural heartland. In 1859, the region produced 46 percent of the nation's wheat and 33 percent of its corn. Moreover, a steadily increasing amount was exported to foreign markets: from 12 percent in 1820 to 27 percent in 1840 to 70 percent in 1860. While Southerners boasted in 1858 that "Cotton is King," in fact the Old Northwest, not the South, had become the export heart of the national economy.

**MAP 12.3**

**Commercial Links: The Old Northwest, 1850**    After 1825, the Erie Canal brought streams of migrants to the upper parts of the Old Northwest, where they quickly built the roads, canals and railroads that made their commercial agriculture possible.

WHAT EFFECT did the opening of various canals, including the Erie Canal, have on cities such as St. Louis, Chicago, and New Orleans?

## TRANSPORTATION CHANGES AFFECT THE CITIES

The changing fortunes of the region's major cities demonstrate the dramatic effects of improvements in transportation. Before 1830, when the easiest way to move goods and people was by water, Ohioans shipped corn and hogs first by flatboat and later by steamboat down the Ohio and Mississippi Rivers to New Orleans. Cincinnati, the center of the Ohio trade, earned the nickname "Porkopolis" because of the importance of its slaughterhouses.

After 1830, with the opening of the Erie Canal and canals in Ohio and Illinois, St. Louis became the distribution point for the flood of goods New York merchants sent westward via the canal system. St. Louis became a magnet for migration: in 1849, the year of the California gold rush (see Chapter 14), 60,000 people passed through the city.

After 1840, with the impact of railroads, the region's distribution system changed again, causing Chicago, barely a dot on the map early in the century, to grow at an incredible rate. By 1860, it had reached a population of 100,000 and, although still smaller than Cincinnati and St. Louis, was clearly destined to become the nation's east–west hub (see Map 12.3).

The loser in this economic redistribution was New Orleans. As early as 1853, only 30 percent of Old Northwest produce was shipped via New Orleans, while 60 percent was exported via the Erie Canal. Railroads increased the disparity, while at the same time they provided easy transportation to New Englanders who wanted to move west. These new transportation links tied the Old Northwest to New York and New England economically and politically, creating, as one Southerner bitterly commented, a "universal Yankee nation" that was a huge factor in the sectional disputes and eventual civil war that were to come (see Chapter 15).

# INDUSTRIALIZATION BEGINS

The most dramatic single aspect of the market revolution was industrialization. Even in its earliest stages, industrialization changed the nature of work itself.

HOW DID industrialization affect workers in early factories?

**myhistorylab**

**Review Summary**

**9–7**
Henry Clay, *Defense of the American System* (1832)

## BRITISH TECHNOLOGY AND AMERICAN INDUSTRIALIZATION

Begun in Britain in the eighteenth century, industrialization was the result of a series of technological changes in the textile trade. In marked contrast to the putting-out system, in which capitalists had dispersed work into many individual households, industrialization required workers to concentrate in factories and pace themselves to the rhythms of power-driven machinery.

The simplest and quickest way for America to industrialize was to copy the British, but the British, well aware of the value of their machinery, enacted laws forbidding its export and even the emigration of skilled workers. Over the years, however, Americans managed to lure a number of British artisans to the United States.

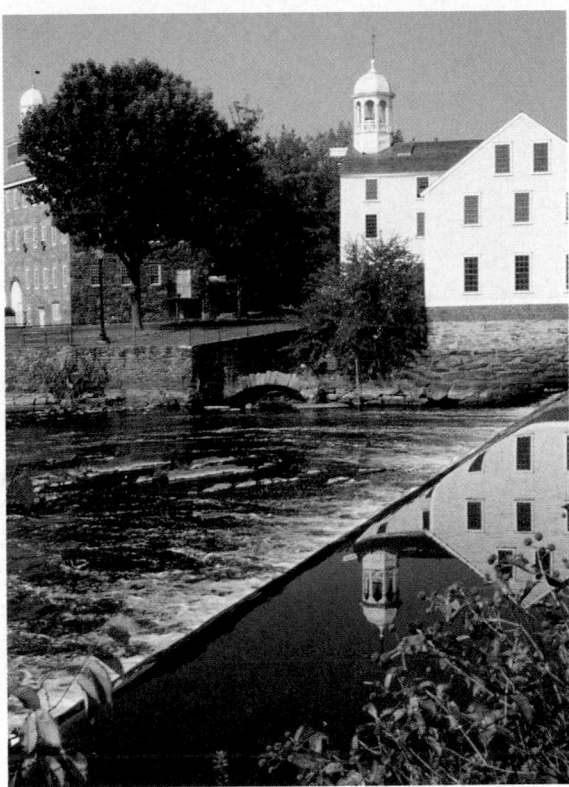

This photograph shows the much restored Slater Mill, the first cotton textile factory in the United States, and the falls that powered its machinery. Built in 1793, the mill—now a National Historic Landmark—, is an example of the way early entrepreneurs used the power potential of New England's swiftly flowing streams.

In 1789, Samuel Slater, who had just finished an apprenticeship in the most up-to-date cotton spinning factory in England, disguised himself as a farm laborer and slipped out of England without even telling his mother good-bye. In Providence, Rhode Island, he met Moses Brown and William Almy, who had been trying without success to duplicate British industrial technology. Having carefully committed the designs to memory before leaving England, Slater promptly built copies of the latest British machinery for Brown and Almy.

Many other merchants and mechanics followed Slater's lead, and the rivers of New England were soon dotted with mills wherever waterpower could be tapped.

## THE LOWELL MILLS

Another way to deal with British competition was to beat the British at their own game. With the intention of designing better machinery, a young Bostonian, Francis Cabot Lowell, made an apparently casual tour of British textile mills in 1810.

When he returned to the United States, he went to work with a Boston mechanic, Paul Moody, to improve on the British models. Lowell and Moody not only made the machinery for spinning cotton more efficient, but they also invented a power loom. This was a great advance, for now all aspects of textile manufacture, from the initial cleaning and carding (combing) to the production of finished lengths of cloth, could be gathered together in the same factory. Such a mill required a much larger capital investment than a small spinning mill such as Slater's, but Lowell's family network gave him access to the needed funds. In 1814, he opened the world's first integrated cotton mill in Waltham, near Boston. It was a great success: in 1815, the Boston Associates (Lowell's partners) made profits of 25 percent, and their efficiency allowed them to survive the intense British competition following the War of 1812. Many smaller New England mills did not survive.

The Boston Associates took the lesson to heart, and when they moved their enterprise to a new location in 1823, they thought big. They built an entire town at the junction of the Concord and Merrimack Rivers where the village of East Chelmsford stood, renaming it Lowell in memory of Francis, who had died, still a young man, in 1817 (see Map 12.4).

## FAMILY MILLS

Lowell was unique. Much more common in the early days of industrialization were small rural spinning mills, on the model of Slater's first mill, built on swiftly running streams near existing farm communities. Because the owners of smaller mills often hired entire families, their operations came to be called family mills. Children aged eight to twelve, whose customary job was "doffing" (changing) bobbins on the spinning machines, made up 50 percent of the workforce. Women and men each made up about 25 percent of the workforce, but men had the most skilled and best-paid jobs. (See Figure 12.1.)

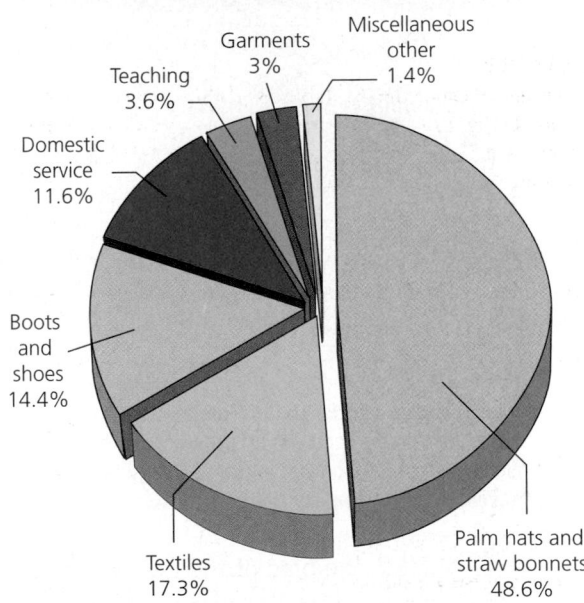

Total women employed
105,977

**Figure 12.1 Occupations of Women Wage Earners in Massachusetts, 1837**
This chart shows how important piecework was for women workers. Textile work in factories occupied less than 20 percent of women, while piecework making palm-leaf hats, straw bonnets, and boots and shoes accounted for over half of the total workforce. Teaching was a new occupation for women in 1837; the small percentage of 3.6 would grow in the future.

Based on Thomas Dublin, *Transforming Women's Work* (Ithaca, NY: Cornell University Press, 1991), Table 1.1, p. 20.

# MAP EXPLORATION

To explore an interactive version of this map, go to **http://www.prenhall.com/faraghertlc/map12.4**

**MAP 12.4**

**Lowell, Massachusetts, 1832**   This town plan of Lowell, Massachusetts, in 1832, illustrates the comprehensive relationship the owners envisaged between the factories and the workforce. The mills are located on the Merrimack River, while nearby are the boardinghouses for the single young female workers, row houses for the male mechanics and their families, and houses for the overseers. Somewhat farther away is the mansion of the company agent.

HOW DID the plan of the town of Lowell affect the people who lived there?

Relations between these small rural mill communities and the surrounding farming communities were often difficult, as the history of the towns of Dudley and Oxford, Massachusetts, shows. Samuel Slater, now a millionaire, built three small mill communities near these towns in the early years of the nineteenth century and Slater's mills provided a substantial amount of work for local people. But in spite of this economic link, relations between Slater and his workers on one side and the farmers and shopkeepers of the Dudley and Oxford communities on the other were stormy. They disagreed over the building of mill dams, over taxes, over the upkeep of local roads, and over schools. The residents of Dudley and Oxford became increasingly hostile to Slater's authoritarian control, which they regarded as undemocratic. Their dislike carried over to the workers as well. Disdaining the mill workers for their poverty and transiency, people in the rural communities began referring to them as "operatives," making them somehow different in their work roles from themselves. Industrial work thus led to new social distinctions.

**American system** A technique of production pioneered in the United States in the first half of the nineteenth century that relied on precision manufacturing with the use of interchangeable parts.

## "THE AMERICAN SYSTEM OF MANUFACTURES"

Not all American industrial technology was copied from British inventions, for there were many homegrown inventors. Perhaps the most important invention was the development of standardized parts.

The concept of interchangeable parts, realized first in gun manufacturing, was so unusual that the British soon dubbed it the "**American system**." In this system, a gun was broken down into its component parts and an exact mold was made for each. All pieces made from the same mold (after being hand filed by inexpensive unskilled laborers) matched a uniform standard. As a result, repairing a gun required only installing a replacement for the defective part rather than laboriously making a new part or perhaps an entirely new gun, as had been the customary practice.

America's early lead in interchangeable parts was a substantial source of national pride. Standardized production quickly revolutionized the manufacture of items as simple as nails and as complicated as clocks.

American businesses mass-produced high-quality goods for ordinary people earlier than manufacturers in Britain or any other European country were able to do. The availability of these goods was a practical demonstration of American beliefs in democracy and equality.

## FROM ARTISAN TO WORKER

The changes wrought by the market revolution had major and lasting effects on ordinary Americans. The proportion of wage laborers in the nation's labor force rose from 12 percent in 1800 to 40 percent by 1860. Most of these workers were employed in the North, and almost half were women.

**HOW DID** the market revolution change the lives of ordinary people?

**myhistorylab**
**Review Summary**

**In 1816, Connecticut** gunsmith Simeon North did what Eli Whitney had only hoped to do. North produced the first gun with interchangeable parts. North's invention, taken up and improved by the national armories at Springfield and Harpers Ferry, formed the basis of the American system of manufactures.

**9–9**
The Harbinger, *Female Workers of Lowell* (1836)

**11–6**
*A Lowell Mill Girl Tells Her Story* (1836)

## PREINDUSTRIAL WAYS OF WORKING

When Lowell began operation, 97 percent of all Americans still lived on farms, and most work was done in or near the home. As had been true in colonial times, the lives of most people were family and community based and depended on local networks of barter and mutual obligation. Work was slow, unscheduled, and task oriented. People did their jobs as they needed to be done, along with the daily household routine. "Home" and "work" were not separate locations or activities but were intermixed. Likewise, in urban areas, skilled craftsmen organized the apprenticeship system in the family-learning model used in farms, training apprentices who became journeymen and skilled workers in turn.

In both rural and urban settings, working families were organized along strictly patriarchal lines. The man had unquestioned authority to direct the lives and work of family members and apprentices and to decide on occupations for his sons and marriages for his daughters. His wife had many crucial responsibilities—feeding, clothing, child rearing, taking care of apprentices, and all the other domestic affairs of the household—but in all these duties she was subject to the direction of her husband. Men were heads of families and bosses of artisanal shops; although entire families were engaged in the enterprise, the husband and father was the trained craftsman, and assistance by the family was informal and generally unrecognized.

## MECHANIZATION AND GENDER

The apprenticeship system was destroyed by the immense increase in productivity made possible by the principles of division of labor and specialization applied in shoe production in Lynn and in other trades elsewhere.

**In the 1840s,** Edward Hicks painted his childhood home, rendering an idealized image of rural harmony that owes more to faith in republican agrarianism than to the artist's accurate memory. The prosperous preindustrial farm had a mixed yield—sheep, cattle, dairy products, and field crops—and had an African American farm worker (perhaps a slave), shown plowing.

"Residence of David Twining," 1787. Oil on canvas. Abby Aldrich Rockefeller Folk Art Museum, Colonial Williamsburg Foundation, Williamsburg, VA.

**This illustration of** seamstresses at work, from *Sartain's Union Magazine*, January 1851, shows an early abuse created by the market revolution. Women workers were crowded into just a few occupations, thereby allowing owners to offer very low wages for very long hours of work. The women in this illustration appear to be gathered together in a central workshop, where they had each other for company. Many other women sewed alone at home, often for even lower wages.

Industrialization posed a further threat to the status and independence of skilled male workers. In trade after trade, mechanization meant that most tasks could be performed by unskilled labor. In fact, the work in the textile mills was so simple that children came to form a large part of the workforce. By 1850, in New York City, many formerly skilled trades were filled with unskilled, low-paid workers who did one specialized operation or tended machinery. Many former artisans were reduced to performing wage labor for others. Because women were so frequently hired in the putting-out system, male workers began to oppose female participation in the workforce, fearing that it would lower their own wages.

These fears appeared to be confirmed by the experience of women in the new garment industry, which emerged in the 1820s. In New York City, employers began hiring women to sew ready-made clothing, at first rough, unfitted clothing for sailors and southern slaves, but later, overalls and shirts for Westerners, and finer items, such as men's shirts. Most women performed this work at low piecework rates in their homes.

Soon the low pay and seasonal nature of the industry became notorious. Overcrowding of the market—all women could sew—led to low wages. To make matters worse, most people believed that "respectable" women did not do factory work, and this disparagement fostered low pay and poor working conditions.

Manufacturers in the garment trade made their profits not from efficient production but by obtaining intensive labor for very low wages. The lower the piece rate, the more each woman, sewing at home, had to produce to earn enough to live.

**myhistorylab**

**Exploring America:** *Machinery*

**QUICK REVIEW**

**Women in the Workforce**

- Industrialization threatened skilled male workers.
- Mechanization created opportunities for women to work outside the home.
- The growing garment industry of the 1820s depended on cheap female labor.

## TIME TABLE OF THE LOWELL MILLS,

### To take effect on and after Oct. 21st, 1851.

The Standard time being that of the meridian of Lowell, as shown by the regulator clock of JOSEPH RAYNES, 43 Central Street.

| | From 1st to 10th inclusive. | | | | From 11th to 20th inclusive. | | | | From 21st to last day of month. | | | |
|---|---|---|---|---|---|---|---|---|---|---|---|---|
| | 1st Bell | 2d Bell | 3d Bell | Eve. Bell | 1st Bell | 2d Bell | 3d Bell | Eve. Bell | 1st Bell | 2d Bell | 3d Bell | Eve. Bell |
| January, | 5.00 | 6.00 | 6.50 | *7.30 | 5.00 | 6 00 | 6.50 | *7.30 | 5.00 | 6.00 | 6.50 | *7.30 |
| February, | 4.30 | 5.30 | 6.40 | *7.30 | 4.30 | 5.30 | 6.25 | *7.30 | 4.30 | 5.30 | 6.15 | *7.30 |
| March, | 5.40 | 6.00 | | *7.30 | 5.20 | 5.40 | | *7.30 | 5.05 | 5.25 | | 6.35 |
| April, | 4.45 | 5.05 | | 6.45 | 4.30 | 4.50 | | 6.55 | 4.30 | 4.50 | | 7.00 |
| May, | 4 30 | 4.50 | | 7·00 | 4.30 | 4.50 | | 7.00 | 4.30 | 4.50 | | 7 00 |
| June, | " | " | | " | " | " | | " | " | " | | " |
| July, | " | " | | " | " | " | | " | " | " | | " |
| August, | " | " | | " | " | " | | " | " | " | | " |
| September, | 4.40 | 5.00 | | 6.45 | 4.50 | 5.10 | | 6.30 | 5.00 | 5.20 | | *7.30 |
| October, | 5.10 | 5.30 | | *7.30 | 5.20 | 5.40 | | *7.30 | 5.35 | 5.55 | | *7.30 |
| November, | 4.30 | 5.30 | 6.10 | *7.30 | 4.30 | 5.30 | 6.20 | *7.30 | 5.00 | 6.00 | 6.35 | *7.30 |
| December, | 5.00 | 6.00 | 6.45 | *7.30 | 5.00 | 6.00 | 6.50 | *7.30 | 5.00 | 6·00 | 6.50 | *7.30 |

* Excepting on Saturdays from Sept. 21st to March 20th inclusive, when it is rung at 20 minutes after sunset.

#### YARD GATES,

Will be opened at ringing of last morning bell, of meal bells, and of evening bells; and kept open Ten minutes.

#### MILL GATES.

Commence hoisting Mill Gates, Two minutes before commencing work.

#### WORK COMMENCES,

At Ten minutes after last morning bell, and at Ten minutes after bell which "rings in" from Meals.

#### BREAKFAST BELLS.

During March "Ring out"........at....7.30 a. m.........."Ring in" at 8:05 a. m.
April 1st to Sept. 20th inclusive.....at....7 00 " " ........ " " at 7.35 " "
Sept. 21st to Oct. 31st inclusive.....at....7.30 " " ........ " " at 8.05 " "
Remainder of year work commences after Breakfast.

#### DINNER BELLS.

"Ring out"...... ............12.30 p. m........."Ring in".... 1.05 p. m.

In all cases, the *first* stroke of the bell is considered as marking the time.

**This timetable from** the Lowell Mills illustrates the elaborate time schedules that the cotton textile mills expected their employees to meet. For workers, it was difficult to adjust to the regimentation imposed by clock time, in contrast to the approximate times common to preindustrial work.

The invention of the sewing machine only made matters worse. Manufacturers dropped their piecework rates still lower, and some women found themselves working fifteen to eighteen hours a day, producing more than they ever had but earning the same pay.

## TIME, WORK, AND LEISURE

Preindustrial work had a flexibility that factory work did not, and it took factory workers a while to get accustomed to the constant pace of work. Factory workers gradually adjusted to having their lives regulated by the sound of the factory bell, but they did not necessarily become the docile "hands" the owners wanted. Absenteeism was common and there was much pilfering. Workers were beginning to think of themselves as a separate community whose interests differed from those of owners, and the tyranny of time over their work was certainly one reason for this.

Another adjustment required by the constant pace was that time now had to be divided into two separate activities—work and leisure. In preindustrial times, the place of work—often the home—and the pace made it possible to stop and have a chat or a friendly drink with a visitor. Now, however, the separation of home and workplace and the pace of production not only squeezed the fun out of the long workday but also left a smaller proportion of time for leisure activities.

For many workingmen, the favored spot for after-hours and Sunday leisure became the local tavern. Community-wide celebrations and casual sociability, still common in rural areas, began to be replaced in cities by spectator sports and by popular entertainments, such as plays, operas, minstrel shows, concerts, and circuses. Some of these diversions, such as plays and horse racing, appealed to all social classes, but others, like parades, rowdy dance halls, and tavern games were favored working-class amusements. The effect of these changes was to make working-class amusements more distinct, and visible, than they had been before.

## FREE LABOR

Another effect of the market revolution was the transformation of a largely barter system into cash payments. For workers, this change was both unsettling and liberating. On the minus side, workers were no longer part of a settled, orderly, and familiar community. On the plus side, they were now free to labor wherever they could, at whatever wages their skills or their bargaining power could command. That workers took their freedom seriously is evidenced by the very high rate of turnover—50 percent a year—in the New England textile mills.

But if moving on was a sign of increased freedom of opportunity for some workers, for others it was an unwanted consequence of the market revolution. In New England, for example, many quite prosperous artisans and farmers faced disruptive competition from factory goods and western commercial agriculture. They could remain where they were only if they were willing to become factory workers or, in the case of farmers, to move west and try to become successful commercial farmers themselves.

At the heart of this industrializing economy was the notion of free labor. Originally, "free" referred to individual economic choice—that is, to the right of workers to move to another job rather than be held to a position by customary obligation or the formal contract of apprenticeship or journeyman labor. But "free labor" soon came to encompass as well the range of attitudes—hard work, self-discipline, and a striving for economic independence—that were necessary for success in a competitive, industrializing economy.

The spread of the factory system and of the ideology of free labor soon became an issue in the growing political battle between the North and the South over slavery. Southern defenders of slavery compared their cradle-to-grave responsibility to their slaves with northern employers' "heartless" treatment of their "wage slaves." Southerners were right: this was a heartless system. But Northerners were also right: industrialization was certainly freer than the slave system, freer even than the hierarchical craft system, although it sometimes offered only the freedom to starve.

## EARLY STRIKES

Rural women workers led some of the first strikes in American labor history. Among the most famous were the strikes led by the women at the model mill at Lowell. The first serious trouble came in 1834, when 800 women participated in a spontaneous turnout to protest a wage cut of 25 percent. The owners were shocked and outraged by the strike, considering it both unfeminine and ungrateful. The workers, however, were bound together by a sense of sisterhood and were protesting not just the attack on their economic independence but also the blow to their position as "daughters of freemen still." Nevertheless, the wage cuts were enforced, as were more cuts in 1836, again in the face of a turnout. Many women simply packed their clothes in disgust and returned home to the family farm. Others who remained formed the New England Female Labor Reform Association in 1845. In 1847, legislators in New Hampshire, responding to a petition from women workers in Nashua, made theirs the first state to enact a ten-hour-day law. For the first time, thanks to women's pioneering role in factory protests, a group of workers had obtained state legislation improving their working conditions.

# THE NEW MIDDLE CLASS

The market revolution reached into every aspect of life, down to the most personal family decisions. As just described, it changed working life. The market revolution also fundamentally changed the social order, creating a new middle class with distinctive habits and beliefs.

## WEALTH AND RANK

There had always been social divisions in America. Since the early colonial period, planters in the South and merchants in the North had comprised a wealthy elite. Somewhere below the elite but above the mass of people were the "middling sort": a small professional group that included lawyers, ministers, schoolteachers, doctors, public officials, some prosperous farmers, prosperous urban shopkeepers and innkeepers, and a few wealthy artisans. "Mechanics and farmers"—artisans and yeoman farmers—made up another large group, and the laboring poor, consisting of ordinary laborers, servants, and marginal farmers, were below them. At the very bottom were the paupers—those dependent on public charity—and the enslaved. This was the "natural" social order that fixed most people in the social rank to which they were born.

WHAT VALUES were promoted by the new middle class?

**Review Summary**

The market revolution ended this stable and hierarchical social order, creating the dynamic and unstable one we recognize today: upper, middle, and working classes, whose members all share the hope of climbing as far up the social ladder as they can. This social mobility was new. The expanding opportunities of the market revolution enriched the already rich. At the other extreme, fully one-third of the population possessed little more than the clothes they wore and some loose change. The major transformation came in the lives of the "middling sort."

The market revolution downgraded many independent artisans. Formerly independent artisans or farmers (or, more frequently, their children) joined the rapidly growing ranks of managers and white-collar workers. These new white-collar workers owed not only their jobs but also their lifestyles to the new structure and organization of industry. The new economic order demanded certain habits and attitudes of workers: sobriety, responsibility, steadiness, and hard work. Inevitably, employers found themselves not only enforcing these new standards but also adopting them themselves.

## RELIGION AND PERSONAL LIFE

Religion, which had undergone dramatic changes since the 1790s, played a key role in the emergence of the new attitudes. The Second Great Awakening had supplanted the orderly and intellectual Puritan religion of early New England. The new evangelical religious spirit, which stressed the achievement of salvation through personal faith, was more democratic and more enthusiastic than the earlier faith. Conversion and repentance were no longer private, because they now took place in huge revival meetings in which an entire congregation focused on the sinners about to be saved and where group support actively encouraged individual conversion. The converted bore a heavy personal responsibility to demonstrate their faith in their own daily lives through morally respectable behavior. In this way, the new religious feeling fostered individualism and self-discipline.

The Second Great Awakening had its greatest initial success on the western frontier in the 1790s, but by the 1820s, evangelical religion was reaching a new audience: the people whose lives were being changed by the market revolution and who needed help in adjusting to the demands made by the new economic conditions. In 1825, in Utica, New York, and in other towns along the recently opened Erie Canal, evangelist Charles G. Finney began a series of dramatic revival meetings. His spellbinding message reached both rich and poor, converting members of all classes to the new evangelistic religion.

Middle-class women in particular carried Finney's message by prayer and pleading to the men of their families, who found that evangelism's stress on self-discipline and individual achievement helped them adjust to new business conditions. The enthusiasm and optimism of evangelism aided what was often a profound personal transformation in the face of the market's stringent new demands. Moreover, it gave businessmen a basis for demanding the same behavior from their workers. Businessmen now argued that traditional paternalism had no role in the new business world. Because achievement depended on individual character, each worker was responsible for making his own way.

## THE NEW MIDDLE-CLASS FAMILY

The economic changes of the market revolution reshaped family roles, first in the middle class and eventually throughout the entire society. As men increasingly concentrated their energies on their careers and occupations, women assumed major new responsibilities for rearing the children and inculcating in them the new attitudes necessary for success in the business world.

11–1
Joshua and Sally Wilson, *Letters to George Wilson* (1823)

When the master craftsman became a small manufacturer, or the small sub-sistence farmer began to manage a large-scale commercial operation, production moved away from both the family home and its members. Husbands and fathers became managers of paid workers—or workers themselves—and although they were still considered the heads of their households, they spent most of the day away from their homes and families. Their wives, on the other hand, remained at home, where they were still responsible for cooking, cleaning, and other domestic tasks but no longer contributed directly to what had previously been the family enter-prise. Instead, women took on a new responsibility, that of providing a quiet, well-ordered, and relaxing refuge from the pressures of the industrial world.

As the work roles of middle-class men and women diverged, so did social attitudes about appropriate male and female characteristics and behavior. Men were expected to be steady, industrious, responsible, and painstakingly attentive to their business. In contrast, women were expected to be nurturing, gentle, kind, moral, and selflessly devoted to their families. They were expected to operate within the "woman's sphere"—the home.

The maintenance or achievement of a middle-class lifestyle required the joint efforts of husband and wife. More cooperation between them was called for than in the preindustrial, patriarchal family. The nature of the new, companion-ate marriage that evolved in response to the market revolution was reflected most clearly in decisions concerning children. Middle-class couples had fewer children than did their predecessors. The dramatic fall in the birthrate during the nine-teenth century (from an average of seven children per woman in 1800 to five in 1860) is evidence of conscious decisions about family limitation, first by members of the new middle class and later by working-class families.

When mutual efforts at birth control failed, married women often sought a surgical abortion, a new technique that was much more reliable than the folk remedies women had always shared among themselves. Surgical abortions were widely advertised after 1830, and widely used, especially by middle-class married women seeking to limit family size. Some historians estimate that one out of every four pregnancies was aborted in the years from 1840 to 1860 (compared to one in six in 2000). The rising rate of abortion by married women (in other words, its use as birth control) prompted the first legal bans; by 1860, twenty states had out-lawed the practice.

Accompanying the interest in family limitation was a redefinition of sexual-ity. Doctors generally recommended that sexual urges be controlled, but they believed that men would have much more difficulty exercising such control than women, partly because they also believed that women were uninterested in sex. Although it is always difficult to measure the extent to which the suggestions in advice books were applied in actual practice, it seems that many middle-class women accepted this new and limited definition of their sexuality because of the desire to limit the number of their pregnancies.

## MIDDLE-CLASS CHILDREN

Child rearing had been shared in the preindustrial household, boys learning farm-ing or craft skills from their fathers while girls learned domestic skills from their mothers. The children of the new middle class, however, needed a new kind of upbringing, one that involved a long period of nurturing in the beliefs and per-sonal habits necessary for success. Mothers assumed primary responsibility for this training, in part because fathers were too busy but also because people believed that women's superior qualities of gentleness, morality, and loving watchfulness were essential to the task.

**11–3**
The Mother's Magazine, "*Early Habits of Industry*" (1834)

Middle-class status required another sharp break with tradition. As late as 1855, artisanal families expected all children over 15 years to work. Middle-class families, in contrast, sacrificed to keep their sons in school or in training for their chosen professions, and they often housed and fed their sons until the young men had "established" themselves financially and could marry. Mothers took the lead in an important informal activity: making sure their children had friends and contacts that would be useful when they were old enough to consider careers and marriage. Matters such as these, rarely considered by earlier generations living in small communities, now became important in the new middle-class communities of America's towns and cities.

Contrary to the growing myth of the self-made man, middle-class success was not a matter of individual achievement. Instead it was usually based on a family strategy in which fathers provided the money and mothers the nurturance. The reorganization of the family described in this section was successful: from its shelter and support emerged generations of ambitious, responsible, and individualistic middle-class men. But although boys were trained for success, this was not an acceptable goal for their sisters. Women were trained to be the silent "support system" that undergirded male success. And women were also expected to ease the tensions of the transition to new middle-class behavior by acting as models and monitors of traditional values.

## SENTIMENTALISM AND TRANSCENDENTALISM

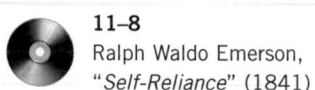

**11–8**
Ralph Waldo Emerson,
"*Self-Reliance*" (1841)

Just as factory workers were forced by the nature of their work to develop new attitudes, so too the new middle class adopted attitudes that suited their new social roles. Two new "isms" soon emerged: sentimentalism, which appealed particularly to women, and transcendentalism, which encouraged men to a new self-reliance.

The individualistic competitiveness brought by the market revolution caused women of the new middle class to place extraordinary emphasis on sincerity and feeling. So-called sentimentalism sprang from nostalgia for the imagined trust and security of the familiar, face-to-face life of the preindustrial village. Middle-class women were expected to counteract the impersonality and hypocrisy of the business world by the example of their own morality and sincere feeling.

For guidance in this new role, women turned to a new literary form, the sentimental novel. Although denounced by ministers and scholars as frivolous, immoral, and subversive of authority, the novel found a ready audience among American women. By 1850, *Harper's Magazine* estimated, four-fifths of the reading public were women, and they were reading novels written by women.

Sentimental novels concentrated on private life. Religious feeling, antipathy toward the dog-eat-dog world of the commercial economy, and the need to be prepared for unforeseen troubles were common themes. Although the heroines usually married happily at the end of the story, few novels concentrated on romantic love. Most of these domestic novels, as they were known, presented readers with a vision of responsibility and community based on moral and caring family life.

Although sentimentalism originally sprang from genuine fear of the dangers individualism posed to community trust, it rapidly hardened into a rigid code of etiquette for all occasions. Moments of genuine and deep feeling, such as death, were smothered in elaborate rules concerning condolences, expressions of grief, and appropriate clothing. Transformed into a set of rules about genteel manners to cover all occasions, sentimentalism itself became a mark of middle-class status. And it became one of the tasks of the middle-class woman to make sure her family conformed to the social code and associated only with other respectable families. In this way, women forged and enforced the distinctive social behavior of the new middle class.

As the new middle class conformed to the rules of sentimental behavior, it also sought a more general intellectual reassurance. Middle-class men, in particular,

## CHRONOLOGY

| | | | | |
|---|---|---|---|---|
| **1790** | Samuel Slater's first mill opens in Rhode Island | | **1823** | Lowell mills open |
| **1798** | Eli Whitney contracts with the federal government for 10,000 rifles, which he undertakes to produce with interchangeable parts | | **1824** | John Hall successfully achieves interchangeable parts at Harpers Ferry armory |
| | | | | Women lead strike at Pawtucket textile mill |
| **1810** | Francis Cabot Lowell tours British textile factories | | **1825** | Erie Canal opens |
| | First steamboat on the Ohio River | | **1830** | Baltimore and Ohio Railroad opens |
| **1812** | Micajah Pratt begins his own shoe business in Lynn, Massachusetts | | | Charles G. Finney's Rochester revivals |
| | | | **1833** | National Road completed to Columbus, Ohio |
| **1813** | Francis Cabot Lowell raises $300,000 to build his first cotton textile factory at Waltham, Massachusetts | | **1834** | First strike at Lowell mills |
| | | | | Cyrus McCormick patents the McCormick reaper |
| **1815** | War of 1812 ends; British competition in manufactures resumes | | **1837** | John Deere invents steel plow |
| **1817** | Erie Canal construction begins | | **1841** | Catharine Beecher's *Treatise on Domestic Economy* published |
| **1818** | National Road completed to Wheeling, Virginia (now West Virginia) | | **1845** | New England Female Reform Association formed |
| **1820s** | Large-scale outwork networks develop in New England | | | |

needed to feel comfortable about their public assertions of individualism and self-interest. One source of reassurance was the philosophy of transcendentalism and its well-known spokesman, Ralph Waldo Emerson. Famous as a writer and lecturer, Emerson popularized transcendentalism, a romantic philosophical theory claiming that there was an ideal, intuitive reality transcending ordinary life. The best place to achieve that individual intuition of the Universal Being, Emerson suggested, was not in church or in society but alone in the natural world. The same assertion of individualism rang through Emerson's stirring polemic "Self-Reliance" (1841). Announcing "Whoso would be a man, must be a nonconformist," Emerson urged that "Nothing is at last sacred but the integrity of your own mind."

Emerson's younger friend, Henry David Thoreau, pushed the implications of individualism further than the more conventional Emerson. Determined to live the transcendental ideal of association with nature, Thoreau lived in solitude in a primitive cabin for two years at Walden Pond, near Concord, Massachusetts, confronting "the essential facts of life." His experience was the basis for *Walden* (1854), a penetrating criticism of the spiritual cost of the market revolution. Margaret Fuller, perhaps the most intellectually gifted of the transcendental circle, was patronized by Emerson because she was a woman. She expressed her sense of women's wasted potential in her pathbreaking work *Woman in the Nineteenth Century* (1845).

Although Thoreau and Fuller were too radical for many readers, Emerson's version of the romantic philosophy of transcendentalism, seemingly so at odds with the competitive and impersonal spirit of the market revolution, was in fact an essential component of it. Individualism, or, as Emerson called it, self-reliance, was at the heart of the personal transformation required by the market revolution. Sentimentalism, transcendentalism, and evangelical religion all helped the new middle class to forge values and beliefs that were appropriate to their social roles.

**Emerson's romantic glorification** of nature included the notion of himself as a "transparent eyeball," as he wrote in "Nature" in 1836. This caricature of Emerson is from "Illustrations of the New Philosophy" by Christopher Pearce Cranch.

## CONCLUSION

The three transformations of the market revolution—improvements in transportation, commercialization, and industrialization—changed the ways people worked, and in time, changed how they thought.

For most people, the changes were gradual. Until midcentury, the lives of rural people were still determined largely by community events, although the spread of democratic politics and the availability of newspapers and other printed material increased their connection to a larger world. Wage earners made up only 40 percent of the working population in 1860, and factory workers made up an even smaller percentage.

The new middle class was most dramatically affected by the market revolution. All aspects of life, including intimate matters of family organization, gender roles, and the number and raising of children, changed. New values—evangelical religion, sentimentalism, and transcendentalism—helped the members of the new middle class in their adjustment. As the next chapter describes, the nation's cities were the first arena where old and new values collided.

## REVIEW QUESTIONS

1. What changes in preindustrial life and work were caused by the market revolution?

2. This chapter argues that when people begin doing new kinds of work, their beliefs and attitudes change. Give three examples of such changes described in the chapter. Can you think of other examples?

3. Discuss the opinion offered by historian David Potter that mass production has been an important democratizing force in American politics. Do you agree? Why or why not?

4. Consider the portrait of the nineteenth-century middle-class family offered in this chapter and imagine yourself as a member of such a family. What new aspects of family relations would you welcome? Which would be difficult? Why?

**myhistorylab**

Flashcard Review

## KEY TERMS

**American system** (p. 309)
**Market revolution** (p. 300)
**Putting-out system** (p. 302)

# RECOMMENDED READING

Jeffrey S. Adler, *Yankee Merchants and the Making of the Urban West* (1991). The importance of New England entrepreneurs in St. Louis.

Peter L. Bernstein, *Wedding of the Waters: The Erie Canal and the Making of a Great Nation* (2005). The economic consequences of one of the first public works projects.

Christopher Clark, *The Roots of Rural Capitalism: Western Massachusetts, 1780–1860* (1990). The most thorough examination to date of how the commercial spirit changed rural life.

Alan Dawley, *Class and Community: The Industrial Revolution in Lynn* (1976). A pathbreaking study of the shift from artisanal to wage labor.

Susan E. Gray, *The Yankee West* (1996). Demonstrates the Yankee connection between capitalism and community in lower Michigan.

David Houndshell, *From the American System to Mass Production, 1800–1932* (1984). How an entire network of New England "mechanics" contributed to the invention of interchangeable parts.

Paul Johnson, *Sam Patch, the Famous Jumper* (2003). Johnson uses the story of Patch, famous for plunging over Niagara Falls, to explore the bumpy transition from independent artisan to wage worker.

Mary Ryan, *The Making of the Middle Class* (1981). A study of Utica, New York, demonstrating the role of women in the family strategies of the new middle class.

Charles Sellers, *The Market Revolution: Jacksonian America, 1815–1846* (1991). A synthesis of the political, religious, and economic changes of the period.

Carol Sheriff, *The Artificial River: The Erie Canal and the Paradox of Progress, 1817–1862* (1996). Shows how the building of the Erie Canal changed personal lives and fostered religious beliefs in human perfectability.

George Rogers Taylor, *The Transportation Revolution, 1815–1860* (1951). The indispensable book on all aspects of the American economy during this period.

For study resources for this chapter, go to **www.myhistorylab.com** and choose *Out of Many, Teaching and Learning Classroom Edition.* You will find a wealth of study and review material for this chapter, including pretests and posttests, customized study plan, key-term review flash cards, interactive map and document activities, and documents for analysis.

# The Second Great Awakening and Religious Diversity in America

One of the reasons that separation of church and state has worked so well in the United States is the wide diversity of religious affiliations within the American population. From the beginning of English colonial efforts to the time of the American Revolution, this happy scenario was not necessarily present. In the northern colonies the Congregationalist Church was the established state religion among Puritan settlers. In the middle and southern colonies the Anglican Church or Church of England was the established church.

**THE SECOND** Great Awakening (1800–1830s) led to the creation of many new religious affiliations and an increased diversity within American religious life. How has this growing diversity impacted American society.

In 1801 the Danbury Baptist Association wrote a letter to newly elected President Thomas Jefferson complaining that the dominant Congregationalist sect in Connecticut was threatening to legislate against them and called for religious freedom. Jefferson responded with a letter outlining what we now call the separation of church and state.

Religious diversity grew slowly in the early years of the American colonies and nation. The First Great Awakening of the 1730s and 1740s strengthened the Presbyterian, Baptist, and Methodist churches in their quest to attract the followers of the Congregationalist and Anglican churches and create diversity of American religions. The Second Great Awakening created even greater diversity.■

REV CHARLES G. FINNEY.

*C. S. Finney*

**▲** Rev. Charles G. Finney – 1839

## Charles Grandison Finney, *Lectures on the Revival of Religion*, 1835

**I would** say nothing to undervalue, or lead you to undervalue a thorough education for ministers. But I do not call that a thorough education, which they get in our colleges and seminaries. It does not fit them for their work…. Those fathers who have the training of our young ministers are good men, but they are ancient men, men of another age and different stamp from what is needed in these days of excitement, when the church and world are rising to new thought and action. Those dear fathers will not, I suppose, see this; and will - perhaps think hard of me for saying it; but it is the cause of Christ.■

## From *Autobiography of Peter Cartwright, The Backwoods Preacher*

*The revival, or "camp meeting," was the signal event of the Second Great Awakening.*
Somewhere between 1800 and 1801, in the upper part of Kentucky, at a memorable place called "Cane Ridge," there was appointed a sacramental meeting by some of the Presbyterian ministers, at which meeting, seemingly unexpected by ministers or people, the mighty power of God was displayed in a very extraordinary manner; many were moved to tears, and bitter and loud crying for mercy. The meeting was protracted for weeks. Ministers of almost all denominations flocked in from far and near. The meeting was kept up by night and day. Thousands heard of the mighty work, and came on foot, on horseback, in carriages and wagons. It was supposed that there were in attendance at times during the meeting from twelve to twenty-five thousand people. Hundreds fell prostrate under the mighty

power of God, as men slain in battle. Stands were erected in the woods from which preachers of different Churches proclaimed repentance toward God and faith in our Lord Jesus Christ, and it was supposed, by eye and ear witnesses, that between one and two thousand souls were happily and powerfully converted to God during the meeting.

### SIMPLE GIFTS

'Tis the gift to be simple, 'tis the gift to be free,

'Tis the gift to come down where we ought to be,

And when we find ourselves in the place just right,

'Twill be in the valley of love and delight.

When true simplicity is gain'd,

To bow and to bend we shan't be asham'd,

To turn, turn will be our delight,

Till by turning, turning we come round right.

"*Simple Gifts*" is a Shaker quick dance or dancing song used in worship services. The hymn was written by Elder Joseph Brackett Jr. in 1848. Although they originated much earlier than the Second Great Awakening, the Shakers benefited from the diversity and growth of religious movements during the first decades of the 19th century. Shakers lived a communal, celibate lifestyle. Men and women lived in separate quarters, used separate stairs, and sat on opposite sides of the room during worship. Their devotions included rituals of trembling, shouting, dancing, shaking, singing, and speaking in unknown tongues. By the end of the 19th century the Shakers were practically extinct.■

## CHURCH OF JESUS CHRIST OF LATTER-DAY SAINTS

Founded in 1830 in New York by Joseph Smith, Jr., the Church of Jesus Christ of Latter-day Saints is based upon the Book of Mormon. Smith moved his followers to Missouri in the 1830's where controversy and persecution resulted in the Mormon War of 1838 after which the governor of the state ordered Smith to move his church elsewhere. Smith settled his people in Illinois and built the town of Navuoo. Mormon practices led to more persecution and the murder of Smith in 1844. Leadership of the church was taken over by Brigham Young who led his followers out of Illinois to the Mexican territories in Utah in 1846. The Mormon Church continued to thrive in Utah and the Southwest and in the 20th century has become one of the faster growing denominations in the U.S.■

Religious camp meeting, ca. 1839

Shaker Dance, Joseph Becker, *Frank Leslie's Illustrated Newspaper*, 1873

Brigham Young, Mormon leader and Second Mormon President

*Our duties originate, not from difference of sex,
but from the diversity of the relations of life,
the various gifts and talents committed to our care,
and the different eras in which we live.*

—Angelina Emily Grimké, October 2, 1837

**An abolitionist freeing a slave from his shackles:** A colored woodcut, c. 1840, from an American antislavery almanac.

PICTORIAL PRIMER

9 and 9 make 18   10 and 10 make 20

STEAMBOAT.

Here is a Steamboat full of passengers, how swift it glides along, and makes the water foam. Steamboats were invented by Robert Fulton, and the first one was built in New-York.

PICTORIAL PRIMER

Boy Flying a Kite.

Here is a boy just coming from school, he has learned his lesson well, and his teacher has rewarded him with a kite. He will raise it very high in the air, it will not fall down while the wind blows are made of

# 13

# MEETING THE CHALLENGES OF THE NEW AGE

## IMMIGRATION, URBANIZATION, SOCIAL REFORM
### 1820S–1850S

**WHO MIGRATED** to America

in the first half of the nineteenth century?

**WHO WERE** the major

proponents of the labor movement?

**WHAT ROLE** did women play

in the development of American education?

**WHO WERE** the abolitionists

and what were their racial attitudes?

**WHAT CONNECTIONS** were there between

the women's rights movement and previous movements

for social reform?

# AMERICAN COMMUNITIES
## Women Reformers of Seneca Falls Respond to the Market Revolution

IN THE SUMMER OF 1848, CHARLOTTE WOODWARD, A NINETEEN-YEAR-old glove maker who did outwork in her rural home, saw a small advertisement in an upstate New York newspaper announcing a "convention to discuss the social, civil, and religious condition and rights of woman," to be held at Seneca Falls on July 19 and 20. Woodward persuaded six friends to join her in the forty-mile journey to the convention. "At first we travelled quite alone," she recalled. "But before we had gone many miles we came on other wagon-loads of women, bound in the same direction. As we reached different crossroads we saw wagons coming from every part of the country, and long before we reached Seneca Falls we were a procession."

To the surprise of the convention organizers, almost 300 people—men as well as women—attended the two-day meeting, which focused on the **Declaration of Sentiments**, a petition for women's rights modeled on the Declaration of Independence. "We hold these truths to be self-evident," it announced: "That all men and women are created equal." As the Declaration of Independence detailed the oppressions King George III had imposed on the colonists, the Declaration of Sentiments detailed, in a series of resolutions, the oppressions men had imposed on women.

The struggle for women's rights was only one of many reform movements that emerged in the United States in the wake of the economic and social disruptions of the market revolution that deeply affected regions like Seneca Falls. Swamped by newcomers (among them a growing number of poor Irish Catholics), the inhabitants of Seneca Falls struggled to maintain a sense of community. They formed volunteer organizations of all kinds—religious, civic, social, educational, and recreational. And they became active participants in reform movements seeking to counteract the effects of industrialization, rapid growth, and the influx of newcomers.

Many reformers belonged to liberal religious groups with wide social perspectives. Perhaps a third of those attending the women's rights convention, for example, were members of the Wesleyan Methodist Society of Seneca Falls, which had broken with the national Methodist organization because it would not take a strong stand against slavery. Another quarter were Progressive Quakers of the nearby town of Waterloo, who had broken with their national organization for the same reason.

The idea for the women's rights convention emerged during a meeting in early July 1848 between Lucretia Mott, a Philadelphia Quaker and the nation's best-known woman reformer, and Elizabeth Cady Stanton of Seneca Falls, wife of a well-known antislavery orator. Stanton first met Mott in 1840 at the World AntiSlavery Conference in London. In 1848, Stanton renewed her acquaintance with Mott and, in this context of friendship and shared concern for reform, the two began planning the convention.

But what of Charlotte Woodward, a local farm girl, unaware of the national reform community? Why was she there? In this age of hopefulness and change, she wanted a better life for herself. She was motivated, she said, by "all the hours that I sat and sewed gloves for a miserable pittance, which, after it was earned, could never be mine." By law and custom, her father, as head of the household, was entitled to her wages. "I wanted to work," she explained, "but I wanted to choose my task and I wanted to collect my wages." The reforming women of Seneca Falls, grouped together on behalf of social improvement, had found in the first women's rights convention a way to speak for the needs of working women such as Charlotte Woodward.

All over the North, in communities like Seneca Falls as well as in cities like New York, Americans gathered together in reform organizations to try to solve the problems that the market revolution posed for work, family life, personal and social values, and urban growth. Through these organizations, local women and men became participants in wider communities of social concern, but in spite of their best efforts, they were rarely able to settle the issues that had brought them together. The aspirations of some, among them women, free blacks, and immigrants, clashed with the social control agendas of other groups. In this fervent atmosphere of reform, many problems were raised but few were resolved.

Seneca Falls

**Declaration of Sentiments** The resolutions passed at the Seneca Falls Convention in 1848 calling for full female equality, including the right to vote.

# IMMIGRATION AND THE CITY

Although the market revolution affected all aspects of American life, nowhere was its impact so noticeable as in the cities. And it was primarily in cities that the startlingly large number of new immigrants clustered.

## THE GROWTH OF CITIES

The market revolution dramatically increased the size of America's cities, with the great seaports leading the way. The proportion of America's population living in cities increased from only 7 percent in 1820 to almost 20 percent in 1860, a rate of growth greater than at any other time in the country's history. The nation's five largest cities in 1850 were the same as in 1800, with one exception. New York, Philadelphia, Baltimore, and Boston still topped the list, but New Orleans had edged out Charleston. The rate of urban growth was extraordinary. All four Atlantic seaports grew at least 25 percent each decade between 1800 and 1860, and often much more. New York, which grew from 60,000 in 1800 to 202,600 in 1830 and to more than 1 million in 1860, emerged as the nation's most populous city, its largest port, and its financial center.

Philadelphia, which had been the nation's largest city in 1800, was half the size of New York in 1850. Nevertheless, its growth was substantial—from 70,000 in 1800 to 389,000 in 1850 and to 565,529 in 1860. Philadelphia became as much an industrial as a commercial city.

Another result of the market revolution was the appearance of "instant" cities at critical points on the new transportation network. Utica, New York, once a frontier trading post, was transformed by the opening of the Erie Canal into a commercial and manufacturing center. Chicago, on the shores of Lake Michigan, was transformed by the coming of the railroad into a major junction for water and rail transport. The city, which emerged as a fur trading center around Fort Dearborn, an army post built in 1803, had become, by the 1850s, a hub of trade boasting grain storage facilities, slaughterhouses, and warehouses of all kinds. Farm implement manufacturers such as Cyrus McCormick built manufacturing plants there to serve the needs of midwestern farmers. By 1860 Chicago had a population of over 100,000, making it the nation's eighth largest city (see Table 13.1).

**WHO MIGRATED** to America in the first half of the nineteenth century?

**myhistorylab**
Review Summary

## QUICK REVIEW

**"Instant" Cities**

- Utica, New York transformed by opening of Erie Canal.
- Railroad made growth of Chicago possible.
- Chicago's population reached 100,000 in 1860.

**TABLE 13.1**

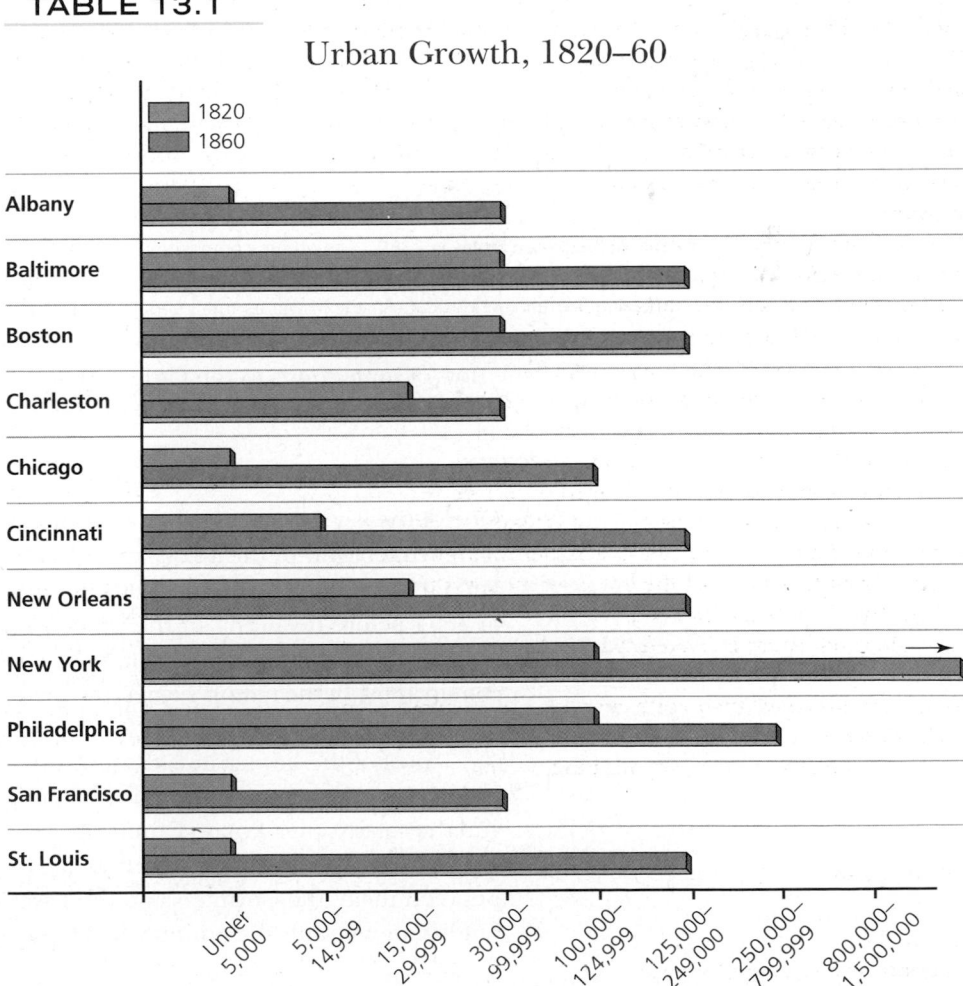

Urban Growth, 1820–60

# MAP EXPLORATION
To explore an interactive version of this map, go to **http://www.prenhall.com/faraghertlc/map13.1**

**MAP 13.1**

**Distribution of Foreign-Born Residents of the United States in 1860**   The ethnic composition of the American population was increased by Irish and German immigration in the 1840s and 1850s, Chinese attraction to the California gold rush, Mormon recruitment of Scottish and English followers to Utah, and the reclassification of Mexicans after the Mexican-American War as foreigners in what had been their own lands.

HOW DID events in Europe affect the flow of immigrants to the United States in the 1840s and 1850s?

## PATTERNS OF IMMIGRATION

One of the key aspects of urban growth was a surge in immigration to the United States that began in the 1820s and accelerated dramatically after 1830. From an annual figure of about 20,000 in 1831, immigration ballooned to a record 430,000 in 1854 before declining in the years prior to the Civil War. The proportion of immigrants in the population jumped from 1.6 percent in the 1820s to 11.2 percent in 1860. In the nation's cities, the proportion was vastly larger: by 1860, nearly half of New York's population (48 percent) was foreign-born (see Map 13.1).

Most of the immigrants to the United States during this period came from Ireland and Germany. Political unrest and poor economic conditions in Germany and the catastrophic Potato Famine of 1845–49 in Ireland were responsible for an enormous surge in immigration from those countries between 1845 and 1854. Between them, the Germans and the Irish represented the largest influx of non-English immigrants the country had known. They were also the poorest: most of the Irish arrived destitute. In addition, most of the Irish and half of the Germans were Catholics, an unwelcome novelty that provoked a nativist backlash among some Protestant Americans, including many leaders of national reform movements (see Chapter 15).

It would be a mistake, however, to think that immigration was unwelcome to everyone. Industries needed willing workers, and western states, among them Wisconsin, Iowa, and Minnesota, actively advertised in Europe for settlers. Many of the changes in industry and transportation that accompanied the market revolution would have been impossible without immigrants.

Few immigrants found life in the United States pleasant or easy. In addition to the psychological difficulties of leaving a home and familiar ways behind, most immigrants endured harsh living and working conditions. America's cities were unprepared for the social problems posed by large numbers of immigrants.

## IRISH IMMIGRATION

The first major immigrant wave to test American cities was caused by the catastrophic Irish Potato Famine of 1845–49. Throughout Ireland, many native Irish subsisted on small landholdings and a diet of potatoes while working as laborers on British-owned farms. Young people who knew they could not hope to own land in Ireland had long looked to America for better opportunities. But in 1845, Ireland's green fields of potato plants turned black with blight. The British government could not cope with the scale of the disaster. The Irish had two choices: starve or leave. One million people died, and another 1.5 million emigrated, the majority to the United States. Starving, diseased, and destitute, hundreds of thousands (250,000 in 1851 alone) disembarked in the East Coast ports of New York, Philadelphia, Boston, and Baltimore. Lacking the money to go inland and begin farming, they remained in the cities. Crowded together in miserable housing, desperate for work at any wages, foreign in their religion and pastimes, tenaciously nationalistic and bitterly anti-British, they created ethnic enclaves of a kind new to American cities.

The largest numbers of Irish came to New York, which managed to absorb them. But Boston, a much smaller and more homogeneous city, was overwhelmed by the Irish influx. By 1850, a quarter of Boston's population was Irish, most of them recent immigrants. Boston, the home of Puritanism and the center of American intellectualism, did not welcome illiterate Irish Catholic peasants. All over the city, in places of business and in homes normally eager for domestic servants, the signs went up: "No Irish Need Apply."

## GERMAN IMMIGRATION

Germans, like the Irish, had a long history of emigration to America. The nineteenth-century immigration of Germans began somewhat later and more slowly than that of the Irish, but by 1854 it had surpassed the Irish influx. The typical German immigrant was a small farmer or artisan dislodged by the same market forces at work in America: the industrialization of production and consolidation, and the commercialization of farming. There was also a small group of middle-class liberal intellectuals who left the German states (Germany was not yet a unified nation) after 1848 when attempts at revolution had failed.

German migrants were not as poor as the Irish, and they could afford to move out of the East Coast seaports to other locations. Many settled in Pittsburgh, Cincinnati, St. Louis, and Milwaukee and on farms in Ohio, Indiana, Missouri, and Texas. In Texas, the nucleus of a German community began with a Mexican land grant in the 1830s. Few Germans settled either in northeastern cities or in the South.

German agricultural communities took a distinctive form that fostered cultural continuity. Immigrants formed predominantly German towns by clustering, or taking up adjoining land. A small cluster could support German churches, German-language schools, and German customs and thereby attract other Germans, some directly from Europe and some from other parts of the United States.

**Wright's Grove, shown** here in an 1868 illustration, was the popular picnic grounds and beer garden for the large German community on Chicago's North Side. Establishments such as this horrified American temperance advocates, who warned about the dangerous foreign notion of mixing alcohol with family fun.

## THE CHINESE IN CALIFORNIA

Another area attracting immigrants in the early nineteenth century was Gold Rush California, which drew, among others, numbers of Chinese (see Chapter 14). The Chinese who came to California worked in the mines, mostly as independent prospectors. Other miners disliked their industriousness and their clannishness. By the mid-1860s, Chinese workers made up 90 percent of the laborers building the Central Pacific Railroad, replacing more expensive white laborers and sowing the seeds of the long-lasting hostility of American workers toward Chinese. In the meantime, however, San Francisco's Chinatown, the oldest Chinese ethnic enclave in America, became a well-established, thriving community and a refuge in times of anti-Chinese violence.

## ETHNIC NEIGHBORHOODS

Ethnic neighborhoods were not limited to the Chinese. Almost all new immigrants preferred to live in neighborhoods where they could find not only family ties and familiar ways but also community support as they learned how to survive in new surroundings. Isolated partly by their religious beliefs, Irish immigrants created their own communities in Boston and New York, their major destinations. They raised the money to erect Catholic churches with Irish priests. They established parochial schools with Irish nuns as teachers and sent their children to them in preference to the openly anti-Catholic public schools. They formed mutual aid societies based on kinship or town of origin in Ireland. Men and women formed religious and social clubs, lodges, and brotherhoods and their female auxiliaries. Irishmen manned fire and militia companies as well. This dense network of associations served the same purpose that social welfare organizations do today: providing help in time of need and offering companionship in a hostile environment.

Germans who settled in urban areas also built their own ethnic enclaves— "Little Germanies"—in which they sought to duplicate the rich cultural life of their homeland. Like the Irish, the Germans formed church societies, mutual benefit societies, and fire and militia companies to provide mutual support. Partly because their communities were more prosperous than those of the Irish, the Germans also formed a network of leisure organizations: singing societies, debating and political clubs, concert halls like New York's Beethoven Hall, theaters, *turnvereins* (gymnastics associations), and beer gardens. They published German-language newspapers as well.

# URBAN PROBLEMS

It was within the new urban environment, with its stimulating and frightening confusion of rapid growth, occupational and ethnic change, and economic competition, that new American political and social forms began to emerge.

## NEW LIVING PATTERNS IN THE CITIES

The preindustrial cities of eighteenth-century America had been small and compact "walking cities," in which people, rich and poor, lived near their work in a dense, small-scale housing pattern that fostered neighborliness and the mingling of social classes. The growth caused by immigration changed the character of urban life by sharpening class differences.

Even though per capita income in America is estimated to have doubled between 1800 and 1850, the gap between rich and poor was glaringly apparent in the nation's cities. Differences in income affected every aspect of urban life. Very poor families, including almost all new immigrants, performed unskilled labor in jobs where the future was uncertain at best, lived in cheap rented housing, moved frequently, and depended on more than one income to survive. Artisans and skilled workers with incomes of $500 or more could live adequately, though often in cramped quarters that also served as their shops. A middle-class family with an income of more than $1,000 a year could live comfortably in a house of four to six rooms complete with carpeting, wallpaper, and good furniture. The very rich built mansions and large town houses and staffed them with many servants. In the summer, they left the cities for country estates or homes at seaside resorts such as Newport, Rhode Island, which attracted wealthy families from all over the country.

Early nineteenth-century cities lacked municipal water supplies, sewers, and garbage collection. Every American city suffered epidemics of sanitation-related diseases such as yellow fever, cholera, and typhus. Philadelphia's yellow fever epidemic of 1793 caused 4,000 deaths and stopped all business with the outside world for more than a month. Major cholera epidemics ravaged New York in 1832 and 1849, and New Orleans suffered repeated episodes of cholera and yellow fever.

WHO WERE the major proponents of the labor movement?

**myhistorylab**
**Review Summary**

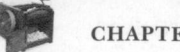
Yet the cities were slow to take action. Mostly, this was due to poor understanding of the links between sanitation and disease, but expense was also a factor. Garbage collection remained a private service, and cities charged property owners for the costs of sewers, water mains, and street paving. Poorer areas of the cities could not afford the costs. When disease struck, wealthier people simply left the cities, leaving the poor to suffer.

Lack of municipal services encouraged residential segregation. Richer people clustered in neighborhoods that had the new amenities. By the 1850s, the middle class began to escape cities completely by moving to the new "streetcar suburbs," named for the new mode of urban transportation that connected these nearby areas to the city itself.

As the middle class left the city, the poor clustered in bad neighborhoods that became known as slums. The worst New York slum in the nineteenth century was Five Points, a stone's throw from City Hall. There, immigrants, free black people, and criminals were crammed into rundown buildings known in the slang of the time as "rookeries." Notorious gangs of thieves and pickpockets with names such as the Plug Uglies and the Shirt Tails dominated the district. Starvation and murder were commonplace.

THE FIVE POINTS IN 1859
Crossing of Baxter [late Orange] Park [late Cross] & Worth [late Anthony] Sts.

**The Five Points** neighborhood in lower Manhattan illustrates the segregated housing patterns that emerged as New York City experienced rapid growth. Immigrants, free African Americans, the poor, and criminals were crowded together in New York's most notorious slum, while wealthier people moved to more prosperous neighborhoods.

With the influx of European immigrants after 1830, middle-class Americans increasingly saw slums as the home of strange and foreign people, who deserved less than American-born citizens did. In this way, residential patterns came to embody larger issues of class and citizenship. Even disease itself was blamed on immigrants. As banker John Pintard reasoned in 1832, the cholera epidemic must be God's judgment on "the lower classes of intemperate dissolute and filthy people huddled together like swine in their polluted habitations."

## ETHNICITY IN URBAN POPULAR CULTURE

Immigrants to American cities contributed to a new urban popular culture, with New York, the largest city, leading the way. In the period 1820–60, New York experienced the replacement of artisanal labor by wagework, two serious depressions (1837–43 and 1857), and a vast influx of immigrant labor (see Figure 13.1). In response to these pressures, working-class amusements became rougher and rowdier.

Irish immigrants, in particular, faced not only employment discrimination but also persistent cultural denigration. It was common for newspapers of the time to caricature the Irish as monkeys, similar to the way cartoonists portrayed African Americans. The Irish response, which was to insist on their "whiteness," played itself out in urban popular culture in violence and mockery.

Theaters, which had been frequented by men of all social classes, provided another setting for violence. Few women, except for the prostitutes who met their customers in the third tier of the balcony, attended.

By the 1830s, middle-class and upper-class men withdrew to more respectable theaters to which they could bring their wives and daughters, and workers found new amusements in theaters such as the Lafayette Circus, which featured dancing girls and horseback riders as well as theatrical acts (see Seeing History).

The new working-class culture flourished especially on the Bowery, a New York City street filled with workshops, small factories, shops with cheap goods, dance halls, theaters, ice cream parlors, and oyster bars. Here working-class youth, the "Bowery b'hoys" (slang pronunciation of "boys") and "gals," found Saturday night amusement and provided it for themselves with outrageous clothing and behavior. The deliberately provocative way they dressed was, in effect, a way of thumbing their noses at the more respectable classes.

## THE LABOR MOVEMENT AND URBAN POLITICS

By the 1830s, the status of artisans and independent craftsmen in the nation's cities had deteriorated. Members of urban workers' associations, increasingly angry over their declining status in the economic and social order, became active defenders of working-class interests in their cities.

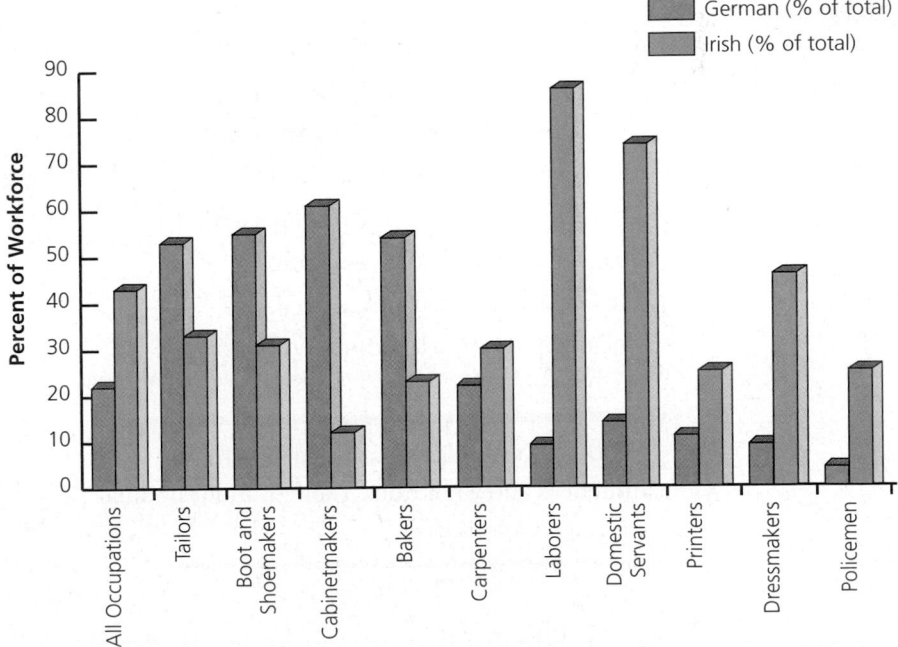

**Figure 13.1 Participation of Irish and German Immigrants in the New York City Workforce for Selected Occupations, 1855**
This chart shows the impact of the new immigrants on the New York's workforce, and the dramatic difference between groups. German workers predominate in the skilled trades, while the Irish are clustered in low-skilled, low paying occupations.

Robert Ernst, *Immigrant Life in New York City 1825–1863* (Syracuse: Syracuse University Press, 1994).

# Thomas "Daddy" Rice, Blackface Minstrel, Dances Jim Crow

In 1832, a young white man in blackface appeared at a variety show at the Bowery Theater where he sang and danced the following:

*First, on de heel tap,*
*Den on the toe*
*Every time I wheel about*
*I jump Jim Crow.*
*Wheel about and turn about*
*En do j's so*
*And every time I wheel about,*
*I jump Jim Crow.*

This performance was so wildly popular that Thomas Rice had to repeat it twenty times before the audience would let him go. In this way, the cruel stereotype of the slow-witted slave, Jim Crow, entered American popular culture and Rice himself became one of the best-known blackface minstrels. He was far from alone, for blackface minstrel shows were among the most popular American entertainments. A full evening's performance by a company of minstrels (all white men with faces blackened by cork) consisted of songs, wisecracks, parodies of politicians and other notable figures, comedy scenes of plantation life, dancing, and music. Minstrel shows were a favorite American entertainment for the rest of the nineteenth century.

**WHAT EXPLAINS** its appeal to white audiences and what does it tell us about popular stereotypes of blacks?

When it first appeared, in the popular culture of the 1830s and 1840s, blackface minstrelsy was a clear indicator of how the issue of slavery permeated all aspects of American life in both the North and South. ■

This cartoon encounter between a newly arrived Irishman and an African American expresses the fear of many immigrants that they would be treated like blacks and denied the privileges of whiteness.

### IRISH EMIGRANT.

*Patrick, (just landing.)* "BY MY SOWL, YOU'RE BLACK, OLD FELLOW! HOW LONG HAVE YE BIN HERE?"

*Nigger, (imitatng the brogue.)* "JIST THREE MONTHS, MY HONEY!"

*Pat.* "BY THE POWERS, I'LL GO BACK TO TIPPERARY IN A JIFFY! I'D NOT BE SO BLACK AS THAT FUR ALL THE WHISKEY IN ROSCREA!"

Between 1833 and 1837, a wave of strikes in New York City cut the remaining ties between master craftsmen and the journeymen who worked for them. In 1833, journeymen carpenters struck for higher wages. Workers in fifteen other trades came to their support, and within a month the strike was won. The same year, representatives from nine different craft groups formed the General Trades Union (GTU) of New York. By 1834, similar groups had sprung up in over a dozen cities. In 1834 also, representatives of several local GTUs met in Baltimore and organized the National Trades Union (NTU). In its founding statement the NTU criticized the "unjustifiable distribution of the wealth of society in the hands of a few individuals," which had created for working people "a humiliating, servile dependency, incompatible with . . . natural equality."

Naturally, employers disagreed with the NTU's criticism of the economic system. In Cincinnati and elsewhere, employers prevailed upon police to arrest strikers even when no violence had occurred. In another case, New York employers took striking journeymen tailors to court in 1836. Judge Ogden Edwards pronounced the strikers guilty of conspiracy and declared unions un-American. The GTU responded with a mass rally at which Judge Edwards was burned in effigy.

A year later, stunned by the effects of the Panic of 1837, the GTU collapsed. The founding of these general unions, a visible sign of a class-based community of interest among workers, is generally considered to mark the beginning of the American labor movement. However, the early unions included only white men in skilled trades, who made up only a small percentage of all workers. The majority of workers—men in unskilled occupations, all free African Americans, and all women—were excluded.

Although workers were unable to create strong unions or stable political parties that spoke for their economic interests, they were a vital factor in urban politics. As America's cities experienced unprecedented growth, the electorate mushroomed. In New York, for example, the number of voters grew from 20,000 in 1825 to 88,900 in 1855. Furthermore, by 1855 half of the voters were foreign-born. Because immigrants clustered in neighborhoods, their impact on politics could be concentrated and manipulated. In New York, for example, the Irish-dominated districts quickly became Democratic Party strongholds. Germans, who were less active politically than the Irish, nevertheless voted heavily for the new Republican Party in the 1850s. Between them, these two new blocs of immigrant voters destroyed the Whig Party that had controlled New York politics before the immigrants arrived.

In New York City, the **Tammany Society**, begun in the 1780s as a fraternal organization of artisans, slowly evolved into the key organization of the new mass politics. Tammany, which was affiliated with the national Democratic Party, reached voters by using many of the techniques of mass appeal made popular earlier by craft organizations—parades, rallies, popular songs, and party newspapers.

## CIVIC ORDER

The challenges to middle-class respectability posed by new immigrants and unruly workers were fostered and publicized by the immensely popular "penny papers," which began publication in 1833, and by the rapidly growing number of political papers. This exuberant urban popular culture was unquestionably a part of the same new democratic political spirit that led to the great upsurge in political participation discussed in Chapter 11.

In New York, the prosperous classes were increasingly frightened by the urban poor and by working-class rowdyism. New York City's tradition of New Year's Eve "frolics," in which laborers, apprentices, and other members of the lower classes paraded through the streets playing drums, trumpets, whistles, and other noisemakers, was an example. By 1828, the revelry had been taken over by gangs of young workers from the lower classes, 4,000 strong, who marched through the city, overturning carts, breaking windows, obstructing traffic, and harassing middle-class citizens. In the following year, the city government banned the traditional New Year's Eve parade.

In colonial days, civic disturbances had been handled informally: members of the city watch asked onlookers for whatever assistance was necessary to keep the peace. New York City's first response in the 1820s and 1830s to increasing civic disorder was to hire more city watchmen and to augment them with constables and marshals. When riots occurred, the militia were called, and deaths were increasingly common as they forcibly restrained mobs. Finally, in 1845, the city created a permanent police force with a mandate to keep the poor in order. Southern cities, because of fear of slave disorder, had police forces much earlier.

But even with police forces in place, the pressures of rapid urbanization, immigration, and the market revolution proved to be too much for America's cities. Beginning in the 1830s, a series of urban riots broke out against the two poorest urban groups: Catholics and free black people. As if their miserable living conditions were not enough, Irish immigrants were met with virulent anti-Catholicism.

**Tammany Society** A fraternal organization of artisans begun in the 1780s that evolved into a key organization of the new mass politics in New York City.

**By 1855, half** the voters in New York City were foreign-born. This 1858 engraving of an Irish bar in the Five Points area appeared in the influential *Harper's Weekly*. It expressed the temperance reformers' dislike of immigrants and their drinking habits and the dismay of political reformers that immigrant saloons and taverns were such effective organizing centers for urban political machines.

In 1834, rioters burned an Ursuline convent in Charlestown, Massachusetts; in 1844, a Philadelphia mob attacked priests and nuns and vandalized Catholic churches; in 1854, a mob destroyed an Irish neighborhood in Lawrence, Massachusetts. Often the Irish replied in kind—for example, in an 1806 riot in New York, when they counterattacked a mob that disrupted their Christmas Eve mass in a Catholic church on Augustus Street. But the most common targets of urban violence were free African Americans.

## FREE AFRICAN AMERICANS IN THE CITIES

By 1860, there were nearly half a million free African Americans in the United States, constituting about 11 percent of the country's total black population. More than half of all free African Americans lived in the North, mostly in cities, where they competed with immigrants and native-born poor white people for jobs as day laborers and domestic servants. Philadelphia and New York had the largest black communities. There were much smaller but still significant black communities in the New England cities of Boston, Providence, and New Haven and in Ohio cities like Cincinnati.

Free African Americans in northern cities faced residential segregation, pervasive job discrimination, segregated public schools, and severe limitations on their civil rights. In addition to these legal restrictions, there were matters of custom: African Americans of all economic classes endured daily affronts, such as exclusion from public concerts, lectures, and libraries, and segregation or exclusion from public transportation. For example, in Massachusetts—which had the reputation

**This appealing portrait** of a musician, *The Bone Player*, evokes the prevalent stereotype of African Americans as innately musical, but it also clearly portrays a man who is proud of his talent.

William Sidney Morris (American, 1807–1868), "The Bone Player," 1856. Oil on canvas, 91.76 × 73.98 cm (36 1/8 × 29 1/8 in.). Courtesy, Museum of Fine Arts, Boston. Bequest of Martha C. Karolik for the M. and M. Karolik Collection of American Paintings. 48.46 Reproduced with permission. Photograph © 2006 Museum of Fine Arts, Boston. All Rights Reserved.

WHAT ROLE did women play in the development of American education?

**myhistorylab**

**Review Summary**

**11–4**
Charles Finney, *What a Revival of Religion Is* (1835)

of being more hospitable to black people than any other northern state—the famed African American abolitionist Frederick Douglass was denied admission to a zoo on Boston Common, a public lecture and revival meeting, a restaurant, and a public omnibus, all within the space of a few days.

In common with Irish and German immigrants, African Americans created defenses against the hostile larger society by building their own community structures. They formed associations for aiding the poorest members of the community, for self-improvement, and for socializing. Tired of being insulted by the white press, African American communities supported their own newspapers. The major community organization was the black Baptist or African Methodist Episcopal (AME) church.

Employment prospects for black men deteriorated from 1820 to 1850. Those who had held jobs as skilled artisans were forced from their positions, and their sons denied apprenticeships, by white mechanics and craftsmen who were themselves suffering from the effects of the market revolution. Limited to day labor, African Americans found themselves in direct competition with the new immigrants, especially the Irish, for jobs. On the waterfront, black men lost their jobs as carters and longshoremen to the Irish. One of the few occupations to remain open to them was that of seaman. More than 20 percent of all American sailors in 1850 were black. Mothers, wives, and daughters worked as domestic servants (in competition with Irishwomen), washerwomen, and seamstresses.

Free African Americans remained committed to their enslaved brethren in the South. In New York, for example, black communities rioted four times—in 1801, 1819, 1826, and 1832—against slave catchers taking escaped slaves back to slavery. But even more frequently, free African Americans were themselves targets of urban violence. Philadelphia, "the City of Brotherly Love," was repeatedly rocked by antiblack riots in the period between 1820 and 1859.

## SOCIAL REFORM MOVEMENTS

The passion for reform that had become such an important part of the new middle-class thinking was focused on the problems of the nation's cities. As the opening of this chapter describes, the earliest response to the dislocations caused by the market revolution was community based and voluntary. Middle-class people tried to deal with social changes in their communities by joining organizations devoted to reforms. The reform message was vastly amplified by inventions such as the steam printing press, which made it possible to publish reform literature in great volume. Soon there were national networks of reform groups.

### RELIGION, REFORM, AND SOCIAL CONTROL

Evangelical religion was fundamental to social reform. Men and women who had been converted to the enthusiastic new faith assumed personal responsibility for making changes in their own lives. Personal reform quickly led to social reform. Religious converts were encouraged in their social activism by such leading revivalists as Charles G. Finney, who preached a doctrine of "perfectionism," claiming it was possible for all Christians to personally understand and live by God's will and thereby become "as perfect as God." This new religious feeling evoked by Finney was intensely hopeful: members of evangelistic religions really did expect to convert the world and create the perfect moral and religious community on earth.

Much of America was swept by this reform-minded religious fervor, and it was the new middle class that set the agenda. Reform efforts arose from the recognition that the traditional methods of small-scale local relief were no longer adequate. Reformers realized that large cities had to make large-scale provisions for social misfits and that institutional rather than private efforts were needed. This thinking was especially true of the institutional reform movements that began in the 1830s, such as the push for insane asylums. At this time, of course, the federal government provided no such relief.

A second characteristic of the reform movements was a belief in the basic goodness of human nature. All reformers believed that the condition of the unfortunate—the poor, the insane, the criminal—would improve in a wholesome environment. Prison reform carried this sentiment to the extreme. On the theory that bad social influences were largely responsible for crime, some "model" prisons completely isolated prisoners from one another, making them eat, sleep, work, and do required Bible reading in their own cells. The failure of these prisons to achieve dramatic changes for the better in their inmates (a number of isolated prisoners went mad, and some committed suicide) or to reduce crime was one of the first indications that reform was not a simple task.

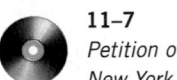

**11–7**
*Petition of the Catholics of New York* (1840)

A third characteristic of the reform movements was their moralistic dogmatism. Reformers were certain they knew what was right and were determined to see their improvements enacted. It was a short step from developing individual self-discipline to imposing discipline on others. The reforms that were proposed thus took the form of social controls. Lazy, sinful, intemperate, or unfit members of society were to be reformed for their own good, whether they wanted to be or not. This attitude was bound to cause controversy; by no means did all Americans share the reformers' beliefs, nor did those for whom it was intended always take kindly to being the targets of the reformers' concern.

Indeed, some aspects of the social reform movements were harmful. The evangelical Protestantism of the reformers promoted a dangerous hostility to Catholic immigrants from Ireland and Germany that, as noted earlier, repeatedly led to urban riots. The temperance movement, in particular, targeted immigrants for their free drinking habits. Seeking uniformity of behavior rather than tolerance, the reformers thus helped to promote the virulent nativism that infected American politics between 1840 and 1860 (see Chapter 15).

Regional and national reform organizations quickly grew from local projects to deal with social problems such as drinking, prostitution, mental illness, and crime. In 1828, for example, Congregationalist minister Lyman Beecher joined other ministers in forming a General Union for Promoting the Observance of the Christian Sabbath; the aim was to prevent business on Sundays. To achieve its goals, the General Union adopted the same methods used by political parties: lobbying, petition drives, fundraising, and special publications.

In effect, Beecher and similar reformers engaged in political action but remained aloof from direct electoral politics, stressing their religious mission. In any case, sabbatarianism was controversial. Workingmen (who usually worked six days a week) were angered when the General Union forced the Sunday closure of their favorite taverns and were quick to vote against the Whigs, the party perceived to be most sympathetic to reform thinking. But in many new western cities, **sabbatarianism** divided the business class itself. In Rochester, a city created by the Erie Canal,

**Sabbatarianism** Reform movement that aimed to prevent business on Sundays.

businessmen who wished to observe Sunday only in religious ways were completely unable to stop the traffic of passenger and freight boats owned by other businessmen. Other reforms likewise muddied the distinction between political and social activity. It is not surprising that women, who were barred from electoral politics but not from moral and social activism, were major supporters of reform.

## EDUCATION AND WOMEN TEACHERS

Women became deeply involved in reform movements through their churches. It was they who did most of the fundraising for the home missionary societies that were beginning to send the evangelical message worldwide—at first by ministers alone, later by married couples. Nearly every church had a maternal association, where mothers gathered to discuss ways to raise their children as true Christians. These associations reflected a new and more positive definition of childhood. The Puritans had believed that children were born sinful and that their wills had to be broken before they could become godly. Early schools reflected these beliefs: teaching was by rote, and punishment was harsh and physical. Educational reformers, however, tended to believe that children were born innocent and needed gentle nurturing and encouragement if they were to flourish. At home, mothers began to play the central role in child rearing. Outside the home, women helped spread the new public education pioneered by Horace Mann, secretary of the Massachusetts State Board of Education.

Although literacy had long been valued, especially in New England, schooling since colonial times had been a private enterprise and a personal expense. In 1827, Massachusetts pioneered compulsory education by legislating that public schools be supported by public taxes. Soon schooling for white children between the ages of five and nineteen was common, although, especially in rural schools, the term might be only a month or so long. Uniformity in curriculum and teacher training, and the grading of classes by ability—measures pioneered by Horace Mann in the 1830s—quickly caught on in other states. In the North and West (the South lagged far behind), more and more children went to school, and more and more teachers, usually young single women, were hired to teach them.

The spread of public education created the first real career opportunity for women. By 1850, women were dominant in primary school teaching, which had come to be regarded as an acceptable occupation for educated young women during the few years between their own schooling and marriage. For some women, teaching was a great adventure; they enthusiastically volunteered to be "schoolmarms" on the distant western frontiers of Wisconsin and Iowa. Still others thought globally. The young women who attended Mary Lyon's Mount Holyoke Female Seminary in Massachusetts, founded in 1837, hoped to be missionary teachers in distant lands. For others, a few years of teaching was quite enough. Low pay (half of what male schoolteachers earned) and strict community supervision (women teachers had to board with families in the community) were probably sufficient to make almost any marriage proposal look appealing.

## TEMPERANCE

Reformers believed not only that children could be molded but also that adults could change. The largest reform organization of the period, the **American Society for the Promotion of Temperance**, founded in 1826, boasted more than 200,000 members by the mid-1830s. Dominated by evangelicals, local chapters used revival methods—lurid **temperance** tracts detailing the evils of alcohol, large prayer and song meetings, and heavy group pressure—to encourage young men to stand up, confess their bad habits, and "take the pledge" not to drink. Here again, women played an important role (see Figure 13.2).

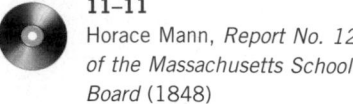

**11–11**
Horace Mann, *Report No. 12 of the Massachusetts School Board* (1848)

---

**QUICK REVIEW**

**Women and Reform**

- Women often became involved in reform through their churches.
- Maternal associations focused on raising of children as true Christians.
- Women helped spread public education of children.

---

**American Society for the Promotion of Temperance** Largest reform organization of its time dedicated to ending the sale and consumption of alcoholic beverages.

**Temperance** Reform movement originating in the 1820s that sought to eliminate the consumption of alcohol.

Excessive drinking was a national problem, and it appears to have been mostly a masculine one, for respectable women did not drink in public. Men drank hard cider and liquor—whiskey, rum—in abundance. Traditionally, drinking had been a basic part of men's working lives. It concluded occasions as formal as the signing of a contract and accompanied such informal activities as card games. Drink was a staple offering at political speeches, rallies, and elections. In the old artisanal workshops, drinking had been a customary pastime. Much of the drinking was well within the bounds of sociability, but the widespread use must have encouraged drunkenness.

There were many reasons to support temperance. Heavy-drinking men hurt their families economically by spending their wages on drink. Women had no recourse: the laws of the time gave men complete financial control of the household, and divorce was difficult as well as socially unacceptable. Excessive drinking also led to violence and crime, both within the family and in the larger society.

But there were other reasons. The new middle class, preoccupied with respectability, morality, and efficiency, found the old easygoing drinking ways unacceptable. Temperance became a social and political issue. Whigs, who embraced the new morality, favored it; Democrats, who in northern cities consisted increasingly of immigrant workers, were opposed. Both German and Irish immigrants valued the social drinking that occurred in beer gardens and saloons and were hostile to temperance reform.

The Panic of 1837 affected the temperance movement. Whereas most temperance crusaders in the 1820s had been members of the middle class, the long depression of 1837–43 prompted artisans and skilled workers to give up or at least cut down substantially on drinking. Forming associations known as Washington Temperance Societies, these workers spread the word that temperance was the workingman's best chance to survive economically and to maintain his independence. Their wives, gathered together in Martha Washington Societies, were frequently even more committed to temperance than their husbands.

By the mid-1840s, alcohol consumption had been more than halved, to about the level of today. Concern over drinking would remain constant throughout the nineteenth century and into the twentieth.

## MORAL REFORM, ASYLUMS, AND PRISONS

Alcohol was not the only "social evil" that reform groups attacked. Another was prostitution, which was common in the nation's port cities. The customary approach of evangelical reformers was to "rescue" prostitutes, offering them the salvation of religion, prayer, and temporary shelter. The success rate was not very high. As an alternative to prostitution, reformers usually offered domestic work, a low-paying and restrictive occupation that many women scorned. Nevertheless, campaigns against prostitution, generally organized by women, continued throughout the nineteenth century.

One of the earliest and most effective antiprostitution groups was the **Female Moral Reform Society**. Founded by evangelical women in New York in 1834 (the first president was Lydia Finney), it boasted 555 affiliates throughout the country by 1840. The societies quickly realized that prostitution was not as much a moral as an economic issue and moved to organize charity and work for poor women and orphans. They also took direct action against the patrons of prostitutes by printing their names in local papers and then successfully lobbied the New York state legislature for criminal penalties against the male clients as well as the women themselves.

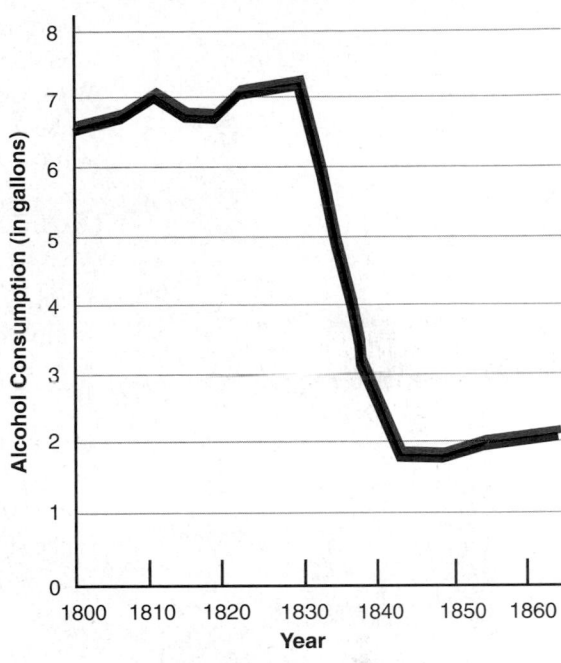

**Figure 13.2 Per Capita Consumption of Alcohol, 1800–60**
The underlying cause of the dramatic fall in alcohol consumption during the 1830s was the changing nature of work brought about by the market revolution. Contributing factors were the shock of the Panic of 1837 and the untiring efforts of temperance reformers.

W. J. Rorabaugh, *The Alcoholic Republic: An American Tradition* (New York: Oxford University Press, 1979).

**11–2**
Lyman Beecher, *Six Sermons on Intemperance* (1828)

**11–5**
*Temperance and the Washingtonians* (1836)

**Female Moral Reform Society**
Antiprostitution group founded by evangelical women in New York in 1834.

**This Currier and** Ives lithograph, *The Drunkard's Progress*, dramatically conveys the message that the first glass leads the drinker inevitably to alcoholism and finally to the grave, while his wife and child (shown under the arch) suffer.

Another dramatic example of reform was the asylum movement, spearheaded by the evangelist Dorothea Dix. In 1843, Dix horrified the Massachusetts state legislature with the results of her several years of study of the conditions to which insane women were subjected. She described in lurid detail how the women were incarcerated with ordinary criminals, locked up in "cages, closets, stalls, pens! Chained, naked, beaten with rods, and lashed into obedience!" Dix's efforts led to the establishment of a state asylum for the insane in Massachusetts and to similar institutions in other states.

Other reformers were active in related causes, such as prison reform and the establishment of orphanages, homes of refuge, and hospitals. Model penitentiaries were built in Auburn and Ossining (known as "Sing Sing"), New York, and in Philadelphia and Pittsburgh. Characterized by strict order and discipline, these prisons were supposed to reform rather than simply incarcerate their inmates, but their regimes of silence and isolation caused despair more often than rehabilitation.

## UTOPIANISM AND MORMONISM

Amid all the political activism and reform fervor of the 1830s, a few people chose to escape into utopian communities and new religions. The upstate New York area along the Erie Canal was the seedbed for this movement, just as it was for evangelical revivals and reform movements like the **Seneca Falls convention**. The area was so notable for its reform enthusiasm that it has been called "the Burned-Over District," a reference to the waves of reform that swept through like forest fires (see Map 13.2).

**Seneca Falls convention**   The first convention for women's equality in legal rights, held in upstate New York in 1848.

# MAP EXPLORATION

To explore an interactive version of this map, go to **http://www.prenhall.com/faraghertlc/map13.2**

**MAP 13.2**

**Reform Movements in the Burned-Over District**   The so-called Burned-Over District, the region of New York State most changed by the opening of the Erie Canal, was a seedbed of religious and reform movements. The Mormon Church originated there and utopian groups and sects like the Millerites and the Fourierists thrived. Charles G. Finney held some of his most successful evangelical revivals in the district. Antislavery feeling was common in the region, and the women's rights movement began at Seneca Falls.

Whitney Cross, *The Burned-Over District* (1950; reprint, New York: Hippocrene Books, 1981).

WHY WERE the many religious revivals and reform movements in the Burned-Over District in the 1830s and 1840s strongest in this region of the country?

Apocalyptic religions tend to spring up in places experiencing rapid social change. The Erie Canal region, which experienced the full impact of the market revolution in the early nineteenth century, was such a place. A second catalyst is hard times, and the prolonged depression that began with the Panic of 1837 led some people to embrace a belief in imminent catastrophe.

The **Shakers**, founded by "Mother" Ann Lee in 1774, were the oldest utopian group. An offshoot of the Quakers, the Shakers espoused a radical social philosophy that called for the abolition of the traditional family in favor of a family of brothers and sisters joined in equal fellowship. Despite its insistence on celibacy, the Shaker movement grew between 1820 and 1830, eventually reaching twenty settlements in eight states with a total membership of 6,000. The Shakers' simple and highly structured lifestyle, their isolation from the changing world, and their belief in equality drew new followers, especially among women. In contrast, another

**11–12**
John Humphrey Noyes, *Speech to the Convention of Perfectionists* (1845) and *Bible Communism* (1849)

**Shakers**   The followers of Mother Ann Lee, who preached a religion of strict celibacy and communal living.

**Begun in 1822**, the castle-like Eastern State Penitentiary in Philadelphia was intended as a model of rational prison reform. Replacing the crowded mass imprisonment of the past, prisoners were held in isolation from other inmates in separate cells. But instead of the expected repentance and reform, isolation bred despair and attempts at suicide.

The Library Company of Philadelphia.

**10–1**
Joseph Smith, *The Beginnings of Mormorism* (1823)

**14–2**
Harriet Beecher Stowe, *Uncle Tom's Cabin* (1852)

**Mormonism**   The doctrines based on the Book of Mormon, taught by Joseph Smith and the succeeding prophets and leaders of the Church.

**WHO WERE** the abolitionists and what were their racial attitudes?

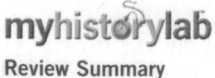

**Review Summary**

utopian community, the Oneida Community, became notorious for its sexual freedom. Founded by John Humphrey Noyes in 1848, the Oneida community, like the Shaker community, viewed itself as one family. But rather than celibacy, members practiced "complex marriage," a system of highly regulated group sexual activity.

Still other forthrightly socialist communities flourished briefly. New Harmony, Indiana, founded by the famous Scottish industrialist Robert Owen in 1825, was to be a manufacturing community without poverty and unemployment. The community survived only three years. Faring little better were the "phalanxes," huge communal buildings structured on the socialist theories of the French thinker Charles Fourier. Based on his belief that there was a rational way to divide work, Fourier suggested, for example, that children would make the best garbage collectors because they didn't mind dirt! The rapid failure of these socialist communities was due largely to inadequate planning and organization. Another reason may have been, as author Louisa May Alcott suggested in her satirical reminiscence, *Transcendental Wild Oats*, that the women were left to do all the work while the men philosophized.

The most successful of the nineteenth-century communitarian movements was also a product of the Burned-Over District. In 1830, a young man named Joseph Smith founded the Church of Jesus Christ of Latter-Day Saints, based on the teachings of the Book of Mormon, which he claimed to have received from an angel in a vision. Initially **Mormonism**, as the new religion became known, seemed little different from the many other new religious groups and utopian communities of the time. But under the benevolent authority of its patriarch, Joseph Smith, it rapidly gained distinction for its extraordinary unity. Close cooperation and hard work made the Mormon community successful, attracting both new followers and the animosity of neighbors.

The Mormons were harassed in New York and driven west to Ohio and then Missouri. Finally they seemed to find an ideal home in Nauvoo, Illinois, where in 1839 they built a model community, achieving almost complete self-government and isolation from non-Mormon neighbors. But in 1844, dissension within the community over Joseph Smith's new doctrine of polygamy (marriage between one man and more than one woman simultaneously) gave outsiders a chance to intervene. Smith and his brother were arrested peacefully but were killed by a mob from which their jailers failed to protect them. The beleaguered Mormon community decided to move beyond reach of harm. Led by Brigham Young, the Mormons migrated in 1846 to the Great Salt Lake in present-day Utah. Their hopes of isolation were dashed, however, by the California Gold Rush of 1849. (See Chapter 14)

## ANTISLAVERY AND ABOLITIONISM

The antislavery feeling that was to play such an important role in the politics of the 1840s and 1850s also had its roots in the religious reform movements that began in the 1820s and 1830s. Three groups—free African Americans, Quakers, and militant white reformers—worked to bring an end to slavery, but each in different ways. Their efforts eventually turned a minor reform movement into the dominant political issue of the day.

## THE AMERICAN COLONIZATION SOCIETY

The first national attempt to "solve" the problem of slavery was a plan for gradual emancipation of slaves (with compensation to their owners) and their resettlement in Africa. This plan was the work of the **American Colonization Society**, formed in 1817 by northern religious reformers (Quakers prominent among them) and a number of southern slave owners, most from the Upper South and the border states (Kentuckian Henry Clay was a supporter). The American Colonization Society was remarkably ineffective; by 1830, it had managed to send only 1,400 black people to a colony in Liberia, West Africa. Critics pointed out that more slaves were born in a week than the society sent back to Africa in a year.

## AFRICAN AMERICANS AGAINST SLAVERY

For free African Americans, the freedom of other black people had always been a goal, but in order to achieve change, they needed white allies. Most free African Americans rejected the efforts of the American Colonization Society, insisting instead on a commitment to the immediate end of slavery and the equal treatment of black people in America. "We are natives of this country," an African American minister in New York pointed out. Then he added bitterly, "We only ask that we be treated as well as foreigners." By 1830, there were at least fifty African American abolitionist societies in the North. The first African American newspaper, founded in 1827 by John Russwurm and Samuel Cornish, announced its antislavery position in its title, *Freedom's Journal*.

In 1829, David Walker, a free African American in Boston, wrote a widely distributed pamphlet, *Appeal to the Colored Citizens of the World*, that encouraged slave rebellion. "We must and shall be free . . . in spite of you," Walker warned whites. "And woe, woe will be it to you if we have to obtain our freedom by fighting." White Southerners blamed pamphlets such as these and the militant articles of African American journalists for stirring up trouble among southern slaves and, in particular, for Nat Turner's revolt in 1831.

## ABOLITIONISTS

The third and best-known group of antislavery reformers was headed by William Lloyd Garrison. In 1831, Garrison broke with the gradualist persuaders of the American Colonization Society and began publishing his own paper, the *Liberator*. Garrison's approach was to mount a sweeping crusade condemning slavery as sinful and demanding its immediate abolition. In reality, Garrison did not expect that all slaves would be freed immediately, but he did want and expect everyone to acknowledge the immorality of slavery. On the other hand, Garrison took the truly radical step of demanding full social equality for African Americans, referring to them individually as "a man and a brother" and "a woman and a sister."

Garrison's moral vehemence radicalized northern antislavery religious groups. Theodore Weld, an evangelical minister, joined Garrison in 1833 in forming the American Anti-Slavery Society. The following year, Weld encouraged a group of students at Lane Theological Seminary in Cincinnati to form an antislavery society. When the seminary's president, Lyman Beecher, sought to suppress it, the students moved en masse to Oberlin College in northern Ohio, where they were joined by revivalist Charles Finney, who became president of the college. Oberlin soon became known as the most liberal college in the country, not only for its antislavery stance but for its acceptance of African American students and of women students as well.

The style of abolitionist writings and speeches was similar to the oratorical style of the religious revivalists. Northern abolitionists believed that a full description of the evils of slavery would force southern slave owners to confront their wrongdoing

---

**QUICK REVIEW**

**The American Colonization Society**

- Formed in 1817 with the goal of resettling slaves in Africa.

- Members included Northern religious reformers and some Southern slave owners.

- By 1830, the Society had only managed to send 1,400 people to Liberia, West Africa.

**American Colonization Society** Organization founded in 1817 by antislavery reformers, that called for gradual emancipation and the removal of freed blacks to Africa.

**The different dates** on these two widely used antislavery images are important. The title page of Thomas Branagan's 1807 book includes an already commonly used image at the time of a male slave. The engraving of a chained female slave was made by Patrick Reason, a black artist, in 1835. The accompanying message saying "Am I Not a Woman and a Sister?" spoke particularly to white female abolitionists in the North, who were just becoming active in antislavery movements in the 1830s.

and lead to a true act of repentance—freeing their slaves. They were confrontational, denunciatory, and personal in their message, much like the evangelical preachers. Southerners, however, regarded abolitionist attacks as libelous and abusive.

Abolitionists adopted another tactic of revivalists and temperance workers when, to enhance their powers of persuasion, they began to publish great numbers of antislavery tracts. In 1835 alone, they mailed more than a million pieces of antislavery literature to southern states. This tactic also drew a backlash: southern legislatures banned abolitionist literature, encouraged the harassment and abuse of anyone distributing it, and looked the other way when (as in South Carolina) proslavery mobs seized and burned it. Most serious, the majority of southern states reacted by toughening laws concerning emancipation, freedom of movement, and all aspects of slave behavior. Hoping to prevent the spread of the abolitionist message, most southern states reinforced laws making it a crime to teach a slave how to read. Ironically, then, the immediate impact of abolitionism in the South was to stifle dissent and make the lives of slaves harder.

Even in the North, controversy over abolitionism was common. Some places were prone to anti-abolitionist violence. The Ohio Valley, settled largely by Southerners, was one such place, as were northern cities experiencing the strains of rapid growth, such as Philadelphia. Immigrant Irish, who found themselves pitted against free black people for jobs, were often violently anti-abolitionist. William Lloyd Garrison was stoned, dragged through the streets, and on one occasion almost hanged by a Boston mob. In a three-day New York riot of 1834, abolitionist Arthur Tappan's home and store were sacked at the same time that black churches and homes were damaged and free blacks attacked. In 1837, antislavery editor Elijah P. Lovejoy of Alton, Illinois, was killed and his press destroyed.

## ABOLITIONISM AND POLITICS

Abolitionism began as a social movement but soon intersected with sectional interests and became a national political issue. In the 1830s, massive abolitionist petition drives gathered a total of nearly 700,000 petitions requesting the abolition of slavery and the slave trade in the District of Columbia but were rebuffed by Congress. At southern insistence and with President Andrew Jackson's approval, Congress passed a "gag rule" in 1836 that prohibited discussion of antislavery petitions.

**In 1837, white** abolitionist Elijah P. Lovejoy had placed the press he used to print his antislavery newspaper in an Alton, Illinois, warehouse in order to protect the press against a mob. This contemporary woodcut depicts the mob's attack on the warehouse. Lovejoy died defending it.

Many Northerners viewed the gag rule and censorship of the mails, which Southerners saw as necessary defenses against abolitionist frenzy, as alarming threats to free speech. First among them was Massachusetts representative John Quincy Adams, the only former president ever to serve in Congress after leaving the executive branch. Adams so publicly and persistently denounced the gag rule as a violation of the constitutional right to petition that it was repealed in 1844. Less well-known Northerners, like the thousands of women who canvassed their neighborhoods with petitions, made personal commitments to abolitionism that they did not intend to abandon.

Although abolitionist groups raised the nation's emotional temperature, they failed to achieve the moral unity they had hoped for, and they began to splinter. Frederick Douglass and William Lloyd Garrison parted ways when Douglass, refusing to be limited to a simple recital of his life as a slave, began to make specific suggestions for improvements in the lives of free African Americans.

Douglass and other free African Americans worked under persistent discrimination, even from antislavery whites; some of the latter refused to hire black people or to meet with them as equals. While many white reformers eagerly pressed for civil equality for African Americans, they did not accept the idea of social equality. On the other hand, black and white "stations" worked closely in the risky enterprise of passing fugitive slaves north over the famous Underground Railroad, as the various routes by which slaves made their way to freedom were called. Contrary to abolitionist legend, however, it was free African Americans, rather than white people, who played the major part in helping the fugitives.

In 1840, the abolitionist movement formally split. The majority moved toward party politics (which Garrison abhorred), founding the **Liberty Party** and choosing James G. Birney (whom Theodore Weld had converted to abolitionism) as their presidential candidate. Thus, the abolitionist movement, which began as an effort at moral reform, took its first major step into politics, and this step in turn led to the formation of the Republican Party in the 1850s and to the Civil War. (See Chapter 15)

For one particular group of antislavery reformers, the abolitionist movement opened up new possibilities for action. Through their participation in antislavery activity, some women came to a vivid realization of the social constraints on their activism.

**Liberty Party**  The first antislavery political party, formed in 1840.

**WHAT CONNECTIONS** were
there between the women's rights
movement and previous movements
for social reform?

**Review Summary**

**Exploring America:** *Angelina Grimké*

**11–0**
*Declaration of Sentiments and
Resolutions, Woman's Rights
Convention, Seneca Falls, New
York* (1848)

**11–13**
Sojourner Truth, *Address to the
Woman's Rights Convention,
Akron, Ohio* (1851)

# THE WOMEN'S RIGHTS MOVEMENT

American women, without the vote or a role in party politics, found a field of activity in social reform movements. There was scarcely a reform movement in which women were not actively involved. The majority of women did not participate in these activities, for they were fully occupied with housekeeping and child rearing (families with five children were the average). A few women— mostly members of the new middle class, who could afford servants—had the time and energy to look beyond their immediate tasks. Touched by the religious revival, these women enthusiastically joined reform movements. Led thereby to challenge social restrictions, some, such as the Grimké sisters, found that their commitment carried them beyond the limits of what was considered acceptable activity for women.

## THE GRIMKÉ SISTERS

Sarah and Angelina Grimké, members of a prominent South Carolina slaveholding family, rejected slavery out of religious conviction and moved north to join a Quaker community near Philadelphia. In the 1830s, these two sisters found themselves drawn into the growing antislavery agitation in the North. Because they knew about slavery firsthand, they were in great demand as speakers. At first they spoke to "parlor meetings" of women only, as was considered proper. But interested men kept sneaking into the talks, and soon the sisters found themselves speaking to mixed gatherings. The meetings got larger and larger, and the sisters became the first female public speakers in America.

The Grimké sisters were criticized for speaking because they were women. A letter from a group of ministers cited the Bible in reprimanding the sisters for stepping out of "woman's proper sphere" of silence and subordination. Sarah Grimké answered the ministers in her 1838 *Letters on the Equality of the Sexes and the Condition of Women*, claiming that "men and women were CREATED EQUAL. . . . Whatever is right for a man to do, is right for woman."

Not all female assertiveness was as dramatic as Sarah Grimké's, but women in the antislavery movement found it a constant struggle to be heard. Some solved the problem of male dominance by forming their own groups, like the Philadelphia Female Anti-Slavery Society. In the antislavery movement and other reform groups as well, men accorded women a secondary role, even when—as was frequently the case—women constituted a majority of the members.

## WOMEN'S RIGHTS

The Seneca Falls Convention of 1848, the first women's rights convention in American history, was an outgrowth of almost twenty years of female activity in social reform. As described in the chapter opener, the long agenda of rights was drawn directly from the discrimination many women had experienced in social reform groups. Every year after 1848, women gathered to hold women's rights conventions and to work for political, legal, and social equality. Over the years, in response to persistent lobbying, states passed property laws more favorable to women, and altered divorce laws to allow women to retain custody of children. Teaching positions in higher education opened up to women, as did jobs in some other occupations, and women gained the vote in some states, beginning with Wyoming Territory in 1869. In 1920, seventy-two years after universal woman suffrage was first proposed at Seneca Falls, a woman's right to vote was at last guaranteed in the Nineteenth Amendment to the Constitution.

Historians have only recently realized how much the reform movements of this "Age of the Common Man" were due to the efforts of the "common woman." Women played a vital role in all the social movements of the day. In doing so, they implicitly

A CONVENTION OF HEMMERS AND STITCHERS HELD AT LYNN, FEB. 28, FOR ADOPTING A LIST OF PRICES; MRS. E. HALL, PRESIDING.—(See page 284.)

**Women's gatherings**, like the first women's rights convention in Seneca Falls in 1848, and this meeting of strikers in Lynn in 1860, were indicators of widespread female activism.

challenged the popular notion of separate spheres for men and women—the public world for him, home and family for her. The separate spheres argument, although it heaped praise on women for their allegedly superior moral qualities, was meant to exclude them from political life. The reforms discussed in this chapter show clearly that women reformers believed they had a right and a duty to propose solutions for the moral and social problems of the day. Empowered by their own religious beliefs and activism, the Seneca Falls reformers spoke for all American women when they demanded an end to the unfair restrictions they suffered as women.

## CONCLUSION

Beginning in the 1820s, the market revolution changed the size and social order of America's preindustrial cities and towns. Immigration, dramatically rapid population growth, and changes in working life and class structure created a host of new urban problems ranging from sanitation to civic order. These changes occurred so rapidly that they seemed overwhelming. Former face-to-face methods of social control no longer worked. To fill the gap, new kinds of associations—the political party, the religious crusade, the reform cause, the union movement—sprang up. These associations were new manifestations of the deep human desire for social connection, for continuity, and—especially in the growing cities—for social order. A striking aspect of these associations was the uncompromising nature of the attitudes and beliefs on which they were based. Most groups were formed of like-minded people who wanted to impose their will on others. Such intolerance boded ill for the future. If political parties, religious bodies, and reform groups were to splinter along sectional lines (as happened in the 1850s), political compromise would be very difficult. In the meantime, however, Americans came to terms with the market revolution by engaging in a passion for improvement. As a perceptive foreign observer, Francis Grund noted, "Americans love their country not as it is but as it will be."

### QUICK REVIEW

**Seneca Falls Convention**

- 1848: First women's rights convention in American history.
- Every year after 1848 conventions gathered to work for equality.
- Efforts resulted in political and legal advances.

## CHRONOLOGY

| | |
|---|---|
| 1817 | American Colonization Society founded |
| 1820s | Shaker colonies grow |
| 1825 | New Harmony founded, fails three years later |
| 1826 | American Society for the Promotion of Temperance founded |
| 1827 | Workingmen's Party founded in Philadelphia |
| | *Freedom's Journal* begins publication |
| | Public school movement begins in Massachusetts |
| 1829 | David Walker's *Appeal to the Colored Citizens of the World* is published |
| 1830 | Joseph Smith founds Church of Jesus Christ of Latter-Day Saints (Mormon Church) |
| | Charles G. Finney's revivals in Rochester |
| 1831 | William Lloyd Garrison begins publishing antislavery newspaper, the *Liberator* |
| 1832 | Immigration begins to increase |
| 1833 | American Anti-Slavery Society founded by William Lloyd Garrison and Theodore Weld |
| 1834 | First Female Moral Reform Society founded in New York |
| | National Trades Union formed |
| 1836 | Congress passes "gag rule" to prevent discussion of antislavery petitions |

| | |
|---|---|
| 1837 | Antislavery editor Elijah P. Lovejoy killed |
| | Angelina Grimké addresses Massachusetts legislature |
| | Sarah Grimké writes *Letters on the Equality of the Sexes and the Condition of Women* |
| | Panic begins seven-year depression |
| 1839 | Theodore Weld publishes *American Slavery As It Is* |
| 1840s | New York and Boston complete public water systems |
| 1840 | Liberty Party founded |
| 1843 | Millerites await the end of the world |
| | Dorothea Dix spearheads asylum reform movement |
| 1844 | Mormon leader Joseph Smith killed by mob |
| 1845 | New York creates city police force |
| | Beginning of Irish Potato Famine and mass Irish immigration into the United States |
| 1846 | Mormons begin migration to the Great Salt Lake |
| 1848 | Women's Rights Convention at Seneca Falls |
| | John Noyes founds Oneida Community |

## REVIEW QUESTIONS

1. What impact did the new immigration of the 1840s and 1850s have on American cities?
2. Why did urbanization produce so many problems?
3. What motivated the social reformers of the period? Were they benevolent helpers or dictatorial social controllers? Study several reform causes and discuss similarities and differences among them.
4. Abolitionism differed little from other reforms in its tactics, but the effects of antislavery activism were politically explosive. Why was this so?
5. Women were active members of almost every reform group. What reasons might women have given for their unusual degree of participation?

# KEY TERMS

American Colonization Society (p. 343)
American Society for the Promotion of
  Temperance (p. 338)
Declaration of Sentiments (p. 324)
Female Moral Reform Society (p. 339)
Liberty Party (p. 345)

Mormonism (p. 342)
Sabbatarianism (p. 337)
Seneca Falls convention (p. 340)
Shakers (p. 341)
Tammany Society (p. 334)
Temperance (p. 338)

myhistorylab
Flashcard Review

# RECOMMENDED READING

Tyler Anbinder, *Five Points* (2001). A social history of New York's most notorious slum.

Paul Boyer, *Urban Masses and the Moral Order in America, 1820–1920* (1978). Interprets reform as an effort to reestablish the moral order of the preindustrial community.

Kathleen Neils Conzen, *Immigrant Milwaukee, 1836–1860: Accommodation and Community in a Frontier City* (1976). Milwaukee rapidly became the most German city in the nation. This book explains how and why.

David Grimsted, *American Mobbing, 1828–1865: Toward Civil War* (1998). A national perspective on mob violence, North and South, including political violence.

James Oliver Horton and Lois E. Horton, *In Hope of Liberty: Culture, Community and Protest Among Northern Free Blacks, 1700–1860* (1997). A fine portrait that adds the perspective of change over time to earlier studies.

Mary Kelley, *Learning to Stand and Speak: Women, Education, and Public Life in America's Republic* (2006). The centrality of education to women's growing role in civic life.

Bruce Laurie, *Beyond Garrison: Antislavery and Social Reform* (2005). Focus on reformers in Massachusetts shows how antislavery and other social reforms were interconnected.

Steven Mintz, *Moralists and Modernizers: America's Pre–Civil War Reformers* (1995). A brief but inclusive study of reforms and reformers.

David Roediger, *The Wages of Whiteness* (1991). Explores the links between artisanal republicanism, labor organization, and white racism.

Mary Ryan, *Civic Wars: Democracy and Public Life in the American City During the Nineteenth Century* (1997). A study of New York, New Orleans, and San Francisco that argues that urban popular culture was "meeting-place democracy" in action.

Deborah Van Broekhoven, *The Devotion of These Women: Rhode Island in the Antislavery Network* (2002). Shows how informal women's activities sustained antislavery protest at the local level.

myhistorylab
Where it's a good time to connect to the past!

For study resources for this chapter, go to www.**myhistorylab.com** and choose *Out of Many*, *Teaching and Learning Classroom Edition*. You will find a wealth of study and review material for this chapter, including pretests and posttests, customized study plan, key-term review flash cards, interactive map and document activities, and documents for analysis.

*They immigrate constantly, hardly no one
to prevent them, and take possession of
the location that best suits them without either
asking leave or going through any formality
other than that of building their homes.*
—José Maria Sánchez

**Albert Bierstadt (1830–1902), "The Oregon Trail" (oil on canvas).**

# AMERICAN COMMUNITIES
## Texans and Tejanos "Remember the Alamo!"

FOR THIRTEEN DAYS IN FEBRUARY AND MARCH 1836, A FORCE OF 187 Texans held the mission fortress known as the Alamo against a siege by 5,000 Mexican troops under General Antonio López de Santa Anna, president of Mexico. Santa Anna had come north to subdue rebellious Texas, the northernmost part of the Mexican province of Coahuila y Tejas, and to place it under central authority. On March 6 he ordered a final assault, and in brutal fighting that claimed over 1,500 Mexican lives, his army took the mission. All the defenders were killed, including Commander William Travis and the well-known frontiersmen Jim Bowie and Davy Crockett. It was a crushing defeat for the Texans. But the cry "Remember the Alamo!" rallied their remaining forces, which, less than two months later, routed the Mexican army and forced Santa Anna to grant Texas independence from Mexico. Today, the Alamo is one of the most cherished historic sites in the United States.

But memory is selective: within a generation of the uprising, few remembered that many Tejanos, Spanish-speaking people born in Texas, had joined with American settlers fighting for Texas independence.

The Tejano community, descended from eighteenth-century Spanish and Mexican settlers, included wealthy rancheros who raised cattle on the shortgrass prairies of southern Texas, as well as the cowboys known as *vaqueros* and the *peónes*, or poor tenant farmers. The Tejano elite, enthusiastic about American plans for the economic development of Texas, welcomed the American immigrants. Many Americans married into elite Tejano families, who hoped that by thus assimilating and sharing power with the Americans, they could not only maintain but also strengthen their community.

The Mexican state, however, was politically and socially unstable during these first years after its successful revolt against Spain in 1821. When, in 1828, the conservative centralists came to power in Mexico City and decided the Americans had too much influence in Texas, many Tejanos rose up with the Americans in opposition. In 1832, the Tejano elite of San Antonio and many prominent rancheros favored provincial autonomy and a strong role for the Americans.

As Santa Anna's army approached from the south, the wealthy ranchero Juan Nepomuceno Seguín recruited a company of Tejano volunteers and joined the American force inside the walls of the Alamo. In April, Seguín led a regiment of Tejanos in the decisive battle of San Jacinto that won independence for Texas.

Pleased with independence, Tejanos played an important political role in the new Republic of Texas at first. The liberal Lorenzo de Zavala was chosen vice president, and Seguín became the mayor of San Antonio. But soon things began to change. Illustrating a recurring pattern in the American occupation of new lands—a striking shift in the relations between different cultures in frontier areas. Most commonly, in the initial stage newcomers blended with native Peoples, creating a "frontier of inclusion." The first hunters, trappers, and traders on every American frontier—west of the Appalachians, in the Southwest, and in the Far West—married into the local community and tried to learn native ways. Outnumbered American settlers—initially invited in by Mexicans and Tejanos—developed an anti-Mexican passion, regarding all Spanish speakers as their Mexican enemies rather than their Tejano allies. Tejanos were attacked and forced from their homes; some of their villages were burned to the ground. "On the pretext that they were Mexicans," Seguín wrote, Americans treated Tejanos "worse than brutes. . . . My countrymen ran to me for protection against the assaults or exactions of these adventurers." But even in his capacity as mayor, Seguín could do little, and in 1842, he and his family, like hundreds of other Tejano families, fled south to Mexico in fear for their lives.

San Antonio

Spanish-speaking communities in Texas, and later in New Mexico and California, like the communities of Indians throughout the West, became conquered peoples. "White folks and Mexicans were never made to live together," a Texas woman told a traveler a few years after the revolution. "The Mexicans had no business here," she said, and the Americans might "just have to get together and drive them all out of the country." The descendants of the first European settlers of the American Southwest had become foreigners in the land their people had lived in for two centuries.

# 14

# THE TERRITORIAL EXPANSION OF THE UNITED STATES
## 1830s–1850s

**WHAT ROLE** did the federal government play in the exploration of the West?

**WHAT WERE** the major differences between the Oregon, Texas, and California frontiers?

**WHAT WERE** the most important consequences of the Mexican-American War?

**WHAT KINDS** of people participated in the California Gold Rush?

**WHAT KEY** factors explain the outcome of the election of 1848?

# EXPLORING THE WEST

There seemed to be no stopping the expansion of the American people. By 1840, they had occupied all of the land east of the Mississippi River and had organized all of it (except for Florida and Wisconsin) into states. The speed and success of this expansion were a source of deep national pride that whetted appetites for further expansion. Many Americans looked eagerly westward to the vast unsettled reaches of the Louisiana Purchase: to Texas, Santa Fé, to trade with Mexico, and even to the Far West, where New England sea captains had been trading for furs since the 1780s. By 1848, the United States had gained all of these coveted western lands. This chapter examines the way the United States became a continental nation, forming many frontier communities in the process. Exploring the vast continent of North America and gaining an understanding of its geography took several centuries and the efforts of many people.

## THE FUR TRADE

The fur trade, which flourished from the 1670s to the 1840s, was an important spur to exploration on the North American continent. In the 1670s, the British Hudson's Bay Company and its French Canadian rival, Montreal's North West Company, began exploring beyond the Great Lakes in the Canadian West in search of beaver pelts. Indeed, Alexander Mackenzie of the North West Company reached the Pacific Ocean in 1793, becoming the first European to make a transcontinental crossing of North America. Traders and trappers for both companies depended on the goodwill and cooperation of the native peoples of the region. From the marriages of European men with native women arose a distinctive mixed-race group, the "métis" (French for "mixed").

**WHAT ROLE** did the federal government play in the exploration of the West?

**myhistorylab**
Review Summary

## IMAGE KEY

for pages 350–351

**a.** A tanned buffalo skin.

**b.** A long wooden pipe of the Mandan tribe.

**c.** Albert Bierstadt (1830–1902), "The Oregon Trail."

**d.** Cactus with a large pink flower.

**e.** A model of a Plains Indian tepee.

**f.** John Gast's "American Progress," c. 1872, depicting America heading westward.

**g.** "The Interior of Fort Laramie," 1858–1860, by Alfred Jacob Miller.

**h.** "General Winfield Scott at the Siege of Vera Cruz, March 1847" by Nathaniel Currier.

**i.** A drawing of an 1855 San Francisco gambling saloon.

**The artist Alfred** Jacob Miller, a careful observer of the western fur trade, shows a mountain man and his Indian wife in his 1837 *Bourgeois Walker and His Wife.* Walker and his wife worked together to trap and prepare beaver pelts for market, as did other European men and their Indian wives.

Alfred Jacob Miller, "Bourgeois Walker and His Wife," 1837. Watercolor. 37.1940.78. The Walters Art Museum, Baltimore.

Most American trappers, like the British and French before them, sought accommodation and friendship with Indian peoples: nearly half of them contracted long-lasting marriages with Indian women, who not only helped in the trapping and curing of furs but also acted as vital diplomatic links between the white and Indian worlds. One legendary trapper adapted so well that he became a Crow chief: the African American Jim Beckwourth, who married a Crow woman and was accepted into her tribe.

For all its adventure, the American fur trade was short-lived. By the 1840s, the population of beaver in western streams was virtually destroyed, and the day of the mountain man was over. But with daring journeys like that of Jedediah Smith, the first American to enter California over the Sierra Nevada Mountains, the mountain men had helped forge a clear picture of western geography. Soon permanent settlers would follow the trails they had blazed.

## GOVERNMENT-SPONSORED EXPLORATION

Following the lead of fur trade explorers like Alexander Mackenzie, David Thompson and others', the federal government played a major role in the exploration and development of the U.S. West. The exploratory and scientific aspects of the Lewis and Clark expedition in 1804–06 set a precedent for many government-financed quasi-military expeditions. In 1806 and 1807, Lieutenant Zebulon Pike led an expedition to the Rocky Mountains in Colorado. Major Stephen Long's exploration and mapping of the Great Plains in the years 1819–20 was part of a show of force meant to frighten British fur trappers out of the West. Then, in 1843 and 1844, another military explorer, John C. Frémont, mapped the overland trails to Oregon and California. In the 1850s, the Pacific Railroad surveys explored possible transcontinental railroad routes (see Map 14.1).

In the wake of the pathfinders came hundreds of government geologists and botanists as well as the surveyors who mapped and plotted the West for settlement according to the Land Ordinance of 1785. The basic pattern of land survey and sale established by these measures (see Chapter 7) was followed all the way to the Pacific Ocean. The federal government sold the western public lands at low prices. The federal government also shouldered the expense of Indian removal by making long-term commitments to compensate the Indian people themselves and supporting the forts and soldiers whose task was to maintain peace between settlers and Indian peoples in newly opened areas.

## EXPANSION AND INDIAN POLICY

While American artists were painting the way of life of western Indian peoples, eastern Indian tribes were being removed from their homelands to Indian Territory (present-day Oklahoma, Kansas, and Nebraska), a region west of Arkansas, Missouri, and Iowa on the eastern edge of the Great Plains, widely regarded as unfarmable and popularly known as the Great American Desert.

Encroachment on Indian Territory was not long in coming (see Map 14.2). The territory was crossed by the **Santa Fé Trail**, established in 1821; in the 1840s, the northern part was crossed by the heavily traveled Overland Trails to California, Oregon, and the Mormon community in Utah. In 1854, the government abolished the northern half of Indian Territory, establishing the Kansas and Nebraska Territories in its place and opening them to immediate white settlement. The tribes of the area—the Potawatomis, Wyandots, Kickapoos, Sauks, Foxes, Delawares, Shawnees, Kaskaskias, Peorias, Piankashaws, Weas, Miamis, Omahas, Otos, and Missouris—signed treaties accepting either vastly reduced reservations or allotments. Those who accepted allotments—sections of private land—

**Santa Fé Trail** The 900-mile trail opened by American merchants for trading purposes following Mexico's liberalization of the formerly restrictive trading policies of Spain.

**Legend:**
- Mackenzie, 1793
- Lewis and Clark, 1804–06
- Zebulon Pike, 1806–07
- Fraser, 1808
- Thompson, 1810–11
- Stephen Long, 1819–20
- Jedediah Smith, 1822–30

**MAP 14.1**

**Exploration of the Continent, 1804–30**   Members of British fur trading companies like Alexander Mackenzie and David Thompson led the way. Lewis and Clark's "voyage of discovery" of 1804–06 was the first of many U.S. government-sponsored western military expeditions. Lieutenant Zebulon Pike crossed the Great Plains in 1806, followed by Major Stephen Long in 1819–20. Meanwhile, American fur trappers, among them the much-traveled Jedediah Smith, became well acquainted with the Far West as they hunted beaver for their pelts.

WHAT ROLE did the routes taken by major expeditions westward between 1804 and 1830 play in shaping United States policy in the West?

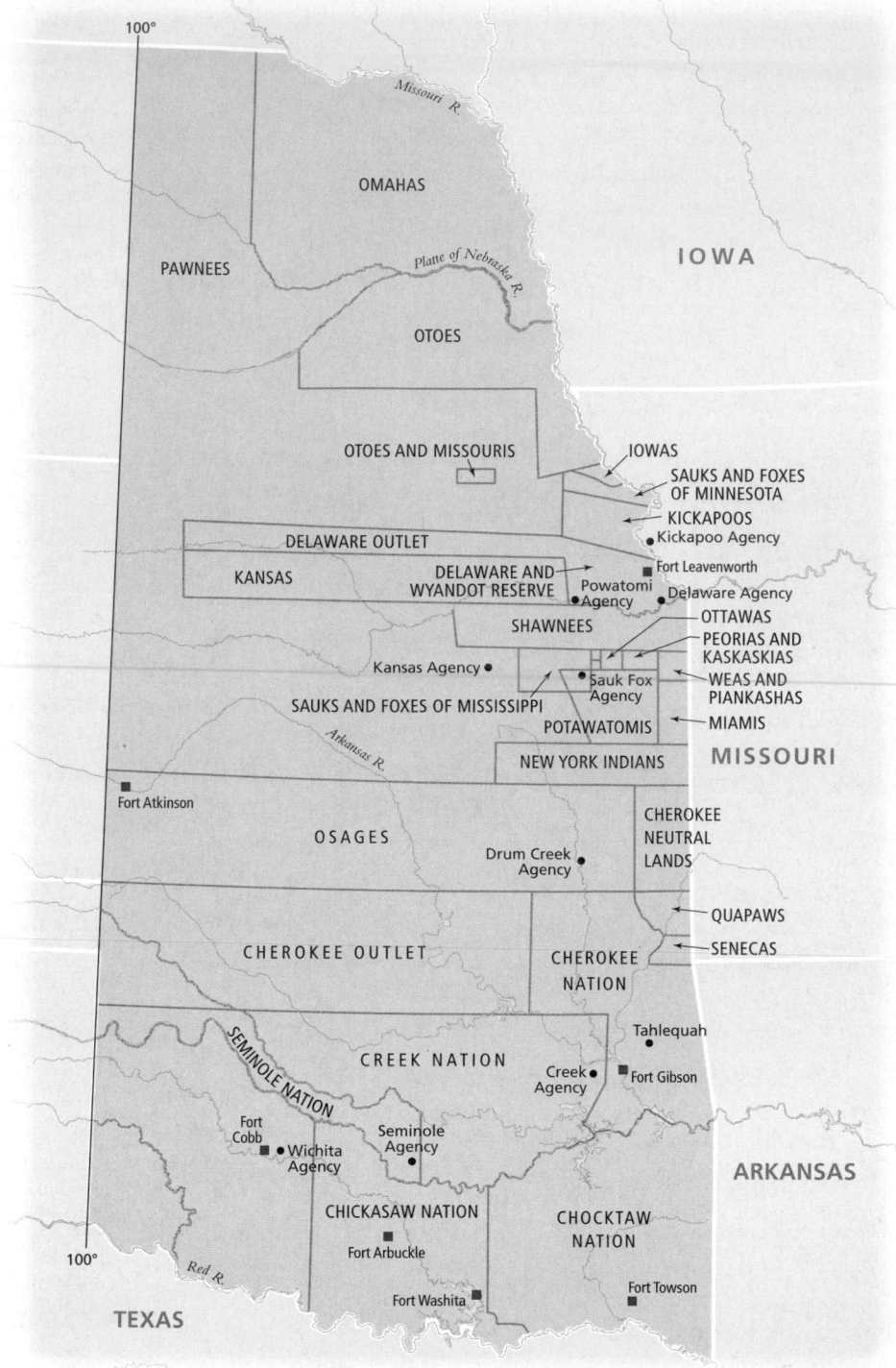

**MAP 14.2**

**Indian Territory Before the Kansas-Nebraska Act of 1854**    Indian Territory lay west of Arkansas, Missouri, and Iowa and east of Mexican Territory. Most of the Indian peoples who lived there in the 1830s and the 1840s had been "removed" from east of the Mississippi River. The southern part (now Oklahoma) was inhabited by peoples from the Old Southwest: the Cherokees, Chickasaws, Choctaws, Creeks, and Seminoles. North of that (in what is now Kansas and Nebraska) lived peoples who had been removed from the Old Northwest. All these Indian peoples had trouble adjusting not only to a new climate and a new way of life but also to the close proximity of some Indian tribes who were their traditional enemies.

DISCUSS THE effect of the Kansas-Nebraska Act on Indian tribes and territories.

often sold them, under pressure, to white people. Thus, many of the Indian people who had hoped for independence and escape from white pressures in Indian Territory lost both their autonomy and their tribal identity.

The people in the southern part of Indian Territory, in what is now Oklahoma, fared somewhat better. Those members of the southern tribes—the Cherokees, Chickasaws, Choctaws, Creeks, and Seminoles—who had survived the trauma of forcible removal from the Southeast in the 1830s, quickly created impressive new communities. Until after the Civil War, these southern tribes were able to withstand outside pressures and remain the self-governing communities that treaties had assured them they would be.

# THE POLITICS OF EXPANSION

America's rapid expansion had many consequences, but perhaps the most significant was that it reinforced Americans' sense of themselves as pioneering people. Ever since the time of Daniel Boone, venturing into the wilderness has held a special place in the American imagination and been seen almost as a right.

## MANIFEST DESTINY, AN EXPANSIONIST IDEOLOGY

How did Americans justify their restless expansionism? After all, the United States was already a very large country with much undeveloped land. In 1845, newspaperman John O'Sullivan provided such a justification. It was, he wrote, "our **manifest destiny** to overspread the continent allotted by Providence for the free development of our yearly multiplying millions." Sullivan argued that Americans had a God-given right to bring the benefits of American democracy to other, more backward peoples—meaning Mexicans and Indians—by force, if necessary. The notion of manifest destiny summed up the powerful combination of pride in what America had achieved and missionary zeal and racist attitudes toward other peoples that lay behind the thinking of many expansionists. Americans were proud of their rapid development: the surge in population, the remarkable canals and railroads, the grand scale of the American enterprise. Why shouldn't America be even bigger?

Expansionism was deeply tied to national politics. O'Sullivan, whose "manifest destiny" became the expansionist watchword, was not a neutral observer: he was the editor of the *Democratic Review,* a party newspaper. Most Democrats were wholehearted supporters of expansion, whereas many Whigs (especially in the North) opposed it. Whigs welcomed most of the changes brought by industrialization but advocated strong government policies that would guide growth and development within the country's existing boundaries. They feared (correctly, as it turned out) that expansion would raise the contentious issue of the extension of slavery to new territories.

On the other hand, many Democrats feared the industrialization that the Whigs welcomed. Where the Whigs saw economic progress, Democrats saw economic depression, uncontrolled urban growth, and growing social unrest. For many Democrats, the answer to the nation's social ills was to continue to follow Thomas Jefferson's vision of establishing agriculture in the new territories in order to counterbalance industrialization. Another factor in the political struggle over expansion in the 1840s was that many Democrats were Southerners, for whom the continual expansion of cotton-growing lands was a matter of social faith as well as economic necessity.

**WHAT WERE** the major differences between the Oregon, Texas, and California frontiers?

myhistorylab
Review Summary

**12–4**
John L. O'Sullivan, *The Great Nation of Futurity* (1845)

**Manifest destiny** Doctrine, first expressed in 1845, that the expansion of white Americans across the continent was inevitable and ordained by God.

**MAP 14.3**

**The Overland Trails, 1840** All the great trails west started at the Missouri River. The Oregon, California, and Mormon Trails followed the Platte River into Wyoming, crossed South Pass, and divided in western Wyoming. The much harsher Santa Fé Trail stretched 900 miles southwest across the Great Plains. All of the trails crossed Indian Territory and, to greater or lesser extent, Mexican possessions as well.

WHAT DANGERS did settlers face as they followed the overland trails?

These were politicians' reasons. The average farmer moved west for many other reasons: land hunger, national pride, plain and simple curiosity, and a sense of adventure.

## THE OVERLAND TRAILS

The 2,000-mile trip on the Overland Trails from the banks of the Missouri River to Oregon and California usually took seven months, sometimes more. Travel was slow, dangerous, tedious, and exhausting. Yet despite the risks, settlers streamed west: 5,000 to Oregon by 1845 and about 3,000 to California by 1848 (before the discovery of gold) (see Map 14.3).

Pioneers had many motives for making the trip. Glowing reports from Oregon's Willamette Valley, for example, seemed to promise economic opportunity and healthy surroundings, an alluring combination to farmers in the malaria-prone Midwest who had been hard hit by the Panic of 1837. But rational motives do not tell the whole story. Many men were motivated by a sense of adventure, by a desire to experience the unknown.

**12–3**
*Across the Plains with Catherine Sager Pringle* (1844)

**17–2**
*Lydia Allen Rudd, Diary of Westward Travel* (1852)

Few pioneers traveled alone, partly because they feared Indian attack (which was rare) but largely because they needed help fording rivers or crossing mountains with heavy wagons. Most Oregon pioneers traveled with their families but usually also joined a larger group, forming a "train." In the earliest years, when the route was still uncertain, trains hired "pilots," generally former fur trappers.

Wagon trains started westward as soon as the prairies were green (thus ensuring feed for the livestock). The daily routine was quickly established. Men took care of the moving equipment and the animals, while the women cooked and kept track of the children. Slowly, at a rate of about fifteen miles a day, the wagon trains moved west. In addition to tedium and exhaustion, wagon trains were beset by such trail hazards as illness and accident. Danger from Indian attack, which all pioneers feared, was actually very small. It appears that unprovoked white attacks on Indians were more common than the reverse.

In contrast, cholera killed at least a thousand people a year in 1849 and in the early 1850s, when it was common along sections of the trail along the Platte River. Drownings were not uncommon, nor were accidental ax wounds or shootings, and children sometimes fell out of wagons and were run over. The members of the wagon train community provided support for survivors: men helped widows drive their wagons onward, women nursed and tended babies whose mothers were dead, and at least one parentless family, the seven Sager children, were brought to Oregon in safety.

By 1860, almost 300,000 people had traveled the Overland Trails to Oregon or California. Ruts from the wagon wheels can be seen in a number of places along the route even today. In 1869, the completion of the transcontinental railroad marked the end of the wagon train era (see Figure 14.1).

**This painting by** William Henry Jackson shows the wagon of westward migrants waiting at Council Bluffs, Iowa, to cross the Missouri River on the ferry established by the Mormons. At the height of the migration this was a major bottleneck: some people waited as long as ten days for their turn to cross.

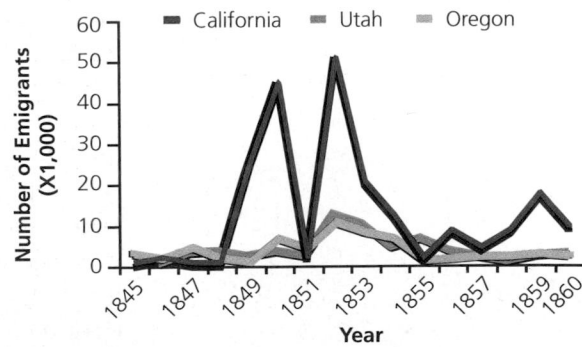

**Figure 14.1 Overland Emigration to Oregon, California, and Utah, 1840–60**

Before 1849, the westward migration consisted primarily of family groups going to Oregon or Utah. The discovery of gold in California dramatically changed the migration: through 1854, most migrants were single men "rushing" to California, which remained the favored destination up until 1860. Over the twenty-year period from 1840 to 1860, the Overland Trails were transformed from difficult and dangerous routes to well-marked and well-served thoroughfares.

John Unruh Jr., *The Plains Across* (Champaign-Urbana: University of Illinois Press, 1979), pp. 119–20.

## OREGON

The American settlement of Oregon provides a capsule example of the stages of frontier development. The first contacts between the region's Indian peoples and Europeans were commercial. Spanish, British, Russian, and American ships traded for sea otter skins from the 1780s to about 1810. Subsequently, land-based groups scoured the region for beaver skins as well. In this first "frontier of inclusion" there were frequent contacts, many of them sexual, between Indians and Europeans.

Both Great Britain and the United States claimed the Oregon Country by right of discovery, but in the Convention of 1818, the two nations agreed to occupy it jointly, postponing a final decision on its disposition. In reality, the British clearly dominated the region. In 1824, the Hudson's Bay Company consolidated Britain's position by establishing a major fur trading post at Fort Vancouver, on the banks of the Columbia River. Like all fur-trading ventures, the post exemplified the racial mixing of a "frontier of inclusion." Fort Vancouver housed a polyglot population of eastern Indians (Delawares and Iroquois), local Chinook Indians, French and métis from Canada, British traders, and Hawaiians. But the effect of the fur trade on native tribes in Oregon was catastrophic; suffering the fate of all Indian peoples after their initial contact with Europeans, they were decimated by European diseases.

The first permanent European settlers in Oregon were retired fur trappers and their Indian wives and families. The next to arrive were Protestant and Catholic. None of these missionaries was very successful. Epidemics had taken the lives of many of the region's peoples, and those who were left were disinclined to give up their nomadic life and settle down as the missionaries wanted them to do.

Finally, in the 1840s, came the Midwest farmers who would make up the majority of Oregon's permanent settlers, carried on the wave of enthusiasm known as "Oregon fever" and lured by free land and patriotism. By 1845, Oregon boasted 5,000 American settlers, most of them living in the Willamette Valley and laying claim to lands to which they had as yet no legal right. Their arrival signaled Oregon's transition away from a "frontier of inclusion."

In June 1846, Britain and the United States concluded a treaty establishing the 49th parallel as the U.S.–Canada border but leaving the island of Vancouver in British hands. The British then quietly wound up their declining fur trade in the region. In 1849, the Hudson's Bay Company closed Fort Vancouver and moved its operations to Victoria, thus ending the Pacific Northwest's largely successful experience with joint occupancy. Oregon's Donation Land Claim Act of 1850 codified the practice of giving 320 acres to each white male age eighteen or over and 640 acres to each married couple to settle in the territory (African Americans, Hawaiians, and American Indians were excluded).

The white settlers realized that they had to forge strong community bonds if they hoped to survive on their distant frontier. Cooperation and mutual aid were the rule. Until well into the 1850s, residents organized yearly parties that traveled back along the last stretches of the **Oregon Trail** to help straggling parties making their way to the territory. Kinship networks were strong and vital: many pioneers came to join family who had migrated before them. Food sharing and mutual labor were essential in the early years when crop and livestock loss to weather or natural predators was common. Help, even to total strangers, was customary in times of illness or death.

Relations with the small and unthreatening disease-thinned local Indian tribes were generally peaceful until 1847, when Cayuse Indians killed the missionaries Marcus and Narcissa Whitman. Their deaths triggered a series of "wars" against the remaining native people. A "frontier of exclusion" had been achieved.

**Oregon Trail** Overland trail of more than two thousand miles that carried American settlers from the Midwest to new settlements in Oregon, California, and Utah.

**This view of** Fort Vancouver on the Columbia River shows established agriculture and thriving commerce, indicated by the large sailing ship on the river, which is probably the Hudson's Bay Company yearly supply ship from England. It was a scene like this that led Narcissa Whitman to call Fort Vancouver "the New York of the Pacific."

Nonetheless, the process by which Oregon became part of the United States (it was admitted as a state in 1859) was relatively peaceful, especially when compared with American expansion into the Spanish provinces of New Mexico and Texas.

## THE SANTA FÉ TRADE

Commerce with Santa Fé, first settled by colonists from Mexico in 1609, and the center of the Spanish frontier province of New Mexico, had long been desired by American traders. But Spain had forcefully resisted American penetration.

When Mexico gained its independence from Spain in 1821, this exclusionary policy changed. American traders were now welcome in Santa Fé, but the trip over the legendary Santa Fé Trail from Independence, Missouri, was a forbidding 900 miles of arid plains, deserts, and mountains. The number of people venturing west in the trading caravans increased yearly because the profits were so great. By the 1840s, a few hundred American trappers and traders (called *extranjeros*, or "foreigners") lived permanently in New Mexico. In Santa Fé, some American merchants married daughters of important local families, suggesting the start of the inclusive stage of frontier contact.

**Tejanos** Persons of Spanish or
Mexican descent born in Texas.

Settlements and trading posts soon grew up along the long Santa Fé Trail. One of the most famous was Bent's Fort, on the Arkansas River in what is now eastern Colorado, which did a brisk trade in beaver skins and buffalo robes. Like most trading posts, it had a multiethnic population. This racially and economically mixed existence was characteristic of all early trading frontiers, but another western frontier, the American agricultural settlement in Texas, was different from the start.

## MEXICAN TEXAS

In 1821, when Mexico gained its independence from Spain, there were 2,240 Tejano (Spanish-speaking) residents of Texas. As was customary throughout New Spain, communities were organized around three centers: missions and *presidios* (forts), which formed the nuclei of towns, and the large cattle-raising ranchos on which rural living depended. As elsewhere in New Spain, society was divided into two classes: the *ricos* (rich), who claimed Spanish descent, and the mixed-blood *pobres* (poor). Most **Tejanos** were neither ricos nor vaqueros but small farmers or common laborers who led hardscrabble frontier lives. But all Tejanos, rich and poor, faced the constant threat of raids by Comanche Indians.

Legendary warriors, the Comanches raided the small Texas settlements at will and even struck deep into Mexico itself. The nomadic Comanches followed the immense buffalo herds on which they depended for food and clothing. Their relentless raids on the Texas settlements rose from a determination to hold onto this rich buffalo territory, for the buffalo provided all that they wanted. They had no interest in being converted by mission priests or incorporated into mixed-race trading communities.

## AMERICANS IN TEXAS

In 1821, seeking to increase the strength of its buffer zone between the heart of Mexico and the marauding Comanches, the Mexican government granted Moses Austin of Missouri an area of 18,000 square miles within the territory of Texas. Moses died shortly thereafter, and the grant was taken up by his son Stephen F. Austin, who became the first American empresario (land agent). From the beginning, the American settlement of Texas differed markedly from that of other frontiers. Elsewhere, Americans frequently settled on land to which Indian peoples still held title, or, as in the case of Oregon, they occupied lands to which other

**Painted by George** Catlin in about 1834, this scene, *Commanche Village Life*, shows how the everyday life of the Comanches was tied to buffalo. The women in the foreground are scraping buffalo hide, and buffalo meat can be seen drying on racks. The men and boys may be planning their next buffalo hunt.

countries also made claim. In contrast, the Texas settlement was fully legal: Austin and other **empresarios** owned their lands as a result of formal contracts with the Mexican government.

Insisting that "no frontiersman who has no other occupation than that of hunter will be received—no drunkard, no gambler, no profane swearer, no idler," Austin chose instead prosperous southern slave owners eager to expand the lands devoted to cotton. Soon Americans (including African American slaves, to whose presence the Mexican government turned a blind eye) outnumbered Tejanos by nearly two to one.

The Austin settlement of 1821 was followed by others, twenty-six in all, concentrating in the fertile river bottoms of eastern Texas (along the Sabine River) and south central Texas (the Brazos and the Colorado Rivers). These large settlements were highly organized farming enterprises whose principal crop was cotton, grown by African American slave labor and sold in the international market.

Austin's colonists and those who settled later were predominantly Southerners who viewed Texas as a natural extension of the cotton frontier in Mississippi and Louisiana. These settlers created "**enclaves**" (self-contained communities) that had little contact with Tejanos or Indian peoples. In fact, although they lived in Mexican territory, most Americans never bothered to learn Spanish. Yet, because of the nature of agreements made by the empresarios, the Americans could not set up local American-style governments like the one created by settlers in Oregon. Like the immigrants who flooded into East Coast cities (see Chapter 13), the Americans in Texas were immigrants to another country—but one to which they did not intend to adapt.

For a brief period, Texas was big enough to hold three communities: Comanche, Tejano, and American. Each group would fight to hold its land: the Comanches, their rich hunting grounds; the Mexicans, their towns and ranchos; and the newcomers, the Americans, their rich land grants.

The balance among the three communities in Texas was broken in 1828, when centrists gained control of the government in Mexico City and, in a dramatic shift of policy, decided to exercise firm control over the northern province. As the Mexican government restricted American immigration, outlawed slavery, levied customs duties and taxes, and planned other measures, Americans seethed and talked of rebellion. Bolstering their cause were as many as 20,000 additional Americans, many of them openly expansionist, who flooded into Texas after 1830.

Many of the post-1830 immigrants were vehemently anti-Mexican. Statements of racial superiority were commonplace, and even Stephen Austin wrote in 1836 that he saw the Texas conflict as one of barbarism on the part of "a mongrel Spanish-Indian and negro race, against civilization and the Anglo-American race."

Between 1830 and 1836, in spite of the mediation efforts of Austin, the mood on both the Mexican and the American-Texan sides became more belligerent. In the fall of 1835, war finally broke out, and a volunteer American and Tejano army assembled. After the disastrous defeat at the **Alamo** described in the chapter opener, Mexican general and president Antonio López de Santa Anna led his army in pursuit of the remaining army of American and Tejano volunteers commanded by General Sam Houston.

On April 21, 1836, at the San Jacinto River in eastern Texas, Santa Anna thought he had Houston trapped at last. Confident of victory against the exhausted Texans, Santa Anna's army rested in the afternoon, failing even to post sentries. Although Houston advised against it, Houston's men voted to attack immediately rather than wait till the next morning. Shouting "Remember the Alamo!" for the first time, the Texans completely surprised their opponents and won an overwhelming victory. On May 14, 1836, Santa Anna signed a treaty fixing the southern boundary of the newly independent Republic of Texas at the Rio Grande. The

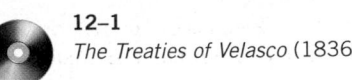

12–1
*The Treaties of Velasco* (1836)

**Empresarios**   Agents who received a land grant from the Spanish or Mexican government in return for organizing settlements.

**Enclave**   Self-contained community.

**Alamo**   Franciscan mission at San Antonio, Texas that was the site in 1836 of a siege and massacre of Texans by Mexican troops.

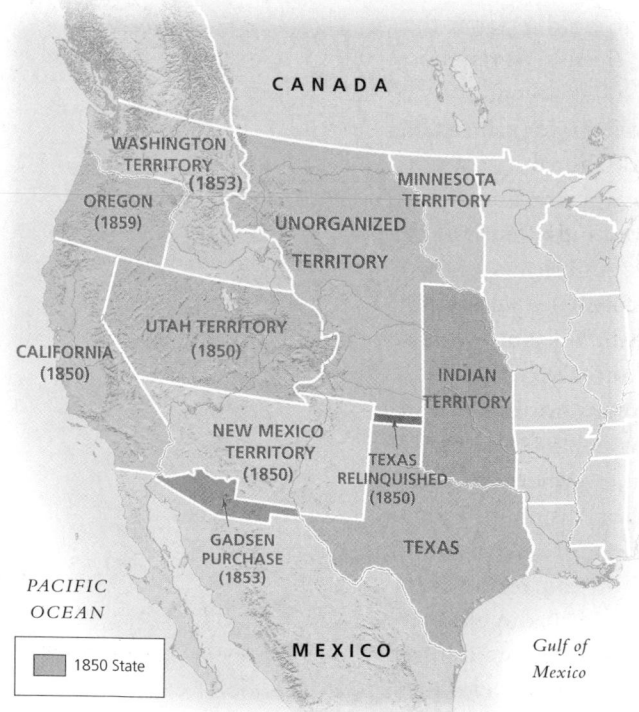

**MAP 14.4**

**Texas: From Mexican Province to U.S. State**   In the space of twenty years, Texas changed shape three times. Initially part of the Mexican province of Coahuila y Tejas, it became the Republic of Texas in 1836, following the Texas Revolt, and was annexed to the United States in that form in 1845. Finally, in the Compromise of 1850 following the Mexican-American War, it took its present shape.

WHO SUPPORTED the formation of the Republic of Texas? What were the forces that resulted in eventual statehood?

Mexican Congress, however, repudiated the treaty and refused to recognize Texan independence (see Map 14.4).

## THE REPUBLIC OF TEXAS

The Republic of Texas was unexpectedly rebuffed in another quarter as well. The U.S. Congress refused to grant it statehood when, in 1837, Texas applied for admission to the Union. Petitions opposing the admission of a fourteenth slave state (there were then thirteen free states) poured into Congress. Congressman (and former president) John Quincy Adams of Massachusetts led the opposition to the admission of Texas. Congress debated and ultimately dropped the Texas application.

The unresolved conflict with Mexico put heavy stress on American–Tejano relations. As before, ambitious Anglos married into the Tejano elite, which made it easier for those Tejano families to adjust to the changes in law and commerce that the Americans quickly enacted. But following a temporary recapture of San Antonio by Mexican forces in 1842, positions hardened. Many more of the Tejano elite fled to Mexico, and Americans discussed banishing or imprisoning all Tejanos until the border issue was settled. This was, of course, impossible. Culturally, San Antonio remained a Mexican city long after the Americans had declared independence.

American control over the other Texas residents, the Indians, was also slow in coming. The Comanches still rode the high plains of northern and western Texas. West of the Rio Grande, equally fierce Apache bands were in control. Both groups soon learned to distrust American promises to stay out of their territory, and they did not hesitate to raid settlements and to kill trespassers. Not until after the Civil War and major campaigns by the U.S. Army were these fierce Indian tribes conquered.

Texans continued to press for annexation to the United States, while at the same time seeking recognition and support from Great Britain. The idea of an independent and expansionist republic on its southern border that might gain the support of America's traditional enemy alarmed many Americans. Annexation thus became an urgent matter of national politics. This issue also added to the troubles of a governing Whig Party that was already deeply divided by the policies of John Tyler, who had become president by default when William Harrison died in office (see Chapter 11). Tyler raised the issue of annexation in 1844, hoping thereby to ensure his reelection, but the strategy backfired. Presenting the annexation treaty to Congress, Secretary of State John Calhoun awakened sectional fears by connecting Texas with the urgent need of southern slave owners to extend slavery.

In a storm of antislavery protest, Whigs rejected the treaty proposed by their own president and ejected Tyler himself from the party. In his place, they chose Henry Clay, the party's longtime standard-bearer, as their presidential candidate. Clay took a noncommittal stance on Texas, favoring annexation, but only if Mexico approved. Since Mexico's emphatic disapproval was well known, Clay's position was widely interpreted as a politician's effort not to alienate voters on either side of the fence.

In contrast, in the Democratic Party, wholehearted and outspoken expansionists seized control. The Democrats nominated their first "dark horse" candidate, James K. Polk of Tennessee. Democrats enthusiastically endorsed Polk's platform, which called for "the re-occupation of Oregon and the re-annexation of Texas at the earliest practicable period."

Polk won the 1844 election by a narrow margin. The 1844 election was widely interpreted as a mandate for expansion. Thereupon, John Tyler, in one of his last actions as president, pushed through Congress a joint resolution (which did not require the two-thirds approval by the Senate necessary for treaties) for the annexation of Texas. When Texas entered the Union in December 1845, it was the twenty-eighth state and the fifteenth slave state.

# THE MEXICAN-AMERICAN WAR

James K. Polk lived up to his campaign promises. In 1846, he peacefully added Oregon south of the 49th parallel to the United States; in 1848, following the **Mexican-American War**, he acquired Mexico's northern provinces of California and New Mexico as well. Thus, with the annexation of Texas, the United States, in the short space of three years, had added 1.5 million square miles of territory, an increase of nearly 70 percent. Polk was indeed the "manifest destiny" president.

## ORIGINS OF THE WAR

In the spring of 1846, just as the controversy over Oregon was drawing to a peaceful conclusion, tensions with Mexico grew more serious. Because the United States supported the Texas claim of all land north of the Rio Grande, it became embroiled

**WHAT WERE** the most important consequences of the Mexican-American War?

**myhistorylab**
Review Summary

Mexican-American War   War fought between Mexico and the United States between 1846 and 1848 over control of territory in southwest North America.

in a border dispute with Mexico. In June 1845, Polk sent General Zachary Taylor to Texas, and by October a force of 3,500 Americans were on the Nueces River with orders to defend Texas in the event of a Mexican invasion.

Polk had something bigger than border protection in mind. He coveted the continent clear to the Pacific Ocean. At the same time that he sent Taylor to Texas, Polk secretly instructed the Pacific naval squadron to seize the California ports if Mexico declared war. He also wrote the American consul in Monterey, Thomas Larkin, that a peaceful takeover of California by its residents—Spanish Mexicans and Americans alike—would not be unwelcome.

In April 1846, a brief skirmish between American and Mexican soldiers broke out in the disputed zone. Polk seized on the event, sending a war message to Congress: "Mexico has passed the boundary of the United States, has invaded our territory and shed American blood upon American soil. . . . War exists, and, notwithstanding all our efforts to avoid it, exists by the act of Mexico herself." This claim of President Polk's was, of course, contrary to fact. On May 13, 1846, Congress declared war on Mexico (see Map 14.5).

## MR. POLK'S WAR

From the beginning, the Mexican-American War was politically divisive. Whig critics in Congress, among them a gawky young congressman from Illinois named Abraham Lincoln, questioned Polk's account of the border incident. They accused the president of misleading Congress and of maneuvering the country into an unnecessary war. As the Mexican-American War dragged on and casualties and costs mounted, opposition increased, especially among northern antislavery Whigs. Many Northerners asked why Polk had been willing to settle for only a part of Oregon but was so eager to pursue a war for slave territory. Thus, expansionist dreams served to fuel sectional antagonisms.

Whigs termed the war with Mexico "Mr. Polk's War," but the charge was not just a Whig jibe. Although he lacked a military background, Polk assumed the overall planning of the war's strategy. By his personal attention to the coordination of civilian political goals and military requirements, Polk gave a new and expanded definition to the

LANDING OF THE AMERICAN FORCES UNDER GENL SCOTT
AT VERA CRUZ MARCH 9th 1847

**General Winfield Scott's** amphibious attack on the Mexican coastal city of Veracruz in March 1847 was greeted with wide popular acclaim in the United States. It was the first successful amphibious attack in U.S. military history. Popular interest in the battles of the Mexican-American War was fed by illustrations such as this in newspapers and magazines.

**MAP 14.5**

**The Mexican-American War, 1846–48**   The Mexican-American War began with an advance by U.S. forces into the disputed area between the Nueces River and the Rio Grande in Texas. The war's major battles were fought by General Zachary Taylor in northern Mexico and General Winfield Scott in Veracruz and Mexico City. Meanwhile Colonel Stephen Kearny secured New Mexico and, with the help of the U.S. Navy and John C. Frémont's troops, California.

WHY WAS the United States more successful than Mexico in achieving its goals?

role of the president as commander in chief during wartime. By the end of 1846, the northern provinces that Polk had coveted were secured, but contrary to his expectations, Mexico refused to negotiate. In March 1847, General Winfield Scott launched an amphibious attack on the coastal city of Veracruz and rapidly captured it. Americans celebrated these twin victories joyously, but they were to be the last easy victories of the war. It took Scott six months of brutal fighting against stubborn Mexican resistance on the battlefield and harassing guerrilla raids to force his way to Mexico City. American troops reacted bitterly to their high casualty rates, retaliating against Mexican citizens with acts of murder, robbery, and rape. In September, Scott took Mexico City, and Mexican resistance came to an end.

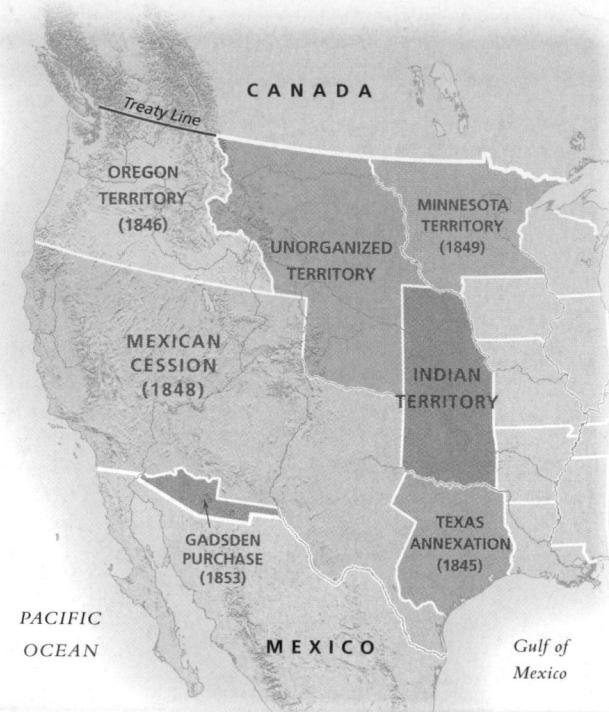

**MAP 14.6**

**Territory Added, 1845–53**    James K. Polk was elected president in 1844 on an expansionist platform. He lived up to most of his campaign rhetoric by gaining the Oregon Country (to the 49th parallel) peacefully from the British, Texas by the presidential action of his predecessor John Tyler, and present-day California, Arizona, Nevada, Utah, New Mexico, and part of Colorado by war with Mexico. In the short space of three years, the size of the United States grew by 70 percent. In 1853, the Gadsden Purchase added another 30,000 square miles.

WHAT CHALLENGES did the United States face as it absorbed substantial new territories?

**12–5**
Thomas Corwin, *Against the Mexican War* (1847)

**WHAT KINDS** of people participated in the California Gold Rush?

**myhistorylab**

**Review Summary**

Californios    Californians of Spanish descent.

With the American army went a special envoy, Nicholas Trist, who delivered Polk's terms for peace. In the Treaty of Guadalupe Hidalgo, signed February 2, 1848, Mexico ceded its northern provinces of California and New Mexico (which included present-day Arizona, Utah, Nevada, and part of Colorado) and accepted the Rio Grande as the boundary of Texas. The United States agreed to pay Mexico $15 million and assume about $2 million in individual claims against that nation.

When Trist returned to Washington with the treaty, however, Polk was furious. He had actually recalled Trist after Scott's sweeping victory, intending to send a new envoy with greater demands, but Trist had ignored the recall order. "All Mexico!" had become the phrase widely used by those in favor of further expansion, Polk among them. But two very different groups opposed further expansion. The first group, composed of northern Whigs. The second group was composed of Southerners who realized that Mexicans could not be kept as conquered people but would have to be offered territorial government as Louisiana had been offered in 1804. Bowing to these political protests, Polk reluctantly accepted the treaty. A later addition, the $10 million Gadsden Purchase of parts of present-day New Mexico and Arizona, added another 30,000 square miles to the United States in 1853 (see Map 14.6).

## THE PRESS AND POPULAR WAR ENTHUSIASM

The Mexican-American War was the first war in which regular, on-the-scene reporting by representatives of the press caught the mass of ordinary citizens up in the war's daily events. Thanks to the recently invented telegraph, newspapers could get the latest news from their reporters, who were among the world's first war correspondents. The "penny press," with more than a decade's experience of reporting urban crime and scandals, was quick to realize that the public's appetite for sensational war news was apparently insatiable. For the first time in American history, accounts by journalists, and not the opinions of politicians, became the major shapers of popular attitudes toward a war. From beginning to end, news of the war stirred unprecedented popular excitement (see Seeing History).

Exciting, sobering, and terrible, war news had a deep hold on the popular imagination. It was a lesson newspaper publishers never forgot.

## CALIFORNIA AND THE GOLD RUSH

In the early 1840s, California was inhabited by many seminomadic Indian tribes whose people numbered approximately 50,000. There were also some 7,000 **Californios**, descendants of the Spanish-Mexican pioneers who had begun to settle in 1769. Even American annexation at the end of the Mexican-American War changed little for the handful of Americans on this remote frontier. But then came the gold rush of 1849, which changed California permanently.

# War News from Mexico

The unprecedented immediacy of the news reporting from the battlefields of the Mexican-American War, transmitted for the first time by telegraph, is captured in this painting by the American artist Richard Caton Woodville, painted in 1848 (the year the war ended). Woodville was one of a number of genre painters who enlivened their depictions of everyday life and ordinary people by focusing on political debates or dramatic moments like the one shown here.

Almost every aspect of this painting is political commentary. The central figure in the painting is standing on the porch of the American Hotel reading the latest war news to the crowd of men gathered around him from a cheap "penny paper" full of sensational stories, war news, and lithographs of battle scenes from the war. Although the audience seems deeply engaged, the range of expressions reminds the viewer that the war was very divisive, with many antislavery Northerners in outright opposition. The placement of the African American man at a lower level on the step is a clear statement of his exclusion from political participation. Don't overlook the woman leaning out of the window on the right side of the painting. She too is excluded from politics but is obviously just as interested and concerned as the men. Woodville's inclusion of the black child in a white smock seems to be an ambiguous statement about the impact of the Mexican-American War on slavery. ∎

**ARE YOU** surprised at the extent of political commentary in this painting? Are paintings an appropriate media for political opinion?

Richard Caton Woodville, "War News from Mexico," Oil on canvas. Manovgian Foundation on loan to the National Gallery of Art, Washington, DC. © Board of Trustees, National Gallery of Art, Washington.

## RUSSIAN–CALIFORNIOS TRADE

The first outsiders to penetrate the isolation of Spanish California were not Americans but Russians. A mutually beneficial barter of California food for iron tools and woven cloth from Russia was established in 1806. This arrangement became even brisker after the Russians settled Fort Ross (near present-day Mendocino) in 1812 and led in time to regular trade with Mission San Rafael and Mission Sonoma. That the Russians in Alaska, so far from their own capital, were better supplied with manufactured goods than the Californios is an index of the latter's isolation.

When Mexico became independent in 1821, the California trade was thrown open to ships of all nations. Nevertheless, Californios continued their special relationship with the Russians, exempting them from the taxes and inspections that they required of Americans. However, agricultural productivity declined after 1832, when the Mexican government ordered the secularization of the California missions, and the Russians regretfully turned to the rich farms of the Hudson's Bay Company in the Pacific Northwest for their food supply. In 1841, they sold Fort Ross, and the Russian–Californio connection came to an end.

## EARLY AMERICAN SETTLEMENT

It was Johann Augustus Sutter, a Swiss who had settled in California in 1839, becoming a Mexican citizen, who served as a focal point for American settlement in the 1840s. In the 1840s, Sutter offered valuable support to the handful of American overlanders who chose California over Oregon, the destination preferred by most pioneers. Most of these Americans, keenly aware that they were interlopers in Mexican territory, settled near Sutter in California's Central Valley, away from the Californios clustered along the coast.

The 1840s' immigrants made no effort to intermarry with the Californios or to conform to Spanish ways. They were bent on taking over the territory. In June 1846, these Americans banded together at Sonoma in the Bear Flag Revolt (so called because their flag bore a bear emblem), declaring independence from Mexico. The American takeover of California was not confirmed until the Treaty of Guadalupe Hidalgo in 1848.

## GOLD!

In January 1848, carpenter James Marshall noticed small flakes of gold in the millrace at Sutter's Mill (present-day Coloma). Soon he and all the rest of John Sutter's employees were panning for gold in California's streams. But not until the autumn of 1848 did the East Coast hear the first rumors about the discovery of gold in California. The spirit of excitement and adventure so recently aroused by the Mexican-American War was now directed toward California, the new El Dorado. Thousands left farms and jobs and headed west, by land and by sea, to make their fortune. Later known as "forty-niners" for the year the gold rush began in earnest, these people came from all parts of the United States—and indeed, from all over the world. They transformed what had been a quiet ranching paradise into a teeming and tumultuous community in search of wealth in California's rivers and streams.

Eighty percent of the forty-niners were Americans. The second largest group of migrants was from nearby Mexico and the western coast of Latin America (13 percent). The remainder came from Europe and Asia (see Figure 14.2).

The presence of Chinese miners surprised many Americans. Several hundred Chinese arrived in California in 1849 and 1850, and in 1852 more than 20,000 landed in San Francisco hoping to share in the wealth of "Gum Sam"

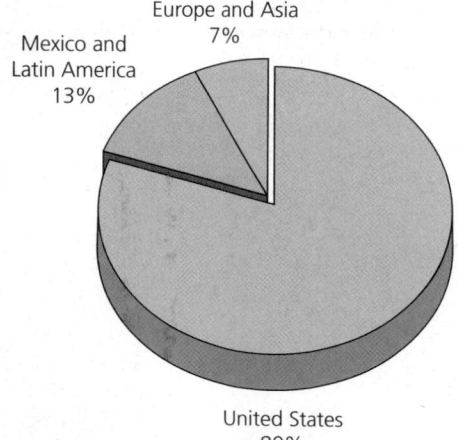

**Figure 14.2  Where the Forty-Niners Came From**

Americans drawn to the California gold rush of 1849 encountered a more diverse population than most had previously known. Nearly as novel to them as the 20 percent from foreign countries was the regional variety from within the United States itself.

Europe and Asia
7%

Mexico and Latin America
13%

United States
80%

This drawing of the bar of a gambling saloon in San Francisco in 1855 shows the effects of the gold rush on California. Men from all parts of the world are gathered at this elegant bar in the large cosmopolitan city of San Francisco, which had been only a small trading post before gold was discovered in 1849.

Frank Marryat, "The Bar of a Gambling Saloon," published 1855. Lithograph. Collection of the New-York Historical Society, New York City.

(Golden Mountain). Most came, like the Americans, as temporary sojourners, intending to return home as soon as they made some money. Again, like most of the American miners, the majority of Chinese were men who left their wives at home. The distinctive appearance of the Chinese, added to the threat of economic competition that they posed, quickly aroused American hostility. A special tax was imposed on foreign miners in 1852, and in the 1870s, Chinese immigration was sharply curtailed.

In 1849, as the gold rush began in earnest, San Francisco, the major entry port and supply point, sprang to life. From a settlement of 1,000 in 1848, it grew

Chinese first came to California in 1849 attracted by the gold rush. Frequently, however, they were forced off their claims by intolerant whites. Rather than enjoy an equal chance in the goldfields, they were often forced to work as servants or in other menial occupations.

## QUICK REVIEW

### Discovery of Gold

- Gold discovered at Sutter's Mill in 1848.
- Most forty-niners were Americans.
- Gold rush led rapid growth of San Francisco.

to a city of 35,000 in 1850. This surge suggested that the real money to be made in California was not in panning for gold but in feeding, clothing, housing, provisioning, and entertaining the miners. The white population of California jumped from an estimated pre–gold rush figure of 11,000 to more than 100,000 by 1852. California was admitted into the Union as a state in 1850.

## MINING CAMPS

As had occurred in San Francisco, most mining camps boomed almost instantly to life, but unlike San Francisco, they were empty again within a few years. Most miners lived in tents or hovels, unwilling to take time from mining to build themselves decent quarters. They cooked monotonous meals of beans, bread, and bacon or, if they had money, bought meals at expensive restaurants and boardinghouses. They led a cheerless, uncomfortable, and unhealthy existence, especially during the long, rainy winter months, with few distractions apart from the saloon, the gambling hall, and the prostitute's bed (see Map 14.7).

Most miners were young, unmarried, and unsuccessful. Only a small percentage ever struck it rich in California. Gold deposits that were accessible with pick and shovel were soon exhausted, and the deeper deposits required capital and machinery. Increasingly, those who stayed on in California had to give up the status of independent miners and become wage earners for large mining concerns.

Every mining community had its saloonkeepers, gamblers, prostitutes, merchants, and restauranteurs. Like the miners themselves, these people were transients, always ready to pick up and move at the word of a new gold strike. The majority of women in the early mining camps were prostitutes. Most of the other women were hardworking wives of miners, and in this predominantly male society, they made good money doing domestic work by keeping boardinghouses, cooking, and doing laundry.

Partly because few people put any effort into building communities violence was endemic in mining areas, and much of it was racial. Discrimination, especially against Chinese, Mexicans, and African Americans, was common.

By the mid-1850s, the immediate effects of the gold rush had passed. California had a booming population, a thriving agriculture, and a corporate mining industry. The gold rush also left California with a population that was larger, more affluent, and (in urban San Francisco) more culturally sophisticated than that in other newly settled territories. And it was significantly more multicultural than the rest of the nation, for many of the Chinese and Mexicans, as well as immigrants from many European countries, remained in California after the gold rush subsided. But the gold rush left some permanent scars, and not just on the foothills landscape: the virtual extermination of the California Indian peoples, the dispossession of many Californios who were legally deprived of their land grants, and the growth of racial animosity toward the Chinese in particular.

**MAP 14.7**

**California in the Gold Rush** This map shows the major gold camps along the mother lode in the western foothills of the Sierra Nevada Mountains. Gold seekers reached the camps by crossing the Sierra Nevada near Placerville on the Overland Trail or by sea via San Francisco. The main area of Spanish-Mexican settlement, the coastal region between Monterey and Los Angeles, was remote from the goldfields.

Warren A. Beck and Ynez D. Haase, *Historical Atlas of California* (Norman: University of Oklahoma Press, 1974), map 50.

WHAT WAS life like in the California gold camps during the gold rush?

**Exploring America:**
*The Unwelcome Mat*

**17–1**
Edward Gould Buffum, *Six Months in the Gold Mines* (1850)

# THE POLITICS OF MANIFEST DESTINY

I n three short years, from 1845 to 1848, the territory of the United States grew an incredible 70 percent, and a continental nation took shape. This expansion, pushed by economic desires and feelings of American cultural superiority, led directly to the emergence of the divisive issue of slavery as the dominant issue in national politics.

## THE WILMOT PROVISO

In 1846, almost all the northern members of the Whig Party opposed Democratic president James Polk's belligerent expansionism on antislavery grounds. Northern Whigs correctly feared that expansion would reopen the issue of slavery in the territories. But the outpouring of popular enthusiasm for the Mexican-American War convinced most Whig congressmen that they needed to vote military appropriations for the war in spite of their misgivings.

Ironically, it was not the Whigs but a freshman Democratic congressman from Pennsylvania, David Wilmot, who opened the door to sectional controversy over expansion. In August 1846, only a few short months after the beginning of the Mexican-American War, Wilmot proposed, in an amendment to a military appropriations bill, that slavery be banned in all the territories acquired from Mexico. In the debate and voting that followed, something new and ominous occurred: southern Whigs joined southern Democrats to vote against the measure, while Northerners of both parties supported it. Sectional interest had triumphed over party loyalty.

The **Wilmot Proviso** was so controversial that it was deleted from the necessary military appropriations bills during the Mexican-American War. But in 1848, following the Treaty of Guadalupe Hidalgo, the question of the expansion of slavery could no longer be avoided or postponed. Antislavery advocates from the North argued with proslavery Southerners in a debate that was much more prolonged and bitter than in the Missouri Crisis debate of 1819. The Wilmot Proviso posed a fundamental challenge to both parties. Neither the Democrats nor the Whigs could

**WHAT KEY** factors explain the outcome of the election of 1848?

**Review Summary**

**Overview:** *Expansion Causes the First Splits in the Second American Party System*

**Wilmot Proviso**   The amendment offered by Pennsylvania Democrat David Wilmot in 1846 which stipulated that "as an express and fundamental condition to the acquisition of any territory from the Republic of Mexico … neither slavery nor involuntary servitude shall ever exist in any part of said territory."

---

## OVERVIEW | Expansion Causes the First Splits in the Second American Party System

| | |
|---|---|
| **1844** | Whigs reject President John Tyler's move to annex Texas and expel him from the Whig Party. |
| | Southern Democrats choose expansionist James K. Polk as their presidential candidate, passing over Martin Van Buren, who is against expansion. |
| | Liberty Party runs abolitionist James Birney for president, attracting northern antislavery Whigs. |
| **1846** | The Wilmot Proviso, proposing to ban slavery in the territories that might be gained in the Mexican-American War, splits both parties: southern Whigs and Democrats oppose the measure; northern Whigs and Democrats support it. |
| **1848** | The new Free-Soil Party runs northern Democrat Martin Van Buren for president, gaining 10 percent of the vote from abolitionists, antislavery Whigs, and some northern Democrats. This strong showing by a third party causes Democrat Lewis Cass to lose the electoral votes of New York and Pennsylvania, allowing the Whig Zachary Taylor to win. |

**In 1848, the** Whigs nominated a hero of the Mexican-American War, General Zachary Taylor, who ran on his military exploits. In this campaign poster, every letter of Taylor's name is decorated with scenes from the recent war, which had seized the popular imagination in a way no previous conflict had done.

---

## QUICK REVIEW

**Slavery and the Election of 1848**

♦ Democratic candidate Lewis Cass argued that territorial residents should decide issue of slavery.

♦ Whig nominee Zachary Taylor remained silent on slavery issue.

♦ Taylor's election gave country first president from Lower South.

**Liberty Party**   The first antislavery political party, formed in 1840.

**Popular sovereignty**   A solution to the slavery crisis suggested by Michigan senator Lewis Cass by which territorial residents, not Congress, would decide slavery's fate.

---

take a strong stand on the amendment because neither party could get its northern and southern wings to agree.

## THE FREE-SOIL MOVEMENT

Why did David Wilmot propose this controversial measure? Wilmot, a northern Democrat, was propelled not by ideology but by the pressure of practical politics. The dramatic rise of the **Liberty Party**, founded in 1840 by abolitionists, threatened to take votes away from both the Whig and the Democratic parties.

The Liberty Party took an uncompromising stance against slavery. The party proposed to prohibit the admission of slave states to the Union, end slavery in the District of Columbia, and abolish the interstate slave trade that was vital to the expansion of cotton growing into the Old Southwest. Liberty Party doctrine was too uncompromising for the mass of northern voters, who immediately realized that the southern states would leave the Union before accepting it. Still, many Northerners opposed slavery. From this sentiment, the Free-Soil Party was born.

The free-soil argument was a calculated adjustment of abolitionist principles to practical politics. It shifted the focus from the question of the morality of slavery to the ways in which slavery posed a threat to northern expansion. The free-soil doctrine thus established a direct link between expansion, which most Americans supported, and sectional politics.

Free-soilers were willing to allow slavery to continue in the existing slave states because they supported the Union, not because they approved of slavery. They were unwilling, however, to allow the extension of slavery to new and unorganized territory. If the South were successful in extending slavery, they argued, northern farmers who moved west would find themselves competing at an economic disadvantage with large planters using slave labor. Free-soilers also insisted that the northern values of freedom and individualism would be destroyed if the slave-based southern labor system were allowed to spread.

Many free-soilers really meant "anti-black" when they said "antislavery." They proposed to ban all African American people from the new territories, Most Northerners were unwilling to consider social equality for African Americans, free or slave. Banning all black people from the western territories seemed a simple solution.

## THE ELECTION OF 1848

A swirl of emotions—pride, expansionism, sectionalism, abolitionism, free-soil sentiment—surrounded the election of 1848. Lewis Cass of Michigan, the Democratic nominee for president (Polk, in poor health, declined to run for a second term), proposed to apply the doctrine of popular sovereignty to the crucial slave–free issue. **Popular sovereignty** was based on the accepted constitutional principle that decisions about slavery should be made at the state rather than the national level. In reality, popular sovereignty was an admission of the national failure to resolve sectional differences.

For their part, the Whigs passed over perennial candidate Henry Clay and turned to a war hero, General Zachary Taylor. Taylor, a Louisiana slaveholder, refused to take a position on the Wilmot Proviso, allowing both northern and southern voters to hope that he agreed with them.

The deliberate vagueness of the two major candidates displeased many northern voters. An uneasy mixture of disaffected Democrats (among them David Wilmot) and Whigs joined former Liberty Party voters to support the candidate

## CHRONOLOGY

| | |
|---|---|
| **1609** | First Spanish settlement in New Mexico |
| **1670s** | British and French Canadians begin fur trade in western Canada |
| **1716** | First Spanish settlements in Texas |
| **1769** | First Spanish settlement in California |
| **1780s** | New England ships begin sea otter trade in Pacific Northwest |
| **1793** | Alexander Mackenzie of the North West Company reaches the Pacific Ocean |
| **1803** | Louisiana Purchase |
| **1804–06** | Lewis and Clark expedition |
| **1806** | Russian–Californio trade begins |
| **1806–07** | Zebulon Pike's expedition across the Great Plains to the Rocky Mountains |
| **1819–20** | Stephen Long's expedition across the Great Plains |
| **1821** | Hudson's Bay Company gains dominance of western fur trade |
| | Mexico seizes independence from Spain |
| | Santa Fé Trail opens, soon protected by U.S. military |
| | Stephen F. Austin becomes first American empresario in Texas |
| **1824** | First fur rendezvous sponsored by Rocky Mountain Fur Company |
| | Hudson's Bay Company establishes Fort Vancouver in Oregon Country |
| **1830** | Indian Removal Act moves eastern Indians to Indian Territory |
| **1833–34** | Prince Maximilian and Karl Bodmer visit Plains Indians |
| **1834** | Jason Lee establishes first mission in Oregon Country |
| **1835** | Texas revolts against Mexico |
| **1836** | Battles of the Alamo and San Jacinto |
| | Republic of Texas formed |
| **1843–44** | John C. Frémont maps trails to Oregon and California |
| **1844** | Democrat James K. Polk elected president on an expansionist platform |
| **1845** | Texas annexed to the United States as a slave state |
| | John O'Sullivan coins the phrase "manifest destiny" |
| **1846** | Oregon question settled peacefully with Britain |
| | Mexican-American War begins |
| | Bear Flag Revolt in California |
| | Wilmot Proviso |
| **1847** | Cayuse War begins in Oregon |
| | Americans win battles of Buena Vista, Veracruz, and Mexico City |
| **1848** | Treaty of Guadalupe Hidalgo |
| | Free-Soil Party captures 10 percent of the popular vote in the North |
| | General Zachary Taylor, a Whig, elected president |
| **1849** | California gold rush |

of the Free-Soil Party, former president Martin Van Buren. In the end, Van Buren garnered 10 percent of the vote (all in the North). The vote for the Free-Soil Party cost Cass the electoral votes of New York and Pennsylvania, and General Zachary Taylor won the election with only 47 percent of the popular vote. This was the second election after 1840 that the Whigs had won by running a war hero who could duck hard questions by claiming to be above politics. Uncannily, history was to repeat itself: Taylor, like William Henry Harrison, died before his term was completed, and the chance he offered to maintain national unity—if ever it existed—was lost.

## CONCLUSION

In the decade of the 1840s, westward expansion took many forms, from relatively peaceful settlement in Oregon, to war with Mexico over Texas, to the overwhelming numbers of gold rushers who changed California forever. Most of these frontiers—in Oregon, New Mexico, and California—began as frontiers of inclusion, in which small numbers of Americans were eager for trade, accommodation, and intermarriage with the original inhabitants. Texas, with its agricultural enclaves, was the exception to this pattern. Yet on every frontier, as the number of American settlers increased, so did the sentiment for exclusion, so that by 1850, whatever their origins, the far-flung American continental settlements were more similar than different, and the success of manifest destiny seemed overwhelming.

The amazing expansion achieved by the Mexican-American War—America's manifest destiny—made the United States a continental nation but stirred up the issue that was to tear it apart. Sectional rivalries and fears now dominated every aspect of politics. Expansion, once a force for unity, now divided the nation into Northerners and Southerners, who could not agree on the community they shared—the federal Union.

# REVIEW QUESTIONS

1. Define and discuss the concept of manifest destiny.

2. Trace the different ways in which the frontiers in Oregon, Texas, and California moved from frontiers of inclusion to frontiers of exclusion.

3. Take different sides (Whig and Democrat) and debate the issues raised by the Mexican-American War.

4. The California gold rush was an unprecedented scramble for riches. What were its effects on its participants, on California, and on the nation as a whole?

5. Referring to Chapter 13, compare the positions of the Liberty Party and the Free-Soil Party. Examine the factors that made the free-soil doctrine politically so acceptable and abolitionism so controversial.

# KEY TERMS

**myhistorylab**

Flashcard Review

**Alamo** (p. 363)
**Californios** (p. 368)
**Empresarios** (p. 363)
**Enclave** (p. 363)
**Liberty Party** (p. 374)
**Manifest destiny** (p. 357)

**Mexican-American War** (p. 365)
**Oregon Trail** (p. 360)
**Popular sovereignty** (p. 374)
**Santa Fé Trail** (p. 354)
**Tejanos** (p. 362)
**Wilmot Proviso** (p. 373)

# RECOMMENDED READING

Sucheng Chan, *This Bittersweet Soil: The Chinese in California Agriculture 1860–1910* (1987). The Chinese in California after the gold rush.

John Mack Faragher, *Women and Men on the Overland Trail* (1979). One of the first books to consider the experience of women on the journey west.

Paul Foos, *A Short, Offhand, Killing Affair: Soldiers and Social Conflict During the Mexican-American War* (2002). The lives and attitudes of ordinary American soldiers.

Robert W. Johannsen, *To the Halls of the Montezumas: The Mexican War in the American Imagination* (1985). A lively book that explores the impact of the Mexican-American War on public opinion.

Susan Johnson, *Roaring Camp: The Social World of the California Gold Rush* (2000). A beautifully written study of the varieties of mining camp experience.

Paul D. Lack, *The Texas Revolutionary Experience: A Political and Social History, 1835–1836* (1992). A political and social history that stresses the chaotic and discordant nature of the Texas Revolt.

Andrés Reséndez, *Changing National Identities at the Frontier: Texas and New Mexico, 1800–1850* (2004). The choices faced by Latinos, American Indians, and Anglos.

Randy Roberts and James S. Olson, *A Line in the Sand: The Alamo in Blood and Memory* (2001). How the battle became a symbol.

Malcolm Rohrbough, *Days of Gold: The California Gold Rush and the American Nation* (1997). A lively history that emphasizes the effects of this "great American epic" on the national self-image.

David J. Weber, *The Mexican Frontier, 1821–1846: The American Southwest under Mexico* (1982). A fine study of the history of the Southwest before American conquest by a leading borderlands historian.

Where it's a good time to connect to the past!

*This horror, this nightmare abomination!*
*Can it be in my country! It lies like lead on*
*my heart, it shadows my life with sorrow . . .*

— Harriet Beecher Stowe, December 16, 1852

Republican night-time parade.

# 15

## THE COMING CRISIS
### THE 1850S

**WHY DID** people in the North and the South tend to see the issue of slavery differently?

**WHAT WAS** the intent of the Compromise of 1850?

**WHAT EXPLAINS** the end of the Second American Party System and the rise of the Republican Party?

**WHAT WAS** the outcome of the *Dred Scott* decision?

**WHY DID** the South secede following the Republican Party victory in the election of 1860?

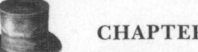
# AMERICAN COMMUNITIES
## Illinois Communities Debate Slavery

"THE PRAIRIES ARE ON FIRE," ANNOUNCED THE *NEW YORK EVENING POST* correspondent who covered the debates. "It is astonishing how deep an interest in politics these people take." The reason was clear: by 1858, the American nation was in political crisis. The decade-long effort to solve the problem of the future of slavery had failed. For most of this time, Washington politicians trying to build broad national parties with policies acceptable to voters in both the North and the South had done their best not to talk about slavery. That the **Lincoln–Douglas debates** were devoted to one issue alone—slavery and the future of the Union—showed how serious matters had become.

Democratic Senator Stephen A. Douglas of Illinois and his Republican challenger, Springfield lawyer Abraham Lincoln, presented their views in three hours of closely reasoned argument. But they did not speak alone. Cheers, boos, groans, and shouted questions from active, engaged listeners punctuated all seven of the now famous confrontations between the two men. Thus, the Lincoln–Douglas debates were community events in which Illinois citizens—who, as did Americans everywhere, held varying political beliefs—took part.

Stephen Douglas was the leading Democratic contender for the 1860 presidential nomination, but before he could mount a campaign for national office, he had first to win reelection to the Illinois seat he had held in the U.S. Senate for twelve years. His vote against allowing slavery in Kansas had alienated him from the strong southern wing of his own party and had put him in direct conflict with its top leader, President James Buchanan. Because the crisis of the Union was so severe and Douglas's role so pivotal, his reelection campaign clearly previewed the 1860 presidential election.

Lincoln had represented Illinois in the House of Representatives in the 1840s but had lost political support in 1848 because he had opposed the Mexican-American War. Developing a prosperous Springfield law practice, he had been an influential member of the Illinois Republican Party since its founding in 1856. Lincoln was radicalized by the issue of the extension of slavery. Even though his wife's family were Kentucky slave owners, Lincoln's commitment to freedom and his resistance to the spread of slavery had now become absolute: for him, freedom and the Union were inseparable.

The first of the seven debates, held in Ottawa, in northern Illinois, on Saturday, August 21, 1858, showed not only the seriousness but also the exuberance of the democratic politics of the time. By early morning, the town was jammed with people. The clouds of dust raised by carriages driving to Ottawa, one observer complained, turned the town into "a vast smoke house." By one o'clock, the town square was filled to overflowing, and the debate enthralled an estimated 12,000 people. Ottawa in northern Illinois, was pro-Republican, and the audience heckled Douglas unmercifully. But as the debates moved south in the state, where Democrats predominated, the tables were turned, and Lincoln sometimes had to plead for a chance to be heard.

Although Douglas won the 1858 senatorial election in Illinois, the acclaim that Lincoln gained in the famous debates helped establish the Republicans' claim to be the only party capable of stopping the spread of slavery and made Lincoln himself a strong contender for the Republican presidential nomination in 1860. But the true winners of the Lincoln–Douglas debates were the people of Illinois who gathered peacefully to discuss the most serious issue of their time. The young German immigrant Carl Schurz, who attended the Quincy debate, was deeply impressed by its democratic character. He noted, "There was no end of cheering and shouting and jostling on the streets of Quincy that day. But in spite of the excitement created by the political contest, the crowds remained very good-natured, and the occasional jibes flung from one side to the other were uniformly received with a laugh."

The Lincoln–Douglas debates are famous for their demonstration of the widespread public belief in commonality and community to resolve disagreements. Unfortunately, differences that could be resolved through conversation and friendship in the local community were less easy to resolve at the national level. In the highly charged and highly public political atmosphere of Congress, politicians struggled in vain to find compromises to hold the national community together.

Illinois

**Lincoln-Douglas debates** Series of debates in the 1858 Illinois senatorial campaign during which Douglas and Lincoln staked out their differing opinions on the issue of slavery.

# AMERICA IN 1850

The America of 1850 was a very different nation from the republic of 1800. Geographic expansion, population increase, economic development, and the changes wrought by the market revolution had transformed the struggling new nation. Economically, culturally, and politically Americans had forged a strong sense of national identity.

## EXPANSION AND GROWTH

America was now a much larger nation than it had been in 1800. Through war and diplomacy, the country had grown to continental dimensions, more than tripling in size from 890,000 to 3 million square miles. Its population had increased enormously from 5.3 million in 1800 to more than 23 million, 4 million of whom were African American slaves and 2 million new immigrants, largely from Germany and Ireland. Comprising just sixteen states in 1800, America in 1850 had thirty-one states, and more than half of the population lived west of the Appalachians. America's cities had undergone the most rapid half century of growth they were ever to experience (see Map 15.1).

America was also much richer: it is estimated that real per capita income doubled between 1800 and 1850 Southern cotton was no longer the major influence on the domestic economy. The growth of manufacturing in the Northeast and the rapid opening up of rich farmlands in the Midwest had serious domestic implications. As the South's share of responsibility for economic growth waned, so did its political importance—at least in the eyes of many Northerners. Thus, the very success of the United States both in geographic expansion and in economic development served to undermine the role of the South in national politics and to hasten the day of open conflict between the slave South and the free-labor North and Midwest.

## POLITICS, CULTURE, AND NATIONAL IDENTITY

Pride in democracy was one unifying theme in a growing sense of national identity and the new middle-class values, institutions, and culture that supported it. Since the turn of the century, American writers had struggled to find distinctive American themes, and these efforts bore fruit in the 1850s in the burst of creative activity termed the "American Renaissance." Newspapers, magazines, and communication improvements of all kinds created a national audience for the American scholars and writers who emerged during this decade.

During the American Renaissance, American writers pioneered new literary forms. Nathaniel Hawthorne, in works like "Young Goodman Brown" (1835), raised the short story to a distinctive American literary form. Poets like Walt Whitman and Emily Dickinson experimented with unrhymed and "off-rhyme" verse. Henry David Thoreau published *Walden* in 1854. A pastoral celebration of his life at Walden Pond, in Concord, Massachusetts, the essay was also a searching meditation on the cost to the individual of the loss of contact with nature that was a consequence of the market revolution.

Indeed, although the midcentury popular mood was one of self-congratulation, most of the writers of the American Renaissance were social critics. In *The Scarlet Letter* (1850) and *The House of the Seven Gables* (1851), Nathaniel Hawthorne brilliantly exposed the repressive and hypocritical aspects of Puritan New England in the colonial period and the often impossible moral choices faced by individuals. Hawthorne's friend Herman Melville, in his great work *Moby Dick* (1851), used the story of Captain Ahab's obsessive search for the white whale to write a profound study of the nature of good and evil and a critique of American society in the 1850s. The strongest social critique, however, was Frederick Douglass's starkly simple autobiography, *Narrative of the Life of Frederick Douglass* (1845), which told of his brutal life as a slave.

**WHY DID** people in the North and the South tend to see the issue of slavery differently?

**myhistorylab**
Review Summary

## IMAGE KEY
for pages 378–379

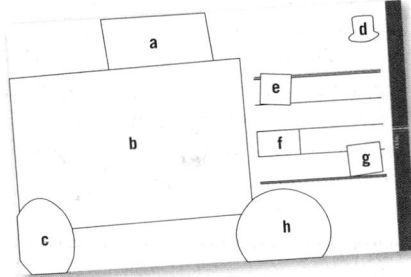

**a.** Dred Scott and his family, c. 1857.

**b.** Republican night-time parade.

**c.** A portrait photo of John Brown (1800–1859).

**d.** An old fashioned black stovepipe hat with a narrow brim like the one worn by Abe Lincoln.

**e.** A poster of *Uncle Tom's Cabin* with an illustration of a slave woman standing in the doorway of a log cabin. The copy describes various editions of the book for sale.

**f.** Robert Marshall Root's painting of the Lincoln-Douglas debate.

**g.** A contemporary colored engraving of the inside of the Armory at Harper's Ferry, Virginia, where John Brown and his men were trapped by the fire of the U.S. Marines under the command of Col. Robert E. Lee, October 18, 1859.

**h.** Gold ore and gravel in a shallow pan like those used by '49ers.

# MAP EXPLORATION

To explore an interactive version of this map, go to **http://www.prenhall.com/faraghertlc/map15.1**

**MAP 15.1**

**U.S. Population and Settlement, 1850**   By 1850, the United States was a continental nation. Its people, whom Thomas Jefferson had once thought would not reach the Mississippi River for forty generations, had not only passed the river but also leapfrogged to the West Coast. In comparison to the America of 1800 (see Map 9.1 on p. 210), the growth was astounding.

WHAT WERE the reasons behind these growth patterns?

**14–2**
Harriet Beecher Stowe, *Uncle Tom's Cabin* (1852)

The most successful American novel of the mid-nineteenth century was also about the great issue of the day—slavery. In writing *Uncle Tom's Cabin*, Harriet Beecher Stowe combined the literary style of the popular women's domestic novels of the time (discussed in Chapter 12) with vivid details of slavery culled from firsthand accounts by northern abolitionists and escaped slaves. Published in 1851, it was a runaway best seller. More than 300,000 copies were sold in the first year, and within ten years, the book had sold more than 2 million copies, becoming the all-time American best seller in proportion to population. Turned into a play that remained popular throughout the nineteenth century, *Uncle Tom's Cabin* reached an even wider audience. *Uncle Tom's Cabin* was more than a heart-tugging story: it was a call to action. In 1863, when Harriet Beecher Stowe was introduced to Abraham Lincoln, the president is said to have remarked, "So you're the little woman who wrote the book that made this great war!"

# CRACKS IN NATIONAL UNITY

Stowe's novel clearly spoke to the growing concern of the American people. The year 1850 opened to the most serious political crisis the United States had ever known. The issue raised by the 1846 Wilmot Proviso—whether slavery should be extended to the new territories—could no longer be ignored (see Chapter 14). Furthermore, California, made rich and populous by the gold rush, applied for statehood in 1850, thereby reopening the issue of the balance between slave and free states.

## THE COMPROMISE OF 1850

The **Compromise of 1850** was actually five separate bills embodying three separate compromises.

First, California was admitted as a free state, but the status of the remaining former Mexican possessions was left to be decided by **popular sovereignty** (a vote of the territory's inhabitants) when they applied for statehood. The result was, for the time being, fifteen slave states and sixteen free states. Second, Texas (a slave state) was required to cede land to New Mexico Territory (free or slave status undecided). Finally, the slave trade, but not slavery itself, was ended in the District of Columbia, but a stronger fugitive slave law, to be enforced in all states, was enacted (see Map 15.2).

Jubilation and relief greeted the news that compromise had been achieved, but analysis of the votes on the five bills that made up the compromise revealed no consistent majority. The sectional splits within each party that had existed before the compromise remained. Antislavery northern Whigs and proslavery southern Democrats, each the larger wing of their party, were the least willing to compromise.

## POLITICAL PARTIES SPLIT OVER SLAVERY

The Second American Party System, forged in the great controversies of Andrew Jackson's presidency (see Chapter 11), was a national party system. At a time when the ordinary person still had very strong sectional loyalties, the mass political party created a national community of like-minded voters. Yet, by the election of 1848, sectional interests were eroding the political "glue" in both parties. Although each party still appeared united, sectional fissures ran deep.

Political splits were preceded by divisions in other social institutions. Disagreements about slavery had already split the country's great religious organizations into northern and southern groups: the Presbyterians in 1837, the Methodists in 1844, and the Baptists in 1845. Theodore Weld, the abolitionist leader, saw these splits as inevitable: "Events . . . have for years been silently but without a moment's pause, settling the basis of two great parties, the nucleus of one slavery, of the other, freedom."

## CONGRESSIONAL DIVISIONS

But was freedom national and slavery sectional, or was it the other way around? In the midst of the debate that preceded the Compromise of 1850, President Zachary Taylor died. A bluff military man, Taylor had been prepared to follow Andrew Jackson's precedent during the Nullification Crisis of 1832 and simply demand that southern dissidents compromise. Vice President Millard Fillmore, who assumed the presidency, was a much weaker man who did not seize the opportunity for presidential action.

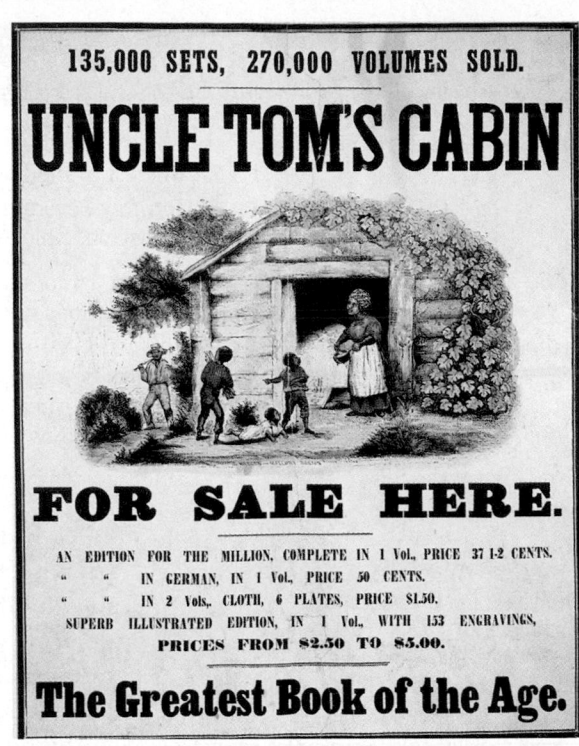

This poster advertises *Uncle Tom's Cabin*, the best-selling novel by Harriet Beecher Stowe. The poignant story of long-suffering African American slaves had an immense impact on northern popular opinion, swaying it decisively against slavery. In that respect, the poster's boast, "The Greatest Book of the Age," was correct.

**WHAT WAS** the intent of the Compromise of 1850?

## myhistorylab
**Review Summary**

**Compromise of 1850** The four-step compromise which admitted California as a free state, allowed the residents of the New Mexico and Utah territories to decide the slavery issue for themselves, ended the slave trade in the District of Columbia, and passed a new fugitive slave law to enforce the constitutional provision stating that a slave escaping into a free state shall be delivered back to the owner.

**Popular sovereignty** A solution to the slavery crisis suggested by Michigan senator Lewis Cass by which territorial residents, not Congress, would decide slavery's fate.

# OVERVIEW | The Great Sectional Compromises

| 1820 | Missouri Compromise | Admits Missouri to the Union as a slave state and Maine as a free state; prohibits slavery in the rest of the Louisiana Purchase Territory north of 36°30′. |
| --- | --- | --- |
| | | Territory Covered: The entire territory of the Louisiana Purchase, exclusive of the state of Louisiana, which had been admitted to the Union in 1812. |
| 1850 | Compromise of 1850 | Admits California to the Union as a free state, settles the borders of Texas (a slave state); sets no conditions concerning slavery for the rest of the territory acquired from Mexico. Enacts national Fugitive Slave Law. |
| | | Territory Covered: The territory that had been part of Mexico before the end of the Mexican-American War and the Treaty of Guadalupe Hidalgo (1848): part of Texas, California, Utah Territory (now Utah, Nevada, and part of Colorado), and New Mexico Territory (now New Mexico and Arizona). |

myhistorylab

**Overview:** *The Great Sectional Compromises*

**14–7**
Hinton Rowan Helper, *A White Southerner Speaks Out Against Slavery* (1857)

**14–4**
John C. Calhoun, *A Dying Statesman Speaks Out Against the Compromise of 1850*

And southerners, personified by John C. Calhoun, were unwilling to compromise. Calhoun, who had uncompromisingly spoken for the slave South since the Nullification Crisis in 1828 (see Chapter 11) insisted that the states rights' doctrine was necessary to protect the legitimate rights of a minority in a democratic system governed by majority rule. Now in 1850 Calhoun broadened his argument to insist that Congress did not have a constitutional right to prohibit slavery in the territories. The territories, he said, were the common property of all the states, North and South, and slave owners had a constitutional right to the protection of their property wherever they moved. Calhon's position on the territories quickly became southern dogma: anything less than full access to the territories was unconstitutional. As Congressman Robert Toombs of Georgia put the case in 1850, the choice was stark: "Give us our just rights and we are ready to stand by the Union. Refuse [them] and for one, I will strike for independence."

Calhoun's failing health served to make his ultimatum all the more ominous. He brought an aura of death with him as he sat on the Senate floor for the last time, listening to the speech that he was too ill to read for himself. He died less than a month later, still insisting on the right of the South to secede if necessary, to preserve its way of life.

The southern threat to secede confirmed for many Northerners the warnings of antislavery leaders that they were endangered by a menacing "slave power." Liberty Party leader James Birney, in a speech in 1844, was the first to add this phrase to the nation's political vocabulary. "The slave power," Birney explained, was a group of aristocratic slave owners who not only dominated the political and social life of the South but conspired to control the federal government as well, posing a danger to free speech and free institutions throughout the nation.

Birney's warning about the "slave power" in 1844 had seemed merely the overheated rhetoric of an extremist group of abolitionists. But the defensive southern political strategies of the 1850s convinced an increasing number of northern voters that "the slave power" did in fact exist. The long-standing proslavery strategy of maintaining supremacy in the Senate by having at least as many slave as free states admitted to the Union (a plan that required slavery expansion) now looked like a conspiracy by sectional interests to control national politics. In northern eyes, the South became a demonic monolith that threatened the national government.

## TWO COMMUNITIES, TWO PERSPECTIVES

Ironically, it was their common commitment to expansion that made the argument between Northerners and Southerners so irreconcilable. Basically, both North and South believed in manifest destiny, but each on its own terms.

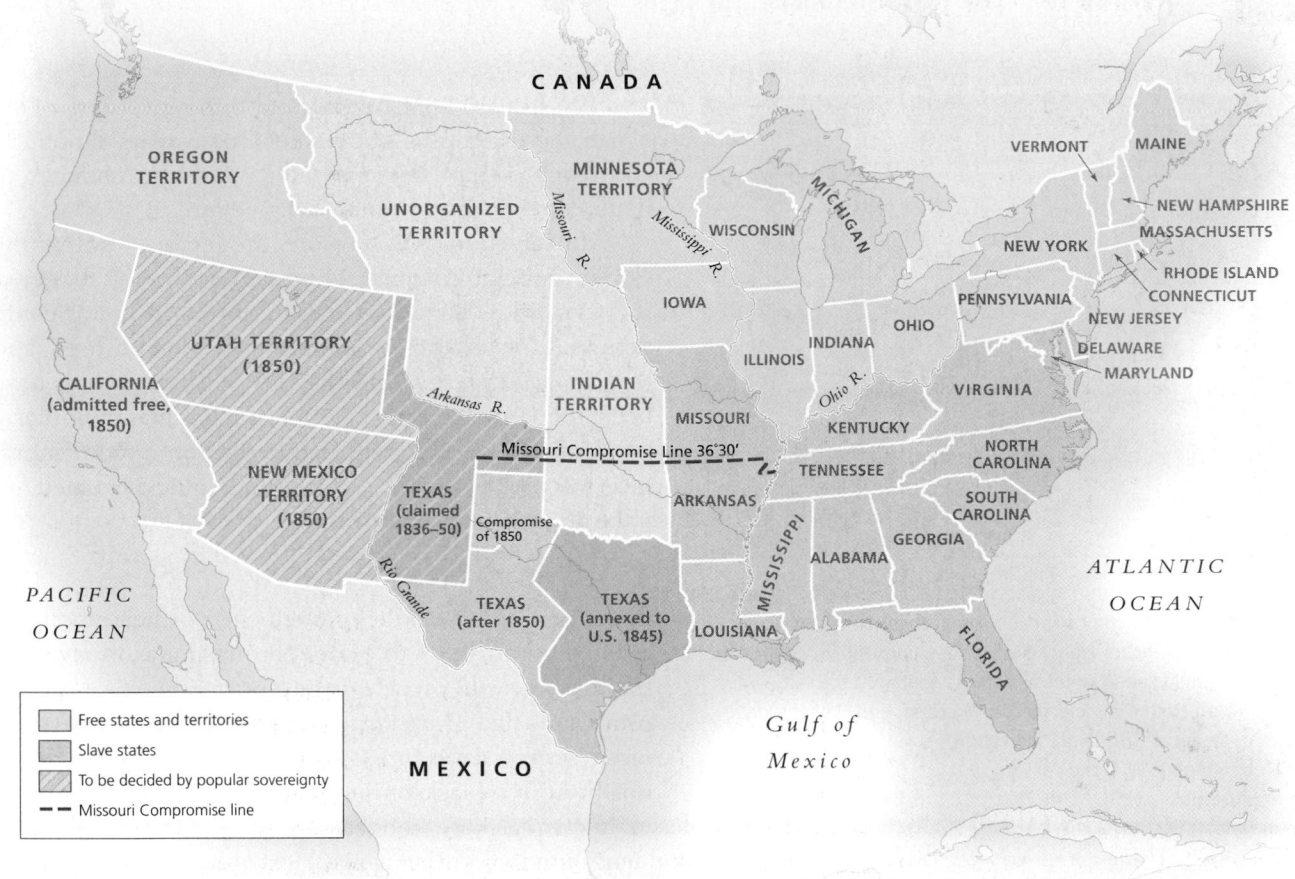

**MAP 15.2**
**The Compromise of 1850**   The Compromise of 1850, messier and more awkward than the Missouri Compromise of 1820, reflected heightened sectional tensions. California was admitted as a free state, the borders of Texas were settled, and the status of the rest of the former Mexican territory was left to be decided later by popular sovereignty. No consistent majority voted for the five separate bills that made up the compromise.

WHAT GROUPS opposed the Compromise of 1850? Why?

Similarly, both North and South used the language of basic rights and liberties in the debate over expansion. But free-soilers were speaking of personal liberty, whereas Southerners meant their right to own a particular kind of property (slaves) and to maintain a way of life based on the possession of that property. In defending its own rights, each side had taken measures that infringed on the rights of the other.

By 1850, North and South had created fixed stereotypes of the other. To antislavery Northerners, the South was an economic backwater dominated by a small slave-owning aristocracy that lived off the profits of forced labor and deprived poor whites of their democratic rights and the fruits of honest work. The slave system was not only immoral but also a drag on the entire nation, for, in the words of Senator William Seward of New York, it subverted the "intelligence, vigor and energy" that were essential for national growth. In contrast, the dynamic and enterprising commercial North boasted a free-labor ideology that offered economic opportunity to the common man and ensured his democratic rights.

Things looked very different through southern eyes. Far from being economically backward, the South, through its export of cotton, was, according to Southerners, the great engine of national economic growth from which the North benefited. Slavery was not only a blessing to an inferior race but also the cornerstone of democracy, for it ensured the freedom and independence of all white men without entailing the bitter class divisions that marked the North. Slave owners accused northern manufacturers of hypocrisy for practicing "wage slavery" without the paternal benevolence they claimed to bestow on their slaves.

In 1850, the three men who had long represented America's three major regions attempted to resolve the political crisis brought on by the application of California for statehood. Henry Clay is speaking; John C. Calhoun stands second from right; and Daniel Webster is seated at the left, with his head in his hand. Both Clay and Webster were ill, and Calhoun died before the Compromise of 1850 was arranged by a younger group of politicians led by Stephen A. Douglas.

**13–5**
De Bow's Review, *"The Stability of the Union,"* (1850)

**Exploring America:** *Anthony Burns*

**Fugitive Slave Law**   Part of the Compromise of 1850 that required the authorities in the North to assist Southern slave catchers and return runaway slaves to their owners.

By the early 1850s, these vastly different visions of the North and the South—the result of many years of political controversy—had become fixed, and the chances of national reconciliation increasingly slim.

In the country as a whole, the feeling was that the Compromise of 1850 had solved the question of slavery in the territories. The *Philadelphia Pennsylvanian* was confident that "peace and tranquillity" had been ensured, and the *Louisville Journal* said that a weight seemed to have been lifted from the heart of America. But many Southerners felt that their only real gain in the contested compromise was the Fugitive Slave Law, which quickly turned out to be an inflammatory measure.

## THE FUGITIVE SLAVE LAW

From the early days of their movement, northern abolitionists had urged slaves to escape, promising assistance and support when they reached the North. Some free African Americans had given far more than verbal support, and most escaped slaves found their most reliable help within northern free black communities. Northerners had long been appalled by professional slave catchers, who zealously seized African Americans in the North and took them south into slavery again. Most abhorrent in northern eyes was that captured black people were at the mercy of slave catchers because they had no legal right to defend themselves. In more than one case, a free African American was captured in his own community and helplessly shipped into slavery.

As a result of stories like this, nine northern states passed personal liberty laws between 1842 and 1850, serving notice that they would not cooperate with federal recapture efforts. These laws enraged Southerners, who had long been convinced that all Northerners, not just abolitionists, were actively hindering efforts to reclaim their escaped slaves. At issue were two distinct definitions of "rights": Northerners were upset at the denial of legal and personal rights to escaped slaves.

The **Fugitive Slave Law**, enacted in 1850, dramatically increased the power of slave owners to capture escaped slaves. The full authority of the federal government now supported slave owners, and although fugitives were guaranteed a hearing before a federal commissioner, they were not allowed to testify on their own behalf. Furthermore, the new law imposed federal penalties on citizens who protected or assisted fugitives or who did not cooperate in their return. A number of free northern blacks, estimated at 30,000 to 40,000, emigrated to Canada to avoid the possibility of capture.

In Boston, the center of the American abolitionist movement, reaction to the Fugitive Slave Law was fierce. In the most famous Boston case, a biracial group of armed abolitionists led by Unitarian clergyman Thomas Wentworth Higginson stormed the federal courthouse in 1854 in an attempt to save escaped slave Anthony Burns. The rescue effort failed, and a federal deputy marshal was killed. President Pierce sent marines, cavalry, and artillery to Boston to reinforce the guard over Burns and ordered a federal ship to be ready to deliver the fugitive back into slavery. When the effort by defense lawyers to argue for Burns's freedom failed, Bostonians raised money to buy his freedom. But the U.S. attorney, ordered by the president to enforce the Fugitive Slave Law in all circumstances, blocked the purchase. The case was lost, and Burns was marched to the docks through streets lined with sorrowing abolitionists. Buildings were shrouded in black and draped with American flags hanging upside down, while bells tolled as if for a funeral.

In this volatile atmosphere, escaped African Americans wrote and lectured bravely on behalf of freedom. Frederick Douglass, the most famous and eloquent of the fugitive slaves, spoke out fearlessly in support of armed resistance. Openly active in the underground network that helped slaves reach safety in Canada, Douglass himself had been constantly in danger of capture until his friends bought his freedom in 1847. Harriet Jacobs, who escaped to the North after seven years in hiding in the South, wrote bitterly in her *Incidents in the Life of a Slave Girl* (1861) that "I was, in fact, a slave in New York, as subject to slave laws as I had been in a slave state . . . I had been chased during half my life, and it seemed as if the chase was never to end." Threatened by owners who came north for her, Jacobs was forced into hiding while northern white friends arranged her purchase. "A gentleman near me said, 'It's true; I have seen the bill of sale.' 'The bill of sale!' Those words struck me like a blow. So I was sold at last! A human being sold in the free city of New York!"

The Fugitive Slave Law made slavery national and forced northern communities to confront the full meaning of slavery. Although most people were still unwilling to grant social equality to the free African Americans who lived in the northern states, more and more had come to believe that the institution of slavery was wrong. The strong northern reaction against the Fugitive Slave Law also had consequences in the South. Northern protests against the Fugitive Slave Law bred suspicion in the South and encouraged secessionist thinking. These new currents of public opinion were reflected in the election of 1852.

**13–7**
George Fitzhugh, *"The Blessings of Slavery"* (1857)

**13–6**
Benjamin Drew, *Narratives of Escaped Slaves* (1855)

**14–5**
Frederick Douglass, *Independence Day Speech* (1852)

JD9512 Recaptured Slave circa 1854
Anthony Burns (1834 - 1862) surrounded by scenes of his capture. He was arrested in Boston in May 1854 on a charge of theft. Recognised as a fugitive slave, his return to Virginia was the cause of riots. After he was bought out of slavery, he later became pastor of a Negro baptist church in St. Catherine's Canada.
PHOTO: HULTON GETTY / LIAISON AGENCY

**Escaped slave Anthony** Burns, shown here surrounded by scenes of his capture in 1854, was the cause of Boston's greatest protest against the Fugitive Slave Law. The injustice of his trial and shipment back to the South converted many Bostonians to the antislavery cause.

# CAUTION!!
## COLORED PEOPLE
### OF BOSTON, ONE & ALL,
You are hereby respectfully CAUTIONED and advised, to avoid conversing with the
### Watchmen and Police Officers of Boston,
For since the recent ORDER OF THE MAYOR & ALDERMEN, they are empowered to act as
# KIDNAPPERS
### AND
## Slave Catchers,
And they have already been actually employed in KIDNAPPING, CATCHING, AND KEEPING SLAVES. Therefore, if you value your LIBERTY, and the *Welfare of the Fugitives* among you, *Shun* them in every possible manner, as so many *HOUNDS* on the track of the most unfortunate of your race.
## Keep a Sharp Look Out for
# KIDNAPPERS, and have
## TOP EYE open.
**APRIL 24, 1851.**

**This handbill warning** free African Americans of danger circulated in Boston following the first of the infamous recaptures under the Fugitive Slave Law, that of Thomas Sims in 1851.

## THE ELECTION OF 1852

The first sign of the weakening of the national party system in 1852 was the difficulty both parties experienced at their nominating conventions. After fifty-two ballots General Winfield Scott (a military hero like two of the party's previous three candidates), rather than the sitting President Fillmore, was nominated. Many southern Whigs were permanently alienated by the choice; although Whigs were still elected to Congress from the South, their loyalty to the national party was strained to the breaking point.

The Democrats had a wider variety of candidates. Lewis Cass, Stephen Douglas, and James Buchanan competed for forty-nine ballots, each strong enough to block the others but not strong enough to win. Finally, the party turned to Franklin Pierce of New Hampshire, who was thought to have southern sympathies. Uniting on a platform pledging "faithful execution" of all parts of the Compromise of 1850, including the Fugitive Slave Law, Democrats polled well in the South and in the North. Most Democrats who had voted for the Free-Soil Party in 1848 voted for Pierce. So, in record numbers, did immigrant Irish and German voters, who were eligible for citizenship after three years' residence. The strong immigrant vote for Pierce was a sign of the strength of Democratic Party organizations in northern cities. Pierce easily won the 1852 election, 254 electoral votes to 42.

## "YOUNG AMERICA": THE POLITICS OF EXPANSION

Pierce entered the White House in 1853 on a wave of good feeling. This goodwill was soon strained by Pierce's support for the expansionist adventures of the "Young America" movement.

The "Young America" movement began as a group of writers and politicians in the New York Democratic Party who believed in the democratic and nationalistic promise of "manifest destiny." By the 1850s, however, their lofty goals had shrunk to a desire to conquer Central America and Cuba. During the Pierce administration, several private "filibusters" (from the Spanish *filibustero*, meaning an "adventurer" or "pirate") invaded Caribbean and Central American countries, usually with the declared intention of extending slave territory.

The Pierce administration, not directly involved in the filibustering, *was* deeply involved in an effort to obtain Cuba. In 1854, Pierce authorized his minister to Spain, Pierre Soulé, to try to force the unwilling Spanish to sell Cuba for $130 million. Soulé met in Ostend, Belgium, with the American ministers to France and England, John Mason and James Buchanan, to compose the offer. At first appealing to Spain to recognize the deep affinities between the Cubans and American Southerners that made them "one people with one destiny," the document went on to threaten to "wrest" Cuba from Spain if necessary. This amazing document, which became known as the Ostend Manifesto, was supposed to be secret but was soon leaked to the press. Deeply embarrassed, the Pierce administration was forced to repudiate it.

In another expansionist gesture in another direction, President Franklin Pierce dispatched Commodore Matthew Perry across the Pacific to Japan, a nation famous for its insularity and hostility to outsiders. The mission resulted in 1854 in a commercial treaty that opened Japan to American trade.

Overall, however, the complicity between the Pierce administration and proslavery expansionists was foolhardy and lost it the northern goodwill with which it had begun. The sectional crisis that preceded the Compromise of 1850 had made obvious the danger of reopening the territorial issue. Ironically, it was not the Young America expansionists but the prime mover of the Compromise of 1850, Stephen A. Douglas, who reignited the sectional struggle over slavery expansion.

# THE CRISIS OF THE NATIONAL PARTY SYSTEM

In 1854, Douglas introduced the **Kansas-Nebraska Act**, proposing to open those lands that had been the northern part of Indian Territory to American settlers under the principle of popular sovereignty. He thereby reopened the question of slavery in the territories. Douglas knew he was taking a political risk, but he believed he could satisfy both his expansionist aims and his presidential ambitions. He was wrong: he pushed the national party system into crisis, first killing the Whigs and then destroying the Democrats.

## THE KANSAS-NEBRASKA ACT

In a stunning example of the expansionist pressures generated by the market revolution, Stephen Douglas introduced the Kansas-Nebraska Act to further the construction of a transcontinental railroad across what was still considered the "Great American Desert" to California. Douglas wanted the rail line to terminate in Chicago, in his own state of Illinois, rather than in the rival St. Louis, but for that to happen, the land west of Iowa and Missouri had to be organized into territories (the first step toward statehood). To get Congress to agree to the organization of the territories, however, Douglas needed the votes of southern Democrats, who were unwilling to support him unless the territories were open to slavery (see Map 15.3).

The Kansas-Nebraska bill passed, but it badly strained the major political parties. Southern Whigs voted with southern Democrats in favor of the measure; northern Whigs rejected it absolutely, creating an irreconcilable split that left Whigs unable to field a presidential candidate in 1856. The damage to the Democratic Party was almost as great. In the congressional elections of 1854, northern Democrats lost two-thirds of their seats (a drop from ninety-one to twenty-five), giving the southern Democrats (who were solidly in favor of slavery extension) the dominant voice both in Congress and within the party.

Douglas had committed one of the greatest miscalculations in American political history. A storm of protest arose throughout the North. Douglas, who confidently

**WHAT EXPLAINS** the end of the Second American Party System and the rise of the Republican Party?

**myhistorylab**
Review Summary

**Kansas-Nebraska Act** Law passed in 1854 creating the Kansas and Nebraska Territories but leaving the question of slavery open to residents, thereby repealing the Missouri Compromise.

**A Japanese painting** shows Commodore Matthew Perry landing in Japan in 1853. The commercial treaty Perry signed with the Japanese government, which opened a formerly closed country to American trade, was viewed in the United States as another fruit of manifest destiny.

"The Landing of Commodore Perry in Japan in 1853." (Detail) Japanese, Edo period, 19th century. Handscroll; ink and color on paper, 10 7/8 × 211 1/8 in. (27.6 × 536.3 cm). Museum of Fine Arts, Boston. William Sturgis Bigelow Collection, RES.11.6054. Photograph © 2006 Museum of Fine Arts, Boston.

This engraving shows "Border Ruffians" from Missouri lining up to vote for slavery in the Kickapoo, Kansas Territory, election of 1855. The widespread practice of illegal voting and of open violence earned Kansas the dreadful nickname of "Bleeding Kansas."

## QUICK REVIEW

**The Kansas-Nebraska Act**

◆ Passed in 1854.

◆ Made the status of slavery in new territories subject to the principal of popular sovereignty.

◆ Act aroused storm of protest in the North.

 **14–6**
Kansas Begins to Bleed (1856)

believed that "the people of the North will sustain the measure when they come to understand it," found himself shouted down more than once at public rallies when he tried to explain the bill.

The Kansas-Nebraska bill shifted a crucial sector of northern opinion: the wealthy merchants, bankers, and manufacturers, called the "Cotton Whigs," who had economic ties with southern slave owners and had always disapproved of abolitionist activity. Convinced that the bill would encourage antislavery feeling in the North, Cotton Whigs urged southern politicians to vote against it, only to be ignored. Passage of the Kansas-Nebraska Act convinced many northern Whigs that compromise with the South was impossible.

In Kansas in 1854, hasty treaties were concluded with the Indian tribes who owned the land. Some, such as the Kickapoos, Shawnees, Sauks, and Foxes, agreed to relocate to small reservations. Others, like the Delawares, Weas, and Iowas, agreed to sell their lands to whites. Once the treaties were signed, both proslavery and antislavery white settlers began to pour in, and the battle was on.

## "BLEEDING KANSAS"

The first to claim land in Kansas were residents of nearby Missouri, itself a slave state. Missourians took up land claims, established proslavery strongholds such as the towns of Leavenworth, Kickapoo, and Atchison, and repeatedly and blatantly swamped Kansas elections with Missouri votes. In 1855, in the second of several notoriously fraudulent elections, 6,307 ballots were cast in a territory that had fewer than 3,000 eligible voters. Most of the proslavery votes were cast by "border ruffians," as they proudly called themselves, from Missouri.

Northerners quickly responded. The first party of New Englanders arrived in the summer of 1854 and established the free-soil town of Lawrence, named for former "Cotton Whig" Amos Lawrence, who financed them. More than a thousand others had joined them by the following summer. Many northern migrants were Free-Soilers, and many were religious reformers as well. The contrast of values between them and the border ruffians was almost total.

Kansas soon became a bloody battleground as the two factions struggled to secure the mandate of "popular sovereignty." Free-Soilers in Lawrence received shipments of heavy crates, innocuously marked "BOOKS" but actually containing Sharps repeating rifles, sent by eastern supporters. For their part, the border ruffians called for reinforcements.

In the summer of 1856, these lethal preparations exploded into open warfare. First, proslavery forces burned and looted the town of Lawrence. In retaliation, a grim old man named John Brown led his sons in a raid on the proslavery settlers of Pottawatomie Creek, killing five unarmed people. A wave of violence ensued. Armed bands roamed the countryside, and burnings and killings became commonplace.

The rest of the nation watched in horror as the residents of Kansas slaughtered each other in the pursuit of sectional goals. Americans' pride in their nation's great achievements was threatened by the endless violence in one small part—but a part that increasingly seemed to represent the divisions of the whole.

## THE POLITICS OF NATIVISM

The violence in Kansas was echoed by increasing violence in the nation's cities. Serious violence marred the elections of 1854 and 1856 in New York. In New Orleans, anger over corrupt elections caused a self-appointed vigilance committee to erect barricades in Jackson Square in the heart of the city, where they skirmished for five

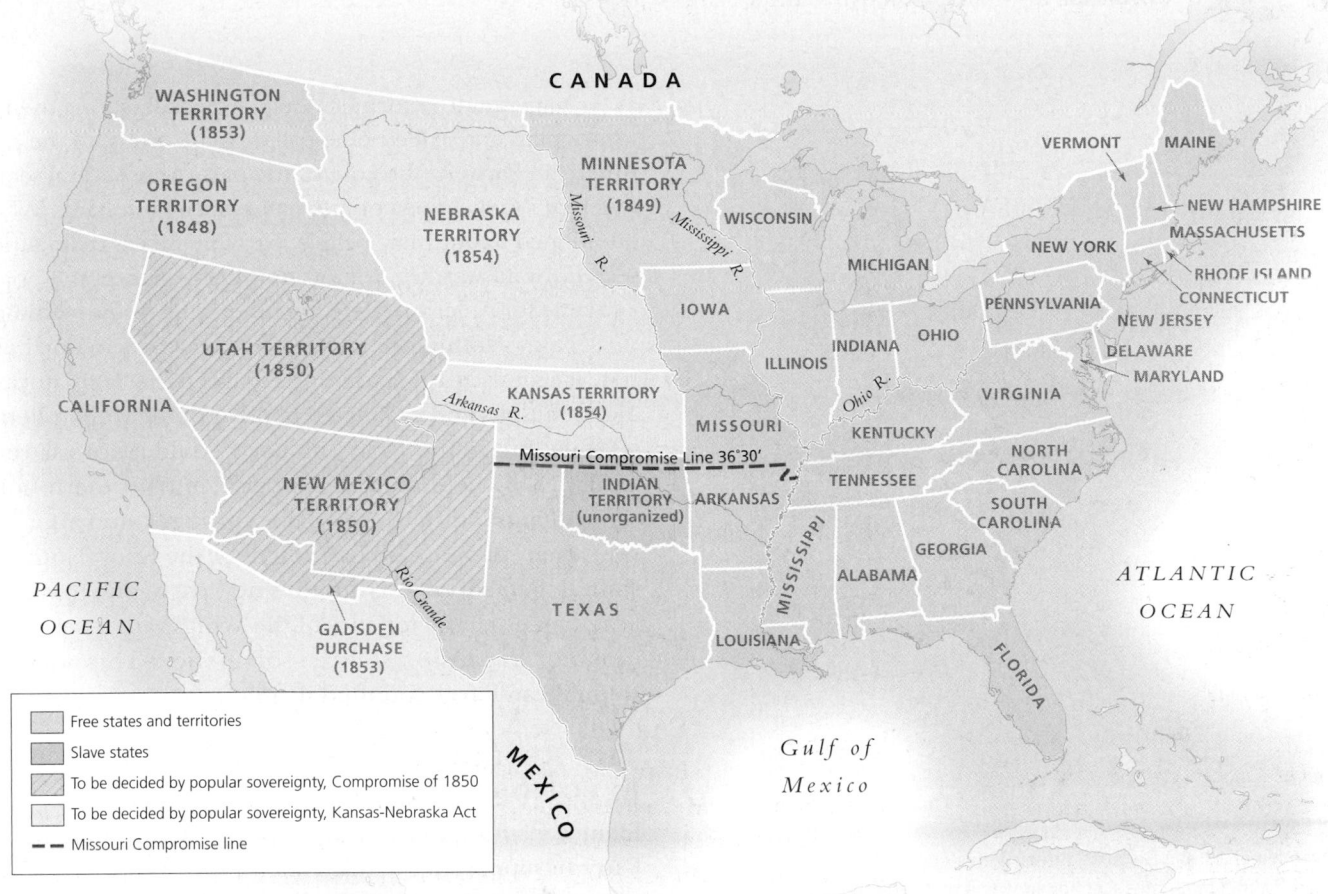

MAP 15.3

**The Kansas-Nebraska Act, 1854**    The Kansas-Nebraska Act, proposed by Steven A. Douglas in 1854, opened the central and northern Great Plains to settlement. The act had two major faults: it robbed Indian peoples of half the territory guaranteed to them by treaty and, because it repealed the Missouri Compromise line, it opened up the lands to warring proslavery and antislavery factions.

WHY DID the act provoke such a passionate response from antislavery activists?

days with an opposing force composed largely of Catholics and immigrants. In Chicago, riots started in 1855, when the mayor attempted to close the saloons on Sunday. German workingmen joined by Irishmen and Swedes paraded in protest and were met by 200 men of the National Guard, militia, and special police. The ensuing "Lager Beer Riots" ended with the imposition of martial law on the entire city.

This urban violence, like that in Kansas, was caused by the breakdown of the two-party system. The breakup of the Whig Party left a political vacuum that was filled by one of the strongest bursts of nativism, or anti-immigrant feeling, in American history, and by the rapid growth of the new American Party, which formed in 1850 to give political expression to nativism. The new party was in part a reaction to the Democratic Party's success in capturing the support of the rapidly growing population of mostly Catholic foreign-born voters. Irish immigrants in particular voted Democratic, both in reaction to Whig hostility (as in Boston) and because of their own antiblack prejudices.

The reformist and individualistic attitudes of many Whigs inclined them toward nativism. Many Whigs disapproved of the new immigrants because they were poor, Catholic, and often disdainful of the temperance movement. Moreover nativist Whigs held immigration to be solely responsible for the increases in crime and the rising cost of relief for the poor that accompanied the astoundingly rapid urban growth of the 1830s and 1840s (see Chapter 13).

**myhistorylab**

**Exploring America:** *The Unwelcome Mat*

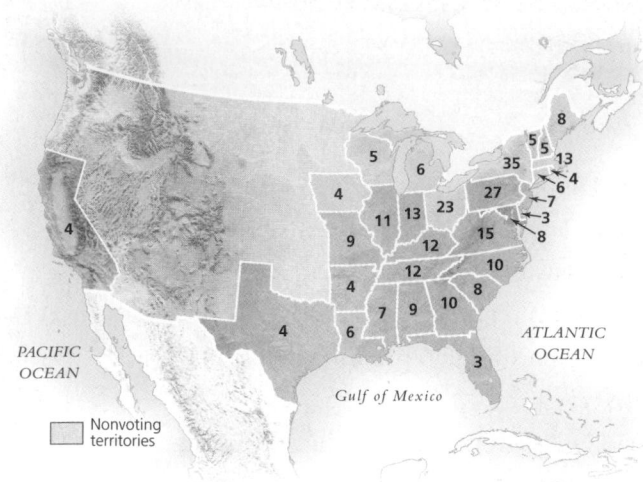

| | Electoral Vote (%) | Popular Vote (%) |
|---|---|---|
| **JAMES BUCHANAN** (Democrat) | 174 (59) | 1,832,955 (45) |
| John C. Frémont (Republican) | 114 (39) | 1,339,932 (33) |
| Millard Fillmore (American) | 8 (3) | 871,731 (22) |

**MAP 15.4**

**The Election of 1856**   Because three parties contested the 1856 election, Democrat James Buchanan was a minority president. Although Buchanan alone had national support, Republican John Frémont won most of the free states, and Millard Fillmore of the American Party gained 40 percent of the vote in most of the slave states.

WHAT GROUPS constituted Buchanan's political base?

**This nighttime meeting** of supporters of the Know-Nothing Party in New York City was dramatically spotlighted by a new device borrowed from the theater, an incandescent calcium light, popularly called a limelight.

Nativism drew former Whigs, especially young men in white-collar and skilled blue-collar occupations, to the new American Party. At the core of the party were several secret fraternal societies open only to native-born Protestants. When questioned about their beliefs, party members maintained secrecy by answering, "I know nothing"—hence, the popular name for American Party members, the **Know-Nothings**.

Know-Nothings scored startling victories in northern state elections in 1854, winning control of the legislature in Massachusetts and polling 40 percent of the vote in Pennsylvania. But in the 1850s, no party could ignore slavery, and in 1855, the American Party split into northern (antislavery) and southern (proslavery) wings. Soon after this split, many people who had voted for the Know-Nothings shifted their support to another new party, one that combined many characteristics of the Whigs with a westward-looking, expansionist, free-soil policy. This was the **Republican Party**, founded in 1854.

## THE REPUBLICAN PARTY AND THE ELECTION OF 1856

Many constituencies found room in the new Republican Party. Its supporters included many former northern Whigs who opposed slavery absolutely, many Free-Soil Party supporters who opposed the expansion of slavery but were willing to tolerate it in the South, and many northern reformers concerned about temperance and Catholicism. The Republicans also attracted the economic core of the old Whig Party—the merchants and industrialists who wanted a strong national government to promote economic growth by supporting a protective tariff, transportation improvements, and cheap land for western farmers.

The immediate question facing the nation in 1856 was which new party, the Know-Nothings or the Republicans, would emerge the stronger. But the more important question was whether the Democratic Party could hold together. The two strongest contenders for the Democratic nomination were President Pierce and Stephen A. Douglas. Douglas had proposed the Kansas-Nebraska Act and Pierce had actively supported it. But it was precisely their support of this act that made Northerners oppose both of them. The Kansas-Nebraska Act's divisive effect on the Democratic Party now became clear: no one who had voted on the bill, either for or against, could satisfy both wings of the party. A compromise candidate was found in James Buchanan of Pennsylvania, the "northern man with southern principles." Luckily for him, he had been ambassador to Great Britain at the time of the Kansas-Nebraska Act and, thus, had not had to commit himself.

The election of 1856 appeared to be a three-way contest that pitted Buchanan against explorer John C. Frémont of the Republican Party and the American (Know-Nothing) Party's candidate, former president Millard Fillmore (see Map 15.4). In fact, the election was two separate contests, one in the North and one in the South. The northern race was between Buchanan and Frémont, the southern

# Brooks Beats Sumner

In a violent episode on the floor of the U.S. Senate in 1856, Senator Charles Sumner of Massachusetts suffered permanent injury in a vicious attack by Congressman Preston Brooks of South Carolina. Trapped at his desk, Sumner was helpless as Brooks beat him so hard with his cane that it broke. A few days earlier, Sumner had given an insulting antislavery speech. Using the abusive, accusatory style favored by abolitionists, he had singled out for ridicule Senator Andrew Butler of South Carolina, charging him with choosing "the harlot, slavery" as his mistress. Senator Butler was Preston Brooks's uncle; in Brooks's mind, he was simply avenging an intolerable affront to his uncle's honor.

So far had the behavioral codes of North and South diverged that each man found his own action perfectly justifiable and the action of the other outrageous. Their attitudes were mirrored in their respective sections. Protest rallies were held in most northern cities; Sumner himself received sympathy letters from hundreds of strangers, all expressing indignation, as one writer put it, over "the most foul, most damnable and dastardly attack," and sympathetic illustrations like this one appeared in northern papers. In contrast, southern newspapers almost unanimously supported Brooks, regarding it as a well-deserved whipping for an intolerable insult. A group of Charleston merchants even bought Brooks a new cane inscribed: "Hit him again." ∎

**WHAT WOULD** a southern version of this episode look like? Which version is "true"?

SOUTHERN CHIVALRY — ARGUMENT versus CLUB'S.

**Know-Nothings** Name given to the antiimmigrant party formed from the wreckage of the Whig Party and some disaffected Northern democrats in 1854.

**Republican Party** Party that emerged in the 1850s in the aftermath of the bitter controversy over the Kansas-Nebraska Act, consisting of former Whigs, some Northern Democrats, and many Know-Nothings.

**WHAT WAS** the outcome of the *Dred Scott* decision?

**myhistorylab**
**Review Summary**

one between Buchanan and Fillmore. Buchanan won the election with only 45 percent of the popular vote, because he was the only national candidate. But the Republicans, after studying the election returns, claimed "victorious defeat," for they realized that in 1860, the addition of just two more northern states to their total would mean victory. Furthermore, the Republican Party had clearly defeated the American Party in the battle to win designation as a major party. These were grounds for great optimism—and great concern—for the Republican Party was a sectional, rather than a national, party; it drew almost all its support from the North. Southerners viewed its very existence as an attack on their vital interests. Thus, the rapid rise of the Republicans posed a growing threat to national unity.

# THE DIFFERENCES DEEPEN

Although James Buchanan firmly believed that he alone could hold together a nation so split by hatred and violence, his self-confidence outran his abilities. He was so deeply indebted to the strong southern wing of the Democratic Party that he could not take the impartial actions necessary to heal "**Bleeding Kansas.**" And his support for a momentous pro-southern decision by the Supreme Court further aggravated sectional differences.

## THE *DRED SCOTT* DECISION

In *Dred Scott* v. *Sandford*, decided on March 6, 1857, two days after James Buchanan was sworn in, a southern-dominated Supreme Court attempted—and failed—to solve the political controversy over slavery. Dred Scott had been a slave all his life. His owner, army surgeon John Emerson, had taken Scott on his military assignments during the 1830s to Illinois (a free state) and Wisconsin Territory (a free territory, north of the Missouri Compromise line). During that time, Scott married another slave, Harriet, and their daughter Eliza was born in free territory. Emerson and the Scotts then returned to Missouri (a slave state) and there, in 1846, Dred Scott sued for his freedom and that of his wife and his daughter born in Wisconsin Territory (who as women had no legal standing of their own) on the grounds that residence in free lands had made them free. It took eleven years for the case to reach the Supreme Court, and by then its importance was obvious to everyone.

Declaring the Missouri Compromise unconstitutional Chief Justice Roger B. Taney asserted that the federal government had no right to interfere with the free movement of property throughout the territories. He then dismissed the *Dred Scott* case on the grounds that only citizens could bring suits before federal courts and that black people—slave or free—were not citizens. With this bold judicial intervention into the most heated issue of the day, Taney intended to settle the controversy over the expansion of slavery once and for all. Instead, he inflamed the conflict.

The five southern members of the Supreme Court concurred in Taney's decision, as did one Northerner, Robert C. Grier. Historians have found that President-elect Buchanan had pressured Grier, a fellow Pennsylvanian, to support the majority. Two of the three other Northerners vigorously dissented, and the last voiced other objections. This was clearly a sectional decision, and the response to it was sectional. Southerners expressed great satisfaction and strong support for the Court.

Northerners disagreed. Many were so troubled by the *Dred Scott* decision that, for the first time, they found themselves seriously questioning the power of the Supreme Court to establish the "law of the land." The

**These sympathetic portraits** of Harriet and Dred Scott and their daughters in 1857 helped to shape the northern reaction to the Supreme Court's decision that denied the Scotts' claim to freedom. The infamous *Dred Scott* decision was intended to resolve the issue of slavery expansion but instead heightened angry feelings in both North and South.

New York legislature passed a resolution declaring that the Supreme Court had lost the confidence and respect of the people of that state and another resolution refusing to allow slavery within its borders "in any form or under any pretense, or for any time, however short."

## THE LECOMPTON CONSTITUTION

In Kansas, the doctrine of popular sovereignty led to continuing civil strife and the political travesty of two territorial governments. The first election of officers to a territorial government in 1855 produced a lopsided proslavery outcome that was clearly the result of illegal voting by Missouri border ruffians. Free-Soilers protested by forming their own government, giving Kansas both a proslavery territorial legislature in Lecompton and a Free-Soil government in Topeka.

Free-Soil voters boycotted a June 1857 election of representatives to a convention called to write a constitution for the territory once it reached statehood. As a result, the convention had a proslavery majority that wrote the proslavery **Lecompton constitution** and then applied to Congress for admission to the Union under its terms. In the meantime, in October, Free-Soil voters had participated in relatively honest elections for the territorial legislature, elections that returned a clear Free-Soil majority. Nevertheless, Buchanan, in the single most disastrous mistake of his administration, endorsed the proslavery constitution, because he feared the loss of the support of southern Democrats. It seemed that Kansas would enter the Union as a sixteenth slave state, making the number of slave and free states equal.

Unexpected congressional opposition came from none other than Stephen Douglas, author of the legislation that had begun the Kansas troubles in 1854. Now, in 1857, in what was surely the bravest step of his political career, Douglas opposed the Lecompton constitution on the grounds that it violated the principle of popular sovereignty. He insisted that the Lecompton constitution must be voted on by Kansas voters in honest elections. Defying James Buchanan, the president of his own party, Douglas voted with the majority in Congress in April 1858 to refuse admission to Kansas under the Lecompton constitution. In a new referendum, the people of Kansas also rejected the Lecompton constitution, 11,300 to 1,788. Kansas was finally admitted as a free state in January 1861.

## THE PANIC OF 1857

Adding to the growing political tensions was the short, but sharp, depression of 1857 and 1858. Technology played a part. In August 1857, the failure of an Ohio investment house—the kind of event that had formerly taken weeks to be widely known—was the subject of a news story flashed immediately over telegraph wires to Wall Street and other financial markets. A wave of panic selling ensued, leading to business failures and slowdowns that threw thousands out of work. The major cause of the panic was a sharp, but temporary, downturn in agricultural exports to Britain, and recovery was well under way by early 1859.

Because it affected cotton exports less than northern exports, the **Panic of 1857** was less harmful to the South than to the North. Southerners took this as proof of the superiority of their economic system to the free-labor system of the North.

It seemed that all matters of political discussion were being drawn into the sectional dispute. The next step toward disunion was an act of violence perpetrated by the grim abolitionist from Kansas, John Brown.

## JOHN BROWN'S RAID

In the heated political mood of the late 1850s, some improbable people became heroes. None was more improbable than John Brown, the self-appointed avenger who had slaughtered unarmed proslavery men in Kansas in 1856. In 1859, Brown

---

14–8
Dred Scott v. Sandford (1857)

**QUICK REVIEW**

**The *Dred Scott* Decision**

- 1857 attempt by Supreme Court to solve the political controversy over slavery.

- Court ruled that slaves were property and government could not restrain free movement of property.

- Decision invalidated the Missouri Compromise.

**Bleeding Kansas**   Violence between pro- and antislavery forces in Kansas Territory after the passage of the Kansas-Nebraska Act in 1854.

***Dred Scott* decision**   Supreme Court ruling, in a lawsuit brought by Dred Scott, a slave demanding his freedom based on his residence in a free state, that slaves could not be U.S. citizens and that Congress had no jurisdiction over slavery in the territories.

**Lecompton constitution**   Proslavery draft written in 1857 by Kansas territorial delegates elected under questionable circumstances; it was rejected by two governors, supported by President Buchanan, and decisively defeated by Congress.

**Panic of 1857**   Banking crisis that caused a credit crunch in the North; it was less severe in the South, where high cotton prices spurred a quick recovery.

# OVERVIEW | Political Parties Split and Realign

| | |
|---|---|
| **Whig Party** | Ran its last presidential candidate in 1852. The candidate, General Winfield Scott, alienated many southern Whigs, and the party was so split it could not field a candidate in 1856. |
| **Democratic Party** | Remained a national party through 1856, but Buchanan's actions as president made southern domination of the party so clear that many northern Democrats were alienated. Stephen Douglas, running as a northern Democrat in 1860, won 29 percent of the popular vote; John Breckinridge, running as a southern Democrat, won 18 percent. |
| **Liberty Party** | Antislavery party; ran James G. Birney for president in 1844. He won 62,000 votes, largely from northern antislavery Whigs. |
| **Free-Soil Party** | Ran Martin Van Buren, former Democratic president, in 1848. Gained 10 percent of the popular vote, largely from Whigs but also from some northern Democrats. |
| **American (Know-Nothing) Party** | Nativist party made striking gains in 1854 congressional elections, attracting both northern and southern Whigs. In 1856, its presidential candidate, Millard Fillmore, won 21 percent of the popular vote. |
| **Republican Party** | Founded in 1854. Attracted many northern Whigs and northern Democrats. Presidential candidate John C. Frémont won 33 percent of the popular vote in 1856; in 1860, Abraham Lincoln won 40 percent and was elected in a four-way race. |

**myhistorylab**

**Overview:** *Political Parties Split and Realign*

proposed a wild scheme to raid the South and start a general slave uprising. He believed that discontent among southern slaves was so great that such an uprising needed only a spark to get going. On October 16, 1859, Brown led a group of twenty-two white and African American men against the arsenal. In less than a day, the raid was over. Eight of Brown's men (including two of his sons) were dead, no slaves had joined the fight, and Brown himself was captured. Moving quickly to prevent a lynching by local mobs, the state of Virginia tried and convicted Brown (while he was still weak from the wounds of battle) of treason, murder, and fomenting insurrection.

Brown's death by hanging on December 2, 1859, was marked throughout northern communities with public rites of mourning not seen since the death of George Washington. Church bells tolled, buildings were draped in black, ministers preached sermons, prayer meetings were held, abolitionists issued eulogies. Naturally, not all Northerners supported Brown's action. But many people, while rejecting Brown's raid, increasingly supported the antislavery cause that he represented.

Brown's raid shocked the South because it aroused the fear of slave rebellion. Southerners believed that northern abolitionists were provoking slave revolts, a suspicion apparently confirmed when documents captured at Harpers Ferry revealed that Brown had the financial support of half a dozen members of the northern elite.

Even more shocking to Southerners than the raid itself was the extent of northern mourning for Brown's death. Although the Republican Party disavowed Brown's actions, Southerners simply did not believe the party's statements. Senator Robert Toombs of Georgia warned that the South would "never permit this Federal government to pass into the traitorous hands of the Black Republican party." Talk of secession as the only possible response became common throughout the South.

## THE SOUTH SECEDES

**WHY DID** the South secede following the Republican Party victory in the election of 1860?

**myhistorylab**

**Review Summary**

By 1860, sectional differences had caused one national party, the Whigs, to collapse. The second national party, the Democrats, stood on the brink of dissolution. Not only the politicians but also ordinary people in both the North and the South were coming to believe there was no way to avoid what in 1858 William Seward (once a Whig, now a Republican) had called an "irrepressible conflict."

# THE ELECTION OF 1860

The split of the Democratic Party into northern and southern wings that had occurred during President Buchanan's tenure became official at the Democratic nominating conventions in 1860. The party convened first in Charleston, South Carolina. Although Stephen Douglas had the support of the plurality of delegates, he did not have the two-thirds majority necessary for nomination. As the price of their support, Southerners insisted that Douglas support a federal slave code—a guarantee that slavery would be protected in the territories. Douglas could not agree without violating his own belief in popular sovereignty and losing his northern support.

After ten days, the convention ended where it had begun: deadlocked. Northern supporters of Douglas were angry and bitter: "I never heard Abolitionists talk more uncharitably and rancorously of the people of the South than the Douglas men," one reporter wrote. "They say they do not care a damn where the South goes."

In June, the Democrats met again in Baltimore. The Douglasites, recognizing the need for a united party, were eager to compromise wherever they could, but most southern Democrats were not. More than a third of the delegates bolted. Later, holding a convention of their own, they nominated Buchanan's vice president, John C. Breckinridge of Kentucky. The remaining two-thirds of the Democrats nominated Douglas, but everyone knew that a Republican victory was inevitable. To make matters worse, some southern Whigs joined with some border-state nativists to form the **Constitutional Union Party**, which nominated John Bell of Tennessee.

Republican strategy was built on the lessons of the 1856 "victorious defeat." The Republicans planned to carry all the states Frémont had won, plus Pennsylvania, Illinois, and Indiana. The two leading Republican contenders were Senator William H. Seward of New York and Abraham Lincoln of Illinois. Seward, the party's best-known figure, had enemies among party moderates, who thought he was too radical, and among nativists with whom he had clashed in the New York Whig Party. Lincoln, on the other hand, appeared new, impressive, more moderate than Seward, and certain to carry Illinois. Lincoln won the nomination on the third ballot.

The election of 1860 presented voters with one of the clearest choices in American history. On the key issue of slavery, Breckinridge supported its extension to the territories; Lincoln stood firmly for its exclusion. Douglas attempted to hold the middle ground with his principle of popular sovereignty; Bell vaguely favored compromise as well. Although they spoke clearly against the extension of slavery, Republicans sought to dispel their radical abolitionist image. The Republican platform condemned John Brown's raid as "the gravest of crimes," repeatedly denied that Republicans favored the social equality of black people, and strenuously affirmed that they sought to preserve the Union. In reality, Republicans simply did not believe the South would secede if Lincoln won.

The only candidate who spoke urgently and openly about the impending threat of secession was Douglas. Breaking with convention, Douglas campaigned personally, in both the North and, bravely, in the hostile South. Realizing his own chances for election were slight, he told his private secretary, "Mr. Lincoln is the next President. We must try to save the Union. I will go South."

In accordance with tradition, Lincoln did not campaign for himself, but many other Republicans spoke for him. The Republicans did not campaign in the South; Breckinridge did not campaign in the North. Each side was, therefore, free to believe the worst about the other.

The mood in the Deep South was close to mass hysteria. Rumors of slave revolts swept the region, and vigilance committees sprang up to counter the

**In a contemporary** engraving, John Brown and his followers are shown trapped inside the armory at Harpers Ferry in October 1859. Captured, tried, and executed, Brown was regarded as a martyr in the North and a terrorist in the South.

**Constitutional Union Party** National party formed in 1860, mainly by former Whigs, that emphasized allegiance to the Union and strict enforcement of all national legislation.

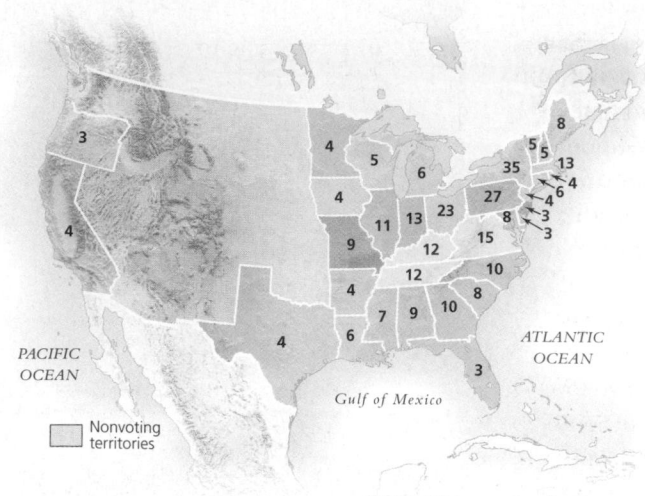

| | Electoral Vote (%) | Popular Vote (%) |
|---|---|---|
| **ABRAHAM LINCOLN** (Republican) | 180 (59) | 1,865,593 (40) |
| John C. Breckinridge (Southern Democrat) | 72 (24) | 848,356 (18) |
| John Bell (Constitutional Union) | 39 (13) | 592,906 (13) |
| Stephen A. Douglas (Northern Democrat) | 12 (4) | 1,382,713 (29) |
| States that Republicans lost in 1856, won in 1860 | | |

**MAP 15.5**

**The Election of 1860**   The election of 1860 was a sectional election. Lincoln won no votes in the South, Breckinridge none in the North. The contest in the North was between Lincoln and Douglas, and although Lincoln swept the electoral vote, Douglas's popular vote was uncomfortably close. The large number of northern Democratic voters opposed to Lincoln was a source of political trouble for him during the Civil War.

WHAT DO the results of the election of 1860 tell us about support for Lincoln in the North on the eve of the Civil War?

supposed threat. In the South Carolina up-country, the question of secession dominated races for the state legislature. Candidates such as A. S. Wallace of York, who advocated "patriotic forbearance" if Lincoln won, were soundly defeated. The very passion and excitement of the election campaign moved Southerners toward extremism.

The election of 1860 produced the second highest voter turnout in U.S. history. The election turned out to be two regional contests: Breckinridge versus Bell in the South, Lincoln versus Douglas in the North. Lincoln won all eighteen of the free states (he split New Jersey with Douglas) and almost 40 percent of the popular vote. Douglas carried only Missouri but gained nearly 30 percent of the popular vote. Lincoln's electoral vote total was overwhelming: 180 to a combined 123 for the other three candidates. But although Lincoln had won 54 percent of the vote in the northern states, his name had not even appeared on the ballot in ten southern states. The true winner of the 1860 election was sectionalism (see Map 15.5).

## THE SOUTH LEAVES THE UNION

The results of the election shocked Southerners. They were humiliated and frightened by the prospect of becoming a permanent minority in a political system dominated by a party pledged to the elimination of slavery. In southern eyes, the Republican triumph meant they would become unequal partners in the federal enterprise, their way of life (the slave system) existing on borrowed time. Mary Boykin Chesnut, member of a well-connected South Carolina family, confided to her diary, "The die is cast—no more vain regrets— sad forebodings are useless. The stake is life or death."

The governors of South Carolina, Alabama, and Mississippi, each of whom had committed his state to secession if Lincoln were elected, immediately issued calls for special state conventions. At the same time, calls went out to southern communities to form vigilance committees and volunteer militia companies. Cooperationists (the term used for those opposed to immediate secession) were either intimidated into silence or simply left behind by the speed of events.

On December 20, 1860, a state convention in South Carolina, accompanied by all the hoopla and excitement of bands, fireworks displays, and huge rallies, voted unanimously to secede from the Union. In the weeks that followed, conventions in six other southern states (Mississippi, Florida, Alabama, Georgia, Louisiana, and Texas) followed suit, with the support, on average, of 80 percent of their delegates. There was genuine division of opinion in the Deep South, especially in Georgia and Alabama, along customary up-country–low-country lines. Yeoman farmers who did not own slaves and workers in the cities of the South were most likely to favor compromise with the North. But secessionists constantly reminded both groups that the Republican victory would lead to the emancipation of the slaves and the end of white privilege. And all Southerners, most of whom were deeply loyal to their state and region, believed that Northerners threatened their way of life. Throughout the South, secession occurred because Southerners no longer believed they had a choice.

In every state that seceded, the joyous scenes of South Carolina were repeated as the decisiveness of action replaced the long years of anxiety and tension. People danced in the streets, most believing the North had no choice but to accept secession peacefully. They ignored the fact that eight other slave states—Delaware, Maryland, Kentucky, Missouri, Virginia, North Carolina, Tennessee, and Arkansas—had not acted, though the latter four states did secede after war broke out (see Map 15.6). Just as Republicans had miscalculated in thinking southern threats a mere bluff, so secessionists now miscalculated in believing they would be able to leave the Union in peace.

## THE NORTH'S POLITICAL OPTIONS

What should the North do? Buchanan, indecisive as always, did nothing. The decision thus rested with Abraham Lincoln, even before he officially became president. One possibility was compromise, and many proposals were suggested, ranging from full adoption of the Breckinridge campaign platform to reinstatement of the Missouri Compromise line. Lincoln cautiously refused them all, making it clear that he would not compromise on the extension of slavery, which was the South's key demand. He hoped, by appearing firm but moderate, to discourage additional southern states from seceding, while giving pro-Union Southerners time to organize. He succeeded in his first aim but not in the second. Lincoln and most of the Republican Party had seriously overestimated the strength of pro-Union sentiment in the South.

A second possibility, suggested by Horace Greeley of the *New York Tribune*, was to let the seven seceding states "go in peace." This is what many secessionists expected, but too many Northerners—including Lincoln himself—believed in the Union for this to happen. As Lincoln said, what was at stake was "the necessity of proving that popular government is not an absurdity. We must settle this question now, whether in a free government the minority have the right to break up the government whenever they choose."

The third possibility was force, and this was the crux of the dilemma. Although he believed their action was wrong, Lincoln was loath to go to war to force the seceding states back into the Union. On the other hand, he refused to give up federal powers over military forts and customs posts in the South. These were precisely the powers the seceding states had to command if they were to function as an independent nation. A confrontation was bound to come.

## ESTABLISHMENT OF THE CONFEDERACY

In February, delegates from the seven seceding states met in Montgomery, Alabama, and created the **Confederate States of America**. They wrote a constitution that was identical to the Constitution of the United States, with a few crucial exceptions: it strongly supported states' rights and made the abolition of slavery practically impossible. These two clauses did much to define the Confederate enterprise. L. W. Spratt of South Carolina confessed as much in 1859: "We stand committed to the South, but we stand more vitally committed to the cause of slavery. It is, indeed, to be doubted whether the South [has] any cause apart from the institution which affects her."

The Montgomery convention chose Jefferson Davis of Mississippi as president and Alexander Stephens of Georgia as vice president of the new nation. Both men were known as moderates. The choice of moderates was deliberate, for the strategy of the new Confederate state was to argue that secession was a normal, responsible, and expectable course of action, and nothing for the North to get upset about. This was the theme that President Jefferson Davis of the Confederate States of America struck in his Inaugural Address, delivered to a crowd of 10,000 from the steps of the State Capitol at Montgomery, Alabama, on February 18, 1861. Secession was a legal and peaceful step that, Davis said, quoting from the Declaration of Independence, "illustrates the American idea that governments rest on the consent

**This special edition** of the *Charleston Mercury* was issued on December 20, 1860, the day South Carolina voted to secede from the Union.

**14–9**
Abraham Lincoln, *A House Divided* (1858)

**Confederate States of America**
Nation proclaimed in Montgomery, Alabama, in February 1861, after the seven states of the Lower South seceded from the United States.

# OVERVIEW | The Irrepressible Conflict

| Year | Event | Description |
|---|---|---|
| 1776 | Declaration of Independence | Thomas Jefferson's denunciation of slavery deleted from the final version. |
| 1787 | Northwest Ordinance | Slavery prohibited in the Northwest Territory (north of the Ohio River). |
| 1787 | Constitution | Slavery unmentioned but acknowledged in Article I, Section 2, counting three-fifths of all African Americans, slave and free, in a state's population; and in Article I, Section 9, which barred Congress from prohibiting the international slave trade for twenty years. |
| 1803 | Louisiana Purchase | Louisiana admitted as a slave state in 1812; no decision about the rest of Louisiana Purchase. |
| 1820 | Missouri Compromise | Missouri admitted as a slave state, but slavery prohibited in Louisiana Purchase north of 36°30'. |
| 1846 | Wilmot Proviso | Proposal to prohibit slavery in territory that might be gained in Mexican-American War causes splits in national parties. |
| 1850 | Compromise of 1850 | California admitted as free state; Texas (already admitted in 1845) is a slave state; the rest of Mexican Cession to be decided by popular sovereignty. Ends the slave trade in the District of Columbia, but a stronger Fugitive Slave Law, leading to a number of violent recaptures, arouses northern antislavery opinion. |
| 1854 | Kansas-Nebraska Act | At the urging of Stephen A. Douglas, Congress opens Kansas and Nebraska Territories for settlement under popular sovereignty. Open warfare between proslavery and antislavery factions breaks out in Kansas. |
| 1857 | Lecompton Constitution | President James Buchanan's decision to admit Kansas to the Union with a proslavery constitution is defeated in Congress. |
| 1857 | Dred Scott Decision | The Supreme Court's denial of Dred Scott's case for freedom is welcomed in the South, condemned in the North. |
| 1859 | John Brown's Raid and Execution | Northern support for John Brown shocks the South. |
| 1860 | Democratic Party Nominating Conventions | The Democrats are unable to agree on a candidate; two candidates, one northern (Stephen A. Douglas) and one southern (John C. Breckinridge) split the party and the vote, thus allowing Republican Abraham Lincoln to win. |

## myhistorylab

**Overview:** *The Irrepressible Conflict*

### QUICK REVIEW

**Northern Response to Secession**

◆ Buchanan did nothing in response to secession.

◆ Lincoln refused calls to compromise on the question of slavery.

◆ Lincoln also rejected proposals to let the seven seceding states leave the Union.

of the governed . . . and that it is the right of the people to alter or abolish them at will whenever they become destructive of the ends for which they were established."

## LINCOLN'S INAUGURATION

The country as a whole waited to see what Abraham Lincoln would do, which at first appeared to be very little. In Springfield, Lincoln refused to issue public statements before his inaugural for fear of making a delicate situation worse. Similarly, during a twelve-day whistle-stopping railroad trip east from Springfield, he was careful to say nothing controversial. Eastern intellectuals, already suspicious of a mere "prairie lawyer," were not impressed. These signs of moderation and caution did not appeal to an American public with a penchant for electing military heroes. Americans wanted leadership and action.

Lincoln continued, however, to offer nonbelligerent firmness and moderation. And at the end of his Inaugural Address on March 4, 1861, as he stood ringed by federal troops called out in case of a Confederate attack, the new president offered unexpected eloquence:

> I am loath to close. We are not enemies, but friends. We must not be enemies. Though passion may have strained, it must not break our bonds of affection. The mystic chords of memory, stretching from every battlefield, and patriot grave, to every living heart and hearthstone, all over this broad land, will yet swell the chorus of the Union, when again touched, as surely they will be, by the better angels of our nature.

# MAP EXPLORATION

To explore an interactive version of this map, go to **http://www.prenhall.com/faraghertlc/map15.6**

Map legend:
- Border states (did not secede)
- Seceded before Fort Sumter
- Seceded after Fort Sumter
- Counties that voted against secession
- No returns

Note: The western counties of Virginia remained loyal to the Union and were admitted as the state of West Virginia in 1863.

**MAP 15.6**

**The South Secedes**   The southern states that would constitute the Confederacy seceded in two stages. The states of the Lower South seceded before Lincoln took office. Arkansas and three states of the Upper South—Virginia, North Carolina, and Tennessee—waited until after the South fired on Fort Sumter. And four border slave states—Delaware, Maryland, Kentucky, and Missouri—chose not to secede. Every southern state (except South Carolina) was divided on the issue of secession, generally along up-country–low-country lines. In Virginia, this division was so extreme that West Virginia split off to become a separate nonslave state admitted to the Union in 1863.

WHY WERE some states quicker to secede than others?

# CONCLUSION

Americans had much to boast about in 1850. Their nation was vastly larger, richer, and more powerful than it had been in 1800. But the issue of slavery was slowly dividing the North and the South, two communities with similar origins and many common bonds. The following decade was marked by frantic efforts at political compromise, beginning with the Compromise of 1850, continuing with the Kansas-Nebraska Act of 1854, and culminating in the Supreme Court's 1859 decision in the *Dred Scott* case. Increasingly, the ordinary people of the two regions demanded resolution of the crisis. The two great parties of the Second American Party System, the Democrats and the Whigs, unable to find a solution, were destroyed. Two new sectional parties—the Republican Party and a southern party devoted to the defense of slavery—fought the 1860 election, but Southerners refused to accept the national verdict. Politics had failed: the issue of slavery was irreconcilable. The only remaining recourse was war. But although Americans were divided, they were still one people. That made the war, when it came, all the more terrible.

**401**

## CHRONOLOGY

| | |
|---|---|
| 1820 | Missouri Compromise |
| 1828–32 | Nullification Crisis |
| 1846 | Wilmot Proviso |
| 1848 | Treaty of Guadalupe Hidalgo ends Mexican-American War |
| | Zachary Taylor elected president |
| | Free-Soil Party formed |
| 1849 | California and Utah seek admission to the Union as free states |
| 1850 | Compromise of 1850 |
| | California admitted as a free state |
| | American (Know-Nothing) Party formed |
| | Zachary Taylor dies; Millard Fillmore becomes president |
| 1851 | North reacts to Fugitive Slave Law |
| | Harriet Beecher Stowe's *Uncle Tom's Cabin* published |
| 1852 | Franklin Pierce elected president |
| 1854 | Ostend Manifesto |
| | Kansas-Nebraska Act |
| | Treaties with Indians in northern part of Indian Territory renegotiated |

| | |
|---|---|
| | Republican Party formed as Whig Party dissolves |
| 1855 | William Walker leads his first filibustering expedition to Nicaragua |
| 1856 | Burning and looting of Lawrence, Kansas |
| | John Brown leads Pottawatomie massacre |
| | Attack on Senator Charles Sumner |
| | James Buchanan elected president |
| 1857 | *Dred Scott* decision |
| | President Buchanan accepts proslavery Lecompton constitution in Kansas |
| | Panic of 1857 |
| 1858 | Congress rejects Lecompton constitution |
| | Lincoln–Douglas debates |
| 1859 | John Brown's raid on Harpers Ferry |
| 1860 | Four parties run presidential candidates |
| | Abraham Lincoln elected president |
| | South Carolina secedes from Union |
| 1861 | Six other Deep South states secede |
| | Confederate States of America formed |
| | Lincoln takes office |

## REVIEW QUESTIONS

1. What aspects of the remarkable economic development of the United States in the first half of the nineteenth century contributed to the sectional crisis of the 1850s?

2. How might the violent efforts by abolitionists to free escaped slaves who had been recaptured and the federal armed enforcement of the Fugitive Slave Law have been viewed differently by northern merchants (the so-called Cotton Whigs), Irish immigrants, and abolitionists?

3. Consider the course of events in "Bloody Kansas" from Douglas's Kansas-Nebraska Act to the congressional rejection of the Lecompton constitution. Were these events the inevitable result of the political impasse in Washington, or could other decisions have been made that would have changed the outcome?

4. The nativism of the 1850s that surfaced so strongly in the Know-Nothing Party was eclipsed by the crisis over slavery. But nativist sentiment has been a recurring theme in American politics. Discuss why it was strong in the 1850s and why it has emerged periodically since then.

5. Evaluate the character and actions of John Brown: Was he the hero proclaimed by northern supporters or the terrorist condemned by the South?

6. Imagine that you lived in Illinois, home state to both Douglas and Lincoln, in 1860. How would you have voted in the presidential election, and why?

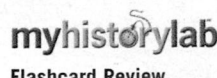

# KEY TERMS

Bleeding Kansas (p. 395)
Compromise of 1850 (p. 383)
Confederate States of America
  (p. 399)
Constitutional Union Party (p. 397)
*Dred Scott* decision (p. 395)
Fugitive Slave Law (p. 386)

Kansas-Nebraska Act (p. 389)
Know-Nothings (p. 394)
Lecompton constitution (p. 395)
Lincoln-Douglas debates (p. 380)
Panic of 1857 (p. 395)
Popular sovereignty (p. 383)
Republican Party (p. 394)

**myhistorylab**
Flashcard Review

# RECOMMENDED READING

William L. Barney, *The Secessionist Impulse: Alabama and Mississippi in 1860*
  (1974). Covers the election of 1860 and the subsequent conventions that
  led to secession.

Nicole Etcheson, *Bleeding Kansas: Contested Liberty in the Civil War Era* (2004).
  A look at the Kansas issue from the perspective of white settlers.

Don E. Fehrenbacher, *The* Dred Scott *Case: Its Significance in American Law and
  Politics* (1978). A major study by the leading historian on this controversial
  decision.

Eric Foner, *Free Soil, Free Labor, Free Men: The Ideology of the Republican Party before
  the Civil War* (1970). One of the first studies to focus on the free labor ideology of the North and its importance in the political disputes of the 1850s.

William A. Link, *Roots of Secession: Slavery and Politics in Antebellum Virginia* (2003).
  Draws connections between the changing circumstances of slavery and politics in the 1850s.

Robert E. May, *Manifest Destiny's Underworld: Filibustering in Antebellum America*
  (2002). A study of the activities and attitudes toward the adventurers.

David S. Reynolds, *John Brown, Abolitionist* (2005). Argues that Brown's extremism became the Civil War norm.

Kenneth M. Stampp, *America in 1857: A Nation on the Brink* (1990). A study of
  the "crucial" year by a leading southern historian.

John Stauffer, *The Black Hearts of Men: Radical Abolitionists and the Transformation
  of Race* (2001). Argues that radical abolitionists rejected the gender and
  racial conventions of their day.

For study resources for this chapter, go to **www.myhistorylab.com** and choose *Out of Many,
Teaching and Learning Classroom Edition.* You will find a wealth of study and review material
for this chapter, including pretests and posttests, customized study plan, key-term review
flash cards, interactive map and document activities, and documents for analysis.

*If it is necessary that I should
fall on the battle-field
for my Country I am ready.*
—Sullivan Ballou

**Awaiting combat, 1861:** Union Soldiers from New York relax
at camp awaiting orders to move to the front. The young men
show great confidence and determination for their coming
engagements, though one fellow to the left of the tent,
perhaps a teenager far from home, seems to long for something
as he stares beyond the camera. Note also the young
African American with a broom sitting apart from the soldiers.

# 16

# THE CIVIL WAR
## 1861–1865

**WHAT ADVANTAGES** did the North possess at the outset of the Civil War?

**HOW DID** the power of the federal government expand as the war progressed?

**WHAT SUCCESSES** did the South enjoy in the early years of the war and how were they achieved?

**HOW DID** the end of slavery affect the war efforts of the North and South?

**WHAT IMPACT** did the war have on northern political, economic, and social life? and on the same aspects of southern life?

**HOW DID** Grant and Sherman turn the tide of the war?

# AMERICAN COMMUNITIES

## Mother Bickerdyke Connects Northern Communities to Their Boys at War

IN MAY 1861, THE REVEREND EDWARD BEECHER INTERRUPTED HIS customary Sunday service at Brick Congregational Church in Galesburg, Illinois, to read a disturbing letter to the congregation. Two months earlier, Galesburg had proudly sent 500 of its young men off to join the Union army. They had not yet been in battle. Yet, the letter reported, an alarming number were dying of diseases caused by inadequate food, medical care, and sanitation at the crowded military camp in Cairo, Illinois. Most army doctors were surgeons trained to operate and amputate on the battlefield. The letter writer, appalled by the squalor and misery he saw around him, complained of abuses by the army. The Union army, however, was overwhelmed with the task of readying recruits for battle and had made few provisions for their health when they were not in combat.

The shocked and grieving members of Beecher's congregation quickly decided to send not only supplies but also one of their number to inspect the conditions at the Cairo camp and to take action. In spite of warnings that army regulations excluded women from encampments, the congregation voted to send their most qualified member, Mary Ann Bickerdyke, a middle-aged widow who made her living as a "botanic physician."

"Mother" Bickerdyke, as she was called, let nothing stand in the way of helping her "boys." When she arrived in Cairo, she immediately set to work cleaning the hospital tents and the soldiers themselves, and finding and cooking nourishing food for them. The hospital director, who resented her interference, ordered her to leave, but she blandly continued her work. When he reported her to the commanding officer, General Benjamin Prentiss, she quickly convinced the general to let her stay.

A plain spoken, hardworking woman, totally unfazed by rank or tender masculine egos, Mother Bickerdyke single-mindedly devoted herself to what she called "the Lord's work." Once, when an indignant officer's wife complained about Bickerdyke's rudeness, General William Tecumseh Sherman joked, "You've picked the one person around here who outranks me. If you want to lodge a complaint against her, you'll have to take it to President Lincoln."

Other communities all over the North rallied to make up for the Army's shortcomings with supplies and assistance. By their actions, Mother Bickerdyke and others like her exposed the War Department's inability to meet the needs of the nation's first mass army. The efforts of women on the local level quickly took on national dimensions. The Women's Central Association of Relief (WCAR) eventually had 7,000 chapters throughout the North. Its volunteers raised funds, made and collected food, clothes, medicine, bandages, and more than 250,000 quilts and comforters, and sent them to army camps and hospitals. All told, association chapters supplied an estimated $15 million worth of goods to the Union troops.

In June 1861, responding to requests by officials of the WCAR for formal recognition of the organization, President Abraham Lincoln created the United States Sanitary Commission and gave it the power to investigate and advise the Medical Bureau.

Although at first she worked independently and remained suspicious of all organizations (and even of many other relief workers), in 1862 Mother Bickerdyke was persuaded to become an official agent of "the Sanitary," as it was known. The advantage to her was access to the commission's warehouses and the ability to order from them precisely what she needed. The advantage to the Sanitary was that Mother Bickerdyke was an unequaled fundraiser. With the help of Bickerdyke's blunt appeals, the Sanitary raised $50 million for the Union war effort.

Illinois

The Civil War was a national tragedy, ripping apart the political fabric of the country and causing more casualties than any other war in the nation's history. The death toll of approximately 620,000 exceeded the number of dead in all the other wars from the Revolution through the Vietnam War. Yet in another sense, it was a community triumph. Local communities directly supported and sustained their soldiers on a massive scale in unprecedented ways. As national unity failed, the strength of local communities, symbolized by Mother Bickerdyke, endured.

# COMMUNITIES MOBILIZE FOR WAR

A neutral observer in March 1861 might have seen ominous similarities. Two nations—the United States of America (shorn of seven states in the Deep South) and the Confederate States of America—each blamed the other for the breakup of the Union. Two new presidents—Abraham Lincoln and Jefferson Davis—each faced the challenging task of building and maintaining national unity. Two regions—North and South—scorned each other and boasted of their own superiority. But the most important similarity was not yet apparent: both sides were unprepared for the ordeal that lay ahead.

## FORT SUMTER: THE WAR BEGINS

Fort Sumter, a federal military installation, sat on a granite island at the entrance to Charleston harbor. So long as it remained in Union hands, Charleston, the center of secessionist sentiment, would be immobilized. Thus, it was hardly surprising that Fort Sumter would provide President Lincoln with his first crisis.

With the fort dangerously low on supplies, Lincoln had to decide whether to abandon it or risk the fight that might ensue if he ordered it resupplied. On April 6, 1861, Lincoln took cautious and careful action, notifying the governor of South Carolina that he was sending a relief force to the fort carrying only food and no military supplies. Now the decision rested with Jefferson Davis. On April 10, he ordered General P. G. T. Beauregard to demand the surrender of Fort Sumter and to attack it if the garrison did not comply. On April 12, Beauregard opened fire. Two days later, the defenders surrendered.

Even before the attack on Fort Sumter, the Confederate Congress had authorized a volunteer army of 100,000 men to serve for twelve months. Men flocked to enlist, and their communities sent them off in ceremonies featuring bands, bonfires, and belligerent oratory.

The "thunderclap of Sumter" startled the North into an angry response. The apathy and uncertainty that had prevailed since Lincoln's election disappeared, to be replaced by strong feelings of patriotism. On April 15, Lincoln issued a proclamation calling for 75,000 state militiamen to serve in the federal army for ninety days. Enlistment offices were swamped with so many enthusiastic volunteers that men were sent home. Free African Americans, among the most eager to serve, were turned away: this was not yet a war for or by black people.

**WHAT ADVANTAGES** did the North possess at the outset of the Civil War?

myhistorylab
**Review Summary**

**15–1**
Jefferson Davis, *Address to the Provisional Congress of the Confederate States of America* (1861)

**15–2**
Alexander Hamilton Stephens, *The "Cornerstone Speech"* (1861)

**15–4**
*Why They Fought* (1861)

**This Currier and** Ives lithograph shows the opening moment of the Civil War. On April 12, 1861, Confederate General P.G.T. Beauregard ordered the shelling of Fort Sumter in Charleston harbor. Two days later, Union Major Robert Anderson surrendered, and mobilization began for what turned out to be the most devastating war in American history.

## IMAGE KEY

for pages 404–405

**a.** A federal flag that flew over Fort Sumter.

**b.** A photo of engineers of the 8th New York State Militia, 1861.

**c.** The battle flag of the Second Battalion Hilliard's Alabama Legion. This flag was pierced 83 times during the charge up Snod Grass Hill at Chickamauga, Georgia.

**d.** The gray cap of a Confederate soldier from the American Civil War.

**e.** A blue Union soldier's hat with a bugle emblem embroidered on the front.

**f.** The opening moment of the Civil War, April 12, 1861, at Fort Sumter in Charleston harbor.

**g.** A painting by William C. Washington, *Jackson Entering the City of Winchester*, shows General "Stonewall" Jackson saving the Virginia town from Union capture in 1862.

**h.** Robert E. Lee (1807–1870), commander-in-chief of the Confederate armies during the Civil War.

**i.** American President Abraham Lincoln presents the Emancipation Proclamation to grateful black slaves and white peasants in a political cartoon about education, freedom, and equality.

**j.** A black family runs through a vacant lot while being chased by white hooligans during the 1863 race riots in New York City.

The mobilization in Chester, Pennsylvania, was typical of the northern response to the outbreak of war. As volunteers marched off to Washington (the gathering place for the Union army), companies of home guards were organized by the men who remained behind. Within a month, the women of Chester had organized a countywide system of war relief. Such relief organizations, some formally organized, some informal, emerged in every community, North and South, that sent soldiers off to the Civil War. These organizations not only played a vital role in supplying the troops, but they also maintained the human, local link on which so many soldiers depended. In this sense, every American community accompanied its young men to war.

### THE BORDER STATES

The first secession, between December 20, 1860, and February 1, 1861, had taken seven Deep South states out of the Union. Now, in April, the firing on Fort Sumter and Lincoln's call for state militias forced the other southern states to take sides. Courted—and pressured—by both North and South, four states of the Upper South (Virginia, Arkansas, Tennessee, and North Carolina) joined the original seven in April and May 1861. Virginia's secession tipped the other three toward the Confederacy. The capital of the Confederacy was now moved to Richmond.

Still undecided was the loyalty of the northernmost tier of slave-owning states: Missouri, Kentucky, Maryland, and Delaware. Each controlled vital strategic assets. Missouri not only bordered the Mississippi River but also controlled the routes to the west. Kentucky controlled the Ohio River. The main railroad link with the West ran through Maryland and the hill region of western Virginia. Delaware controlled access to Philadelphia. Finally, were Maryland to secede, the nation's capital would be completely surrounded by Confederate territory.

Delaware was loyal to the Union (less than 2 percent of its population were slaves), but Maryland's loyalty was divided, as an ugly incident on April 19 showed. When the Sixth Massachusetts Regiment marched through Baltimore, a hostile crowd of 10,000 southern sympathizers, carrying Confederate flags, pelted the troops with bricks, paving stones, and bullets. Finally, in desperation, the troops fired on the crowd, killing twelve people and wounding others. In retaliation, southern sympathizers burned the railroad bridges to the North and destroyed the telegraph line to Washington, cutting off communication between the capital and the rest of the Union for six days.

Lincoln's response was swift and stern. He stationed Union troops along Maryland's crucial railroads, declared martial law in Baltimore, and arrested the suspected ringleaders of the pro-Confederate mob and held them without trial. The arrests in Maryland were the first of a number of violations of basic civil rights during the war, all of which the president justified on the basis of national security.

An even bloodier division occurred in Missouri, where old foes from "Bleeding Kansas" faced off. The proslavery governor and most of the legislature fled to Arkansas, where they declared a Confederate state government in exile, while Unionists remained in control in St. Louis. Consequently, Missouri was plagued by guerrilla battles throughout the war. In Kentucky, division took the form of a huge illegal trade with the Confederacy through neighboring Tennessee.

That Delaware, Maryland, Missouri, and Kentucky chose to stay in the Union was a severe blow to the Confederacy. Among them, the four states could have added 45 percent to the white population and military manpower of the Confederacy and 80 percent to its manufacturing capacity.

## THE BATTLE OF BULL RUN

Once sides had been chosen and the initial flush of enthusiasm had passed, the nature of the war, and the mistaken notions about it, soon became clear. The event that shattered the illusions was the First Battle of Bull Run, at Bull Run Creek near Manassas in Virginia in July 1861. Confident of a quick victory, a Union army of 35,000 men marched south. The troops were accompanied not only by journalists but also by a crowd of politicians and sightseers. At first the Union troops held their ground against the 25,000 Confederate troops. But when 2,300 fresh Confederate troops arrived as reinforcements, the untrained northern troops broke ranks in an uncontrolled retreat that swept up the frightened sightseers as well.

## THE RELATIVE STRENGTHS OF NORTH AND SOUTH

Bull Run was sobering—and prophetic. The Civil War was the most lethal military conflict in American history, leaving a legacy of devastation on the battlefield and desolation at home. It claimed the lives of nearly 620,000 soldiers, more than the First and Second World Wars combined. One out of every four soldiers who fought in the war never returned home.

Overall, in terms of both population and productive capacity, the Union seemed to have a commanding edge over the Confederacy. The North had two and a half times the South's population and enjoyed an even greater advantage in industrial capacity (nine times that of the South). These advantages were ultimately to prove decisive: by the end of the war, the Union had managed to field and equip more than 2 million soldiers as compared to the Confederacy's 800,000. The Confederacy's problems of supply, however, were due mostly to a poor railroad system. But in the short term, the South had important assets to counter the advantage of the North (see Figure 16.1).

The first was the nature of the struggle. For the South, this was a defensive war, in which the basic principle of the defense of home and community united almost all white citizens, regardless of their views about slavery. The North would have to invade the South and then control it against guerrilla opposition in order to win.

Second, the military disparity was less extreme than it appeared. Although the North had manpower, its troops were mostly untrained. Moreover, the South appeared to have an advantage in military leaders, the most notable of which was Robert E. Lee.

Finally, it was widely believed that slavery would work to the South's advantage, for slaves could continue to do the vital plantation work while their masters

**15–3**
Mary Boykin Chesnut,
*A Confederate Lady's Diary*
(1861)

**15–5**
*A Confederate General Assesses First Bull Run*
(1861)

### QUICK REVIEW

**The First Battle of Bull Run**

- July 1861: Beauregard (Confederacy) and McDowell (Union) meet at Manassas.
- Confederate troops repulse a strong Union attack.
- Battle foreshadowed war to come.

### QUICK REVIEW

**Northern Advantages**

- Two and a half times the South's population.
- North controlled much of nation's industrial capacity.
- Could field a much larger army.

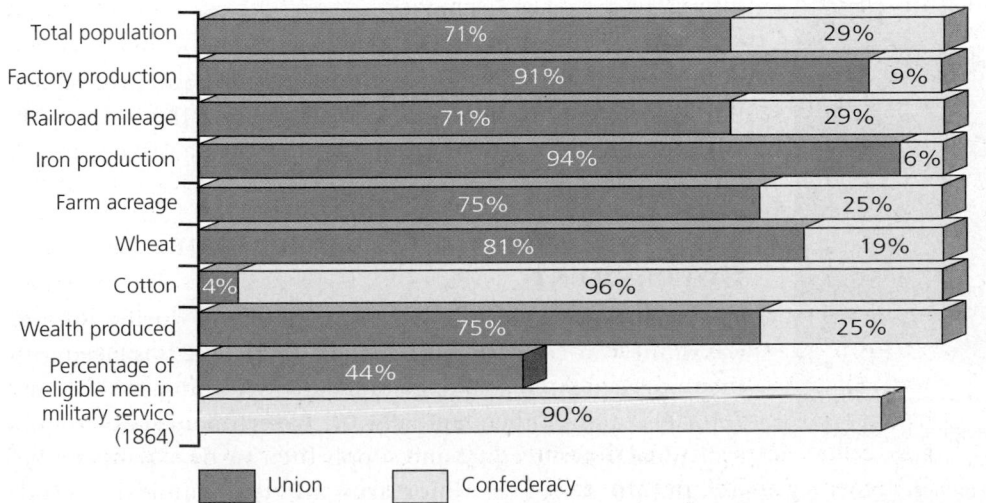

| | Union | Confederacy |
|---|---|---|
| Total population | 71% | 29% |
| Factory production | 91% | 9% |
| Railroad mileage | 71% | 29% |
| Iron production | 94% | 6% |
| Farm acreage | 75% | 25% |
| Wheat | 81% | 19% |
| Cotton | 4% | 96% |
| Wealth produced | 75% | 25% |
| Percentage of eligible men in military service (1864) | 44% | 90% |

**Figure 16.1**
As this chart shows, the North far surpassed the South in the resources necessary to support a large, long war. Initially, however, these strengths made little difference in a struggle that began as a traditional war of maneuver in which the South held the defensive advantage. Only slowly did the Civil War become a modern war in which all the resources of society, including the property and lives of civilians, were mobilized for battle.

*The Times Atlas of World History* (Maplewood, New Jersey: Hammond, 1978).

went off to war. But above all, the South had the weapon of cotton. Because of the crucial role of cotton in industrialization, Southerners were confident that the British and French need for southern cotton would soon bring those countries to recognize the Confederacy as a separate nation.

# THE GOVERNMENTS ORGANIZE FOR WAR

HOW DID the power of the federal government expand as the war progressed?

**myhistorylab**

**Review Summary**

The Civil War forced the federal government to assume powers unimaginable just a few years before. Abraham Lincoln took as his primary task leading and unifying the nation in his role as commander in chief. He found the challenge almost insurmountable. Jefferson Davis's challenge was even greater. He had to create a Confederate nation out of a loose grouping of eleven states, each believing strongly in states' rights. Yet in the Confederacy, as in the Union, the conduct of the war required central direction.

## LINCOLN TAKES CHARGE

Lincoln's first task as president was to assert control over his own cabinet. Because he had few national contacts outside the Republican Party, Lincoln chose to staff his cabinet with other Republicans, including, most unusually, several who had been his rivals for the presidential nomination. That the Republican Party was a not-quite-jelled mix of former Whigs, abolitionists, moderate Free-Soilers, and even some prowar Democrats made Lincoln's task as party leader much more difficult than it might otherwise have been.

After the fall of Fort Sumter, military necessity prompted Lincoln to call up the state militias, order a naval blockade of the South, and vastly expand the military budget. Breaking with precedent, he took these actions without congressional sanction because Congress was not in session. Military necessity—the need to hold the border states—likewise prompted other early actions, such as the suspension of habeas corpus and the acceptance of Kentucky's ambiguous neutrality. The president also repudiated an unauthorized declaration issued by General John C. Frémont, military commander in Missouri, in August 1861 that would have freed Missouri's slaves. Lincoln feared that such an action would lead to the secession of Kentucky and Maryland.

Lincoln was the first president to act as commander in chief in both a practical and a symbolic way. He actively directed military policy, because he realized that a civil war presented problems different from those of a foreign war of conquest. Lincoln wanted above all to persuade the South to rejoin the Union, and his every military order was dictated by the hope of eventual reconciliation—hence, his caution and his acute sense of the role of public opinion. At the same time, he presided over a vast expansion of the powers of the federal government.

## EXPANDING THE POWER OF THE FEDERAL GOVERNMENT

The greatest expansion in government power during the war was in the War Department, which by early 1862 was faced with the unprecedented challenge of feeding, clothing, and arming 700,000 Union soldiers. Initially, the government relied on the individual states to equip and supply their vastly expanded militias. But the size of the Union army and the complexity of fully

This **photograph, taken** a month before his inauguration, shows Lincoln looking presidential. It was clearly intended to reassure a public still doubtful about his abilities.

supplying it demanded constant efforts at all levels—government, state, and community—throughout the war. Thus, in the matter of procurement and supply, as in mobilization, the battlefront was related to the home front on a scale that Americans had not previously experienced.

The need for money for the vast war effort was pressing. Treasury Secretary Salmon P. Chase worked closely with Congress to develop ways to finance the war. With the help of Philadelphia financier Jay Cooke, the Treasury used patriotic appeals to sell war bonds to ordinary people in amounts as small as $50. By the war's end, the United States had borrowed $2.6 billion for the war effort, the first example in American history of the mass financing of war.

Most radical of all was Chase's decision to print and distribute Treasury notes (paper money). Until then, the money in circulation had been a mixture of coins and state bank notes issued by 1,500 different state banks. The **Legal Tender Act** of February 1862 created a national currency. In 1863, Congress passed the **National Bank Act**, which prohibited state banks from issuing their own notes and forced them to apply for federal charters. The switch to a national currency was widely recognized as a major step toward centralization of economic power in the hands of the federal government.

Although the outbreak of war overshadowed everything else, the Republican Party in Congress was determined to fulfill its campaign pledge of a comprehensive program of economic development. Republicans quickly passed the **Morrill Tariff Act** (1861). In 1862 and 1864, Congress created two federally chartered corporations to build a transcontinental railroad thus fulfilling the dreams of the many expansionists who believed America's economic future lay in trade with Asia across the Pacific Ocean. The **Homestead Act** (1862) gave 160 acres of public land to any citizen who agreed to live on the land for five years, improve it by building a house and cultivating some of the land, and pay a small fee. The **Morrill Land Grant Act** (1862) gave states public land that would allow them to finance land-grant colleges offering education to ordinary citizens in practical skills such as agriculture, engineering, and military science. Coupled with this act, the establishment of a federal Department of Agriculture in 1862 gave American farmers a big push toward modern commercial agriculture.

The enactment of the Republican program increased the role of the federal government in national life. Although many of the executive war powers lapsed when the battles ended, the accumulation of strength by the federal government was never reversed.

## DIPLOMATIC OBJECTIVES

To Secretary of State William Seward fell the job of making sure that Britain and France did not extend diplomatic recognition to the Confederacy. Although Southerners had been certain that King Cotton would gain them European support, they were wrong. British public opinion would not countenance the recognition of a new nation based on slavery. British cotton manufacturers found economic alternatives to southern cotton. In spite of Union protests, however, both Britain and France did allow Confederate vessels to use their ports, and British shipyards sold six ships to the Confederacy. But in 1863, when the Confederacy commissioned Britain's Laird shipyard to build two ironclad ships, the Union threatened war, and the British government made sure that the Laird ironclads were never delivered.

## JEFFERSON DAVIS TRIES TO UNIFY THE CONFEDERACY

Although Jefferson Davis had held national cabinet rank (as secretary of war under President Franklin Pierce), had experience as an administrator, and was a former military man, he was unable to hold the Confederacy together.

**Legal Tender Act**  Act creating a national currency in February 1862.

**National Bank Act**  Act prohibiting state banks from issuing their own notes and forcing them to apply for federal charters.

**Morrill Tariff Act**  Act that raised tariffs to more than double their prewar rate.

**Homestead Act**  Law passed by Congress in May 1862 providing homesteads with 160 acres of free land in exchange for improving the land within five years of the grant.

**Morrill Land Grant Act**  Law passed by Congress in July 1862 awarding proceeds from the sale of public lands to the states for the establishment of agricultural and mechanical colleges.

Davis's first cabinet of six men, appointed in February 1861, included a representative from each of the states of the first secession except Mississippi, which was represented by Davis himself. This careful attention to the equality of the states pointed to the fundamental problem Davis was unable to overcome. A shared belief in states' rights—that is, in their own autonomy—was a poor basis on which to build a unified nation. Although Davis saw the need for unity, he was unable to impose it. Soon his style of leadership—micromanagement—angered his generals, alienated cabinet members, and gave southern governors reason to resist his orders. After the first flush of patriotism had passed, the Confederacy never lived up to its hope of becoming a unified nation.

## CONTRADICTIONS OF SOUTHERN NATIONALISM

The failure of "cotton diplomacy" was a crushing blow. White Southerners were stunned that Britain and France would not recognize their claim to independence. Well into 1863, the South hoped that a decisive battlefield victory would change the minds of cautious Europeans.

Perhaps the greatest southern failure was in the area of finances. At first, the Confederate government tried to raise money from the states, but governors refused to impose new taxes. By the time uniform taxes were levied in 1863, it was too late. Heavy borrowing and the printing of great sums of paper money produced runaway inflation (a ruinous rate of 9,000 percent by 1865, compared with 80 percent in the North). Inflation, in turn, caused incalculable damage to morale and prospects for unity.

**15–6**
Charles Harvey Brewster, *Three Letters from the Civil War Front* (1862)

After the initial surge of volunteers, enlistment in the military fell off, as it did in the North also. In April 1862, the Confederate Congress passed the first draft law in American history, and the Union Congress followed suit in March 1863. The southern law declared that all able-bodied men between eighteen and thirty-five were eligible for three years of military service. Purchase of substitutes was allowed, as in the North. The most disliked part of the draft law was a provision exempting one white man on each plantation with twenty or more slaves. This provision not only seemed to disprove the earlier claim that slavery freed white men to fight, but also it aroused class resentments.

In the early days of the war, Jefferson Davis successfully mobilized feelings of regional identity and patriotism. Many Southerners felt part of a beleaguered region that had been forced to resist northern tyranny. But most felt loyalty to their own state and local communities, not to a Confederate nation. The strong belief in states' rights and aristocratic privilege undermined the Confederate cause. Some southern governors resisted potentially unifying actions such as moving militias outside their home states. Broader measures, such as general taxation, were widely evaded by rich and poor alike.

The inequitable draft was only one of many things that convinced the ordinary people of the South that this was a war for privileged slave owners, not for them. With its leaders and

**This painting by** William C. Washington, *Jackson Entering the City of Winchester*, shows the dashing Confederate General "Stonewall" Jackson saving the Virginia town from Union capture in 1862. Jackson and other Confederate generals evoked fierce loyalty to the Confederacy. Unfortunately, by the time this victory was commemorated, Jackson himself was dead from wounds caused by friendly fire at the Battle of Chancellorsville in May of 1863.

William Washington, "Stonewall Jackson Entering the City of Winchester, Virginia." Oil painting. Valentine Museum Library, Richmond, Virginia.

**The contrast between** the hope and valor of these young southern volunteer soldiers, photographed shortly before the First Battle of Bull Run, and the later advertisements for substitutes (at right), is marked. Southern exemptions for slave owners and lavish payment for substitutes increasingly bred resentment among the ordinary people of the South.

(above) Cook Collection. Valentine Museum Library/Richmond History Center.

## SUBSTITUTE NOTICES.

WANTED—A SUBSTITUTE for a conscript, to serve during the war. Any good man over the age of 35 years, not a resident of Virginia, or a foreigner, may hear of a good situation by calling at Mr. GEORGE BAGBY'S office, Shockoe Slip, to-day, between the hours of 9 and 11 A. M.   [Jy 9—1t*]   A COUNTRYMAN.

WANTED—Two SUBSTITUTES—one for artillery, the other for infantry or cavalry service. Also, to sell, a trained, thoroughbred cavalry HORSE.   Apply to   DR. BROOCKS, Corner Main and 12th streets, or to T. T. BROOCKS, jy 9—3t*   Petersburg, Va.

WANTED—Immediately, a SUBSTITUTE. A man over 35 years old, or under 18, can get a good price by making immediate application to Room No. 50, Monument Hotel, or by addressing "J. W.," through Richmond P. O.   jy 9—1t*

WANTED—A SUBSTITUTE, to go into the 24th North Carolina State troops, for which a liberal price will be paid. Apply to me at Dispatch office this evening at 4 o'clock P. M.   jy 9—1t*   R. R. MOORE.

WANTED—A SUBSTITUTE, to go in a first-rate Georgia company of infantry, under the heroic Jackson. A gentleman whose health is impaired, will give a fair price for a substitute. Apply immediately at ROOM, No. 13, Post-Office Department, third story, between the hours of 10 and 3 o'clock.   jy 9—6t*

WANTED—Two SUBSTITUTES for the war. A good bonus will be given. None need apply except those exempt from Conscript. Apply to-day at   GEORGE I. HERRING'S, jy 9—1t*   Grocery store, No. 56 Main st.

citizens fearing (perhaps correctly) that centralization would destroy what was distinctively southern, the Confederacy was unable to mobilize the resources—financial, human, and otherwise—that might have prevented its destruction by northern armies.

# THE FIGHTING THROUGH 1862

Just as political decisions were often driven by military necessity, the basic northern and southern military strategies were affected by political considerations as much as by military ones. The initial policy of limited war, thought to be the best route to ultimate reconciliation, ran into difficulties because of the public's impatience for victories. But victories, as the mounting slaughter made clear, were not easy to achieve.

## THE WAR IN NORTHERN VIRGINIA

The initial northern strategy, dubbed by critics the Anaconda Plan (after the constrictor snake), envisaged slowly squeezing the South with a blockade at sea and on the Mississippi River. The plan avoided invasion and conquest in the hope that a strained South would recognize the inevitability of defeat and thus surrender. Lincoln accepted the basics of the plan, but public clamor for a fight pushed him to agree to the disastrous Battle of Bull Run and then to a major buildup of Union troops in northern Virginia under General George B. McClellan (see Map 16.1).

**WHAT SUCCESSES** did the South enjoy in the early years of the war and how were they achieved?

**myhistorylab**
Review Summary

# MAP EXPLORATION

To explore an interactive version of this map, go to **http://www.prenhall.com/faraghertlc/map16.1**

**1861–62**

| | |
|---|---|
| ☐ Area controlled by Union | ← Union advance |
| ☐ Area gained by Union | ✦ Union victory |
| ☐ Area controlled by Confederacy | ✦ Confederate victory |

**1863**

**1864–65**

SCOTT'S GREAT SNAKE.

## MAP 16.1

**Overall Strategy of the Civil War**   The initial northern strategy for subduing the South, the so-called Anaconda Plan (see cartoon above), entailed strangling it by a blockade at sea and obtaining control of the Mississippi River. But at the end of 1862, it was clear that the South's defensive strategy could only be broken by the invasion of southern territory. In 1864, Sherman's "March to the Sea" and Grant's hammering tactics in northern Virginia brought the war home to the South. Lee's surrender to Grant at Appomattox Courthouse on April 9, 1865, ended the bloodiest war in the nation's history.

HOW DID the military strategies of the North and the South reflect each side's larger goals?

In March 1862, after almost a year spent drilling the raw Union recruits and after repeated exhortations by an impatient Lincoln, McClellan committed 120,000 troops to what became known as the **Peninsular campaign**. The objective was to capture Richmond, the Confederate capital. Inching up the James Peninsula, he tried to avoid battle, hoping his overwhelming numbers would convince the South to surrender. In a series of battles known as the Seven Days, Robert E. Lee boldly counterattacked, repeatedly catching McClellan off guard. Taking heavy losses as well as inflicting them, Lee drove McClellan back. In August, Lee routed another Union army, commanded by General John Pope, at the Second Battle of Bull Run (Second Manassas).

Lincoln, alarmed at the threat to Washington and disappointed by McClellan's inaction, ordered him to abandon the Peninsular campaign and return to the capital.

Jefferson Davis, like Abraham Lincoln, was an active commander in chief. And like Lincoln, he responded to a public that clamored for more action than a strictly defensive war entailed. After the Seven Days victories, Davis supported a Confederate march into Maryland. At the same time, he issued a proclamation urging the people of Maryland to make a separate peace. But in the brutal battle of Antietam on September 17, 1862, which claimed more than 5,000 dead and 19,000 wounded, McClellan's army checked Lee's advance. Lee retreated to Virginia, inflicting terrible losses on northern troops at Fredricksburg when they again made a thrust toward Richmond in December 1862. The war in northern Virginia was stalemated: neither side was strong enough to win, but each was too strong to be defeated (see Map 16.2).

## SHILOH AND THE WAR FOR THE MISSISSIPPI

Although most public attention was focused on the fighting in Virginia, battles in Tennessee and along the Mississippi River proved to be the key to eventual Union victory. In February 1862, General Ulysses S. Grant captured Fort Henry and Fort Donelson, on the Tennessee and Cumberland Rivers, establishing Union control of much of Tennessee and forcing Confederate troops to retreat into northern Mississippi.

Moving south with 28,000 men, Grant met a 40,000-man Confederate force at Shiloh Church in April 1862. Seriously outnumbered on the first day, Grant's forces were reinforced by the arrival of 35,000 troops. After two days of bitter and bloody fighting in the rain, the Confederates withdrew. The losses on both sides were enormous: the North lost 3,000 men, the South 11,000. Nevertheless, Union forces kept moving, capturing Memphis in June and beginning a campaign to eventually capture Vicksburg. Grant and other Union generals faced strong Confederate resistance, and progress was slow. Earlier that year, naval forces under Admiral David Farragut had captured New Orleans and then continued up the Mississippi River. By the end of 1862, it was clearly only a matter of time before the entire river would be in Union hands. Arkansas, Louisiana, and Texas would then be cut off from the rest of the Confederacy (see Map 16.3).

## THE WAR IN THE TRANS–MISSISSIPPI WEST

Although only one western state, Texas, seceded from the Union, the Civil War was fought in small ways in many parts of the West. A Confederate force led by General Henry H. Sibley occupied Santa Fé and Albuquerque early in 1862 without resistance, thus posing a serious threat to the entire Southwest. Confederate hopes were dashed,

**MAP 16.2**

**Major Battles in the East, 1861–62** Northern Virginia was the most crucial and the most constant theater of battle. The prizes were the two opposing capitals, Washington and Richmond, only 70 miles apart. By the summer of 1862, George B. McClellan, famously cautious, had achieved only stalemate in the Peninsular campaign. He did, however, turn back Robert E. Lee at Antietam in September.

WHAT WAS the Anaconda Plan? Why did it fail?

**Peninsular campaign** Union offensive led by McClellan with the objective of capturing Richmond.

**MAP 16.3**

**Major Battles in the Interior, 1862–63** Ulysses S. Grant waged a mobile war, winning at Fort Henry and Fort Donelson in Tennessee in February 1862, at Shiloh in April, and capturing Memphis in June. He then laid siege to Vicksburg, as Admiral David Farragut captured New Orleans and began to advance up the Mississippi River.

WHAT ROLE did Indians Play in the Fighting in the West?

however, by a ragtag group of 950 miners and adventurers organized into the first Colorado Volunteer Infantry Regiment. After an epic march of 400 miles from Denver, which was completed in thirteen days despite snow and high winds, the Colorado militia stopped the unsuspecting Confederate troops in the Battle of Glorieta Pass on March 26–28, 1862. This dashing action, coupled with the efforts of California militias to safeguard Arizona and Utah from seizure by Confederate sympathizers, secured the Far West for the Union.

Another civil war took place in Indian Territory, south of Kansas. The southern Indian tribes who had been removed there from the Old Southwest in the 1830s included many who were still bitter over the horrors of their removal by federal troops, and they sympathized with the Confederacy. The Confederacy actively sought Indian support by offering Indian people representation in the Confederate Congress. Consequently, many Indians fought for the South. Union victories at Pea Ridge (in northwestern Arkansas) in 1862 and near Fort Gibson (in Indian Territory) in 1863 secured the area for the Union but did little to stop dissension among the Indian groups themselves. After the Civil War, the victorious federal government used the tribes' wartime support for the Confederacy as a justification for demanding further land cessions.

Elsewhere in the West, other groups of Indians found themselves caught up in the wider war. An uprising by the Santee Sioux in Minnesota occurred in August 1862, just as McClellan conceded defeat in the Peninsular campaign in Virginia. Alarmed whites, certain that the uprising was a Confederate plot, ignored legitimate Sioux grievances and responded in kind to Sioux ferocity. In little more than a month, 500 to 800 white settlers and an even greater number of Sioux were killed. Thirty-eight Indians were hanged in a mass execution in Mankato on December 26, 1862, and subsequently all Sioux were expelled from Minnesota. In 1863, U.S. Army Colonel Kit Carson invaded Navajo country in Arizona in retaliation for Indian raids on U.S. troops. Eight thousand Navajos were forced on the brutal "Long Walk" to Bosque Redondo on the Pecos River in New Mexico, where they were held prisoner until a treaty between the United States and the Navajos was signed in 1868.

## THE NAVAL WAR

The Union's naval blockade of the South, intended to cut off commerce between the Confederacy and the rest of the world, was initially unsuccessful. The U.S. Navy had only thirty-three ships with which to blockade 189 ports along 3,500 miles of coastline. Beginning in 1863, however, as the Union navy became larger, the blockade began to take effect. As a result, fewer and fewer supplies reached the South.

North and South also engaged in a brief duel featuring the revolutionary new technology of ironcladding. The Confederacy refitted a scuttled Union vessel, the *Merrimac*, with iron plating and renamed it the *Virginia*. On March 8, 1862, the *Virginia* steamed out of Norfolk harbor to challenge the Union blockade. The iron plating protected the *Virginia* from the fire of the Union ships, which found themselves defenseless against its ram and its powerful guns. Two Union ships went down, and the blockade seemed about to be broken. But the North had an experimental ironclad of its own, the *Monitor*, which was waiting for the *Virginia* when it emerged from port on March 9. The historic duel between these first two ironclads was inconclusive. But this brief duel prefigured the naval and land battles of the world wars of the twentieth century as much as did the massing of huge armies on the battlefield.

For the Union, the most successful naval operation in the first two years of the war was not the blockade but the seizing of exposed coastal areas. The Sea Islands of South Carolina were taken, as were some of the North Carolina islands and Fort Pulaski, which commanded the harbor of Savannah, Georgia. Most damaging to the South was the capture of New Orleans.

## THE BLACK RESPONSE

The capture of Port Royal in the South Carolina Sea Islands in 1861 was important for another reason. Whites fled at the Union advance, but 10,000 slaves greeted the troops with jubilation and shouts of gratitude. Union troops had unwittingly freed these slaves in advance of any official Union policy on the status of slaves in captured territory.

Early in the war, an irate Southerner who saw three of his slaves disappear behind Union lines at Fortress Monroe, Virginia, demanded the return of his property, citing the Fugitive Slave Law. The Union commander, Benjamin Butler, replied that the Fugitive Slave Law no longer applied and that the escaped slaves were "contraband of war." Two days later, eight runaway slaves appeared; the next day, fifty-nine black men and women arrived at the fort. Union commanders had found an effective way to rob the South of its basic workforce. The "contrabands," as they were known, were put to work building fortifications and doing other useful work in northern camps.

# THE DEATH OF SLAVERY

As Union troops drove deeper into the South, the black response grew. When Union General William Tecumseh Sherman marched his army through Georgia in 1864, 18,000 slaves—entire families, people of all ages—flocked to the Union lines. By the war's end, nearly a million black people, fully a quarter of all the slaves in the South, had "voted with their feet" for the Union. The overwhelming response of black slaves to the Union advance changed the nature of the war. As increasing numbers of slaves flocked to Union lines, the conclusion that the South refused to face was unmistakable: the southern war to defend the slave system did not have the support of the slaves themselves. Any northern policy that ignored the issue of slavery and the wishes of the slaves themselves was unrealistic.

**HOW DID** the end of slavery affect the war efforts of the North and South?

**myhistorylab**
Review Summary

## THE POLITICS OF EMANCIPATION

In 1862, as the issue of slavery loomed ever larger, Abraham Lincoln, acutely aware of divided northern opinion, inched his way toward a declaration of emancipation. Lincoln was correct to be worried about opinion in the North. Before the war, within the Republican Party, only a small group of abolitionists had favored freeing the slaves. There was also the question of what would become of slaves who were freed. Northern Democrats effectively played on racial fears in the 1862 congressional elections, warning that freed slaves would pour into northern cities and take jobs from white laborers.

Nevertheless, the necessities of war demanded that Lincoln adopt a policy to end slavery. Even as Radical Republicans chafed at Lincoln's slow pace, he was edging toward a new position. Following the Union victory at Antietam in September 1862, Lincoln issued a preliminary decree: unless the rebellious states returned to the Union by January 1, 1863, he would declare their slaves "forever free." Although Lincoln did not expect the Confederate States to surrender because of his proclamation, the decree increased the pressure on the South by directly linking the slave system to the war effort.

On January 1, 1863, Lincoln duly issued the final **Emancipation Proclamation**, which turned out to be less than sweeping. The proclamation freed the slaves in the areas of rebellion—the areas the Union did not control—but specifically exempted slaves in the border states and in former Confederate areas conquered by the Union. Lincoln's purpose was to meet the abolitionist demand for a war against slavery while not losing the support of conservatives, especially in the border states.

One group greeted the Emancipation Proclamation with open celebration. On New Year's Day, hundreds of African Americans gathered outside the White House and cheered the president. Free African Americans predicted that the news would encourage southern slaves either to flee to Union lines or refuse to work for their masters. Both of these things were already happening as African Americans seized on wartime changes to reshape white–black relations in the South. In one sense, then, the Emancipation Proclamation simply gave a name to a process already in motion.

Abolitionists set about moving Lincoln beyond his careful stance in the Emancipation Proclamation. Reformers such as Elizabeth Cady Stanton and Susan B. Anthony lobbied and petitioned for a constitutional amendment outlawing slavery. Congress, at Lincoln's urging, approved and sent to the states a statement banning slavery throughout the United States. Quickly ratified by the Union states in 1865, the statement became the **Thirteenth Amendment** to the Constitution. (The southern states, being in a state of rebellion, could not vote.) Lincoln's firm support for this amendment is a good indicator of his true feelings about slavery when he was freed of the kinds of military and political considerations necessarily taken into account in the Emancipation Proclamation.

## BLACK FIGHTING MEN

As part of the Emancipation Proclamation, Lincoln gave his support for the first time to the recruitment of black soldiers. Early in the war, eager black volunteers had been bitterly disappointed at being turned away. Many, like Robert Fitzgerald, a free African American from Pennsylvania, found other ways to serve the Union cause. Fitzgerald first drove a wagon and mule for the Quartermaster Corps, and later, in spite of persistent seasickness, he served in the Union navy. After the Emancipation Proclamation, however, Fitzgerald was able to do what he had wanted to do all along: be a soldier. He enlisted in the Fifth Massachusetts Cavalry, a regiment that, like all the units in which black soldiers served, was 100 percent African American but commanded by white officers (see Seeing History).

In Fitzgerald's company of eighty-three men, half came from slave states and had run away to enlist. Other regiments had volunteers from Africa. The proportion of volunteers from the loyal border states (where slavery was still legal) was upwards of 25 percent—a lethal blow to the slave system in those states.

Black volunteers, eager and willing to fight, made up 10 percent of the Union army. Nearly 200,000 African Americans (one out of every five black males in the nation) served in the Union army or navy. A fifth of them—37,000—died defending their own freedom and the Union.

# Come and Join Us Brothers

This is a recruitment poster for the Massachusetts 54th Infantry regiment, one of the first official black regiments in the U.S. Army. Organized in March 1863, the 600-man unit led the charge against Fort Wagner, South Carolina, in July, resulting in 116 deaths, including that of the white commanding officer, Colonel Robert Gould Shaw, and many casualties. The bravery of the recruits at Fort Wagner and in other battles changed the minds of many Union officers, who had previously disparaged the fighting abilities of African Americans.

**COMPARE THE** portraits of the men in this recruiting poster with the caricatures of African Americans shown in Chapter 13. What has changed? Frederick Douglass said, "Once let the black man get upon his person the brass letters, U.S., let him get an eagle on his button and a musket on his shoulder and bullets in his pocket," Douglass continued, and "there is no power on earth that can deny that he has earned the right to citizenship." Was Douglass right?

A general belief in African American inferiority was rampant in the North, but the army service of black men made a dent in white racism. Massachusetts enacted the first law forbidding discrimination against African Americans in public facilities. Some major cities, among them San Francisco, Cincinnati, Cleveland, and New York, desegregated their streetcars. Some states—Ohio, California, Illinois—repealed statutes that had barred black people from testifying in court or serving on juries. ■

PUBLISHED BY THE SUPERVISORY COMMITTEE FOR RECRUITING COLORED REGIMENTS
1210 CHESTNUT ST. PHILADELPHIA.

E. Sachse and Company, "The Shackle Broken by the Genius of Freedom", Baltimore, Md.; 1874, Chicago Historical Society.

**myhistorylab**

**Exploring America:** *Fort Pillow*

**15–8**
James Henry Gooding, *Letter to President Lincoln* (1863)

**WHAT IMPACT** did the war have on northern political, economic, and social life? and on the same aspects of southern life?

**myhistorylab**

**Review Summary**

**15–12**
Susie King Taylor, *Reminiscences of an Army Laundress* (1902)

Military service was something no black man could take lightly. African American soldiers faced prejudice within the army and had to prove themselves in battle. Moreover, the Confederates hated and feared African American troops and threatened to treat any captured black soldier as an escaped slave subject to execution. In 1864, Confederate soldiers massacred 262 black soldiers at Fort Pillow, Tennessee, after they had surrendered. Although large-scale episodes such as this were rare (especially after President Lincoln threatened retaliation), smaller ones were not.

Another extraordinary part of the story of the African American soldiers was their reception by black people in the South, who were overjoyed at the sight of armed black men, many of them former slaves themselves, wearing the uniform of the Union army. As his regiment entered Wilmington, North Carolina, one soldier wrote, "Men and women, old and young, were running throughout the streets, shouting and praising God. We could then truly see what we have been fighting for."

African American soldiers were not treated equally by the Union army. They were segregated in camp, given the worst jobs, and paid less than white soldiers ($10 a month rather than $13). Although they might not be able to do much about the other kinds of discrimination, the men of the Fifty-fourth Massachusetts found an unusual way to protest their unequal pay: they refused to accept it, preferring to serve the army for free until it decided to treat them as free men. The protest was effective; in June 1864, the War Department equalized the wages of black and white soldiers.

# THE FRONT LINES AND THE HOME FRONT

Civil War soldiers wrote millions of letters home, more proportionately than in any American war. Their letters and the ones they received in return were links between the front lines and the home front, between the soldiers and their home communities. They are a testament to the patriotism of both Union and Confederate troops, for the story they tell is frequently one of slaughter and horror.

## THE TOLL OF WAR

In spite of early hopes for what one might call a "brotherly" war, one that avoided excessive brutality, Civil War battles were appallingly deadly (see Figure 16.2). One reason was technology: improved weapons, particularly modern rifles, had much greater range and accuracy than the muskets they replaced.

Civil War generals, however, were slow to adjust to this new reality. Almost all Union and Confederate generals remained committed to the conventional military doctrine of massed infantry offensives. Part of this strategy had been to "soften up" a defensive line with artillery before an infantry assault, but now the range of the new rifles made artillery itself vulnerable to attack. As a result, generals relied less on "softening up" than on immense numbers of infantrymen, hoping that enough of them would survive the withering rifle fire to overwhelm the enemy line.

Medical ignorance was another factor in the casualty rate. Because the use of antiseptic procedures was in its infancy, men often died because minor wounds became infected. Disease was an even more frequent killer, taking twice as many men as were lost in battle.

Both North and South were completely unprepared to handle the supply and health needs of their large armies. Nor were the combatants prepared to deal with masses of war prisoners, as the shocking example of the Confederate prison camp at Andersonville in northern Georgia demonstrated. Andersonville was an open stockade with no shade or shelter, erected early in 1864 to hold 10,000 northern prisoners. But by midsummer, it held 33,000.

| Battles, by date | Union | Confederacy | Total |
|---|---|---|---|
| Fort Donelson 2/13–16/1862 Tennessee | 2,832 | 16,623 | 19,455 |
| Shiloh 4/6–7/1862 Tennessee | 13,047 | 10,694 | 23,741 |
| 2nd Manassas 8/29–30/1862 Virginia | 16,054 | 9,197 | 25,251 |
| Antietam 9/17/1862 Maryland | 12,410 | 13,723 | 26,134 |
| Stone's River 12/31/1862 Tennessee | 12,906 | 11,739 | 24,645 |
| Chancellorsville 5/1–4/1863 Virginia | 17,278 | 12,821 | 30,099 |
| Gettysburg 7/1–3/1863 Maryland | 23,049 | 28,063 | 51,112 |
| Chickamagua 9/19–20/1863 Georgia | 16,170 | 18,454 | 34,624 |
| Wilderness 5/5–7/1864 Virginia | 17,666 | 7,750 | 24,624 |
| Spotsylvania 5/8–19/1864 Virginia | 18,399 | 9,000 | 27,399 |

Casualities in thousands   0   4,000   8,000   12,000   16,000   20,000   24,000   28,000   32,000   36,000   40,000   44,000   48,000   52,000   56,000   60,000

**Figure 16.2 The Casualties Mount Up**
This chart of the ten costliest battles of the Civil War shows the relentless toll of casualties (killed, wounded, missing, captured) on both the Union and Confederate sides.

## ARMY NURSES

There was an urgent need for skilled nurses to care for wounded and convalescent soldiers. Under the pressure of wartime necessity, and over the objections of most army doctors, women became army nurses. Hospital nursing, previously considered a job only disreputable women would undertake, now became a suitable vocation for middle-class women. By the war's end more than 3,000 northern women had worked as paid army nurses and many more as volunteers.

Southern women were also active in nursing and otherwise aiding soldiers, though the South never boasted a single large-scale organization like the Sanitary Commission. As in the North, middle-class women at first faced strong resistance from army doctors and even their own families, who believed that a field hospital was "no place for a refined lady." Kate Cumming of Mobile, who nursed in Corinth, Mississippi, after the Battle of Shiloh, faced down such reproofs, though she confided to her diary that nursing wounded men was very difficult: "Nothing that I had ever heard or read had given me the faintest idea of the horrors witnessed here." She and her companion nurses persisted and became an important part of the Confederate medical services. For southern women, who had been much less active in the public life of their communities than their northern reforming sisters, this Civil War activity marked an important break with prewar tradition.

15–7
Clara Barton, *Medical Life at the Battlefield* (1862)

**Nurse Ann Bell** shown preparing medicine for a wounded soldier. Prompted by the medical crisis of the war, women such as Bell and "Mother" Bickerdyke actively participated in the war effort as nurses.

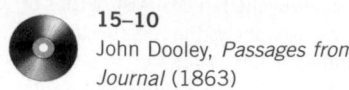

15–10
John Dooley, *Passages from a Journal* (1863)

## THE LIFE OF THE COMMON SOLDIER

The conditions experienced by the eager young volunteers of the Union and Confederate armies included massive, terrifying, and bloody battles, apparently unending, with no sign of victory in sight. Soldiers suffered from the uncertainty of supply, which left troops, especially in the South, without uniforms, tents, and sometimes even food. They endured long marches over muddy, rutted roads while carrying packs weighing fifty or sixty pounds. Disease was rampant in their dirty, verminous, and unsanitary camps, and hospitals were so dreadful that more men left them dead than alive. As a result, desertion was common: an estimated one of every nine Confederate soldiers and one of every seven Union soldiers deserted. Unauthorized absence was another problem. At Antietam, Robert E. Lee estimated that unauthorized absence reduced his strength by a third to a half.

## WARTIME POLITICS

In the earliest days of the war, Northerners had joined together in support of the war effort. Democrat Stephen A. Douglas, Lincoln's defeated rival, paid a visit to the White House to offer Lincoln his support, then traveled home to Illinois, where he addressed a huge rally of Democrats in Chicago: "There can be no neutrals in this war, only patriots—or traitors!" Within a month, Douglas was dead at age forty-eight. By 1862, Democrats had split into two factions: the War Democrats and the Peace Democrats, derogatorily called "**Copperheads**" (from the poisonous snake).

Despite the split in the party in 1860 and the secession of the South, the Democratic Party remained a powerful force in northern politics. It had received 44 percent of the popular vote in the North in the 1860 election, and its united opposition to the emancipation of slaves explains much of Lincoln's equivocal action on this issue.

The leader of the Copperheads, Clement Vallandigham, a former Ohio congressman, advocated an armistice and a negotiated peace that would "look only to the welfare, peace and safety of the white race, without reference to the effect that settlement may have on the African." Western Democrats, he threatened, might form their own union with the South, excluding New England with its radical abolitionists and high-tariff industrialists. Indeed, in the fall and winter of 1862–63 rumors swirled that the Northwest was ready to secede. Lincoln could not afford to take these threats and rumors lightly. In 1862, Lincoln proclaimed that all people who discouraged enlistments in the army or otherwise engaged in disloyal practices would be subject to martial law. More than 13,000 people, most of them deserters and war profiteers, were arrested, tried in military courts, and imprisoned. Some, however, were convicted in military courts on charges of "declaring sympathy for the enemy." Lincoln rejected all protests, claiming that his arbitrary actions were necessary for national security.

Lincoln also faced challenges from the radical faction of his own party. As the war continued, the Radicals gained strength: it was they who pushed for emancipation in the early days of the war and for harsh treatment of the defeated South after it ended. The most troublesome Radical was Salmon P. Chase, who in December 1862 caused a cabinet crisis when he encouraged Senate Republicans to complain that Secretary of State William Seward was "lukewarm" in his support for emancipation. This Radical challenge was a portent of the party's difficulties after the war, which Lincoln did not live to see—or prevent.

## ECONOMIC AND SOCIAL STRAINS ON THE NORTH

Wartime needs caused a surge in northern economic growth, but the gains were unequally distributed. Early in the war, some industries suffered: textile manufacturers could not get cotton, and shoe factories that had made cheap shoes for

**Copperheads**   A term Republicans applied to Northern war dissenters and those suspected of aiding the Confederate cause during the Civil War.

slaves were without a market. But other industries boomed—boot making, ship-building, and the manufacture of woolen goods such as blankets and uniforms, to give just three examples. Coal mining expanded, as did ironmaking, especially the manufacture of iron rails for railroads. Agricultural goods were in great demand, promoting further mechanization of farming. Women, left to tend the family farm while the men went to war, found that with mechanized equipment, they could manage the demanding task of harvesting.

Meeting wartime needs enriched some people honestly, but speculators and profiteers also flourished, as they have in every war. By the end of the war, government contracts had exceeded $1 billion. Not all of this business was free from corruption. New wealth was evident in every northern city.

For most people, however, the war brought the day-to-day hardship of inflation. During the four years of the war, the North suffered an inflation rate of 80 percent, or nearly 15 percent a year. Wages rose only half as much as prices, and workers responded by joining unions and striking. Manufacturers, bitterly opposed to unions, freely hired strikebreakers (many of whom were African Americans, women, or immigrants) and formed organizations of their own to prevent further unionization and to blacklist union organizers. Thus, both capital and labor moved far beyond the small, localized confrontations of the early industrial period. The formation of large-scale organizations, fostered by wartime demand, laid the groundwork for the national battle between workers and manufacturers that would dominate the last part of the nineteenth century.

Another major source of social tension was conscription. The Union introduced a draft in March 1863. Especially unpopular was a provision in the draft law that allowed the hiring of substitutes or the payment of a commutation fee of $300. Substitutes were mostly recent immigrants who had not yet filed for citizenship and were thus not yet eligible to be drafted. It is estimated that immigrants (some of whom were citizens) made up 20 percent of the Union army.

As practiced in the local communities, conscription was indeed often marred by favoritism and prejudice. Local officials called up many more poor than rich men and selected a higher proportion of immigrants than nonimmigrants. In reality, however, only 7 percent of all men called to serve actually did so. About 25 percent hired a substitute, another 45 percent were exempted for "cause" (usually health reasons), and another 20 to 25 percent simply failed to report to the community draft office. Nevertheless, by 1863, many northern urban workers believed that the slogan "a rich man's war but a poor man's fight," though coined in the South, applied to them as well.

## THE NEW YORK CITY DRAFT RIOTS

In the spring of 1863, there were protests against the draft throughout the North. Riots and disturbances broke out in many cities, and several federal enrollment officers were killed. The greatest trouble occurred in New York City between July 13 and July 16, 1863, where a wave of working-class looting, fighting, and lynching claimed the lives of 105 people, many of them African American. The rioting, the worst up to that time in American history, was quelled only when five units of the U.S. Army were rushed from the battlefield at Gettysburg, where they had been fighting Confederates the week before.

The riots had several causes. Anger at the draft and racial prejudice were what most contemporaries saw. From a historical perspective, however, the riots were at least as much about the urban growth and tensions described in Chapter 13. The Civil War made urban problems worse and heightened the visible contrast between the lives of the rich and those of the poor. These tensions exploded, but were not solved, during those hot days in the summer of 1863.

15–11
*A Firsthand Account of the New York Draft Riots* (1863)

Ironically, African American men, a favorite target of the rioters' anger, were a major force in easing the national crisis over the draft. Though they had been barred from service until 1863, in the later stages of the war African American volunteers filled much of the manpower gap that the controversial draft was meant to address.

## THE FAILURE OF SOUTHERN NATIONALISM

The war brought even greater changes to the South. As in the North, war needs led to expansion and centralization of government control over the economy. The expansion of government brought sudden urbanization, a new experience for the predominantly rural South. The population of Richmond, the Confederate capital, almost tripled, in large part because the Confederate bureaucracy grew to 70,000 people. Because of the need for military manpower, a good part of the Confederate bureaucracy consisted of women, who were referred to as "government girls." All of this—government control, urban growth, women in the paid workforce—was new to Southerners, and not all of it was welcomed.

Even more than in the North, the voracious need for soldiers fostered class antagonisms. When small yeoman farmers went off to war, their wives and families struggled to farm on their own, without the help of mechanization, which they could not afford, and without the help of slaves, which they had never owned. But wealthy men could be exempted from the draft if they had more than twenty slaves. Furthermore, many upper-class Southerners—at least 50,000—avoided military service by paying liberally ($5,000 and more) for substitutes. Worst of all was the starvation. The North's blockade and the breakdown of the South's transportation system restricted the availability of food in the South, and these problems were vastly magnified by runaway inflation. Prices in the South rose by an unbelievable 9,000 percent from 1861 to 1865. Speculation and hoarding by the rich made matters even worse. In the spring of 1863, food riots broke out in four Georgia cities (Atlanta among them) and in North Carolina. In Richmond, more than a thousand people, mostly women, broke into bakeries and snatched loaves of bread, crying "Bread! Bread! Our children are starving while the rich roll in wealth!"

Increasingly, the ordinary people of the South, preoccupied with staying alive, refused to pay taxes, to provide food, or to serve in the army. Soldiers were drawn home by the desperation of their families as well as by the discouraging course of the war. By January 1865, the desertion rate had climbed to 8 percent a month.

At the same time, the life of the southern ruling class was irrevocably altered by the changing nature of slavery. By the end of the war, one-quarter of all slaves had fled to the Union lines, and those who remained often stood in a different relationship to their owners. As white masters and overseers left to join the army, white women were left behind on the plantation to cope with shortages, grow crops, and manage the labor of slaves. Lacking the patriarchal authority of their husbands, white women found that white–black relationships shifted, sometimes drastically (as when slaves fled) and sometimes more subtly. Slaves increasingly made their own decisions about when and how they would work. One black woman, implored by her mistress not to reveal the location of a trunk of money and silver plate when the invading Yankees arrived, looked her in the eye and said, "Mistress, I can't lie over that; you bought that silver plate when you sold my three children."

Peace movements in the South were motivated by a confused mixture of realism, war weariness, and the animosity of those who supported states' rights and opposed Jefferson Davis. The anti-Davis faction was led by his own vice president, Alexander Stephens, who early in 1864 suggested a negotiated peace. Peace sentiment was especially strong in North Carolina, where more than a hundred public meetings in support of negotiations were held in the summer of 1863. Davis would have none of it, and he commanded enough votes in the Confederate Congress to enforce his will and to suggest that peace sentiment was traitorous.

## THE TIDE TURNS

As Lincoln's timing of the Emancipation Proclamation showed, by 1863 the nature of the war was changing. The proclamation freeing the slaves struck directly at the southern home front and the civilian workforce. That same year, the nature of the battlefield war changed as well. The Civil War became the first total war.

### THE TURNING POINT OF 1863

In the summer of 1863, the moment finally arrived when the North could begin to hope for victory. But for the Union army, the year opened with stalemate in the East and slow and costly progress in the West. For the South, 1863 represented its highest hopes for military success and for diplomatic recognition by Britain or France.

Attempting to break the stalemate in northern Virginia, General Joseph "Fighting Joe" Hooker and a Union army of 130,000 men attacked a Confederate army half that size at Chancellorsville in May. In response, Robert E. Lee daringly divided his forces, sending General Thomas "Stonewall" Jackson and 30,000 men on a day-long flanking movement that caught the Union troops by surprise. Chancellorsville was a great Confederate victory; there were 17,000 Union losses. However, Confederate losses were also great: 13,000 men, representing more than 20 percent of Lee's army.

Though weakened, Lee moved to the attack. In June, in his second and most dangerous single thrust into Union territory, he moved north into Maryland and Pennsylvania. His purpose was as much political as military: he hoped that a great Confederate victory would lead Britain and France to intervene in the war and demand a negotiated peace. The ensuing Battle of Gettysburg, July 1–3, 1863, was another horrible slaughter.

Lee retreated from the field, leaving more than one-third of his army behind—28,000 men killed, wounded, or missing. Union general George Meade elected not to pursue with his battered Union army (see Map 16.4).

The next day, July 4, 1863, Ulysses S. Grant took Vicksburg, Mississippi, after a costly siege. The combined news of Gettysburg and Vicksburg dissuaded Britain and France from recognizing the Confederacy and checked the northern peace movement. It also tightened the North's grip on the South, for the Union now controlled the entire Mississippi River. In November, Generals Grant and Sherman broke the Confederate hold on Chattanooga, Tennessee, thereby opening the way to Atlanta.

**HOW DID** Grant and Sherman turn the tide of the war?

**myhistorylab**
**Review Summary**

## MAP EXPLORATION

To explore an interactive version of this map, go to
**http://www.prenhall.com/faraghertlc/map16.4**

**MAP 16.4**
**The Turning Point, 1863**   In June, Lee boldly struck north into Maryland and Pennsylvania, hoping for a victory that would cause Britain and France to demand a negotiated peace on Confederate terms. Instead, he lost the hard-fought battle of Gettysburg, July 1–3. The very next day, Grant's long siege of Vicksburg succeeded. These two great Fourth of July victories turned the tide in favor of the Union. The Confederates never again mounted a major offensive. Total Union control of the Mississippi now exposed the Lower South to attack.

WHAT WAS Lee hoping to achieve with his campaign northward and why was his defeat at Gettysburg the war's turning point?

A black man is lynched during the New York City Draft Riots in July 1863. Free black people and their institutions were major victims of the worst rioting in American history until then. The riots were more than a protest against the draft; they were also an outburst of frustration over urban problems that had been festering for decades.

**15–9**
Abraham Lincoln, *Gettysburg Address* (1863)

**15–13**
*General William Tecumseh Sherman on War* (1864)

## QUICK REVIEW

**Grant's Strategy**

♦ Better coordination of Union effort and the application of steady pressure.

♦ The waging of nonstop warfare.

♦ Grant's plan worked in the long run, but at a high cost.

## GRANT AND SHERMAN

In March 1864, President Lincoln called Grant east and appointed him general-in-chief of all the Union forces. Grant devised a plan of strangulation and annihilation. While he took on Lee in northern Virginia, he sent General William Tecumseh Sherman to defeat Confederate general Joe Johnston's Army of Tennessee, which was defending the approach to Atlanta. Both Grant and Sherman exemplified the new kind of warfare. They aimed to inflict maximum damage on the fabric of southern life, hoping that the South would choose to surrender rather than face total destruction. This decision to broaden the war so that it directly affected civilians was new in American military history and prefigured the total wars of the twentieth century.

In northern Virginia, Grant pursued a policy of destroying civilian supplies. He said he "regarded it as humane to both sides to protect the persons of those found at their homes, but to consume everything that could be used to support or supply armies." One of those supports was slaves. Grant welcomed fleeing slaves to Union lines and encouraged army efforts to put them to work or enlist them as soldiers.

The most famous example of the new strategy of total war was General Sherman's 1864 march through Georgia. Sherman captured Atlanta on September 2, 1864, and the rest of Georgia now lay open to him. In November, Sherman set out to march the 285 miles to the coastal city of Savannah, living off the land and destroying everything in his path. His military purpose was to tighten the noose around Robert E. Lee's army in northern Virginia by cutting off Mississippi, Alabama, and Georgia from the rest of the Confederacy. But his second purpose, openly stated, was to "make war so terrible" to the people of the South, to "make them so sick of war that generations would pass away before they would again appeal to it." Accordingly, he told his men to seize, burn, or destroy everything in their path (but, significantly, not to harm civilians).

It was estimated that Sherman's army did $100 million worth of damage. "They say no living thing is found in Sherman's track," Mary Boykin Chesnut wrote, "only chimneys, like telegraph poles, to carry the news of [his] attack backwards."

Terrifying to white southern civilians, Sherman was initially hostile to black Southerners as well. In the interests of speed and efficiency, his army turned away many of the 18,000 slaves who flocked to it in Georgia, causing a number to be recaptured and reenslaved. This callous action caused such a scandal in Washington that Secretary of War Edwin Stanton arranged a special meeting in Georgia with Sherman and twenty African American ministers who spoke for the freed slaves. This meeting in itself was extraordinary: no one had ever before asked slaves what they wanted. Equally extraordinary was Sherman's response in Special Field Order 15, issued in January 1865: he set aside more than 400,000 acres of Confederate land to be given to the freed slaves in forty-acre parcels. This was war of a kind that white Southerners had never imagined.

## THE 1864 ELECTION

The war complicated the 1864 presidential election. Lincoln was renominated during a period when the war was going badly. Opposed by the Radicals, who thought he was too conciliatory toward the South, and by Republican conservatives, who disapproved of the Emancipation Proclamation, Lincoln had little support within his own party.

In contrast, the Democrats had an appealing candidate: General George McClellan, a war hero (always a favorite with American voters) who was known to be sympathetic to the South. Democrats played shamelessly on the racist fears of the urban working class, accusing Republicans of being "negro-lovers" and warning that racial mixing lay ahead.

A deeply depressed Lincoln fully expected to lose the election. "I am going to be beaten," he told an army officer in August 1864, "and unless some great change takes place badly beaten." A great change did take place: Sherman captured Atlanta on September 2. Lincoln won the election with 55 percent of the popular vote. The vote probably saved the Republican Party from extinction. Ordinary people and war-weary soldiers had voted to continue a difficult and divisive conflict. The election was important evidence of northern support for Lincoln's policy of unconditional surrender for the South. There would be no negotiated peace; the war would continue.

## NEARING THE END

As Sherman devastated the lower South, Grant was locked in struggle with Lee in northern Virginia. Grant did not favor subtle strategies. He bluntly said, "The art of war is simple enough. Find out where your enemy is. Get at him as soon as you can. Strike at him as hard as you can, and keep moving on." Following this plan, Grant eventually hammered Lee into submission but at enormous cost. Lee inflicted heavy losses on the Union army in a succession of bloody encounters in the spring and summer of 1864: almost 18,000 at the battle of the Wilderness, more than 8,000 at Spotsylvania, and 12,000 at Cold Harbor. At Cold Harbor, Union troops wrote their names and addresses on scraps of paper and pinned them to their backs, so certain were they of being killed or wounded in battle.

Grim and terrible as Grant's strategy was, it proved effective. Rather than pulling back after his failed assaults, he kept moving South, finally settling in for a prolonged siege of Lee's forces at Petersburg. The North's great advantage in population finally began to tell. There were more Union soldiers to replace those lost in battle, but there were no more white Confederates (see Map 16.5).

In desperation, the South turned to what had hitherto been unthinkable: arming slaves to serve as soldiers in the Confederate army. But—and this was the bitter irony—the African American soldiers and their families would have to be promised freedom or they would desert to the Union at the first chance they had. The Confederate Congress balked at first. As one member said, the idea was "revolting to Southern sentiment, Southern pride, and Southern honor." Another candidly admitted, "If slaves make good soldiers our whole theory of slavery is wrong." Finally, on March 13, the Confederate Congress authorized a draft of black soldiers—without mentioning freedom.

**This striking photograph** by Thomas C. Roche shows a dead Confederate soldier, killed at Petersburg on April 3, 1865, only six days before the surrender at Appomattox. The new medium of photography conveyed the horror of the war with a gruesome reality to the American public.

**MAP 16.5**
**The Final Battles in Virginia, 1864–65**   In the war's final phase early in 1865, Sherman closed one arm of a pincers by marching north from Savannah, while Grant attacked Lee's last defensive positions in Petersburg and Richmond. Lee retreated from them on April 2 and surrendered at Appomattox Court House on April 9, 1865.

WHAT DESPERATE measures did the South resort to as the war came to an end?

By the spring of 1865, public support for the war simply disintegrated in the South. Starvation, inflation, dissension, and the prospect of military defeat were too much. In February, Jefferson Davis sent his vice president, Alexander Stephens, to negotiate terms at a peace conference at Hampton Roads. Lincoln would not countenance anything less than full surrender, although he did offer gradual emancipation with compensation for slave owners. Davis, however, insisted on southern independence at all costs. Consequently, the Hampton Roads conference failed and southern resistance faded away. In March 1865, Mary Boykin Chesnut recorded in her diary: "I am sure our army is silently dispersing. Men are going the wrong way all the time. They slip by now with no songs nor shouts. They have given the thing up."

## APPOMATTOX

In the spring of 1865, Lee and his remaining troops, outnumbered two to one, still held Petersburg and Richmond. Starving, short of ammunition, and losing men in battle or to desertion every day, Lee retreated from Petersburg on April 2. The Confederate government fled Richmond, stripping and burning the city. Seven days later, Lee and his 25,000 troops surrendered to Grant at Appomattox Court House. Grant treated Lee with great respect and set a historic precedent by giving the Confederate troops parole. This meant they could not subsequently be prosecuted for treason. Grant then sent the starving army on its way with three days' rations for every man. Jefferson Davis, who had hoped to set up a new government in Texas, was captured in Georgia on May 10. The war was finally over.

Sensing that the war was near its end, Abraham Lincoln visited Grant's troops when Lee withdrew from Petersburg on April 2. Thus it was that Lincoln came to visit Richmond, and to sit briefly in Jefferson Davis's presidential office, soon after Davis had left it. As Lincoln walked the streets of the burned and pillaged city, black people poured out to see him and surround him, shouting "Glory to God! Glory! Glory! Glory!"

## DEATH OF A PRESIDENT

Lincoln had only the briefest time to savor the victory. On the night of April 14, President and Mrs. Lincoln went to Ford's Theater in Washington. There Lincoln was shot at point-blank range by John Wilkes Booth, a Confederate sympathizer.

**The 55th Massachusetts** Colored Regiment is shown entering Charleston, February 21, 1865, greeted by happy crowds of African Americans. For white Charlestonians, the sight of victorious black troops in the cockpit of the Confederacy must have been devastating.

Harper's Weekly, March 18, 1865. Courtesy of William C. Hine.

## CHRONOLOGY

**1861**   March: Morrill Tariff Act

April: Fort Sumter falls; war begins

April: Mobilization begins

April–May: Virginia, Arkansas, Tennessee, and North Carolina secede

June: United States Sanitary Commission established

July: First Battle of Bull Run

December: French troops arrive in Mexico, followed by British and Spanish forces in January

**1862**   February: Legal Tender Act

February: Battles of Fort Henry and Fort Donelson

March: Battle of Pea Ridge

March: Battle of the *Monitor* and the *Merrimack* (renamed the *Virginia*)

March–August: George B. McClellan's Peninsular campaign

March: Battle of Glorieta Pass

April: Battle of Shiloh

April: Confederate Conscription Act

April: David Farragut captures New Orleans

May: *El Cinqo de Mayo:* Mexican troops repel French invaders

May: Homestead Act

June–July: Seven Days Battles

July: Pacific Railway Act

July: Morrill Land Grant Act

August: Santee Sioux Uprising, Minnesota

September: Battle of Antietam

December: Battle of Fredericksburg

**1863**   January: Emancipation Proclamation

February: National Bank Act

March: Draft introduced in the North

March: Colonel Kit Carson sends 8,000 Navajos on the "Long Walk" to Bosque Redondo, New Mexico Territory

April: Richmond bread riot

May: Battle of Chancellorsville

June: French occupy Mexico City

July: Battle of Gettysburg

July: Surrender of Vicksburg

July: New York City Draft Riots

November: Battle of Chattanooga

November: Union troops capture Brownsville, Texas

**1864**   March: Ulysses S. Grant becomes general-in-chief of Union forces

April: Fort Pillow massacre

May: Battle of the Wilderness

May: Battle of Spotsylvania

June: Battle of Cold Harbor

June: Maximilian becomes Emperor of Mexico

September: Atlanta falls

October: St. Albans incident

November: Abraham Lincoln reelected president

November–December: William Tecumseh Sherman's march to the sea

**1865**   April: Richmond falls

April: Robert E. Lee surrenders at Appomattox

April: Lincoln assassinated

December: Thirteenth Amendment to the Constitution becomes law

He died the next day. After a week of observances in Washington, Lincoln's coffin was loaded on a funeral train that slowly carried him back to Springfield. All along the railroad route, day and night, in small towns and large, people gathered to see the train pass and to pay their last respects. At that moment, the Washington community and the larger Union community were one and the same.

The nation as a whole was left with Lincoln's vision for the coming peace, expressed in the unforgettable words of his Second Inaugural Address:

With malice toward none, with charity for all, with firmness in the right as God gives us to see the right, let us strive on to finish the work we are in, to bind up the nation's wounds, to care for him who shall have borne the battle and for his widow and his orphan, to do all which may achieve and cherish a just and lasting peace among ourselves and with all nations.

# CONCLUSION

In 1865, a divided people were forcibly reunited by battle. Their nation, the United States of America, had been permanently changed by civil war. Devastating losses among the young men of the country—the greatest such losses the nation was ever to suffer—would affect not only their families but also all of postwar society. Politically, the deepest irony of the Civil War was that only by fighting it had America become completely a nation. For it was the war that broke down local isolation. Ordinary citizens in local communities, North and South, developed a national perspective as they sent their sons and brothers to be soldiers, their daughters to be nurses and teachers. Then, too, the federal government, vastly strengthened by wartime necessity, reached the lives of ordinary citizens more than ever before. The question now was whether this strengthened but divided national community, forged in battle, could create a just peace.

## REVIEW QUESTIONS

1. At the outset of the Civil War, what were the relative advantages of the North and the South, and how did they affect the final outcome?

2. In the absence of the southern Democrats, in the early 1860s, the new Republican Congress was able to pass a number of party measures with little opposition. What do these measures tell you about the historical roots of the Republican Party? More generally, how do you think we should view legislation passed in the absence of the customary opposition, debate, and compromise?

3. The greatest problem facing Jefferson Davis and the Confederacy was the need to develop a true feeling of nationalism. Can the failure of this effort be blamed on Davis's weakness as a leader alone, or are there other causes?

4. In what ways can it be said that the actions of African Americans, both slave and free, came to determine the course of the Civil War?

5. Wars always have unexpected consequences. List some of those consequences both for soldiers and for civilians in the North and in the South.

6. Today Abraham Lincoln is considered one of our greatest presidents, but he did not enjoy such approval at the time. List and evaluate some of the contemporary criticisms of Lincoln.

**myhistorylab**

Flashcard Review

## KEY TERMS

Copperheads (p. 422)

Emancipation Proclamation (p. 418)

Homestead Act (p. 411)

Legal Tender Act (p. 411)

Morrill Land Grant Act (p. 411)

Morrill Tariff Act (p. 411)

National Bank Act (p. 411)

Peninsular campaign (p. 415)

Thirteenth Amendment (p. 418)

# RECOMMENDED READING

Edward Ayers, *In the Presence of Mine Enemies: War in the Heart of America, 1859–1863* (2003). A study of two counties, one Confederate, one Union, in the war.

Paul A. Cimbala and Randall M. Miller, *Union Soldiers and the Northern Home Front: Wartime Experiences, Postwar Adjustments* (2002). The effects of the Civil War on ordinary people.

Paul Escott, *After Secession: Jefferson Davis and the Failure of Confederate Nationalism* (1978). A thoughtful study of Davis's record as president of the Confederacy.

Drew Gilpin Faust, *Mothers of Invention: Women of the Slaveholding South in the American Civil War* (1996). A major study that considers the importance of gender at the white South's "moment of truth."

James M. Mc Pherson, *Battle Cry of Freedom: The Civil War Era* (1988). An acclaimed, highly readable synthesis of much scholarship on the war.

—, *The Atlas of the Civil War* (1994). Detailed battle diagrams with clear descriptions.

Pauli Murray, *Proud Shoes: The Story of an American Family* (1956). Murray tells the proud story of her African American family and her grandfather, Robert Fitzgerald.

Nina Silbar, *Daughters of the Union: Northern Women Fight the Civil War* (2005). Argues that women found a new sense of self and citizenship in wartime.

Keith P. Wilson, *Campfires of Freedom: The Camp Life of Black Soliders During the Civil War* (2002). Camp life examined to show the soldiers' personal transition from slavery to freedom.

Where it's a good time to connect to the past!

For study resources for this chapter, go to **www.myhistorylab.com** and choose *Out of Many, Teaching and Learning Classroom Edition.* You will find a wealth of study and review material for this chapter, including pretests and posttests, customized study plan, key-term review flash cards, interactive map and document activities, and documents for analysis.

*The war passed from words to stones which the white children began to hurl at the colored. Several colored children were hurt and, as they had not resented the rock throwing . . . , the white children became more aggressive and abusive.*

— T. Thomas Fortune, from Norfolk Journal and Guide, *1866*

**Women and children escaping slavery.**

Theo. Kaufmann, "On to Liberty," 1867, Oil on canvas. The Metropolitan Museum of Art. Gift of Erving and Joyce Wolf, 1982 (1982.443.3) Photograph © 1982 The Metropolitan Museum of Art.

# AMERICAN COMMUNITIES
## Hale County, Alabama: From Slavery to Freedom in a Black Belt Community

ON A BRIGHT SATURDAY MORNING IN MAY 1867, 4,000 FORMER SLAVES streamed into the town of Greensboro to hear speeches from two delegates to a recent freedmen's convention in Mobile and to find out about the political status of black people under the Reconstruction Act just passed by Congress. Tensions mounted in the days following this unprecedented gathering, as military authorities began supervising voter registration for elections to the upcoming constitutional convention that would rewrite the laws of Alabama. On June 13, John Orrick, a local white, confronted Alex Webb, a politically active freedman, on the streets of Greensboro and shot Webb dead. Hundreds of armed and angry freedmen formed a posse to search for Orrick but failed to find him. Galvanized by Webb's murder, 500 local freedmen formed a chapter of the Union League, the Republican Party's organizational arm in the South. The chapter functioned as both a militia company and a forum to agitate for political rights.

West-central Alabama had emerged as a fertile center of cotton production just two decades before the Civil War. There African Americans, as throughout the South's black belt, constituted more than three-quarters of the population. With the arrival of federal troops in the spring of 1865, African Americans in Hale County, like their counterparts elsewhere, began to challenge the traditional organization of plantation labor.

Above all, freed people wanted more autonomy. Overseers and owners grudgingly allowed them to work the land "in families," letting them choose their own supervisors and find their own provisions. The result was a shift from the gang labor characteristic of the antebellum period, in which large groups of slaves worked under the harsh and constant supervision of white overseers, to the sharecropping system, in which African American families worked small plots of land in exchange for a small share of the crop. This shift represented less of a victory for newly freed African Americans than a defeat for plantation owners, who resented even the limited economic independence it forced them to concede to their black workforce.

Local African Americans also organized politically. In 1866, Congress had passed the Civil Rights Act and sent the Fourteenth Amendment to the Constitution to the states for ratification; both promised full citizenship rights to former slaves. Hale County freedmen joined the Republican Party and local Union League chapters. They used their new political power to press for better labor contracts, demand greater autonomy for the black workforce, and agitate for the more radical goal of land confiscation and redistribution. "The colored people are very anxious to get land of their own to live upon independently; and they want money to buy stock to make crops," reported one black Union League organizer. "The only way to get these necessaries is to give our votes to the [Republican] party." Two Hale County former slaves, Brister Reese and James K. Green, won election to the Alabama state legislature in 1869.

It was not long before these economic and political gains prompted a white counterattack. In the spring of 1868, the Ku Klux Klan came to Hale County. Disguised in white sheets, armed with guns and whips, and making nighttime raids on horseback, Klansmen flogged, beat, and murdered freed people. They intimidated voters and silenced political activists. Planters used Klan terror to dissuade former slaves from leaving plantations or organizing for higher wages.

With the passage of the Ku Klux Klan Act in 1871, the federal government cracked down on the Klan, breaking its power temporarily in parts of the former Confederacy. But no serious effort was made to stop Klan terror in the west Alabama black belt, and planters there succeeded in reestablishing much of their social and political control.

The events in Hale County illustrate the struggles that beset communities throughout the South during the Reconstruction era after the Civil War. The destruction of slavery and the Confederacy forced African Americans and white people to renegotiate their old roles. These community battles both shaped and were shaped by the victorious and newly expansive federal government in Washington. But the new arrangements of both political power sharing and the organization of labor had to be worked out within local communities. In the end, Reconstruction was only partially successful. Not until the "Second Reconstruction" of the twentieth-century civil rights movement would the descendants of Hale County's African Americans begin to enjoy the full fruits of freedom—and even then not without challenge.

# 17

# RECONSTRUCTION
## 1863–1877

**WHAT WERE** the competing political plans for reconstructing the defeated Confederacy?

**WHAT WERE** the most important changes in the lives of African Americans in the years immediately following the war?

**WHAT MAJOR** groups made up the Southern Republicans?

**WHAT PRECIPITATED** the electoral crisis of 1876?

# THE POLITICS OF RECONSTRUCTION

lthough President Abraham Lincoln insisted early on that the purpose of the war was to preserve the Union, by 1863 it had evolved as well into a struggle for African American liberation. Indeed, the political, economic, and moral issues posed by slavery were the root cause of the Civil War, and the war ultimately destroyed slavery, although not racism, once and for all.

The Civil War also settled the Constitutional crisis provoked by the secession of the Confederacy and its justification in appeals to states' rights. The old notion of the United States as a voluntary union of sovereign states gave way to the new reality of a single nation, in which the federal government took precedence over the individual states. The key historical developments of the Reconstruction era revolved around precisely how the newly strengthened national government would define its relationship with the defeated Confederate states and the 4 million newly freed slaves.

## THE DEFEATED SOUTH

The white South paid an extremely high price for secession, war, and defeat. In addition to the battlefield casualties, the Confederate states sustained deep material and psychological wounds. Much of the best agricultural land lay waste. Many towns and cities were in ruins. By 1865, the South's most precious commodities, cotton and African American slaves, no longer were measures of wealth and prestige.

Emancipation proved the most bitter pill for white Southerners to swallow, especially the planter elite. Conquered and degraded, and in their view robbed of their slave property, white people responded by regarding African Americans, more than ever, as inferior to themselves. In the antebellum South, white skin had defined a social bond that transcended economic class. It gave even the lowliest poor white a badge of superiority over even the most skilled slave or prosperous free African American. Emancipation, however, forced white people to redefine their world. The specter of political power and social equality for African Americans made racial order the consuming passion of most white Southerners during the Reconstruction years. In fact, racism can be seen as one of the major forces driving Reconstruction and, ultimately, undermining it.

**WHAT WERE** the competing political plans for reconstructing the defeated Confederacy?

**myhistorylab**
Review Summary

**16–2**
Carl Schurz, *Report on the Condition of the South* (1865)

**16–9**
The Nation, *"The State of the South"* (1872)

**"Decorating the Graves** of Rebel Soldiers," *Harper's Weekly,* August 17, 1867. After the Civil War, both Southerners and Northerners created public mourning ceremonies honoring fallen soldiers. Women led the memorial movement in the South that, by establishing cemeteries and erecting monuments, offered the first cultural expression of the Confederate tradition. This engraving depicts citizens of Richmond, Virginia, decorating thousands of Confederate graves with flowers at the Hollywood Memorial Cemetery on the James River. A local women's group raised enough funds to transfer over 16,000 Confederate dead from northern cemeteries for reburial in Richmond.

**Photography pioneer Timothy** O'Sullivan took this portrait of a multi-generational African American family on the J. J. Smith plantation in Beaufort, South Carolina, in 1862. Many white plantation owners in the area had fled, allowing slaves like these to begin an early transition to freedom before the end of the Civil War.

**16–1**
*"Address from the Colored Citizens of Norfolk, Virginia, to the People of the United States"* (1865)

**Radical Republicans** A shifting group of Republican congressmen, usually a substantial minority, who favored the abolition of slavery from the beginning of the Civil War and later advocated harsh treatment of the defeated South.

**Field Order 15** Order by General William T. Sherman in January 1865 to set aside abandoned land along the southern Atlantic coast for forty-acre grants to freedmen; rescinded by President Andrew Johnson later that year.

# ABRAHAM LINCOLN'S PLAN

By late 1863, Union military victories had convinced President Lincoln of the need to fashion a plan for the reconstruction of the South (see Chapter 16). Lincoln based his reconstruction program on bringing the seceded states back into the Union as quickly as possible. His Proclamation of Amnesty and Reconstruction of December 1863 offered "full pardon" and the restoration of property, not including slaves, to white Southerners willing to swear an oath of allegiance to the United States and its laws, including the Emancipation Proclamation. Prominent Confederate military and civil leaders were excluded from Lincoln's offer, though he indicated that he would freely pardon them.

The president also proposed that when the number of any Confederate state's voters who took the oath of allegiance reached 10 percent of the number who had voted in the election of 1860, this group could establish a state government that Lincoln would recognize as legitimate. Fundamental to this Ten Percent Plan was acceptance by the reconstructed governments of the abolition of slavery. Lincoln's plan was designed less as a blueprint for reconstruction than as a way to shorten the war and gain white people's support for emancipation.

Lincoln's amnesty proclamation angered those Republicans—known as **Radical Republicans**—who advocated not only equal rights for the freedmen but also a tougher stance toward the white South. In July 1864, Senator Benjamin F. Wade of Ohio and Congressman Henry W. Davis of Maryland, both Radicals, proposed a harsher alternative to the Ten Percent Plan. The Wade–Davis bill required 50 percent of a seceding state's white male citizens to take a loyalty oath before elections could be held for a convention to rewrite the state's constitution. Lincoln wanted to weaken the Confederacy by creating new state governments that could win broad support from southern white people. The Wade–Davis bill threatened his efforts to build political consensus within the southern states. Lincoln, therefore, pocket-vetoed the bill by refusing to sign it within ten days of the adjournment of Congress.

As Union armies occupied parts of the South, commanders improvised a variety of arrangements involving confiscated plantations and the African American labor force. For example, in 1862 General Benjamin F. Butler began a policy of transforming slaves on Louisiana sugar plantations into wage laborers under the close supervision of occupying federal troops.

In January 1865, General William T. Sherman issued Special **Field Order 15**, setting aside the Sea Islands off the Georgia coast and a portion of the South Carolina low-country rice fields for the exclusive settlement of freed people. Each family would receive forty acres of land and the loan of mules from the army. By the summer of 1865 some 40,000 freed people, eager to take advantage of the general's order, had been settled on 400,000 acres of "Sherman land."

Conflicts within the Republican Party prevented the development of a systematic land distribution program. Still, Lincoln and the Republican Congress supported other measures to aid the emancipated slaves. In March 1865 Congress established the **Freedmen's Bureau**. Along with providing food, clothing, and fuel to destitute former slaves, the bureau was charged with supervising and managing "all the abandoned lands in the South and the control of all subjects relating to refugees and freedmen." The act that established the bureau also stated that forty acres of abandoned or confiscated land could be leased to freed slaves or white Unionists, who would have an option to purchase after three years.

On the evening of April 14, 1865, while attending the theater in Washington, President Lincoln was shot by John Wilkes Booth and died of his wounds several hours later. At the time of his assassination, Lincoln's reconstruction policy remained unsettled and incomplete. In its broad outlines the president's plans had seemed to favor a speedy restoration of the southern states to the Union and a minimum of federal intervention in their affairs. But with his death the specifics of postwar Reconstruction had to be hammered out by a new president, Andrew Johnson of Tennessee, a man whose personality, political background, and racist leanings put him at odds with the Republican-controlled Congress.

## ANDREW JOHNSON AND PRESIDENTIAL RECONSTRUCTION

Throughout his career, Andrew Johnson had championed yeoman farmers and viewed the South's plantation aristocrats with contempt. He was the only southern member of the U.S. Senate to remain loyal to the Union, and he held the planter elite responsible for secession and defeat. In 1862, Lincoln appointed Johnson to the difficult post of military governor of Tennessee. There he successfully began wartime Reconstruction and cultivated Unionist support in the mountainous eastern districts of that state.

In 1864, the Republicans, in an appeal to northern and border state "**War Democrats**," nominated Johnson for vice president. But despite Johnson's success in Tennessee and in the 1864 campaign, many Radical Republicans distrusted him. In the immediate aftermath of Lincoln's murder, however, Johnson appeared to side with those Radical Republicans who sought to treat the South as a conquered province. But support for Johnson quickly faded as the new president's policies unfolded. Johnson defined Reconstruction as the province of the executive, not the legislative branch, and he planned to restore the Union as quickly as possible. He blamed individual Southerners—the planter elite—rather than entire states for leading the South down the disastrous road to secession. In line with this philosophy, Johnson outlined mild terms for reentry to the Union.

In the spring of 1865, Johnson granted amnesty and pardon, including restoration of property rights except slaves, to all Confederates who pledged loyalty to the Union and support for emancipation. Fourteen classes of Southerners, mostly major Confederate officials and wealthy landowners, were excluded. But these men could apply individually for presidential pardons. (During his tenure Johnson pardoned roughly 90 percent of those who applied.) Significantly, Johnson instituted this plan while Congress was not in session.

By the fall of 1865, ten of the eleven Confederate states claimed to have met Johnson's requirements to reenter the Union. But a serious division within the federal government was taking shape, for the Congress was not about to allow the president free rein in determining the conditions of southern readmission. Johnson's open sympathy for his fellow white Southerners, his antiblack bias, and his determination to control the course of Reconstruction placed him on a collision course with the powerful Radical wing of the Republican Party.

## FREE LABOR AND THE RADICAL REPUBLICAN VISION

Most Radicals were men whose careers had been shaped by the slavery controversy. One of the most effective rhetorical weapons used against slavery and its

**Freedmen's Bureau**  Agency established by Congress in March 1865 to provide social, educational, and economic services, advice, and protection to former slaves and destitute whites; lasted seven years.

**War Democrats**  Those from the North and the border states who broke with the Democratic Party and supported the Abraham Lincoln's military policies during the Civil War.

## QUICK REVIEW

**Johnson's Reconstruction Plan**

- Johnson extended pardons to Southerners who swore an oath of allegiance.
- He restored property rights to Southerners who swore an oath of allegiance.
- His plan had nothing to say about the voting and civil rights of former slaves.

**Black codes** Laws passed by states and municipalities denying many rights of citizenship to free black people before the Civil War.

**Civil Rights Bill** 1866 act that gave full citizenship to African Americans.

**16–3**
Clinton B. Fisk, *Plain Counsels for Freedmen* (1865)

**16–4**
*Mississippi Black Codes* (1865)

**16–7**
*The Fourteenth Amendment* (1868)

spread had been the ideal of a society based upon free labor. The model of free individuals, competing equally in the labor market and enjoying equal political rights, formed the core of this worldview.

Radicals now looked to reconstruct southern society along these same lines, backed by the power of the national government. They argued that once free labor, universal education, and equal rights were implanted in the South, that region would be able to share in the North's material wealth, progress, and social mobility. In the Radicals' view, the power of the federal government would be central to the remaking of southern society, especially in guaranteeing civil rights and suffrage for freedmen.

Northern Republicans were especially outraged by the stringent "**black codes**" passed by South Carolina, Mississippi, Louisiana, and other states. These were designed to restrict the freedom of the black labor force and keep freed people as close to slave status as possible. Laborers who left their jobs before contracts expired would forfeit wages already earned and be subject to arrest by any white citizen. Vagrancy, very broadly defined, was punishable by fines and involuntary plantation labor. Apprenticeship clauses obliged black children to work without pay for employers. Some states attempted to bar African Americans from land ownership. Other laws specifically denied African Americans equality with white people in civil rights, excluding them from juries and prohibiting interracial marriages.

The Radicals, although not a majority of their party, were joined by moderate Republicans as growing numbers of Northerners grew suspicious of white southern intransigence and the denial of political rights to freedmen. When the Thirty-ninth Congress convened in December 1865, the large Republican majority prevented the seating of the white Southerners elected to Congress under President Johnson's provisional state governments.

In the spring of 1866, Congress passed two important bills designed to aid African Americans. The landmark **Civil Rights Bill**, which bestowed full citizenship on African Americans, overturned the 1857 *Dred Scott* decision and the black codes. It defined all persons born in the United States (except Indian peoples) as national citizens, and it enumerated various rights, including the rights to make and enforce contracts, to sue, to give evidence, and to buy and sell property. Under this bill,

**"Office of the** Freedmen's Bureau, Memphis, Tennessee,** *Harper's Weekly*, June 2, 1866. Established by Congress in 1865, the Freedmen's Bureau provided economic, educational, and legal assistance to former slaves in the post–Civil War years. Bureau agents were often called on to settle disputes between black and white Southerners over wages, labor contracts, political rights, and violence. Although most southern whites only grudgingly acknowledged the bureau's legitimacy, freed people gained important legal and psychological support through testimony at public hearings like this one.

African Americans acquired "full and equal benefit of all laws and proceedings for the security of person and property as is enjoyed by white citizens."

Congress also voted to enlarge the scope of the Freedmen's Bureau, empowering it to build schools and pay teachers, and also to establish courts to prosecute those charged with depriving African Americans of their civil rights. The bureau achieved important, if limited, success in aiding African Americans. Bureau-run schools helped lay the foundation for southern public education. The bureau's network of courts allowed freed people to bring suits against white people in disputes involving violence, nonpayment of wages, or unfair division of crops. The very existence of courts hearing public testimony by African Americans provided an important psychological challenge to traditional notions of white racial domination.

An angry President Johnson vetoed both of these bills. But Johnson's intemperate attacks on the Radicals—he damned them as traitors unwilling to restore the Union—united moderate and Radical Republicans and they succeeded in overriding the vetoes. Congressional Republicans, led by the Radical faction, were now unified in challenging the president's power to direct Reconstruction and in using national authority to define and protect the rights of citizens.

In June 1866, fearful that the Civil Rights Act might be declared unconstitutional, and eager to settle the basis for the seating of southern representatives, Congress passed the Fourteenth Amendment. The amendment defined national citizenship to include former slaves and prohibited the states from violating the privileges of citizens without due process of law. It also empowered Congress to reduce the representation of any state that denied the suffrage to males over twenty-one. Republicans adopted the Fourteenth Amendment as their platform for the 1866 congressional elections and suggested that southern states would have to ratify it as a condition of readmission.

For their part, the Republicans skillfully portrayed Johnson and northern Democrats as disloyal and white Southerners as unregenerate. Republicans began an effective campaign tradition known as "waving the bloody shirt"—reminding northern voters of the hundreds of thousands of Yankee soldiers left dead or maimed by the war. In the November 1866 elections, the Republicans increased their majority in both the House and the Senate and gained control of all the northern states. The stage was now set for a battle between the president and Congress. Was it to be Johnson's "restoration" or **Congressional Reconstruction**?

## CONGRESSIONAL RECONSTRUCTION AND THE IMPEACHMENT CRISIS

In March 1867, Congress passed the **First Reconstruction Act** over Johnson's veto. This act divided the South into five military districts subject to martial law. To achieve restoration, southern states were first required to call new constitutional conventions, elected by universal manhood suffrage. Once these states had drafted new constitutions, guaranteed African American voting rights, and ratified the Fourteenth Amendment, they were eligible for readmission to the Union. Supplementary legislation, also passed over the president's veto, invalidated the provisional governments established by Johnson, empowered the military to administer voter registration, and required an oath of loyalty to the United States (see Map 17.1).

Congress also passed several laws aimed at limiting Johnson's power. One of these, the **Tenure of Office Act**, stipulated that any officeholder appointed by the president with the Senate's advice and consent could not be removed until the Senate had approved a successor. In August 1867, with Congress

**Congressional Reconstruction** Name given to the period 1867–1870 when the Republican-dominated Congress controlled Reconstruction-era policy.

**First Reconstruction Act** 1877 act that divided the South into five military districts subject to martial law.

**Tenure of Office Act** Act stipulating that any officeholder appointed by the president with the Senate's advice and consent could not be removed until the Senate had approved a successor.

QUICK REVIEW

**Key Components of the Radical Agenda**

- Free labor.
- Universal education.
- Equal rights.

QUICK REVIEW

**The Tenure of Office Act and Johnson's Impeachment**

- Act prohibited the president from removing certain officeholders without the Senate's approval of a successor.
- Johnson deliberately violated the act in February 1868.
- Johnson escaped impeachment by one vote.

# MAP EXPLORATION

To explore an interactive version of this map, go to
http://www.prenhall.com/faraghertlc/map17.1

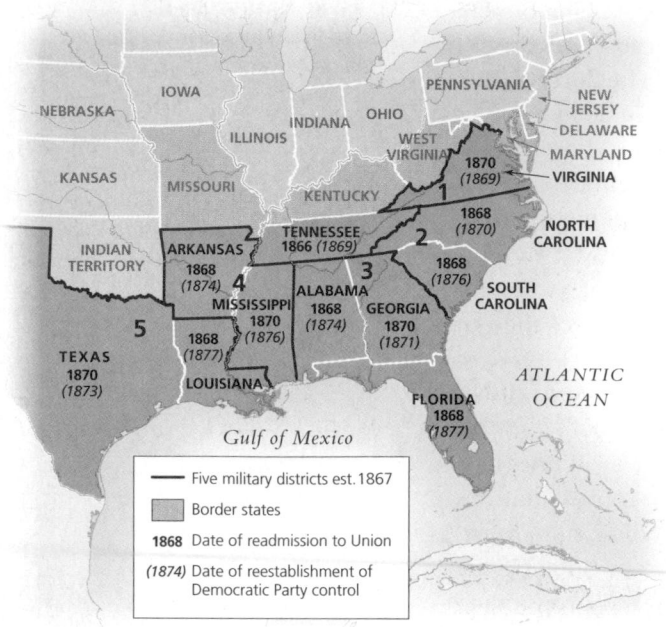

**MAP 17.1**

**Reconstruction of the South, 1866–77** Dates for the readmission of former Confederate states to the Union and the return of Democrats to power varied according to the specific political situations in those states.

WHAT WERE the competing plans for reconstructing the Southern states?

adjourned, Johnson suspended Stanton and appointed General Ulysses S. Grant interim secretary of war. This move enabled the president to remove generals in the field that he judged to be too radical and replace them with men who were sympathetic to his own views. It also served as a challenge to the Tenure of Office Act. In January 1868, when the Senate overruled Stanton's suspension, Grant broke openly with Johnson and vacated the office. Stanton resumed his position and barricaded himself in his office when Johnson attempted to remove him once again.

Outraged by Johnson's relentless obstructionism, and seizing upon his violation of the Tenure of Office Act as a pretext, moderate and Radical Republicans in the House of Representatives again joined forces and voted to impeach the president by a vote of 126 to 47 on February 24, 1868, charging him with eleven counts of high crimes and misdemeanors. To ensure the support of moderate Republicans, the articles of impeachment focused on violations of the Tenure of Office Act.

An influential group of moderate Senate Republicans feared the damage a conviction might do to the constitutional separation of powers. They also worried about the political and economic policies that might be pursued by Benjamin Wade, the president pro tem of the Senate and a leader of the Radical Republicans, who, because there was no vice president, would succeed to the presidency if Johnson were removed from office. Behind the scenes during his Senate trial, Johnson agreed to abide by the Reconstruction Acts. In May, the Senate

**The Fifteenth Amendment,** ratified in 1870, stipulated that the right to vote could not be denied "on account of race, color, or previous condition of servitude." This illustration expressed the optimism and hopes of African Americans generated by this consitutional landmark aimed at protecting black political rights. Note the various political figures (Abraham Lincoln, John Brown, Frederick Douglass) and movements (abolitionism, black education) invoked here, providing a sense of how the amendment ended a long historical struggle.

voted 35 for conviction, 19 for acquittal—one vote shy of the two-thirds necessary for removal from office. Johnson's narrow acquittal established the precedent that only criminal actions by a president—not political disagreements—warranted removal from office.

## THE ELECTION OF 1868

By the summer of 1868, seven former Confederate states (Alabama, Arkansas, Florida, Louisiana, North Carolina, South Carolina, and Tennessee) had ratified the revised constitutions, elected Republican governments, and ratified the Fourteenth Amendment. They had thereby earned readmission to the Union. In 1868 Republicans nominated Ulysses S. Grant, the North's foremost military hero, as their nominee for President. Grant enjoyed tremendous popularity after the war, especially when he broke with Johnson. Totally lacking in political experience, Grant admitted, after receiving the nomination, that he had been forced into it in spite of himself.

Significantly, at the very moment that the South was being forced to enfranchise former slaves as a prerequisite for readmission to the Union, the Republicans rejected a campaign plank endorsing black suffrage in the North. State referendums calling for black suffrage failed in eight northern states between 1865 and 1868, succeeding only in Iowa and Minnesota. The Democrats, determined to reverse Congressional Reconstruction, nominated Horatio Seymour, former governor of New York and a longtime foe of emancipation and supporter of states' rights.

The **Ku Klux Klan** emerged as a potent instrument of terror (see the opening of this chapter). In Louisiana, Arkansas, Georgia, and South Carolina, the Klan threatened, whipped, and murdered black and white Republicans to prevent them from voting. This terrorism enabled the Democrats to carry Georgia and Louisiana, but it ultimately cost the Democrats votes in the North. In the final tally, Grant carried twenty-six of the thirty-four states for an electoral college victory of 214 to 80. Significantly, more than 500,000 African American voters cast their ballots for Grant, demonstrating their overwhelming support for the Republican Party. The Republicans also retained large majorities in both houses of Congress.

In February 1869, Congress passed the **Fifteenth Amendment**, providing that "the right of citizens of the United States to vote shall not be denied or abridged on account of race, color, or previous condition of servitude." To enhance the chances of ratification, Congress required the four remaining unreconstructed states—Mississippi, Georgia, Texas, and Virginia—to ratify both the Fourteenth and Fifteenth Amendments before readmission. They did so and rejoined the Union in early 1870. The Fifteenth Amendment was ratified in February 1870. In the narrow sense of simply readmitting the former Confederate states to the Union, Reconstruction was complete.

## WOMAN SUFFRAGE AND RECONSTRUCTION

Many women's rights advocates had long been active in the abolitionist movement. The Fourteenth and Fifteenth Amendments, which granted citizenship and the vote to freedmen, both inspired and frustrated these activists. Insisting that the causes of the African American vote and the women's vote were linked, Elizabeth Cady Stanton, Susan B. Anthony, and Lucy Stone founded the American Equal Rights Association in 1866. The group launched a series of lobbying and petition campaigns to remove racial and sexual restrictions on voting from state constitutions. Throughout the nation, the old abolitionist organizations and the Republican Party

**Ku Klux Klan**    Perhaps the most prominent of the vigilante groups that terrorized black people in the South during Reconstruction era, founded by the Confederate veterans in 1866.

**Fifteenth Amendment**    Passed by Congress in 1869, guaranteed the right of American men to vote, regardless of race.

**16–8**
Albion W. Tourgee, *Letter on Ku Klux Klan Activities* (1870)

**Susan B. Anthony** (1820–1906) and Elizabeth Cady Stanton (1815–1902), the two most influential leaders of the woman suffrage movement. As founders of the militant National Woman Suffrage Association, Stanton and Anthony established an independent woman suffrage movement with a broader spectrum of goals for women's rights and drew millions of women into public life during the late nineteenth century.

# OVERVIEW | Reconstruction Amendments to the Constitution, 1865–1870

| Amendment and Date Passed by Congress | Main Provisions | Ratification Process (3/4 of all States Including Ex-Confederate States Required) |
|---|---|---|
| 13 (January 1865) | • Prohibited slavery in the United States | December 1865 (27 states, including 8 southern states) |
| 14 (June 1866) | • Conferred national citizenship on all persons born or naturalized in the United States<br>• Reduced state representation in Congress proportionally for any state disfranchising male citizens<br>• Denied former Confederates the right to hold state or national office<br>• Repudiated Confederate debt | July 1868 (after Congress made ratification a prerequisite for readmission of ex-Confederate states to the Union) |
| 15 (February 1869) | • Prohibited denial of suffrage because of race, color, or previous condition of servitude | March 1870 (ratification required for readmission of Virginia, Texas, Mississippi, and Georgia) |

**myhistorylab**

**Overview:** *Reconstruction Amendments to the Constitution, 1865–1870*

**16–10**
*Susan B. Anthony and the "New Departure" for Women* (1873)

**WHAT WERE** the most important changes in the lives of African Americans in the years immediately following the war?

**myhistorylab**

**Review Summary**

emphasized passage of the Fourteenth and Fifteenth Amendments and withdrew funds and support from the cause of woman suffrage. Disagreements over these amendments divided suffragists for decades and by 1869 woman suffragists had split into two competing organizations: the moderate American Woman Suffrage Association (AWSA), which sought the support of men, and the more radical all-female National Woman Suffrage Association (NWSA).

Although women did not win the vote in this period, they did establish an independent suffrage movement that eventually drew millions of women into political life. The NWSA in particular demonstrated that self-government and democratic participation in the public sphere were crucial for women's emancipation. The failure of woman suffrage after the Civil War was less a result of factional fighting than of the larger defeat of Radical Reconstruction and the ideal of expanded citizenship.

## THE MEANING OF FREEDOM

For nearly 4 million slaves, freedom arrived in various ways in different parts of the South. In many areas, slavery had collapsed long before Lee's surrender at Appomattox. In regions far removed from the presence of federal troops, African Americans did not learn of slavery's end until the spring of 1865. But regardless of specific regional circumstances, the meaning of "freedom" would be contested for years to come. The deep desire for independence from white control formed the underlying aspiration of newly freed slaves. For their part, most southern white people sought to restrict the boundaries of that independence.

### MOVING ABOUT

The first impulse of many emancipated slaves was to test their freedom. The simplest, most obvious way to do this involved leaving home. Throughout the summer and fall of 1865, observers in the South noted enormous numbers of freed

People on the move. When urged to stay on with the South Carolina family she had served for years as a cook, a slave woman replied firmly: "No, Miss, I must go. If I stay here I'll never know I am free."

Yet many who left their old neighborhoods returned soon afterward to seek work in the general vicinity or even on the plantation they had left. Many wanted to separate themselves from former owners, but not from familial ties and friendships. Others moved away altogether, seeking jobs in nearby towns and cities. Many former slaves left predominantly white counties, where they felt more vulnerable and isolated, for new lives in the relative comfort of predominantly black communities. In most southern states, there was a significant population shift toward black belt plantation counties and towns after the war. Many African Americans, attracted by schools, churches, and fraternal societies as well as the army, preferred the city.

Disgruntled planters had difficulty accepting African American independence. The deference and humility white people expected from African Americans could no longer be taken for granted. Indeed, many freed people went out of their way to reject the old subservience. Moving about freely was one way of doing this, as was refusing to tip one's hat to white people, ignoring former masters or mistresses in the streets, and refusing to step aside on sidewalks.

## THE AFRICAN AMERICAN FAMILY

Emancipation allowed freed people to strengthen family ties. For many former slaves, freedom meant the opportunity to find long-lost family members. To track down these relatives, freed people trekked to faraway places, put ads in newspapers, sought the help of Freedmen's Bureau agents, and questioned anyone who might have information about loved ones. Many thousands of family reunions, each with its own story, took place after the war. One North Carolina slave, who had seen his parents separated by sale, recalled many years later what for him had been the most significant aspect of freedom. "I has got thirteen great-gran' chilluns an' I know whar dey ever'one am. In slavery times dey'd have been on de block long time ago." Thousands of African American couples who had lived together under slavery streamed to military and civilian authorities and demanded to be legally married. By 1870, the two-parent household was the norm for a large majority of African Americans.

Emancipation brought changes to gender roles within the African American family as well. By serving in the Union army, African American men played a more direct role than women in the fight for freedom. In the political sphere, black men could now serve on juries, vote, and hold office; black women, like their white counterparts, could not. Freedmen's Bureau agents designated the husband as household head and established lower wage scales for women laborers.

African American men asserted their male authority, denied under slavery, by insisting their wives work at home instead of in the fields. African American women generally wanted to devote more time than they had under slavery to caring for their children and to performing such domestic chores as cooking, sewing, gardening, and laundering. Yet African American women continued to work outside the home, engaging in seasonal field labor for wages or working a family's rented plot. The key difference from slave times was that African American families themselves, not white masters and overseers, decided when and where women and children worked.

## AFRICAN AMERICAN CHURCHES AND SCHOOLS

The creation of separate African American churches proved the most lasting and important element of the energetic institution building that went on in post-emancipation years. Before the Civil War, southern Protestant churches had

### QUICK REVIEW

**Black Churches**

- Many African Americans found inspiration and courage in their religious faith.
- Most black churches split from white-dominated congregations after the war.
- Black churches created a variety of organizations that served the black community.

**rflow congregation** crowds into mond's First African Baptist Church 1874. Despite their poverty, freed people struggled to save money, buy land, and erect new buildings as they organized hundreds of new black churches during Reconstruction. As the most important African American institution outside the family, the black church, in addition to tending to spiritual needs, played a key role in the educational and political life of the community.

relegated slaves and free African Americans to second-class membership. Black worshipers were required to sit in the back during services, they were denied any role in church governance, and they were excluded from Sunday schools. Even in larger cities, where all-black congregations sometimes built their own churches, the law required white pastors.

In communities around the South, African Americans now pooled their resources to buy land and build their own churches. Churches became the center not only for religious life but also for many other activities that defined the African American community: schools, picnics, festivals, and political meetings. The church became the first social institution fully controlled by African Americans. In nearly every community, ministers, respected for their speaking and organizational skills, were among the most influential leaders. By 1877, the great majority of black Southerners had withdrawn from white-dominated churches.

The rapid spread of schools reflected African Americans' thirst for self-improvement. Southern states had prohibited education for slaves. But many free black people managed to attend school, and a few slaves had been able to educate themselves. Still, over 90 percent of the South's adult African American population was illiterate in 1860. Access to education thus became a central part of the meaning of freedom. Freedmen's Bureau agents repeatedly expressed amazement at the number of makeshift classrooms organized by African Americans in rural areas.

African American communities received important educational aid from outside organizations. By 1869, the Freedmen's Bureau was supervising nearly 3,000 schools serving over 150,000 students throughout the South. Over half of the roughly 3,300 teachers in these schools were African Americans, many of whom had been free before the Civil War. Other teachers included dedicated northern white women, volunteers sponsored by the American Missionary Association (AMA). The bureau and the AMA also assisted in the founding of several black colleges, including Tougaloo, Hampton, and Fisk, designed to train black teachers. Black self-help proved crucial to the education effort. Throughout the South in 1865 and 1866, African Americans raised money to build schoolhouses, buy supplies, and pay teachers. Black artisans donated labor for construction, and black families offered room and board to teachers.

## LAND AND LABOR AFTER SLAVERY

Most newly emancipated African Americans aspired to quit the plantations and to make new lives for themselves. Some freed people did find jobs in railroad building, mining, ranching, or construction work. Others raised subsistence crops and tended vegetable gardens as squatters. White planters, however, tried to retain African Americans as permanent agricultural laborers. Restricting the employment of former slaves was an important goal of the black codes.

The majority of African Americans hoped to become self-sufficient farmers. Many former slaves believed they were entitled to the land they had worked throughout their lives. This perception was not merely a wishful fantasy. Frequent reference in the Congress and the press to the question of land distribution made the idea of "forty acres and a mule" not just a pipe dream but a matter of serious public debate. But by 1866, the federal government had already pulled back from the various wartime experiments involving the breaking up of large plantations and the leasing of small plots to individual families. President Johnson directed General Oliver O. Howard of the Freedmen's Bureau to evict tens of thousands of freed people settled on confiscated and abandoned land in southeastern Virginia, southern Louisiana, and the Georgia and South Carolina low country.

In communities throughout the South, freed people and their former masters negotiated new arrangements for organizing agricultural labor (see Map 17.2). By the late 1860s, **sharecropping** and tenant farming had emerged as the dominant form of working the land. Sharecropping represented a compromise between planters and former slaves. Under sharecropping arrangements that were usually very detailed, individual families contracted with landowners to be responsible for a specific plot. Large plantations were thus broken into family-sized farms. Generally, sharecropper families received one-third of the year's crop if the owner furnished implements, seed, and draft animals or one-half if they provided their own supplies. African Americans preferred sharecropping to gang labor, as it allowed families to set their own hours and tasks and offered freedom from white supervision and control. For planters, the system stabilized the workforce by requiring sharecroppers to remain until the harvest and to employ all family members. It also offered a way around the chronic shortage of cash and credit that plagued the postwar South. Freed people did not aspire to sharecropping. Owning land outright or tenant farming (renting land) were both more desirable. But though black sharecroppers clearly enjoyed more autonomy than in the past, the vast majority never achieved economic independence or land ownership. They remained a largely subordinate agricultural labor force.

## THE ORIGINS OF AFRICAN AMERICAN POLITICS

Inclusion, rather than separation, was the objective of early African American political activity. The greatest political activity by African Americans occurred in areas occupied by Union forces during the war. In 1865 and 1866, African Americans throughout the South organized scores of mass meetings, parades, and petitions that demanded civil equality and the right to vote. In the cities, the growing web of churches and fraternal societies helped bolster early efforts at political organization.

Hundreds of African American delegates, selected by local meetings or churches, attended statewide political conventions held

**16–5**
James C. Beecher, *Report on Land Reform in the South Carolina Islands* (1865, 1866)

**16–11**
James T. Rapier, *Testimony Before U.S. Senate Regarding the Agricultural Labor Force in the South* (1880)

*A Sharecrop Contract* (1882)

**Sharecropping**   Labor system that evolved during and after Reconstruction whereby landowners furnished laborers with a house, farm animals, and tools and advanced credit in exchange for a share of the laborers' crop.

**"The First Vote,"** *Harper's Weekly*, November 16, 1867, reflected the optimism felt by much of the northern public as former slaves began to vote for the first time. The caption noted that freedmen went to the ballot box "not with expressions of exultation or of defiance of their old masters and present opponents depicted on their countenances, but looking serious and solemn and determined."

**MAP 17.2**

**The Barrow Plantation, Oglethorpe County, Georgia, 1860 and 1881 (approx. 2,000 acres)**   These two maps, based on drawings from *Scribner's Monthly*, April 1881, show some of the changes brought by emancipation. In 1860, the plantation's entire black population lived in the communal slave quarters, right next to the white master's house. In 1881, black sharecropper and tenant families lived on individual plots, spread out across the land. The former slaves had also built their own school and church.

WHAT CHANGES in the lives of Black Southerners are reflected in the two maps of the Barrow Plantation?

throughout the South in 1865 and 1866. Previously free African Americans, as well as black ministers, artisans, and veterans of the Union army, tended to dominate these proceedings, setting a pattern that would hold throughout Reconstruction. Convention debates sometimes reflected the tensions within African American communities, such as friction between poorer former slaves and better-off free black people, or between lighter- and darker-skinned African Americans. But most of these state gatherings concentrated on passing resolutions on issues that united all African Americans. The central concerns were suffrage and equality before the law.

The passage of the First Reconstruction Act in 1867 encouraged even more political activity among African Americans. The military started registering the South's electorate, ultimately enrolling approximately 735,000 black and 635,000 white voters in the ten unreconstructed states. Five states—Alabama, Florida, Louisiana, Mississippi, and South Carolina—had black electoral majorities. Four-fifths of the

# Changing Images of Reconstruction

After the Civil War, northern journalists and illustrators went south to describe Reconstruction in action. They took a keen interest in how the newly freed slaves were reshaping local and national politics. A drawing by *Harper's Weekly* illustrator William L. Sheppard titled "Electioneering in the South" clearly approved of the freedmen's exercise of their new citizenship rights. "Does any man seriously

**HOW DOES** the portrayal of the larger African American community in "Electioneering in the South" reflect the political point being made? What do the caricatures in "The Ignorant Vote" suggest about Reconstruction era ideas about the meaning of "whiteness"?

doubt," the caption asked, "whether it is better for this vast population to be sinking deeper and deeper in ignorance and servility, or rising into general intelligence and self-respect? They can not be pariahs; they can not be peons; they must be slaves or citizens."

Thomas Nast was the nation's best-known political cartoonist during the 1860s and 1870s. During the Civil War he strongly supported the Union cause and the aspirations of the newly freed slaves. But by 1876, like many Northerners originally sympathetic to guaranteeing blacks full political and civil rights, Nast had turned away from the early ideals of Reconstruction. Nast used grotesque racial caricature to depict southern African Americans and northern Irish

immigrants as undeserving of the right to vote. The aftermath of the disputed 1876 presidential election included charges of widespread vote fraud from both Republicans and Democrats. Nast's view—published in *Harper's Weekly* in December 1876, while the election's outcome was still in doubt—reflected concerns among many middle-class Northerners that the nation's political system was tainted by the manipulation of "ignorant" voters in both the South and the North. ■

registered black voters cast ballots in these elections. Much of this new African American political activism was channeled through local **Union League** chapters throughout the South.

Begun during the war as a northern, largely white middle-class patriotic club, the Union League now became the political voice of the former slaves. Union League chapters brought together local African Americans, soldiers, and Freedmen's Bureau agents to demand the vote and an end to legal discrimination against African Americans. It brought out African American voters, instructed freedmen in the rights and duties of citizenship, and promoted Republican candidates. Not surprisingly, newly enfranchised freedmen voted Republican and formed the core of the Republican Party in the South. For most ordinary African Americans, politics was inseparable from economic issues, especially the land question. Grassroots political organizations frequently intervened in local disputes with planters over the terms of labor contracts. African American political groups closely followed the congressional debates over Reconstruction policy and agitated for land confiscation and distribution. Perhaps most important, politics was the only arena where black and white Southerners might engage each other on an equal basis.

## SOUTHERN POLITICS AND SOCIETY

By the summer of 1868, when the South had returned to the Union, the majority of Republicans believed the task of Reconstruction to be finished. Ultimately, they put their faith in a political solution to the problems facing the vanquished South. Most Republican congressmen were moderates, conceiving Reconstruction in limited terms. They rejected radical calls for confiscation and redistribution of land, as well as permanent military rule of the South. The Reconstruction Acts of 1867 and 1868 laid out the requirements for the readmission of southern states, along with the procedures for forming and electing new governments.

Yet over the next decade, the political structure created in the southern states proved too restricted and fragile to sustain itself. To most southern whites, the active participation of African Americans in politics seemed extremely dangerous. Federal troops were needed to protect Republican governments and their supporters from violent opposition. Congressional action to monitor southern elections and protect black voting rights became routine. Despite initial successes, southern Republicanism proved an unstable coalition of often conflicting elements, unable to sustain effective power for very long. By 1877, Democrats had regained political control of all the former Confederate states.

### SOUTHERN REPUBLICANS

Three major groups composed the fledgling Republican coalition in the postwar South. African American voters made up a large majority of southern Republicans throughout the Reconstruction era. Yet African Americans outnumbered whites in only three southern states; Republicans would have to attract white support to win elections and sustain power.

A second group consisted of white Northerners, derisively called "**carpetbaggers**" by native white Southerners. Most were veterans of the Union army who stayed in the South after the war. Others included Freedmen's Bureau agents and businessmen who had invested capital in cotton plantations and other enterprises. Although they made up a tiny percentage of the population, carpetbaggers played

---

**WHAT MAJOR** groups made up the Southern Republicans?

**myhistorylab**
Review Summary

**Union League**   Republican party organizations in Northern cities that became an important organizing device among freedmen in Southern cities after 1865.

**Carpetbaggers**   Northern transplants to the South, many of whom were Union soldiers who stayed in the South after the war.

a disproportionately large role in southern politics. They won a large share of Reconstruction offices, particularly in Florida, South Carolina, and Louisiana and in areas with large African American constituencies.

The third major group of southern Republicans were the native whites pejoratively termed "**scalawags.**" They had even more diverse backgrounds and motives than the northern-born Republicans. Some were prominent prewar Whigs who saw the Republican Party as their best chance to regain political influence. Others viewed the party as an agent of modernization and economic expansion. Loyalists during the war and traditional enemies of the planter elite (most were small farmers), these white Southerners looked to the Republican Party for help in settling old scores and relief from debt and wartime devastation.

Southern Republicanism also reflected prewar political divisions. Its influence was greatest in those regions that had long resisted the political and economic power of the plantation elite. Yet few white Southerners identified with the political and economic aspirations of African Americans. Moderate elements more concerned with maintaining white control of the party, and encouraging economic investment in the region, outnumbered and defeated "confiscation radicals" who focused on obtaining land for African Americans.

**Scalawags** Southern whites, mainly small landowning farmers and well-off merchants and planters, who supported the Southern Republican party during Reconstruction.

**The Ku Klux** Klan emerged as a potent political and social force during Reconstruction, terrorizing freed people and their white allies. An 1868 Klan warning threatens Louisiana governor Henry C. Warmoth with death. Warmoth, an Illinois-born "carpetbagger," was the state's first Republican governor. Two Alabama Klansmen, photographed in 1868, wear white hoods to hide their identities.

## RECONSTRUCTING THE STATES: A MIXED RECORD

With the old Confederate leaders barred from political participation, and with carpetbaggers and newly enfranchised African Americans representing many of the plantation districts, Republicans managed to dominate the ten southern constitutional conventions from 1867 to 1869. Most of these conventions produced constitutions that expanded democracy and the public role of the state. The new documents guaranteed the political and civil rights of African Americans, and they abolished property qualifications for officeholding and jury service as well as imprisonment for debt. They created the first state-funded systems of education in the South to be administered by state commissioners. The new constitutions also mandated establishment of orphanages, penitentiaries, and homes for the insane. In 1868, only three years after the end of the war, Republicans came to power in most of the southern states. By 1869, new constitutions had been ratified in all the old Confederate states.

Republican governments in the South faced a continual crisis of legitimacy that limited their ability to legislate change. They had to balance reform against the need to gain acceptance, especially by white Southerners. Their achievements were thus mixed. In the realm of race relations there was a clear thrust toward equal rights and against discrimination. Republican legislatures followed up the federal Civil Rights Act of 1866 with various antidiscrimination clauses in new constitutions and laws prescribing harsh penalties for civil rights violations.

Segregation, though, became the norm in public school systems. African American leaders often accepted segregation because they feared that insistence on integrated education would jeopardize funding for the new school systems. Segregation in railroad cars and other public places was more objectionable. By the early 1870s, as black influence and assertiveness grew, laws guaranteeing equal access to transportation and public accommodation were passed in many states. By and large, though, such civil rights laws were difficult to enforce in local communities.

In economic matters, Republican governments failed to fulfill African Americans' hopes of obtaining land. Few former slaves possessed the cash to buy land in the open market, and they looked to the state for help. Republicans tried to weaken the plantation system and promote black ownership by raising taxes on land. Yet even when state governments seized land for nonpayment of taxes, the property was never used to help create black homesteads.

Republican leaders envisioned promoting northern-style capitalist development—factories, large towns, and diversified agriculture—through state aid. Much Republican state lawmaking was devoted to encouraging railroad construction. But in spite of all the new laws, it proved impossible to attract significant amounts of northern and European investment capital. The obsession with railroads withdrew resources from education and other programs. As in the North, it also opened the doors to widespread corruption and bribery of public officials. Railroad failures eroded public confidence in the Republicans' ability to govern.

## WHITE RESISTANCE AND "REDEMPTION"

The emergence of a Republican Party in the reconstructed South brought two parties, but not a two-party system, to the region. The opponents of Reconstruction, the Democrats, refused to acknowledge Republicans' right to participate in southern political life. Republicans were split between those who urged conciliation in an effort to gain white acceptance and those who emphasized consolidating the party under the protection of the military.

From its founding in 1868 through the early 1870s, the Ku Klux Klan fought an ongoing terrorist campaign against Reconstruction governments and local leaders. Just as the institution of slavery had depended on violence and the threat of violence, the Klan acted as a kind of guerrilla military force in the service of the Democratic Party, the planter class, and all those who sought the restoration of white supremacy. It employed a wide array of terror tactics: destroying ballot boxes, issuing death threats, the beating and murdering of politically active blacks and their white allies. Freedmen and their allies sometimes resisted the Klan. In Hale County, Alabama, Union Leaguers set up a warning system using buglers to signal the activities of Klan raiders. But violence and intimidation decimated Union League leadership in the countryside by 1869.

In October 1870, after Republicans carried Laurens County in South Carolina, bands of white people drove 150 African Americans from their homes and murdered thirteen white and black Republican activists. In March 1871, three African Americans were arrested in Meridian, Mississippi, for giving "incendiary" speeches. At their court hearing, Klansmen killed two of the defendants and the Republican judge, and thirty more African Americans were murdered in a day of rioting. The single bloodiest episode of Reconstruction era violence took place in Colfax, Louisiana, on Easter Sunday 1873. Nearly 100 African Americans were murdered after they failed to hold a besieged courthouse during a contested election.

Southern Republicans looked to Washington for help. In 1870 and 1871, Congress passed three Enforcement Acts designed to counter racial terrorism. These declared that interference with voting was a federal offense. The acts provided for federal supervision of voting and authorized the president to send the army and to suspend the writ of habeas corpus in districts declared to be in a state of insurrection. The most sweeping measure was the Ku Klux Klan Act of April 1871, which made the violent infringement of civil and political rights a federal crime punishable by the national government. By the election of 1872, the federal government's intervention had helped break the Klan and restore a semblance of law and order.

The Civil Rights Act of 1875 outlawed racial discrimination in theaters, hotels, railroads, and other public places. But the law proved more an assertion of principle than a direct federal intervention in southern affairs. Enforcement required African Americans to take their cases to the federal courts, a costly and time-consuming procedure.

As wartime idealism faded, northern Republicans became less inclined toward direct intervention in southern affairs. They had enough trouble retaining political control in the North. In 1874, the Democrats gained a majority in the House of Representatives for the first time since 1856. Key northern states also began to fall to the Democrats. Northern Republicans slowly abandoned the freedmen and their white allies in the South. Southern Democrats were also able to exploit a deepening fiscal crisis by blaming Republicans for excessive extension of public credit and the sharp increase in tax rates.

Gradually, conservative Democrats "redeemed" one state after another. Virginia and Tennessee led the way in 1869, North Carolina in 1870, Georgia in 1871, Texas in 1873, and Alabama and Arkansas in 1874. In Mississippi, white conservatives employed violence and intimidation to wrest control in 1875 and "redeemed" the state the following year. Republican infighting in Louisiana in 1873 and 1874 led to a series of contested election results, including bloody clashes between black militia and armed whites, and finally to "redemption" by the Democrats in 1877.

Several Supreme Court rulings involving the Fourteenth and Fifteenth Amendments effectively constrained federal protection of African American civil rights. In

**Slaughterhouse cases** Group of cases resulting in one sweeping decision by the U.S. Supreme Court in 1873 that contradicted the intent of the Fourteenth Amendment by decreeing that most citizenship rights remained under state, not federal, control.

the so-called **Slaughterhouse cases** of 1873, the Court issued its first ruling on the Fourteenth Amendment. The cases involved a Louisiana charter that gave a New Orleans meatpacking company a monopoly over the city's butchering business on the grounds of protecting public health. A rival group of butchers had sued, claiming the law violated the Fourteenth Amendment, which prohibited states from depriving any person of life, liberty, or property without due process of law. The Court held that the Fourteenth Amendment protected only the former slaves, not butchers, and that it protected only national citizenship rights, not the regulatory powers of states. It separated national citizenship from state citizenship and declared that most of the rights that Americans enjoyed on a daily basis—freedom of speech, fair trials, the right to sit on juries, protection from unreasonable searches, and the right to vote—were under the control of state law. The ruling in effect denied the original intent of the Fourteenth Amendment—to protect against state infringement of national citizenship rights as spelled out in the Bill of Rights.

Three other decisions curtailed federal protection of black civil rights. In *United States* v. *Reese* (1876) and *United States* v. *Cruikshank* (1876), the Court restricted congressional power to enforce the Ku Klux Klan Act. Future prosecution would depend on the states rather than on federal authorities. In these rulings, the Court held that the Fourteenth Amendment extended the federal power to protect civil rights only in cases involving discrimination by states; discrimination by individuals or groups was not covered. The Court also ruled that the Fifteenth Amendment did not guarantee a citizen's right to vote; it only barred certain specific grounds for denying suffrage—"race, color, or previous condition of servitude." This interpretation opened the door for southern states to disenfranchise African Americans for allegedly nonracial reasons. States back under Democratic control began to limit African American voting by passing laws restricting voter eligibility through poll taxes and property requirements.

Finally, in the 1883 Civil Rights Cases decision, the Court declared the Civil Rights Act of 1875 unconstitutional, holding that the Fourteenth Amendment gave Congress the power to outlaw discrimination by states but not by private individuals. The majority opinion held that black people must no longer "be the special favorite of the laws." Together, these Supreme Court decisions marked the end of federal attempts to protect African American rights until well into the next century.

## KING COTTON: SHARECROPPERS, TENANTS, AND THE SOUTHERN ENVIRONMENT

The Republicans' vision of a "New South" remade along the lines of the northern economy failed to materialize. In the post–Civil War years, "King Cotton" expanded its realm, as greater numbers of small white farmers found themselves forced to switch from subsistence crops to growing cotton for the market (see Map 17.3).

A chronic shortage of capital and banking institutions made local merchants and planters the sole source of credit. They advanced loans and supplies to small owners, tenant farmers, and sharecroppers in exchange for a lien, or claim, on the year's cotton crop. At the end of the year, sharecroppers and tenants found themselves deep in debt to stores for seed, supplies, and clothing. The spread of the "crop lien" system as the South's main form of agricultural credit forced more and more farmers into cotton growing.

As the "crop lien" system spread, and as more and more farmers turned to cotton growing as the only way to obtain credit, expanding production depressed cotton prices. Competition from new cotton centers in the world market, such as Egypt and India, accelerated the downward spiral. As cotton prices declined, per

---

**QUICK REVIEW**

**The End of Federal Intervention: Key Supreme Court Cases**

- Slaughterhouse cases (1873).
- *United States* v. *Reese* (1876).
- *United States* v. *Cruikshank* (1876).
- Civil Rights Cases (1883).

# MAP EXPLORATION

To explore an interactive version of this map, go to **http://www.prenhall.com/faraghertlc/map17.3**

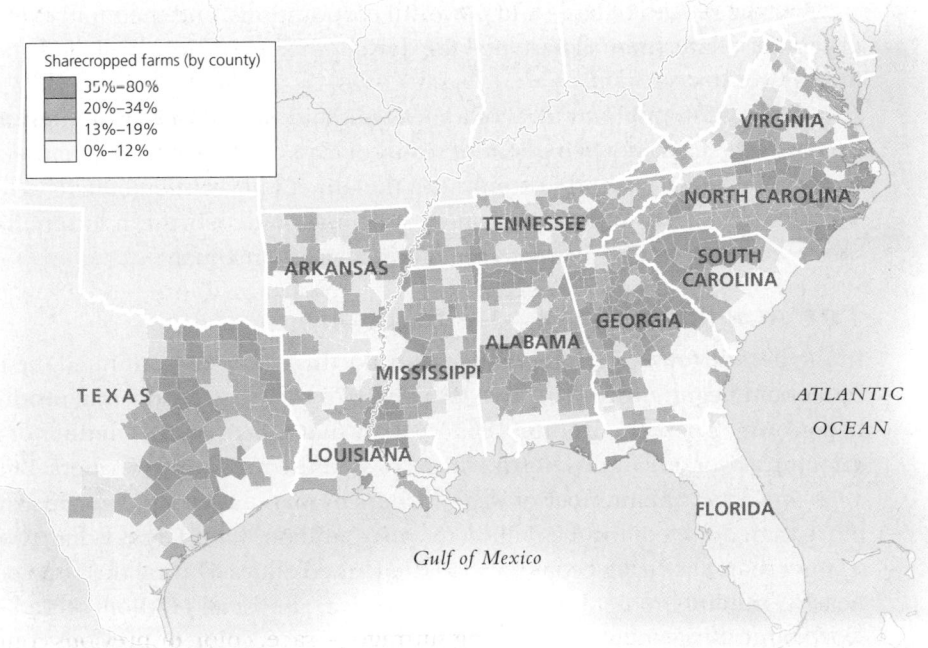

**MAP 17.3**

**Southern Sharecropping and the Cotton Belt, 1880**    The economic depression of the 1870s forced increasing numbers of southern farmers, both white and black, into sharecropping arrangements. Sharecropping was most pervasive in the cotton belt regions of South Carolina, Georgia, Alabama, Mississippi, and eastern Texas.

HOW DID this new form of labor affect the lives of former slaves?

capita wealth in the South fell steadily, equaling only one-third that of the East, Midwest, or West by the 1890s. Small farmers caught up in a vicious cycle of low cotton prices, debt, and dwindling food crops found their old ideal of independence sacrificed to the cruel logic of the cotton market.

To obtain precious credit, most southern farmers, both black and white, found themselves forced to produce cotton for market and, thus, became enmeshed in the debt-ridden crop lien system. In traditional cotton producing areas, especially the black belt, landless farmers growing cotton had replaced slaves growing cotton. In the up-country and newer areas of cultivation, cotton-dominated commercial agriculture, with landless tenants and sharecroppers as the main workforce, had replaced the more diversified subsistence economy of the antebellum era. By 1900, over roughly half of the South's 2,620,000 farms were operated by tenants, who rented land, or sharecroppers, who pledged a portion of the crop to owners in exchange for some combination of work animals, seed, and tools. Over one-third of the white farmers and nearly three-quarters of the African American farmers in the cotton states were tenants or sharecroppers. Large parts of the southern landscape would remain defined by this system well into the twentieth century: small farms operated by families who did not own their land, mired in desperate poverty and debt.

# RECONSTRUCTING THE NORTH

**WHAT PRECIPITATED** the electoral crisis of 1876?

**myhistorylab**
Review Summary

The triumph of the North brought with it fundamental changes in the economy, labor relations, and politics. The spread of the factory system, the growth of large and powerful corporations, and the rapid expansion of capitalist enterprise all hastened the development of a large unskilled and routinized workforce.

The old Republican ideal of a society bound by a harmony of interests had become overshadowed by a grimmer reality of class conflict. A violent national railroad strike in 1877 was broken only with the direct intervention of federal troops. That conflict struck many Americans as a turning point. Northern society, like the society of the South, appeared more hierarchical than equal.

## THE AGE OF CAPITAL

In the decade following Appomattox, the North's economy continued the industrial boom begun during the Civil War. By 1873, America's industrial production had grown 75 percent over the 1865 level. By that time, too, the number of nonagricultural workers in the North had surpassed the number of farmers. Between 1860 and 1880, the number of wage earners in manufacturing and construction more than doubled, from 2 million to over 4 million. Only Great Britain boasted a larger manufacturing economy than the United States. During the same period, nearly 3 million immigrants arrived in America, almost all of whom settled in the North and West.

The railroad business both symbolized and advanced the new industrial order. Shortly before the Civil War, enthusiasm mounted for a transcontinental line. Private companies took on the huge and expensive job of construction, but the federal government funded the project, providing the largest subsidy in American history. The Pacific Railway Act of 1862 granted the Union Pacific and the

**Chinese immigrants, like** these section gang workers, provided labor and skills critical to the successful completion of the first transcontinental railroad. This photo was taken in Promontory Point, Utah Territory, in 1869.

Central Pacific rights to a broad swath of land extending from Omaha, Nebraska, to Sacramento, California. An 1864 act bestowed a subsidy of $15,000 per mile of track laid over smooth plains country and varying larger amounts up to $48,000 per mile in the foothills and mountains of the Far West. The Union Pacific employed gangs of Irish American and African American workers to lay track heading west from Omaha.

Meanwhile the Central Pacific, pushing east from California, had a tougher time finding workers, and began recruiting thousands of men from China. Some 12,000 Chinese laborers (about 90 percent of the workforce) bore the brunt of the difficult conditions in the Sierra Nevada where blizzards, landslides, and steep rock faces took an awful toll. But after completion of the transcontinental line threw thousands of Chinese railroad workers onto the California labor market, these workers faced a virulent tide of anti-Chinese agitation among western politicians and labor unions. In 1882, Congress passed the Chinese Exclusion Act, suspending any further Chinese immigration for ten years.

Railroad corporations became America's first big businesses. Railroads required huge outlays of investment capital, and their growth increased the economic power of banks and investment houses centered in Wall Street. Bankers often gained seats on the boards of directors of railroad companies, and their access to capital sometimes gave them the real control of the corporations. By the early 1870s the Pennsylvania Railroad was the nation's largest single company with more than 20,000 employees. A new breed of aggressive entrepreneur sought to ease cutthroat competition by absorbing smaller companies and forming "pools" that set rates and divided the market.

Some of the nation's most prominent politicians routinely accepted railroad largesse. Republican senator William M. Stewart of Nevada, a member of the Committee on Pacific Railroads, received a gift of 50,000 acres of land from the Central Pacific for his services. The worst scandal of the Grant administration grew out of corruption involving railroad promotion. When the scandal broke in 1872, it politically ruined Vice President Schuyler Colfax and led to the censure of two congressmen.

Other industries also boomed in this period, especially those engaged in extracting minerals and processing natural resources. Railroad growth stimulated expansion in the production of coal, iron, stone, and lumber, and these also received significant government aid. For example, under the National Mineral Act of 1866, mining companies received millions of acres of free public land. Oil refining enjoyed a huge expansion in the 1860s and 1870s. As with railroads, an early period of fierce competition soon gave way to concentration.

## LIBERAL REPUBLICANS AND THE ELECTION OF 1872

With the rapid growth of large-scale, capital-intensive enterprises, Republicans increasingly identified with the interests of business rather than the rights of freedmen or the antebellum ideology of "free labor." State Republican parties now organized themselves around the spoils of federal patronage rather than grand causes such as preserving the Union or ending slavery. Republicans had no monopoly on political scandal. In 1871 New York City newspapers reported the shocking story of how Democratic Party boss William M. Tweed and his friends had systematically stolen tens of millions from the city treasury. But to many, the scandal represented only the most extreme case of the routine corruption that now plagued American political life.

**"The Tramp,"** *Harper's Weekly,* September 2, 1876. The depression that began in 1873 forced many thousands of unemployed workers to go "on the tramp" in search of jobs. Men wandered from town to town, walking or riding railroad cars, desperate for a chance to work for wages or simply for room and board. The "tramp" became a powerful symbol of the misery caused by industrial depression and, as in this drawing, an image that evoked fear and nervousness among the nation's middle class.

By the end of President Grant's first term, a large number of disaffected Republicans sought an alternative. The **Liberal Republicans**, as they called themselves, emphasized the doctrines of classical economics. They called for a return to limited government, arguing that bribery, scandal, and high taxes all flowed from excessive state interference in the economy.

Liberal Republicans were also suspicious of expanding democracy. They believed that politics ought to be the province of "the best men"—educated and well-to-do men like themselves, devoted to the "science of government." They proposed civil service reform as the best way to break the hold of party machines on patronage.

Although most Liberal Republicans had enthusiastically supported abolition, the Union cause, and equal rights for freedmen, they now opposed continued federal intervention in the South. The national government had done all it could for the former slaves; they must now take care of themselves. In the spring of 1872 a diverse collection of Liberal Republicans nominated Horace Greeley to run for president. A longtime foe of the Democratic Party, Greeley nonetheless won that party's presidential nomination as well. All Americans, Greeley urged, must put the Civil War behind them and "clasp hands across the bloody chasm."

Grant easily defeated Greeley, carrying every state in the North and winning 56 percent of the popular vote. But the 1872 election accelerated the trend toward federal abandonment of African American citizenship rights. The Liberal Republicans quickly faded as an organized political force. But their ideas helped define a growing conservative consciousness among the northern public. Their agenda included retreat from the ideal of racial justice, hostility toward trade unions, suspicion of immigrant and working-class political power, celebration of competitive individualism, and opposition to government intervention in economic affairs.

## THE DEPRESSION OF 1873

In the fall of 1873 the postwar boom came to an abrupt halt as a severe financial panic triggered a deep economic depression. The collapse resulted from commercial overexpansion, especially speculative investing in the nation's rail-

**Liberal Republicans** Disaffected Republicans that emphasized the doctrines of classical economics.

road system. By 1876 half the nation's railroads had defaulted on their bonds. Over the next two years more than 100 banks folded and 18,000 businesses shut their doors. The depression that began in 1873 lasted sixty-five months—the longest economic contraction in the nation's history until then.

The human toll was enormous. As factories began to close across the nation, the unemployment rate soared to about 15 percent. In many cities the jobless rate was much higher. The Pennsylvania Bureau of Labor Statistics noted that never before had "so many of the working classes, skilled and unskilled, been moving from place to place seeking employment that was not to be had." Farmers were also hard hit by the depression. Agricultural output continued to grow, but prices and land values fell sharply.

Mass meetings of workers in New York and other cities issued calls to government officials to create jobs through public works. But these appeals were rejected. Indeed, many business leaders and political figures denounced even meager efforts at charity. They saw the depression as a natural, if painful, part of the business cycle, one that would allow only the strongest enterprises (and workers) to survive.

The depression of the 1870s prompted workers and farmers to question the old free-labor ideology that celebrated a harmony of interests in northern society. More people voiced anger at and distrust of large corporations that exercised great economic power from outside their communities.

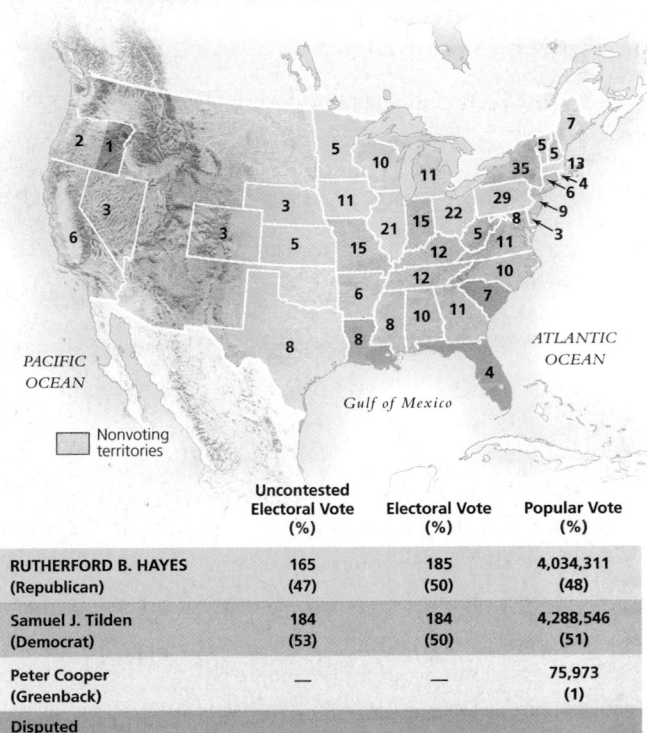

| | Uncontested Electoral Vote (%) | Electoral Vote (%) | Popular Vote (%) |
|---|---|---|---|
| **RUTHERFORD B. HAYES** (Republican) | 165 (47) | 185 (50) | 4,034,311 (48) |
| **Samuel J. Tilden** (Democrat) | 184 (53) | 184 (50) | 4,288,546 (51) |
| **Peter Cooper** (Greenback) | — | — | 75,973 (1) |
| Disputed | | | |

**MAP 17.4**

**The Election of 1876**   The presidential election of 1876 left the nation without a clear-cut winner.

WHAT LED to the electoral crisis of 1876?

## THE ELECTORAL CRISIS OF 1876

With the economy mired in depression, Democrats looked forward to capturing the White House in 1876. Democrats nominated Governor Samuel J. Tilden of New York, who brought impeccable reform credentials to his candidacy. In 1871 he had helped expose and prosecute the "Tweed Ring" in New York City. As governor he had toppled the "Canal Ring," a graft-ridden scheme involving inflated contracts for repairs on the Erie Canal. In their platform, the Democrats linked the issue of corruption to an attack on Reconstruction policies.

Republican nominee Rutherford B. Hayes, governor of Ohio, also sought the high ground. As a lawyer in Cincinnati he had defended runaway slaves. Later he had distinguished himself as a general in the Union army. Hayes promised, if elected, to support an efficient civil service system, to vigorously prosecute officials who betrayed the public trust, and to introduce a system of free universal education.

On an election day marred by widespread vote fraud and violent intimidation, Tilden received 250,000 more popular votes than Hayes. But Republicans refused to concede victory, challenging the vote totals in the electoral college. Tilden garnered 184 uncontested electoral votes, one shy of the majority required to win, while Hayes received 165 (see Map 17.4). The problem centered on twenty disputed votes from Florida, Louisiana, South Carolina, and Oregon.

The crisis was unprecedented. In January 1877 Congress moved to settle the deadlock, establishing an Electoral Commission composed of five senators, five representatives, and five Supreme Court justices; eight were Republicans and seven

## QUICK REVIEW

**The Depression of 1873**

- End of postwar boom brought depression.
- Collapse resulted from commercial overexpansion.
- Longest economic contraction in the nation's history until then.

## CHRONOLOGY

**1865** Freedmen's Bureau established

Abraham Lincoln assassinated

Andrew Johnson begins Presidential Reconstruction

Black codes begin to be enacted in southern states

Thirteenth Amendment ratified

**1866** Civil Rights Act passed

Congress approves Fourteenth Amendment

Ku Klux Klan founded

**1867** Reconstruction Acts, passed over President Johnson's veto, begin Congressional Reconstruction

Tenure of Office Act

Southern states call constitutional conventions

**1868** President Johnson impeached by the House but acquitted in Senate trial

Fourteenth Amendment ratified

Most Southern states readmitted to the Union

Ulysses S. Grant elected president

**1869** Congress approves Fifteenth Amendment

Union Pacific and Central Pacific tracks meet at Promontory Point in Utah Territory

Suffragists split into National Woman Suffrage Association and American Woman Suffrage Association

**1870** Fifteenth Amendment ratified

**1871** Ku Klux Klan Act passed

"Tweed Ring" in New York City exposed

**1872** Liberal Republicans break with Grant and Radicals, nominate Horace Greeley for president

Crédit Mobilier scandal

Grant reelected president

**1873** Financial panic and beginning of economic depression

Slaughterhouse cases

**1874** Democrats gain control of House for first time since 1856

**1875** Civil Rights Act

**1876** Disputed election between Samuel Tilden and Rutherford B. Hayes

**1877** Electoral Commission elects Hayes president

President Hayes dispatches federal troops to break Great Railroad Strike and withdraws last remaining federal troops from the South

---

were Democrats. The commission voted along strict partisan lines to award all the contested electoral votes to Hayes. Outraged by this decision, Democratic congressmen threatened a filibuster to block Hayes's inauguration. Violence and stalemate were avoided when Democrats and Republicans struck a compromise in February. In return for Hayes's ascendance to the presidency, the Republicans promised to appropriate more money for southern internal improvements, to appoint a Southerner to Hayes's cabinet, and to pursue a policy of noninterference ("home rule") in southern affairs.

Shortly after assuming office, Hayes ordered removal of the remaining federal troops in Louisiana and South Carolina. Without this military presence to sustain them, the Republican governors of those two states quickly lost power to Democrats. "Home rule" meant Republican abandonment of freed people, Radicals, carpetbaggers, and scalawags. It also effectively nullified the Fourteenth and Fifteenth Amendments and the Civil Rights Act of 1866. The **Compromise of 1877** completed repudiation of the idea, born during the Civil War and pursued during Congressional Reconstruction, of a powerful federal government protecting the rights of all American citizens.

**Compromise of 1877** The Congressional settling of the 1876 election which installed Republican Rutherford B. Hayes in the White House and gave Democrats control of all state governments in the South.

# CONCLUSION

Reconstruction succeeded in the limited political sense of reuniting a nation torn apart by the Civil War. The Radical Republican vision, emphasizing racial justice, equal civil and political rights guaranteed by the Fourteenth and Fifteenth Amendments, and a new southern economy organized around independent small farmers, never enjoyed the support of the majority of its party or the northern public. By 1877, the political force of these ideals was spent and the national retreat from them nearly complete.

The end of Reconstruction left the way open for the return of white domination in the South. The freed people's political and civil equality proved only temporary. It would take a "Second Reconstruction," the civil rights movement of the next century, to establish full black citizenship rights once and for all. Yet the newly autonomous black family, along with black-controlled churches, schools, and other social institutions, provided the foundations for the modern African American community. If the federal government was not yet fully committed to protecting equal rights in local communities, the Reconstruction era at least pointed to how that goal might be achieved. Even as the federal government retreated from the defense of equal rights for black people, it took a more aggressive stance as the protector of business interests. In the aftermath of Reconstruction, the struggle between capital and labor had clearly replaced "the southern question" as the number one political issue of the day.

## REVIEW QUESTIONS

1. How did various visions of a "reconstructed" South differ? How did these visions reflect the old political and social divisions that had led to the Civil War?

2. What key changes did emancipation make in the political and economic status of African Americans? Discuss the expansion of citizenship rights in the post–Civil War years. To what extent did women share in the gains made by African Americans?

3. What role did such institutions as the family, the church, the schools, and the political parties play in the African American transition to freedom?

4. How did white Southerners attempt to limit the freedom of former slaves? How did these efforts succeed, and how did they fail?

5. Evaluate the achievements and failures of Reconstruction governments in the southern states.

6. What were the crucial economic changes occurring in the North and South during the Reconstruction era?

## KEY TERMS

Black codes (p. 438)

Carpetbaggers (p. 448)

Civil Rights Bill (p. 438)

Congressional Reconstruction (p. 439)

Compromise of 1877 (p. 458)

Field Order 15 (p. 436)

Fifteenth Amendment (p. 441)

First Reconstruction Act (p. 439)

Freedmen's Bureau (p. 437)

Ku Klux Klan (p. 441)

Liberal Republicans (p. 456)

Radical Republicans (p. 436)

Scalawags (p. 449)

Sharecropping (p. 445)

Slaughterhouse cases (p. 452)

Tenure of Office Act (p. 439)

Union League (p. 448)

War Democrats (p. 437)

## RECOMMENDED READING

David W. Blight, *Race and Reunion: The Civil War in American Memory* (2001). An elegantly written and deeply researched inquiry into how Americans "remembered" the Civil War in the half century after Appomattox, arguing that sectional reconciliation came at the cost of racial division.

Thomas J. Brown, ed., *Reconstructions: New Perspectives on the Postbellum United States* (2006). A wide-ranging collection of essays that explores Reconstruction from a broadly national perspective, including economic, political, and cultural impacts.

Jane Dailey, *Before Jim Crow: The Politics of Race in Postemancipation Virginia* (2000). A fine study that focuses on the tension between the drive to establish white supremacy and the struggle for biracial coalitions in post–Civil War Virginia politics.

Laura F. Edwards, *Gendered Strife & Confusion: The Political Culture of Reconstruction* (1997). An ambitious analysis of how gender ideologies played a key role in shaping the party politics and social relations of the Reconstruction era south.

Michael W. Fitzgerald, *The Union League Movement in the Deep South* (1989). Uses the Union League as a lens through which to examine race relations and the close connections between politics and economic change in the post–Civil War South.

Eric Foner, *Forever Free: The Story of Emancipation and Reconstruction* (2005). An excellent brief one-volume overview that condenses Foner's more comprehensive work on Reconstruction. It also includes several striking "visual essays" by Joshua Brown, documenting the changes in visual representations of African Americans in popular media of the era.

Eric Foner, *Reconstruction: America's Unfinished Revolution, 1863–1877* (1988). The most comprehensive and thoroughly researched overview of the Reconstruction era.

Steven Hahn, *A Nation Under Our Feet: Black Political Struggles in the Rural South from Slavery to the Great Migration* (2003). This Pulitzer Prize–winning history includes excellent chapters detailing the political activism of recently freed slaves and the violent resistance they encountered throughout the rural South.

Elizabeth Regosin, *Freedom's Promise: Ex-Slave Families and Citizenship in the Age of Emancipation* (2002). A thoughtful analysis of how freedmen and freedwomen asserted familial relationships as a means to claiming citizenship rights after emancipation, based on research into federal pension applications made by dependent survivors of Civil War soldiers.

Scott Reynolds Nelson, *Iron Confederacies: Southern Railways, Klan Violence, and Reconstruction* (1999). Pathbreaking analysis of how conservative southern and northern business interests rebuilt the South's railroad system and also achieved enormous political power within individual states.

Heather Cox Richardson, *West From Appomattox: The Reconstruction of America After the Civil War* (2007). A new interpretation of the era that both emphasizes post–Civil War change in the nation's West and large cities and locates the origins of current political divisions in the Reconstruction period.

For study resources for this chapter, go to **www.myhistorylab.com** and choose *Out of Many, Teaching and Learning Classroom Edition.* You will find a wealth of study and review material for this chapter, including pretests and posttests, customized study plan, key-term review flash cards, interactive map and document activities, and documents for analysis.

# Realities of Freedom

The Freedmen's Bureau established in 1865 by Congress provided freedmen with clothing, temporary shelter, food, and series of freedmen's schools across the South. Southern response was to fall into the use of terror to deter blacks from becoming economically independent using the agencies of groups like the Ku Klux Klan. Sharecropping, tenant farming, and peonage were insidious economic arrangements that placed whites and blacks in a form of economic slavery to large land holders in the South of the post-Civil War era.

**FOLLOWING EMANCIPATION**, what economic and social opportunities existed for African Americans in the United States? How did these opportunities change the lives of freedmen after the official end to slavery?

The story of African Americans after the end of slavery is complex and varied. Some blacks attempted to seek out better places to establish their new lives while others remained in the security of the only home they had known as slaves.■

## AN ACT TO ESTABLISH A BUREAU FOR THE RELIEF OF FREEDMEN AND REFUGEES, 1865

BE IT enacted, That there is hereby established in the War Department, to continue during the present war of rebellion, and for one year thereafter, a bureau of refugees, freedmen, and abandoned lands, to which shall be committed, as hereinafter provided, the supervision and management of all abandoned lands, and the control of all subjects relating to refugees and freedmen from rebel states, or from any district of country within the territory embraced in the operations of the army, under such rules and regulations as may be prescribed by the head of the bureau and approved by the President. The said bureau shall be under the management and control of a commissioner to be appointed by the President, by and with the advice and consent of the Senate...■

◄ African-American family working together in the cotton fields.

# WHEN WE WORKED ON SHARES, WE COULDN'T MAKE NOTHING

AFTER SLAVERY we had to get in before night too. If you didn't, Ku Klux would drive you in. They would come and visit you anyway. . . . When he got you good and scared he would drive on away. They would whip you if they would catch you out in the night time. . . .

I've forgot who it is that that told us that we was free. Somebody come and told us we're free now. I done forgot who it was.

After freedom, we worked on shares a while. Then we rented. When we worked on shares, we couldn't make nothing, just overalls and something to eat. Half went to the other man and you would destroy your half if you weren't careful. A man that didn't know how to count would always lose. He might lose anyhow. They didn't give no itemized statement. No, you just had to take their word. They never give you no details. They just say you owe so much. No matter how good account you kept, you had to go by their account and now, Brother, I'm tellin' you the truth about this. It's been that way for a long time. You had to take the white man's work on note, and everything. Anything you wanted, you could git if you were a good hand. You could git anything you wanted as long as you worked. If you didn't make no money, that's all right; they would advance you more. But

Share croppers and their families were evicted from the plantation they were working after being convicted of engaging in a conspiracy to retain their homes. This picture was taken just after the evictions before the families were moved into a tent colony.

you better not leave him, you better not try to leave and get caught. They'd keep you in debt. They were sharp. Christmas come, you could take up twenty dollar, in somethin' to eat and much as you wanted in whiskey. You could buy a gallon of whiskey. . . . Anything that kept you a slave because he was always right and you were always wrong it there was difference. If there was an argument, he would get mad and there would be a shooting take place. . . . ■

# SHARE CROPPER CONTRACT, 1882

TO EVERY one applying to rent land upon shares, the following conditions must be read, and agreed to.

To every 30 or 35 acres, I agree to furnish the team, plow, and farming implements, except cotton planters, and I do not agree to furnish a cart to every cropper. The croppers are to have half of the cotton, corn and fodder (and peas and pumpkins and potatoes if any are planted. . .

Croppers are to have no part or interest in the cotton seed raised from the crop planted and worked by them. No vine crops of any description, that is, no watermelons, muskmelons,...squashes or anything of that kind, except peas and pumpkins, and potatoes, are to be planted in the cotton or corn. All must work under my direction. All plantation work to be done by the croppers. . . .

For every mule or horse furnished by me there must be 1000 good sized rails...hauled, and the fence repaired as far as they will go, the fence to be torn down and put up from the bottom if I so direct. All croppers to haul rails and work on fence whenever I may order. Rails to be split when I may say. . . .

Each cropper must keep in good repair all bridges in his crop or over ditches that he has to clean out and when a bridge needs repairing that is outside of all their crops, then any one that I call on must repair it. . . .

No cropper to work off the plantation when there is any work to be done on the land he has rented, or when his work is needed by me or other croppers. Trees to be cut down on Orchard, House field & Evanson fences, leaving such as I may designate. . . . ■

Interpreting the Past

*The two locomotives then moved up until they touched each other, . . .and at one p.m., under an almost cloudless sky, and in the presence of about one thousand one hundred people, the completion of the greatest railroad on earth was announced.*

—*Andrew J. Russel, from* Frank Leslie's Illustrated Railroad, *June 5, 1869*

**This engraving, showing passengers shooting buffalo from a train crossing the plains,** suggests the often casual approach Americans took toward the Western Environment. The destruction of the buffalo herds, for both profit and "sport," also destroyed the basis of the Plains Indians' economy and culture.

# 18

## CONQUEST AND SURVIVAL
### THE TRANS–MISSISSIPPI WEST, 1860–1900

**WHAT WAS** the impact of U.S. western expansion on Indian Society?

**HOW DID** the mining industry develop in the United States?

**WHAT WAS** life like for a cowboy in the late nineteenth century?

**WHO TOOK** advantage of the Homestead Act?

**HOW DID** agribusiness differ from more traditional forms of farming?

**WHAT PLACE** did the West hold in the national imagination?

**WHAT KIND** of Indian society did reformers envision?

# AMERICAN COMMUNITIES
## The Oklahoma Land Rush

DECADES AFTER THE EVENT, COWBOY EVAN G. BARNARD VIVIDLY recalled the preparations made by settlers when Oklahoma territorial officials announced the biggest "land rush" in American history. "Thousands of people gathered along the border. . . . As the day for the race drew near, the settlers practiced running their horses and driving carts." Finally, the morning of April 22, 1889, arrived. Like many others, Barnard displayed his guns prominently on his hips, determined to discourage competitors from claiming the 160 acres of prime land that he intended to grab for himself.

Evan Barnard's story was one strand in the larger tale of the destruction and creation of communities in the trans–Mississippi West. In the 1830s, the federal government designated what was to become the state of Oklahoma as Indian Territory, reserved for the Five Civilized Tribes (Cherokees, Chickasaws, Choctaws, Creeks, and Seminoles) who had been forcibly removed from their eastern lands. All five tribes had reestablished themselves as sovereign republics in Indian Territory. The Cherokees and Choctaws became prosperous cotton growers. The Creeks managed large herds of hogs and cattle, and the Chickasaws grazed not only cattle but also sheep and goats on their open fields. The Five Tribes also ran sawmills, gristmills, and cotton gins. Indian merchants were soon dealing with other tribespeople as well as licensed white traders and even contracting with the federal government.

The Civil War, however, took a heavy toll on their success. Some tribes, slaveholders themselves, sided with the Confederacy; others with the Union. When the war ended, more than 10,000 people—nearly one-fifth of the population of Indian Territory—had died. To make matters worse, new treaties required the Five Civilized Tribes to cede the entire western half of the territory, including the former northern Indian territory of Nebraska and Kansas, for the resettlement of tribes from other regions.

Western Oklahoma thereby became home to thousands of newly displaced peoples, including the Pawnees, Peorias, Ottawas, Wyandots, and Miamis. Many small tribes readily took to farming and rebuilt their communities. But the nomadic, buffalo-hunting Kiowas, Cheyennes, Comanches, and Arapahoes did not settle so peacefully. They continued to traverse the plains until the U.S. Army finally forced them onto reservations.

Eventually, more than 80,000 tribespeople were living on twenty-one separate reservations in western Oklahoma, all governed by agents appointed by the federal government.

The opening of the unassigned far western district of Oklahoma (No Man's Land) however, signaled the impending end of Indian sovereignty. Many non-Indians saw this almost 2-million-acre strip as a Promised Land, perfect for dividing into thousands of small farms. Meanwhile, the railroads, seeing the potential for lucrative commerce, put constant pressure on the federal government to open No Man's Land for settlement. In 1889, the U.S. Congress finally gave in.

Cowboy Barnard was just one of thousands to pour into No Man's Land on April 22, 1889. In a little over two months, after 6,000 homestead claims had been filed, the first sod houses appeared, sheltering growing communities of non-Indian farmers, ranchers, and other entrepreneurs. Some Indian leaders petitioned the federal government for the right to resettle on new land distant from white settlers, but nothing came from their efforts.

Dramatic as it was, the land rush of 1889 was only one in a series of events that soon dispossessed Oklahoma's Indians of their remaining lands. First, the federal government broke up the estates held collectively by various tribes in western Oklahoma, assigning to individuals the standard 160-acre allotment and allowing non-Indian homesteaders to claim the rest. Then, in 1898, Congress passed the Curtis Act, which abolished tribal jurisdiction over all Indian Territory.

By this time, in 1907, tribespeople were outnumbered in Oklahoma by ten to one. By this time also, nearly one-quarter of the entire population of the United States lived west of the Mississippi River. Hundreds of new communities, supported primarily by cattle ranching, agriculture, mining, or other industries, had not only grown with the emerging national economy but also helped to shape it in the process. The newcomers had displaced communities that had formed centuries earlier. They also drastically transformed the physical landscape. Through their activities and the support of Easterners, the United States realized an ambition that John L. O'Sullivan had described in 1845 as the nation's "manifest destiny to overspread the continent" and remake it in a new image.

Indian Territory (Oklahoma)

# INDIAN PEOPLES UNDER SIEGE

The Indians living west of the Mississippi River keenly felt the pressure of the gradual incorporation of the West into the American nation. California became a state in 1850, Oregon in 1859. Congress consolidated the national domain in the next decades by granting territorial status to Utah, New Mexico, Washington, Dakota, Colorado, Nevada, Arizona, Idaho, Montana, and Wyoming. The purchase of Alaska in 1867 added an area twice the size of Texas.

A series of events brought large numbers of white settlers into these new states and territories: the discovery of gold in California in 1848, the opening of western lands to homesteaders in 1862, and the completion of the transcontinental railroad in 1869. With competition for the land and its resources escalating into violent skirmishes and small wars, federal officials became determined to end tribal rule and bring Indians into the American mainstream.

## INDIAN TERRITORY

Before the European colonists reached the New World, various Indian tribes had occupied western lands for more than 20,000 years. Invasion by the English, Spanish, and other Europeans brought disease, religious conversion, and new patterns of commerce. But geographic isolation still gave many tribes a margin of survival unknown in the East. At the close of the Civil War, approximately 360,000 Indian peoples still lived in the trans–Mississippi West, the majority of them in the Great Plains (see Map 18.1).

The surviving tribes adapted to changing conditions. The Plains Indians learned to ride the horses and shoot the guns introduced by Spanish and British traders. The Pawnees migrated farther westward to evade encroaching non-Indian settlers, while the Sioux and the Comanches fought neighboring tribes to gain control of large stretches of the Great Plains. The southwestern Hopis and Zunis,

**WHAT WAS** the impact of U.S. western expansion on Indian Society?

**myhistorylab**
Review Summary

**17–6**
*Congressional Report on Indian Affairs* (1887)

## IMAGE KEY
for pages 464–465

a. A feather fan carried by Yuchi dancers.
b. Passengers and the train crew shooting buffalo on the line of the Kansas-Pacific Railroad in this colored line engraving of 1871.
c. Confederate cavalry spurs from the American Civil War.
d. An old fashioned steam locomotive engine.
e. Wooly Head's wife and child.
f. A Chinese mine worker steadies a water cannon in a shallow riverbed in Idaho with a fellow laborer standing nearby.
g. Buffalo Bill Cody from an 1899 poster for his "Wild West Show."
h. Nebraska homesteaders in 1886.
i. Thirty-three horse team harvester, cutting, threshing, and sacking wheat, c. 1902.

**NO MAN'S LAND**
*Added to Oklahoma Territory by Organic Act, May 2, 1890*

1  Opened by run, Sept 22, 1891
2  Tonkawa lands by allotment, 1891
3  Pawnee lands by allotment, 1892
4  Opened by run, May 23, 1895
5  Ponces and Oto-Missouri lands by allotment, 1904
6  Kaw lands by allotment, 1906
7  Osage lands by allotment, 1906
8  Unassigned lands opened by run, Apr 22, 1889
9  Opened by run, Sept 16, 1893
10  Opened by lottery, July 9–Aug 6, 1901
11  Opened by sealed bids, Dec, 1906

*Attached to Oklahoma by decision of U.S. Supreme Court, Mar 16, 1896*

**MAP 18.1**
**Oklahoma Territory**    Land openings to settlers came at different times, making new land available through various means.

From *Historical Atlas of Oklahoma*, 3rd edition, by John W. Morris, Charles R. Goins, and Edwin C. McReynolds. Copyright © 1965, 1976, 1986 by the University of Oklahoma Press, Norman. Reprinted by permission of the publisher. All rights reserved.

WHAT WAS the impact of the land rush on Indian settlements?

conquered earlier by the Spanish, continued to trade with the Mexicans who lived near them. Some tribes took dramatic steps toward accommodation with white ways. Even before they were uprooted and moved across the Mississippi River, the Cherokees had learned English, converted to Christianity, established a constitutional republic, and become a nation of farmers.

Legally, the federal government had long regarded Indian tribes as autonomous nations residing within American boundaries and had negotiated numerous treaties with them over land rights and commerce. But pressured by land-hungry whites, several states had violated these federal treaties so often that the U.S. Congress passed the Indian Removal Act of 1830 (see Chapter 10), which provided funds to relocate all eastern tribes by force if necessary. The Cherokees challenged this legislation, and the Supreme Court ruled in their favor in *Cherokee Nation* v. *Georgia* (1831). Ignoring the Court's decision, President Andrew Jackson, known as a hardened Indian fighter, forced many tribes to cede their land and remove to Indian Territory. But soon, the onslaught of white settlers, railroad entrepreneurs, and prospectors rushing for gold pressured tribes to cede millions of their acres to the United States. As demand for resources and land accelerated, the entire plan for a permanent Indian Territory fell apart.

## THE RESERVATION POLICY AND THE SLAUGHTER OF THE BUFFALO

As early as the 1840s, highly placed officials had outlined a plan to subdue the intensifying rivalry over natural resources and land. Under the terms of their proposal, individual tribes would agree to live within clearly defined zones—reservations. In exchange, the Bureau of Indian Affairs would provide guidance, while U.S. military forces ensured protection. By the end of the 1850s, eight western reservations had been established where Indian peoples were induced to speak English, take up farming, and convert to Christianity (see Map 18.2).

Those tribes that moved to reservations often found federal policies inadequate to their needs. The Medicine Lodge Treaty of 1867 assigned reservations in existing Indian Territory to Comanches, Plains (Kiowa) Apaches, Kiowas, Cheyennes, and Arapahoes, bringing these tribes together with Sioux, Shoshones, and Bannocks. All told, more than 100,000 people found themselves competing intensely for survival. Corrupt officials of the Bureau of Indian Affairs routinely diverted funds for their own use and reduced food supplies, a policy promoting malnutrition, demoralization, and desperation. Meanwhile, white prospectors and miners continued to flood the Dakota Territory.

The mass slaughter of the buffalo brought this crisis to a peak. In earlier eras, vast herds of buffalo had literally darkened the western horizon. As gunpowder and the railroad moved west, the number of buffalo fell rapidly. Non-Indian traders avidly sought fur for coats, hide for leather, bones for fertilizer, and heads for trophies. New rifles, like the .50 caliber Sharps, could kill at 600 feet; one sharpshooter bragged of killing 3,000 buffalo. Army commanders encouraged the slaughter, accurately predicting that starvation would break tribal resistance to the reservation system. With their food sources practically destroyed, diseases such as smallpox and cholera (brought by fur traders) sweeping through their villages, and their way of life undermined, many Great Plains tribes, including many Sioux, concluded that they could only fight or die.

## THE INDIAN WARS

In 1864, large-scale war erupted. Having decided to terminate all treaties with tribes in eastern Colorado, territorial governor John Evans encouraged a group

**QUICK REVIEW**

**White Migration and the Plains Indians**

◆ Desire by whites for land led to violations of treaties.

◆ Buffalo were eliminated from tribal hunting grounds.

◆ Many Indian peoples decided they could only fight or die.

of white civilians, the Colorado Volunteers, to stage raids through Cheyenne camp-grounds. Seeking protection, Chief Black Kettle brought a band of 800 Cheyennes to a U.S. fort and received orders to set up camp at Sand Creek. Feeling secure in this arrangement, Black Kettle sent out most of his young warriors to hunt. Several weeks later, on November 29, 1864, the Colorado Volunteers and soldiers attacked. While Black Kettle held up a U.S. flag and a white truce banner, a disorderly group of 700 men, many of them drunk, slaughtered 105 Cheyenne women and children and 28 men. They mutilated the corpses and took scalps back to Denver to exhibit as trophies. Months after the **Sand Creek Massacre**, bands of Cheyennes, Sioux, and Arapahoes were still retaliating, burning civilian outposts and sometimes killing whole families.

The Sioux played the most dramatic roles in the Indian Wars. In 1851, believing the U.S. government would recognize their own rights of conquest over other Indian tribes, the Sioux relinquished large tracts of land as a demonstration of good faith. But within a decade, a mass invasion of miners and the construction of military forts along the Bozeman Trail in Wyoming, the Sioux's principal buffalo range, threw the tribe's future into doubt. During the **Great Sioux War** of 1865–67, the Oglala Sioux warrior Red Cloud fought the U.S. Army to a stalemate and forced the government to abandon its forts, which the Sioux then burned to the ground. The Treaty of Fort Laramie, signed in 1868, restored only a temporary peace to the region.

The **Treaty of Fort Laramie** granted the Sioux the right to occupy the Black Hills, or Paha Sapa, their sacred land, "as long as the grass shall grow," but the discovery of gold soon undermined this guarantee. White prospectors hurriedly invaded the territory. Directed to quash rumors of fabulous deposits of the precious metal, Lieutenant Colonel George Armstrong Custer organized a surveying expedition to the Black Hills during the summer of 1874, but, contrary to plan, the Civil War hero described rich veins of ore that could be cheaply extracted. The U.S. Congress then pushed to purchase the territory for Americans. To protect their land, thousands of Sioux, Cheyenne, and Arapaho warriors moved into war camps during the summer of 1876 and prepared for battle (see Map 18.2).

After several months of skirmishes between the U.S. Army and Indian warriors, Lieutenant Colonel Custer decided to rush ahead to a site in Montana that was known to white soldiers as Little Bighorn and to Lakotas as Greasy Grass. This foolhardy move offered the allied Cheyenne and Sioux warriors a perfect opportunity to cut off Custer's logistical and military support. On June 25, 1876, Custer and his troops were wiped out by one of the largest Indian contingents ever assembled, an estimated 2,000 to 4,000 warriors.

"Custer's Last Stand" gave Indian-haters the emotional ammunition to whip up public excitement. The U.S. Army tracked down the disbanded Indian contingents one by one and forced them to surrender. In February 1877, Sioux leadership in the Indian Wars ended.

Among the last to hold out against the reservation system were the Apaches in the Southwest. Most Apache bands had abided by the Medicine Lodge Treaty of 1867, but in 1874, some of the Apache bands, unable to tolerate the harsh conditions on the reservation, returned to their old ways of seizing territory and stealing cattle.

Pursued by the U.S. Army, the Apaches earned a reputation as intrepid warriors. Brilliant strategists like Geronimo and skilled horse-riding braves became legendary for lightning-swift raids against the white outposts in the rugged Arizona terrain. In 1874–75, the Kiowas and the Comanches, both powerful tribes, joined the Apaches in one of the bloodiest conflicts of the era, the Red

**myhistorylab**

**Exploring America:** *Dakota Sioux Conflict*

**Sand Creek Massacre**  The near annihilation in 1864 of Black Kettle's Cheyenne band by Colorado troops under Colonel John Chivington's orders to "kill and scalp all, big and little."

**Great Sioux War**  From 1865 to 1867 the Oglala Sioux warrior Red Cloud waged war against the U.S. Army, forcing the U.S. to abandon its forts built on land relinquished to the government by the Sioux.

**Treaty of Fort Laramie**  The treaty acknowledging U.S. defeat in the Great Sioux War in 1868 and supposedly guaranteeing the Sioux perpetual land and hunting rights in South Dakota, Wyoming, and Montana.

## MAP EXPLORATION

To explore an interactive version of this map, go to **http://www.prenhall.com/faragherlc/map18.2**

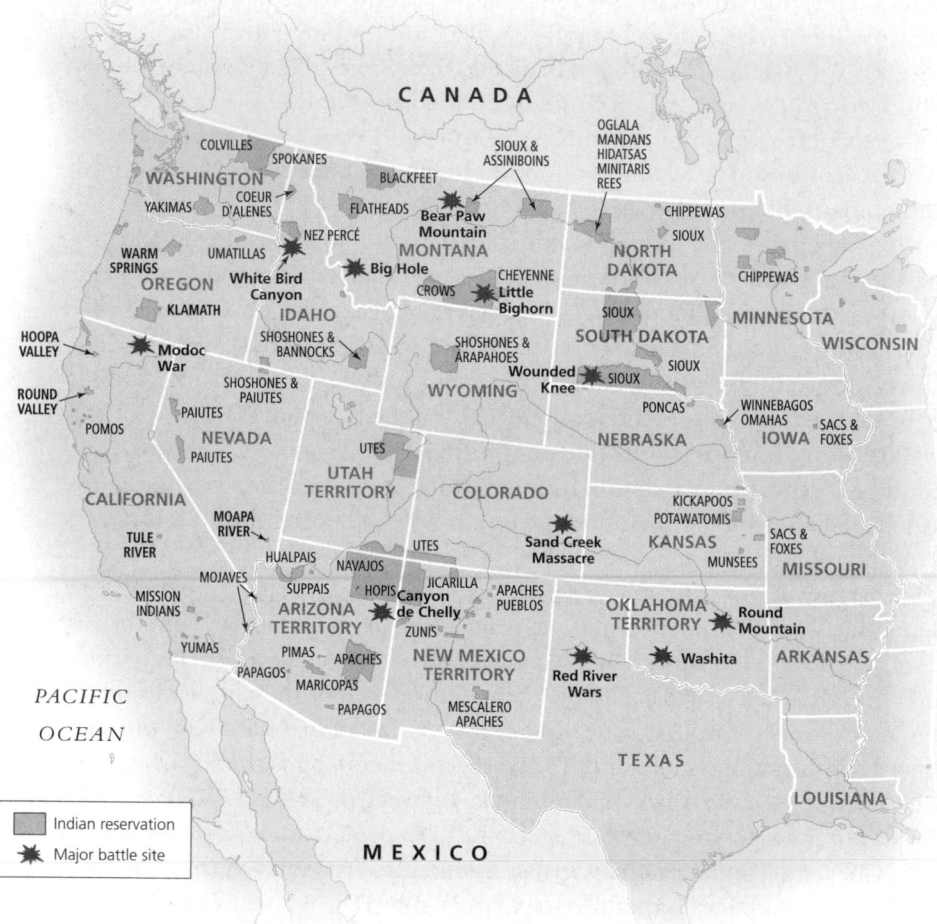

**MAP 18.2**

**Major Indian Battles and Indian Reservations, 1860–1900**  As commercial routes and white populations passed through and occupied Indian lands, warfare inevitably erupted. The displacement of Indians to reservations opened access by farmers, ranchers, and investors to natural resources and to markets.

WHY WERE the Indians forcibly removed to reservations?

River War. The U.S. Army ultimately prevailed, although less by military might than by denying Indians access to food. Small-scale warfare sputtered on until September 1886, when Geronimo, his band reduced to only thirty people, finally surrendered, thereby ending the Indian Wars.

### THE NEZ PERCÉ

For generations, the Nez Percé had regarded themselves as good friends to white traders and settlers. Living in the plateau where Idaho, Washington, and Oregon now meet, they had saved the Lewis and Clark expedition from starvation in 1803.

**The Oglala Sioux** spiritual leader, Chief Red Cloud, in an 1868 photograph. Here he is seen with (l. to r.) Red Dog, Little Wound, interpreter John Bridgeman (standing), (Red Cloud), American Horse, and Red Shirt. He ventured to Washington with this delegation to discuss with President Ulysses S. Grant the various provisions of the peace treaty, just signed, to end the violent conflict over the Bozeman Trail.

But the discovery of gold on Nez Percé territory in 1860 changed their relations with whites for the worse. Pressed by prospectors and mining companies, government officials demanded, in the treaty of 1863, that the Nez Percé cede 6 million acres, nine-tenths of their land, at less than ten cents per acre. Some of the Nez Percé leaders agreed to the terms of the treaty, which had been fraudulently signed on behalf of the entire tribe, but others refused. At first, federal officials listened to Nez Percé complaints against the treaty and decided to allow them to remain on their land. But responding to pressure from settlers and politicians, they almost immediately reversed their decision, ordering the Nez Percé, including Chief Joseph and his followers, to sell their land and to move onto a reservation.

Intending to comply, Chief Joseph's band set out from the Wallowa Valley with their livestock and all the possessions they could carry. Along the way, some young members of another Indian band traveling with them rode away from camp to avenge the death of one of their own by killing several white settlers. Hoping to explain the situation, a Nez Percé truce team approached U.S. troops. The troops opened fire, and the Indian riders fired back, killing one-third of the soldiers. Brilliantly outmaneuvering vengeful U.S. troops sent to intercept them, the 750 Nez Percé retreated for some 1,400 miles into Montana and Wyoming through mountains and prairies and across the Bitterroot Range. U.S. troops finally trapped the Nez Percé in the Bear Paw Mountains of northern Montana, just thirty miles from the Canadian border. Suffering from hunger and cold, they surrendered.

Promised they would be returned to Oregon, the Nez Percé were sent instead to disease-ridden bottomland near Fort Leavenworth in Kansas, and then to Oklahoma. Arguing for the right of his people to return to their Oregon reservation, Joseph spoke eloquently, through an interpreter, to Congress in 1879: "Treat all men alike. Give them all the same law. Give them all an even chance to live and grow. All men were made by the same Great Spirit Chief." The last remnant of

Joseph's band were deported under guard to a non–Nez Percé reservation in Washington, where Chief Joseph died in 1904 "of a broken heart," and where his descendants continue to live in exile to this day.

# THE INTERNAL EMPIRE

**HOW DID** the mining industry develop in the United States?

myhistorylab

**Review Summary**

Determined to make their fortunes, be it from copper in Arizona, wheat in Montana, or oranges in California, numerous adventurers traveled west. As a group, they carried out the largest migration and greatest commercial expansion in American history.

But the settlers themselves also became the subjects of a huge "internal empire" whose financial, political, and industrial centers of power remained in the East. Only a small number of settlers actually struck it rich. Meanwhile, older populations—Indian peoples, Hispanic peoples, and more recently settled communities like the Mormons—struggled to create places for themselves in this new expansionist order.

## MINING TOWNS

The discovery of gold in California in 1848 attracted fortune seekers from as far away as Chile and China; just ten years later, approximately 35,000 Chinese men were working in western mines. Meanwhile, prospecting parties overran the territories, setting a pattern for intermittent rushes for gold, silver, and copper that extended from the Colorado mountains to the Arizona deserts, from California to Oregon and Washington, and from Alaska to the Black Hills of South Dakota. Mining camps and boomtowns soon dotted what had once been thinly

**Kiowa Preparing for** a War Expedition, ca. 1887. This sketch on paper was made by an Indian artist, Silverhorn, who had himself taken part in the final revolt of the Kiowas in 1874. He later became a medicine man and then served as a private in the U.S. Cavalry at Fort Sill, Oklahoma Territory.

Silverhorn (Native American), "Kiowa Preparing for a War Expedition." From "Sketchbook," 1887. Graphite, ink and crayon on paper. Collection of the McNay Art Museum, Gift of Mrs. Terrell Bartlett.

settled regions and speeded the urban development of the West. Mining soon brought the West into a vast global market for capital, commodities, and labor (see Map 18.3).

 # MAP EXPLORATION

To explore an interactive version of this map, go to **http://www.prenhall.com/faraghertlc/map18.3**

**MAP 18.3**

**Railroad Routes, Cattle Trails, Gold and Silver Rushes, 1860–1900**   By the end of the nineteenth century, the vast region of the West was crosscut by hundreds of lines of transportation and communication. The trade in precious metals and in cattle helped build a population almost constantly on the move, following the rushes for gold or the herds of cattle.

*Encyclopedia of American Social History.*

HOW DID the growth of railroads and mining impact the environment and the lives of native peoples?

**Caminetti Act** 1893 act giving the state the power to regulate the mines.

---

### QUICK REVIEW

**Technology and Mining**

- Mining began as an individual enterprise.
- Deeper mining required expensive equipment.
- As mining became more complex and costly, it came under corporate control.

---

The mining industry quickly grew from its treasure-hunt origins into a grand corporate enterprise. The most successful mine owners bought out the smaller claims and built an entire industry around their stakes. They purchased the latest in extractive technology. They gained access to timber to fortify their underground structures and water to feed the hydraulic pumps that washed down mountains. They built smelters to refine the crude ore into ingots and often financed railroads to transport the product to distant markets.

The mining corporations laid the basis for a new economy as well as an interim government and established many of the region's first white settlements. Before the advent of railroads, ore had to be brought out of, and supplies brought into, mining areas by boats, wagons, and mules traveling hundreds of miles over rough territory. The railroad made transportation of supplies and products easier and faster. The shipping trade meanwhile grew into an important industry of its own, employing thousands of merchants, peddlers, and sailors.

The many boomtowns, known as "Helldorados," flourished, if only temporarily, as ethnically diverse communities. Men outnumbered women by as much as ten to one, and very few lived with families or stayed very long. The Chinese men, the sojourners who hoped to find riches in the "Gold Mountain" of America before returning home, clustered together and created their own institutions such as social clubs, temples, and fraternal societies known as tongs. The town center was usually the saloon.

The western labor movement began in these camps, partly as a response to dangerous working conditions. Miners began to organize in the 1860s, demanding good pay for dangerous and life-shortening work. By the end of the century, they had established the strongest unions in the West.

The unions fought hard, but they did so exclusively for the benefit of white workers. The native-born and the Irish and Cornish immigrants (from Cornwall, England) far outnumbered other groups before the turn of the century, when Italians, Slavs, and Greeks began to replace them. Labor unions eventually admitted these new immigrants but refused Chinese, Mexican, Indian, and African American workers.

When prices and ore production fell sharply, not even unions could stop the owners from shutting down the mines and leaving ghost towns in their wake. Often they also left behind an environmental disaster. Hydraulic mining, which used water cannons to blast hillsides and expose gold deposits, drove tons of rock and earth into the rivers and canyons. By the late 1860s, California's rivers were clogged, producing floods that wiped out towns and farms. In 1893, Congress finally passed the **Caminetti Act**, giving the state the power to regulate the mines. Underground mining continued unregulated, using up whole forests for timbers and filling the air with dangerous, sulfurous smoke.

**William Henry Jackson** (1843–1942) was the first person to photograph the Yellowstone region in Wyoming Territory. Documenting the Grand Tetons, including the magnificent waterfalls and geysers, his images caught the public's attention and likewise helped to convince Congress to create the Yellowstone National Park in 1872. Jackson then joined up with the U.S. Geological Survey to photograph various sites in the Rocky Mountains. Here he captures "John, the Cook" baking slapjacks in a mining camp in 1874.

## MORMON SETTLEMENTS

Led by their new prophet, Brigham Young, the Mormons migrated in 1846–47 from the Midwest to the Great Salt Lake Basin to form an independent theocratic state called Deseret and to affirm the sanctity of plural marriage, or polygamy. By 1870, more than 87,000 Mormons lived in Utah Territory, creating relatively sizable communities complemented by satellite villages joined to communal farmlands and a common pasture. Eventually, nearly 500 Mormon communities spread from Oregon to Idaho to northern Mexico (see Map 18.4).

As territorial rule tightened, the Mormons saw their unique way of life once again threatened. The Supreme Court finally ruled against polygamy in the 1879 case of *United States* v. *Reynolds,* which granted the freedom of belief but not the freedom of practice. In 1882, Congress passed the **Edmunds Act**, which effectively disenfranchised those who believed in or practiced polygamy and threatened them with fines and imprisonment. Equally devastating was the **Edmunds-Tucker Act**, passed five years later, which destroyed the temporal power of the Mormon Church by confiscating all assets over $50,000 and establishing a federal commission to oversee all elections in the territory. By the early 1890s, Mormon leaders officially renounced the practice of plural marriage.

The "celestial" law of plural marriage had been central to the Mormons' messianic mission. Forced to give up the right to the practice, they gave up many other aspects of their distinctive communal life, including the common ownership of land. By the time Utah became a state in 1896, Mormon communities resembled in some ways the society that the original settlers had sought to escape. Nevertheless, they combined their religious cohesion with leadership in the expanding regional economy to become a major political force in the West.

## MEXICAN BORDERLAND COMMUNITIES

The Treaty of Guadalupe Hidalgo, which ended the Mexican-American War in 1848, allowed the Hispanic people north of the Rio Grande to choose between immigrating to Mexico or staying in what was now the United States. But the new Mexican-American border, one of the longest unguarded boundaries in the world, did not sever communities that had been connected for centuries. What gradually emerged was an economically and socially interdependent zone, the Anglo-Hispanic borderlands linking the United States and Mexico.

Although under the treaty all Hispanics were formally guaranteed citizenship and the "free enjoyment of their liberty and property," local Anglos (as the Mexicans called white Americans) often violated these provisions and, through fraud or coercion, took control of the land. The Sante Fe Ring, a group of lawyers, politicians, and land speculators, stole millions of acres from the public domain and grabbed over 80 percent of the Mexicano landholdings in New Mexico alone.

**MAP 18.4**

**Mormon Cultural Diffusion, ca. 1883**    Mormon settlements permeated many sparsely populated sections of Idaho, Nevada, Arizona, Wyoming, Colorado, and New Mexico. Built with church backing and the strong commitment of community members, they survived and even prospered in adverse climates.

*Mormon Cultural Diffusion, ca. 1883,* Donald W. Meinig, "The Geography of the American West, 1847–1964" from *The Annals of the Association of American Geographers* 55, no. 2, June 1965.

WHY WERE many western parks and national Forests established before eastern ones?

**Edmunds Act**   1882 act that effectively disenfranchised those who believed in or practiced polygamy and threatened them with fines and imprisonment.

**Edmunds-Tucker Act**   1887 act which destroyed the temporal power of the Mormon Church by confiscating all assets over $50,000 and establishing a federal commission to oversee all elections in the Utah territory.

**Hispanic-American Alliance**
Organization formed to protect and fight for the rights of Spanish Americans.

For a time, Arizona and New Mexico seemed to hold out hope for a mutually beneficial interaction between Mexicanos and Anglos. A prosperous class of Hispanic landowners, with long-standing ties to Anglos through marriage, had established itself in cities like Albuquerque and Tucson, old Spanish towns that had been founded in the seventeenth and eighteenth centuries. These Mexican elites, well integrated into the emerging national economy, continued to wield political power as ranchers, landlords, and real estate developers until the end of the century. They secured passage of bills for education in their regions and often served as superintendents of local schools. Several prominent merchants became territorial delegates to Congress.

But the majority of Mexicans who had lived in the mountains and deserts of the Southwest for well over two centuries were less prepared for these changes. With the Anglos came land closures as well as commercial expansion, prompted by railroad, mining, and timber industries. Many poor families found themselves crowded onto plots too small for subsistence farming. Many turned to seasonal labor on the new Anglo-owned commercial farms, where they became the first of many generations of poorly paid migratory workers. Other Mexicanos adapted by taking jobs on the railroad or in the mines. Meanwhile, their wives and daughters moved to the new towns and cities in such numbers that by the end of the century, Mexicanos had become a predominantly urban population, dependent on wages for survival.

Women were quickly drawn into the expanding network of market and wage relations. They tried to make ends meet by selling produce from their backyard gardens; more often they worked as seamstresses or laundresses. Formerly at the center of a communal society, Mexicanas found themselves with fewer options in the cash economy. What wages they could now earn fell below even the low sums paid to their husbands, and women lost status within both the family and community.

Occasionally, Mexicanos organized to reverse these trends or at least to limit the damage done to their communities. In the 1880s, Las Gorras Blancas, a band of agrarian rebels in New Mexico, destroyed railroad ties and farm machinery and posted demands for justice on fences of the new Anglo farms and ranches. In 1890, Las Gorras turned from social banditry to political organization, forming *El Partido del Pueblo Unido* (The People's Party). Organized along similar lines, *El Alianzo Hispano-Americano* (The **Hispanic-American Alliance**) was formed "to protect and fight for the rights of Spanish Americans" through political

**Mexican Americans in** San Antonio continued to conduct their traditional market bazaar well after the incorporation of this region into the United States. Forced off the land and excluded from the better-paying jobs in the emerging regional economy, many Mexicanos, and especially women, sought to sell the products of their own handiwork for cash or for bartered food and clothing.

Thomas Allen, "Market Plaza," 1878–1879. Oil on canvas, 26 × 39 1/2. Witte Museum, San Antonio, Texas.

action. *Mutualistes* (mutual aid societies) provided sickness and death benefits to Mexican families.

Despite many pressures, Mexicanos preserved much of their cultural heritage. Many persisted in older ways simply because they had few choices. In addition, the influx of new immigrants from Mexico helped to reinforce traditional cultural norms. Beginning in the late 1870s, the modernizing policies of Porfirio Diaz, the president of Mexico from 1876 to 1911, brought deteriorating living conditions to the masses of poor people and prompted a migration northward that accelerated through the first decades of the twentieth century. These newcomers revitalized old customs and rituals associated with family and religion. Spanish language and Spanish place names continued to distinguish the Southwest.

# THE OPEN RANGE

The slaughter of the buffalo made way for the cattle industry, one of the most profitable businesses in the West. Texas longhorns, introduced by the Spanish, numbered over 5 million at the close of the Civil War and represented a potentially plentiful supply of beef for eastern consumers. In the spring of 1866, entrepreneurs such as Joseph G. McCoy began to build a spectacular cattle market in the eastern part of Kansas, where the Kansas Pacific Railroad provided crucial transportation links to slaughtering and packing houses and commercial distributors in Kansas City, St. Louis, and Chicago.

## THE LONG DRIVES

The great cattle drives depended on the cowboy, a seasonal or migrant worker. After the Civil War, cowboys rounded up herds of Texas cattle and drove them as much as 1,500 miles north to grazing ranches or to the stockyards where they were readied for shipping by rail to eastern markets. In return for his labor, the cowboy received at the best of times about $30 per month. Wages were usually paid in one lump sum at the end of a drive, a policy that encouraged cowboys to spend their money quickly and recklessly in the booming cattle towns. In the 1880s, when wages began to fall along with the price of beef, cowboys fought back by stealing cattle or by forming unions. Aided by the legendary camaraderie fostered in the otherwise desolate conditions of the long drive, cowboys, along with miners, were among the first western workers to organize against employers.

Like other parts of the West, the cattle range was ethnically diverse. Between one-fifth and one-third of all workers were Indian, Mexican, or African American. Indian cowboys worked mainly on the northern plains and in Indian Territory; the *vaqueros,* who had previously worked on the Mexican cattle *haciendas,* or huge estates, predominated in South Texas and California. African American cowboys worked primarily in Texas, where the range cattle industry was founded (see Seeing History).

Like the vaqueros, African American cowboys were highly skilled managers of cattle. Unlike Mexicans, they earned wages comparable to those paid to Anglos and, especially during the early years, worked in integrated drover parties. By the 1880s, as the center of the cattle industry shifted to the more settled regions around the northern ranches, African Americans were forced out, and they turned to other kinds of work.

**WHAT WAS** life like for a cowboy in the late nineteenth century?

**myhistorylab**
Review Summary

**17–3**
Horace Greeley, *An Overland Journey* (1860)

**17–4**
Joseph G. McCoy, *Historic Sketches of the Cattle Trade of the West and Southwest* (1874)

Very few women participated in the long drives. Most women stayed back at the ranch. Occasionally, a husband and wife worked as partners, sharing even the labor of wrangling cattle, and following her husband's death, a woman might take over altogether. The majority of wives attended to domestic chores, caring for children and maintaining the household. Their daughters, however, often tagged along after their fathers and learned to love outdoor work. They were soon riding astride, "clothespin style," roping calves, branding cattle or cutting their ears to mark them, and castrating bulls. But not until 1901 did a woman dare to enter an official rodeo contest.

## THE SPORTING LIFE

In cattle towns as well as mining camps, saloons, gambling establishments, and dance halls were regular features on the horizon. Although prostitution was illegal in most towns, the laws were rarely enforced until the end of the century, when reformers led campaigns to shut down the red-light districts.

Like the cowboys who bought their services, most prostitutes were unmarried and in their teens or twenties. Often fed up with underpaid jobs in dressmaking or domestic service, they found few alternatives to prostitution in the cattle towns, where the cost of food and lodging was notoriously high. Still, earnings in prostitution were slim, except during the cattle-shipping season when young men outnumbered women by as much as three to one. Injury or even death from violent clients, addiction to narcotics such as cocaine or morphine, and venereal disease were workaday dangers.

## FRONTIER VIOLENCE AND RANGE WARS

The combination of prostitution, gambling, and drinking discouraged the formation of stable communities. Personal violence was notoriously commonplace on the streets and in the barrooms of cattle towns and mining camps populated mainly by young, single men. Many western towns such as Wichita outlawed the carrying of handguns, but enforcement usually lagged. Local specialty shops and mail-order catalogues continued to sell weapons with little regulation.

After the Civil War, violent crime, assault, and robbery rose sharply throughout the United States. In the West, the most prevalent crimes were horse theft and cattle rustling, which peaked during the height of the open range period and then fell back by the 1890s.

The "range wars" of the 1870s produced violent conflicts. By this time, both farmers and sheepherders were encroaching on the fields where cattle had once grazed freely. Sheep chew grass down to its roots, making it practically impossible to raise cattle on land they have grazed. Farmers meanwhile set about building fences to protect their domestic livestock and property. Great cattle barons fought back against farmers by ordering cowboys to cut the new barbed-wire fences.

The cattle barons helped to bring about their own demise, but they did not go down quietly. Eager for greater profits, and often backed by foreign capital, they overstocked their herds, and eventually the cattle began to deplete the

**As early as** 1879, the local newspaper described Leadville, Colorado, as a town that never sleeps: "The dancing houses and liquoring shops are never shut . . . . The streets are full of drunken carousers taking the town." This photograph of a typical saloon was taken shortly before the silver mining town reached its peak, with a population topping 60,000 in 1893. That year, the repeal of the Sherman Silver Act forced thousands of out-of-work miners to search for jobs elsewhere in the West.

# The Legendary Cowboy:
## Nat Love, Deadwood Dick

Nat Love was born a slave in 1854 and spent his childhood on a plantation in Tennessee. In 1907 he published a short autobiography, *The Life and Adventures of Nat Love, Better Known in the Cattle Country as "Deadwood Dick,"* recounting his "unusually adventurous" life during the decades after emancipation. He worked as a cowboy, a ranch hand, an Indian fighter, and a rodeo performer. His most famous episode occurred in the boomtown of Deadwood, South Dakota, where in 1876 he won a cowboy tournament. It began with a roping contest, in which Love roped, saddled, and mounted a mustang in just nine minutes, winning the almost unbelievably large prize of $200. In the second part of this competition, a shooting contest, Love once again came out on top, hitting the bull's-eye in ten out of twelve shots. He boasted that the miners and gamblers who had gathered for the tournament were so awed that they called him "Deadwood Dick," a name he proudly claimed until his death in 1921.

That name became familiar to the many readers of Edward Wheeler's *Deadwood Dick* dime novels, and at least five of Love's contemporaries claimed to be that character. Wheeler published the first installment in this popular series in 1877 as *Deadwood Dick, the Prince of the Road, or, The Black Rider of the Black Hills*. It is said that Love's autobiography reads like a dime novel, packed with adventures that no historian has yet been able to authenticate.

The photograph illustrating Love's popular autobiography captures the standard image of the cowboy of the legendary Wild West—the chaps, firearm, and ammunition in the cartridge belt circling his waist, the tack on the floor (saddle, harness, rope), and the assertive body language. But in Love's case, the cowboy is a black man. ∎

**HOW DOES** Nat Love fit into the legendary Wild West? How readily would you expect nineteenth-century readers of the *Deadwood Dick* dime novels to accept the hero's identity as a black man?

How does Nat Love's identity as an African American line up with the image of the heroic cowboy in modern American popular culture?

limited supply of grass. Finally, during 1885–87, a combination of summer drought and winter blizzards killed 90 percent of the cattle in the northern Plains. Many ranchers went bankrupt. Along the way, they often took out their grievances against the former cowboys who had gathered small herds for themselves. They charged these small ranchers with cattle rustling, taking them to court or, in some cases, rounding up lynching parties.

# FARMING COMMUNITIES ON THE PLAINS

The vision of a huge fertile garden extending from the Appalachians to the Pacific Ocean had inspired Americans since the early days of the republic. But the first explorers who actually traveled through the Great Plains quashed this dream. "The Great Desert" was the name they gave to the region stretching west from Kansas and Nebraska, north to Montana and the Dakotas, and south again to Oklahoma and Texas. It took massive improvements in both transportation and farm technology—as well as unrelenting advertising and promotional campaigns—to open the Great Plains to widescale agriculture.

## THE HOMESTEAD ACT

The **Homestead Act of 1862** offered the first incentive to prospective white farmers. This act granted a quarter section (160 acres) of the public domain free to any settler who lived on the land for at least five years and improved it; or a settler could buy the land for $1.25 per acre after only six months' residence. Restricting its provisions to household heads, the Homestead Act encouraged adventurous and hardworking unmarried women to file between 5 and 15 percent of the claims.

Homesteaders achieved their greatest success in the central and upper Midwest, where the soil was rich and weather relatively moderate. But those settlers lured to the Great Plains by descriptions of land "carpeted with soft grass—a sylvan paradise" found themselves locked in a fierce struggle with the harsh climate and arid soil.

Rather than filing a homestead claim with the federal government, most settlers acquired their land outright. State governments and land companies usually held the most valuable land near transportation and markets, and the majority of farmers were willing to pay a hefty price for those benefits. The big-time land speculators did even better, plucking choice locations at bargain prices and selling high. And the railroads, which received land grants from the federal government, did best, selling off the holdings near their routes at top dollar.

## POPULATING THE PLAINS

The rapid settlement of the West could not have taken place without the railroad. Although the Homestead Act offered prospective farmers free land, it was the railroad that promoted settlement, brought people to their new homes, and carried crops and cattle to eastern markets. The railroads, therefore, wielded tremendous economic and political power.

Along with providing transportation links between the East and the West and potential markets as distant as Russia and China, the western railroads directly encouraged settlement. Unlike the railroads built before the Civil War, which followed the path of villages and towns, the western lines preceded settlement. Bringing people west became their top priority, and the railroad companies conducted aggressive promotional and marketing campaigns. Agents enticed Easterners and Europeans alike with long-term loans and free transportation by rail to distant

---

**WHO TOOK** advantage of the Homestead Act?

**Review Summary**

**17–15**
*Homestead Act of 1862*
(1874)

## QUICK REVIEW

**The Homestead Act**

- 1862 Act granted 160 acres to any settler who lived on land for five years and improved it.

- Achieved greatest success in the central and upper Midwest.

- Most settlers acquired their land outright, rather than filing a homestead claim.

**Homestead Act of 1862** 1862 act which granted a quarter section (160 acres) of the public domain free to any settler who lived on the land for at least five years and improved it.

points in the West. The Santa Fe Railroad sent agent C. B. Schmidt to Germany, where he managed to entice nearly 60,000 Germans to settle along the rail line. The railroads also sponsored land companies to sell parcels of their own huge allotments from the federal government. The National Land Company, founded in Chicago in 1869, alone organized sixteen colonies of mainly European immigrants in parts of Kansas and Colorado.

In 1887, Lizzie Chrisman filed the first homestead claim on Lieban Creek in Custer County, Nebraska. Joined by her three sisters, she is shown here standing in front of her sod cabin. "Soddies," as these small houses were called, were constructed of stacked layers of cut prairie turf, which were eventually fortified by a thick network of roots. The roofs, often supported by timber, were usually covered with more sod, straw, and small branches.

More than 2 million Europeans, many recruited by professional promoters, settled the Great Plains between 1870 and 1900. Some districts in Minnesota seemed to be virtual colonies of Sweden; others housed the largest number of Finns in the New World. Nebraska, whose population as early as 1870 was 25 percent foreign-born, concentrated Germans, Swedes, Danes, and Czechs. But Germans outnumbered all other immigrants by far. A smaller portion of European immigrants reached Kansas, still fewer the territories to the south where Indian and Hispanic peoples and African Americans remained the major ethnic populations.

Having traveled the huge distance with kin or members of their Old World villages, immigrants tended to form tight-knit communities on the Great Plains. Many married only within their own group. For example, only 3 percent of Norwegian men married women of a different ethnic background. Like many Mexicanos in the Southwest, several immigrant groups retained their languages well into the twentieth century, usually by sponsoring parochial school systems and publishing their own newspapers. A few groups closed their communities to outsiders. The Poles who migrated to central Nebraska in the 1880s, for example, formed an exclusive settlement; and the German Hutterites, who disavowed private property, lived in seclusion as much as possible in the Bon Homme colony of South Dakota, established in 1874.

Among the native-born settlers of the Great Plains, the largest number had migrated from states bordering the Mississippi River. Settling as individual families rather than as whole communities, they faced an exceptionally solitary life on the Great Plains. To stave off isolation, homesteaders sometimes built their homes on the adjoining corners of their homestead plots. Still, the prospect of doing better, which brought most homesteaders to the Great Plains in the first place, caused many families to keep seeking greener pastures. Mobility was so high that between one-third and one-half of all households pulled up stakes within a decade.

Communities eventually flourished in prosperous towns like Grand Island, Nebraska; Coffeyville, Kansas; and Fargo, North Dakota, that served the larger agricultural region. Built alongside the railroad, they grew into commercial centers, home to banking, medical, legal, and retail services. Town life fostered a special intimacy. But closeness did not necessarily promote social equality or even friendship. A social hierarchy based on education (for the handful of doctors and lawyers) and, more important, investment property (held mainly by railroad agents and bankers) governed relationships between individuals and families. Reinforced by family ties and religious and ethnic differences, this hierarchy often persisted across generations.

## WORK, DAWN TO DUSK

Most farm families survived, and prospered if they could, through hard work, often from dawn to dusk. Men's activities in the fields tended to be seasonal, with heavy work during planting and harvest. At other times, their labor centered on construction or repair of buildings and on taking care of livestock. Women's activities were usually far more routine, week in and week out: cooking and canning of seasonal fruit and vegetables, washing, ironing, churning cream for butter, and keeping chickens for their eggs. Women tended to the young children, and they might occasionally take in boarders, usually young men working temporarily in railroad construction.

Milking the cows, hauling water, and running errands to neighboring farms could be done by the children, once they had reached the age of nine or so. The "one-room school," where all grades learned together, taught the basics of literacy and arithmetic that a future farmer or commercial employee would require.

The harsh climate and unyielding soil nevertheless forced all but the most reclusive families to seek out friends and neighbors. Neighbors might agree to work together haying, harvesting, and threshing grain. A well-to-do farmer might "rent" his threshing machine in exchange for a small cash fee and, for instance, three days' labor. His wife might barter her garden produce for her neighbor's bread and milk or for help during childbirth or disability. Women often combined work and leisure in quilting bees and sewing circles, where they made friends while sharing scraps of material and technical information. Whole communities turned out for special events, such as the seasonal husking bees and apple bees, which were organized mainly by women.

Much of this informal barter, however, resulted from lack of cash rather than from a lasting desire to cooperate. When annual harvests were bountiful, even the farm woman's practice of bartering goods with neighbors and local merchants—butter and eggs in return for yard goods or seed—diminished sharply, replaced by cash transactions.

For many farmers, the soil simply would not yield a livelihood, and they often owed more money than they took in. Start-up costs, including the purchase of land and equipment, put many farmers deep in debt to local creditors. Some lost their land altogether. By the turn of the century, more than one-third of all farmers in the United States were tenants on someone else's land.

The Garden of Eden was not to be found on the prairies or on the plains, no matter how hard the average farm family worked. Again and again, foreclosures wiped out the small landowner through dips in commodity prices, bad decisions, natural disasters, or illness. The swift growth of rural population soon ended. Although writers and orators alike continued to celebrate the family farm as the source of virtue and economic well-being, the hard reality of big money and political power told a far different story.

**HOW DID** agribusiness differ from more traditional forms of farming?

**myhistorylab**
Review Summary

# THE WORLD'S BREADBASKET

During the second half of the nineteenth century, commercial farms employed the most intensive and extensive methods of agricultural production in the world. Hardworking farmers brought huge numbers of acres under cultivation, while new technologies allowed them to achieve unprecedented levels of efficiency in the planting and harvesting of crops. As a result, farming became increasingly tied to international trade, and modern capitalism soon ruled western agriculture, as it did the mining and cattle industries.

## NEW PRODUCTION TECHNOLOGIES

Only after the trees had been cleared and grasslands cut free of roots could the soil be prepared for planting. But as farmers on the Great Plains knew so well, the sod west of the Mississippi did not yield readily to cultivation and often broke the cast-iron plows typically used by eastern farmers. Farther west, some farmers resorted to drills to plant seeds for crops such as wheat and oats. Even in the best locations, where loamy, fertile ground had built up over centuries into eight or more inches of decayed vegetation, the preliminary breaking, or "busting," of the sod required hard labor.

This **"thirty-three** horse team harvester" was photographed at the turn of the century in Walla Walla, Washington. Binding the grain into sheaves before it could hit the ground, the "harvester" cut, threshed, and sacked wheat in one single motion.

Agricultural productivity depended as much on new technology as on the farmers' hard labor. In 1837, John Deere had designed his famous "singing plow," which easily turned prairie grasses under and turned up even highly compacted soils. Around the same time, Cyrus McCormick's reaper began to be used for cutting grain; by the 1850s, his factories were turning out reapers in mass quantities. The harvester, invented in the 1870s, drew the cut stalks upward to a platform where two men could bind them into sheaves; by the 1880s, an automatic knotter tied them together. Drastically reducing the number of people traditionally required for this work, the harvester increased the pace many times over. The introduction of mechanized corn planters and mowing or raking machines for hay all but completed the technological arsenal (see Table 18.1). The improvements allowed an average farmer to produce up to ten times more than was possible with the old implements.

Scientific study of soil, grain, and climate conditions was another factor in the record output. Beginning in the mid-nineteenth century, federal and state

### QUICK REVIEW

**Changes in Farming**

- Increased emphasis on production for exchange.
- International demand for wheat supported wheat farming in U.S.
- New technology encouraged the consolidation of land into large farms.

## TABLE 18.1

### Hand v. Machine Labor on the Farm, ca. 1880

| Crop | Time Worked | | Labor Cost | |
|------|------|------|------|------|
| | Hand | Machine | Hand | Machine |
| Wheat | 61 hours | 3 hours | $3.55 | $0.66 |
| Corn | 39 hours | 15 hours | 3.62 | 1.51 |
| Oats | 66 hours | 7 hours | 3.73 | 1.07 |
| Loose Hay | 21 hours | 4 hours | 1.75 | 0.42 |
| Baled Hay | 35 hours | 12 hours | 3.06 | 1.29 |

governments added inducements to the growing body of expertise, scientific information, and hands-on advice. Through the **Morrill Act of 1862**, "land-grant" colleges acquired space for campuses in return for promising to institute agricultural programs. The Department of Agriculture, which attained cabinet-level status in 1889, and the Weather Bureau (transferred from the War Department in 1891) also made considerable contributions to farmers' knowledge. The federal Hatch Act of 1887, which created a series of state experimental stations, provided for basic agricultural research, especially in the areas of soil minerals and plant growth. Many states added their own agricultural stations, usually connected with state colleges and universities.

Nature nevertheless often reigned over technological innovation and seemed in places to take revenge against these early successes. West of the 98th meridian—a north–south line extending through western Oklahoma, central Kansas and Nebraska, and eastern Dakota—perennial dryness due to an annual rainfall of less than 20 inches constantly threatened to turn soil into dust and to break plows on the hardened ground. Summer heat burned out crops and ignited grass fires. Mountains of winter snows turned rivers into spring torrents that flooded fields; heavy fall rains washed crops away. Even good weather invited worms and flying insects to infest the crops. During the 1870s, grasshoppers in clouds a mile long ate everything organic, including tree bark and clothes.

After the Civil War, the veteran John Wesley Powell set off to explore much of the trans–Mississippi West and soon concluded that the shortage of water would remain a huge problem unless settlers worked together to plan irrigation projects. His *Report on the Lands of the Arid Region,* published in 1878, advised prospective farmers to settle near watersheds and to construct, where necessary, dams and canals. Congress ignored his suggestions, fearing that such planning would inhibit free enterprise.

## PRODUCING FOR THE GLOBAL MARKET

Farming changed in important ways during the last third of the nineteenth century. Although the family remained the primary source of labor, farmers tended to put more emphasis on production for exchange rather than for home use. They continued to plant vegetable gardens and often kept fowl or livestock for the family's consumption but raised crops mainly for a market that stretched across the world.

The new machines and expanding market did not necessarily guarantee success. Land, draft animals, and equipment remained very expensive, and start-up costs could keep a family in debt for decades. A year of good returns often preceded a year of financial disaster. Weather conditions, international markets, and railroad and steamship shipping prices all proved equally unpredictable and heartless.

The new technology and scientific expertise favored the large, well-capitalized farmer over the small one. The majority of farmers with fewer resources expanded at more modest rates. Between 1880 and 1900, average farm size in the seven leading grain-growing states increased from 64.4 acres to more than 100 acres.

## CALIFORNIA AGRIBUSINESS

The trend toward bonanza farming reached an apex in California, where farming as a business surpassed farming as a way of life. Bankers, railroad magnates, and other Anglos made rich by the gold rush took possession of the best farming land in the state. They introduced the latest technologies, built dams and canals, and invested huge amounts of capital, setting the pattern for the state's prosperous agribusiness.

**Morrill Act of 1862** Act by which "land-grant" colleges acquired space for campuses in return for promising to institute agricultural programs.

**This painting by** the British-born artist Thomas Hill (1829–1908) depicts workers tending strawberry fields in the great agricultural valley of northern California. Chinese field hands, such as the two men shown here, supplied not only cheap labor but also invaluable knowledge of specialized fruit and vegetable crops.

Thomas Hill, "Irrigating at Strawberry Farm, Santa Clara," 1888. Courtesy of the Bancroft Library, University of California, Berkeley.

Farms of nearly 500 acres dominated the California landscape in 1870; by the turn of the century, two-thirds of the state's arable land was in 1,000-acre farms.

By 1900, California had become the model for American agribusiness—not the home of self-sufficient homesteaders but the showcase of heavily capitalized farm factories that employed a huge tenant and migrant workforce, including many Chinese. After the mines gave out and work on the transcontinental railroad ended, thousands of Chinese helped to bring new lands under cultivation. Chinese tenant farmers specialized in labor-intensive crops, such as vegetables and fruits, and peddled their crops door-to-door or sold them in roadside stands. Others worked in packing and preserving in all the major agricultural regions of the state. However, the Chinese, like the majority of field hands, rarely rose to the ranks of agricultural entrepreneurs. By the turn of the century, amid intense legislative battles over land and irrigation rights, it was clear that the rich and powerful dominated California agribusiness.

## THE TOLL ON THE ENVIRONMENT

Viewing the land as a resource to command, the new inhabitants often looked past the existing flora and fauna toward a landscape remade strictly for commercial purposes. The changes they produced in some areas were nearly as cataclysmic as those that occurred during the Ice Age.

Farmers "improved" the land by introducing exotic plants and animals—that is, biological colonies indigenous to other regions and continents. Farmers also unintentionally introduced new varieties of weeds, insect pests, and rats. Surviving portions of older grasslands and meadows eventually could be found only alongside railroad tracks, in graveyards, or inside national parks.

Numerous species disappeared altogether or suffered drastic reduction. The grizzly bear, for example, an animal exclusive to the West, could once be found in large numbers from the Great Plains to California and throughout much of Alaska; by the early decades of the twentieth century, one nature writer estimated that only 800 survived, mostly in Yellowstone National Park. At the same time, the number of wolves declined from perhaps as many as 2 million to just 200,000. By the mid-1880s, no more than 5,000 buffalo survived in the entire United States.

The slaughter of the buffalo had a dramatic impact, not only on the fate of the species, but also on the grasslands of the Great Plains. Overall, the biological diversity of the region had been drastically reduced. Having killed off the giant herds, ranchers and farmers quickly shifted to cattle and sheep production. Unlike the roaming buffalo, these livestock did not range widely and soon devoured the native grasses down to their roots. With the ground cover destroyed, the soil eroded and became barren. By the end of the century, huge dust storms swept across the plains.

Large-scale commercial agriculture also took a heavy toll on inland waters. Before white settlement, rainfall had drained naturally into lakes and underground aquifers, and watering spots were abundant throughout the Great Plains. Farmers mechanically rerouted and dammed water to irrigate their crops, causing many bodies of water to disappear and the water table to drop significantly. In the 1870s, successful ranchers in California pressed for ever greater supplies of water and contracted Chinese work gangs to build the largest irrigation canal in the West. In 1887, the state of California formed irrigation districts, securing bond issues for the construction of canals, and other western states followed. But by the 1890s, irrigation had seemed to reach its limit without federal support. The Newlands or **National Reclamation Act** of 1902 added 1 million acres of irrigated land, and state irrigation districts added more than 10 million acres. Expensive to taxpayers, and ultimately benefiting corporate farmers rather than small landowners, these projects further diverted water and totally transformed the landscape.

Although western state politicians and federal officials debated water rights for decades, they rarely considered the impact of water policies on the environment. Lake Tulare in California's Central Valley, for example, had occupied up to 760 square miles. After farmers began to irrigate their land by tapping the rivers that fed Tulare, the lake shrank dramatically, covering a mere 36 square miles by the early twentieth century. Finally the lake, which had supported rich aquatic and avian life for thousands of years, disappeared entirely. The land left behind, now wholly dependent on irrigation, grew so alkaline in spots that it could no longer be used for agricultural purposes.

The need to maintain the water supply indirectly led to the creation of national forests and the Forest Service. Western farmers supported the **General Land Revision Act of 1891**, which gave the president the power to establish forest reserves to protect watersheds against the threats posed by lumbering, overgrazing, and forest fires. In the years that followed, President Benjamin Harrison established fifteen forest reserves exceeding 16 million acres, and President Grover Cleveland added more than 21 million acres. But only in 1897 did the secretary of the interior finally gain the authority to regulate the use of these reserves.

The **Forest Management Act** of 1897 and the National Reclamation Act of 1902 set the federal government on the path of large-scale regulatory activities. The Forest Service was established in 1905, and in 1907, forest reserves were transferred from the Department of the Interior to the Department of Agriculture. The federal government would now play an even larger role in economic development of the West, dealing mainly with corporate farmers and ranchers eager for improvements.

**National Reclamation Act** 1902 act which added 1 million acres of irrigated land to the United States.

**General Land Revision Act of 1891** Act which gave the president the power to establish forest reserves to protect watersheds against the threats posed by lumbering, overgrazing, and forest fires.

**Forest Management Act** 1897 act which, along with the National Reclamation Act, set the federal government on the path of large-scale regulatory activities.

# THE WESTERN LANDSCAPE

Throughout the nineteenth century, many Americans viewed western expansion as the nation's "manifest destiny," and just as many marveled at the region's natural and cultural wonders. The public east of the Mississippi craved stories about the West and visual images of its sweeping vistas. Artists and photographers built their reputations on what they saw and imagined. Scholars, from geologists and botanists to historians and anthropologists, toured the trans–Mississippi West in pursuit of new data. The region and its peoples came to represent what was both unique and magnificent about the American landscape.

## NATURE'S MAJESTY

Moved by such evidence, reports of the West's natural beauty, the federal government began to set aside huge tracts of land as nature reserves. In 1864, Congress passed the Yosemite Act, which placed the spectacular cliffs and giant sequoias under the management of the State of California. Meanwhile, explorers returned to the East awestruck by the varied terrain of the Rocky Mountains, the largest mountain chain in North America, and described huge sky-high lakes, boiling mud, and spectacular waterfalls. In 1872, Congress named Yellowstone the first national park. Yosemite and Sequoia in California, Crater Lake in Oregon, Mount Rainier in Washington, and Glacier in Montana all became national parks between 1890 and 1910 (see Map 18.5).

Landscape painters, particularly the group that became known as the Rocky Mountain School, also piqued the public's interest in western scenery. In the 1860s, German-born Albert Bierstadt's "earthscapes"—huge canvases with exacting details of animals and plants—thrilled viewers and sold for tens of thousands of dollars.

**WHAT PLACE** did the West hold in the national imagination?

myhistorylab
Review Summary

**QUICK REVIEW**

**National Parks**

♦ 1864: Congress passed the Yosemite Act placing area under management of state of California.

♦ 1872: Yellowstone named first national park.

♦ Five new national parks named between 1890 and 1910.

**Albert Bierstadt became** one of the first artists to capture on enormous canvases the vastness and rugged terrain of western mountains and wilderness. Many other artists joined Bierstadt to form the Rocky Mountain School. In time, the camera largely replaced the paintbrush, and most Americans formed an image of these majestic peaks from postcards and magazine illustrations.

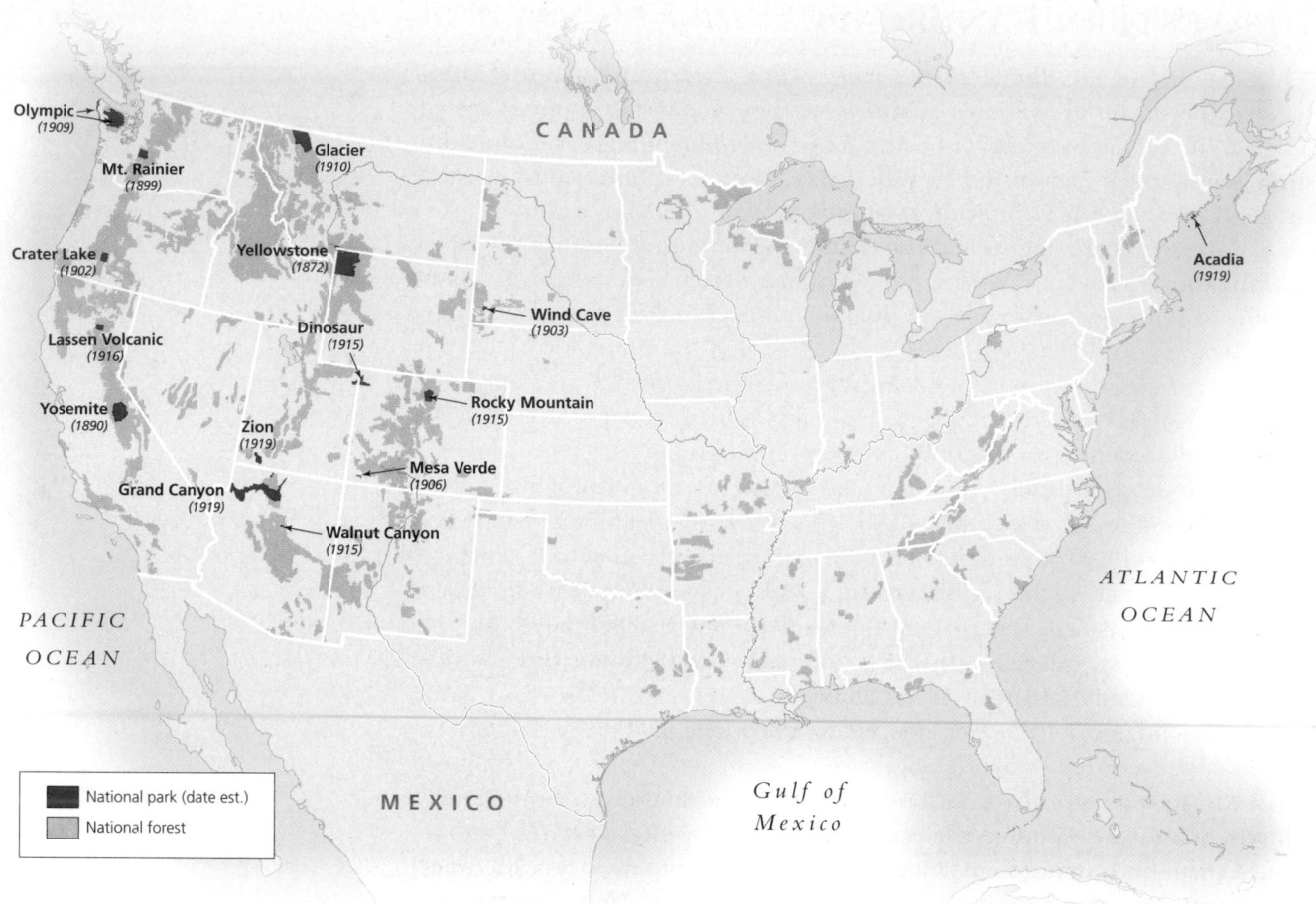

**MAP 18.5**

**The Establishment of National Parks and Forests**    The setting aside of land for national parks saved large districts of the West from early commercial development and industrial degradation, setting a precedent for the later establishment of additional parks in economically marginal, but scenic, territory. The West, home to the vast majority of park space, became a principal site of tourism by the end of the nineteenth century.

WHAT IF any factors in the West provided a more conducive environment in which the Mormons could flourish?

## THE LEGENDARY WILD WEST

By the end of the century, many Americans, rich and poor alike, imagined the West as a land of promise and opportunity and, above all, of excitement and adventure. Future president Theodore Roosevelt helped to promote this view. Soon after his election to the New York State Assembly in 1882, Roosevelt was horrified to see himself lampooned in the newspapers as a dandy and a weakling. A year later, after buying a ranch in North Dakota, he began to reconstruct his public image. He wrote three books recounting his adventures in the West, claiming that they had instilled in him not only personal bravery and "hardihood" but also self-reliance. The West, Roosevelt insisted, meant "vigorous manhood."

The first "westerns," the "dime novels" that sold in the 1860s in editions of 50,000 or more, reflected these myths. Edward Zane Carroll Judson's *Buffalo Bill, the King of the Border Men,* first published in 1869, spawned hundreds of other novels, thousands of stories, and an entire magazine devoted to Buffalo Bill.

The former Pony Express rider, army scout, and famed buffalo hunter William F. Cody hit upon the idea of an extravaganza that would bring the legendary West to those who could never experience it in person. "Buffalo Bill" Cody made sharpshooter Annie Oakley a star performer. Entrancing crowds with her stunning accuracy with pistol or rifle, Oakley shot dimes in midair and cigarettes from her husband's mouth. Cody also hired Sioux Indians and hundreds of cowboys to perform in mock stagecoach robberies and battles.

Cody's Wild West Show attracted masses of fairgoers at the World's Columbian Exposition, the spectacular celebration of the 400th anniversary of Columbus's landing in the New World held in Chicago in 1893. Less well attended but nonetheless significant was the annual meeting of the American Historical Association, the leading professional society of historians, and the presentation of an essay that one historian has deemed "the single most influential piece of writing in the history of American history."

At this meeting, Frederick Jackson Turner, a young historian at the University of Wisconsin, read a paper that, like Cody's Wild West Show, celebrated the West. "The Significance of the Frontier in American History" made a compelling argument that the continuous westward movement of settlement allowed Americans to develop new standards for democracy. Turner reasoned that each generation, in its move westward, mastered the "primitive conditions" and thereby developed a distinctive American character.

What became known as the "frontier thesis" also sounded a warning bell. The 1890 federal census revealed that the "free land" had been depleted, prompting Turner to conclude that the "closing" of the frontier marked the end of the formative period of American history. The "frontier thesis" lived on, although most historians no longer consider the frontier as the key to all American history. Many have pointed out that the concept of "the frontier" has meaning only to Euro-Americans and not to the tribal people who had occupied this land for centuries. Nevertheless, many of Turner's contemporaries found in his thesis the rationale for seeking new "frontiers" through overseas expansion.

## THE "AMERICAN PRIMITIVE"

New technologies of graphic reproduction encouraged painters and photographers to provide new images of the West, authentic as well as fabricated. A young German American artist, Charles Schreyvogel, saw Buffalo Bill's tent show in Buffalo and decided to make the West his life's work. His canvases depicted Indian warriors and U.S. cavalry fighting furiously but without blood and gore. Charles Russell, a genuine cowboy, painted the life he knew but also indulged in imaginary scenarios, producing paintings of buffalo hunts and first encounters between Indian peoples and white explorers.

Frederic Remington, the most famous of all the western artists, left Yale Art School to visit Montana in 1881, became a Kansas sheepherder and tavern owner, and then returned to painting. Inspired by newspaper stories of the army's campaign against the Apaches, he made himself into a war correspondent and captured vivid scenes of battle in his sketches. Painstakingly accurate in physical details, especially of horses, his paintings celebrated the "winning of the West" from the Indian peoples.

**Born Phoebe Ann** Moses in 1860, Annie Oakley was a star attraction in Buffalo Bill's Wild West show. Dubbed "Little Sure Shot" by Chief Sitting Bull, Oakley traveled with Cody's show for seventeen years. This poster from 1901 advertises her sharp-shooting talents.

Photographers often produced highly nuanced portraits of Indian peoples. Dozens of early photographers from the Bureau of American Ethnology captured the gaze of noble tribespeople or showed them hard at work digging clams or grinding corn. President Theodore Roosevelt praised Edward Sheriff Curtis for vividly conveying tribal virtue.

Painters and photographers led the way for scholarly research on the various Indian societies. The early ethnographer and pioneer of fieldwork in anthropology Lewis Henry Morgan devoted his life to the study of Indian family or kinship patterns, mostly of eastern tribes such as the Iroquois, who adopted him into their Hawk Clan. In 1851, he published *League of the Ho-de-no-sau-nee, or Iroquois*, considered the first scientific account of an Indian tribe.

One of the most influential interpreters of the cultures of living tribespeople was the pioneering ethnographer Alice Cunningham Fletcher. In 1879, Fletcher met Susette (Bright Eyes) La Flesche of the Omaha tribe, who was on a speaking tour to gain support for her people, primarily to prevent their removal from tribal lands. Fletcher, then forty-two years old, accompanied La Flesche to Nebraska, telling the Omahas that she had come "to learn, if you will let me, something about your tribal organization, social customs, tribal rites, traditions and songs. Also to see if I can help you in any way." After transcribing hundreds of songs, Fletcher became well known as an expert on Omaha music. She also promoted assimilation through the allotment of individual claims to 160-acre homesteads, eked out of tribal lands, and helped to draft the model legislation that was enacted by Congress as the **Omaha Act of 1882**. In 1885, Fletcher produced for the U.S. Senate a report titled *Indian Education and Civilization*, one of the first general statements on the status of Indian peoples. As a founder of the American Anthropological Society and president of the American Folklore Society, she encouraged further study of Indian societies.

# THE TRANSFORMATION OF INDIAN SOCIETIES

In 1871, the U.S. government formally ended the treaty system, eclipsing without completely abolishing the sovereignty of Indian nations. Still, the tribes persisted. Using a mixture of survival strategies from farming and trade to the leasing of reservation lands, they both adapted to changing conditions and maintained old traditions.

## REFORM POLICY AND POLITICS

By 1880, many Indian tribes had been forcibly resettled on reservations, but very few had adapted to white ways. For decades, reformers, mainly from the Protestant churches, had lobbied Congress for a program of salvation through assimilation, and they looked to the Board of Indian Commissioners, created in 1869, to carry out this mission. The board often succeeded in mediating conflicts among the various tribes crowded onto reservations but made far less headway in converting them to Christianity or transforming them into prosperous farming communities.

The majority of Indian peoples lived in poverty and misery, deprived of their traditional means of survival and, more often than not, subjected to fraud by corrupt government officials and private suppliers. Reformers who observed

---

**WHAT KIND** of Indian society did reformers envision?

myhistorylab

**Review Summary**

 **17–5**
Helen Hunt Jackson, from *A Century of Dishonor* (1881)

**Omaha Act of 1882** Act which allowed the establishment of individual title to tribal lands.

## OVERVIEW | Major Indian Treaties and Legislation of the Late Nineteenth Century

| 1863 | Nez Percé Treaty | Signed illegally on behalf of the entire tribe, in which the Nez Percé abandoned 6 million acres of land in return for a small reservation in northeastern Oregon. Led to Nez Percé wars, which ended in 1877 with the surrender of Chief Joseph. |
|---|---|---|
| 1867 | Medicine Lodge Treaty | Assigned reservations in existing Indian Territory to Comanches, Plains (Kiowa), Apaches, Kiowas, Cheyennes, and Arapahoes, bringing these tribes together with Sioux, Shoshones, Bannocks, and Navajos. |
| 1868 | Treaty of Fort Laramie | Successfully ended Red Cloud's war by evacuating federal troops from Sioux Territory along the Bozeman Trail; additionally granted Sioux ownership of the western half of South Dakota and rights to use Powder River country in Wyoming and Montana. |
| 1871 | | Congress declares end to treaty system. |
| 1887 | Dawes Severalty Act | Divided communal tribal land, granting the right to petition for citizenship to those Indians who accepted the individual land allotment of 160 acres. Successfully undermined sovereignty. |

these conditions firsthand nevertheless remained unshaken in their belief that tribespeople must be raised out of the darkness of ignorance into the light of civilization. Some conceded, however, that the reservation system might not be the best means to this end.

Unlike most Americans, who saw the conquest of the West as a means to national glory, some reformers were genuinely outraged by the government's continuous violation of treaty obligations and the military enforcement of the reservation policy. One of the most influential was Helen Hunt Jackson, a noted poet and author of children's stories. In 1879, Jackson had attended a lecture in Hartford, Connecticut, by a chief of the Ponca tribe whose destitute people had been forced from their Dakota homeland.

Jackson threw herself into the Indian Rights Association, an offshoot of the Women's National Indian Association (WNIA), which had been formed in 1874 to rally public support for a program of assimilation. The two organizations helped to place Protestant missionaries in the West to work to eradicate tribal customs as well as to convert Indian peoples to Christianity. By 1882, the WNIA had gathered 100,000 signatures on petitions urging Congress to phase out the reservation system, to establish universal education for Indian children, and to award title to 160 acres to any Indian individual willing to work the land.

The **Dawes Severalty Act**, passed by Congress in 1887, incorporated many of these measures and established federal Indian policy for decades to come. The act allowed the president to distribute land, not to tribes, but to individuals legally "severed" from their tribes. The commissioner of Indian affairs rendered the popular interpretation that "tribal relations should be broken up, socialism destroyed and the family and autonomy of the individual substituted. The allotment of land in severalty, the establishment of local courts and police, the development of a personal sense of independence and the universal adoption of the English language are means to this end."

**myhistorylab**

**Overview:** *Major Indian Treaties and Legislation of the Late Nineteenth Century*

**Dawes Severalty Act** An 1887 law terminating tribal ownership of land and allotting some parcels of land to individual Indians with the remainder opened for white settlement.

Those individuals who accepted the land allotment of 160 acres and agreed to allow the government to sell unallotted tribal lands (with some funds set aside for education) could petition to become citizens of the United States. A little over a decade after its enactment, many reformers believed that the Dawes Act had resolved the basis of the "Indian problem." Hollow Horn Bear, a Sioux chief, offered a different opinion, judging the Dawes Act to be "only another trick of the whites."

The Dawes Act successfully undermined tribal sovereignty but offered little compensation. Indian religions and sacred ceremonies were banned, the telling of legends and myths forbidden, and shaman and medicine men imprisoned or exiled for continuing their traditional practices. "Indian schools" forbade Indian languages, clothing styles, and even hair fashions.

These and other measures did little to integrate Indians into white society. Treated as savages, Indian children fled most white schools. Nor did adults receive much encouragement to become property holders. Government agencies allotted them inferior farmland, inadequate tools, and little training for agricultural self-sufficiency. Seeing scant advantage in assimilating, only a minority of adults dropped their tribal religion for Christianity or their communal ways for the accumulation of private property. Within the next forty years, the Indian peoples lost 60 percent of the reservation land remaining in 1887 and 66 percent of the land allotted to them as homesteaders. The tenets of the Dawes Act were not reversed until 1934. In that year, Congress passed the Indian Reorganization Act, which affirmed the integrity of Indian cultural institutions and returned some land to tribal ownership (see Chapter 24).

## THE GHOST DANCE

After the passage of the Dawes Severalty Act, one more cycle of rebellion remained for the Sioux. In 1888, the Paiute prophet Wovoka, ill with scarlet fever, had a vision during a total eclipse of the sun. In his vision, the Creator told him that if the Indian peoples learned to love each other, they would be granted a special place in the afterlife. The Creator also gave him the Ghost Dance, which the prophet performed for others and soon spread throughout the tribe. The Sioux came to believe that when the day of judgment came, all Indian peoples who had ever lived would return to their lost world and white peoples would vanish from the earth.

Many white settlers and federal officials feared the Ghost Dancers, even though belief in a sudden divine judgment was common among Christians and Jews. Before the Civil War, Protestant groups such as the Millerites, who had renounced personal property and prepared themselves for the millennium, were tolerated by other Americans. But after decades of Indian warfare, white Americans took the Ghost Dance as a warning of tribal retribution rather than a religious ceremony. As thousands of Sioux danced to exhaustion, local whites intolerantly demanded the practice be stopped. The U.S. Seventh Cavalry, led in part by survivors of the Battle of Little Bighorn, rushed to the Pine Ridge Reservation, and a group of the Sioux led by Big Foot, now fearing

**The celebrated artist** Frederic Remington (1861–1909) produced this sketch of Oglala Sioux at the Pine Ridge Indian Reservation in South Dakota. Published in the popular magazine *Harper's Weekly,* Remington's depiction of the ghost dance of 1890 showed dancers in vividly patterned robes and shirts, some decorated with stars symbolizing the coming of a new age for the Indians.

Ogallala Sioux performing the Ghost Dance at the Pine Ridge Indian Agency, South Dakota. Illustration by Frederic Remington, 1890. The Granger Collection.

mass murder, moved into hiding in the Bad Lands of South Dakota. After a skirmish, the great leader Sitting Bull and his young son lay dead.

The Seventh Cavalry pursued the Sioux Ghost Dancers and 300 undernourished Sioux, freezing and without horses, to Wounded Knee Creek on the Pine Ridge Reservation. There, on December 29, 1890, while the peace-seeking Big Foot, who had personally raised a white flag of surrender, lay dying of pneumonia, they were surrounded by soldiers armed with automatic guns. The U.S. troops expected the Sioux to surrender their few remaining weapons, but an accidental gunshot from one deaf brave who misunderstood the command caused panic on both sides.

Within minutes, 200 Sioux had been cut down and dozens of soldiers wounded, mostly by their own cross fire. For two hours soldiers continued to shoot at anything that moved—mostly women and children straggling away. Many of the injured froze to death in the snow; others were transported in open wagons and finally laid out on beds of hay under Christmas decorations at the Pine Ridge Episcopal church. The massacre, which took place almost exactly 400 years after Columbus "discovered" the New World for Christian civilization, seemed to mark the final conquest of the continent's indigenous peoples.

## ENDURANCE AND REJUVENATION

The most tenacious tribes were those occupying land rejected by white settlers or those distant from their new communities. Still, not even an insular, peaceful agricultural existence on semiarid, treeless terrain necessarily provided protection. Nor did a total willingness to peacefully accept white offers prevent attack.

The Pimas of Arizona, for instance, had a well-developed agricultural system adapted to a scarce supply of water, and they rarely warred with other tribes. After the arrival of white settlers, they integrated Christian symbolism into their religion, learned to speak English, and even fought with the U.S. cavalry against the Apaches. Still, the Pimas saw their lands stolen, their precious waterways diverted, and their families impoverished.

The similarly peaceful Yana tribes of California, hunters and gatherers rather than farmers, were even less fortunate. Suffering enslavement, prostitution, and multiple new diseases from white settlers, they faced near extinction within a generation. One Yana tribe, the Yahi, chose simply to disappear. For more than a decade, they lived in caves and avoided all contact with white settlers.

A majority of tribes, especially smaller ones, sooner or later reached numbers too low to maintain their collective existence. Intermarriage, although widely condemned by the white community, drew many young people outside their Indian communities. Some tribal leaders also deliberately chose a path toward assimilation. The Quapaws, for example, formally disbanded in the aftermath of the Dawes Severalty Act. The minority that managed to prosper in white society as tradespeople or farmers abandoned their language, religious customs, and traditional ways of life.

For those tribes who remained on reservations, the aggressively assimilationist policies of the Office of Indian Affairs (OIA) challenged their traditional ways. The Southern Ute, for example, at one time hunted, fished, and gathered throughout a huge region spanning the Rocky Mountains and the Great Basin. In 1848, they began to sign a series of treaties in accord with the reservation policy of the U.S. government. Twenty years later their territory had been reduced to approximately one-quarter of Colorado Territory, and in 1873, they had further relinquished about one-quarter of this land. After the passage of the Dawes Act, the U.S. government, pressured by white settlers, gave the tribe two choices: they could break up their communal land holdings and accept the 160 acres granted to the male heads of families, or they could maintain their tribal status and move to a reservation in Utah.

**17–7**
*Tragedy at Wounded Knee* (1890)

**17–8**
*Benjamin Harrison, Report on Wounded Knee Massacre and the Decrease in Indian Land Acreage* (1891)

The Utes divided over the issue, but a considerable number chose to live on reservations under the administration of the OIA.

Under the terms of the Dawes Act, Southern Ute men and women endured continuous challenges to their egalitarian practices. The OIA assumed, for example, that Ute men would represent the tribe in all official matters, a policy that forced Ute women to petition the U.S. government to recognize their rights and concerns. Similarly, Ute women struggled to hold on to their roles as producers within the subsistence family economy against the efforts of the OIA agents to train them for homemaking alone.

A small minority of tribes, grown skillful in adapting to dramatically changing circumstances, managed to persist and even grow. Never numbering more than a few thousand people, during the late eighteenth century the Cheyennes had found themselves caught geographically between aggressive tribes in the Great Lakes region and had migrated into the Missouri area, where they split into small village-sized communities. By the mid-nineteenth century, they had become expert horse traders on the Great Plains.

The Navajos experienced an extraordinary renewal, largely because they built a life in territory considered worthless by whites. Having migrated to the Southwest from the northwestern part of the continent perhaps 700 years ago, the Diné ("the People"), as they called themselves, had already survived earlier invasions by the Spanish. In 1863, they had been conquered again through the cooperation of hostile tribes led by the famous Colonel Kit Carson. Their crops burned, their fruit trees destroyed, 8,000 Navajo were forced in the 300-mile "Long Walk" to the desolate Bosque Redondo reservation, where they nearly starved. Four years later, the Indian Bureau allowed the severely reduced tribe to return to a fraction of its former lands.

By 1880, the Navajos' population had returned to nearly what it had been before their conquest by white Americans. Quickly depleting the deer and antelope on their hemmed-in reservation, they had to rely on sheep alone as a food reserve during years of bad crops. With their wool rugs and blankets much in demand in the East, the Navajos increasingly turned to crafts, eventually including silver jewelry as well as weaving, to survive. Although living on the economic margin, they persevered to become the largest Indian nation in the United States.

The nearby Hopis, like the Navajos, survived by stubbornly clinging to lands unwanted by white settlers, and by adapting to drastically changing conditions. The Hopis' highly developed theological beliefs, peaceful social system, sand paintings, and kachina dolls interested many educated and influential whites. The resulting publicity helped them gather the public supporters and financial resources needed to fend off further threats to their reservations.

Fortunate northwestern tribes remained relatively isolated from white settlers until the early twentieth century, although they had begun trading with white visitors centuries earlier. Northwestern peoples relied largely on salmon and other resources of the region's rivers and bays. In potlatch ceremonies, leaders redistributed tribal wealth and maintained their personal status and the status of their tribe by giving lavish gifts to invited guests. Northwestern peoples also made intricate wood carvings, including commemorative "totem" poles that recorded their history and identified their regional status. Northwestern peoples maintained their cultural integrity in part through connections with kin in Canada, as did southern tribes with kin in Mexico. In Canada and Mexico, native populations suffered less pressure from new populations and retained more tribal authority than in the United States.

## QUICK REVIEW

**Adaptation**

- Cheyenne became expert horse traders.

- Navajos turned to crafts for survival.

- Interest of influential whites helped Hopis fend off threats.

## CHRONOLOGY

| | |
|---|---|
| 1848 | Treaty of Guadalupe Hidalgo |
| 1853 | Gadsden Purchase |
| 1862 | Homestead Act makes free land available<br>Morrill Act authorizes "land-grant" colleges |
| 1865–67 | Great Sioux War |
| 1866 | Texas cattle drives begin |
| 1867 | Medicine Lodge Treaty established reservation system<br>Alaska purchased |
| 1869 | Board of Indian Commissioners created<br>*Buffalo Bill, the King of the Border Men* sets off "Wild West" publishing craze |
| 1870s | Grasshopper attacks on the Great Plains |
| 1872 | Yellowstone National Park created |
| 1873 | Timber Culture Act |
| 1874–75 | Sioux battles in Black Hills of Dakotas<br>Red River War |
| 1876 | Custer's Last Stand |
| 1877 | Defeat of the Nez Percé |
| 1878 | John Wesley Powell published *Report on the Lands of the Arid Region* |
| 1881 | Helen Hunt Jackson, *A Century of Dishonor* |
| 1882 | Edmunds Act outlaws polygamy |
| 1885–87 | Droughts and severe winters cause the collapse of the cattle boom |
| 1887 | Dawes Severalty Act |
| 1890 | Sioux Ghost Dance movement<br>Massacre of Lakota Sioux at Wounded Knee<br>Census Bureau announces the end of the frontier line |
| 1893 | Frederick Jackson Turner presents his "frontier thesis" |
| 1897 | Forest Management Act gives the federal government authority over forest reserves |

Indian nations approached their nadir as the nineteenth century came to a close. The descendants of the great pre-Columbian civilizations had been conquered by foreigners, their population reduced to fewer than 250,000. Under the pressure of assimilation, the remaining tribespeople became known to non-Indians as "the vanishing Americans." It would take several generations before Indian sovereignty experienced a resurgence.

## CONCLUSION

The West, rich in natural resources, soon served the nation in supplying ore and timber for its expanding industries and agricultural products for the growing urban populations. Envisioning the West as a cornucopia whose boundless treasures would offer themselves to the willing pioneer, most of the new residents failed to calculate the odds against their making a prosperous livelihood as miners, farmers, or petty merchants. Nor could they appreciate the long-term consequences of the violence they brought with them from the battlefields of the Civil War to the far reaches of the West.

The new settlers adapted their political and legal systems, as well as many of their economic and cultural institutions, to western circumstances. Ironically though, even after statehood, they would still be only distant representatives of an empire whose financial, political, and industrial centers remained in the Northeast. They were often frustrated by their isolation and enraged at the federal regulations that governed them and at the eastern investors and lawyers who seemed poised on all sides to rob them of the fruits of their labor. Embittered Westerners, along with Southerners, would form the core of a nationwide discontent that would soon threaten to uproot the American political system.

## REVIEW QUESTIONS

1. Discuss the role of federal legislation in accelerating and shaping the course of westward expansion.

2. How did the incorporation of western territories into the United States affect Indian nations such as the Sioux or the Nez Percé? Discuss the causes and consequences of the Indian Wars. Discuss the significance of reservation policy and the Dawes Severalty Act for tribal life.

3. What were some of the major technological advances in mining and in agriculture that promoted the development of the western economy?

4. Describe the unique features of Mexicano communities in the Southwest before and after the mass immigration of Anglos. How did changes in the economy affect the patterns of labor and the status of women in these communities?

5. What role did the Homestead Act play in western expansion? How did farm families on the Great Plains divide chores among their members? What factors determined the likelihood of economic success or failure?

6. Describe the responses of artists, naturalists, and conservationists to the western landscape. How did their photographs, paintings, and stories shape perceptions of the West in the East?

## KEY TERMS

**Flashcard Review**

| | |
|---|---|
| **Caminetti Act** (p. 474) | **Hispanic-American Alliance** (p. 476) |
| **Dawes Severalty Act** (p. 491) | **Homestead Act of 1862** (p. 480) |
| **Edmunds Act** (p. 475) | **Morrill Act of 1862** (p. 484) |
| **Edmunds-Tucker Act** (p. 475) | **National Reclamation Act** (p. 486) |
| **Forest Management Act** (p. 486) | **Omaha Act of 1882** (p. 490) |
| **General Land Revision Act of 1891** (p. 486) | **Sand Creek Massacre** (p. 469) |
| | **Treaty of Fort Laramie** (p. 469) |
| **Great Sioux War** (p. 469) | |

## RECOMMENDED READING

Jon Gjerde, *The Minds of the West: Ethnocultural Evolution in the Rural Middle West, 1830–1917* (1997). A combination cultural and economic history that weighs the importance of ethnicity in the shaping of American identities in the farming regions of the Middle West. Gjerde pays close attention to the religious institutions and systems of belief of European immigrants as the basis of community formation.

Robert V. Hine and John Mack Faragher, *The American West: A New Interpretive History* (2000). A sweeping, amply illustrated survey of western history with reference to recent scholarship. The authors emphasize Native Americans and include rich material on ethnicity, the environment, and the role of women.

John C. Hudson, *Making the Corn Belt: A Geographical History of Middle-Western Agriculture* (1994). An ecologically oriented study of corn growing that traces its development from Indians to Southerners moving westward.

Andrew C. Isenberg, *The Destruction of the Bison: An Environmental History, 1750–1920* (2000). A rich study of the forces behind the near-extinction of the bison, with special attention to the interplay among Indians, Euroamericans, and the environment of the Great Plains. Isenberg constructs a narrative that is as much cultural as economic in framing the problem.

Karl Jacoby, *Crimes Against Nature: Squatters, Poachers, Thieves, and the Hidden History of American Conservation* (2001). A complex analysis of the origins of national parks in the Adirondacks, Yellowstone, and the Grand Canyon. Rather than focusing on the individuals and groups that led the conservation of vast public lands, Jacoby switches perspective to focus on those who were dispossessed by the process.

Elizabeth Jameson and Susan Armitage, eds., *Writing the Range* (1997). A collection of essays on women in the West that presents an inclusive historical narrative based on the experiences of women of differing backgrounds, races, and ethnic groups.

Valerie Sherer Mathes and Richard Lowitt, *The Standing Bear Controversy: Prelude to Indian Reform* (2003). A fascinating account of the Ponca chief's efforts to bring attention to the injustices surrounding the forced removal of the Poncas from their tribal lands.

Katherine M. B. Osburn, *Southern Ute Women: Autonomy and Assimilation on the Reservation, 1887–1934* (1998). Presents a careful analysis of the impact of the Dawes Act on the role and status of women among the Southern Ute. Osburn acknowledges the changes brought by the Office of Indian Affairs programs on the reservations but emphasizes the resistance of the Ute and the retention of old ways.

Glenda Riley, *Building and Breaking Families in the American West* (1996). Essays covering the variety of cultures in the American West, organized topically to highlight courtship, marriage and intermarriage, and separation and divorce.

Thomas E. Sheridan, *Los Tucsonenses: The Mexican Community in Tucson, 1854–1941* (1986). A highly readable account of Mexican American communities in the Southwest. Sheridan shows how a midcentury accommodation of Anglos and Mexicanos faded with the absorption of the region into the national economy and with the steady displacement of the Mexicano community from its agricultural landholdings.

Louis S. Warren, *Buffalo Bill's America: William Cody and the Wild West Show* (2005). Deals with many of the legends Cody created about himself and his performers and relates his celebrity at the turn of the twentieth century to continuing forms of mass entertainment.

Liping Zhu, *A Chinaman's Chance: The Chinese on the Rocky Mountain Mining Frontier* (1997). Studies the mining communities of Chinese in the Boise Basin of Idaho. Zhu emphasizes the success the Chinese enjoyed not only as miners but also as merchants in the face of discriminatory practices and laws.

myhistorylab
Where it's a good time to connect to the past!

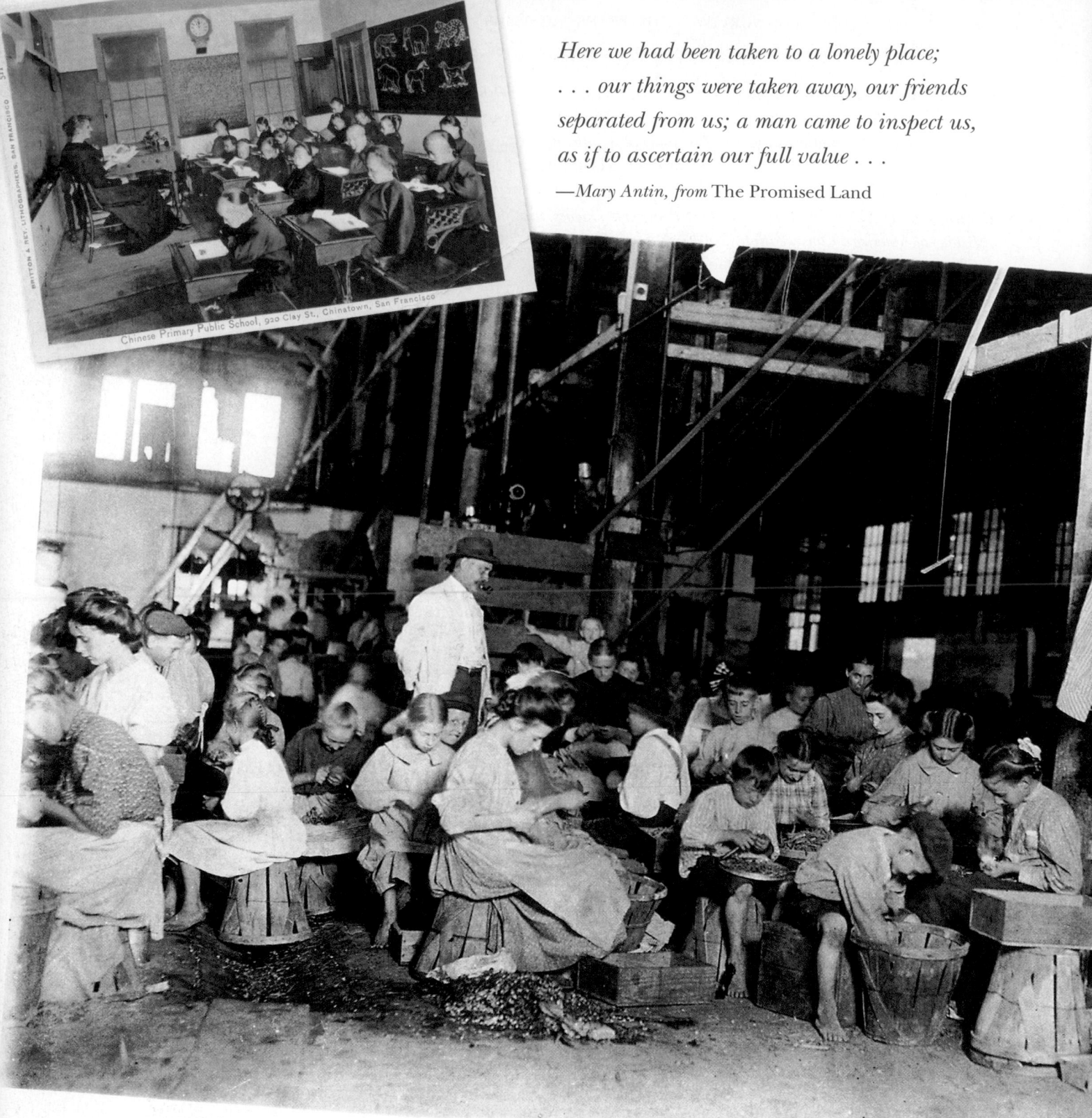

Chinese Primary Public School, 920 Clay St., Chinatown, San Francisco

*Here we had been taken to a lonely place;*
*. . . our things were taken away, our friends*
*separated from us; a man came to inspect us,*
*as if to ascertain our full value . . .*

—Mary Antin, *from* The Promised Land

**Noted urban photographer Lewis Hines** captures the cramped working conditions
and child labor in this late nineteenth-century canning factory. Women and children
provided a cheap and efficient work force for labor-intensive industries.

# 19

# PRODUCTION AND CONSUMPTION IN THE GILDED AGE
## 1865–1900

**WHAT WAS** the effect of the expansion in the production of both capital goods and consumer goods?

**WHAT WERE** the sources of the new labor being recruited for factory work in Gilded Age America?

**HOW DID** the development of Southern industry affect the lives of African Americans living in the South?

**WHAT CONTRIBUTED** to the growing population of American cities?

**WHAT ACCOUNTS** for the rise of a consumer society and how did various groups participate in its development?

**WHAT ROLE** did public spaces play in late nineteenth-century popular culture?

# AMERICAN COMMUNITIES
## Haymarket Square, Chicago, May 4, 1886

As Rain approached the City, approximately 1,500 People gathered for a mass meeting in Haymarket Square to protest the brutality of the previous day, when Chicago police killed four strikers at the fiercely antiunion McCormick Reaper Works. The crowd listened peacefully as several speakers denounced the violence. Around 10:00 P.M., when the winds picked up, most headed for home, including the city's longtime mayor, Democrat Carter Harrison. According to newspaper reports, the crowd quickly dwindled to only 600 people. The final speaker, stone hauler Samuel Fielden, jumped up on the hay wagon that served as a make-shift stage and concluded on an ominous note. He warned that "war has been declared on us" and advised the crowd "to get hold of anything that will help you to resist the onslaught of the enemy and the usurper."

Within minutes, a column of 176 police marched down the street, pushing what remained of the crowd onto the wooden sidewalks and commanding them to disperse. Then, according to the city's leading newspaper, the *Tribune*, "something like a miniature rocket suddenly rose out of the crowd on the east sidewalk." The bomb exploded "with terrific force, shaking buildings on the street and creating havoc among the police." One policeman died immediately, provoking others to open fire into the scattering crowd. At the end of just a few minutes of chaos, seven policemen had received mortal wounds and as many as sixty more were injured, many in their own cross fire. Several civilians were killed, and dozens were injured.

Those who attended the rally were mainly disgruntled workers, recent immigrants from central and eastern Europe who had come to Chicago to take advantage of the city's growing industries. They were determined to establish unions and a workday shorter than the customary ten or twelve hours.

Since early in the year, an eight-hour campaign had been sweeping the nation, with its center in Chicago. Workers and sympathetic consumers alike boycotted brands of beer, tobacco, bread, and other products made in longer-hour shops.

With more than wages at stake, workers were joining unions and striking so often that the era became known as the "Great Upheaval." Their leaders responded to this upsurge by calling for a general strike across all industries on May 1, 1886.

A community of radical workers who had emigrated from Germany and settled in Chicago's near North Side made up the most militant contingent of the movement. They called themselves "revolutionary socialists," seeking a government of working people in place of politicians and corporate power. Writing in the *Arbeiter-Zeitung* (*Workers' Newspaper*), the local German-language newspaper, editor August Spies greeted May 1, hailed as "Emancipation Day," calling: "Workmen, let your watchword be: No compromise! Cowards to the Rear! Men to the front!"

On May Day, Spies renewed the cry of "eight for ten" and helped to lead the spectacular parade of 80,000 men, women, and children up Michigan Avenue, Chicago's main street. A Saturday, the day passed peacefully. However, when the workweek resumed on Monday, May 3, the deadly confrontation of strikers and police at the McCormick Reaper Works set the stage for virtual class warfare.

Feelings of animosity on all sides intensified. In the days following the tragedy at Haymarket Square, Chicago police arrested hundreds of working people, rounded up known leaders, and searched their homes and detained them without warrants. Meanwhile, newspapers denounced them as "enemy forces" and the "scum" of Europe. Sentiment swung sharply against immigrants. Many prominent citizens called for a ban on "foreign savages who might come to America with their dynamite bombs and anarchic purposes."

Ultimately, eight men were charged with incitement to murder. In the most celebrated trial of the nineteenth century, a jury of middle-class men pronounced all eight guilty despite the lack of evidence linking the defendants to the bombing. Three of the eight had not even been at Haymarket Square on the evening of May 4. The judge sentenced them to death by hanging.

By the final decades of the nineteenth century, the nation's eyes were fixed on Chicago because the city was marking the steps being taken by the nation as a whole. If class differences sharpened and led to violence, the rise in living standards provided a different, more appealing focus. The city with the most technologically advanced industries in the world seemed to be leading the way—but to what?

Chicago

# THE RISE OF INDUSTRY, THE TRIUMPH OF BUSINESS

At the time of the Civil War, the typical American business firm was a small enterprise, owned and managed by a single family, and producing goods for a local or regional market. By the turn of the century, businesses depending on large-scale investments had organized as corporations and grown to unforeseen size. These mammoth firms could afford to mass-produce goods for national and even international markets. At the helm stood unimaginably wealthy men, powerful representatives of a new national business community, who led in the transformation of the United States from a rural to an urban industrial nation.

## MECHANIZATION TAKES COMMAND

The second industrial revolution (1871–1914) proceeded at a pace that was not only unprecedented but also previously unimaginable. In 1865, the annual production of goods was estimated at $2 billion; by 1900, it stood at $13 billion, transforming the United States from fourth to first in the world in terms of productivity. American industry had outstripped its European rivals, Germany and Great Britain, and manufactured one-third of the world's goods.

A major force behind economic growth was the completion of the most extensive transportation network in the world. As the nation's first big business and recipient of generous government subsidies, railroads linked cities in every state and served as a nationwide distributor of goods. Freight trains carried the bountiful natural resources, such as iron, coal, and minerals that supplied the raw materials for industry, as well as food and other commodities for the growing urban populations (see Map 19.1).

No factor was more important in promoting economic growth than the application of new technologies to increase the productivity of labor and the volume of goods. Machines, factory managers, and workers together created a system of continuous production by which more could be made—and faster—than anywhere else on earth. Higher productivity depended not only on machinery and technology but also on economies of scale and speed, reorganization of factory labor and business management, and the unparalleled growth of a market for goods of all kinds.

New systems of mass production replaced wasteful and often chaotic practices and speeded up the delivery of finished goods. Within a generation, continuous production—the assembly line—became standard in most areas of manufacturing, revolutionizing the making of furniture, cloth, grain products, soap, and canned goods; the refining, distilling, and processing of animal and vegetable fats; and eventually, the manufacture of automobiles.

## EXPANDING THE MARKET FOR GOODS

To distribute the growing volume of goods and to create a dependable market, businesses demanded new techniques of merchandising on a national and, in some cases, international scale. For generations, legions of sellers, or "drummers," had worked their routes, pushing goods, especially hardware and patent medicines, to individual buyers and local retail stores. After the Civil War, the appearance of mail-order houses, which accompanied the consolidation of the railroad lines and the expansion of the postal system, helped to get new products to consumers.

Growing directly out of these services, the successful Chicago-based mail-order houses drew rural and urban consumers into a common marketplace. Sears,

# MAP EXPLORATION

To explore an interactive version of this map, go to **http://www.prenhall.com/faraghertlc/map19.1**

**MAP 19.1**

**Patterns of Industry, 1900** Industrial manufacturing concentrated in the Northeast and Midwest, whereas the raw materials for production came mostly from other parts of the nation.

WHY DID industrial patterns differ from region to region?

## QUICK REVIEW

### Growth of Industry

- 1865: $2 billion annual production of goods.

- 1900: $13 billion annual production of goods.

- Revolutions in technology and transportation made growth possible.

Roebuck and Company and Montgomery Ward offered an enormous variety of goods, from shoes to buggies to gasoline stoves and cream separators. The mail-order catalogue also returned to rural folks the fruits of their own labor, now processed and packaged for easy use. In turn, the purchases made by farm families through the Sears catalogue sent cash flowing into Chicago.

The chain store achieved similar economies of scale. By 1900, a half-dozen grocery chains had sprung up. Other chains selling drugs, costume jewelry, shoes, cigars, and furniture soon appeared, offering a greater selection of goods and lower prices than the small, independent stores.

Opening shortly after the Civil War, department stores began to take up much of the business formerly enjoyed by specialty shops, offering a spectrum of services that included restaurants, rest rooms, ticket agencies, nurseries, reading rooms, and post offices. Elegantly appointed with imported carpets, sweeping marble staircases, and crystal chandeliers, the department store raised retailing to new heights.

Advertising lured customers to the department stores, the chains, and the independent neighborhood stores. The advertising revolution began in 1869, when Francis Wayland Ayer founded the earliest advertising agency. Ayer's managed the accounts of such companies as Montgomery Ward, Wanamaker's Department Store, Singer Sewing Machines, and the National Biscuit Company. With the help of this new sales tool, gross revenues of retailers raced upward from $8 million in 1860 to $102 million in 1900.

## INTEGRATION, COMBINATION, AND MERGER

The business community aspired to exercise greater control of the economy and to enlarge the commercial empire. From the source of raw materials to the organization of production, from the conditions of labor to the climate of public opinion, business leaders acted shrewdly. Economic cycles alternating between rapid growth and sharp decline also promoted the rise of big business. Major economic setbacks in 1873 and 1893 wiped out weaker competitors, allowing the strongest firms to rebound swiftly and to expand their sales and scale of operation during the recovery period.

Businesses grew in two distinct, if overlapping, ways. Through *vertical integration* a firm gained control of production at every step of the way—from raw materials through processing to the transporting and merchandising of the finished items. In 1899, the United Fruit Company began to build a network of wholesale houses in the United States, and within two years it had opened distribution centers in twenty-one major cities. Eventually, it controlled an elaborate system of Central American plantations and temperature-controlled shipping and storage facilities for its highly perishable bananas.

The second means of growth, *horizontal combination*, entailed gaining control of the market for a single product. The most famous case was the Standard Oil Company, founded by John D. Rockefeller in 1870. Operating out of Cleveland in a highly competitive but lucrative field, Rockefeller first secured preferential rates from railroads eager to ensure a steady supply of oil. He then convinced or coerced other local oil operators to sell their stock to him. The Standard Oil Trust, established in 1882, controlled over 90 percent of the nation's oil-refining industry (see Seeing History).

In 1890, Congress passed the Sherman Antitrust Act to restore competition by encouraging small business and outlawing "every . . . combination . . . in restraint of trade or commerce." Ironically, the courts interpreted the law in ways that inhibited the organization of trade unions and actually helped the consolidation of business. More than 2,600 firms vanished between 1898 and 1902 alone.

## THE GOSPEL OF WEALTH

Ninety percent of the nation's business leaders were Protestant, and the majority attended church services regularly. They attributed their personal achievement to hard work and perseverance and made these the principal tenets of a new faith that imbued the pursuit of wealth with old-time religious zeal.

One version of this "**gospel of wealth**" justified the ruthless behavior of the entrepreneurs who accumulated unprecedented wealth and power through shady deals and conspiracies. Speculator Jay Gould, known in the popular press as the

**The Marshall Field** building constructed in Chicago's Loop between 1893 and 1915 came to occupy an entire block to reign as the world's largest department store. In addition to all kinds of fine goods, the retail store offered a host of personal amenities, such as lunch and tea rooms, travel agencies, hair salons, and even personal shoppers. The photograph here features its 6,000 square foot mosaic dome, which was surfaced with 1.6 million pieces of iridescent Tiffany art glass.

 **18–2**
Henry George, *Progress and Poverty* (1879)

**Vertical integration** The consolidation of numerous production functions, from the extraction of the raw materials to the distribution and marketing of the finished products, under the direction of one firm.
**Horizontal combination** The merger of competitors in the same industry.
**Gospel of wealth** Thesis that hard work and perseverance lead to wealth, implying that poverty is a character flaw.

"Worst Man in the World," wrung his fortune, it was widely believed, from the labor of others. He rose quickly from his modest origins through a series of unsavory financial maneuvers. At his death, one obituary described Jay Gould as "an incarnation of cupidity and sordidness," whose life symbolized "idolatrous homage [to] the golden calf."

Andrew Carnegie—the "Richest Man in the World"—offered a strikingly different model. Carnegie built an empire in steel. A genius at vertical integration, he undercut his competitors by using the latest technology and designing his own system of cost analysis. By 1900, Carnegie managed the most efficient steel mills in the world, which accounted for one-third of the nation's output. When he sold out to J. P. Morgan's new United States Steel Corporation in 1901, his personal share of the proceeds came to $225 million.

Carnegie was well known as a civic leader. From one point of view, he was a factory despot who underpaid his employees and ruthlessly managed their working conditions. But to the patrons of the public libraries, art museums, concert halls, colleges, and universities that he funded, Carnegie appeared to be the single greatest philanthropist of the age. Late in his life, he outlined his personal philosophy in a popular essay, *The Gospel of Wealth* (1889), explaining that "there is no genuine, praiseworthy success in life if you are not honest, truthful, and fair-dealing." By the time he died, he had given away his massive personal fortune.

Whether following the rough road of Gould or the smooth path of Carnegie, the business community worked together to fashion the new conservative ideology of social Darwinism, which purportedly explained, and justified, why some Americans grew rich while others remained poor. Grafted on the biological theory of evolution propounded by the famed British naturalist Charles Darwin, social Darwinism raised the principle of the "survival of the fittest" as an ideal for modern society. In 1883, the Yale professor William Graham Sumner published an essay entitled *What Social Classes Owe to Each Other*, wherein he argued that to tamper with the "natural" order by establishing welfare programs to help the poor or redistributing wealth in any way would be hazardous to society.

# LABOR IN THE AGE OF BIG BUSINESS

L ike the gospel of wealth, the "gospel of work" affirmed the dignity of hard work, the virtue of thrift, and the importance of individual initiative. But unlike business leaders, the philosophers of American working people did not believe in riches as the proof of work well done or in the lust for power as the driving force of progress. On the contrary, they contended that honesty and competence should be the badge of all morally responsible citizens.

Behind the "gospel of work" stood the reality of the rising industrial order, especially its new systems of production that were, in turn, enabled by new technologies. The impact of the new order on the lives of working people would be nothing less than revolutionary. Increasingly, Americans made their livelihoods by producing, not for their own subsistence, but exclusively for the market, and they earned wages in return for their labor. Big business thus found its mirror image in the labor movement spawned by the consolidation of the wage system.

## THE WAGE SYSTEM

The accelerating growth of industry, especially the steady mechanization of production, dramatically changed employer–employee relations and created new categories of workers. Both in turn fostered competition among workers and created conditions often hazardous to health. In many occupations—meat processing,

---

**WHAT WERE** the sources of the new labor being recruited for factory work in Gilded Age America?

**myhistorylab**

Review Summary

# The Standard Oil Company

John D. Rockefeller, who formed the Standard Oil Company in 1870, sought to control all aspects of the industry, from the transportation of crude oil to the marketing and distribution of the final products.

Rockefeller's best-known critic was Ida Tarbell. In 1904 she published *The History of the Standard Oil Company*, first in serial form in the popular *McClure's Magazine* and later as a book. Tarbell's muckraking exposé attracted a great deal of attention. But even more popular were political cartoons depicting Rockefeller's stranglehold on the entire oil industry.

*Puck* magazine, which had been founded in 1871 by Joseph Keppler, an immigrant from Austria, held up Rockefeller and his company to ridicule. This cartoon, published in *Puck* in 1904, shows Standard Oil as a sinister octopus, wrapping its arms around the White House and Congress as well as workers and even the denizens of Wall Street. In 1911, in response to an antitrust suit, the Supreme Court ordered the company to break up. The modern corporations Exxon, Mobil, Chevron, Amoco, and Sohio (some of which have recently merged) all descended from Rockefeller's Standard Oil.

**WHAT DOES** this cartoon tell us about Rockefeller's reputation at the turn of the twentieth century? What does it suggest about Americans' feelings about the trusts?

This engraving of steel manufacturing at Andrew Carnegie's plant in 1886 features a Bessemer Converter, which converts molten pig iron into steel. The process was named after Sir Henry Bessemer of Sheffield, England, who first patented the process in 1855.

**myhistorylab**

**Exploring America:** *French Canadian Controversy*

**19–1**
*Memorial of the Chinese Six Companies to U.S. Grant, President of the United States* (1876)

**Chinese Exclusion Act** Act which suspended Chinese immigration, limited the civil rights of resident Chinese, and forbade their naturalization.

clothing and textile manufacturing, cigar making, and mining, for example—immigrants from Europe and Asia predominated by the end of the century.

For most craft workers, the new system destroyed long-standing practices and chipped away at their customary autonomy. Managers now constantly supervised workers, set the pace of production and rate of payment, and introduced new, faster machinery that made many skills obsolete. In the woodworking trades, highly skilled cabinetmakers, who for generations had brought their own tools to the factory, were largely replaced with "green hands"—immigrants, including many women—who with only minimal training and close supervision could operate new woodworking machines at cheaper rates of pay.

Not all trades conformed to this pattern. The garment industry, for example, grew at a very fast pace in New York, Boston, Chicago, Philadelphia, Cleveland, and St. Louis but retained older systems of labor along with the new. The highly mechanized factories employed hundreds of thousands of young immigrant women, while the outwork system, established well before the Civil War, contracted ever-larger numbers of families to work in their homes on sewing machines or by hand.

Industrial expansion also offered new opportunities for women to work outside the home, and many young women fled the family farm for the factory. African American and immigrant women found employment in trades least affected by technological advances, such as domestic service. In contrast, English-speaking white women moved into the better-paying clerical and sales positions in the rapidly expanding business sector. After the typewriter and telephone came into widespread use in the 1890s, the number of women employed in office work rose even faster. At the turn of the century, 8.6 million women worked outside their homes—nearly triple the number in 1870.

By contrast, African American men found themselves excluded from many fields. In Cleveland, for example, the number of black carpenters declined after 1870, just as the volume of construction was rapidly increasing. African American men were also systematically driven from restaurant service and barred from newer trades such as boilermaking, plumbing, electrical work, and paperhanging, which European immigrants secured for themselves.

Discriminatory or exclusionary practices fell hardest on workers recruited earlier from China. A potent and racist anti-Chinese movement organized to protest "cheap" Chinese labor and to demand a halt to Chinese immigration. By the 1870s white rioters were insistently calling for deportation measures and razing Chinese neighborhoods. In 1882, Congress passed the **Chinese Exclusion Act**, which restricted Chinese immigration by barring laborers, limited the civil rights of resident Chinese, and forbade their naturalization.

For even the best-placed wage earners, the new work-place could be unhealthy, even dangerous. Factory owners often failed to mark high-voltage wires, locked fire doors, and allowed the emission of toxic fumes. Moreover, machines ran faster in American factories than anywhere else in the world, and workers who could not keep up or suffered serious injury found themselves without a job.

Even under less hazardous conditions, workers complained about the tedium of performing repetitive tasks for many hours each day. Although federal employees had been granted the eight-hour day in 1868, most workers still toiled upward of ten to twelve hours. "Life in a factory," one textile operative grumbled, "is perhaps, with the exception of prison life, the most monotonous life a human being can live." Nor could glamour be found in the work of saleswomen in the elegant department stores. Clerks could not sit down, despite workdays as long as sixteen hours in the busy season, or hold "unnecessary conversations" with customers or other clerks.

Moreover, steady employment was rare. Between 1866 and 1897, fourteen years of prosperity stood against seventeen years of hard times. The major depressions of 1873–79 and 1893–97 were the worst in the nation's history up to that time. Three "minor" recessions (1866–67, 1883–85, and 1890–91) did not seem insignificant to the millions who lost their jobs.

## THE KNIGHTS OF LABOR

The Noble and Holy Order of the **Knights of Labor**, founded by a group of Philadelphia garment cutters in 1869, grew to become the largest labor organization in the nineteenth century. The order sought to bring together wage earners, regardless of skill. The Knights endorsed a variety of reform measures—the restriction of child labor, a graduated income tax, more land set aside for homesteading, the abolition of contract labor, and monetary reform—to offset the power of the industrialists. They believed that the "producing classes," once freed from the grip of corporate monopoly and the curses of ignorance and alcohol, would transform the United States into a genuinely democratic society.

The Knights sought to overturn the wage system and, as an alternative, they promoted producers' cooperatives. In these factories, workers collectively made all decisions on prices charged for goods and shared all the profits. Local assemblies launched thousands of small co-ops. The Knights also ran small cooperative cigar shops and grocery stores, often housed in their own assembly buildings. Successful for a time, most cooperatives could not compete against the heavily capitalized enterprises and ultimately failed.

For women, the Knights of Labor created a special department within the organization "to investigate the abuses to which our sex is subjected by unscrupulous employers, to agitate the principles which our Order teaches of equal pay for equal work and the abolition of child labor." At the 1886 convention, delegates approved this plan. With perhaps 65,000 women members at its peak, the Knights ran daycare centers and occasionally even set up cooperative kitchens to reduce the drudgery of cooking.

E PLURIBUS UNUM (EXCEPT THE CHINESE).

**Thomas Nast (1840–1902),** the most famous political cartoonist of the late nineteenth century, used his art to comment on pressing political issues, such as the plight of former slaves during Reconstruction, the evils of machine politics, and the rivalry between the national political parties. His drawings were made into wood engravings that were then printed in newspapers and popular magazines. In this cartoon, published in *Harper's Weekly*, April 1, 1882, Nast shows America welcoming all immigrants except Chinese.

**Knights of Labor** Labor union founded in 1869 that included skilled and unskilled workers irrespective of race or gender.

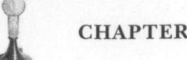

The Knights reached their peak during the great campaign for a shorter workday. The organization grew from a few thousand in 1880 to nearly three-quarters of a million six years later. The Knights welcomed workers usually excluded by other unions. Nearly 3,000 women formed their own "ladies assemblies" or joined mixed locals. The Knights also organized African American workers—20,000 to 30,000 nationally—mainly in separate assemblies within the organization. Chinese workers, however, were barred from membership.

The Haymarket affair in Chicago, where the Knights were headquartered, virtually crushed the organization. Local employers' associations successfully pooled funds to rid their factories of troublesome organizers and announced that companies would no longer bargain with unions. The wage system had triumphed.

## THE AMERICAN FEDERATION OF LABOR

The events of 1886 also signaled the rise of a very different kind of organization, the **American Federation of Labor (AFL)**. Unlike the Knights, the AFL accepted the wage system. Following a strategy of "pure and simple unionism," the AFL sought recognition of its union status to bargain with employers for better working conditions, higher wages, and shorter hours. In return, it offered compliant firms the benefit of amenable day-to-day relations with the most highly skilled wage earners. Only if companies refused to bargain in good faith would union members resort to strikes.

The new federation rapidly pushed ahead of the rival Knights by organizing craft workers. AFL president Samuel Gompers disregarded unskilled workers, racial minorities, and immigrants, believing they were impossible to organize and even unworthy of membership. He also believed in the "family wage," a wage paid to a male household head that would keep women and children comfortable

**American Federation of Labor (AFL)** Union formed in 1886 that organized skilled workers along craft lines and emphasized a few workplace issues rather than a broad social program.

**At the 1886** General Assembly of the Knights of Labor, which met in Richmond, Virginia, sixteen women attended as delegates. Elizabeth Rodgers, the first woman in Chicago to join the Knights and the first woman to serve as a master workman in a district assembly, attended with her two-week-old daughter. The convention established a Department of Women's Work and appointed Leonora M. Barry, a hosiery worker, as general investigator.

within the confines of domesticity. Women, Gompers insisted, did not belong in the factory, where they would serve only to lower wages.

Rank-and-file AFL members did not always share Gompers's opinions, and they often revived some of the best qualities of the Knights of Labor. They provided support to strikers, gathered votes for pro-labor political candidates, sponsored social activities, and published their own weekly newspapers.

Although the AFL represented only a small minority of working Americans—about 10 percent at the end of the century—local unions often played important roles in their communities. They may not have been able to slow the steady advance of mass production, which diminished the craft worker's autonomy and eliminated some of the most desirable jobs, but AFL members managed to make their presence felt. Local politicians courted their votes, and Labor Day, first celebrated in the 1880s, became a national holiday in 1894.

## THE NEW SOUTH

Physically and financially devastated by the war, the South remained economically stagnant, its per capita wealth only 27 percent of that of the northeastern states. While a few urban centers moved very slowly into the era of modern industry, the countryside receded into greater isolation and poverty. The southern economy in general was held back by dependence on northern finance capital, continued reliance on cotton production, and the legacy of slavery.

### AN INTERNAL COLONY

Northern investors secured huge concessions from southern state legislatures, including land, forest, and mineral rights and large tax exemptions. Exploiting the incentives, railroad companies laid more than 22,000 miles of new track, connecting the region to national markets and creating new cities. By 1890, a score of large railroad companies, centered mainly in New York, held more than half of all the track in the South.

Northerners also employed various means to protect their investments from southern competition. By the late 1870s, southern merchants, with help from foreign investors, had begun to run iron factories around Birmingham, Alabama. Southern iron production was soon encroaching on the northeastern market. To stave off this competition, Andrew Carnegie ordered the railroads to charge higher freight fees to Birmingham's iron producers. New York bankers later succeeded in expatriating Birmingham's profits through stock ownership in southern firms. After the turn of the century, U.S. Steel simply bought out the local merchants and took over much of Birmingham's production.

Beyond iron or steel and textiles, southern industry remained largely extractive and, like the South itself, rural. Turpentine and lumbering businesses pushed ever farther into diminishing pine forests, the sawmills and distilleries moving with them. Toward the end of the century, fruit canning and sugar refining flourished. For the most part, southern enterprises mainly produced raw materials for consumption or use in the North, thereby perpetuating the economic imbalance between the sections.

The governing role of capital investments from outside the region reinforced long-standing relationships. Even rapid industrialization—in iron, railroads, and textiles—did not carry the same consequences achieved in the North. Industrialization in the South reinforced, rather than diminished, the region's status as the nation's internal colony.

**HOW DID** the development of Southern industry affect the lives of African Americans living in the South?

**myhistorylab**
Review Summary

## SOUTHERN LABOR

The advance of southern industry did little to improve the working lives of most African Americans, who made up more than one-third of the region's population. Although the majority continued to work in agriculture, large numbers found jobs in industries such as the railroad. In booming cities like Atlanta, they even gained skilled positions as bricklayers, carpenters, and painters. For the most part, however, African Americans were limited to unskilled, low-paying jobs. Nearly all African American women who earned wages did so as household workers; girls as young as ten worked as domestics or as nurses for white children.

Most trade unions refused membership to black workers. Locals of the all-white carpenters' union maintained a segregation policy so absolute that if too few members were available for a job, the union would send for out-of-town white workers rather than employ local members of the black carpenters' union. In an Atlanta mill in 1897, 1,400 white women operatives went on strike when the company proposed to hire two black spinners.

Wages throughout the South were low for both black and white workers. Southern textile workers' wages were barely half those of New Englanders. Black men earned at or below the poverty line of $300 per year, while black women rarely earned more than $120 and white women about $220 annually. The poorest paid workers were children, the mainstay of southern mill labor.

As industry expanded throughout the nation, so too did the number of children earning wages. This was especially so in the South. Traditions rooted in the agricultural economy reinforced the practice of using the labor of all family members, even the very young. Seasonal labor, such as picking crops or grinding sugarcane, put families on the move, making formal education all but impossible. Not until well into the twentieth century did compulsory school attendance laws effectively restrict child labor in the South.

A system of convict labor also thrived in the South. Bituminous coal mines and public work projects of all kinds, especially in remote areas, employed disciplinary methods and created living and working conditions reminiscent of slavery. African Americans constituted up to 90 percent of the convict workforce.

## THE TRANSFORMATION OF PIEDMONT COMMUNITIES

The impact of modern industry was nowhere greater than in the Piedmont, the region extending from southern Virginia and the central Carolinas into northern Alabama and Georgia. After 1870, long-established farms and plantations gave way to railroad tracks, textile factories, numerous mill villages, and a few sizable cities. Once the South's backcountry, the Piedmont now surpassed New England in the production of yarn and cloth to stand first in the world.

Rural poverty and the appeal of a new life encouraged many farm families to strike out for a mill town. Those with the least access to land and credit—mainly widows and their children and single women—were the first to go into the mills. Then families sent their children. Some families worked in the mills on a seasonal basis, between planting and harvesting.

**The processing of** raw tobacco employed thousands of African American women, who sorted, stripped, stemmed, and hung tobacco leaves as part of the redrying process. After mechanization was introduced, white women took jobs as cigarette rollers, but black women kept the worst, most monotonous jobs in the tobacco factories. The women shown in this photograph are stemming tobacco in a Virginia factory while their white male supervisor oversees their labor.

But as the agricultural crisis deepened, more and more people abandoned the countryside entirely for what they called "public work."

A typical mill community was made up of rows of single-family houses, a small school, several churches, a company-owned store, and the home of the super-intendent, who governed everyone's affairs. Millworkers frequently complained that they had no private life at all. A federal report published shortly after the turn of the century concluded that "all the affairs of the village and the conditions of living of all the people are regulated entirely by the mill company. Practically speaking, the company owns everything and controls everything, and to a large extent controls everybody in the mill village."

Mill superintendents also relied on schoolteachers and clergy to set the tone of community life. They hired and paid the salaries of Baptist and Methodist min-isters to preach a faith encouraging workers to be thrifty, orderly, temperate, and hardworking. The schools, similarly subsidized by the company, reinforced the lesson of moral and social discipline required of industrial life and encouraged stu-dents to follow their parents into the mill. But it was mainly young children between six and eight years old who attended school. When more hands were needed in the mill, superintendents plucked out those youngsters and sent them to join their older brothers and sisters who were already at work.

## THE INDUSTRIAL CITY

Before the Civil War, manufacturing had centered in the countryside, in new factory towns such as Lowell, Massachusetts, and Troy, New York. By the end of the nineteenth century, 90 percent of all manufacturing took place in cities. The metropolis stood at the center of the growing industrial economy, a magnet drawing raw material, capital, and labor, and a key distribution point for manufactured goods throughout the nation and worldwide. The industrial city became the home of nearly 20 million immigrants, mainly the so-called "new immigrants" from southern and eastern Europe, who hoped to escape famine, political upheaval, or religious persecution in their homelands or simply make a better life for themselves and their families.

### POPULATING THE CITY

The population of cities grew at double the rate of the nation's population as a whole. In 1860, only sixteen cities had more than 50,000 residents. By 1890, one-third of all Americans were city dwellers. Eleven cities claimed more than 250,000 people (see Table 19.1).

### TABLE 19.1

## A Growing Urban Population

|  | 1870 | 1880 | 1890 | 1900 |
|---|---|---|---|---|
| U.S. population | 35,558,000 | 50,156,000 | 62,947,000 | 75,995,000 |
| Urban population | 9,902,000 | 14,130,000 | 22,106,000 | 30,160,000 |
| Percent urban | 25.7 | 28.2 | 35.1 | 39.7 |
| Percent rural | 74.3 | 71.8 | 64.9 | 60.3 |

Note that during each decade, the U.S. population as a whole grew between 20 and 30 percent. Figures in the table have been rounded to the nearest thousand.

Robert G. Barrows, "Urbanizing America," in Charles W. Calhoun, ed., *The Gilded Age* (Wilmington DE, 1996), 93, 95.

The nation's largest cities—New York, Chicago, Philadelphia, St. Louis, Boston, and Baltimore—achieved international fame for the size and diversity of their populations. Many of their new residents had migrated from rural communities within the United States. Between 1870 and 1910, an average of nearly 7,000 African Americans moved north each year, hoping to escape the poverty and oppression in the South and to find better-paying jobs. By the end of the century, nearly 80 percent of African Americans in the North lived in urban areas.

Immigrants and their children were the major source of urban population growth in the late nineteenth century. Most of those in the first wave of immigration, before the Civil War, had settled in the countryside. In contrast, in the last half of the nineteenth century, it was the industrial city that drew the so-called new immigrants, who came primarily from eastern and southern Europe. By the turn of the century, Chicago had more Germans than all but a few German cities and more Poles than most Polish cities; New York had more Italians than a handful of the largest Italian cities, and Boston had nearly as many Irish as Dublin. In almost every group except the Irish, men outnumbered women (see Map 19.2).

Like rural migrants, immigrants came to the American city to take advantage of the expanding opportunities for employment. Many intended to work hard, save money, and return to their families in the Old Country. In the 1880s, for example, nearly half of all Italian, Greek, and Serbian men returned to their native lands. Others could not return to their homelands or did not wish to. Jews, for instance, had emigrated to escape persecution in Russia and Russian-dominated Polish and Romanian lands.

Of all groups, Jews had the most experience with urban life. Forbidden to own land in most parts of Europe and boxed into *shtetls* (villages), Jews had also formed thriving urban communities in Vilna, Berlin, London, and Vienna. Many had worked in garment manufacturing, in London's East End, for example, and followed a path to American cities like New York, Rochester, Philadelphia, or Chicago where the needle trades flourished.

Other groups, the majority coming from rural parts of Europe, sought out their kinfolk in American cities, where they could most easily find housing and employment. Bohemians settled largely in Chicago, Pittsburgh, and Cleveland. Still other groups tended toward cities dominated by fishing, shoemaking, or even glassblowing, a craft carried directly from the Old Country. Italians, the most numerous among the new immigrants, settled mainly in northeastern cities, laying railroad track, excavating subways, and erecting buildings.

Resettlement in an American city did not necessarily mark the end of the immigrants' travels. Newcomers, both native-born and immigrant, moved frequently from one neighborhood to another and from one city to another. As manufacturing advanced outward from the city center, working populations followed. American cities experienced a total population turnover three or four times during each decade of the last half of the century.

## THE URBAN LANDSCAPE

Faced with a population explosion and an unprecedented building boom, the cities encouraged the creation of many beautiful and useful structures, including commercial offices, sumptuous homes, and efficient public services. At the same time, cities did little to improve the conditions of the majority of the population, who worked in dingy factories and lived in crowded **tenements**. Open space decreased as American cities grew. City officials usually lacked any master plan, save the idea of endless expansion. Factories often occupied the best sites, typically near waterways, where goods could be easily transported and chemical wastes dumped.

---

**QUICK REVIEW**

**Big Cities**

- Cities grew at double the rate of the nation as a whole.
- Immigrants and their children were the major source of urban population growth.
- After the Civil War, most new immigrants settled in cities.

**Tenements**  Four- to six-story residential dwellings, once common in New York, built on tiny lots without regard to providing ventilation or light.

## MAP EXPLORATION

To explore an interactive version of this map, go to **http://www.prenhall.com/faraghertlc/map19.2**

**MAP 19.2**

**Population of Foreign Birth by Region, 1880**    European immigrants after the Civil War settled primarily in the industrial districts of the northern Midwest and parts of the Northeast. French Canadians continued to settle in Maine, Cubans in Florida, and Mexicans in the Southwest.

Clifford L. Lord and Elizabeth H. Lord, *Lord & Lord Historical Atlas of the United States* (New York: Holt, 1953).

WHY DID immigrants tend to settle in some regions and not in others?

Built after the Civil War, the tenement was designed to maximize the use of space. A typical tenement sat on a lot 25 by 100 feet and rose to five stories. There were four families on each floor, each with three rooms. By 1890, New York's Lower East Side packed more than 700 people per acre into back-to-back buildings, producing one of the highest population densities in the world.

The industrial city established a new style of commercial and civic architecture. Using fireproof materials, expanded foundations, and internal metal construction, the era's talented architects focused on the factory and office building. Concentrating as many offices as possible in the downtown areas, they fashioned hundreds of buildings from steel, sometimes decorating them with elaborate wrought-iron facades. The office building could rise seven, ten, even twenty stories high, and with the invention of the safety elevator, people and goods could easily be moved vertically.

Architects played a key role in the late nineteenth-century City Beautiful movement. Influenced by American wealth and its enhanced role in the global

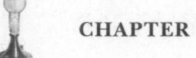

economy, they turned to the monumental or imperial style common in European cities, laying grand concrete boulevards at enormous public cost. New sports amphitheaters spread pride in the city's accomplishments. New schools, court-houses, capitol buildings, hospitals, museums, and huge new art galleries, muse-ums, and concert halls promoted urban excitement as well as cultural uplift. The imperial style also increased congestion and noise, making the city a more desir-able place to visit than to live.

Like the railroad, but on a smaller scale, streetcars and elevated railroads changed business dramatically, because they moved traffic of many different kinds—information, people, and goods—faster and farther than before. By 1895, more than 800 communities operated systems of electrically powered cars or trol-leys. In 1902, New York opened its subway system, which would grow to become the largest in the nation.

## THE CITY AND THE ENVIRONMENT

By making it possible for a great number of workers to live in communities distant from their place of employment, mass transportation allowed the metropolitan region to grow dramatically. By the end of the nineteenth century, suburban trains were bringing nearly 100,000 riders daily into the city of Chicago. Suburbs sprang up outside the major cities, offering many professional workers quiet residential retreats from the city's busy and increasingly polluted downtown.

Electric trolleys eliminated the tons of waste from horsecars that had for decades fouled city streets. But the new rail systems also increased congestion and created new safety hazards for pedestrians. During the 1890s, 600 people were killed each year by Chicago's trains. Elevated trains, designed to avoid these prob-lems, placed entire communities under the shadow of noisy and rickety wooden platforms. Despite many technological advances, the quality of life in the nation's cities did not necessarily improve.

Modern water and sewer systems now constituted a hidden city of pipes and wires, mirroring the growth of the visible city above ground. These advances, which brought indoor plumbing to most homes, did not, however, eradicate seri-ous environmental or health problems. Most cities continued to dump sewage into nearby bodies of water. Moreover, most municipal governments established separate clean-water systems through the use of reservoirs rather than outlawing upriver dump-ing by factories. Downriver communities began to complain about unendurable stench from the polluted rivers and streams.

The unrestricted burning of coal to fuel the railroads and to heat factories and homes after 1880 greatly intensified urban air pollution. Noise levels continued to rise in the most com-pacted living and industrial areas. Overcrowded conditions and inadequate sanitary facilities bred tuberculosis, smallpox, and scarlet fever, among other contagious diseases. Children's diseases like whooping cough and measles spread rapidly through poor neighborhoods. Only after the turn of the century, amid an intensive campaign against municipal corruption, did laws and administrative practices address the serious prob-lems of public health (see Chapter 21).

**18–10**
United States Sanitary Commission, *Sketch of Its Purposes* (1864)

**In his watercolor** *The Bowery at Night*, painted in 1885, W. Louis Sonntag Jr. shows a New York City scene trans-formed by electric light. Electricity transformed the city in other ways as well, as seen in the electric streetcars and elevated railroad.

Meanwhile, the distance between the city and the countryside narrowed. Nearby rural lands not destined for private housing or commercial development became sites for water treatment and sewage plants, garbage dumps, and grave-yards—services essential to the city's growing population.

# THE RISE OF CONSUMER SOCIETY

The growth of industry and the spread of cities promoted—and depended on—the consumption of mass-produced goods. During the final third of the nineteenth century, the standard of living climbed, although unevenly and erratically. Real wages (pay in relation to the cost of living) rose, fostering improvements in nutrition, clothing, and housing. Meanwhile, prices dropped. More and cheaper products came into the reach of all but the very poor. Food from the farms became more abundant and varied—grains for bread or beer; poultry, pork, and beef; fresh fruits and vegetables from California. Although many Americans continued to acknowledge the moral value of hard work, thrift, and self-sacrifice, the explosion of consumer goods and services promoted sweeping changes in behavior and beliefs, although in vastly and increasingly different ways.

## "CONSPICUOUS CONSUMPTION"

Labeled the **"Gilded Age"** by humorist and social critic Mark Twain, the era following the Civil War favored the growth of a new business class that pursued both money and leisure and formed national networks to consolidate their power. Business leaders built diverse stock portfolios and often served simultaneously on the boards of several corporations. Similarly, they intertwined their interests by joining the same religious, charitable, athletic, and professional societies. Their wives and children vacationed together in the sumptuous new seashore and mountain resorts, while they themselves made deals in the exclusive social clubs and on the golf links of suburban country clubs. Just as Dun and Bradstreet ranked the leading corporations, the Social Register identified the 500 families that controlled most of the nation's wealth.

According to economist and social critic Thorstein Veblen, the rich had created a new style of **"conspicuous consumption."** The Chicago mansion of real estate tycoon Potter Palmer, for example, was constructed without exterior door-knobs. Not only could no one enter uninvited, but a visitor's calling card supposedly passed through the hands of twenty-seven servants before admittance was allowed. The women who oversaw these elaborate households served as measures of their husbands' status, according to Veblen, by adorning themselves in jewels, furs, and dresses of the latest Paris design.

Toward the end of the century, the wealthy added a dramatic public dimension to the "high life." New York's Waldorf-Astoria hotel, which opened in 1897, incorporated the grandeur of European royalty but with an important difference. Because rich Americans wanted to be watched, the elegantly appointed corridors and restaurants were visible to the public through huge windows. The New York rich also established a unique custom to welcome the New Year: they opened wide the curtains of their Fifth Avenue mansions so that passersby could marvel at the elegant decor.

The wealthy became the leading patrons of the arts as well as the chief procurers of art treasures from Europe and Asia. They provided the bulk of funds for the new symphonies, operas, and ballet companies, which soon rivaled those of Continental Europe. Nearly all major museums and art galleries, including the Boston Museum of Fine Arts, the Philadelphia Museum of Art, the Art Institute of Chicago, and the Metropolitan Museum of Art in New York, were founded during the last decades of the nineteenth century.

WHAT ACCOUNTS for the rise of a consumer society and how did various groups participate in its development?

**myhistorylab**
Review Summary

 **18–3**
*The Gilded Age* (1880)

 **18–6**
Edward Bellamy, from *Looking Backward* (1888)

**Gilded Age**   Term applied to late nineteenth-century America that refers to the shallow display and worship of wealth characteristic of that period.

**Conspicuous consumption**   Highly visible displays of wealth and consumption.

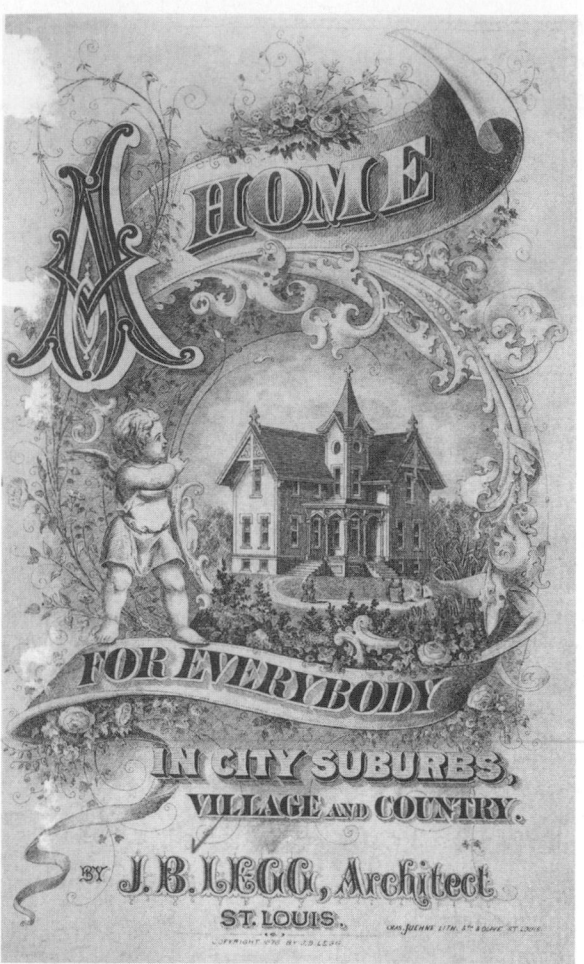

**Taken from J. B.** Legg's architecture book, this page illustrates the ideal suburban home. His book, published in 1876, was aimed at the prospering middle class.

## SELF-IMPROVEMENT AND THE MIDDLE CLASS

A new middle class, very different from its predecessor, formed during the last half of the century. The older middle class comprised the owners or superintendents of small businesses, doctors, lawyers, teachers, and ministers and their families. The new middle class included these professionals but also the growing number of salaried employees—the managers, technicians, clerks, and engineers who worked in the complex web of corporations and government. Long hours of labor earned their families a modest status and sufficient income to live securely in style and comfort.

By the end of the century, many middle-class families were nestled in suburban retreats far from the noise, filth, and dangers of the city. This peaceful domestic setting, with its manicured lawns and well-placed shrubs, afforded both privacy and rejuvenation as well as the separation of business from leisure and the breadwinner from his family for most of the day. Assisted by modern transportation systems, men often traveled one to two hours each day, five or six days a week, to their city offices and back again. Women and children stayed behind.

Middle-class women devoted a large part of their day to care of the home. They frequently employed one or two servants but relied increasingly on the many new appliances to get their work done. Improvements in the kitchen stove, such as the conversion from wood fuel to gas, saved a lot of time. Yet, simultaneously, with the widespread circulation of cookbooks and recipes in newspapers and magazines, as well as the availability of new foods, the preparation of meals became more complex and time-consuming. New devices such as the eggbeater speeded some familiar tasks, but the era's fancy culinary practices offset any gains in saving time. Similarly, the new carpet sweepers surpassed the broom in efficiency, but the fashionable high-napped carpeting demanded more care. Thus, rather than diminishing with technological innovation, household work expanded to fill the time available.

Almost exclusively white, Anglo-Saxon, and Protestant, the new middle class embraced "culture" not for purposes of conspicuous consumption but as a means of self-improvement. Whole families visited the new museums and art galleries. The middle class also provided the bulk of patrons for the new public libraries.

Middle-class families applied the same standards to their leisure activities. What one sporting-goods entrepreneur rightly called the "gospel of exercise" involved men and women in calisthenics and outdoor activities, not so much for pleasure as for physical and mental discipline. Hiking was a favorite among both men and women and required entirely new outfits: for women, loose upper garments and skirts short enough to prevent dragging; for men, rugged outerwear and jaunty hats. Soon men and women began camping out, with almost enough amenities to recreate a middle-class home in the woods.

Leisure became the special province of middle-class childhood. Removed from factories and shops and freed from many domestic chores, children enjoyed creative play and physical activity. The toy market boomed, and lower printing prices helped children's literature flourish. Uplifting classics such as *Little Women* and *Black Beauty* were popular.

## LIFE IN THE STREETS

Immigrants often weighed the material abundance they found in the United States against their memories of the Old Country. One could "live better" here, but only by working much harder. Embittered German immigrants called their new land *Malhuerica,* "misfortune"; Jews called it *Ama Reka,* Hebrew for "without soul"; and Slavs referred to it as *Dollaryka.*

Many newcomers, having little choice about their place of residence, concentrated in urban districts marked off by racial or ethnic lines. In San Francisco, city ordinances prevented Chinese from operating laundries in most of the city's neighborhoods, and the city's schools excluded their children. In the 1880s, Chinese San Franciscans, representing 10 percent of the city's population, crowded into a dozen blocks of restaurants, shops, and small factories known as Chinatown. In Los Angeles and San Antonio, Mexicans lived in distinctive barrios. In most cities, African American families were similarly compelled to remain in the dingiest, most crime ridden, and dangerous sections of town.

The working-class home did not necessarily ensure privacy or offer protection from the dangers of the outside world. In the tenements, families often shared their rooms with other families or paying boarders. During the summer heat, adults, children, and boarders alike competed for a sleeping place on the fire escape or roof, and all year round, noise resounded through paper-thin walls.

Whether it was a small cottage or a tenement flat, the working-class home involved women and children in routines of household labor without the aid of new mechanical devices. In addition to cooking and cleaning, women used their cramped domestic space for work that provided a small income. They gathered their children—and their husbands after a hard day's labor—to sew garments, wrap cigars, string beads, or paint vases for a contractor who paid them by the piece. And they cooked and cleaned for the boarders whose rent supplemented the family income.

Despite working people's slim resources, their combined buying power created new and important markets for consumer goods. Often they bought shoddy replicas of products sold to the middle class. Several leading clothing manufacturers specialized in inexpensive ready-to-wear items, usually copied from patterns designed for wealthier consumers but constructed hastily from flimsy materials.

The close quarters of the urban neighborhood allowed immigrants to preserve many Old World customs. In immigrant communities such as Chicago's German North Side, Pittsburgh's Poletown, New York's Lower East Side, or San Francisco's Chinatown, people usually spoke their native language while visiting friends and relatives. No organization was as important as the fraternal society, which sponsored social clubs and provided insurance benefits. Social organizations, known as *huiguan,* were especially important in preserving clan and dialect among the largely male unmarried population of Chinese San Francisco. Immigrants also re-created Old World religious institutions such as the temple, church, or synagogue, or secular institutions such as German family-style saloons or Russian Jewish tearooms. Chinese theaters, in inexpensive daily and nightly performances, presented dramas depicting historical events or explicating moral teachings and thereby preserved much of Chinese native culture. Immigrants also replicated their native cuisine and married, baptized children, and buried their dead according to Old World customs.

**The intersection of** Orchard and Hester Streets on New York's Lower East Side, photographed ca. 1905. Unlike the middle classes, who worked and played hidden away in offices and private homes, the Jewish lower-class immigrants who lived and worked in this neighborhood spent the greater part of their lives on the streets.

In the cosmopolitan cities, immigrants, by being innovative entrepreneurs as well as the best customers, helped to shape the emerging popular culture. German immigrants, for example, created Tin Pan Alley, the center of the popular music industry. They also became the first promoters of ragtime, which found its way north from Storyville, the red-light district of New Orleans. Created by African American and Creole bands, ragtime captivated those teenage offspring of immigrants who rushed to the new dance halls.

When developers realized that "wholesome fun" for the masses could pay better than upper-class leisure or lower-class vice, in 1895 they decided to transform Coney Island into a magnificent seaside park filled with ingenious amusements such as water slides, mechanized horse races, carousels, roller coasters, and fun houses. On the rides or at the nearby beach, young men and women could easily meet apart from their parents, cast off their inhibitions, and enjoy a hug or kiss. At Coney Island or at Riverview, Chicago's oldest amusement park, located on the city's North Side, millions of working-class people enjoyed cheap thrills that offset the hardships of their working lives.

# CULTURES IN CONFLICT, CULTURE IN COMMON

**WHAT ROLE** did public spaces play in late nineteenth-century popular culture?

**myhistorylab**
Review Summary

The new commercial entertainments gave Americans from various backgrounds more in common than they would otherwise have had. On New York's Lower East Side, for instance, theater blossomed with dramas that Broadway would adopt years later, while children dreamed of going "uptown" where the popular songs they heard on the streets were transcribed onto sheet music and sold in stores throughout the city. Even so, just as the changes in production fostered conflict in the forms of strikes and workers' protests, so too did the accompanying changes in the daily life of the community. Competing claims to the resources of the new urban, industrial society, such as public schools and urban parks, became more intense as the century moved to a close.

## EDUCATION

Business and civic leaders realized that the welfare of society now depended on an educated population, one possessing the skills and knowledge required to keep both industry and government running. In the last three decades of the nineteenth century, the idea of universal free schooling, at least for white children, took hold.

Public high schools, which were rare before the Civil War, increased in number, from 160 in 1870 to 6,000 by the end of the century. In Chicago alone, average daily attendance multiplied sixfold. Despite this spectacular growth, which was concentrated in urban industrial areas, as late as 1890 only 4 percent of children between the ages of fourteen and seventeen were enrolled in school, the majority of them girls planning to become teachers or office workers (See Figure 19.1) Most high schools continued to serve mainly the middle class. The expected benefits of this kind of a high school education rarely outweighed the immediate needs of working-class families who depended on their children's wages.

Higher education also expanded along several lines. Agricultural colleges formed earlier in the century developed into institutes of technology and took their places alongside the prestigious liberal arts colleges. To extend learning to the "industrial classes," Representative Justin Morrill (R., Vermont) sponsored the Morrill Federal Land Grant Act of 1862, which funded a system of state colleges and universities for teaching agriculture and mechanics "without excluding other scientific and classic studies." Still, as the overall number of colleges and universities grew from 563 in 1870 to nearly 1,000 by 1910, only 3 percent of the college-age population took advantage of these new opportunities.

This expansion benefited women, who previously had had little access to higher education. After the Civil War, a number of women's colleges were founded, beginning in 1865 with Vassar, which set the academic standard for the remainder of the century. Smith and Wellesley followed in 1875, Bryn Mawr in 1885. By the end of the century, 125 women's colleges offered a first-rate education comparable to that given to men at Harvard, Yale, or Princeton. Meanwhile, coeducation grew at an even faster rate; by 1890, 47 percent of the nation's colleges and universities admitted women. The proportion of women college students changed dramatically. Women constituted 21 percent of undergraduate enrollments in 1870, 32 percent in 1880, and 40 percent in 1910.

An even greater number of women enrolled in vocational courses. Normal schools, which offered one- or two-year programs for women who planned to become elementary school teachers, developed a collegiate character after the Civil War and had become accredited state teachers' colleges by the end of the century. Other institutions, many founded by middle-class philanthropists, also prepared women for vocations. Founded in 1877, the **Women's Educational and Industrial Union** offered a multitude of classes to Boston's wage-earning women, ranging from elementary French and German to drawing, watercolor, and oil and china paintings; to dressmaking and millinery, stenography and typing; as well as crafts less familiar to women, such as upholstering, cabinetmaking, and carpentry.

The leaders of the business community had also begun to promote manual training for working-class and immigrant boys. Trade unionists often opposed this development, preferring their own methods of apprenticeship to training programs they could not control. But local associations of merchants and manufacturers lobbied hard for "industrial education" and raised funds to supplement the public school budget. By 1895, all elementary and high schools in Chicago offered courses that trained boys for future jobs in industry and business.

The expansion of education did not benefit all Americans or benefit them all in the same way. Because African Americans were often excluded from colleges attended by white students, special colleges were founded shortly after the Civil War. All-black Atlanta and Fisk Universities both soon offered rigorous curricula in the liberal arts. Other institutions, such as Hampton, founded in 1868, specialized in vocational training, mainly in manual trades. Educator Booker T. Washington encouraged African Americans to resist "the craze for Greek and Latin learning" and to strive for practical instruction. In 1881, he founded the Tuskegee Institute in Alabama to provide industrial education and moral uplift. Black colleges, including Tuskegee, trained so many teachers that by the century's end the majority of black schools were staffed by African Americans.

## LEISURE AND PUBLIC SPACE

Most large cities set aside open land for leisure-time use by residents. New York's Central Park opened for ice-skating in 1858, providing a model for urban park systems across the United States. These parks were rolling expanses, cut across by

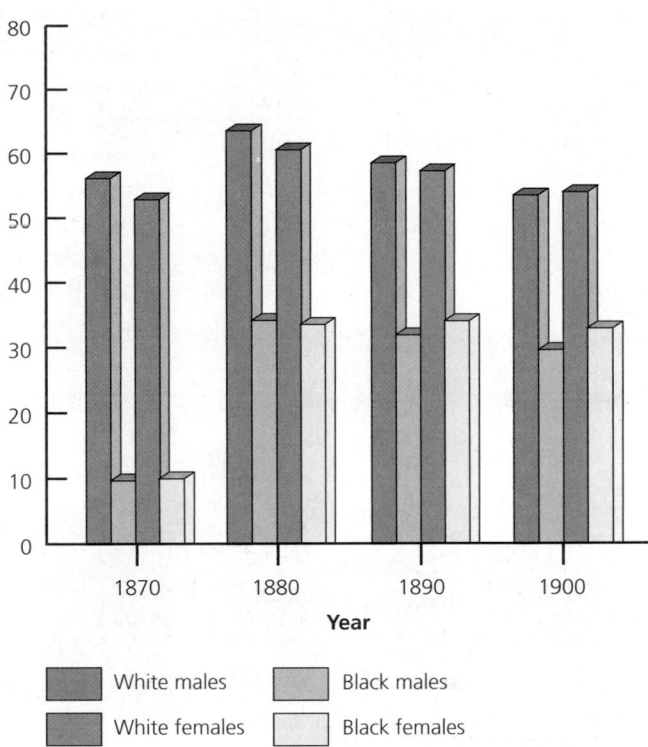

**Figure 19.1  School Enrollment of 5- to 19-Year-Olds, 1870–1900**
In the final decades of the nineteenth century, elementary and high school enrollments grew across the board but especially so for children of color and for girls.

U.S. Department of Commerce, Bureau of the Census, *Historical Statistics of the United States, Colonial Times to 1970.* U.S. Department of Education, Office of Educational Research and Improvement.

**George Washington Carver** (1864–1943), who had been born in slavery, had been invited by Booker T. Washington to direct agricultural research at the Tuskegee Institute in Alabama. A leader in development of agriculture in the New South, Carver promoted crop diversification to rejuvenate soil that was depleted by the continuous planting of cotton and encouraged the cultivation of alternative, high-protein crops such as peanuts and soybeans.

**18–4**
Richard K. Fox, from *Coney Island Frolics* (1883)

streams and pathways and footbridges and set off by groves of trees, ornamental shrubs, and neat flower gardens. According to the designers' vision, the urban middle class might find here a respite from the stresses of modern life.

The working classes had their own ideas about the use of parks and open land in their communities. Trapped in overcrowded tenements or congested neighborhoods, they wanted space for sports, picnics, and lovers' trysts. Young people openly defied ordinances that prohibited play on the grassy knolls, while their elders routinely voted against municipal bonds that did not include funds for more recreational space. Immigrant ward representatives on the Pittsburgh City Council, for instance, argued that band shells for classical music meant little to their constituents, while spaces suitable for sports meant much.

Toward the end of the century, many park administrators relaxed the rules and expanded the range of permitted activities. By this time, large numbers of the middle class had become sports enthusiasts and pressured municipal governments to turn meadowlands into tennis courts and golfing greens. In the 1890s, bicycling brought many women into the parks. Still, not all city residents enjoyed these facilities. Officials in St. Louis, for example, barred African Americans from the city's grand Forest Park and set aside the smaller Tandy Park for their use. After challenging this policy in court, African Americans won a few concessions, such as the right to picnic at any time in Forest Park and to use the golf course on Monday mornings.

## NATIONAL PASTIMES

Toward the end of the century, the younger members of the urban middle class had begun to find common ground in lower-class pastimes, especially ragtime music. Introduced to many Northerners by the African American composer Scott Joplin at the Chicago World's Fair of 1893, "rag" quickly became the staple of entertainment in the new cabarets and nightclubs. Middle-class urban dwellers began to seek out ragtime bands and congregated in nightclubs and even on the rooftops of posh hotels to listen and dance and even to drink.

Vaudeville, the most popular form of commercial entertainment since the 1880s, also bridged middle- and working-class tastes. Drawing on a variety-show tradition of singers, dancers, comedians, jugglers, and acrobats who had entertained Americans since colonial days, "vaude" became a big business that made ethnic and racial stereotypes and the daily frustrations of city life into major topics of amusement.

Sports, however, outdistanced all other commercial entertainments in appealing to all kinds of fans and managing to create a sense of national community. Baseball clubs formed in many cities, and shortly after the Civil War traveling teams with regular schedules made baseball a professional sport. The formation of the National League in 1876 encouraged other spectator sports, but for generations baseball remained the most popular.

Rowdy behavior gave the game a working-class ambience. Team owners, themselves often proprietors of local breweries, counted heavily on beer sales in the parks. Having to contend with hundreds of drunken fans, officials maintained order only with great difficulty. To attract more subdued middle-class fans, the National League raised admission prices, banned the sale of alcohol, and observed Sunday blue laws. Catering to a working-class audience, the American Association kept the price of admission low, sold liquor, and played ball on Sunday.

Baseball, like many other sports, soon became incorporated into the larger business economy. In Chicago, local merchants, such as Marshall Field, supported teams, and by the end of the 1860s there were more than fifty company-sponsored teams playing in the local leagues. By 1870, a Chicago Board of Trade team emerged as the city's first professional club, the White Stockings. Capitalized as a joint stock company, the White Stockings soon succeeded in recruiting a star pitcher from the Boston Red Stockings, Albert Spalding, who eventually became manager and then president of the team.

Spalding tightened the rules of participation in the sport. In 1879, he dictated the "reserve clause," which prevented players from negotiating a better deal and leaving the team that originally signed them. He encouraged his player-manager "Cap" Anson to forbid the White Stockings from playing against any team with an African American member. The firing of Moses "Fleet" Walker, an African American, from the Cincinnati Red Stockings in 1884 marked the first time the color line had been drawn in a major professional sport. Effectively excluded, African Americans organized their own traveling teams. In the 1920s, they formed the Negro Leagues, which produced some of the nation's finest ball players.

Players occasionally organized to regain control over their sport. They frequently complained about low wages and arbitrary rules, and like the Knights of Labor in the 1880s, they formed their own league, the Brotherhood of Professional Base Ball Players, with profits divided between participants and investors. This effort failed, partly because fans would not desert the established leagues, but mostly because successful baseball franchises demanded large quantities of capital. American sports had become big business.

As attendance continued to grow, the enthusiasm for baseball straddled major social divisions, bringing together Americans of many backgrounds, if only on a limited basis. By the end of the century, no section of the daily newspaper drew more readers than the sports pages. Although it interested relatively few women, sports news riveted the attention of men from all social classes. Loyalty to the "home team" helped to create an urban identity, while individual players became national heroes.

*Spalding's Base Ball* Guide offered fans nothing less than "the official records of America's national game." The first issue came out in 1877 and by 1889 the publication grew to 180 pages packed with statistics, editorials by players, photographs, and overall assessments of teams in the major and minor leagues.

## CONCLUSION

By the end of the nineteenth century, industry and the growing cities had opened a new world for Americans. Fresh from Europe or from the native countryside, ordinary urban dwellers struggled to form communities of fellow newcomers through both work and leisure, in the factory, the neighborhood, the ballpark, and the public school. Meanwhile, their "betters," the wealthy and the new middle class, made and executed the decisions of industry and marketing, established the era's grand civic institutions, and set the tone for high fashion and art. Rich and poor alike shared many aspects of the new order. Yet inequality not only persisted but also increased and prompted new antagonisms.

The Haymarket tragedy highlighted the often strained relationships between Chicago's immigrant working population and civic leaders, precipitating violence, which included the public hanging of four of the eight men brought to trial,

## CHRONOLOGY

**1862**    Morrill Act authorizes "land-grant" colleges

**1869**    Knights of Labor founded

**1870**    Standard Oil founded

**1873**    Financial panic brings severe depression

**1876**    Baseball's National League founded

        Alexander Graham Bell patents the telephone

**1879**    Thomas Edison invents the incandescent bulb

        Depression ends

**1881**    Tuskegee Institute founded

**1882**    Peak of immigration to the United States (1.2 million) in the nineteenth century

        Chinese Exclusion Act passed

        Standard Oil Trust founded

**1883**    William Graham Sumner published the social Darwinist classic *What Social Classes Owe to Each Other*

**1886**    Campaigns for eight-hour workday peak

        Haymarket riot and massacre discredit the Knights of Labor

        American Federation of Labor founded

**1889**    Andrew Carnegie's *The Gospel of Wealth* recommends honesty and fair dealing

**1890**    Sherman Antitrust Act passed

**1893**    Stock market panic precipitates severe depression

**1895**    Coney Island opens

**1901**    U.S. Steel Corporation formed

---

including August Spies. Although the new governor of Illinois, Peter Altgeld, pardoned the three who had their sentences commuted to life in prison, his attempt at amelioration did not signal a shift in the political climate. In the 1890s, hopes for a peaceful reconciliation of these tensions had worn thin, and the lure of overseas empire appeared as one of the few goals that held together a suffering and divided nation.

## REVIEW QUESTIONS

1. Discuss the sources of economic growth in the decades after the Civil War. Historians often refer to this period as the era of the "second industrial revolution." Do you agree with this description?

2. Describe the impact of new technologies and new forms of production on the routines of industrial workers. How did these changes affect African American and women workers in particular? What role did trade unions play in this process?

3. Discuss the role of northern capital in the development of the New South. How did the rise of industry affect the lives of rural Southerners? Analyze these changes from the point of view of African Americans.

4. How did urban life change during the Gilded Age? How did economic development affect residential patterns? How did the middle class aspire to live during the Gilded Age? How did their lifestyles compare with those of working-class urbanites?

5. How did the American educational system change to prepare children for their adult roles in the new industrial economy?

6. How did the rise of organized sports and commercial amusements reflect and shape social divisions at the end of the century? Which groups were affected most (or least) by new leisure activities?

# KEY TERMS

American Federation of Labor (AFL)
(p. 508)
Chinese Exclusion Act (p. 506)
Conspicuous consumption (p. 515)
Gilded Age (p. 515)
Gospel of wealth (p. 503)

Horizontal combination (p. 503)
Knights of Labor (p. 507)
Tenements (p. 512)
Vertical integration (p. 503)
Women's Educational and
Industrial Union (p. 519)

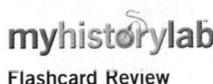
Flashcard Review

# RECOMMENDED READING

Sarah Deutsch, *Women and the City: Gender, Space, and Power in Boston, 1870–1940*
(2000). A close study of women's struggle to define the shape of the modern city and to ease the oppressive quality of spacial divisions along lines of gender, race, and class. Deutsch illustrates the efforts of women to exert their own principles of "moral geography" in shaping Boston's urban landscape.

Rebecca Edwards, *New Spirits: Americans in the Gilded Age, 1865–1905* (2006). A synthesis of recent scholarship with a thematic arrangement that takes the shape of an engaging essay. Edwards provides regional coverage and links domestic events—political, cultural, and social—to overseas expansion.

James Green, *Death in the Haymarket* (2006). Examines the Haymarket event within the context of changing class relations in Chicago and explores its significance as the first act of bombing for political purposes.

Tera W. Hunter, *To 'Joy My Freedom: Southern Black Women's Lives and Labors after the Civil War* (1997). A careful study of African American working women in the New South city of Atlanta. Hunter covers their various occupations in the modern urban economy without sacrificing attention to their pursuits of pleasure in the emerging world of mass entertainments and leisure.

Susan Strasser, *Satisfaction Guaranteed: The Making of the American Mass Market* (1989). A clear and concise explanation of marketing and distribution during the rise of consumer society. Illustrated with examples of early advertising.

Alan Trachtenberg, *The Incorporation of America: Culture and Society in the Gilded Age*, Twenty-Fifth Anniversary ed. (2007). One of the best and most readable overviews of the post–Civil War era. Trachtenberg devotes great care to describing the rise of the corporation to the defining institution of national life and the reorientation of culture to reflect the new middle classes employed by the corporation.

Where it's a good time to connect to the past!

For study resources for this chapter, go to **www.myhistorylab.com** and choose *Out of Many, Teaching and Learning Classroom Edition.* You will find a wealth of study and review material for this chapter, including pretests and posttests, customized study plan, key-term review flash cards, interactive map and document activities, and documents for analysis.

*Dear Father, In the 5th, 8th, and 19th Wards . . .
the negroes were driven away from the polls, beaten
and wounded . . . No colored votes were polled in
those precincts after twelve o'clock.*

—William Taft, October 22, 1894

Destruction of the battleship Maine in Havana harbor.

# 20

DEMOCRACY AND EMPIRE
1870–1900

**WHAT FACTORS** contributed to the growth of government in the late nineteenth century?

**HOW AND** why did workers and farmers organize to participate in politics during this era?

**WHAT CRISES** of the 1890s paved the way to political reform?

**IN WHAT** ways did the election of 1896 represent a turning point in U.S. political history?

**HOW DID** proponents of imperialism justify colonization?

**WHAT CRITIQUES** of empire were put forward in the years after the Spanish-American War?

1870   1900

# AMERICAN COMMUNITIES
## The Annexation of Hawai'i

ON JANUARY 17, 1891, LILI'UOKALANI SUCCEEDED HER BROTHER, KING Kalakaua, to become the queen of Hawai'i. Raised a Christian and fluent in English, the fifty-two-year-old monarch was nevertheless intensely loyal to the Hawaiian people and to their language and customs. This allegiance—and her strong opposition to a movement to annex Hawai'i to the United States—brought her downfall. On January 17, 1893, the queen was deposed in a plot carried out by an American diplomat and his co-conspirators.

This event followed more than a half century of intense economic and diplomatic maneuvering by the United States and other nations. Both American and British missionaries, who had arrived in the 1820s to convert Hawaiians to Christianity, had bought up huge parcels of land, and they and their children—known as the *haole* to native Hawaiians—had grown into a large and powerful community of planters. The missionaries in turn encouraged American businesses to buy into the sugar plantations, and by 1875 U.S. corporations dominated the sugar trade. Within a year Hawaiian sugar was entering the United States duty free. Hawai'i was beginning to appear, in the opinion of Secretary of State James G. Blaine, to be "an outlying district of the state of California," and he pushed for formal annexation.

In 1888 American planters forced on the weak King Kalakaua a new constitution that severely limited his power and established wealth and property qualifications for voting. This so-called Bayonet Constitution, because it implied the use of U.S. arms to implement it, allowed noncitizens, Europeans as well as Americans, to vote but denied the right of suffrage to poor native Hawaiians and the Chinese and Japanese who had come to work in the sugar fields.

In the name of democracy, the haole planters had secured a constitutional government that was closely allied to their economic interests—until King Kalakaua died in 1891. After ascending to the throne, Queen Lili'uokalani struck back. She decided she must empower native Hawaiians and limit the political influence of the haole elite and noncitizens.

The U.S.-led annexation forces first denounced the queen for attempting to abrogate the Bayonet Constitution and then welcomed Blaine's decision to send in U.S. troops to protect American lives and property. With no shots fired or documents signed, Lili'uokalani was deposed and a new provisional government installed. Sanford B. Dole, Honolulu-born son of Protestant missionaries, stepped in as the president of the new provisional government of Hawai'i, now a protectorate of the United States.

Lili'uokalani immediately protested to President Grover Cleveland, explaining that she had yielded "to the superior force of the United States of America" only to avoid a serious armed confrontation and the loss of life. She called on President Cleveland to recognize her authority as "the constitutional sovereign of the Hawaiian Islands" and to reinstate her as queen. After investigating the situation, Cleveland agreed and ordered Lili'uokalani's reinstatement as queen. Ironically, Dole, who had been a major force for annexation, countered by refusing to recognize the right of the U.S. president "to interfere in our domestic affairs." On July 3, 1894, he proclaimed Hawai'i an independent republic, with himself retaining the office of president.

After Lili'uokalani's supporters attempted an unsuccessful military uprising in 1895, the deposed queen was arrested, tried by a military tribunal, and convicted of misprision of treason (having knowledge of treason but not informing the authorities).

President Cleveland later declared privately that he was "ashamed of the whole affair" and stubbornly refused to listen to arguments for annexation. But he was powerless to stop the process before William McKinley succeeded him as president in 1896. Although more than a hundred members of Congress voted against annexation, an improper joint resolution passed to annex Hawai'i. In 1900, at McKinley's urging, Hawai'i became a territory. The people of Hawai'i were never consulted about this momentous change in their national identity.

The path to empire was paved with major changes in government and the party system. As the 1890s culminated in the acquisition of new territories, it also witnessed a decisive realignment of the party system. Voters not only changed affiliations that had been in place since the Civil War but also waged significant challenges to the two-party system at the local, regional, and national levels. While Queen Lili'uokalani was trying to regain control of her government, a mass political movement was forming in the United States to revive the nation's own democratic impulse.

Oahu

# TOWARD A NATIONAL GOVERNING CLASS

The basic structure of government changed dramatically in the last quarter of the nineteenth century. Mirroring the fast-growing economy, public administration expanded at all levels—municipal, county, state, and federal—and took on greater responsibility for regulating society, especially market and property relations. Growing numbers of citizens for the first time looked to the government, from the local level upward, for public education, military veterans' pensions, and other social services. The leaders of the business community looked just as eagerly, and with far more influence, for protection of their property and sometimes for personal gain.

Reformers mobilized to rein in corruption and to promote both efficiency and professionalism in the multiplying structures of government. Meanwhile, some notable politicians acted to benefit directly, competing with one another for control of the new mechanisms of power. A lot was at stake.

## THE GROWTH OF GOVERNMENT

Before the Civil War, local governments attended mainly to the promotion and regulation of trade and relied on private enterprise to supply vital services such as fire protection and water supplies. Cities gradually introduced professional police and firefighting forces and began to finance expanding school systems, public libraries, roads, and parks, an expansion requiring huge increases in local taxation. State governments grew in tandem, consolidating oversight of banking, transportation systems such as the railroads, and major enterprises such as the construction of dams and canals. By the end of the nineteenth century, city halls and state capitols had become beehives of activity.

At the national level, mobilization for the Civil War and Reconstruction had demanded an unprecedented degree of resources and their coordination, as both revenues and administrative bureaucracy grew quickly. At the end of Reconstruction, various aspects of federal government were trimmed at Congressional order, and the army was reduced to a fraction of its swollen size. Despite these particular reductions, the federal government as a whole continued to expand under the weight of new tasks and responsibilities.

The modern apparatus of departments, bureaus, and cabinets took shape amid this upswing. The Department of the Interior, created in 1849, grew into the largest and most important federal office other than the Post Office. It consisted of some twenty agencies, including the Bureau of Indian Affairs and the U.S. Geological Survey. Through its authority, the federal government was the chief landowner of all the West. The Department of the Treasury, responsible for collecting federal taxes and customs as well as printing money and stamps, quadrupled its own size from 1873 to 1900, to nearly 25,000 employees.

Regulatory agencies sprung up: foremost among them was the **Interstate Commerce Commission (ICC)**. The ICC was created in 1887 to bring order to the growing patchwork of state laws concerning railroads. The five-member commission appointed by the president approved freight and passenger rates set by the railroads. The ICC remained weak in the period, its rate-setting policies usually voided by the Supreme Court. But ICC commissioners could take public testimony on possible violations, examine company records, and generally oversee enforcement of the law. This set a precedent for future regulation of trade as well as for positive government, making rules for business while superseding state laws with federal power—that is, for the intervention of the federal government into the affairs of private enterprise.

**WHAT FACTORS** contributed to the growth of government in the late nineteenth century?

**myhistorylab**
Review Summary

## IMAGE KEY
for pages 524–525

a. 1892 Benjamin Harrison presidential campaign ribbon.
b. Susan B. Anthony medal for the New York State Suffrage Assn. Convention.
c. Destruction of the battleship Maine in Havana harbor.
d,e. Campaign buttons for William McKinley, 1896.
f. A Benjamin Harrison presidential campaign souvenir.
g. Madison Square Garden during the Democratic National Convention of 1888.
h. A poster of Grange artists, from *Kingfisher Reformer*, May 3, 1894.
i. Coxey's Army marching with a band.
j. William Jennings Bryan at the 1896 Democratic Convention.
k. Chinese refugee women studying with a Protestant missionary.
l. An 1898 American magazine cover honoring the U.S.A.'s victory in the Spanish-American War.
m,n. Campaign paraphernalia.

**Interstate Commerce Commission (ICC)** The 1887 law that expanded federal power over business by prohibiting pooling and discriminatory rates by railroads and establishing the first federal regulatory agency, the Interstate Commerce Commission.

## THE MACHINERY OF POLITICS

Only gradually did Republicans and Democrats adapt to the demands of government expansion. The Republican Party continued to run on its Civil War record, pointing to its achievements in reuniting the nation and in passing new reform legislation. Democrats, by contrast, sought to reduce the influence of the federal government, slash expenditures, repeal legislation, and protect states' rights. While Republicans held on to their longtime constituencies, Democrats gathered support from southern white voters and immigrants newly naturalized in the North. But neither party commanded a clear majority of votes until the century drew to a close.

Presidents in the last quarter of the century customarily yielded power to Congress and the state legislatures. Democrats usually held a majority in the House and Republicans a majority in the Senate. With neither party sufficiently strong to govern effectively, Congress passed little legislation before 1890.

One major political issue that separated the two parties was the tariff. Manufacturing regions, especially the Northeast, favored a protective policy, while the southern and western agricultural regions opposed high tariffs as unfair to farmers and ranchers who had to pay the steep fees on imported necessities. Democrats, with a stronghold among southern voters, argued for sharp reductions in the tariff as a way to save the rural economy and to give a boost to workers. Republicans, who represented mainly business interests, raised tariffs to new levels on a wide array of goods during the Civil War and retained high tariffs as long as they held power. Despite the importance of the tariff in setting apart Republicans and Democrats, the two political parties operated essentially as state or local organizations.

By the 1870s partisan politics had become a full-time occupation, with local officials usually running for office every two years. "We work through one campaign," quipped one candidate, "take a bath and start in on the next." Election paraphernalia—leaflets or pamphlets, banners, hats, flags, buttons, inscribed playing cards, or clay pipes featuring a likeness of a candidate's face or the party symbol—became a major expense for both parties. And voters did turn out. During the last quarter of the century, participation in presidential elections peaked at nearly 80 percent of those eligible to vote.

**19–10**
William T. Riordon, *Plunkitt of Tammany Hall* (1905)

**19–13**
George Washington Plunkitt, *Honest Graft* (1905)

The rising costs of maintaining local organizations and orchestrating mammoth campaigns drove party leaders to seek ever-larger sources of revenue. Winners often seized and added to the "spoils" of office through an elaborate system of payoffs and patronage. Legislators who supported government subsidies for railroad corporations, for instance, commonly received stock in return and sometimes cash bribes. At the time, few politicians or business leaders regarded these practices as unethical.

At the local level, where a combination of ethnicity, race, and religion determined party loyalty, powerful bosses and political machines dominated both parties. Democrats William Marcy Tweed of New York's powerful political organization, Tammany Hall, and Michael "Hinky Dink" Kenna of Chicago, specialized in giving municipal jobs to loyal voters and holiday food baskets to their families.

A large number of federal jobs, meanwhile, changed hands each time the presidency passed from one party to another. More than 50 percent of all federal jobs were patronage positions, jobs that could be awarded to loyal supporters as part of the "spoils" of the "victor."

Upon taking office, President James Garfield encountered loyal Republicans "lying in wait" for him "like vultures for a wounded bison." His colleagues in Congress were no less besieged. Observers estimated that decisions about patronage filled one-third of their time. Garfield himself served as president

**In 1888, Grover** Cleveland, with his running mate, Allen G. Thurman, led a spirited campaign for reelection to the presidency. Although he played up his strong record on civil service reform and tariff reduction, Cleveland, an incumbent, lost the election to his Republican challenger, Benjamin Harrison. Cleveland tallied the greatest number of popular votes, but Harrison easily won in the electoral college by a margin of 233 to 168. In this lithograph campaign poster, the Democratic ticket invokes the legacy of Thomas Jefferson and the patriotism of Uncle Sam.

for only four months before being mortally wounded by a disgruntled office seeker, an event that prompted his successor, Chester A. Arthur, to encourage reform of the civil service system.

## THE SPOILS SYSTEM AND CIVIL SERVICE REFORM

In January 1883, a bipartisan congressional majority passed the **Pendleton Civil Service Reform Act.** This measure allowed the president to create, with Senate approval, a three-person commission to draw up a set of guidelines for executive and legislative appointments. The commission established a system of standards for various federal jobs and instituted "open, competitive examinations for testing the fitness of applicants for public service." The Pendleton Act also barred political candidates from funding their campaigns by assessing a "tax" on the salaries of holders of party-sponsored government jobs.

Although patronage did not disappear entirely, many departments of the federal government took on a professional character similar to that which doctors, lawyers, and scholars were imposing on their fields through regulatory societies such as the American Medical Association and the American Historical Association. At the same time, the federal judiciary began to act more aggressively to establish the parameters of government. With the Circuit Courts of Appeals Act of 1891, Congress granted the U.S. Supreme Court the right to review all cases at will. Despite these reforms, many observers still viewed government as a sinkhole of self-interest and corruption.

# FARMERS AND WORKERS ORGANIZE THEIR COMMUNITIES

**HOW AND** why did workers and farmers organize to participate in politics during this era?

**myhistorylab**
**Review Summary**

Farmers and workers began to build regional as well as national organizations to oppose, as a Nebraska newspaper put it, "the wealthy and powerful classes who want the control of government to plunder the people." Over the course of the last quarter of the nineteenth century, they gradually developed a distinctively radical agenda that spoke directly to the increasing power of elected officials and government. By the 1890s, farmers and workers had formed a mass movement that presented the most significant challenge to the two-party system since the Civil War—**Populism**—and pledged themselves to restore the reins of government to "the hands of the people."

## THE GRANGE

In 1867, white farmers in the Midwest formed the Patrons of Husbandry for their own "social, intellectual, and moral improvement." Led by Oliver H. Kelley, this fraternal society resembled the secretive Masonic order. In many farming communities, the headquarters of the local chapter, known as the **Grange** (a word for "farm"), became the main social center.

**Populism** A mass movement of the 1890s formed on the basis of the Southern Farmers' Alliance and other reform organizations.

**Grange** The National Grange of the Patrons of Husbandry, a national organization of farm owners formed after the Civil War.

**The symbols chosen** by Grange artists represented their faith that all social value could be traced to honest labor and most of all to the work of the entire farm family. The hardworking American required only the enlightenment offered by the Grange to build a better community.

The Granger movement spread rapidly, especially in areas where farmers were experiencing their greatest hardships (see Figure 20.1). Grangers blamed hard times on a band of "thieves in the night"—especially railroads and banks—that charged exorbitant fees for service. They fumed at American manufacturers, such as Cyrus McCormick, who sold farm equipment more cheaply in Europe than in the United States. They raged at the banks that charged high interest rates for the money farmers had to borrow to pay the steep prices for equipment and raw materials.

Grangers mounted their greatest assault on the railroad corporations. By bribing state legislators, railroads enjoyed a highly discriminatory rate policy, commonly charging farmers more to ship their crops short distances than over long hauls. In 1874, several midwestern states responded to pressure and passed a series of so-called **Granger laws** establishing maximum shipping rates. Grangers also complained to their lawmakers about the price-fixing policies of grain wholesalers and operators of grain elevators. In 1873, the Illinois legislature passed a Warehouse Act establishing maximum rates for storing grains. Chicago firms challenged the legality of this measure, but in *Munn* v. *Illinois* (1877), the Supreme Court upheld the law, ruling that states had the power to regulate privately owned businesses like the railroads in the public interest.

Determined to buy less and produce more, Grangers created a vast array of cooperative enterprises for both the purchase of supplies and the marketing of crops. They established local grain elevators, set up retail stores, and even manufactured some of their own farm machinery. Grangers ran banks as well as fraternal life and fire insurance companies.

The deepening depression of the late 1870s wiped out most of these cooperative programs, and Grange membership fell. In the mid-1880s, the Supreme Court overturned most of the key legislation regulating railroads. Despite these setbacks, the Patrons of Husbandry had nonetheless effectively promoted the idea of an activist government with primary responsibility to its producer-citizens. This idea would remain at the heart of farmer-worker protest movements until the end of the century.

## THE FARMERS' ALLIANCE

Agrarian unrest did not end with the downward turn of the Grange but instead moved south. In the South, the falling price of cotton underscored the need for action, and farmers readily translated their anger into intense loyalty to the one organization pledged to improve their lot. With more than 500 chapters in Texas alone, and cooperative stores complemented by the cooperative merchandising of crops, the **Southern Farmers' Alliance** became a viable alternative to the capitalist marketplace—if only temporarily.

The Northern Farmers' Alliance took shape in the Great Plains states, drawing on larger organizations in Minnesota, Nebraska, Iowa, Kansas, and the Dakota Territory. During 1886 and 1887, summer drought followed winter blizzards and ice storms, reducing wheat harvests by one-third on the plains. Locusts and cinch bugs ate much of the rest. As if this were not enough, prices for wheat on the world market fell sharply for what little remained.

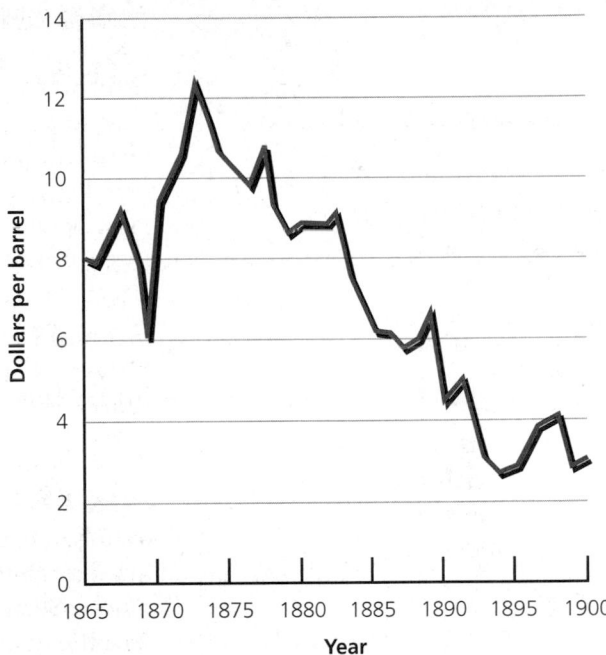

**Figure 20.1 Falling Price of Wheat Flour, 1865–1900**
The falling price of wheat was often offset by increased productivity, giving farmers a steady, if not higher, income. Nevertheless, in the short term farmers often carried more debt and faced greater risk, both factors in sparking the populists protest by the end of the century.

**Granger laws** State laws enacted in the Midwest in the 1870s that regulated rates charged by railroads, grain elevator operators, and other middlemen.

**Southern Farmers' Alliance** The largest of several organizations that formed in the post-Reconstruction South to advance the interests of beleaguered small farmers.

In 1889, the regional organizations joined forces to create the National Farmers' Alliance and Industrial Union. Within a year the combined movement claimed 3 million white members. Excluded from the all-white chapters, the Colored Farmers' Alliance and Cooperative Union organized separately and quickly spread across the South; from its beginnings in Texas and Arkansas it grew to more than a million members.

Grangers had only rarely put up candidates for office. In comparison, the Farmers' Alliance had few reservations about entering electoral races. At the end of the 1880s, regional alliances put up candidates on platforms demanding state ownership of the railroads, a graduated income tax, lower tariffs, restriction of land ownership to citizens, and easier access to money through "the free and unlimited coinage of silver." By 1890, the alliances had won several local and state elections, gained control of the Nebraska legislature, and held the balance of power in Minnesota and South Dakota.

## WORKERS SEARCH FOR POWER

Before the end of the century, more than 6 million workers would strike in industries ranging from New England textiles to southern tobacco factories to western mines. Some of the largest strikes were against the corporations targeted by farmers: the railroads. Although most of these strikes ended in failure, they revealed the readiness of workers to spell out their grievances in a direct and dramatic manner. They also suggested how strongly many townspeople, including merchants who depended on workers' wages, would support local strikes and turn them into community uprisings (see Map 20.1).

# MAP EXPLORATION

To explore an interactive version of this map, go to **http://www.prenhall.com/faraghertlc/map20.1**

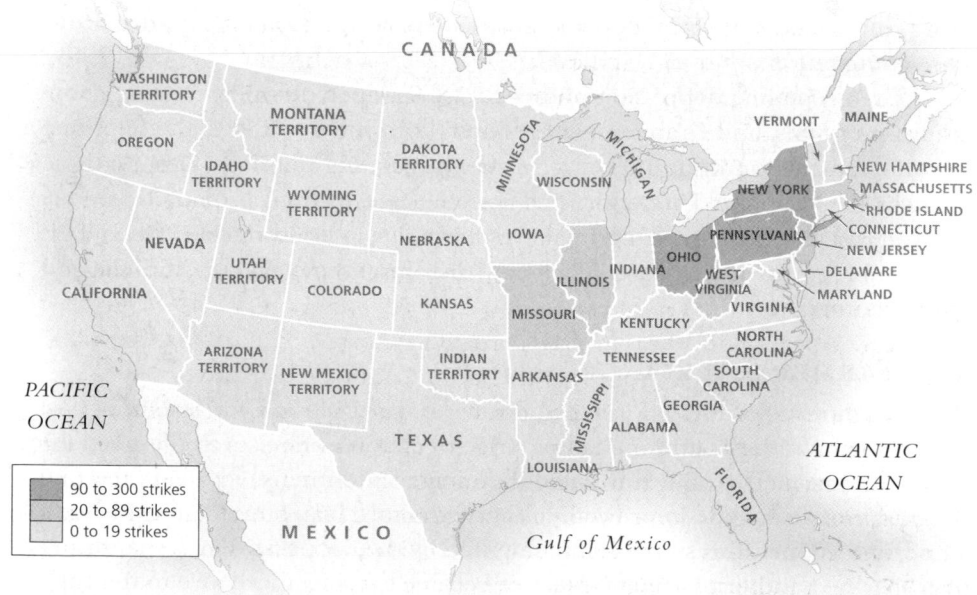

**MAP 20.1**

**Strikes by State, 1880**   Most strikes after the Uprising of 1877 could be traced to organized trades, concentrated in the manufacturing districts of the Northeast and Midwest.

Carville Earle, *Geographical Inquiry and American Historical Problems* (Stanford, CA: Stanford University Press, 1992).

WHAT WERE the most important elements of McKinley's campaign platform?

**The Great Uprising** of 1877, which began as a strike of railroad workers, spread rapidly to communities along the railroad routes. Angry crowds defied the armed militia and the vigilantes hired to disperse them. In Philadelphia, for example, strikers set fire to the downtown, destroying many buildings before federal troops were brought in to stop them. More than a hundred people died before the strike ended, and the railroad corporations suffered a $10 million loss in property.

While the Farmers' Alliance put up candidates in the South and Plains states, workers launched labor parties in dozens of industrial towns and cities. In New York City, popular economist and land reformer Henry George put himself forward in 1886 as candidate for mayor on the United Labor Party ticket. George called on "all honest citizens" to join in independent political action as "the only hope of exposing and breaking up the extortion and speculation by which a standing army of professional politicians corrupt the people whom they plunder."

Tammany Hall delivered many thousands of the ballots cast for George straight into the Hudson River. Nevertheless, George managed to finish a respectable second with 31 percent of the vote. Although his campaign ended in defeat, George had issued a stern warning to the entrenched politicians. Equally important, his impressive showing encouraged labor groups in other cities to form their own parties.

In the late 1880s, labor parties won seats on many city councils and state legislatures. The victories of local labor parties caught the attention of farmers, who began to weigh their prospects for a political alliance with discontented urban workers. For the 1888 presidential election, they formed a coalition to sponsor the Union Labor Party, which ran on a plank of government ownership of the railroads. The new party made no headway against the two-party system, polling little more than 1 percent of the vote. Still, the successes in local communities nurtured hopes for a viable political alliance of the "producing classes," rural as well as urban.

## WOMEN BUILD ALLIANCES

Women activists helped build both the labor and agrarian protest movements while campaigning for their own rights as citizens.

The Grangers issued a charter to a local chapter only when women were well represented on its rolls, and in the 1870s, delegates to its conventions routinely gave speeches endorsing woman suffrage and even dress reform. In both the

**Great Uprising of 1877**
Unsuccessful railroad strike to protest wage cuts and the use of federal troops against strikers, the first nationwide work stoppage in American history.

FRANCES WILLARD                    598-10

**Frances E. Willard** (1839–1898) became a full-time activist for the national Woman's Christian Temperance Union (WCTU) in 1874. From 1879 until her death, she served as president, pushing the organization to expand its interests beyond temperance under the rubric of her "do-everything" policy. Under her leadership, the WCTU established 39 departments promoting a wide array of reform causes ranging from the establishment of free kindergartens to the prohibition of the manufacture of cigarettes.

**19–5**
*The People's Party Platform*
(1892)

**Woman's Christian Temperance Union (WCTU)**  Women's organization whose members visited schools to educate children about the evils of alcohol, addressed prisoners, and blanketed men's meetings with literature.

**National American Woman Suffrage Association (NAWSA)**  The organization, formed in 1890, that coordinated the ultimately successful campaign to achieve women's right to vote.

Northern and Southern Farmers' Alliances, women made up perhaps one-quarter of the membership, and several advanced through the ranks to become leading speakers and organizers.

Women in both the Knights of Labor and the Farmers' Alliance found their greatest leader in Frances E. Willard, the most famous woman of the nineteenth century and a shrewd politician in her own right. Willard argued that women, who guarded their families' physical and spiritual welfare, could have only a beneficial impact on the world outside their homes. From 1878 until her death in 1897, she presided over the **Woman's Christian Temperance Union (WCTU)**. By the 1880s, the most militant branches had joined the campaign for an activist government, demanding an overhaul of the prison system, the eradication of prostitution, changes in the age of consent, and even the elimination of the wage system. Willard went so far as to draw up plans for a new system of government whereby all offices, right up to the presidency, would be shared jointly by men and women. By 1890, she had mobilized nearly 200,000 paid members into the largest organization of women in the world.

Willard understood that for women to participate in politics they needed the right to vote. Under her leadership, the WCTU grew into the major force for woman suffrage, far surpassing the American Woman Suffrage Association and the National Woman Suffrage Association. By 1890, when the two rival suffrage associations merged to form the **National American Woman Suffrage Association**, the WCTU had already pushed the heart of the suffrage campaign into the Great Plains states and the West.

## POPULISM AND THE PEOPLE'S PARTY

In December 1890, the Farmers' Alliance called a meeting at Ocala, Florida, to press for the creation of a national third party. This was a risky proposition because the Southern Alliance hoped to capture control of the Democratic Party, whereas many farmers in the Plains states voted Republican. In some areas, however, the Farmers' Alliance established its own parties, put up full slates of candidates for local elections, won majorities in state legislatures, and even sent a representative to Congress. Reviewing these successes, delegates at Ocala decided to push ahead and form a national party, and they appealed to other farm, labor, and reform organizations to join them.

In February 1892, 1,300 representatives from the Farmers' Alliance, the Knights of Labor, and the Colored Farmers' Alliance, among others, met in St. Louis under a broad banner that read: "We do not ask for sympathy or pity. We ask for justice." The new People's Party called for government ownership of railroads, banks, and telegraph lines, prohibition of large landholding companies, a graduated income tax, an eight-hour workday, and restriction of immigration. The most ambitious plan called for the national government to build local warehouses—"subtreasuries"—where farmers could store their crops until prices reached acceptable levels. The People's Party convened again in Omaha in July 1892 and nominated James Baird Weaver of Iowa for president and, to please the South, the Confederate veteran James G. Field from Virginia for vice president.

The Populists, as supporters of the People's Party styled themselves, quickly became a major factor in American politics. Although Democrat Grover Cleveland regained the presidency in 1892 (he had previously served from 1885 to

1889), Populists scored a string of local victories. In Idaho, they elected three governors, ten representatives to Congress, and five senators. Despite poor showings among urban workers east of the Mississippi, Populists looked forward to the next round of state elections in 1894. But the great test would come with the presidential election in 1896.

# THE CRISIS OF THE 1890S

A series of events in the 1890s shook the confidence of many citizens in the reigning political system. But nothing was more unsettling than the severe economic depression that consumed the nation and lasted for five years. Many feared—while others hoped—that the entire political system would topple.

## FINANCIAL COLLAPSE AND DEPRESSION

By the spring of 1893, the nation was drawn into a depression that had been plaguing European nations since the late 1880s. Their market for imported goods, including those manufactured in the United States, sharply contracted. Financial panic in England spread across the Atlantic, as British investors began to sell off their American stocks to obtain funds. Other factors—tight credit, falling agricultural prices, a weak banking system, and overexpansion, especially in railroad construction—all helped to bring about the collapse of the U.S. economy. In May and June a crash in the stock market sent waves of panic splashing over business and financial institutions across the country. Agricultural prices meanwhile continued to plummet until they reached new lows. The business boom of nearly two decades ended, and the entire economy ground to a halt. The new century arrived before prosperity returned.

In many cities, unemployment rates reached 25 percent; Samuel Gompers, head of the American Federation of Labor (AFL), estimated nationwide unemployment at 3 million. Few people starved but millions suffered. Inadequate diets prompted a rise in communicable diseases, such as tuberculosis and pellagra. Unable to buy food, clothes, or household items, families learned to survive with the barest minimum.

**WHAT CRISES** of the 1890s paved the way to political reform?

myhistorylab
Review Summary

**After five weeks** the main body of Coxey's Army reached Washington, DC, where on May 1, 1894, the leaders were immediately arrested for trespassing on government property. Fifty years later, on May 1, 1944, the ninety-year-old Coxey finally gave his speech advocating public works programs on the steps of the nation's capitol.

The popular magazine *Harper's Weekly* published this illustration of workers and their families protesting the use of a private security force at the Carnegie Steel Company in Homestead, Pennsylvania, in July 1892.

**19–6**
*The Secret Oath of the American Protective Association* (1893)

**myhistorylab**

**Exploring America:** *Homestead Strike of 1892*

**Coxey's Army** A protest march of unemployed workers, led by Populist businessman Jacob Coxey, demanding inflation and a public works program during the depression of the 1890s.

**Protective association** Organizations formed by mine owners in response to the formation of labor unions.

As the depression deepened so did demands on the federal government for positive action. Populist Jacob Sechler Coxey decided to gather the masses of unemployed into a huge army and then to march to Washington, DC. Far in advance of the New Deal, Coxey proposed that Congress fund a public work program in order to give jobs to the unemployed. On Easter Sunday, 1894, Coxey left Massillon, Ohio, with several hundred followers. Meanwhile, brigades from across the country joined his "petition in boots." Only 600 men and women reached the nation's capital, where the police first clubbed and then arrested the leaders for trespassing on the grass. **"Coxey's Army"** quickly disbanded but not before voicing the public's expectation of federal responsibility for the welfare of its citizens, especially in times of crisis.

## STRIKES: COEUR D'ALENE, HOMESTEAD, AND PULLMAN

Even before the onset of the depression, the conflict between labor and capital had escalated to the brink of civil war. In the 1890s, three major strikes dramatized the extent of collusion between the corporations and government. In each case, state or federal troops were deployed to crush the labor uprising, providing a vivid lesson to workers on the growing role of government in this era.

Wage cuts in the silver and lead mines of northern Idaho led to one of the most bitter conflicts of the decade. To put a brake on organized labor, mine owners had formed a **"protective association,"** and in March 1892, they announced a wage cut throughout the Coeur d'Alene district. After the miners' union refused to accept the cut, the owners locked out all union members and brought in strikebreakers by the trainload. Unionists tried peaceful methods of protest. But after three months of stalemate, they loaded a railcar with explosives and blew up a mine. The governor proclaimed martial law and dispatched a combined state-federal force of about 1,500 troops, who broke the strike. But the miners' union survived, and most members became active in the Populist Party, which at the next session of the Idaho legislature allied with Democrats to cut back all appropriations to the National Guard.

At Homestead, Pennsylvania, members of the Amalgamated Iron, Steel and Tin Workers, the most powerful union of the AFL, had carved out an admirable position for themselves in the Carnegie Steel Company. But, determined to gain control over every stage of production, Carnegie and his chairman, Henry C. Frick, decided not only to lower wages but also to break the union.

In 1892, when Amalgamated's contract expired, Frick announced a drastic wage cut. He also ordered a wooden stockade built around the factory, with grooves for rifles and barbed wire on top. When Homestead's city government—the mayor and police chief were both union members—refused to assign police to disperse the strikers, Frick dispatched a barge carrying a private army armed to the teeth. Gunfire broke out and continued throughout the day. Finally, the governor stepped in and sent the Pennsylvania National Guard, 8,000 strong, to restore order, and Carnegie's factory reopened with strikebreakers doing the work.

After four months, the union was forced to concede a crushing defeat, not only for itself but, in effect, for all steelworkers as well. The Carnegie company reduced its workforce by 25 percent, lengthened the workday, and cut wages 25 percent for those who remained on the job. Within a decade, every major steel company operated without union interference.

Pullman, Illinois, just south of Chicago, had been constructed as a model industrial community. Its creator and proprietor, George M. Pullman, had manufactured luxurious "sleeping cars" for railroads since 1881. He built his company as a self-contained community, with the factory at the center, surrounded by modern cottages, a library, churches, parks, an independent water supply, even its own cemetery, but no saloons. The Pullman Palace Car Company deducted rent, library fees, and grocery bills from each worker's weekly wages.

When times grew hard, the company cut wages by as much as one-half, in some cases down to less than $1 a day. Charges for food and rent remained unchanged. Furthermore, factory supervisors sought to make up for declining profits by driving workers to produce more. In May 1894, after Pullman fired members of a committee that had drawn up a list of grievances, workers voted to strike.

Pullman workers found their champion in Eugene V. Debs, who had recently formed the American Railway Union (ARU). Debs, the architect of the ARU's victory over the Great Northern rail line just one month earlier, advised caution, but delegates to an ARU convention voted to support a nationwide boycott of all Pullman cars. This action soon turned into a sympathy strike by railroad workers across the country.

Compared to the Great Uprising of 1877, the orderly Pullman strike at first produced little violence. ARU officials urged strikers to ignore all provocations and hold their ground peacefully. But Richard C. Olney, a former railroad lawyer, used his current office as attorney general, claiming that the ARU was disrupting mail shipments, to issue a blanket injunction against the strike. On July 4, President Cleveland sent army units to Chicago, over the pro-labor Illinois governor John Peter Altgeld's objections. After a bitter confrontation that left thirteen people dead and more than fifty wounded, the army dispersed the strikers. For the next week, railroad workers in twenty-six other states resisted federal troops, and a dozen more people were killed. On July 17, the strike finally ended when federal marshals arrested Debs and other leaders.

Assailing the arrogance of class privilege that encouraged the government to use brute force against its citizens, Debs concluded that the labor movement could not regain its dignity without seizing the reigns of government. He came out of jail committed to the ideals of socialism, and in 1898 helped to form a political party dedicated to its principles.

## THE SOCIAL GOSPEL

"What is socialism?" Debs once asked. "Merely Christianity in action. It recognizes the equality in men." During the 1890s, especially as hard times spread across the nation, a growing number of Protestant and Catholic clergy and lay theologians came close to sharing his perspective, noting a discrepancy between the ideals of Christianity and prevailing attitudes toward the poor.

Social gospel ministers called on the government to be more responsible toward its most impoverished and unprotected citizens. Supporting labor's right to organize and, if necessary, to strike, they petitioned government officials to regulate corporations and place a limit on profits. Women guided the social gospel movement in their communities. In the midst of the depression, women activists were well placed to respond to the plight of the poor and dispossessed. In nearly every sizable city, groups of white women affiliated with various evangelical Protestant sects raised money to establish inexpensive residential hotels for working women, whose low wages rarely covered the price of safe, comfortable shelter. At the forefront of this movement was the Young Women's Christian Association (YWCA), which by 1900 had more than 600 local chapters. The "Y" sponsored a range of services for needy Christian women, ranging from homes for the elderly and for unmarried mothers to elaborate programs of vocational instruction and physical fitness. Meanwhile, Catholic laywomen and nuns served the poor women of their faith, operating numerous schools, hospitals, and orphanages.

Affiliated principally with the Baptist Church, African American women sponsored dozens of self-help programs and, in addition, emphasized the importance of education to racial uplift. Excluded by the whites-only policy of the YWCA in most localities, they organized their own chapters and branched out to form nurseries, orphanages, hospitals, and nursing homes. In Chicago, for example, African American women established the Phyllis Wheatley Home, which opened in 1908 to provide, in the founders' words, a "Christian influence" for the working women and college students who boarded there.

# POLITICS OF REFORM, POLITICS OF ORDER

The severe hardships of the 1890s, following a quarter century of popular unrest and economic uncertainty, led to a crisis in the two-party system. The presidential election of 1896, considered a turning point in American politics, marked both a dramatic realignment of voters and the centrality of economic issues. It also sanctioned the popular call for a stronger government, making the question of control vital to the nation's voters as well as the composition of the electorate. Ultimately, the election of 1896 brought to national office politicians who perceived a clear link between domestic problems and the expansion of markets overseas and were willing to act aggressively to implement this vision.

## THE FREE SILVER ISSUE

For generations, reformers had advocated "soft" currency, that is, an increase in the money supply that would loosen credit. During the Civil War the federal government took decisive action, replacing state bank notes with a national paper currency popularly called "greenbacks" (from the color of the bills). Then in 1873 the Coinage Act tightened the money supply by eliminating silver from circulation, prompting farmers who depended on credit to call it "the Crime of '73." This measure actually had little real impact on the economy but opened the door to yet more tinkering.

The **Sherman Silver Purchase Act** of 1890 directed the Treasury to increase the amount of currency coined from silver mined in the West and also permitted the U.S. government to print paper currency backed by silver. In turn Westerners, who stood to benefit most from this reform, agreed to support the McKinley Tariff of 1890 which, by establishing the highest import duties yet on foreign goods, pleased the business community.

Following the crash of 1893, a desperate President Cleveland demanded the repeal of the Sherman Act, insisting that only the gold standard could pull the nation out of depression. By exerting intense pressure on congressional Democrats, Cleveland succeeded in October 1893, but not without ruining his chances for renomination. The midterm elections of 1894 brought the largest shift in congressional power in American history: the Republicans gained 117 seats, while the Democrats lost 113. The "Silver Democrats" of Cleveland's own party vowed revenge and began to look to the Populists, mainly Westerners and farmers who favored "free silver," that is, the unlimited coinage of silver. Republicans confidently began to prepare for the presidential election of 1896, warming to what they called the "battle of the standards."

**Free silver** Philosophy that the government should expand the money supply by purchasing and coining all the silver offered to it.

## POPULISM'S LAST CAMPAIGNS

Populists had been buoyed by the 1894 elections, which delivered to their candidates nearly 1.5 million votes—a gain of 42 percent over their 1892 totals. As Populists prepared for the 1896 presidential campaign, they found themselves at a crossroad: what were they to do with the growing popularity of the Democratic candidate, William Jennings Bryan? A spellbinding orator, Bryan won a congressional seat in 1890. After seizing the Populist slogan "Equal Rights to All, Special Privilege to None," the thirty-six-year-old lawyer from Nebraska became a major contender for president of the United States.

Noting the surging interest in free silver, Bryan became its champion. For two years before the 1896 election, he wooed potential voters in a speaking tour that took him to every state in the nation. Pouring new life into his divided party, Bryan pushed Silver Democrats to the forefront.

At the 1896 party convention, Bryan thrilled delegates with his evocation of agrarian ideals. "Burn down your cities and leave our farms," Bryan preached, "and your cities will spring up again as if by magic; but destroy our farms and the grass will grow in the streets of every city in the country." Bryan carried the Democratic presidential nomination.

The Populists realized that by nominating Bryan the Democrats had stolen their thunder. They also feared that the growing emphasis on currency would overshadow their more important planks calling for government ownership of the nation's railroads and communications systems. As the date of their own convention approached, delegates divided over strategy: they could endorse Bryan and give up their independent status, or they could run an independent campaign and risk splitting the silver vote. In the end, Populists nominated Bryan for president and one of their own, Georgian Tom Watson, for vice president. Most of the state Democratic Party organizations, however, refused to put the "fusion" ticket on the ballot, and Bryan and his Democratic running mate Arthur Sewall simply ignored the Populist campaign.

## THE REPUBLICAN TRIUMPH

After Cleveland's blunders, Republicans anticipated an easy victory in 1896, but Bryan's nomination, as party stalwart Mark Hanna warned, "changed everything." Luckily, they had their own handsome, knowledgeable, courteous, and ruthless candidate, Civil War veteran William McKinley.

The Republican campaign in terms of sheer expense and skill of coordination outdid all previous campaigns and established a precedent for future presidential elections. Hanna guided a strategy that raised up to $7 million and outspent Bryan more than ten to one. Fearful that the silver issue would divide their own ranks, Republicans stepped around it while emphasizing the tariff. Delivering a hard-hitting negative campaign, they consistently cast Bryan as a nay-sayer.

**This Republican campaign** poster of 1896 depicts William McKinley standing on sound money and promising a revival of prosperity. The depression of the 1890s shifted the electorate into the Republican column.

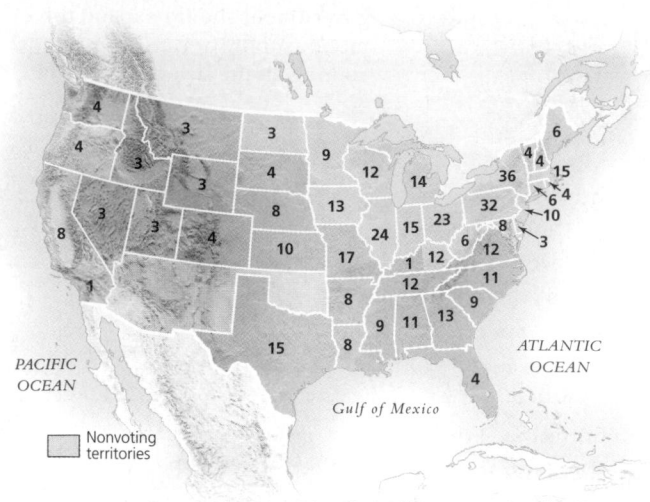

| | Electoral Vote (%) | Popular Vote (%) |
|---|---|---|
| **WILLIAM McKINLEY** (Republican) | 271 (61) | 7,102,246 (51) |
| **William J. Bryan** (Democrat) | 176 (39) | 6,492,559 (47) |
| **Minor parties** | — | 315,398 (2) |

**MAP 20.2**

**Election of 1896**   Democratic candidate William Jennings Bryan carried most of rural America but could not overcome Republican William McKinley's stronghold in the populous industrial states.

WHAT WERE the most important elements of McKinley's campaign platform?

**18–9**
Booker T. Washington, *Atlanta Exposition Address* (1895)

**17–10**
*Plessy* v. *Ferguson* (1896)

**Nativism**   Favoring the interests and culture of native-born inhabitants over those of immigrants.

**Jim Crow laws**   Segregation laws that became widespread in the South during the 1890s.

**Segregation**   A system of racial control that separated the races, initially by custom but increasingly by law during and after Reconstruction.

***Plessy* v. *Ferguson***   Supreme Court decision holding that Louisiana's railroad segregation law did not violate the Constitution as long as the railroads or the state provided equal accommodations.

McKinley triumphed in the most important presidential election since Reconstruction. Bryan managed to win 46 percent of the popular vote but failed to carry the Midwest, West Coast, or Upper South (see Map 20.2). Moreover, the free silver campaign rebuffed traditionally Democratic urban voters who feared that soft money would bring higher prices. Many Catholics uncomfortable with Bryan's Protestant moral piety also deserted the Democrats. Finally, neither the reform-minded middle classes nor impoverished blue-collar workers were convinced that Bryan's grand reform vision really included them. The Populist following, disappointed and disillusioned, dwindled away.

Once in office, McKinley strengthened the executive branch and actively promoted a mixture of probusiness and expansionist measures. McKinley's triumph ended the popular challenge to the nation's governing system. With prosperity returning by the end of the century and nationalism rising swiftly, McKinley encouraged Americans to go for "a full dinner pail," the winning Republican slogan of the 1900 presidential campaign. With news of his second triumph, stock prices on Wall Street skyrocketed.

## NATIVISM AND JIM CROW

Campaign rhetoric aside, McKinley and Bryan had differed only slightly on the major problems facing the nation in the 1890s. Neither Bryan, the reformer, nor McKinley, the prophet of prosperity, addressed the escalation of racism and **nativism** (anti-immigrant feeling) throughout the nation.

Toward the end of the century, many political observers noted, the nation's patriotic fervor took on a strongly nationalistic and antiforeign tone. Striking workers and their employers alike tended to blame "foreigners" for the hard times. Semisecret organizations such as the American Protective Association sprang up to defend American institutions. Fourth of July orators continued to celebrate freedom and liberty but more often boasted about the might and power of their nation.

In the South, local and state governments codified racist ideology by passing discriminatory and segregationist legislation, which became known as **Jim Crow laws**. The phrase, dating from the early decades of the nineteenth century, was made popular by a white minstrel in blackface who used the name "Jim Crow" to demean all African Americans. By the end of the century, "Jim Crow" referred to the customs of **segregation** that were becoming secured by legislation throughout the South. With nine of every ten black Americans living in this region, the significance of this development was sweeping.

To secure their privileges, white Southerners acted directly to impose firm standards of segregation and domination and to forestall any appearance of social equality. State after state in the South enacted new legislation to cover facilities such as restaurants, public transportation, and even drinking fountains.

The United States Supreme Court upheld the new discriminatory legislation. Its decisions in the *Civil Rights Cases* (1883) overturned the Civil Rights Act of 1875; in ***Plessy* v. *Ferguson*** (1896), the Court upheld a Louisiana state law formally segregating railroad passenger cars on the basis of the "separate but equal" doctrine. The majority opinion, delivered by Justice Henry Billings Brown, stated that political equality and social equality are distinct: "Legislation is powerless to eradicate racial instincts or to abolish distinctions based on physical differences. If one race be inferior to the other socially, the Constitution of the United States cannot put them on the same plane."

This ruling established the legal rationale for segregation, North as well as South, for the next fifty years. In *Cumming* v. *Richmond County Board of Education* (1899), the Court allowed separate schools for blacks and whites, even where facilities for African American children did not exist. This ruling reverberated in other parts of the country. For example, a year later, in 1900, the New Orleans school board decided to eliminate all schools for black children beyond the fifth grade, reasoning that African Americans needed only minimal education to fit them for menial jobs "to which they are best suited and seem ordained by the proper fitness of things."

Southern states enacted new literacy tests and property qualifications for voting. Loopholes permitted poor whites to vote even under these conditions, except where they threatened the Democratic Party's rule. "**Grandfather clauses**," invented in Louisiana, exempted from all restrictions those who had been entitled to vote on January 1, 1867, together with their sons and grandsons, a measure that effectively enfranchised whites while barring African Americans (see Figure 20.2).

Racial violence escalated. Race riots, which took the lives of hundreds of African Americans, broke out in small towns like Rosewood, Florida, and Phoenix, South Carolina, and in large cities like New Orleans and Tulsa. In November 1898, in Wilmington, North Carolina, where a dozen African Americans had ridden out the last waves of the Populist insurgency to win appointments to minor political offices, a group of white opponents organized to root them out and ultimately staged a violent coup, restoring white rule and forcing black leaders to leave town. "It come so," a black woman explained, "that we in this town is afraid of a white face." As many as 100 African Americans were killed in what came to be known as the Wilmington massacre.

Not only race riots but also thousands of lynchings took place. Between 1882 and the turn of the century, the number of lynchings usually exceeded 100 each year; 1892 produced a record 230 deaths (161 black, 69 white). Mobs often burned or dismembered victims in order to drag out their agony and entertain the crowd of onlookers. Announced in local newspapers, lynchings in the 1890s became public spectacles for entire white families, and railroads sometimes offered special excursion rates for travel to these events.

Antilynching became the one-woman crusade of Ida B. Wells, young editor of a black newspaper in Memphis. Wells launched an international movement against lynching, lecturing across the country and in Europe, demanding an end to the silence about this barbaric crime. Her work also inspired the growth of a black women's club movement. The National Association of Colored Women, founded in 1896, took up the antilynching cause and also fought to protect black women from sexual exploitation by white men.

Few white reformers rallied to defend African Americans. Even the National American Woman Suffrage Association, in an attempt to appease its southern members at its 1899 convention, voted down a resolution condemning racial segregation in public facilities. More than a few Americans had come to believe that their future welfare hinged on white supremacy, not only in their own country but across the globe as well.

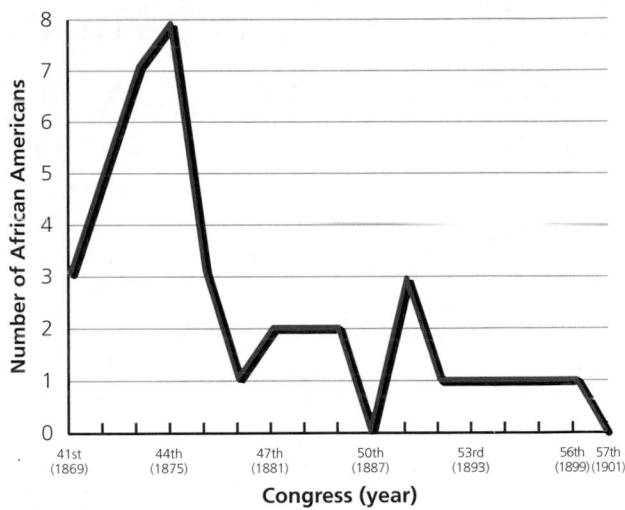

**Figure 20.2 African American Representation in Congress, 1867–1900**
Black men served in the U.S. Congress from 1870 until 1900. All were Republicans.

## QUICK REVIEW

**Jim Crow**

- Neither major party addressed problem of racism and nativism in campaign of 1896.
- Local and state governments in the South codified racism in Jim Crow laws.
- The Supreme Court upheld the new discriminatory legislation.

 **18–8**
Ida B. Wells-Barnett, *A Red Record* (1895)

**Grandfather clauses**   Rules that required potential voters to demonstrate that their grandfathers had been eligible to vote; used in some Southern states after 1890 to limit the black electorate.

HOW DID proponents of
imperialism justify colonization?

myhistorylab
Review Summary

# THE PATH TO IMPERIALISM

Many Americans attributed the economic crisis of 1893–97 not simply to the collapse of the railroads and banks but also to basic structural problems: an overbuilt economy and an insufficient market for goods. Profits from total sales of manufactured and agricultural products had grown substantially over levels achieved in the 1880s, but output increased even more rapidly. Although the number of millionaires shot up from 500 in 1860 to more than 4,000 in 1892, the majority of Americans did not have enough money to buy a significant portion of what they produced. To find new markets for American goods, many Americans looked abroad.

## ALL THE WORLD'S A FAIR

The World's Columbian Exposition, held in Chicago, commemorated the four hundredth anniversary of Columbus's landing and answered Congress's call for "an exhibition of the progress of civilization in the New World." On May Day 1893, less than two months after the nation's economy had collapsed, crowds began to flock to the fair, a complex of more than 400 buildings newly constructed in beaux arts design.

The section known as "The White City" celebrated the achievements of American business in the global economy. Agriculture Hall showcased the production of corn, wheat, and other crops and featured a gigantic globe encircled by samples of American-manufactured farm machinery. Another building housed a model of a canal cut across Nicaragua, suggesting the ease with which American traders might reach Asian markets if transport ships could travel directly from the Caribbean to the Pacific. The symbolism was evident: all eyes were on international trade as a marker of American prowess.

In contrast to the White City was the Midway, a strip nearly a mile long and more than 600 feet wide that offered entertainment. The Midway also offered amusement in the form of "displays" of "uncivilized" people from foreign lands. One enormous sideshow re-created Turkish bazaars and South Sea island huts. There were Javanese carpenters, Dahomean drummers, Egyptian swordsmen, and Hungarian Gypsies, as well as Eskimos, Syrians, Samoans, and Chinese. According to the guidebook, all these peoples had come "from the nightsome North and the splendid South, from the wasty West and the effete East, bringing their manners, customs, dress, religions, legends, amusements, that we might know them better."

By celebrating the brilliance of American industry and simultaneously presenting the "uncivilized" people of the world as a source of exotic entertainment, the planners of the fair delivered a powerful message. Former abolitionist Frederick Douglass, who attended the fair on "Colored People's Day," recognized it immediately. Douglass objected to the stark contrast setting off Anglo-Saxons from people of color, an opposition between "civilization" and "savagery." He and Ida B. Wells also objected to the exclusion of African Americans from representation among the exhibits at the White City. Wells boycotted the special day set aside for African Americans, while Douglass attended, using the occasion to deliver a speech upbraiding white Americans for their racism.

Also speaking at the fair was Frederick Jackson Turner, who read his famous essay about the disappearance of the frontier. Having passed "from the task of filling up the vacant spaces of the continent," the young historian warned, the nation is now "thrown back upon itself." His message was clear: if democracy were to survive, Americans required a new "frontier."

The Chicago World's Fair, which attracted 27 million visitors from all over the world, reassured Turner by marking the coming to age of the United States as a global power and by making a deliberate case for commercial expansion abroad. The exposition also gave material shape to prevalent ideas about the pre-eminence of American civilization as well as the superiority of the Anglo-Saxon race (see Seeing History).

## THE "IMPERIALISM OF RIGHTEOUSNESS"

**20–1**
Josiah Strong, *Our Country*
(1885)

Social gospeler Josiah Strong, a Congregational minister who had begun his career hoping to "civilize" the Indians by converting them to Christianity, provided a prescient commentary in 1885. Linking economic and spiritual expansion, he advocated an "imperialism of righteousness." He identified white Americans, who, with "their genius for colonizing," as the best agents for "Christianizing" and "civilizing" the people of Africa and the Pacific and beyond.

The push for overseas expansion coincided with a major wave of religious evangelism and foreign missions. Early in the nineteenth century, Protestant missionaries, hoping to fulfill what they believed to be a divine command to carry God's message to all peoples and to win converts for their church, had focused on North America. As early as the 1820s, however, a few missionaries had traveled to the Sandwich Islands (Hawai'i) in an effort to supplant the indigenous religion with Christianity. After the Civil War, the major evangelical Protestant denominations all sponsored missions directed at foreign lands.

By the 1890s, college campuses blazed with missionary excitement, and the intercollegiate Student Volunteers for Foreign Missions spread rapidly under the slogan "The Evangelicization of the World in This Generation." By the turn of the century, some 23 American Protestant churches had established missions in China, the majority staffed by women.

Young Protestant women rushed to join foreign missionary societies. Since the early part of the nineteenth century, Protestant women had headed "cent" and "mite" societies, which gathered money to support overseas missionaries. By 1820, women were accompanying their minister husbands to distant parts to convert the "heathens" to Christianity. After the Civil War, in tandem with the expansion of higher educational opportunities, unmarried women petitioned church leaders to request their own missionary assignments. By 1900, the various Protestant denominations were supporting forty-one women's missionary boards; several years later more than 3 million women had enrolled in societies to support this work, together surpassing in size all other women's organizations in the United States.

**By the end** of the nineteenth century, women represented 60 percent of the American missionary force in foreign lands. This photograph shows two Methodist women using "back chairs," a traditional form of transportation, at Mount Omei in Szechwan, China.

Outside the churches, the YMCA and YWCA, which had set up nondenominational missions for the working poor in many American cities, also embarked on a worldwide crusade to reach non-Christians. By the turn of the century, the YWCA had foreign branches in Ceylon (present-day Sri Lanka) and China. After foreign branches multiplied in the next decade, a close observer ironically suggested that the United States had three great occupying forces: the army, the navy, and the "Y." He was not far wrong.

Missionaries played an important role both in generating public interest in foreign lands and in preparing the way for American economic expansion. As Josiah Strong aptly put it, "Commerce follows the missionary."

**20–2**
Henry Cabot Lodge,
*The Business World vs. the Politicians* (1895)

**20–3**
Albert Beveridge, *The March of the Flag* (1898)

## THE QUEST FOR EMPIRE

Not only missionaries but also business and political leaders had set their sights on distant lands, which in turn meant new markets. In the 1860s, Secretary of State William Henry Seward, under Abraham Lincoln and then under Andrew Johnson, correctly predicted that foreign trade would play an increasingly important part in the American economy. Between 1870 and 1900, exports more than tripled, from about $400 million to over $1.5 billion, with textiles and agricultural products leading the way. But as European markets for American goods began to contract, business and political leaders, of necessity, looked more eagerly to Asia as well as to lands closer by.

Since the American Revolution, many Americans had regarded all nearby nations as falling naturally within their own territorial realm, destined to be acquired when opportunity allowed. Seward advanced these imperialist principles in 1867 by negotiating the purchase of Alaska. Meanwhile, with European nations launched on their own imperialist missions in Asia and Africa, the United States increasingly viewed the Caribbean as an "American lake" and all of Latin America as a vast potential market for U.S. goods. The crisis of the 1890s transformed this long-standing desire into a perceived economic necessity.

Americans focused their expansionist plans on the Western Hemisphere, determined to dislodge the dominant power, Great Britain. In 1867, when Canada became a self-governing dominion, American diplomats hoped to annex their northern neighbor, believing that Great Britain would gladly accede in order to concentrate its imperial interests in Asia. But Great Britain refused to give up Canada, and the United States backed away. Central and South America proved more accommodating to American designs (see Map 20.3).

Republican stalwart James G. Blaine, secretary of state under presidents Garfield and Harrison, determined to work out a Good Neighbor policy (a phrase coined by Henry Clay in 1820). Bilateral treaties with Mexico, Colombia, the British West Indies, El Salvador, and the Dominican Republic allowed American business to dominate local economies, importing their raw materials at low prices and flooding their local markets with goods manufactured in the United States.

The Good Neighbor policy depended, Blaine knew, on peace and order in the Latin American states. As early as 1875, when revolt shook Venezuela, the Department of State warned European powers not to meddle. If popular uprisings proved too much for local officials, the U.S. Navy would intervene and return American allies to power.

In 1883, wishing to enforce treaties and protect overseas investments, Congress appropriated funds to build up American sea power and in 1884 established the Naval War College in Newport, Rhode Island, to train the officer corps. Beginning with ninety small ships, over one-third of them wooden, the

## QUICK REVIEW

**The Good Neighbor Policy**

- Spearheaded by James G. Blaine, secretary of state under Garfield and Harrison.

- Allowed U.S. to dominate local economies in Central America and the Caribbean.

- U.S. expanded navy to help enforce control of Latin American states.

# The White Man's Burden

In 1899, the British poet Rudyard Kipling published "The White Man's Burden" in the American magazine *McClure's* with the subtitle "The United States and the Philippine Islands." Some interpreted the poem as an endorsement of the U.S. imperialist ventures in the Pacific; others read it as a cautionary note warning against taking on colonies. Those who favored expansion embraced the notion of the "white man's burden" as means to justify their position as a noble enterprise, that is, in "uplifting" those people of color who had not yet enjoyed the benefits of "civilization."

The concept even made its way into advertising for soap. In 1789, London soapmaster Andrew Pears began producing a distinctive oval bar of a transparent amber glycerin and marketing it as a luxury item under the name Pears Soap. Barratt's advertising presented Pears Soap as safe and beneficial but suitable only for discerning consumers. Pears Soap

The first step towards lightening

## The White Man's Burden

is through teaching the virtues of cleanliness.

## Pears' Soap

is a potent factor in brightening the dark corners of the earth as civilization advances, while amongst the cultured of all nations it holds the highest place—it is the ideal toilet soap.

promised a smooth, white complexion, underscoring this message by associating dark skins with "uncivilized" people. The advertisement appeared first in 1899 in *McClure's*—the same magazine in which Kipling's poetic exhortation was published.

**WHAT DID** the readers of *McClure's* magazine understand as "the white man's burden"? How did this responsibility relate to the belief in a hierarchy of races and civilizations expressed in Kipling's poem?

> *Take up the White Man's burden—*
> *Send forth the best ye breed—*
> *Go bind your sons to exile*
> *To serve your captives' need;*
> *To wait in heavy harness,*
> *On fluttered folk and wild—*

> *Your new-caught, sullen peoples,*
> *Half-devil and half-child.*
> *Take up the White Man's burden—*
> *In patience to abide,*
> *To veil the threat of terror*
> *And check the show of pride...* ■

*Seeing History*

# MAP EXPLORATION

To explore an interactive version of this map, go to **http://www.prenhall.com/faraghertlc/map20.3**

RUSSIA

Alaska
1867

CANADA

CHINA

KOREA

JAPAN

Aleutian Islands
1867

UNITED
STATES

Midway
Islands
1867

Tropic of Cancer

Hawaiian
Islands
1898

U.S. acquires exclusive
rights to lease naval
bases, 1898

DOMINICAN
REPUBLIC

Wake Island 1899

MEXICO

CUBA

Santiago

Puerto Rico
1898

Philippine
Islands
1898

Guam 1898

Johnston Island 1858

ATLANTIC

OCEAN

Kingman Reef 1858

GUATEMALA
HONDURAS
NICARAGUA
PANAMA

VENEZUELA

Equator

Howland Island 1856

Palmyra Island 1898

Baker
Island
1856

Jarvis Island 1856

PACIFIC

American Samoa 1899

OCEAN

Tropic of Capricorn

AUSTRALIA

CHILE

Valparaiso

NEW
ZEALAND

United States involvement

United States territory

**MAP 20.3**

**The American Domain, ca. 1900**   The United States claimed numerous islands in the South Pacific and intervened repeatedly in Latin America to secure its own economic interests.

WHAT FUELED America's expansion overseas?

navy grew quickly to include modern steel fighting ships. The force behind this build-up of the U.S. Navy was Captain Alfred Thayer Mahan, one of the first presidents of the Naval War College.

Mahan achieved international fame for outlining an imperialist strategy based on command of the seas. His book, *The Influence of Sea Power upon History, 1660–1873* (1890), helped to define foreign policy not only for the United States but also for Great Britain, Japan, and Germany by identifying sea power as the key to world dominance. For the United States to achieve global preeminence, he prescribed not only open markets but also the control of colonies out for the annexation of Hawai'i, claiming the United States, with its continental border extending to the Pacific Ocean, was "the proper guardian for this most important position." The Hawaiian archipelago, he insisted, held key strategic value as stepping-stone to Asia and beyond.

# ONTO A GLOBAL STAGE

Influenced by Alfred Thayer Mahan, McKinley became an advocate of expansion as a means to make the United States first in international commerce and as a means to implement its humanitarian and democratic goals. He also hoped to achieve these ends peacefully. He was pleased, therefore, to grease the wheels for the annexation of Hawai'i and in June 1898 agreed with representatives from the Republic on a treaty of annexation. Soon, however, McKinley found himself embroiled in a war with Spain that would establish the United States as a strong player in global imperialism (see Map 20.4). By the end of the century, the United States had joined Europe and Japan in the quest for empire and claimed territories spread out from the Caribbean Sea across the Pacific.

## A "SPLENDID LITTLE WAR" IN CUBA

Before the Civil War, Southerners pushed for the acquisition of Cuba, a possession of Spain, for the expansion of slavery into its sugar mills, tobacco plantations, and mines. After failing several times to buy the island outright, the United

**WHAT CRITIQUES** of empire were put forward in the years after the Spanish-American War?

**Review Summary**

**20–4**
*The Spanish-American War (1898)*

# MAP EXPLORATION

To explore an interactive version of this map, go to **http://www.prenhall.com/faraghertlc/map20.4**

Legend:
- ← American forces
- ← Spanish forces
- ✳ American victories
- ▼▼▼ U.S. naval blockade
- ▢ Spanish possessions

UNITED STATES

Tampa

Gulf of Mexico

*ATLANTIC OCEAN*

Bahama Islands (Br)

Spanish fleet destroyed, July 3, 1898

Havana

Cuba (Spanish possession)

Santiago

HAITI    DOMINICAN REPUBLIC

San Juan

Puerto Rico (Spanish possession)

Cayman Islands (Br)

Jamaica (Br)

*Caribbean Sea*

HONDURAS

NICARAGUA

COSTA RICA    PANAMA

VENEZUELA

COLOMBIA

CHINA

Canton    Hong Kong (Br.)

Formosa (Taiwan) (Japanese)

*PACIFIC OCEAN*

Gulf of Tonkin    Hainan

Dewey

Luzon

Manila Bay – Spanish fleet destroyed, May 1, 1898

South China Sea

FRENCH INDOCHINA

Manila

*Philippines* (Spanish possession)

Leyte

BRITISH NORTH BORNEO

Sulu Sea

Mindanao

BRUNEI

SARAWAK

BORNEO

**MAP 20.4**
**The Spanish-American War**   In two theaters of action, the United States used its naval power adeptly against a weak foe.

WHAT DID the United States gain from victories in each of these conflicts?

**Brought to power** with the assistance of American businessmen, Queen Lili'uokalani sought to limit outsider influence. American Marines, Christian missionaries, and sugar planters joined in 1893 to drive her from her throne. A century later, the U.S. government apologized to native Hawaiians for this illegal act.

## QUICK REVIEW

### Cuba Libre

♦ At the end of the Spanish-American war, the United States gained effective control over Cuba.

♦ Platt amendment spelled out Cuban subservience to the United States.

♦ Terms of the amendment incorporated in the Cuban-American Treaty of 1903.

States settled for the continuation of the status quo and resolved to protect Spain's sovereignty over Cuba against the encroachment of other powers, including Cuba itself.

In the mid-1860s, a movement for independence began in Cuba when Spain, its empire in ruins, began to impose stiff taxes on the island. After a series of defeats, insurgents rallied in the 1890s under the nationalist leadership of José Martí. In May 1895 Spanish troops ambushed and killed Martí, turning him into a martyr and fanning the flames of rebellion. In February 1896 Spain appointed General Valeriano Weyler as governor and gave him full authority to crush the rebellion. Weyler instituted a policy *of reconcentrado,* forcing civilians from the countryside into concentration camps so they could not aid the rebels. Thousands starved or died from the diseases that swept these crowded, dirty camps.

In the United States, the popular press whipped up support for the movement for *Cuba Libre,* circulating sensationalistic and even false stories of the atrocities that Weyler, "the butcher," perpetrated against the insurgents. Newspapers ran stories on mass executions in the "death camps" and featured drawings of emaciated children.

Public sympathy, again whipped up by the press, turned into frenzy on February 15, 1898, when an explosion ripped through the battleship USS *Maine,* stationed in Havana harbor to protect American interests. The newspapers ran banner headlines charging a Spanish conspiracy, although there was no proof. The impatient public, meanwhile, demanded revenge for the death of 266 American sailors. Within days, a new slogan appeared: "Remember the Maine! To Hell with Spain!"

Finally, on April 11, President McKinley asked Congress for a declaration of war against Spain. Yet Congress barely passed the war resolution on April 25, and only with the inclusion of an amendment by Senator Henry Teller (Rep., Colorado) that disclaimed "any disposition or intention to exercise sovereignty, jurisdiction or control over said island, except for the pacification thereof."

Ten weeks later the war was all but over. On land, Lieutenant Colonel Theodore Roosevelt—who boasted of killing Spaniards "like jackrabbits"—led his Rough Riders to victory. On July 3, the main Spanish fleet near Santiago Bay was destroyed; two weeks later Santiago itself surrendered, and the war drew to a close. Roosevelt felt invigorated by the conflict, agreeing with McKinley's Secretary of State John Hay that it had been a "splendid little war."

On August 12, at a small ceremony in McKinley's office marking Spain's surrender, the United States secured Cuba's independence from Spain, but not its own sovereignty. American businesses proceeded to tighten their hold on Cuban sugar plantations, while U.S. military forces oversaw the formation of a constitutional convention that made Cuba a protectorate of the United States. Under the Platt Amendment, sponsored by Republican senator Orville H. Platt of Connecticut in 1901, Cuba was required to provide land for American bases, including a navy base at Guantanomo Bay; to devote national revenues to pay back debts to the United States; to sign no treaty that would be detrimental to American interests; and to acknowledge the right of the United States to intervene at any time to protect its interests in Cuba. After the U.S. withdrawal of troops, the terms of the Platt

Amendment were incorporated into the Cuban-American Treaty of 1903. This treaty, which remained in place until 1934, paved the way for American domination of the island's sugar industry and contributed to anti-American sentiment among Cuban nationalists.

## WAR IN THE PHILIPPINES

The Philippines, another of Spain's colonies, seemed an especially attractive prospect, its 7,000 islands a natural way station to the markets of mainland Asia. Shortly after Congress declared war on Spain, on May 4, McKinley dispatched 5,000 troops to occupy the Philippines. During the first week of the conflict, the Spanish fleet was demolished in Manila Bay through seven hours of unimpeded target practice. Once the war ended, McKinley refused to sign the armistice unless Spain relinquished all claims to its Pacific islands. When Spain conceded, McKinley quickly drew up plans for colonial administration. He pledged "to educate the Filipinos, and to uplift and civilize and Christianize them." But after centuries of Spanish rule, the majority of islanders—already Christians—were eager to create their own nation.

The Filipino rebels, like the Cubans, at first welcomed American troops and fought with them against Spain. But when the Spanish-American War ended and they perceived that American troops were not preparing to leave, the rebels, led by Emilio Aguinaldo, turned against their former allies and attacked the American base of operations in Manila in February 1899. Predicting a brief skirmish, American commanders seriously underestimated the population's capacity to endure great suffering for the sake of independence.

U.S. troops had provoked this conflict in various ways. Military leaders, the majority veterans of the Indian Wars, commonly described the natives as "gugus," and reported themselves, as one said, as "just itching to get at the niggers." While awaiting action, American soldiers repeatedly insulted or physically abused civilians, raped Filipino women, and otherwise whipped up resentment.

The resulting conflict took the form of modern guerrilla warfare, with brutalities on both sides. By the time the fighting slowed down in 1902, 4,300 American lives had been lost, and one of every five Filipinos had died in battle or from starvation or disease. On some of the Philippine islands, intermittent fighting lasted until 1935.

The conquest of the Philippines, which remained a U.S. colony until 1946, evoked for its defenders the vision of empire. The Philippines joined Hawai'i as yet another stepping-stone for U.S. merchants en route to China. The acquisition of Pacific territories, including Guam, marked the emergence of the United States as a global colonial power.

20–5
William McKinley, *Decision on the Philippines* (1900)

## CRITICS OF EMPIRE

No mass movement formed to forestall U.S. expansion, but distinguished figures like Mark Twain, Andrew Carnegie, William Jennings Bryan, and Harvard philosopher William James voiced their opposition strongly. To protest military action in the Philippines, a small group of prominent Bostonians organized the Anti-Imperialist League.

The *National Labor Standard* expressed its common hope that all those "who believe in the Republic against Empire should join." By 1899, the league claimed a half-million members.

20–8
Mark Twain, *Incident in the Philippines* (1924)

**"Uncle Sam Teaches** the Art of Self-Government," editorial cartoon, 1898. Expressing a popular sentiment of the time, a newspaper cartoonist shows the rebels as raucous children who constantly fight among themselves and need to be brought into line by Uncle Sam. The Filipino leader, Emilio Aguinaldo, appears as a dunce for failing to learn properly from the teacher. The two major islands where no uprising took place, Puerto Rico and Hawai'i, appear as passive but exotically dressed women, ready to learn their lessons.

Within the press, which overwhelmingly supported the Spanish-American War, the voices of opposition appeared primarily in African American and labor papers. The *Indianapolis Recorder* asked rhetorically in 1899, "Are the tender-hearted expansionists in the United States Congress really actuated by the desire to save the Filipinos from self-destruction or is it the worldly greed for gain?" The *Railroad Telegrapher* similarly commented, "The wonder of it all is that the working people are willing to lose blood and treasure in fighting another man's battle."

Most Americans put aside their doubts and welcomed the new era of imperialism. Untouched by the private tragedies of dead or wounded American soldiers and the mass destruction of civilian society in the Philippines, the vast majority could approve Theodore Roosevelt's defense of armed conflict: "No triumph of peace is quite so great as the supreme triumphs of war."

## CONCLUSION

The conflicts marking the last quarter of the nineteenth century that pitted farmers, workers, and the proprietors of small businesses against powerful national interests had offered Americans an important moment of democratic promise. By the end of the century, however, the rural and working-class campaigns to retain a large degree of self-government in their communities had been defeated, their organizations destroyed, their autonomy eroded. The rise

# CHRONOLOGY

| | |
|---|---|
| **1867** | Grange founded |
| | Secretary of State Seward negotiates the purchase of Alaska |
| **1874** | Granger laws begin to regulate railroad shipping rates |
| **1877** | Rutherford B. Hayes elected president. |
| | Great Uprising of 1877 |
| **1879** | Henry George publishes *Progress and Poverty* |
| **1881** | President James A. Garfield assassinated; Chester A. Arthur becomes president |
| **1882** | Chinese Exclusion Act |
| **1883** | Pendleton Act passed |
| **1884** | Grover Cleveland elected president |
| **1887** | Interstate Commerce Act creates the Interstate Commerce Commission |
| **1888** | Colored Farmers' Alliance formed |
| | Benjamin Harrison elected president |
| **1889** | National Farmers' Alliance formed |
| **1890** | Sherman Silver Purchase Act |
| | McKinley Tariff enacted |
| | National American Woman Suffrage Association formed |
| **1892** | Populist (People's) Party formed |
| | Coeur d'Alene miners' strike |

| | |
|---|---|
| | Homestead strike |
| | Ida B. Wells begins crusade against lynching |
| **1893** | Western Federation of Miners formed |
| | Financial panic and depression |
| | World's Columbian Exhibition opens in Chicago |
| **1894** | "Coxey's Army" marches on Washington, DC |
| | Pullman strike and boycott |
| **1896** | *Plessy* v. *Ferguson* upholds segregation |
| | William McKinley defeats William Jennings Bryan for president |
| **1897** | Dingley Tariff again raises import duties to an all-time high |
| **1898** | Eugene V. Debs helps found Social Democratic Party |
| | Hawai'i is annexed |
| | Spanish-American War begins |
| | Anti-Imperialist League formed |
| | Wilmington, North Carolina, massacre |
| **1899** | *Cumming* v. *Richmond County Board of Education* sanctions segregated education |
| | Guerrilla war begins in the Philippines |
| **1900** | Gold Standard Act |
| | Josiah Strong publishes *Expansion* |

of a national governing class and its counterpart, the large bureaucratic state, established new rules of behavior, new sources of prestige, and new rewards for the most successful citizens.

But the nation would eventually pay a steep price for the failure of democratic reform. Regional antagonisms, nativist movements against the foreign-born, and above all deepening racial tensions blighted American society. As the new century opened, progressive reformers moved to correct flaws in government while accepting the framework of a corporate society and its overseas empire. So, too, did the majority of citizens who shared their president's pride in expansion.

William Jennings Bryan made another bid for the presidency in 1900 on a strong anti-imperialist platform and was roundly defeated at the polls. The dream of Queen Lili'uokalani for an independent Hawai'i was likewise crushed, although a century after her overthrow, in 1993 President William Clinton signed a joint congressional resolution apologizing for the "alleged role the United States had played" in deposing her. But in 1900, Americans would find the widening divisions in their own society difficult—if not impossible—to overcome.

# REVIEW QUESTIONS

1. Discuss some of the problems accompanying the expansion of government during the late nineteenth century. What role did political parties play in this process? Explain how a prominent reformer such as James Garfield might become a leading "machine" politician.

2. What were the major causes and consequences of the Populist movement of the 1880s and 1890s? Why did the election of 1896 prove so important to the future of American politics?

3. Discuss the role of women in both the Grange and the People's Party. What were their specific goals?

4. Discuss the causes and consequences of the financial crisis of the 1890s. How did various reformers and politicians respond to the event? What kinds of programs did they offer to restore the economy or reduce poverty?

5. How did the exclusion of African Americans affect the outcome of populism? Explain the rise of Jim Crow legislation in the South and discuss its impact on the status of African Americans.

6. Describe American foreign policy during the 1890s. Why did the United States intervene in Cuba and the Philippines? What were some of the leading arguments for and against overseas expansion?

Flashcard Review

# KEY TERMS

**Coxey's Army** (p. 536)
**Free silver** (p. 539)
**Grandfather clauses** (p. 541)
**Grange** (p. 530)
**Granger laws** (p. 531)
**Great Uprising of 1877** (p. 533)
**Interstate Commerce Commission (ICC)** (p. 527)
**Jim Crow laws** (p. 540)
**National American Woman Suffrage Association (NAWSA)** (p. 534)

**Nativism** (p. 540)
**Pendleton Civil Service Reform Act** (p. 529)
*Plessy* v. *Ferguson* (p. 540)
**Populism** (p. 530)
**Protective association** (p. 536)
**Segregation** (p. 540)
**Sherman Silver Purchase Act** (p. 538)
**Southern Farmers' Alliance** (p. 531)
**Woman's Christian Temperance Union (WCTU)** (p. 534)

# RECOMMENDED READING

Steven Hahn, *A Nation Under Our Feet: Black Political Struggles in the Rural South from Slavery to the Great Migration* (2003). A sweeping history of African American politics with an eye on its influence in shaping the South and the nation in the last half of the nineteenth century. Hahn emphasizes the emergence of political communities and highlights the 1880s as a period of exceptional assertiveness on the part of southern African Americans.

Evelyn Brooks Higginbotham, *Righteous Discontent: The Women's Movement in the Black Baptist Church, 1880–1920* (1993). Documents the central role of women in shaping the theology and racial uplift programs of the National Baptist Convention, the largest denomination of African Americans at the end of the nineteenth century.

Matthew Frye Jacobson, *Barbarian Virtues: The United States Encounters Foreign Peoples at Home and Abroad, 1876–1917* (2000). Links the histories of immigration and empire-building to examine public discussions about foreign people, especially their "fitness" for self-government. Jacobson casts the search for markets as backdrop for cultural history.

Michael Kazin, *A Godly Hero: The Life of William Jennings Bryan* (2006). Makes a strong case for the relevance of Bryan to the history of American liberalism. Kazin explores the sources of Bryan's popularity among the nation's poor and working classes.

Walter LaFeber, *The New Empire: An Interpretation of American Expansion, 1860–1898* (1963, 1998). The best overview of U.S. imperial involvement in the late nineteenth century. LaFeber shows how overseas commitments grew out of the economic expansionist assumptions of American leaders and expanded continuously, if often chaotically, with the opportunities presented by the crises experienced by the older imperial powers.

Leon F. Litwack, *Trouble in Mind: Black Southerners in the Age of Jim Crow* (1998). An expansive social history of the first generation of African Americans born in freedom and surviving a period of extraordinary violent and repressive race relations in the South. Litwack examines the retrenchment of their political and civil rights but emphasizes their resourcefulness and resistance.

Eric T. L. Love, *Race over Empire and U.S. Imperialism, 1865–1900* (2004). An engaging narrative of expansion in the late nineteenth century and a keen analysis of the policies supporting and opposing annexation of territories and the assimilation of new populations.

Noenoe K. Silva, *Aloha Betrayed: Native Hawaiian Resistance to American Colonialism* (2004). Highlights the active role native Hawaiians played in the face of U.S. annexation pressures. Silva breaks ground by using Hawaiian-languages newspapers and sources.

John Lawrence Tone, *War and Genocide in Cuba, 1895–1898* (2006). Provides a new perspective on the Cuban rebellion from Spain and a careful study of Spanish policy in the hand of General Varleriano Weyler.

William Appleman Williams, *Empire as a Way of Life: An Essay on the Causes and Character of America's Present Predicament* (1982). A lucid general exploration of American views of empire. Williams shows that Americans allowed the idea of empire and, more generally, economic expansion to dominate their concept of democracy, especially in the last half of the nineteenth century.

**myhistorylab**
Where it's a good time to connect to the past!

For study resources for this chapter, go to **www.myhistorylab.com** and choose *Out of Many, Teaching and Learning Classroom Edition*. You will find a wealth of study and review material for this chapter, including pretests and posttests, customized study plan, key-term review flash cards, interactive map and document activities, and documents for analysis.

# Currency Reform

During the Civil War, farmers in the Midwest had gone deeply into debt to expand their crop production and meet the profitable demand for grain and other crops created by war. During the wild financial swings of booms and busts between 1865 and 1900, farmers again borrowed heavily to meet the demand for grains created by various world events. Farmers frequently had to borrow yearly to obtain the seeds and materials to plant their crops. If crop prices were low at harvest or a crop failure occurred, farmers were in deep financial trouble. Radical variations in international crop prices impacted the farmer's bottom line. Panics or depressions would also drive indebted farmers to the wall resulting in mortgage foreclosures and loss of their farms. Looking for simplistic explanations to complicated problems, farmers decided that the railroads and eastern financial interests were in a conspiracy to reduce them to economic slavery to the industrial East.

**EXPLAIN AND** describe the powerful political lure of currency reform in American presidential campaigns between 1874 and 1900. Where did various political groups and candidates stand on this issue and to whom did they attempt to appeal?

Simplistic explanations led to simplistic answers and currency reform became the central focus of many farmer political movements. After silver was dropped from the list of authorized coins for the U.S., farmers decided that was the focus of their problems and began demanding the free coinage of silver to create an artificial inflation that would raise crop prices and free them from debt, or so they believed. Currency reform became an emotional issue in politics between 1874 and 1900.■

⚑ McKinley stands upon the platform of a gold dollar coin supported by cheering workers, clerks, bankers and industrialists. Shipping and industry thrives behind the President under the banner: "Prosperity at Home, Prestige Abroad."

## COINAGE ACT, FEBRUARY 12, 1873

**AN ACT** revising and amending the Laws relative to the Mints, Assay- offices, and Coinage of the United States.

*Called the "Crime of '73" by farmers and Populists, the Coinage Act of 1873 demonetized silver by removing it from the list of dollar coins and relegating it to the minor coinage of the United States. Silver had become too expensive to coin, so the Treasury had ceased minting silver dollars. Demonetizing silver was really simply a housekeeping action by Congress, but farmers considered it a conspiracy mounted by eastern bankers to keep them in peonage to the industrial East. It is this law that launches the issue of free coinage of silver.*

SEC. 14. That the gold coins of the United States shall be a One-dollar piece… a quartereagle, or two-and-a-half dollar piece; a three dollar piece; a half-eagle, or five-dollar piece; an eagle, or ten-dollar piece; and a double eagle, or twenty dollar piece… which coins shall be a legal tender in all payments at their nominal value….

SEC. I5. That the silver coins of the United States shall be… a half dollar, or fifty-cent piece, a quarter-dollar, or twenty five-cent piece, a dime, or ten-cent piece;… and said coins shall be a legal tender at their nominal value for any amount not exceeding five dollars in any one payment….

SEC. I7. That no coins, either of gold, silver, or minor coinage, shall hereafter be issued from the mint other than those of the denominations, standards, and weights herein set forth.■

## POPULIST PLATFORM, 1892

**AUTHORED BY** *Ignatius Donnelly, leader in the Grange movement and later with the Populists, this statement of demands along with others was adopted by the Populists at their 1892 convention in Omaha, Nebraska. Populists hoped to democratize the nation's economic system, but they never succeeded in their goal.*

Silver, which has been accepted as coin since the dawn of history, has been demonetized to add to the purchasing power of gold by decreasing the value of all forms of property as well as human labor, and the supply of currency is purposely abridged to fatten usurers, bankrupt enterprise, and enslave industry. A vast conspiracy against mankind has been organized on two continents, and it is rapidly taking possession of the world. If not met and overthrown at once it forebodes terrible social convulsions, the destruction of civilization, or the establishment of an absolute despotism.We demand a national currency, safe, sound, and flexible issued by the general government only, a full legal tender for all debts, public and private…. We demand free and unlimited coinage of silver and gold at the present legal ratio of 16 to 1.■

---

## WILLIAM H. HARVEY, *COIN'S FINANCIAL SCHOOL*, 1893

**HARVEY WROTE** Coin's Financial School *to explain to farmers the complicated economic issue of bimetallism and the demand for free coinage of silver.*

Hard times are with us; the country is distracted; very few things are marketable at a price above the cost of production; tens of thousands are out of employment; the jails, penitentiaries, workhouses and insane asylums are full… the cry of distress is heard on every hand…

Up to 1873 we were on what was known as a bimetallic basis, but what was in fact a silver basis, with gold as a companion metal enjoying the same privileges as silver, except that silver fixed the unit, and the value of gold was regulated by it. This was bimetallism….

Gold was considered the money of the rich. It was owned, principally by that class of people, and the poor people seldom handled it, and… seldom ever saw any of it….

It is proposed by the bimetallists to remonetize silver, and add it to the quantity of money that is to be used for measuring the value of all other property….

You increase the value of all property by adding to the number of money units in the land. You make it possible for the debtor to pay his debts; business to start anew, and revivify all the industries of the country, which must remain paralyzed so long as silver as well as all other property is measured by a gold standard….

The money lenders in the United States, who own substantially all our money, have a selfish interest in maintaining the gold standard. They, too, will not yield….

With silver remonetized, and gold at a premium, not one-tenth the hardships could result that now afflict us…. The bimetallic standard will make the United States the most prosperous nation on the globe.■

---

## WILLIAM JENNINGS BRYAN, "CROSS OF GOLD SPEECH," OFFICIAL PROCEEDINGS OF THE DEMOCRATIC NATIONAL CONVENTION, CHICAGO, ILLINOIS, JULY 9, 1896.

**BRYAN BECAME** *the champion of farmers and a candidate for president with this "Cross of Gold" speech, which advocated the free silver position of the earlier Populist movement.*

You come to us and tell us that the great cities are in favor of the gold standard. I tell you that the great cities rest upon these broad and fertile prairies. Burn down your cities and leave our farms, and your cities will spring up again as if by magic. But destroy our farms and the grass will grow in the streets of every city in the country….

If they dare to come out in the open field and defend the gold standard as a good thing, we shall fight them to the uttermost, having behind us the producing masses of the nation and the world. Having behind us the commercial interests and the laboring interests and all the toiling masses, we shall answer their demands for a gold standard by saying to them, you shall not press down upon the brow of labor this crown of thorns. You shall not crucify mankind upon a cross of gold.■

Grant Hamilton, *Judge Magazine,* October 13, 1900 ➤
The cartoonist emphasizes the free silver issue in this cartoon that criticizes Bryan as "worth 53 cents only in free silver."

*The women, trudging stoutly along under great difficulties, were able to complete their march only when troops of cavalry from Fort Meyers were rushed into Washington . . . No inauguration has ever produced such scenes . . .*

—Washington Post, *March 4, 1913*

THE JUNGLE

UPTON SINCLAIR

VOTES FOR US WHEN ARE WOMEN

**Suffragettes display signs** and American flags, while piled into a festooned car.

VOTES FOR WOMEN

# 21

# URBAN AMERICA AND THE PROGRESSIVE ERA

## 1900–1917

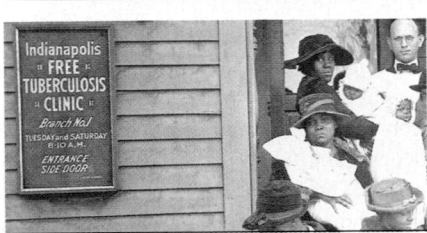

**WHAT WERE** the social and intellectual roots of progressive reform?

**TO WHAT** extent did progressives redefine the role of the state in American politics?

**HOW DID** tensions between social justice and social control divide progressives?

**HOW DID** the impact of new immigration transform American cities?

**WHAT NEW** forms of activism emerged among the working class, women, and African Americans?

**WHAT ROLE** did Theodore Roosevelt envision the federal government playing in the national economy?

# AMERICAN COMMUNITIES

## The Henry Street Settlement House: Women Settlement House Workers Create a Community of Reform

A SHY AND FRIGHTENED YOUNG GIRL APPEARED IN THE DOORWAY OF A weekly home-nursing class for women on Manhattan's Lower East Side. The teacher beckoned her to come forward. Tugging on the teacher's skirt, the girl pleaded in broken English for the teacher to come home with her. "Mother," "baby," "blood," she kept repeating. The teacher gathered up the sheets that were part of the interrupted lesson in bed making. The two hurried through narrow, garbage-strewn, foul-smelling streets, then groped their way up a pitch-dark, rickety staircase. They reached a cramped, two-room apartment, home to an immigrant family of seven and several boarders. There, in a vermin-infested bed, encrusted with dried blood, lay a mother and her newborn baby. The mother had been abandoned by a doctor because she could not afford his fee.

The teacher, Lillian Wald, had enjoyed a comfortable upbringing in a middle-class German Jewish family in Rochester. Despite her parents' objections, she had moved to New York City to become a professional nurse. Resentful of the disdainful treatment nurses received from doctors, and horrified by the inhumane conditions at a juvenile asylum she worked in, Wald determined to find a way of caring for the sick in their neighborhoods and homes. With nursing school classmate Mary Brewster, Wald rented a fifth-floor walk-up apartment on the Lower East Side and established a visiting nurse service. In 1895, philanthropist Jacob Schiff generously donated a red brick Georgian house on Henry Street as a new base of operation.

The Henry Street Settlement stood in the center of perhaps the most overcrowded neighborhood in the world, New York's Lower East Side. Roughly 500,000 people were packed into an area only as large as a midsized Kansas farm. Population density was about 500 per acre, roughly four times the figure for the rest of New York City, and far more concentrated than even the worst slums of London or Calcutta. A single city block might have as many as 3,000 residents. Home for most Lower East Siders was a small tenement apartment that might include paying boarders squeezed in alongside the immediate family. Residents were mostly recent immigrants from southern and eastern Europe: Jews, Italians, Germans, Greeks, Hungarians, Slavs. Men, women, and children toiled in the garment shops, small factories, retail stores, breweries, and warehouses to be found on nearly every street.

The Henry Street Settlement became a model for a new kind of reform community composed essentially of college-educated women who encouraged and supported one another in a wide variety of humanitarian, civic, and political activities. These included support for organized labor, campaigns for better sanitation and more parks, lobbying state legislatures for tougher laws regulating tenement construction and factory safety, and pushing for women's right to vote. Settlement house living arrangements closely resembled those in the dormitories of such new women's colleges as Smith, Wellesley, and Vassar. Like these colleges, the settlement house was an "experiment," but one designed, in settlement house pioneer Jane Addams's words, "to aid in the solution of the social and industrial problems which are engendered by the modern conditions of urban life." Unlike earlier moral reformers, who tried to impose their ideas from outside, settlement house residents lived in poor communities and worked for immediate improvements in the health and welfare of those communities. Yet, as Addams and others repeatedly stressed, the college-educated women were beneficiaries as well. The settlement house allowed them to preserve a collegial spirit, satisfy the desire for service, and apply their academic training.

With its combined moral and social appeal, the settlement house movement attracted many educated young women and grew rapidly. Few women made settlement work a career, but those who did typically chose not to marry, and most lived together with female companions. As the movement flourished, settlement house residents called attention to the plight of the poor and fostered respect for different cultural heritages in countless articles and lectures. Leaders of the movement, including Jane Addams, Lillian Wald, and Florence Kelley, emerged as influential political figures during the progressive era.

During the first two decades of the twentieth century, millions of Americans identified themselves as "progressives" and most, like Lillian Wald, were first drawn to causes and campaigns rooted in their local communities. But many soon saw that confronting the grim realities of an urban and industrial society required national and even global strategies for pursuing reform. It was no cliché for Wald to say, as she did on many occasions, "The whole world is my neighborhood." By the time America entered World War I in 1917, despite its contradictions, the progressive movement had reshaped the political and social landscape of the entire nation.

New York City

# THE ORIGINS OF PROGRESSIVISM

Between the 1890s and World War I, a large and diverse number of Americans claimed the political label "progressive." Progressives could be found in all classes, regions, and races. They shared a fundamental belief that America needed a new social consciousness to cope with the problems brought on by the enormous rush of economic and social change in the post–Civil War decades. The devastating depression of the 1890s, the often bloody labor conflicts of that decade, and the Populist revolt caused many Americans to look for a stronger government response to economic and social ills. Yet **progressivism** was no unified movement with a single set of principles. It is best understood as a varied collection of reform communities, often fleeting, uniting citizens in a host of political, professional, and religious organizations, some of which were national in scope.

## UNIFYING THEMES

Three basic attitudes underlay the various progressive crusades and movements. The first was anger over the excesses of industrial capitalism and urban growth. Unlike Populist era reformers, who were largely rural and small-town oriented, progressives focused their energies on the social and political ills experienced by Americans in factories or mines and in dreary city tenements or filthy streets. At the same time, progressives shared an essential optimism about the ability of citizens to improve social and economic conditions. They were reformers, not revolutionaries, who believed in using the democratic institutions available to them—the vote, the courts, the legislature—to address social problems. Second, progressives emphasized social cohesion and common bonds as a way of understanding how modern society and economics actually worked. They largely rejected the ideal of individualism that had informed nineteenth-century economic and political theory. For progressives, poverty and success hinged on more than simply individual character; the economy was more than merely a sum of individual calculations. Society's problems, in this view, were structural rather than simply the result of individual failures. Third, progressives believed in the need for citizens to intervene actively, both politically and morally, to improve social conditions. They looked to convert personal outrage into civic activism and to mobilize public opinion in new ways. Progressives thus called for expansion of the legislative and regulatory powers of the state. They moved away from the nineteenth-century celebration of minimal government as the surest way to allow all Americans to thrive.

*(margin handwriting: didn't believe in individual failure)*

*(margin handwriting: wanted)*

Progressive rhetoric and methods drew on two distinct sources of inspiration. One was evangelical Protestantism, particularly the late nineteenth-century social gospel movement. Social gospelers rejected the idea of original sin as the cause of human suffering. They emphasized both the capacity and the duty of Christians to purge the world of poverty, inequality, and economic greed. Many progressive activists with roots in the evangelical tradition adapted the old emphasis on individual salvation into a new social activism more focused on finding the common good. A second strain of progressive thought looked to natural and social scientists to develop rational measures for improving the human condition. They believed that experts trained in statistical analysis, engineering, and the sciences could make government and industry more efficient and set new standards for personal behavior. Progressivism thus offered an uneasy combination of social justice and social control, a tension that would characterize American reform for the rest of the twentieth century.

**WHAT WERE** the social and intellectual roots of progressive reform?

**Review Summary**

**21–12**
Herbert Croly, *Progressive Democracy* (1914)

## IMAGE KEY

for pages 556–557

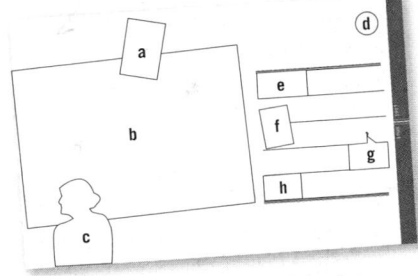

a. Cover, featuring a factory, of "The Jungle" by Upton Sinclair.
b. Suffragettes display signs and American flags, while piled into a festooned car.
c. Suffragette Dorothy Newell has "Votes for Women" written on her back.
d. Bull Moose Party campaign paraphernalia.
e. The Flanner House Baby Clinic, about 1918.
f. Publicity poster for 1913 pageant organized by John Reed and other Greenwich Village radicals supporting the striking silk workers in Paterson, New Jersey.
g. Detail of photo of Women's suffrage parade in Washington, D.C. in 1913.
h. Cartoon showing President Theodore Roosevelt slaying bad trusts and restraining good trusts.

**Progressivism**   A national movement focused on a variety of reform initiatives, including ending corruption, a more business like approach to government, and legislative responses to industrial excess.

## NEW JOURNALISM: MUCKRAKING

Changes in journalism helped fuel a new reform consciousness by drawing the attention of millions to urban poverty, political corruption, the plight of industrial workers, and immoral business practices. As early as 1890, journalist Jacob Riis had shocked the nation with his landmark book *How the Other Half Lives*, a portrait of New York City's poor. Riis's book included a remarkable series of photographs he had taken in tenements, lodging houses, sweatshops, and saloons. These striking pictures, combined with Riis's analysis of slum housing patterns, had a powerful impact on a whole generation of urban reformers (see Seeing History).

Within a few years, magazine journalists had turned to uncovering the seamier side of American life. The key innovator was S. S. McClure, a young midwestern editor who in 1893 started America's first large-circulation magazine, *McClure's*. Charging only a dime for his monthly, McClure effectively combined popular fiction with articles on science, technology, travel, and recent history. He attracted a new readership among the urban middle class through aggressive subscription and promotional campaigns, as well as newsstand sales.

In 1902, McClure began hiring talented reporters to write detailed accounts of the nation's social problems. *McClure's* and other magazines discovered that "exposure journalism" paid off handsomely in terms of increased circulation. The middle-class public responded to this new combination of factual reporting and moral exhortation. Between 1902 and 1908, magazines were full of articles exposing insurance scandals, patent medicine frauds, and stock market swindles.

**Muckraking** crusades could take many forms. In the 1890s the young African American newspaper editor Ida B. Wells set out to investigate an upsurge in lynchings around the city of Memphis. She paid special attention to the common white defense of lynching—that it was a necessary response to attempts by black men to rape white women. Her 1895 pamphlet *A Red Record* showed that the vast majority of black lynching victims had not even been accused of sexual transgression. Instead, Wells found that lynching was primarily a brutal device to eliminate African Americans who competed with white businesses or who had become too prosperous or powerful (see Chapter 20).

In 1906, David Graham Phillips, in a series for *Cosmopolitan* called "The Treason of the Senate," argued that many conservative U.S. senators were no more than mouthpieces for big business. President Theodore Roosevelt, upset by Phillips's attack on several of his friends and supporters, coined a new term when he angrily denounced Phillips and his colleagues as "muckrakers" who "raked the mud of society and never looked up." Partly due to Roosevelt's outburst, the muckraking vogue began to wane. But muckraking had demonstrated the potential for mobilizing public opinion on a national scale.

## INTELLECTUAL TRENDS PROMOTING REFORM

On a deeper level than muckraking, early twentieth-century thinkers challenged several of the core ideas in American intellectual life. Their new theories of education, law, economics, and society provided effective tools for reformers. The emergent fields of the social sciences—sociology, psychology, anthropology, and economics—emphasized observation of how people actually lived and behaved in their communities. Progressive reformers linked the systematic analysis of society and the individual characteristic of these new fields of inquiry to the project of improving the material conditions of Americans. Significantly, many of these intellectual currents transcended national boundaries. American progressives engaged in running dialogues with European counterparts who also contended with crafting effective and rational responses to the needs of overcrowded cities,

**18–11**
Lincoln Steffens, from *The Shame of the Cities* (1904)

**Muckraking** Journalism exposing economic, social, and political evils, so named by Theodore Roosevelt for its "raking the muck" of American society.

# Photographing Poverty in the Slums of New York

"Five Cents a Spot: Lodgers in a Bayard Street Tenement". c. 1899. Museum of the City of New York, Jacob A. Riis Collection.

J acob A. Riis was a twenty-year-old Danish immigrant when he arrived in New York City in 1870. After several years wandering the country as a casual laborer, he returned to New York and began a career as a reporter covering the police beat. By the early 1880s Riis found himself drawn to report on the deteriorating conditions of tenement house life. Riis's reports on the tenement districts reflected a keen outrage and new sense of purpose. "It was upon my midnight trips with the sanitary police," he recalled, "that the wish kept cropping up in me that there were some way of putting before the people what I saw there."

In 1888 Riis taught himself the rudiments of photography. He shot many of these photographs in the dead of the night, taking his subjects by surprise. Other photographs were carefully staged to ensure maximum emotional impact. He spent two years touring the country, presenting an illustrated lecture called "The Other Half: How It Lives and Dies in New York." The use of photography would become a key element for reform crusades in the progressive era and beyond. ■

**HERE ARE** two Riis photographs, "Five Cents a Spot" and "Home of an Italian Ragpicker." What visual information does each communicate about tenement life? How do they differ in their depiction of New York City's immigrant poor? How do you imagine Riis set up the scene for each of these photographs?

The Jacob A. Riis Collection 157, Museum of the City of New York.

**Lewis Hine, one** of the pioneers of social documentary photography, made this evocative 1908 portrait of "Mamie," a typical young spinner working at a cotton mill in Lancaster, South Carolina. The National Child Labor Committee hired Hine to help document, publicize, and curb the widespread employment of children in industrial occupations. "These pictures," Hine wrote, "speak for themselves and prove that the law is being violated."

Lewis Hine (American, 1874–1940), "A Carolina Spinner," 1908. Gelatin silver print, 4 3/4 × 7 in. Milwaukee Art Museum, Gift of the Sheldon M. Barnett Family. M1973.83.

**Social Darwinism** The application of Charles Darwin's theory of biological evolution to society, holding that the fittest and wealthiest survive, the weak and the poor perish, and government action is unable to alter this "natural" process.

impoverished industrial workers, and unresponsive political systems. Jane Addams's original inspiration for the Hull House settlement in Chicago had come when she visited Toynbee Hall in London. Housing reformers in Glasgow and Manchester, as well as workmen's compensation reformers in Berlin, and old age insurance experts in Copenhagen provided important international forums for progressives here and around the world. Despite their national differences, progressives around the world searched for new ways to reinforce social bonds in the modern era.

Sociologist Lester Frank Ward, in his pioneering work *Dynamic Sociology* (1883), offered an important critique of **social Darwinism**, the orthodox theory that attributed social inequality to natural selection and the "survival of the fittest." Ward argued that the conservative social theorists responsible for social Darwinism, such as Herbert Spencer and William Graham Sumner, had wrongly applied evolutionary theory to human affairs. They had confused organic evolution with social evolution. Nature's method was genetic: unplanned, involuntary, automatic, and mechanical. By contrast, civilization had been built on successful human intervention in the natural processes of organic evolution.

Philosopher John Dewey criticized the excessively rigid and formal approach to education found in most American schools. Dewey advocated developing what he called "creative intelligence" in students, which could then be put to use in improving society. Schools ought to be "embryonic communities," miniatures of society, where children were encouraged to participate actively in different types of experiences. By cultivating imagination and openness to new experiences, schools could develop creativity and the habits required for systematic inquiry. Dewey's belief that education was the "fundamental method of social progress and reform" inspired generations of progressive educators.

At the University of Wisconsin, John R. Commons founded the new field of industrial relations and organized a state industrial commission that became a model for other states. Working closely with Governor Robert M. La Follette, Commons and his students helped draft pioneering laws in worker compensation and public utility regulation. Another Wisconsin faculty member, economist Richard Ely, argued that the state was "an educational and ethical agency whose positive aim is an indispensable condition of human progress." Ely believed the state must intervene directly to help solve public problems. He rejected the doctrine of laissez-faire as merely "a tool in the hands of the greedy." Like Commons, Ely worked with Wisconsin lawmakers to apply his expertise in economics to reforming the state's labor laws.

Progressive legal theorists began challenging the conservative view of constitutional law that had dominated American courts. Since the 1870s, the Supreme Court had interpreted the Fourteenth Amendment (1868) as a guarantee of broad rights for corporations. That amendment, which prevented states from depriving "any person of life, liberty, or property, without due process of law," had been designed to protect the civil rights of African Americans against violations by the states. But the Court, led by Justice Stephen J. Field, used the due process clause to strike down state laws regulating business and labor conditions. The Supreme Court and state courts had thus made the Fourteenth Amendment a bulwark for big business and a foe of social welfare measures.

The most important dissenter from this view was Oliver Wendell Holmes Jr. A scholar and Massachusetts judge, Holmes believed the law had to take into account changing social conditions. And courts should take care not to invalidate social legislation enacted democratically. Before the late 1930s, Holmes's pragmatic views of the law seldom convinced a majority of the Court. But his views influenced a generation of lawyers who began practicing what came to be called sociological jurisprudence. In *Muller v. Oregon* (1908), the Court upheld an Oregon law limiting the maximum hours for working women, finding that the liberty of contract "is not absolute." Noting that "woman's physical structure and the performance of maternal functions place her at a disadvantage," the Court found that "the physical well-being of woman becomes an object of public interest and care." Louis Brandeis, the state's attorney, amassed statistical, sociological, and economic data, rather than traditional legal arguments, to support his arguments. The "Brandeis Brief" became a common strategy for lawyers defending the constitutionality of progressive legislation.

## THE FEMALE DOMINION

In the 1890s, the settlement house movement had begun to provide an alternative to traditional concepts of private charity and humanitarian reform. Settlement workers found they could not transform their neighborhoods without confronting a host of broad social questions: chronic poverty, overcrowded tenement houses, child labor, industrial accidents, public health. They soon discovered the need to engage the political and cultural life of the larger community. As on Henry Street, college-educated, middle-class women were a key vanguard in the crusade for social justice.

**21–6**
Jane Addams, *Twenty Years at Hull House* (1910)

Jane Addams founded one of the first settlement houses, Hull House, in Chicago in 1889, after years of struggling to find work and a social identity equal to her talents. A member of one of the first generations of American women to attend college, Addams was a graduate of Rockford College. Many educated women were dissatisfied with the life choices conventionally available to them: early marriage or the traditional female professions of teaching, nursing, and library work. Settlement work provided an attractive alternative. Addams often spoke of the "subjective necessity" of settlement houses. By this she meant that they gave young, educated women a way to satisfy their powerful desire to connect with the real world. "There is nothing after disease, indigence and guilt," she wrote, "so fatal to life itself as the want of a proper outlet for active faculties."

Lillian Wald and her allies convinced the New York Board of Health to assign a nurse to every public school in the city. They lobbied the board of education to create the first school lunch programs. They persuaded the city to set up municipal milk stations to ensure the purity of milk. Henry Street also pioneered tuberculosis treatment and prevention. Its leaders became powerful advocates for playground construction, improved street cleaning, and tougher housing inspection. Lillian Wald became a national figure—an outspoken advocate of child labor legislation and woman suffrage and a vigorous opponent of American involvement in World War I.

**A portrait of** the young Jane Addams, probably taken around the time she founded Hull House in Chicago, in 1889.

# OVERVIEW | Currents of Progressivism

|  | Key Figures | Issues |
|---|---|---|
| **Local Communities** | Jane Addams, Lillian Wald, Florence Kelley, Frederic C. Howe, Samuel Jones | • Improving health, education, welfare in urban immigrant neighborhoods<br>• Child labor, eight-hour day<br>• Celebrating immigrant cultures<br>• Reforming urban politics<br>• Municipal ownership/regulation of utilities |
| **State** | Robert M. La Follette, Hiram Johnson, Al Smith | • Limiting power of railroads, other corporations<br>• Improving civil service<br>• Direct democracy<br>• Applying academic scholarship to human needs |
| **National** | James K. Vardaman, Hoke Smith, Theodore Roosevelt, Woodrow Wilson | • Disfranchisement of African Americans<br>• Trust-busting<br>• Conservation and western development<br>• National regulation of corporate and financial excesses<br>• Reform of national banking |
| **Intellectual/Cultural** | Jacob Riis, Lincoln Steffens, Ida Tarbell, Upton Sinclair, S. S. McClure | • Muckraking |
|  | John Dewey, Louis Brandeis, Edwin A. Ross | • Education reform<br>• Sociological jurisprudence<br>• Empowering "ethical elite" |

## myhistorylab

**Overview:** *Currents of Progressivism*

**19–11**
John Spargo, *The Bitter Cry of Children* (1906)

She offered Henry Street as a meeting place to the National Negro Conference in 1909, out of which emerged the National Association for the Advancement of Colored People.

Social reformer Florence Kelley helped direct the support of the settlement house movement behind groundbreaking state and federal labor legislation. In 1893, she wrote a report detailing the dismal conditions in sweatshops and the effects of long hours on the women and children who worked in them. This report became the basis for landmark legislation in Illinois that limited women to an eight-hour workday, barred children under fourteen from working, and abolished tenement labor. Illinois governor John Peter Altgeld appointed Kelley as chief inspector for the new law. In 1895, Kelley published *Hull House Maps and Papers*, the first scientific study of urban poverty in America. Moving to the Henry Street Settlement in 1898, Kelley served as general secretary of the new National Consumers' League. With Lillian Wald, she established the New York Child Labor Committee and pushed for the creation of the U.S. Children's Bureau, established in 1912. Its director, the first woman to head a federal bureau, was Julia Lathrop, another alumna of Hull House.

New female-dominated occupations, such as social work, public health nursing, and home economics, allowed women to combine professional aspirations with the older traditions of moral reform, especially those centered on child welfare. The new professionalism, in turn, sustained reform commitments and a female dominion that simultaneously expanded the social welfare function of the state and increased women's public authority and influence.

Kelley, Addams, Wald, Lathrop, and their circle consciously used their power as women to reshape politics in the progressive era. Electoral politics and the state were historically male preserves, but female social progressives turned their gender into an advantage. Activists like Kelley used their influence in civil society to create new state powers in the service of social justice. "Women's place is Home," wrote reformer Rheta Childe Dorr, "but Home is not contained within the four walls of an individual home. Home is the community."

# PROGRESSIVE POLITICS IN CITIES AND STATES

Progressive reformers poured much of their zeal and energy into local political battles. In cities and states across the nation, progressive politicians became a powerful force, often balancing the practical need for partisan support with nonpartisan appeals to the larger citizenry. Although their motives and achievements were mixed, progressives were united in their attacks on corruption in government, the need to reign in corporate power, and calls for more activist city and state governments.

## THE URBAN MACHINE

By the turn of the century, Democratic Party machines, usually dominated by first- and second-generation Irish, controlled the political life of most large American cities. The keys to machine strength were disciplined organization and the delivery of essential services to both immigrant communities and business elites. The successful machine politician viewed his work as a business, and he accumulated his capital by serving people who needed assistance. In exchange for votes, machine politicians offered their constituents a variety of services. These included municipal jobs in the police and fire departments, work at city construction sites, intervention with legal problems, and food and coal during hard times. In exchange for valuable franchises and city contracts, businessmen routinely bribed machine politicians and contributed liberally to their campaign funds.

The machines usually had close ties to organized prostitution and gambling, as well as more legitimate commercial entertainments. Vaudeville and burlesque theater, boxing, horse racing, and professional baseball were other urban enterprises with economic and political links to machines. Entertainment and spectacle made up a central element in the machine political style as well. Constituents looked forward to the colorful torchlight parades, free summer picnics, and riverboat excursions regularly sponsored by the machines.

In the early twentieth century, to expand their base of support, political machines in the Northeast began concentrating more on passing welfare legislation beneficial to working-class and immigrant constituencies. In this way, machine politicians often allied themselves with progressive reformers in state legislatures. In New York, for example,

**TO WHAT** extent did progressives redefine the role of the state in American politics?

**Review Summary**

**21–8**
Helen M. Todd, *Getting Out the Vote* (1911)

**Timothy D. "Big** Tim" Sullivan, the popular and influential Democratic Party machine boss of the Bowery and Lower East Side districts of New York City, ca. 1901.

**19–10**
William T. Riordon, *Plunkitt of Tammany Hall* (1905)

**21–9**
Walker Percy, *Birmingham under the Commission Plan* (1911)

---

### QUICK REVIEW

**Municipal Reform**

◆ Urban reformers sought to break alliances between city bosses and business leaders.

◆ Urban reformers developed the concept of the city commission and the city manager.

◆ Business groups often promoted these reforms.

Tammany Hall figures such as Robert Wagner, Al Smith, and Big Tim Sullivan worked with middle-class progressive groups to pass child labor laws, factory safety regulations, worker compensation plans, and other efforts to make government more responsive to social needs. As Jewish and Catholic immigrants expanded in number and proportion in the city population, urban machines also began to champion cultural pluralism, opposing prohibition and immigration restrictions and defending the contributions made by new ethnic groups in the cities.

## PROGRESSIVES AND URBAN REFORM

Political progressivism originated in the cities. It was both a challenge to the power of machine politics and a response to deteriorating urban conditions. Reformers placed much of the blame for urban ills on the machines and looked for ways to restructure city government. The "good government" movement, led by the National Municipal League, fought to make city management a nonpartisan, even nonpolitical, process by bringing the administrative techniques of large corporations to cities. Reformers revised city charters in favor of stronger mayoral power and expanded use of appointed administrators and career civil servants. They drew up blueprints for model charters, ordinances, and zoning plans designed by experts trained in public administration.

Progressive politicians who focused on the human problems of the industrial city championed a different kind of reform, one based on changing policies rather than the political structure. In Cleveland, for example, wealthy businessman Thomas L. Johnson served as mayor from 1901 to 1909. He emphasized both efficiency and social welfare. His popular program included lower streetcar fares, public baths, milk and meat inspection, and an expanded park and playground system.

## STATEHOUSE PROGRESSIVES

On the state level progressives focused on two major reform themes that sometimes coexisted uneasily. On the one hand they looked to make politics more open and accessible by pushing through procedural reforms. The *direct primary*, for example, promised to take the selection of electoral candidates out of the smoke-filled backrooms of party bosses and into the hands of party voters. In 1902 Oregon was the first state to adopt two other reforms: the *initiative*, the popular power to initiate legislation, and the ***referendum***, the right to a popular vote on proposed legislation. Several states also adopted a related reform, the "Australian," or secret ballot, which took the mechanics of ballot printing and distribution from the parties and made it the responsibility of the government. California and other states also established the *recall*: the power to remove elected officials from office. And in 1913 the states and Congress ratified the Seventeenth Amendment, shifting the selection of U.S. senators from the state legislatures to direct election by voters. On the other hand, progressive activists sought to remove some decisions from the electoral process entirely. They believed that judgments about railroad regulations, improving a city's sewer system, or establishing tax rates might best be made by informed, unbiased experts appointed to boards and commissions charged with setting policy. Many progressive states became political laboratories for testing both more democratic procedures and a greater reliance on professional expertise.

In Wisconsin, Republican dissident Robert M. La Follette forged a coalition of angry farmers, small businessmen, and workers with his fiery attacks on railroads and other large corporations. Leader of the progressive faction of the state Republicans, "Fighting Bob" won three terms as governor (1900–06), then served as a

**Referendum** Submission of a law, proposed or already in effect, to a direct popular vote for approval or rejection.

U.S. senator until his death in 1925. As governor, he pushed through tougher corporate tax rates, a direct primary, an improved civil service code, and a railroad commission designed to regulate freight charges. La Follette used faculty experts at the University of Wisconsin to help research and write his bills. Other states began copying the "Wisconsin Idea," the application of academic scholarship and theory to the needs of the people.

In New York Theodore Roosevelt won the governor's race in 1898, propelled by his fame as a Spanish-American War hero. Although supported by the Republican Party machine, Roosevelt embraced the progressive view that the people's interest ought to be above partisan politics, and he used his personal popularity with voters to assert independence from party leaders. As governor he held frequent press conferences to communicate more directly with voters and gain support for progressive legislation. Roosevelt's administration strengthened the state's civil service system, set wage and hour standards for state employees, raised teachers' salaries, and placed a franchise tax on corporations controlling public utilities. Roosevelt also championed progressive conservation measures by expanding New York's forest preserves and reforming the fish and game service, thus anticipating his strong support of environmental regulation as president.

Western progressives targeted railroads, mining and timber companies, and public utilities for reform. Large corporations such as Pacific Gas and Electric and the Southern Pacific Railroad had amassed enormous wealth and political influence. They were able to corrupt state legislatures and charge consumers exorbitant rates. An alliance between middle-class progressives and working-class voters reflected growing disillusionment with the ideology of individualism that had helped pave the way for the rise of the big corporation. Between 1905 and 1909, nearly every southern state moved to regulate railroads by mandating lower passenger and freight rates.

Southern progressives also directed their energies at the related problems of child labor and educational reform. In 1900, at least one-quarter of all southern cotton mill workers were between the ages of ten and sixteen, and many worked over sixty hours per week. Led by reform-minded ministers Edgar Gardner Murphy and Alexander McKelway and drawing on the activism of white club women, reformers attacked child labor by focusing on the welfare of children and their mothers and emphasizing the degradation of "Anglo Saxons." In 1903, Alabama and North Carolina enacted the first state child labor laws, setting twelve as a minimum age for employment. But the laws were weakened by many exemptions and no provisions for enforcement, as lawmakers also heard the loud complaints from parents and mill owners who resented the efforts of reformers to limit their choices.

But southern progressivism was for white people only. Indeed, southern progressives believed that the disenfranchisement of black voters and the creation of a legally segregated public sphere were necessary preconditions for political and social reform. With African Americans removed from political life, white southern progressives argued, the direct primary system of nominating candidates would give white voters more influence. Between 1890 and 1910, southern states passed a welter of statutes specifying poll taxes, literacy tests, and property qualifications with the explicit goal of preventing voting by blacks. This systematic disenfranchisement of African American voters stripped black communities of any political power.

Southern progressives also supported the push toward a fully segregated public sphere. Between 1900 and 1910, southern states strengthened Jim Crow laws requiring separation of races in restaurants, streetcars, beaches, and theaters.

The legacy of southern progressivism was thus closely linked to the strengthening of the legal and institutional guarantees of white supremacy.

Contradictions in the progressive approach to political reform were not limited to the South. Undermining party control of voting and elections may have also weakened politicians' incentives to get out the vote. Greater reliance on city commissions and other experts meant less in the way of promised favors for voters, which may have also made voters less interested in elections. Tightening up on residency requirements and voter registration rules in the cities cut into turnout in immigrant and ethnic neighborhoods. The effort to make politics more open, nonpartisan, and voter friendly also led, ironically, to a decline in voter participation and interest around the country. Whereas in the 1890s voter participation in national elections was routinely close to 90 percent, by World War I that figure had fallen to barely 60 percent, where it would stay for most of the rest of the century.

# SOCIAL CONTROL AND ITS LIMITS

HOW DID tensions between social justice and social control divide progressives?

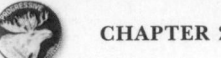

**Review Summary**

Many middle- and upper-class Protestant progressives feared that immigrants and large cities threatened the stability of American democracy. Progressives often believed they had a mission to frame laws and regulations for the "benefit" of immigrants, industrial workers, and African Americans. These efforts at social control usually required some form of coercion. This was the moralistic and frequently xenophobic side of progressivism, and it provided a powerful source of support for the regulation of drinking, prostitution, leisure activities, and schooling.

## THE PROHIBITION MOVEMENT

During the last two decades of the nineteenth century, the Woman's Christian Temperance Union (WCTU) had grown into a powerful mass organization. The WCTU appealed especially to women angered by men who used alcohol and then abused their wives and children. It directed most of its work toward ending the production, sale, and consumption of alcohol. But local WCTU chapters put their energy into nontemperance activities as well, including homeless shelters, Sunday schools, prison reform, child nurseries, and woman suffrage. The WCTU thus provided women with a political forum in which they could fuse their traditional moral posture as guardians of the home with broader public concerns. By 1911, the WCTU, with a quarter million members, was the largest women's organization in American history.

Other **temperance groups** had a narrower focus. The Anti-Saloon League, founded in 1893, began by organizing local-option campaigns in which rural counties and small towns banned liquor within their geographical limits. It drew much of its financial support from local businessmen, who saw a link between closing a community's saloons and increasing the productivity of workers. The league was a one-issue pressure group that played effectively on anti-urban and anti-immigrant prejudice. League lobbyists hammered away at the close connections among saloon culture, liquor dealers, brewers, and big-city political machines.

The battle to ban alcohol revealed deep ethnic and cultural divides within America's urban communities. Opponents of alcohol were generally "pietists," who viewed the world from a position of moral absolutism. These included native-born, middle-class Protestants associated with evangelical churches, along with some old-stock Protestant immigrant denominations. Opponents of prohibition

**Prohibition** A ban on the production, sale, and consumption of liquor, achieved temporarily through state laws and the Eighteenth Amendment.

**Temperance groups** Groups dedicated to reducing the sale and consumption of alcohol.

were generally "ritualists" with less arbitrary notions of personal morality. These were largely new-stock, working-class Catholic and Jewish immigrants, along with some Protestants, such as German Lutherans.

## THE SOCIAL EVIL

Many of the same reformers who battled the saloon and drinking also engaged in efforts to eradicate prostitution. Crusades against "the social evil" had appeared at intervals throughout the nineteenth century, but they reached a new level of intensity between 1895 and 1920. Antiprostitution campaigns epitomized the diverse makeup and mixed motives of so much progressive reform. Male business and civic leaders joined forces with feminists, social workers, and clergy to eradicate "commercialized vice."

Between 1908 and 1914, exposés of the "white slave traffic" became a national sensation. Dozens of books, articles, and motion pictures alleged an international conspiracy to seduce and sell girls into prostitution. Most of these materials exaggerated the practices they attacked. They also made foreigners, especially Jews and southern Europeans, scapegoats for the sexual anxieties of native-born whites.

Reformers had trouble believing that any woman would freely choose to be a prostitute; such a choice was antithetical to conventional notions of female purity and sexuality. But for wage-earning women, prostitution was a rational choice in a world of limited opportunities. The antivice crusades succeeded in closing down many urban red-light districts and larger brothels, but these were replaced by the streetwalker and call girl, who were more vulnerable to harassment and control by policemen and pimps. Rather than eliminating prostitution, reform efforts transformed the organization of the sex trade.

## THE REDEMPTION OF LEISURE

Progressives faced a thorny issue in the growing popularity of commercial entertainment. For large numbers of working-class adults and children, leisure meant time and money spent at vaudeville and burlesque theaters, amusement parks, dance halls, and motion picture houses. These competed with municipal parks, libraries, museums, YMCAs, and school recreation centers. "Commercialized leisure," warned Frederic C. Howe in 1914, "must be controlled by the community, if it is to become an agency of civilization rather than the reverse."

By 1908, movies had become the most popular form of cheap entertainment in America. As the films themselves became more sophisticated and as "movie palaces" began to replace cheap storefront theaters, the new medium attracted a large middle-class clientele as well. Progressive reformers seized the chance to help regulate the new medium as a way of improving the commercial recreation of the urban poor. In 1909, New York City movie producers and exhibitors joined with the reform-minded People's Institute to establish the voluntary National Board of Censorship (NBC). A revolving group of civic activists reviewed new movies, passing them, suggesting changes, or condemning them. Local censoring committees all over the nation subscribed to the board's weekly bulletin. They aimed at achieving what John Collier of the NBC called "the redemption of leisure." By 1914, the NBC was reviewing 95 percent of the nation's film output.

## STANDARDIZING EDUCATION

The most important educational trends in these years were the expansion and bureaucratization of the nation's public school systems. In most cities, centralization served to consolidate the power of older urban elites who felt threatened by

***Movies,* by John Sloan,** 1913, the most talented artist among the so-called Ashcan realist school of painting. Active in socialist and bohemian circles, Sloan served as art editor for *The Masses* magazine for several years. His work celebrated the vitality and diversity of urban working-class life and leisure, including the new commercial culture represented by the motion picture.

John Sloan, "Movies," 1913. Oil painting. The Toledo Museum of Art.

the large influx of immigrants. Children began school earlier and stayed there longer. Kindergartens spread rapidly in large cities. They presented, as one writer put it in 1903, "the earliest opportunity to catch the little Russian, the little Italian, the little German, Pole, Syrian, and the rest and begin to make good American citizens of them." By 1918, every state had some form of compulsory school attendance. High schools also multiplied, extending the school's influence beyond the traditional grammar school curriculum.

High schools reflected a growing belief that schools should be comprehensive, multifunctional institutions. In 1918, the National Education Association offered a report defining Cardinal Principles of Secondary Education. These included instruction in health, family life, citizenship, and ethical character. Academic programs prepared a small number of students for college. Vocational programs trained boys and girls for a niche in the new industrial order. Boys took shop courses in metal trades, carpentry, and machine tools. Girls learned typing, bookkeeping, sewing, cooking, and home economics. The Smith-Hughes Act of 1917 provided federal grants to support these programs and set up a Federal Board for Vocational Education.

# CHALLENGES TO PROGRESSIVISM

While most progressive reformers had roots in Protestantism and the middle-class professions, other Americans vigorously challenged their political vision. Organized workers often invoked progressive rhetoric and ideals but for quite different, sometimes radical, ends.

All these industrial workers shared the need to sell their labor for wages in order to survive. At the same time, differences in skill, ethnicity, and race proved powerful barriers to efforts at organizing trade unions that could bargain for improved wages and working conditions. So, too, did the economic and political power of the large corporations that dominated much of American industry. Yet there were also small, closely knit groups of skilled workers, such as printers and brewers, who exercised real control over their lives and labors. And these years saw many labor struggles that created effective trade unions or laid the groundwork for others. Industrial workers also became a force in local and national politics, adding a chorus of insistent voices to the calls for social justice.

## THE NEW GLOBAL IMMIGRATION

On the eve of World War I, close to 60 percent of the industrial labor force was foreign-born. Most of these workers were among the roughly 9 million new immigrants from southern and eastern Europe who arrived in the United States between

HOW DID the impact of new immigration transform American cities?

Review Summary

19–12
Mary Antin, *The Promised Land* (1912)

**Newly landed European** immigrant families on the dock at Ellis Island in New York harbor, 1900. Originally a black-and-white photograph, this image was later color tinted for reproduction as a postcard or book illustration.

1900 and 1914. Nearly all the new Italian, Polish, Hungarian, Jewish, and Greek immigrants lacked industrial skills. They thus entered the bottom ranks of factories, mines, mills, and sweatshops.

These new immigrants had been driven from their European farms and towns by several forces, including the undermining of subsistence farming by commercial agriculture; a falling death rate that brought a shortage of land; and religious and political persecution. American corporations also sent agents to recruit cheap labor. Except for Jewish immigrants, a majority of whom fled virulent anti-Semitism in Russia and Russian Poland, most newcomers planned on earning a stake and then returning home (see Map 21.1).

The decision to migrate usually occurred through social networks—people linked by kinship, personal acquaintance, and work experience. These "chains," extending from places of origin to specific destinations in the United States, helped migrants cope with the considerable risks entailed by the long and difficult journey. A study conducted by the U.S. Immigration Commission in 1909 found that about 60 percent of the new immigrants had their passage arranged by immigrants already in America.

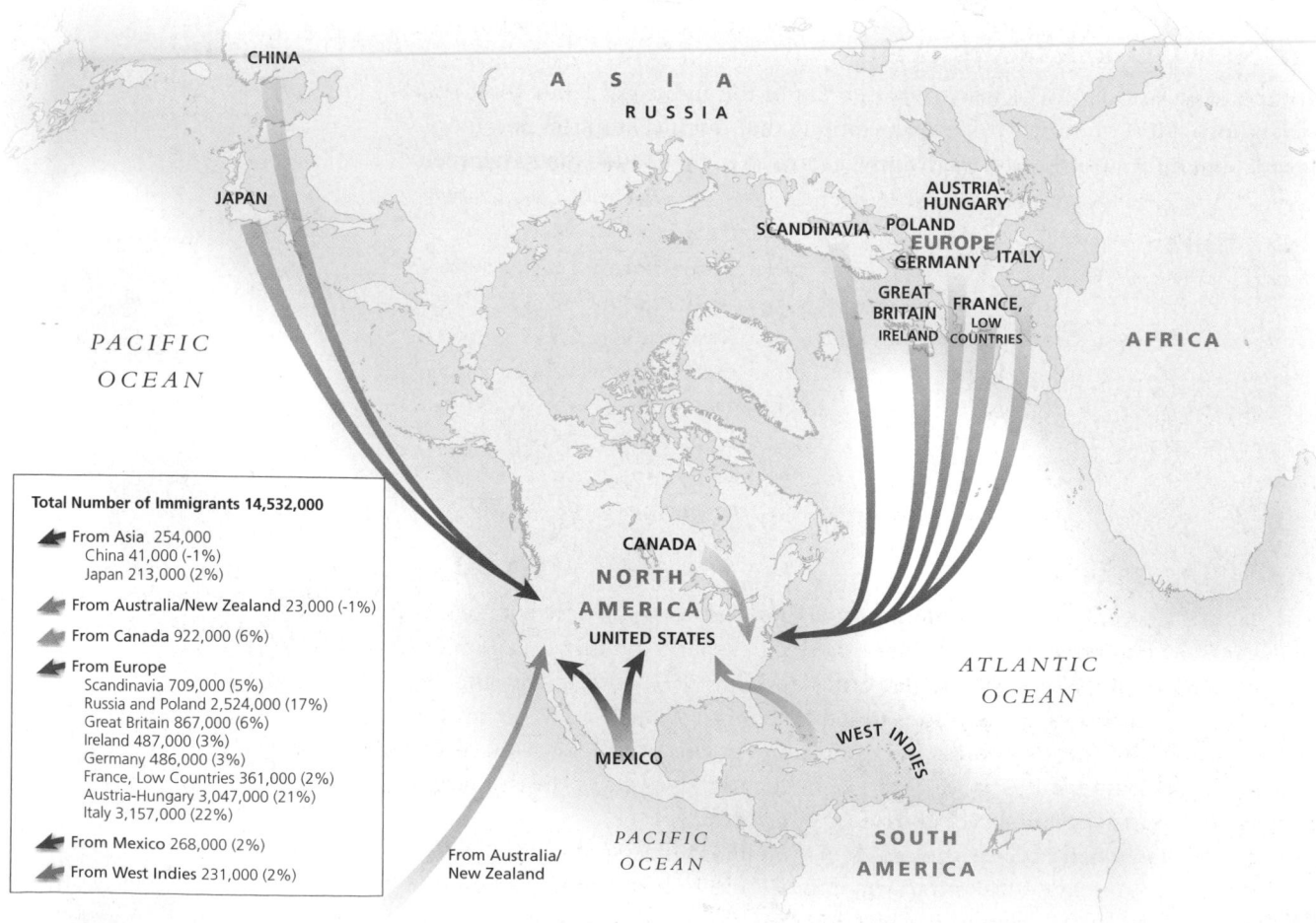

**Total Number of Immigrants 14,532,000**

From Asia 254,000
  China 41,000 (-1%)
  Japan 213,000 (2%)

From Australia/New Zealand 23,000 (-1%)

From Canada 922,000 (6%)

From Europe
  Scandinavia 709,000 (5%)
  Russia and Poland 2,524,000 (17%)
  Great Britain 867,000 (6%)
  Ireland 487,000 (3%)
  Germany 486,000 (3%)
  France, Low Countries 361,000 (2%)
  Austria-Hungary 3,047,000 (21%)
  Italy 3,157,000 (22%)

From Mexico 268,000 (2%)

From West Indies 231,000 (2%)

**MAP 21.1**
**Immigration to the United States, 1901–20**

WHAT FORCES propelled so many people to emigrate from European countries?

The low-paid, backbreaking work in basic industry became nearly the exclusive preserve of the new immigrants. In 1907, of the 14,359 common laborers employed at Pittsburgh's U.S. Steel mills, 11,694 were eastern Europeans. One-third of the immigrant steelworkers were single, and among married men who had been in the country less than five years, about two-thirds reported that their wives were still in Europe. Workers with families generally supplemented their incomes by taking in single men as boarders.

Not all of the new immigrants came from Europe, as hemispheric migration increased sharply as well. Over 300,000 French Canadians arrived in the United States between 1900 and 1930, settling mostly in New England. But the maturing continental railroad system had widened the choice of destinations to communities in upstate New York and Detroit, which had the largest number of French Canadian migrants outside of New England. The pull of jobs in New England's textile industry, along with its physical proximity, attracted male farmers and laborers unable to make a living in the rural districts of Quebec. Roughly one-third of female migrants were domestic servants looking for the higher pay and greater independence associated with factory labor.

Mexican immigration also grew in these years, providing a critical source of labor for the West's farms, railroads, and mines. Between 1900 and 1914, the number of people of Mexican descent living and working in the United States tripled, from roughly 100,000 to 300,000. Economic and political crises spurred tens of thousands of Mexico's rural and urban poor to emigrate north. Large numbers of seasonal agricultural workers regularly came up from Mexico to work in the expanding sugar beet industry and then returned. But a number of substantial resident Mexican communities also emerged in the early twentieth century. Throughout Texas, California, New Mexico, Arizona, and Colorado, western cities developed *barrios*, distinct communities of Mexicans.

Between 1898 and 1907, more than 80,000 Japanese entered the United States. The vast majority were young men working as contract laborers in the West, mainly in California. American law prevented Japanese immigrants (the *Issei*) from obtaining American citizenship because they were not white. This legal discrimination, along with informal exclusion from many occupations, forced the Japanese to create niches for themselves within local economies. Most Japanese settled near Los Angeles, where they established small communities centered around fishing, truck farming, and the flower and nursery business.

## URBAN GHETTOS

In large cities, new immigrant communities took the form of densely packed ghettos. The sheer size and dynamism of these cities made the immigrant experience more complex than in smaller cities and more isolated communities. Workers in the urban garment trades toiled for low wages and suffered layoffs, unemployment, and poor health. But conditions in the small, labor-intensive shops of the clothing industry differed significantly from those in the large-scale, capital-intensive industries like steel.

New York City had become the center of both Jewish immigration and America's huge ready-to-wear clothing industry. Most of the industry operated on the grueling piece-rate, or task, system, in which manufacturers and subcontractors paid individuals or teams of workers to complete a certain quota of labor within a specific time.

The garment industry was highly seasonal. A typical workweek was sixty hours with seventy common during the busy season. But there were long stretches of unemployment in slack times. Often forced to work in cramped, dirty, and badly

**21–1**
Frederick Winslow Taylor, *A Piece-Rate System* (1896)

**New York City** police set up this makeshift morgue to help identify victims of the disastrous Triangle Shirtwaist Company fire, March 25, 1911. Unable to open the locked doors of the sweatshop and desperate to escape from smoke and flames, many of the 146 who died had leaped eight stories to their death.

---

### QUICK REVIEW

**Triangle Shirtwaist Fire**

◆ 1911: fire kills 146 workers.

◆ Managers had locked the exits.

◆ Tragedy led to the enactment of new industrial safety laws.

---

lit rooms, garment workers strained under a system in which time equaled money.

In November 1909, two New York garment manufacturers responded to strikes by unskilled women workers by hiring thugs and prostitutes to beat up pickets. The strikers won the support of the Women's Trade Union League, a group of sympathetic female reformers that included Lillian Wald, Mary Dreier, and prominent society figures. The Uprising of the 20,000, as it became known, swept through the city's garment district. The strikers demanded union recognition, better wages, and safer and more sanitary conditions. They drew support from thousands of suffragists, trade unionists, and sympathetic middle-class women as well. Hundreds of strikers were arrested, and many were beaten by police. After three cold months on the picket line, the strikers returned to work without union recognition. But the International Ladies Garment Workers Union (ILGWU), founded in 1900, did gain strength and negotiated contracts with some of the city's shirtwaist makers. The strike was an important breakthrough in the drive to organize unskilled workers into industrial unions.

On March 25, 1911, the issues raised by the strike took on new urgency when a fire raced through three floors of the Triangle Shirtwaist Company. As the flames spread, workers found themselves trapped by exit doors that had been locked from the outside. Fire escapes were too narrow and too weak to withstand the heat. Within half an hour, 146 people, mostly young Jewish women, had been killed by smoke or had leaped to their deaths. In the bitter aftermath, women progressives led by Florence Kelley and Frances Perkins of the National Consumers' League joined with Tammany Hall leaders Al Smith, Robert Wagner, and Big Tim Sullivan to create a New York State Factory Investigation Commission. Under Perkins's vigorous leadership, the commission conducted an unprecedented round of public hearings and on-site inspections, leading to a series of state laws that dramatically improved safety conditions and limited the hours for working women and children.

## COMPANY TOWNS

Immigrant industrial workers and their families often established their communities in a company town, where a single large corporation was dominant. Cities such as Lawrence, Massachusetts; Gary, Indiana; and Butte, Montana, revolved around the industrial enterprises of Pacific Woolen, U.S. Steel, and Anaconda Copper. Workers had little or no influence over the economic and political institutions of these cities. In the more isolated company towns, residents often had no alternative but to buy their food, clothing, and supplies at company stores, usually for exorbitantly high prices. But they did maintain some community control in other ways. Family and kin networks, ethnic lodges, saloons, benefit societies, churches and synagogues, and musical groups affirmed traditional forms of community in a setting governed by individualism and private capital.

On the job, modern machinery and industrial discipline meant high rates of injury and death. A 1910 study of work accidents revealed that nearly a fourth of all new steelworkers were killed or injured each year. Mutual aid associations, organized around ethnic groups, offered some protection through cheap insurance and death benefits.

In steel and coal towns, women not only maintained the household and raised the children, but they also boosted the family income by taking in boarders, sewing, and laundry. Many women also tended gardens and raised chickens, rabbits, and goats. Their produce and income helped reduce dependence on the company store. Working class women felt the burdens of housework more heavily than their middle-class sisters. Pump water, indoor plumbing, and sewage disposal were often available only on a pay-as-you-go basis. Many women struggled with the effects of their husbands' excessive drinking and faced early widowhood.

The power of large corporations in the life of company towns was most evident among the mining communities of the West, as was violent labor conflict. The Colorado Fuel and Iron Company (CFI) employed roughly half of the 8,000 coal miners who labored in that state's mines. In mining towns such as Ludlow and Trinidad, the CFI thoroughly dominated the lives of miners and their families. By the early twentieth century, new immigrants, such as Italians, Greeks, Slavs, and Mexicans, composed a majority of the population in these western mining communities.

In September 1913, the United Mine Workers led a strike in the Colorado coalfields, calling for improved safety, higher wages, and recognition of the union. Thousands of miners' families moved out of company housing and into makeshift tent colonies provided by the union. In October, Governor Elias Ammons ordered the Colorado National Guard into the tense strike region to keep order. The troops, supposedly neutral, proceeded to ally themselves with the mine operators. By spring, the strike had bankrupted the state, forcing the governor to remove most of the troops. The coal companies then brought in large numbers of private mine guards who were extremely hostile toward the strikers. On April 20, 1914, a combination of guardsmen and private guards surrounded the largest of the tent colonies at Ludlow, where more than a thousand mine families lived. A shot rang out (each side accused the other of firing), and a pitched battle ensued that lasted until the poorly armed miners ran out of ammunition. At dusk, the troops burned the tent village to the ground, routing the families and killing fourteen, eleven of them children. Enraged strikers attacked mines throughout southern Colorado in an armed rebellion that lasted ten days, until President Woodrow Wilson ordered the U.S. Army into the region. News of the Ludlow Massacre shocked millions and aroused widespread protests and demonstrations against the policies of Colorado Fuel and Iron and its owner, John D. Rockefeller Jr.

## The AFL: "Unions, Pure and Simple"

Following the depression of the 1890s, the American Federation of Labor (AFL) emerged as the strongest and most stable organization of workers. Samuel Gompers's strategy of recruiting skilled labor into unions organized by craft had paid off. Union membership climbed from under 500,000 in 1897 to 1.7 million by 1904.

But the strength of craft organization also gave rise to weakness. In 1905, Gompers told a union gathering in Minneapolis that "caucasians" would not "let their standard of living be destroyed by negroes, Chinamen, Japs, or any others." Those "others" included the new immigrants from eastern and southern Europe, men and women, who labored in the steel mills and garment trades. Each trade looked mainly to the welfare of its own. Many explicitly barred women and African Americans from membership.

AFL unions had a difficult time holding on to their gains. Economic slumps, technological changes, and aggressive counterattacks by employer organizations could be devastating. Trade associations using management-controlled efficiency drives fought union efforts to regulate output and shop practices. The National

Association of Manufacturers (NAM), a group of smaller industrialists founded in 1903, launched an "open shop" campaign to eradicate unions altogether. "Open shop" was simply a new name for a workplace where unions were not allowed. Unfriendly judicial decisions also hurt organizing efforts. Not until the 1930s and New Deal legislation would unions be able to count on legislative and legal protections for collective bargaining and the right to strike.

## THE IWW: "ONE BIG UNION"

Some workers developed more radical visions of labor organizing. The Western Federation of Miners (WFM) had gained strength in the metal mining regions of the West by leading several strikes marred by violence. In 1899, during a strike in the silver mining district of Coeur d'Alene, Idaho, the Bunker Hill and Sullivan Mining Company had enraged the miners by hiring armed detectives and firing all union members. Desperate miners retaliated by destroying a company mill with dynamite. Idaho's governor declared martial law and obtained federal troops to enforce it. In a pattern that would become familiar in western labor relations, the soldiers served as strikebreakers, rounding up hundreds of miners and imprisoning them for months in makeshift bullpens.

In response to the brutal realities of labor organizing in the West, most WFM leaders embraced socialism and industrial unionism. In 1905, leaders of the WFM, the Socialist Party, and various radical groups gathered in Chicago to found the Industrial Workers of the World (IWW). The IWW charter proclaimed bluntly, "The working class and the employing class have nothing in common. . . . Between these two classes a struggle must go on until the workers of the world unite as a class, take possession of the earth and the machinery of production, and abolish the wage system."

William D. "Big Bill" Haywood, an imposing, one-eyed, hard-rock miner, emerged as the most influential and flamboyant spokesman for the IWW, or **Wobblies**, as they were called. Haywood, a charismatic speaker and effective organizer, regularly denounced the AFL for its conservative emphasis on organizing skilled workers by trade. He insisted that the IWW would exclude no one from its ranks. The Wobblies concentrated their efforts on miners, lumberjacks, sailors, "harvest stiffs," and other casual laborers.

The IWW briefly became a force among eastern industrial workers, tapping the rage and growing militance of the immigrants and unskilled. Wobbly leaders such as Haywood, Elizabeth Gurley Flynn, and Joseph Ettor used class-conscious rhetoric and multilingual appeals to forge unity among the ethnically diverse Lawrence workforce of 25,000.

The IWW failed to establish permanent organizations in the eastern cities, but it remained a force in the lumber camps, mines, and wheat fields of the West. In spite of its militant rhetoric, the IWW concerned itself with practical gains. "The final aim is revolution," said one Wobbly organizer, "but for the present let's see if we can get a bed to sleep in, water enough to take a bath in and decent food to eat." But when the United States entered World War I, the Justice Department used the IWW's anticapitalist rhetoric and antiwar stance to crush it.

## REBELS IN BOHEMIA

During the 1910s, a small but influential community of painters, journalists, poets, social workers, lawyers, and political activists coalesced in the New York City neighborhood of Greenwich Village. These cultural radicals, nearly all of middle-class background and hailing from provincial American towns, shared a deep sympa-

**Wobblies**  Popular name for the members of the Industrial Workers of the World (IWW).

thy toward the struggles of labor, a passion for modern art, and an openness to socialism and anarchism.

The term **"bohemian"** referred to anyone who had artistic or intellectual aspirations and who lived with disregard for conventional rules of behavior. Other American cities, notably Chicago at the turn of the century, had supported bohemian communities. But the Village scene was unique, if fleeting. The worldview of the Village's bohemian community found expression in *The Masses*, a monthly magazine founded in 1911 by socialist critic Max Eastman, who was also its editor. "The broad purpose of *The Masses*," wrote John Reed, one of its leading writers, "is a social one—to everlastingly attack old systems, old morals, old prejudices—the whole weight of outworn thought that dead men have saddled upon us."

For some, Greenwich Village offered a chance to experiment with sexual relationships or work arrangements. For others, it was an escape from small-town conformity, or a haven for like-minded artists and activists. Yet the Village bohemians were united in their search for a new sense of community. Intellectuals and artists, as well as workers, feeling alienated from the rest of society, sought shelter in the collective life and close-knit social relations of the Village community.

The Village bohemia lasted only a few years, a flame snuffed out by the chill political winds accompanying America's entry into World War I. Yet for decades, Greenwich Village remained a mecca for young men and women searching for alternatives to conventional ways of living.

Publicity poster for the 1913 pageant, organized by John Reed and other Greenwich Village radicals, supporting the cause of striking silk workers in Paterson, New Jersey. This poster drew on aesthetic styles associated with the Industrial Workers of the World, typically including a heroic, larger-than-life image of a factory laborer.

## WOMEN'S MOVEMENTS AND BLACK ACTIVISM

Like working-class radicals, politically engaged women and African American activists often found themselves at odds with more moderate and mainstream progressive reformers. They contested both gender and racial assumptions inherited from the nineteenth century. Some progressives supported the challenges in one or both of these spheres. They helped shape an agenda for social justice that would echo throughout the rest of the twentieth century.

In fighting racial discrimination, African Americans had a more difficult task. As racism gained ground in the political and cultural spheres, black progressives fought defensively to prevent the rights they had secured during Reconstruction from being further undermined. Still, they managed to produce leaders, ideas, and organizations that would have a long-range impact on American race relations.

### THE NEW WOMAN

The settlement house movement discussed in the opening of this chapter was just one of the new avenues of opportunity opened to progressive-era women. A steady proliferation of women's organizations attracted growing numbers of educated, middle-class women. With more men working in offices, more children attending school, and family size declining, the middle-class home was emptier. At the same time, more middle-class women were graduating from high school and college.

WHAT NEW forms of activism emerged among the working class, women, and African Americans?

**myhistorylab**

**Review Summary**

Bohemian   Artistic individual who lives with disregard for the conventional rules of behavior.

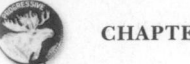
Single-sex clubs brought middle-class women into the public sphere by celebrating the distinctive strengths associated with women's culture: cooperation, uplift, service. The women's club movement combined an earlier focus on self-improvement and intellectual pursuits with newer benevolent efforts on behalf of working women and children. The Buffalo Union, for example, sponsored art lectures for housewives and classes in typing, stenography, and bookkeeping for young working women. It also maintained a library, set up a "noon rest" downtown where women could eat lunch, and ran a school for training domestics.

For many middle-class women, the club movement provided a new kind of female-centered community. Club activity often led members to participate in other civic ventures, particularly "child-saving" reforms, such as child labor laws and mothers' pensions. Some took up the cause of working-class women, fighting for protective legislation and offering aid to trade unions. As wives and daughters of influential and well-off men in their communities, club women had access to funds and could generate support for projects they undertook.

Other women's associations made even more explicit efforts to bridge class lines between middle-class homemakers and working-class women. The National Consumers' League (NCL), started in 1898 by Maud Nathan and Josephine Lowell, sponsored a "white label" campaign in which manufacturers who met safety and sanitary standards could put NCL labels on their food and clothing. Under the dynamic leadership of Florence Kelley, the NCL took an even more aggressive stance by publicizing labor abuses in department stores and lobbying for maximum-hour and minimum-wage laws in state legislatures. In its efforts to protect home and housewife, worker and consumer, the NCL embodied the ideal of "social housekeeping."

## BIRTH CONTROL

The phrase "birth control," coined by Margaret Sanger around 1913, described her campaign to provide contraceptive information and devices for women. Sanger had seen her own mother die at age forty-nine after bearing eleven children. In 1910, Sanger was a thirty-year-old nurse and housewife living with her husband and three children in a New York City suburb. Excited by a socialist lecture she had

**A supportive crowd** surrounds birth control pioneer Margaret Sanger and her sister, Ethel Byrne, as they leave the Court of Special Services in New York City in 1917. Police had recently closed Sanger's first birth control clinic in the immigrant neighborhood of Brownsville, New York, and Sanger herself had spent a month in jail.

attended, she convinced her husband to move to the city, where she threw herself into the bohemian milieu. She became an organizer for the IWW, and in 1912, she wrote a series of articles on female sexuality for a socialist newspaper.

When postal officials confiscated the paper for violating obscenity laws, Sanger left for Europe to learn more about contraception. She returned to New York determined to challenge the obscenity statutes with her own magazine, the *Woman Rebel*. When she distributed her pamphlet *Family Limitation*, postal inspectors confiscated copies and she found herself facing forty-five years in prison. In October 1914, she fled to Europe again. In her absence, anarchist agitator Emma Goldman and many women in the Socialist Party took up the cause.

An older generation of feminists had advocated "voluntary motherhood," or the right to say no to a husband's sexual demands. The new birth control advocates embraced contraception as a way of advancing sexual freedom for middle-class women, as well as responding to the misery of those working-class women who bore numerous children while living in poverty. Sanger returned to the United States in October 1915. After the government dropped the obscenity charges, she embarked on a national speaking tour. In 1916, she again defied the law by opening a birth control clinic in a working-class neighborhood in Brooklyn and offering birth control information without a physician present. Arrested and jailed, she gained more publicity for her crusade. Within a few years, birth control leagues and clinics could be found in every major city and most large towns in the country.

## RACISM AND ACCOMMODATION

At the turn of the century, four-fifths of the nation's 10 million African Americans still lived in the South, where most eked out a living working in agriculture. In the cities, most blacks were relegated to menial jobs, but a small African American middle class of entrepreneurs and professionals gained a foothold by selling services and products to the black community. They all confronted a racism that was growing in both intensity and influence in American politics and culture. White racism came in many variants and had evolved significantly since slavery days. The more virulent strains, influenced by Darwin's evolutionary theory, held that blacks were a "degenerate" race, genetically predisposed to vice, crime, and disease and destined to lose the struggle for existence with whites.

African Americans also endured a deeply racist popular culture that made hateful stereotypes of black people a normal feature of political debate and everyday life. Benjamin Tillman, a U.S. senator from South Carolina, denounced the African American as "a fiend, a wild beast, seeking whom he may devour." In northern cities "coon songs," based on gross caricatures of black life, were extremely popular in theaters and as sheet music.

Southern progressives articulated a more moderate racial philosophy. They also assumed the innate inferiority of blacks, but they believed that black progress was necessary to achieve the economic and political progress associated with a vision of the New South. Their solution to the "race problem" stressed paternalist uplift.

Amid this political and cultural climate, Booker T. Washington won recognition as the most influential black leader of the day. Born a slave in 1856, Washington was educated at Hampton Institute in Virginia, one of the first freedmen's schools devoted to industrial education. In 1881, he founded Tuskegee Institute, a black school in Alabama devoted to industrial and moral education. He became the leading spokesman for racial accommodation, urging blacks to focus on economic improvement and self-reliance, as opposed to political and civil rights. In an 1895 speech delivered at the Cotton States Exposition in Atlanta, Washington outlined the key themes of accommodationist philosophy. "Cast down your buckets

18–9
Booker T. Washington, *Atlanta Exposition Address* (1895)

In July 1905, a group of African American leaders met in Niagara Falls, Ontario, to protest legal segregation and the denial of civil rights to the nation's black population. This portrait was taken against a studio backdrop of the falls. In 1909, the leader of the Niagara movement, W. E. B. Du Bois (second from right, middle row) founded and edited *The Crisis*, the influential monthly journal of the National Association for the Advancement of Colored People.

Photographs and Prints Division, Schomburg Center for Research in Black Culture, The New York Public Library, Astor, Lenox and Tilden Foundations.

**17–11**
W. E. B. Du Bois, *Of Mr. Booker T. Washington and Others* (1903)

**21–4**
*Platform Adopted by the National Negro Committee* (1909)

**Niagara movement** African American group organized in 1905 to promote racial integration, civil and political rights, and equal access to economic opportunity.

**National Association for the Advancement of Colored People** Interracial organization co-founded by W. E. B. Du Bois in 1910 dedicated to restoring African American political and social rights.

where you are," Washington told black people, meaning they should focus on improving their vocational skills as industrial workers and farmers. "In all things that are purely social," he told attentive whites, "we can be as separate as the fingers, yet one as the hand in all things essential to mutual progress."

Washington's message won him the financial backing of leading white philanthropists and the respect of progressive whites. But Washington also gained a large following among African Americans, especially those who aspired to business success. With the help of Andrew Carnegie, he founded the National Negro Business League to preach the virtue of black business development in black communities.

Washington also had a decisive influence on the flow of private funds to black schools in the South. Publicly he insisted that "agitation of questions of social equality is the extremest folly." But privately, Washington also spent money and worked behind the scenes trying to halt disfranchisement and segregation. He offered secret financial support, for example, for court cases that challenged Louisiana's grandfather clause, the exclusion of blacks from Alabama juries, and railroad segregation in Tennessee and Georgia.

## RACIAL JUSTICE, THE NAACP, AND BLACK WOMEN'S ACTIVISM

In the early 1900s, scholar and activist W. E. B. Du Bois created a significant alternative to Washington's leadership. A product of the black middle class, Du Bois had been educated at Fisk University and Harvard, where in 1895, he became the first African American to receive a Ph.D. In *The Souls of Black Folk* (1903), Du Bois declared prophetically that "the problem of the twentieth century is the problem of the color line." Through essays on black history, culture, education, and politics, Du Bois explored the concept of "double consciousness." Black people, he argued, would always feel the tension between an African heritage and their desire to assimilate as Americans. *Souls* represented the first effort to embrace African American culture as a source of collective black strength and something worth preserving.

Du Bois criticized Booker T. Washington's philosophy for its acceptance of "the alleged inferiority of the Negro." The black community, he argued, must fight for the right to vote, for civic equality, and for higher education for the "talented tenth" of their youth. In 1905, Du Bois and editor William Monroe Trotter brought together a group of educated black men to oppose Washington's conciliatory views. Discrimination they encountered in Buffalo, New York, prompted the men to move their meeting to Niagara Falls, Ontario. The **Niagara movement** protested legal segregation, the exclusion of blacks from labor unions, and the curtailment of voting and other civil rights.

The Niagara movement failed to generate much change. But in 1909, many of its members, led by Du Bois, attended a National Negro Conference held at the Henry Street Settlement in New York. The group included a number of white progressives sympathetic to the idea of challenging Washington's philosophy. A new interracial organization emerged from this conference, the **National Association for the Advancement of Colored People**. Du Bois, the only black officer of the original NAACP, founded and edited *The Crisis*, the influential NAACP monthly journal. For the next several decades, the NAACP would lead struggles to overturn legal and economic barriers to equal opportunity.

The disenfranchisement of black voters in the South severely curtailed African American political influence. In response, African American women created new strategies to challenge white supremacy and improve life in their communities. Founded in 1900, the Women's Convention of the National Baptist Convention, the largest black denomination in the United States, offered African American women a new public space to pursue reform work and "racial uplift." They organized settlement houses and built playgrounds; they created daycare facilities and kindergartens; they campaigned for women's suffrage, temperance, and advances in public health. In effect, they transformed church missionary societies into quasi–social service agencies.

# NATIONAL PROGRESSIVISM

On the presidential level, both Republican Theodore Roosevelt and Democrat Woodrow Wilson laid claim to the progressive mantle—a good example of how on the national level, progressivism animated many perspectives. In their pursuit of reform agendas, both significantly reshaped the office of the president. As progressivism moved to Washington, nationally organized interest groups and public opinion began to rival the influence of the old political parties in shaping the political landscape.

## THEODORE ROOSEVELT AND PRESIDENTIAL ACTIVISM

The assassination of William McKinley in 1901 made forty-two-year-old Theodore Roosevelt the youngest man to ever hold the office of president. Roosevelt viewed the presidency as a "bully pulpit"—a platform from which he could exhort Americans to reform their society—and he aimed to make the most of it.

Roosevelt was a uniquely colorful figure, a shrewd publicist, and a creative politician. His three-year stint as a rancher in the Dakota Territory; his fondness for hunting and nature study; his passion for scholarship, which resulted in ten books before he became president—all these set "T. R." apart from most of his upper-class peers. Roosevelt preached the virtues of "the strenuous life," and he believed that educated and wealthy Americans had a special responsibility to serve, guide, and inspire those less fortunate. But he believed the nation was at a crossroads that required the national state to play a more active role in curbing the power of wealthy industrialists.

Roosevelt made key contributions to national progressivism and to changing the office of the president. He knew how to inspire and guide public opinion. In 1902, Roosevelt demonstrated his unique style of activism when he personally intervened in a bitter dispute in the anthracite coal industry. Using public calls for conciliation, a series of White House meetings, and private pressure on the mine owners, Roosevelt secured an arbitrated settlement that won better pay and working conditions for the miners but without recognition of their union. Roosevelt also pushed for efficient government as the solution to social problems. Administrative agencies run by experts, he believed, could find rational solutions that would satisfy everyone.

## TRUST-BUSTING AND REGULATION

One of the first issues Roosevelt faced was growing public concern with the rapid business consolidations taking place in the American economy. In 1902, he directed

**WHAT ROLE** did Theodore Roosevelt envision the federal government playing in the national economy?

**myhistorylab**
Review Summary

 **21–7**
Theodore Roosevelt, *The New Nationalism* (1910)

**This 1909 cartoon** by Clifton Berryman depicts President Theodore Roosevelt slaying those trusts he considered "bad" for the public interest while restraining those whose business practices he considered "good" for the economy. The image also plays on T. R.'s well-publicized fondness for big-game hunting.

the Justice Department to begin a series of prosecutions under the **Sherman Antitrust Act**. The first target was the Northern Securities Company, a huge merger of transcontinental railroads. The Justice Department fought the case all the way through a hearing before the Supreme Court. In *Northern Securities* v. *United States* (1904), the Court held that the stock transactions involved in the merger constituted an illegal combination in restraint of interstate commerce.

This case established Roosevelt's reputation as a "trust-buster." During his two terms, the Justice Department filed forty-three cases under the Sherman Antitrust Act to restrain or dissolve business monopolies. Roosevelt viewed these suits as necessary to publicize the issue and assert the federal government's ultimate authority over big business. But he did not really believe in the need to break up large corporations. "Trust-busting" might be good politics, but unlike many progressives, who were nostalgic for smaller companies and freer competition, Roosevelt accepted centralization as a fact of modern economic life. Indeed many of the legal cases against trusts were dropped after business executives met privately with Roosevelt in the White House. What was most important, in T. R.'s view, was to insist on the right and power of the federal government to reign in excessive corporate behavior.

After easily defeating Democrat Alton B. Parker in the 1904 election, Roosevelt felt more secure in pushing for regulatory legislation. In 1906, Roosevelt responded to public pressure for greater government intervention and, overcoming objections from a conservative Congress, signed three important measures into law. The **Hepburn Act** strengthened the Interstate Commerce Commission (ICC) by authorizing it to set maximum railroad rates and inspect financial records.

Two other laws passed in 1906 also expanded the regulatory power of the federal government. The battles surrounding these reforms demonstrate how progressive measures often attracted supporters with competing motives. The **Pure Food and Drug Act** established the Food and Drug Administration (FDA), which tested and approved drugs before they went on the market. The Meat Inspection Act empowered the Department of Agriculture to inspect and label meat products. In both cases, supporters hailed the new laws as providing consumer protection against adulterated or fraudulently labeled food and drugs.

But regulatory legislation found advocates among American big business as well. Large meatpackers such as Swift and Armour strongly supported stricter federal regulation as a way to drive out smaller companies that could not meet tougher standards. The new laws also helped American packers compete more profitably in the European export market by giving their meat the official seal of federal inspectors. Large pharmaceutical manufacturers similarly supported new regulations that would eliminate competitors and patent medicine suppliers.

## THE BIRTH OF ENVIRONMENTALISM

As a naturalist and outdoorsman, Theodore Roosevelt also believed in the need for government regulation of the natural environment. The conservation of forest and water resources, he argued, was a national problem of vital import. In 1905, he created the U.S. Forest Service and named conservationist Gifford Pinchot to

**Sherman Antitrust Act**   The first federal antitrust measure, passed in 1890; sought to promote economic competition by prohibiting business combinations in restraint of trade or commerce.

**Hepburn Act**   Act that strengthened the Interstate Commerce Commission (ICC) by authorizing it to set maximum railroad rates and inspect financial records.

**Pure Food and Drug Act**   Act that established the Food and Drug Administration (FDA), which tested and approved drugs before they went on the market.

head it. Pinchot recruited a force of forest rangers to manage the reserves. By 1909, total timber and forest reserves had increased from 45 to 195 million acres, and more than 80 million acres of mineral lands had been withdrawn from public sale.

On the broad issue of managing America's natural resources, the Roosevelt administration took the middle ground between preservation and unrestricted commercial development. But other voices championed a more radical vision of conservation, emphasizing the preservation of wilderness lands against the encroachment of commercial exploitation. The most influential and committed of these was John Muir, an essayist and founder of the modern environmentalist movement. Muir made a passionate and spiritual defense of the inherent value of the American wilderness. He served as first president of the Sierra Club, founded in 1892 to preserve and protect the mountain regions of the West Coast as well as Yellowstone National Park in Wyoming, Montana, and Idaho.

A bitter, drawn-out struggle over new water sources for San Francisco revealed the deep conflicts between conservationists, represented by Pinchot, and preservationists, represented by Muir. After a devastating earthquake in 1906, San Francisco sought federal approval to dam and flood the spectacular Hetch Hetchy Valley, located 150 miles from the city in Yosemite National Park. Conservationists and their urban progressive allies argued that developing Hetch Hetchy would be a victory for the public good over greedy private developers, since the plan called for municipal control of the water supply. To John Muir and the Sierra Club, Hetch Hetchy was a "temple" threatened with destruction by the "devotees of ravaging commercialism." Although, in the end, they lost the battle for Hetch Hetchy, the preservationists gained much ground in the larger campaign of alerting the nation to the dangers of a vanishing wilderness. They began to use their own utilitarian rationales, arguing that national parks would encourage economic growth through tourism and provide Americans with a healthy escape from urban and industrial areas. In 1916, the preservationists obtained their own bureaucracy in Washington with the creation of the National Park Service.

**my**history**lab**

**Exploring America:** *Hetchy Hetchy*

## REPUBLICAN SPLIT

In 1908, Roosevelt kept his promise to retire after a second term. He chose Secretary of War William Howard Taft as his successor. Taft easily defeated Democrat William Jennings Bryan in the 1908 election. During Taft's presidency, the gulf between "insurgent" progressives and the "stand pat" wing split the Republican Party wide open. To some degree, the battles were as much over style as substance. Compared with Roosevelt, the reflective and judicious Taft brought a much more restrained concept of the presidency to the White House. He supported some progressive measures, including the constitutional amendment legalizing a graduated income tax (ratified in 1913), safety codes for mines and railroads, and the creation of a federal Children's Bureau (1912). But in a series of bitter political fights involving tariff, antitrust, and conservation policies, Taft alienated Roosevelt and many other progressives.

After returning from an African safari and a triumphant European tour in 1910, Roosevelt threw himself back into national politics. He directly challenged Taft for the Republican Party leadership. Although Roosevelt won most of the state primaries, the old guard still controlled the national convention, and renominated Taft in June 1912. Roosevelt's supporters stormed out, and in August, the new Progressive Party nominated Roosevelt and Hiram Johnson of California as its presidential ticket. Roosevelt's "New Nationalism" presented a vision of a strong federal

**New Freedom** Woodrow Wilson's 1912 program for limited government intervention in the economy to restore competition by curtailing the restrictive influences of trusts and protective tariffs, thereby providing opportunities for individual achievement.

**21–11**
Woodrow Wilson, *The New Freedom* (1913)

**21–3**
Eugene V. Debs, *The Outlook for Socialism in the United States* (1900)

government, led by an activist president, regulating and protecting the various interests in American society. The platform called for woman suffrage, the eight-hour day, prohibition of child labor, minimum-wage standards for working women, and stricter regulation of large corporations.

## THE ELECTION OF 1912: A FOUR-WAY RACE

With the Republicans so badly divided, the Democrats sensed a chance for their first presidential victory in twenty years. They chose Governor Woodrow Wilson of New Jersey as their candidate. Although not nearly as well known nationally as Taft and Roosevelt, Wilson had built a strong reputation as a reformer. After teaching history and political science at several schools, he became president of Princeton University in 1902. In 1910, he won election as New Jersey's governor, running against the state Democratic machine. He won the Democratic nomination for president with the support of many of the party's progressives, including William Jennings Bryan.

Wilson declared himself and the Democratic Party to be the true progressives. Viewing Roosevelt rather than Taft as his main rival, Wilson contrasted his **New Freedom** campaign with Roosevelt's New Nationalism. Crafted largely by progressive lawyer Louis Brandeis, Wilson's platform was far more ambiguous than Roosevelt's. The New Freedom emphasized restoring conditions of free competition and equality of economic opportunity. Wilson did favor a variety of progressive reforms for workers, farmers, and consumers. But in sounding older, nineteenth-century Democratic themes of states' rights and small government, Wilson argued against allowing the federal government to become as large and paternalistic as Roosevelt advocated. Socialist Party nominee Eugene V. Debs offered the fourth and most radical choice to voters. The party's 1912 platform called for collective ownership of all large-scale industry and all means of transportation and communication. It demanded shorter working hours, an end to child labor, and the vote for women.

An inspiring orator who drew large and sympathetic crowds wherever he spoke, Debs proved especially popular in areas with strong labor movements and populist traditions. He wrapped his socialist message in an apocalyptic vision. Socialists would "abolish this monstrous system and the misery and crime which flow from it." Debs and the Socialists also took credit for pushing both Roosevelt and Wilson further toward the left. Both the Democratic and Progressive Party platforms contained proposals that had been considered extremely radical only ten years earlier.

In the end, the divisions in the Republican Party gave the election to Wilson (see Map 21.2). In several respects, the election of 1912 was the first "modern" presidential race. It featured the first direct primaries, challenges to traditional party loyalties, an issue-oriented campaign, and a high degree of interest-group activity.

## WOODROW WILSON'S FIRST TERM

As president, Wilson followed Roosevelt's lead in expanding the activist dimensions of the office. He became more responsive to pressure for a greater federal role in regulat-

**This political cartoon,** drawn by Charles Jay Budd, appeared on the cover of *Harper's Weekly*, September 28, 1912. It employed the imagery of autumn county fairs to depict voters as unhappy with their three choices for president. Note that the artist did not include the fourth candidate, Socialist Eugene V. Debs, who was often ignored by more conservative publications such as *Harper's*.

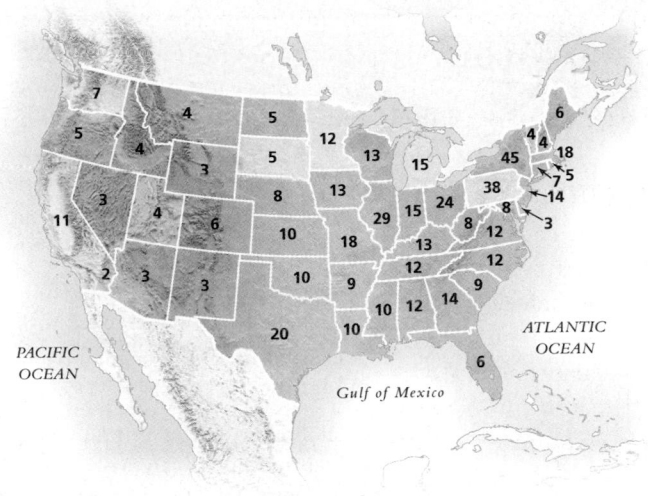

| | Electoral Vote (%) | Popular Vote (%) |
|---|---|---|
| **WOODROW WILSON** (Democrat) | 435 (82) | 6,296,547 (42) |
| **Theodore Roosevelt** (Progressive) | 88 (17) | 4,118,571 (27) |
| **William Taft** (Republican) | 8 (1) | 3,486,720 (23) |
| **Eugene Debs** (Socialist) | — | 900,672 (6) |

**MAP 21.2**
**The Election of 1912**   The split within the Republican Party allowed Woodrow Wilson to become only the second Democrat since the Civil War to be elected president. Eugene Debs's vote was the highest ever polled by a Socialist candidate.

WHAT CAUSED the split in the Republican Party?

ing business and the economy. This increase in direct lobbying—from hundreds of local and national reform groups, Washington-based organizations, and the new Progressive Party—was itself a new and defining feature of the era's political life. With the help of a Democratic-controlled Congress, Wilson pushed through a significant battery of reform proposals.

The **Underwood-Simmons Act of 1913** substantially reduced tariff duties on a variety of raw materials and manufactured goods, including wool, sugar, agricultural machinery, shoes, iron, and steel. Taking advantage of the newly ratified **Sixteenth Amendment**, which gave Congress the power to levy taxes on income, it also imposed the first graduated tax (up to 6 percent) on personal incomes. The **Federal Reserve Act** that same year restructured the nation's banking and currency system. It created twelve Federal Reserve Banks, regulated by a central board in Washington. Member banks were required to keep a portion of their cash reserves in the Federal Reserve Bank of their district.

Wilson also supported the **Clayton Antitrust Act** of 1914, which replaced the old Sherman Act of 1890 as the nation's basic antitrust law. The Clayton Act reflected the growing political clout of the American Federation of Labor. It exempted unions from being construed as illegal combinations in restraint of trade, and it forbade federal courts from issuing injunctions against strikers. But Wilson adopted the view that permanent federal regulation was necessary for checking the abuses of big business. The **Federal Trade Commission (FTC)**, established in 1914, sought to give

**QUICK REVIEW**

**Democratic Victory in 1912**

- Republicans split between Taft and Roosevelt.
- Democrats put themselves forward as the "true progressives."
- Wilson won with only 42 percent of the popular vote.

**Underwood-Simmons Act of 1913** Reform law that lowered tariff rates and levied the first regular federal income tax.

**Sixteenth Amendment** Authorized a federal income tax.

**Federal Reserve Act** The 1913 law that revised banking and currency by extending limited government regulation through the creation of the Federal Reserve System.

## CHRONOLOGY

**1889** Jane Addams founds Hull House in Chicago

**1890** Jacob Riis publishes *How the Other Half Lives*

**1895** Booker T. Washington addresses Cotton States Exposition in Atlanta, emphasizing an accommodationist philosophy

Lillian Wald establishes Henry Street Settlement in New York

**1898** Florence Kelley becomes general secretary of the new National Consumers' League

**1900** Robert M. La Follette is elected governor of Wisconsin

**1901** Theodore Roosevelt succeeds the assassinated William McKinley as president

**1903** Lincoln Steffens publishes *The Shame of the Cities*

**1905** President Roosevelt creates U.S. Forest Service and names Gifford Pinchot head

Industrial Workers of the World is founded in Chicago

**1906** Upton Sinclair's *The Jungle* exposes conditions in the meatpacking industry

Congress passes Pure Food and Drug Act and Meat Inspection Act and establishes Food and Drug Administration

**1908** In *Muller* v. *Oregon* the Supreme Court upholds a state law limiting maximum hours for working women

**1909** Uprising of 20,000 garment workers in New York City's garment industries helps organize unskilled workers into unions

National Association for the Advancement of Colored People (NAACP) is founded

**1911** Triangle Shirtwaist Company fire kills 146 garment workers in New York City

Socialist critic Max Eastman begins publishing *The Masses*

**1912** Democrat Woodrow Wilson wins presidency, defeating Republican William H. Taft, Progressive Theodore Roosevelt, and Socialist Eugene V. Debs

"Bread and Roses" strike involves 25,000 textile workers in Lawrence, Massachusetts

Margaret Sanger begins writing and speaking in support of birth control for women

**1913** Sixteenth Amendment, legalizing a graduated income tax, is ratified.

Seventeenth Amendment, shifting the selection of U.S. senators to direct election by voters

**1914** Clayton Antitrust Act exempts unions from being construed as illegal combinations in restraint of trade

Federal Trade Commission is established

Ludlow Massacre occurs

**1916** National Park Service is established

---

**Clayton Antitrust Act** Replaced the old Sherman Act of 1890 as the nation's basic antitrust law. It exempted unions from being construed as illegal combinations in restraint of trade, and it forbade federal courts from issuing injunctions against strikers.

**Federal Trade Commission (FTC)** Government agency established in 1914 to provide regulatory oversight of business activity.

the federal government the same sort of regulatory control over corporations that the ICC had over railroads.

On social issues, Wilson proved more cautious in his first two years. His initial failure to support federal child labor legislation and rural credits to farmers angered many progressives. A Southerner, Wilson also issued an executive order that instituted legal segregation in federal employment, requiring African Americans to work separately from white employees in government offices around Washington, DC. As the reelection campaign of 1916 approached, Wilson worried about defections from the labor and social justice wings of his party. He proceeded to support a rural credits act providing government capital to federal farm banks, as well as federal aid to agricultural extension programs in schools. He also came out in favor of a worker compensation bill for federal employees, and he signed the landmark Keating-Owen Act, which banned children under fourteen from working in enterprises engaged in interstate commerce. But by 1916, the dark cloud of war in Europe had already begun to cast its long shadow over progressive reform.

## CONCLUSION

In her memoirs Lillian Wald summarized the growth of the Henry Street Settlement she had founded in 1895 as a home health and visiting nurse service on New York's Lower East Side. "Our experience in one small East Side section," she recalled in 1934, "a block perhaps, has led to a next contact, and a next, in widening circles, until our community relationships have come to include the city, the state, the national government, and the world at large." Much the same could be said of the progressive movement. What had begun as a series of interlocking, sometimes contradictory, reform initiatives had come to redefine Americans' relationship to government itself. Cities and state legislatures now routinely made active interventions to improve the lives of their citizens. Real advances had been made through a range of social legislation covering working conditions, child labor, minimum wages, and worker compensation. Social progressives, too, had discovered the power of organizing into extraparty lobbying groups, such as the National Consumers' League and the National American Woman Suffrage Association. But the national government had now become the focus of political power and reform energy. The president was now expected to provide leadership in policymaking, and new federal bureaucracies exerted more influence over the day-to-day lives of Americans.

Yet many progressive reforms had uneven or unintended consequences. The tensions between fighting for social justice and the urge toward social control remained unresolved. The emphasis on efficiency, uplift, and rational administration often collided with humane impulses to aid the poor, the immigrant, the slum dweller. The large majority of African Americans, blue-collar workers, and urban poor remained untouched by federal assistance programs. The drive for a more open and democratic political process, in particular, had the effect of excluding some people from voting while including others. For African Americans, progressivism largely meant disenfranchisement from voting altogether. Stricter election laws made it more difficult for third parties to get on the ballot. Voting itself steadily declined after 1916. Overall, party voting became a less important form of political participation. Interest-group activity, congressional and statehouse lobbying, and direct appeals to public opinion gained currency as ways of influencing government. Business groups and individual trade associations were among the most active groups pressing their demands on government. Political action often shifted from legislatures to the new administrative agencies and commissions created to deal with social and economic problems. Popular magazines and journals grew significantly in both number and circulation, becoming more influential in shaping and appealing to national public opinion. America's entry into World War I effectively drained the energy out of progressive reform. But the progressive movement, with all its contradictions and internal tensions, had profoundly changed the landscape of American political and social life.

# REVIEW QUESTIONS

1. Discuss the tensions within progressivism between the ideals of social justice and the urge for social control. What concrete achievements are associated with each wing of the movement? What were the driving forces behind them?

2. Describe the different manifestations of progressivism at the local, state, and national levels.

3. How did workers use their own values and communities to restrain the power of large corporations during the progressive era?

4. How did the era's new immigration reshape America's cities and workplaces? What connections can you draw between the new immigrant experience and progressive era politics?

5. Analyze the progressive era from the perspective of African Americans. What political and social developments were most crucial, and what legacies did they leave?

6. How do the goals, methods, and language of progressives still find voice in contemporary America?

**myhistorylab**

Flashcard Review

# KEY TERMS

**Bohemian** (p. 577)
**Clayton Antitrust Act** (p. 586)
**Federal Reserve Act** (p. 585)
**Federal Trade Commission (FTC)** (p. 586)
**Hepburn Act** (p. 582)
**Muckraking** (p. 560)
**National Association for the Advancement of Colored People** (p. 580)
**New Freedom** (p. 584)
**Niagara movement** (p. 580)

**Progressivism** (p. 559)
**Prohibition** (p. 568)
**Pure Food and Drug Act** (p. 582)
**Referendum** (p. 566)
**Sherman Antitrust Act** (p. 582)
**Sixteenth Amendment** (p. 585)
**Social Darwinism** (p. 562)
**Temperance groups** (p. 568)
**Underwood-Simmons Act of 1913** (p. 585)
**Wobblies** (p. 576)

# RECOMMENDED READING

James Chace, *1912: Wilson, Roosevelt, Taft & Debs—The Election That Changed the Country* (2004). Narrative account of this pivotal presidential election that revolved around competing visions of progressivism.

Alan Dawley, *Struggles for Justice: Social Responsibility and the Liberal State* (1991). Offers an important interpretation of progressivism that focuses on how the working class and women pushed the state toward a more activist role in confronting social problems.

David von Drehle, *Triangle: The Fire That Changed America* (2003). Superb, deeply researched narrative of the disastrous Triangle Fire that re-creates the world of the victims and the reform movement that ensued.

Maureen Flanagan, *America Reformed: Progressives and Progressivisms, 1890s–1920s* (2007). An excellent new overview of progressive era achievements, including fine analysis of the contradictions within the movement.

Louise W. Knight, *Citizen: Jane Addams and the Struggle for Democracy* (2005). Beautifully written new biography of this key progressive figure, focusing on Addams's early life and the evolution of her political thought.

Michael McGerr, *A Fierce Discontent: The Rise and Fall of the Progressive Movement in America, 1870–1920* (2003). A new synthesis arguing that the heart of progressivism lay in the efforts of the urban middle class to reshape the behavior of both the poor and the wealthy.

Michael Perman, *Struggle for Mastery: Disfranchisement in the South, 1888–1908* (2001). A comprehensive, state-by-state overview of the campaigns to remove African Americans from the electoral process.

Daniel T. Rodgers, *Atlantic Crossings: Social Politics in a Progressive Age* (1998). A magisterial work of comparative history focusing on the transnational conversations that deeply influenced American progressive thinkers and reformers.

Christine Stansell, *American Moderns: Bohemian New York and the Creation of a New Century* (2000). Vividly written account that places radical politics and "New Women" at the center of the shaping of modernism.

myhistorylab™

Where it's a good time to connect to the past!

For study resources for this chapter, go to **www.myhistorylab.com** and choose *Out of Many, Teaching and Learning Classroom Edition*. You will find a wealth of study and review material for this chapter, including pretests and posttests, customized study plan, key-term review flash cards, interactive map and document activities, and documents for analysis.

*On the other hand, if there is little enthusiasm, the people everywhere are taking the war as a grim necessity, feeling that they have been forced into it by events beyond their control . . .*

—Ray Stannard Baker, June 17, 1917

**Female workers build a vehicle** in an engineering shop in 1917.

# 22

# A GLOBAL POWER
## THE UNITED STATES IN THE ERA OF THE GREAT WAR
### 1901–1920

**HOW DID** Theodore Roosevelt use force as component of U.S. foreign policy?

**WHY DID** most Americans oppose U.S. involvement in World War I in 1914?

**HOW DID** the federal government try to change public opinion about U.S. involvement in World War I?

**WHAT WERE** the domestic effects in the United States of World War I?

**WHAT STEPS** did the federal government take to suppress the antiwar movement?

**HOW CAN** we explain Woodrow Wilson's failure to win the peace?

# AMERICAN COMMUNITIES
## The American Expeditionary Force in France

AT 5:30 A.M. ON SEPTEMBER 26, 1918, SOME 600,000 SOLDIERS OF the American Expeditionary Force (AEF) pulled themselves out of the mud and headed into the dense grey fog on a twenty-mile front between the Meuse River and the Argonne Forest in northern France. The biggest and costliest American operation of World War I had begun. In sheer size and scale, the Meuse-Argonne offensive dwarfed anything an American army had ever attempted. American commander General John J. Pershing aimed to overwhelm the undermanned and dispirited German lines with massive numbers and swift movement and thereby force a German surrender. Pershing hoped to put a distinctively American stamp on ending the war with the Meuse-Argonne offensive.

But the individual infantryman had little time or use for grand strategy. Each man carried a rifle and bayonet, steel helmet, and gas mask, along with 250 rounds of ammunition. His two days of "iron rations" consisted of two cans of corned beef, six boxes of hard crackers, and a quart canteen of water. The American thrust quickly stalled as the Germans put up fierce resistance with well-placed machine gun nests and artillery batteries, spread out amidst a ghostly landscape littered with abandoned trenches, tangled barbed wire fences, water-filled craters, and dead and mangled bodies everywhere. The scene was nothing like the storybooks of war, recalled Lieutenant Maury Maverick. "There were no bugles, no flags, no drums, and as far as we knew, no heroes. . . . I have never read in any military history a description of the high explosives that break overhead. There is a great swishing scream, a smash-bang, and it seems to tear everything loose from you. The intensity of it simply enters your heart and brain and tears every nerve to pieces."

As members of the AEF shipped off for the front, they carried with them vague and often romantic notions of what to expect on the battlefield. By the summer of 1918, when most American soldiers traveled to France, the carnage across Europe

was no secret. Nor was the grim reality of death associated with machine guns, tanks, and trench warfare. But the blizzard of posters, films, war bond drives, and other propaganda activities coordinated by the Committee on Public Information (CPI) mostly avoided this side of war. Instead it emphasized appeals to patriotism, manhood, heroism, and the fight for democracy. And many doughboys carried to France images of war shaped by their grandfathers' stories about the Civil War or romantic accounts of medieval knights.

Their experiences in the Meuse-Argonne offensive brought them face-to-face with the very different reality of mass mechanized killing. Rather than the swift victory General Pershing had hoped for, the campaign turned into a slow, sometimes chaotic slog. American combat units measured their gains in yards as they found their advances blunted by tough German defenders. Between September 25 and the Armistice ending the fighting on November 11, each day claimed an average of over 550 Americans dead, with a total of 26,000 Americans killed in the campaign.

In early 1919, encouraged by some senior officers, a group of AEF veterans founded the American Legion, "to preserve the memories and incidents of our association in the great war . . . to consecrate and sanctify our comradeship." American Legion halls soon became a familiar sight in communities across America. But the Legion had a political mission as well, one that would play out during the postwar "Red Scare." Legion leaders saw it as a way to counter radical ideas that might "infect" returning veterans, especially those who suffered from unemployment or had trouble readjusting to civilian life. It would commemorate the war, celebrate sacrifice, and honor the dead, all in the name of promoting "100 percent Americanism" and fighting against "dangerous" socialists and other radical groups. As much a political lobby as a veterans' organization, the American Legion would extend the memory and life of the AEF community well into the twentieth century.

Verdun

# BECOMING A WORLD POWER

In the first years of the new century, the United States pursued a more vigorous and aggressive foreign policy than it had in the past. In addition to its new-found imperial presence in Asia, the United States marked out the Western Hemisphere—especially the Caribbean, Mexico, and Central America—as a site for establishing American hegemony. Presidents Theodore Roosevelt, William Howard Taft, and Woodrow Wilson all contributed to "progressive diplomacy," in which commercial expansion was backed by a growing military presence in the hemisphere. This policy reflected a view of world affairs that stressed the links between ensuring American commercial expansion and a foreign policy couched in terms of moralism, order, and a special, even God-given, role for the United States. By 1917, when the United States entered the Great War, the nation was just as complicit in building empire as were the European states and Japan.

## ROOSEVELT: THE BIG STICK

Theodore Roosevelt left a strong imprint on the nation's foreign policy. Like many of his class and background, "T.R." took for granted the superiority of Protestant Anglo-American culture and the goal of spreading its values and influence. He believed that to maintain and increase its economic and political stature, America must be militarily strong. In 1900, Roosevelt summarized his activist views, declaring, "I have always been fond of the West African proverb, 'Speak softly and carry a big stick, you will go far.'"

Roosevelt brought the "big stick" approach to disputes in the Caribbean region. Since the 1880s, several British, French, and American companies had pursued plans for building a canal across the Isthmus of Panama, thereby connecting the Atlantic and Pacific Oceans. The canal was a top priority for Roosevelt, and he tried to negotiate a leasing agreement with Colombia, of which Panama was a province. But when the Colombian Senate rejected a final American offer in the fall of 1903, Roosevelt invented a new strategy. A combination of native forces and foreign promoters associated with the canal project plotted a revolt against Colombia. Roosevelt kept in touch with at least one leader of the revolt, Philippe Bunau-Varilla, an engineer and agent for the New Panama Canal Company, and the president let him know that U.S. warships were steaming toward Panama.

On November 3, 1903, just as the USS *Nashville* arrived in Colón harbor, the province of Panama declared itself independent of Colombia. The United States immediately recognized the new Republic of Panama. Less than two weeks later, Bunau-Varilla, serving as a minister from Panama, signed a treaty granting the United States full sovereignty in perpetuity over a ten-mile-wide canal zone.

"The inevitable effect of our building the Canal," wrote Secretary of State Elihu Root in 1905, "must be to require us to police the surrounding premises." Roosevelt agreed. He was especially concerned that European powers might step in if America did not. In 1903, Great Britain, Germany, and Italy had imposed a blockade on Venezuela in a dispute over debt payments owed to private investors. To prevent armed intervention by the Europeans, in 1904 Roosevelt proclaimed what became known as the **Roosevelt Corollary** to the **Monroe Doctrine**. "Chronic wrongdoing, or an impotence which results in a general loosening of the ties of civilized society," the statement read, justified "the exercise of an international police power" anywhere in the hemisphere. Roosevelt and later presidents cited the corollary to justify armed intervention in the internal affairs of the Dominican Republic, Cuba, Haiti, Nicaragua, and Mexico.

**HOW DID** Theodore Roosevelt use force as component of U.S. foreign policy?

**myhistorylab**

**Review Summary**

## IMAGE KEY
for pages 590–591

a. British Prime Minister Lloyd George, French Prime Minister George Clemenceau, and U.S. President Woodrow Wilson in Versailles, France in 1919.

b. Women war workers working in an engineering shop, 1917.

c. The *New York Times:* the sinking of the *Lusitania* in 1915.

d. A British World War I biplane being shot down.

e. A 1905 cartoon from *Judge* magazine.

f. President Woodrow Wilson reading his war message to Congress, April, 1917.

g. An American World War I Liberty Loan poster.

h. Women draft protesters at New York's City Hall June 1917.

i. A portrait of Woodrow Wilson (1856–1924).

**Roosevelt Corollary**   President Theodore Roosevelt's policy asserting U.S. authority to intervene in the affairs of Latin American nations; an expansion of the Monroe Doctrine.

**Monroe Doctrine**   In December 1823, Monroe declared to Congress that Americans "are henceforth not to be considered as subjects for future colonization by any European power."

THE WORLD'S CONSTABLE.

**This 1905 cartoon** portraying President Theodore Roosevelt, "The World's Constable," appeared in *Judge* magazine. In depicting the president as a strong but benevolent policeman bringing order in a contentious world, the artist Louis Dalrymple drew on familiar imagery from Roosevelt's earlier days as a New York City police commissioner.

With the outbreak of the Russo-Japanese War in 1904, Roosevelt worried about the future of the **Open Door** policy in Asia. (See Chapter 20.) A total victory by Russia or Japan could upset the balance of power in East Asia and threaten American business enterprises there. He became especially concerned after the Japanese scored a series of military victories over Russia and began to loom as a dominant power in East Asia. Roosevelt mediated a settlement of the Russo-Japanese War at Portsmouth, New Hampshire, in 1905 (for which he was awarded the 1906 Nobel Peace Prize). In this settlement, Japan won recognition of its dominant position in Korea and consolidated its economic control over Manchuria. Yet repeated incidents of anti-Japanese racism in California kept American–Japanese relations strained. In 1907, in the so-called Gentlemen's Agreement, Japan agreed not to issue passports to Japanese male laborers looking to emigrate to the United States, and Roosevelt promised to fight anti-Japanese discrimination.

But Roosevelt did not want these conciliatory moves to be interpreted as weakness. He thus built up American naval strength in the Pacific, and in 1908, he sent battleships to visit Japan in a muscle-flexing display of sea power. In that same year, the two burgeoning Pacific powers reached a reconciliation. The Root-Takahira Agreement affirmed the "existing status quo" in Asia, mutual respect for territorial possessions in the Pacific, and the Open Door trade policy in China.

**Open Door** American policy of seeking equal trade and investment opportunities in foreign nations or regions.

## TAFT: DOLLAR DIPLOMACY

Roosevelt's successor, William Howard Taft, believed he could replace the militarism of the big stick with the more subtle and effective weapon of business investment. Taft and his secretary of state, corporate lawyer Philander C. Knox, followed a strategy (called "dollar diplomacy" by critics) in which they assumed that political influence would follow increased U.S. trade and investment. As Taft explained in 1910, he advocated "active intervention to secure for our merchandise and our capitalists opportunity for profitable investment."

Overall American investment in Central America grew rapidly, from $41 million in 1908 to $93 million by 1914. Most of this money went into railroad construction, mining, and plantations. The United Fruit Company alone owned about 160,000 acres of land in the Caribbean by 1913. But dollar diplomacy ended up requiring military support. The Taft administration sent the navy and the marines to intervene in political disputes in Honduras and Nicaragua, propping up factions pledged to protect American business interests. A contingent of U.S. Marines remained in Nicaragua until 1933. The economic and political structures of Honduras and Nicaragua were controlled by both the dollar and the bullet (see Map 22.1).

In China, Taft and Knox pressed for a greater share of the pie for U.S. investors. They gained a place for U.S. bankers in the European consortium, building the massive new Hu-kuang Railway in southern and central China. But Knox blundered by attempting to "neutralize" the existing railroads in China. He tried to secure a huge international loan for the Chinese government that would allow it to buy up all the foreign railways and develop new ones. Both Russia and Japan, which had fought wars over their railroad interests in Manchuria, resisted this plan as a threat to the arrangements hammered out at Portsmouth with the help of Theodore Roosevelt. Knox's "neutralization" scheme, combined with U.S. support for the Chinese Nationalists in their 1911 revolt against the ruling Manchu dynasty, prompted Japan to sign a new friendship treaty with Russia. The Open Door to China was now effectively closed, and American relations with Japan began a slow deterioration that ended in war thirty years later.

## WILSON: MORALISM AND INTERVENTION IN MEXICO

Wilson, like most corporate and political leaders of the day, emphasized foreign investments and industrial exports as the keys to the nation's prosperity. He believed that the United States, with its superior industrial efficiency, could achieve supremacy in world commerce if artificial barriers to free trade were removed. Wilson often couched his vision of a dynamic, expansive American capitalism in terms of a moral crusade. As he put it in a speech to a congress of salesmen, "[Since] you are Americans and are meant to carry liberty and justice and the principles of humanity wherever you go, go out and sell goods that will make the world more comfortable and more happy, and convert them to the principles of America." Yet he quickly found that the complex realities of power politics could interfere with moral vision.

Wilson's policies toward Mexico, which foreshadowed the problems he would encounter in World War I, best illustrate his difficulties. The 1911 Mexican Revolution had overthrown the brutally corrupt dictatorship of Porfirio Díaz, and popular leader Francisco Madero had won wide support by promising democracy and economic reform for millions of landless peasants. But the U.S. business community was nervous about the future of its investments which, in the previous generation, had come to dominate the Mexican economy.

Wilson at first gave his blessing to the revolutionary movement, expressed regret over the Mexican-American War of 1846–48, and disavowed any interest in

# MAP EXPLORATION

To explore an interactive version of this map, go to **http://www.prenhall.com/faraghertic/map22.1**

| | |
|---|---|
| ☐ | United States and U.S. possessions |
| ☐ | Countries influenced by U.S. activities |
| ☐ | European possessions |
| ■ | U.S. military bases |
| ✳ | U.S. military actions |

U.S. expeditionary force, 1916–17

Santa Ysabel

Parral

**UNITED STATES**

*Gulf of Mexico*

Platt Amendment, 1903–34
U.S. exports to equal
$1.6 billion by 1917

*ATLANTIC OCEAN*

Bahama Islands (Br.)

**MEXICO**

Tampico

Mexico City

Veracruz
U.S. seizure, 1914

Sinking of Maine, 1898 • Havana

**CUBA**

U.S. troops, 1898–1902,
1906–09, 1912, 1917–22

Guantanamo, 1903

U.S. control of customs houses, 1905,
U.S. troops, 1916–24

Virgin Islands
**1917 (U.S.)**

Jamaica (Br.)

**HAITI** **DOMINICAN REPUBLIC**

U.S. troops,
1915–34

Financial supervision,
1905–41

Puerto Rico
**1898 (U.S.)**

Guadeloupe (Fr.)

Martinique (Fr.)

Americans control 43% of
Mexican property, 1910
U.S. exports to equal
$1.3 billion by 1917

**GUATEMALA**

British Honduras (Br.)

**HONDURAS**

U.S. troops, 1907,
1924–25

*Caribbean Sea*

Trinidad (Br.)

Barbados (Br.)

United Fruit Co.
organized 1899

**EL SALVADOR**

**NICARAGUA**
Financial supervision, 1911–24

U.S. troops, 1909–10,
1912–25, 1926–33

Caracas

*PACIFIC OCEAN*

**COSTA RICA**
Canal option, 1916

**PANAMA**
Acquired Canal Zone, 1903
Canal completed 1914

**COLOMBIA**

**VENEZUELA**
Debt crisis, 1903–04

**BRAZIL**

**MAP 22.1**

**The United States in the Caribbean, 1865–1933** An overview of U.S. economic and military involvement in the Caribbean during the late nineteenth and early twentieth centuries. Victory in the Spanish-American War, the Panama Canal project, and rapid economic investment in Mexico and Cuba all contributed to a permanent and growing U.S. military presence in the region.

WHAT WERE the arguments for and against the repeated United States intervention in the Caribbean?

another war. But right before he took office, Wilson was stunned by the ousting and murder of Madero by his chief lieutenant, General Victoriano Huerta. Other nations, including Great Britain and Japan, recognized the Huerta regime, but Wilson refused. He announced that the United States would support only governments that rested on the rule of law. An armed faction opposed to Huerta, known as the Constitutionalists and led by Venustiano Carranza, emerged in northern Mexico. Both sides rejected an effort by Wilson to broker a compromise between them. Carranza, an ardent nationalist, pressed for the right to buy U.S. arms, which he won in 1914. Wilson also isolated Huerta diplomatically by persuading the British to withdraw their support in exchange for American guarantees of English property interests in Mexico.

But Huerta stubbornly remained in power. In April 1914, Wilson used a minor insult to U.S. sailors in Tampico as an excuse to invade. American naval forces bombarded and then occupied Veracruz, the main port through which Huerta received arms shipments. Nineteen Americans and 126 Mexicans died in the battle, which brought the United States and Mexico close to war, and provoked anti-American demonstrations in Mexico and throughout Latin America. Wilson accepted the offer of the ABC Powers—Argentina, Brazil, and Chile—to mediate the dispute. Huerta rejected a plan for him to step aside in favor of a provisional government. But then in August, Carranza managed to overthrow Huerta. Playing to nationalist sentiment, Carranza too denounced Wilson for his intervention.

As war loomed in Europe, Mexico's revolutionary politics continued to frustrate Wilson. For a brief period, Wilson threw his support behind Francisco "Pancho" Villa, Carranza's former ally, who now led a rebel army of his own in northern Mexico. But Carranza's forces dealt Villa a major setback in April 1915. In October, its attention focused on the war in Europe, the Wilson administration recognized Carranza as Mexico's de facto president. Meanwhile, Pancho Villa, feeling betrayed, turned on the United States and tried to provoke a crisis that might draw the United States into war with Mexico.

In March 1916, enraged by Villa's defiance, Wilson dispatched General John J. Pershing and an army that eventually numbered 15,000 to capture him. For a year, Pershing's troops chased Villa in vain, penetrating 300 miles into Mexico. The invasion made Villa a symbol of national resistance in Mexico, and his army grew from 500 men to 10,000 by the end of 1916.

Skirmishes between American forces and Carranza's army brought the two nations to the brink of war again in June 1916. Although Wilson prepared a message to Congress asking permission for American troops to occupy all of northern Mexico, he never delivered it. There was fierce opposition to war with Mexico throughout the country. Perhaps more important, mounting tensions with Germany caused Wilson to hesitate. Wilson thus accepted negotiations by a face-saving international commission.

Wilson's attempt to guide the course of Mexico's revolution and protect U.S. interests left a bitter legacy of suspicion and distrust in Mexico. It also suggested the limits of a foreign policy tied to a moral vision rooted in the idea of American exceptionalism. **Militarism** and **imperialism**, Wilson had believed, were hallmarks of the old European way. American liberal values—rooted in capitalist development, democracy, and free trade—were the wave of the future. Wilson believed the United States could lead the world in establishing a new international system based on peaceful commerce and political stability. In both the 1914 invasion and the 1916 punitive expedition, Wilson declared that he had no desire to interfere with Mexican sovereignty. But in both cases, that is exactly what he did. The United States, he argued, must actively use its enormous moral and material power to create the new order. That principle would soon engage America in Europe's bloodiest war and its most momentous revolution.

**This 1914 political** cartoon comments approvingly on the interventionist role adopted by the United States in Latin American countries. By depicting President Woodrow Wilson as a schoolteacher giving lessons to children, the image captures the paternalistic views that American policy makers held toward nations like Mexico, Venezuela, and Nicaragua.

## QUICK REVIEW

**Wilson and Mexico**

◆ Wilson refused to recognize the regime of General Victoriano Huerta.

◆ 1914: Wilson used the excuse of a minor event to attack Veracruz.

◆ Wilson's efforts to control events in Mexico led to the brink of war.

◆ Policies resulted in enduring distrust of the United States in Mexico.

**Militarism** The tendency to see military might as the most important and best tool for the expansion of a nation's power and prestige.

**Imperialism** The policy and practice of exploiting nations and peoples for the benefit of an imperial power either directly through military occupation and colonial rule or indirectly through economic domination of resources and markets.

WHY DID most Americans oppose U.S. involvement in World War I in 1914?

**myhistorylab**

Review Summary

**22–1**
*The Great War* (1914)

---

**QUICK REVIEW**

**The Outbreak of War**

◆ June 28, 1914: Archduke Franz Ferdinand assassinated.

◆ July 28, 1914: Austria declares war on Serbia with German support.

◆ Chain reaction draws all European powers into the war.

**Allies** In World War I, Britain, France, Russia, and other belligerent nations fighting against the Central Powers but not including the United States.

# THE GREAT WAR

World War I, or the Great War, as it was originally called, took an enormous human toll on an entire generation of Europeans. At the war's start in August 1914, both sides had confidently predicted a quick victory. Instead, the killing dragged on for more than four years, and in the end, transformed the old power relations and political map of Europe.

## THE GUNS OF AUGUST

Only a complex and fragile system of alliances had kept the European powers at peace with each other since 1871. Two great competing camps had evolved by 1907: the Triple Alliance (also known as the Central Powers), which included Germany, Austria-Hungary, and Italy; and the Triple Entente (also known as the **Allies**), which included Great Britain, France, and Russia. The alliance system managed to keep small conflicts from escalating into larger ones for most of the late nineteenth and early twentieth centuries. But its inclusiveness was also its weakness: the alliance system threatened to entangle many nations in any war that did erupt. On June 28, 1914, Archduke Franz Ferdinand, heir to the throne of the unstable Austro-Hungarian Empire, was assassinated in Sarajevo, Bosnia. The archduke's killer was a Serbian nationalist who believed the Austro-Hungarian province of Bosnia ought to be annexed to neighboring Serbia. Germany gave Austria-Hungary a blank check to stamp out the Serbian threat, and the Serbians in turn asked Russia for help.

That summer both sides began mobilizing their armies, and by early August they had exchanged declarations of war. Germany invaded Belgium and prepared to move across the French border. At the beginning, most Europeans supported the war effort, believing there would be quick and glorious victories. But after the German armies were stopped at the River Marne in September, the war settled into a long, bloody stalemate.

## AMERICAN NEUTRALITY

The outbreak of war in Europe shocked Americans. President Wilson issued a formal proclamation of neutrality and urged citizens to be "impartial in thought as well as in action." In practice, powerful cultural, political, and economic factors made the impartiality advocated by Wilson impossible. The U.S. population included many ethnic groups with close emotional ties to the Old World. Out of a total population of 92 million in 1914, about one-third were "hyphenated" Americans, either foreign-born or having one or both parents who were immigrants. Strong support for the Central Powers could be found among the 8 million German-Americans, as well as the 4 million Irish-Americans, who shared their ancestral homeland's historical hatred of English rule. On the other side, many Americans were at least mildly pro-Allies due to cultural and language bonds with Great Britain and the tradition of Franco-American friendship.

Economic ties between the United States and the Allies were perhaps the greatest barrier to true neutrality. Early in the war, Britain imposed a blockade on all shipping to Germany. The United States, as a neutral country, might have insisted on the right of nonbelligerents to trade with both sides, as required by international law. But in practice, although Wilson protested the blockade, he wanted to avoid antagonizing Britain and disrupting trade between the United States and the Allies. Trade with Germany all but ended while trade with the Allies increased dramatically. As America's annual export trade jumped from $2 billion in 1913 to nearly $6 billion in 1916, the nation enjoyed a great economic boom and the United States became neutral in name only.

## PREPAREDNESS AND PEACE

In February 1915, Germany declared the waters around the British Isles to be a war zone, a policy that it would enforce with unrestricted submarine warfare. All enemy shipping, despite the requirements of international law to the contrary, would be subject to surprise submarine attack. Neutral powers were warned that the problems of identification at sea put their ships at risk. The United States issued a sharp protest to this policy, calling it "an indefensible violation of neutral rights," and threatened to hold Germany accountable.

**Patriotic marchers carry** on over-sized American flag past spectators, as part of a "preparedness parade" in downtown Mobile Alabama, before American entry into World War I.

University of South Alabama Archives.

On May 7, 1915, a German U-boat sank the British liner *Lusitania* off the coast of Ireland. Among the 1,198 people who died were 128 American citizens. The *Lusitania* was, in fact, secretly carrying war materials, and passengers had been warned about a possible attack. Wilson nevertheless denounced the sinking as illegal and inhuman, and the American press loudly condemned the act as barbaric.

Tensions heated up again in March 1916 when a German U-boat torpedoed the *Sussex*, an unarmed French passenger ship, injuring four Americans. President Wilson threatened to break off diplomatic relations with Germany unless it abandoned its submarine warfare. He won a temporary diplomatic victory when Germany promised that all vessels would be visited prior to attack. But the crisis also prompted Wilson to begin preparing for war. The National Security League, active in large eastern cities and bankrolled by conservative banking and commercial interests, helped push for a bigger army and navy and, most important, a system of universal military training. In June 1916, Congress passed the National Defense Act, which more than doubled the size of the regular army to 220,000 and integrated the state National Guards under federal control. In August, Congress passed a bill that dramatically increased spending for new battleships, cruisers, and destroyers.

Not all Americans supported these preparations for battle, and opposition to military buildup found expression in scores of American communities. As early as August 29, 1914, 1,500 women clad in black had marched down New York's Fifth Avenue in the Woman's Peace Parade. Out of this gathering evolved the American Union against Militarism, which lobbied against the **preparedness** campaign and against intervention in Mexico. Antiwar feeling was especially strong in the South and Midwest.

A group of thirty to fifty House Democrats, led by majority leader Claude Kitchin of North Carolina, stubbornly opposed Wilson's military buildup. Jane Addams, Lillian D. Wald, and many other prominent progressive reformers spoke out for peace.

Wilson acknowledged the active opposition to involvement in the war by adopting the winning slogan "He Kept Us Out of War" in the 1916 presidential campaign. He made a point of appealing to progressives of all kinds, stressing his support for the eight-hour day and his administration's efforts on behalf of farmers. The war-induced prosperity no doubt helped him to defeat conservative Republican Charles Evans.

**QUICK REVIEW**

**Anglo-American Ties**

◆ 1915: United States gave tacit support to British naval blockade of Germany.

◆ May 1915: German submarine sank the *Lusitania*.

◆ Americans demanded a tough stand against Germany but did not want to be drawn into the war.

**Preparedness**   Military buildup in preparation for possible U.S. participation in World War I.

THE NAVY
NEEDS YOU!
DON'T READ
AMERICAN HISTORY—
MAKE IT!

U·S·NAVY RECRUITING STATION
34 EAST 23rd ST., NEW YORK

**James Montgomery Flagg's** Navy recruiting poster from 1918 combined appeals to patriotism, the opportunity to "make history," and traditional images depicting liberty as a woman.

22–2
Boy Scouts of America, *Boy Scouts Support the War Effort* (1917)

## SAFE FOR DEMOCRACY

By the end of January 1917, Germany's leaders had decided against a negotiated peace settlement, placing their hopes instead in a final decisive offensive against the Allies. On February 1, 1917, with the aim of breaking the British blockade, Germany declared unlimited submarine warfare, with no warnings, against all neutral and belligerent shipping. This strategy went far beyond the earlier, more limited use of the U-boat. The decision was made with full knowledge that it might bring America into the conflict. In effect, German leaders were gambling that they could destroy the ability of the Allies to fight before the United States would be able to effectively mobilize manpower and resources.

Wilson was indignant and disappointed. He still hoped for peace, but Germany had made it impossible for him to preserve his twin goals of U.S. neutrality and freedom of the seas. Reluctantly, Wilson broke off diplomatic relations with Germany and called on Congress to approve the arming of U.S. merchant ships. On March 1, the White House shocked the country when it made public a recently intercepted coded message, sent by German foreign secretary Arthur Zimmermann to the German ambassador in Mexico. The Zimmermann note proposed that an alliance be made between Germany and Mexico if the United States entered the war. Zimmermann suggested that Mexico take up arms against the United States and receive in return the "lost territory in New Mexico, Texas, and Arizona." The specter of a German-Mexican alliance helped turn the tide of public opinion in the Southwest, where opposition to U.S. involvement in the war had been strong.

Revelation of the Zimmermann note stiffened Wilson's resolve. He issued an executive order in mid-March, authorizing the arming of all merchant ships and allowing them to shoot at submarines. In that month, German U-boats sank seven U.S. merchant ships, with a heavy death toll. Anti-German feeling increased, and thousands took part in prowar demonstrations in New York, Boston, Philadelphia, and other cities. Wilson finally called a special session of Congress to ask for a declaration of war.

On April 2, on a rainy night, before a packed and very quiet assembly, Wilson made his case. He reviewed the escalation of submarine warfare, which he called "warfare against mankind," and said that neutrality was no longer feasible or desirable. But the conflict was not merely about U.S. shipping rights, Wilson argued. He employed highly idealistic language to make the case for war, reflecting his deeply held belief that America had a special mission as the world's most enlightened and advanced nation. In effect, Wilson wrapped together American commercial and diplomatic interests in the language of universal principles like freedom of the seas and neutral rights. He expressed the realist ambition of making America a world power in terms of an absolute moral imperative. The Senate adopted the war resolution 82 to 6, the House 373 to 50. Wilson's eloquent speech won over not only the Congress, but also most of the press, and even his bitterest political critics, such as Theodore Roosevelt. Upper-class conservatives supported the language emphasizing national interest, while most progressives responded to the appeal of an idealistic mission. On April 6, President Wilson signed the declaration of war. All that remained was to win over the American public.

# AMERICAN MOBILIZATION

The overall public response to Wilson's war message was enthusiastic. Most newspapers, religious leaders, state legislatures, and prominent public figures endorsed the call to arms. But the Wilson administration was less certain about the feelings of ordinary Americans and their willingness to fight in Europe. It therefore took immediate steps to win over public support for the war effort, to place a legal muzzle on antiwar dissenters, and to establish a universal military draft. War mobilization was, above all, a campaign to unify the country.

**HOW DID** the federal government try to change public opinion about U.S. involvement in World War I?

**myhistorylab**
Review Summary

## SELLING THE WAR

Just a week after signing the war declaration, Wilson created the **Committee on Public Information (CPI)** to organize public opinion. It was dominated by its civilian chairman, the journalist and reformer George Creel. He had become a personal friend of Wilson's while handling publicity for the 1916 Democratic campaign. Creel quickly transformed the CPI from its original function as coordinator of government news into a sophisticated and aggressive agency for promoting the war. To sell the war, Creel adapted techniques from the emerging field of public relations. He enlisted more than 150,000 people to work on a score of CPI committees. They produced more than 100 million pieces of literature—pamphlets, articles, books—that explained the causes and meaning of the war. Across the nation, a volunteer army of 75,000 "Four Minute Men" gave brief patriotic speeches before stage and movie shows. The CPI also created posters, slides, newspaper advertising, and films to promote the war. It called upon movie stars such as Charlie Chaplin, Mary Pickford, and Douglas Fairbanks to help sell war bonds at huge rallies. Famous journalists like the muckraker Ida Tarbell and well-known artists like Charles Dana Gibson were recruited. Many popular entertainers injected patriotic themes into their work as well, as when Broadway composer George M. Cohan wrote the rousing prowar anthem "Over There," sung by the great opera tenor Enrico Caruso (see Seeing History).

The CPI led an aggressively negative campaign against all things German. Posters and advertisements depicted the Germans as Huns, bestial monsters outside the civilized world. German music and literature, indeed the German language itself, were suspect and were banished from the concert halls, schools, and libraries of many communities. Many restaurants now offered "liberty cabbage" and "liberty steaks" instead of sauerkraut and hamburgers. The CPI also urged ethnic Americans to abandon their Old World ties, to become "unhyphenated Americans." The CPI's push for conformity would soon encourage thousands of local, sometimes violent, campaigns of harassment against German-Americans, radicals, and peace activists.

**22–6**
Newton B. Baker, *The Treatment of German-Americans* (1918)

## FADING OPPOSITION TO WAR

By defining the call to war as a great moral crusade, President Wilson was able to win over many Americans who had been reluctant to go to war. In particular, many liberals and progressives were attracted to the possibilities of war as a positive force for social change. Although some progressives—notably Senator Robert M. La Follette of Wisconsin—continued to oppose the war, many more identified with President Wilson's definition of the war as an idealistic crusade to defend democracy, spread liberal principles, and redeem European decadence and militarism.

**Committee on Public Information (CPI)** Government agency during World War I that sought to shape public opinion in support of the war effort through newspapers, pamphlets, speeches, films, and other media.

**African American officers** of the 367th Infantry Regiment, 77th Division, pose with a girl in France, 1918. Nicknamed the "Buffalos" a reference to the black "buffalo soldiers" who had served in the U.S. Army during the late nineteenth century campaigns against Indians, this was one of only two army units that commissioned African American officers.

The Woman's Peace Party, founded in 1915 by feminists opposed to the preparedness campaign, dissolved. Most of its leading lights—Florence Kelley, Lillian D. Wald, and Carrie Chapman Catt—threw themselves into volunteer war work. Catt, leader of the huge National American Woman Suffrage Association (NAWSA), believed that supporting the war might help women win the right to vote. She joined the Women's Committee of the Council of National Defense and encouraged suffragists to mobilize women for war service of various kinds. A few lonely feminist voices, such as Jane Addams, continued steadfastly to oppose the war effort. But war work proved very popular among activist middle-class women. It gave them a leading role in their communities—selling bonds, coordinating food conservation drives, and working for hospitals and the Red Cross.

## "YOU'RE IN THE ARMY NOW"

The central military issue facing the administration was how to raise and deploy U.S. armed forces. When war was declared, there were only about 200,000 men in the army. Traditionally, the United States had relied on volunteer forces organized at the state level. But volunteer rates after April 6 were less than they had been for the Civil War or the Spanish-American War, reflecting the softness of prowar sentiment. The administration thus introduced the **Selective Service Act**, which provided for the registration and classification for military service of all men between ages twenty-one and thirty-five.

The vast, polyglot army posed unprecedented challenges of organization and control. But progressive elements within the administration also saw opportunities for pressing reform measures, especially for the one-fifth of U.S. soldiers born in another country. Army psychologists gave the new Stanford-Binet intelligence test to all recruits and were shocked to find illiteracy rates as high as 25 percent. The low test scores among recent immigrants and rural African Americans undoubtedly reflected the cultural biases embedded in the tests and a lack of proficiency in English for many test takers. After the war, intelligence testing became a standard feature of America's educational system.

## RACISM IN THE MILITARY

African Americans who served found severe limitations in the U.S. military. They were organized into totally segregated units, barred entirely from the marines and the Coast Guard, and largely relegated to working as cooks, laundrymen, stevedores, and the like in the army and navy. Thousands of black soldiers endured humiliating, sometimes violent treatment, particularly from southern white officers. African American servicemen faced hostility from white civilians as well, North and South. The ugliest incident occurred in Houston, Texas, in August 1917. Black infantrymen, incensed over continual insults and harassment by local whites, seized weapons from an armory and killed seventeen civilians. The army executed thirty black soldiers and imprisoned forty-one others for life, denying any of them a chance for appeal.

---

### QUICK REVIEW

**African American Soldiers**

◆ 200,000 African Americans served in France.

◆ One in five saw combat.

◆ African American combat units served with distinction in the French army.

**Selective Service Act**   The law establishing the military draft for World War I.

# Selling War

The world War I posters generally defined the war as a clear struggle between good and evil, in which American democracy and freedom opposed German militarism and despotism. Yet artists used a wide range of visual themes to illustrate these stark contrasts. World War I posters drew upon traditional ideas about gender differences (men as soldiers, women as nurturers), but they also illustrated the new wartime expectations of women working outside the home in support of the war effort. Appeals to American patriotism cutting across lines of ethnic and religious difference were common, as was the demonizing of the German enemy. And just as the wartime economy blurred the boundaries between public and private enterprises, businesses adapted patriotic appeals to their own advertising.

Creel aptly titled the memoir of his war experience *How We Advertised America*. These three images illustrate the range of World War I propaganda posters. ∎

**HOW WOULD** you contrast the different kind of patriotic appeals made by "Pershing's Crusaders," "Americans All," and "And They Thought We Couldn't Fight"? Which of these posters do you think makes the most compelling case for supporting the war? How do the artists portray gender differences as part of a visual strategy for winning the war?

http://www.
firstworldwar.com/
posters/images

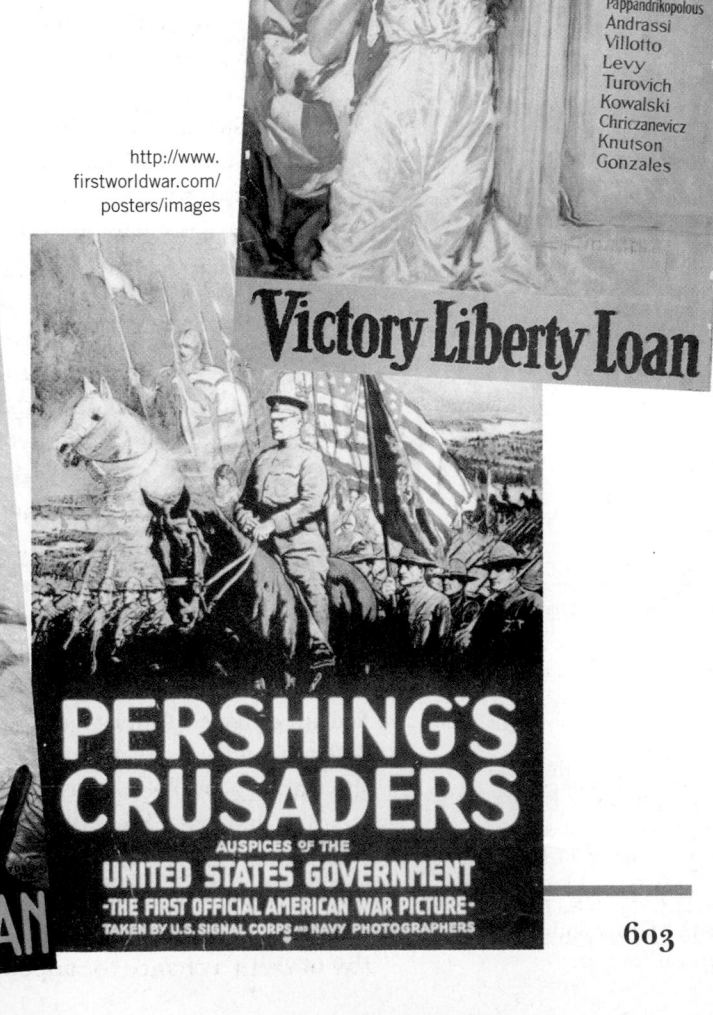

More than 200,000 African Americans eventually served in France, but only about one in five saw combat, as opposed to two out of three white soldiers. Black combat units served with distinction in various divisions of the French army. The French government awarded the Croix de Guerre to the all-black 369th U.S. Infantry regiment, and 171 officers and enlisted men were cited individually for exceptional bravery in action. African American soldiers by and large enjoyed a friendly reception from French civilians as well. The contrast with their treatment at home would remain a sore point with these troops upon their return to the United States.

## AMERICANS IN BATTLE

President Wilson appointed General John J. Pershing, recently returned from pursuing Pancho Villa in Mexico, as commander of the American Expeditionary Force (AEF). Pershing insisted that the AEF maintain its own identity, distinct from that of the French and British armies. He was also reluctant to send American troops into battle before they had received at least six months' training. The AEF's combat role would be brief but intense: not until early 1918 did AEF units reach the front in large numbers; eight months later, the war was over (see Map 22.2).

By the time the guns went silent on November 11, some 2 million men had served in the AEF. Overall 60,000 Americans had died in battle with 206,000 wounded. Another 60,000 died from diseases, mainly influenza. These figures paled in comparison to the millions lost by the European nations. Yet the American contribution to winning the war was substantial, and both the Allies and the Germans attested to the bravery and enthusiasm that American soldiers displayed on the front. Still, the American impact in the Meuse-Argonne campaign was best understood not in terms of individual heroism or tactical brilliance. Rather, it was the prospect of facing seemingly unlimited quantities of American men and supplies that convinced the exhausted German army to surrender.

## THE RUSSIAN REVOLUTION, THE FOURTEEN POINTS, AND ALLIED VICTORY

Since early 1917, the turmoil of the Russian Revolution had changed the climate of both foreign affairs and domestic politics. The repressive and corrupt regime of Czar Nicholas II had been overthrown in March 1917 by a coalition of forces demanding change. The new provisional government vowed to keep Russia in the fight against Germany. But the war had taken a terrible toll on Russian soldiers and civilians and had become very unpopular. The radical **Bolsheviks**, led by V. I. Lenin, gained a large following by promising "peace, land, and bread," and they began plotting to seize power. The Bolsheviks followed the teachings of German revolutionary Karl Marx, emphasizing the inevitability of class struggle and the replacement of capitalism by communism. In November 1917, the Bolsheviks took control of the Russian government.

Although sympathetic to the March revolution overthrowing the czar, President Wilson refused to recognize the authority of the Bolshevik regime. Bolshevism represented a threat to the liberal-capitalist values that Wilson believed to be the foundation of America's moral and material power. Thus, in January 1918 Wilson outlined American war aims, known as the **Fourteen Points**, in a speech before Congress. He wanted to counter a fierce Bolshevik campaign to discredit the war as a purely imperialist venture, their sensational publication of secret treaties that the czar had signed with the Allies, and their revelations about annexationist plans across Europe. In effect, Wilson's response to the Bolsheviks was the opening shot of the Soviet-American Cold War that would dominate so much of American domestic politics and foreign affairs for the remainder of the century.

**22–4**
*American Troops in the Trenches* (1918)

**22–7**
*An Official Report* (1917)

**22–8**
Woodrow Wilson, *The Fourteen Points* (1918)

**Bolsheviks**   Members of the Communist movement in Russia that established the Soviet government after the 1917 Russian Revolution.

**Fourteen Points**   Goals outlined by Woodrow Wilson for war.

**MAP 22.2**
**The Western Front, 1918**    American units saw their first substantial action in late May, helping to stop the German offensive at the Battle of Cantigny. By September, more than 1 million American troops were fighting in a counteroffensive campaign at St. Mihiel, the largest single American engagement of the war.

HOW DID the entrance of the United States help turn the tide of World War I?

As a blueprint for peace, the Fourteen Points contained three main elements. First, Wilson offered a series of specific proposals for setting postwar boundaries in Europe and creating new countries out of the collapsed Austro-Hungarian and Ottoman empires. The key idea here was the right of all peoples to "national self-determination." Second, Wilson listed general principles for governing international conduct, including freedom of the seas, free trade, open covenants instead of secret treaties, reduced armaments, and mediation for competing colonial claims. Third, and most important, Wilson called for a **League of Nations** to help implement these principles and resolve future disputes. The Fourteen Points offered a plan for world order deeply rooted in the liberal progressivism long associated with Wilson. The plan reflected a faith in efficient government and the rule of law as means for solving international problems. It advocated a dynamic democratic capitalism as a middle ground between Old World autocracy and revolutionary socialism.

**League of Nations**  International organization created by the Versailles Treaty after World War I to ensure world stability.

QUICK REVIEW

**Wilson's Fourteen Points**

◆ Wilson articulated U.S. war aims in his Fourteen Points.

◆ The Allies did not explicitly support Wilson's program.

◆ Domestic political failures undermined Wilson's position at the Paris Peace Conference.

**22–5**
Eugene Kennedy, *A "Doughboy" Describes the Fighting Front* (1918)

**WHAT WERE** the domestic effects in the United States of World War I?

myhistorylab

Review Summary

In March 1918, to the dismay of the Allies, the new Bolshevik government followed through on its promise and negotiated a separate peace with Germany, the Treaty of Brest-Litovsk. Russia was now lost as a military ally, and its defection made possible a massive shift of German troops to the western front. In the early spring of 1918, the Germans launched a major offensive that brought them within fifty miles of Paris. In early June, about 70,000 AEF soldiers helped the French stop the Germans in the battles of Château-Thierry and Belleau Wood. In July, Allied forces led by Marshal Ferdinand Foch of France began a counteroffensive designed to defeat Germany once and for all. American reinforcements began flooding the ports of Liverpool in England and Brest and Saint-Nazaire in France. The **"doughboys"** (a nickname for soldiers dating back to Civil War–era recruits who joined the army for the money) streamed in at a rate of over 250,000 a month. By September, General Pershing had more than a million Americans in his army.

In late September 1918, the AEF took over the southern part of a twenty-mile front in the Meuse-Argonne offensive. In seven weeks of fighting, most through terrible mud and rain, U.S. soldiers used more ammunition than the entire Union army had in the four years of the Civil War. The Germans, exhausted and badly outnumbered, began to fall back and look for a cease-fire. On November 11, 1918, the war ended with the signing of an armistice.

# OVER HERE

In one sense, World War I can be understood as the ultimate progressive crusade: an opportunity to expand the powers of the federal government in order to win the war. Nearly all the reform energy of the previous two decades now turned toward that central goal. The federal government would play a larger role than ever in managing and regulating the wartime economy. Planning, efficiency, scientific analysis, and cooperation were key principles for government agencies and large volunteer organizations. Although much of the regulatory spirit was temporary, the war experience started some important and lasting organizational trends in American life.

## ORGANIZING THE ECONOMY

In the summer of 1917, President Wilson established the **War Industries Board (WIB)** as a clearinghouse for industrial mobilization to support the war effort. Led by the successful Wall Street speculator Bernard M. Baruch, the WIB proved a major innovation in expanding the regulatory power of the federal government. Given broad authority over the conversion of industrial plants to wartime needs and the manufacture of war materials, the WIB had to balance price controls against war profits. Only by ensuring a fair rate of return on investment could it encourage stepped-up production.

In August 1917, Congress passed the Food and Fuel Act, authorizing the president to regulate the production and distribution of the food and fuel necessary for the war effort. To lead the Food Administration (FA), Wilson appointed Herbert Hoover. He became one of the best-known figures of the war administration. Hoover imposed price controls on certain agricultural commodities, such as sugar, pork, and wheat. These were purchased by the government and then sold to the public through licensed dealers. The FA also raised the purchase price of grain, so that farmers would increase production. But Hoover stopped short of imposing mandatory food rationing, preferring to rely on persuasion, high prices, and voluntary controls.

**Doughboys** Nickname for soldiers during the Civil War era who joined the army for money.

**War Industries Board (WIB)** The federal agency that reorganized industry for maximum efficiency and productivity during World War I.

Hoover's success, like George Creel's at the CPI, depended on motivating hundreds of thousands of volunteers in thousands of American communities. These efforts resulted in a sharp cutback in the consumption of sugar and wheat as well as a boost in the supply of livestock. The resultant increase in food exports helped sustain the Allied war effort.

The enormous cost of fighting the war, about $33 billion, required unprecedentedly large expenditures for the federal government. The tax structure shifted dramatically as a result. Taxes on incomes and profits replaced excise and customs levies as the major source of revenue. The bulk of war financing came from government borrowing, especially in the form of the popular **Liberty Bonds** sold to the American public. Bond drives became highly organized patriotic campaigns that ultimately raised a total of $23 billion for the war effort. The administration also used the new Federal Reserve Banks to expand the money supply, making borrowing easier. The federal debt jumped from $1 billion in 1915 to $20 billion in 1920.

## THE GOVERNMENT–BUSINESS PARTNERSHIP

Overall, the war meant expansion and high profits for American business. Total capital expenditure in U.S. manufacturing jumped from $600 million in 1915 to $2.5 billion in 1918. Corporate profits as a whole nearly tripled between 1914 and 1919, and many large businesses did much better than that. The total value of farm produce rose from $9.8 billion in 1914 to $21.3 billion by 1918. Expanded farm acreage and increased investment in farm machinery led to a jump of 20 to 30 percent in overall farm production.

The most important and long-lasting economic legacy of the war was the organizational shift toward corporatism in American business. The wartime need for efficient management, manufacturing, and distribution could be met only by a greater reliance on the productive and marketing power of large corporations. Never before had business and the federal government cooperated so closely. Under war administrators like Baruch and Hoover, entire industries (such as radio manufacturing) and economic sectors (such as agriculture and energy) were organized, regulated, and subsidized. War agencies used both public and private power—legal authority and voluntarism—to hammer out and enforce agreements. Here was the genesis of the modern bureaucratic state.

Some Americans worried about the wartime trend toward a greater federal presence in their lives. As *The Saturday Evening Post* noted, "All this government activity will be called to account and reexamined in due time." Although many aspects of the government–business partnership proved temporary, some institutions and practices grew stronger in the postwar years. Among these were the Federal Reserve Board, the income tax system, the Chamber of Commerce, the Farm Bureau, and the growing horde of lobbying groups that pressed Washington for special interest legislation.

## LABOR AND THE WAR

Organized labor's power and prestige, though by no means equal to those of business or government, clearly grew during the war. The expansion of the economy, combined with army mobilization and a decline in immigration from Europe, caused

**FOOD WILL WIN THE WAR**

You came here seeking Freedom
You must now help to preserve it
**WHEAT is needed for the allies**
**Waste nothing**

**A Food Administration** poster blended a call for conservation of wheat with an imaginative patriotic appeal for recent immigrants to support the war effort.

**Liberty Bonds** Interest-bearing certificates sold by the U.S. government to finance the American World War I effort.

a growing wartime labor shortage. As the demand for workers intensified, the federal government was forced to recognize that labor, like any other resource or commodity, would have to be more carefully tended to than in peacetime. For the war's duration, working people generally enjoyed higher wages and a better standard of living. Trade unions, especially those affiliated with the American Federation of Labor (AFL), experienced a sharp rise in membership. In effect, the government took in labor as a junior partner in the mobilization of the economy.

Samuel Gompers, president of the AFL, pledged the organization's support for the war effort, and in April 1918, President Wilson appointed him to the National War Labor Board (NWLB). During 1917, the nation had seen thousands of strikes involving more than a million workers. Wages were usually at issue, reflecting workers' concerns with spiraling inflation and higher prices. The NWLB, cochaired by labor attorney Frank Walsh and former president William H. Taft, acted as a kind of supreme court for labor, arbitrating disputes and working to prevent disruptions in production. The great majority of these interventions resulted in improved wages and reduced hours of work. Most important, the NWLB supported the right of workers to organize unions and furthered the acceptance of the eight-hour day for war workers—central aims of the labor movement.

Yet the war also brought widespread use of federal troops under the War Department's new "public utilities" doctrine, under which any private business remotely connected to war production was defined as a public utility. An influx of federal troops poured into lumber camps, coal districts, mining towns, and rail junctions across the nation, as employers requested help in guarding against threatened strikes or alleged "sabotage" by militant workers. Wartime conditions often meant severe disruptions and discomfort for America's workers as well. Overcrowding, rapid workforce turnover, and high inflation rates were typical in war-boom communities.

In the Southwest, the demand for wartime labor temporarily eased restrictions against the movement of Mexicans into the United States. The Immigration Act of 1917, requiring a literacy test and an $8 head tax, had cut Mexican immigration nearly in half, down to about 25,000 per year. But employers complained of severe shortages of workers.

Responding to these protests, in June 1917, the Department of Labor suspended the immigration law for the duration of the war and negotiated an agreement with the Mexican government permitting some 35,000 Mexican contract laborers to enter the United States. Mexicans let in through this program had to demonstrate they had a job waiting before they could cross the border. They received identification cards and transportation to their place of work from American labor contractors. Pressure from southwestern employers kept the exemptions in force until 1921, well after the end of the war, demonstrating the growing importance of cheap Mexican labor to the region's economy.

If the war boosted the fortunes of the AFL, it also spelled the end for more radical elements of the U.S. labor movement. The Industrial Workers of the World (IWW), unlike the AFL, had concentrated on organizing unskilled workers into all-inclusive industrial unions. The Wobblies denounced capitalism as an unreformable system based on exploitation, and they opposed U.S. entry into the war. In September 1917 the Wilson administration responded to appeals from western business leaders for a crackdown on the Wobblies. Justice Department agents, acting under the broad authority of the recently passed **Espionage Act**, swooped down on IWW offices in more than sixty towns and cities, arresting more than 300 people and confiscating files. The mass trials and convictions that followed broke the back of America's radical labor movement and marked the beginning of a powerful wave of political repression.

QUICK REVIEW

**National War Labor Board**

♦ Federal and state governments created agencies to oversee the wartime economy.
♦ The National War Labor Board guaranteed the rights of unions to organize and bargain collectively.
♦ Labor unions sharply increased their membership under this protection.

**Espionage Act** Law whose vague prohibition against obstructing the nation's war effort was used to crush dissent and criticism during World War I.

**Women workers at** the Midvale Steel and Ordnance Company in Pennsylvania, 1918. Wartime labor shortages created new opportunities for over 1 million women to take high-wage manufacturing jobs like the women shown here. The opportunities proved temporary, however, and with the war's end, nearly all of these women lost their jobs. By 1920, the number of women employed in manufacturing was lower than it had been in 1910.

## WOMEN AT WORK

For many of the 8 million women already in the labor force, the war meant a chance to switch from low-paying jobs, such as domestic service, to higher-paying industrial employment. About a million women workers joined the labor force for the first time. Of the estimated 9.4 million workers directly engaged in war work, some 2.25 million were women. World War I also marked the first time that women were mobilized directly into the armed forces. Over 16,000 women served overseas with the AEF in France, where most worked as nurses, clerical workers, telephone operators, and canteen operators. Another 12,000 women served stateside in the navy and U.S. Marine Corps, and tens of thousands of civilian women were employed in army offices and hospitals. But the war's impact on women was greatest in the broader civilian economy.

In response to the widened range of female employment, the Labor Department created the Women in Industry Service (WIS). Directed by Mary Van Kleeck, the service advised employers on using female labor and formulated general standards for the treatment of women workers. The WIS represented the first attempt by the federal government to take a practical stand on improving working conditions for women.

At war's end, women lost nearly all their defense-related jobs. But the war accelerated female employment in fields already dominated by women. By 1920, more women who worked outside the home did so in white-collar occupations— as telephone operators, secretaries, and clerks, for example—than in manufacturing or domestic service. The new awareness of women's work led Congress to create the Women's Bureau in the Labor Department, which continued the WIS wartime program of education and investigation through the postwar years.

# MAP EXPLORATION

To explore this interactive map, go to **http://www.prenhall.com/faraghertlc/map22.3**

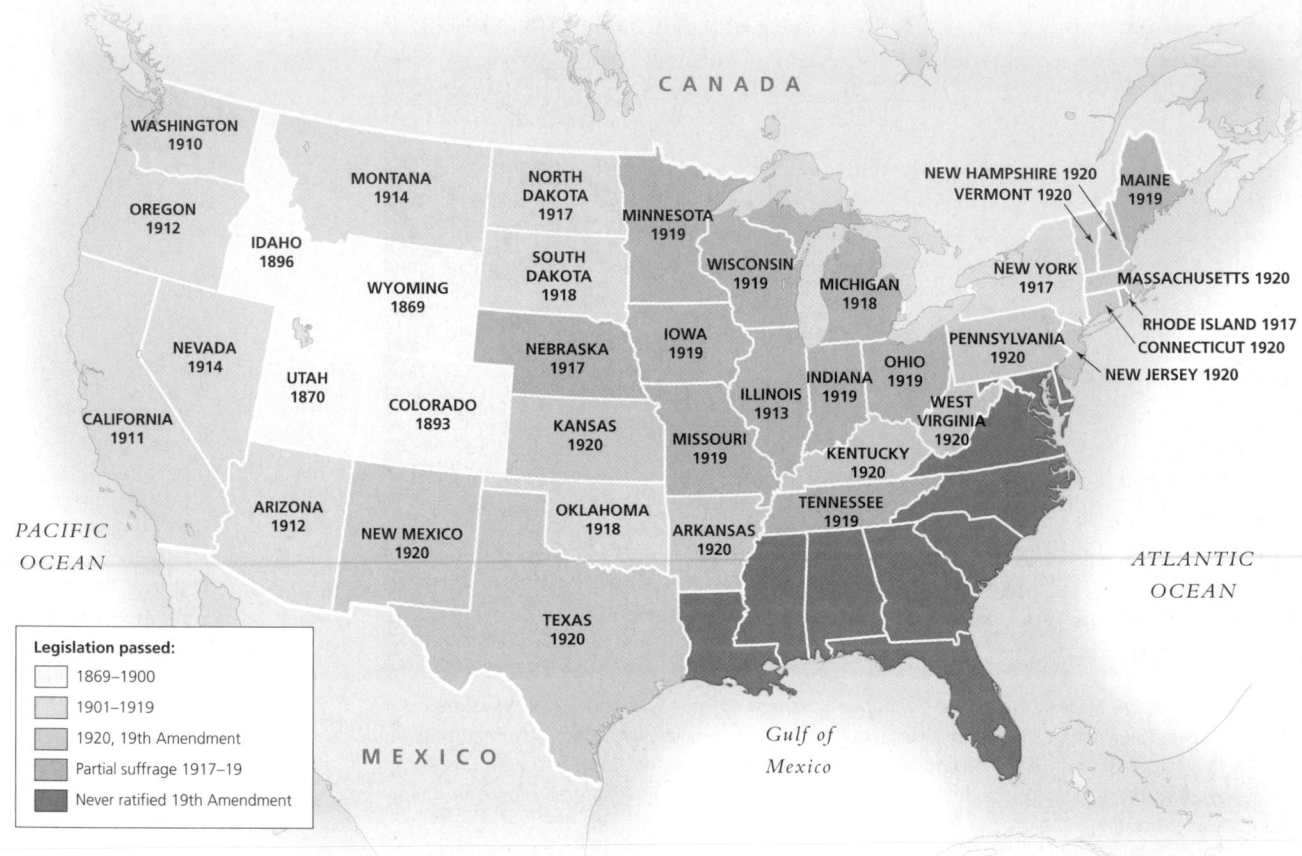

**MAP 22.3**

**Woman Suffrage by State, 1869–1919**   Dates for the enactment of woman suffrage in the individual states. Years before ratification of the Nineteenth Amendment in 1920, a number of western states had legislated full or partial voting rights for women. In 1917, Montana suffragist Jeannette Rankin became the first woman elected to Congress.

Barbara G. Shortridge, *Atlas of American Women* (New York: Macmillan, 1987).

WHAT WERE the reasons behind the regional differences in support of woman suffrage?

## WOMAN SUFFRAGE

Until World War I, the fight for woman suffrage had been waged largely within individual states. Western states and territories had led the way. Various forms of woman suffrage had become law in Wyoming in 1869, followed by Utah (1870), Colorado (1893), and Idaho (1896). Rocky Mountain and Pacific Coast states did not have the sharp ethnocultural divisions between Catholics and Protestants that hindered suffrage efforts in the East. For example, the close identification in the East between the suffrage and prohibition movements led many Catholic immigrants and German Lutherans to oppose the vote for women, because they feared it would lead to prohibition (see Map 22.3).

The U.S. entry into the war provided a unique opportunity for suffrage groups to shift their strategy to a national campaign for a constitutional amendment granting the vote to women. The most important of these groups was the National American Woman Suffrage Association (NAWSA). Before 1917, most American suffragists had opposed the war. Under the leadership of Carrie Chapman Catt, the NAWSA threw its support behind the war effort and doubled its membership to 2 million. Catt gambled that a strong show of patriotism would help clinch the century-old fight to win the vote for women.

At the same time, more militant suffragists, led by the young Quaker activist Alice Paul, injected new energy and more radical tactics into the movement. Dissatisfied with the NAWSA's conservative strategy of quiet lobbying and orderly demonstrations, Paul left the organization in 1916. She joined forces with western women voters to form the National Woman's Party. Borrowing from English suffragists, this party pursued a more aggressive and dramatic strategy of agitation. In one demonstration, they chained themselves to the White House fence, and after their arrest, went on a hunger strike in jail. The militants generated a great deal of publicity and sympathy.

Although some in the NAWSA objected to these tactics, Paul's radical approach helped make the NAWSA position more acceptable to Wilson. In 1917, the president urged Congress to pass a woman suffrage amendment as "vital to the winning of the war." The House did so in January 1918 and a more reluctant Senate approved it in June 1919. Another year of hard work was spent convincing the state legislatures. In August 1920, Tennessee gave the final vote needed to ratify the Nineteenth Amendment to the Constitution, finally making woman suffrage legal nationwide.

## PROHIBITION

Another reform effort closely associated with women's groups triumphed at the same time. The movement to eliminate alcohol from American life had attracted many Americans, especially women, since before the Civil War. Temperance advocates saw drinking as the source of many of the worst problems faced by the working class, including family violence, unemployment, and poverty. By the early twentieth century, the Woman's Christian Temperance Union, with a quarter-million members, had become the single largest women's organization in American history.

The moral fervor that accompanied America's entry into the war provided a crucial boost to the cause. In 1917, a coalition of progressives and rural fundamentalists in Congress pushed through a constitutional amendment providing for a national ban on alcoholic drinks. The Eighteenth Amendment was ratified by the states in January 1919 and became the law of the land one year later. Although Prohibition would create a host of problems in the postwar years, especially as a stimulus for the growth of organized crime, many Americans, particularly native Protestants, considered it a worthy moral reform.

## PUBLIC HEALTH AND THE INFLUENZA PANDEMIC

Wartime mobilization brought deeper government involvement with public health issues, especially in the realm of sex hygiene, child welfare, and disease prevention. The rate of venereal disease among draftees was as high as 6 percent in some states, presenting a potential manpower problem for the army. In April 1917, the War Department mounted a vigorous campaign against venereal disease, which attracted the energies of progressive-era sex reformers—social hygienists and antivice crusaders.

**A nurse takes** a patient's pulse in the influenza ward at Walter Reed Hospital, Washington, DC, November 1, 1918. Intensified by the crowded conditions on the battlefield, in training camps, and on troop ships, the influenza pandemic killed over half a million Americans and some 21 million people worldwide.

The wartime boost to government health work continued into the postwar years. The Children's Bureau, created in 1912 as a part of the Labor Department, undertook a series of reports on special problems growing out of the war: the increase in employment of married women, the finding of day care for children of working mothers, and the growth of both child labor and delinquency. Julia C. Lathrop, chief of the bureau, proposed a plan to institutionalize federal aid to the states for protection of mothers and children. Congress finally passed the Maternity and Infancy Act in 1921, appropriating over $1 million a year to be administered to the states by the Children's Bureau. In the postwar years, clinics for prenatal and obstetrical care grew out of these efforts and greatly reduced the rate of infant and maternal mortality and disease.

The disastrous influenza pandemic of 1918–19 offered the most serious challenge to national public health during the war years. It was part of a global scourge that originated in South China, then spread to the Philippines and moved across the United States, over to Europe, and then back with returning troops. Wartime conditions—large concentrations of people in military camps, on transport ships, and at the front—made its impact especially devastating. With no cure for the lethal combination of the "flu" and respiratory complications (mainly pneumonia), the pandemic killed over 21 million people worldwide. Few Americans paid attention to the disease until it swept through military camps and eastern cities in September 1918 and killed roughly 550,000 Americans in ten months. Most victims were young adults between the ages of twenty and forty. Much of the care for the sick and dying came from Red Cross nurses and volunteers working in local communities across the nation. With a war on, and the nation focused on reports from the battlefront, even a public health crisis of this magnitude went relatively unnoticed.

## REPRESSION AND REACTION

World War I exposed and intensified many of the deepest social tensions in American life. On the local level, vigilantes increasingly took the law into their own hands to punish those suspected of disloyalty. The push for national unity led the federal government to crack down on a wide spectrum of dissenters. The war inflamed racial hatred, and the worst race riots in the nation's history exploded in several cities. At war's end, a newly militant labor movement briefly asserted itself in mass strikes around the nation. Over all these developments loomed the 1917 Bolshevik Revolution in Russia. From 1918 through 1920, the federal government directed a repressive antiradical campaign that had crucial implications for the nation's future.

**WHAT STEPS** did the federal government take to suppress the antiwar movement?

myhistorylab
**Review Summary**

### MUZZLING DISSENT: THE ESPIONAGE AND SEDITION ACTS

The Espionage Act of June 1917 became the government's key tool for the suppression of antiwar sentiment. It set severe penalties (up to twenty years' imprisonment and a $10,000 fine) for anyone found guilty of aiding the enemy, obstructing recruitment, or causing insubordination in the armed forces. The act also empowered the postmaster general to exclude from the mails any newspapers or magazines he thought treasonous. Within a year, the mailing rights of forty-five newspapers had been revoked.

To enforce the Espionage Act, the government had to increase its overall police and surveillance machinery. Civilian intelligence was coordinated by the newly created Bureau of Investigation in the Justice Department. In May 1918, the **Sedition Act**, an amendment to the Espionage Act, outlawed "any disloyal, profane, scurrilous, or abusive language intended to cause contempt, scorn, contumely, or disrepute" to the government, Constitution, or flag.

These acts became a convenient vehicle for striking out at socialists, pacifists, radical labor activists, and others who resisted the patriotic tide. The Supreme Court upheld the constitutionality of the acts in several 1919 decisions.

In many western communities local vigilantes used the superpatriotic mood to settle scores with labor organizers and radicals. In July 1917, for example, 2,000 armed vigilantes swept through the mining town of Bisbee, Arizona, acting on behalf of the Phelps-Dodge mining company and local businessmen. They wanted to break an IWW-led bitter strike that had crippled Bisbee's booming copper industry. The vigilantes seized miners in their homes, on the street, and in restaurants and stores, delivering an ultimatum that any miner who refused to return to work would be deported. Some 1,400 miners refused to end their walkout; they were forced at gunpoint onto a freight train, which took them to Columbus, New Mexico, where they were dumped in the desert.

In thousands of other instances government repression and local vigilantes reinforced each other. The American Protective League, founded with the blessing of the Justice Department, mobilized 250,000 self-appointed "operatives" in more than 600 towns and cities. Members of the league, mostly businessmen, bankers, and former policemen, spied on their neighbors and staged a series of well-publicized "slacker" raids on antiwar protesters and draft evaders. Many communities, inspired by Committee on Public Information campaigns, sought to ban the teaching of the German language in their schools or the performance of German music in concert halls.

## THE GREAT MIGRATION AND RACIAL TENSIONS

Economic opportunity brought on by war prosperity triggered a massive migration of rural black Southerners to northern cities. From 1914 to 1920, between 300,000 and 500,000 African Americans left the rural South for the North. Acute labor shortages led northern factory managers to recruit black migrants to the expanding industrial centers. Black workers eagerly left low-paying jobs as field hands and domestic servants for the chance at relatively high-paying work in meatpacking plants, shipyards, and steel mills (see Table 22.1).

Kinship and community networks were crucial in shaping what came to be called the **Great Migration**. They spread news about job openings, urban residential districts, and boardinghouses in northern cities. Black clubs, churches, and fraternal lodges in southern communities frequently sponsored the migration of their members, as well as return trips to the South. Single African American women often made the trip first, because they could more easily obtain steady work as maids, cooks, and laundresses. Relatively few African American men actually secured high-paying skilled jobs in industry or manufacturing. Most had to settle for such low-paying occupations as construction laborers, teamsters, janitors, or porters.

**22–3**
*Letters from the Great Migration* (1917)

**Sedition Act** Broad law restricting criticism of America's involvement in World War I or its government, flag, military, taxes, or officials.

**Great Migration** The mass movement of African Americans from the rural South to the urban North, spurred especially by new job opportunities during World War I and the 1920s.

**TABLE 22.1**

## The Great Migration: Black Population Growth in Selected Northern Cities, 1910–20

| Northern Cities | 1910 | | 1920 | | Percent Increase |
|---|---|---|---|---|---|
| | No. | Percent | No. | Percent | |
| New York | 91,709 | 1.9% | 152,467 | 2.7% | 66.3% |
| Chicago | 44,103 | 2.0 | 109,458 | 4.1 | 148.2 |
| Philadelphia | 84,459 | 5.5 | 134,229 | 7.4 | 58.9 |
| Detroit | 5,741 | 1.2 | 40,838 | 4.1 | 611.3 |
| St. Louis | 43,960 | 6.4 | 69,854 | 9.0 | 58.9 |
| Cleveland | 8,448 | 1.5 | 34,451 | 4.3 | 307.8 |
| Pittsburgh | 25,623 | 4.8 | 37,725 | 6.4 | 47.2 |
| Cincinnati | 19,739 | 5.4 | 30,079 | 7.5 | 53.2 |

U.S. Department of Commerce.

But rigid residential segregation of African Americans laid the foundation for the sprawling segregated ghettoes characteristic of twentieth-century northern cities. Shut out of white neighborhoods by a combination of custom and law (such as restrictive covenants forbidding homeowners to sell to non-whites), African American migrants found themselves forced to squeeze into less desirable and all-black neighborhoods. In 1920, for example, approximately 85 percent of Chicago's 110,000 black citizens lived within a narrow strip roughly three miles long and a quarter mile wide. The city's South Side ghetto—surrounded on all sides by railroad tracks—had been born.

The persistence of lynching and other racial violence in the South no doubt contributed to the Great Migration. But racial violence was not limited to the South. Two of the worst race riots in American history occurred as a result of tensions brought on by wartime migration. On July 2, 1917, in East St. Louis, Illinois, a ferocious mob of whites attacked African Americans, killing at least 200. Before this riot, some of the city's manufacturers had been steadily recruiting black labor as a way to keep local union demands down. Unions had refused to allow black workers as members, and politicians had cynically exploited white racism in appealing for votes. In Chicago, on July 27, 1919, antiblack rioting broke out on a Lake Michigan beach. For two weeks, white gangs hunted African Americans in the streets and burned hundreds out of their homes. Twenty-three African Americans and fifteen whites died, and more than 500 were injured. Yet in both East St. Louis and Chicago, local authorities held African Americans responsible for the violence.

African Americans had supported the war effort as faithfully as any group. In 1917, despite a segregated army and discrimination in defense industries, most African Americans thought the war might improve their lot. But black disillusionment with the war grew quickly, as did a newly militant spirit. A heightened sense of race consciousness and activism was evident among black veterans and the growing black communities of northern cities. Taking the lead in the fight against bigotry and injustice, the NAACP held a national conference in 1919 on lynching. It pledged to defend persecuted African Americans, publicize the horrors of lynch law, and seek federal legislation against "Judge Lynch."

## LABOR STRIFE

The relative labor peace of 1917 and 1918 dissolved after the armistice. In 1919 alone more than 4 million American workers were involved in some 3,600 strikes. This unprecedented strike wave had several causes. Most of the modest wartime wage gains were wiped out by spiraling inflation and high prices for food, fuel, and housing. With the end of government controls on industry, many employers withdrew their recognition of unions. Difficult working conditions, such as the twelve-hour day in steel mills, were still routine in some industries.

Several of the postwar strikes received widespread national attention. They seemed to be more than simple economic conflicts, and they provoked deep fears about the larger social order. In February 1919, a strike in the shipyards of Seattle, Washington, over wages escalated into a general citywide strike involving 60,000 workers. The local press and Mayor Ole Hanson denounced the strikers as revolutionaries. Hanson effectively ended the strike by requesting federal troops to occupy the city. In September, Boston policemen went out on strike when the police commissioner rejected a citizens' commission study that recommended a pay raise. Massachusetts governor Calvin Coolidge called in the National Guard to restore order and won a national reputation by crushing the strike. The entire police force was fired.

The biggest strike took place in the steel industry and involved some 350,000 steelworkers. Centered in several midwestern cities, this epic struggle lasted from September 1919 to January 1920. The AFL had hoped to build on wartime gains in an industry that had successfully resisted unionization before the war. The steel companies used black strikebreakers and armed guards to keep the mills running. Elbert Gary, president of U.S. Steel, directed a sophisticated propaganda campaign that branded the strikers as revolutionaries. Public opinion turned against the strike and condoned the use of state and federal troops to break it. The failed steel strike proved to be the era's most bitter and devastating defeat for organized labor.

# AN UNEASY PEACE

The armistice of November 1918 ended the fighting on the battlefield, but the war continued at the peace conference. In the old royal palace of Versailles near Paris, delegates from twenty-seven countries spent five months hammering out a settlement. Yet neither Germany nor Russia was represented. The proceedings were dominated by leaders of the "Big Four": David Lloyd George (Great Britain), Georges Clemenceau (France), Vittorio Orlando (Italy), and Woodrow Wilson (United States).

**This southern African** American family is shown arriving in Chicago around 1910. Black migrants to northern cities often faced overcrowding, inferior housing, and a high death rate from disease. But the chance to earn daily wages of $6 to $8 (the equivalent of a week's wages in much of the South), as well as the desire to escape persistent racial violence, kept the migrants coming.

## QUICK REVIEW

**Strikes**

◆ 1919: American workers involved in 3,600 strikes.

◆ Large strikes received national attention.

◆ Breaking of 1919–1920 steel strike was a bitter defeat for organized labor.

**HOW CAN** we explain Woodrow Wilson's failure to win the peace?

**Review Summary**

## PEACEMAKING AND THE SPECTER OF BOLSHEVISM

Even before November 1918, the Allies struggled with how to respond to the revolutionary developments in Russia. British and French leaders wanted to help counterrevolutionary forces overthrow the new Bolshevik regime. President Wilson refused to recognize the authority of the Bolshevik regime. Bolshevism represented a threat to the liberal-capitalist values that Wilson believed to be the foundation of America's moral and material power, and that provided the basis for the Fourteen Points. At the same time, however, Wilson at first resisted British and French pressure to intervene in Russia, citing his commitment to national self-determination and noninterference in other countries' internal affairs.

By August 1918, as the Russian political and military situation became increasingly chaotic, Wilson agreed to British and French plans for sending troops to Siberia and northern Russia. Meanwhile, Japan poured troops into Siberia and northern Manchuria in a bid to control the commercially important Chinese Eastern and Trans-Siberian railways. After the Wilson administration negotiated an agreement that placed these strategic railways under international control, the restoration and protection of the railways became the primary concern of American military forces in Russia.

**Woodrow Wilson,** Georges Clemenceau, and David Lloyd George are among the central figures depicted in John Christen Johansen's *Signing of the Treaty of Versailles.* But all the gathered statesmen appear dwarfed by their surroundings.

John Christen Johansen (1876–1964), "Signing of the Treaty of Versailles," 1919, oil on canvas, 249 cm × 224.5 cm (98-1/16 × 88-3/8"). Gift of an anonymous donor through Mrs. Elizabeth Rogerson, 1926. National Portrait Gallery, Smithsonian Institution, Washington, DC/Art Resource, New York.

The Allied armed intervention widened the gulf between Russia and the West. In March 1919, Russian Communists established the Third International, or Comintern. Their call for a worldwide revolution deepened Allied mistrust, and the Paris Peace Conference essentially ignored the new political reality posed by the Russian Revolution.

## WILSON IN PARIS

Wilson arrived in Paris with the United States delegation in January 1919. He believed the Great War revealed the bankruptcy of diplomacy based on alliances and the "balance of power." He believed that peacemaking, based on the framework put forward in his Fourteen Points, meant an opportunity for America to lead the rest of the world toward a new vision of international relations. The most controversial element, both at home and abroad, would prove to be the League of Nations.

Despite Wilson's devotion to "open covenants," much of the negotiating in Paris was in fact done in secret among the Big Four. The ideal of **self-determination** found limited expression. The independent states of Austria, Hungary, Poland, Yugoslavia, and Czechoslovakia were carved out of the homelands of the defeated **Central Powers.** But the Allies resisted Wilson's call for independence for the colonies of the defeated nations. A compromise mandate system of protectorates gave the French and British control of parts of the old German and Turkish empires in Africa and western Asia. Japan won control of former German colonies in China. Among those trying, but failing, to influence the treaty negotiations were the sixty-odd delegates to the first Pan African Congress, held in Paris at the same time as the peace talks. The group included Americans W. E. B. Du Bois and William Monroe Trotter as well as representatives from Africa and the West Indies. All were disappointed with the failure of the peace conference to grant self-determination to thousands of Africans living in former German colonies.

**Self-determination** The right of a people or a nation to decide on its own political allegiance or form of government without external influence.

**Central Powers** Germany and its World War I allies in Austria, Italy, Turkey, and Bulgaria.

Another disappointment for Wilson came with the issue of war guilt. He had strongly opposed the extraction of harsh economic reparations from the Central Powers. But the French and British, with their awful war losses fresh in mind, insisted on making Germany pay. The final treaty contained a clause attributing the war to "the aggression of Germany," and a commission later set German war reparations at $33 billion. Bitter resentment in Germany over the punitive treaty helped sow the seeds for the Nazi rise to power in the 1930s.

The final treaty was signed on June 28, 1919, in the Hall of Mirrors at the Versailles palace. The Germans had no choice but to accept its harsh terms. President Wilson had been disappointed by the secret deals and the endless compromising of his ideals. He had nonetheless won a commitment to the League of Nations, the centerpiece of his plan, and he was confident that the American people would accept the treaty.

## THE TREATY FIGHT

Preoccupied with peace conference politics in Paris, Wilson had neglected politics at home. His troubles had actually started earlier. Republicans had captured both the House and the Senate in the 1918 elections. Wilson had then made a tactical error by including no prominent Republicans in the U.S. peace delegation. He therefore faced a variety of tough opponents to the treaty he brought home.

Wilson's most extreme enemies in the Senate were a group of about sixteen **"irreconcilables"** who were opposed to a treaty in any form. The less dogmatic, but more influential, opponents were led by Republican Henry Cabot Lodge of Massachusetts, powerful majority leader of the Senate. They had strong reservations about the League of Nations, especially the provisions for collective security in the event of a member nation's being attacked. Lodge argued that this provision impinged on congressional authority to declare war and placed unacceptable restraints on the nation's ability to pursue an independent foreign policy. Lodge proposed a series of amendments that would have weakened the League. But Wilson refused to compromise, motivated in part by the long-standing hatred he and Lodge felt toward each other.

In September, Wilson set out on a speaking tour across the country to drum up support for the League and the treaty. The crowds were large and responsive, but they did not change any votes in the Senate. The strain took its toll. On September 25, after speaking in Pueblo, Colorado, the sixty-three-year-old Wilson collapsed from exhaustion. A week later, back in Washington, the president suffered a stroke that left him partially paralyzed. With Wilson badly incapacitated, his wife and his doctor exercised significant decision-making authority, and they reinforced his refusal to agree to any amendments on the Treaty and the League Covenant. In November, Lodge brought the treaty out of committee for a vote, having appended to it fourteen reservations—that is, recommended changes. A bedridden Wilson stubbornly refused to compromise and instructed Democrats to vote against the Lodge version of the treaty. On November 19, Democrats joined with the "irreconcilables" to defeat the amended treaty, 39 to 55.

Wilson refused to budge. In January, he urged Democrats to either stand by the original treaty or vote it down. The 1920 election, he warned, would be "a great and solemn referendum" on the whole issue. In the final vote, on March 19, 1920, twenty-one Democrats broke with the president and voted for the Lodge version, giving it a majority of 49 to 35. But this was seven votes short of the two-thirds needed for ratification. As a result, the United States never signed

---

**QUICK REVIEW**

**Defeat of the Treaty**

◆ Most Democrats favored the treaty.

◆ Republicans led by Henry Cabot Lodge wanted amendments.

◆ Wilson's refusal to compromise doomed the treaty.

**Irreconcilables** Group of U.S. senators adamantly opposed to ratification of the Treaty of Versailles after World War I.

the **Versailles Treaty**, nor did it join the League of Nations. The absence of the United States weakened the League and made it more difficult for the organization to realize Wilson's dream of a peaceful community of nations.

## THE RED SCARE

The revolutionary changes taking place in Russia became an important backdrop for domestic politics. In the United States, it became common to blame socialism, the IWW, trade unionism in general, and even racial disturbances on foreign radicals and alien ideologies. The accusation of Bolshevism became a powerful weapon for turning public opinion against strikers and political dissenters of all kinds. In the spring of 1919, a few extremists mailed bombs to prominent business and political leaders. That June, simultaneous bombings in eight cities killed two people and damaged the residence of Attorney General A. Mitchell Palmer. With public alarm growing, state and federal officials began a coordinated campaign to root out subversives and their alleged Russian connections.

Palmer used the broad authority of the 1918 Alien Act, which enabled the government to deport any immigrant found to be a member of a revolutionary organization prior to or after coming to the United States. In a series of raids in late 1919, Justice Department agents in eleven cities arrested and roughed up several hundred members of the IWW and the Union of Russian Workers. Little evidence of revolutionary intent was found, but 249 people were deported, including prominent anarchists Emma Goldman and Alexander Berkman. In early 1920, some 6,000 people in thirty-three cities, including many U.S. citizens and non-Communists, were arrested and herded into prisons and bullpens. Again, no evidence of a grand plot was found, but another 600 aliens were deported.

Palmer's popularity had waned by the spring of 1920, when it became clear that his predictions of revolutionary uprisings were wildly exaggerated. A report prepared by a group of distinguished lawyers questioned the legality of the attorney general's tactics. As part of the resistance to Palmer's policies, a group of progressive activists formed the American Civil Liberties Union (ACLU) in 1920. Its founders included Clarence Darrow, Felix Frankfurter, Jane Addams, Helen Keller, and John Dewey. For progressives dispirited by the wartime political repression, the ACLU offered a new political front stressing the militant defense of civil liberties just when they seemed most fragile.

The **Red Scare** left an ugly legacy: wholesale violations of constitutional rights, deportations of hundreds of innocent people, fuel for the fires of nativism and intolerance. The Red Scare took its toll on the women's movement as well. Before the war, many suffragists and feminists had maintained ties and shared platforms with socialist and labor groups. The suffrage movement in particular had brought together women from very different class backgrounds and political perspectives. But the calls for "100 percent Americanism" during and after the war destroyed the fragile alliances that had made a group such as the National American Woman Suffrage Association so powerful. Hostility to radicalism marked the political climate of the 1920s, and this atmosphere narrowed the political spectrum for women activists.

## THE ELECTION OF 1920

Woodrow Wilson had wanted the 1920 election to be a "solemn referendum" on the League of Nations and his conduct of the war. Ill and exhausted, Wilson did not run for reelection. A badly divided Democratic Party compromised on Governor James M. Cox of Ohio as its candidate.

**Versailles Treaty**   The treaty ending World War I and creating the League of Nations.

**Red Scare**   Post–World War I public hysteria over Bolshevik influence in the United States directed against labor activism, radical dissenters, and some ethnic groups.

## CHRONOLOGY

| | |
|---|---|
| **1903** | United States obtains Panama Canal rights |
| **1905** | President Theodore Roosevelt mediates peace treaty between Japan and Russia at Portsmouth Conference |
| **1908** | Root-Takahira Agreement with Japan affirms status quo in Asia and Open Door policy in China |
| **1911** | Mexican Revolution begins |
| **1914** | U.S. forces invade Mexico |
| | Panama Canal opens |
| | World War I begins in Europe |
| | President Woodrow Wilson issues proclamation of neutrality |
| **1915** | Germany declares war zone around Great Britain |
| | German U-boat sinks *Lusitania* |
| **1916** | Pancho Villa raids New Mexico and is pursued by General Pershing |
| | Wilson is reelected |
| | National Defense Act establishes preparedness program |
| **1917** | February: Germany resumes unrestricted submarine warfare |
| | March: Zimmermann note, suggesting a German-Mexican alliance, shocks Americans |
| | April: United States declares war on the Central Powers |

| | |
|---|---|
| | May: Selective Service Act is passed |
| | June: Espionage Act is passed |
| | November: Bolshevik Revolution begins in Russia |
| **1918** | January: Wilson unveils Fourteen Points |
| | May: Sedition Act is passed |
| | June: U.S. troops begin to see action in France |
| | September: Influenza outbreaks among AEF troops in France |
| | November: Armistice ends war |
| **1919** | January: Eighteenth Amendment (Prohibition) is ratified |
| | Wilson serves as chief U.S. negotiator at Paris Peace Conference |
| | June: Versailles Treaty is signed in Paris |
| | July: Race riot breaks out in Chicago |
| | Steel strike begins in several midwestern cities |
| | November: Palmer raids begin |
| **1920** | March: Senate finally votes down Versailles Treaty and League of Nations |
| | August: Nineteenth Amendment (woman suffrage) is ratified |
| | November: Warren G. Harding is elected president |

The Republicans nominated Senator Warren G. Harding of Ohio. A political hack, the handsome and genial Harding had virtually no qualifications to be president, except that he looked like one. Harding's campaign was vague and ambiguous about the Versailles Treaty and almost everything else. "America's present need," he said, "is not heroics but healing; not nostrums but normalcy; not revolution but restoration."

The notion of a "return to normalcy" proved very attractive to voters exhausted by the war, inflation, big government, and social dislocation. Harding won the greatest landslide in history to that date, carrying every state outside the South and taking the popular vote by 16 million to 9 million. Republicans retained their majorities in the House and Senate as well. The overall vote repudiated Wilson and the progressive movement. Americans seemed eager to pull back from moralism in public and international controversies. Yet many of the economic, social, and cultural changes wrought by the war would accelerate during the 1920s. In truth, there could never be a "return to normalcy."

**22–9**
Warren G. Harding, *Campaign Speech at Boston* (1920)

# CONCLUSION

The global impact of the Great War, including the United States' place in relation to the rest of the world, was profound. The war created economic, social, and political dislocations that helped reshape American life long after Armistice Day. The ability to raise and deploy the massive American Expeditionary Force overseas so quickly had proved decisive to ending the fighting. The government's direct intervention in every aspect of the wartime economy was unprecedented, and wartime production needs contributed to a "second industrial revolution" that transformed the economy in the decade following the war. Republican administrations invoked the wartime partnership between government and industry to justify an aggressive peacetime policy fostering cooperation between the state and business. Although the United States would not join the League of Nations, the war turned the United States into a major global force: the world's new leading creditor nation would now also take its place as a powerful commercial and industrial engine in the global economy.

Patriotic fervor and the exaggerated threat of Bolshevism were used to repress radicalism, organized labor, feminism, and the entire legacy of progressive reform. The wartime measure of national prohibition evolved into perhaps the most contentious social issue of peacetime. Sophisticated use of sales techniques, psychology, and propaganda during the war helped define the newly powerful advertising and public relations industries of the 1920s. The growing visibility of immigrants and African Americans, especially in the nation's cities, provoked a xenophobic and racist backlash in the politics of the 1920s. More than anything else, the desire for "normalcy" reflected the deep anxieties evoked by America's wartime experience.

# REVIEW QUESTIONS

1. What central issues drew the United States deeper into international politics in the early years of the century? How did American presidents justify a more expansive role? What diplomatic and military policies did they exploit for these ends?

2. Compare the arguments for and against American participation in the Great War. Which Americans were most likely to support entry? Which were more likely to oppose it?

3. How did mobilizing for war change the economy and its relationship to government? Which of these changes, if any, spilled over to the postwar years?

4. How did the war affect political life in the United States? What techniques were used to stifle dissent? What was the war's political legacy?

5. Analyze the impact of the war on American workers. How did the conflict affect the lives of African Americans and women?

6. What principles guided Woodrow Wilson's Fourteen Points? How would you explain the United States' failure to ratify the Treaty of Versailles?

**myhistorylab**

Flashcard Review

# KEY TERMS

Allies (p. 598)

Bolsheviks (p. 604)

Central Powers (p. 616)

Committee on Public Information (CPI) (p. 601)

Doughboys (p. 606)

Espionage Act (p. 608)

Fourteen Points (p. 604)

Great Migration (p. 613)

Imperialism (p. 597)

# RECOMMENDED READING

Alan Dawley, *Changing the World: American Progressives in War and Revolution* (2003). Thoughtful analysis that traces the interplay between progressive politics and America's involvement in the Great War.

James H. Hallas, *Doughboy War: The American Expeditionary Force in World War I* (2000). Excellent and wide-ranging account of the AEF told entirely from first-person accounts—letters, diaries, and interviews—of the doughboys themselves.

Robert Hannigan, *The New World Power: American Foreign Policy, 1898–1917* (2002). An ambitious analysis of how the American policy-making elite sought to impose political and economic order around the globe.

Paul L. Murphy, *World War I and the Origin of Civil Liberties* (1979). A good overview of the various civil liberties issues raised by the war and government efforts to suppress dissent.

Ronald Schaffer, *America in the Great War: The Rise of the War Welfare State* (1991). Excellent material on how the war transformed the relationship between business and government and spurred improved conditions for industrial workers.

Richard Slotkin, *Lost Battalions: The Great War and the Crisis of Nationality* (2006). A beautifully written and imaginative account of two AEF units: the African American 369th Infantry (the "Harlem Hellfighters") and the 77th Division (the "Melting Pot"). Slotkin explores the tensions inherent in the wartime mobilization that included large groups of citizens—in these cases blacks and immigrants—who were deemed inferior yet also promised the benefits of full citizenship rights.

Joe William Trotter Jr., ed., *The Great Migration in Historical Perspective* (1991). An excellent collection of essays examining the Great Migration, with special attention to issues of class and gender within the African American community.

Susan Zeiger, *In Uncle Sam's Service: Women Workers with the American Expeditionary Force, 1917–1919* (1999). The first in-depth study of American women's experiences with the armed forces overseas.

Robert H. Zieger, *America's Great War: World War I and the American Experience* (2000). The best recent one-volume synthesis on how the war transformed the United States and its role in the world.

For study resources for this chapter, go to **www.myhistorylab.com** and choose *Out of Many, Teaching and Learning Classroom Edition.* You will find a wealth of study and review material for this chapter, including pretests and posttests, customized study plan, key-term review flash cards, interactive map and document activities, and documents for analysis.

*Happy times were here again.*
—*Upton Sinclair, from* The Flivver King

**Toward a Modern America:** The 1920s. "More than a car. FORD: A National Institution" poster, 1923.

# 23

# THE TWENTIES
## 1920–1929

**HOW DID** the widespread use of automobiles change American society in the 1920s?

**HOW AND** why did the Republican Party dominate 1920s' politics?

**HOW DID** the new mass media reshape American culture?

**WHAT POLITICAL** and cultural movements opposed modern cultural trends?

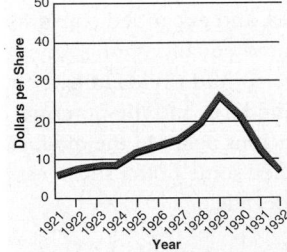

**WHICH AMERICANS** were less likely to share in postwar prosperity and why?

# AMERICAN COMMUNITIES
## The Movie Audience and Hollywood:
## Mass Culture Creates a New National Community

INSIDE MIDTOWN MANHATTAN'S MAGNIFICENT NEW ROXY THEATER, A sellout crowd eagerly settled in for opening night. Outside, thousands of fans cheered wildly at the arrival of movie stars such as Charlie Chaplin, Gloria Swanson, and Harold Lloyd. A squadron of smartly uniformed ushers guided patrons under a five-story-tall rotunda to some 6,200 velvet-covered seats. The audience marveled at the huge gold and rose-colored murals, classical statuary, plush carpeting, and Gothic-style windows. It was easy to believe newspaper reports that the theater had cost $10 million to build. Suddenly, light flooded the orchestra pit and 110 musicians began playing "The Star Spangled Banner." A troupe of 100 performers took the stage, dancing ballet numbers and singing old southern melodies such as "My Old Kentucky Home" and "Swanee River." Congratulatory telegrams from President Calvin Coolidge and other dignitaries flashed on the screen. Finally, the evening's feature presentation, *The Love of Sunya*, starring Gloria Swanson, began. Samuel L. "Roxy" Rothapfel, the theater's designer, had realized his grand dream—to build "the cathedral of the motion picture."

When Roxy's opened in March 1927, nearly 60 million Americans "worshiped" each week at movie theaters across the nation. The "movie palaces" of the 1920s were designed to transport patrons to exotic places and different times. As film pioneer Marcus Loew put it, "We sell tickets to theaters, not movies." Every large community boasted at least one opulent movie theater. Houston's Majestic was built to represent an ancient Italian garden; it had a ceiling made to look like an open sky, complete with stars and cloud formations. The Tivoli in Chicago featured French Renaissance decor; Grauman's Egyptian in Los Angeles recreated the look of a pharaoh's tomb; and Albuquerque's Kimo drew inspiration from Navajo art and religion.

Hollywood's emergence might be thought of as part of a broader "second industrial revolution" that modernized industrial production and greatly expanded the availability of consumer goods in the postwar years. The studios concentrated on producing big-budget feature films designed for mass audiences, with the "star system" providing the industry's version of product branding. Movie stars like Charlie Chaplin, Mary Pickford, Rudolph Valentino, Gloria Swanson, and Douglas Fairbanks became popular idols as much for their highly publicized private lives as for their roles on screen. Many accumulated great wealth, becoming the nation's experts on how to live well. Americans embraced the culture of celebrity, voraciously consuming fan magazines, gossip columns, and news of the stars. Indeed during the 1920s there was a tight connection between celebrity and the rapid growth of new networks of mass culture—movies, radio, advertising, musical recordings, and big-time sports.

Ordinary Americans found it easy to identify with movie stars despite their wealth and status. Unlike industrialists or politicians, stars had no social authority over large groups of employees or voters. They, too, had to answer to a boss, and most had risen from humble beginnings. But above all, Hollywood, like the movies it churned out, represented for millions of Americans new possibilities: freedom, material success, upward mobility, and the chance to remake one's very identity.

By the end of the decade, the Hollywood "dream factory" had helped forge a national community whose collective aspirations and desires were increasingly defined by those possibilities, even if relatively few Americans realized them during the 1920s.

Of course, Hollywood films offered nothing near an accurate reflection of the complexities of American society. As American culture became increasingly defined by an urban-based mass media that claimed the entire nation for its audience, resentment toward and resistance against the new popular culture was widespread. Movies celebrated prosperity, new technologies, and expanded consumerism, but these were by no means shared equally among Americans in the decade following World War I. And while Hollywood films touted the promise of the modern, and the potential for people to remake themselves, tenacious belief in the old-fashioned verities of prewar America fueled some of the strongest political and cultural currents of the decade.

Hollywood

# POSTWAR PROSPERITY AND ITS PRICE

Republican Warren G. Harding won the presidency in 1920, largely thanks to his nostalgic call for a "return to normalcy." But in the decade following the end of World War I, the American economy underwent profound structural changes that guaranteed life would never be "normal" again.

**HOW DID** the widespread use of automobiles change American society in the 1920s?

**myhistorylab**
Review Summary

## THE SECOND INDUSTRIAL REVOLUTION

The prosperity of the 1920s rested on what historians have called the "second industrial revolution" in American manufacturing, in which technological innovations made it possible to increase industrial output without expanding the labor force. Electricity replaced steam as the main power source for industry in these years, making possible the replacement of older machinery with more efficient and flexible electric machinery.

Much of the newer, automatic machinery could be operated by unskilled and semiskilled workers, and it boosted the overall efficiency of American industry. Thus, in 1929, the average worker in manufacturing produced roughly three-quarters more per hour than he or she had in 1919.

During the late nineteenth century, heavy industries such as machine tools, railroads, iron, and steel had pioneered mass-production techniques. These industries manufactured what economists call producer-durable goods. In the 1920s, modern mass-production techniques were increasingly applied to newer consumer-durable goods—automobiles, radios, washing machines, and telephones—permitting firms to make large profits while keeping prices affordable. With more efficient management, greater mechanization, intensive product research, and ingenious sales and advertising methods, the consumer-based industries helped to nearly double industrial production in the 1920s.

The watchword for all this was efficiency, a virtue that progressives had emphasized in their prewar efforts to improve urban life and the mechanics of government itself. But efficiency was now an obsession for American businessmen, who thought it defined modernity as well. American success in mechanization and the mass production of consumer goods evoked admiration and envy in much of the industrialized (and industrializing) world.

## THE MODERN CORPORATION

In the late nineteenth century, individual entrepreneurs such as John D. Rockefeller in oil and Andrew Carnegie in steel had provided a model for success. They maintained both corporate control (ownership) and business leadership (management) in their enterprises. In the 1920s, a managerial revolution increasingly divorced ownership of corporate stock from the everyday control of businesses (see Figure 23.1). A growing class of salaried executives, plant managers, and engineers formed a new elite, who made corporate policy without themselves having a controlling interest in the companies they worked for. They stressed scientific management and the latest theories of behavioral psychology in their effort to make their workplaces

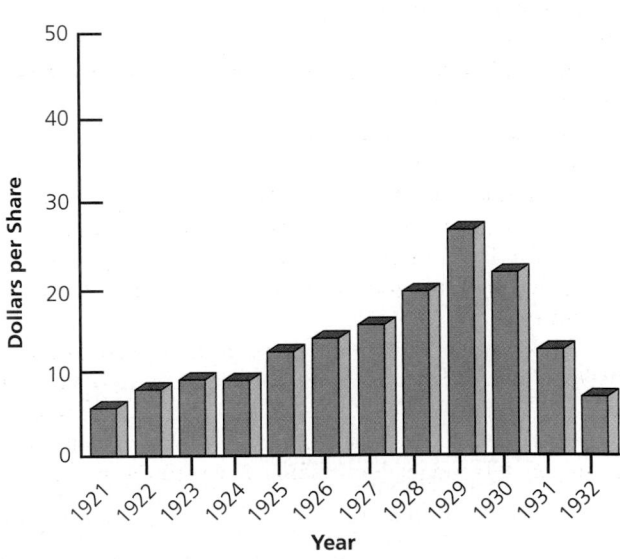

**Figure 23.1 Stock Market Prices, 1921–32**
Common stock prices rose steeply during the 1920s. Although only about 4 million Americans owned stocks during the period, "stock watching" became something of a national sport.

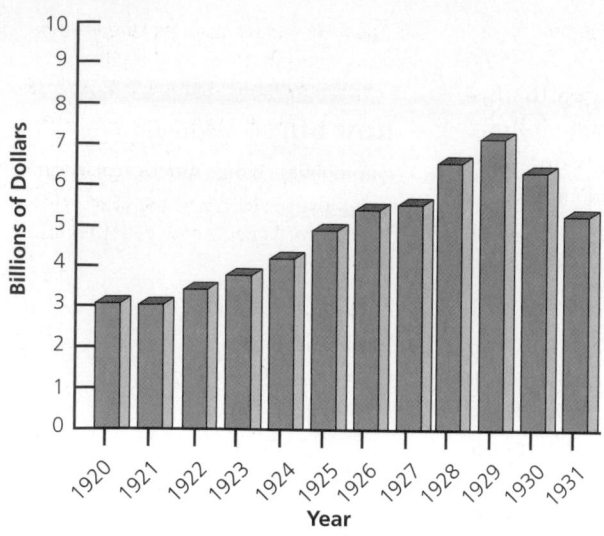

**Figure 23.2 Consumer Debt, 1920–31**
The expansion of consumer borrowing was a key component of the era's prosperity. These figures do not include mortgages or money borrowed to purchase stocks. They reveal the great increase in "installment buying" for such consumer durable goods as automobiles and household appliances.

more productive, stable, and profitable (see Figure 23.2). Modern managers also brought a more sophisticated understanding of global markets to their management. Exploiting overseas markets, especially in Europe, became a key element in corporate strategy, especially for car manufacturers, chemical companies, and businesses engaged in the new world of modern mass media. During the 1920s, the most successful corporations were those that led in three key areas: the integration of production and distribution, product diversification, and the expansion of industrial research.

By 1929, the 200 largest corporations owned nearly half the nation's corporate wealth—that is, physical plant, stock, and property. Half the total industrial income—revenue from sales of goods—was concentrated in 100 corporations. Oligopoly—the control of a market by a few large producers—became the norm. Four companies packed almost three-quarters of all American meat. Another four rolled nine out of every ten cigarettes. National chain grocery stores, clothing shops, and pharmacies began squeezing out local neighborhood businesses. These changes meant that Americans were increasingly members of national consumer communities, buying the same brands all over the country, as opposed to locally produced goods.

## WELFARE CAPITALISM

The wartime gains made by organized labor, and the active sympathy shown to trade unions by government agencies such as the National War Labor Board (NWLB), troubled most corporate leaders. Shortly after the war's end, largely as a result of pressure from business leaders, the Wilson administration dismantled the NWLB and other mechanisms aimed at mediation of labor disputes. To challenge the power and appeal of trade unions and collective bargaining, large employers aggressively promoted a variety of new programs designed to improve worker well-being and morale while also fending off unionization. These schemes, collectively known as **welfare capitalism**, became a key part of corporate strategy in the 1920s.

Large corporations mounted an effective antiunion campaign in the early 1920s called "the American plan" as an alternative to trade unionism and the class antagonism associated with European labor relations. Backed by powerful business lobbies such as the National Association of Manufacturers and the Chamber of Commerce, campaign leaders called for the **open shop**, in which no employee would be compelled to join a union. In effect, an "open shop" meant that no known union member would be hired. If a union existed, nonmembers would still get whatever wages and rights the union had won—a policy that put organizers at a disadvantage in signing up new members.

The open shop undercut the gains won in a union shop, where new employees had to join an existing union, or a closed shop, where employers agreed to hire only union members. As alternatives, large employers such as U.S. Steel and International Harvester began setting up company unions. Their intent was to substitute largely symbolic employee representation in management conferences for the more confrontational process of collective bargaining. These management strategies contributed to a sharp decline in the ranks of organized labor. Total union membership dropped from about 5 million in 1920 to 3.5 million in 1926. A large proportion of the remaining union members were concentrated in the skilled crafts of the building and printing trades.

**Welfare capitalism** A paternalistic system of labor relations emphasizing management responsibility for employee well-being.

**Open shop** Factory of business employing workers whether or not they are union members; in practice, such a business usually refuses to hire union members and follows antiunion policies.

**The A&P grocery** chain expanded from 400 stores in 1912 to more than 15,000 by the end of the 1920s, making it a familiar sight in communities across America. A&P advertisements, like this one from 1927, emphasized cleanliness, order, and the availability of name-brand goods at discount prices.

## IMAGE KEY

for pages 622–623

a. Silent film star Gertrude Olmstead wears a ruffled flapper dress with a striped hat in 1925.
b. "More than a car. FORD: A National Institution" poster, 1923.
c. A clarinet like those used during "the Jazz Age" of the 1920s.
d. An old football symbolizes the exuberance of the times.
e. Men are shown piecing together automobiles on an assembly line in the Rouge plant of the Ford Motor Company.
f. Campbell's Tomato Soup advertisement.
g. The price of stocks through the 1920s and early 1930s.
h. Women dressed in the white robes and hoods of the Ku Klux Klan in 1924.

Another approach encouraged workers to acquire property through stock-purchase plans or, less frequently, home-ownership plans. By 1927, 800,000 employees had more than $1 billion invested in more than 300 companies. Other programs offered workers insurance policies covering accidents, illness, old age, and death. By 1928, some 6 million workers had group insurance coverage valued at $7.5 billion. Many plant managers and personnel departments consciously worked to improve safety conditions, provide medical services, and establish sports and recreation programs for workers. Employers hoped such measures would encourage workers to identify personally with the company and discourage complaints on the job. To some extent they succeeded. But welfare capitalism could not solve the chronic problems faced by industrial workers: seasonal unemployment, low wages, long hours, and unhealthy factory conditions. Indeed corporate policy reinforced economic insecurity for millions of workers and advanced growing income inequality. The failure of the 1920s' economy to distribute gains in productivity more equally would help set the stage for the Great Depression of the 1930s.

## THE AUTO AGE

The auto industry offered the clearest example of the rise to prominence of consumer durables. During the 1920s, America made approximately 85 percent of all the world's passenger cars. By 1929, the motor vehicle industry was the most productive in the United States in terms of value. In that year, the industry added 4.8 million new cars to the more than 26 million—roughly one for every five people—already on American roads.

**Finished automobiles roll** off the moving assembly line at the Ford Motor Company, Highland Park, Michigan, ca. 1920. During the 1920s, Henry Ford achieved the status of folk hero, as his name became synonymous with the techniques of mass production. Ford cultivated a public image of himself as the heroic genius of the auto industry, greatly exaggerating his personal achievements.

## QUICK REVIEW

**The Automobile Industry**

- 1920s: America made 85 percent of the world's passenger cars.
- By 1925, Ford's assembly line produced one new car every ten seconds.
- Auto industry provided a market for steel, rubber, glass, and petroleum products.

This extraordinary new industry had mushroomed in less than a generation. Its great pioneer, Henry Ford, had shown how the use of a continuous assembly line could drastically reduce the number of worker hours required to produce a single vehicle. In 1913, it took thirteen hours to produce one automobile. In 1914, at his sprawling new Highland Park assembly plant just outside Detroit, Ford's system finished one car every ninety minutes. By 1925, cars were rolling off his assembly line at the rate of one every ten seconds.

In 1914, Ford startled American industry by inaugurating a new wage scale: $5 for an eight-hour day. This was roughly double the going pay rate for industrial labor, along with a shorter workday as well. But in defying the conventional economic wisdom of the day, Ford acted less out of benevolence than out of shrewdness. He understood that workers were consumers as well as producers, and the new wage scale helped boost sales of Ford cars. It also reduced the high turnover rate in his labor force and increased worker efficiency. Roughly two-thirds of the labor force at Ford consisted of immigrants from southern and eastern Europe. By the early 1920s Ford also employed about 5,000 African Americans, more than any other large American corporation. Ford's mass-production system and economies of scale permitted him to progressively reduce the price of his cars, bringing them within the reach of millions of Americans.

By 1927, Ford had produced 15 million Model Ts. But by then, the company faced stiff competition from General Motors (GM), which had developed an effective new marketing strategy. Under the guidance of Alfred P. Sloan, GM organized into separate divisions, each of which appealed to a different market segment. The GM business structure, along with its attempts to match production with demand through sophisticated market research and sales forecasting, became a widely copied model for other large American corporations. Both Ford and GM also pushed the idea of purchasing cars on credit, thus helping to make "installment buying" an underpinning of the new consumer culture.

The auto industry provided a large market for makers of steel, rubber, glass, and petroleum products. It stimulated public spending for good roads and extended the housing boom to new suburbs. Showrooms, repair shops, and gas stations appeared in thousands of communities. New small enterprises, from motels to billboard advertising to roadside diners, sprang up as motorists took to the highway. Automobiles widened the experience of millions of Americans. They made the exploration of the world outside the local community easier and more attractive. For some, the car merely reinforced old social patterns, making it easier for them to get to church on Sunday, for example, or visit neighbors. Others used their cars to go to new places, shop in nearby cities, or take vacations. The automobile made leisure, in the sense of getting away from the routines of work and school, a more regular part of everyday life. It undoubtedly also changed the courtship practices of America's youth. Young people took advantage of the car to gain privacy and distance from their parents, and many had their first sexual experiences in automobiles.

## CITIES AND SUBURBS

Cars also promoted urban and suburban growth. The federal census for 1920 was the first in American history in which the proportion of the population that lived in urban places (those with 2,500 or more people) exceeded the proportion of the population living in rural areas. More revealing of urban growth was the steady increase in the number of big cities. In 1910, there were sixty cities with more than 100,000 inhabitants; in 1920, there were sixty-eight; and by 1930, there were ninety-two.

Cities promised business opportunity, good jobs, cultural richness, and personal freedom. They attracted millions of Americans, white and black, from small towns and farms, as well as immigrants from abroad. Immigrants were drawn to cities by the presence there of family and people of like background in already

**Until 1924, Henry Ford** had disdained national advertising for his cars. But as General Motors gained a competitive edge by making yearly changes in style and technology, Ford was forced to pay more attention to advertising. This ad was directed at "Mrs. Consumer," combining appeals to female independence and motherly duties.

established ethnic communities. In a continuation of the Great Migration that began during World War I, roughly 1.5 million African Americans from the rural South migrated to cities in search of economic opportunities during the 1920s, doubling the black populations of New York, Chicago, Detroit, and Houston.

Houston offers a good example of how the automobile shaped an urban community. In 1910, it was a sleepy railroad town with a population of about 75,000 that served the Texas Gulf coast and interior. The enormous demand for gasoline and other petroleum products helped transform the city into a busy center for oil refining. Its population soared to 300,000 by the end of the 1920s. Abundant cheap land and the absence of zoning ordinances, combined with the availability of the automobile, pushed Houston to expand horizontally rather than vertically. It became the archetypal decentralized, low-density city, sprawling miles in each direction from downtown and thoroughly dependent upon automobiles and roads for its sense of community. Suburban communities grew at twice the rate of their core cities, also thanks largely to the automobile boom. Undeveloped land on the fringes of cities became valuable real estate. All the new "automobile suburbs" differed in important ways from earlier suburbs built along mass transit lines. The car allowed for a larger average lot size and, in turn, lower residential density.

# THE STATE, THE ECONOMY, AND BUSINESS

**HOW AND** why did the Republican Party dominate 1920s' politics?

**myhistorylab**
Review Summary

Throughout the 1920s, a confident Republican Party dominated national politics, certain that it had ushered in a "new era" in American life. A new and closer relationship between the federal government and American business became the hallmark of Republican policy in both domestic and foreign affairs during the administrations of three successive Republican presidents: Warren Harding (1921–23), Calvin Coolidge (1923–29), and Herbert Hoover (1929–33).

## HARDING AND COOLIDGE

Handsome, genial, and well-spoken, Warren Harding may have looked the part of a president—but acting like one was another matter. Harding was a product of small-town Marion, Ohio, and the machine politics in his native state. Republican Party officials had made a point of keeping Senator Harding, a compromise choice, as removed from the public eye as possible in the 1920 election. They correctly saw that active campaigning could only hurt their candidate by exposing his shallowness and intellectual weakness.

Harding surrounded himself with a close circle of friends, the "Ohio gang," delegating to them a great deal of administrative power. In the summer of 1923, Harding began to get wind of the scandals for which his administration is best remembered.

Soon after Harding's death from a heart attack in 1923, a series of congressional investigations revealed a deep pattern of corruption. The worst affair was the Teapot Dome scandal involving Interior Secretary Albert Fall. Fall received hundreds of thousands of dollars in payoffs when he secretly leased navy oil reserves in Teapot Dome, Wyoming, and Elk Hills, California, to two private oil developers. He eventually became the first cabinet officer ever to go to jail.

But the Harding administration's legacy was not all scandal. Andrew Mellon, an influential Pittsburgh banker, served as secretary of the treasury under all three Republican presidents of the 1920s. Mellon believed government ought to be run on the same conservative principles as a corporation. He was a leading voice for trimming the federal budget and cutting taxes on incomes, corporate profits, and inheritances. Mellon's program sharply cut taxes for both higher-income brackets and for businesses. By 1926, a person with an income of a million a year paid less than a third of the income tax he or she had paid in 1921.

When Calvin Coolidge succeeded to the presidency, he seemed to most people the temperamental opposite of Harding. Taciturn, genteel, and completely honest, Coolidge believed in the least amount of government possible. He spent only four hours a day at the office. His famous aphorism, "The business of America is business," perfectly captured the core philosophy of the Republican new era.

Coolidge easily won election on his own in 1924. He benefited from the general prosperity and the contrast he provided with the disgraced Harding. Coolidge defeated little-known Democrat John W. Davis, the compromise choice of a party badly divided between its rural and urban wings. Also running was Progressive Party candidate Robert M. La Follette of Wisconsin, who mounted a reform campaign that attacked economic monopolies and called for government ownership of utilities. In his full term, Coolidge showed most interest in reducing federal spending, lowering taxes, and blocking congressional initiatives. He saw his primary function as clearing the way for American businessmen. They, after all, were the agents of the era's unprecedented prosperity.

## HERBERT HOOVER AND THE "ASSOCIATIVE STATE"

The most influential figure of the Republican new era was Herbert Hoover, who as secretary of commerce dominated the cabinets of Harding and Coolidge before becoming president himself in 1929. A successful engineer, administrator, and politician, Hoover had earned an enviable reputation as wartime head of the U.S. Food Administration and director general of relief for Europe. He effectively embodied the belief that enlightened business, encouraged and informed by the government, would act in the public interest. In this sense Hoover maintained an essentially progressive outlook. But in the modern industrial age, Hoover believed, the government needed only to advise private citizens' groups about what national or international polices to pursue.

Hoover thus fused a faith in old-fashioned individualism with a strong commitment to the progressive possibilities offered by efficiency and rationality. Unlike an earlier generation of Republicans, Hoover wanted not just to create a favorable climate for business but also to actively assist the business community. He spoke of creating an "associative state," in which the government would encourage voluntary cooperation among corporations, consumers, workers, farmers, and small businessmen. This became the central occupation of the Department of Commerce under Hoover's leadership. The Bureau of Standards became one of the nation's leading research centers, setting engineering standards for key American industries such as machine tools and automobiles. The bureau also helped standardize the styles, sizes, and designs of many consumer products, such as canned goods and refrigerators.

Hoover actively encouraged the creation and expansion of national trade associations. By 1929, there were about 2,000 of them. At industrial conferences called by the Commerce Department, government officials explained the advantages of mutual cooperation in figuring prices and costs and then publishing the information. The idea was to improve efficiency by reducing competition. To some, this practice violated the spirit of antitrust laws, but in the 1920s, the Justice Department's Antitrust Division took a very lax view of its responsibility. In addition, the

Supreme Court consistently upheld the legality of trade associations. The government thus provided an ideal climate for the concentration of corporate wealth and power.

## WAR DEBTS, REPARATIONS, KEEPING THE PEACE

Rejection of the Treaty of Versailles and the League of Nations did not mean disengagement from the rest of the globe. The United States emerged from World War I as the strongest economic power in the world. The war transformed it from the world's leading debtor nation to its most important creditor. New York replaced London as the center of international finance and capital markets. Yet America's postwar policies included a great contradiction: protectionism. The rest of the world owed the United States billions of dollars, but high tariffs on both farm products and manufactured goods made it much more difficult for debtor nations to repay by selling exports.

During the 1920s, war debts and reparations were the single most divisive issue in international economics. In France and Great Britain, which both owed the United States large amounts in war loans, many concluded that the Uncle Sam who had offered assistance during wartime was really a loan shark in disguise. In turn, many Americans viewed Europeans as ungrateful debtors. In 1922, the U.S. Foreign Debt Commission negotiated an agreement with the debtor nations that called for them to repay $11.5 billion over a sixty-two-year period. But by the late 1920s, the European financial situation had become so desperate that the United States agreed to cancel a large part of these debts. Continued insistence by the United States that the Europeans pay at least a portion of the debt fed anti-American feeling in Europe and isolationism at home.

The Germans believed that war reparations, set at $33 billion by the Treaty of Versailles, not only unfairly punished the losers of the conflict but, by saddling their civilian economies with such massive debt, also deprived them of the very means to repay. In 1924, Herbert Hoover and Chicago banker Charles Dawes worked out a plan to aid the recovery of the German economy. The Dawes Plan reduced Germany's debt, stretched out the repayment period, and arranged for American bankers to lend funds to Germany. These measures helped stabilize Germany's currency and allowed it to make reparations payments to France and Great Britain. The Allies, in turn, were better able to pay their war debts to the United States.

In addition to the Dawes Plan and the American role in naval disarmament, the United States joined the league-sponsored World Court in 1926 and was represented at numerous league conferences. In 1928, with great fanfare, the United States and sixty-two other nations signed the Pact of Paris (better known as the Kellogg-Briand Pact), which grandly and naively renounced war in principle. Peace groups, such as the Woman's Peace Party and the Quaker-based Fellowship of Reconciliation, hailed the pact for formally outlawing war. But critics charged that the Kellogg-Briand Pact was essentially meaningless, since it lacked powers of enforcement and relied solely on the moral force of world opinion.

## GLOBAL COMMERCE AND U.S. FOREIGN POLICY

Throughout the 1920s, Secretary of State Charles Evans Hughes and other Republican leaders pursued policies designed to expand American economic activity abroad. They understood that capitalist economies must be dynamic; they must expand their markets if they were to thrive. The focus must be on friendly nations and investments that would help foreign citizens to buy American goods. Toward this end, Republican leaders urged close cooperation between bankers and the government as a strategy for expanding American investment and economic influence abroad.

The strategy of maximum freedom for private enterprise, backed by limited government advice and assistance, significantly boosted the power and profits of American overseas investors. But in Central and Latin America, in particular, aggressive U.S. investment also fostered chronically underdeveloped economies, dependent on a few staple crops (sugar, coffee, cocoa, bananas) grown for export. American investments in Latin America more than doubled between 1924 and 1929, from $1.5 billion to over $3.5 billion. A large part of this money went to taking over vital mineral resources, such as Chile's copper and Venezuela's oil. The growing wealth and power of U.S. companies made it more difficult for these nations to grow their own food or diversify their economies. U.S. economic dominance in the hemisphere also hampered the growth of democratic politics by favoring autocratic, military regimes that could be counted on to protect U.S. investments.

## WEAKENED AGRICULTURE, AILING INDUSTRIES

Amid prosperity and progress, there were large pockets of the country that lagged behind. Advances in real income and improvements in the standard of living for workers and farmers were uneven at best. In 1920, some 32 million Americans still lived on farms, out of a total population of 106 million. Yet during the 1920s the farm sector failed to share in the general prosperity. The years 1914–19 had been a kind of golden age for the nation's farmers. But with the war's end, American farmers began to suffer from a chronic worldwide surplus of such farm staples as cotton, hogs, and corn.

In the South, farmers' dependency on "King Cotton" deepened, as the region lagged farther behind the rest of the nation in both agricultural diversity and standard of living. Cotton acreage expanded, as large and heavily mechanized farms opened up new land in Oklahoma, west Texas, and the Mississippi-Yazoo delta. But in most of the South, from North Carolina to east Texas, small one- and two-mule cotton farms, most under 50 acres, still dominated the countryside. With few large urban centers and inadequate transportation, even those southern farmers who had access to capital found it extremely difficult to find reliable markets for vegetables, fruit, poultry, or dairy products. Some 700,000 southern farmers, roughly half white and half black, still labored as sharecroppers. Modern conveniences such as electricity, indoor plumbing, automobiles, and phonographs remained far beyond the reach of the great majority of southern farmers. Widespread rural poverty, poor diet, little access to capital—the world of southern agriculture had changed very little since the days of the Populist revolt in the 1890s.

The most important initiatives for federal farm relief were the McNary-Haugen bills, a series of complicated measures designed to prop up and stabilize farm prices. The basic idea, borrowed from the old Populist proposals of the 1890s, was for the government to purchase farm surpluses and either store them until prices rose or sell them on the world market. But President Calvin Coolidge viewed these measures as unwarranted federal interference in the economy and vetoed the McNary-Haugen Farm Relief bill of 1927 when it finally passed

**23–2**
H. L. Mencken, *The Sahara of the Bozart* (1920)

Congress. American farmers hoping to export produce abroad also suffered from the high tariffs imposed by European countries trying to protect their own devastated economies.

To be sure, some farmers thrived. Improved transportation and chain supermarkets allowed for a wider and more regular distribution of such foods as oranges, lemons, and fresh green vegetables. Citrus, dairy, and truck farmers in particular profited from the growing importance of national markets. Wheat production jumped more than 300 percent during the 1920s. Across the plains of Kansas, Nebraska, Colorado, Oklahoma, and Texas, wheat farmers brought the methods of industrial capitalism to the land. They hitched disc plows and combined harvester-threshers to gasoline-powered tractors, tearing up millions of acres of grassland to create a vast wheat factory. With prices averaging above $1 per bushel over the decade, mechanized farming created a new class of large-scale wheat entrepreneurs on the plains.

Overall, per capita farm income remained well below what it had been in 1919, and the gap between farm and nonfarm income widened. By 1929, the average income per person on farms was $223, compared with $870 for nonfarm workers. By the end of the decade, hundreds of thousands had quit farming altogether for jobs in mills and factories. And fewer farmers owned their land. In 1930, 42 percent of all farmers were tenants, compared with 37 percent in 1919.

Large sectors of American industry also failed to share in the decade's general prosperity. As oil and natural gas gained in importance, America's coal mines became a less important source of energy. A combination of shrinking demand, new mining technology, and a series of losing strikes reduced the coal labor force by one-quarter. The United Mine Workers, perhaps the strongest AFL union in 1920, with 500,000 members, had shrunk to 75,000 by 1928. Economic hardship was widespread in many mining communities dependent on coal, particularly Appalachia and the southern Midwest. And those miners who did work earned lower hourly wages.

In textiles, shrinking demand and overcapacity (too many factories) were chronic problems. To improve profit margins, textile manufacturers in New England and other parts of the Northeast began a long-range shift of operations to the South, where nonunion shops and substandard wages became the rule. Older New England manufacturing centers such as Lawrence, Lowell, Nashua, Manchester, and Fall River were hard hit by this shift. The center of the American textile industry shifted permanently to the Piedmont region of North and South Carolina. By 1933, factories there employed nearly 70 percent of the workers in the industry.

# THE NEW MASS CULTURE

New communications media reshaped American culture in the 1920s, and much of the new mass culture was exported to the rest of the economically developed world. The phrase "Roaring Twenties" captures the explosion of image- and sound-making machinery that came to dominate so much of American life.

## MOVIE-MADE AMERICA

The early movie industry, centered in New York and a few other big cities, had made moviegoing a regular habit for millions of Americans, especially immigrants and

HOW DID the new mass media reshape American culture?

Review Summary

the working class. They flocked to cheap, storefront theaters, called nickelodeons, to watch short Westerns, slapstick comedies, melodramas, and travelogues. By 1914, there were about 18,000 "movie houses" showing motion pictures, with more than 7 million daily admissions and $300 million in annual receipts. With the shift of the industry westward to Hollywood, movies entered a new phase of business expansion. Large studios such as Paramount, Fox, Metro-Goldwyn-Mayer (MGM), Universal, and Warner Brothers dominated the business with longer and more expensively produced movies—feature films. Each studio combined the three functions of production, distribution, and exhibition, and each controlled hundreds of movie theaters around the country.

**23-11**
*Motion Picture Diaries* (1920s)

The era of silent films ended when Warner Brothers scored a huge hit in 1927 with *The Jazz Singer*, starring Al Jolson, which successfully introduced sound. New genres—musicals, gangster films, and screwball comedies—soon became popular. To maintain their hold on European markets, the major studios established production facilities abroad that used foreign actors for the "dubbing" of American films into other languages. The higher costs associated with "talkies" also increased the studios' reliance on Wall Street investors and banks for working capital.

At the heart of Hollywood's success was the star system and the accompanying cult of celebrity, both of which help define American popular culture to this day (see Seeing History). Stars became vital to the fantasy lives of millions of fans. For many in the audience, there was only a vague line separating the on-screen and off-screen adventures of the stars. Studio publicity, fan magazines, and gossip columns reinforced this ambiguity. Film idols, with their mansions, cars, parties, and private escapades, became the national experts on leisure and consumption. Their movies generally emphasized sexual themes and celebrated youth, athleticism, and the liberating power of consumer goods. Young Americans in particular looked to movies to learn how to dress, wear their hair, talk, or kiss.

But many Americans, particularly in rural areas and small towns, worried about Hollywood's impact on traditional sexual morality. They attacked the permissiveness associated with Hollywood life, and many states created censorship boards to screen movies before allowing them to be shown in theaters. To counter growing calls for government censorship, Hollywood's studios came up with a plan to censor themselves. In 1922, they hired Will Hays to head the Motion Picture Producers and Distributors of America. As the movie industry's czar, Hays lobbied against censorship laws, wrote pamphlets defending the movie business, and began setting guidelines for what could and could not be depicted on the screen. He insisted that movies be treated like any other industrial enterprise, for he understood the relationship between Hollywood's success and the growth of the nation's consumer culture.

## RADIO BROADCASTING

In the fall of 1920, Westinghouse executive Harry P. Davis noticed that amateur broadcasts from the garage of an employee had attracted attention in the local Pittsburgh press. A department store advertised radio sets capable of picking up these "wireless concerts." Davis converted this amateur station to a stronger one at the Westinghouse main plant. Beginning with the presidential election returns that November, station KDKA offered regular nightly broadcasts that were probably heard by only a few hundred people. Radio broadcasting, begun as a service for selling cheap radio sets left over from World War I, would soon sweep the nation.

Before KDKA, wireless technology had been of interest only to the military, the telephone industry, and a few thousand "ham" (amateur) operators who enjoyed communicating with each other. The "radio mania" of the early 1920s was a response to the new possibilities offered by broadcasting. By 1923, nearly 600 stations had been licensed by the Department of Commerce, and about 600,000 Americans had bought radios. For millions of Americans, especially in rural areas and small towns, radio provided a new and exciting link to the larger national community of consumption.

Who would pay for radio programs? In the early 1920s, owners and operators of radio stations included radio equipment manufacturers, newspapers, department stores, state universities, cities, ethnic societies, labor unions, and churches. But by the end of the decade, commercial (or "toll") broadcasting emerged as the answer. The dominant corporations in the industry—General Electric, Westinghouse, Radio Corporation of America (RCA), and American Telephone and Telegraph (AT&T)—settled on the idea that advertisers would foot the bill for radio. Millions of listeners might be the consumers of radio shows, but sponsors were to be the customers. AT&T leased its nationwide system of telephone wires to allow the linking of many stations into powerful radio networks, such as the National Broadcasting Company (NBC) in 1926 and the Columbia Broadcasting System (CBS) in 1928. The rise of network radio squeezed out many of the stations and programs aimed at ethnic communities or broadcast in languages other than English, thus promoting a more homogenized culture.

NBC and CBS led the way in creating popular radio programs that relied heavily on older cultural forms. The variety show, hosted by vaudeville comedians, became network radio's first important format. Radio's first truly national hit, *The Amos 'n' Andy Show* (1928), was a direct descendant of nineteenth-century "blackface" minstrel entertainment. Radio did more than any previous medium to publicize and commercialize once isolated forms of American music such as country-and-western, blues, and jazz. Broadcasts of baseball and college football games proved especially popular. In 1930, some 600 stations were broadcasting to more than 12 million homes with radios, or roughly 40 percent of American families. By that time, all the elements that characterize the present American system of broadcasting—regular daily programming paid for and produced by commercial advertisers, national networks carrying shows across the nation, and mass ownership of receiver sets in American homes—were in place.

Radio broadcasting created a national community of listeners, just as motion pictures created one of viewers. And like movies it also transcended national boundaries. Broadcasting had a powerful hemispheric impact. In both Canada and Mexico, governments established national broadcasting systems to bolster cultural and political nationalism. Yet American shows—and advertising—continued to dominate Canadian airwaves. Large private Mexican radio stations were often started in partnership with American corporations such as RCA, as a way to create demand for receiving sets. Language barriers limited the direct impact of U.S. broadcasts, but American advertisers became the backbone of commercial radio in Mexico. Radio broadcasting thus significantly amplified the influence of American commercialism throughout the hemisphere.

# Creating Celebrity

A common definition for "celebrity" is one who is famous for being famous. Although politics, the arts, science, and the military have produced famous people for centuries, the celebrity is a twentieth-century phenomenon, one closely linked to the emergence of modern forms of mass media. In the 1920s Hollywood's "star system," along with tabloid newspapers and the new profession of public relations, created the modern celebrity. Film producers were at first wary of identifying screen actors by name, but they soon discovered that promoting popular leading actors would boost the box office for their movies. The use of "close-ups" in movies and the fact that screen images were literally larger than life distinguished the images of film actors from, say, stage performers or opera singers.

Fans identified with their favorites in contradictory ways. Stars like Charlie Chaplin and Mary Pickford were like royalty. Audiences were also curious about the stars' private lives. Film studios took advantage of this curiosity by carefully controlling the public image of their stars through press releases, planted stories in newspapers, and carefully managed interviews and public appearances. By the 1920s film stars were essentially studio owned and operated commodities, requiring enormous capital investment. ■

**WHAT VISUAL** themes strike you as most powerful in the accompanying images? How do they compare to celebrity images of today? Why do you think male stars such as Valentino and Fairbanks were so often portrayed as exotic foreigners?

## NEW FORMS OF JOURNALISM

A new kind of newspaper, the tabloid, became popular in the postwar years. The *New York Daily News*, founded in 1919 by Joseph M. Patterson, was the first to develop the tabloid style. Its folded-in-half page size made it convenient to read on buses or subways. The *Daily News* devoted much of its space to photographs and other illustrations. With a terse, lively reporting style that emphasized sex, scandal, and sports, *Daily News* circulation reached 400,000 in 1922 and 1.3 million by 1929.

This success spawned a host of imitators in New York and elsewhere. The circulation of existing dailies was little affected. Tabloids had instead discovered an audience of millions who had never read newspapers before. Most of these new readers were poorly educated working-class city dwellers, many of whom were immigrants or children of immigrants.

The tabloid's most popular new feature was the gossip column, invented by Walter Winchell, an obscure former vaudevillian who began writing his column "Your Broadway and Mine" for the *New York Daily Graphic* in 1924. Winchell described the secret lives of public figures with a distinctive, rapid-fire, slangy style that made the reader feel like an insider. He chronicled the connections among high society, show business stars, powerful politicians, and the underworld. By the end of the decade, scores of newspapers "syndicated" Winchell's column, making him the most widely read—and imitated—journalist in America.

Journalism followed the larger economic trend toward consolidation and merger. Newspaper chains like Hearst, Gannett, and Scripps-Howard flourished during the 1920s. There was a sizable increase in the number of these chains and in the percentage of total daily circulation that was chain-owned. By the early 1930s, the Hearst organization alone controlled twenty-six dailies in eighteen cities, accounting for 14 percent of the nation's newspaper circulation. One of every four Sunday papers sold in America was owned by the Hearst group.

## ADVERTISING MODERNITY

**23–4**
*Advertisements* (1925, 1927)

A thriving advertising industry both reflected and encouraged the growing importance of consumer goods in American life. Previously, advertising had been confined mostly to staid newspapers and magazines and offered little more than basic product information. The most creative advertising was usually for dubious products, such as patent medicines. The successful efforts of the government's Committee on Public Information, set up to "sell" World War I to Americans, suggested that new techniques using modern communication media could convince people to buy a wide range of goods and services. As a profession, advertising reached a higher level of respectability, sophistication, and economic power in American life during the 1920s.

The larger ad agencies moved toward a more scientific approach by sponsoring market research and welcoming the language of psychology to their profession. Indeed psychology's growing prestige as a field in the 1920s was reflected throughout the world of mass culture. Advertisers began focusing on the needs, desires, and anxieties of the consumer, rather than on the qualities of the product. "There are certain things that most people believe," noted one ad agency executive in 1927. "The moment your copy is linked to one of those beliefs, more than half your battle is won."

Ad agencies and their clients invested extraordinary amounts of time, energy, and money trying to discover and, to some extent, shape those beliefs. Leading agencies such as Lord and Thomas in Chicago and J. Walter Thompson in New

York combined knowledge gained from market research and consumer surveys with carefully prepared ad copy and graphics to sell their clients' wares. High-powered ad campaigns made new products like Fleischmann's Yeast, Kleenex, and Listerine household words across the country. Above all, advertising celebrated consumption itself as a positive good. In this sense, the new advertising ethic was a therapeutic one, promising that products would contribute to the buyer's physical, psychic, or emotional well-being.

## THE PHONOGRAPH AND THE RECORDING INDUSTRY

Like radio and movies, the phonograph came into its own in the 1920s as a popular entertainment medium. Dance crazes such as the fox trot, tango, and grizzly bear, done to complex ragtime and Latin rhythms, boosted the record business tremendously. Dixieland jazz, which recorded well, also captured the public's fancy in the early 1920s, and records provided the music for new popular dances like the Charleston and the black bottom. In 1921, more than 200 companies produced some 2 million records, and annual record sales exceeded $100 million.

Record sales declined toward the end of the decade, due to competition from radio. But in a broader cultural sense, records continued to transform American popular culture. Record companies discovered lucrative regional and ethnic markets for country music, which appealed primarily to white Southerners, and blues and jazz, which appealed primarily to African Americans. Country musicians like the Carter Family and Jimmie Rodgers, and blues singers like Blind Lemon Jefferson and Ma Rainey and Bessie Smith, had their performances put on records for the first time. Their records sold mainly in specialized "hillbilly" and "race" markets. Yet they were also played over the radio, and millions of Americans began to hear musical styles and performers who had previously been isolated from the general population. Jazz records by such African American artists as Louis Armstrong and Duke Ellington found a wide audience overseas as well, and jazz emerged as a uniquely American cultural form with broad appeal around the globe. The combination of records and radio started an extraordinary cross-fertilization of American musical styles that continues to this day.

## SPORTS AND CELEBRITY

During the 1920s, spectator sports enjoyed an unprecedented growth in popularity and profitability. As radio, newspapers, magazines, and newsreels exhaustively documented their exploits, athletes took their place alongside movie stars in defining a new culture of celebrity. Big-time sports, like the movies, entered a new corporate phase. Yet it was the athletes themselves, performing extraordinary feats on the field and transcending their often humble origins, who attracted millions of new fans. The image of the modern athlete—rich, famous, glamorous, and often a rebel against social convention—came into its own during the decade.

Major league baseball had more fans than any other sport, and its greatest star, George Herman "Babe" Ruth, embodied the new celebrity athlete. Aided by the new "live ball," Ruth's prodigious home run hitting completely changed baseball strategy and attracted legions of new fans to the sport. Ruth was a larger-than-life character off the field as well. In New York, media capital of the nation, newspapers and magazines chronicled his enormous appetites—for food, whiskey, expensive cars, and big-city nightlife. He hobnobbed with politicians, movie stars, and gangsters, and he regularly visited sick children in hospitals. Ruth became the first athlete avidly sought after by manufacturers for celebrity endorsement of their products.

Baseball attendance exploded during the 1920s, reaching a one-year total of 10 million in 1929. The attendance boom prompted urban newspapers to increase their baseball coverage, and the larger dailies featured separate sports sections. The best sportswriters, such as Grantland Rice, Heywood Broun, and Ring Lardner, brought a poetic sensibility to descriptions of the games and their stars. William K. Wrigley, owner of the Chicago Cubs, discovered that by letting local radio stations broadcast his team's games, the club could win new fans, especially among housewives.

**Babe Ruth, baseball's** biggest star, shakes hands with President Warren G. Harding at the Opening Day of the brand new Yankee Stadium, Bronx, New York, April 4, 1923. The new celebrity culture of the 1920s routinely brought together public figures from the worlds of politics, sports, show business, and even organized crime.

Among those excluded from major league baseball were African Americans, who had been banned from the game by an 1890s "gentleman's agreement" among owners. During the 1920s, black baseball players and entrepreneurs developed a world of their own, with several professional and semi-professional leagues catering to expanding African American communities in cities. The largest of these was the Negro National League, organized in 1920 by Andrew "Rube" Foster. Black ballclubs also played exhibitions against, and frequently defeated, teams of white major leaguers. African Americans had their own baseball heroes, such as Josh Gibson and Satchel Paige, who no doubt would have been stars in the major leagues if not for racial exclusion.

The new media configuration of the 1920s created heroes in other sports as well. Radio broadcasts and increased journalistic coverage made college football a big-time sport. The center of college football shifted from the old elite schools of the Ivy League to the big universities of the Midwest and Pacific Coast, where most of the players were now second-generation Irish, Italians, and Slavs. Athletes like boxers Jack Dempsey and Gene Tunney, tennis players Bill Tilden and Helen Wills, golfer Bobby Jones, and swimmers Gertrude Ederle and Johnny Weissmuller became household names who brought legions of new fans to their sports.

## A NEW MORALITY?

Movie stars, radio personalities, sports heroes, and popular musicians became the elite figures in a new culture of celebrity defined by the mass media. They were the model for achievement in the new age. Great events and abstract issues were made real through movie close-ups, radio interviews, and tabloid photos. The new media relentlessly created and disseminated images that are still familiar today: Babe Ruth trotting around the bases after hitting a home run; the wild celebrations that greeted Charles Lindbergh after he completed the first solo transatlantic airplane flight in 1927; the smiling gangster Al Capone, bantering with reporters who transformed his criminal exploits into important news events.

But images do not tell the whole story. Consider one of the most enduring images of the "Roaring Twenties," the flapper. She was usually portrayed on screen, in novels, and in the press as a young, sexually aggressive woman with bobbed hair, rouged cheeks, and short skirt. She loved to dance to jazz music, enjoyed smoking cigarettes, and drank bootleg liquor in cabarets and dance halls. She could also be competitive, assertive, and a good pal. As writer Zelda Fitzgerald put it in 1924: "I think a woman gets more happiness out of being gay, light-hearted, unconventional, mistress of her own fate. . . . I want [my daughter] to be a flapper, because flappers are brave and gay and beautiful."

Was the flapper a genuine representative of the 1920s? Did she embody the "new morality" that was so widely discussed and chronicled in the media of the day? The flapper certainly did exist, but she was neither as new nor as widespread a phenomenon as the image would suggest. The delight in sensuality, personal pleasure, and rhythmically complex dance and music had long been key elements of subcultures on the fringes of middle-class society. In the 1920s, these activities

**A woman in** a man's shirt and necktie wears a pair of Paul Jones knickers in this 1922 advertisement. Her boyish, almost androgynous look reflects one way that notions of the "new woman" intersected with the worlds of fashion and advertising.

**23–5**
Margaret Sanger, *Family Planning* (1926)

**23–9**
Eleanor Wembridge, *Petting and Necking* (1925)

**WHAT POLITICAL** and cultural movements opposed modern cultural trends?

**myhistorylab**
**Review Summary**

**Volstead Act** The 1920 law defining the liquor forbidden under the Eighteenth Amendment and giving enforcement responsibilities to the Prohibition Bureau of the Department of the Treasury.

became normative for a growing number of white middle-class Americans, including women. Jazz, sexual experimentation, heavy makeup, and cigarette smoking spread to college campuses.

Several sources, most of them rooted in earlier years, can be found for the increased sexual openness of the 1920s. Troops in the armed forces during World War I had been exposed to government-sponsored sex education. New psychological and social theories like those of Havelock Ellis, Ellen Key, and Sigmund Freud stressed the central role of sexuality in human experience, maintaining that sex is a positive, healthy impulse that, if repressed, could damage mental and emotional health. The pioneering efforts of Margaret Sanger in educating women about birth control had begun before World War I (see Chapter 21). In the 1920s, Sanger campaigned vigorously—through her journal *Birth Control Review*, in books, and on speaking tours—to make contraception freely available to all women.

Sociological surveys also suggested that genuine changes in sexual behavior began in the prewar years among both married and single women. A 1938 survey of 777 middle-class females found that among those born between 1890 and 1900, 74 percent were virgins before marriage; for those born after 1910, the figure dropped to 32 percent. Women born after the turn of the century were twice as likely to have had premarital sex as those born before 1900. The critical change took place in the generation that came of age in the late teens and early twenties. By the 1920s, male and female "morals" were becoming more alike.

The emergence of homosexual subcultures also reflected the newly permissive atmosphere of the postwar years. Although such subcultures had been a part of big city life since at least the 1890s, they had been largely confined to working-class saloons associated with the urban underworld. By the 1920s, the word "homosexual" had gained currency as a scientific term for describing romantic love between women or between men, and middle-class enclaves of self-identified homosexuals took root in cities like New York, Chicago, and San Francisco. But if these enclaves provided some sense of community and safety for homosexuals, the repressive shadow of the larger culture was never far away. Psychologists of the era, with Freud in the lead, condemned "perversion" as a mental illness and counseled the need for a "cure."

# MODERNITY AND TRADITIONALISM

One measure of the profound cultural changes of the 1920s was the hostility and opposition expressed toward them by large sectors of the American public. Deep and persistent tensions, with ethnic, racial, and geographical overtones, characterized much of the decade's politics.

## PROHIBITION

The Eighteenth Amendment, banning the manufacture, sale, and transportation of alcoholic beverages, took effect in January 1920. Prohibition was the culmination of a long campaign that associated drinking with the degradation of working-class family life and the worst evils of urban politics. Supporters, a coalition of women's temperance groups, middle-class progressives, and rural Protestants, hailed the new law as "a noble experiment." But it became clear rather quickly that enforcing the new law would be extremely difficult. The **Volstead Act** of 1920 established a federal Prohibition Bureau to enforce the Eighteenth Amendment. Yet the bureau was severely understaffed with only about 1,500 agents to police the entire country.

The public demand for alcohol, especially in the big cities, led to widespread lawbreaking. Drinking was such a routine part of life for so many Americans that bootlegging quickly became a big business. Nearly every town and city had at least one "speakeasy," where people could drink and enjoy music and other entertainment. Local law enforcement personnel, especially in the cities, were easily bribed to overlook these illegal establishments. By the early 1920s, many eastern states no longer made even a token effort at enforcing the law.

But because liquor continued to be illegal, Prohibition gave an enormous boost to violent organized crime. The profits to be made in the illegal liquor trade dwarfed the traditional sources of criminal income—gambling, prostitution, and robbery. The pattern of organized crime in the 1920s closely resembled the larger trends in American business: smaller operations gave way to larger and more complex combinations. Successful organized crime figures, like Chicago's Al "Scarface" Capone, became celebrities in their own right and received heavy coverage in the mass media. Capone himself shrewdly used the rhetoric of the Republican new era to defend himself: "Everybody calls me a racketeer. I call myself a businessman. When I sell liquor it's bootlegging. When my patrons serve it on a silver tray on Lake Shore Drive, it's hospitality."

Organized crime, based on its huge profits from liquor, also made significant inroads into legitimate businesses, labor unions, and city government, especially in large cities. By the time Congress and the states ratified the Twenty-First Amendment in 1933, repealing Prohibition, organized crime was a permanent feature of American life.

## IMMIGRATION RESTRICTION

Sentiment for restricting immigration, growing since the late nineteenth century, reached its peak immediately after World War I. Barriers against Asian immigrants were already in place with the Chinese Exclusion Act of 1882 and the so-called Gentleman's Agreement with Japan in 1907. The movement to curb European immigration reflected the growing preponderance after 1890 of "new immigrants"—those from southern and eastern Europe—over the immigrants from northern and western Europe, who had predominated before 1890. Between 1891 and 1920, roughly 10.5 million immigrants arrived from southern and eastern Europe. This was nearly twice as many as arrived during the same years from northern and western Europe (see Figure 23.3).

The "new immigrants" were mostly Catholic and Jewish, and they were darker-skinned than the "old immigrants." To many old-stock Americans, they seemed more exotic, more foreign, and less willing and able to assimilate the nation's political and cultural values. They were also relatively poorer, more physically isolated in the nation's cities, and less politically strong than earlier immigrants. In the 1890s, the anti-Catholic American Protective Association called for a curb on immigration, and by exploiting the economic depression of that decade, it reached a membership of 2.5 million. In 1894, a group of prominent Harvard graduates, including Senator Henry Cabot Lodge (Rep., Massachusetts) and John Fiske, founded the Immigration Restriction League, providing an influential forum for the fears of the nation's elite. The league used newer scientific arguments, based on a flawed application of Darwinian evolutionary theory and genetics, to support its call for immigration restriction. The new immigration, Lodge argued, "is bringing to the country people whom it is very difficult to assimilate and who do not promise well for the standard of civilization in the United States."

Theories of scientific racism, which had become more popular in the early 1900s, reinforced anti-immigrant bias. Eugenicists, who enjoyed considerable

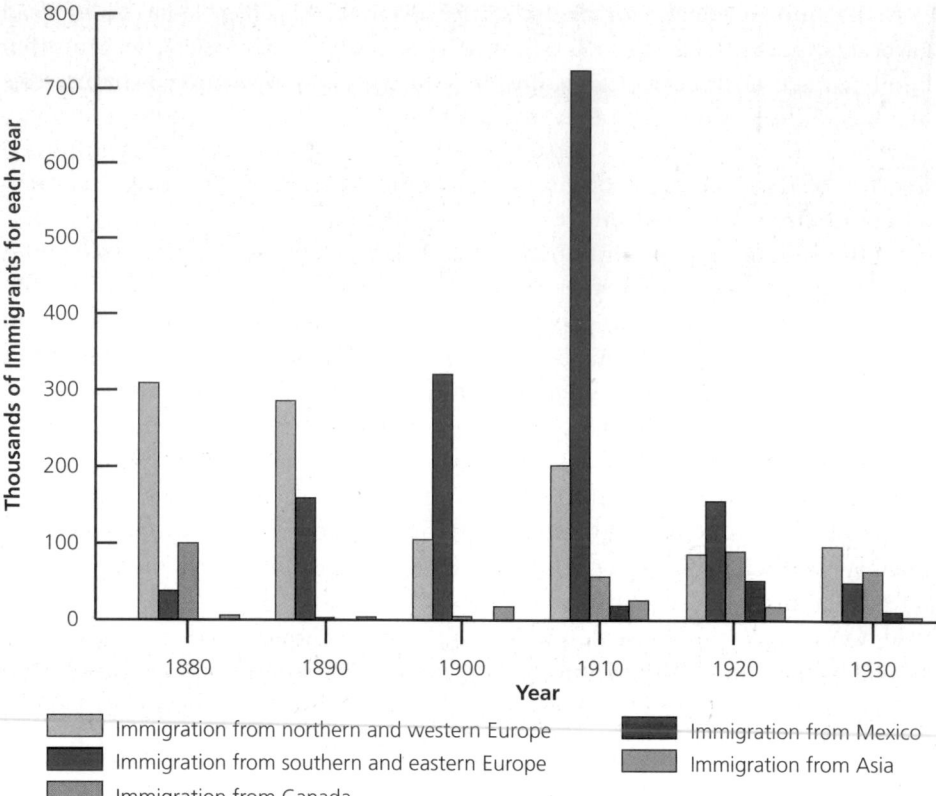

**Figure 23.3 Immigration trends to the United States by contingent/region 1880–1930.**

Adapted from Historical Statistics of the United States, Millenial Edition (NY: Cambridge University Press, 2006).

vogue in those years, held that heredity determined almost all of a person's capacities and that genetic inferiority predisposed people to crime and poverty. Such pseudoscientific thinking sought to explain historical and social development solely as a function of "racial" differences.

Against this background, the war and its aftermath provided the final push for the restriction of European immigration. The "100 percent American" fervor of the war years fueled nativist passions. So did the Red Scare of 1919–20, which linked foreigners with Bolshevism and radicalism of all kinds in the popular mind. The postwar depression coincided with the resumption of massive immigration, bringing much hostile comment on the relationship between rising unemployment and the new influx of foreigners. The American Federation of Labor proposed stopping all immigration for two years. Sensational press coverage of organized crime figures, many of them Italian or Jewish, also played a part.

In 1921, Congress passed the **Immigration Act**, setting a maximum of 357,000 new immigrants each year. Quotas limited annual immigration from any European country to 3 percent of the number of its natives counted in the 1910 U.S. census. But restrictionists complained that the new law still allowed too many southern and eastern Europeans in, especially since the northern and western Europeans did not fill their quotas. The Reed-Johnson National Origins Act of 1924 revised the quotas to 2 percent of the number of foreign-born counted for each nationality in the census for 1890, when far fewer southern or eastern Europeans were present in the United States. The maximum total allowed each year was also cut to 164,000. A *Los Angeles Times* headline expressed both the fundamental premise and flawed science of the new law: "Nordic Victory Is Seen in Drastic Restrictions."

The 1924 National Origins Act in effect limited immigration to white Europeans eligible for immigration by country of origin (nationality), while it divided

**23–3**
*National Origins Quota Act* (1924)

**23–12**
US Congress, *Debating Immigration Restriction* (1921)

**Immigration Act**   1921 act setting a maximum of 357,000 new immigrants each year.

**Women members of** the Ku Klux Klan in New Castle, Indiana, August 1, 1923. The revived Klan was a powerful presence in scores of American communities during the early 1920s, especially among native-born white Protestants, who feared cultural and political change. In addition to preaching "100 percent Americanism," local Klan chapters also served a social function for members and their families.

the rest of the world into "five colored races" (black, mulatto, Chinese, and Indian) who were ineligible for immigration. These new restrictions dovetailed with two recent Supreme Court decisions, *Ozawa* v. *U.S.* (1922) and *U.S.* v. *Thind* (1923), in which the Court held that Japanese and Asian Indians were unassimilable aliens and racially ineligible for U.S. citizenship. By the 1920s, American law had thus created the peculiar new racial category of "Asian" and codified the principle of racial exclusion in immigration and naturalization law.

## THE KU KLUX KLAN

If immigration restriction was resurgent nativism's most significant legislative expression, a revived Ku Klux Klan (KKK) was its most effective mass movement. The original Klan had been formed in the Reconstruction South as an instrument of white racial terror against newly freed slaves (see Chapter 17). It had died out in the 1870s. The new Klan, born in Stone Mountain, Georgia, in 1915, was inspired by D. W. Griffith's racist spectacle *The Birth of a Nation*, a film released in that year depicting the original KKK as a heroic organization. The new Klan patterned itself on the secret rituals and antiblack hostility of its predecessor and, until 1920, it was limited to a few local chapters in Georgia and Alabama.

When Hiram W. Evans, a dentist from Dallas, became imperial wizard of the Klan in 1922, he transformed the organization. Evans hired professional fundraisers and publicists and directed an effective recruiting scheme that paid a commission to sponsors of new members. The Klan advocated "100 percent Americanism" and "the faithful maintenance of White Supremacy." It staunchly supported the enforcement of Prohibition, and it attacked birth control and Darwinism. The new Klan made a special target of the Roman Catholic Church, labeling it a hostile and dangerous alien power.

The new Klan presented itself as the righteous defender of the embattled traditional values of small-town Protestant America. But ironically, to build its membership rolls, it relied heavily on the publicity, public relations, and business techniques associated with modern urban culture. By 1924, the new Klan counted more than 3 million members across the country. "Native, White, Protestant Supremacy," proved especially attractive in the Midwest and South, including many cities. Klansmen boycotted businesses, threatened families, and sometimes resorted to violence—public whippings, arson, and lynching—against their chosen enemies. The Klan's targets sometimes included white Protestants accused of sexual promiscuity, blasphemy, or drunkenness, but most victims were African Americans, Catholics, and Jews. Support for Prohibition enforcement probably united Klansmen more than any single issue.

On another level, the Klan was a popular social movement, a defensive bastion against forces of modernity. Perhaps a half million women joined the Women of the Ku Klux Klan, and women constituted nearly half of the Klan membership in some states. Klanswomen drew on family and community traditions, such as church suppers, kin reunions, and gossip campaigns, to defend themselves and their families against what they saw as corruption and immorality. The Klan's power was strong in many communities precisely because it fit so comfortably into the everyday life of white Protestants.

At its height, the Klan also became a powerful force in Democratic Party politics, and it had a strong presence among delegates to the 1924 Democratic National Convention. The Klan began to fade in 1925, when its Indiana leader, Grand Dragon David C. Stephenson, became involved in a sordid personal affair. With one of its most famous leaders disgraced and in jail, the new Klan began to lose members and influence.

## FUNDAMENTALISM IN RELIGION

Paralleling political nativism in the 1920s was the growth of religious fundamentalism. In many eastern Protestant churches, congregations focused less on religious practice and worship than on progressive social and reform activities in the larger community. By the early 1920s, a fundamentalist revival had developed in reaction to these tendencies, particularly in the South and Midwest. The fundamentalists emphasized a literal reading of the Bible, and they rejected the tenets of modern science as inconsistent with the revealed word of God. Fundamentalist publications and Bible colleges flourished, particularly among southern Baptists.

One special target of the fundamentalists was the theory of evolution, first set forth by Charles Darwin in his landmark work *The Origin of Species* (1859). By 1925, five southern state legislatures had passed laws restricting the teaching of evolution.

A young biology teacher, John T. Scopes, deliberately broke the Tennessee law prohibiting the teaching of Darwinism in 1925, in order to challenge it in court. The resulting trial that summer in Dayton, a small town near Chattanooga, drew international attention to the controversy. Scopes's defense team included attorneys from the American Civil Liberties Union and Clarence Darrow, the most famous trial lawyer in America. The prosecution was led by William Jennings Bryan, the old Democratic standard-bearer who had thrown himself into the fundamentalist and antievolutionist cause. Held in a circus atmosphere in sweltering heat, the trial attracted thousands of reporters and partisans to Dayton and was broadcast across the nation by the radio.

The Scopes "monkey trial"—so called because fundamentalists trivialized Darwin's theory into a claim that humans were descended from monkeys—became one of the most publicized and definitive moments of the decade. Scopes's guilt was never in question. The jury convicted him quickly, although the verdict was later thrown out on a technicality. The struggle over the teaching of evolution continued in an uneasy stalemate; state statutes were not repealed, but prosecutions for teaching evolution ceased. Fundamentalism, a religious creed and a cultural defense against the uncertainties of modern life, continued to have a strong appeal for millions of Americans.

# PROMISES POSTPONED

The prosperity of the 1920s was unevenly distributed and enjoyed across America. Older progressive reform movements that had pointed out inequities faltered in the conservative political climate. But the new era did inspire a range of critics deeply troubled by unfulfilled promises in American life.

## FEMINISM IN TRANSITION

The achievement of the suffrage removed the central issue that had given cohesion to the disparate forces of female reform activism. In addition, female activists of all persuasions found themselves swimming against a national tide of hostility to political idealism. During the 1920s, the women's movement split into two main wings over a fundamental disagreement about female identity. Should activists stress women's differences from men—their vulnerability and the double burden of work and family—and continue to press for protective legislation, such as laws that limited the length of the workweek for women? Or should they emphasize the ways that women were like men—sharing similar aspirations—and push for full legal and civil equality?

In 1920, the National American Woman Suffrage Association reorganized itself as the **League of Women Voters**. The league represented the historical mainstream of the suffrage movement, those who believed that the vote for women would bring a nurturing sensibility and a reform vision to American politics. This view was rooted in politicized domesticity, the notion that women had a special role to play in bettering society: improving conditions for working women, abolishing child labor, humanizing prisons and mental hospitals, and serving the urban poor. Most league members continued working in a variety of reform organizations, and the league itself concentrated on educating the new female electorate, encouraging women to run for office, and supporting laws for the protection of women and children.

A newer, smaller, and more militant group was the National Woman's Party (NWP), founded in 1916 by militant suffragist Alice Paul. The NWP downplayed the significance of suffrage and argued that women were still subordinate to men in every facet of life. The NWP opposed protective legislation for women, claiming that such laws reinforced sex stereotyping and prevented women from competing with men in many fields. Largely representing the interests of professional and business women, the NWP focused on passage of a brief Equal Rights Amendment (ERA) to the Constitution, introduced in Congress in 1923: "Men and women shall have equal rights throughout the United States and every place subject to its jurisdiction." Many of the older generation of women reformers opposed the ERA as elitist, arguing that far more women benefited from protective laws than were injured by them. ERA supporters countered that maximum-hours laws or laws prohibiting women from night work prevented women from getting many lucrative jobs.

**WHICH AMERICANS** were less likely to share in postwar prosperity and why?

myhistorylab
**Review Summary**

League of Women Voters   League formed in 1920 advocating for women's rights, among them the right for women to serve on juries and equal pay laws.

**Sheppard-Towner Act** The first federal social welfare law, passed in 1921, providing federal funds for infant and maternity care.

But most women's groups did not think there was a "fair field." Positions solidified. The League of Women Voters, the National Consumers' League, and the Women's Trade Union League opposed the ERA. ERA supporters generally stressed individualism, competition, and the abstract language of "equality" and "rights." ERA opponents emphasized the grim reality of industrial exploitation and the concentration of women workers in low-paying jobs in which they did not compete directly with men. ERA advocates dreamed of the labor market as it might be, one in which women might have the widest opportunity. Anti-ERA forces looked at the labor market as it was, insisting it was more important to protect women from existing exploitation. The NWP campaign failed to get the ERA passed by Congress, but the debates it sparked would be echoed during the feminist movement of the 1970s, when the ERA became a central political goal of a resurgent feminism.

The most significant, if limited, victory for feminist reformers was the 1921 **Sheppard-Towner Act**, which established the first federally funded health care program, providing matching funds for states to set up prenatal and child health care centers. These centers also provided public health nurses for house calls. Although hailed as a genuine reform breakthrough, especially for women in rural and isolated communities, the act aroused much opposition. Many Republicans, including President Harding, had supported it as a way to curry favor with newly enfranchised women voters. But their support faded when it became clear that there was little "gender gap" in voting patterns. The NWP disliked Sheppard-Towner for its assumption that all women were mothers. Birth control advocates such as Margaret Sanger complained that contraception was not part of the program. The American Medical Association (AMA) objected to government-sponsored health care and to nurses who functioned outside the supervision of physicians. By 1929, largely as a result of intense AMA lobbying, Congress cut off funds for the program.

**Figure 23.4 Mexican Immigration to the United States in the 1920s** Many Mexican migrants avoided official border crossing stations so they would not have to pay visa fees. Thus, these official figures probably underestimated the true size of the decade's Mexican migration. As the economy contracted with the onset of the Great Depression, immigration from Mexico dropped off sharply.

## MEXICAN IMMIGRATION

While immigration restriction sharply cut the flow of new arrivals from Europe, the 1920s also brought a dramatic influx of Mexicans to the United States. Mexican immigration, which was not included in the immigration laws of 1921 and 1924, had picked up substantially after the outbreak of the Mexican Revolution in 1911, when politically inspired violence and economic hardships provided incentives to cross the border to *El Norte* (see Figure 23.4).

The primary pull was the tremendous agricultural expansion occurring in the American Southwest. Irrigation and large-scale agribusiness had begun transforming California's Imperial and San Joaquin Valleys from arid desert into lucrative fruit and vegetable fields. Cotton pickers were needed in the vast plantations of Lower Rio Grande Valley in Texas and the Salt River Valley in Arizona. The sugar beet fields of Michigan, Minnesota, and Colorado attracted many Mexican farm workers. American industry had also begun recruiting Mexican workers, first to fill wartime needs and later to fill the gap left by the decline in European immigration.

The new Mexican immigration appeared more permanent than previous waves—that is, more and more newcomers stayed—and, like other immigrants, settled in cities. This was partly the unintended consequence of new policies designed to make immigration

**Mexican workers gathered** outside a San Antonio labor bureau in 1924. These employment agencies contracted Mexicans to work for Texas farmers, railroads, and construction companies. Note the three Anglo men in front (wearing suits and ties), who probably owned and operated this agency. During the 1920s, San Antonio's Mexican population doubled from roughly 40,000 to over 80,000, making it the second largest *colonia* in *El Norte* after Los Angeles.

more difficult. As the Border Patrol (established in 1924) made border crossing more difficult (through head taxes, visa fees, literacy tests, and document checks), what had once been a two-way process for many Mexicans became a one-way migration. Permanent communities of Mexicans in the United States grew rapidly. Many of the immigrants alternated between agricultural and factory jobs, depending on the seasonal availability of work. Mexican women often worked in the fields alongside their husbands. They also had jobs as domestics and seamstresses, or took in laundry and boarders.

Racism and local patterns of residential segregation confined most Mexicans to barrios. Housing conditions were generally poor, particularly for recent arrivals, who were forced to live in rude shacks without running water or electricity. Disease and infant mortality rates were much higher than average, and most Mexicans worked at low-paying, unskilled jobs and received inadequate health care. Legal restrictions passed by states and cities made it difficult for Mexicans to enter teaching, legal, and other professions. Mexicans were routinely banned from local public works projects as well. Many felt a deep ambivalence about applying for American citizenship. Loyalty to the Old Country was strong, and many cherished dreams of returning to live out their days in Mexico.

Nativist efforts to limit Mexican immigration were thwarted by the lobbying of powerful agribusiness interests. The Los Angeles Chamber of Commerce typically employed racist stereotyping in arguing to keep the borders open. Mexicans, it claimed, were naturally suited for agriculture, "due to their crouching and bending habits, . . . while the white is physically unable to adapt himself to them."

Mutual aid societies—*mutualistas*—became key social and political institutions in the Mexican communities of the Southwest and Midwest. They provided death benefits and widows' pensions for members and also served as centers of resistance to civil rights violations and discrimination. In 1928, the Federation of Mexican Workers Unions formed in response to a large farm labor strike in the Imperial Valley of California. A group of middle-class Mexican professionals in Texas organized the League of United Latin American Citizens (LULAC) in 1929. The founding of these organizations marked only the beginnings of a long struggle to bring economic, social, and racial equality to Mexican Americans.

## THE "NEW NEGRO"

The Great Migration spurred by World War I showed no signs of letting up during the 1920s, and African American communities in northern cities grew rapidly. By far the largest and most influential of these communities was New York City's Harlem. Previously a residential suburb, Harlem began attracting middle-class African Americans in the prewar years. After the war, heavy black migration from the South and the Caribbean encouraged real estate speculators and landlords to remake Harlem as an exclusively black neighborhood (see Map 23.1).

# MAP EXPLORATION

To explore an interactive version of this map, go to **http://www.prenhall.com/faraghertlc/map23.1**

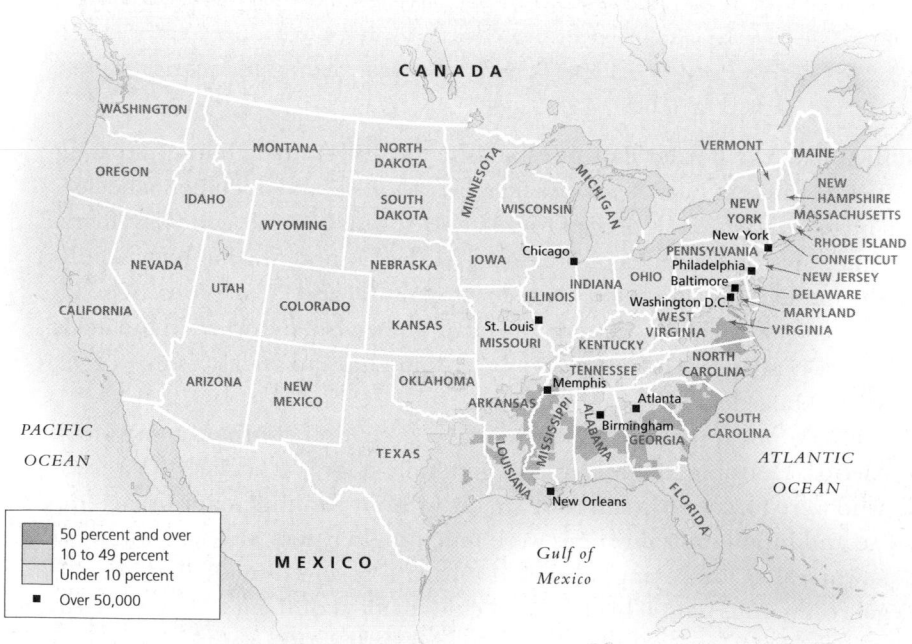

**MAP 23.1**

**Black Population, 1920** Although the Great Migration had drawn hundreds of thousands of African Americans to the urban North, the southern states of the former Confederacy still remained the center of the African American population in 1920.

WHY WERE African Americans drawn to Northern cities?

Harlem emerged as the demographic and cultural capital of black America, but its appeal transcended national borders, as mass migration from the Caribbean helped reshape the community. Between 1900 and 1930, some 300,000 West Indians emigrated to the United States, roughly half of whom settled in New York City. Some of the leading cultural, business, and political figures of the era—poet Claude McKay, newspaper publisher P. M. H. Savory, labor organizer Hubert Harrison, black nationalist Marcus Garvey—had roots in the West Indies. Most black Caribbean migrants came from societies where class differences mattered more than racial ones, and many refused to accept racial bigotry without protest. A large number also carried with them entrepreneurial experience that contributed to their success in running small businesses. Intraracial tensions and resentment between American-born blacks and an increasingly visible West Indian population were reflections of Harlem's transformation into a hemispheric center for black people.

Harlem was also headquarters to Marcus Garvey's Universal Negro Improvement Association. An ambitious Jamaican immigrant who had moved to Harlem in 1916, Garvey created a mass movement that stressed black economic self-determination and unity among the black communities of the United States, the Caribbean, and Africa. With colorful parades and rallies and a central message affirming pride in black identity, Garvey attracted as many as a million members worldwide. Garvey's best-publicized project was the Black Star Line, a black-owned and -operated fleet of ships that would link people of African descent around the world. But insufficient capital and serious financial mismanagement resulted in the spectacular failure of the enterprise. In 1923, Garvey was found guilty of mail fraud in his fundraising efforts; he later went to jail and was subsequently deported to England. Despite the disgrace, Harlem's largest newspaper, the *Amsterdam News*, explained Garvey's continuing appeal to African Americans: "In a world where black is despised, he taught them that black is beautiful. He taught them to admire and praise black things and black people."

The demand for housing in this restricted geographical area led to skyrocketing rents, but most Harlemites held low-wage jobs. This combination produced extremely overcrowded apartments, unsanitary conditions, and the rapid deterioration of housing stock. Disease and death rates were abnormally high. Harlem was well on its way to becoming a slum. Yet Harlem also boasted a large middle-class population and supported a wide array of churches, theaters, newspapers and journals, and black-owned businesses. It became a mecca, as poet and essayist James Weldon Johnson wrote, for "the curious, the adventurous, the enterprising, the ambitious, and the talented of the entire Negro world."

Harlem became the political and intellectual center for what writer Alain Locke called the "New Negro." Locke was referring to a new spirit in the work of black writers and intellectuals, an optimistic faith that encouraged African Americans to develop and celebrate their distinctive culture, firmly rooted in the history, folk culture, and experiences of African American people. This faith was the common denominator uniting the disparate figures associated with the **Harlem Renaissance**. The assertion of cultural independence resonated in the poetry of Langston Hughes and Claude McKay, the novels of Zora Neale Hurston and Jessie Fauset, the essays of Countee Cullen and James Weldon Johnson, the acting of Paul Robeson, and the blues singing of Bessie Smith.

There was a political side to the "New Negro" as well. The newly militant spirit that black veterans had brought home from World War I matured and found a variety of expressions in the Harlem of the 1920s. New leaders and movements began to appear alongside established organizations like the National Association

**Exploring America:** *Harlem Renaissance*

 **23–14**
Charles S. Johnson, *The City Negro* (1925)

**Harlem Renaissance**   A new African American cultural awareness that flourished in literature, art, and music in the 1920s.

for the Advancement of Colored People. A. Philip Randolph began a long career as a labor leader, socialist, and civil rights activist in these years, editing the *Messenger* and organizing the Brotherhood of Sleeping Car Porters.

Through the new mass media of radio and phonograph records, millions of Americans now listened and danced to a distinctively African American music, as jazz began to enter the cultural mainstream. Jazz found wildly enthusiastic fans in European capitals like Berlin and Paris, and noted classical composers such as Maurice Ravel and Igor Stravinsky treated it as a serious art form. The best jazz bands of the day, led by artists such as Duke Ellington, Fletcher Henderson, Cab Calloway, and Louis Armstrong, often had their performances broadcast live from such Harlem venues as the Cotton Club and Small's Paradise. Yet these clubs themselves were rigidly segregated. Black dancers, singers, and musicians provided the entertainment, but no African Americans were allowed in the audience. Chronicled in novels and newspapers, Harlem became a potent symbol to white America of the ultimate good time. Yet the average Harlemite never saw the inside of a nightclub. For the vast majority of Harlem residents, working menial jobs for low wages and forced to pay high rents, the day-to-day reality was depressingly different.

## ALIENATED INTELLECTUALS

War, Prohibition, growing corporate power, and the deep currents of cultural intolerance troubled many intellectuals in the 1920s. Some felt so alienated from the United States that they left to live abroad. In the early 1920s, Gertrude Stein, an American expatriate writer living in Paris, told the young novelist Ernest Hemingway: "All of you young people who served in the war, you are a lost generation." The phrase "a lost generation" was widely adopted as a label for American writers, artists, and intellectuals of the postwar era. Yet it is difficult to generalize about so diverse a community. For one thing, living abroad attracted only a handful of American writers. Alienation and disillusion with American life were prominent subjects in the literature and thought of the 1920s, but artists and thinkers developed these themes in very different ways.

The mass slaughter of World War I provoked revulsion and a deep cynicism about the heroic and moralistic portrayal of war so popular in the nineteenth century. Novelists Ernest Hemingway and John Dos Passos, who both served at the front as ambulance drivers, depicted the war and its aftermath in world-weary and unsentimental tones. The search for personal moral codes that would allow one to endure life with dignity and authenticity was at the center of Hemingway's fiction. In the taut, spare language of *The Sun Also Rises* (1926) and *A Farewell to Arms* (1929), he questioned idealism, abstractions, and large meanings.

Hemingway and F. Scott Fitzgerald were the most influential novelists of the era. Fitzgerald joined the army during World War I but did not serve overseas. His work celebrated the youthful vitality of the "Jazz Age" (a phrase he coined) but was also deeply distrustful of the promises of American prosperity and politics. Fitzgerald's finest work, *The Great Gatsby* (1925), written in the south of France, depicted the glamorous parties of the wealthy, while evoking the tragic limits of material success.

At home, many American writers engaged in sharp attacks on small-town America and what they viewed as its provincial values. Essayist H. L. Mencken, caustic editor of the *American Mercury*, heaped scorn on fundamentalists, Prohibition, and nativists, while ridiculing what he called the "American booboisie."

The most popular and acclaimed writer of the time was novelist Sinclair Lewis. In a series of novels satirizing small-town life, such as *Main Street* (1920) and especially *Babbitt* (1922), Lewis affectionately mocked his characters. His treatment of the central character in *Babbitt*—George Babbitt of Zenith—also had a strong element of self-mockery, for Lewis could offer no alternative set of values to Babbitt's crass self-promotion, hunger for success, and craving for social acceptance. In 1930, Lewis became the first American author to win the Nobel Prize for literature.

In the aftermath of the postwar Red Scare, American radicalism found itself on the defensive throughout the 1920s. But one *cause célèbre* did attract a great deal of support from intellectuals. In 1921, two Italian American immigrants, Nicola Sacco and Bartolomeo Vanzetti, were tried and convicted for murder in the course of robbing a shoe factory in South Braintree, Massachusetts. Neither Sacco, a shoemaker, nor Vanzetti, a fish peddler, had criminal records, but both had long been active in militant anarchist circles, labor organizing, and antiwar agitation. Their trial took place amidst an intense atmosphere of nativist and antiradical feeling, and both the judge and prosecuting attorney engaged in clearly prejudicial conduct toward the defendants. A six-year struggle to save Sacco and Vanzetti following the trial failed, despite attracting support from a broad range of liberal intellectuals, including Harvard law professor and future Supreme Court justice Felix Frankfurter. The two men were finally executed in 1927, and for many years, their case would remain a powerful symbol of how the criminal justice system could be tainted by political bias and anti-immigrant fervor.

Another side of intellectual alienation was expressed by writers critical of industrial progress and the new mass culture. The most important of these was a group of poets and scholars centered in Vanderbilt University in Nashville, Tennessee, collectively known as the Fugitives. They included Allen Tate, John Crowe Ransom, Donald Davidson, and Robert Penn Warren, all of whom invoked traditional authority, respect for the past, and older agrarian ways as ideals to live by.

## THE ELECTION OF 1928

The presidential election of 1928 served as a kind of national referendum on the Republican new era. It also revealed just how important ethnic and cultural differences had become in defining American politics. The contest reflected many of the deepest tensions and conflicts in American society in the 1920s: native-born versus immigrant; Protestant versus Catholic; Prohibition versus legal drinking; small-town life versus the cosmopolitan city; fundamentalism versus modernism; traditional sources of culture versus the new mass media (see Map 23.2).

The 1928 campaign featured two politicians who represented profoundly different sides of American life. Al Smith, the Democratic nominee for president, was a pure product of New York City's Lower East Side. Smith came from a background that included Irish, German, and Italian ancestry, and he was raised as a Roman Catholic. He rose through the political ranks of New York's Tammany Hall machine. A personable man with a deep sympathy for poor and working-class people, Smith served four terms as governor of New York, pushing through an array of laws

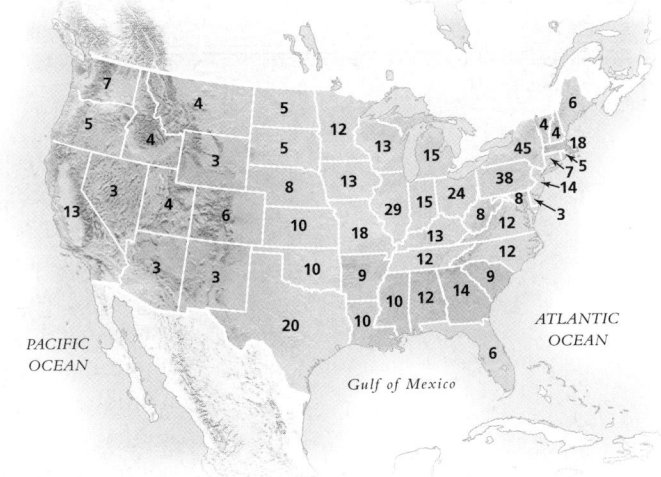

| | Electoral Vote (%) | Popular Vote (%) |
|---|---|---|
| **HERBERT HOOVER** (Republican) | 444 (82) | 21,391,993 (58.2) |
| **Alfred E. Smith** (Democrat) | 87 (17) | 15,016,169 (40.9) |
| **Norman Thomas** (Socialist) | — | 267,835 (0.7) |
| **Other parties** (Socialist Labor, Prohibition) | — | 62,890 (0.2) |

**MAP 23.2**

**The Election of 1928** Although Al Smith managed to carry the nation's twelve largest cities, Herbert Hoover's victory in 1928 was one of the largest popular and electoral landslides in the nation's history.

WHAT VALUES did Hoover claim to stand for in the election of 1928?

## CHRONOLOGY

**1920** Prohibition takes effect

Warren G. Harding is elected president

Station KDKA in Pittsburgh goes on the air

Census reports that urban population is greater than rural population for the first time

**1921** First immigration quotas are established by Congress

Sheppard-Towner Act establishes first federally funded health care program

**1923** Equal Rights Amendment is first introduced in Congress

Harding dies in office; Calvin Coolidge becomes president

**1924** Ku Klux Klan is at height of its influence

Dawes Plan for war reparations stabilizes European economies

Reed-Johnson Immigration Act tightens quotas established in 1921

**1925** Scopes trial pits religious fundamentalism against modernity

F. Scott Fitzgerald publishes *The Great Gatsby*

**1926** National Broadcasting Company establishes first national radio network

**1927** McNary-Haugen Farm Relief bill finally passed by Congress but is vetoed by President Coolidge as unwarranted federal interference in the economy

Warner Brothers produces *The Jazz Singer*, the first feature-length motion picture with sound

Charles Lindbergh makes first solo flight across the Atlantic Ocean

**1928** Kellogg-Briand Pact renounces war

Herbert Hoover defeats Al Smith for the presidency

**1929** Robert and Helen Lynd publish their classic community study, *Middletown*

---

reforming factory conditions, housing, and welfare programs. Two of his closest advisers were the progressives Frances Perkins and Belle Moskowitz. Smith thus fused older-style machine politics with the newer reform emphasis on state intervention to solve social problems.

Herbert Hoover easily won the Republican nomination after Calvin Coolidge announced he would not run for reelection. Hoover epitomized the successful and forward-looking American. An engineer and self-made millionaire, he offered a unique combination of experience in humanitarian war relief, administrative efficiency, and probusiness policies. Above all, Hoover stood for a commitment to voluntarism and individualism as the best method for advancing the public welfare. He was one of the best-known men in America and promised to continue the Republican control of national politics.

Smith himself quickly became the central issue of the campaign. His sharp New York accent, jarring to many Americans who heard it over the radio, marked him clearly as a man of the city. So did his brown derby and fashionable suits, as well as his promise to work for the repeal of Prohibition. As the first Roman Catholic nominee of a major party, Smith also drew a torrent of anti-Catholic bigotry, especially in the South and Midwest. For his part, Smith ran a largely conservative race. He appointed John Raskob, a Republican vice president of General Motors, to manage his campaign and tried to outdo Hoover in his praise for business. Democrats remained regionally divided over Prohibition, Smith's religion, and the widening split between rural and urban values. Hoover did not have to do much, other than take credit for the continued prosperity.

Hoover polled 21 million votes to Smith's 15 million, and swept the electoral college 444 to 87, including New York State. Even the Solid South, reliably

Democratic since the Civil War, gave five states to Hoover—a clear reflection of the ethnocultural split in the party. Yet the election offered important clues to the future of the Democrats. Smith ran better in the big cities of the North and East than any Democrat in modern times. He outpolled Hoover in the aggregate vote of the nation's twelve largest cities and carried six of them, thus pointing the way to the Democrats' future dominance with urban, northeastern, and ethnic voters.

## CONCLUSION

America's big cities, if not dominant politically, now defined the nation's cultural and economic life as never before. With Hollywood movies leading the way, the new mass media brought cosmopolitan entertainment and values to the remotest small communities. The culture of celebrity knew no geographic boundaries. New consumer durable goods associated with mass-production techniques—automobiles, radios, telephones, household appliances—were manufactured largely in cities. The advertising and public relations companies that sang their praises were also distinctly urban enterprises. Even with the curtailing of European immigration, big cities attracted a kaleidoscopic variety of migrants: white people from small towns and farms, African Americans from the rural South, Mexicans from across the border, and intellectuals and professionals looking to make their mark.

Many Americans, of course, remained deeply suspicious of postwar cultural and economic trends. Yet the partisans of Prohibition, members of the Ku Klux Klan, and religious fundamentalists usually found themselves on the defensive against what they viewed as alien cultural and economic forces centered in the cities. Large sectors of the population did not share in the era's prosperity. But the large numbers who did—or at least had a taste of good times—ensured Republican political dominance throughout the decade. Thus, America in the 1920s balanced dizzying change in the cultural and economic realms with conservative politics. The reform crusades that attracted millions during the progressive era were a distant memory. Political activism was no match for the new pleasures promised by technology and prosperity.

## REVIEW QUESTIONS

1. Describe the impact of the "second industrial revolution" on American business, workers, and consumers. Which technological and economic changes had the biggest impact on American society?

2. Analyze the uneven distribution of the 1920s' economic prosperity. Which Americans gained the most, and which were largely left out?

3. How did an expanding mass culture change the contours of everyday life in the decade following World War I? What role did new technologies of mass communication play in shaping these changes? What connections can you draw between the "culture of consumption" then and today?

4. What were the key policies and goals articulated by Republican political leaders of the 1920s? How did they apply these to both domestic and foreign affairs?

5. How did some Americans resist the rapid changes taking place in the post–World War I world? What cultural and political strategies did they employ?

6. Discuss the 1928 election as a mirror of the divisions in American society.

Flashcard Review

## KEY TERMS

**Harlem Renaissance** (p. 651)
**Immigration Act** (p. 644)
**League of Women Voters** (p. 647)
**Open shop** (p. 626)
**Sheppard-Towner Act** (p. 648)
**Volstead Act** (p. 642)
**Welfare capitalism** (p. 626)

## RECOMMENDED READING

Roger Daniels, *Guarding the Golden Door: American Immigration Policy and Immigrants Since 1882* (2002). A comprehensive overview by a pioneering scholar in the field, with special emphasis on how racism and ethnocentrism have shaped American immigration policy.

Victoria De Grazia, *Irresistible Empire: America's Advance through Twentieth Century Europe* (2005). A sophisticated analysis of how and why American commercial culture made such strong inroads into postwar Europe.

Lynn Dumenil, *The Modern Temper: America in the 1920s* (1995). An excellent synthesis of recent scholarship, which emphasizes the ambivalence that many Americans felt toward the emergence of modern society.

David J. Goldberg, *Discontented America: The United States in the 1920s* (1999). Focuses on Americans' continuing discomfort with racial, ethnic, religious, and class differences during the decade.

Desmond King, *Making Americans: Immigration, Race, and the Origins of Diverse Democracy* (2000). Fine analysis of the shift of U.S. immigration policies in the 1920s, with special attention to the influence of eugenics, and the long-term consequences of the new restrictive legislation.

Charles L. Ponce de Leon, *Self Exposure: Human Interest Journalism and the Emergence of Celebrity in America, 1890–1940* (2002). A thoughtful cultural history that explores the intersection of new mass media, journalism, and the American fascination with celebrity.

Susan Smulyan, *Selling Radio: The Commercialization of American Broadcasting, 1920–1934* (1994). The best analysis of the rise of commercial radio broadcasting in the 1920s.

Joshua Zeitz, *Flapper* (2006). A lively and well-researched new account of "the flapper" phenomenon, with emphasis on how a wide variety of women contributed to new cultural images for females.

For study resources for this chapter, go to **www.myhistorylab.com** and choose *Out of Many, Teaching and Learning Classroom Edition*. You will find a wealth of study and review material for this chapter, including pretests and posttests, customized study plan, key-term review flash cards, interactive map and document activities, and documents for analysis.

# The Scopes Monkey Trial as a Harbinger of Change

The Roaring '20's was a decade of turmoil and change in the United States on many levels. All this insecurity unsettled American traditionalists, especially religious fundamentalists. In rural states fundamentalists possessed a majority and control of the state legislature. John Washington Butler, a part time preacher and full time farmer served in the Tennessee legislature, had never read anything about evolution, but heard it denied the teachings of the Bible. He formulated a bill to forbid the teaching of evolution in the schools of Tennessee titled "AN ACT prohibiting the teaching of the Evolution Theory in all the Universities, Normals and all other public schools of Tennessee…"

The Butler Act immediately provoked a reaction from the American Civil Liberties Union. To challenge the law, John T. Scopes, part time biology teacher from Dayton, Tennessee, agreed to be arrested and placed on trial. The Scopes Monkey Trial, as it soon came to be known, became the first trial ever broadcast live on national radio. William Jennings Bryan, a prominent fundamentalist Christian, was seeking the Democratic presidential nomination again for the 1928 election and saw this trial as a vehicle to promote his candidacy. Clarence Darrow, nationally famous criminal lawyer, liberal, and agnostic, took the role of the defense. A circus of a trial followed.

**EXAMINE THE** history and impact of Tennessee's Butler Act (1925) and the trial of John T. Scopes that followed. Would contemporary observers have considered the jury decision to be the final decision on the issue of teaching evolution in the public schools of America-or did they have an inkling of the future of this issue?

John T. Scopes was found guilty and fined. The sentence was appealed to the Tennessee Supreme Court, which upheld the Dayton sentence, but set the sentence aside on a legal technicality that the jury had not set the fine levied against Scopes. The Butler Act would not be repealed by the Tennessee state legislature until 1967. The U.S. Supreme Court would declare similar laws to be unconstitutional in an Arkansas case in 1968. ■

Scopes trial in Tennessee in 1925. Clarence Darrow (standing) and John T. Scopes (seated behind Darrow, in a white shirt staring straight ahead).

## Butler Act, 1925

**That is** shall be unlawful for any teacher in any of the Universities, Normals and all other public schools of the State which are supported in whole or in part by the public school funds of the State, to teach any theory that denies the story of the Divine Creation of man as taught in the Bible, and to teach instead that man has descended from a lower order of animals.

In the national media Clarence Darrow and William Jennings Bryan were the chief protagonists of the trial. Darrow, the famous criminal lawyer, agnostic, and liberal stood for the defense. William Jennings Bryan volunteered for the prosecution and was given the honorary title of "colonel." During the trial a famous confrontation between Darrow and Bryan occurred when Bryan offered to testify as a biblical expert. Darrow demolished Bryan's arguments and even forced him to contradict the fundamentalist literal interpretation of Genesis as a seven-day creation event.■

## H. L. Mencken, Aftermath (of the Scopes Trial), *Baltimore Evening Sun*, September 14, 1925

**True enough**, even a superstitious man has certain inalienable rights. He has a right to harbor and indulge his imbecilities as long as he pleases, provided only he does not try to inflict them upon other men by force. He has a right to argue for them as eloquently as he can, in season and out of season. He has a right to teach them to his children. But certainly he has no right to be protected against the free criticism of those who do not hold them. He has no right to demand that they be treated as sacred. He has no right to preach them without challenge....

The meaning of religious freedom, I fear, is sometimes greatly misapprehended. It is taken to be a sort of immunity, not merely from governmental control but also from public opinion. A dunderhead gets himself a long-tailed coat, rises behind the sacred desk, and emits such bilge as would gag a Hottentot. Is it to pass unchallenged? If so, then what we have is not religious freedom at all, but the most intolerable and outrageous variety of religious despotism. Any fool, once he is admitted to holy orders, becomes infallible. Any half-wit, by the simple device of ascribing his delusions to revelation, takes on an authority that is denied to all the rest of us.■

▲ What Would Their Verdict Be? *The Daily Star* (Montreal), reprinted in the *Literary Digest*, July 25, 1925

## Epperson V. Arkansas, 393 U.S. 97 (1968)

**In the** present case, there can be no doubt that Arkansas has sought to prevent its teachers from discussing the theory of evolution because it is contrary to the belief of some that the Book of Genesis must be the exclusive source of doctrine as to the origin of man. No suggestion has been made that Arkansas' law may be justified by considerations of state policy other than the religious views of some of its citizens. It is clear that fundamentalist sectarian conviction was and is the law's reason for existence. Its antecedent, Tennessee's "monkey law," candidly stated its purpose: to make it unlawful "to teach any theory that denies the story of the Divine Creation of man as taught in the Bible, and to teach instead that man has descended from a lower order of animals." Perhaps the sensational publicity attendant upon the Scopes trial induced Arkansas to adopt less explicit language. It eliminated Tennessee's reference to "the story of the Divine Creation of man" as taught in the Bible, but there is no doubt that the motivation for the law was the same: to suppress the teaching of a theory which, it was thought, "denied" the divine creation of man.

Arkansas' law cannot be defended as an act of religious neutrality. Arkansas did not seek to excise from the curricula of its schools and universities all discussion of the origin of man. The law's effort was confined to an attempt to blot out a particular theory because of its supposed conflict with the Biblical account, literally read. Plainly, the law is contrary to the mandate of the First, and in violation of the Fourteenth, Amendment to the Constitution.

The judgment of the Supreme Court of Arkansas is Reversed.■

*I remembered seeing the people passing on their way to California . . . It hurt me to see the people in their rickety old cars, their clothes in tatters, escaping from the drought and the dust bowls.*

—Carlotta Silvas Martin, January 1936

**NRA** MEMBER U.S.

**WE DO OUR PART**

CIVILIAN CONSERVATION CORPS U S Co. 272

Work Pays America!
PROSPERITY
WORKS PROGRESS ADMINISTRATION

**Hands in their pockets,** hungry men stand numbly in one of New York City's breadlines. Said one observer: "The wretched men, many without overcoats or decent shoes, usually began to line up soon after six o'clock— in good weather or bad, rain or snow."

# 24

# THE GREAT DEPRESSION
# AND THE NEW DEAL
## 1929–1940

**WHAT WERE** the causes of the Great Depression, and what were its consequences?

**WHAT DID** FDR hope to accomplish in his first hundred days in office?

**WHAT GROUPS** formed the New Deal coalition?

**HOW DID** the New Deal expand the scope of the federal government in the South and West?

**YEARS OF DUST**

RESETTLEMENT ADMINISTRATION
Rescues Victims
Restores Land to Proper Use

**WHAT WERE** the limits of the New Deal's reforms, and what legacy did they leave?

**HOW DID** the Great Depression affect American cultural life during the 1930s?

# AMERICAN COMMUNITIES
## Sit-Down Strike at Flint:
## Automobile Workers Organize a New Union

IN THE GLOOMY EVENING OF FEBRUARY 11, 1937, 400 TIRED, unshaven, but very happy strikers marched out of the sprawling automobile factory known as Fisher Body Number 1 in Flint, Michigan. A makeshift banner on top of the plant announced "Victory Is Ours." A wildly cheering parade line of a thousand supporters greeted the strikers at the gates. Shouting with joy, honking horns, and singing songs, the celebrants marched to two other factories to greet other emerging strikers. After forty-four days, the great Flint sit-down strike was over.

Flint was the heart of production for General Motors, the largest corporation in the world. Originally a center for lumbering and then carriage making, Flint had boomed with the auto industry during the 1920s. Thousands of migrants streamed into the city, attracted by assembly-line jobs averaging about $30 a week.

The Great Depression hit Flint very hard. Employment at GM fell from a 1929 high of 56,000 to fewer than 17,000 in 1932. As late as 1938, close to half the city's families were receiving some kind of emergency relief. By that time, as in thousands of other American communities, Flint's private and county relief agencies had been overwhelmed by the needs of the unemployed and their families. Two new national agencies based in Washington, DC, the Federal Emergency Relief Administration and the Works Progress Administration, had replaced local sources of aid during the economic crisis. These New Deal programs embodied a new federal approach to providing relief and employment to American communities unable to cope with the enormity of mass unemployment.

The United Automobile Workers (UAW) came to Flint in 1936, seeking to organize GM workers into one industrial union. The previous year, Congress had passed the National Labor Relations Act (also known as the Wagner Act), which made union organizing easier by guaranteeing the right of workers to join unions and bargain collectively. But the obstacles to labor organizing were still enormous.

Unemployment was high, and GM had maintained a vigorous antiunion policy for years. By the fall of 1936, the UAW had signed up only a thousand members. The key moment came with the seizure of two Flint GM plants by a few hundred

auto workers on December 30, 1936. The idea was to stay in the factories until strikers could achieve a collective bargaining agreement with General Motors. "We don't aim to keep the plants or try to run them," explained one sit-downer to a reporter, "but we want to see that nobody takes our jobs. We don't think we're breaking the law, or at least we don't think we're doing anything really bad."

As the strike continued through January, support in Flint and around the nation grew. Overall production in the GM empire dropped from 53,000 vehicles per week to 1,500. Reporters and union supporters flocked to the plants. On January 11, in the so-called Battle of Running Bulls, strikers and their supporters clashed violently with Flint police and private GM guards. Michigan governor Frank Murphy, sympathetic to the strikers, brought in the National Guard to protect them. He refused to enforce an injunction obtained by GM to evict the strikers. In the face of determined unity by the sit-downers, GM gave in and recognized the UAW as the exclusive bargaining agent in all sixty of its factories.

The strike was perhaps the most important in American labor history, sparking a huge growth in union membership in the automobile and other mass-production industries. Out of the tight-knit, temporary community of the sit-down strike emerged a looser yet more permanent kind of community: a powerful, nationwide trade union of automobile workers. The UAW struggled successfully to win recognition and collective bargaining rights from other carmakers, such as Chrysler and Ford. The national UAW, like other new unions in the mass-production industries, was composed of locals around the country. The permanent community of unionized auto workers won significant improvements in wages, working conditions, and benefits. Locals also became influential in the political and social lives of their larger communities—industrial cities such as Flint, Detroit, and Toledo.

More broadly, the Flint sit-down embodied the new political and economic dynamics of Depression-era America. Workers, farmers, and consumers hard hit by the worst economic catastrophe in U.S. history called for a more activist federal government to relieve suffering and offer greater economic security for Americans.

Flint

# HARD TIMES

No twentieth-century event more profoundly affected American life than the Great Depression—the worst economic crisis in American history.

## UNDERLYING WEAKNESSES OF THE 1920S' ECONOMY

It would be oversimplifying to say that the 1929 stock market collapse "caused" the **Great Depression**. Signs of deep economic weakness had already begun to surface amid the general prosperity of the 1920s. First, workers and consumers received too small a share of the enormous increases in labor productivity. Between 1923 and 1929, manufacturing output per worker-hour increased by 32 percent, while wages rose only 8 percent. Gains in wages and salaries were extremely uneven. While workers in newer industries such as automobiles and electrical manufacturing enjoyed pay increases, those in textiles and coal mining watched their wages fall. Moreover, the rise in productivity itself had encouraged overproduction in many industries, and the farm sector had never been able to regain the prosperity of the World War I years (see Chapter 23).

To be sure, Americans overall in the 1920s had more money to spend on consumer goods. But economic insecurity was a brutal fact of life for millions of families, especially in rural communities. Most industrial workers endured regular bouts of unemployment and seasonal layoffs. Eighty percent of the nation's families had no savings at all, and an old age spent in poverty was far more likely for the average worker than "retirement." The most important weakness in the economy was the extremely unequal distribution of income, yielding the greatest concentration of wealth in the nation's history (see Table 24.1).

## THE BULL MARKET AND THE CRASH

Stock trading in the late 1920s captured the imagination of the broad American public. The stock market resembled a sporting arena, millions following stock prices as avidly as the exploits of Babe Ruth or Jack Dempsey.

During the bull market of the 1920s, stock prices increased at roughly twice the rate of industrial production. By the end of the decade, stocks that had been bought mainly on the basis of their earning power, which was passed on to stockholders in the form of dividends, now came to be purchased only for the resale value after their prices rose.

Yet only about 3 million Americans—out of a total population of 120 million—owned any stocks at all. Many of these stock buyers had been lured into the market through easy-credit margin accounts, which allowed investors to purchase stocks with a small down payment (as low as 10 percent), borrowing the rest from a broker and using the shares as collateral on the loan. Just as installment plans had stimulated the automobile and other industries, "buying on the margin" brought new customers to the stock market. Investment trusts, similar to today's mutual funds, attracted many new investors with promises of high returns. Corporations found that lending excess capital to stockbrokers was more profitable than investing in new technologies. All these factors fed an expansive and optimistic atmosphere on Wall Street.

Although often portrayed as a one- or two-day catastrophe, the Wall Street crash of 1929 was actually a steep slide. The bull market peaked in early September, and prices drifted downward. Once expectations of an endless boom began to melt, the market had to decline. On Monday, October 28, the Dow lost 38 points—13 percent of its value. The next day—"Black Tuesday," October 29—the

**Review Summary**

## IMAGE KEY
for pages 660–661

a. The National Recovery Agency seal with an eagle holding a cog in one talon and lightning bolts in the other over the slogan "We Do Our Part."
b. The Civilian Conservation Corps' emblem.
c. Hungry men stand in a bread line in New York City.
d. A Works Progress Administration poster, depicting a farmer and a miner shaking hands.
e. An old fashioned box radio in a wooden cabinet.
f. Anxious citizens crowd along Wall Street sidewalks while automobiles edge down the street on Black Tuesday, October 29, 1929.
g. Gov. Franklin D. Roosevelt shakes hands with a poor mine worker during a campaign trip.
h. Ben Shahn's 1936 poster for the Resettlement Administration.
i. Isaac Soyer's "Employment Agency," oil on canvas.

**Great Depression**   The nation's worst economic crisis, extending through the 1930s, producing unprecedented bank failures, unemployment, and industrial and agricultural collapse.

TABLE 24.1

## Distribution of Total Family Income Among Various Segments of the Population, 1929–44 (in Percentages)

| Year | Poorest Fifth | Second Poorest Fifth | Middle Fifth | Second Wealthiest Fifth | Wealthiest Fifth | Wealthiest 5 Percent |
|------|---------------|----------------------|--------------|-------------------------|------------------|----------------------|
| 1929 | 12.5 | | 13.8 | 19.3 | 54.4 | 30.0 |
| 1935–36 | 4.1 | 9.2 | 14.1 | 20.9 | 51.7 | 26.5 |
| 1941 | 4.1 | 9.5 | 15.3 | 22.3 | 48.8 | 24.0 |
| 1944 | 4.9 | 10.9 | 16.2 | 22.2 | 45.8 | 20.7 |

Adapted from U.S. Bureau of the Census, *Historical Statistics of the United States, Colonial Times to 1970*, Bicentennial Edition (Washington, DC: U.S. Government Printing Office, 1975), 301.

bottom fell out and panic selling took hold. For many stocks, no buyers were available at any price.

The situation worsened. The market's fragile foundation of credit, based on the margin debt, quickly crumbled. Many investors with margin accounts had to sell when stock values fell. Since the shares themselves represented the security for their loans, more money had to be put up to cover the loans when prices declined.

The stock market crash undermined the confidence, investment, and spending of businesses and the well-to-do. Manufacturers cut production and began laying off workers, which brought further declines in consumer spending, and so another round of production cutbacks ensued. A spurt of consumer spending might have checked this downward spiral, but consumers had less to spend as industries laid off workers and reduced work hours. With a shrinking market for products, businesses feared to expand. A large proportion of the nation's banking funds had been tied to the speculative bubble. Many banks began to fail as anxious depositors withdrew their funds, which were uninsured, costing thousands of families all their savings. And an 86 percent plunge in agricultural prices between 1929 and 1933, compared to a decline in agricultural production of only 6 percent, brought terrible suffering to America's farmers.

## MASS UNEMPLOYMENT

At a time when unemployment insurance did not exist and public relief was completely inadequate, the loss of a job could mean economic catastrophe for workers and their families. Massive unemployment across America became the most powerful sign of a deepening depression. In 1930, the Department of Labor estimated that roughly 9 percent of the labor force was out of work. By 1933, 12.6 million workers—over one-quarter of the labor force—were without jobs. (Other sources put the figure that year above 16 million, or nearly one out of every three workers.) No statistics tell us how long people were unemployed or how many Americans found only part-time work.

Many Americans, raised believing that they were responsible for their own fate, blamed themselves for their failure to find work. Unemployment upset the psychological balance in many families by undermining the traditional authority of the male breadwinner. Women, because their labor was cheaper than men's,

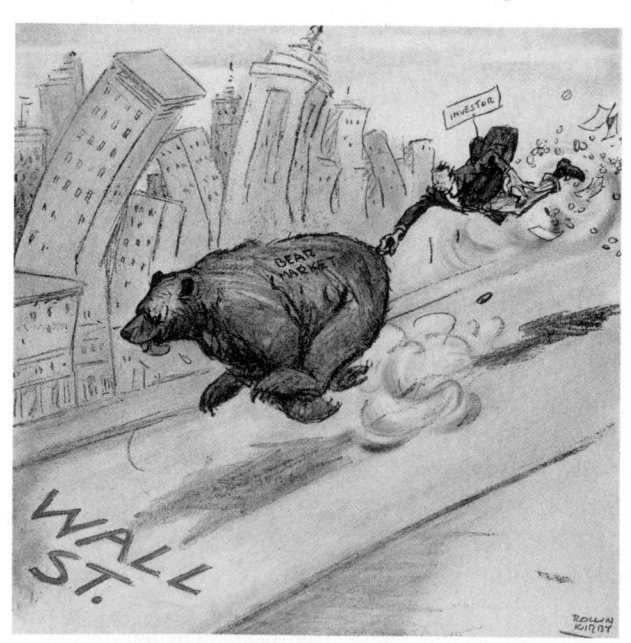

**Rollin Kirby's 1929** cartoon depicts an individual investor losing his money as he clings to a bear running down Wall Street. The bear symbolizes an atmosphere of panic selling and heavy losses, the opposite of a "bull" market in which investor confidence spurs buying and faith in the future.

found it easier to keep jobs. Female clerks, secretaries, maids, and waitresses earned much less than male factory workers, but their jobs were more likely to survive hard times. Men responded in a variety of ways to unemployment. Some withdrew emotionally; others became angry or took to drinking. A few committed suicide. In 1934, one Chicago social worker summed up the strains she found in families: "Fathers feel they have lost their prestige in the home; there is much nagging, mothers nag at the fathers, parents nag at the children. Children of working age who earn meager salaries find it hard to turn over all their earnings and deny themselves even the greatest necessities and as a result leave home." Fear of unemployment and a deep desire for security marked the Depression generation.

## HOOVER'S FAILURE

The enormity of the Great Depression overwhelmed traditional—and meager—sources of relief. In most communities across America, these sources were a patchwork of private agencies and local government units, such as towns, cities, or counties. They simply lacked the money, resources, and staff to deal with the worsening situation.

There was great irony, even tragedy, in President Hoover's failure to respond to human suffering. During World War I he had effectively administered Belgian war relief abroad and won wide praise for his leadership of the Food Administration at home. As a leader of the progressive wing of the Republican Party, Hoover had long championed a kind of cooperative individualism that relied upon public-spirited citizens. Failing to face the facts of the depression, Hoover worried more about undermining individual initiative than providing actual relief for victims. He ignored all mounting evidence to the contrary when he claimed, in his 1931 State of the Union Address, "Our people are providing against distress from unemployment in true American fashion by magnificent response to public appeal and by action of the local governments."

Hoover's plan for recovery centered on restoring business confidence. His administration's most important institutional response to the depression was the Reconstruction Finance Corporation (RFC), established in early 1932 and based on the War Finance Corporation of the World War I years. The RFC was designed to make government credit available to ailing banks, railroads, insurance companies, and other businesses, thereby stimulating economic activity. The key assumption here was that the problem was one of supply (for businesses) rather than demand (from consumers). But given the public's low purchasing power, most businesses were not interested in obtaining loans for expansion. In July 1932, congressional Democrats pushed through the Emergency Relief Act, which authorized the RFC to lend $300 million to states that had exhausted their own relief funds. Hoover grudgingly signed the bill, but less than $30 million had actually been given out by the end of 1933.

Two other federal actions—in each case, the opposite of what should have been done—worsened the situation. First, the Federal Reserve, whose policies of low interest rates and easy credit in the late 1920s had helped fuel the speculative

**Dorothea Lange captured** the lonely despair of unemployment in *White Angel Breadline, San Francisco, 1933.* During the 1920s, Lange had specialized in taking portraits of wealthy families, but by 1932, she could no longer stand the contradiction between her portrait business and "what was going on in the street." She said of this photograph: "There are moments such as these when time stands still and all you can do is hold your breath and hope it will wait for you."

Dorothea Lange, "White Angel Breadline, San Francisco, 1933." Copyright the Dorothea Lange Collection, The Oakland Museum of California, City of Oakland. Gift of Paul S. Taylor.

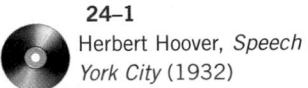

**24–1**
Herbert Hoover, *Speech at New York City* (1932)

**Isaac Soyer's** *Employment Agency*, a 1937 oil painting, offered one of the decade's most sensitive efforts at depicting the anxiety and sense of isolation felt by millions of depression-era job hunters.

Isaac Soyer, "Employment Agency," 1937. Oil on canvas, 34 1/2" × 45". Whitney Museum of American Art.

boom in stock buying, now tightened credit sharply. That caused interest rates to spike, putting heavy pressure on the nation's banking system, especially the smaller banks on which farmers, merchants, and local businessmen relied. Without any state or federal insurance, more than 5,000 rural banks and ethnic-group-oriented savings and loans institutions failed between 1929 and 1932, and more than 9 million depositors lost their savings. Second, in 1930 Congress passed (and Hoover signed) the Smoot-Hawley Tariff, raising import duties to their highest levels in American history. Supporters, including the president, claimed that this would protect American farmers from global competition and raise farm prices. But as other nations responded by raising their own tariffs world trade declined steeply, exacerbating the economic collapse.

## A Global Crisis and the Election of 1932

By 1931 the depression had spread not only across the United States but also throughout the world, a sign of how interdependent the global economy had become. The immediate problem was the highly unstable system of international finance. The 1919 peace settlement had saddled Germany with $33 billion in war reparations, owed largely to Great Britain and France. The United States had loaned money to the British and French during the war, and American banks had loaned large sums to Germany in the 1920s. Germany used these loans to pay reparations to the British and French, who in turn used these reparations to repay their American debts. The 1929 stock market crash put an end to American loans for Germany, thus removing a critical link in the international cash flow. When Germany then defaulted on its reparations, Great Britain and France in turn stopped paying what they owed to this country. As German banks collapsed and unemployment swelled, nervous European investors sold their American stocks, depressing the stock market even further. Great Britain and several other European nations also abandoned the gold standard and devalued (lowered) their currency relative to the dollar. This made American goods more difficult to sell abroad, further dampening production at home. With many nations also raising their tariffs to protect national industries, international trade slowed to a crawl. The total

## QUICK REVIEW

**The 1932 Election**

◆ Republicans renominated Hoover.

◆ The Democratic platform differed little from the Republican platform.

◆ Franklin D. Roosevelt's victory was a repudiation of Hoover.

volume of global trade declined from about $36 billion in 1929 to roughly $12 billion by 1932. American banks, badly hurt by both domestic depositors clamoring for their money and the foreign withdrawal of capital, began failing in record numbers. In 1931 alone, 2,294 U.S. banks failed, double the number that had collapsed in 1930.

By 1932 the desperate mood of many Americans was finding expression in direct, sometimes violent, protests that were widely covered in the press. On March 7, communist organizers led a march of several thousand Detroit auto workers and unemployed in Dearborn. Ford-controlled police fired tear gas and bullets, killing four demonstrators and seriously wounding fifty others.

The spring of 1932 also saw the **"Bonus Army"** begin descending on Washington, DC. This protest took its name from Congress's promise in 1924 to pay every veteran of World War I a $1,000 bonus—in the form of a bond that would not mature until 1945. The veterans who were gathering in Washington demanded immediate payment of the bonus in cash. By summer, they and their families numbered around 20,000 strong and were camping out all over the capital city. The House passed a bill for immediate payment, but when the Senate refused to agree, most of the downcast veterans left. At the end of July, U.S. Army troops, led by Chief of Staff General Douglas MacArthur, forcibly evicted the remaining 2,000 veterans. The spectacle of these unarmed and unemployed men, the heroes of 1918, being driven off by bayonets and bullets, provided the most disturbing evidence yet of the failure of Hoover's administration.

In 1932, Democrats nominated Franklin D. Roosevelt, governor of New York, for the presidency. Roosevelt's plans for recovery were vague and contradictory. He frequently attacked Hoover for reckless and extravagant spending and accused him of concentrating too much power in Washington, but he also spoke of the need for government to meet "the problem of underconsumption" and to help in "distributing wealth and products more equitably." Above all, Roosevelt stressed, "the country demands bold, persistent experimentation." Hoover bitterly condemned Roosevelt's ideas as a "radical departure" from the American way of life. But with the depression growing worse every day, probably any Democrat would have defeated Hoover. The Democratic victory was overwhelming. Roosevelt carried forty-two states, taking the electoral college 472 to 59 and the popular vote by about 23 million to 16 million. Democrats won big majorities in both the House and the Senate. The stage was set for FDR's "new deal" (see Map 24.1).

# FDR and the First New Deal

No twentieth-century president had a greater impact on American life and politics than Franklin Delano Roosevelt (FDR). To a large degree, the New Deal was a product of his astute political skills and the sheer force of his personality. The only president ever elected to four terms, FDR would

## MAP EXPLORATION
To explore an interactive version of this map, go to
http://www.prenhall.com/faraghertlc/map24.1

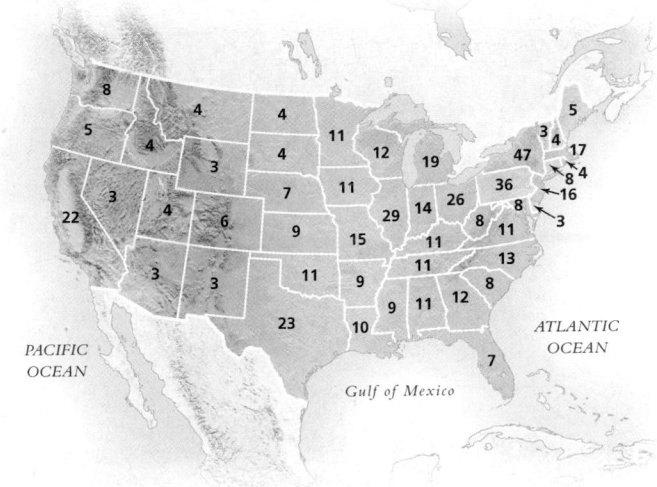

| | Electoral Vote (%) | Popular Vote (%) |
|---|---|---|
| **FRANKLIN D. ROOSEVELT** (Democrat) | 472 (89) | 22,809,638 (57) |
| **Herbert Hoover** (Republican) | 59 (11) | 15,758,901 (40) |
| **Minor parties** | — | 1,153,306 (3) |

**MAP 24.1**
**The Election of 1932** Democrats owed their overwhelming victory in 1932 to the popular identification of the depression with the Hoover administration. Roosevelt's popular vote was about the same as Hoover's in 1928, and FDR's electoral college margin was even greater.

DID THE election of 1932 represent a repudiation of Hoover or an affirmation of Roosevelt?

**24–3**
Franklin Delano Roosevelt, *Speech at San Francisco* (1932)

**WHAT DID** FDR hope to accomplish in his first hundred days in office?

**myhistorylab**
**Review Summary**

**Bonus Army** Unemployed veterans of World War I gathering in Washington in 1932 demanding payment of service bonuses not due until 1945.

This *New Yorker* magazine cover depicted an ebullient Franklin D. Roosevelt riding to his 1933 inauguration in the company of a glum Herbert Hoover. This drawing typified many mass media images of the day, contrasting the different moods and temperaments of the new president and the defeated incumbent.

**24–2**
Franklin Delano Roosevelt, *First Inaugural Address* (1933)

**24–7**
Mrs. Henry Weddington, *Letter to President Roosevelt* (1938)

**Fireside chat** Speeches broadcast nationally over the radio in which President Franklin D. Roosevelt explained complex issues and programs in plain language, as though his listeners were gathered around the fireside with him.

**Emergency Banking Act** 1933 act which gave the president broad discretionary powers over all banking transactions and foreign exchange.

loom as the dominant personality in American political life through twelve years of depression and global war.

## FDR THE MAN

Franklin Delano Roosevelt was born in 1882 in Dutchess County, New York, where he grew up an only child, secure and confident, on his family's vast estate. Roosevelt's education at private school, Harvard, and Columbia Law School reinforced his aristocratic family's sense of civic duty. In 1905, he married his distant cousin, Anna Eleanor Roosevelt, a niece of President Theodore Roosevelt. He was elected as a Democrat to the New York State Senate in 1910, served as assistant secretary of the navy from 1913 to 1920, and was nominated for vice president by the Democrats in the losing 1920 campaign.

In the summer of 1921, Roosevelt was stricken with polio; he was never to walk again without support. His illness proved the turning point in his life. The wealthy aristocrat, for whom everything had come relatively easily, now personally understood the meaning of struggle and hardship.

Elected governor of New York in 1928, Roosevelt served two terms and won a national reputation for reform. As governor, he instituted unemployment insurance, strengthened child labor laws, enacted tax relief for farmers, and provided pensions for the old.

## "THE ONLY THING WE HAVE TO FEAR": RESTORING CONFIDENCE

In the first days of his administration, Roosevelt conveyed a sense of optimism and activism that helped restore the badly shaken confidence of the nation. "First of all," he told Americans in his Inaugural Address on March 4, 1933, "let me assert my firm belief that the only thing we have to fear is fear itself." The very next day, as people lined up to pull savings out of failing banks and hoarded cash under their mattresses, he issued an executive order calling for a four-day "bank holiday" to stop the collapse of the country's financial system.

The new Congress was not scheduled to convene until the end of 1933, but Roosevelt convened a special session to deal with the banking crisis, unemployment aid, and farm relief. On March 12, he broadcast his first **"fireside chat"** to explain the steps he had taken to meet the financial emergency. These radio broadcasts became a standard part of Roosevelt's political technique, and they proved enormously successful. They gave courage to ordinary Americans and communicated a genuine sense of compassion from the White House.

Congress immediately passed the **Emergency Banking Act**, which gave the president broad discretionary powers over all banking transactions and foreign exchange. By the middle of March, about half the country's banks, holding about 90 percent of the nation's deposits, were open for business again.

Roosevelt assembled a group of key advisers, the "brains trust," to counsel him in the White House. They gave conflicting advice. Some advocated fiscal conservatism to restore confidence in the dollar; others pushed for central planning to manage the economy. But the "brain trusters" shared a basic belief in expert-directed government–business cooperation. Structural economic reform, they argued, must accept the modern reality of large corporate enterprise based on mass production and distribution.

## THE HUNDRED DAYS

From March to June 1933—"the Hundred Days"—FDR pushed through Congress an extraordinary amount of depression-fighting legislation. Roosevelt's enormous political skill—as a power broker, as a coalition builder, and as a communicator with the American public—was crucial. What came to be called the **New Deal** was no unified program to end the depression but rather an improvised series of reform and relief measures, some of which completely contradicted each other. Still, all the New Deal programs were united by the fundamental goals of relief, reform, and recovery.

Five measures were particularly important and innovative. The Civilian Conservation Corps (CCC), established in March as an unemployment relief effort, provided work for jobless young men in protecting and conserving the nation's natural resources. Road construction, reforestation, flood control, and national park improvements were some of the major projects performed in work camps across the country.

In May, Congress authorized $500 million for the Federal Emergency Relief Administration (FERA). Half the money went as direct relief to the states; the rest was distributed on the basis of a dollar of federal aid for every three dollars of state and local funds spent for relief. This system of outright federal grants differed significantly from Hoover's loans-only approach. Establishment of work relief projects, however, was left to state and local governments.

The Agricultural Adjustment Administration (AAA) was set up to provide immediate relief to the nation's farmers. The AAA established a new federal role in agricultural planning and price setting. It established parity prices for basic farm commodities. The concept of parity pricing was based on the purchasing power that farmers had enjoyed during the prosperous years of 1909 to 1914. That period now became the benchmark for setting "floor"— that is, minimum—prices for farm commodities. The AAA also incorporated the principle of subsidy, whereby farmers received benefit payments in return for reducing acreage or otherwise cutting production where surpluses existed. New taxes on food processing were to pay for these programs.

The **Tennessee Valley Authority (TVA)** proved to be one of the most unique and controversial projects of the New Deal era. The TVA, an independent public corporation, built dams and power plants, produced cheap fertilizer for farmers, and, most significantly, for the first time brought low-cost electricity to thousands of people in six southern states. Denounced by some as a dangerous step toward socialism, the TVA stood for decades as a model of how careful government planning could dramatically improve the social and economic welfare of an underdeveloped region.

On the very last of the Hundred Days, Congress passed the **National Industrial Recovery Act**, the closest attempt yet at a systematic plan for economic recovery. In theory, each industry would be self-governed by a code hammered out by

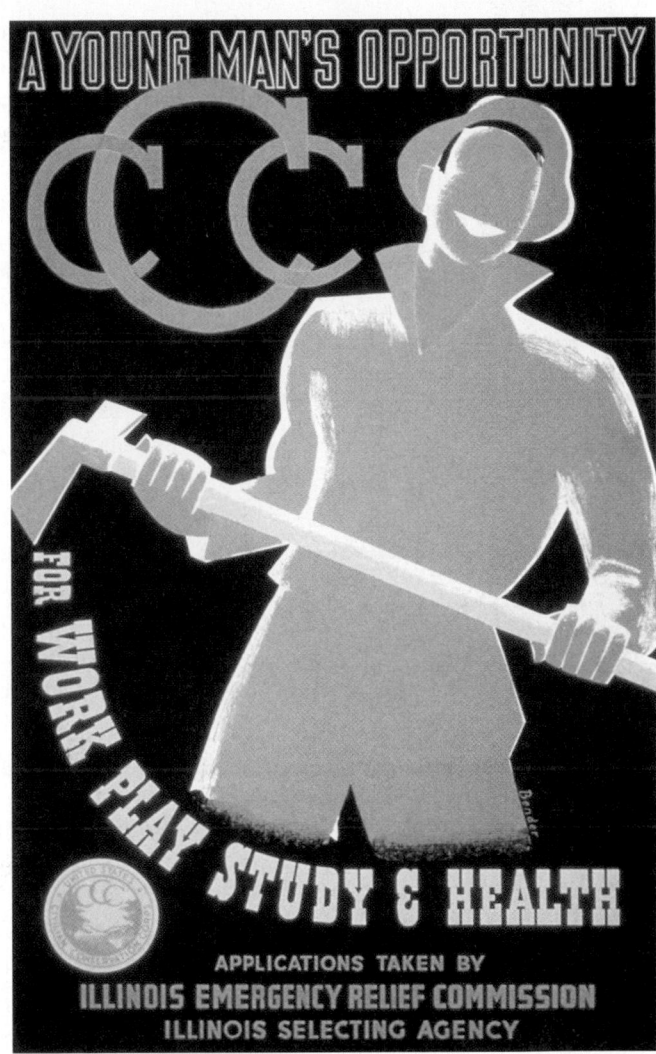

**A recruitment poster** represents the Civilian Conservation Corps (CCC) as much more than simply an emergency relief measure, stressing character building and the opportunity for self-improvement. By the time the CCC expired in 1942, it had become one of the most popular of all the New Deal programs.

**New Deal**  The economic and political policies of the Roosevelt administration in the 1930s.

**Tennessee Valley Authority (TVA)** Federal regional planning agency established to promote conservation, produce electric power, and encourage economic development in seven Southern states.

**National Industrial Recovery Act** 1933 act which was meant to be a systematic plan for economic recovery.

representatives of business, labor, and consumers. Once approved by the National Recovery Administration (NRA) in Washington, the codes would have the force of law. In practice, almost all the National Recovery Administration codes were written by the largest firms in any given industry; labor and consumers got short shrift. The sheer administrative complexities involved with code writing and compliance made a great many people unhappy with the NRA's operation.

Finally, the Public Works Administration (PWA), led by Secretary of the Interior Harold Ickes, authorized $3.3 billion for the construction of roads, public buildings, and other projects. The idea was to provide jobs and, through increased consumer spending, stimulate the economy. "Priming the pump," this strategy was called, borrowing a phrase from what an old-time farmer had to do to get his well pump going. Eventually the PWA spent over $4.2 billion building roads, schools, post offices, bridges, courthouses, and other public buildings, which in thousands of communities today remain tangible reminders of the New Deal era.

During the Hundred Days and the months immediately following, Congress passed other legislation that would have important long-range effects. The Glass-Steagall Act created the Federal Deposit Insurance Corporation (FDIC), which provided protection to individual depositors by guaranteeing accounts of up to $5,000 in case of bank failure. Congress also established the Securities and Exchange Commission (SEC) to regulate stock exchanges and brokers, require full financial disclosures, and curb the speculative practices that had contributed to the 1929 crash. The 1934 National Housing Act, aimed at stimulating residential construction and making home financing more affordable, set up the Federal Housing Administration (FHA). The FHA insured loans made by banks and other private lenders for home building and home buying.

## ROOSEVELT'S CRITICS, RIGHT AND LEFT

From the beginning, the New Deal had loud and powerful critics on the right who complained bitterly that FDR had overstepped the traditional boundaries of government action. From the left came angry cries that Roosevelt had not done nearly enough.

### QUICK REVIEW

**The National Recovery Administration (NRA)**

- Sought to halt the slide in prices, wages, and employment.
- Tended to help business, often at the expense of labor.
- Declared unconstitutional in 1935.

**myhistorylab**

**Overview:** *Key Legislation of the First New Deal*

---

# OVERVIEW | Key Legislation of the First New Deal ("Hundred Days," March 9–June 16, 1933)

| Legislation | Purpose |
|---|---|
| Emergency Banking Relief Act | Enlarged federal authority over private banks. |
| | Government loans to private banks. |
| Civilian Conservation Corps | Unemployment relief. |
| | Conservation of natural resources. |
| Federal Emergency Relief Administration | Direct federal money for relief, funneled through state and local governments. |
| Agricultural Adjustment Administration | Federal farm aid based on parity pricing and subsidy. |
| Tennessee Valley Authority | Economic development and cheap electricity for Tennessee Valley. |
| National Industrial Recovery Act | Self-regulating industrial codes to revive economic activity. |
| Public Works Administration | Federal public works projects to increase employment and consumer spending. |

Pro-Republican newspapers and the American Liberty League, a group of conservative businessmen organized in 1934, vehemently attacked the administration for what they considered its attack on property rights, the growing welfare state, and the alleged decline of personal liberty. But in the 1934 election, Democrats crushed their right-wing critics and—countering the losses that incumbent parties usually suffer at midterm—increased their majorities in both houses of Congress.

More troublesome for Roosevelt were the vocal and popular movements on the left. These found the New Deal too timid. In California, the well-known novelist and socialist Upton Sinclair entered the 1934 Democratic primary for governor by running on a program he called EPIC ("End Poverty in California"). He proposed a monthly pension of $50 for all poor people over age sixty and championed a government-run system of "production for use" (rather than profit) workshops for the unemployed. Sinclair shocked local and national Democrats by winning the primary easily. He lost a close general election only because the Republican candidate received heavy financial and tactical support from wealthy Hollywood studio executives and frightened regular Democrats.

Huey Long, Louisiana's flamboyant backcountry orator, posed the greatest potential threat to Roosevelt's leadership. Long had captured Louisiana's governorship in 1928 by attacking the state's entrenched oil industry and calling for a radical redistribution of wealth. In office, he significantly improved public education, roads, medical care, and other public services, winning the loyalty of the state's poor farmers and industrial workers. Elected to the U.S. Senate in 1930, Long came to Washington with national ambitions. He at first supported Roosevelt, but in 1934, his own presidential ambitions and his impatience with the pace of New Deal measures led to a break with FDR.

Long organized the Share Our Wealth Society. Its purpose, he thundered, "was to break up the swollen fortunes of America and to spread the wealth among all our people." Although Long's economics were fuzzy, his "Every Man a King" slogan touched a deep popular nerve. A secret poll in the summer of 1935 stunned the Democratic National Committee by showing that Long might attract 3 or 4 million votes for president. Only his assassination that September by a political enemy of his corrupt political machine prevented Long's third-party candidacy, which might have proved disastrous for FDR.

A newly militant labor movement also loomed as a force to be reckoned with. Unemployed Councils, organized largely by the Communist Party in industrial cities, held marches and rallies demanding public works projects and relief payments. Section 7a of the National Industrial Recovery Act required that workers be allowed to bargain collectively with employers through representatives of their own choosing. Although this provision of the NIRA was not enforced, it did help raise expectations and sparked union organizing. Almost 1.5 million workers took part in some 1,800 strikes in 1934.

## LEFT TURN AND THE SECOND NEW DEAL

The popularity of Coughlin, Sinclair, and Long suggested Roosevelt might be losing electoral support among workers, farmers, the aged, and the unemployed. In addition, FDR had to contend with a conservative Supreme Court that did not share the public's enthusiasm for the New Deal. In May 1935, in *Schecter* v. *United States*, the Court found the NRA unconstitutional in its entirety. In early 1936, ruling in *Butler* v. *United States*, the Court invalidated the AAA, declaring it an unconstitutional attempt at regulating agriculture. Looking

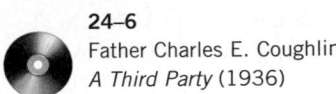
**24–6**
Father Charles E. Coughlin,
*A Third Party* (1936)

**24–4**
Huey Long, *Share The Wealth*
(1935)

**WHAT GROUPS** formed the New Deal coalition?

**Review Summary**

**Social Security Act of 1935** Act establishing federal old-age pensions and unemployment insurance.

**National Labor Relations Act** Act establishing Federal guarantee of right to organize trade unions and collective bargaining.

**24–12**
*Investigation of Strikebreaking*
(1939)

---

**QUICK REVIEW**

**The Social Security Act**

♦ Provided unemployment compensation, old-age pensions, and aid for dependent mothers and children and the blind.

♦ The law excluded more than a fourth of all workers.

♦ Funded by a payroll tax.

---

**myhistorylab**

**Overview:** *Key Legislation of the Second New Deal (1935–38)*

---

toward the 1936 election and eager for a popular mandate, Roosevelt and his closest advisers responded by turning left and offering new social-reform programs.

## THE SECOND HUNDRED DAYS

In April 1935 the administration pushed through Congress the Emergency Relief Appropriation Act, which allocated $5 billion for large-scale public works programs for the jobless. New Deal economists argued that each government dollar spent had a multiplier effect, pumping two or three dollars into the depressed gross domestic product. Over the next seven years, the WPA, under Harry Hopkins's leadership, oversaw the employment of more than 8 million Americans on a vast array of construction projects: roads, bridges, dams, airports, and sewers. Among the most innovative WPA programs were community service projects that employed thousands of jobless artists, musicians, actors, and writers.

The landmark **Social Security Act of 1935** provided for old-age pensions and unemployment insurance. The old-age pensions were quite small at first, as little as $10 a month. And no one could collect unemployment who had not first lost a job. But the law, which has subsequently been amended many times, established the crucial principle of federal responsibility for America's most vulnerable citizens.

In July 1935, Congress passed the **National Labor Relations Act**, often called the Wagner Act for its chief sponsor, Democratic senator Robert F. Wagner of New York. For the first time, the federal government guaranteed the right of American workers to join, or form, independent labor unions and to bargain collectively for improved wages, benefits, and working conditions. The law also defined and prohibited unfair labor practices by employers, including firing workers for union activity. The Wagner Act, described as "the Magna Carta for labor," quickly proved a boon to union growth, especially in previously unorganized industries such as automobiles, steel, and textiles.

## LABOR'S UPSURGE: RISE OF THE CIO

The Wagner Act greatly facilitated union organizing and galvanized the moribund labor movement. In 1932, only 2.8 million workers were union members, a half-million fewer than in 1929 and more than 2 million fewer than in 1920. Yet by 1942,

---

# OVERVIEW | Key Legislation of the Second New Deal (1935–38)

| Legislation | Purpose |
|---|---|
| **Emergency Relief Appropriations Act (1935)** | Large-scale public works program for the jobless (includes Works Progress Administration). |
| **Social Security Act (1935)** | Federal old-age pensions and unemployment insurance. |
| **National Labor Relations Act (1935)** | Federal guarantee of right to organize trade unions and collective bargaining. |
| **Resettlement Administration (1935)** | Relocation of poor rural families. |
| | Reforestation and soil erosion projects. |
| **National Housing Act (1937)** | Federal funding for public housing and slum clearance. |
| **Fair Labor Standards Act (1938)** | Federal minimum wage and maximum hours. |

unions claimed more than 10.5 million members, nearly a third of the total nonagricultural work force. This remarkable turnaround was one of the key events of the depression era. The growth in the size and power of the labor movement permanently changed the work lives and economic status of millions, as well as the national and local political landscapes.

At the core of this growth was a series of dramatic successes in the organization of workers in large-scale, mass-production industries such as automobiles, steel, rubber, electrical goods, and textiles. The conservative, craft-oriented unions that dominated the American Federation of Labor (AFL) had largely ignored workers in these industries. At the 1935 AFL convention, a group of more militant union officials led by John L. Lewis (of the United Mine Workers) and Sidney Hillman (of the Amalgamated Clothing Workers) formed the **Congress for Industrial Organizations** and set about organizing mass-production workers by industry—regardless of a worker's level of skill. They differed from nearly all old-line AFL unions by calling for the inclusion of black and women workers.

**Photographer Milton Brooks** won the first Pulitzer Prize for photography with this 1941 image for the *Detroit News*. He captured a violent labor confrontation in front of the Ford Motor Company's River Rouge plant, as private armed guards, employed by Ford, assault and beat organizers for the United Automobile Workers.

The gruff son of a Welsh miner, Lewis was articulate, ruthless, and very ambitious. He saw the new legal protection given by the Wagner Act as a historic opportunity. Lewis knew that establishing permanent unions in the mass-production industries would be a bruising battle. He committed the substantial resources of the United Mine Workers to a series of organizing drives, focusing first on the steel and auto industries. Many CIO organizers were communists or radicals of other kinds, and their dedication, commitment, and willingness to work within disciplined organizations proved invaluable in the often dangerous task of creating industrial unions. After the dramatic breakthrough in a 1937 sit-down strike against General Motors at Flint, Michigan, membership in CIO unions grew rapidly. In eight months, membership in the United Automobile Workers (UAW) alone soared from 88,000 to 400,000. CIO victories in the steel, rubber, and electrical industries followed, but often at a very high cost. One bloody example of the perils of union organizing was the 1937 Memorial Day Massacre in Chicago. In a field near the struck Republic Steel Mill in South Chicago, police fired into a crowd of union supporters, killing ten workers and wounding scores more.

In 1938, CIO unions, now boasting nearly 4 million members, withdrew from the AFL and reorganized themselves as the Congress of Industrial Organizations. For the first time ever, the labor movement had gained a permanent place in the nation's mass-production industries. Organized labor took its place as a key power broker in Roosevelt's New Deal and the national Democratic Party.

## THE NEW DEAL COALITION AT HIGH TIDE

Both major political parties looked forward to the 1936 elections as a national referendum, and the campaign itself was exciting and hard fought. The Republicans nominated Governor Alfred M. Landon of Kansas, who had gained attention by surviving the Democratic landslide of 1934. His campaign served as a lightning rod for all those, including many conservative Democrats, who were dissatisfied with Roosevelt and the direction he had taken.

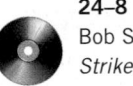

**24–8**
Bob Stinson, *Flint Sit-Down Strike* (1936)

**Congress for Industrial Organizations**
An alliance of industrial unions that spurred the 1930s organizational drive among the mass-production industries.

Huge and enthusiastic crowds greeted Roosevelt, especially in large cities. Still, the vast majority of the nation's newspapers endorsed Landon. And a widely touted "scientific" poll by the *Literary Digest* forecast a Republican victory in November.

Election day erased all doubts: Roosevelt carried every state but Maine and Vermont, polling 61 percent of the popular vote. Democrats increased their substantial majorities in the House and Senate as well. The *Literary Digest*, it turned out, had polled only people with addresses in telephone directories and car registration records, thus omitting poorer Americans who had no telephones or cars—and who supported Roosevelt. In 1936, the Democrats drew millions of new voters into the political process, and at the same time, forged a new coalition of voters that would dominate national politics for two generations.

This **"New Deal coalition,"** as it came to be known, included white Southern Democrats, ethnics who supported big-city political machines, unionized workers (including those being organized by the CIO), and many depression-hit farmers. Black voters in the North and West, long affiliated with the Republicans as "the party of Lincoln," went Democratic in record numbers. (Of course, blacks were largely barred from voting in the South.)

The Great Depression was by no means over. But the New Deal's active response to the nation's misery, particularly its bold initiatives in 1935, had obviously struck a powerful chord with the American electorate. Roosevelt was especially popular among first- and second-generation immigrants of Catholic and Jewish descent, and the New Deal drew enthusiastic support from millions who had never bothered with politics. Popular federal programs like Social Security, the WPA, and Home Owners Loan Corporation mortgages changed the consciousness of a generation of the ethnic working class. In exchange for their votes, they now looked to the state—especially the federal government—for relief, protection, and help in achieving the American dream.

## THE NEW DEAL IN THE SOUTH AND WEST

The New Deal had its profoundest impact in the South and the West. From Great Plains farming communities to Pacific Coast cities, federal subsidy and management became an integral part of western life. In the process, the New Deal helped propel both the South and the West into the modern era and laid the groundwork for the postwar "Sunbelt."

### MODERNIZING SOUTHERN FARMING AND LANDHOLDING

In 1930, less than half of all southern farmers owned their own land; over three-quarters of the region's African American farmers and nearly half its white farmers were sharecroppers or tenants. The continued dominance of a few crops—mainly cotton and tobacco—had only intensified the depression by glutting the market and keeping crop prices at rock bottom. The Agricultural Adjustment Administration succeeded in boosting prices by paying farmers to "plow under"—take their land out of production. But particularly in the South, these federal subsidies went overwhelmingly to large landowners, who controlled local county committees charged with administering AAA programs. Most planters did not share these payments with sharecroppers and tenants, and individual protest was usually futile.

New Deal policies helped destroy the old sharecropping and tenant system largely by helping landowners prosper. Those farmers who had access to government funds were able to diversify their crops, consolidate holdings, and work their

---

**HOW DID** the New Deal expand the scope of the federal government in the South and West?

**myhistorylab**
**Review Summary**

**New Deal coalition** Coalition that included traditional-minded white Southern Democrats, big-city political machines, industrial workers of all races, trade unionists, and many Depression-hit farmers.

land more efficiently with laborsaving machinery, such as tractors and mechanical harvesters. Mechanized farming and government-subsidized reductions of cultivated land cut the demand for labor and increased evictions. Uprooted tenants, sharecroppers, and day laborers found themselves on the road in search of work; many thousands migrated to cities and towns.

No New Deal initiative had more impact on southern communities than electrification. In the early 1930s, only about 3 percent of rural Southerners had access to electric power and, hence, to household appliances and farm machinery. The Tennessee Valley Authority and the Rural Electrification Administration (REA) helped millions of southern households move into the modern era by making electricity available for the first time. It built sixteen dams across some 800 miles of the Tennessee River basin, bringing flood control and electric power to hundreds of thousands of families in seven southern states. It also significantly reduced consumer electric rates in many cities and towns by providing a cheaper alternative to private utilities. By 1944, the TVA was the largest power producer in the United States.

## AN ENVIRONMENTAL DISASTER: THE DUST BOWL

An ecological and economic catastrophe of unprecedented proportions struck the southern Great Plains in the mid-1930s. The region had suffered several drought years in the early 1930s. Such dry spells occurred regularly, in roughly twenty-year cycles. But this time, the parched earth became swept up in violent dust storms, the likes of which had never been seen before. The dust storms were largely the consequence of years of stripping the landscape of its natural vegetation. During World War I, wheat brought record-high prices on the world market, and for the next twenty years Great Plains farmers turned the region into a vast wheat factory.

Great Plains farmers had created an ecological time bomb that exploded when drought returned in the early 1930s. With native grasses destroyed to grow wheat, there was nothing left to prevent soil erosion. Dust storms blew away tens of millions of acres of rich topsoil, and thousands of farm families left the region. Those who stayed suffered calamitous economic and psychological losses. The hardest-hit regions were western Kansas, eastern Colorado, western Oklahoma, the Texas Panhandle, and eastern New Mexico—an area that a Denver journalist named the "Dust Bowl" (see Map 24.2).

Black blizzards of dust a mile and a half high rolled across the landscape, darkening the sky and whipping the earth into great drifts that settled over hundreds of miles. Dust storms made it difficult for humans and livestock to breathe, and destroyed crops and trees over vast areas. "Dust pneumonia" and other respiratory infections afflicted thousands, and many travelers found themselves stranded in automobiles and trains unable to move.

myhistorylab

**Exploring America:** *The Dust Bowl*

## MAP EXPLORATION

To explore an interactive version of this map, go to
**http://www.prenhall.com/faraghertlc/map24.2**

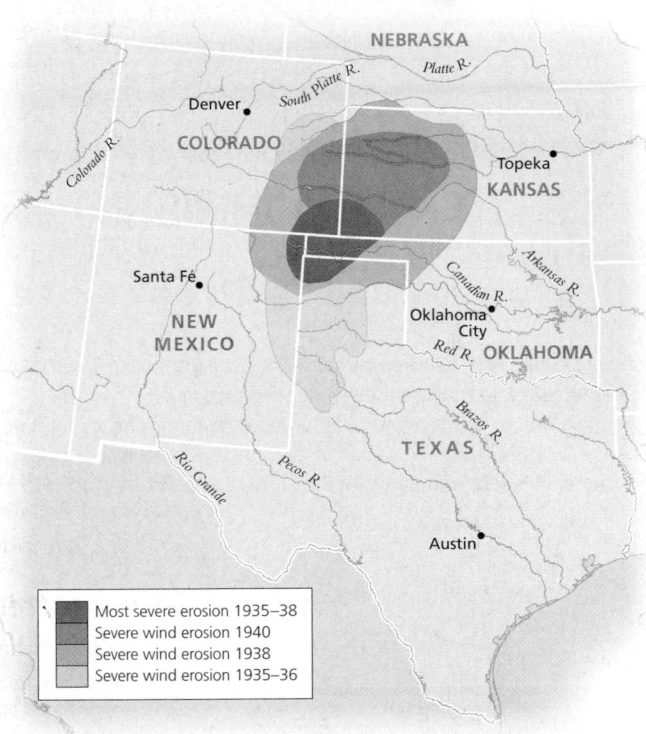

Most severe erosion 1935–38
Severe wind erosion 1940
Severe wind erosion 1938
Severe wind erosion 1935–36

**MAP 24.2**

**The Dust Bowl, 1935–40**   This map shows the extent of the Dust Bowl in the southern Great Plains. Federal programs designed to improve soil conservation, water management, and farming practices could not prevent a mass exodus of hundreds of thousands out of the Great Plains.

WHAT WERE the reasons for this ecological disaster and why was it particularly damaging to people in the region?

**YEARS OF DUST**

**RESETTLEMENT ADMINISTRATION**
**Rescues Victims**
**Restores Land to Proper Use**

*Years of Dust.* This 1936 poster by the artist and photographer Ben Shahn, served to publicize the work of Resettlement Administration, which offered aid to destitute farm families hit hard by the Dust Bowl. Shahn's stark imagery here was typical of the documentary aesthetic associated with the Depression-era art and photography.

 **24–14**
Carey McWilliams, *Okies in California* (1939)

### QUICK REVIEW

**The SCS**
- Soil Conservation Service created in response to soil erosion in the Dust Bowl.
- SCS energetically enforced new agricultural practices.
- 1940: Affected area had been reduced from 50 million acres to 4 million acres.

In most Great Plains counties, from one-fifth to one-third of the families applied for relief; in the hardest-hit communities, as many as 90 percent of the families received direct government aid. Several federal agencies intervened directly to relieve the distress. Many thousands of Great Plains farm families were given direct emergency relief by the Resettlement Administration. Other federal assistance included crop and seed loans, moratoriums on loan payments, and temporary WPA jobs. The AAA paid wheat farmers millions of dollars not to grow what they could not sell and encouraged the diversion of acreage from soil-depleting crops like wheat to soil-enriching crops such as sorghum.

The federal government also pursued longer-range policies designed to alter land-use patterns, reverse soil erosion, and restore grasslands. The Department of Agriculture, under Secretary Henry A. Wallace, sought to change farming practices through the Soil Conservation Service (SCS), which conducted research into controlling wind and water erosion, set up demonstration projects, and offered technical assistance, supplies, and equipment to farmers engaged in conservation work on farms and ranches.

While large landowners and ranchers were reaping sizable benefits from New Deal programs, thousands of tenant farmers and sharecropper families were being forced off the land in cotton-growing regions of Texas, Oklahoma, Missouri, and Arkansas. They became part of a stream of roughly 300,000 people, disparagingly called "Okies," who migrated to California in the 1930s. California migrants included victims of the Dust Bowl, but the majority were blue-collar workers and small businessmen hoping to improve their economic lot. California suffered from the depression along with the rest of the nation, but it still offered more jobs, higher wages, and higher relief payments than the southern plains. Most Okies could find work only as poorly paid agricultural laborers in the fertile San Joaquin and Imperial Valley districts, facing scorn as "poor white trash" while they struggled to create communities amid the squalor of migrant labor camps. Only the outbreak of World War II and the pressing demand for labor allowed migrants to improve their situation significantly.

Mexican farm laborers faced stiff competition from Dust Bowl refugees. By the mid-1930s, they no longer dominated California's agricultural workforce. In 1936, an estimated 85 to 90 percent of the state's migratory workers were white Americans, as compared to less than 20 percent before the depression. Mexican farm worker families who managed to stay employed in California, Texas, and Colorado saw their wages plummet.

Southwestern communities, responding to racial hostility from unemployed whites and looking for ways to reduce their welfare burden, campaigned to deport Mexicans and Mexican Americans. Employers, private charities, and the Immigration and Naturalization Service joined in this effort. Authorities made little effort to distinguish citizens from aliens; most of the children they deported had been born in the United States and, hence, were citizens. Los Angeles County had the most aggressive campaign, using boxcars to ship out more than 13,000 Mexicans between 1931 and 1934. The hostile climate convinced thousands more to leave voluntarily.

## WATER POLICY

The New Deal ushered in the era of large-scale water projects, designed to provide irrigation and cheap power and to prevent floods. The long-range impact of these undertakings on western life was enormous. The key government agency in this realm was the Bureau of Reclamation of the Department of the Interior, established in 1902. The bureau's original responsibility had been to construct dams and irrigation works and thereby to encourage the growth of small farms throughout the arid regions of the West. Until the late 1920s, its efforts had been of little consequence. But its fortunes changed when its focus shifted to building huge multipurpose dams designed to control entire river systems (see Map 24.3).

 MAP EXPLORATION

To explore an interactive version of this map, go to **http://www.prenhall.com/faraghertlc/map24.3**

**MAP 24.3**

**The New Deal and Water**   This map illustrates U.S. drainage areas and the major large-scale water projects begun or completed by federal agencies in them during the New Deal.

WHAT WAS the impact of irrigation, cheap power, flood control, and recreation areas on America's western communities?

The first of these projects, Boulder Dam (later renamed Hoover Dam), was completed in 1935 with the help of funds from the Public Works Administration. Its total cost was $114 million, to be offset by the sale of its hydroelectric power. Los Angeles and neighboring cities built a 259-mile aqueduct, costing $220 million, to channel water to their growing populations. Lake Mead, created by construction of the dam, became the world's largest artificial lake, extending 115 miles up the canyon and providing a popular new recreation area. The dam's irrigation water helped make the Imperial Valley, covering over 500,000 acres, one of the most productive agricultural districts in the world.

The success of Boulder Dam transformed the Bureau of Reclamation into a major federal agency commanding huge resources. In 1938, it completed the All-American Canal—an 80-mile channel connecting the Colorado River to the Imperial Valley and with a 130-mile branch to the Coachella Valley. This opened up more than a million acres of desert land to the cultivation of citrus fruits, melons, vegetables, and cotton. Irrigation districts receiving water promised to repay, without interest, the cost of the canal over a forty-year period.

The largest power and irrigation project of all was Grand Coulee Dam, northwest of Spokane, Washington. Completed in 1941, it was designed to convert the power of the Columbia River into cheap electricity and to irrigate previously uncultivated land, thereby stimulating economic development in the Pacific Northwest. Tens of thousands of workers built Grand Coulee, and the project pumped millions of dollars into the region's badly depressed economy. Between 1933 and 1940, Washington State ranked first in per-capita federal expenditures. In the longer run, Grand Coulee provided the cheapest electricity in the United States and helped attract new manufacturing to a region previously dependent on the export of lumber and ore.

These technological marvels and the new economic development they stimulated were not without an environmental and human cost. Grand Coulee and smaller dams nearby reduced the Columbia River, long a potent symbol of the western wilderness, to a string of lakes. Spawning salmon could no longer run the river above the dam. In California, the federal guarantee of river water made a relative handful of large farmers fabulously wealthy. But tens of thousands of farm workers, mostly of Mexican descent, labored in the newly fertile fields for very low wages, and pesticides undermined their health. The Colorado River, its flow into the sea drastically diminished, began to build up salt deposits, making its water increasingly unfit for drinking or irrigation. Water pollution in the form of high salinity continues to plague the 2,000-mile river.

## A NEW DEAL FOR INDIANS

The New Deal brought important changes and some limited improvements to the lives of Indians. In 1933, some 320,000 Indian people, belonging to about 200 tribes, lived on reservations, mostly in Oklahoma, Arizona, New Mexico, and South Dakota. Indians were the nation's poorest people with an infant mortality rate twice that of whites. Alcoholism, tuberculosis, and measles were at much higher rates on the reservation than off. Half of all those on reservations were landless. The Bureau of Indian Affairs (BIA) had a long history of corruption and mismanagement. For years it had tried to assimilate Indians through education, in the process routinely interfering with Indian religious and tribal customs.

In 1933, Roosevelt appointed John Collier to bring change to the BIA. As the new BIA head, Collier pledged to "stop wronging the Indians and to rewrite the cruel and stupid laws that rob them and crush their family lives." Collier became the driving force behind the Indian Reorganization Act (IRA) of 1934. The IRA reversed the allotment provisions of the Dawes Severalty Act of 1887, which had weakened tribal sovereignty by shifting the distribution of land from tribes to individuals (see Chapter 18). The new legislation permitted the restoration of surplus reservation lands to tribal ownership, and it allocated funds to purchase additional lands and for economic development. At its heart, the IRA sought to restore tribal structures by making the tribes instruments of the federal government. Any tribe that ratified the IRA could then elect a tribal council that would enjoy federal recognition as the legal tribal government. Collier fought first to get the legislation through a reluctant Congress, uneasy with reversing the longstanding policy of Indian assimilation.

The more difficult battle involved winning approval by Indian peoples. Collier's efforts to win acceptance of the IRA met with mixed results on the reservations. Under Collier, the BIA became much more sensitive to Indian cultural and religious freedom. The number of Indian people employed by the BIA itself increased from a few hundred in 1933 to more than 4,600 in 1940. Collier trumpeted the principle of Indian political autonomy, a radical idea for the day. But in practice both the BIA and Congress regularly interfered with reservation governments, especially in money matters. For the long run, Collier's most important legacy was the reassertion of the status of Indian tribes as semisovereign nations. In 1934, a Department of the Interior lawyer, Nathan Margold, wrote a legal opinion that tribal governments retained all their original powers—their "internal sovereignty"—except when these were specifically limited by acts of Congress. Decades later, U.S. courts would uphold the Margold opinion, leading to a significant restoration of tribal rights and land to Indian peoples of the West.

# THE LIMITS OF REFORM

In his second Inaugural Address, Roosevelt emphasized that much remained to be done to remedy the effects of the depression. With his stunning electoral victory, the future for further social reform seemed bright. Yet by 1937, the New Deal was in retreat. A rapid political turnaround over the next two years put continuing social reform efforts on the defensive.

## COURT PACKING

After his landslide reelection, and still smarting from the Supreme Court having struck down the NRA and the AAA, Roosevelt wanted more friendly justices. In February 1937, he asked Congress to allow him to make new Supreme Court appointments whenever a justice failed to retire upon reaching age seventy. This would expand the Court from nine to a maximum of fifteen justices, the majority presumably sympathetic to the New Deal. Newspapers almost unanimously denounced FDR's "court-packing bill."

Even more damaging was the determined opposition from a congressional coalition of conservatives and outraged New Dealers. The president gamely fought on, disingenuously insisting that his purpose was simply to reduce the workload of elderly Supreme Court justices. But as the battle dragged on through the spring and summer, FDR's claims weakened. Then a conservative justice retired, permitting Roosevelt to make his first Court appointment. More important, several justices began voting for rather than against Roosevelt's law, so that the Court upheld the constitutionality of key measures from the second New Deal, including the Social Security Act and the National Labor Relations Act. At the end of August 1937,

WHAT WERE the limits of the New Deal's reforms, and what legacy did they leave?

Review Summary

FDR backed off his court-packing scheme and accepted a compromise bill that reformed lower court procedures but left the Supreme Court untouched.

FDR lost the battle for his judiciary proposal, but he may have won the war for a more responsive Court. Still, the political price was very high. The Court fight badly weakened Roosevelt's relations with Congress. Many more conservative Democrats now felt free to oppose further New Deal measures.

## THE WOMEN'S NETWORK

The New Deal brought a measurable, if temporary, increase in women's political influence. For those women associated with social reform, the New Deal opened up possibilities to effect change. A "women's network," linked by personal friendships and professional connections, made its presence felt in national politics and government. Most of the women in this network had deep roots in progressive era movements promoting suffrage, labor law reform, and welfare programs (see Chapter 21).

The center of the women's network, First Lady Eleanor Roosevelt became a powerful political figure, using her prominence to fight for liberal causes. She revolutionized the role of the political wife by taking a position involving no institutional duties and turning it into a base for independent action. Privately, she enjoyed great influence with her husband, and behind the scenes she supported a wide network of women professionals and reformers whom she had come to know in the 1920s. As a strong supporter of protective labor legislation for women, she owed much to the social reform tradition of the women's movement.

Eleanor Roosevelt worked vigorously for antilynching legislation, compulsory health insurance, and child-labor reform, and she fought racial discrimination in New Deal relief programs. She saw herself as the guardian of "human values" within the administration, a buffer between depression victims and government bureaucracy. She frequently testified before legislative committees, lobbied her husband privately and the Congress publicly, and wrote a widely syndicated newspaper column.

Mrs. Roosevelt's closest political ally was Molly Dewson. A longtime social worker and suffragist, Dewson wielded great political clout as director of the Women's Division of the national Democratic Party. Under her leadership, women for the first time played a central role in shaping the party platform and running election campaigns. Dewson proved a tireless organizer, traveling to cities and towns around the country and educating women about Democratic policies and candidates. Her success impressed the president, and he relied on her judgment in recommending political appointments. Dewson placed more than a hundred women in New Deal positions.

Perhaps Dewson's most important success came in persuading FDR to appoint Frances Perkins secretary of labor—the first woman cabinet member in U.S. history. As labor secretary, Perkins embodied the gains made by women in appointive offices. Her department was responsible for creating the Social Security Act and the Fair Labor Standards Act of 1938, both of which incorporated protective measures long advocated by women reformers. Perkins defined feminism as "the movement of women to participate in service to society." New Deal agencies opened up spaces for scores of women in the federal bureaucracy. These women were concentrated in Perkins's Labor Department, the FERA and WPA, and the Social Security Board. In addition, the social work profession, which remained roughly two-thirds female in the 1930s, grew enormously in response to the massive relief

**24–9**
Meridel Le Sueur, *Women on the Breadlines* (1932)

and welfare programs. In sum, although the 1930s saw no radical challenges to existing male and female roles, working-class women and professional women held their own and managed to make some gains.

During the Great Depression, most women continued to perform unpaid domestic labor, work that was not covered by the Social Security Act. A growing minority, however, also worked outside the home for wages and salaries. By 1940, 25.1 percent of the workforce was female. Hard times increased the ranks of married working women. But sexual stereotyping still routinely forced most women into low-paying, low-status jobs.

## A NEW DEAL FOR MINORITIES?

Long near the bottom of the American economic ladder, African Americans suffered disproportionately in the Great Depression. The old saying among black workers that they were "last hired, first fired" was never truer than during times of high unemployment.

Overall, the Roosevelt administration made little overt effort to combat the racism and segregation entrenched in American life. FDR was especially worried about offending the powerful Southern Democratic congressmen. And local administration of many federal programs meant that most early New Deal programs routinely accepted discrimination. The CCC established separate camps for African Americans. The NRA labor codes tolerated lower wages for black workers doing the same jobs as white workers. African Americans could not get jobs with the TVA. When local AAA committees in the South reduced acreage and production to boost prices, thousands of black sharecroppers and farm laborers were forced off the land. Racism was also embedded in the entitlement provisions of the Social Security Act, which excluded domestics and casual laborers—whose ranks were disproportionately African American and Hispanic—from old-age insurance.

Yet some limited gains were made. Roosevelt issued an executive order in 1935 banning discrimination in WPA projects. In cities, the WPA enabled thousands of jobless African Americans to survive, at minimum wages of $12 a week. Between 15 and 20 percent of all WPA employees were black people, although African Americans made up less than 10 percent of the nation's population. The Public Works Administration, under Harold Ickes, constructed a number of integrated housing complexes and employed more than its fair share of black workers in construction.

FDR appointed several African Americans to second-level positions in his administration. This group became known as "the Black Cabinet." Mary McLeod Bethune proved a superb leader of the Office of Minority Affairs in the National Youth Administration. Her most successful programs substantially reduced black illiteracy. Harvard-trained Robert Weaver advised the president on economic affairs, and in 1966, became the first black cabinet member when he was appointed secretary of housing and urban development.

Hard times were equally trying for Mexican Americans. As the Great Depression drastically reduced the demand for their labor, they faced massive layoffs, deepening poverty, and deportation. The New Deal programs did little to help. The AAA benefited large growers, not laborers. Neither the National Labor Relations Act nor the Social Security Act made any provisions for farm laborers. The FERA and the WPA did, at first, provide relief and jobs to the needy, irrespective of citizenship status. But after 1937, the WPA eliminated aliens from eligibility, causing great hardship for thousands of Mexican families.

---

**QUICK REVIEW**

**Blacks and the New Deal**

- Black unemployment rate was twice the rate for white people.
- Black people had less access to state and private aid and relief.
- New federal policies produced some limited gains for black people.

**First Lady Eleanor Roosevelt** rides with miners in a flag-decorated car during a visit to the mining town of Bellaire, Ohio, in 1935. Mrs. Roosevelt was more outspoken than the president in championing the rights of labor and African Americans, and she actively used her prestige as First Lady in support of social justice causes.

The New Deal made no explicit attempt to attack the deeply rooted patterns of racism and discrimination in American life. The entrenched power of white Southern Democrats in the Congress and the exclusion of black voters from southern politics made such an assault unthinkable. But there were occasional symbolic victories for racial equality. In 1939 the conservative Daughters of the American Revolution (DAR) refused to permit the world-renowned African American classical singer Marian Anderson to perform in the DAR's Washington hall. Eleanor Roosevelt and Interior Secretary Harold Ickes intervened to arrange for Anderson to perform on Easter Sunday at the Lincoln Memorial before an integrated audience of 75,000. More broadly, African Americans, especially in the cities, benefited from New Deal relief and work programs, even though this assistance was not color-blind. Black industrial workers made inroads into labor unions affiliated with the CIO. By 1936 an important political shift had begun: For the first time, a majority of black voters abandoned "the party of Lincoln" and voted Democratic. This was concrete evidence that African Americans supported the directions taken by FDR's New Deal. Black voters and hardened white segregationists would coexist uneasily as partners in the New Deal coalition, a tension that would strain the Democratic Party for decades to come.

## THE ROOSEVELT RECESSION AND THE EBBING OF THE NEW DEAL

The nation's economy had improved significantly by 1937. Unemployment had declined to "only" 14 percent (9 million people), farm prices had improved to 1930 levels, and industrial production was slightly higher than the 1929 mark. Roosevelt, always uneasy about the growing national debt, called for large reductions in federal spending, and the Fed, worried about inflation, tightened credit policies.

This retrenchment caused a steep recession. The stock market plunged in August 1937, and industrial output and farm prices plummeted. Unemployment shot up alarmingly; by March 1938, it hovered around 20 percent, with more than 13 million people looking for work.

The blunt reality was that even after five years, the New Deal had not brought about economic recovery. Throughout 1937 and 1938, the administration drifted. Roosevelt received conflicting advice on the economy. Some advisers, suspicious of the reluctance of business to make new investments, urged a massive antitrust campaign against monopolies. Others urged more federal spending. Emergency spending bills in the spring of 1938 put new life into the WPA and the PWA. But Republican gains in the 1938 congressional elections made it harder than ever to get new reform measures through. Conservative Southern Democrats increasingly allied themselves with Republicans in a coalition that would dominate Congress until the mid-1960s.

There were a couple of important exceptions. The 1938 Fair Labor Standards Act established the first federal minimum wage (twenty-five cents an hour) and set a maximum workweek of forty-four hours for all employees engaged in interstate commerce. The National Housing Act of 1937, also known as the Wagner-Steagall Act, funded public housing construction and slum clearance and provided rent subsidies for low-income families. But by and large, by 1938, the reform whirlwind of the New Deal was over.

# DEPRESSION-ERA CULTURE

The Great Depression profoundly affected American culture, as it did all other aspects of national life. Yet contradictory messages coexisted, sometimes within the same novel or movie. With American capitalism facing its worst crisis in history, radical expressions of protest and revolution became more frequent. But there were also strong celebrations of individualism, nostalgia for a simpler, rural past, and many attempts to define American core virtues.

## A NEW DEAL FOR THE ARTS

The depression hit America's writers, artists, and teachers just as hard as it did blue-collar workers. In 1935, the WPA allocated $300 million for the unemployed in these fields. Over the next four years, Federal Project No. 1, an umbrella agency covering writing, theater, music, and the visual arts, proved to be one of the most innovative and successful New Deal programs.

At its height, the Federal Writers Project employed 5,000 writers on a variety of programs. Most notably, it produced a popular (and still useful) series of state and city guidebooks. The 150-volume "Life in America" series included valuable oral histories of former slaves, studies of ethnic and Indian cultures, and pioneering collections of American songs and folk tales. Work on the Writers Project helped many American writers to survive, to hone their craft, and later to achieve prominence—among them Ralph Ellison, Richard Wright, Margaret Walker, John Cheever, Saul Bellow, and Zora Neale Hurston. The Federal Theater Project (FTP) reached as many as 30 million Americans with its productions, expanding the audience for theater beyond the regular patrons of the commercial stage. The parallel Federal Music Project, under Nikolai Sokoloff of the Cleveland Symphony Orchestra, employed 15,000 musicians and financed hundreds of thousands of low-priced public concerts by touring orchestras. The Composers' Forum Laboratory commissioned new works by important young American classical composers.

Among the struggling painters, later world famous, who received government assistance through the Federal Art Project (FAP) were Willem de Kooning, Jackson Pollock, and Louise Nevelson. It also commissioned artists to paint hundreds of murals on the walls of post offices, meeting halls, courthouses, and other government buildings.

## THE DOCUMENTARY IMPULSE

During the 1930s, an enormous number of artists, novelists, journalists, photographers, and filmmakers tried to document the devastation wrought by the depression in American communities. They also depicted people's struggles to cope with, and reverse, hard times. Mainstream mass media, such as *Life* magazine with its photo essays or "March of Time" newsreels, also adapted this stance.

HOW DID the Great Depression affect American cultural life during the 1930s?

myhistorylab
Review Summary

QUICK REVIEW

**The FWP**
- Federal Writers Project employed 5,000 writers.
- Produced a series of state and city guidebooks.
- The FWP helped many notable American writers survive the Depression.

**Fletcher Martin painted** *Mine Rescue* (1939) in the Kellogg, Idaho, post office. The work was part of a Treasury Department program that employed unemployed artists to beautify government buildings. The mural was eventually removed under pressure from local citizens who worried that it might upset those who had lost loved ones in mine accidents.

Fletcher Martin (1904–1979), "Mine Rescue," 1939, mural study for Kellog, Idaho Post Office; tempera on panel, 15-3/4 x 36-1/2 in (40.0 x 92.7 cm). Copyright Smithsonian American Art Museum, Washington, DC/Art Resource, NY.

The "documentary impulse" became a prominent style in 1930s' cultural expression. The most direct and influential expression of the documentary style was the photograph. In 1935, Roy Stryker, chief of the Historical Section of the Resettlement Administration, gathered a remarkable group of photographers to help document the work of the agency. Stryker encouraged them to photograph whatever caught their interest, even if the pictures had no direct connection with RA projects. These photographers, including Dorothea Lange and Walker Evans, left the single most significant visual record of the Great Depression. They traveled through rural areas, small towns, and migrant labor camps, and they produced powerful images of despair and resignation, of hope and resilience (see Seeing History).

That double vision, combining a frank portrayal of pain and suffering with a faith in the possibility of overcoming disaster, could be found in many other cultural works of the period. John Steinbeck's *Grapes of Wrath* (1939), soon made into an acclaimed film, sympathetically portrayed the hardships of Oklahoma Dust Bowl migrants on their way to California. "We ain't gonna die out," Ma Joad asserts near the end of the book. "People is goin' on—changing' a little, maybe, but goin' right on." Many writers interrupted their work to travel around the country and discover the thoughts and feelings of ordinary people. "With real events looming larger than any imagined happenings," novelist Elizabeth Noble wrote, "documentary films and still photographs, reportage and the like have taken the place once held by the grand invention."

## WAITING FOR LEFTY

For some, capitalism itself was responsible for the Great Depression. Relatively few Americans became communists or socialists in the 1930s (at its height, the Communist Party of the United States had perhaps 100,000 members), and many of these remained active for only a brief time. Yet Marxist analysis, with its emphasis on class conflict and the failures of capitalism, had a wide influence on thought and writing.

# Documenting Hard Times in Black and White and Color

Between 1935 and 1942, photographers working for the Farm Security Administration (FSA) created a remarkable pictorial record of depression life. The photography project had a political goal as well: to prod New Deal agricultural policy into providing greater support for the poorest agricultural workers. The photographers thus took aim at social, economic, and racial inequalities within American agriculture.

Many FSA photographs were published in newspapers and popular magazines as part of the agency's campaign to win public support for a greater federal role in building more migrant worker camps. Some of these photographs, such as those by Dorothea Lange and Walker Evans, have become among the most widely circulated images in the history of the medium. But even though Lange's "Migrant Mother" became a kind of universal symbol of suffering, its context and social-science origins have been lost. Her original caption simply read, "Destitute pea pickers in California. Mother of seven children. Age thirty-two." ■

**HOW DOES** Lee's portrait of the homesteader couple compare to Lange's portrait of the "Migrant Mother" as a document of rural life in the Great Depression? Are there differences beyond black and white and color?

Some writers joined the Communist Party, seeing in the Soviet Union an alternative to an American system mired in exploitation, racial inequality, and human misery. Communist writers sought to radicalize art and literature and celebrated collective struggle rather than individual achievement.

A more common pattern for intellectuals, especially young ones, was brief flirtation with communism. Many African American writers, attracted by the Communist Party's militant opposition to lynching, job discrimination, and segregation, briefly joined the party or found their first supportive audiences there. These included Richard Wright, Ralph Ellison, and Langston Hughes. Playwrights and actors associated with New York's influential Group Theater were often part of the Communist Party orbit in those years.

Left-wing influence reached its height after 1935 during the "Popular Front" period. Alarmed by the rise of fascism in Europe (see Chapter 25), communists around the world followed the Soviet line of aligning with liberals and other antifascists. Some 3,000 American men and women volunteered for the Communist Party–organized Abraham Lincoln Brigade, which fought in the Spanish Civil War on the republican side against the fascists led by Francisco Franco. The Lincolns' sense of commitment and sacrifice appealed to millions of Americans sympathetic to the republican cause. At home, the American Communist Party adopted the slogan "Communism is Twentieth-Century Americanism," and Communists proclaimed strong support of Roosevelt's New Deal (which before they had denounced). Their influence became especially strong within the labor movement as Communists and other radicals, known for their dedication and effectiveness, played a leading role in the difficult CIO unionizing drives in the auto, steel, and electrical industries. The radical presence was also strong within certain WPA arts projects. A decade later, many young idealists who came into the Communist Party orbit, no matter how briefly, would pay a heavy price.

## RAISING SPIRITS: FILM, RADIO, AND THE SWING ERA

Despite the depression, the mass-culture industry expanded enormously during the 1930s. If mass culture offered little in the way of direct responses to the economic and social problems of the day, it nonetheless played a more integral role than ever in shaping the rhythms and desires of the nation's everyday life.

Toward the end of the 1920s, the coming of "talking pictures" helped make movies the most popular entertainment form of the day. More than 60 percent of Americans attended one of the nation's 20,000 movie houses each week, and millions followed the lives and careers of movie stars more avidly than ever. At the same time, the movie studios themselves, responding to pressure from the Roman Catholic Church and other advocates of traditional morality, instituted a more stringent Production Code in 1933. For the next three decades American filmmakers had to work within very narrow parameters of what was acceptable to depict on screen.

With so many movies being churned out by Hollywood studios for so many fans, it is difficult to generalize about the cultural impact of individual films. Some 1930s' filmmakers expressed highly personal visions of core American values. Two who succeeded in capturing both popular and critical acclaim were Walt Disney and Frank Capra. By the mid-1930s, Disney's animated cartoons (including Mickey Mouse) had become moral tales that preached following the rules. Capra's comedies idealized a small-town America, with close families and comfortable homes. Although Capra's films dealt with contemporary problems more than most, he seemed to suggest that most of the country's ills could be

**Reginald Marsh,** *Twenty Cent Movie*, 1936. Marsh documented the urban landscape of the 1930s with great empathy, capturing the city's contradictory mix of commercialism, optimism, energy, and degradation. The popularity of Hollywood films and their stars reached new heights during the Great Depression.

Reginald Marsh, "Twenty Cent Movie," 1936. Egg tempera on composition board. 40" × 40".
Whitney Museum of American Art/Artists Rights Society, New York.

solved if only its leaders learned the old-fashioned values of "common people"—kindness, loyalty, and charity.

Radio broadcasting emerged as the most powerful medium of communication in the home, profoundly changing the rhythms and routines of everyday life. In 1930, roughly 12 million American homes (40 percent of the total) had radio sets; by the end of the decade, 90 percent had them. Advertisers dominated the structure and content of American radio, forming a powerful alliance with the two large networks, the National Broadcasting Company (NBC) and the Columbia Broadcasting System (CBS). The Federal Communications Commission, established in 1934, continued long-standing policies that favored commercial broadcasting over other arrangements, such as municipal or university programming.

The depression actually helped radio expand. An influx of talent arrived from the weakened worlds of vaudeville, ethnic theater, and the recording industry. The well-financed networks offered an attractive outlet to advertisers seeking

## CHRONOLOGY

| | |
|---|---|
| **1929** | Stock market crash |
| **1930** | Democrats regain control of the House of Representatives |
| **1932** | Reconstruction Finance Corporation established to make government credit available |
| | "Bonus Army" marches on Washington |
| | Franklin D. Roosevelt elected president |
| **1933** | Roughly 13 million workers unemployed |
| | The "Hundred Days" legislation of the First New Deal |
| | Twenty-First Amendment repeals Prohibition (Eighteenth Amendment) |
| **1934** | Indian Reorganization Act repeals Dawes Severalty Act and reasserts the status of Indian tribes as semisovereign nations |
| | Growing popularity of Father Charles E. Coughlin and Huey Long, critics of Roosevelt |
| **1935** | Second New Deal |
| | Committee for Industrial Organization (CIO) established |
| | Dust storms turn the southern Great Plains into the Dust Bowl |
| | Boulder Dam completed |
| **1936** | Roosevelt defeats Alfred M. Landon in reelection landslide |
| | Sit-down strike begins at General Motors plants in Flint, Michigan |
| **1937** | General Motors recognizes United Automobile Workers |
| | Roosevelt's "Court-packing" plan causes controversy |
| | Memorial Day Massacre in Chicago demonstrates the perils of union organizing |
| | "Roosevelt recession" begins |
| **1938** | CIO unions withdraw from the American Federation of Labor to form the Congress of Industrial Organizations |
| | Fair Labor Standards Act establishes the first federal minimum wage |

a national audience. Radio programming achieved a regularity and professionalism absent in the 1920s, making it much easier for a listener to identify a show with its sponsor. Much of network radio was based on older cultural forms. The variety show, hosted by comedians and singers, and based on the old vaudeville format, was the first important style. Its stars constantly plugged the sponsor's product. The use of an audible studio audience re-created the human interaction so necessary in vaudeville. The popular comedy show *Amos 'n' Andy* adapted the minstrel "blackface" tradition to the new medium. Its two white comedians used only their voices to invent a world of stereotyped African Americans for millions of listeners.

Daytime serials, dubbed "soap operas," dominated radio drama. Aimed at women working in the home, these serials alone constituted 60 percent of all daytime shows by 1940. Soaps revolved around strong, warm female characters who provided advice and strength to weak, indecisive friends and relatives. Action counted very little; the development of character and relationships was all-important.

Radio news arrived in the 1930s, showing the medium's potential for direct and immediate coverage of political events. Network news and commentary shows multiplied rapidly. Father Couglin's radio demagoguery for a while had a powerful political impact, and FDR always used the radio to great effect. Complex political and economic issues and the impending European crisis (see Chapter 25) fueled a news hunger among Americans.

One measure of radio's cultural impact was its role in popularizing jazz. Before the 1930s, jazz was heard largely among African Americans and a small coterie of white fans. Regular broadcasts of live performances exposed a broader public to the music. Bands led by black artists such as Duke Ellington and Count Basie began to enjoy reputations outside of traditional jazz centers like Chicago, Kansas City, and New York.

Benny Goodman became the key figure in the "swing era," largely through radio exposure. Goodman, a white, classically trained clarinetist, had been inspired by African American bandleaders who created big-band arrangements that combined harmonic call-and-response patterns with breaks for improvised solos. Goodman purchased a series of these arrangements, smoothing out the sound but keeping the strong dance beat. His band's late Saturday night broadcasts began to attract attention, and in 1935, at the Palomar Ballroom in Los Angeles, made the breakthrough that established his enormous popularity. When his band started playing, the young crowd, primed by radio broadcasts, roared its approval and began to dance wildly. Goodman's music was perfect for doing the jitterbug or lindy hop, dances borrowed from African American culture. As the "King of Swing," Goodman helped make big-band jazz a hit with millions of teenagers and young adults from all backgrounds. In the late 1930s, big-band music by artists like Goodman, Ellington, and Basie accounted for the majority of million-selling records.

## CONCLUSION

Far from being the radical program its conservative critics charged, the New Deal did little to alter fundamental property relations or the distribution of wealth. Indeed, most of its programs largely failed to help the most powerless groups in America—migrant workers, tenant farmers and sharecroppers, African Americans, and other minorities. But the New Deal profoundly changed many areas of American life. Overall, it radically increased the role of the federal government in American lives and communities, creating a new kind of liberalism defined by an activist state. Social Security, unemployment insurance, and federal relief programs established at least the framework for a welfare state. The FDIC and the SEC established important new federal rules protecting individuals from financial ruin and unregulated stock markets. For the first time in American history, the national government took responsibility for assisting its needy citizens. And also for the first time, the federal government guaranteed the rights of workers to join trade unions, and it set standards for minimum wages and maximum hours. Western and southern communities in particular were transformed through federal intervention in water, power, and agricultural policies. In politics, the New Deal established the Democrats as the majority party. Some version of the Roosevelt New Deal coalition would dominate the nation's political life for another three decades.

The New Deal's efforts to end racial and gender discrimination were modest at best. Some of the more ambitious programs, such as subsidizing the arts or building model communities, enjoyed only brief success. Other reform proposals, such as national health insurance, never got off the ground. Conservative counterpressures, especially after 1937, limited what could be changed. Still, the New Deal did more than strengthen the presence of the national government in people's lives. It also fed expectations that the federal presence would intensify. Washington became a much greater center of economic regulation and political power, and the federal bureaucracy grew in size and influence. With the coming of World War II, the direct role of national government in shaping American communities would expand beyond the dreams of even the most ardent New Dealer.

## REVIEW QUESTIONS

1. What were the underlying causes of the Great Depression? What consequences did it have for ordinary Americans, and how did the Hoover administration attempt to deal with the crisis?

2. Analyze the key elements of Franklin D. Roosevelt's first New Deal program. To what degree did these succeed in getting the economy back on track and in providing relief to suffering Americans?

3. How did the so-called Second New Deal differ from the first? What political pressures did Roosevelt face that contributed to the new policies?

4. How did the New Deal reshape western communities and politics? What specific programs had the greatest impact in the region? How are these changes still visible today?

5. Evaluate the impact of the labor movement and radicalism on the 1930s. How did they influence American political and cultural life?

6. To what extent were the grim realities of the depression reflected in popular culture? To what degree were they absent?

7. Discuss the long- and short-range effects of the New Deal on American political and economic life. What were its key successes and failures? What legacies of New Deal–era policies and political struggles can you find in contemporary America?

**myhistorylab**
Flashcard Review

## KEY TERMS

**Bonus Army** (p. 667)
**Congress for Industrial Organizations** (p. 673)
**Emergency Banking Act** (p. 668)
**Fireside chat** (p. 668)
**Great Depression** (p. 663)
**National Industrial Recovery Act** (p. 669)

**National Labor Relations Act** (p. 672)
**New Deal** (p. 669)
**New Deal coalition** (p. 674)
**Social Security Act of 1935** (p. 672)
**Tennessee Valley Authority (TVA)** (p. 669)

## RECOMMENDED READING

Anthony J. Badger, *The New Deal: The Depression Years, 1933–1940* (1989). Very useful overview that emphasizes the limited nature of New Deal reforms.

Alan Brinkley, *The End of Reform: New Deal Liberalism in Recession and War* (1995). A sophisticated analysis of the political and economic limits faced by New Deal reformers from 1937 through World War II.

Lizabeth Cohen, *Making a New Deal: Industrial Workers in Chicago, 1919–1939* (1990). A brilliant study that demonstrates the transformation of immigrant and African American workers into key actors in the creation of the CIO, and in New Deal politics, and illuminates the complex relationship between ethnic cultures and mass culture.

Michael Denning, *The Cultural Front: The Laboring of American Culture in the Twentieth Century* (1997). A provocative reinterpretation of 1930s' culture, emphasizing the impact of the Popular Front and its lasting influence on American modernism and mass culture.

Ronald Edsforth, *The New Deal: America's Response to the Great Depression* (2000). A concise political history of the 1930s, offering an excellent synthesis of the massive secondary literature.

David M. Kennedy, *Freedom From Fear: The American People in Depression and War* (1999). An absorbing narrative account of the U.S. experience in depression and war.

Richard Lowitt, *The New Deal and the West* (1984). A comprehensive study of the New Deal's impact in the West, with special attention to water policy and agriculture.

Robert S. McElvaine, *The Great Depression: America, 1929–1941* (1984). The best one-volume overview of the Great Depression. It is especially strong on the origins and early years of the worst economic calamity in American history.

Jason Scott Smith, *Building New Deal Liberalism: The Political Economy of Public Works, 1935–1956* (2006). Argues for the centrality of public works programs such as the PWA and WPA for understanding how the New Deal transformed governmental priorities and remade the economy and landscape.

For study resources for this chapter, go to **www.myhistorylab.com** and choose *Out of Many, Teaching and Learning Classroom Edition*. You will find a wealth of study and review material for this chapter, including pretests and posttests, customized study plan, key-term review flash cards, interactive map and document activities, and documents for analysis.

*The event was not spectacular, no fuses burned, no lights flashed. But to us it meant that release of atomic energy on a large scale would be only a matter of time.*

—*Enrico Fermi, from* The First Reactor

**GARDENS**

**FOR**

**VICTORY**

**GROW VITAMINS AT YOUR KITCHEN DOOR**

**Enter VICTORY GARDEN CONTEST**

REGISTER 404 S. 8th ST. MAY 1-15

CONSUMER INTEREST DIVISION. MINNEAPOLIS DEFENSE COUNCIL - A WAR CHEST AGENCY

**On June 6, 1944,** American, British, and Canadian forces seized a beachhead in German-occupied France. The landings began the final phase of World War II in Europe, which ended eleven months later with German surrender to the U.S., Britain, the Soviet Union, and their allies.

# 25

# WORLD WAR II
## 1941–1945

**WHAT STEPS** did Roosevelt take in the late 1930s to prepare the United States for war?

**WHAT WERE** the economic consequences of the war for the United States?

**WHAT MAJOR** changes occurred in American society as a consequence of wartime mobilization?

**WHAT ROLE** did women play in the armed forces during World War II?

**WHAT WERE** the main elements of the Allied war strategy?

**WHAT WERE** the factors behind the decision to deploy the atomic bomb against Japan?

1941 1945

# AMERICAN COMMUNITIES
## Los Alamos, New Mexico

ON MONDAY, JULY 16, 1945, AT 5:29:45 A.M., MOUNTAIN WAR TIME, the first atomic bomb exploded in a brilliant flash visible in three states. Within just seven minutes, a huge, multicolored, bell-shaped cloud soared 38,000 feet into the atmosphere and threw back a blanket of smoke and soot to the earth below. The heat generated by the blast was four times the temperature at the center of the sun, and the light produced rivaled that of nearly twenty suns. Even ten miles away people felt a strong surge of heat. The giant fireball ripped a crater a half-mile wide in the ground, fusing the desert sand into glass. The shock wave blew out windows in houses more than 200 miles away. The blast killed every living creature—squirrels, rabbits, snakes, plants, and insects—within a mile and the smells of death lingered for nearly a month.

President Franklin D. Roosevelt, convinced by Albert Einstein and other physicists that the Nazis might successfully develop an atomic bomb, had inaugurated a small nuclear research program in 1939. Then, after the United States entered World War II in 1941, the president released resources to create the Manhattan Project and placed it under the direction of the Army Corps of Engineers. By December 1942 a team headed by Italian-born Nobel Prize winner Enrico Fermi had produced the first chain reaction in uranium under the University of Chicago's football stadium. Now the mission was to build a new formidable weapon, the atomic bomb.

In March 1943, the government moved the key researchers and their families to Los Alamos, New Mexico, a remote and sparsely populated region of soaring peaks, ancient Indian ruins, modern Pueblos, and villages occupied by the descendants of the earliest Spanish settlers. Most were young, with an average age of twenty-seven, and quite a few were recently married. Many couples began their families at Los Alamos, producing a total of nearly a thousand babies between 1943 and 1949.

The scientists and their families formed an exceptionally close-knit community, united by the need for secrecy and their shared antagonism toward their army guardians. The military atmosphere was oppressive. Homes and laboratories were cordoned off by barbed wire and guarded by military police. Everything, from linens to food packages, was stamped "Government Issue." The scientists were followed by security personnel whenever they left Los Alamos. Several scientists were reprimanded for discussing their work at home, although many of their wives worked forty-eight hours a week in the Technical Area. All outgoing mail was censored. Well-known scientists commonly worked under aliases—Fermi became "Eugene Farmer"—and code names were used for such terms as *atom, bomb,* and *uranium fission.* Los Alamos children were registered without surnames at nearby public schools. Even automobile accidents, weddings, and deaths went unreported. Only a group thoroughly committed to the war effort could accept such restrictions on personal liberty.

A profound urgency motivated the research team, which included refugees from Nazi Germany and Fascist Italy and a large proportion of Jews. The director of the project, California physicist J. Robert Oppenheimer, promoted a scientific élan that offset the military style of commanding general Leslie Groves. Just thirty-eight, slightly built, and deeply emotional, "Oppie" personified the idealism that helped the community of scientists overcome whatever moral reservations they held about placing such a potentially terrible weapon in the hands of the government.

In the Technical Area of Los Alamos, Oppenheimer directed research. At seven o'clock each workday morning, the siren dubbed "Oppie's Whistle" called the other scientists to their laboratories to wrestle with the theoretical and practical problems of building an atomic device. From May to November 1944, after the bomb had been designed, the key issue was testing it. Many scientists feared a test might fail, scattering the precious plutonium at the bomb's core and discrediting the entire project. Finally, with plutonium production increasing, the Los Alamos team agreed to test "the gadget" at a site 160 miles away.

The United States nevertheless emerged from World War II far stronger than its European allies, who bore the brunt of the fighting. Indeed, the nation was now strong enough to claim a new role as the world's leading superpower.

Los Alamos

25–3
Franklin D. Roosevelt,
*The Four Freedoms* (1941)

# THE COMING OF WORLD WAR II

The worldwide depression helped to undermine a political order that had been shaky since World War I. Political unrest spread across Europe and Asia as international trade dropped by as much as two-thirds and unemployment rose. Demagogues played on national and racial hatreds, fueled by old resentments and current despair, and offered solutions in the form of territorial expansion by military conquest.

Preoccupied with restoring the domestic economy, President Franklin D. Roosevelt had no specific plan to deal with growing conflict elsewhere in the world. Moreover, the majority of Americans strongly opposed foreign entanglements. But as debate over diplomatic policy heated up, terrifying events overseas pulled the nation steadily toward war.

## THE SHADOWS OF WAR ACROSS THE GLOBE

Two major threats to peace gathered force in the 1930s in East Asia and in Central Europe. In Japan, devastated by the depression, military leaders decided that imperialism would make their nation the richest in the world, and in 1931 the army seized Manchuria from China. When the League of Nations objected, Japan simply quit the league. A full-scale Japanese invasion of China proper followed in 1937, and the world watched in horror the Rape of Nanking (today, Nanjing)—the destruction of what was then China's capital and the slaughter of as many as 300,000 Chinese men, women, and children. Within a year, Japan controlled most of coastal China.

In Europe, fanatical and tyrannical fascist leaders were taking power—first in Italy and later in Germany. "We have buried the putrid corpse of liberty," boasted Italy's Fascist dictator Benito Mussolini in the 1920s. In Germany, nationalist resentment over the Treaty of Versailles fueled Adolf Hitler's National Socialist (Nazi) movement with its racist doctrine of "Aryan" supremacy that condemned nonwhites and Jews as "degenerate races." In January 1933, by political intrigue, Hitler became chancellor. He posed as the last bastion against Communism and had the backing of German industrialists but only about one-third of the voters. With his brown-shirted storm troopers ruling the streets, Hitler quickly destroyed opposition parties and made himself absolute dictator. Renouncing the disarmament provisions imposed by the Versailles peace treaty, he began to rebuild Germany's armed forces. No European powers opposed him.

Soon enough, Mussolini and Hitler began to act on their imperial visions. In 1935 Italy conquered Ethiopia and turned the African nation into a colony. In 1936 Hitler sent 35,000 troops to occupy the formerly demilitarized Rhineland region. In the Spanish Civil War that broke out later that year, Italy and Germany both supported General Francisco Franco's fascist rebels against the democratic republican regime. In November, Germany and Italy forged an alliance, the Rome–Berlin Axis.

Hitler was now nearly ready to put into operation his plan to secure *Lebensraum*—living space for the "Aryan" population—through territorial expansion. In 1938 he annexed Austria and then turned his attention to Czechoslovakia, the one remaining democracy in Central Europe, which Britain and France had pledged to assist. War seemed imminent. But Britain and France surprised the world by agreeing, at Munich on September 30, 1938, to allow Germany to annex the Sudetenland—the German-speaking parts of Czechoslovakia. "Appeasement," this was called: Hitler pledged that he would make no more territorial demands. But within six months, in March 1939, Germany seized the rest of the country.

**WHAT STEPS** did Roosevelt take in the late 1930s to prepare the United States for war?

**myhistorylab**
Review Summary

## IMAGE KEY
for pages 692–693

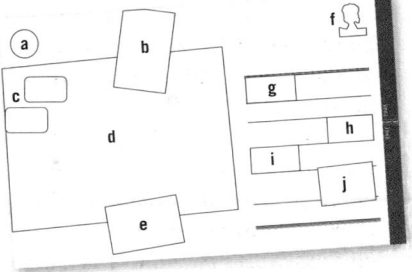

a. A cloth patch with a yellow Star of David that all Jews had to wear under the Nazi regime.
b. A Victory Garden contest poster.
c. POWs identification (ID) tags.
d. American soldiers landing on the coast of France at Normandy on June 6, 1944.
e. Unusually addressed letters to Winston Churchill.
f. The mushroom cloud produced by the explosion of an atomic bomb.
g. The Pearl Harbor attack, December 7, 1941.
h. Japanese-Americans were forced into internment camps during the war.
i. New recruits to the Women's Army Corps (WAC) during World War II.
j. The D-Day invasion of the beaches of Normandy, France, June 6, 1944.

By then, much of the world was aware of the horror of Hitler's racist regime. On the night of November 9, 1938, Nazi storm troopers rounded up Jews, beating them mercilessly and murdering an untold number. From the smashed windows of Jewish shops and burned synagogues, this attack came to be known as *Kristallnacht,* the "Night of Broken Glass." The Nazi government expropriated Jewish property and excluded Jews from all but the most menial jobs. Pressured by Hitler, his allies Hungary and Italy also enacted laws curtailing the civil rights of Jews.

On September 27, 1938, Germany, Italy, and Japan signed the anti-Communist Tripartite Pact and pledged to "stand by and co-operate with one another" for the next ten years.

## ISOLATIONISM

World War I had left a legacy of strong isolationist yearnings in the United States. In 1937, nearly 70 percent of Americans responding to a Gallup poll agreed that U.S. involvement in World War I had been a mistake.

Antiwar sentiment won strong support in Congress. In 1934, a committee headed by Republican senator Gerald P. Nye of North Dakota charged weapons manufacturers with driving the United States into World War I to make windfall profits. (Many in fact many did.) In 1935, Congress passed the first of five Neutrality Acts to deter entanglements in future foreign wars. It required the president to embargo the sale and shipment of munitions to all belligerents.

Isolationism spanned the political spectrum. In 1938 socialist Norman Thomas gathered leading liberals and trade unionists into the Keep America Out of War Congress; the communist-influenced American League against War and Fascism claimed more than 1 million members. In 1940 the arch-conservative Committee to Defend America First formed to oppose U.S. intervention. Some America Firsters were openly anti-Semitic and championed the Nazis as "anti-Communists."

## ROOSEVELT READIES FOR WAR

FDR's instincts were to stand with other threatened democracies, but he knew that the American public was strongly isolationist. In October 1937 he had called for international cooperation to "quarantine the aggressors." But two-thirds of Congress opposed economic sanctions as a "back door to war." Forced to draw back, Roosevelt nevertheless won from Congress $1 billion to enlarge the navy. Another less stringent Neutrality Act in 1939 permitted wartime arms sales to Great Britain, France, and China.

War broke out in Europe in the fall of 1939. In August, Germany and the Soviet Union, hitherto mortal enemies, stunned the world by signing a nonaggression pact. A week later, on September 1, Hitler invaded Poland. Within days, Poland's allies, Great Britain and France, declared war on Germany. On September 17, Soviet troops invaded Poland too. Warsaw capitulated, and Hitler and Stalin divided Poland between them. Fighting slowed to a near halt as French and German troops did not even exchange fire. Soviet forces, however, attacked Finland and seized the tiny Baltic republics.

Hitler began a crushing offensive against Western Europe in April 1940. In a *blitzkrieg* (lightning war), fast-moving columns of German tanks supported by air power struck first at Denmark and Norway and soon thereafter conquered Holland, Belgium, and Luxembourg. More than 338,000 British troops had to escape across the English Channel. Hitler's army, joined at the last minute by the Italians, then easily overran France in June 1940. When Britain refused to surrender, Hitler launched the Battle of Britain. Nazi bombers pounded cities while U-boats tried to cut off incoming supplies.

*Blitzkrieg* German war tactic in World War II ("lightning war") involving the concentration of air and armored firepower to punch and exploit holes in opposing defensive lines.

The American public desperately hoped to stay out of the war, but they also agreed with Roosevelt that the nation's security depended on both a strong defense and Hitler's defeat. Invoking the **Neutrality Act of 1939**, which permitted the sale of arms to Britain, France, and China, the president affirmed his position: "All aid to the Allies short of war." In May 1940, when France collapsed, he began to transfer surplus U.S. warships and equipment to Britain, in exchange for West Indies naval bases. In September, while the Battle of Britain raged, Roosevelt and Congress enacted the nation's first peacetime military draft, which sent 1.4 million young men to army training camps by July 1941.

FDR could not yet admit the inevitability of U.S. involvement—especially during an election year. His popularity had dropped with the 1937 "Roosevelt recession," and the Republicans had nominated a popular former Democrat turned anti–New Dealer, Wendell L. Willkie, from Indiana. Although isolationists who hated Roosevelt flocked to the folksy yet successful Wall Street industrialist, Wilkie pushed away many potential voters by supporting aid to Britain and rearming America and by waging a campaign enlivened primarily by his slurs on the Roosevelt family. When FDR promised voters not to "send your boys to any foreign wars," he clinched an unprecedented third term.

Reelected, Roosevelt moved more aggressively to aid hard-pressed Great Britain. In his annual message to Congress in early 1941, he proposed a bill allowing the president to sell, exchange, or lease arms to any country whose defense he judged vital to U.S. security. Passed in March 1941, the **Lend-Lease Act** made Great Britain the first beneficiary of massive aid. Congress also authorized the merchant marine to sail fully armed while conveying Lend-Lease supplies directly to Britain.

In August 1941 Roosevelt met on a warship off Newfoundland with Winston Churchill, the embattled British prime minister. Roosevelt evaded Churchill's pleas to enter the war—he knew that Congress and the American public still hoped to stay out—but the two leaders declared common goals for the postwar world in what was called the **Atlantic Charter**, a lofty proclamation calling for all peoples to live in freedom from fear, want, and tyranny.

The European war now widened. Having conquered the Balkans, Hitler broke the Nazi–Soviet Pact and in June 1941 invaded the Soviet Union. Roosevelt sent Lend-Lease supplies to the Soviets and ordered U.S. warships to "sink on sight" any lurking German submarines. The result was an undeclared and unpublicized naval war between the United States and Nazi Germany on the North Atlantic.

## PEARL HARBOR

While throughout 1940 and 1941 Americans watched with dread the widening European struggle, war also escalated in East Asia. Anticipating trouble in the Pacific, in May 1940 Roosevelt transferred the Pacific fleet from its California bases to a forward position at Pearl Harbor in Hawai'i. Less than five months later, Japan formally joined Germany and Italy as a full Axis ally.

Both the United States and Japan were playing for time. Roosevelt wanted to bank

**Neutrality Act of 1939** Permitted the sale of arms to Britain, France, and China.

**Lend-Lease Act** An arrangement for the transfer of war supplies, including food, machinery, and services to nations whose defense was considered vital to the defense of the United States in Word War II.

**Atlantic Charter** Statement of common principles and war aims developed by President Franklin Roosevelt and British Prime Minister Winston Churchill at a meeting in August 1941.

 **25–4**
Franklin Delano Roosevelt, *Annual Message to Congress* (1941)

**On December 7,** 1941, Japanese attack planes devastated the U.S. fleet stationed at Pearl Harbor, on the Hawaiian island of Oahu. This photograph shows the explosion of the USS *Shaw*, a dry-docked destroyer, during the second wave of Japanese attack. The "sneak" attack on Pearl Harbor became a symbol of Japanese treachery and the necessity for U.S. revenge.

**On the day** after the attack on Pearl Harbor, President Franklin D. Roosevelt addressed a joint session of Congress and asked for an immediate declaration of war against Japan. The resolution passed with one dissenting vote, and the United States entered World War II.

## QUICK REVIEW

**Undeclared War**

◆ March 1941: Lend-lease program approved by Congress.

◆ FDR ordered navy to offer support to Britain.

◆ August 1941: Atlantic Charter lays out British and American war aims.

resources to fight Germany (the greater danger, he thought); Japan's leaders gambled that America's preoccupation with Europe might allow them to conquer all Southeast Asia, including France's Indochinese colonies (today, Vietnam, Cambodia, and Laos), British outposts like Hong Kong and Singapore, and the oil-rich Dutch East Indies (today, Indonesia). Lacking petroleum, Japan was desperate to obtain a reliable source for oil; without that, its navy and huge land army in China could not fight. When Japan occupied French Indochina in July 1941, Roosevelt moved from economic sanctions, which had been in place for several months, to freezing Japanese assets in the United States and cutting off its oil supplies.

War with Japan now looked likely. The Japanese military decided to hit the Americans with a knock-out blow that would give them time to seize Southeast Asia and the western Pacific; the United States, they hoped, would be too shaken to fight back. But American intelligence had broken the Japanese secret diplomatic code, and the president knew that Japan was preparing to strike somewhere, most likely the Philippines. By the end of November, all American Pacific forces were put on high alert.

Early on Sunday morning, December 7, 1941, carrier-borne Japanese bombers struck the Pacific fleet at Pearl Harbor. Americans were caught completely off guard. No one expected such a skillful attack. Within two hours, Japanese pilots destroyed nearly 200 American planes and badly damaged the fleet; more than 2,400 Americans were killed and nearly 1,200 wounded. (Fortunately, the U.S. carriers were spared, being out to sea on the morning of the attack.) That same day, Japan bombed U.S. bases on the Philippines, Guam, and Wake Island and attacked the British fleet and colonies in East Asia.

On December 8, declaring the attack on Pearl Harbor a day that "will live in infamy," Roosevelt asked Congress for a declaration of war against Japan. With only one dissenting vote Congress agreed. The United States did not declare war on Germany; it was Hitler who made that fateful decision when he ordered his puppet Reichstag on December 11 to proclaim war against "half Judaized and the half Negrified" America. Mussolini chimed in. World War II had now begun for Americans.

# THE GREAT ARSENAL OF DEMOCRACY

As early as 1938, the American economy had begun to benefit from sales to the British and French when those countries started rearming. In 1940, Roosevelt told Americans in a radio "fireside chat" that the nation must become a "great arsenal of democracy," and by the time the United States entered the war the U.S. economy had already geared up for military purposes.

## MOBILIZING FOR WAR

A few days after the United States declared war, Congress passed the **War Powers Act**, establishing a precedent for executive authority that would endure long after the war's end. Under the new law, the president could reorganize the federal government and create new agencies, censor all news and information and abridge civil liberties, seize foreign-owned property, and even award government contracts without competitive bidding.

Roosevelt promptly used his authority to create special wartime agencies. At the top of his agenda was a massive reorientation and management of the economy, and to do that an alphabet soup of new agencies appeared. For example, the Supply Priorities and Allocation Board (SPAB) oversaw the use of scarce materials and resources vital to the war, adjusting domestic consumption to military needs, even ending it for some products such as automobiles. The Office of Price Administration (OPA) used price controls to check inflation. The National War Labor Board (NWLB) mediated labor–management disputes. The War Manpower Commission (WMC) directed the mobilization of military and civilian services. And the Office of War Mobilization (OWM) coordinated operations among all these new agencies.

Several new agencies took on the responsibility of creating propaganda to promote a war that was being fought 3,000 miles away. Although Pearl Harbor brought an outpouring of rage against Japan and ended all talk of isolationism, the government nevertheless fanned patriotic fires and tried to shape public opinion. In June 1942 the president created the Office of War Information (OWI) to engage the press, radio, and film industry in selling the war to the American people, as well as to publish leaflets for the armed services and to flood enemy ranks with subversive propaganda. Domestic propaganda also fueled the selling of war bonds.

In mid-1942 Roosevelt established an agency that would prove vital to the Allied victory and change the way science was conducted in the United States. The Office of Scientific Research and Development (OSRD) brought together government, business, and scientific leaders to coordinate military research. It developed better radar and early warning systems, more effective medicines and pesticides, and improved weapons.

With the creation of these new agencies, the size of the federal government increased many times over its New Deal level. It cost about $250 million a day to fight the war, and the government spent twice as much during the war as it had during its entire history up to then. The number of federal employees nearly quadrupled, from a little over 1 million in 1940 to nearly 4 million by the war's end.

The New Deal itself, however, withered away. "Dr. New Deal" had been replaced by "Dr. Win the War," said Roosevelt in 1942. With the depression over and chronic unemployment giving way to acute labor shortages, FDR's administration directed all its resources toward securing the planes, ships, guns, and food—and the war workers—required for victory. Moreover, the 1942 elections weakened the New Deal coalition by unseating many liberal Democrats while sending fifty-five

---

**WHAT WERE** the economic consequences of the war for the United States?

**myhistorylab**
Review Summary

**War Powers Act** Gave the U.S. president the power to reorganize the federal government and create new agencies; to establish programs censoring news, information, and abridging civil liberties; to seize foreign-owned property; and award government contracts without bidding.

new and mostly conservative Republicans to Congress. Republicans now quashed proposals to extend the social programs instituted during the 1930s, including the WPA and the CCC. One of the hallmarks of the New Deal, the Farm Security Administration, managed to hang on but only after severe cuts to its budget, as was the case with the Rural Electrification Administration, which the private power companies despised. One by one, New Deal agencies vanished.

## ORGANIZING THE WAR ECONOMY

Victory, many experts agreed, would ultimately depend less on military prowess and superior strategy than on the ability of the United States to outproduce its enemies. The nation enjoyed incomparable advantages: freedom from bombing and invasions, a huge industrial base, abundant natural resources, and a civilian population large enough to swell both its labor force and its armed forces. But first the entire civilian economy had to be both expanded and transformed for the production of arms and other military supplies.

Even before Pearl Harbor, by the summer of 1941, the federal government was pouring vast sums into defense production. Six months after the attack, allocations topped $100 billion for equipment and supplies, which exceeded what American firms had produced in all previous wars. Facing war orders too large to fill, American industries were primed for all-out production. Once-idled factories operated around-the-clock, seven days a week.

Defense production transformed entire regions. The impact was strongest in the West—the major staging area for the war in the Pacific—where the federal government spent nearly $40 billion for military and industrial expansion. The South benefited from having 60 of the army's 100 new military camps, and its textile factories hummed: the army alone required nearly 520 million pairs of socks and 230 million pairs of pants. Much of the South's sharecropping and tenant-farming population—already thinned by New Deal economic policies (see Chapter 24)—migrated into well-paid urban industrial jobs, and unprecedented profits poured into southern businesses.

Across the nation, the rural population decreased by almost 20 percent, and American farmers could not keep up with the rising international—or even the domestic—demand for milk, potatoes, fruits, and sugar. The Department of Agriculture reached its goals only in areas such as livestock production, thanks to skyrocketing wholesale meat prices. The war speeded the development of large-scale and mechanized crop production, including the first widespread use of chemical fertilizers and pesticides. By 1945 farm income had doubled, but thousands of small farms had disappeared.

Much like large-scale commercial agriculture, many big businesses did well during the war. Military contracts allowed huge profits. The government provided low-interest loans and even direct subsidies for the expansion of facilities, with generous tax write-offs for retooling. The 100 largest corporations, which manufactured 30 percent of all goods in 1940, garnered 70 percent of all war and civilian contracts and the bulk of war profits. On the other hand, many small businesses closed.

## NEW WORKERS

The wartime economy required an unprecedented number of new workers. The *bracero* program, negotiated by the United States and Mexico in 1942, brought more than 200,000 Mexicans into the United States for short-term employment, mainly as farm and railroad workers. Sioux and Navajos were hired in large numbers to build ordnance depots and military training centers. African Americans secured in just four years a greater variety of jobs than in the seven decades since the outbreak of the Civil War. They joined white workers in defense industries—in iron and steel plants, shipyards and aircraft factories, and numerous government agencies. The number of black workers rose from 2.9 million to 3.8 million.

The war most dramatically altered the wage-earning patterns of women. The female labor force grew by more than 50 percent, reaching 19.5 million in 1945. The rate of growth proved especially high for white women over thirty-five, and for the first time married women became the majority of female wage earners. The employment rate changed comparatively little for African American women; fully 90 percent had been in the labor force in 1940. However, many black women left domestic service for higher-paying industrial jobs.

Compared to the Great Depression, when married women were barred from many jobs, World War II opened up new fields. The number of women automobile workers jumped from 29,000 to 200,000, that of women electrical workers from 100,000 to 374,000. Polled near the end of the war, 75 percent of women workers said they wanted to keep working, preferably at the same jobs (see Seeing History).

Although the war generated 17 million new jobs, the economic gains were not evenly distributed. Wages increased by as much as 50 percent, but never as fast as profits or prices. This widely reported disparity produced one of the most turbulent periods in American labor history (see Table 25.1). More workers went on strike in 1941, before the United States entered the war, than in any previous year except 1919.

**Facing a shortage** of workers and increased production demands, the War Manpower Commission and the Office of War Information conducted a campaign to recruit women into the labor force. Women were encouraged to "take a job for your husband/son/brother" and to "keep the world safe for your children." Higher wages also enticed many women to take jobs in factories. In this photograph, women are shown packaging powdered milk.

### QUICK REVIEW

**Rosie the Riveter**

- Demand for labor drew women into the workplace.
- Companies opened positions for women in nontraditional jobs.
- Most women were forced to leave industrial jobs after the war.

## TABLE 25.1

### Strikes and Lockouts in the United States, 1940–45

| Year | Number of Strikes | Number of Workers Involved | Number of Man-Days Idle | Percent of Total Employed |
| --- | --- | --- | --- | --- |
| 1940 | 2,508 | 576,988 | 6,700,872 | 2.3 |
| 1941 | 4,288 | 2,362,620 | 23,047,556 | 8.4 |
| 1942 | 2,968 | 839,961 | 4,182,557 | 2.8 |
| 1943 | 3,752 | 1,981,279 | 13,500,529 | 6.9 |
| 1944 | 4,956 | 2,115,637 | 8,721,079 | 7.0 |
| 1945 | 4,750 | 3,467,000 | 38,025,000 | 12.2 |

Despite "no-strike" pledges, workers staged wildcat strikes in the war years. Union leaders negotiated shorter hours, higher wages, and seniority rules and helped to build union membership to a new height. When the war ended, nearly 30 percent of all nonagricultural workers were union members.

"Work Stoppages Caused by Labor–Management Disputes in 1945," *Monthly Labor Review*, May 1946, p. 720; and Martin Glaberman, *War Time Strikes* (Detroit: Bewick, 1980), p. 36.

# Norman Rockwell's "Rosie, the Riveter"

D uring his long career as an artist-illustrator, Norman Rockwell published forty-seven covers of the popular family magazine *The Saturday Evening Post*, all venerating various aspects of American life. "Rosie, the Riveter" appeared on the magazine's cover May 29, 1943, and virtually enshrined women's contribution to the war effort.

Now an iconic image, Rosie was modeled on a real-life woman, a telephone operator in Vermont. Rockwell took advantage of his artistic license by making Rosie older and more muscular than his slight nineteen-year-old model. There is no doubt, though, that Rockwell captured the spirit of wartime patriotism. The self-confident Rosie takes obvious pride in her work, keeping her riveter on her ample lap even during lunchtime. A halo encircles her head, the American flag waves in the background. To seal the message, Rockwell shows Rosie crushing Hitler's autobiography, *Mein Kampf*, under her penny loafer.

In calling attention to Rosie's impressive biceps, Rockwell nevertheless attended to the small details that assure viewers that his defense worker has lost none of her femininity. Moreover, Rockwell does not show Rosie riveting but instead eating a ham sandwich that she undoubtedly made at home. ■

Library of Congress restricted copyright w/Curtic Publishing.

**IN WHAT** ways does Rockwell's painting convey ideals related to gender roles during the war?

Printed by permission of the Norman Rockwell Family Agency. Copyright © 1943 the Norman Rockwell Family Entities.

Once the United States entered the war, the major unions patriotically agreed to no-strike pledges for the duration. Nevertheless, rank-and-file union members sporadically staged illegal "wildcat" strikes. The most dramatic, a walkout of more than a half-million coal miners in 1943 led by the rambunctious John L. Lewis, withstood the attacks of the government and the press. Roosevelt repeatedly ordered the mines seized, only to find, as Lewis retorted, that coal could not be mined with bayonets. The Democratic-majority Congress passed the first federal antistrike bill, giving the president power to penalize or even draft strikers. And yet the strikes reached a level greater than in any other four-year period in American history.

# THE HOME FRONT

Alone among the major combatants, the homelands of the United States and Canada were neither invaded nor bombed, except for remote Pearl Harbor. On the U.S. mainland, most civilians—unless they had loved ones serving in the armed forces or relocated to distant parts—experienced the war mainly in terms of inconveniences: rationing, long workdays, and a sharp increase in income taxes. Nevertheless, Americans were not immune to the social upheavals that accompany war.

## FAMILIES IN WARTIME

"Economic conditions were ripe for a rush to the altar," quipped one social scientist. Men and women rushed into marriage, despite (or maybe because of) wartime uncertainties. The wartime boom sent personal incomes surging, allowing many young couples to set up separate households for the first time since the depression struck. The prospect of wartime separation pushed other couples into marriage. The marriage rate peaked in 1946—but by then divorces were also setting records.

Housing shortages were acute and rents were high. Landlords were free to discriminate against families with children—and, even more so, against racial minorities.

Wartime wages made many Americans eager to stock up on consumer goods, including a few luxuries, but they soon discovered that even supplying a household was difficult. Shopping had to be squeezed in between long work hours. Rationing required extra planning for purchasing meat, cheese, sugar, milk, coffee, gasoline, and shoes, and such staples were often in short supply. One homemaker said she and her friends referred to butter as "twenty-four karat gold." Illegal black markets flourished despite the high prices charged for scarce or rationed goods.

Caring for small children became a major problem. Wartime employment or military service often separated husbands and wives, leaving children in the care of only one parent. Even when families stayed together, both adults often worked long hours, sometimes on different shifts. In most communities, the limited facilities sponsored by industry or municipal governments could not keep up with the growing number of "latchkey" children.

Juvenile delinquency rose. With employers relaxing minimum age requirements, many teenagers—too young for the draft—quit school for high-wage factory jobs. Runaways drifted from city to city, finding temporary work at wartime plants or military installations. Urban gangs spawned brawling, prostitution, and automobile thefts for joy rides. To curb this trend, the U.S. Office of Education and the Children's Bureau sponsored a back-to-school campaign and appealed to employers to hire only older workers.

Public health improved greatly. Forced to forgo medical care during the Great Depression, many Americans spent large portions of their wartime paychecks on doctors, dentists, and prescription drugs. Some families ate lots of

WHAT MAJOR changes occurred in American society as a consequence of wartime mobilization?

myhistorylab
Review Summary

**More than 110,000** Japanese Americans were interned during World War II, some for up to four years. This photograph, taken in May 1942 by Dorothea Lange (1895–1965), the famed photographer of depression-era migrant families, shows young boys waiting in the baggage-inspection line at the Assembly Center in Turlock, California.

**25–6**
*Japanese Relocation Order* (1942)

## QUICK REVIEW

**Internment**

- December 8, 1941: Financial assets of Issei frozen.
- February 19, 1942: Civil rights of Japanese Americans suspended and 112,000 people relocated to internment camps.
- 1944: Supreme Court upheld constitutionality of relocation.

**25–7**
Sterling A. Brown, *Out of Their Mouths* (1942)

healthy fresh vegetables raised in their backyard "victory gardens." Even more important were the medical benefits provided to the more than 16 million men inducted into the armed forces and their dependents. Nationally, the infant death rate fell by more than a third, and life expectancy increased by three years. In the South and Southwest, however, racism and poverty combined to halt or even reverse these trends. These regions continued to have the nation's highest infant and maternal mortality rates.

## THE INTERNMENT OF JAPANESE AMERICANS

No families suffered more from wartime dislocations than Japanese Americans who were interned for the duration. After Pearl Harbor, military officials feared an invasion of the mainland and suspected Japanese Americans of secret disloyalty. On December 8, 1941, the federal government froze the financial assets of those born in Japan, called Issei, who had been barred from U.S. citizenship. Meanwhile, in the name of national defense, a coalition of politicians, patriotic organizations, business groups, and military officials called for the removal of all Americans of Japanese descent from Pacific coastal areas.

Charges of sedition against the Japanese unleashed deep racial prejudices. Headlines freely blared the word *Jap*, while political cartoonists and the popular culture employed blatant racial stereotypes.

On February 19, 1942, Roosevelt signed Executive Order 9066, which banned more than 120,000 Japanese American men, women, and children from designated military areas, mainly in California, but also in Oregon, Washington, and southern Arizona. The army prepared for forced evacuation, rounding up and removing Japanese Americans from communities where they had lived and worked, sometimes for generations.

During the spring of 1942, Japanese American families received one week's notice to close up their businesses and homes. Told to bring only what they could carry, they were then transported to one of the ten internment camps managed by the War Relocation Authority. The guarded camps were located as far away as Arkansas, although the majority had been set up in the remote desert areas of Utah, Colorado, Idaho, Arizona, Wyoming, and California.

By August, virtually every West Coast resident with at least one Japanese grandparent had been interned. The Japanese American Citizens League charged that "racial animosity," not military necessity, motivated the internment policy. Despite the protest of the American Civil Liberties Union and several church groups, the Supreme Court in *Korematsu* v. *United States* (1944) upheld the constitutionality of relocation on grounds of national security. In protest, nearly six thousand Japanese Americans renounced their U.S. citizenship. Japanese Americans had lost homes and businesses valued at $500 million in what many historians judge as being the worst violation of American civil liberties during the war. Not until 1988 did Congress vote to award each of the 60,000 surviving victims reparations of $20,000 and a public apology.

## "DOUBLE V": VICTORY AT HOME AND ABROAD

Throughout the war, African American activists conducted a "Double V" campaign, mobilizing not only for Allied victory but also for their own rights as citizens.

Black militants demanded, at a minimum, fair housing and equal employment opportunities, laying the foundation for the postwar civil rights movement.

Even before the United States entered the war, the foremost black labor leader—A. Philip Randolph, president of both the Brotherhood of Sleeping Car Porters and the National Negro Congress—began to mobilize against discrimination. At a planning meeting in Chicago a black woman proposed sending African Americans to Washington, DC. African Americans across the country began to prepare for a "great rally" of no less than 100,000 people at the Lincoln Memorial on the Fourth of July.

Eager to stop the March on Washington movement, Roosevelt met with Randolph, who proposed an executive order "making it mandatory that Negroes be permitted to work in [defense] plants." Randolph reviewed several drafts before approving the text that became, on June 25, 1941, Executive Order 8802, banning discrimination in defense industries and government. The president later appointed a Fair Employment Practices Committee to hear complaints and redress grievances. Randolph called off the march but remained determined to "shake up white America."

Other civil rights organizations formed during wartime to fight discrimination and Jim Crow, including segregation in the armed forces. The interracial Congress of Racial Equality (CORE), formed by pacifists in 1942, staged sit-ins at Chicago, Detroit, and Denver restaurants that refused to serve African Americans. Membership in the NAACP, which fought discrimination in defense plants and the military, grew from 50,000 in 1940 to 450,000 in 1946. The Supreme Court ruling in *Smith* v. *Albright* (1944) "white primaries" used in southern states to exclude black voters was a major victory paving the way for future civil rights struggles.

Approximately 1.2 million African Americans left the rural South to take wartime jobs, and they faced not only serious housing shortages but also whites intent on keeping them out of their own jobs and neighborhoods. "Hate strikes" broke out in defense plants across the country when African Americans were hired or upgraded to "white" positions. In February 1942, when twenty black families attempted to move into new federally funded apartments adjacent to a Polish American community in Detroit, a mob of 700 armed white protesters halted the moving vans and burned a cross on the project's grounds. The police ignored the white rioters but arrested black youths. Finally, two months later, 1,000 state troopers supervised the move of these families into the Sojourner Truth Housing Project, named after the famous abolitionist and former slave.

Racial violence reached its wartime peak during the summer of 1943, when 274 conflicts broke out in nearly fifty cities. In Detroit, where the black population had grown by more than a third since the beginning of the war, twenty-five blacks and nine whites were killed and more than 700 were injured.

**This painting is** by Horace Pippin, a self-taught African American artist who began painting as therapy for an injury suffered while serving with the U.S. Army's 369th Colored Infantry Regiment during World War I. It is one of a series drawn during World War II illustrating the contradiction between the principles of liberty and justice, for which Americans were fighting abroad, and the reality of racial prejudice at home.

Horace Pippin (1888–1946), "Mr. Prejudice", 1943. Oil on canvas, 18 × 14 inches. Philadelphia Museum of Art, Gift of Dr. and Mrs. Matthew T. Moore. Photo by Graydon Wood. 1984–108–1.

 **25–5**
A. Philip Randolph,
*Why Should We March?*
(1942)

## ZOOT-SUIT RIOTS

On the night of June 4, 1943, sailors poured into nearly 200 cars and taxis to drive through the streets of East Los Angeles in search of Mexican Americans dressed in "zoot suits." The sailors assaulted their victims at random, even chasing one youth into a movie theater and stripping him of his clothes while the audience cheered. Riots broke out and continued for five days.

Two communities had collided with tragic results. The sailors had only recently been uprooted from their hometowns and regrouped under the strict discipline of boot camp. Stationed in southern California while awaiting deployment overseas, they came face-to-face with Mexican American teenagers wearing long-draped coats, pegged pants, pocket watches with oversized chains, and big floppy hats. To the sailors, the zoot suit was not just a flamboyant fashion. Unlike the uniform the young sailors wore, the zoot suit signaled defiance and a lack of patriotism.

The zoot-suiters, however, represented less than 10 percent of the Hispanic community's youth. More than 300,000 Mexican Americans were serving in the armed forces (a number representing a greater proportion of their draft-age population than other Americans), often in the most hazardous branches, as paratroops and Marines. Many others were employed in war industries in Los Angeles, which had become home to the nation's largest Mexican American community. For the first time, Mexican Americans were finding well-paying jobs, and like African Americans, they expected their government to protect them from discrimination.

Military and civilian authorities eventually contained the zoot-suit riots by ruling several sections of Los Angeles off-limits to military personnel, and the city council passed legislation making the wearing of a zoot suit in public a criminal offense.

## POPULAR CULTURE AND "THE GOOD WAR"

Global events shaped the lives of American civilians but appeared to touch them only indirectly in their everyday activities. Food shortages, long hours in the factories, and even fears for loved ones abroad did not take away all the pleasures of full employment and prosperity.

Despite the sharpening racial divisions of the neighborhood and the workplace, popular music crossed racial lines. Transplanted southern musicians, black and white, brought their regional styles to northern cities. Played on jukeboxes in bars, bus stations, and cafés, "country" and "rhythm & blues" not only won new audiences but also inspired musicians to crisscross old boundaries. War themes pervaded popular music, meshing personal experiences with government directives to enshrine World War II as a "good war" that justified massive sacrifice.

**25–2**
Charles Lindbergh,
*Radio Address* (1941)

Hollywood mobilized, as one screenwriters group explained, "to build morale" and to "stimulate...initiative and responsibility." Combat films such as *Action in the North Atlantic* made heroes of ordinary Americans under fire, depicting GIs of different races and ethnicities discovering their common humanity. With military cooperation, wartime movies encouraged Americans to think well of all the Allies—including the Soviet Union. Several films, such as *Tender Comrade*, plugged pro-Soviet views that would be abruptly reversed in the postwar years. Other films such as the Oscar-winning *Since You Went Away* portrayed the loyalty and resilience of American families with servicemen stationed overseas. Hollywood aided the war effort in additional ways. Frank Capra directed the government-sponsored *Why We Fight*, a series of documentaries to explain the war's aims to soldiers. Meanwhile, movie stars led the war bond campaign, selling nearly $1 billion worth in 1942 alone.

The wartime spirit infected even the juvenile world of comics. The climbing sales of nickel "books" spawned a proliferation of patriotic superheroes such as the Green Lantern, Captain Marvel, and Wonder Woman. Even Bugs Bunny put on a uniform and fought sinister-looking enemies.

For many civilians, including civil defense volunteers and Red Cross workers, wearing a uniform demonstrated patriotism, and padded shoulders and straight lines became popular among fashion-conscious men and women. Women employed in defense plants wore slacks, often for the first time in their lives.

Much of this war fervor was spontaneous, but the government did all it could to encourage self-sacrificing patriotism. The Office of War Information screened all popular music, movies, radio programs, and advertisements to ensure that everyone got the message: only the collective effort of all Americans could preserve democracy at home and save the world from fascism. Washington tried to make sure that the public saw the daily inconveniences and shortages of wartime, and above all the drafting of young men to serve and die abroad, as sacrifices essential to victory. And in the government's zeal to popularize sacrifice among the citizenry, no one was excluded and no action considered insignificant. The government even worried about war workers' casual conversations. People were told that snooping Nazi spies lurked everywhere; posters and advertisements warned "Loose Lips Sink Ships."

By the mid-1940s, popular culture had helped to shape a collective memory of World War II as "the good war," the standard by which the nation's subsequent wars would be judged. It also played an important part in bringing diverse and sometimes antagonistic communities together, not only in support of the war but also as steadfast consumers of mass entertainment.

# MEN AND WOMEN IN UNIFORM

World War II mobilized 16.4 million Americans into the armed forces. Although only 34 percent of men who served in the army saw combat—the majority during the final year of the war—the experience had a powerful impact on nearly everyone. For those who survived, the war often proved to be the defining experience of their lives.

## CREATING THE ARMED FORCES

Neither the army nor the navy was prepared for the scale of combat World War II entailed. Only the U.S. Marine Corps, which had been planning since the 1920s to seize the western Pacific from Japan in the event of war, was ready to fight.

On October 16, 1940, National Registration Day, all men between twenty-one and thirty-six had to register for military service. After the United States entered the war, the draft age was lowered to eighteen, and local boards were instructed to choose the youngest first.

One-third of the men examined by the Selective Service were rejected. Surprising numbers were refused induction as physically unfit. For the first time, men were screened for "neuropsychiatric disorders or emotional problems," and approximately 1.6 million were rejected for that reason. At a time when only one American in four graduated from high school, many conscripts were turned away as functionally illiterate.

The democratic rhetoric of the war and the sudden massive expansion of the armed forces contributed to this transformation of the officer corps. A shortage of officers during World War I had prompted a huge expansion of the Reserve Officer Training Corps (ROTC) on campuses, but it still could not meet the demand. Racing to make up for the deficiency, Army Chief of Staff George Marshall opened schools for officer candidates. In 1942, in seventeen-week training periods, these schools produced more than 54,000 platoon leaders.

## WOMEN ENTER THE MILITARY

With the approach of World War II, Massachusetts Republican congresswoman Edith Nourse Rogers proposed legislation for the formation of a women's corps. The army instead drafted its own bill, which both Rogers and Eleanor Roosevelt

WHAT ROLE did women play in the armed forces during World War II?

myhistorylab
Review Summary

**New recruits to** the Women's Army Corps (WAC) pick up their clothing "issue" (allotment). These volunteers served in many capacities, from nursing men in combat to performing clerical and communication duties "stateside" (within the United States). Approximately 140,000 women served in the WACS during World War II.

supported, creating in May 1942 the Women's Army Auxiliary Corps (WAAC), later changed to Women's Army Corps (WAC). In 1942–43 other bills established a women's division of the navy (WAVES), the Women's Air Force Service Pilots, and the Marine Corps Women's Reserve.

Overall, more than 350,000 women served in World War II, two-thirds of them in the WACS and WAVES. As a group, they were better educated and more skilled—although paid less—than the average enlisted man. However, military policy prohibited women from supervising male workers, even in desk jobs.

Barred from combat, women were not necessarily protected from danger. Nurses accompanied troops into combat, treated men under fire, and dug their own foxholes. More than 1,000 women flew planes, although not in combat missions. Others worked as photographers and cryptoanalysts. But the vast majority remained far from battlefronts. Stationed mainly within the United States, most women worked in familiar jobs, serving in administration, communications, clerical, or health care facilities.

The WACS and WAVES were both subject to hostile commentary and bad publicity. The overwhelming majority of soldiers believed that most WACS were prostitutes; the War Department itself, fearing "immorality" among women in the armed forces, closely monitored their conduct and established much stricter rules for women than for men. The U.S. Marine Corps even used intelligence officers to ferret out suspected lesbians or women who showed "homosexual tendencies" (as opposed to homosexual acts), both causes for dishonorable discharge.

## OLD PRACTICES AND NEW HORIZONS

The Selective Service Act, in response to the demands of African American leaders, specified that "there shall be no discrimination against any person on account of race or color." The draft brought hundreds of thousands of young black men into the army, and African Americans enlisted at a rate 60 percent above their proportion of the general population. By 1944, black soldiers represented 10 percent of the army's troops, and overall approximately 1 million African Americans served in the armed forces during World War II. The army, however, channeled black recruits into segregated, poorly equipped units, commanded by white officers. The majority of African Americans served mainly in construction or stevedore work. Only toward the end of the war, when the shortage of infantry neared a crisis, were African Americans permitted to rise to combat status. The all-black 761st Tank Battalion, the first African American unit in combat, won a Medal of Honor after 183 days in action. And despite the very small number of African Americans admitted to the Air Force, the 99th Pursuit Squadron, trained at the new base in Tuskegee, Alabama, earned high marks in action against the feared German Luftwaffe. Even the Marine Corps and the Coast Guard agreed to end their historic exclusion of African Americans, although they recruited and promoted only a small number.

The ordinary black soldier, sailor, or Marine experienced few benefits from these late-in-the-war gains. They encountered discrimination everywhere.

Even the blood banks kept blood segregated by race. The year 1943 marked the peak of unrest, with violent confrontations between blacks and whites breaking out at military installations, especially in the South, where the majority of African American soldiers were stationed. Toward the end of the war, to improve morale among black servicemen the army relaxed its policy of segregation, mainly in recreational facilities.

The army also grouped Japanese Americans into segregated units, sending most to fight far from the Pacific Theater. Better educated than the average soldier, many **Nisei** soldiers who knew Japanese served stateside as interpreters and translators. When the army decided to create a Nisei regiment, more than 10,000 volunteers stepped forward, although only one in five was accepted. The Nisei 442nd fought heroically in Italy and France and became the most decorated regiment in the war.

Despite segregation, the armed forces ultimately pulled Americans of all varieties out of their separate communities. Many Jews and other second-generation European immigrants, for example, described their military stint as an "Americanizing" experience. For the first time in their lives, many Indian peoples left reservations as approximately 25,000 served in the armed forces. In the Pacific war, Navajo "code talkers" used their native language (a complex, unwritten language unknown to the Japanese) to transmit information from the front lines and also improved their English in special classes. For many African Americans, military service provided a bridge to postwar civil rights agitation.

Many homosexuals also discovered a wider world in the service. Despite rules barring them from the military, most slipped through at the induction centers. Moreover, the emotional pressures of wartime, especially the fear of death, encouraged close friendships, and homosexuals in the military often found more room than in civilian life to express their sexual orientation openly.

## THE MEDICAL CORPS

By the time the war ended, the army reported 949,000 casualties, including 175,000 killed in action. Although the European Theater produced the most casualties, the Pacific held grave dangers beyond enemy fire. For soldiers in humid jungles, malaria, typhus, diarrhea, or dengue fever posed the most common threat to their lives.

The prolonged stress of combat also took a toll in "battle fatigue"—the official army term for combat stress and what would today be called posttraumatic stress. Despite rigorous screening, more than 1 million soldiers suffered at one time or another from debilitating psychiatric symptoms, and the number of men discharged for neuropsychiatric reasons was 2.5 times greater than in previous wars. The cause, psychiatrists concluded, was not individual weakness but long stints in the front lines. In France, for example, where soldiers spent up to 200 days in the field without a break from fighting, thousands cracked, occasionally wounding themselves in order to be sent home. In 1944 the army concluded that eight months in combat was the maximum. When replacements were available, it instituted a rotation system to relieve exhausted soldiers.

In basic training soldiers received first-aid instruction, and they went into battle with bandages to treat minor wounds. For anything more serious, however, they needed physicians and medics. Army Medical Corps doctors went to the front lines.

**The Marines recruited** more than 400 Navajos to serve as code talkers by communicating in their own language. Deployed mainly to the Pacific Theater, they used radio and telegraph to transmit quickly vital information about battlefield activities, including troop movements. This photograph, taken in December 1943, shows Corporal Henry Bake, Jr., and Private First Class George H. Kirk operating a portable radio unit in a jungle clearing near the front lines.

**Nisei**    U.S. citizens born of immigrant Japanese parents.

There, in makeshift tent hospitals, these physicians advanced surgical techniques and used new "wonder drugs" such as penicillin to save many wounded soldiers who in earlier wars would have died. Of the soldiers who underwent emergency field surgery, more than 85 percent survived. Overall, less than 4 percent of all soldiers who received medical care died of their injuries.

Grateful for the care of skilled surgeons, many soldiers nevertheless named medics the true heroes of the battlefront. Thirty to forty medics were attached to each infantry battalion, and under fire they gave emergency first aid and transported the wounded to the aid station and, if necessary, the field hospital.

In the military hospitals, American nurses gave the bulk of care to recovering soldiers. Like medics, army nurses went first to training centers in the United States, learning how to dig foxholes and dodge bullets before being sent overseas. By 1945, approximately 56,000 women, including 500 African American women, were on active duty in the Army Nurse Corps, staffing medical facilities in every theater of the war.

# THE WORLD AT WAR

WHAT WERE the main elements of
the Allied war strategy?

myhistorylab
Review Summary

The Allies remained on the defensive almost until the end of 1942. During this time, from the Atlantic to deep in Russia, Hitler and his allies controlled most of continental Europe and continued to pound Great Britain from the air. A German army also swept across North Africa and almost took the Suez Canal from the British.

In the Pacific and East Asia the situation was just as dire. Just two hours after the attack on Pearl Harbor, Japanese planes struck the main U.S. airbase in the Philippines and demolished half the warplanes commanded by General Douglas MacArthur. Japanese troops soon conquered the entire Philippines. MacArthur retreated to the Bataan Peninsula and then fled by submarine to Australia. When his stranded troops on Bataan finally surrendered, they were subjected to a horrific "death march" into POW camps; where they would face abuse, disease, and starvation until liberated. The Japanese easily overran Britain's Southeast Asian colonies, the Dutch East Indies, and the entire western Pacific. Although China officially joined the Allies, Japanese forces on the Chinese mainland remained on the offensive. Roosevelt called the news "all bad," and his military advisers predicted a long fight to victory (see Map 25.1).

## SOVIETS HALT NAZI DRIVE

World War II was a war of offensive maneuvers punctuated by surprise attacks. Its chief weapons—tanks and planes on land and aircraft carriers and submarines at sea—combined mobility and concentrated firepower. Also of major importance were artillery and explosives, which according to some estimates accounted for more than 30 percent of casualties. Major improvements in communication systems, mainly two-way radio transmission and radiotelephony that permitted commanders to stay in contact with division leaders, played a decisive role throughout the war.

From the beginning of the European war in 1939, Hitler had used these methods to seize the advantage, purposefully striking terror among stricken populations of Western Europe as he routed opposing armies. The Royal Air Force, however, fought the Luftwaffe to a standstill in the Battle of Britain, frustrating Hitler's hopes of invading England. By the spring of 1941, he had turned his attention eastward, planning to conquer the Soviet Union. But he had to delay the invasion to rescue Mussolini, whose weak army faced defeat in North Africa and Greece. Not until June 22, 1941, six weeks behind schedule, did Hitler invade the Soviet Union.

# MAP EXPLORATION

To explore an interactive version of this map, go to **http://www.prenhall.com/faraghertlc/map25.1**

**MAP 25.1**

**The War in Europe**   The Allies remained on the defensive during the first years of the war, but by 1943 the British and Americans, with an almost endless supply of resources, had turned the tide.

WHAT WERE the key turning points of the war in Europe?

Hitler's forces initially devastated the Red Army. The brutality of the Nazis—from the beginning they intended to kill all the Jews and reduce the Russian population to slave laborers—kindled a desperate civilian resistance. The German army in Russia found its supply lines overextended and the brutal Russian winter just beginning, while Stalin was able to send every available resource to his troops concentrated just outside Moscow. The Red Army launched a massive counterattack, catching the frostbitten German troops off guard and driving them to retreat. For the first time, the Nazi war machine had suffered a major setback.

In 1942, German troops had a new objective: occupying the rich oil fields of the Caucasus. But at Stalingrad (now Volgograd), a major Soviet industrial city on the Volga River, Hitler met his nemesis. In the battle for that city alone, the Soviets suffered more casualties than Americans did during the entire war. House-to-house fighting and a massive Red Army counterattack inflicted an even greater toll on the Nazis. Hitler ordered to his troops to die rather than surrender. But in February 1943 the German Sixth Army at last gave up.

Already in retreat but plotting one last desperate attempt to halt the Red Army, the Germans threw most of their remaining armored vehicles into action at Kursk in July 1943. The clash quickly spiraled into the greatest tank battle in history, involving more than 2 million troops and 6,000 tanks. After another stunning defeat, the Germans had decisively lost the initiative. Their only option was to delay the advance of the Red Army toward their own homeland.

Meanwhile, the Soviet Union had begun to recover from its early losses, even as tens of millions of its people remained homeless and near starvation. Assisted by Lend-Lease, by 1942 the Soviets were outproducing Germany in many types of weapons and other supplies. Nazi officers and German civilians alike began to doubt that Hitler could win.

Soviet victories had turned the tide; the Soviet Union, not the Western Allies, bore by far the heaviest burden in stopping what had once seemed an unstoppable Nazi advance. The American and British people were grateful for this immense Soviet contribution (the full extent of which they did not know at the time), and the British and American governments found themselves under enormous pressure from Stalin to open a second front in the west. But to do so required complex strategic planning and the assembling of immense material and human resources.

## PLANNING AND INITIATING THE ALLIED OFFENSIVE

Despite the huge territories that Nazi Germany and Japan controlled in 1942, the Axis momentum was flagging. After Stalingrad, Hitler lost ground. In the Pacific that summer, Japan's plans to invade Hawai'i and Australia were stopped by the U.S. Navy. In the course of 1942 as well, American shipbuilding began to outpace the punishment Nazi U-boats could inflict on Allied shipping; that advance kept open the vital Lend-Lease supply lanes to Britain and Russia, while submarine-hunting destroyers greatly reduced the German undersea threat. The United States far outstripped Germany in building landing craft and amphibious vehicles, two of the most important innovations of the war. Now outnumbered by the Allies, the German Luftwaffe was increasingly limited to defensive action.

Against this backdrop, Roosevelt, Churchill, and their generals hammered out a strategy to defeat the Axis. They saw Japan as the lesser threat—one that for the moment should be contained rather than attacked all-out (although MacArthur, the U.S. Navy, and the American public all clamored for a "Japan-first" strategy of avenging Pearl Harbor). Germany, Roosevelt and Churchill agreed, must be beaten first, which meant eventually invading Europe and fighting Hitler's Reich from the west, while the Red Army advanced from the east.

But the Allies disagreed about where to attack Germany. Remembering the terrible bloodletting on the western front during World War I, the British dreaded another long, stalemated struggle in France. Churchill and his generals wanted to strike through what he called "Europe's soft under-belly," the Mediterranean. The American generals retorted that only a direct, though meticulously prepared, assault through France would bring down Nazi Germany.

In the end, Roosevelt and Churchill compromised: they would first send smaller armies into the Mediterranean, while gathering a huge Anglo-American invasion army in Britain. This strategy was set in motion in late 1942. On October 23–24, near El Alamein in the desert of western Egypt, the British Eighth Army halted a major offensive by the German Afrika Korps, headed by the famed "Desert Fox," General Erwin Rommel. Although suffering heavy losses, British forces destroyed the Italian North African Army and much of the Afrika Korps. Then, in November, American troops for the first time went into action in the European Theater by joining the British in **Operation Torch**, an invasion of Morocco and Algeria. While at the eastern end the British drove Rommel back from El Alamein, from the west, a mostly American army, still inexperienced and mistake-prone, forced the Germans out of Tunisia. In six months, North Africa was cleared of Axis troops.

Allied aerial bombing was increasing the pressure on Germany. Bombing missions over the Rhineland and the Ruhr did take out many German factories, while also costing tens of thousands of civilian lives, but the Germans successfully relocated many industrial plants to the countryside.

Determined to break German resistance, the Royal Air Force redirected its main attack away from military targets to cities, fuel dumps, and transportation lines. Indiscriminate bombing practically leveled the great city of Hamburg, killing between 60,000 and 100,000 people and destroying 300,000 buildings. Sixty other cities were hit hard, leaving 20 percent of Germany's total residential area in ruins. Americans joined in the very worst air raid of the war—650,000 incendiary bombs dropped on Dresden in 1945 destroying 8 square miles and killing perhaps 135,000 civilians (no one knows for sure, for the city sheltered uncounted refugees). Dresden, famous for its architecture and art galleries, had no military value. This was terror bombing. Hitler had started it, but the Allies more than repaid in kind.

Though the air war disappointed those who saw in it the means of a bloodless—to the attackers—victory, the Allied strategic air offensive did weaken the German economy and did terrorize (but also enrage) German civilians. Moreover, in trying to defend German cities and factories, the Luftwaffe sacrificed most of its remaining fighter planes and aircraft fuel. When the Allies finally invaded Western Europe in the summer of 1944, they would enjoy total air superiority.

## THE ALLIED INVASION OF EUROPE

In the summer of 1943, the Allies continued their Mediterranean offensive by attacking southern Italy. On July 10, British and American troops stormed Sicily and by mid-August conquered the island. King Vittorio Emmanuel fired Mussolini, calling him "the most despised man in Italy." After Allied troops landed near

**Operation Torch** The Allied invasion of Axis-held North Africa in 1942.

**As part of** the air war on Germany, Allied bombers launched a devastating attack on Dresden, a major economic center, in February 1945. Of the civilians who died, most from burns or smoke inhalation during the firestorm, a large number were women and children, refugees from the eastern front. The city was left in ruins.

**Operation Overlord**   United States and British invasion of France in June 1944 during World War II.

**D-Day**   June 6, 1944, the day of the first paratroop drops and amphibious landings on the coast of Normandy, France, in the first stage of Operation Overlord during World War II.

Naples, Italy surrendered to the Western Allies on September 8. But Hitler sent new divisions into northern and central Italy, stalling the Allied campaign. Almost until the end of the European war, a large Allied army was still bogged down on Italy's rugged terrain, battling a much smaller German force.

All across occupied Europe, resistance to the Nazis spread. Jews walled off in the Nazi-built Warsaw ghetto, realizing that they were marked for extermination, revolted in the summer of 1943 and fought to the death. Scattered revolts followed in the Nazi labor camps, where military prisoners of war and civilians were being worked on starvation rations. Underground fighters, known as partisans, resisted the Nazis from Norway to Greece and from Poland to France. Untrained and lightly armed, men, women, and children risked their lives to distribute antifascist propaganda, committed sabotage, rescued downed Allied bomber crews, and killed Nazi collaborators. They smuggled food and weapons to clandestine resistance groups and prepared the way for the offensive that, in shortwave radio broadcasts, the Allies promised.

Allied preparations for that offensive were thorough and time-consuming. As a huge American army gathered and trained in Britain, Churchill's objections to invading France gradually wore down, while Stalin ceaselessly demanded a second front. (To him, the stalled invasion of Italy was no substitute.) By early 1944, Anglo-American plans were being readied for **Operation Overlord**, a campaign to retake the Continent with a decisive counterattack through France. General Dwight D. Eisenhower, who was put in command, displayed great skill not only in strategizing but also in dealing with contentious British, Americans, and the prickly Free French leader, General Charles de Gaulle.

**D-Day**—the start of the Allied invasion—finally came on June 6, 1944. Much depended on surprise and even the right mix of tides, moonlight, and clear weather. After receiving a forecast of a short break in storms that otherwise might have doomed the operation, "Ike" made the courageous decision: "Go." Under heavy German machine-gun and mortar fire, wave after wave of American, British, Canadian, and Free French troops hit the Normandy beaches, the tides swelling with the dead and the wounded. Some 2,500 men died in the initial assault, many before they could fire a shot. At Omaha Beach the Germans had prepared their defense almost perfectly, and the Americans who landed there had a particularly difficult time gaining a toehold. Within days, though, more than 175,000 Allied troops and 20,000 vehicles were battling the Germans—the largest landing operation in history. Over the next six weeks, nearly 1 million more Allied soldiers came ashore. But not until mid-July did this invasion army finally break out of Normandy and drive into the French interior.

All eyes now turned to Paris. Allied bombers pounded roads, bridges, rail lines, and factories that were producing German munitions all around the French capital. As demoralized German soldiers retreated, hoping only to survive, the French Resistance unfurled the French flag at impromptu demonstrations on Bastille Day, July 14. On August 10, railway workers staged one of the first successful strikes against Nazi occupiers, and three days later the Paris police defected to the Resistance, which

**D-Day landing, June** 6, 1944, marked the greatest amphibious maneuver in military history. Troop ships ferried Allied soldiers from England to Normandy beaches. Within a month, nearly 1 million men had assembled in France, ready to retake western and central Europe from German forces.

distributed leaflets proclaiming that "the hour of liberation has come." With Free French and Allied troops, de Gaulle entered Paris on August 25 and announced a reconstituted French Republic. Belgium also fell swiftly to the liberators. But Allied troops had only reached a resting place between bloody battles, their supply lines stretched thin and German resistance stiffening.

## THE HIGH COST OF EUROPEAN VICTORY

By September 1944 Allied commanders were searching for a way to end the war quickly. Missing a spectacular chance to move through largely undefended territory and on to Berlin, they turned north instead, intending to strike through the Netherlands into Germany's industrial heartland. Faulty intelligence reports overlooked a well-armed German division at the Dutch town of Arnhem, waiting to cut Allied paratroops to pieces. The Germans captured 6,000 Americans.

That winter, making a final, desperate effort to break the Allied momentum, Hitler sent his last reserves, a quarter-million men, against American lines in Belgium's dense Ardennes forest. In this so-called **Battle of the Bulge**, the Germans surprised the Americans, driving them fifty miles back before literally running out of gas. This last effort exhausted the German capacity for counterattack. After Christmas Day 1944, the Germans had to retreat into their own territory.

In March 1945, discovery of a single intact bridge across the Rhine allowed the Allies to roll into the heart of Germany, taking the heavily industrialized Ruhr Valley. By now, Soviet offenses were crushing the German army in the east. The Red Army had reached Warsaw in the midsummer of 1944 but then stood by while the anti-Russian Polish resistance rose up—only to be destroyed (along with most of the city) by the Nazis. While that tragedy unfolded, the Soviets occupied the Balkans and battled the Germans in Hungary. Only in January 1945 did the Red Army sweep across Poland and by April besiege Berlin, where Hitler had holed up. The defense of Germany, now hopeless, had fallen into the hands of teenagers, terrified elderly men, and a few desperate Nazis.

## THE WAR IN ASIA AND THE PACIFIC

Six months after Pearl Harbor, the United States began regaining naval superiority in the central Pacific. The Americans had been supremely lucky that their aircraft carriers were out at sea during the Pearl Harbor attack; that luck was spectacularly demonstrated in the great naval battle of the Coral Sea on May 7–8, 1942, in which carrier-based American aircraft blocked a Japanese thrust at Australia. A month later, on June 4, the Japanese fleet converged on Midway Island, an outpost vital to American communications and to the defense of Hawai'i. And there the Americans had another lucky break, for intelligence officers had broken the Japanese codes and thus knew when and where the attack would fall. Still separated by hundreds of miles of open sea, the Japanese and American carrier fleets clashed at long distance. Descending from the clouds, American warplanes sank four Japanese carriers and destroyed hundreds of planes, ending Japan's offensive threat to Hawai'i and the West Coast. These two battles signaled an historic shift in naval warfare: now aircraft carriers, not huge battleships, would rule the waves.

Even so, Japan controlled a vast arc of the western Pacific. That perimeter stretched from the outermost Aleutians (off Alaska) to northern New Guinea and the Solomon Islands (off Australia). Japan also dominated all of coastal China and the European colonies of Southeast Asia: Indochina, Malaya, present-day Indonesia, and Burma (see Map 25.2). In much of East Asia (except China), nationalistic and anticolonial sentiment played into Japanese hands at first. With only 200,000 troops, Japan easily overran Southeast Asia because so few people

**Battle of the Bulge**   German offensive in December 1944 that penetrated deep into Belgium (creating a "bulge"). Allied forces, while outnumbered, attacked from the north and south. By January 1945, the German forces were destroyed or routed, but not without some 77,000 Allied casualties.

# MAP EXPLORATION

To explore an interactive version of this map, go to **http://www.prenhall.com/faraghertlc/map25.2**

**ALASKA (US)**

**SOVIET UNION**
*(entered war against Japan Aug 8, 1945)*

*Bering Sea*

*Sea of Okhotsk*

**Attu,** *(May 11–20, 1943)*

*Sakhalin*

← **Kiska**

*Aleutian Islands*

*Kurile Islands*

*PACIFIC OCEAN*

**OUTER MONGOLIA**

*Harbin*
*Mukden*

**Peking**
**Port Arthur**

*Sea of Japan*

**CHINA**

**KOREA**

**JAPAN**
**Tokyo,** *(firebombed May 23, 1945)*
**Tokyo Bay,** *(surrender signed Sept 2, 1945)*

**Midway Island,** *(Jun 4–5, 1942)*

**Pearl Harbor,** *(Dec 7, 1941)*

*Hawaiian Islands*

**BHUTAN**
*Chungking*
*Nanking*
*Shanghai*
*Hankow*

**Okinawa,** *(Apr 1–Jun 22, 1945)*

**Iwo Jima,** *Feb 19–Mar 16, 1945)*

**Wake Island,** *(Dec 23, 1941)*

*Mariana Islands*

**FRENCH INDOCHINA**
*Canton*
**Hong Kong**
*Formosa*

**Burma (Br)**
*Hanoi*
**Lingayen Gulf,** *(Jan 9, 1945)*

**Bataan,** *(Jan 9–Apr 3, 1942)*
*Manila*

**Philippine Sea,** *(Jun 19–21, 1944)*

**Tinian,** *(Jul 24–Aug 1, 1944)*

*Rangoon*
**THAILAND**
**Corregidor,** *(US surrender May 5, 1942) (US counterattack Jan 22–Mar 2, 1945)*
**Leyte Gulf,** *(Oct 23–26, 1944)*
**Saipan**
**Guam,** *(Jul 21, 1944)*

*Bangkok*
*Philippine Islands*

*South China Sea*

**Ngulu,** *(Oct 16, 1944)*

**Eniwetok,** *(Feb 17–20, 1944)*

**Kwajalein,** *(Feb 1–6, 1944)*

*Marshall Islands*

**MALAYA**
**Borneo,** *(May–Aug, 1945)*
**Palau,** *(Sept 15– Oct 13, 1944)*
*Caroline Islands*

**Makin,** *(Nov 20–23, 1943)*

*Singapore*
*Sumatra*
*Borneo*
*Celebes*

**Bismarck Sea,** *(Mar 2–4, 1943)*

**Tarawa,** *(Nov 20–23, 1943)*

*Gilbert Islands*

**NETHERLANDS EAST INDIES**
*New Guinea*

*Java*
*Solomon Islands*

**Guadalcanal,** *(Aug 7, 1942– Feb 9, 1943)*

**Java Sea,** *(Feb–Mar 1942)*

*Port Moresby*

*New Hebrides (Br and Fr)*

**Lombok Strait,** *(Feb 18–19, 1942)*

**Coral Sea,** *(May 7–11, 1942)*

*Fiji Islands (Br)*

*INDIAN OCEAN*

**AUSTRALIA**

*New Caledonia (Br)*

*PACIFIC OCEAN*

Legend:
- ········· Extent of Japanese control (Aug 1942)
- Japanese-held territory (Aug 1942)
- ← Japanese forces
- ← Allied forces
- ✸ Japanese victories
- ✸ Allied victories
- ▼ Atomic bombs, Aug 6 and Aug 9, 1945

**MAP 25.2**

**War in the Pacific** Across an ocean battlefield utterly unlike the European Theater, Allies battled Japanese troops near their homeland.

HOW DID strategies in the Pacific differ from those in Europe?

in the British, French, and Dutch colonies would fight for their imperial masters. Japan installed puppet governments in Burma and the Philippines, and independent Thailand became a Japanese ally. But the new Japanese empire proved terrifyingly cruel. Local nationalists from Indochina to the Philippines turned against the Japanese, forming guerrilla bands that harassed the invaders. In China, Japan's huge land army bogged down fighting both the Nationalist forces of Chiang Kai shek and the Communist People's Liberation Army led by Mao Zedong.

Thus, in mid-1942 the war for the Pacific was still only beginning. Pulling back their offensive operations, the Japanese concentrated their remaining forces. Their commanders calculated that bitter fighting, with high casualties on both sides, would wear down the American military and public. The U.S. command, divided between MacArthur in the southwest Pacific and Admiral Chester Nimitz in the central Pacific, developed a strategy to strangle the Japanese import-dependent economy and to **"island-hop"** from one strategic outpost to another, closing in on the home islands.

In the Solomons and New Guinea, American and Australian ground troops began the counterattack. On Guadalcanal in the Solomons, American Marines struck at one Japanese stronghold, and during a six-month struggle endured tropical diseases, dangerous parasites, food and ammunition shortages, and very high casualty rates against Japanese defenders who fought to the death. Finally, with strong supply lines secured by a string of costly naval battles, in February 1943 the Americans finally prevailed, proving that they could defeat Japanese forces in brutal jungle combat.

For the next two years, the U.S. Navy and Marine Corps opened a path to Japan, capturing a series of important Pacific atolls but bypassing others, helplessly stranding well-armed Japanese defenders. In October of that year, MacArthur led an American force of 250,000 to retake the Philippines. Trying to hold the islands, practically all that remained of the Japanese navy threw itself at the Americans in the Battle of Leyte Gulf, the largest naval battle in history. The Japanese lost eighteen capital ships, leaving the United States in control of the Pacific. While MacArthur mopped up operations in the Philippines—at a cost of 100,000 Filipino lives and leaving Manila devastated—the small but strategically important island of Iwo Jima, south of Japan, fell. Here too, the American death toll was high; casualties were estimated at nearly 27,000.

Even bloodier was the struggle for Okinawa, an island 350 miles southwest of the Japanese home islands and the site of vital airbases. The invasion—the largest American amphibious operation in the Pacific war—began on Easter Sunday, April 1, 1945. Waves of Japanese *kamikaze* ("divine wind") pilots, flying suicide missions with a 500-pound bomb and only enough fuel for a one-way flight, met the Marines on the beaches. The U.S. troops who survived this onslaught used flame-throwers, each with 300 gallons of napalm, to incinerate dug-in Japanese defenders. On Okinawa, more Americans died or were wounded than at Normandy. But at the end of June, when the ghastly struggle ended, 140,000 Japanese were dead, including 42,000 civilians.

The war was now over in Europe, and the Allies could concentrate on Japan alone. Tokyo and other Japanese cities were targeted by B-17s and new B-29s flying from Guam with devastating results. Massive fire bombings burned thousands of civilians alive in their mostly wooden or bamboo houses, and hundreds of thousands were left homeless. Meanwhile U.S. submarines cut the home islands off from supplies on the East Asian mainland.

**Island-hop** The Pacific campaigns of 1944 that were the American naval versions of the Blitzkrieg.

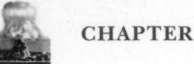

Japan could not hold out forever. Without a navy or air force, critically important oil, tin, rubber, and grain could not be transported to maintain its soldiers or feed its people. Great Britain and particularly the United States, however, pressed for a quick and unconditional surrender. They had special reasons to hurry. Earlier they had sought a commitment from the Soviet Union to invade Japan, but now they looked beyond the war, determined to prevent the Red Army from taking any Japanese-held territories. These calculations, as well as chilling forecasts of the bloody cost of invading and subjugating the home islands, set the stage for unleashing the top-secret weapon that American scientists had been building: the atomic bomb.

## THE LAST STAGES OF WAR

From the attack on Pearl Harbor until mid-1943, Roosevelt and his advisers had focused on military strategy rather than on postwar plans. But once the defeat of Nazi Germany appeared in sight, high government officials began to consider long-range objectives.

### THE HOLOCAUST

Another fact also became clear, at least to the American public, as the European war entered its final stages: the full horror of Nazi atrocities. As part of a comprehensive plan for achieving Aryan superiority and the "final solution of the Jewish question," Hitler had ordered the extermination of "racial enemies" and others deemed undesirable, including mentally retarded and crippled German children and adults. The toll included some 6 million Jews, 250,000 Romany (Gypsies), 60,000 homosexuals, members of other "inferior races" (such as Slavs), and indeed anyone else deemed an enemy of the German Reich and its "master race." Beginning in 1933, but accelerating from 1941 onward, the Nazis murdered millions of people in Germany and all the European nations they conquered. Gruesome "medical experiments" were also performed on Jews and Soviet prisoners of war (POWs).

WHAT WERE the factors behind the decision to deploy the atomic bomb against Japan?

**myhistorylab**
**Review Summary**

***Belsen Camp: The*** *Compound for Women*, painted by American artist Leslie Cole, depicts Belsen as the Allied troops found it when they invaded Germany in 1945.

Leslie Cole, "Belsen Camp: The Compound for Women". Imperial War Museum, London.

These policies had begun at the outset of the Hitler regime in 1933, and at the beginning of 1942 the Nazis initiated mass murder in death camps like Auschwitz in Poland. Very soon, word was leaking out of occupied Europe of what the Nazis were doing. But throughout almost the entire war, the U.S. government released little information about what came to be known as the **Holocaust**. Although liberal magazines such as *The Nation* and small committees of intellectuals tried to call attention to what was happening in the Nazi camps, major news media like the *New York Times* and *Time* magazine treated reports of genocide as minor news items. As late as 1943, only 43 percent of Americans polled believed that Hitler was systematically murdering European Jews.

Leaders of the American Jewish community, however, were better informed than the general population, and since the mid-1930s they had been petitioning the government to suspend immigration quotas that barred significant numbers of German Jews from taking refuge in the United States. Backed by public opinion (fixated on foreigners threatening American jobs), Roosevelt and Congress refused. Even after the United States entered the war, the president maintained that the liberation of European Jews and other oppressed peoples depended on a speedy and total Allied victory. Not until January 1944 did Roosevelt agree to change government policy. At that time, Secretary of the Treasury Henry Morgenthau, himself Jewish, reported to the president on "one of the greatest crimes in history, the slaughter of the Jewish people in Europe," and suggested that anti-Semitism in the State Department had stalled the development of an aggressive plan of action. Within a week, in part to avoid scandal, Roosevelt issued an executive order creating the War Refugee Board. However, when American Jews pleaded for bombing rail lines leading to the notorious death camp at Auschwitz, in occupied Poland, both Roosevelt and the War Department refused. Attempts to rescue civilians—such was the government's unshaken position—would divert resources from military operations. The extent of Nazi depravity was finally revealed to Americans when Allied troops invaded Germany and began liberating the Nazi camps.

## THE YALTA CONFERENCE

Roosevelt was elected to a fourth term in November 1944, defeating the moderately liberal Republican governor of New York, Thomas E. Dewey. Many loyal Democrats looked forward to a revival of the New Deal after the war was won. Elected with FDR was a new vice president, a middle-of-the-road Missouri senator named Harry S Truman, who replaced ultraliberal Henry Wallace. Unknown to the public, however, Roosevelt was now exhausted and gravely ill—though, as was his habit, he kept his vice president totally uninformed of his plans and of the most important wartime secrets.

In early 1945, with the end of the war in sight, Allied leaders began to reassess their goals. The Atlantic Charter of 1941 had stated noble objectives for the world after the defeat of fascism: national self-determination, no territorial aggrandizement, equal access of all peoples to raw materials and collaboration for the improvement of economic opportunities, freedom of the seas, disarmament, and "freedom from fear and want." Now, four years later, Roosevelt realized that neither Great Britain nor the Soviet Union intended to abide by any code of conduct that compromised their national security or conflicted with their economic interests. Stalin and Churchill soon reached a new agreement, one projecting their respective spheres of influence in Eastern Europe.

In early February 1945, Roosevelt held still another wartime meeting with Churchill and Stalin, this time at Yalta, a Crimean resort on the Black Sea.

**Holocaust**  The systematic murder of millions of European Jews and others deemed undesirable by Nazi Germany.

**Yalta Conference**  Meeting of U.S. President Franklin Roosevelt, British Prime Minister Winston Churchill, and Soviet Premier Joseph Stalin held in February 1945 to plan the final stages of World War II and postwar arrangements.

Seeking his partners' cooperation, the president recognized that prospects for postwar peace also depended on compromise. Neither the United States nor Great Britain raised serious objections to Stalin's demand to retain the Baltic states and eastern Poland—booty from the time of the Nazi–Soviet pact—and to create an East European "buffer zone" protecting Russia against future German aggression. In return, Churchill insisted on restoring the British Empire in Asia, and the United States hoped to retain captured Pacific islands from which Japanese military resurgence could be checked. Roosevelt hoped to ease the harshness of these imperialistic goals by creating a global peacekeeping organization, the United Nations, and by using promises of postwar American economic aid to persuade Stalin to behave with restraint in countries, like Poland, that the Red Army was liberating and occupying.

The biggest and most controversial item on the agenda at Yalta was the Soviet entry into the Pacific war, which Roosevelt believed necessary for a timely Allied victory. After driving a hard bargain involving Soviet rights to territory in China, Stalin agreed to declare war against Japan within three months of Germany's surrender. Roosevelt told Congress that the Yalta meeting had been a "great success," proof that the wartime alliance remained intact. Privately, however, the president concluded that the outcome of the conference revealed that the Atlantic Charter had been nothing more than "a beautiful idea."

The death of Franklin Roosevelt of a massive stroke on April 12, 1945, cast a dark shadow over all hopes for long-term, peaceful solutions to global problems. The president did not live to learn of Hitler's suicide in his Berlin bunker on April 30, 1945, or the unconditional surrender of Germany one week later, on May 8.

## THE ATOMIC BOMB

Roosevelt's death made Allied cooperation even more difficult. Harry Truman, an honest and plainspoken product of Kansas City machine politics, made a national reputation as a U.S. senator investigating wartime corruption, but he lacked foreign-policy experience and had none of FDR's finesse and prestige.

The wartime Big Three—now Stalin, Truman, and Churchill (the latter soon replaced as prime minister by Clement Atlee when the British voted in a Labour Party government)—held their final conference at Potsdam, just outside Berlin, from July 17 to August 2, 1945. The meeting lacked the spirited give-and-take of the conferences in which Roosevelt and Churchill had participated. A huge agenda of thorny issues confronted the victorious leaders: the future of defeated and occupied Germany and other former **Axis powers**, the Soviet occupation of Eastern Europe, reparations and economic aid to rebuild a shattered Europe, and crucial details about organizing the new United Nations, on which the Americans set great store. The Big Three clashed sharply over most of these issues, but they held fast in demanding the unconditional surrender of reeling but still defiant Japan.

It was while wrangling with Stalin at Potsdam that Truman learned a closely guarded secret: that on July 16 the United States had successfully tested an atomic bomb in New Mexico. As a senator and as vice president, Truman had not been informed of the existence of the Manhattan Project; he first heard about it upon Roosevelt's death. Until the moment of the test, Truman had been pressing Stalin to make good his Yalta promise to enter the Pacific war three months after Germany's surrender—a deadline that would fall on August 8. The president was eager to get Soviet participation in what everyone said would be a horrendously bloody U.S. invasion of Japan, and indeed he did extract Stalin's promise to attack Japan on schedule. But then Secretary of War Stimson received a cable: "Babies

**Axis powers** The opponents of the United States and its allies in World War II.

satisfactorily born." Truman and his advisers concluded that Soviet assistance was no longer needed to end the war.

On August 3, 1945, Japan announced its refusal to surrender. Its military leaders still demanded a fight to the death, and Japanese civilian politicians wanted Allied guarantees that the emperor, considered sacred, would keep his throne. This response the Americans deemed unsatisfactory: they still demanded unconditional surrender, preferably before the Red Army moved against Japan. Three

## CHRONOLOGY

**1931**  September: Japan occupies Manchuria

**1933**  March: Adolf Hitler seizes power
May: Japan quits League of Nations

**1935**  October: Italy invades Ethiopia

**1935–1937**  Neutrality Acts authorize the president to block the sale of munitions to belligerent nations

**1936**  July: Spanish Civil War begins

**1937**  August: Japan invades China
October: Franklin D. Roosevelt calls for international cooperation against aggression

**1938**  March: Germany annexes Austria
September: Munich Agreement lets Germany annex Sudetenland of Czechoslovakia
November: *Kristallnacht*, Nazis attack Jews and destroy Jewish property

**1939**  March: Germany annexes remainder of Czechoslovakia
August: Germany and the Soviet Union sign nonaggression pact
September: Germany invades Poland; World War II begins
November: Soviet Union invades Finland

**1940**  April–June: Germany's *bliztkrieg* sweeps over Western Europe
September: Germany, Italy, and Japan—the Axis powers—conclude a military alliance
First peacetime military draft in American history
November: Roosevelt defeats Wendall Willkie and is elected to an unprecedented third term

**1941**  March: Lend-Lease Act extends aid to Great Britain
May: German troops secure the Balkans
A. Philip Randolph plans March on Washington movement for July

June: Germany invades Soviet Union
Fair Employment Practices Committee formed
August: The United States and Great Britain agree to the Atlantic Charter
December: Japanese attack Pearl Harbor; United States enters the war

**1942**  January: War mobilization begins
February: Executive order mandates internment of Japanese Americans
May–June: Battles of Coral Sea and Midway give the United States naval superiority in the Pacific
August: Manhattan Project begins
November: United States stages amphibious landing in North Africa; Operation Torch begins

**1943**  January: Casablanca Conference announces unconditional surrender policy
February: Soviet victory over Germans at Stalingrad
April–May: Coal miners strike
May: German Afrika Korps troops surrender in Tunis
July: Allied invasion of Italy
Summer: Race riots break out in nearly fifty cities

**1944**  June–August: Operation Overlord and liberation of Paris
November: Roosevelt elected to fourth term, defeating Thomas E. Dewey

**1945**  February: Yalta Conference renews American-Soviet alliance
February–June: United States captures Iwo Jima and Okinawa in Pacific
April: Roosevelt dies in office; Harry Truman becomes president
May: Germany surrenders
July–August: Potsdam Conference
August: United States drops atomic bombs on Hiroshima and Nagasaki; Japan surrenders

CHAPTER 25    WORLD WAR II, 1941–1945

days later, the B-29 bomber nicknamed *Enola Gay* dropped the five-ton uranium bomb that destroyed the Japanese city of Hiroshima. Instantly, some 40,000 people died; in the following weeks, 100,000 more perished from radiation poisoning or burns. By 1950, the death toll reached 200,000.

Americans first heard of the atomic bomb on August 7, when the news reported the destruction and death it had brought to Hiroshima. But fears about the implications of the awesome new weapon were overwhelmed by an outpouring of relief: Japan surrendered—still not unconditionally—on August 14, several days after a second nuclear bomb destroyed Nagasaki, killing another 73,000. (On schedule between these cataclysmic events, the Soviet army invaded Japanese-occupied Manchuria.)

Allied insistence on unconditional surrender and the decision to atom-bomb Japan remain two of the most controversial political and moral questions about the conduct of World War II. Although Truman insisted in his memoirs (written years later) that he gave the order so as to save "a half a million American lives" in ground combat, no such official estimate exists. An intelligence document of April 30, 1946, stated that "the dropping of the bomb was the pretext seized upon by all [American] leaders as the reason for ending the war, but [even if the bomb had not been used] the Japanese would have capitulated upon the entry of Russia into the war." There is no question, however, that the use of nuclear weapons did strengthen U.S. policymakers' hand. It certainly did force caution upon Stalin, soon to emerge as America's primary adversary. Truman and his advisers knew that their nation's atomic monopoly would not last, but they hoped that in the meantime the United States could play the leading role in building the postwar world.

## CONCLUSION

The new tactics and weapons of World War II, such as massive air raids and the atomic bomb produced by the Los Alamos scientists, made warfare incomparably more deadly than before to both military and civilian populations. Between 40 and 50 million people died in World War II—four times the number in World War I—and half the casualties were women and children. More than 405,000 Americans died, and more than 670,000 were wounded. Although slight compared to the casualties suffered by other Allied nations—more than 20 million Soviets died during the war—the human cost of World War II for Americans was second only to that of the Civil War.

Coming at the end of two decades of resolutions to avoid military entanglements, the war pushed the nation's leaders to the center of global politics and into risky military and political alliances that would not outlive the war. The United States emerged the strongest nation in the world, but in a world where the prospects for lasting peace appeared increasingly remote. If World War II raised the nation's international commitments to a new height, its impact on ordinary Americans was not so easy to gauge. Many new communities formed as Americans migrated in mass numbers to new regions that were booming as a result of the wartime economy. Enjoying a rare moment of full employment, many workers new to well-paying industrial jobs anticipated further advances against discrimination. Exuberant at the Allies' victory over fascism and the return of the troops, the majority were optimistic as they looked ahead.

# REVIEW QUESTIONS

1. How did President Franklin D. Roosevelt ready the nation for war?

2. What role did the federal government, business, and labor play in gearing up the economy for wartime production?

3. How did the war affect the lives of American women?

4. Discuss the causes and consequences of the Japanese American internment program.

5. Describe the role of popular culture in promoting the war effort at home.

6. How did military service affect the lives of those who served in World War II?

7. What were the main points of Allied military strategy in both Europe and Asia?

8. How successful were diplomatic efforts in ending the war and in establishing the terms of peace?

# KEY TERMS

**Atlantic Charter** (p. 697)
**Axis powers** (p. 720)
**Battle of the Bulge** (p. 715)
*Blitzkrieg* (p. 696)
**D-Day** (p. 714)
**Holocaust** (p. 719)
**Island-hop** (p. 717)

**Lend-Lease Act** (p. 697)
**Neutrality Act of 1939** (p. 697)
**Nisei** (p. 709)
**Operation Overlord** (p. 714)
**Operation Torch** (p. 713)
**War Powers Act** (p. 699)
**Yalta Conference** (p. 719)

**myhistorylab**
Flashcard Review

# RECOMMENDED READING

Philip D. Beidler, *The Good War's Greatest Hits: World War II and American Remembering* (1998). Examines the popular culture produced about World War II, such as movies, photographs, cartoons, and books, to show how these sources created a lasting image of World War II as the "good war."

Kenneth S. Davis, *FDR, the War President, 1940–1943* (2000). The fifth volume in Davis's biography of Franklin D. Roosevelt, this massive text examines the president's frenetic efforts to create a coherent policy for American involvement in World War II.

Linda Gordon and Gary Y. Okihiro, *Impounded: Dorothea Lange and the Censored Images of Japanese Internment* (2006). An anthology of 100 images from the relocation camps by the famed WPA photographer. Gordon and Okohiro provide essays discussing the production of the photographs and the impact of internment on the Japanese American community.

Laura Hein and Mark Selden, eds., *Living With the Bomb: American and Japanese Cultural Conflict in the Nuclear Age* (1997). Essays dealing with the ambiguous legacy of the atomic bomb in both the United States and Japan. Reviews the "official story" of the bomb as the symbol of U.S. triumph in the "good war" in light of the growing number of dissenting voices and the impact of both views on memorials and museum exhibits.

John W. Jeffries, *Wartime America: The World War II Homefront* (1996). Provides a useful synthesis of scholarship and assesses the major differences in the interpretations of leading historians.

David M. Kennedy, *The American People in World War II* (1999). The second volume in Kennedy's Pulitzer Prize–winning *Freedom from Fear*, this book examines U.S. strategy to win the war from the perspective of the nation's leader as well as its citizens. The narrative interweaves overseas military events and home front experiences.

Gerald F. Linderman, *The World within War: America's Combat Experience in World War II* (1997). Emphasizes the less glamorous aspects of war, mainly the strains placed on the combat soldiers on the front lines. Linderman examines in especially close detail the grim experiences of army infantrymen and the marine riflemen who fought in the Pacific campaign and provides a nuanced analysis of their complex responses to the horror of war.

Katrina R. Mason, *Children of Los Alamos: An Oral History of the Town Where the Atomic Age Began* (1995). Recollections of those who spent their childhood in Los Alamos. They describe their affection for the geographical setting as well as sense of safety growing up in a community so well protected. They also comment on the ethnic diversity of those who populated the town and on the pride they took in their parents' contribution to building the bomb and ending the war.

Neil R. McMillen, ed., *Remaking Dixie: The Impact of World War II on the American South* (1997). A collection of essays on the impact of World War II on the South that pay special attention to the experiences of African Americans and women. Several authors question the degree to which southern society was transformed by wartime mobilization.

Eduardo Obregón Pagán, *Murder at the Sleepy Lagoon: Zoot Suits, Race, and Riot in Wartime L.A.* (2003). Examines the 1942 murder trial of seventeen young Chicanos for an alleged gang slaying and the zoot-suit riots that followed just several months later. Pagán provides a rich portrait of urban culture as well as race relations as the setting for the murder and court trial.

Emily Rosenberg, *A Date Which Will Live: Pearl Harbor in American Memory* (2004). Examines the circulation of memories of Pearl Habor in American life and the media's role in shaping them. Rosenberg includes the impact of the fiftieth anniversary commemorations of Pearl Harbor.

Mark A. Stoler, *Allies in War; Britain and America Against the Axis Powers, 1940–1945* (2005). A compact overview of wartime military strategy and diplomatic missions. Stoler provides a useful synthesis of new scholarship on the war.

Ronald Takaki, *Double Victory: A Multicultural History of America in World War II* (2000). A history of the war years told from the perspective of ethnically diverse Americans. Takaki examines the tension between the "good war" and the treatment of people of color and the response to the Holocaust.

Kenneth William Townsend, *World War II and the American Indian* (2000). A close study of the policies developed by the Bureau of Indian Affairs to bring American Indians into the war effort.

Emily Yellin, *Our Mothers' War: American Women at Home and at the Front During World War II* (2004). Makes a convincing case, based on a wealth of primary courses, that the war greatly changed the expectations for many American women.

For study resources for this chapter, go to **www.myhistorylab.com** and choose *Out of Many, Teaching and Learning Classroom Edition*. You will find a wealth of study and review material for this chapter, including pretests and posttests, customized study plan, key-term review flash cards, interactive map and document activities, and documents for analysis.

*To my mind we are in a situation no less dangerous than the one we were facing in 1939, and it is of the greatest importance that we realize it. We must realize . . . that democracy will not be saved by ideals alone.*

—Edward Teller

**As international tensions rose with the onset of the Cold War,** Americans wondered how to prepare for a possible nuclear war. Many families stocked extra food and water and bought a battery-powered radio, but few actually installed backyard bomb shelters like the one being tested by this family in a Long Island suburb not far from Levittown.

# 26

FALLOUT SHELTER

# THE COLD WAR BEGINS
## 1945–1952

**WHAT STEPS** did the allies take to promote growth in the postwar global economy?

**HOW DID** the Truman Doctrine shape U.S. postwar foreign policy?

**HOW DID** the "Fair Deal" differ from the "New Deal"?

**WHAT FACTORS** contributed to the rise of McCarthyism?

**WHAT WERE** the most important demographic trends in the 1950s?

**WHAT ISSUES** were at the center of the election of 1952?

1945 | 1952

# AMERICAN COMMUNITIES

## University of Washington, Seattle: Students and Faculty Face the Cold War

IN MAY 1948, A PHILOSOPHY PROFESSOR AT THE UNIVERSITY OF Washington in Seattle answered a knock on his office door. Two state legislators, members of the state's Committee on Un-American Activities, entered. "Our information," they charged, "puts you in the center of a Communist conspiracy."

The accused professor, Melvin Rader, had never been a Communist. A self-described liberal, Rader drew fire because he had joined several organizations supported by Communists. During the 1930s, alarmed by the rise of fascism, Rader had become a prominent political activist in his community. At one point he served as president of the University of Washington Teacher's Union, which had formed during the upsurge of labor organizing during the New Deal. When invited to join the Communist Party, Rader bluntly refused. "The experience of teaching social philosophy had clarified my concepts of freedom and democracy," he later explained. "I was an American in search of a way—but it was not the Communist way."

Despite this disavowal, Rader was caught up in a second Red Scare—the first had been that of 1919–20 (see Chapter 22)—that curtailed free speech and political activity on campuses throughout the United States. At some universities, such as Yale, the FBI set up camp with the consent of the college administration, spying on students and faculty, screening the credentials of job or scholarship applicants, and enticing students to report on friends or roommates. The University of Washington administration turned down the Physics Department's recommendation to hire J. Robert Oppenheimer, the famed atomic scientist and former director of Los Alamos Scientific Laboratory who had become a vocal opponent of the arms race.

Although one state legislator claimed that "not less than 150 members" of the University of Washington faculty were subversives, the state's Committee on Un-American Activities turned up just six Communist Party members. These six were hauled before the university's Faculty Committee on Tenure and Academic Freedom, charged with violations ranging from neglect of duty to failing to inform the university administration of their party membership. Three were ultimately dismissed, while the other three were placed on probation.

What had provoked this paranoia? Instead of peace in the wake of World War II, "Cold War"—tense, icy relations but no outright fighting—prevailed between the United States and the Soviet Union. Uneasy wartime allies, the two superpowers now viewed each other as archenemies, and nearly all other nations lined up with one or the other. Within the United States, the Cold War demanded pledges of absolute loyalty from citizens in every institution, from universities to unions and from the media to government itself.

FBI director J. Edgar Hoover testified that the college campuses were centers of "red propaganda," full of teachers "tearing down respect for agencies of government, belittling tradition and moral custom and . . . creating doubts in the validity of the American way of life." Due to "Communistic" teachers and "Communist-line textbooks," a senator wailed, thousands of parents sent "their sons and daughters to college as good Americans," only to see them return home "four years later as wild-eyed radicals."

These extravagant charges were far from true. The overwhelming majority of college graduates in the late 1940s and 1950s were conservative and conformist. Nevertheless, several states, including Washington, enacted or revived loyalty-security programs, obligating all state employees to swear in writing their loyalty to the United States and to disclaim membership in any subversive organization. Nationwide, approximately 200 "radical" faculty members were dismissed outright and many others were denied tenure. Thousands of students simply left school, dropped out of organizations, or changed friends after "visits" from FBI agents or interviews with administrators. The main effect on campus was the restraint of free speech generally and fear of criticizing U.S. racial, military, or diplomatic policies in particular.

Seattle

# GLOBAL INSECURITIES AT WAR'S END

The war that had engulfed the world from 1939 to 1945 created an international interdependence that no country could ignore. Never before, not even at the end of World War I, had hopes been so strong for a genuine "community of nations." But, as a 1945 opinion poll indicated, most Americans believed that prospects for a durable peace rested to a large degree on one factor: Soviet–American harmony.

## FINANCING THE FUTURE

Americans had good reason to be confident about their prospects for setting the terms of reconstruction. Unlike Great Britain, France, and the Soviet Union, the United States had not only escaped the ravages of the war but had actually prospered. By June 1945, the capital assets of manufacturing had increased 65 percent over prewar levels to equal in value approximately half the entire world's goods and services.

Yet many Americans recognized that massive wartime government spending, not the New Deal, had ended the nightmare of the Great Depression. A stark question loomed: What would happen when wartime production slowed and millions of troops returned home to claim jobs?

Just to maintain the current level of growth, the United States needed to export—to a war-ravaged world—a staggering $14 billion in goods and services. During the war, many business leaders had looked to the Soviet Union as a future customer. With that prospect vanishing, with potential Eastern European markets threatened, and with the enormous European colonies closed to American enterprise, U.S. business and government leaders decided to integrate Western Europe, Latin America, and Asia into an international economy open to American trade and investment.

During the final stages of the war, President Roosevelt's advisers laid plans to establish U.S. primacy in the postwar global economy. In July 1944, representatives from forty-four Allied nations met at Bretton Woods, New Hampshire, and established the International Bank for Reconstruction and Development (the World Bank) and the **International Monetary Fund (IMF)**. These institutions were expected to help rebuild war-torn Europe and Asia. By stabilizing exchange rates to permit the expansion of international trade, the IMF would deter currency conflicts and trade wars. The United States was the principal supplier of funds for the IMF and the World Bank and thus, by determining the allocation of loans, could unilaterally reshape the global economy.

The Soviet Union participated at Bretton Woods but refused to ratify the agreements. From Stalin's perspective, the United States intended to rebuild the world economy along capitalist lines; accepting World Bank and IMF aid would, he believed, make the Soviet Union an economic colony of the capitalist West. By spurning this aid, the Soviet Union economically isolated itself and its East European satellites.

## THE DIVISION OF EUROPE

In the Atlantic Charter of 1941, the United States and Great Britain proclaimed the right of all nations to self-determination and renounced claims to new territories as spoils of war. Before the war ended, though, Churchill and Roosevelt violated the charter by dividing Europe into spheres of influence (see Chapter 25 and Map 26.1).

**WHAT STEPS** did the allies take to promote growth in the postwar global economy?

## myhistorylab
**Review Summary**

## IMAGE KEY
for pages 726–727

a. A man reading "The Mirror" newspaper with a headline about actress Lucille Ball.

b. A photo of parents and their three children in a home-based fallout shelter. "The Cold War at Home and Abroad, 1946–1952."

c. The North Atlantic Treaty Organization (NATO) treaty with signatures and seal.

d. A fallout shelter sign directing the populace to safety during a nuclear attack.

e. Civilians atop the bombed out ruins of buildings watching American C-54 cargo planes fly overhead during the Allied airlift to bring food and supplies to besieged citizens of Soviet-controlled Berlin.

f. American President Harry Truman shakes hands with supporters from a train car during a rally in the 1948 presidential campaign.

g. Senator Joseph McCarthy points to Oregon on an organizational map implying Communist Party organizations in the United States.

h. An unidentified model displays a kitchen interior circa 1950s.

i. Soldiers in the Korean conflict endured frigid conditions in winter and blistering summers.

**International Monetary Fund (IMF)**
International organization established in 1945 to assist nations in maintaining stable currencies.

## QUICK REVIEW

**The IMF and the World Bank**

♦ July 1944: Allies met at Bretton Woods, New Hampshire.

♦ International Monetary Fund and World Bank created to help rebuild and stabilize postwar economy.

♦ United States gained effective control of the new institutions.

From the earliest days of fighting Hitler, the Soviet Union was intent on reestablishing its 1941 borders. At the Potsdam Conference in July 1945, Stalin not only regained but also extended his territory, annexing eastern Poland with Western approval and the little Baltic nations without it. Soviet influence quickly became paramount in all East European countries that the Red Army had occupied. The question remained: Did Stalin aim to bring all of Europe into the Communist domain?

At the Potsdam Conference, when the wartime allies began to plan Germany's future, that question loomed over all deliberations. They decided to divide the conquered nation into four occupation zones, each temporarily ruled by one of the Allied nations. But they could not agree on long-term plans. Having borne the brunt of German aggression, France and the Soviet Union both opposed reunification. Stalin, moreover, demanded heavy reparations and a limit on postwar German reindustrialization. Truman shared Churchill's hope of rebuilding Germany into a powerful counterweight to the Soviet Union and a strong market for U.S. and British exports.

After the war, continuing disagreements about the future of Germany darkened hopes for Soviet-American cooperation. By July 1946, Americans had begun to withhold reparations due to the Soviets from their occupation zone and began to grant amnesty to some former Nazis. Then, in December, the Americans and British merged their zones and invited France and the Soviet Union to join. France agreed; Stalin, fearing a resurgence of a united Germany, refused.

The United States and the Soviet Union were now at loggerheads. Twice in the twentieth century, Germany had invaded Russia, and the Soviet Union interpreted any moves toward German reunification as menacing. For their part, American policymakers, assuming Stalin to be aggressively expansionist, envisioned a united Germany as a bulwark against further Soviet encroachments.

## THE UNITED NATIONS AND HOPES FOR COLLECTIVE SECURITY

In 1944 at the Dumbarton Oaks Conference in Washington, and again in April 1945 at San Francisco, the Allies worked to shape the United Nations (UN) as a world organization that would arbitrate disputes among member nations and stop aggressors, by force if necessary.

The terms of membership, however, limited the UN's ability to mediate disputes. Although all fifty nations that signed the UN charter voted in the General Assembly, only five (the United States, Great Britain, the Soviet Union, France, and China) served permanently on the Security Council, which had the "primary responsibility for the maintenance of international peace and security," and each had absolute veto power over the Council's decisions.

The UN achieved its greatest success with its humanitarian programs. Its relief agency gave war-torn European and Asian countries billions of dollars for medical supplies, food, and clothing. The UN also dedicated itself to protecting human rights, and the high principles enunciated by its 1948 Universal Declaration of Human Rights owed much to lobbying by Eleanor Roosevelt, one of the first delegates from the United States.

On other issues, however, the UN operated strictly along lines dictated by the emerging **Cold War**. The Western nations allied with the United States held the balance of power and controlled the admission of new members. For example, when in 1949 the Communists won the Chinese civil war (discussed later), the

**Cold War** The political and economic confrontation between the Soviet Union and the United States that dominated world affairs from 1946 to 1989.

# MAP EXPLORATION

To explore an interactive version of this map, go to **http://www.prenhall.com/faraghertlc/map26.1**

EAST GERMANY

French
Tegel
WEST
British
BERLIN
Gatow
BERLIN
Tempelhof
American

EAST BERLIN

Soviet

EAST GERMANY

ICELAND

SWEDEN   FINLAND

NORWAY

North
Sea

Baltic Sea

GREAT
BRITAIN

IRELAND

DENMARK

ATLANTIC
OCEAN

NETHERLANDS

Berlin

POLAND

EAST
GERMANY

BELGIUM

WEST

LUXEMBOURG   GERMANY

CZECHOSLOVAKIA

Bay of
Biscay

FRANCE

SWITZERLAND   AUSTRIA

HUNGARY

ROMANIA

SOVIET UNION

Caspian
Sea

PORTUGAL

SPAIN

Corsica

ITALY

YUGOSLAVIA

BULGARIA

Black Sea

Sardinia

ALBANIA

GREECE

TURKEY

IRAN

Mediterranean   Sea

Sicily

Crete

Cyprus

LEBANON

ISRAEL

SYRIA

IRAQ

JORDAN

NATO countries
Warsaw Pact countries
Nonparticipants

AFRICA

**MAP 26.1**

**Divided Europe**   During the Cold War, Europe was divided into opposing military alliances, the North American Treaty Organization (NATO) and the Warsaw Pact (Communist bloc).

WHICH COUNTRIES were aligned with the United States, and which with the Soviet Union?

Western powers would block the new People's Republic from claiming China's UN seat, held by the defeated Nationalists on Taiwan. East–West polarization made negotiated settlements virtually impossible.

# THE POLICY OF CONTAINMENT

HOW DID the Truman Doctrine

shape U.S. postwar foreign policy?

**myhistorylab**

Review Summary

**26–1**
George F. Kennan, *Long Telegram* (1946)

**26–4**
George Kennan, *Containment* (1947)

---

## QUICK REVIEW

**Postwar Foreign Policy**

- Truman launched the nation into a global battle against communism.
- The United States pledged to help countries that faced external pressure or internal revolution.
- The United States played a decisive role in the rebuilding of Europe.

In March 1946, in a speech delivered in Fulton, Missouri, Winston Churchill spoke to the end of wartime cooperation. With President Truman at his side, the former British prime minister solemnly intoned: "An iron curtain has descended across the [European] continent." He called directly upon the United States, standing "at this time at the pinnacle of world power," to recognize its "awe-inspiring accountability to the future" and, in alliance with Great Britain, act vigorously to stop Soviet expansion.

### THE TRUMAN DOCTRINE

Many Americans believed that Franklin D. Roosevelt, had he lived, could have smoothed tensions between the Soviet Union and the United States. His successor sorely lacked FDR's diplomatic talent and experience. More comfortable with machine politicians than with polished New Dealers, Truman liked to talk tough and act defiantly.

Truman's distrust of the Soviet Union was not always consistent; during the first years after the war, at times he also attempted to be conciliatory. But among U.S. policymakers an anti-Soviet consensus was growing, fed by perceptions that Stalin was taking a hard line. In February 1946, George F. Kennan, the nation's premier diplomat in dealing with the Soviet Union, sent an 8,000-word "long telegram" from Moscow to the State Department, insisting that Soviet fanaticism made cooperation impossible. The Soviet Union intended to extend its realm not by military means alone, he explained, but by "subversion" within "free" nations. Tough-minded realism, not idealistic hopes, should govern America's relations with the Soviet Union. In the long run, Kennan predicted, the Soviet system would collapse from within, but until that happened the West should pursue a policy of containment.

**Appointed to the** UN delegation by President Harry Truman in 1946, Eleanor Roosevelt (1884–1962) pressured the organization to adopt the Declaration of Human Rights in 1948. In this photograph, taken in 1946, the former First Lady is exchanging ideas with Warren Austin, also a delegate to the United Nations.

# OVERVIEW | Major Cold War Policies

| Date | Policy | Provisions |
| --- | --- | --- |
| 1947 | Truman Doctrine | Pledged the United States to the containment of communism in Europe and elsewhere. The doctrine was the foundation of Truman's foreign policy. It impelled the United States to support any nation whose stability was threatened by communism or the Soviet Union. |
| 1947 | Federal Employees Loyalty and Security Program | Established by Executive Order 9835, this barred Communists and fascists from federal employment and outlined procedures for investigating current and prospective federal employees. |
| 1947 | Marshall Plan | U.S. program to aid war-torn Europe, also known as the European Recovery Program. The Marshall Plan was a cornerstone in the U.S. use of economic policy to contain communism. |
| 1947 | National Security Act | Established Department of Defense (to coordinate the three armed services), the National Security Council (to advise the president on security issues), and the Central Intelligence Agency (to gather and evaluate intelligence data). |
| 1948 | Smith-Mundt Act | Launched an overseas campaign of anti-Communist propaganda. |
| 1949 | North Atlantic Treaty Organization (NATO) | A military alliance of twelve nations formed to deter possible aggression of the Soviet Union against Western Europe. |
| 1950 | NSC-68 | National Security Council Paper calling for an expanded and aggressive U.S. defense policy, including greater military spending and higher taxes. |
| 1950 | Internal Security Act (also known as the McCarran Act and the Subversive Activities Control Act) | Legislation providing for the registration of all Communist and totalitarian groups and authorizing the arrest of suspect persons during a national emergency. |
| 1951 | Psychological Strategy Board created | Created to coordinate anti–Communist propaganda campaigns. |
| 1952 | Immigration and Nationality Act (also known as McCarran Walter Immigration Act) | Reaffirmed the national origins quota system but tightened immigration controls, barring homosexuals and people considered subversive from entering the United States. |

**myhistorylab**

**Overview:** *Major Cold War Policies*

A perceived crisis in the Mediterranean marked the turning point. On February 21, 1947, amid a civil war in Greece, Great Britain informed the U.S. State Department that it could no longer afford to prop up the anti-Communist government there and announced its intention to withdraw all aid. Without U.S. intervention, Truman concluded, Greece, Turkey, and perhaps the entire oil-rich Middle East would fall under Soviet control. But, warned an influential Republican senator, Congress would not act unless president "scare[d] hell out of the American people."

On March 12, 1947, the president made his case in a speech to Congress. Never naming the Soviet Union, he appealed for all-out resistance to a "certain ideology" wherever it appeared in the world. The preservation of peace and the freedom of all Americans depended, the president insisted, on containing communism.

**26–5**
Harry S Truman, *The Truman Doctrine* (1947)

**26–3**
George Marshall, *The Marshall Plan* (1947)

Congress approved $400 million to aid Greece and Turkey, which helped conservative forces in those countries crush left-wing rebels. By dramatically opposing communism, Truman somewhat buoyed his sagging popularity and helped generate popular support for an anti-communist crusade at home and abroad.

The significance of what became known as the **Truman Doctrine** far outlasted events in the Mediterranean: the United States had declared its right to intervene to save other nations from communism. In advocating containment of the Soviet Union, Kennan called for political and economic, not military, countermeasures. But Truman and his advisers were willing to consider military responses too. It was now the responsibility of the United States, the White House insisted, to safeguard what was coming to be called the Free World by any means necessary. They had fused anticommunism and internationalism into a strong foreign policy.

## THE MARSHALL PLAN

The Truman Doctrine complemented the European Recovery Program, commonly known as the **Marshall Plan**. Considered by many historians the most successful postwar U.S. diplomatic venture, the Marshall Plan improved the climate for a viable capitalist economy in Western Europe and, in effect, brought aid recipients into bilateral agreements with the United States. In addition, the United States and seventeen Western European nations ratified the tariff-cutting General Agreement on Tariffs and Trade pact opening all to U.S. trade and investment. (Today, GATT has been renamed the World Trade Organization, or WTO.)

The Marshall Plan was costly to Americans. In its initial year it accounted for 12 percent of the federal budget. But much of that aid was American-made goods, produced by American workers. In the European nations covered by the plan, industrial production increased by 35 percent between 1947 and 1952, living standards improved, and American consumer goods and the American lifestyle became familiar.

The Marshall Plan drove a deeper wedge between the United States and the Soviet Union. Although invited to participate, Stalin denounced the plan for what it was—an American scheme to rebuild Germany and incorporate it into an anti-Soviet bloc. Soon after the announcement of the Marshall Plan, the Soviet Union tightened its grip in Eastern Europe. In February 1948, as the U.S. Congress formally approved by the Marshall Plan, a Soviet-supported coup d'état established a communist government in Czechoslovakia.

## THE BERLIN CRISIS AND THE FORMATION OF NATO

Within a year of the start of the Marshall Plan, the United States and Britain moved closer to the goal of economically integrating their occupation zones in Germany into the western sphere of influence. A common currency was established for these zones. Stalin reacted on June 24, 1948, by halting all traffic to the western occupation zones of Berlin, deep within Soviet-occupied eastern Germany (see Map 26.1).

The **Berlin blockade** created both a crisis and an opportunity for the Truman administration. With help from the Royal Air Force, the United States began an unprecedented around-the-clock airlift. "Operation Vittles" delivered nearly 2 million tons of supplies (including food and coal) to West Berliners. Stalin finally lifted the blockade in May 1949, clearing the way for the western powers to merge their occupation zones into a single nation, the Federal Republic of Germany. The Soviet Union countered by turning its zone into the communist-dominated German Democratic Republic.

**Truman Doctrine** President Harry Truman's statement in 1947 that the United States should assist other nations that were facing external pressure or internal revolution.

**Marshall Plan** Secretary of State George C. Marshall's European Recovery Plan of June 5, 1947, committing the United States to help in the rebuilding of post-World War II Europe.

**Berlin blockade** Three-hundred-day Soviet blockade of land access to United States, British, and French occupation zones in Berlin, 1948–1949.

**Located deep within** communist East Germany, West Berlin was suddenly cut off from the West when Josef Stalin blockaded all surface traffic in an attempt to take over the war-torn city. Between June 1948 and May 1949, British and U.S. pilots made 272,000 flights, dropping food and fuel to civilians. The Berlin airlift successfully foiled the blockade, and the Soviet Union reopened access on May 12, 1949.

The Berlin Crisis had made a U.S.-led military alliance against the Soviet Union attractive to noncommunist Western Europeans. In April 1949 ten European nations, Canada, and the United States formed the **North Atlantic Treaty Organization (NATO)**. NATO complemented the Marshall Plan, strengthening economic ties among the member nations. It also deepened divisions between Eastern and Western Europe, making a permanent military mobilization on both sides almost inevitable.

Global implications flowed from the forging of the North Atlantic alliance. Several Western European allies ruled valuable but restive colonial empires. During the war, FDR had urged British and French leaders to start dismantling their empires, a suggestion welcomed neither by Churchill nor by France's Charles de Gaulle. In 1947, a financially strapped Britain granted independence to India and Pakistan, and under U.S. pressure the Dutch gave up Indonesia in 1949, but the French were determined to regain Indochina, lost to Japan before Pearl Harbor (see Chapter 25). Cold War anticommunism now trumped traditional American anticolonialism. Because the most important fighter against France's attempt to reconquer Indochina was Vietnamese communist Ho Chi Minh, Truman decided that France deserved American support and helped persuade France to join NATO. The first seeds had been planted of what would eventually become an American commitment to fight communism in Vietnam.

The Truman administration took Latin America for granted and was satisfied when the right-wing dictators ruling much of that region proclaimed

**North Atlantic Treaty Organization (NATO)**  Organization of ten European countries, Canada, and the United States whom together formed a mutual defense pact in April 1949.

themselves staunchly anticommunist. But Latin Americans complained that the United States' preoccupation with rebuilding Western Europe was depriving them of American investment capital desperately needed for economic development. The most positive gesture that the United States made toward Latin opinion was designating Puerto Rico a self-governing "commonwealth" in 1952. A rising Puerto Rican independence movement—extremist members of which attempted to assassinate Truman in 1950—prompted this move to make U.S. sovereignty over the island look less colonialist. Beneath the surface, though, trouble was brewing for the United States throughout the hemisphere.

Between 1947 and 1949, the Truman administration had defined the policies that would shape the Cold War for decades to come. The Truman Doctrine explained the ideological basis of containment, not just in Europe but also around the globe; the Marshall Plan put into place its economic underpinnings in Western Europe; and NATO created the mechanisms for military defense. When NATO extended membership to a rearmed West Germany in May 1955, the Soviet Union responded by creating a counterpart, the Warsaw Pact, including East Germany.

## ATOMIC DIPLOMACY

The containment policy depended on the ability of the United States to back its commitments through military force, and Truman invested his faith in the U.S. monopoly of atomic weapons. After 1945, the United States began to build an atomic stockpile and to conduct tests on remote Pacific islands.

Despite warnings to the contrary by leading scientists, U.S. military analysts estimated it would take the Soviet Union three to ten years to produce an atomic bomb. In August 1949, the Soviet Union proved them wrong by testing its own atomic bomb.

**Police and strikers** confront each other in Los Angeles during one of many postwar strikes in 1946. Employers wanted to cut wages, and workers refused to give up the higher living standard achieved during the war.

The arms race that scientists had feared since 1945 was now under way. By the early 1950s, both the United States and the Soviet Union were testing hydrogen bombs a thousand times more powerful than the weapons dropped on Hiroshima and Nagasaki in 1945. By the late 1950s, stockpiles of nuclear bombs were being supplemented by nuclear-armed missiles.

The United States and the Soviet Union were now firmly locked into the Cold War. The nuclear arms race risked global catastrophe, diverted economic resources, and fed public fears of impending doom. Despite the Allied victory in World War II, the world had again divided into hostile camps.

# Cold War Liberalism

Truman wanted to enlarge the New Deal but settled on a modest domestic agenda to promote social welfare and an anti-isolationist, anti-Communist foreign policy. Fatefully, during his administration domestic and foreign policy became increasingly entangled. Out of that entanglement emerged a distinctive brand of liberalism—Cold War liberalism.

## "To Err Is Truman"

Within a year of assuming office, Harry Truman's poll ratings were among the lowest of any twentieth-century president. The responsibilities of reestablishing peacetime conditions seemed to overwhelm the new president. "To err is Truman," critics sneered.

The task of reconverting from a wartime to a peace-time economy was enormous. Truman faced millions of restless would-be consumers tired of rationing and eager to spend their wartime savings on shiny cars, new furniture, choice cuts of meat, and stylish clothing. The demand for consumer items rapidly outran supply, fueling inflation and a huge black market.

In 1945 and 1946, the country appeared ready to explode. While homemakers protested rising prices by boycotting neighborhood stores, industrial workers struck in unprecedented numbers. Employers, fearing a rapid decline to depression-level profits, determined to slash wages; workers wanted a bigger cut of the huge war profits they had heard about.

Congress defeated most of Truman's proposals to revive the New Deal. One week after Japan's surrender, the president introduced a twenty-one-point program that included greater unemployment compensation, higher minimum wages, and housing assistance. Later he added national health insurance and atomic-energy legislation. Congress rejected most of these bills and passed the Employment Act of 1946 but only with substantial modification. The act created the **Council of Economic Advisers**, a panel of three experts who would counsel the president and formulate policies for maintaining employment, production, and purchasing power. But no funding mechanisms guaranteed the full employment to which the government committed itself. "Had enough?" Republicans, anticipating victory in the midterm elections, asked voters that simple question. The voters had. They gave Republicans majorities in both houses of Congress and many state capitols. Symbolically repudiating FDR, Republican-dominated state legislatures ratified the Twenty-Second Amendment, limiting future presidents to two terms.

The Republicans, dominant in Congress for the first time since 1931, mounted a counterattack on the New Deal, beginning with organized labor. Unions had peaked in size and prestige; membership topped 15 million and encompassed nearly 40 percent of all wage earners. Claiming that "Big Labor" had gone too

**HOW DID** the "Fair Deal" differ from the "New Deal"?

myhistorylab
Review Summary

**Council of Economic Advisers**  Board of three professional economists established in 1946 to advise the president on economic policy.

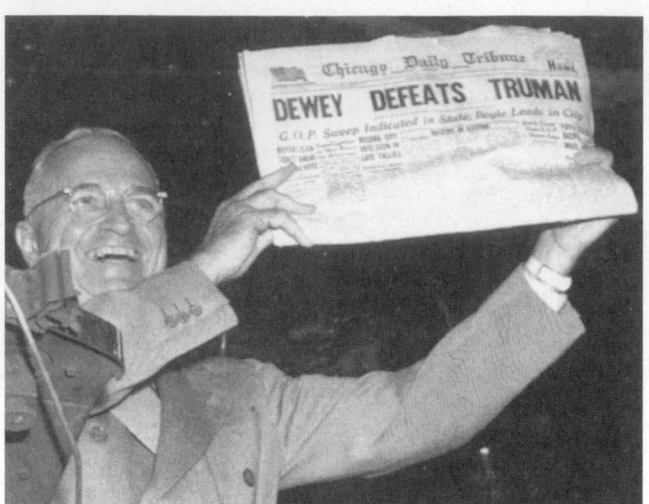

President Truman waves a copy of the *Chicago Daily Tribune*, printed before the election results were in.

far, the Eightieth Congress aimed at abolishing many practices legalized by the Wagner Act of 1935 (see Chapter 24). The resultant **Taft-Hartley Act** of 1947, passed over Truman's veto, outlawed the closed shop, the secondary boycott, and the use of union dues for political activities; mandated an eighty-day cooling-off period in the case of strikes affecting "national safety or health"; and required all union officials to swear that they were not Communists—a Cold War mandate abridging First Amendment freedoms. Truman himself would later invoke the act against strikers.

## THE 1948 ELECTION

Harry Truman had considered some of Roosevelt's advisers "crackpots and the lunatic fringe." By 1946 he forced out many of the remaining social planners who had staffed the Washington bureaus for more than a decade. Truman also fired Roosevelt's secretary of commerce and former vice president, Henry Wallace, for advocating a more conciliatory policy toward the Soviet Union.

Wallace, refusing to fade away, vowed to run against Truman for president. He pledged to expand New Deal programs by moving boldly to establish full employment, racial equality, and stronger unions. He also promised peace with the Soviet Union. As the 1948 election neared, Wallace appeared a viable candidate on the new Progressive Party ticket.

Truman shrewdly repositioned himself. He deflated Wallace by branding him a tool of the Communists (who in fact were part of a coalition of ex–New Dealers who encouraged Wallace to run). Truman also attacked the conservative congressional Republicans, proposing federal funds for education, housing, and medical insurance. Summoning Congress back for a special session after the summertime political conventions of 1948, he dared it to enact the Republican platform—and when it predictably failed—lambasted the "do-nothing Congress."

Wallace and the Republican nominee, New York governor Thomas E. Dewey, had taken strong leads on civil rights, but Truman outflanked them. In July 1948 he issued executive decrees desegregating the armed forces and banning discrimination in the federal civil service. In response, some 300 southern delegates bolted from the Democratic National Convention and named a States' Rights ("**Dixiecrat**") ticket, headed by the staunchly segregationist governor of South Carolina, J. Strom Thurmond. With the South looking as good as lost, with Wallace threatening to siphon off left-leaning Democrats, and with soothing Dewey heading the Republicans, Truman appeared doomed.

But "Give 'em Hell Harry's" vigorous campaign slowly revived the New Deal coalition. Fear of Republicans who had passed Taft-Hartley won back the bulk of organized labor, and Truman's decision in May 1948 immediately to recognize the new State of Israel kept many liberal Jews loyally Democratic. The success of the Berlin airlift buoyed the president's popularity, and by Election Day growing anti-Communist sentiment among liberals was limiting the Wallace vote to the extreme left. Meanwhile Dewey, who in 1944 had run a hard-hitting but unsuccessful campaign against Roosevelt, this time tried to coast to victory by appearing bland and "presidential."

Polls predicted a Dewey victory—but the pollsters stopped taking samples several weeks before Election Day and so missed a late Democratic surge. Truman won the popular vote by a 5 percent margin. Democrats regained majorities in both houses of Congress. But Truman had hit the apex of his popularity. A long downhill slide was about to begin (see Map 26.2).

**Taft-Hartley Act**   Federal legislation of 1947 that substantially limited the tools available to labor unions in labor-management disputes.

**Dixiecrat**   States' Rights Democrats.

## THE FAIR DEAL

"Every segment of our population and every individual has a right," Truman announced in January 1949, "to expect from our Government a fair deal." Democratic congressional majorities would, he hoped, translate campaign promises into laws and expand the New Deal. But a powerful bloc of conservative southern Democrats and midwestern Republicans turned back his domestic agenda.

The National Housing Act of 1949 provided federally funded low-income housing. Congress also raised the minimum wage (from 40 to 75 cents per hour) and brought an additional 10 million people under Social Security coverage. Otherwise Truman made no headway. He and congressional liberals introduced a variety of bills to weaken southern racism. Southern-led filibusters killed them all, while conservative-dominated congressional committees bottled up his initiatives for national health insurance, federal aid to education, and a repeal or modification of Taft-Hartley.

Truman's greatest domestic achievement was to articulate the basic principles of Cold War liberalism, which would remain the northern Democratic agenda for decades to come. Toning down visionary New Deal rhetoric about economic equality and reapportioning wealth and power, his Fair Deal promoted bread-and-butter issues and economic growth. His administration insisted, therefore, on an ambitious program of expanded foreign trade, while relying on the federal government to encourage higher productivity. Equally important, Truman reshaped liberalism by making anticommunism a key element in both foreign policy and domestic affairs.

# THE COLD WAR AT HOME

All global powers engage in espionage, and the Soviet Union, like the United States, placed intelligence-gathering agents in foreign governments. However, subversion by American-bred Communists was relatively insignificant. By the late 1940s the Communist Party, U.S.A., formed in 1919 and at the peak of its influence in the 1930s, was steadily losing ground. By this time, anticommunism held center stage in domestic politics. The federal government, with help from the media, led the crusade, using the threat of communism to reorder its operation and to quell dissent. Seeking absolute security, Americans permitted a greater concentration of power in government and, while promising to lead the Free World, allowed many of their own rights to be circumscribed.

## THE NATIONAL SECURITY ACT OF 1947

The imperative of national security destroyed old-fashioned isolation, forcing the United States into unprecedented alliances such as NATO and global leadership. Such responsibility required massive resources. Truman demanded a substantial

## MAP EXPLORATION

To explore an interactive version of this map, go to
**http://www.prenhall.com/taragherllc/map26.2**

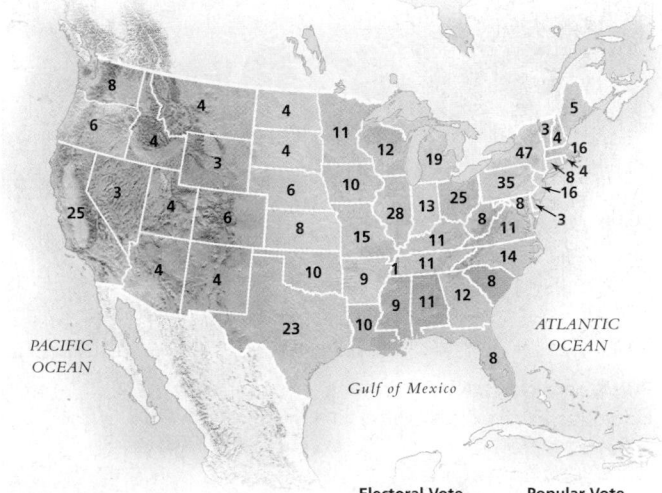

| | Electoral Vote (%) | Popular Vote (%) |
|---|---|---|
| **HARRY S. TRUMAN** (Democrat) | 303 (57) | 24,105,812 (49.5) |
| **Thomas E. Dewey** (Republican) | 189 (36) | 21,970,065 (45.1) |
| **Strom Thurmond** (States' Rights) | 39 (7) | 1,169,063 (2.4) |
| **Henry A. Wallace** (Progressive) | — | 1,157,172 (2.4) |
| **Other candidates** (Socialist, Prohibition, Socialist Labor, Socialist Workers) | — | 272,713 (0.6) |

**MAP 26.2**

**The Election of 1948**   Harry Truman holds up a copy of the *Chicago Daily Tribune* with headlines confidently and mistakenly predicting the victory of his opponent, Thomas E. Dewey (opposite page). An initially unpopular candidate, Truman made a whistle-stop tour of the country by train to win 49.5 percent of the popular vote to Dewey's 45.1 percent.

WHY WAS Truman relatively unpopular at the beginning of the 1948 campaign?

**WHAT FACTORS** contributed to the rise of McCarthyism?

**Review Summary**

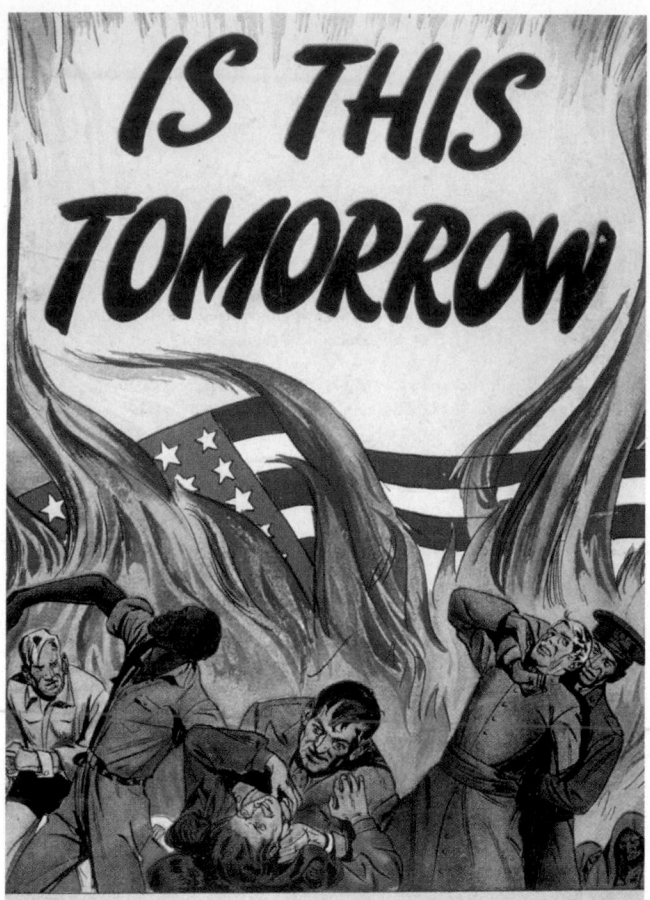

**IS THIS TOMORROW**

**AMERICA UNDER COMMUNISM!**

**Published in 1947,** this full-color comic book appeared as one of many sensationalistic illustrations of the threat of the "commie menace" to Americans at home. Approximately 4 million copies of *Is This Tomorrow?* were printed, the majority distributed to church groups or sold for ten cents a copy.

**National Security Council (NSC)** The formal policymaking body for national defense and foreign relations, created in 1947 and consisting of the president, the secretary of defense, the secretary of state, and others appointed by the president.

**Central Intelligence Agency (CIA)** Agency established in 1947 that coordinates the gathering and evaluation of military and economic information on other nations.

**Executive Order 9835** Signed by Harry Truman in 1947 to establish a loyalty program requiring federal employees to sign loyalty oaths and undergo security checks.

increase in the size of the federal government in both military forces and surveillance agencies. Security measures designed to keep the nation in a steady state of preparedness, readily justified during wartime, were now extended indefinitely into the very uneasy peacetime.

The sweeping National Security Act, passed by Congress in July 1947, established the Department of Defense and the **National Security Council (NSC)** to administer and coordinate defense policies and advise the president. The Department of Defense combined the old War and Navy Departments, bringing the Army, the Navy, and the new Air Force under a single cabinet-level secretary. Ties between the armed forces and the State Department grew closer. The act also created the National Security Resources Board (NSRB) to coordinate plans throughout the government "in the event of war" and, for the first time in American history, to maintain military preparedness in peacetime.

The Department of Defense and the NSRB became the principal sponsor of scientific research during the first ten years of the Cold War. It was commonly recognized at the time that World War II had been the "physicists' war." Scientists had built the ultimate weapon, the atom bomb, and achieved major advances in military navigation and detection, strategic targeting, and communication. Federal agencies tied to military projects supplied well over 90 percent of the funding for research in the physical sciences, much of it in major universities.

The **Central Intelligence Agency (CIA)** was another product of the National Security Act. With roots in the wartime Office of Strategic Services (OSS), the new CIA became a permanent operation devoted to collecting political, military, and economic information for security purposes throughout the world. (It was barred from domestic intelligence gathering: that was the domain of its rival, the FBI.) Although information about the CIA was classified—that is, kept secret from both Congress and the public—historians have estimated that the agency soon dwarfed the State Department in number of employees and size of budget.

The national-security state required a huge workforce. Before World War II, approximately 900,000 civilians worked for the federal government, about 10 percent of them in security work; by the beginning of the Cold War, nearly 4 million people were on the government's payroll, 75 percent of them in national-security agencies.

National security absorbed increasingly large portions of the nation's resources. By the end of Truman's second term, defense allocations accounted for 10 percent of GNP, directly or indirectly employed hundreds of thousands of well-paid workers, and subsidized some of the nation's most profitable corporations. This vast financial outlay created the rationale for permanent, large-scale military spending and powerfully stimulated economic growth.

## THE LOYALTY-SECURITY PROGRAM

National security required increased surveillance at home. Within two weeks of proclaiming the Truman Doctrine, the president signed **Executive Order 9835** on March 21, 1947, establishing a civilian loyalty program for all federal employees.

The new Federal Employees Loyalty and Security Program, directed at members of the Communist Party—as well as fascists and anyone guilty of "sympathetic association" with either—in effect established a political test for federal employment. It also outlined procedures for investigating current and prospective federal employees. The loyalty review boards often asked employees about their opinions of the Soviet Union, the Marshall Plan, or NATO and whether they would report fellow workers if they found out they were Communists. Any employee could be dismissed merely on "reasonable grounds," including guilt by association (that is, knowing or being related to a "subversive" person), rather than on proof of disloyalty. Later amendments added homosexuals as potential security risks on grounds that they might succumb to enemy blackmail.

Many state and municipal governments enacted loyalty programs and required public employees, including teachers at all levels, to sign loyalty oaths. In all, some 6.6 million people underwent loyalty and security checks. An estimated 500 government workers were fired, and perhaps as many as 6,000 more chose to resign. Numerous private employers and labor unions also instituted loyalty programs.

Attorney General Tom C. Clark aided this effort by publishing a list of hundreds of potentially subversive organizations. There was no right of appeal for organizations so listed. The famous "Attorney General's List" effectively outlawed many political and social organizations, stigmatizing hundreds of thousands of individuals who had done nothing illegal. Church associations, civil rights organizations, musical groups, and even summer camps appeared on the list.

In 1950 Congress overrode the president's veto to pass a bill that Truman called "the greatest danger to freedom of press, speech, and assembly since the Sedition Act of 1798." The Internal Security (or McCarran) Act required Communist organizations to register with the Subversive Activities Control Board—if they did not register, they were prosecuted—and authorized the arrest of suspect persons during a national emergency. The Immigration and Nationality Act, also sponsored by Republican senator Pat McCarran of Nevada and adopted in 1952, again over Truman's veto, barred people deemed "subversive" or "homosexual" from becoming citizens or even visiting the United States. It also empowered the attorney general to deport immigrants who were members of Communist organizations, even if they had become citizens. Challenged repeatedly on constitutional grounds, the Subversive Activities Control Board remained in place until 1973, when it was terminated.

## THE SECOND RED SCARE

Renamed and made a permanent standing committee in 1945, the **House Un-American Activities Committee (HUAC)** had the power to subpoena witnesses and to compel them to answer all questions or face contempt of Congress charges. In well-publicized hearings held in Hollywood in October 1947, the mother of actress Ginger Rogers defended her daughter by saying that she had been duped into appearing in the 1943 pro-Soviet wartime film *Tender Comrade* and "had been forced" to read the subversive line "Share and share alike, that's democracy." HUAC encouraged such testimony by other "friendly witnesses," including actors Ronald Reagan and Gary Cooper. The committee intimidated many others, who feared loss of their careers, into naming former friends and co-workers in order to be cleared for future work in Hollywood.

A small but prominent minority refused to cooperate with HUAC. By claiming the freedoms of speech and association guaranteed by the First and Sixth

---

**26–6**
Ronald Reagan, *Testimony Before the House Un-American Activities Committee* (1947)

**House Un-American Activities Committee (HUAC)** Originally intended to ferret out pro-Fascists, it later investigated "un-American propaganda" that attacked constitutional government.

Amendments, they became known as "unfriendly witnesses," and a handful served prison sentences for refusing to "name names."

Hollywood studios would not employ any writer, director, or actor who refused to cooperate with HUAC. The resulting blacklist remained in effect until the 1960s and limited the production of films dealing with "controversial" social or political issues. Meanwhile the privately published *Red Channels: The Report of Communist Influence in Radio and Television* (1950) persuaded advertisers to cancel their accounts with many programs considered friendly to the Soviet Union, the UN, or liberal causes.

The labor movement also became a victim of this second Red Scare. Like the Hollywood film industry, a sizable portion of its leaders and members had affiliated with the Communist Party or supported liberal causes in the 1930s, and they emerged from their wartime experiences even more deeply committed to social justice. The Food, Tobacco, Agricultural, and Allied Workers-Congress of Industrial Organizations (FTA-CIO) organized a postwar campaign against discriminatory practices within southern industry and allied with local civil rights activists to spearhead a major organizing drive. In 1947 the R.J. Reynolds Tobacco Company struck back by characterizing union organizers and supporters as Moscow's pawns. A year later, CIO president Philip Murray decided to rid his organization of all Communists. Soon, eleven unions representing more than a million workers were expelled. This "purge" succeeded in eliminating Communist influence and with it the commitment to industrial democracy that had buoyed the CIO since the 1930s.

## SPY CASES

In August 1948, *Time* magazine editor Whittaker Chambers appeared before HUAC to name Alger Hiss as a fellow Communist in the Washington underground during the 1930s. Hiss, then president of the prestigious Carnegie Endowment for International Peace and a former member of FDR's State Department, denied the charges and sued his accuser for slander. Chambers then revealed his trump card, a cache of films of secret documents that he claimed Hiss had passed them to him for transmission to the Soviet Union. The statute of limitations for espionage having run out, a federal grand jury in January 1950 convicted Hiss of perjury for denying he knew Chambers. He received a five-year prison term. Hiss was released two years later proclaiming his innocence, a position he held throughout his life. Historians remain divided on the question of his spying.

Many Democrats, including Truman, dismissed the allegations against Hiss—conveniently publicized at the start of the 1948 election campaign—as a Republican slander. Nevertheless, the highly publicized allegations against Hiss hurt the Democrats, suggesting that FDR and Truman had allowed Communists to infiltrate the federal government.

The most dramatic spy case of the era involved Julius Rosenberg, a former government engineer, and his wife Ethel, who were accused of conveying atomic secrets to Soviet agents during World War II. The government had only a weak case against Ethel but hoped that her conviction would "break" her husband, forcing him to name other spies. Although the Rosenbergs maintained their innocence to the end, in March 1951 a jury found them both guilty. The American press showed them no sympathy, but the death sentence drew large protest demonstrations in the United States and abroad. Julius and Ethel Rosenberg died in the electric chair on June 19, 1953. Documents declassified in the 1990s provided evidence of Julius (but not Ethel) Rosenberg's guilt.

## McCARTHYISM

In a sensational Lincoln Day speech to the Republican Women's Club of Wheeling, West Virginia, on February 9, 1950, Republican senator Joseph R. McCarthy of Wisconsin announced that the United States had been sold out by the "traitorous actions" of men holding important positions in the federal government. These acted as part of a conspiracy, he charged, of 205 card-carrying Communists in the State Department.

McCarthy refused to reveal names because, in reality, he had none. Although investigations uncovered not a single Communist in the State Department, McCarthy launched a flamboyant offensive against New Deal Democrats and the Truman administration for failing to defend the nation's security. He gave his name to the era: **McCarthyism**.

Behind the blitz of publicity, the previously obscure junior senator from Wisconsin had struck a chord. Communism seemed to many Americans to be much more than a military threat—nothing less than a demonic force undermining all basic values. It compelled patriots to prepare Americans even for atomic warfare: "Better Dead Than Red."

Civil rights organizations faced the worst persecution since the 1920s. But attacks on women's organizations and homosexuals, which cloaked deep fears about changing sexual mores, took a huge toll. Aided by FBI reports, the federal government fired up to sixty homosexuals per month in the early 1950s. Dishonorable discharges from the U.S. armed forces for homosexuality, an administrative procedure without appeal, also increased dramatically.

Joseph McCarthy and his fellow Red-hunters eventually burned themselves out. During nationally televised congressional hearings in 1954, not only did McCarthy fail to prove his wild charges of Communist infiltration of the Army, but also in the glare of television he appeared deranged. Cowed for four years, the Senate finally censured him for "conduct unbecoming a member."

**26–7**
Joseph R. McCarthy, *Speech Delivered to the Women's Club of Wheeling, West Virginia* (1950)

**26–9**
Joseph McCarthy, *Telegram to President Truman Following the 'Wheeling (W.Va.) Speech'* (1950)

**myhistorylab**

**Exploring America:** *How to Lie with Statistics*

**McCarthyism** Anti-Communist attitudes and actions associated with Senator Joe McCarthy in the early 1950s, including smear tactics and innuendo.

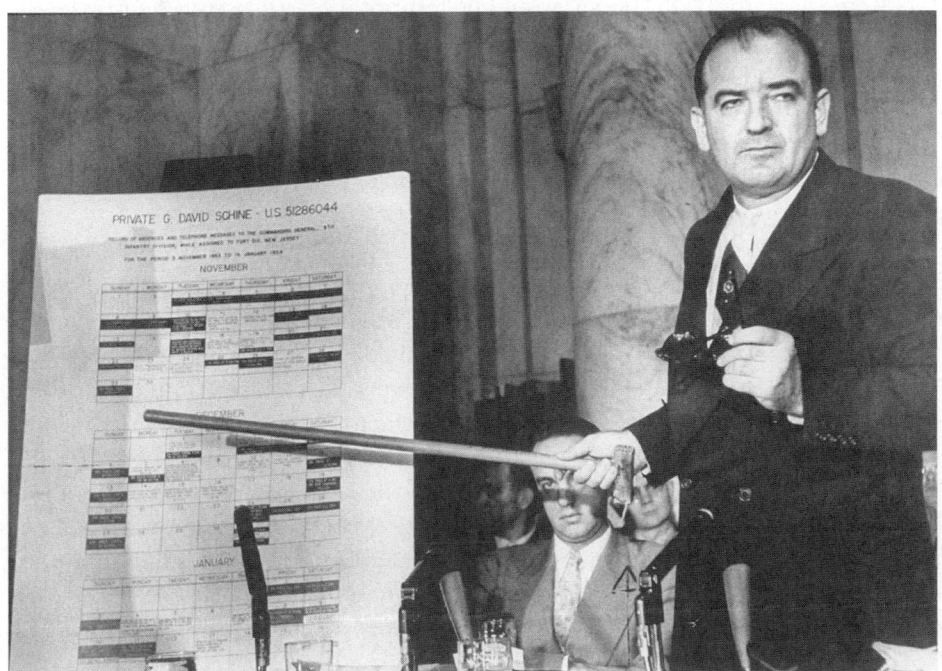

**The tables turned** on Senator Joseph McCarthy (1908–57) after he instigated an investigation of the U.S. Army for harboring Communists. A special congressional committee then investigated McCarthy for attempting to make the Army grant special privileges to his staff aide, Private David Schine. During the televised hearings, Senator McCarthy discredited himself. In December 1954, the Senate voted to censure him, thus robbing him of his power. He died three years later.

# COLD WAR CULTURE

As the Truman Doctrine revealed, the Cold War did not necessarily mean military confrontation. Nor was it defined exclusively by a quest for economic supremacy. The Cold War embodied the struggle of one "way of life" against another. It was, in short, a contest of values.

## AN ANXIOUS MOOD

"We have about 50 percent of the world's wealth," Kennan noted in 1948, "but only 3.6 percent of its population." However, many Americans feared an economic backslide. If wartime production had ended the hardships of the Great Depression, how would the economy fare in peacetime? No one could say. Peace itself seemed precarious.

The genre of *film noir* (French for "black film") deepened this postwar moodiness into a pessimistic aesthetic. American movies like *Out of the Past, Detour,* and *They Live by Night* told stories of relentless fate and ruthless betrayal. Their protagonists were loners running from a bad past, falsely accused of transgressions, or trapped into committing crimes. The high-contrast lighting of these black-and-white films accentuated the difficulty of distinguishing friend from foe.

Serious literature vividly captured a sense of anxious alienation. Playwright Arthur Miller in *Death of a Salesman* (1949) sketched an exacting portrait of self-destructive individualism. The novel was (and remains) very controversial: conservatives accused Salinger of encouraging disrespect for adults as "phonies," while for many young people he precisely articulated their alienation.

*Should mention Catcher in the Rye*

*Print error*

## THE FAMILY AS BULWARK

Postwar prosperity helped to strengthen the ideal of domesticity, although many Americans interpreted their rush toward marriage and parenthood, as one writer put it, as a "defense—an impregnable bulwark" against the era's anxieties.

Young couples were marrying younger and producing more children than at any time in the past century. The Census Bureau predicted that the "baby boom" would be temporary. To everyone's surprise, the birthrate continued to grow at a record pace, peaking at more than 118 per 1,000 women in 1957 (see Figure 26.1).

The new families who enjoyed postwar prosperity inaugurated a spending spree of trailblazing proportions. By the time Truman left office, two-thirds of all American households claimed at least one television set.

These two trends—the baby boom and high rates of consumer spending—encouraged a major change in the middle-class family. Having worked during World War II, often in occupations traditionally closed to them, many women wished to continue in full-time employment. Reconversion to peacetime production forced the majority from their factory positions, but most women quickly returned, taking jobs at a faster rate than men and providing half the total growth of the labor force. By 1952, 2 million more wives worked than during the war. Gone, however, were the high-paying unionized jobs in manufacturing. Instead, most women found low-wage jobs in the expanding service sector: clerical work, health care and education, and restaurant, hotel, and retail

**27–3**
Ladies Home Journal, *Young Mother* (1956)

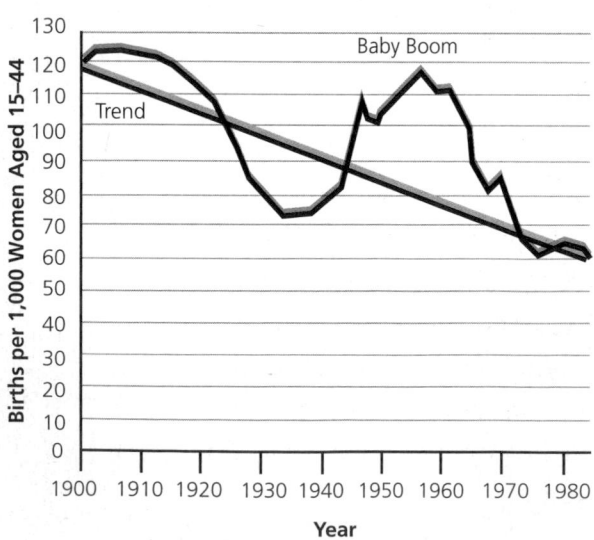

**Figure 26.1  U.S. Birthrate, 1900–1980**
The bulge of the "baby boom," a leading demographic factor in the postwar economy, stands out for this fifty-year period.

National Archives and Records Administration.

# The Hollywood Film
## *Invasion, U.S.A.*

*nvasion, U.S.A.* was the first of the genre of Red-scare films to do well at the box office. Shot in just seven days and released by Columbia Pictures in 1952, the film opens by depicting a group of well-off Americans, drinking casually in a New York bar and showing no particular concern about the imminent threat to their nation. Suddenly, they hear the news of horrific attacks by The Enemy. After atomic bombs fall and The Enemy approaches the nation's capital, they have all learned a potent lesson about complacency and begin to renounce their selfish ways. The group disperses, each character now understanding that freedom carries with it the price of vigilance.

The Enemy is never named, but Slavic accents and references to the "People's Government" that takes over Manhattan strongly suggest that the evildoers are Russian Communists.

THEY PUSH A BUTTON AND VAST CITIES VANISH BEFORE YOUR VERY EYES!

INVASION U.S.A.

GERALD MOHR · PEGGIE CASTLE · DAN O'HERLIHY

The poster builds on the foundation of fear. Studio publicists also advised local movie theaters to promote the movie along the same line: "Dress a young man in full paratroop regalia and have him walk through the principal streets of town in advance of playdate with a sign on his back reading HERE'S HOW IT WOULD HAPPEN IF IT HAPPENED NOW! SEE COLUMBIA PICTURES' *INVASION, U.S.A.* AT THE STATE THEATER FRIDAY!" The studio also suggested that blasts by air raid sirens and the use of local Civil Defense workers would be good choices to advertise the film. ■

**HOW DID** Hollywood and other forms of mass media help to shape Cold War culture in the late 1940s and early 1950s?

TABLE 26.1

Distribution of Total Personal Income Among Various Segments of the Population, 1947–70 (in Percentages)*

Year	Poorest Fifth	Second Poorest Fifth	Middle Fifth	Second Wealthiest Fifth	Wealthiest Fifth	Wealthiest 5 Percent
1947	3.5	10.6	16.7	23.6	45.6	18.7
1950	3.1	10.5	17.3	24.1	45.0	18.2
1960	3.2	10.6	17.6	24.7	44.0	17.0
1970	3.6	10.3	17.2	24.7	44.1	16.9

Despite the general prosperity of the postwar era, the distribution of income remained essentially unchanged.
*Monetary income only.

Adapted from U.S. Bureau of the Census, *Historical Statistics of the United States, Colonial Times to 1970*, Bicentennial ed. (Washington, DC: U.S. Government Printing Office, 1975), p. 292.

services. Older women whose children were grown might work because they had come to value a job for its own sake. Younger women often worked out of "economic necessity" that is, to maintain a middle-class standard of living that now required more than one income. Indeed, mothers of young children were the most likely to be employed (see Table 26.1).

Even though most women sought employment primarily to support their families, they ran up against popular opinion and expert advice urging them to go home. Polls registered resounding disapproval—by 86 percent of those surveyed—of a married woman working if jobs were scarce and her husband could support her. Noting that most Soviet women worked outside the home, many commentators appealed for a return to an imaginary "traditional" American family where men alone were breadwinners and women were exclusively homemakers.

Patterns of women's higher education reflected this conservative trend. Having made slight gains during World War II, when college-age men were serving in the armed forces or working in war industries, women lost ground after the **G.I. Bill** created a huge upsurge in male enrollment. Women represented 40 percent of all college graduates in 1940 but only 25 percent a decade later.

QUICK REVIEW

Working Wives

- 1952: More wives worked than during the war but held lower paying jobs.
- Many women worked to maintain a middle-class standard of living.
- Working women faced criticism by advocates of return to "traditional" family.

Military-Industrial Communities in the American West

All regions of the United States felt the impact of the Cold War, but none so directly as the West. World War II defense spending had stimulated the western economy and encouraged a mass westward migration of people eager to find wartime jobs. Following the war, many cities successfully converted to peacetime production; Los Angeles, for example, attracted one-eighth of all new business in the nation during the late 1940s. It was the Cold War, however, that by reviving defense funding gave the western economy its most important boost.

So much defense money—nearly 10 percent of the entire military budget—was poured by the federal government into California that the state's rate of economic growth between 1949 and 1952 outpaced that of the nation as a whole. Ten years later, an estimated one-third of all Los Angeles workers were employed by defense industries, particularly aerospace, and the absolute number of defense workers far exceeded those of the peak production years in World War II. The

G.I. Bill Legislation in June 1944 that eased the return of veterans into American society by providing educational and employment benefits.

Bay Area also benefited economically from defense spending, and cities such as San Jose began their rise as home to the nation's budding high-technology industry.

The Cold War pumped new life into communities that had grown up during World War II. Hanford, Washington, and Los Alamos, New Mexico, both centers of the **Manhattan Project**, employed more people in the construction of the Cold War nuclear arsenal than in the development of the atom bomb.

New communities accompanied the growth of the U.S. military bases and training camps in the West. Many of these installations, as well as hospitals and supply depots, not only survived but also expanded during the transition from the actual warfare of World War II to the threatened warfare of the Cold War. The availability of public lands with areas of sparse population made western states especially attractive to military planners designing such dangerous and secretive installations as the White Sands Missile Range in the New Mexican desert.

Local politicians, real estate agents, and merchants usually welcomed these developments as sources of revenue and employment. There were, however, heavy costs for speedy and unplanned federally induced growth. To accommodate the new populations, the government poured money into new highway systems but did little for public transportation. Uncontrolled sprawl, traffic congestion, air pollution, and strains on limited water and energy resources all grew with the military-industrial communities in the West. For those populations living near nuclear testing grounds, environmental degradation complemented the ultimate threat to their own physical well-being: over the next forty years, cancer rates soared.

## ZEAL FOR DEMOCRACY

Following the massive and spontaneous V-J Day celebrations, Americans began to retreat from public displays of patriotism, but soon new organizations, like the Freedoms Foundation of Valley Forge and the American Heritage Foundation, were joining such stalwarts as the American Legion and the Chamber of Commerce in scolding about "national apathy."

Patriotic messages also permeated public education. Following guidelines set down by the Truman administration, teachers were to "strengthen national security through education," designing their lesson plans to illustrate the superiority of the American democratic system over Soviet communism. In 1947 the federal Office of Education launched a "Zeal for Democracy" program for implementation by school boards nationwide. The program veered toward propaganda, announcing its intention to "promote and strengthen democratic thinking and practice, just as the schools of totalitarian states have so effectively promoted the ideals of their respective cultures." Meanwhile, in a national civil defense program, schoolchildren learned to "duck" under their desks and "cover" their heads in the event of a surprise Soviet nuclear attack.

Voices of protest were raised. A brave minority of scholars protested infringements on academic freedom by refusing to sign loyalty oaths and by writing books pointing out the potential dangers of aggressively nationalistic foreign and domestic policies. But the chilling atmosphere made many individuals reluctant to express contrary opinions or ideas.

This photograph, taken in 1955, presents an ideal image of domestic life for American women during the Cold War. This young mother sits with her three small children in a well-equipped kitchen that depicts the high standard of living that symbolized the "American way of life."

**26–2**
Kenneth MacFarland, *The Unfinished Work* (1946)

**Manhattan Project** Scientific research project during World War II specifically devoted to developing the atomic bomb.

# STALEMATE FOR THE DEMOCRATS

WHAT ISSUES were at the center
of the election of 1952?

**myhistorylab**

Review Summary

With Cold War tensions festering in Europe, neither the United States nor the Soviet Union would have predicted that events in Asia would bring them to the brink of a new world war. Yet in China, the most populous land on earth, Communists completed their seizure of power in late 1949. A few months later, in June 1950, Communist armies threatened to conquer all of Korea.

Truman sent American forces to conduct a "police action" in Korea, which within a few years absorbed more than 1.8 million U.S. troops with no victory in sight. For Truman, the "loss" of China and the Korean stalemate proved political suicide, ending the twenty-year Democratic lock on the presidency and the greatest era of reform in U.S. history.

## DEMOCRATIZING JAPAN AND "LOSING" CHINA

At the close of World War II, the United States acted deliberately to secure Japan firmly within its sphere of influence. General Douglas MacArthur directed an interim Japanese government in a modest reconstruction program that included land reform, creation of independent trade unions, abolition of contract marriages, granting of woman suffrage, sweeping demilitarization, and eventually a constitutional democracy that renounced war and barred Communists from all posts. American leaders worked to rebuild the nation's economy along capitalist lines and integrate Japan, like West Germany, into an anti-Soviet bloc. Japan also housed huge U.S. military bases, placing U.S. troops and weapons on the doorstep of the Soviet Union's Asian rim.

China could not be handled so easily. After years of civil war, the pro–Western Nationalist government of Jiang Jeishi (Chiang Kai-shek) collapsed. Since World War II, the United States had been aiding Jiang's unpopular and corrupt regime, while warning him that without major reforms and a coalition with his political opponents, the Nationalists were heading for defeat. Jiang refused any concessions, and in the late 1940s the Truman administration cut off virtually all aid and then watched as Nationalist troops surrendered to the Communists, led by Mao Zedong. Mao's Communists had the support of the Chinese countryside, where 85 percent of the population lived. Abandoning the entire mainland, the defeated Nationalists fled to the island of Taiwan. On October 1, 1949, Mao proclaimed the People's Republic of China, and in February 1950 the Soviet Union and the People's Republic of China signed an alliance.

China's "fall" to communism set off an uproar in the United States. The Asia First wing of the Republican Party, which saw the Far East rather than Europe as the primary target of U.S. trade and investment, blamed Truman for the "loss" of China. The president's adversaries, pointing to the growing menace of "international communism," called the Democrats the "party of treason."

## THE KOREAN WAR

At the end of World War II, the Allies had divided the Korean peninsula, surrendered by Japan, at the 38th Parallel. Although all Koreans hoped to reunite their nation under an independent government, the line between North and South hardened. While the United States backed the unpopular southern government of Syngman Rhee (the Republic of Korea), the Soviet Union sponsored a rival government in North Korea under Communist Kim Il-Sung (see Map 26.3).

On June 25, 1950, the U.S. State Department received a cablegram reporting an invasion of South Korea by the Communist North. While the Soviet Union apparently regarded the invasion as Kim's affair, China supported and perhaps incited Kim to invade South Korea. Truman sought the Security Council's approval to send troops to defend South Korea under the UN's collective-security provisions. With the Soviet delegate (who could have cast a veto) unaccountably absent, the Security Council agreed.

Military events seemed at first to justify the president's decision. Seoul, the capital of South Korea, fell to North Korean troops within weeks, and Communist

 MAP EXPLORATION

To explore an interactive version of this map, go to **http://www.prenhall.com/faraghertlc/map26.3**

Farthest UN advance
(Nov 1950)

CHINA

Yalu River

NORTH
KOREA

Sea of
Japan

Pyongyang
(Sept 1950)

Armistice line
(Nov 1951–July 1953)

International
boundary 1950

38th parallel

Panmunjon

Inchon,
(Sept 1950)

Seoul

SOUTH
KOREA

Farthest North Korean
advance (Sept 1950)

Yellow Sea

Pusan    Pusan
(Aug–Sept 1950)

North Korean invasion
UN offensive
Communist Chinese offensive
Battles

JAPAN

**MAP 26.3**
**The Korean War**    The intensity of battles underscored the strategic importance of Korea in the Cold War.

HOW DID the United States' military campaign in Korea reflect Truman's doctrine of containment?

**By midcentury, General** Douglas MacArthur (1880–1964) had earned a reputation as one of the most flamboyant and controversial American generals. This photograph, taken in September 1950, shows him during his finest hour as commander of the UN troops during the Korean War. He is observing the shelling of enemy forces shortly before he led a brilliant and successful amphibious landing at the Inchon peninsula. Nearly 1.8 million Americans served in Korea.

forces pushed south, occupying most of the peninsula. The situation appeared grim until Truman authorized MacArthur to carry out an amphibious landing at Inchon, near Seoul, on September 15, 1950. With tactical brilliance and good fortune, the general's campaign not only halted the Communist drive but also sent the North Koreans fleeing. By October, UN troops had retaken South Korea.

Basking in victory, the Truman administration could not resist the temptation to expand its war aims. To prove that Democrats were not "soft on communism," the president decided to roll back the Communists beyond the 38th Parallel, uniting Korea as a showcase for democracy. China, not yet directly involved in the war, warned that crossing that dividing line would threaten its national security. Truman flew to Wake Island in the Pacific on October 15 to confer with MacArthur, who assured him of a speedy victory.

MacArthur had sorely miscalculated. Chinese troops massed along the Yalu River, the border between Korea and China. As the UN forces approached the Yalu, suddenly and without air support a Chinese "human wave" attack began. MacArthur, who had foolishly divided his forces, suffered a crushing defeat. The Chinese drove the UN troops back into South Korea, where they regrouped south of the 38th Parallel. Finally, by the summer of 1951 a stalemate had been reached very near the old dividing line.

MacArthur tried to convince Truman to prepare for a new invasion of Communist territory. Encouraged by strong support at home, and defying the American tradition of civilian control over the military, MacArthur publicly criticized the president's policy, calling for bombing supply lines in China and blockading the Chinese coast. Such actions would certainly have led to a Chinese-American war. Finally, on April 10, 1951, Truman fired MacArthur for insubordination.

## THE PRICE OF NATIONAL SECURITY

The Korean conflict had profound implications for the use of executive power. By unilaterally instituting a peacetime draft in 1948 and in 1950 ordering American troops into Korea without a declaration of war, Truman had bypassed congressional authority. Republican Senator Robert Taft called the president's actions "evidence of an 'imperial presidency'" that was guilty of "a complete usurpation" of checks and balances. For a while, Truman sidestepped such criticisms and their constitutional implications by declaring a national emergency and by carefully referring to the military deployment not as a U.S. "war" but as a UN-sanctioned "police action."

The president was acting at the prompting of **National Security Council Paper 68 (NSC-68)**, a sweeping declaration of Cold War policy. This lengthy document was submitted to Truman by the National Security Council in April 1950. NSC-68 declared it necessary and expedient not only to repel Communist influence wherever it appeared but also to "foster the seeds of destruction within the Soviet Union." The document defined the struggle between the United States and the Soviet Union as "permanent" and the era one of "total war." American citizens, it declared, must be willing to sacrifice—"to give up some of the benefits which they have come to associate with their freedom"—to defend their way of life. NSC-68 articulated the intellectual and psychological rationale behind U.S. national security policies for the next forty years.

**26–8**
*National Security Council Memorandum Number 68*
(1950)

**National Security Council Paper 68 (NSC-68)** Policy statement that committed the United States to a military approach to the Cold War.

Initially hesitant, after the outbreak of the Korean war Truman accepted the policies outlined in NSC-68 and agreed to a rapid and permanent military buildup. At the same time, the federal government accelerated development of both conventional and nonconventional weapons.

The Korean war also provided the rationale to expand anti-Communist propaganda. At the end of World War II, Truman had taken steps to transform the Office of War Information into a peace-time program with a much smaller budget. But by 1948 Congress was ready to pass with bipartisan support the Smith-Mundt Act, designed "to promote the better understanding of the United States among the peoples of the world and to strengthen cooperative international relations." Within a year, Congress doubled the budget for such programming, granting $3 million to revive the Voice of America, the shortwave international radio program that had been established in 1942. The new legislation also funded films, print media, cultural exchange programs, and exhibitions, and it created a foundation to disseminate anti-Communist propaganda throughout the world. By 1951 a massive "Campaign of Truth" was reaching 93 nations, and the Voice of America was broadcasting anti-Communist programming in 45 languages.

In the end, the Korean conflict did nothing to roll back communism, and it cost the United States approximately $100 billion, inaugurating an era of huge federal budget deficits. In Korea, peace negotiations and fighting proceeded in tandem until the summer of 1953, when a settlement was reached returning North and South Korea to almost the same territory each had held at the start of the war. Approximately 54,000 Americans died in Korea; North Korea and China lost well over 2 million. The UN troops had employed both "carpet bombing" (an intense, destructive attack on a small area) and napalm (jellied gasoline bombs), destroying most of the housing and food supplies in both North and South Korea. True to patterns of modern warfare that emerged during World War II, the majority of civilians killed were women and children. Nearly a million Koreans were left homeless.

The Korean conflict enlarged the geographical range of the Cold War to include East Asia. "Red China" and the United States would be implacable enemies for the next twenty years. Moreover, Korea did much to establish an ominous tradition of "unwinnable" conflicts that left many Americans skeptical of official policy.

## "I LIKE IKE": THE ELECTION OF 1952

Korea dominated the election campaign of 1952. Truman's popularity had wavered continually since he took office in 1945, but it sank to an all-time low in the early 1950s shortly after he fired MacArthur.

The case against Truman widened. The Asia First lobby argued that if in the late 1940s the president had aggressively turned back communism in China, there would have been no "limited war" in Korea. Large-scale corruption came to light in Truman's administration. Business and organized labor complained about Korean war price and wage freezes. A late 1951 Gallup poll showed the president's approval rating at 23 percent. In March 1952, Truman announced he would not run for reelection, even though he was constitutionally permitted another term.

Accepting political defeat and disgrace, Truman endorsed the uncharismatic governor of Illinois, Adlai E. Stevenson Jr. Admired for his eloquence, wit, honesty, and intelligence, Stevenson offered no solutions to the conflict in Korea, the accelerating arms race, or the Cold War generally. Accepting the Democratic

**On December 23,** 1952, Republican vice-presidential candidate Richard M. Nixon appeared on national television to defend himself against charges that he had taken illegal campaign contributions. This photograph shows him with one of those gifts, a black-and-white spotted cocker spaniel. He said: "And our little girl Tricia, the six year old, named it 'Checkers.' And you know, the kids, like all kids, love the dog, and I just want to say this, right now, that regardless of what they say about it, we're gonna keep it." This speech, which was simulcast on radio, won the hearts of many voters.

nomination, he candidly admitted that "the ordeal of the twentieth century is far from over."

The Republicans made the most of the Democrats' dilemma. Without proposing any sweeping answers of their own, they zeroed in on "$K_1C_2$"—Korea, Communism, and Corruption. When opinion polls showed retired General Dwight D. Eisenhower with an "unprecedented" 64 percent approval rating, they found in "Ike" the perfect candidate.

Eisenhower styled himself the voice of "modern Republicanism." He wisely avoided the negative impressions made in 1948 by Dewey, who had seemed as aggressive as Truman abroad and bent on repealing the New Deal at home. Eisenhower knew better: voters wanted peace and a limited welfare state. Richard Nixon, Eisenhower's vice presidential candidate, meanwhile waged a relentless and defamatory attack on "Adlai the Appeaser."

The Republican campaign was itself not scandal-free: Nixon was caught accepting personal gifts from wealthy benefactors. On national television, he pathetically described his wife Pat's "good Republican cloth coat" and their struggling life but then contritely admitted to indeed accepting one gift: a puppy named Checkers that his little daughters loved and that he refused to give back. "The Poor Richard Show," as critics called this masterfully maudlin "Checkers Speech," defused the scandal without answering the most important charges. And it underscored how important television was becoming in molding voters' perceptions.

Soaring above the scandal, Eisenhower inspired voters as the peace candidate. Ten days before the election he dramatically announced: "I shall go to Korea." Eisenhower carried 55 percent of the vote and thirty-nine states in normally Democratic areas, such as the South, and in New York, Chicago, Boston, and Cleveland. Riding his coattails, the Republicans regained narrow control of Congress. The New Deal coalition—ethnic minorities, northern blacks, unionized workers, liberals, Catholics, Jews, and white southern conservatives—no longer commanded a majority.

## CONCLUSION

In his farewell address, in January 1953, Harry Truman reflected: "I suppose that history will remember my term in office as the years when the 'cold war' began to overshadow our lives. I have hardly had a day in office that has not been dominated by this all-embracing struggle."

The election of Dwight Eisenhower helped to diminish the intensity of this dour mood without actually bringing a halt to the conflict. The new president pledged himself to liberate the world from communism by peaceful means rather than force. "Our aim is more subtle," he announced during his campaign, "more pervasive, more complete. We are trying to get the world, by peaceful means, to believe the truth. . . ." Increasing the budget of the CIA, Eisenhower took the Cold War out of the public eye by relying to a far greater extent than Truman on psychological warfare and covert operations.

"The Eisenhower Movement," wrote journalist Walter Lippmann, was a "mission in American politics" to restore a sense of community among the American people. In a larger sense, many of the issues of the immediate post–World War II years seemed to have been settled or put off for a distant future. The international boundaries of communism were frozen with the Chinese Revolution, the Berlin Crisis, and now the Korean war. Meanwhile, at home Cold War defense spending had become a permanent part of the national budget, an undeniable drain on tax revenues but an important element in the government contribution to economic prosperity. If the nuclear arms race remained a cause for anxiety, joined by

# CHRONOLOGY

**1941** Henry Luce forecasts the dawn of "the American Century."

**1944** G.I. Bill of Rights benefits World War II veterans.

International Monetary Fund and World Bank founded.

**1945** Franklin D. Roosevelt dies in office; Harry S. Truman becomes president.

United Nations charter signed.

World War II ends.

Strike wave begins.

Truman proposes program of economic reforms.

**1946** Employment Act creates Council of Economic Advisers.

Churchill's Iron Curtain speech.

Atomic Energy Act establishes Atomic Energy Commission.

Republicans win control of Congress.

Benjamin Spock publishes *Baby and Child Care.*

**1947** Truman Doctrine announced; Congress appropriates $400 million in aid for Greece and Turkey.

Federal Employees Loyalty and Security Program established and attorney general's list of subversive organizations authorized.

Marshall Plan announced.

Taft-Hartley Act restricts union activities.

National Security Act establishes Department of Defense, the National Security Council, and the Central Intelligence Agency.

House Un-American Activities Committee hearings in Hollywood.

**1948** Smith-Mundt Act passed by Congress.

Ferdinand Lundberg and Marynia Farnham publish *Modern Woman: The Lost Sex.*

State of Israel founded; immediately recognized by the United States.

Berlin blockade begins.

Henry Wallace nominated for president on Progressive Party ticket.

Truman announces peacetime draft and desegregates U.S. armed forces and civil service.

Truman elected president, defeating Dewey, Wallace, and Thurmond; Democrats sweep both houses of Congress.

**1949** Truman announces Fair Deal.

North Atlantic Treaty Organization (NATO) created.

Communists, led by Mao Zedong, take power in China.

Berlin blockade ends.

Soviet Union detonates atomic bomb.

**1950** Alger Hiss convicted of perjury.

Senator Joseph McCarthy begins anti-Communist crusade.

Soviet Union and the People's Republic of China sign an alliance.

Adoption of NSC-68 consolidates presidential war powers.

Korean war begins.

Internal Security (McCarran) Act requires registration of Communist organizations and arrest of Communists during national emergencies.

**1951** Truman dismisses General Douglas MacArthur.

Psychological Strategy Board created.

Armistice talks begin in Korea.

**1952** Immigration and Nationality Act retains quota system, lifts ban on immigration of Asian and Pacific peoples, but bans "subversives" and homosexuals.

United States detonates first hydrogen bomb.

Dwight D. Eisenhower wins presidency, defeating Adlai Stevenson; Richard Nixon becomes vice president.

**1953** Julius and Ethel Rosenberg executed for atomic espionage.

Armistice ends fighting in Korea.

**1954** Army-McCarthy hearings end, discrediting McCarthy.

**1955** Warsaw Pact created.

more personal worries about the changing patterns of family life, a sense of relative security nevertheless spread. Prospects for world peace had dimmed, but the worst nightmares of the 1940s had eased as well.

## REVIEW QUESTIONS

1. Discuss the origins of the Cold War and the sources of growing tensions between the United States and the Soviet Union at the close of World War II.

2. Describe the basic elements of President Harry Truman's policy of containment. How did the threat of atomic warfare affect this policy?

3. Compare the presidencies of Franklin D. Roosevelt and Harry S Truman, both Democrats.

4. Describe the impact of McCarthyism on American political life. How did the anti-Communist campaigns affect the media? What were the sources of Senator Joseph McCarthy's popularity? What brought about his downfall?

5. How did the Cold War shape mid-twentieth-century American culture?

6. Discuss the role of the United States in Korea in the decade after World War II. How did the Korean war affect the 1952 presidential election?

7. Why did Dwight D. Eisenhower win the 1952 presidential election?

## KEY TERMS

**Flashcard Review**

**Berlin blockade** (p. 734)
**Central Intelligence Agency (CIA)**
  (p. 740)
**Cold War** (p. 730)
**Council of Economic Advisers**
  (p. 737)
**Dixiecrat** (p. 738)
**Executive Order 9835** (p. 740)
**G.I. Bill** (p. 746)
**House Un-American Activities**
  **Committee (HUAC)** (p. 741)
**International Monetary Fund (IMF)**
  (p. 729)

**Manhattan Project** (p. 747)
**Marshall Plan** (p. 734)
**McCarthyism** (p. 743)
**National Security Council (NSC)**
  (p. 740)
**National Security Council Paper 68**
  **(NSC-68)** (p. 750)
**North Atlantic Treaty Organization**
  **(NATO)** (p. 735)
**Taft-Hartley Act** (p. 738)
**Truman Doctrine** (p. 734)

## RECOMMENDED READING

Mark S. Byrnes, *The Truman Years, 1945–1953* (2000). A concise history of the Truman administration and its role at the moment when the United States became the dominant economic power in the world. Byrnes covers this transformation with particular attention to the way the president helped to shape a view of the world that presented the United States and the Soviet Union as permanent enemies in a struggle for domination. Includes a set of twenty-one key documents and a detailed chronology of events.

Kevin J. Fernlund, ed., *The Cold War American West, 1945–1989* (1998). Ten es-
    says illustrating the impact of the Cold War on the region of the United
    States that housed the bulk of military bases, airfields, nuclear testing
    grounds, and toxic waste dumps. Presenting a variety of interpretations,
    the contributors ask a common question: Was the West transformed or de-
    formed by the policies of the growing national security state?

David Halberstam, *The Coldest Winter: America and the Korean War* (2007). The
    journalist David Halberstam conducted dozens of interviews with veterans
    to create a huge history of the Korean War that looks ahead to future U.S
    involvement in Southeast Asia and the Middle East.

David K. Johnson, *The Lavender Scare: The Cold War Persecution of Gays and Les-
    bians in the Federal Government* (2004). Goes beyond McCarthy and the per-
    secution of Communists to examine the role of the national-security state
    in purging homosexuals from positions in federal government. Johnson
    also covers the gay subculture of Washington, DC, which grew with the ex-
    pansion of government during the New Deal and World War II.

Elaine Tyler May, *Homeward Bound: American Families in the Cold War Era* (1988).
    A lively account of the effects on family life and women's roles of the na-
    tional mood of "containment." May argues that government policy be-
    came part of a popular culture that solidified the Cold War era's
    "feminine mystique."

Ellen Schrecker, *The Age of McCarthyism: A Brief History with Documents,* 2nd ed.
    (2002). A useful collection of primary sources on internal security and an-
    ticommunism by one of the foremost scholars of the field.

Judith E. Smith, *Visions of Belonging: Family Stories, Popular Culture, and Postwar
    Democracy, 1940–1960* (2004). Creatively uses literature, drama, and film to
    examine the ways public life and private experience were reshaped in the
    aftermath of World War II.

Where it's a good time to connect to the past!

# Cold War Fears and Nuclear Holocaust

In the 1950s and 1960s a multitude of grade B motion pictures appeared with a single theme, the total destruction of the United States by a nuclear holocaust. Some films focused on life after the holocaust in a radioactive nightmare of starvation, crazed mobs, and ruined cities. Others had radioactive spawned monsters of human, reptilian, or aquatic origin ravaging the survivors in a burned out world. The origin of these movies was the Cold War fear of total war or what the Eisenhower administration referred to as MAD (mutual assured destruction). By the middle 1950s the Soviet Union and the

**TO WHAT** extent did Cold War confrontations stimulate fear of world war and nuclear holocaust among the American people?

United States could deliver a complete knockout blow to each other by nuclear bombs carried by aircraft. By the late 1960s scientists were warning of a phenomenon called "nuclear winter" or a world-wide holocaust following any significant nuclear exchange among the world powers.

This was the great fear that motivated so much concern during the Cold War.■

Test Mike—First Hydrogen Bomb Test—Eniwetok Atoll, October 31. 1952

## Leo Szilard, a Petition to the President of the United States, July 3, 1945

DISCOVERIES OF which the people of the United States are not aware may affect the welfare of this nation in the near future. The liberation of atomic power which has been achieved places atomic bombs in the hands of the Army. It places in your hands, as Commander-in-Chief, the fateful decision whether or not to sanction the use of such bombs in the present phase of the war against Japan.

We, the undersigned scientists, have been working in the field of atomic power for a number of years. Until recently we have had to reckon with the possibility that the United States might be attacked by atomic bombs during this war and that her only defense might lie in a counterattack by the same means. Today with this danger averted we feel impelled to say what follows:

The war has to be brought speedily to a successful conclusion and the destruction of Japanese cities by means of atomic bombs may very well be an effective method of warfare. We feel, however, that such an attack on Japan could not be justified in the present circumstances. We believe that the United States ought not to resort to the use of atomic bombs in the present phase of the war, at least not unless the terms which will be imposed upon Japan after

the war are publicly announced and subsequently Japan is given an opportunity to surrender.

If such public announcement gave assurance to the Japanese that they could look forward to a life devoted to peaceful pursuits in their homeland and if Japan still refused to surrender, our nation would then be faced with a situation which might require a re-examination of her position with respect to the use of atomic bombs in the war.

Atomic bombs are primarily a means for the ruthless annihilation of cities. Once they were introduced as an instrument of war it would be difficult to resist for long the temptation of putting them to such use. . . .

Our use of atomic bombs in this war would carry the world a long way further on this path of ruthlessness.

In view of the foregoing, we, the undersigned, respectfully petition that you exercise your power as Commander-in-Chief to rule that the United States shall not, in the present phase of the war, resort to the use of atomic bombs.■

*Letter signed by Leo Szilard and 58 co-signers.*

# Dwight D. Eisenhower, Atoms for Peace Speech, December 8, 1953

On July 16, 1945, the United States set off the world's first atomic explosion. Since that date in 1945, the United States of America has conducted 42 test explosions.

Atomic bombs today are more than 25 times as powerful as the weapons with which the atomic age dawned, while hydrogen weapons are in the ranges of millions of tons of TNT equivalent.

Today, the United States' stockpile of atomic weapons, which, of course, increases daily, exceeds by many times the explosive equivalent of the total of all bombs and all shells that came from every plane and every gun in every theatre of war in all of the years of World War II. . . .

But the dread secret, and the fearful engines of atomic might, are not ours alone. . . .

The secret is also known by the Soviet Union. . . .

Should such an atomic attack be launched against the United States, our reactions would be swift and resolute. But for me to say that the defense capabilities of the United States are such that they could inflict terrible losses upon an aggressor–for me to say that the retaliation capabilities of the United States are so great that such an aggressor's land would be laid waste–all this, while fact, is not the true expression of the purpose and the hope of the United States. . . .

Surely no sane member of the human race could discover victory in such desolation. . . . ■

# Eisenhower's Farewell Address, January 17, 1961

. . . A vital element in keeping the peace is our military establishment. Our arms must be mighty, ready for instant action, so that no potential aggressor may be tempted to risk his own destruction.

Our military organization today bears little relation to that known by any of my predecessors in peace time, or indeed by the fighting men of World War II or Korea.

Until the latest of our world conflicts, the United States had no armaments industry. American makers of plowshares could, with time and as required, make swords as well. But now we can no longer risk emergency improvisation of national defense; we have been compelled to create a permanent armaments industry of vast proportions. Added to this, three and a half million men and women are directly engaged in the defense establishment. We annually spend on military security more than the net income of all United States corporations. . . .

In the councils of government, we must guard against the acquisition of unwarranted influence, whether sought or unsought, by the military-industrial complex.

Hiroshima in ruins following the atomic bomb, dropped at end of WWII

The potential for the disastrous rise of misplaced power exists and will persist.

We must never let the weight of this combination endanger our liberties or democratic processes. . . . ■

# John F. Kennedy, Cuban Missile Address, October 22, 1962

. . . This Government, as promised, has maintained the closest surveillance of the Soviet military build-up on the island of Cuba. Within the past week unmistakable evidence has established the fact that a series of offensive missile sites is now in preparation on that imprisoned island. . . .

The characteristics of these new missile sites indicate two distinct types of installations. Several of them include medium-range ballistic missiles capable of carrying a nuclear warhead for a distance of more than 1,000 nautical miles. Each of these missiles, in short, is capable of striking Washington, D.C., the Panama Canal, Cape Canaveral, Mexico City, or any other city in the southeastern part of the United States, in Central America, or in the Caribbean area.

Additional sites not yet completed appear to be designed for intermediate-range ballistic missiles capable of traveling more than twice as far—and thus capable of striking most of the major cities in the Western Hemisphere,

ranging as far north as Hudson Bay, Canada, and as far south as Lima, Peru. In addition, jet bombers, capable of carrying nuclear weapons, are now being uncrated and assembled in Cuba, while the necessary air bases are being prepared.

This urgent transformation of Cuba into an important strategic base—by the presence of these large, long-range, and clearly offensive weapons of sudden mass destruction—constitutes an explicit threat to the peace and security of all the Americas . . . This action also contradicts the repeated assurances of Soviet spokesmen . . . that the arms build-up in Cuba would retain its original defensive character . . .

In that sense missiles in Cuba add to an already clear and present danger . . . But this secret, swift, and extraordinary build up of Communist missiles is a deliberately provocative and unjustifiable change in the status quo which cannot be accepted by this country if our courage and our commitments are ever to be trusted again by either friend or foe. ■

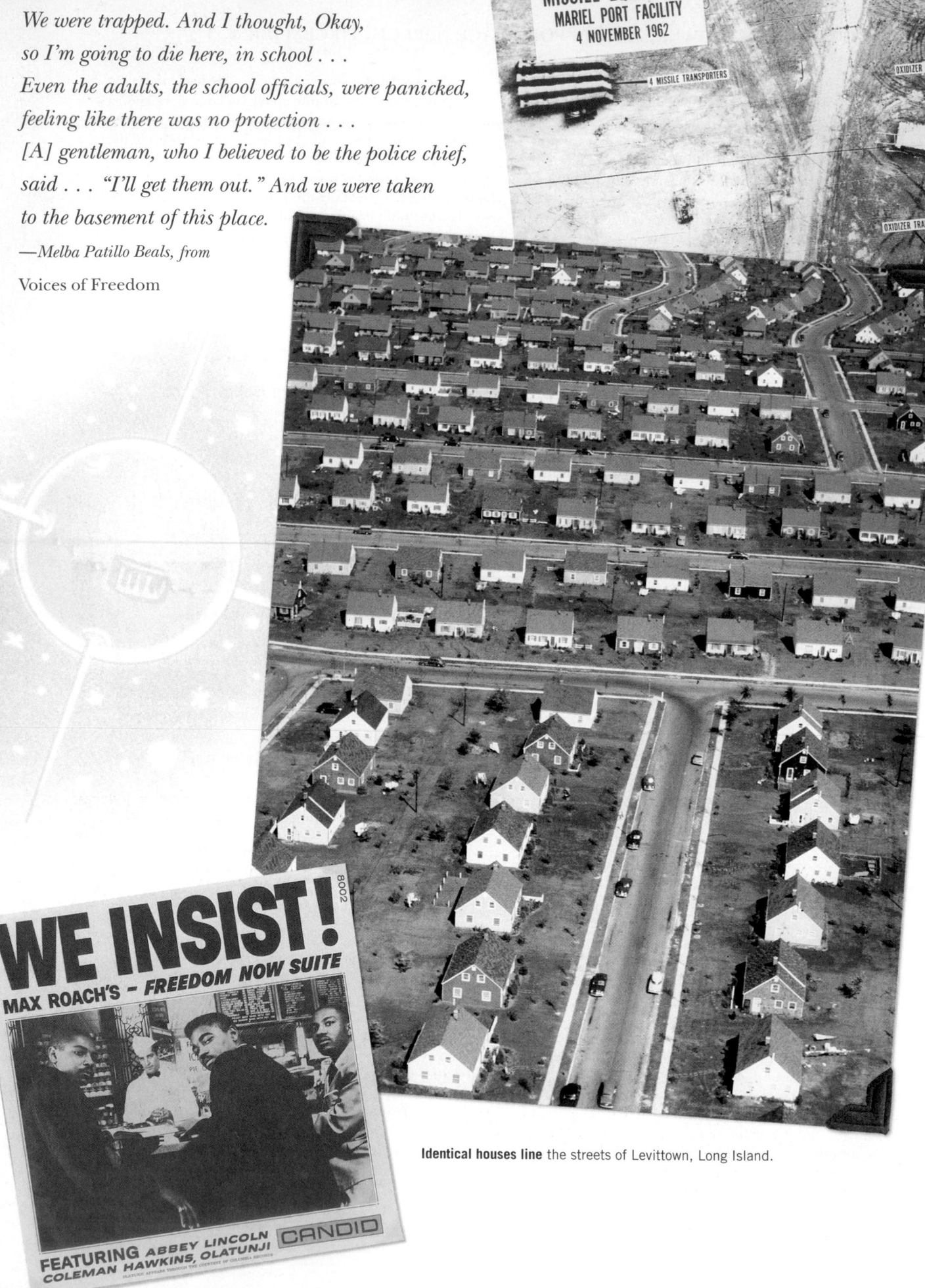

*We were trapped. And I thought, Okay,
so I'm going to die here, in school . . .
Even the adults, the school officials, were panicked,
feeling like there was no protection . . .
[A] gentleman, who I believed to be the police chief,
said . . . "I'll get them out." And we were taken
to the basement of this place.*

—*Melba Patillo Beals, from*
Voices of Freedom

MISSILE EQUIPMENT
MARIEL PORT FACILITY
4 NOVEMBER 1962

4 MISSILE TRANSPORTERS

OXIDIZER TRAILERS

OXIDIZER TRAILERS

**Identical houses line** the streets of Levittown, Long Island.

8002

# WE INSIST!
## MAX ROACH'S — FREEDOM NOW SUITE

CANDID

FEATURING ABBEY LINCOLN
COLEMAN HAWKINS, OLATUNJI

# 27

# AMERICA AT MIDCENTURY
## 1952–1963

**HOW DID** the Eisenhower administration's foreign policy respond to Cold War challenges?

**WHAT IDEALS** did America's suburban life evoke, and how did those ideals correspond to suburban realities?

**WHY DID** the youth market expand so rapidly at midcentury?

**WHAT EXPLAINS** the emergence of a distinct youth culture in 1950s' America?

**WHO WAS** John F. Kennedy, and why did his New Frontier seem so promising to many Americans?

# AMERICAN COMMUNITIES
## Popular Music in Memphis

THE NINETEEN-YEAR-OLD MISSISSIPPIAN PEERED NERVOUSLY OUT OVER the large crowd at Overton Park, Memphis's outdoor amphitheater. He knew that people had come that hot, sticky July day in 1954 to hear the headliner, country music star Slim Whitman. Sun Records, a local Memphis label, had just released the unknown young man's first record, and it had begun to receive some airplay on local radio. He and his two bandmates had never played in a setting even remotely as large as this one. And their music defied categories: it wasn't black and it wasn't white; it wasn't pop and it wasn't country. But when he launched into his version of a black blues song called "That's All Right," the crowd went wild. "I came offstage," he later recalled, "and my manager told me that they was hollering because I was wiggling my legs. I went back out for an encore, and I did a little more, and the more I did, the wilder they went." Elvis Presley had arrived.

Elvis Presley's life and career personified many of the themes and tensions of postwar American life. Elvis was born in Tupelo, Mississippi, in 1935, but like many thousands of other poor rural whites the Presley family moved to Memphis in 1949. Elvis's father found work in a munitions plant. The Presleys were poor enough to qualify for an apartment in Lauderdale Courts, a Memphis public housing project built during the New Deal. Located halfway between St. Louis and New Orleans on the Mississippi River, Memphis enjoyed healthy growth during World War II, with lumber mills, furniture factories, and chemical manufacturing supplementing the cotton market as sources of jobs and prosperity. Memphis also boasted a remarkable diversity of popular theater and music, including a large opera house, numerous brass bands, vaudeville and burlesque, minstrel shows, jug bands, and blues clubs. And like the rest of the South, Memphis was a legally segregated city; whites and blacks lived, went to school, and worked apart. But music—in live clubs and on the radio—was an important means of breaking through the barriers of racial segregation.

As a boy, Elvis turned to music for emotional release and spiritual expression. He soaked up the wide range of musical styles available in Memphis. The all-white Assembly of God

Church his family attended featured a renowned hundred-voice choir. Elvis and his friends went to marathon all-night "gospel singings" at Ellis Auditorium, where they enjoyed the tight harmonies and emotional style of white gospel quartets. Elvis also drew from the sounds he heard on Beale Street, the main black thoroughfare of Memphis and one of the nation's most influential centers of African American music. Elvis himself understood his debt to black music and black performers. "The colored folks," he told an interviewer in 1956, "been singing and playing it just like I'm doing now, man, for more years than I know. They played it like that in the shanties and in their juke joints and nobody paid it no mind until I goosed it up. I got it from them."

Dissatisfied with the cloying pop music of the day, white teenagers across the nation were increasingly turning to the rhythmic drive and emotional intensity of black rhythm and blues. They quickly adopted rock 'n' roll (the term had long been African American slang for dancing and sexual intercourse) as their music. But it was more than just music: it was also an attitude, a celebration of being young, and a sense of having something that adult authority could not understand or control. For millions of young people, rock 'n' roll was an expression of revolt against the conformity and blandness found in so many new postwar suburbs.

Memphis

By helping to accustom white teenagers to the style and sound of black artists, Elvis helped establish rock 'n' roll as an interracial phenomenon. The considerable adult opposition to rock 'n' roll revolved largely around fears of race mixing. To a remarkable degree the new music anticipated and contributed to the collapse of segregation, at least in the realm of popular culture. Institutional racism would continue to plague the music business—many black artists were routinely cheated out of royalties and severely underpaid—but the music of postwar Memphis at least pointed the way toward the exciting cultural possibilities that could emerge from breaking down the barriers of race. It also gave postwar American teenagers a newfound sense of community. In a broader sense, rock 'n' roll heralded a generational shift in American society.

# UNDER THE COLD WAR'S SHADOW

By the time Dwight D. Eisenhower—universally called "Ike"—entered the White House in 1953, the confrontation with communism was already providing the framework for America's relations with the world. Eisenhower developed new strategies for the containment of what he called "international communism," including a greater reliance on nuclear deterrence and aggressively using the CIA for covert action. Yet Eisenhower also resolved to do everything possible to forestall an all-out nuclear conflict.

## THE EISENHOWER PRESIDENCY

As he had promised during his campaign, in December 1952 Eisenhower traveled to Korea just after his election and spent three days at the front. He returned home determined to end the fighting. The death of Soviet leader Joseph Stalin in March 1953, along with the exhaustion of Chinese and North Korean forces, created conditions favorable for a truce. In July 1953 a cease-fire agreement—not a peace settlement—brought the fighting to an uneasy end, freezing the division of North and South Korea near the 38th Parallel.

Eisenhower's success in ending the Korean fighting set the tone for his administration and increased his popularity. As president, Eisenhower kept up anticommunist Cold War rhetoric while persuading Americans to accept the East–West stalemate as a more or less permanent fact. At home, Ike became the reassuring symbol of moderation and stability in a nation worried by threats ranging from communism and nuclear war to a new depression.

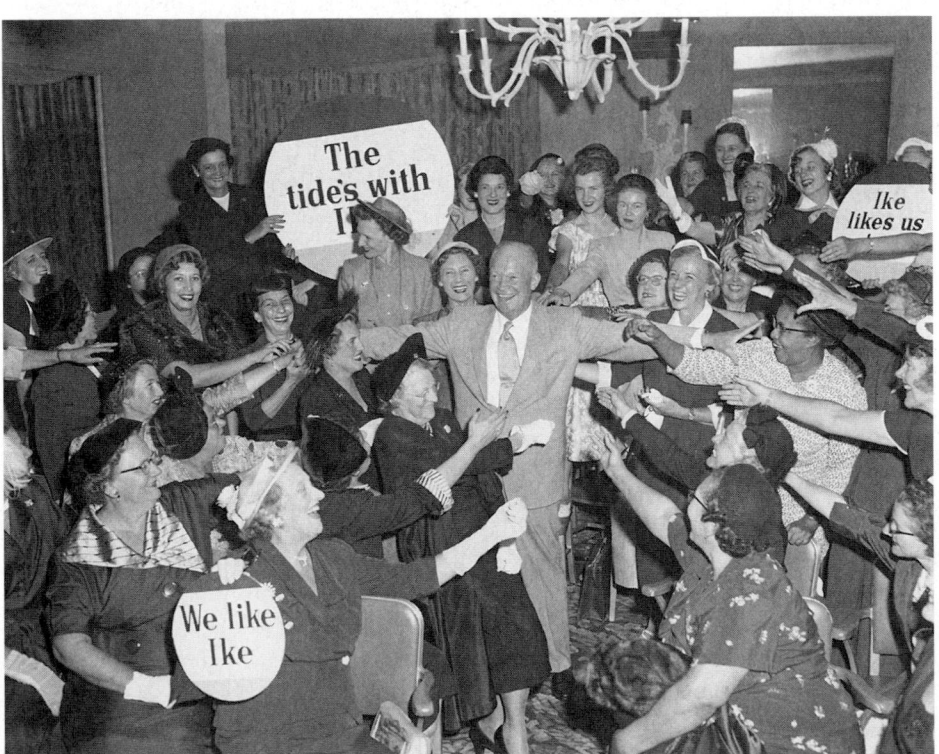

Presidential contender Dwight D. Eisenhower hosts a group of Republican National Committee women at his campaign headquarters in 1952. Ike's status as America's biggest war hero, along with his genial public persona, made him an extremely popular candidate with voters across party lines.

**HOW DID** the Eisenhower administration's foreign policy respond to Cold War challenges?

**myhistorylab**
Review Summary

## IMAGE KEY

for pages 758–759

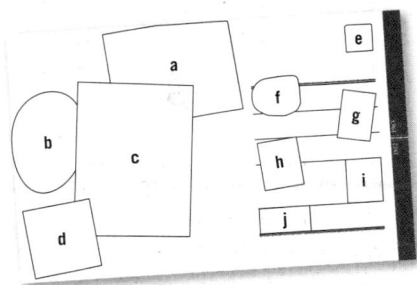

**a.** Russian nuclear missiles photographed at Mariel Port facility in Cuba, with illustrative tags describing various offensive equipment.

**b.** A drawing of the Sputnik satellite appears on a playing card from a game about the space race.

**c.** Identical houses line the streets of Levittown, Long Island.

**d.** The album cover of "We Insist!" by Max Roach depicts African American men at a lunch counter during a sit-in.

**e.** 1960 presidential candidates Richard M. Nixon and John F. Kennedy during a televised debate shown on a vintage television set.

**f.** A suburban family standing in front of their 1948 Levittown house in 1950.

**g.** Rock and roll legend Chuck Berry performs his trademark "duck walk" maneuver with a Gibson semi-solid body guitar.

**h.** A scene from the long-running 1950s television sitcom "Ozzie and Harriet."

**i.** President Dwight D. Eisenhower (1890–1969) sitting at his desk while signing a document.

**j.** President Kennedy's television address on the Cuban Missile Crisis.

A conservative vision of community lay at the core of Eisenhower's political philosophy. He saw America as a corporate commonwealth, similar to Herbert Hoover's "associative state" of a generation before (see Chapter 23). Eisenhower believed the industrial strife, high inflation, and fierce partisan politics of the Truman years could be corrected only through cooperation, self-restraint, and disinterested public service. As president, Eisenhower sought to limit New Deal trends that had expanded federal power, and he encouraged a voluntary, as opposed to a regulatory, government–business partnership. To him, social harmony and "the good life" at home were closely linked to maintaining a stable, American-led international order abroad.

In running his White House staff and his administration, Eisenhower adapted the staff system with which he had effectively managed unwieldy Allied forces during World War II. His "hidden hand presidency" relied on letting the states and corporate interests guide domestic policy and the economy. He appointed nine businessmen—three with ties to General Motors—to his first cabinet. He appointed men congenial to the corporate interests they were supposed to regulate to the Federal Trade Commission, the Federal Communications Commission, and the Federal Power Commission.

At the same time, Eisenhower accepted the New Deal legacy of greater federal responsibility for social welfare. He rejected conservative Republican appeals to dismantle Social Security. His administration agreed to a modest expansion of Social Security and unemployment insurance and small increases in the minimum wage. Ike also created the Department of Health, Education and Welfare, appointing as its head the second woman in history to hold a cabinet position, Oveta Culp Hobby. In agriculture, Eisenhower continued to sustain farm prices—and the interests of agribusiness—by means of New Deal–style parity payments. Between 1952 and 1960, federal spending on agriculture jumped from about $1 billion to $7 billion, and government storage facilities bulged with surpluses.

Eisenhower, a fiscal conservative in Hoover's mold, hesitated to use fiscal policy (government spending) to pump up the economy when it twice went into recession: after the Korean war and again in 1958. In that year, though unemployment hit 7.5 percent, the administration refused to cut taxes or increase spending. Eisenhower feared inflation more than unemployment or poverty—and indeed, by the time he left office he could boast that on his watch the average family's real wages (that is, factoring in inflation) had risen by 20 percent. With low inflation and steady, if modest, growth, the Eisenhower years were prosperous for most Americans.

## THE "NEW LOOK" IN FOREIGN AFFAIRS

The death of Joseph Stalin in 1953, just two months after Eisenhower's inauguration, brought an internal power struggle in the Soviet Union. It also opened up the prospects for a thaw in the Cold War, giving Eisenhower hope for peaceful coexistence between the two superpowers. Although Eisenhower recognized that the United States was engaged in a long-term struggle with the Soviet Union, he feared that permanent Cold War mobilization might overburden the American economy and create a "garrison state." He therefore pursued a high-tech, capital-intensive defense policy that emphasized America's qualitative advantage in strategic weaponry and sought cuts in the military budget.

Secretary of State John Foster Dulles gave shape to the "new look" in American foreign policy in the 1950s. A devout Presbyterian lawyer, Dulles had been involved in diplomacy since World War I. He brought to the job a strong sense of righteousness, an almost missionary belief in America's responsibility to preserve the Free World from godless, immoral communism. Dulles called not simply for "containing" communism but for a "rollback." The key would be greater reliance on America's nuclear superiority. As part of a new strategic doctrine, Dulles emphasized the capacity of the Strategic Air Command to inflict devastating destruction with thermonuclear H-bombs. This would be "massive retaliation . . . at times and places of our own choosing" to deter Soviet aggression.

But the limits of a policy based on nuclear strategy became painfully clear when American leaders faced tense situations that offered no clear way to intervene without provoking full-scale war. U.S. leaders faced the same dilemma in 1956 when Hungary revolted against Communist rule. The United States opened its gates to thousands of Hungarian refugees, but despite desperate appeals on the rebel radio it refused to intervene against Soviet tanks and troops. Eisenhower recognized that the Soviets would defend not just their own borders, but also their domination of Eastern Europe, by all-out war if necessary.

Nikita Khrushchev, who had emerged as Stalin's successor, in 1955 withdrew Soviet troops from eastern Austria in a conciliatory gesture. This first real rollback had been achieved by negotiation and a spirit of common hope, not by threats or force. In 1958 Khrushchev, probing American intentions and hoping to redirect the Soviet economy toward the production of more consumer goods, unilaterally suspended nuclear testing. Khrushchev made a twelve-day trip to America in 1959, visiting an Iowa farm, touring Hollywood, and conferring with Eisenhower at Camp David, the presidential retreat in Maryland. If nothing else, such "summit" diplomacy offered a psychological thaw in the Cold War. In early 1960 Khrushchev called for another summit in Paris, to discuss German reunification and nuclear disarmament. Eisenhower prepared for a friendship tour of the Soviet Union.

All that collapsed in May 1960. The Soviets shot down an American U-2 spy plane gathering intelligence on nuclear facilities. Secret American surveillance and probes of Soviet air defenses had been going on for years—justified in American officials' eyes by Moscow's refusal to allow international inspections as part of any disarmament agreement. A deeply embarrassed Eisenhower at first denied the existence of U-2 flights, but then the Soviets produced the American pilot, who readily confessed. The summit collapsed when Eisenhower refused Khrushchev's demands for an apology and an end to spy flights. The U-2 incident demonstrated the limits of personal diplomacy in resolving the deep structural rivalry between the superpowers.

Eisenhower often provided a moderating voice on issues of defense spending and missile development. The Soviet Union's dramatic launch of *Sputnik*, the first Earth-orbiting satellite, in October 1957 upset Americans' precarious sense of security. Critics attacked the Eisenhower administration for failure to keep up with the enemy. In addition to huge increases in defense spending, some panic-stricken pundits urged a massive program to build fallout shelters for the entire population in case of nuclear attack.

Eisenhower rejected these radical responses. He knew from U-2 evidence that the Soviet Union in fact trailed far behind the United States in ICBM development, but he kept this knowledge secret so as not to reveal to the Soviets the sources of American intelligence. Instead of panicking before *Sputnik*, he held to a doctrine of "sufficiency": maintaining enough military strength to survive any attack and enough nuclear capability to deliver a massive counterattack.

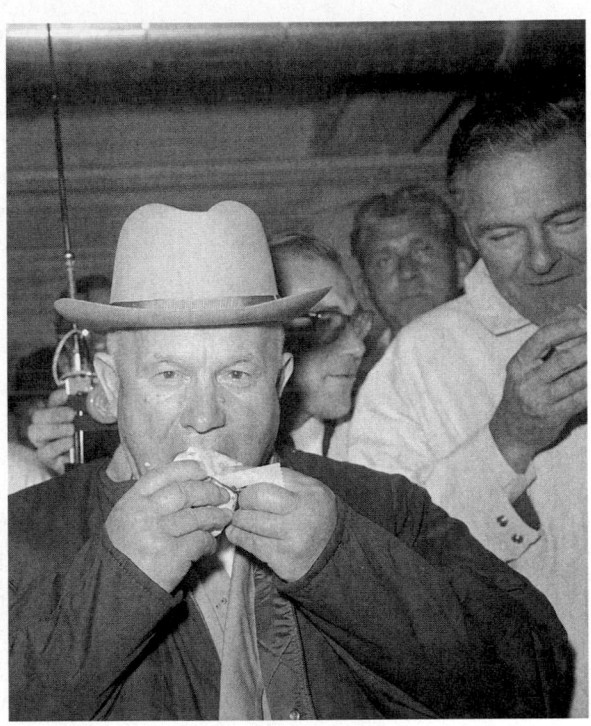

**Soviet Premier Nikita** Khrushchev enjoys a bite to eat during his tour of an Iowa farm in 1959. A colorful, earthy, and erratic man, Khrushchev loomed as the most visible human symbol of the Soviet Union for Americans. On this trip he called for Soviet–American friendship, yet he also boasted "We will bury you.".

## COVERT ACTION

A heavy reliance on covert CIA operations was the other side of Eisenhower's "New Look" defense policy of threatening massive retaliation on America's foreign enemies. He had been an enthusiastic supporter of covert operations during World War II, and during his presidency secret CIA-sponsored paramilitary operations became a key element of American foreign policy. With the American public wary of direct U.S. military interventions, the CIA promised a cheap, quick, and quiet way to depose hostile or unstable regimes, or to prop up conservative governments under siege by indigenous radicals, reformers, or revolutionaries.

Eisenhower's new CIA chief was Allen Dulles, John Foster's brother and an important figure in the OSS, the CIA's World War II precursor. Under Dulles's command, the CIA far exceeded its mandate to collect and analyze information. All over the world, thousands of covert agents carried out operations that included making large, secret payments to friendly political parties (such as conservative Christian Democrats in Italy and Latin America) or to foreign trade unions that opposed the Communist Party.

Independence movements by now were shaking the European colonial empires throughout Asia and Africa, just as in Latin America dislike of U.S. hegemony was surging. To the Eisenhower administration's alarm, the Soviet Union began winning influence in the "Third World," appealing to allegedly common anti-imperialist solidarity and by offering modest foreign aid. Communists played only small roles in most Third World independence movements. But widespread anti-Western feelings in these lands were fanned by publicity about America's racial problems and by resentment against foreign investors' control of natural resources, including oil and mineral wealth. But if emerging nations questioned U.S. regional security arrangements by opting for neutrality—or, worse, expropriated American property—the Eisenhower administration was apt to try covert countermeasures and military intervention.

## GLOBAL INTERVENTIONS

In Iran in 1953 the CIA produced a swift, major victory. The popular Iranian prime minister, Mohammed Mossadegh, had nationalized Britain's Anglo-Iranian Oil Company, and the State Department worried that this might set a precedent throughout the oil-rich Middle East. Kermit Roosevelt, the CIA chief in Iran, organized and financed opposition to Mossadegh within the Iranian army and on the streets of Teheran. This CIA-sponsored movement drove Mossadegh from office and put in power an autocratic monarch (shah), Riza Pahlavi. The shah proved his loyalty to his American sponsors by renegotiating oil contracts, assuring American companies 40 percent of Iran's oil concessions. But U.S. identification with the shah's repressive regime in the long run created a groundswell of anti-Americanism among Iranians.

U.S. policy throughout the Middle East was complicated by the conflict between Israel and its Arab neighbors. Immediately after the United States and the Soviet Union recognized the newborn Jewish state in 1948, the Arab countries launched an all-out attack. Israel repulsed the attack, drove thousands of Palestinians from their homes, and seized territory considerably beyond the lines of the projected UN partition of Palestine into a Jewish and an Arab state. While the Arab world boycotted Israel economically and refused to recognize its right to exist, hundreds of thousands of Palestinians languished in squalid refugee camps.

Guatemala saw the most publicized CIA intervention of the Eisenhower years (see Map 27.1). In that impoverished Central American country—where the American-based United Fruit Company owned vast banana plantations—a fragile democ-

# MAP EXPLORATION

To explore an interactive version of this map, go to **http://www.prenhall.com/faraghertlc/map27.1**

| | |
|---|---|
| | Countries influenced by U.S.- Latin American activities |
| ■ | U.S. military bases |
| ✹ | Overt military actions |
| | Dates indicate year of independence |

Cape Canaveral

**UNITED STATES**

*Gulf of Mexico*

Key West

*Bahama Islands* **(Br.)**

*ATLANTIC OCEAN*

*1962 U.S. naval blockade, missile crisis*

**CUBA**

*1964 Revolution*

1961 CIA–sponsored Bay of Pigs invasion

Guantanamo Bay

Virgin Islands (U.S.)  Virgin Islands (Br.)

**DOMINICAN REPUBLIC**  Ramey AFB

**HAITI**

1959 Fidel Castro assumes power

**MEXICO**

Roosevelt Roads NS

*Puerto Rico* **(U.S.)**

Barbuda **(Br.)**

Antigua **(Br.)**

*Leeward Islands*

Guadeloupe **(Fr.)**

**BELIZE**

**JAMAICA (1962)**

1965 U.S. Marine landing

Dominica **(Br.)**

Martinique **(Fr.)**

*Caribbean Sea*

St. Lucia **(Br.)**

**GUATEMALA**  **HONDURAS**

*Windward Islands*

**BARBADOS (1966)**

St. Vincent **(Br.)**

Curaçao **(Neth.)**

**EL SALVADOR**

Aruba **(Neth.)**

Bonaire **(Neth.)**

Grenada **(Br.)**

**NICARAGUA**

1954 CIA–directed overthrow of Arbenz government

**TRINIDAD AND TOBAGO (1962)**

Canal Zone riots, 1964

**COSTA RICA**

**V E N E Z U E L A**

*PACIFIC OCEAN*

Rodman NS Albrook AFB

**GUYANA (1966)**

**PANAMA**  **COLOMBIA**

**MAP 27.1**
**The United States in the Caribbean, 1948–66**   U.S. military intervention and economic presence grew steadily in the Caribbean following World War II. After 1960, opposition to the Cuban Revolution dominated U.S. Caribbean policies.

WHAT ARE the similarities and differences between American intervention in the Caribbean from 1948–1966 and intervention in this region earlier in the twentieth century?

racy took root in 1944. President Jácobo Arbenz Guzmán, elected in 1950, aggressively pursued land reform, encouraged the formation of trade unions, and tried to buy (at assessed value) enormous acreage that United Fruit owned but did not cultivate. The company demanded far more compensation for this land than Guatemala offered and, having powerful friends in the administration (CIA director Dulles had sat on United Fruit's board of directors), it began lobbying intensively for U.S. intervention, linking land-reform programs to international communism. The CIA spent $7 million training Guatemalan dissidents in neighboring Honduras.

U.S. intervention began when the Navy stopped Guatemala-bound ships and seized their cargoes, and on June 14, 1954, the U.S.-trained antigovernment force invaded from Honduras. Guatemala appealed in vain to the United Nations for help, while Eisenhower publicly denied any knowledge of CIA involvement. A newly appointed Guatemalan leader, Carlos Castillo Armas, flew to the Guatemalan capital in a U.S. embassy plane. In the widespread terror that followed, unions were outlawed and thousands were arrested. In 1957 Castillo Armas was assassinated, initiating a decades-long civil war between military factions and peasant guerrillas.

The global anticommunist strategy that the Truman and Eisenhower administrations embraced led to American backing of France's desperate attempt to maintain its colonial empire in Indochina (see Chapter 26). From 1950 to 1954, the United States poured $2.6 billion in military aid (about three-quarters of the total French costs) and CIA assistance into the fight against the nationalist Vietminh movement, led by Communist Ho Chi Minh. When in March 1954 Vietminh forces surrounded 25,000 French troops at Dien Bien Phu, France pleaded for direct American intervention. Secretary of State Dulles and Vice President Nixon, among others, called for using tactical nuclear weapons and U.S. ground troops to rescue the French. But Eisenhower, remembering Korea, refused. "I can conceive of no greater tragedy," he said, "than for the United States to become engaged in all-out war in Indochina."

Still, Eisenhower feared that the loss of one country to communism would inevitably lead to the loss of others. In his view, the "loss" of Vietnam would threaten other Southeast Asian nations (Laos, Thailand, and the Philippines) and perhaps even India and Australia. After the French surrender at Dien Bien Phu, an international conference in Geneva established a cease-fire and a "temporary" division into a communist northern state and a noncommunist southern state. National elections and reunification were promised in 1956. But the United States refused to sign the accord.

Ngo Dinh Diem, who quickly emerged as South Vietnam's president, was a former Japanese collaborator and a Catholic in a 90 percent Buddhist country. Supported by Eisenhower, Diem refused to permit the promised 1956 elections, knowing that the popular hero Ho Chi Minh would easily win. American economic and military aid, along with covert CIA activity, kept the increasingly isolated Diem in power. His corrupt and repressive policies alienated many peasants. By 1959, his Saigon regime faced a civil war against the thousands of peasants who were joining guerrilla bands to drive him out. Eisenhower's commitment of military advisers and economic aid to South Vietnam, based on Cold War assumptions, had laid the foundation for the Vietnam war of the 1960s.

**28–1**
Dwight D. Eisenhower, *Decision Not to Intervene at Dien Bien Phu* (1954)

**WHAT IDEALS** did America's suburban life evoke, and how did those ideals correspond to suburban realities?

Review Summary

## QUICK REVIEW

### U.S. Intervention Abroad

- U.S. policy shaped by Secretary of State John Foster Dulles.
- Eisenhower used the CIA to subvert democratically elected governments in Iran and Guatemala.
- The United States replaced France as the supporter of pro–Western Vietnamese in the south.

# THE AFFLUENT SOCIETY

With the title of his influential book *The Affluent Society* (1958), economist John Kenneth Galbraith labeled postwar America. Americans, he argued, needed to spend less on personal consumption and devote more public funds to schools, medical care, culture, and social services. For most Americans, however, strong economic growth was the defining fact of the postwar period, and a fierce desire for consumer goods and the "good life" permeated American culture. The deeply held popular belief in the right to a continuously expanding economy and a steadily rising standard of living shaped American social and political life.

## SUBSIDIZING PROSPERITY

During the Eisenhower years the federal government played a crucial role in subsidizing programs that helped millions of Americans achieve middle-class status. Federal aid helped people to buy homes, attend colleges and technical schools, and live in new suburbs. Much of this assistance expanded on programs begun during the New Deal and World War II. The Federal Housing Administration (FHA), established in 1934, extended the government's role in subsidizing the housing industry by insuring long-term mortgage loans to private lenders for home building. In addition, homeowners benefited from the provision in the Internal Revenue Code (dating back to 1913) that allowed the deduction of all forms of interest payments from taxes. The mortgage interest deduction was the most important middle-class tax benefit for millions of postwar home buyers.

Yet FHA policies had long-range drawbacks. FHA insurance went overwhelmingly to new residential developments. FHA policy favored the construction of single-family projects while discouraging multiunit housing, refused loans to repair older structures and rental units, and required for any loan guarantee an "unbiased professional estimate" rating of the property, the prospective borrower, and the neighborhood. In practice, these estimates resulted in blatant discrimination against racially mixed communities.

Most suburbs were built as planned communities. One of the first, Levittown, opened in 1947 in Hempstead, Long Island, on 1,500 acres of former potato fields. Developer William Levitt, who described his firm as "the General Motors of the housing industry," was the first entrepreneur to bring mass-production techniques to home building. Eventually, Levittown encompassed more than 17,000 houses and 82,000 people. Yet in 1960 not one of Levittown's residents was African American, and owners who rented out their homes were told to specify that their houses would not be "used or occupied by any person other than members of the Caucasian race."

The impact on American life of the 1944 Servicemen's Readjustment Act—the G.I. Bill of Rights—reached far beyond higher education (see Chapter 26). In addition to educational grants, the act gave returning veterans low-interest mortgages and business loans, thus subsidizing suburban growth as much as the postwar expansion of higher education. Through 1956, nearly 10 million veterans received G.I. Bill tuition and training benefits. Veterans Administration–insured loans totaled more than $50 billion and assisted millions of former G.I.s in starting businesses.

Another key boost to postwar growth, especially in suburbs, came from the National Interstate and Defense Highways Act of 1956. Significantly, the program was sold to the country partly as a civil defense measure (supposedly to facilitate evacuating American cities in case of nuclear attack). Federal subsidies for interstate highway construction stimulated both the automobile industry and suburb building, while helping transform the American landscape with motels, fast-food outlets, and other businesses servicing road-tripping Americans. It also accelerated the decline of American mass transit and of older cities. By 1970, the nation possessed the world's best roads—and one of the world's worst public transportation systems.

Cold War jitters also prompted the federal government to launch new initiatives to aid education. The Soviet launch of the *Sputnik* satellite in the fall of 1957 dealt a body-blow to Americans' confidence in the superiority of their technology and education; officials, pundits, and educators alike worried that the country might be lagging behind the Soviets in training scientists and engineers. With bipartisan congressional support, the administration pledged to strengthen support for educating American students in mathematics, science, and technology.

**A family poses** before their Cape Cod style home in Levittown, New York, 1950. The photo, taken by *Life Magazine* photographer Bernard Hoffman, embodies the postwar domestic ideal of the white suburban family.

**27–8**
John K. Galbraith, *The Affluent Society* (1958)

In a broader sense, the postwar economy floated on a sea of Cold War–justified military spending. At the height of the Korean war, defense expenditures swallowed up about half the federal budget, or 14 percent of GNP; after Korea, though military spending declined, by 1960 defense contracts still constituted about 10 percent of GNP. That spending provided an enormous boost to defense-industry employers like Boeing and Douglas Aircraft and created hundreds of thousands of new jobs. New military bases, along with the growing aviation industry, spurred enormous economic and population growth across communities in southern California, around Seattle and Charleston, and on New York's Long Island. Military spending, which many associated with high-paying jobs and prosperous communities, thus acquired enormous local political support and powerful patrons in Congress, all devoted to keeping federal contracts flowing into their districts.

## SUBURBAN LIFE

29–2
Betty Friedan, *The Feminist Mystique* (1963)

For millions of Americans, the Great Depression and World War II had meant squeezing into cramped apartments or rundown houses, often sharing space with relatives and boarders. Unquestionably, suburban living meant a huge improvement in material conditions for many postwar American families, and the suburban boom strengthened the domestic ideal of the nuclear family as the model for American life. The image of the perfect suburban wife—efficient, patient, always charming—permeated television, movies, and magazines.

That glowing image often masked a stifling existence defined by housework, child care, and boredom. In the late 1950s, Betty Friedan, a wife, mother, and journalist, began a systematic survey of her Smith College classmates. Extending her research, in 1963 Friedan published her landmark book *The Feminine Mystique,* which gave voice to the silent frustrations of suburban women and helped to launch a new feminist movement.

For millions of suburban families, only two incomes could yield the middle-class life. The expansion of the female labor force—from 17 million in 1946 to 22 million in 1958—was a central economic fact of the post–World War II years. By 1960, 40 percent of women were employed full-time or part-time, and 30 percent of married women looked to supplement the family income and ensure a solidly middle-class standard of living (see Figure 27.1).

The powerful postwar rebirth of American religion was strongly associated with suburban living. In 1940, less than half the American population belonged to institutional churches; by the mid-1950s nearly three-quarters called themselves church members. Most popular religious writers emphasized the importance of belonging, of fitting in—an appeal that meshed perfectly with the conventional aspirations of suburban social life and with the ideal of family-centered domesticity.

Contemporary journalists, novelists, and social scientists fed the popular image of suburban life as essentially dull, conformist, and peopled exclusively by the educated middle class. Yet these writers (who were largely urban by birth and residence) tended to obscure the real class and ethnic differences among and between different suburban communities. Many new suburbs had a distinctively blue-collar cast. Milpitas, California, for example, grew up around a Ford auto plant about fifty miles outside San Jose. Its residents were blue-collar assembly-line workers and their families, not the stereotypical salaried, college-educated,

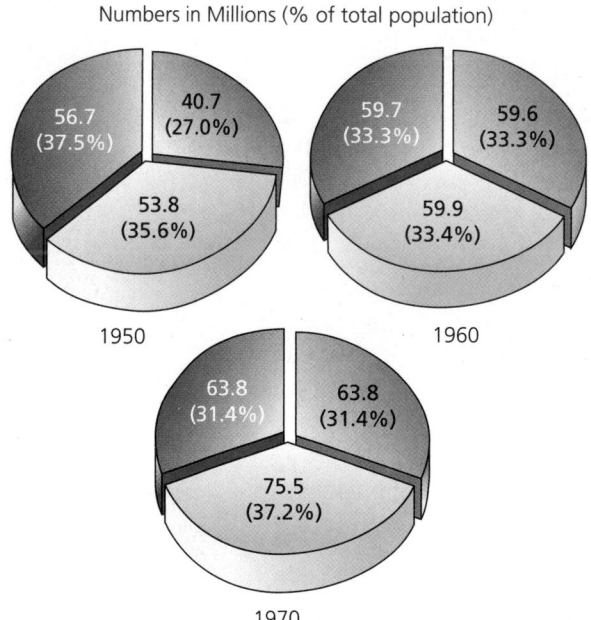

Numbers in Millions (% of total population)

1950

1960

1970

■ Rural and Small Towns
□ Suburbs
■ Central Cities

**Figure 27.1 The Growth of the Suburbs, 1950–70**
Suburban growth, at the expense of older inner cities, was one of the key social trends in the twenty-five years following World War II. By 1970, more Americans lived in suburbs than in either inner cities or rural areas.

Adapted from U.S. Bureau of the Census, *Current Censuses, 1930–1970* (Washington, DC: U.S. Government Printing Office, 1975).

white-collar employees. Self-segregation and zoning ordinances gave some new suburbs distinctively Italian, Jewish, or Irish ethnic identities, similar to older urban neighborhoods. For millions of new suburbanites, architectural and psychological conformity was an acceptable price to pay for the comforts of home ownership, a small plot of land, and a sense of security and status.

## ORGANIZED LABOR AND THE AFL-CIO

By the mid-1950s American trade unions reached an historic high point in their penetration of the labor market, reflecting enormous gains made during the organizing drives in core mass-production industries during the New Deal era and World War II. Whereas only one in eight nonagricultural workers were union members on the eve of the Great Depression, twenty-five years later the figure stood at one in three. Union influence in political life, especially within the Democratic Party, had also increased. Yet the Republican sweep to power in 1952 meant that for the first time in a generation organized labor was without an ally in the White House. New leaders in the nation's two major labor organizations, the American Federation of Labor (dominated by old-line construction and craft unions) and the Congress of Industrial Organizations (new unions in mass-production industry), now pushed for a merger of the two rival groups as the way to protect and build on the movement's recent gains. In 1955 the newly combined AFL-CIO brought some 12.5 million union members under one banner.

The merger marked the apex of trade union membership, and after 1955 its share of the labor market began a slow but steady decline. For millions of workers and their families in well-paying manufacturing jobs, union membership helped bring the trappings of middle-class prosperity: home ownership, higher education for children, travel, and a comfortable retirement. But the AFL-CIO showed little commitment to bringing unorganized workers into the fold. Scandals involving union corruption and racketeering hurt the labor movement's public image. In 1959, after highly publicized hearings into union corruption, Congress passed the **Landrum-Griffin Act**, which widened government control over union affairs and further restricted union use of picketing and secondary boycotts during strikes.

While union membership as a percentage of the total workforce declined, important growth did take place in new areas, reflecting a broader shift in the American workplace from manufacturing to service jobs. During the 1950s and 1960s, union membership among public sector employees, especially at the state and local levels, increased dramatically.

## LONELY CROWDS AND ORGANIZATION MEN

Perhaps the most ambitious and controversial critique of postwar suburban America was sociologist David Riesman's *The Lonely Crowd* (1950). Riesman argued that modern America had given birth to a new kind of character type, the "other-directed" man. For the "other-directed" person morality and ideals came from the overarching desire to conform. Americans, Riesman thought, were now less likely to take risks or act independently. Their thinking and habits had come to be determined by cues they received from the mass media.

Similarly, William H. Whyte's *Organization Man* (1956), a study of the Chicago suburb of Park Forest, offered a picture of people obsessed with fitting into their communities and jobs. In place of the old Protestant ethic of hard work, thrift, and competitive struggle, Whyte believed, middle-class suburbanites now strove mainly for a comfortable, secure niche in the system.

**Landrum-Griffin Act**   1959 Act that widened government control over union affairs and further restricted union use of picketing and secondary boycotts during strikes.

The most radical critic of postwar society, and the one with the most enduring influence, was Texas-reared sociologist C. Wright Mills. In *White Collar* (1951), Mills analyzed the job culture that typified life for middle-class salaried employees, office workers, and bureaucrats. "When white collar people get jobs," he wrote, "they sell not only their time and energy, but their personalities as well. They sell by the week or month their smiles and their kindly gestures, and they must practice the prompt repression of resentment and aggression." In *The Power Elite* (1956), Mills argued that a small, interconnected group of corporate executives, military men, and political leaders had come to dominate American society. The arms race in particular, pursued in the name of Cold War policies, had given an unprecedented degree of power to what President Eisenhower later termed the military-industrial complex.

## THE EXPANSION OF HIGHER EDUCATION

American higher education grew explosively after the war, creating the system of postsecondary training that still exists. This expansion both reflected and reinforced other postwar social trends. The number of students enrolled in colleges and universities climbed from 2.6 million in 1950 to 3.2 million in 1960, and then more than doubled—to 7.5 million—by 1970, as the baby boomers reached college age. Most of these new students attended greatly enlarged state university systems.

College students enjoyed a deferment from the draft, which normally faced young men soon after they finished high school. (If college graduates married and became fathers, or entered graduate or professional school, they could usually count on being deferred until they were past draft age, at twenty-six.) In this sense college marked an important class line in postwar America. Colleges and universities by and large accepted the values of postwar corporate culture. By the mid-1950s, 20 percent of all college graduates majored in business or similar fields.

A college degree was a gateway to the middle class. It became a requirement for a whole range of expanding white-collar occupations in banking, insurance, real estate, advertising and marketing, and corporate management in general. Most administrators accommodated large business interests, which were well represented on university boards of trustees. Universities themselves were increasingly run like businesses, with administrators adopting the language of input-output, cost effectiveness, and quality control.

## HEALTH AND MEDICINE

Dramatic improvements in medical care allowed many Americans to enjoy longer and healthier lives. New antibiotics such as penicillin, the "wonder drug" of World War II, became widely available to the general population. Federal support for research continued after the war with the reorganization of the National Institutes of Health in 1948.

Perhaps the most celebrated achievement of postwar medicine was the victory over poliomyelitis. In 1955 Jonas Salk pioneered the first effective vaccine against the disease, using a preparation of killed virus. A nationwide program of polio vaccination, later supplemented by the oral Sabin vaccine, virtually eliminated polio by the 1960s.

Yet access to "wonder drugs" and advanced medical techniques was not shared equally. More sophisticated treatments and expensive new hospital facilities sharply increased the costs of health care. Poor and many elderly Americans found themselves unable to afford modern medicine. Thousands of communities, especially in rural areas and small towns, lacked doctors or decent hospital facilities.

The American Medical Association (AMA), which certified medical schools, did nothing to increase the flow of new doctors. The number of physicians per

**QUICK REVIEW**

**Growth of Higher Education**

♦ 1950: 2.6 million students enrolled in college.

♦ 1960: 3.2 million students enrolled in college.

♦ 1970: 7.5 million students enrolled in college.

100,000 people actually declined between 1950 and 1960; doctors trained in other countries made up the shortfall. The AMA also lobbied hard against efforts to expand government responsibility for the public's health. Truman proposed national health insurance, to be run along the lines of Social Security, and Eisenhower had proposed a program that would offer government assistance to private health insurance companies. Both proposals were denounced as "socialized medicine" by the AMA. Until 1965, with the advent of Medicare (for the elderly) and Medicaid (for the poor)—both of which it also opposed—the AMA successfully fought any form of direct federal involvement in health care.

# YOUTH CULTURE

During the fifteen years after World War II, unprecedented attention was paid to America's adolescents. Adults expressed deep fears about everything from teenage sexuality and juvenile delinquency to young people's driving habits, hairstyles, and choice of clothing. At the same time, advertisers and businesses pursued the disposable income of America's affluent youth with a vengeance.

## THE YOUTH MARKET

Birthrates had accelerated gradually during the late 1930s and more rapidly during the war years. The children born in those years had by the late 1950s grown into the original teenagers, the older siblings of the celebrated baby boomers of 1946–64. They came of age in a society that, compared with that of their parents and the rest of the world, was uniquely affluent. Converging, the demographic growth of teens and the postwar economic expansion created an explosive and profitable youth market. Manufacturers and advertisers rushed to cash in on the special needs and desires of young consumers: cosmetics, clothing, radios and phonographs, and cars.

In addition, advertisers and market researchers found that teenagers often played a critical, if hard to measure, role as "secret persuaders" in a family's large purchase decisions. Throughout the 1950s and into the 1960s, teenagers had a major, sometimes dominant, voice in determining America's cultural fads.

The special status of teenagers was also made apparent to the public by the increasing uniformity of public school education. Traditional sources of adult authority and socialization—the marketplace, schools, child-rearing manuals, the mass media—all reinforced the notion of teenagers as a special community, united by age, rank, and status.

## "HAIL! HAIL! ROCK 'N' ROLL!"

The demands of the new teen market, combined with structural changes in the postwar American mass media, reshaped the nation's popular music. As television broadcasting rapidly replaced radio as the center of family entertainment, people began using radios in new ways. There was a rapid rise in the production of car radios and portable transistor radios as listeners increasingly tuned them in for diversion from or an accompaniment to other activities. By 1956, some 2,700 AM radio stations were on the air across the United States, with about 70 percent of their broadcast time devoted to record shows.

In the recording industry, change was in the air. Small independent record labels led the way in aggressively recording African American rhythm-and-blues artists. On radio, over jukeboxes, and in record stores, all these African American artists "crossed over," adding millions of white teenagers to their solid base of black fans. The older, more established record companies had largely ignored black

WHY DID the youth market expand so rapidly at midcentury?

Review Summary

27–5
*The Teenage Consumer* (1959)

## QUICK REVIEW

**Teenagers**

- Teenagers became consumers in the 1950s.
- Advertisers directed their message at the youth market.
- Teenagers developed a shared culture.

**As much as** anyone, Chuck Berry created music that defined what it meant to be young in postwar America.

**Elvis Presley performs** on an outdoor stage before a wildly enthusiastic audience during the Mississippi State Fair in the early 1950s.

music. They responded to the new trend with slick, toned-down "cover" versions of rhythm-and-blues originals by white pop singers. These were invariably pallid, artistically inferior imitations.

But while African American artists began to enjoy newfound mass acceptance, there were limits to how closely white kids could identify with black performers. Racism, especially in so sexually charged an arena as musical performance, was a powerful force in American life. The major labels' superior promotional power, as well as institutional racism in the music business, ensured that white cover versions almost always outsold the black originals. But at live shows, white and black teenagers often listened and danced together to the music of African American performers.

The stage was thus set for the arrival of white rock 'n' roll artists who could exploit the new sounds and styles. As a rock 'n' roll performer and recording artist, Elvis Presley reinvented American popular music. His success challenged the old lines separating black music from white and pop from rhythm and blues or country. As a symbol of rebellious youth and as the embodiment of youthful sexuality, Elvis revitalized American popular culture. In his wake came a host of white rock 'n' rollers, many (like him) white Southerners: Jerry Lee Lewis, Buddy Holly, the Everly Brothers, Roy Orbison. But the greatest songwriter and most influential guitarist to emerge from this first "golden age of rock 'n' roll" was Chuck Berry, an African American from St. Louis who worked part-time as a beautician and house painter. With humor, irony, and passion, Berry proved especially adept at capturing the teen spirit.

## ALMOST GROWN

Teenage consumers remade into their own turf the landscape of popular music. The dollar value of annual record sales nearly tripled between 1954 and 1959, from $213 million to $603 million. New magazines aimed exclusively at teens flourished in the postwar years. Most teen magazines, like rock 'n' roll music, focused on the rituals, pleasures, and sorrows surrounding teenage courtship. Paradoxically, behavior patterns among white middle-class teenagers in the 1950s and early 1960s exhibited a new kind of youth orientation and at the same time a more pronounced identification with adults.

While parents were worrying about the separate world inhabited by their teenage children, many teens seemed determined to become adults as quickly as possible. Postwar affluence multiplied the number of two-car families, making it easier for sixteen-year-olds to win driving privileges formerly reserved for eighteen-year-olds. Girls began dating, wearing brassieres and nylon stockings, and using cosmetics at an earlier age than before—twelve or thirteen rather than fifteen or sixteen. Several factors contributed to this trend, including a continuing decline in the age of menarche (first menstruation), the sharp drop in the age of marriage after World War II, and the precocious social climate of junior high schools (institutions that became widespread only after 1945). "Going steady," derived from the college custom of fraternity and sorority pinning, became commonplace among high schoolers. By the late 1950s, eighteen had become the most common age at which American females married.

## DEVIANCE AND DELINQUENCY

Many adults blamed rock 'n' roll for the apparent decline of parental control over teens. Much of the opposition to rock 'n' roll, particularly in the South, played on long-standing racist fears of white females being attracted to black music and black performers. The undercurrent beneath all this opposition was a deep anxiety over the more open expression of sexual feelings by both performers and audiences.

Paralleling the rise of rock 'n' roll was a growing concern with an alleged increase in juvenile delinquency. An endless stream of magazine articles, books, and newspaper stories asserted that criminal behavior among the nation's young was chronic. Gang fights, drug and alcohol abuse, car theft, and sexual offenses drew the most attention. The U.S. Senate established a special subcommittee on juvenile delinquency. Highly publicized hearings in 1955 and 1956 convinced much of the public that youthful criminals were terrorizing the country. Although crime statistics do suggest an increase in juvenile crime during the 1950s, particularly in the suburbs, the public perception of the severity of the problem was surely exaggerated.

In retrospect, the juvenile delinquency controversy tells us more about anxieties over family life and the erosion of adult authority than about crime patterns. Teenagers seemed more defined by and loyal to their peer culture than to their parents. A great deal of their music, speech, dress, and style seemed alien and threatening. The growing importance of the mass media in defining youth culture brought efforts to regulate or censor media forms believed to cause juvenile delinquency.

As reactions to two of the most influential "problem youth" movies of the postwar era indicate, teens and their parents frequently interpreted depictions of youthful deviance in the mass media in very different ways. In *The Wild One* (1954), Marlon Brando played the crude, moody leader of a vicious motorcycle gang. Most adults thought of the film as a critique of mindless gang violence, but many teenagers identified with the Brando character, who, when asked, "What are you rebelling against?" coolly replied, "Whattaya got?" In *Rebel Without a Cause* (1955), James Dean, Natalie Wood, and Sal Mineo played emotionally troubled youths in an affluent California suburb. The movie suggests that parents can cause delinquency when they fail to conform to conventional roles—Dean's father does housework wearing an apron, and his mother is domineering.

Elvis, Brando, and Dean (who died in a car crash at the height of his popularity) were probably the most popular and widely imitated teen idols of the era. For most parents, they were vaguely threatening figures whose sexual energy and lack of discipline placed them outside the bounds of middle-class respectability. For teens, however, they offered an irresistible combination of rough exterior and sensitive core. They embodied, as well, the contradiction of individual rebellion versus the attractions of a community defined by youth.

# MASS CULTURE AND ITS DISCONTENTS

**WHAT EXPLAINS** the emergence of a distinct youth culture in 1950s' America?

myhistorylab

**Review Summary**

No mass medium ever achieved such power and popularity as rapidly as television. By 1960, nearly nine in ten American families owned at least one set, which was turned on an average of more than five hours a day. Television reshaped leisure time and political life. It also helped create a new kind of national community defined by the buying and selling of consumer goods.

Dissident voices challenged the economic trends and cultural conformity of the postwar years. Academics, journalists, novelists, and poets offered a variety of works criticizing the overall direction of American life. These critics of what was dubbed "mass society" were troubled by the premium American culture put on conformity, status, and material consumption.

## TELEVISION: TUBE OF PLENTY

Television was a radical change from radio, and its development as a mass medium was quicker and less chaotic. The three main television networks—NBC, CBS, and ABC—grew directly from radio corporations. The networks led the industry from the start, rather than following individual stations, as radio had done.

Television not only depended on advertising, but it also transformed the advertising industry. The television business, like radio, was based on the selling of time to advertisers who wanted to reach the mass audiences tuning into specific shows. Radio had offered entire shows produced by and for single sponsors, usually advertisers who wanted a close identification between their product and a star. But the higher costs of television production forced key changes. Sponsors left the production of programs to the networks, independent producers, and Hollywood studios.

Sponsors now bought scattered time slots for spot advertisements instead of bankrolling an entire show. Ad agencies switched their creative energy to producing slick thirty-second commercials rather than entertainment programs. A shift from broadcasting live shows to filming them opened up lucrative opportunities for reruns and exports.

**A 1950s' family** watching *I Love Lucy*, one of the most popular situation comedies in the early days of television. Manufacturers designed and marketed TV sets as living room furniture and emphasized their role in fostering family togetherness.

Set largely among urban ethnic families, early shows like *I Remember Mama, The Goldbergs, The Life of Riley, Life with Luigi,* and *The Honeymooners* often featured working-class families struggling with the dilemmas posed by a consumer society. Most plots turned around comic tensions created and resolved by consumption: contemplating home ownership, going out on the town, moving to the suburbs, buying on credit, purchasing a new car. Generational discord and the loss of ethnic identity were also common themes. To some degree, these early shows mirrored and spoke to the real dilemmas facing families that had survived the Great Depression and World War II and were now finding their place in a prosperous consumer culture.

By the late 1950s, all the urban ethnic comedy shows were off the air. A new breed of situation comedies presented nonethnic white, affluent, and insular suburban middle-class families. Shows like *Father Knows Best, Leave It to Beaver, The Adventures of Ozzie and Harriet,* and *The Donna Reed Show* epitomized the ideal suburban American family of the day. Their plots focused on genial crises, usually brought on by children's mischief or wives' inability to cope with money matters, but patiently resolved by kindly fathers. In retrospect, what is most striking about these shows is what is absent: virtually unrepresented were politics, social issues, cities, white ethnic groups, African Americans, and Latinos.

## TELEVISION AND POLITICS

Prime-time entertainment shows carefully avoided any references to the political issues of the day. Network executives bowed to the conformist climate created by the Cold War. Any hint of political controversy could scare off sponsors, ever wary of public protest. Anti-Communist crusaders set themselves up as private watchdogs, warning of alleged subversive influence in the broadcasting industry. Television and advertising executives responded by effectively blacklisting many talented individuals.

As in Hollywood, the Cold War chill severely restricted the range of political discussion on television. Any honest treatment of the conflicts in American society threatened the consensus mentality at the heart of the television business. Even public affairs and documentary programs were largely devoid of substantial political debate. But some of the ways that TV would alter the nation's political life were already emerging in the 1950s. Television made Democratic senator Estes Kefauver of Tennessee a national political figure through live coverage of his 1951 Senate investigation into organized crime. In 1952, Republican vice presidential candidate Nixon's rambling, emotionally manipulative television appeal to voters—the famous "Checkers" speech (see Chapter 26)—saved his career.

The 1952 election brought the first use of TV political advertising for presidential candidates. The Republican Party hired a high-powered ad agency, Batten, Barton, Durstine & Osborn (BBD&O), to create a series of short, sophisticated advertisements touting Ike. The BBD&O campaign saturated TV with twenty-second Eisenhower spots for two weeks before Election Day. Ever since, Television image-making has been the single most important element in American electoral politics.

## CULTURE CRITICS

Critics argued that the audiences for the mass media were atomized, anonymous, and detached. The media themselves had become omnipotent, capable of manipulating the attitudes and behavior of the isolated individuals in the mass. Many of these critics achieved great popularity themselves, suggesting that the public was deeply ambivalent about mass culture. These critics undoubtedly overestimated the media's power. They ignored the preponderance of research suggesting that most people watched and responded to mass media in family, peer group, and other social settings. The critics also missed the genuine vitality and creative brilliance to be found within mass culture: African American music; the films of Nicholas Ray, Elia Kazan, and Howard Hawks; the experimental television of Ernie Kovacs; even the madcap satire of teen-oriented *Mad* magazine.

Some of the sharpest dissents from the cultural conformity of the day came from a group of writers known collectively as the **Beats**. Led by the novelist Jack Kerouac and the poet Allen Ginsberg, the Beats shared a distrust of the American virtues of progress, power, and material gain. The Beats sensibility celebrated spontaneity, friendship, jazz, open sexuality, drug use, and the outcasts of American society.

**Fess Parker, the** actor who starred as Davy Crockett in Walt Disney's popular television series, greets young fans at New York's Idlewild Airport in 1955. The series generated enormous sales of coonskin caps and other Crockett-inspired merchandise, demonstrating the extraordinary selling power of the new medium of television.

 **27–10**
Jack Kerouac, *On the Road* (1957)

### QUICK REVIEW

**The Beats**

- Led by Jack Kerouac and Allen Ginsberg.
- Distrusted progress, power, and material gain.
- Found a receptive audience in American youth.

**Beats**   A group of writers from the 50s whose writings challenged American culture.

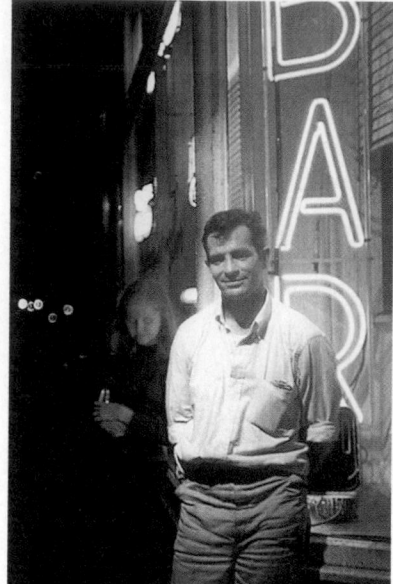

**Jack Kerouac, founding** voice of the Beat literary movement, in front of a neon-lit bar, ca. 1950. Kerouac's public readings, often to the accompaniment of live jazz music, created a performance atmosphere underlining the connections between his writing style and the rhythms and sensibility of contemporary jazz musicians.

**WHO WAS** John F. Kennedy, and why did his New Frontier seem so promising to many Americans?

**myhistorylab**
**Review Summary**

*Beatnik* Term used to designate members of the Beats.

Beat writers received a largely antagonistic, even virulent reception from the literary establishment, and the mass media soon trivialized them. A San Francisco journalist coined the word *beatnik*, which by the late 1950s had become popularly associated with scruffy, bearded men and promiscuous women, all dressed in black, sporting sunglasses and berets, and acting rebellious and alienated. But by challenging America's official culture, Beat writers foreshadowed the mass youth rebellion and counterculture of the 1960s.

# THE COMING OF THE NEW FRONTIER

In personality, temperament, and public image, no one could have less resembled Dwight Eisenhower—or, for that matter, the beatniks—than John Fitzgerald Kennedy. The handsome son of a prominent, wealthy Irish American diplomat, husband of a fashionable, trendsetting heiress, forty-two-year-old JFK embodied youth, excitement, and sophistication. As only the second Catholic candidate for president—the first was Al Smith in 1928—Kennedy ran under the banner of his self-proclaimed "New Frontier." His liberalism inspired idealism and hope in millions of young people at home and abroad, and his presidency seemed to embody the call for a new sense of national purpose beyond simply enjoying affluence.

## THE ELECTION OF 1960

John F. Kennedy's political career began in Massachusetts, which elected him to the House in 1946 and then the Senate in 1952. Kennedy won the Democratic nomination after a bruising series of primaries in which he defeated party stalwarts Hubert Humphrey of Minnesota and Lyndon B. Johnson of Texas. Vice President Richard M. Nixon, the Republican nominee, had faithfully served the Eisenhower administration for eight years and was far better known than his younger opponent. The Kennedy campaign stressed its candidate's youth and

**Presidential candidates John** F. Kennedy and Richard M. Nixon during the second of three televised debates held during the 1960 election campaign. Moderator Frank McGee sits at a desk upstage, facing a panel of newsmen. Eighty-five million viewers watched at least one of the first-ever televised debates, which both reflected and increased the power of television in the electoral process.

his war-hero image. During his World War II tour of duty in the Pacific, Kennedy had bravely rescued one of his crew after their PT boat had been sunk. Kennedy's supporters made much of his intellectual ability. JFK had won the Pulitzer Prize in 1957 for his book *Profiles in Courage,* which in fact had been written largely by his aides.

Kennedy squeaked to victory in the closest election since 1884 (see Map 27.2). He won by a little more than 100,000 votes out of nearly 69 million cast. By solemnly promising to keep church and state separate, he had countered residual anti-Catholic prejudice among conservative Protestants and suspicious liberals. Still, he ran poorly in the South, but by overwhelmingly winning the Catholic vote he carried most of the Northeast and Midwest. Tiny though his margin of victory might be, Kennedy was a glorious winner. Surrounding himself with prestigious Ivy League academics, Hollywood movie stars, and talented artists and writers, he imbued the presidency with an aura of celebrity. The new administration promised to be exciting and stylish, a modern-day Camelot peopled by heroic young men and beautiful women. The new president's ringing inaugural address ("Ask not what your country can do for you—ask what you can do for your country") resonated through a whole generation of young Americans.

## IKE'S WARNING: THE MILITARY-INDUSTRIAL COMPLEX

Just before Kennedy took office, President Eisenhower delivered a televised farewell address that included a stark and unexpected warning against what he called (coining a phrase) "the military-industrial complex." Throughout the 1950s, the small numbers of peace advocates in the United States had pointed to the ultimate illogic of Ike's "new look" in national-defense policy. Increasing reliance on nuclear weapons, they argued, did not strengthen national security—it threatened the entire planet with extinction.

Eisenhower came to share some of the protesters' anxiety and doubts about the arms race, for he had found it difficult to rein in the "New Look" system he helped create. Frustrated—and disturbed by the incoming Democrats' demands for increased military spending to close the "missile gap"—he used his farewell address to express alarm at the growing influence of a large military and defense-industry establishment. "We annually spend on military security more than the net income of all United States corporations," Eisenhower warned the country. "We recognize the imperative need for this development. Yet we must not fail to comprehend its grave implications. Our toil, resources and livelihood are all involved; so is the very structure of our society."

The old soldier understood better than most the dangers of raw military force, and in later years the sentiments behind this language would be adapted by critics of American foreign policy and budget priorities.

## MAP EXPLORATION

To explore an interactive version of this map, go to
**http://www.prenhall.com/faraghertlc/map27.2**

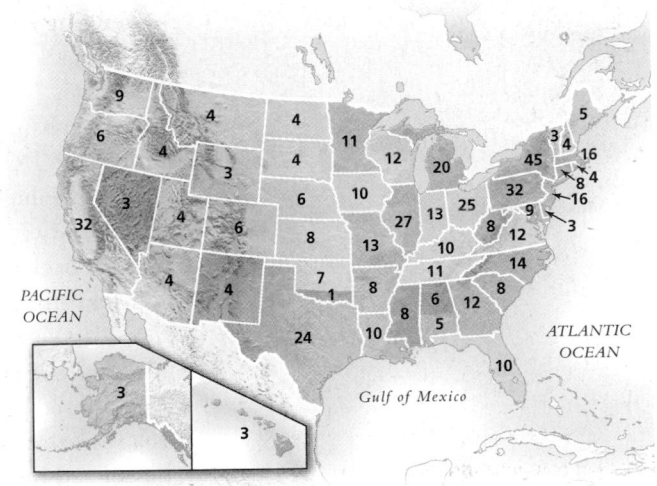

| | Electoral Vote (%) | Popular Vote (%) |
|---|---|---|
| **JOHN F. KENNEDY** (Democrat) | 303 (56) | 34,227,096 (49.7) |
| Richard M. Nixon (Republican) | 219 (41) | 34,108,546 (49.5) |
| Harry F. Byrd (Independent) | 15 (3) | 501,643 (0.7) |

**Map 27.2**

**The Election of 1960**   Kennedy's popular vote margin over Nixon was only a little over 100,000 votes, making this one of the closest elections in American history.

WHAT ROLE did religion play in 1960 election?

 **29–1**
John F. Kennedy, *Inaugural Address* (1961)

## NEW FRONTIER LIBERALISM

As president, John F. Kennedy promised to revive the liberal domestic agenda, stalled since Truman's presidency. His **New Frontier** advocated such liberal programs as medical care for the elderly, greater federal aid for education and public housing, raising Social Security benefits and the minimum wage, and various antipoverty measures. Yet the thin margin of his victory and stubborn opposition by conservative southern Democrats in Congress made it difficult to achieve these goals.

There were a few New Frontier achievements: modest increases in the minimum wage (to $1.25 per hour), Social Security benefits, and $5 billion appropriated for public housing. The Manpower Retraining Act provided $435 million to train the unemployed. The Area Redevelopment Act provided federal funds for rural, depressed Appalachia. The Higher Education Act of 1963 offered aid to colleges for constructing buildings and upgrading libraries.

The Peace Corps was the New Frontier's best-publicized initiative sending thousands of mostly young men and women overseas for two-year stints to provide technical and educational assistance to underdeveloped Third World countries. As a force for change, the Peace Corps produced modest results, but it epitomized Kennedy's promise to provide opportunities for service for a new generation of idealistic young people.

Kennedy's Presidential Commission on the Status of Women, led by Eleanor Roosevelt, helped revive attention to women's rights issues. The commission's 1963 report was the most comprehensive study of women's lives ever produced by the federal government. It documented the ongoing discrimination faced by American women in the workplace and in the legal system, as well as the inadequacy of social services such as day care. It called for federally supported day-care programs, continuing education programs for women, and an end to sex bias in Social Security and unemployment benefits. The commission also insisted that more women be appointed to policy-making positions in government. The **Equal Pay Act of 1963**, a direct result of the commission's work, mandated equal wages for men and women employed in industries engaged in interstate commerce. Kennedy also directed executive agencies to prohibit sex discrimination in hiring and promotion. The work of the commission contributed to a new generation of women's rights activism.

Kennedy took a more aggressive stance on stimulating economic growth and creating new jobs than had Eisenhower. The administration pushed lower business taxes through Congress, even at the cost of a higher federal deficit. The Revenue Act of 1962 encouraged new investment and plant renovation by easing tax depreciation schedules for business. Kennedy also gained approval for lower U.S. tariffs as a way to increase foreign trade. To help keep inflation down, he intervened in the steel industry in 1961 and 1962, pressuring labor to keep its wage demands low and management to curb price increases.

A wholly new realm of government spending also won Kennedy's enthusiastic backing: the space program. In panicky reaction to the Soviets' *Sputnik*, under Eisenhower the **National Aeronautics and Space Administration (NASA)** had been established. In 1961 Kennedy announced the goal of landing an American on the moon by the end of the decade. NASA eventually spent $33 billion before reaching this objective in 1969.

**New Frontier** John F. Kennedy's domestic and foreign policy initiatives, designed to reinvigorate sense of national purpose and energy.

**Equal Pay Act of 1963** Act that made it illegal for employers to pay men and women different wages for the same job.

**National Aeronautics and Space Administration (NASA)** Federal agency created in 1958 to manage American space flights and exploration.

Kennedy's longest-lasting achievement as president may have been his strengthening of the executive branch itself. He insisted on direct presidential control of details that Eisenhower had left to advisers and appointees. Moreover, under Kennedy the White House staff assumed many of the decision-making and advisory functions previously held by cabinet members. This arrangement increased Kennedy's authority, since these appointees, unlike cabinet secretaries, escaped congressional oversight and confirmation proceedings. White House aides lacked independent constituencies; their power derived solely from their ties to the president. Kennedy intensified a pattern whereby American presidents increasingly operated through small groups of fiercely loyal aides, often in secret.

## KENNEDY AND THE COLD WAR

During Kennedy's three years as president, his approach to foreign policy shifted from aggressive containment to efforts at easing U.S.–Soviet tensions. Certainly when he first entered office, Kennedy and his chief aides saw their main task as confronting the Communist threat. In his first State of the Union Address, Kennedy told Congress that America must seize the initiative in the Cold War. The nation must "move outside the home fortress, and . . . challenge the enemy in fields of our own choosing."

Between 1960 and 1962 defense appropriations increased by nearly a third, from $43 billion to $56 billion. JFK expanded Eisenhower's policy of covert operations, deploying the Army's elite Special Forces to supplement covert CIA operations against Third World guerrillas. These soldiers, fighting under the direct orders of the president, could provide "rapid response" to "brush-fire" conflicts

**President John F.** Kennedy, sitting before a television camera in the Oval Office, delivers an address to the nation during the Cuban missile crisis in October 1962. Kennedy's presidency coincided with the emergence of television as the nation's dominant mass medium.

where Soviet influence threatened American interests. The Special Forces, authorized by Kennedy to wear the green berets that gave them their unofficial name, reflected the president's desire to acquire greater flexibility, secrecy, and independence in the conduct of foreign policy.

But Southeast Asia showed the limits of advancing American interests with covert actions and Green Berets. In Laos, the United States had ignored the 1954 Geneva agreement and installed a friendly, CIA-backed military regime, but it could not defeat Soviet-supported Pathet Lao guerrillas. The president had to arrange with the Soviets to neutralize Laos. In neighboring South Vietnam, a more difficult situation developed when Communist Vietcong guerrillas launched an insurgency against the U.S.-supported Diem regime. Kennedy began sending hundreds of Green Berets and other military advisers to bolster Diem. In May 1961, in response to North Vietnamese aid to the Vietcong, Kennedy ordered a covert action against Ho Chi Minh's northern regime that included sabotage and intelligence gathering.

Kennedy's approach to Vietnam reflected an analysis of the situation in that country by two aides, General Maxwell Taylor and Walt Rostow, who saw things solely through Cold War spectacles. "The Communists are pursuing a clear and systematic strategy in Southeast Asia," Taylor and Rostow concluded, ignoring the inefficiency, corruption, and unpopularity of the Diem government. By 1963, with Diem's army unable to contain the Vietcong rebellion, Kennedy had sent nearly 16,000 support and combat troops to South Vietnam. By then, a wide spectrum of South Vietnamese society had joined the revolt against the hated Diem, including highly respected Buddhist monks and their students. Americans watched in horror as evening newscasts showed Buddhists burning themselves to death on the streets of Saigon—the ultimate protest against Diem's repressive rule. American press and television also reported the mounting casualty lists of U.S. forces in Vietnam. The South Vietnamese army, bloated by U.S. aid and weakened by corruption, continued to disintegrate. In the fall of 1963, American military officers and CIA operatives stood aside with approval as a group of Vietnamese generals toppled Diem, killing him and his top advisers. It was the first of many coups that racked the South Vietnamese government over the next few years.

In Latin America, where millions of impoverished peasants were forced to relocate to already overcrowded cities, various revolutionary movements were also gaining ground—and Kennedy looked for ways to forestall them. In 1961 he unveiled the **"Alliance for Progress,"** a ten-year, $100 billion plan to spur economic development in Latin America. The United States committed $20 billion to the project with the Latin nations responsible for the rest. The main goals included greater industrial growth and agricultural productivity, a more equitable distribution of income, and improved health and housing.

Kennedy saw the Alliance for Progress as a Marshall Plan that would benefit Latin America's poor and middle classes. It did help raise growth rates in Latin American economies. But the expansion in export crops and in consumption by the tiny upper class did little to aid the poor or encourage democracy. The United States hesitated to challenge the dictators and extreme conservatives who were its staunchly anti-Communist allies. Thus, the alliance soon degenerated into just another foreign-aid program, incapable of generating genuine social change.

**Alliance for Progress** Program of economic aid to Latin America during the Kennedy administration.

## THE CUBAN REVOLUTION AND THE BAY OF PIGS

The direct impetus for the Alliance for Progress was the 1959 Cuban Revolution, which loomed over Latin America—inspiring the left and alarming the right. The U.S. economic domination of Cuba, beginning with the Spanish-American War (see Chapter 20), had continued through the 1950s. American-owned businesses controlled all of Cuba's oil production, 90 percent of its mines, and roughly half of its railroads and sugar and cattle industries. Havana, the island's capital, was an attractive tourist center for Americans, but U.S. crime syndicates shared control—with dictator Fulgencio Batista—of the island's lucrative gambling, prostitution, and drug trade. As a response, in the early 1950s a peasant-based revolutionary movement, led by a middle-class student named Fidel Castro, began gaining strength in the rural districts and mountains outside Havana.

On New Year's Day 1959, after years of guerrilla war, the rebels entered Havana and amid great public rejoicing seized power. For a brief time, Castro seemed a hero in North America as well. *The New York Times* had conducted sympathetic interviews with Castro in 1958, while he was still fighting in Cuba's mountains. The CIA and President Eisenhower shared none of this exuberance. Castro's land-reform program, involving the seizure of acreage from the tiny minority that controlled much of the fertile land, threatened to set an example for other Latin American countries. Although Castro had not yet joined the Cuban Communist Party, he turned to the Soviet Union after the United States withdrew economic aid. He began to sell sugar to the Soviets and soon nationalized American-owned oil companies and other enterprises. Eisenhower established an economic boycott of Cuba in 1960 and then severed diplomatic relations.

Kennedy inherited from Eisenhower plans for a U.S. invasion of Cuba, including the secret arming and training of Cuban exiles. The CIA drafted the invasion plan, which was based on the assumption that a U.S.-led invasion would trigger a popular uprising and bring down Castro. Kennedy went along with the plan, but at the last moment decided not to supply Air Force cover for the invaders. On April 17, 1961, a ragtag army of 1,400 counterrevolutionaries led by CIA operatives landed at the **Bay of Pigs** on Cuba's southern coast. Castro's efficient and loyal army easily subdued them.

The debacle revealed that the CIA, blinded by Cold War assumptions, had failed to understand the Cuban Revolution. There was no popular uprising against Castro. An embarrassed Kennedy reluctantly took the blame for the disaster. Despite the failure, Kennedy remained committed to getting rid of Castro.

The botched invasion had strengthened "Fidel's" standing among the urban poor and peasants, already attracted by his programs of universal literacy and medical care. As Castro stifled internal opposition, many Cuban intellectuals and professionals fled to the United States. These middle-class émigrés would transform Miami from a retirement resort into a bustling entrepreneurial center, but the growing Cuban presence in electoral-vote-rich Florida also created a powerful lobby for rigid anti-Castro U.S. policies. Even before the end of Kennedy's administration, the CIA's support for anti-Castro operations included at least eight attempts to assassinate Fidel, and the U.S. economic embargo against Cuba continues to this day.

**Bay of Pigs** Site in Cuba of an unsuccessful landing by fourteen hundred anti-Castro Cuban refugees in April 1961.

**28–3**
John F. Kennedy, *Cuban Missile Address* (1962)

## THE 1962 MISSILE CRISIS

The aftermath of the Bay of Pigs led to the Cold War's most serious superpower confrontation: the **Cuban missile crisis** of October 1962. Frightened by U.S. belligerency, Castro asked Soviet Premier Khrushchev for military help. Khrushchev responded in the summer of 1962 by shipping to Cuba a large amount of sophisticated weaponry, including intermediate-range nuclear missiles capable of hitting Washington, the Northeast, and the Midwest. In early October, American U-2 reconnaissance planes found camouflaged missile silos dotting the island. Several Kennedy aides and the Joint Chiefs of Staff demanded an immediate bombing of these missile sites, arguing that the Soviet move had decisively eroded the United States' strategic global advantage. The president and his advisers pondered their options in a series of tense meetings. Kennedy's aggressive attempts to exploit Cuba in the 1960 election and the Bay of Pigs disaster came back to haunt him: He worried that critics would accuse him of weakness in failing to stand up to the Soviets. Even some prominent Democrats, including Senator J. William Fulbright, chairman of the Senate Foreign Relations Committee, called for invading Cuba. What no one in the United States knew was that Khrushchev had already sent tactical nuclear weapons to Cuba and authorized the Soviet commander on the island to use them to repel an American invasion; that was revealed only in the 1990s. Invasion would have meant nuclear war.

Kennedy went on national television on October 22 to announce discovery of the missile sites. He publicly demanded the removal of all missiles and proclaimed a naval "quarantine" of offensive military equipment shipped to Cuba. Requesting an emergency meeting of the UN Security Council, he promised that any missiles launched from Cuba would bring "a full retaliatory response upon the Soviet Union." For a grim week, Americans wondered whether the long-dreaded nuclear Armageddon was imminent. Eyeball to eyeball, each superpower waited for the other to blink. On October 26 and 27 Khrushchev blinked, ordering twenty-five Soviet ships off their course to Cuba, thus avoiding a challenge to the U.S. Navy.

Khrushchev offered to remove the missiles in return for a pledge from the United States not to invade Cuba and later added a demand for removal of American weapons from Turkey, as close to the Soviet Union as Cuba is to the United States. Secretly, Kennedy assured Khrushchev that the United States would dismantle its obsolete missiles in Turkey. On November 20, after weeks of delicate negotiations, Kennedy announced the withdrawal of Soviet missiles and bombers from Cuba. He also pledged to respect Cuban sovereignty and promised not to invade the island.

The crisis had passed. The Soviets, determined not to be intimidated again, began the largest weapons buildup in their history. For his part Kennedy, perhaps chastened by this brush with nuclear disaster, made important gestures toward peaceful coexistence with the Soviets. In a June 1963 address at American University, Kennedy called for a rethinking of Cold War diplomacy. Both sides, he said, had been "caught up in a vicious and dangerous cycle in which suspicion on one side breeds suspicion on the other, and new weapons beget counterweapons."

Shortly after, Washington and Moscow set up a "hot line"—a direct phone connection to permit instant communication during times of crisis. More substantial was the **Limited Nuclear Test-Ban Treaty**, signed in August 1963 by the United States, the Soviet Union, and Great Britain. The treaty prohibited above-ground, outer-space, and underwater nuclear weapons tests, easing global anxieties about

---

**QUICK REVIEW**

**The Cuban Missile Crisis**

- October 15, 1962: United States acquired evidence of construction of missile launching sites in Cuba.
- In response, Kennedy imposed a blockade.
- The Soviets removed the launchers in exchange for removal of U.S. missiles from Turkey and a U.S. promise not to invade Cuba.

**Cuban missile crisis** Crisis between the Soviet Union and the United States over the placement of Soviet nuclear missiles in Cuba.

**Limited Nuclear Test-Ban Treaty** Treaty, signed by the United States, Britain, and the Soviet Union, outlawing nuclear testing in the atmosphere, in outer space, and under water.

radioactive fallout. But underground testing continued to accelerate for years. The limited test ban was perhaps more symbolic than substantive, a psychological breakthrough in East–West relations after three particularly tense years.

By November 1963, the situation in South Vietnam was deteriorating; Diem's overthrow and murder in a U.S.-backed coup was symptomatic of U.S. failure to secure an anticommunist alternative to Ho Chi Minh's revolutionary movement. Kennedy understood this. There are some indications that he was thinking of cutting losses, perhaps after winning reelection in 1964; there are other signs that he was preparing to escalate the U.S. commitment. Most likely, he meant to keep all options open. But we will never know what he would have done about Vietnam.

## THE ASSASSINATION OF PRESIDENT KENNEDY

The assassination of John F. Kennedy in Dallas on November 22, 1963, sent the entire nation into shock and mourning. Just forty-six years old and president for only three years, Kennedy quickly ascended to martyrdom in the nation's consciousness. Millions had identified his strengths—intelligence, optimism, wit, charm, coolness under fire—as those of American society. In life, Kennedy had helped put television at the center of American politics. Now in the aftermath of his death, television riveted a badly shocked nation. One day after the assassination, the president's accused killer, an obscure misfit named Lee Harvey Oswald, was himself gunned down before television cameras covering his arraignment in Dallas. Two days later, tens of millions watched the televised spectacle of Kennedy's funeral, trying to make sense of the brutal murder (see Seeing History). Although a special commission headed by Chief Justice Earl Warren found the killing to be the work of Oswald acting alone, many Americans doubted this conclusion. Kennedy's death gave rise to a host of conspiracy theories, none of which seems provable.

We will never know, of course, what Kennedy might have achieved in a second term. But in his 1,000 days as president, he demonstrated a capacity to change and grow in office. Having gone to the brink during the missile crisis, he managed to launch new initiatives toward peaceful coexistence. At the time of his death, relations between the United States and the Soviet Union were more amicable than at any time since the end of World War II. Much of the domestic liberal agenda of the New Frontier would be finally implemented by Kennedy's successor, Lyndon B. Johnson, who dreamed of creating a **Great Society**.

## CONCLUSION

America in 1963 still enjoyed its postwar economic boom. To be sure, millions of Americans, particularly African Americans and Latinos, did not share in the good times. But millions had managed to reach the middle class since the early 1950s. An expanding economy, cheap energy, government subsidies, and dominance in the global marketplace had made the "the good life" available to more Americans than ever. The postwar "American dream" promised home ownership, college education, secure employment at decent wages, affordable appliances, and the ability to travel—for one's children if not for one's self. The nation's public culture—its schools, mass media, politics, advertising—presented a powerful consensus based on the idea that the American dream was available to all who would work for it.

**Great Society** Theme of Lyndon Johnson's administration, focusing on poverty, education, and civil rights.

# Televising a National Tragedy

The assassination of President John F. Kennedy on Friday, November 22, 1963, marked the emerging power of television as a medium capable of focusing the entire nation's attention on an extraordinary news event.

Kennedy had traveled to Texas on November 21 to shore up popularity in a state crucial to his reelection hopes for 1964. Only local stations covered the presidential arrival and motorcade. But once the president had been shot and declared dead, the networks cut into regular programming. The hasty inauguration of Vice President Lyndon B. Johnson aboard *Air Force One* was not televised, but widespread dissemination of still photos showed Americans the constitutional process of succession proceed side by side with and the personal grief of Jacqueline Kennedy.

On Sunday, November, 24, NBC offered live coverage of the accused assassin, Lee Harvey Oswald, being transferred from police custody to the county jail. Millions were stunned to suddenly see Jack Ruby, a shadowy Dallas underworld figure, emerge from the crowd and shoot Oswald to death—the first nationally televised murder.

On Monday, November 25, virtually the entire nation watched Kennedy's televised funeral. The images of the Kennedy family, especially five-year-old Caroline and three-year-old John Jr. saluting, lent a quiet dignity amid deep mourning. ∎

**WHAT STRIKES** you as most powerful about these images from more than four decades ago? What recent national events have brought the nation together via television coverage? How has that coverage changed—or remained similar—in terms of both techniques and subjects covered?

## CHRONOLOGY

| | | | |
|---|---|---|---|
| **1950** | David Riesman publishes *The Lonely Crowd* | **1958** | National Defense Education Act authorizes grants and loans to college students |
| **1952** | Dwight D. Eisenhower is elected president, defeating Adlai Stevenson | **1959** | Nikita Khrushchev visits the United States |
| **1953** | CIA installs Riza Shah Pahlavi as monarch of Iran | **1960** | Soviets shoot down U-2 spy plane and cancel planned summit meeting with Eisenhower |
| **1954** | Vietminh force French surrender at Dien Bien Phu | | John F. Kennedy is elected president, defeating Richard Nixon |
| | CIA overthrows government of Jácobo Arbenz Guzmán in Guatemala | | Almost 90 percent of American homes have television |
| | United States explodes first hydrogen bomb | **1961** | President Kennedy creates "Green Berets" |
| **1955** | Jonas Salk pioneers vaccine for polio | | Bay of Pigs invasion of Cuba fails |
| | James Dean stars in the movie *Rebel Without a Cause* | **1962** | Cuban missile crisis brings the world to the brink of a superpower confrontation |
| **1956** | Congress passes the National Interstate and Defense Highways Act | **1963** | Report by the Presidential Commission on the Status of Women documents ongoing discrimination |
| | Elvis Presley signs with RCA | | Betty Friedan publishes *The Feminine Mystique* |
| | Eisenhower is reelected, defeating Stevenson a second time | | Limited Nuclear Test-Ban Treaty is signed |
| | Allen Ginsberg publishes *Howl* | | President Kennedy is assassinated; Lyndon B. Johnson becomes president |
| **1957** | Soviet Union launches *Sputnik*, first space-orbiting satellite | | |
| | Jack Kerouac publishes *On the Road* | | |

The presidential transition of 1961—from grandfatherly war hero Dwight Eisenhower to charismatic young war hero Jack Kennedy—symbolized for many a generational shift as well. By 1963, young people had more influence than ever before in shaping the nation's political life, its media images, and its burgeoning consumer culture. Kennedy himself inspired millions of young Americans to pursue public service and to express their idealism. But even by the time of Kennedy's death, the postwar consensus and the conditions that nurtured it were beginning to unravel.

# REVIEW QUESTIONS

1. How did Cold War politics and assumptions shape American foreign policy in these years? What were the key interventions the United States made in Europe and the Third World?

2. How did postwar economic prosperity change the lives of ordinary Americans? Which groups benefited most and which were largely excluded from "the affluent society"?

3. What role did federal programs play in expanding economic opportunities?

4. Analyze the origins of postwar youth culture. How was teenage life different in these years from previous eras? How did popular culture both reflect and distort the lives of American youth?

5. How did mass culture become even more central to American everyday life in the two decades following World War II? What problems did various cultural critics identify with this trend?

6. Evaluate the domestic and international policies associated with John F. Kennedy and the New Frontier. What continuities with Eisenhower-era politics do you find in the Kennedy administration? How did JFK break with past practices?

## KEY TERMS

**myhistorylab**

Flashcard Review

**Alliance for Progress** (p. 780)

**Bay of Pigs** (p. 781)

*Beatnik* (p. 776)

**Beats** (p. 775)

**Cuban missile crisis** (p. 782)

**Equal Pay Act of 1963** (p. 778)

**Great Society** (p. 783)

**Landrum-Griffin Act** (p. 769)

**Limited Nuclear Test-Ban Treaty** (p. 782)

**New Frontier** (p. 778)

**National Aeronautics and Space Administration (NASA)** (p. 778)

## RECOMMENDED READING

Glenn C. Altschuler, *All Shook Up: How Rock 'n' Roll Changed America* (2003). The best new social history of rock 'n' roll, with excellent coverage of the generational and racial controversies surrounding the new music.

James L. Baughman, *Same Time, Same Station: Creating American Television, 1948–1961* (2007). The best new account of the emergence of television as the nation's dominant mass medium with emphasis on the influence of advertising.

Lizabeth Cohen, *A Consumers' Republic: The Politics of Mass Consumption in Postwar America* (2003). An ambitious, deeply researched overview of how postwar Americans negotiated the tensions between expanding opportunities for consumption and traditional ideals of citizenship and political activism.

Gary Donaldson, *The First Modern Campaign: Kennedy, Nixon, and the Election of 1960* (2007). New and deeply researched analysis of the 1960 election as the template for our media-dominated politics.

Lawrence Freedman, *Kennedy's Wars: Berlin, Cuba, Laos, and Vietnam* (2000). A new analysis of JFK's foreign policy, emphasizing the context of Cold War liberalism.

Edward Humes, *Over Here: How the GI Bill Transformed the American Dream* (2006). Comprehensive history of this crucial postwar legislation, including its discriminatory impact on women and racial minorities.

Kenneth T. Jackson, *Crabgrass Frontier* (1985). The most comprehensive overview of the history of American suburbs. Jackson provides a broad historical context for understanding postwar suburbanization and offers an excellent analysis of the impact of government agencies such as the Federal Housing Administration.

David E. Kaiser, *American Tragedy: Kennedy, Johnson, and the Origins of the Vietnam War* (2000). The most detailed account yet of how the contradictions of Cold War thinking pushed policymakers in three administrations toward an unnecessary and unwinnable war.

Elaine Tyler May, *Homeward Bound: American Families in the Cold War* (1988). A thoughtful social history linking family life of the 1950s with the political shadow of the Cold War.

Grace Palladino, *Teenagers: An American History* (1996). A lively and witty narrative account of the emergence of teenagers as a new social class.

myhistorylab
Where it's a good time to connect to the past!

For study resources for this chapter, go to **www.myhistorylab.com** and choose *Out of Many, Teaching and Learning Classroom Edition*. You will find a wealth of study and review material for this chapter, including pretests and posttests, customized study plan, key-term review flash cards, interactive map and document activities, and documents for analysis.

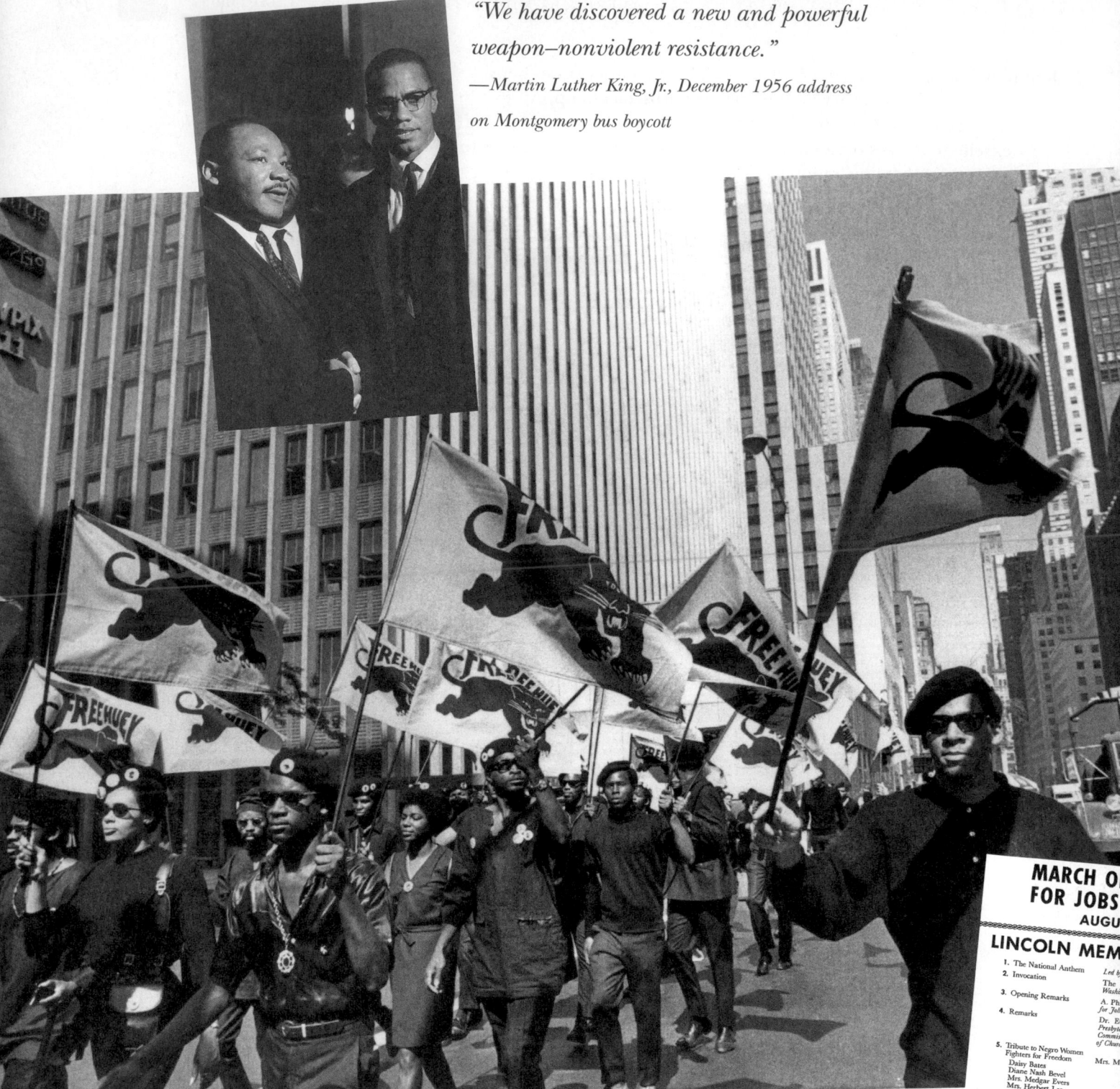

*"We have discovered a new and powerful weapon—nonviolent resistance."*
—*Martin Luther King, Jr., December 1956 address*
*on Montgomery bus boycott*

**The Black Panthers** march in New York City.

# 28

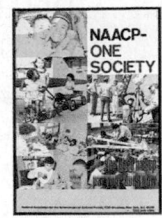

## THE CIVIL RIGHTS MOVEMENT
### 1945–1966

**WHAT WERE** the legal and political origins of the African American civil rights struggle?

**HOW DID** student protesters and direct action shape the civil rights struggle in the South?

**HOW DID** the civil rights movement intersect with national politics in the 1950s and 1960s?

**HOW DID** America's other minorities respond to the African American struggle for civil rights?

# AMERICAN COMMUNITIES

## The Montgomery Bus Boycott: An African American Community Challenges Segregation

ON DECEMBER 1, 1955, ROSA PARKS, A SEAMSTRESS AND WELL-KNOWN activist in the African American community of Montgomery, Alabama, was taken from a bus, arrested, and jailed for refusing to give up her seat to a white passenger. Composing roughly half the city's 100,000 people, Montgomery's black community had long endured the humiliation of a strictly segregated bus system. Drivers could order a whole row of black passengers to stand for one white person. Black people had to pay their fares at the front of the bus, then step back outside and reenter through the rear door.

Protesting Mrs. Parks's arrest, more than 30,000 African Americans answered a hastily organized call to boycott the city's buses. On the day of the boycott, a steady stream of cars and pedestrians jammed the streets around Holt Street Baptist Church. By early evening a patient, orderly, and determined crowd of more than 5,000 African Americans packed the church and spilled over onto the sidewalks. Loudspeakers had to be set up for the thousands who could not squeeze inside. After a brief prayer and a reading from Scripture, all attention focused on the twenty-six-year-old minister, the Reverend Martin Luther King Jr., who rose to address the gathering. "We are here this evening," he began slowly, "for serious business. We are here in a general sense because first and foremost we are American citizens, and we are determined to apply our citizenship to the fullness of its means."

Sensing the crowd's expectant mood, Dr. King got down to specifics and described Mrs. Parks's arrest. As he quickened his cadence and drew shouts of encouragement, he seemed to gather strength and confidence from the crowd. "You know, my friends, there comes a time when people get tired of being trampled over by the iron feet of oppression. There comes a time, my friends, when people get tired of being flung across the abyss of humiliation, when they experience the bleakness of nagging despair."

Even before Dr. King concluded, it was clear to all that the bus boycott would continue for more than just a day. The minister laid out the key principles that would guide the boycott—nonviolence, Christian love, unity. His brief but stirring address created a powerful sense of communion. "If we are wrong, justice is a lie," he told the clapping and shouting throng. "And we are determined here in Montgomery to work and fight until justice runs down like water and righteousness like a mighty stream." Dr. King made his way out of the church amid waves of applause and rows of hands reaching out to touch him.

Dr. King's prophetic speech catapulted him into leadership of the Montgomery bus boycott—but he had not started what would become known simply as the Movement. When Rosa Parks was arrested, local activists with deep roots in the black protest tradition galvanized the community with the idea of a boycott. Mrs. Parks herself had served for twelve years as secretary of the local NAACP chapter. She was a committed opponent of segregation and was thoroughly respected in the city's African American community. E. D. Nixon, president of the Alabama NAACP and head of the local Brotherhood of Sleeping Car Porters union, saw Mrs. Parks's arrest as the right case on which to make a stand. It was Nixon who brought Montgomery's black ministers together on December 5 to coordinate an extended boycott of city buses. They formed the Montgomery Improvement Association (MIA) and chose Dr. King as their leader. Significantly, Mrs. Parks's lawyer was Clifford Durr, a white liberal with a history of representing black clients. His politically active wife Virginia, for whom Mrs. Parks worked as a seamstress, had been a longtime crusader against the poll tax, which prevented many blacks from voting. And two white ministers, Rev. Robert Graetz and Rev. Glenn Smiley, would offer important support to the MIA.

While Nixon organized black ministers, Jo Ann Robinson, an English teacher at Alabama State College, spread the word to the larger black community. Robinson led the Women's Political Council (WPC), an organization of black professional women founded in 1949. With her WPC allies, Robinson wrote, mimeographed, and distributed 50,000 copies of a leaflet telling the story of Mrs. Parks's arrest and urging all African Americans to stay off city buses on December 5. They did. Now the MIA faced the more difficult task of keeping the boycott going. Success depended on providing alternate transportation for the 30,000 to 40,000 maids, cooks, janitors, and other black working people who needed to get to work.

The MIA coordinated an elaborate system of car pools, using hundreds of private cars and volunteer drivers to provide as many as 20,000 rides each day. Many people walked. Local authorities, although shocked by the discipline and sense of purpose shown by Montgomery's African American community, refused to engage in serious negotiations. With the aid of the NAACP, the MIA brought suit in federal court against bus segregation in Montgomery. Police harassed boycotters with traffic tickets and arrests. White racists exploded bombs in the homes of Dr. King and E. D. Nixon. The days turned into weeks, then months, but still the boycott continued. All along, mass meetings in Montgomery's African American churches helped boost morale with singing, praying, and stories of individual sacrifice. The spontaneous remark of one elderly woman, refusing all suggestions that she drop out of the boycott on account of her age, became a classic refrain of the Movement: "My feets is tired, but my soul is rested."

Montgomery

The boycott reduced the bus company's revenues by two-thirds. In February 1956, city officials obtained indictments against King, Nixon, and 113 other boycotters under an old law forbidding hindrance to business without "just cause or legal excuse." A month later King went on trial. A growing contingent of newspaper reporters and TV crews from around the country watched as the judge found King guilty, fined him $1,000, and released him on bond pending appeal. But on June 4, a panel of three federal judges struck down Montgomery's bus segregation ordinances as unconstitutional. On November 13 the Supreme Court affirmed the district court ruling. After eleven hard months and against all odds, the boycotters had won.

# Origins of the Movement

The civil rights movement arose out of the aspirations and community strength of African Americans. Its deepest roots lay in the historic injustices of slavery, racism, and segregation. African Americans' experiences during and immediately after World War II laid the foundation for the civil rights struggle of the 1950s and 1960s.

## Civil Rights after World War II

The wartime boom spurred a mass northward migration of nearly a million black Southerners. Forty-three northern and western cities saw their black population double during the 1940s. With the growth of African American communities in cities like New York, Chicago, and Detroit, black people gained significant influence in urban political machines. Within industrial unions such as the United Automobile Workers and the United Steel Workers, white and black workers learned the power of biracial unity in fighting for better wages and working conditions.

After the war, civil rights issues returned to the national political stage for the first time since Reconstruction. Black voters had already begun to switch their allegiance from the Republicans to the Democrats during the New Deal. A series of symbolic and substantive acts by the Truman administration solidified that shift.

Truman and his advisers walked a political tightrope on civil rights. They understood that black voters in several key northern states would be pivotal in the 1948 election. At the same time, they worried about the loyalty of white southern Democrats adamantly opposed to changing the racial status quo. In July 1948, the president made his boldest move on behalf of civil rights, issuing an executive order ending segregation in the armed forces. Later that summer, when liberals forced the Democratic National Convention to adopt a strong civil rights plank, outraged southern delegates walked out and nominated Governor Strom Thurmond of South Carolina for president on a States' Rights ticket. Thurmond carried four southern states in the election. But with the help of more than 70 percent of the northern black vote, Truman barely managed to defeat Republican Thomas E. Dewey in November. The deep split over race issues would continue to wrack the national Democratic Party for a generation.

Electoral politics was not the only arena for civil rights work. During the war, membership in the National Association for the Advancement of Colored People had mushroomed from 50,000 to 500,000. Working- and middle-class urban black people provided the backbone of this new membership. The NAACP conducted voter registration drives and lobbied against discrimination in housing and employment. Its Legal Defense and Education Fund, vigorously led by special counsel Thurgood Marshall, mounted several significant legal challenges to segregation laws.

**WHAT WERE** the legal and political origins of the African American civil rights struggle?

**Review Summary**

**28–12**
Jo Ann Gibson Robinson, *The Montgomery Bus Boycott* (1955)

## IMAGE KEY

for pages 788–789

a. Martin Luther King, Jr. and Malcolm X.

b. Black Panthers in trademark berets marching in New York City, July 22, 1968.

c. Official program for the March on Washington for "jobs and freedom," August 28, 1963.

d. A poster for the National Association for the Advancement of Colored People (NAACP) features ballplayer Larry Doby, workers, children, and students.

e. The album cover for *Cotton Club Days, Volume 2* by Duke Ellington, featuring a photo of the jazz bandleader.

f. Elizabeth Eckford is heckled by white students while integrating Central High School in Little Rock, Arkansas in 1957.

g. Young black men carrying signs bearing slogans In Tallahassee, Florida in March, 1964.

h. A Native American man standing guard during the American Indian Movement's 1973 occupation of the reservation town at Wounded Knee, South Dakota.

In *Morgan* v. *Virginia* (1946), the Supreme Court used the interstate-commerce clause to declare segregation on interstate buses unconstitutional. Other Supreme Court decisions struck down all-white election primaries, racially restrictive housing covenants, and the exclusion of blacks from law and graduate schools.

The NAACP's legal work demonstrated the potential for using federal courts in attacking segregation. Courts were one place where black people, using the constitutional language of rights, could make forceful arguments that could not be voiced in Congress or at political conventions. But federal enforcement of court decisions was often lacking.

Two symbolic "firsts" raised black expectations and inspired pride. In 1947 Jackie Robinson broke the color barrier in major league baseball, winning rookie-of-the-year honors with the Brooklyn Dodgers. Robinson's courage in the face of racist taunts from fans and players paved the way for the other black ballplayers who soon followed him into the big leagues. In 1950 United Nations diplomat Ralph Bunche won the Nobel Peace Prize for arranging the 1948 Arab-Israeli truce. Bunche, however, later declined an appointment as undersecretary of state because he did not want to subject his family to Washington, D.C.'s humiliating segregation laws.

Cultural change could have political implications as well. In the 1940s, African American musicians created a new form of jazz that revolutionized American music and asserted a militant black consciousness. Although black musicians had pioneered swing and earlier styles of jazz, white bandleaders and musicians had reaped most of the recognition and money. Black artists such as Charlie Parker, Dizzy Gillespie, Thelonius Monk, Bud Powell, and Miles Davis revolted against the standard big-band format of swing, preferring small groups and competitive

**Charlie Parker (alto sax)** and Miles Davis (trumpet) with their group in 1947, at the Three Deuces Club in New York City. Parker and Davis were two creative leaders of the "bebop" movement of the 1940s. Working in northern cities, boppers reshaped jazz music and created a distinct language and style that were widely imitated by young people. They challenged older stereotypes of African American musicians by insisting that they be treated as serious artists.

jam sessions to express their musical visions. The new music, dubbed "bebop," demanded a much more sophisticated knowledge of harmony and melody and featured more complex rhythms and extended improvisation than did previous jazz styles. These black artists insisted on independence from the white-defined norms of show business. Serious about both their music and the way it was presented, they refused to cater to white stereotypes of grinning, easygoing black performers.

## THE SEGREGATED SOUTH

In the postwar South, still home to over half the nation's 15 million African Americans, the racial situation had changed little since the Supreme Court sanctioned "separate but equal" segregation in *Plessy* v. *Ferguson* (see Chapter 20). In practice, segregation meant separate but unequal.

In the late 1940s only about 10 percent of eligible southern black people voted, most of these in urban areas. A combination of legal and extralegal measures kept all but the most determined blacks disenfranchised. African Americans who insisted on exercising their right to vote, especially in remote rural areas, faced physical violence—beatings, shootings, and lynchings.

Outsiders often noted that despite Jim Crow laws (see Chapter 20), contact between blacks and whites was ironically close. The mass of black Southerners worked on white-owned farms or in white households. One black preacher neatly summarized the nation's regional differences this way: "In the South, they don't care how close you get as long as you don't get too big; in the North, they don't care

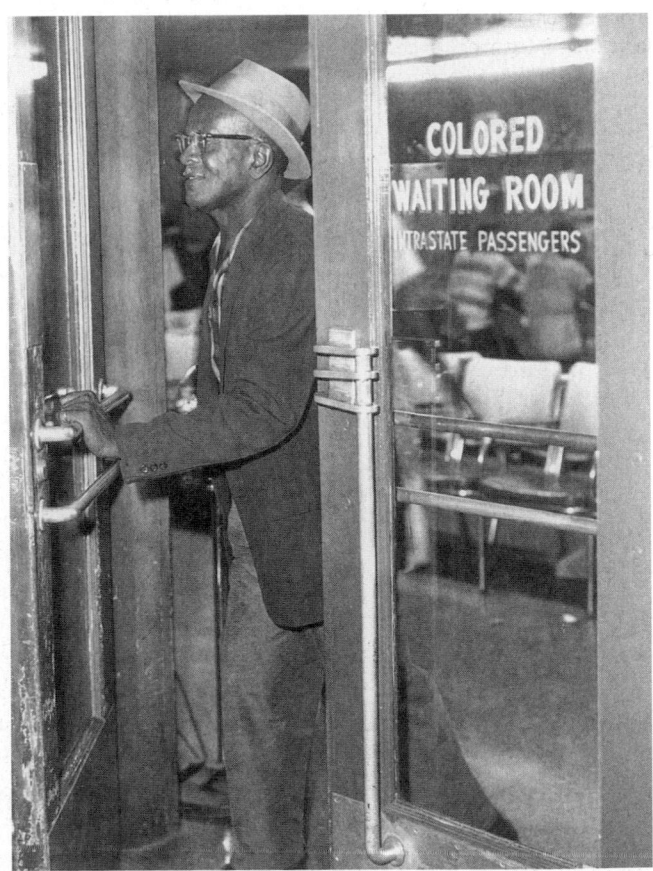

**Signs designating "White"** and "Colored" rest rooms, waiting rooms, entrances, benches, and even water fountains were a common sight in the segregated South. They were a constant reminder that legal separation of the races in public spaces was the law of the land.

how big you get as long as you don't get too close." The South's racial code forced African Americans to accept, at least outwardly, social conventions that reinforced their low standing with whites.

The consequences of violating the code could be fatal. In the summer of 1955 a fourteen-year-old African American boy from Chicago, unaccustomed to local "folkways," was visiting relatives near Money, Mississippi. Leaving a store with some friends, Emmett Till spoke in an informal tone to the white wife of the store owner. Several days later Till was kidnapped from his uncle's house in the middle of the night, and shortly thereafter his body was dragged out of the Tallahatchie River. Back in Chicago, Till's mother, Mamie Bradley, insisted on an open-casket funeral, and the photographs of his horribly mutilated body profoundly shocked African American readers of *Jet* magazine and other black publications around the country. No white publications carried these photos. Till's murderers were acquitted in a trial that attracted national attention and underlined the stark realities of southern segregation. It also reminded northern blacks that racist violence could touch their lives as well.

But broad demographic and economic changes were also remaking the postwar South. On the eve of World War II, more than 40 percent of Southerners lived on farms; two-thirds of its 35 million people resided in places with less than 2,500 inhabitants. During the 1950s, tens of thousands of nonagricultural jobs were created in factories, mills, and office buildings across the region. More and more national corporations, attracted by the region's cheaper labor costs, began establishing a southern presence, and the region's towns and cities competed to lure them. A more highly mechanized agriculture and rapid industrialization pushed more Southerners, black and white, into cities and suburbs. By 1960, roughly half of all Southerners inhabited metropolitan districts and only 15 percent lived on farms.

## BROWN V. BOARD OF EDUCATION

Since the late 1930s, the NAACP had chipped away at the legal foundations of segregation. Rather than making a frontal assault on the *Plessy* separate-but-equal rule, civil rights attorneys launched a series of suits seeking complete equality in segregated facilities. Their strategy was to make segregation so prohibitively expensive that the South would be forced to dismantle it. In the 1939 case *Missouri v. ex rel. Gaines*, the Supreme Court ruled that the University of Missouri law school must either admit African Americans or build another, fully equal law school for them. NAACP lawyers pushed their arguments further, asserting that equality could not be measured simply by money or physical plant. In *McLaurin* v. *Oklahoma State Regents* (1950), the Court agreed with Thurgood Marshall's argument that regulations forcing a black law student to sit, eat, and study in areas apart from white students inevitably created a "badge of inferiority."

By 1951, Marshall had begun coordinating the NAACP's legal resources for a direct attack on the separate-but-equal doctrine, aiming to overturn *Plessy* and the constitutionality of segregation itself. For a test case, Marshall combined five lawsuits challenging segregation in public schools. One of these suits argued the case of Oliver Brown of Topeka, Kansas, who sought to overturn a state law permitting cities to maintain segregated schools. Topeka's ordinance, sanctioned by this law, forced Brown's eight-year-old daughter Linda to travel by bus to a black school even though she lived only three blocks from an all-white elementary school. The Supreme Court heard initial arguments on the cases, grouped together as **Brown v. Board of Education**, in December 1952. The *Brown* case offered an important reminder that segregation was not a purely southern phenomenon.

**27–2**
*Brown v. Board of Education*
(1954)

*Brown v. Board of Education*
Supreme Court decision in 1954 that declared that "separate but equal" schools for children of different races violated the Constitution.

Roughly 40 percent of America's 28 million schoolchildren attended legally segregated schools in the South and border states, while millions more were educated in northern communities where *de facto* segregation—created by housing
patterns and school districting—was the norm.

When Chief Justice Fred Vinson died suddenly in 1953, President Dwight
Eisenhower appointed California Governor Earl Warren to fill the post. After hearing further arguments, the Court remained divided on the issue of overturning
*Plessy*. Warren, eager for a unanimous decision, patiently worked at convincing two
holdouts. Using his political skills to persuade and achieve compromise, Warren
urged his colleagues to affirm a simple principle as the basis for the decision.

On May 17, 1954, Warren read aloud the Court's unanimous decision. "Does
segregation of children in public schools solely on the basis of race . . . deprive the
children of the minority group of equal educational opportunities?" The chief
justice paused. "We believe that it does." In summation, Warren stated the court's
opinion that in the field of public education the doctrine of 'separate but equal'
has no place. Separate educational facilities are inherently unequal . . . Any language in *Plessy* v. *Ferguson* contrary to this finding is rejected."

African Americans and their liberal allies around the country hailed the
decision and the legal genius of Thurgood Marshall. Marshall himself predicted
that all segregated schools would be abolished within five years. Black newspapers
were full of stories on the imminent dismantling of segregation. The *Chicago
Defender* called the decision "a second emancipation proclamation." But the issue
of enforcement soon dampened this enthusiasm. To gain a unanimous decision,
Warren had to agree to let the Court delay for one year its ruling on how to implement desegregation. This second *Brown* ruling, handed down in May 1955, assigned
responsibility for desegregation plans to local school boards. The Court left it to
federal district judges to monitor compliance, requiring only that desegregation
proceed "with all deliberate speed." Thus, although the Court had made a momentous and clear constitutional ruling, the need for compromise dictated gradual
enforcement by unspecified means.

## CRISIS IN LITTLE ROCK

Resistance to *Brown* took many forms. Most affected states passed laws transferring
authority for pupil assignment to local school boards. This prevented the NAACP
from bringing statewide suits against segregated school systems. Counties and
towns created layers of administrative delays designed to stop implementation of
*Brown*. Some school boards transferred public school property to new, all-white private "academies." State legislatures in Virginia, Alabama, Mississippi, and Georgia,
resurrecting pre–Civil War doctrines, passed resolutions declaring their right to
"interpose" themselves between the people and the federal government and to "nullify" federal laws. In 1956, 101 members of Congress from the former Confederate states signed the **Southern Manifesto**, urging their states to refuse compliance
with desegregation. President Eisenhower declined to publicly endorse *Brown*,
contributing to the southern resistance.

In Little Rock, Arkansas, the tense controversy over school integration became
a test case of state versus federal power. A federal court ordered public schools to begin
desegregation in September 1957, and the local school board made plans to comply.
But Governor Orval Faubus, facing a tough reelection fight, decided to make a campaign issue out of defying the court order. He dispatched Arkansas National Guard
troops to Central High School to prevent nine black students from entering. For
three weeks, armed troops stood guard at the school. Screaming crowds, encouraged
by Faubus, menaced the black students, beat up two black reporters.

**28–13**
*Southern Manifesto on
Integration* (1956)

**Southern Manifesto** A document
signed by 101 members of Congress
from Southern states in 1956 that
argued that the Supreme Court's
decision in *Brown* v. *Board of
Education of Topeka* itself
contradicted the Constitution.

**Four African American** students walk swiftly past barricaded sidewalks as they integrate Central High School in Little Rock, Arkansas, in September 1957. Soldiers from the 101st Airborne Division, sent to Little Rock by President Eisenhower, protect the students during the tense racial confrontation.

**HOW DID** student protesters and direct action shape the civil rights struggle in the South?

**myhistorylab**

**Review Summary**

At first, Eisenhower tried to intervene quietly, gaining Faubus's assurance that he would protect the nine black children. But when Faubus suddenly withdrew his troops, leaving the black students at the mercy of the white mob, Eisenhower had to move. On September 24 he placed the Arkansas National Guard under federal command and ordered a thousand paratroopers of the 101st Airborne Division to Little Rock. The nine black students arrived in a U.S. Army car. With fixed bayonets, the soldiers protected the students as they finally integrated Central High School in Little Rock. Eisenhower, the veteran military commander, justified his actions on the basis of upholding federal authority and enforcing the law. He also defended his intervention as crucial to national prestige abroad, noting the propaganda victory Faubus was handing the Communist world (see Seeing History). Yet as the first president since Reconstruction to use armed federal troops in support of black rights, Eisenhower demonstrated that the federal government could, indeed, protect civil rights. Unfazed, Governor Faubus kept Little Rock high schools closed during the 1958–59 academic year to prevent what he called "violence and disorder."

# No Easy Road to Freedom, 1957–62

The legal breakthrough represented by the *Brown* decision heartened opponents of segregation everywhere. Most important, *Brown* demonstrated the potential for using the federal court system as a weapon against discrimination and as a means of protecting the full rights of citizenship. Yet widespread opposition to *Brown* showed the limits of a strictly legal strategy. As the Montgomery bus boycott had proved, black communities would have to help themselves first.

## MARTIN LUTHER KING JR. AND THE SCLC

When it ended with the Supreme Court decision in November 1956, the 381-day Montgomery bus boycott had made Martin Luther King Jr. a national figure. King himself was an extraordinary and complex man. Born in 1929 in Atlanta, he enjoyed a middle-class upbringing as the son of a prominent Baptist minister. After graduating from prestigious Morehouse College, an all-black school, King earned a divinity degree at Crozer Theological Seminary in Pennsylvania and a Ph.D. in theology from Boston University.

In graduate school he was drawn to the Social Christianity of American theologian Walter Rauschenbusch, who insisted on connecting religious faith with struggles for social justice. Above all, King admired Mohandas Gandhi, a lawyer turned ascetic who had led a successful nonviolent resistance movement against British colonial rule in India. Gandhi taught his followers to confront authorities with a readiness to suffer in order to expose injustice and force those in power to end it. This tactic of nonviolent civil disobedience required discipline and sacrifice from its followers, who were sometimes called upon to lay their lives on the line against armed police and military forces. Crucially, King believed Gandhian

# Civil Rights on the World Stage

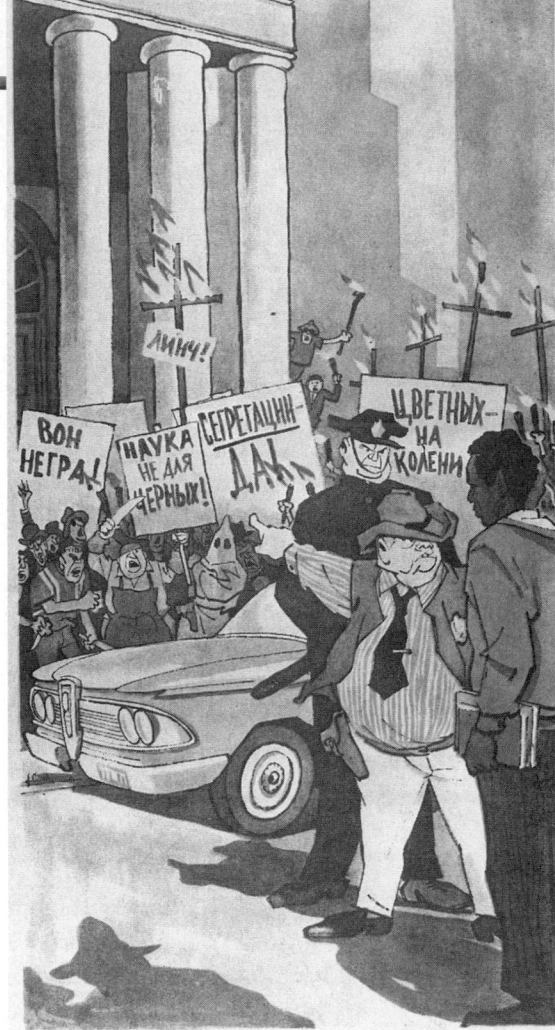

A s the civil rights struggle gained momentum through the late 1950s and early 1960s, it evolved from a regional effort aimed at ending southern segregation to a movement with national and ultimately international implications. The United States and the Soviet Union, locked in the Cold War, were both especially eager to win influence in the new Third World nations of Africa and Asia that emerged from the post–World War II collapse of European colonial empires. Because these nations were home to hundreds of millions of people of color, the increasingly tense racial conflicts in local American communities assumed global significance. The Eisenhower and Kennedy administrations were acutely sensitive to the negative impact these images had on an American foreign policy that touted itself as the beacon of freedom around the world.

These two political cartoons illustrate the ongoing commentary that put the civil rights movement on the world stage. The *Oakland Tribune* published "Right into Their Hands," on September 11, 1957, during the integration crisis at Central High School in Little Rock, Arkansas. The cartoon published in the Soviet satirical magazine *Krokodil* on August 24, 1963, comments on the contemporary attempts to integrate American higher education. It depicts an African American student stopped by police from entering an American university, amid protest signs saying (in Russian) "Nigger Go Away," "Lynch Him," "We Want Segregation," and "Put the Colored on Their Knees." ■

— Хочешь учиться в университете? А читать умеешь?

Рисунок Л. САМОЙЛОВА

**WHAT TECHNIQUES** did these cartoons share in their depiction of forces opposed to integration? How does the *Oakland Tribune* cartoon seek to counter the kind of sentiments evoked in the Soviet cartoon?

797

nonviolence to be not merely a moral imperative but a potent political strategy. A unique blend of traditional African American folk preacher and erudite intellectual, King used his passion and intelligence to help transform a community's pain into a powerful moral force for change.

In a December 1956 address celebrating the Montgomery bus boycott victory, King laid out six key lessons from the yearlong struggle: "(1) We have discovered that we can stick together for a common cause; (2) our leaders do not have to sell out; (3) threats and violence do not necessarily intimidate those who are sufficiently aroused and nonviolent; (4) our church is becoming militant, stressing a social gospel as well as a gospel of personal salvation; (5) we have gained a new sense of dignity and destiny; (6) we have discovered a new and powerful weapon—nonviolent resistance."

King recognized the need to exploit the momentum of the Montgomery movement. In early 1957, with the help of Bayard Rustin of the War Resisters' League and others, he brought together nearly 100 black ministers to found the **Southern Christian Leadership Conference (SCLC)**. The clergymen elected King president and his close friend, the Reverend Ralph Abernathy, treasurer. The SCLC called upon black people "to understand that nonviolence is not a symbol of weakness or cowardice, but as Jesus demonstrated, nonviolent resistance transforms weakness into strength and breeds courage in the face of danger."

But King and other black leaders also understood that the white South was no monolith. They believed white Southerners could be divided roughly into three groups: first, a tiny minority—often with legal training, social connections, and money—that might be counted on to help overthrow segregation; second, extreme segregationists who were willing and able to use violence and terror in defense of white supremacy; and third, a broad middle group who favored and benefited from segregation but were unwilling to take personal risks to prevent its destruction. In the battles to come, civil rights leaders made this nuanced view of the white South central to their larger political strategy. Extreme segregationists could be counted on to overreact, often violently, to civil rights campaigns, and thereby help to win sympathy and support for the cause. White moderates, especially in the business community, might be reluctant to initiate change, but they would try to distance themselves from the desperate violence of extremists and present themselves as pragmatic supporters of order and peace.

The SCLC gained support among black ministers, and King vigorously spread his message in speeches and writings. But the organization failed to generate the kind of mass, direct-action movement that had made history in Montgomery. Instead, the next great spark to light the fire of protest came from what seemed at the time a most unlikely source: black college students.

## Sit-Ins: Greensboro, Nashville, Atlanta

On Monday, February 1, 1960, four black freshmen from North Carolina Agricultural and Technical College in Greensboro sat down at the whites-only lunch counter in Woolworth's. As the students had anticipated while planning the action in their dorm rooms, they were refused service. But the four students stayed at the counter until closing time. Word of their actions spread quickly, and the next day they returned with more than two dozen supporters. On the third day, students occupied sixty-three of the sixty-six lunch counter seats. By Thursday they had been joined by three white students from the Women's College of the University of North Carolina in Greensboro. Scores of sympathizers overflowed Woolworth's

**Southern Christian Leadership Conference (SCLC)** Black civil rights organization founded in 1957 by Martin Luther King Jr., and other clergy.

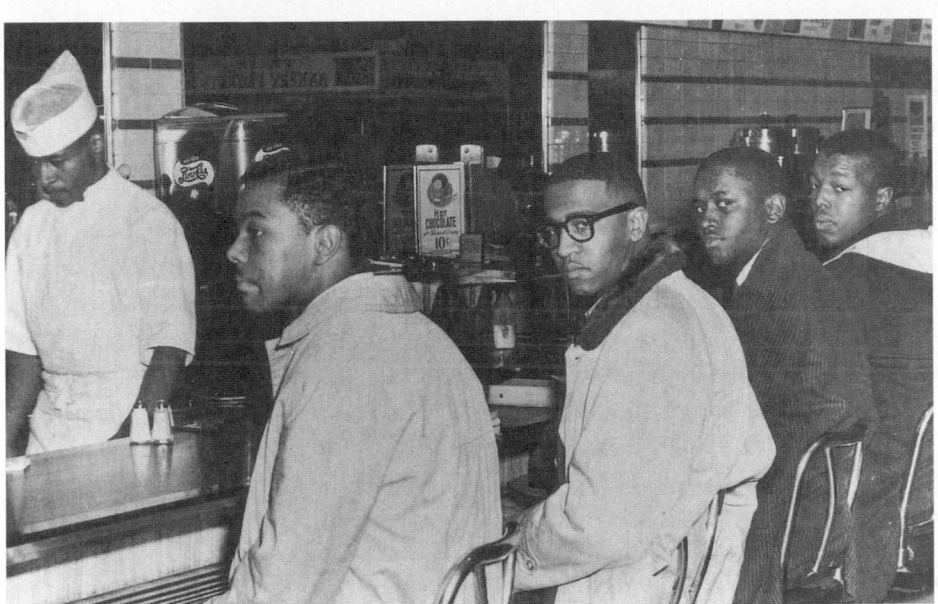

**The second day** of the sit-in at the Greensboro, North Carolina, Woolworth lunch counter, February 2, 1960. From left: Joseph McNeil, Franklin McCain, Billy Smith, and Clarence Henderson. The Greensboro protest sparked a wave of sit-ins across the South, mostly by college students, demanding an end to segregation in restaurants and other public places.

and started a sit-in down the street in S. H. Kress. On Friday, hundreds of black students and a few white sympathizers jammed the lunch counters.

The week's events made Greensboro national news. City officials, looking to end the protest, offered to negotiate in exchange for an end to demonstrations. But white business leaders and politicians proved unwilling to change the racial status quo, and the sit-ins resumed on April 1. In response to the April 21 arrest of forty-five students for trespassing, an outraged African American community organized a boycott of targeted stores that cut deeply into merchants' profits. Greensboro's leaders reluctantly gave in. On July 25, 1960, the first African American ate a meal at Woolworth's.

The Greensboro sit-in sent a shock wave throughout the South. During the next eighteen months, 70,000 people—most of them black students, a few of them white allies—participated in sit-ins against segregation in dozens of communities. More than 3,000 were arrested. African Americans had discovered a new form of direct-action protest, dignified and powerful, that white people could not ignore. The sit-in movement also transformed participants' self-image, empowering them psychologically and emotionally.

In Nashville, Reverend James Lawson, a northern-born black minister, had led workshops in nonviolent resistance since 1958. Lawson gathered around him a group of deeply committed black students from Fisk and Vanderbilt universities and other Nashville colleges. The psychological pressures were enormous. To be successful, practitioners of nonviolent resistance had to learn and practice strict self-control needed to resist lashing back at the angry crowds that would abuse them. Young activists there talked not only of ending segregation but also of creating a "Beloved Community" based on Christian idealism and Gandhian principles.

In the spring of 1960, more than 150 Nashville students were arrested in disciplined sit-ins aimed at desegregating downtown lunch counters. Lawson, who preached the need for sacrifice in the cause of justice, found himself expelled from the divinity school at Vanderbilt. Lawson and other veterans of the Nashville sit-ins, such as John Lewis, Diane Nash, and Marion Barry, would go on to play influential roles in the national civil rights movement. The Nashville group developed rules of conduct that became a model for protesters elsewhere: "Don't strike back or curse if abused. . . . Show yourself courteous and friendly at all times. . . . Report all serious incidents to your leader in a polite manner. Remember love and nonviolence."

The most ambitious sit-in campaign unfolded in Atlanta, the South's largest and wealthiest city, home to the region's most powerful and prestigious black community. Students from Morehouse, Spelman, and the other all-black schools that made up Atlanta University took the lead. On March 15, 1960, 200 young black people staged a well-coordinated sit-in at restaurants in City Hall, the State Capitol, and other government offices. Police arrested and jailed seventy-six demonstrators that day, but the experience only strengthened the activists' resolve. Led by Julian Bond and Lonnie King, two Morehouse undergraduates, the students formed the Committee on an Appeal for Human Rights. Over the summer they planned a fall campaign of large-scale sit-ins at major Atlanta department stores and a boycott of downtown merchants. In October 1960 Martin Luther King Jr. and thirty-six students were arrested when they sat down in the all-white Magnolia Room restaurant in Rich's Department Store. As in Greensboro and Montgomery, the larger African American community in Atlanta supported the continuing sit-ins, picketing, and boycotts. The campaign stretched on for months, and hundreds of protesters went to jail. The city's business leaders finally relented in September 1961, and desegregation came to Atlanta.

## SNCC AND THE "BELOVED COMMUNITY"

The sit-in movement pumped new energy into the civil rights cause, creating a new generation of activists and leaders. Mass arrests, beatings, and vilification in the southern white press only strengthened the resolve of those in the Movement. Students also had to deal with the fears of their families, many of whom had made great sacrifices to send them to college.

The new student militancy also caused discord within black communities. The authority of local African American elites had traditionally depended on their influence and cooperation with the white establishment. Black lawyers, schoolteachers, principals, and businessmen had to maintain regular and cordial relations with white judges, school boards, and politicians. Student calls for freedom disturbed many community leaders worried about upsetting traditional patronage networks. Some black college presidents, pressured by trustees and state legislators, sought to moderate or stop the Movement altogether.

An April 1960 conference of 120 black student activists in Raleigh, North Carolina, underlined the generational and radical aspects of the new movement. The meeting had been called by Ella Baker, executive director of the SCLC, to help the students assess their experiences and plan future actions. With Baker's encouragement, the conference voted to establish a new group, the **Student Nonviolent Coordinating Committee** (**SNCC**, pronounced "Snick"). The strong influence of the Nashville students, led by James Lawson, could be found in the SNCC statement of purpose:

> We affirm the philosophical or religious ideal of nonviolence as the foundation of our purpose, the presupposition of our faith, and the manner of our action. Nonviolence as it grows from Judaic-Christian tradition seeks a social order of justice permeated by love.
> Integration of human endeavor represents the crucial first step towards such a society.

In the fall of 1960 SNCC established an organizational structure, a set of principles, and a new style of civil rights protest. The emphasis was on fighting segregation

**27–4**
*Student Nonviolent Coordinating Committee, Statement of Purpose* (1960)

**Student Nonviolent Coordinating Committee (SNCC)** Black civil rights organization founded in 1960 and drawing heavily on younger activists and college students.

through direct confrontation, mass action, and civil disobedience. SNCC field-workers initiated and supported local, community-based activity. Three-quarters of the first field-workers were less than twenty-two years old. Leadership was vested in a nonhierarchical Coordinating Committee, but local groups were free to determine their own direction. SNCC people distrusted bureaucracy and structure; they stressed spontaneity and improvisation. A small but dedicated group of young white Southerners, inspired by SNCC's idealism and activism, joined the cause. Over the next few years SNCC was at the forefront of nearly every major civil rights battle.

## THE ELECTION OF 1960 AND CIVIL RIGHTS

The race issue was kept from center stage during the very close presidential campaign of 1960. As vice president, Richard Nixon had been a leading Republican voice for stronger civil rights legislation, whereas Democratic nominee Senator John F. Kennedy had played virtually no role in the 1950s' congressional battles over civil rights. But during the campaign, their roles reversed. Kennedy praised the sit-in movement as part of a revival of national reform spirit. While the Republican platform contained a strong civil rights plank, Nixon, eager to court southern white voters, minimized his own identification with the Movement.

Kennedy won 70 percent of the black vote, which helped put him over the top in such critical states as Illinois, Texas, Michigan, and Pennsylvania and secure his narrow victory over Nixon. Many civil rights activists optimistically looked forward to a new president who would have to acknowledge his political debt to the black vote.

But the very closeness of his victory constrained Kennedy on race. Democrats had lost ground in the House and Senate, and Kennedy had to worry about alienating conservative Southern Democrats who chaired key congressional committees. Passage of major civil rights legislation would be virtually impossible. The president did appoint some forty African Americans to high federal positions, including Thurgood Marshall to a federal appellate court. He established a Committee on Equal Employment Opportunity, chaired by Vice President Lyndon B. Johnson, to fight discrimination in the federal civil service and in corporations that received government contracts.

Most significantly, the Kennedy administration sought to invigorate the Civil Rights Division of the Justice Department. Robert Kennedy, the new attorney general, began assembling a staff of brilliant and committed attorneys, headed by Washington lawyer Burke Marshall. Kennedy encouraged them to get out of Washington and into the field wherever racial troubles arose. The new, more aggressive mood at Justice could not solve the central political dilemma: how to move forward on civil rights without alienating southern Democrats. Pressure from the newly energized southern civil rights movement soon revealed the true difficulty of that problem. The movement would also provoke murderous outrage from white extremists determined to maintain the racial status quo (see Map 28.1).

## FREEDOM RIDES

In the spring of 1961 James Farmer, national director of **Congress of Racial Equality (CORE)**, announced plans for an interracial Freedom Ride through the South. The goal was to test compliance with court orders banning segregation in interstate travel and terminal accommodations. "Our intention," Farmer declared, "was to provoke the southern authorities into arresting us and thereby prod the Justice Department into enforcing the law of the land." CORE received financial

**Congress of Racial Equality (CORE)**
Civil rights group formed in 1942 and committed to nonviolent civil disobedience.

# MAP EXPLORATION

To explore an interactive version of this map, go to **http://www.prenhall.com/faraghertlc/map28.1**

**1954:** *Brown v. Board of Education* decision

Topeka

Nashville

**1957:** Federal troops integrate Central High School

Little Rock

Memphis

Oxford

Anniston

Atlanta

Birmingham

**1962:** James Meredith integrates U. Miss.

Jackson

Selma

Montgomery

Albany

**1963:** Medgar Evers assassinated

**1964:** Volunteers arrive for Freedom Summer

**1955–56:** Boycott of bus system

**1965:** Bloody Sunday and march to Montgomery

Washington DC

**1963:** March on Washington

**1960:** Sit-in movement begins, spreads to Nashville and Atlanta

Greensboro

**1961:** Freedom Ride to Mississippi meets with violence in Anniston and Montgomery

**1963:** SCLC launches Project C

**1962:** Martin Luther King and SCLC fail in Albany

*ATLANTIC OCEAN*

*Gulf of Mexico*

— Civil rights marches

**MAP 28.1**

**The Civil Rights Movement**    Key battlegrounds in the struggle for racial justice in communities across the South.

HOW DID the *Brown* decision pave the way for subsequent events?

and tactical support from the SCLC and several NAACP branches. It also informed the Justice Department and the FBI of its plans but received no reply.

On May 4 seven blacks and six whites split into two interracial groups and left Washington on public buses bound for Alabama and Mississippi. At first the two buses encountered only isolated harassment and violence as they headed south. But when one bus entered Anniston, Alabama, on May 14, an angry mob surrounded it, smashing windows and slashing tires. Six miles out of town, the tires went flat. A firebomb tossed through a window forced the passengers out. The mob then beat the Freedom Riders with blackjacks, iron bars, and clubs, and the bus burst into flames. A caravan of cars organized by the Birmingham office of the SCLC rescued the wounded. Another mob attacked the second bus in Anniston, leaving one Freedom Rider near death and permanently brain-damaged.

The violence escalated. In Birmingham, a mob of forty whites waited on the loading platform and attacked the bus that managed to get out of Anniston. Although police had been warned to expect trouble, they did nothing to stop the mob from beating the Freedom Riders with pipes and fists, nor did they make any arrests. FBI agents observed and took notes but did nothing. The remaining Freedom Riders decided to travel as a single group on the next lap, from Birmingham to Montgomery, but no bus would take them. Stranded and frightened, they reluctantly boarded a special flight to New Orleans arranged by the Justice Department. On May 17 the CORE-sponsored Freedom Ride disbanded.

That was not the end of the Freedom Rides. SNCC leaders in Atlanta and Nashville assembled a fresh group of volunteers to continue the trip. On May 20, twenty-one Freedom Riders left Birmingham for Montgomery. The bus station in the Alabama capital was eerily quiet and deserted as they pulled in. But when the passengers left the bus a mob of several hundred whites rushed them, yelling "Get those niggers!" and clubbing people to the ground. It took police more than an hour to halt the rioting. Montgomery's police commissioner later said, "We have no intention of standing guard for a bunch of troublemakers coming into our city."

**A Freedom Riders'** bus burns after being firebombed in Anniston, Alabama, May 14, 1961. After setting the bus afire, whites attacked the passengers fleeing the smoke and flames. Violent scenes like this one received extensive publicity in the mass media and helped compel the Justice Department to enforce court rulings banning segregation on interstate bus lines.

The mob violence and the indifference of Alabama officials made the Freedom Ride first-page news around the country and throughout the world. Newspapers in Europe, Africa, and Asia denounced the hypocrisy of the federal government. The Kennedy administration, preparing for the president's first summit meeting with Soviet premier Nikita Khrushchev, saw the situation as a threat to the nation's global prestige. The attorney general, Robert Kennedy, called for a cooling-off period, but King, Farmer, and the SNCC leaders announced that the Freedom Ride would continue. A bandaged but spirited group of twenty-seven Freedom Riders prepared to leave Montgomery for Jackson, Mississippi, on May 24. To avoid further violence Robert Kennedy arranged a compromise through Mississippi's Senator James Eastland. In exchange for a guarantee of safe passage through Mississippi, the federal government promised not to interfere with the arrest of the Freedom Riders in Jackson. Sticking to a policy of "jail, no bail," Freedom Riders clogged the prison, where they endured beatings and intimidation by prison guards that went largely unreported in the press. Their jail experiences turned most of them into committed core leaders of the student movement.

The Freedom Rides exposed the ugly face of southern racism to the world and inspired grassroots activists around the South. But they also reinforced white resistance to desegregation and showed the limits of federal action against Jim Crow. Eventually the Justice Department did petition the Interstate Commerce Commission to issue clear rules prohibiting segregation on interstate carriers. At the end of 1962, CORE proclaimed victory in the battle against Jim Crow interstate travel. By creating a crisis, the Freedom Rides had forced the Kennedy administration to act. But they also revealed the unwillingness of the federal government to fully enforce the law of the land. The jailings and brutality experienced by Freedom Riders made clear to the civil rights community the limits of moral persuasion alone for effecting change.

**Albany Movement** Coalition formed in 1961 in Albany, a small city in southwest Georgia, of activists from SNCC, the NAACP, and other local groups.

**28–2**
Charles Sherrod, *Student Nonviolent Coordinating Committee Memorandum* (1961)

## THE ALBANY MOVEMENT: THE LIMITS OF PROTEST

Where the federal government chose not to enforce the constitutional rights of black people, segregationist forces tenaciously held their ground, especially in the more remote areas of the Deep South. One such place was Albany, a small city in southwest Georgia, where activists from SNCC, the NAACP, and other local groups formed a coalition known as the **Albany Movement**. For more than a year, beginning in October 1961, thousands of Albany's black citizens marched, sat in, and boycotted as part of a citywide campaign to integrate public facilities and win voting rights. More than a thousand people spent time in jail. In December, the arrival of Martin Luther King Jr. and the SCLC transformed Albany into a national symbol of the struggle.

But the gains at Albany proved minimal. Most important, Albany police chief Laurie Pritchett shrewdly deprived the movement of the kind of national sympathy won by the Freedom Riders. Pritchett filled the jails with black demonstrators, kept their mistreatment to a minimum, and prevented white mobs from running wild. King himself was twice arrested in the summer of 1962, but Albany officials quickly freed him to avoid negative publicity. The Kennedy administration kept clear of the developments in Albany, hoping to help the gubernatorial campaign of "moderate" Democrat Carl Sanders. By late 1962 the Albany movement had collapsed. Albany showed that mass protest without violent white reaction and direct federal intervention could not end Jim Crow.

In contrast to the failure at Albany, a successful battle to integrate the University of Mississippi reinforced the importance of federal intervention for guaranteeing African American civil rights. In the fall of 1962 James Meredith, an Air Force veteran and a student at all-black Jackson State College, tried to register as the first black student at lily-white "Ole Miss." Defying a federal court order, Governor Ross Barnett personally blocked Meredith at the admissions office. When Barnett refused to assure Robert Kennedy that Meredith would be protected, the attorney general dispatched 500 federal marshals to the campus. Over the radio, Barnett encouraged resistance to the "oppressive power of the United States," and an enraged mob of several thousand whites, many of them armed, laid siege to the campus on September 30. A night of violence left two people dead and 160 marshals wounded, 28 from gunfire. President Kennedy ordered 5,000 Army troops onto the campus to stop the riot. A federal guard remained to protect Meredith, who graduated the following summer.

## THE MOVEMENT AT HIGH TIDE, 1963–65

**HOW DID** the civil rights movement intersect with national politics in the 1950s and 1960s?

myhistorylab
**Review Summary**

The tumultuous events of 1960–62 convinced civil rights strategists that segregation could not be dismantled merely through orderly protest and moral persuasion. Only comprehensive civil rights legislation, backed by federal power, could guarantee full citizenship rights for African Americans. To build the national consensus needed for new laws, civil rights activists looked for ways to gain broader support for their cause. By 1963, their sense of urgency had led them to plan dramatic confrontations that would expose the violence and terror routinely faced by southern blacks. With the whole country—indeed, the whole world—watching, the Movement reached the peak of its political and moral power.

### BIRMINGHAM

At the end of 1962, King and his SCLC allies decided to launch a new campaign against segregation in Birmingham, Alabama. Having failed in Albany, King and his aides looked for a way to shore up his leadership and inject new momentum into the freedom struggle. They needed a major victory. Birmingham, the most segregated big city in America, had a deep history of racial violence.

Working closely with local civil rights groups led by the longtime Birmingham activist Reverend Fred Shuttlesworth, the SCLC carefully planned its campaign. The strategy was to fill the city jails with protesters, boycott downtown department stores, and enrage Public Safety Commissioner Eugene "Bull" Connor, a die-hard segregationist. In April, King arrived with a manifesto demanding an end to racist hiring practices and segregated public accommodations and the creation of a biracial committee to oversee desegregation. Connor's police began jailing hundreds of demonstrators, including King himself, who defied a state court injunction against further protests. Held in solitary confinement for several days, King managed to write a response to a group of Birmingham clergy who had deplored the protests. King's "Letter from a Birmingham Jail" was soon widely reprinted and circulated as a pamphlet. It set out the key moral issues at stake, and scoffed at those who claimed the campaign was illegal and ill timed.

**28–14**
Martin Luther King Jr., *Letter from a Birmingham Jail* (1963)

After King's release on bail, the campaign intensified. The SCLC kept up the pressure by recruiting thousands of Birmingham's young students for a "children's crusade." In early May, Connor unleashed high-powered water cannons, billy clubs, and snarling police dogs to break up demonstrations. Millions of Americans reacted with horror to the violent scenes from Birmingham shown on national television. Many younger black people, especially from the city's poor and working-class districts, began to fight back, hurling bottles and bricks at police. On May 10, mediators from the Justice Department negotiated an uneasy truce. The SCLC agreed to an immediate end to the protests. In exchange, businesses would desegregate and begin hiring African Americans over the next three months, and a biracial city committee would oversee desegregation of public facilities.

King claimed the events in Birmingham represented "the most magnificent victory for justice we've ever seen in the Deep South." But white leaders such as Connor and Alabama's governor George Wallace denounced the agreement. A few days after the announcement, more than a thousand robed Ku Klux Klansmen burned a cross in a park on the outskirts of Birmingham. When bombs rocked SCLC headquarters and the home of King's brother, a Birmingham minister, enraged blacks took to the streets and pelted police and firefighters with stones and bottles. President Kennedy ordered 3,000 Army troops into the city and prepared to nationalize the Alabama National Guard. The violence receded, and white businesspeople and politicians began to carry out the agreed-upon pact. But in September a bomb killed four black girls in a Birmingham Baptist church, reminding the city and the world that racial harmony was still a long way off.

The Birmingham campaign and the other protests it sparked over the next seven months engaged more than 100,000 people and led to nearly 15,000 arrests. The civil rights community now drew support from millions of Americans, black and white, all inspired by the protesters and repelled by southern bigotry. At the same time, Birmingham changed the nature of black protest. The black unemployed and working poor who joined in the struggle brought a different perspective from that of the students, professionals, and members of the religious middle class who had dominated the Movement before Birmingham. They cared less about the philosophy of nonviolence and more about immediate gains in employment and housing and an end to police brutality.

## JFK AND THE MARCH ON WASHINGTON

The growth of black activism and of white support convinced President Kennedy the moment had come to press for sweeping civil rights legislation. On June 11 the president went on national television and offered his personal endorsement of the civil rights activism. The next week Kennedy asked Congress for a broad law that would ensure voting rights, outlaw segregation in public facilities, and bolster federal authority to deny funds for discriminatory programs. Knowing they would face a stiff fight from congressional conservatives, administration officials began an intense lobbying effort in support of the law. After three years of fence sitting, Kennedy finally committed his office and his political future to the civil rights cause.

Movement leaders lauded the president's initiative. Yet they understood that racial hatred still haunted the nation. Only hours after Kennedy's television speech, a gunman murdered Medgar Evers, leader of the Mississippi NAACP, outside his home in Jackson, Mississippi. To pressure Congress and demonstrate the urgency of their cause, a broad coalition of civil rights groups planned a massive, nonviolent **March on Washington**.

The Kennedy administration originally opposed the march, fearing it would jeopardize support for the president's civil rights bill in Congress. But as plans for the rally solidified, Kennedy reluctantly gave his approval. Leaders from the SCLC, the NAACP, SNCC, the Urban League, and CORE—the leading organizations in the civil rights community—put aside their tactical differences to forge a broad consensus for the event.

On August 28, 1963, more than a quarter of a million people, including 50,000 whites, gathered at the Lincoln Memorial to rally for "jobs and freedom." Union members, students, teachers, clergy, professionals, musicians, actors— Americans from all walks of life joined the largest political assembly in the nation's history until then. The sight of all those people holding hands and singing "We Shall Overcome," led by white folksinger Joan Baez, would not be easily forgotten, either by participants or by millions of television viewers. Martin Luther King Jr. provided the emotional climax to the march. Combining the democratic promise of the Declaration of Independence with the religious fervor of his Baptist heritage, King stirred the crowd and the nation with his dream for America.

The following year, at age 35, King received the Nobel Peace Prize, which both solidified his reputation as the premier voice of the Movement and added greatly to his stature within mainstream American culture. The award also demonstrated the truly global impact of the Movement he led.

## LBJ AND THE CIVIL RIGHTS ACT OF 1964

An extraordinary demonstration of interracial unity, the March on Washington stood as the high-water mark in the struggle for civil rights. It buoyed the spirits of Movement leaders, as well as of liberals pushing the new civil rights bill through Congress. But the assassination of John F. Kennedy on November 22, 1963, in Dallas threw an ominous cloud over the whole nation and the civil rights movement in particular.

Lyndon Baines Johnson (LBJ), Kennedy's successor, had never been much of a friend to civil rights. As a senator from Texas (1948–60, including six years as majority leader), Johnson had been one of the shrewdest and most powerful Democrats in Congress. Throughout the 1950s he had worked to obstruct the passage and enforcement of civil rights laws. But as vice president he had ably chaired Kennedy's working group on equal employment. Civil rights activists looked upon Johnson warily as he took over the Oval Office.

As president, Johnson realized that he faced a new political reality, created by the civil rights movement. Eager to unite the Democratic Party and prove

**28–5**

John Lewis, *Address at the March on Washington* (1963)

**March on Washington**   Historic gathering of over 250,000 people in Washington D.C. in 1963 marching for jobs and freedom.

himself as a national leader, he seized on civil rights as a golden political opportunity. Throughout the early months of 1964, the new president let it be known publicly and privately that he would brook no compromise on civil rights. Working with the president, the fifteen-year-old Leadership Conference on Civil Rights coordinated a sophisticated lobbying effort in Congress. Groups such as the NAACP, the AFL-CIO, the National Council of Churches, and the American Jewish Congress made the case for a strong civil rights bill. The House passed the bill in February by a 290–130 vote. The more difficult fight would be in the Senate, where a southern filibuster promised to block or weaken the bill. But by June, Johnson's persistence paid off. The southern filibuster collapsed.

On July 2, 1964, Johnson signed the **Civil Rights Act of 1964**. Every major provision had survived intact. This landmark law represented the most significant civil rights legislation since Reconstruction. It prohibited discrimination in most places of public accommodation; it banned discrimination in employment on the basis of race, color, religion, sex, or national origin; it outlawed bias in federally assisted programs; it authorized the Justice Department to institute suits to desegregate public schools and other facilities; and it provided technical and financial aid to communities desegregating their schools. The act also created the Equal Employment Opportunity Commission (EEOC) to investigate and litigate cases of job discrimination.

There were important unintended consequences of this landmark legislation as well. It gave legal foundation to affirmative action policies and to the assertion of equal rights for women and nonblack minorities. The EEOC, for example, became an important site for contesting both gender and racial discrimination in the workplace, receiving over 100,000 complaints a year by the 1970s. And on a political level LBJ was perhaps more prescient than he realized when he commented after signing the bill that the Civil Rights Act "delivered the South to the Republican Party." It took real political courage for Johnson, a Southern Democrat, to support the legislation as vigorously as he did, for the new law did indeed initiate a long-term political realignment that would transform the South from a solidly Democratic region to a solidly Republican one.

## MISSISSIPPI FREEDOM SUMMER

While Johnson and his liberal allies won the congressional battle for the new civil rights bill, activists in Mississippi mounted a far more radical and dangerous campaign than any yet attempted in the South. In the spring of 1964, a coalition of

**Civil Rights Act of 1964** Federal legislation that outlawed discrimination in public accommodations and employment on the basis of race, skin color, sex, religion, or national origin.

**28-6**
*The Civil Rights Act of 1964*

### QUICK REVIEW

**Johnson and Civil Rights**

- Johnson had worked to obstruct civil rights legislation in the 1950s.
- Saw civil rights for African Americans as a way of uniting the Democratic Party.
- Applied personal political skills to passage of Civil Rights Act of 1964.

**28-16**
*Letters from Mississippi Freedom Summer* (1964)

**Part of the** huge throng of marchers at the historic March on Washington for "jobs and freedom," August 28, 1963. The size of the crowd, the stirring oratory and song, and the live network television coverage produced one of the most memorable political demonstrations in the nation's history.

# OVERVIEW | Landmark Civil Rights Legislation, Supreme Court Decisions, and Executive Orders

| Year | Decision, Law, or Executive Order | Significance |
|------|-----------------------------------|--------------|
| 1939 | *Missouri* v. *ex. rel. Gaines* | Required University of Missouri Law School either to admit African Americans or build another fully equal law school |
| 1941 | Executive Order 8802 (by President Roosevelt) | Banned racial discrimination in defense industry and government offices; established Fair Employment Practices Committee to investigate violations |
| 1946 | *Morgan* v. *Virginia* | Ruled that segregation on interstate buses violated federal law and created an "undue burden" on interstate commerce |
| 1948 | Executive Order 9981 (by President Truman) | Desegregated the U.S. armed forces |
| 1950 | *McLaurin* v. *Oklahoma State Regents* | Ruled that forcing an African American student to sit, eat, and study in segregated facilities was unconstitutional because it inevitably created a "badge of inferiority" |
| 1950 | *Sweatt* v. *Painter* | Ruled that an inferior law school created by the University of Texas to serve African Americans violated their right to equal protection and ordered Herman Sweatt to be admitted to University of Texas Law School |
| 1954 | *Brown* v. *Board of Education of Topeka I* | Declared "separate educational facilities are inherently unequal," thus overturning *Plessy* v. *Ferguson* (1896) and the "separate but equal" doctrine as it applied to public schools |
| 1955 | *Brown* v. *Board of Education of Topeka II* | Ordered school desegregation to begin with "all deliberate speed," but offered no timetable |
| 1957 | Civil Rights Act | Created Civil Rights Division within the Justice Department |
| 1964 | Civil Rights Act | Prohibited discrimination in employment and most places of public accommodation on basis of race, color, religion, sex, or national origin; outlawed bias in federally assisted programs; created Equal Employment Opportunity Commission |
| 1965 | Voting Rights Act | Authorized federal supervision of voter registration in states and counties where fewer than half of voting age residents were registered; outlawed literacy and other discriminatory tests in voter registration |

**myhistorylab**

**Overview:** *Landmark Civil Rights Legislation, Supreme Court Decisions, and Executive Orders*

**Freedom Summer**  Voter registration effort in rural Mississippi organized by black and white civil rights workers in 1964.

workers led by SNCC launched the Freedom Summer project, an ambitious effort to register black voters and directly challenge the iron rule of segregation. Mississippi stood as the toughest test for the civil rights movement. It was the nation's poorest state and by most statistical measures the most backward, and it had remained largely untouched by the freedom struggle.

Bob Moses of SNCC and Dave Dennis of CORE planned **Freedom Summer** as a way of opening up this closed society. The project recruited over 900 volunteers, mostly white college students, to aid in voter registration, teach in "freedom schools," and help build a "Freedom Party" as an alternative to Mississippi's all-white Democratic Party. Organizers expected violence, which was precisely why they wanted white volunteers. Dave Dennis later explained their reasoning: "The death of a white college student would bring on more attention to what was going on than for a black college student getting it. That's cold, but that was also in another sense speaking the language of this country." Mississippi authorities prepared for the civil rights workers as if expecting a foreign army, beefing up state highway patrols and local police forces.

On June 21, while most project volunteers were still training in Ohio, three activists disappeared in Neshoba County, Mississippi, when they went to investigate the burning of a black church that was supposed to serve as a freedom school. Six weeks later, after a massive search belatedly ordered by President Johnson, FBI agents discovered the bodies of the three—northern white students Michael Schwerner and Andrew Goodman, and a local black activist, James Chaney—buried in an earthen dam. Over the summer, at least three other civil rights workers died violently. Project workers suffered 1,000 arrests, 80 beatings, 35 shooting incidents, and 30 bombings in homes, churches, and schools.

The project did manage to rivet national attention on Mississippi racism, and it won enormous sympathy from northern liberals. Among their concrete accomplishments, the volunteers could point with pride to more than forty freedom schools that brought classes in reading, arithmetic, politics, and African American history to thousands of black children. Some 60,000 black voters signed up to join the Mississippi Freedom Democratic Party (MFDP). In August 1964 the MFDP sent a slate of delegates to the Democratic National Convention looking to challenge the credentials of the all-white regular state delegation.

At the Democrats' Atlantic City convention, the idealism of Freedom Summer collided with the more cynical needs of the national Democratic Party. Concerned that Republicans might carry a number of southern states in November, Johnson opposed seating the MFDP because he wanted to avoid a divisive floor fight. Led by Senator Hubert Humphrey, whom LBJ had already picked as his running mate, Johnson's forces offered a compromise that would have given the MFDP two token seats on the floor. Bitter over what they saw as a betrayal, the MFDP delegates turned the offer down. Within SNCC, the defeat of the MFDP intensified African American disillusionment with the Democratic Party and the liberal establishment.

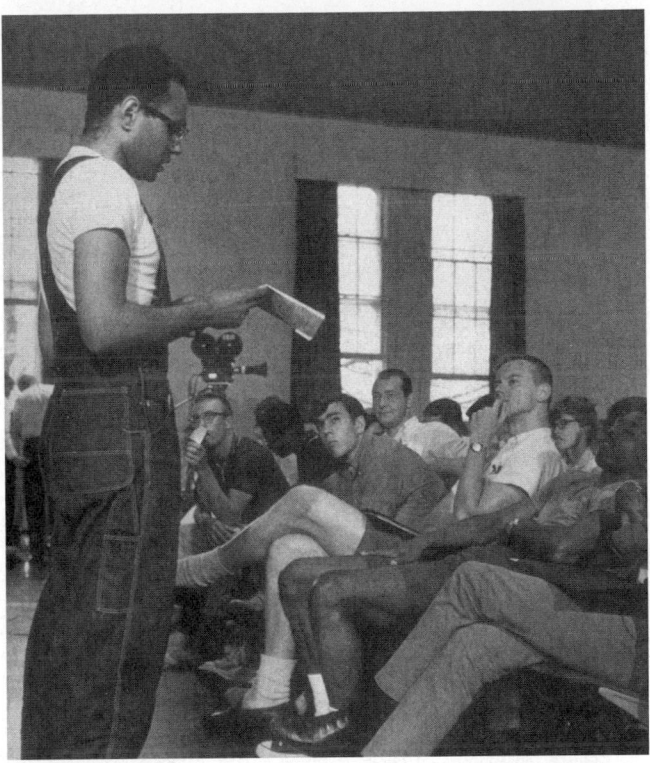

**Bob Moses of** the Student Nonviolent Coordinating Committee was one of the driving forces behind the 1964 Freedom Summer Project. Here he instructs student volunteers gathered in Oxford, Ohio, before they leave for voter registration and other community organizing work in Mississippi. Moses, who had been working for voting rights in Mississippi since 1961, played a key role in persuading SNCC to accept white volunteers from the North.

**28–15**
Fannie Lou Hamer, *Voting Rights in Mississippi* (1962–1964)

## MALCOLM X AND BLACK CONSCIOUSNESS

Frustrated with the limits of nonviolent protest and electoral politics, younger activists within SNCC found themselves increasingly drawn to the militant rhetoric and vision of Malcolm X, who since 1950 had been the preeminent spokesman for the black nationalist religious sect, the **Nation of Islam (NOI)**. Founded in depression-era Detroit by Elijah Muhammad, the NOI, like the followers of black-nationalist leader Marcus Garvey in the 1920s (see Chapter 23), aspired to create a self-reliant, highly disciplined, and proud community—a separate "nation" for black people. Elijah Muhammad preached a message of racial solidarity and self-help, criticized crime and drug use, and castigated whites as "blue-eyed devils" responsible for the world's evil. During the 1950s the NOI (also called Black Muslims) successfully organized in northern black communities, appealing especially to criminals, drug addicts, and others on the margins of urban life. It operated restaurants, retail stores, and schools as models for black economic self-sufficiency.

**Nation of Islam (NOI)** Religious movement among black Americans that emphasizes self-sufficiency, self-help, and separation from white society.

**Malcolm X (1925–65)** emerged in the early 1960s as the foremost advocate of racial unity and black nationalism. The Black Power movement, initiated in 1966 by SNCC members, was strongly influenced by Malcolm X.

The man known as Malcolm X had been born Malcolm Little in 1925 and raised in Lansing, Michigan. His father, a preacher and a follower of Marcus Garvey, was killed in a racist attack by local whites. In his youth, Malcolm led a life of petty crime, eventually serving a seven-year prison term for burglary. While in jail he educated himself and converted to the Nation of Islam. He took the surname "X" to symbolize his original African family name, lost through slavery. Emerging from jail in 1952, he became a dynamic organizer, editor, and speaker for the Nation of Islam. He spoke frequently on college campuses as well on the street corners of black neighborhoods like New York's Harlem. He encouraged his audiences to take pride in their African heritage and to consider armed self-defense rather than relying solely on nonviolence—in short, to break free of white domination "by any means necessary."

Malcolm ridiculed the integrationist goals of the civil rights movement. Black Muslims, he told audiences, do not want "to integrate into this corrupt society, but to separate from it, to a land of our own, where we can reform ourselves, lift up our moral standards, and try to be godly."

In 1964, Malcolm X broke with the Nation of Islam. He made the pilgrimage to Mecca, the Muslim holy city, where he met Islamic peoples of all colors and underwent a "radical alteration in my whole outlook about 'white' men." He returned to the United States as El-Hajj Malik El-Shabazz, abandoned his black separatist views, and founded the Organization of Afro-American Unity. Malcolm now looked for common ground with the civil rights movement, addressing a Mississippi Freedom Democrats rally in Harlem and meeting with SNCC activists. He stressed the international links between the civil rights struggle in America and the problems facing emerging African nations. On February 21, 1965, Malcolm X was assassinated while giving a speech at Harlem's Audubon Ballroom. His assailants were members of a New Jersey branch of the NOI, possibly infiltrated by the FBI.

In his death he became a martyr for the idea that soon became known as Black Power. As much as anyone, Malcolm X pointed the way to a new black consciousness that celebrated black history, black culture, African heritage, and black self-sufficiency.

## SELMA AND THE VOTING RIGHTS ACT OF 1965

28–8
Lyndon B. Johnson,
*Commencement Address at
Howard University* (1965)

Lyndon Johnson won reelection in 1964 by a landslide, capturing 61 percent of the popular vote. Of the 6 million black people who voted in the election—2 million more than in 1960—an overwhelming 94 percent cast their ballots for Johnson. Republican candidate Barry Goldwater managed to carry only his home state of Arizona and five Deep South states, where fewer than 45 percent of eligible black people could vote. With Democrats in firm control of both the Senate and the House, civil rights leaders believed the time was ripe for further legislative gains. There had already been some progress toward guaranteeing voting rights with the 1964 ratification of the Twenty-Fourth Amendment to the Constitution, outlawing the poll tax or any other tax as a condition of voting. Now Johnson and his staff began drafting a tough voting rights bill in late 1964, partly with an eye toward countering Republican gains among Deep South whites with newly registered black Democratic voters (see Map 28.2).

# MAP EXPLORATION

To explore an interactive version of this map, go to **http://www.prenhall.com/faraghertlc/map28.2**

Percentages by state: Virginia 23%/52%, North Carolina 38%/44%, Tennessee 59%/66%, Arkansas 37%/81%, South Carolina 16%/46%, Georgia 29%/64%, Alabama 14%/55%, Mississippi 5%/59%, Louisiana 31%/57%, Texas 35%/68%, Florida 39%/53%

*Gulf of Mexico*   *ATLANTIC OCEAN*

% Registered Voters, Black Voting-age Population
1960
1971

**MAP 28.2**
**Impact of the Voting Rights Act of 1965**  Voter registration among African Americans in the South increased significantly between 1960 and 1971.

IN WHICH states was the increase in registered African American voters particularly dramatic?

Once again, Movement leaders decided to create a crisis that would arouse national indignation, pressure Congress, and force federal action. King and his aides chose Selma, Alabama, as their target. Selma, a city of 27,000 some fifty miles west of Montgomery, had a notorious record of preventing black voting. In 1963, local activists had invited SNCC workers to aid voter registration efforts in the community. But they had met a violent reception from county sheriff Jim Clark. King arrived in Selma in January 1965, just after accepting the Nobel Peace Prize in Oslo. "We are not asking, we are demanding the ballot," he declared. King, the SCLC staff, and SNCC workers led daily marches on the Dallas County Courthouse, where hundreds of black citizens tried to get their names added to voter lists. By early February, Clark had imprisoned more than 3,000 protesters.

Despite the brutal beating of Reverend James Bevel, a key SCLC strategist, and the killing of Jimmy Lee Jackson, a young black demonstrator in nearby Marion, the SCLC failed to arouse the level of national indignation it sought. Consequently, in early March SCLC staffers called on black activists to march from Selma to Montgomery, where they planned to deliver a list of grievances to Governor Wallace. On Sunday, March 7, while King preached to his church in Atlanta,

**Voting Rights Act** Legislation in 1965 that overturned a variety of practices by which states systematically denied voter registration to minorities.

a group of 600 marchers crossed the Pettus Bridge on the Alabama River, on their way to Montgomery. A group of mounted, heavily armed county and state lawmen blocked their path and ordered them to turn back. When the marchers did not move, the lawmen attacked with billy clubs and tear gas, driving the protesters back over the bridge in a bloody rout. More than fifty marchers had to be treated in local hospitals.

The dramatic "Bloody Sunday" attack received extensive coverage on network television, prompting a national uproar. Demands for federal intervention poured into the White House from all over the country. King issued a public call for civil rights supporters to come to Selma for a second march on Montgomery. But a federal court temporarily enjoined the SCLC from proceeding with the march. King found himself trapped. He reluctantly accepted a face-saving compromise: in return for a promise from Alabama authorities not to harm marchers, King would lead his followers across the Pettus Bridge, stop, pray briefly, and then turn back. This plan outraged the more militant SNCC activists and sharpened their distrust of King and the SCLC.

But just when it seemed the Selma movement might die, white racist violence revived it. A gang of white toughs attacked four white Unitarian ministers who had come to Selma to participate in the march. One of them, Reverend James J. Reeb of Boston, died of multiple skull fractures. On March 15, President Johnson delivered a televised address to a joint session of Congress to request passage of a voting rights bill. Johnson also prevailed upon federal judge Frank Johnson to issue a ruling allowing the march to proceed, and he warned Governor Wallace not to interfere.

In August 1965 President Johnson signed the **Voting Rights Act** into law. It authorized federal supervision of registration in states and counties where fewer than half of voting-age residents were registered. It also outlawed literacy and other discriminatory tests that had been used to prevent blacks from registering to vote. Between 1964 and 1968, black registrants in Mississippi leaped from 7 percent to 59 percent of the statewide black population; in Alabama, from 24 percent to 57 percent. In those years the number of southern black voters grew from 1 million to 3.1 million. For the first time in their lives, black Southerners in hundreds of small towns and rural communities could enjoy full participation in American politics. Ten years after the Montgomery bus boycott, the civil rights movement had reached a peak of national influence and interracial unity.

Yet even amid this triumph, the growing mood of desperation among African Americans in northern ghettoes suggested the limits of the Movement and interracial unity. There had been a violent uprising in New York's Harlem in the summer of 1964 and a far more widespread and destructive rebellion in the Watts section of Los Angeles in August 1965 (see Chapter 29). These marked the first of the "long, hot summer" uprisings that would alienate many white citizens who had been sympathetic to the nonviolent civil rights struggle. They served notice as well that the growing frustration and alienation of northern blacks, increasingly defined by a militant turn to the rhetoric of "black power," could not be addressed with the same principles, tactics, and solutions that had made the southern civil rights movement successful.

## CIVIL RIGHTS BEYOND BLACK AND WHITE

**HOW DID** America's other minorities respond to the African American struggle for civil rights?

**myhistorylab**
Review Summary

Other minorities as well had long been denied their civil rights. After World War II, Latinos, Indian peoples, and Asian Americans began making their own halting efforts to improve their political, legal, and economic status. They faced strong opposition from institutional racism and various economic interests that benefited from keeping these groups in a subordinate position.

## MEXICAN AMERICANS AND MEXICAN IMMIGRANTS

The Mexican American community in the West and Southwest included both long-time U.S. citizens—who found white authorities nonetheless unwilling to recognize their rights—and noncitizen immigrants from Mexico. After World War II, several Mexican American political organizations sought to secure equal rights and equal opportunity for their community by stressing its American identity. The most important of these groups were the League of United Latin American Citizens (LULAC), launched in Texas in 1928, and the GI Forum, founded in Texas in 1948 by Mexican American veterans of World War II. Both emphasized learning English, assimilating into American society, improving education, and voting to gain political power. LULAC successfully pursued two important legal cases that anticipated *Brown* v. *Board of Education*. In *Mendez* v. *Westminster*, a 1947 California case, and in the 1948 *Delgado* case in Texas, the Supreme Court upheld lower-court rulings that declared segregation of Mexican Americans unconstitutional. Like *Brown*, these two decisions did not immediately end segregation, but they offered pathbreaking legal and psychological victories to Mexican American activists.

Mexican migration to the United States increased dramatically during and after World War II. The *bracero* program, a cooperative effort between the U.S. and Mexican governments, brought some 300,000 Mexicans to the United States during the war as temporary agricultural and railroad workers. American agribusiness came to depend on Mexicans as a key source of cheap farm labor, and the program continued after the war. Many *braceros* and their children became American citizens, but most returned to Mexico. Another group of postwar Mexican immigrants were the *mojados*, or "wetbacks," so called because many swam the Rio Grande to enter the United States illegally.

This continued flow of immigrant workers into the Southwest heightened tensions within the Mexican American community. Both LULAC and the GI Forum contended that Mexican American civil rights activists needed to focus their efforts on American citizens of Mexican descent. Yet within Mexican American communities, where citizens and noncitizens shared language and work experience and made families together, this distinction had always been blurry.

In 1954, trying to curb the flow of undocumented immigrants from Mexico, the Eisenhower administration launched the massive "Operation Wetback." For three years, Immigration and Naturalization Service (INS) agents rounded up some 3.7 million allegedly undocumented migrants and sent them back over the border. INS agents made little effort to distinguish so-called illegals from *braceros*

**Delegates to the** 1948 National Convention of the League of United Latin American Citizens met in Kingsville, Texas. After World War II, LULAC grew to about 15,000 members active in 200 local councils, mostly in Texas and California.

and Mexican American citizens. Many families were broken up, and thousands who had lived in the United States for a decade or more found themselves deported. Many deportees were denied basic civil liberties, such as due process, and suffered physical abuse and intimidation.

The government campaign against aliens pushed LULAC, the GI Forum, and other activist groups to change their strategy in a critical way. The campaign to win full civil rights for American citizens of Mexican descent would increasingly be linked to improving the lives—and asserting the rights—of all Mexican immigrants, both documented and undocumented. By the 1960s a new civil rights movement emerged, *la raza*, based on the shared ethnicity and historical experiences of the broader Mexican American community.

## PUERTO RICANS

The United States seized Puerto Rico in 1898, during the final stages of the Spanish-American War. The Jones Act of 1917 made the island an unincorporated territory of the United States and granted U.S. citizenship to all Puerto Ricans. Over the next several decades, Puerto Rico's economic base shifted from a diversified, subsistence-oriented agriculture to a single export crop—sugar. U.S. absentee owners dominated the sugar industry, claiming most of the island's arable land, previously tilled by small farmers growing crops for local consumption. Puerto Rico's sugar industry grew enormously profitable, but few island residents benefited from this expansion. By the 1930s, unemployment and poverty were widespread and the island was forced to import its foodstuffs.

Small communities of Puerto Rican migrants had begun to form in New York City during the 1920s. During World War II, labor shortages led the federal government to sponsor the recruitment of Puerto Rican workers for industrial jobs in New Jersey, Philadelphia, and Chicago. But the "great migration" took place from 1945 to 1964. During these two decades the number of Puerto Ricans living on the mainland jumped from less than 100,000 to roughly 1 million. Economic opportunity was the chief impetus for this migration, for the island suffered from high unemployment and low wages.

The advent of direct air service between Puerto Rico and New York in 1945 made the city easily accessible. By 1970 there were about 800,000 Puerto Ricans in New York—more than 10 percent of the city's population. New Puerto Rican communities also took root in Connecticut, Massachusetts, New Jersey, and the Midwest. Puerto Ricans frequently circulated between the island and the mainland, often returning home when economic conditions on the mainland were less favorable.

The experience of Puerto Rican migrants both resembled and differed from that of other immigrant groups in significant ways. Like Mexican immigrants, Puerto Ricans were foreign in language, culture, and experience, yet unlike Mexicans they entered the continental United States as citizens. Many Puerto Ricans were also black. In New York, Puerto Ricans found themselves barred from most craft unions, excluded from certain neighborhoods, and forced to take jobs largely in the low-paying garment industry and service trades. Puerto Rican children were not well served by a public school system insensitive to language differences and too willing to track Spanish-speaking students into obsolete vocational programs.

By the early 1970s, Puerto Rican families were substantially poorer on average than the total U.S. population, and they had the lowest median income of any Latino group. The steep decline in manufacturing jobs and in the garment industry in New York during the 1960s and 1970s hit the Puerto Rican community especially hard. So did the city's fiscal crisis, which brought sharp cuts in funding for schools, health care, libraries, government jobs, and other public services traditionally avail-

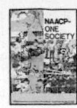

able to immigrant groups. The structural shift in the U.S. economy away from manufacturing and toward service and high-technology jobs reinforced the Puerto Rican community's goal of improving educational opportunities for its members.

## JAPANESE AMERICANS

The harsh relocation program of World War II devastated the Japanese American community on the West Coast (see Chapter 25). But the war against Nazism also helped weaken older notions of white superiority and racism. During the war, the state of California had aggressively enforced an alien land law by confiscating property declared illegally held by Japanese. In November 1946 a proposition supporting the law appeared on the state ballot. Thanks in part to a campaign by the Japanese American Citizens League (JACL) reminding voters of the wartime contributions of Nisei (second-generation Japanese American) soldiers, voters overwhelmingly rejected the referendum.

The 1952 Immigration and Nationality Act (see Chapter 26) removed the old ban against Japanese immigration and also made Issei (first-generation Japanese Americans) eligible for naturalized citizenship. By 1965 some 46,000 immigrant Japanese, most of them elderly Issei, had taken their citizenship oaths.

## INDIAN PEOPLES

The postwar years also brought significant changes in the status and lives of Indian peoples. Congress reversed New Deal policies that had stressed Indian sovereignty and cultural independence. Responding to a variety of pressure groups, including mining and other economic interests wishing to exploit natural resources on reservations, Congress adopted a policy known as "termination," designed to cancel Indian treaties and terminate sovereignty rights. In 1953, Congress passed **House Concurrent Resolution 108**, which allowed Congress to terminate a tribe as a political entity by passing legislation specific to that tribe. Supporters of termination had varied motives, but the policy added up to the return of enforced assimilation for solving the "Indian problem."

Between 1954 and 1962, Congress passed twelve termination bills covering more than sixty tribes, nearly all in the West. Even when tribes consented to their own termination, they discovered that dissolution brought unforeseen problems. For example, members of the Klamaths of Oregon and the Paiutes of Utah received large cash payments from the division of tribal assets. But after these one-time payments were spent, members had to take poorly paid, unskilled jobs to survive. Many Indian peoples became dependent on state social services and slipped into poverty and alcoholism.

Along with termination, the federal government gave greater emphasis to a relocation program aimed at speeding up assimilation. The Bureau of Indian Affairs encouraged reservation Indians to relocate to cities, where they were provided with housing and jobs. For some, relocation meant assimilation, intermarriage with whites, and loss of tribal identity. Others, homesick and unable to adjust to an alien culture and place, either returned to reservations or wound up on the margins of city life. Still others regularly traveled back and forth. In some respects, this urban migration paralleled the larger postwar shift of rural peoples to cities and suburbs.

Indians increasingly came to see termination as a policy geared mainly to exploiting resources on Indian lands. By the early 1960s, a new movement was emerging to defend Indian sovereignty. The National Congress of American Indians (NCAI) condemned termination, calling for a review of federal policies and a return to self-determination. The NCAI led a political and educational campaign that challenged the goal of assimilation and created a new awareness among

**House Concurrent Resolution 108**
Resolution passed in 1953 that allowed Congress to pass legislation to terminate a specific tribe as a political entity.

**A Korean couple** working behind the counter of their newly opened restaurant in Los Angeles, ca. 2000. In the thirty-five years after the Immigration and Nationality Act of 1965, the city's Asian American population had grown to over 1.2 million, including the largest Korean community outside of Korea.

**Termination**

◆ Cancellation of treaties and sover-eignty rights under pressure from mining and other economic interests.

◆ 1954–1962: Termination bills passed covering sixty tribes.

◆ Termination contributed to poverty and social problems among Indian peoples.

**Immigration and Nationality Act**
Act passed in 1965 that abolished national origin quotas and established overall hemisphere quotas.

white people that Indians had the right to remain Indians. When the termination policy ended in the early 1960s, it had affected only about 3 percent of federally recognized Indian peoples.

Taking their cue from the civil rights movement, Indian activists used the court system to reassert sovereign rights. A series of Supreme Court decisions, culminating in *United States* v. *Wheeler* (1978), reasserted the principle of "unique and limited" sovereignty. The Court recognized tribal independence except where limited by treaty or Congress.

The Indian population had been growing since the early years of the century, but most reservations had trouble making room for a new generation. Indians suffered increased rates of poverty, chronic unemployment, alcoholism, and poor health. The average Indian family in the early 1960s earned only one-third of the average family income in the United States. Those who remained in the cities usually became "ethnic Indians," identifying themselves more as simply "Indians" than as members of specific tribes. By the late 1960s, ethnic Indians had begun emphasizing civil rights over tribal rights, making common cause with African Americans and other minorities.

## REMAKING THE GOLDEN DOOR: THE IMMIGRATION AND NATIONALITY ACT OF 1965

The egalitarian political climate created by the civil rights movement nurtured efforts to modernize and reform the country's immigration policies. In 1965 Congress passed a new **Immigration and Nationality Act**, abolishing the national origins quotas that had been in place since the 1920s and substituting overall hemispheric limits: 120,000 visas annually for immigrants from the Western Hemisphere and 170,000 for those from the Eastern Hemisphere (with a 20,000 limit from any single country). The act was intended to redress the grievances of Eastern and Southern European ethnic groups who had been largely shut out since 1924.

Exempted from numerical quotas were immigrants seeking family reunification with American citizens or resident aliens. In addition, preferences to those with specialized job skills and training, in fields like medicine and engineering, were extended to people from the nations of the Eastern Hemisphere. The high priority given family reunification created an unprecedented cycle of "chain immigration and sponsorship" of people seeking to join relatives already in the United States. As initial immigrants attained permanent resident or citizenship status, they would sponsor family members and relatives to come over. Once these family members and relatives arrived in the United States and became resident aliens or citizens, they in turn could sponsor their family members, and so on.

The consequences for Asian American communities in particular were profound. The number of Asian Americans soared from about 1 million in 1965 to 11 million by the end of the century. Immigrants from India and the Philippines included a high percentage of health care professionals, whereas many Chinese and Korean immigrants found work in professional and managerial occupations as well as their own small businesses. At the same time, low-skilled and impover-

## CHRONOLOGY

**1941** Executive Order 8802 forbids racial discrimination in defense industries and government

**1946** *In Morgan* v. *Virginia*, U.S. Supreme Court rules that segregation on interstate buses is unconstitutional

President Harry Truman creates the President's Committee on Civil Rights

**1947** Jackie Robinson becomes the first African American on a major league baseball team

**1948** President Truman issues executive order desegregating the armed forces

**1954** In *Brown* v. *Board of Education*, Supreme Court rules segregated schools inherently unequal

**1955** Supreme Court rules that school desegregation must proceed "with all deliberate speed"

Montgomery bus boycott begins

**1956** Montgomery bus boycott ends in victory as the Supreme Court affirms a district court ruling that segregation on buses is unconstitutional

**1957** Southern Christian Leadership Conference (SCLC) is founded

President Dwight Eisenhower sends in federal troops to protect African American students integrating Little Rock, Arkansas, high school

**1960** Sit-in movement begins as four college students sit at a lunch counter in Greensboro, North Carolina, and ask to be served

Student Nonviolent Coordinating Committee (SNCC) founded

Board of Indian Commissioners is created

**1961** Freedom Rides begin

**1962** James Meredith integrates the University of Mississippi

The Albany movement fails to end segregation in Albany, Georgia

**1963** SCLC initiates campaign to desegregate Birmingham, Alabama

Medgar Evers, leader of the Mississippi NAACP, is assassinated

March on Washington; Martin Luther King Jr. delivers his historic "I Have a Dream" speech

**1964** Mississippi Freedom Summer project brings students to Mississippi to teach and register voters

President Johnson signs the Civil Rights Act of 1964

Civil rights workers Michael Schwerner, James Chaney, and Andrew Goodman are found buried in Philadelphia, Mississippi

Mississippi Freedom Democratic Party (MFDP) is denied seats at the 1964 Democratic Presidential Convention

**1965** SCLC and SNCC begin voter registration campaign in Selma, Alabama

Malcolm X is assassinated

Civil rights marchers walk from Selma to Montgomery

Voting Rights Act of 1965 is signed into law

Immigration and Nationality Act

---

ished Asians poured into the "Chinatowns" and "Koreatowns" of cities like New York and Los Angeles, taking jobs in restaurants, hotels, and garment manufacturing. Four times as many Asians settled in the United States in this period as in the entire previous history of the nation.

The 1965 act also created conditions that increased undocumented immigration from Latin America. The new limits on Western Hemisphere migration, along with the simultaneous ending of the *bracero* program, tempted many thousands to enter the United States illegally. The Immigration and Naturalization Service arrested and deported 500,000 undocumented aliens each year in the decade following the act, most of them from Mexico, Central America, and the Caribbean. By the 1980s, more than 80 percent of all legal immigrants to the United States came from either Asia or Latin America; if one included illegal immigrants, the figure would surpass 90 percent.

## CONCLUSION

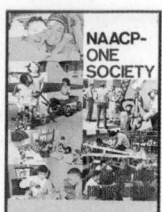

The mass movement for civil rights was arguably the most important domestic event in twentieth-century American history. The struggle that began in Montgomery, Alabama, in December 1955 ultimately transformed race relations in thousands of American communities. By the early 1960s this community-based movement had placed civil rights at the very center of national political life. It achieved its greatest successes by invoking the Constitution—the supreme law of the land—to destroy legal segregation and win individual freedom for African Americans. The Civil Rights Act of 1964 and the Voting Rights Act of 1965 testified to the power of an African American and white liberal coalition. Yet the persistence of racism, poverty, and ghetto slums challenged a central assumption of liberalism: that equal protection of constitutional rights would give all Americans equal opportunities in life. By the mid-1960s, many black people had begun to question the core values of liberalism, the benefits of alliance with whites, and the philosophy of nonviolence. At the same time, a conservative white backlash against the gains made by African Americans further weakened the liberal political consensus.

In challenging the persistence of widespread poverty and institutional racism, the civil rights movement called for deep structural changes in American life. By 1967, Martin Luther King Jr. was articulating a broad and radical vision linking the struggle against racial injustice to other defects in American society. "The black revolution," he argued, "is much more than a struggle for the rights of Negroes. It is forcing America to face all its interrelated flaws—racism, poverty, militarism, and materialism. It is exposing evils that are deeply rooted in the whole structure of our society." Curing these ills would prove far more difficult than ending legal segregation.

## REVIEW QUESTIONS

1. What were the key legal and political antecedents to the civil rights struggle in the 1940s and early 1950s? What organizations played the most central role? Which tactics continued to be used, and which were abandoned?

2. How did African American communities challenge legal segregation in the South? Compare the strategies of key organizations, such as the NAACP, SNCC, SCLC, and CORE.

3. Discuss the varieties of white resistance to the civil rights movement. Which were most effective in slowing the drive for equality?

4. Analyze the civil rights movement's complex relationship with the national Democratic Party between 1948 and 1964. How was the party transformed by its association with the movement? What political gains and losses did that association entail?

5. What legal and institutional impact did the movement have on American life? How did it change American culture and politics? Where did it fail?

6. What relationship did the African Americans who struggled for civil rights have with other American minorities? How—if at all—did these minorities benefit? Did they build their own versions of the movement?

## KEY TERMS

Flashcard Review

Albany Movement (p. 804)
*Brown* v. *Board of Education* (p. 794)
Civil Rights Act of 1964 (p. 807)

Congress of Racial Equality (CORE) (p. 801)
Freedom Summer (p. 808)

## RECOMMENDED READING

Raymond Arsenault, *Freedom Riders: 1961 and the Struggle for Racial Justice* (2006). A new and definitive account of this pivotal moment in Movement history, Arsenault demonstrates how the Freedom Rides both galvanized national and international attention and inspired local activists around the South.

Thomas Borstelmann, *The Cold War and the Color Line: American Race Relations in the Global Arena* (2001). Analyzes how presidents from Harry S. Truman to George H. W. Bush have responded to the civil rights movement in the context of Cold War politics and the fight against colonialism and white supremacy in Africa.

Taylor Branch, *Parting the Waters: America in the King Years, 1954–1963* (1988); *Pillar of Fire: America in the King Years, 1963–1965* (1998). A deeply researched and monumental narrative history of the southern civil rights movement organized around the life and influence of Reverend Martin Luther King Jr.

Clayborne Carson et al., eds., *Reporting Civil Rights* (2003). A wide-ranging compilation of contemporary reportage on the movement and resistance to it.

Roger Daniels, *Guarding the Golden Door: American Immigration Policy and Immigrants Since 1882* (2004). A comprehensive history, including excellent coverage of the legislative and political battles behind post–World War II changes in immigration laws.

Mary L. Dudziak, *Cold War Civil Rights: Race and the Image of American Democracy* (2000). Excellent analysis of the connections between the struggle for racial equality in America and the nation's contest with communism abroad.

Aldon D. Morris, *The Origins of the Civil Rights Movement: Black Communities Organizing for Change* (1984). An important study combining history and social theory. Morris emphasizes the key role of ordinary black people, acting through their churches and other community organizations before 1960.

Howell Raines, *My Soul Is Rested: Movement Days in the Deep South Remembered* (1977). The best oral history of the civil rights movement, drawing from a wide range of participants and points of view. It is brilliantly edited by Raines, who covered the events as a journalist.

Jason Sokol, *There Goes My Everything: White Southerners in the Age of Civil Rights, 1945–1975* (2006). A sophisticated new study examining the range and complexity of white Southerners' encounters with the civil rights movement and the momentous changes it wrought.

myhistorylab™
Where it's a good time to connect to the past!

For study resources for this chapter, go to **www.myhistorylab.com** and choose *Out of Many, Teaching and Learning Classroom Edition.* You will find a wealth of study and review material for this chapter, including pretests and posttests, customized study plan, key-term review flash cards, interactive map and document activities, and documents for analysis.

# The Quest for African American Equality

Booker T. Washington was a leading African American educator in the late 19th century. Born into slavery, he would rise to the position of principal of the Tuskegee Normal Institute (teacher's college) in Alabama, later Tuskegee University. Washington's proposed that African Americans accept the racial separation of Jim Crow laws and the refusal of southern states to grant them voting rights for the time being in exchange for immediate guarantees of economic security and the right to work in industry and agriculture. Against critics angered by his temporary acceptance of Jim Crow, Washington explained that any attempt to challenge segregation would be disastrous for blacks who could later use their enhanced economic status to effect permanent change.

IN THE late 19th and early 20th centuries, Booker T. Washington and W.E.B. Du Bois both held strong positions of leadership in a segregationist society. How and in what manner were the goals of either man like those of Dr. Martin Luther King, Jr. during the civil rights movement of the 1950s and 1960s? How do the style and techniques of both men compare to those used by Dr. King?

W. E. B. Du Bois was among Washington's strongest critics and a founder of the Niagara Movement. Du Bois was the first black graduate of Harvard University. He was a principal in establishing the National Association for the Advancement of Colored People (NAACP) in 1909 and became its director of publications in 1910. Du Bois argued that segregation should be confronted directly and aggressively and was in complete opposition to a position of accommodation.

The Reverend Dr. Martin Luther King, Jr., was the foremost civil rights leader of the 20th century. Beginning with the Montgomery Bus Boycott (Alabama) in 1955 that ended with a U.S. Supreme Court decision banning segregation in all forms of public transportation, King conducted an activist civil rights movement that challenged Jim Crow on both the social and political fronts in the South. King was instrumental in the establishment of the Southern Christian Leadership Conference in 1957 and a civil rights program that was founded on the philosophy of nonviolent civil disobedience based on the teachings of both Mahatma Gandhi and Henry David Thoreau. ■

---

## JUSTICE JOHN MARSHALL HARLAN, DISSENTING OPINION, *PLESSY V. FERGUSON* (1896)

IF EVILS will result from the commingling of the two races upon public highways established for the benefit of all, they will be infinitely less than those that will surely come from state legislation regulating the enjoyment of civil rights upon the basis of race. We boast of the freedom enjoyed by our people above all other peoples. But it is difficult to reconcile that boast with a state of the law which, practically, puts the brand of servitude and degradation upon a large class of our fellow citizens,-our equals before the law. The thin disguise of 'equal' accommodations for passengers in railroad coaches will not mislead any one, nor atone for the wrong this day done....

'People of the United States,' for whom, and by whom through representatives, our government is administered. Such a system is inconsistent with the guaranty given by the constitution to each state of a republican form of government, and may be stricken down by congressional action, or by the courts in the discharge of their solemn duty to maintain the supreme law of the land, anything in the constitution or laws of any state to the contrary notwithstanding.

For the reason stated, I am constrained to withhold my assent from the opinion and judgment of the majority. ■

## Booker T. Washington, Atlanta Compromise Speech, 1895

**The wisest** among my race understand that the agitation of questions of social equality is the extremist folly, and that progress in the enjoyment of all the privileges that will come to us must be the result of severe and constant struggle rather than of artificial forcing. No race that has anything to contribute to the markets of the world is long in any degree ostracized. It is important and right that all privileges of the law be ours, but it is vastly more important that we be prepared for the exercise of these privileges. The opportunity to earn a dollar in a factory just now is worth infinitely more than the opportunity to spend a dollar in an opera-house. ∎

## W.E.B. Du Bois, Of Mr. Booker T. Washington and Others (1903)

**The black** men of America have a duty to perform, a duty stern and delicate, - a forward movement to oppose a part of the work of their greatest leader. So far as Mr. Washington preaches Thrift, Patience, and Industrial Training for the masses, we must hold up his hands and strive with him, rejoicing in his honors and glorying in the strength of this Joshua called of God and of man to lead the headless host. But so far as Mr. Washington apologizes for injustice, North or South, does not rightly value the privilege and duty of voting, belittles the emasculating effects of caste distinctions, and opposes the higher training and ambition of our brighter minds, – so far as he, the South, or the Nation, does this, - we must unceasingly and firmly oppose them. By every civilized and peaceful method we must strive for the rights which the world accords to men, clinging unwaveringly to those great words which the sons of the Fathers would fain forget: "We hold these truths to be self-evident: That all men are created equal; that they are endowed by their Creator with certain unalienable rights; that among these are life, liberty, and the pursuit of happiness." ∎

## Martin Luther King, Jr., I have a Dream, August 28, 1963

**Go back** to Mississippi, go back to Alabama, go back to South Carolina, go back to Georgia, go back to Louisiana, go back to the slums and ghettos of our northern cities, knowing that somehow this situation can and will be changed....

I have a dream that one day this nation will rise up and live out the true meaning of its creed: "We hold these truths to be self-evident: that all men are created equal."

I have a dream that one day on the red hills of Georgia the sons of former slaves and the sons of former slave owners will be able to sit down together at the table of brotherhood.

I have a dream that one day even the state of Mississippi, a state sweltering with the heat of injustice, sweltering with the heat of oppression, will be transformed into an oasis of freedom and justice....

I have a dream that one day, down in Alabama, with its vicious racists, with its governor having his lips dripping with the words of interposition and nullification; one day right there in Alabama, little black boys and black girls will be able to join hands with little white boys and white girls as sisters and brothers....

This is our hope. This is the faith that I go back to the South with. With this faith we will be able to hew out of the mountain of despair a stone of hope....

And when this happens, when we allow freedom to ring, when we let it ring from every village and every hamlet, from every state and every city, we will be able to speed up that day when all of God's children, black men and white men, Jews and Gentiles, Protestants and Catholics, will be able to join hands and sing in the words of the old Negro spiritual, "Free at last! free at last! thank God Almighty, we are free at last!" ∎

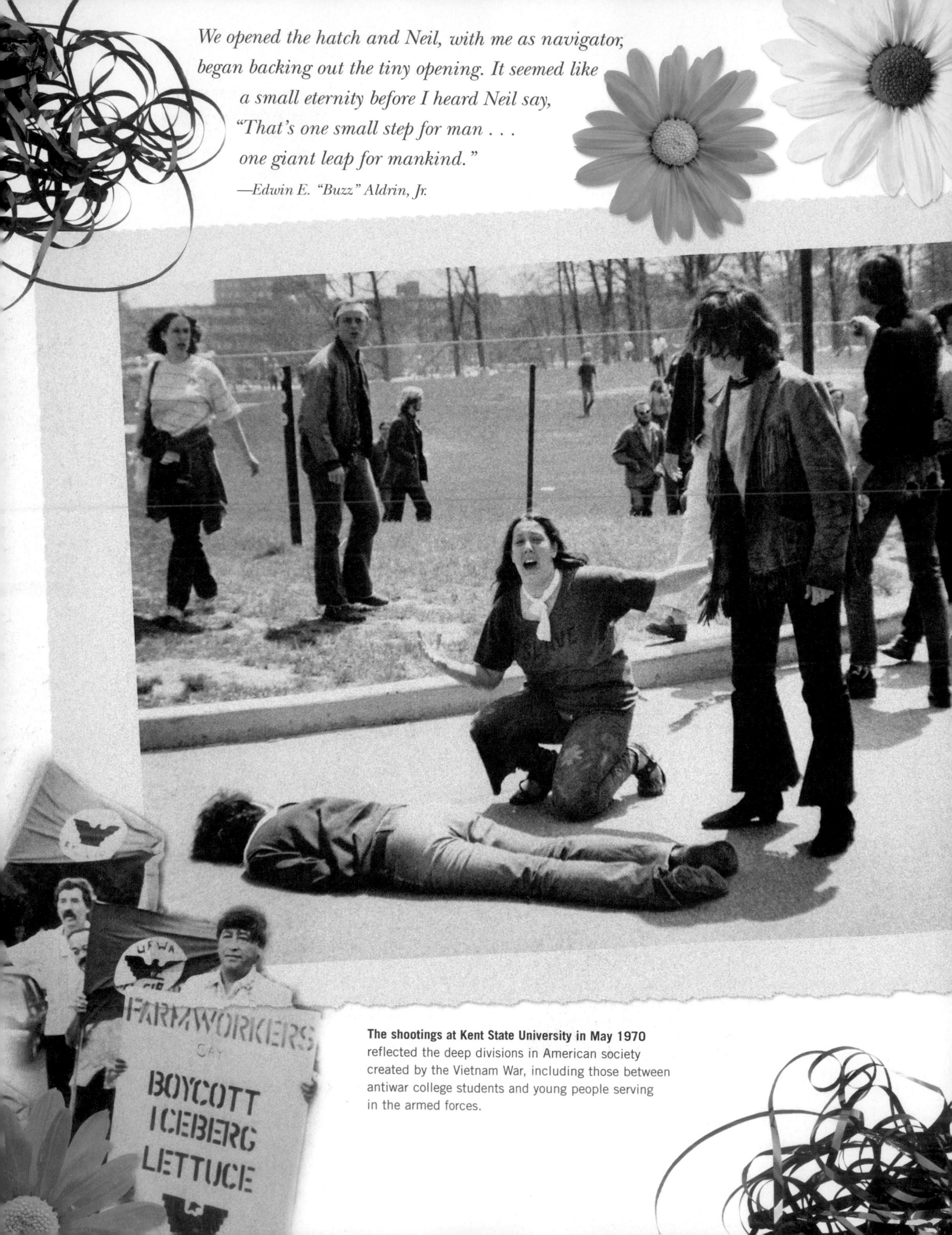

*We opened the hatch and Neil, with me as navigator,
began backing out the tiny opening. It seemed like
a small eternity before I heard Neil say,
"That's one small step for man . . .
one giant leap for mankind."*
—Edwin E. "Buzz" Aldrin, Jr.

FARMWORKERS
DAY
BOYCOTT
ICEBERG
LETTUCE

**The shootings at Kent State University in May 1970**
reflected the deep divisions in American society
created by the Vietnam War, including those between
antiwar college students and young people serving
in the armed forces.

# 29

WAR ABROAD, WAR AT HOME
1965–1974

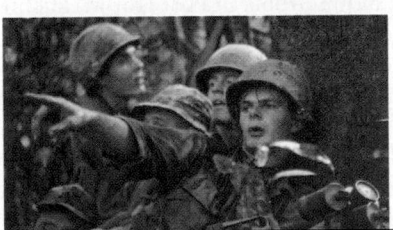

**WHY DID** Johnson escalate the war in Vietnam?

**HOW DID** campus protests shape national political debate?

**WHAT WERE** the goals of Johnson's Great Society?

**WHAT DIVIDED** the Democratic Party in 1968?

**WHAT IS** meant by the "politics of identity"?

**HOW DID** Nixon win the White House in 1968?

# AMERICAN COMMUNITIES

## Uptown, Chicago, Illinois

DURING THE FREEDOM SUMMER OF 1964, WHILE TEAMS OF NORTHERN college students traveled south to join voter registration campaigns among African Americans, a small group moved to Chicago to help the city's poor people take control of their communities. They targeted a neighborhood known as Uptown, a one-mile-square section five miles north of the Loop, the city center. The residents, many transplanted from the poverty of the Appalachian South, lived in crowded tenements or in once elegant mansions now subdivided into tiny, run-down apartments. The student organizers hoped to mobilize the community "so as to demand an end to poverty and the construction of a decent social order."

With the assistance of the Packinghouse Workers union, the students formed Jobs or Income Now (JOIN), opened a storefront office, and invited local residents to work with them to demand jobs and better living conditions. They spent hours listening to people, drawing out their ideas, and helping them develop scores of programs. They campaigned against Mayor Richard Daley's policy of "police omnipresence" that had a fleet of squad cars and paddy wagons continually patrolling the neighborhood. They also helped establish new social clubs, a food-buying cooperative, a community theater, and a health clinic. Within a few years, Uptown street kids had formed the Young Patriots organization, put out a community newspaper, *Rising Up Angry*, and staffed free breakfast programs.

Chicago JOIN was one of ten similar projects sponsored by **Students for a Democratic Society (SDS)**. Impatient with the nation's chronic poverty and Cold War politics, twenty-nine students from nine universities had met in June 1960 to form a new kind of campus-based political organization. SDS soon caught on with liberal students, encouraging them, as part of the nation's largest college population to date, to make their

voices heard. By its peak in 1968, SDS had 350 chapters and between 60,000 and 100,000 members. Its principle of participatory democracy—with its promise to give people control over the decisions affecting their lives—appealed to a wider following of more than a million students.

In June 1962, in Port Huron, Michigan, SDS issued a declaration of principles, drafted mainly by graduate student Tom Hayden. "We are people . . . bred in at least modest comfort, housed now in universities," *The Port Huron Statement* opened, "looking uncomfortably to the world we inherit." Poverty and social injustice, it continued, were not the only problems. A deeper ailment plagued American society. Everyone, including middle-class students with few material wants, suffered from a sense of "loneliness, estrangement, and alienation." *The Port Huron Statement* defined SDS as a new kind of political movement that would bring people "out of isolation and into community" so that not just the poor but all Americans could overcome their feelings of "powerlessness [and hence] resignation before the enormity of events."

SDS began with a campaign to reform the university, especially to disentangle the financial ties between campus-based research programs and the military-industrial complex. SDS also sent small groups of students to live and organize in the poor communities of Boston, Louisville, Cleveland, and Newark as well as Chicago. Ultimately, none of these projects recruited large numbers of people. Protests against local government did little to combat unemployment, and campaigns for better garbage collection or more playgrounds rarely evolved into lasting movements. Nevertheless, organizers did succeed, to some degree, in realizing the goal specified in its slogan: "Let the People Decide." By late 1967, SDS prepared to leave JOIN in the hands of the people it had organized, which was its intention from the beginning.

Chicago

 **28–4**
Students for a Democratic Society, *The Port Huron Statement* (1962)

**Students for a Democratic Society (SDS)** The leading student organization of the New Left of the early and mid-1960s.

# VIETNAM: AMERICA'S LONGEST WAR

The Vietnam War had its roots in the Truman Doctrine and its goal of containing communism (see Chapter 26). In 1954, after the Communist forces of Ho Chi Minh defeated the French colonialists and created a new government in the north, Vietnam emerged as a major zone of Cold War contention. The United States ultimately paid a huge price for its determination to turn back communism in Indochina. More than 58,000 Americans died in an unwinnable overseas war that only deepened divisions at home.

## JOHNSON'S WAR

Although President Kennedy had greatly increased the number of military advisers and Special Forces in South Vietnam (see Chapter 27), it was his successor, Lyndon B. Johnson, who made the decision to engage the United States in a major war there. At first, Johnson simply hoped to stay the course. Facing election in November 1964, he knew that a major military setback would cripple his campaign. But he was equally determined to avoid the fate of President Truman, who had been damaged politically after "losing" China to communism and producing a stalemate in Korea.

Throughout the winter and spring of 1964, as conditions worsened in South Vietnam, Johnson and his advisers quietly laid the groundwork for a sustained bombing campaign against North Vietnam. In early August, they found a pretext to set this plan in motion. The National Security Agency—decades later admitting to faulty intelligence—reported two attacks against U.S. destroyers by North Vietnamese patrol boats in the Gulf of Tonkin, off the coast of North Vietnam. Although the second alleged attack never took place, the report gave Johnson a reason to order retaliatory air strikes against bases in North Vietnam.

Johnson appealed to Congress to give him the authority "to take all necessary measures" to defend U.S. armed forces and to protect Southeast Asia "against aggression or subversion." This **Gulf of Tonkin resolution**, secretly drafted six weeks before the alleged incident, passed the Senate on August 7 with only two dissenting votes and moved unanimously through the House. It served, in Undersecretary of State Nicholas Katzenbach's words, as the "functional equivalent" of a declaration of war.

Ironically, Johnson continued his presidential campaign in 1964 with a call for restraint in Vietnam. This strategy helped him win a landslide victory over conservative Republican Barry Goldwater of Arizona, who had proposed the deployment of "tactical" nuclear weapons in Vietnam.

With the election behind him, Johnson faced a hard decision. The limited bombing raids against North Vietnam had failed to slow Communist forces moving across the border into the South. Meanwhile, the government in Saigon, the capital city of South Vietnam, appeared near collapse. Faced with the prospect of a Communist victory, the president chose to escalate U.S. involvement in Vietnam.

## DEEPER INTO THE QUAGMIRE

In early February 1965, Johnson found a rationale to justify massive bombing of the North. The Vietcong had fired at American soldiers at a military base at Pleiku in the central highlands of Vietnam, killing nine and wounding more than 100 Americans. Johnson ordered immediate reprisal bombing and one week later, on February 13, authorized Operation Rolling Thunder, a campaign of gradually intensifying air attacks.

**WHY DID** Johnson escalate the war in Vietnam?

**Review Summary**

   **28–7**
*The Tonkin Gulf Incident*
(1964)

## IMAGE KEY

for pages 822–823

**a.** Damaged cassette tape evocative of the Watergate scandal's secret Oval Office tapes.

**b.** Daisies represent the "Flower Power" mindset.

**c.** A weeping young woman kneels beside the body of a protester during the 1970 riots at Kent State University in Ohio.

**d.** Labor activist Caesar Chavez.

**e.** An antiwar peace button.

**f.** American soldiers atop captured Hill 875 near Dak To, Vietnam.

**g.** Antiwar protesters marching on the Pentagon and burning draft cards, October 1967.

**h.** A male student puts flowers in the guns of a row of soldiers during a protest at the Pentagon in Washington, D.C.

**i.** Crowds gather to hear Martin Luther King, Jr. speak.

**j.** President Nixon announces he will resign effective noon Friday during a broadcast from the Oval Office of the White House, in this August 8, 1974 file photo.

**The massive bombing** and ground combat created huge numbers of civilian casualties in Vietnam. The majority killed were women and children.

**Gulf of Tonkin resolution**  Request to Congress from President Lyndon Johnson in response to North Vietnamese torpedo boat attacks in which he sought authorization for "all necessary measures" to protect American forces and stop further aggression.

Once Rolling Thunder began, President Johnson hesitated to speak frankly with the American public about his plan of action on the ground. The strategy pursued by the Johnson administration and implemented by General William Westmoreland—a war of attrition—was based on the premise that continuous use of heavy artillery and air power would eventually exhaust North Vietnam's resources. Meanwhile, U.S. ground forces would defeat the Vietcong in South Vietnam and thereby restore political stability to South Vietnam's pro-Western government.

In practice, the United States wreaked havoc in South Vietnam, tearing apart its society and bringing ecological devastation to its land. By late 1968, the United States had dropped more than 3 million tons of bombs on Vietnam and eventually delivered more than three times the tonnage dropped by the Allies on all fronts during World War II. Using herbicides such as Agent Orange to defoliate forests, the United States also conducted the most destructive chemical warfare in history.

Several advisers urged the president to keep the American people informed about his decisions in Vietnam, even to declare a state of national emergency. But Johnson feared he would lose momentum on domestic reform, including his antipoverty programs, if he drew attention to foreign policy. Seeking to avoid "undue excitement in the Congress and in domestic public opinion," he held to a course of intentional deceit.

## THE CREDIBILITY GAP

Every night network television news tallied the soaring American body count, from 26 per week in 1965 to 180 in 1967. No president worked so hard to control the news media, but Johnson found himself badgered by reporters who accused him of creating a credibility gap.

During the early 1960s, network news had either ignored Vietnam or unquestioningly supported U.S. policy. Beginning with a CBS News report by Morley Safer in August 1965, however, the tenor changed. Although government officials described the U.S. operation in the South Vietnamese village Cam Ne as an attack on "fortified Vietcong bunkers," the *CBS Evening News* showed Marines setting fire to the thatched homes of civilians. More unfavorable news commentary soon followed. By 1967, according to a noted media observer, "every subject tended to become Vietnam."

The most vocal congressional critic of Johnson's war policy was Democratic Senator J. William Fulbright of Arkansas, who chaired the Senate Foreign Relations Committee and who had personally speeded the passage of the Gulf of Tonkin resolution. A strong supporter of the Cold War, Fulbright had nevertheless concluded that the war in Vietnam was both unwinnable and destructive to domestic reform. He also persuaded prominent Democrats to put aside their personal loyalty to Johnson and push through Congress a nonbinding resolution appealing to the United Nations to help negotiate an end to hostilities. Meanwhile, some of the nation's most trusted European allies called for restraint in Vietnam.

The impact of the war, which cost Americans $21 billion per year, was also felt by Americans at home. Johnson convinced Congress to levy a 10 percent surcharge on individual and corporate taxes. Later adjustments tapped the Social Security fund, heretofore safe from interference. Inflation raced upward, fed by spending on the war. Johnson replaced advisers who questioned his policy, but as casualties multiplied, more and more Americans began to mistrust his handling of the war.

# A GENERATION IN CONFLICT

As the Vietnam war escalated, Americans from all walks of life protested U.S. involvement. But between 1965 and 1971, a peace movement took shape that had a distinctly generational character. At the forefront were the baby boomers who were just coming of age.

## "THE TIMES THEY ARE A-CHANGIN'"

The first sign of a new kind of protest was the **free speech movement** at the University of California at Berkeley. In the fall of 1964, civil rights activists returned to the 27,000-student campus from Freedom Summer in Mississippi and decided to picket Bay Area stores that practiced discrimination in hiring. When the university administration tried to stop them from setting up information booths on campus, eighteen groups objected, including the archconservative Students for Goldwater, claiming that their right to free speech had been abridged. The administration sent police to break up the protest rally and arrest participants. After university president Clark Kerr, under pressure from conservative regents, announced his intention to press charges against the free speech movement's leaders, a huge crowd gathered. Nearly 1,000 people marched toward the university's administration building, where they planned to stage a sit-in until Kerr rescinded his order. The police moved in, detaining nearly 800 protestors in the largest mass arrest in California history.

Mario Savio, a Freedom Summer volunteer and philosophy student, explained that the free speech movement aspired to more than just the right to conduct political activity on campus. They wanted, in the phrase coined by SDS, participatory democracy. Across the country—and in many nations around the world—college students began to demand a say in their education. Students also spoke out against campus rules that treated students as children instead of as adults.

Across the bay in San Francisco, other young adults staked out a new form of community—a **counterculture**. In 1967, the "Summer of Love," the population of the Haight-Ashbury district swelled by 75,000 as youthful adventurers from around the world gathered for a huge "be-in." In the fall, the majority returned to their own communities, bringing with them the new hippie lifestyle.

The generational rebellion took many forms, including a revolution in sexual behavior that triggered countless quarrels between parents and their maturing sons and daughters. During the 1960s more teenagers experienced premarital sex—by the decade's end three-quarters of all college seniors had engaged in sexual intercourse—and far more talked about it openly than in previous eras. With birth control widely available, including the newly developed "pill," many young women were no longer deterred from sex by fear of pregnancy. Many heterosexual couples chose to live together outside marriage, a practice few parents condoned. A much smaller but significant number formed communes—approximately 4,000 by 1970—where members could share housekeeping and child care as well as sexual partners.

Mood-altering drugs played a large part in this counterculture. Marijuana, illegal yet readily available, was often paired with rock music in a collective ritual of love and laughter.

**HOW DID** campus protests shape national political debate?

**myhistorylab**
**Review Summary**

**Free speech movement** Student movement at the University of California, Berkeley, formed in 1964 to protest limitations on political activities on campus.

**Counterculture** Various alternatives to mainstream values and behaviors that became popular in the 1960s, including experimentation with psychedelic drugs, communal living, a return to the land, Asian religions, and experimental art.

**The nationally acclaimed** photographer Peter Simon was something of a hippie himself in the 1960s and took many photographs of the "alternative culture." Here he captures a group of hippies in the typically rural setting of back-to-the-land communes.

Music played a large part in defining the counterculture. With the emergence of rock 'n' roll in the 1950s, popular music had begun to express a deliberate generational identity (see Chapter 27), a trend that gained international momentum with the emergence of the British rock group the Beatles in 1964. Folk music, popular on campuses since the early 1960s, served as a voice of protest.

At a farm near Woodstock, New York, more than 400,000 people gathered in August 1969 for a three-day rock concert celebrating the counterculture. Thousands took drugs while security officials and local police stood by, some stripped off their clothes to dance or swim, and a few even made love in the grass.

The Woodstock Nation, as the counterculture was mythologized, did not actually represent the sentiments of most young people. But its attitudes and styles, especially its efforts to create a new community, did speak for the large minority seeking a peaceful alternative to the intensifying climate of war. The slogan "Make Love, Not War" linked generational rebellion and opposition to the U.S. war in Vietnam.

## FROM CAMPUS PROTEST TO MASS MOBILIZATION

Three weeks after the announcement of Operation Rolling Thunder in 1965, peace activists called for a daylong boycott of classes so that students and faculty might meet to discuss the war. At the University of Michigan in Ann Arbor, more than 3,000 students turned out. "Teach-ins" soon spread across the United States and to Europe and Japan. Meanwhile, SDS mobilized 20,000 people in an antiwar march on the nation's capital.

Students also protested against war-related research on their campuses. In October 1967, the Dow Chemical Company, manufacturers of napalm, a form of jellied gasoline that produces internal as well as external burns, sent job recruiters to the University of Wisconsin at Madison despite warnings that antiwar activists would try to disrupt interviews. A few hundred students sat-in at the building where the recruitment interviews were scheduled, and 2,000 onlookers gathered outside. Ordered by university administrators to disperse the crowd, the city's police broke glass doors, dragged students through the debris, and clubbed those who refused to move. During the next three years, the momentum grew, and demonstrations took place on campuses in every region of the country.

The peace movement spread well beyond the campus. In April 1967, a day-long antiwar rally in Manhattan's Central Park drew more than 300,000 people. Meanwhile, 60,000 protesters turned out in San Francisco. By summer, Vietnam Veterans Against the War had begun to organize returning soldiers and sailors, encouraging them to cast off the medals and ribbons they had won in battle.

Many demonstrators themselves, concluding that peaceful protest alone had little impact on U.S. policy, decided to change tactics—"from protest to resistance"—and serve as moral witnesses. Despite a 1965 congressional act providing for a five-year jail term and a $10,000 fine for destroying a draft card, thousands of young men burned their draft cards. Approximately a half-million more refused induction. Two Jesuit priests, Daniel and Philip Berrigan, raided the draft board offices in Catonsville, Maryland, in May 1968 and poured homemade napalm over records. Other activists determined to "bring the war home" went beyond civil disobedience. An estimated 40,000 bombing incidents or bomb threats took place from January 1969 to April 1970; more than $21 million of property was damaged, and forty-three people were killed.

Parallel wars were now being fought, one between two systems of government in Vietnam, another between the American government and masses of its citizens. Those Americans sent to Vietnam were caught in between.

**On May 8**, 1970, New York construction workers surged into Wall Street in Lower Manhattan, violently disrupting an antiwar rally and attacking the protesters with lead pipes and crowbars. Known as the "hard hat riots," the well-publicized event was followed later in the month by a march, 100,000 strong, of hard-hat workers unfurling American flags and chanting "All the way U.S.A."

## TEENAGE SOLDIERS

The average age of soldiers who fought in Vietnam hovered around nineteen. Until late 1969 the Selective Service System—the draft—gave deferments to college students and to workers in selected occupations while recruiting hard in poor communities by advertising the armed forces as a provider of vocational training and social mobility. Working-class young men, disproportionately African American and Latino, signed up in large numbers under these inducements. They also bore the brunt of combat. Whereas college graduates constituted only 12 percent of the 2.5 million men who served in Vietnam and 9 percent of those who were killed in combat, high school dropouts were the most likely to serve in Vietnam and by far the most likely to die there. The casualty rate for African Americans was approximately 30 percent higher than the overall death rate for U.S. forces in Southeast Asia. These disparities created a rupture that would last well past the end of the war.

Yet the soldiers were not entirely isolated from the changes affecting their generation. Many G.I.s smoked marijuana, listened to rock music, hung psychedelic posters in their barracks, and participated in the sexual revolution, but most condemned antiwar protest as the self-indulgent behavior of their privileged peers who did not have to fight. As the war dragged on, however, some soldiers showed their frustration. By 1971 many G.I.s were putting peace symbols on their combat helmets, joining antiwar demonstrations, and staging their own events such as "Armed Farces Day." Sometimes entire companies refused to carry out duty assignments or even to enter battle. A smaller number took revenge by "fragging" reckless commanding officers with grenades meant for the enemy. Some African American soldiers complained about fighting "a white man's war" and emblazoned their helmets with slogans like "No Gook Ever Called Me Nigger."

The war's course fed these feelings of disaffection. U.S. troops entering South Vietnam encountered anti-American demonstrations and placards with slogans like "End Foreign Dominance of Our Country." Patently false U.S. government press releases that heralded glorious victories and extolled the gratitude of Vietnamese civilians deepened bitterness on the front lines.

**African American Troops** in Vietnam, 1970. Many black soldiers echoed the growing racial militancy in the United States and increasingly chose to spend their off-duty time apart from white soldiers.

Vietnam veterans returned to civilian life quietly and without fanfare, denied the glory earned by the combat veterans of previous wars. They reentered a society divided over the cause for which they had risked their lives. Tens of thousands suffered debilitating physical injuries. As many as 40 percent of the 8.6 million who served came back with drug dependencies or symptoms of posttraumatic stress disorder, haunted and depressed by troubling memories of atrocities. Moreover, finding and keeping a job proved to be particularly hard in the shrinking economy of the 1970s.

# WARS ON POVERTY

Hoping to build on Kennedy's legacy, President Johnson pledged to expand the antipoverty program that he had inherited. Over the next several years, he used the political momentum of the civil rights movement and the overwhelming Democratic majorities in the House and Senate to push through the most ambitious reform program since the New Deal. Ironically, violence at home as well as abroad ultimately undercut his aspiration to wage "an unconditional **war on poverty**."

### THE GREAT SOCIETY

The cornerstone of Johnson's plan for a Great Society was the Economic Opportunity Act, enacted in August 1964. The legislation established the **Office of Economic Opportunity (OEO)**, which coordinated a network of community-based programs designed to help the poor help themselves by providing opportunities for education and employment. The results were mixed. The Job Corps provided vocational training mostly for urban black youth considered unemployable. Housed in dreary barracks-like camps far from home, trainees often found themselves learning factory skills that were already obsolete. The Neighborhood Youth Corps provided work for about 2 million young people aged sixteen to twenty-one, but nearly all the jobs were low paying and dead-end. Educational programs proved more successful. VISTA (Volunteers in Service to America), a kind of domestic Peace Corps, brought several thousand idealistic volunteers into poor communities for social service work.

The most innovative and controversial element of the OEO was the Community Action Program (CAP), which mandated "maximum feasible participation" of local residents. In theory, community action would empower the poor by giv-

**WHAT WERE** the goals of Johnson's Great Society?

**myhistorylab**
**Review Summary**

**War on poverty** Set of programs introduced by Lyndon Johnson between 1963 and 1966 designed to break the cycle of poverty by providing funds for job training, community development, nutrition, and supplementary education.

**Office of Economic Opportunity (OEO)** Federal agency that coordinated many programs of the War on Poverty between 1964 and 1975.

ing them a direct say in mobilizing resources. What often resulted was a tug-of-war between local government officials and the poor over who should control funding and decision-making.

More successful and popular were the so-called national-emphasis programs, designed in Washington and administered according to federal guidelines. The Legal Services Program, staffed by attorneys, helped millions of poor people in legal battles with housing authorities, welfare departments, police, and slumlords. Head Start and Follow Through reached more than 2 million poor children and significantly improved the long-range educational achievement of participants. Comprehensive Community Health Centers provided basic medical services to patients who could not afford to see doctors. Upward Bound helped low-income teenagers develop the skills and confidence needed for college. Birth control programs dispensed contraceptive supplies and information to hundreds of thousands of poor women (see Figure 29.1).

But the root cause of poverty lay in the unequal distribution of power as well as of income. The Johnson administration never committed itself to reallocating income or wealth. Spending on social welfare jumped from 7.7 percent of the GNP in 1960 to 16 percent in 1974. But roughly three-quarters of social welfare payments went to the nonpoor. The largest sums went to **Medicare**, established by Congress in 1965 to provide basic health care for the aged, and to expanded Social Security payments and unemployment compensation. Having made the largest commitment to federal spending on social welfare since the New Deal, Johnson could take pride in the number of programs passed by Congress. At the same time, he had raised expectations higher than could be reached without a more drastic redistribution of economic and political power. Even in the short run, the president could not sustain the welfare programs and simultaneously fight a lengthy and expensive war abroad.

## CRISIS IN THE CITIES

With funds for new construction limited during the Great Depression and World War II, and the postwar building boom taking place in the suburbs, the housing stock in the nation's cities declined. The Federal Housing Administration encouraged this trend by redlining poor urban neighborhoods (see Chapter 27). Slumlords took advantage of this situation, collecting high rents while allowing their properties to deteriorate. City officials meanwhile spearheaded civic revitalization programs that more often than not sliced up poor neighborhoods with new superhighways, demolished them to build new office complexes, or, as in Chicago's Uptown, favored residential developments for the middle class rather than for the poor. In 1968 a federal survey showed that 80 percent of those displaced under these programs—dubbed "Negro removal" by former residents—were people of color.

Employment opportunities declined along with the housing stock. Black unemployment, however, was nearly twice that of white unemployment. Moreover, the proportion working in the low-paying service sector continued to rise. In short, African Americans were steadily falling further behind whites.

## URBAN UPRISINGS

These conditions brought urban pressures to the boiling point. During the "long, hot summers" of 1964 to 1968, more than 100 urban uprisings rocked the nation. Unlike the race riots of the 1920s and 1940s, when angry whites assaulted blacks, masses of African Americans now took revenge for the white domination of their communities and specifically for police abuse (see Map 29.1).

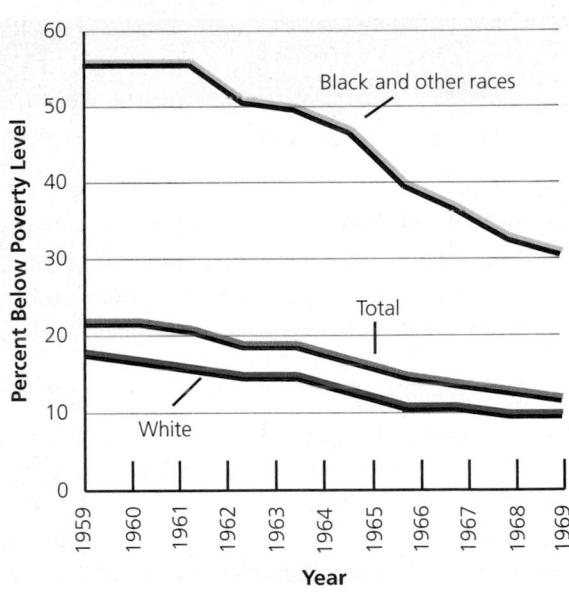

**Figure 29.1 Percent of Population Below Poverty Level, by Race, 1959–69**

NOTE: The poverty threshold for a nonfarm family of four was $3,743 in 1969 and $2,973 in 1959.

*Congressional Quarterly, Civil Rights: A Progress Report*, 1971, p. 46.

## QUICK REVIEW

**The Great Society**

♦ Most ambitious reform program since the New Deal.
♦ Office of Economic Opportunity launched a War on Poverty.
♦ Programs had mixed results.

**Medicare**  Basic medical insurance for the elderly, financed through the federal government; program created in 1965.

# OVERVIEW | The Great Society

## MAJOR LEGISLATION

### CIVIL RIGHTS

**Civil Rights Act of 1964**, forbidding segregation in public accommodations and banning job discrimination

**Voting Rights Act of 1965**, ensuring minority voter registration in places where patterns of past discrimination existed

**Immigration and Nationality Services Act of 1965**, abolishing national-original quotas in immigration law

**Civil Rights Act of 1968**, banning discrimination in housing and extending constitutional protections to Native Americans on reservations

### THE WAR ON POVERTY

**Economic Opportunity Act of 1964**, establishing the Office of Economic Opportunity to oversee such community-based antipoverty programs as the **Job Corps**, the **Neighborhood Youth Corps, VISTA**, the **Model Cities Program, Upward Bound**, the **Community Action Program**, and **Project Head Start**

### EDUCATION

**Elementary and Secondary Education Act of 1965**, providing federal funds for programs to schools in low-income areas

**Bilingual Education Act of 1968**, providing federal aid to school districts with large numbers of children needing to learn English as a second language

### HEALTH

**Social Security Act of 1965**, funding Medicare to help cover costs of health care for older Americans and Medicaid to provide funds for medical care of welfare recipients

### CULTURE

**National Foundation on the Arts and Humanities Act of 1965**, creating the National Endowment for the Arts and the National Endowment for the Humanities

**Public Broadcasting Act of 1967**, chartering the Corporation for Public Broadcasting, which later established the Public Broadcasting Services (PBS) and National Public Radio (NPR)

### TRANSPORTATION

**Urban Mass Transportation Act of 1964**, funding large-scale urban public and private rail projects

**National Traffic and Motor Vehicle Safety Act of 1966**, laying the foundation for the National Highway Traffic Safety Administration to effect policy to reduce traffic injuries and fatalities

**Highway Safety Act of 1966**, permitting the federal government to set standards for motor vehicles and highways

**Department of Transportation**, established in 1966

### CONSUMER PROTECTION

**Nine major enactments between 1965 and 1968, covering such areas as cigarette warning labels, motor safety, "fair packaging and labeling," child safety and flammable fabrics, meat and poultry packaging, "truth in lending," and radiation safety**

### ENVIRONMENT

Nine major enactments between 1964 and 1968, covering such areas as wilderness and endangered species protection, land and water conservation, solid waste disposal, air pollution, aircraft noise abatement, and historic preservation

**National Environmental Policy Act of 1969**, consolidating many of these gains, was passed in the first year of the Nixon administration

---

**myhistorylab**

**Overview:** *The Great Society*

**28–10**
Donald Wheeldin,
*The Situation in Watts Today*
(1967)

The first major uprising erupted in August 1965 in the Watts section of Los Angeles. It took only a minor arrest to set off the uprising, which quickly spread outward for fifty miles. Throwing rocks and bottles through store windows, participants reportedly shouted, "This is for Selma! This is for Birmingham!" and "Burn, baby, burn!" Nearly 50,000 people turned out, and 20,000 National Guard troops were sent in. After six days, 34 people lay dead, 900 were injured, and 4,000 more had been arrested.

The following summer, large-scale uprisings occurred in San Francisco, Milwaukee, Dayton, and Cleveland. On July 12, 1967, in Newark, New Jersey, a city with severe housing shortages and the nation's highest black unemployment

# MAP EXPLORATION

To explore an interactive version of this map, go to **http://www.prenhall.com/faraghertlc/map29.1**

**MAP 29.1**
**Urban Uprisings, 1965–1968**    After World War II, urban uprisings precipitated by racial conflict increased in African American communities. In Watts in 1965 and in Detroit and Newark in 1967, rioters struck out at symbols of white control of their communities, such as white-owned businesses and residential properties.

WHAT WERE the main factors behind urban unrest?

rate, the beating and arrest of a black taxi driver by a white police officer sparked the protest. Five days of looting and burning of buildings ended with 25 people dead. One week later Detroit police raided a bar and arrested the after-hours patrons. Army tanks and paratroopers were brought in to quell the disturbance, which lasted a week and left 34 people dead and 7,000 under arrest.

In July 1967 President Johnson created the National Advisory Commission on Civil Disorders to investigate the riots. Headed by Illinois Governor Otto Kerner, the eleven-member commission indicted "white racism" for creating an "explosive mixture" of poverty and police brutality. But the Johnson administration and Congress put aside the commission's warning that "our nation is moving toward two societies, one black, one white—separate and unequal" and disregarded its advice to direct funds into housing and jobs and to reduce segregation. By this time, the escalating costs of the Vietnam War left little federal money for antipoverty programs.

WHAT DIVIDED the Democratic

Party in 1968?

**myhist⊘rylab**

Review Summary

# 1968: YEAR OF TURMOIL

The urban uprisings of the summer of 1967 marked the most drawn-out violence in the United States since the Civil War. Rather than offering a respite, 1968 proved to be even more turbulent. But it was not just the United States that experienced 1968 as a year of turmoil. In May, hundreds of thousands of students and workers barricaded the streets of Paris in protest against their government. A sweeping series of liberal reforms in Czechoslovakia, known as the "Prague Spring," was followed in August by a massive invasion staged by Eastern-bloc countries. In October, an estimated 300 people were killed in the Tlatelolco section of Mexico City when government forces, using tanks and armored cars, broke up a student-led demonstration. And in China, Mao Zedong was deep into the "Cultural Revolution," a campaign to strengthen the Communist government against liberal reforms.

## THE TET OFFENSIVE

On January 30, 1968, the North Vietnamese and their Vietcong allies launched the Tet Offensive (named for the Vietnamese lunar New Year holiday), stunning the U.S. military command in South Vietnam. The Vietcong pushed into the major cities and provincial capitals of the South, as far as the courtyard of the U.S. embassy in Saigon. U.S. troops ultimately halted the offensive, suffering comparatively modest casualties (see Map 29.2).

The Tet Offensive, despite the U.S. success in stopping it, weakened the resolve of many Americans. News coverage—including scenes of U.S. personnel shooting from the embassy windows in Saigon—dismayed the nation. The United States chalked up a major military victory but lost the war at home. For the first time, polls showed strong opposition to the war. Sectors of the antiwar movement shifted from resistance to open rebellion.

President Johnson, facing the 1968 election campaign, watched his popularity plummet to an all-time low. On March 31 he announced he would not seek the Democratic Party's nomination. He also declared a bombing halt over North Vietnam and called Hanoi to peace talks, which began in Paris in May. Like Truman almost thirty years earlier, and despite his determination not to repeat that bit of history, Johnson had lost his presidency in Asia.

## KING, THE WAR, AND THE ASSASSINATION

By 1968 the civil rights leadership stood firmly against the war, and Martin Luther King Jr. had reached a turning point in his life. King abandoned his customary caution in criticizing U.S. policy in Vietnam. He now became yet more outspoken in his opposition to the war, even if it meant losing the support of those liberal Democrats loyal to Johnson. King refused to compromise.

In the spring of 1968 King chose Memphis, Tennessee, home of striking sanitation workers, to launch a Poor People's Campaign for peace and justice. There he delivered, in what was to be his final speech, a message of hope. The next evening, April 4, 1968, as he stood on the balcony of his motel, King was shot and killed.

Throughout the world crowds turned out to mourn King's death. Riots broke out in more than a hundred cities. Chicago Mayor Richard Daley ordered his police to shoot to kill. In Washington, DC, U.S. Army units set up machine guns outside the Capitol and the White House. King's dream of the nation as a "Beloved Community" died with him.

## THE DEMOCRATS IN DISARRAY

The dramatic events of the first part of the year had a direct impact on the presidential campaign. For those liberals dissatisfied with Johnson's conduct of the war, and

**MAP 29.2**
**The Southeast Asian War**   The Indo-Chinese subcontinent, home to long-standing regional conflict, became the center of a prolonged war with the United States.

WHAT LED to the escalation of U.S. involvement in Vietnam?

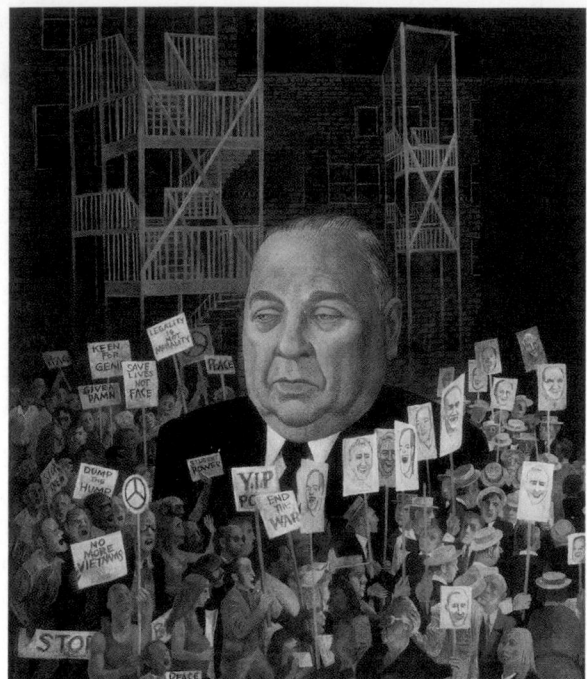

In 1968, Richard J. Daley had been elected mayor of Chicago four times and held power as a traditional city boss. In December of that year, the National Commission on Violence released a report that concluded that Chicago police, acting under Mayor Daley's orders, had been "unrestrained and indiscriminate" in their attacks on demonstrators at the National Democratic Convention held the previous August. In response, Mayor Daley brazenly announced a 22 percent salary increase for members of the city's police and fire personnel.

## QUICK REVIEW

### The 1968 Democratic Convention

- August 26–29: Democrats met to nominate Hubert Humphrey.
- Antiwar protesters marched on the convention hall.
- Undisciplined police helped precipitate violence between the police and the protesters.

**Black Power**   Philosophy emerging after 1965 that real economic and political gains for African Americans could come only through self-help, self-determination, and organizing for direct political influence.

**Black Panther Party**   Political and social movement among black Americans, founded in Oakland, California, in 1966 and emphasizing black economic and political power.

especially for African Americans suffering the loss of their greatest leader, Senator Robert F. Kennedy of New York emerged as the candidate of choice. Kennedy enjoyed a strong record on civil rights, and, like King, he had begun to interpret the war as a mirror of injustice at home.

Ironically, Kennedy faced an opponent who agreed with him, Senator Eugene McCarthy of Minnesota. The race for the Democratic nomination positioned McCarthy, the witty philosopher, against Kennedy, the charismatic campaigner. McCarthy did well with liberal Democrats and white suburbanites. On college campuses his popularity with antiwar students was so great that his campaign became known as the "children's crusade." Kennedy reached out successfully to African Americans and Latinos and won all but the Oregon primary.

Kennedy appeared to be the Democratic Party's strongest candidate as June 4, the day of the California primary, dawned. But as the final tabulation of his victory came in just past midnight, Robert Kennedy was struck down by an assassin's bullet.

Vice President Hubert H. Humphrey, who had announced his candidacy in April, was now the sole Democrat with the credentials to succeed Johnson. He simultaneously courted Democrats who grimly supported the war and the King-Kennedy wing, which was sickened by it. He also skillfully cultivated the Democratic power brokers. Without entering a single state primary, he lined up delegates loyal to city bosses, labor leaders, and conservative southern Democrats. As the candidate least likely to rock the boat, he had secured his party's nomination well before delegates met in convention.

## "THE WHOLE WORLD IS WATCHING!"

The events surrounding the Democratic convention in Chicago, August 21–26, demonstrated how deep the divisions within the United States had become. Mayor Richard Daley, still reeling from the riots following King's assassination, refused to issue parade permits to the antiwar activists, who had called for a massive demonstration at the convention center. According to later accounts, he sent hundreds of undercover police into the crowds to encourage rock throwing and generally to incite violence so that retaliation would appear necessary and reasonable. Daley's strategy boomeranged when his officers staged what a presidential commission later termed a "police riot," randomly assaulting demonstrators, casual passersby, and the television crews broadcasting the events.

Inside the convention hall, a raging debate over a peace resolution underscored the depth of the division within the party. When the resolution failed, McCarthy delegates put on black armbands and sang "We Shall Overcome." Later, as tear gas used against the demonstrators outside turned the amphitheater air acrid, the beaming Humphrey praised Mayor Daley and Johnson's conduct of the Vietnam War. When Senator Abraham Ribicoff of Connecticut protested the "Gestapo tactics" of the Chicago police, television cameras focused on Mayor Daley saying, "You Jew son of a bitch . . . , go home!" The crowd outside chanted, "The whole world is watching! The whole world is watching!" Indeed, through satellite transmission, it was.

Protest had spread worldwide. Across the United States the antiwar movement picked up steam. Meanwhile, demonstrations in Japan, Italy, Ireland, Germany, and England all brought young people into the streets to demand democratic reforms in their own countries and an end to the U.S. war in Vietnam.

## THE REPUBLICAN VICTORY

The Republicans stepped into the breech. Presidential contender Richard Nixon deftly built on voter hostility toward youthful protesters and the counterculture. Nixon claimed to be the one candidate who could restore law and order. (see Map 29.3).

After signing the landmark Civil Rights Act of 1964, President Johnson said privately, "I think we just delivered the South to the Republicans for a long time to come." Republican strategists moved quickly to make this prediction come true. They also recognized the growing electoral importance of the Sunbelt, where populations grew with the rise of high-tech industries and retirement communities. A powerful conservatism dominated this region, home to many military bases, defense plants, and an increasingly influential religious right. Nixon took advantage of this trend.

Nixon squeaked to victory, capturing the popular vote by the slim margin of 43.6 percent to Democrat Hubert Humphrey and Maine senator Edmund Muskie's 42.7 percent but taking nearly all the West's electoral votes. Bitterly divided by the campaign, the Democrats would remain out of presidential contention for more than two decades, except when the Republicans suffered scandal and disgrace. The Republicans in 1968 had paved the way for the conservative ascendancy.

## THE POLITICS OF IDENTITY

Richard Nixon campaigned promising to "bring Americans together again." But, if anything, the divisions among Americans, especially among the young, grew sharper during his presidency. The tragic events of 1968 brought whole sectors of the counterculture to political activism. With great media fanfare, gay liberation and women's liberation movements took shape while young Latinos, Asian Americans, and Indian peoples pressed their own claims.

## BLACK POWER

Impatient with tactics based on voting rights and integration, many young activists spurned the civil disobedience of King's generation for direct action and militant self-defense. In 1966, Stokely Carmichael, who had helped turn SNCC into an all-black organization, began to advocate **Black Power** as a means for African Americans to take control of their own communities.

The **Black Panther Party**, founded in Oakland, California, in 1966 by Huey P. Newton and Bobby Seale, demanded "land, bread, housing, education, clothing, and justice." They adopted a paramilitary style that infuriated the authorities. Monitoring local police was their major activity. In several communities, volunteers also ran free breakfast programs for schoolchildren, established medical clinics, and conducted educational classes. Persecuted by police and the FBI their leaders were arrested, prosecuted, and sentenced to long terms in jail that effectively destroyed the organization.

## MAP EXPLORATION

To explore an interactive version of this map, go to
**http://www.prenhall.com/faraghertic/map29.3**

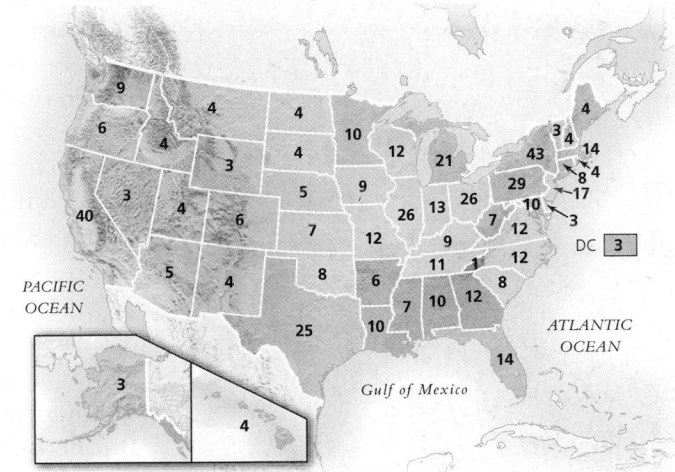

| | Electoral Vote (%) | Popular Vote (%) |
|---|---|---|
| **RICHARD M. NIXON** (Republican) | 301 (56) | 31,785,480 (43.4) |
| Hubert H. Humphrey (Democrat) | 191 (36) | 31,275,165 (42.7) |
| George C. Wallace (American Independent) | 46 (8) | 9,906,473 (13.5) |
| Other candidates (Dick Gregory, Socialist Labor; Fred Halstead and Paul Boutelle, Socialist Workers; Eugene McCarthy, Peace and Freedom; E. Harold Munn and Rolland E. Fisher, Prohibition) | — | 221,134 (0.3) |

**MAP 29.3**

**The Election of 1968**   Although the Republican Nixon-Agnew team won the popular vote by only a small margin, the Democrats lost in most of the northern states that had voted Democratic since the days of FDR. Segregationist Governor George Wallace of Alabama polled more than 9 million votes.

WHAT WERE the most important factors in Nixon's victory in 1968?

WHAT IS meant by the "politics of identity"?

**myhistorylab**
**Review Summary**

 **28–9** Stokely Carmichael and Charles Hamilton, *Black Power* (1967)

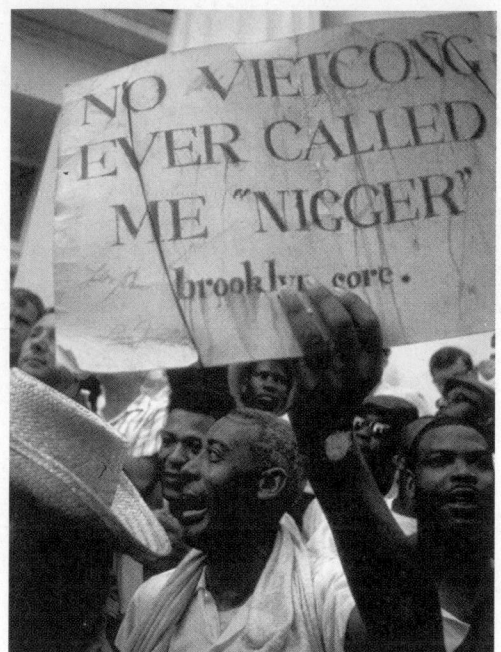

**The war in** Vietnam contributed to the growing racial militancy in the United States. African Americans served on the front lines in Vietnam in disproportionate numbers, and many came to view the conflict as a "white man's war."

## QUICK REVIEW

**Black Panthers**

◆ Founded in 1966 by Huey P. Newton and Bobby Seale.

◆ Adopted a strategy of armed self-defense, combined with community programs.

◆ Panthers faced raids, arrests, and prosecution.

**29–2**
Betty Friedan, *The Feminist Mystique* (1963)

**National Organization for Women (NOW)** Organization founded to campaign for the enforcement of laws related to women's issues.

Black Power nevertheless continued to grow into a multifaceted movement. The Reverend Jesse Jackson, for example, rallied African Americans in Chicago to boycott the A&P supermarket chain until the firm hired 700 black workers. A dynamic speaker and skillful organizer, Jackson encouraged African Americans to support their own businesses and services.

Cultural nationalism became the most enduring component of Black Power. In their popular book *Black Power* (1967), Stokely Carmichael and Charles V. Hamilton urged African Americans "to assert their own definitions, to reclaim their history, their culture; to create their own sense of community and togetherness." Thousands of college students responded by calling for more scholarships and for more classes on African American history and culture.

Meanwhile, trendsetters put aside Western dress for African-style dashikis and hairdos, and black parents gave their children African names. Many well-known activists and artists such as Imamu Amiri Baraka (formerly LeRoi Jones), Muhammad Ali (formerly Cassius Clay), and Kwame Touré (formerly Stokely Carmichael) rejected their "slave names." The new holiday Kwanzaa followed Christmas as a weeklong celebration of African heritage and culture. This deepening sense of racial pride was summed up in the popular slogan "Black Is Beautiful."

## SISTERHOOD IS POWERFUL

In 1966, Betty Friedan's best-selling *Feminine Mystique* (see Chapter 27) sparked the formation of the **National Organization for Women (NOW)**. Members campaigned for the enforcement of laws banning sex discrimination in work and in education, for maternity leaves, and for government funding of day-care centers. NOW also backed the Equal Rights Amendment, first introduced in Congress in 1923, and demanded the repeal of legislation that prohibited abortion or restricted birth control.

By the time Nixon took office, a different kind of movement had emerged: women's liberation. The women's liberation movement attracted young women who had been active in civil rights, SDS, and campus antiwar movements. Impatient with NOW's legislative agenda, angered by the sexism of male activists, these women organized separately under the slogan "Sisterhood Is Powerful."

The women's liberation movement issued a scathing critique of patriarchy—that is, the power of men to dominate all institutions, from the family to business and government to the protest movements themselves. Outraged and sometimes outrageous, one New York group created a lot of publicity for the movement by storming the 1968 Miss America Beauty Pageant in Atlantic City. They crowned a live sheep as queen and threw "implements of female torture" (bras, girdles, curlers, and copies of the *Ladies' Home Journal*) into a "freedom trash can."

The media focused on such audacious acts and brazen pronouncements, but the majority of activists were less flamboyant women simply trying to rise above the limitations imposed on them because of their gender. They met more often outside the limelight in consciousness-raising groups, where they examined the relationship between public events and private lives. Believing that no aspect of life lacked a political dimension, most emphatically including sexuality, consciousness-raising groups explored the power dynamics of the family and marriage as well as the workforce and government.

Women's liberation activism ranged widely. Some feminists staged sit-ins at *Newsweek* to protest demeaning media depictions of women. Others established

# OVERVIEW | Protest Movements of the 1960s

| Year | Organization/ Movement | Description |
|---|---|---|
| 1962 | **Students for a Democratic Society (SDS)** | Organization of college students that became the largest national organization of left-wing white students. Calling for "participatory democracy," SDS involved students in community-based campaigns against poverty and for citizens' control of neighborhoods. SDS played a prominent role in the campaign to end the war in Vietnam. |
| 1964 | **Free Speech Movement** | Formed at the University of California at Berkeley to protest the banning of on-campus political fundraising. Decried the bureaucratic character of the "multiuniversity" and advocated an expansion of student rights. |
| 1965 | **Anti–Vietnam War Movement** | Advocated grassroots opposition to U.S. involvement in Southeast Asia. By 1970 a national mobilization committee organized a demonstration of a half-million protesters in Washington, DC. |
| 1965 | **La raza** | A movement of Chicano youth to advance the cultural and political self-determination of Mexican Americans. *La raza* included the Brown Berets, which addressed community issues, and regional civil rights groups such as the Crusade for Social Justice, formed in 1965. |
| 1966 | **Black Power** | Militant movement that emerged from the civil rights campaigns to advocate independent institutions for African Americans and pride in black culture and African heritage. The idea of Black Power, a term coined by Stokely Carmichael, inspired the formation of the paramilitary Black Panthers. |
| 1968 | **American Indian Movement (AIM)** | Organization formed to advance the self-determination of Indian peoples and challenge the authority of the Bureau of Indian Affairs. Its most effective tactic was occupation. In February 1973, AIM insurgents protesting land and treaty violations occupied Wounded Knee, South Dakota, the location of an 1890 massacre, until the FBI and BIA agents drove them out. |
| 1968 | **Women's Liberation** | Movement of mainly young women that took shape following a protest at the Miss America Beauty Pageant. Impatient with the legislative reforms promoted by the National Organization for Women, founded in 1966, activists developed their own agenda shaped by the slogan "The Personal Is Political." Activities included the formation of "consciousness-raising" groups and the establishment of women's studies programs. |
| 1968 | **Asian American Political Alliance (AAPA)** | Formed at the University of California at Berkeley, the AAPA was one of the first pan-Asian political organizations to struggle against racial oppression. The AAPA encouraged Asian Americans to claim their own cultural identity and to protest the war against Asian peoples in Vietnam. |
| 1969 | **Gay Liberation** | Movement to protest discrimination against homosexuals and lesbians that emerged after the Stonewall Riots in New York City. Unlike earlier organizations such as the Mattachine Society, which focused on civil rights, gay liberationists sought to radically change American society and government, which they believed were corrupt. |

health clinics, day-care centers, rape crisis centers, and shelters for women fleeing abusive husbands or lovers. By the early 1970s, campus activists were demanding women's studies programs and women's centers. Like black studies, women's studies programs included traditional academic goals, such as the generation of new scholarship, but also encouraged personal change and self-esteem. Programs were established; by 1980 nearly 30,000 women's studies courses were offered at colleges

**Overview:** *Protest Movements of the 1960s*

**29–4**
National Organization for Women, *Statement of Purpose* (1966)

**This is the** Statue of Liberty as it appeared after nearly 100 women from various women's liberation groups demonstrated on the island, August 10, 1970. The demonstration was to show support for the proposed equal rights amendment which is currently before the Congress. Shortly after noon, park rangers made the women remove the banner from the base of the statue.

**29–5**
The Gay Liberation Front,
*Come Out* (1970)

and universities throughout the United States. And the number of women in the workforce continued to increase (see Figure 29.2).

The women's liberation movement remained, however, a bastion of white middle-class women. The appeal to sisterhood did not unite women across race or class or even sexual orientation. Lesbians, who charged the early NOW leaders with homophobia, found large pockets of "heterosexism" in the women's liberation movement and broke off to form their own organizations. The majority of African American women remained wary of white women's appeals to sisterhood. African American women formed their own "womanist" movement to address their distinct cultural and political concerns. Similarly, by 1970 a Latina feminist movement addressed issues uniquely relevant to women of color in an Anglo-dominated society.

## GAY LIBERATION

During the tumultuous late 1960s that a sizeable movement formed to encourage gays and lesbians to "come out": "Say It Loud, Gay Is Proud."

The major event prompting gays to organize followed repeated police raids of gay bars. On Friday, June 27, 1969, New York police raided the Stonewall Inn, a well-known gay bar in Greenwich Village, and provoked an uprising that lasted the entire night. The day after the Stonewall Riot, as it was called, "Gay Power" graffiti appeared throughout the neighborhood.

Taking a stand against the war in Vietnam, the GLF quickly adopted the forms of public protest, such as street demonstrations and sit-ins, developed by civil rights activists and given new direction by antiwar protesters.

Changes in public opinion and policies followed. Several churches opened their doors to gay activists; the San Francisco–based Council on Religion and Homosexuality established a network for clergy sympathetic to gay and lesbian parishioners. In 1973 the American Psychiatric Association, which

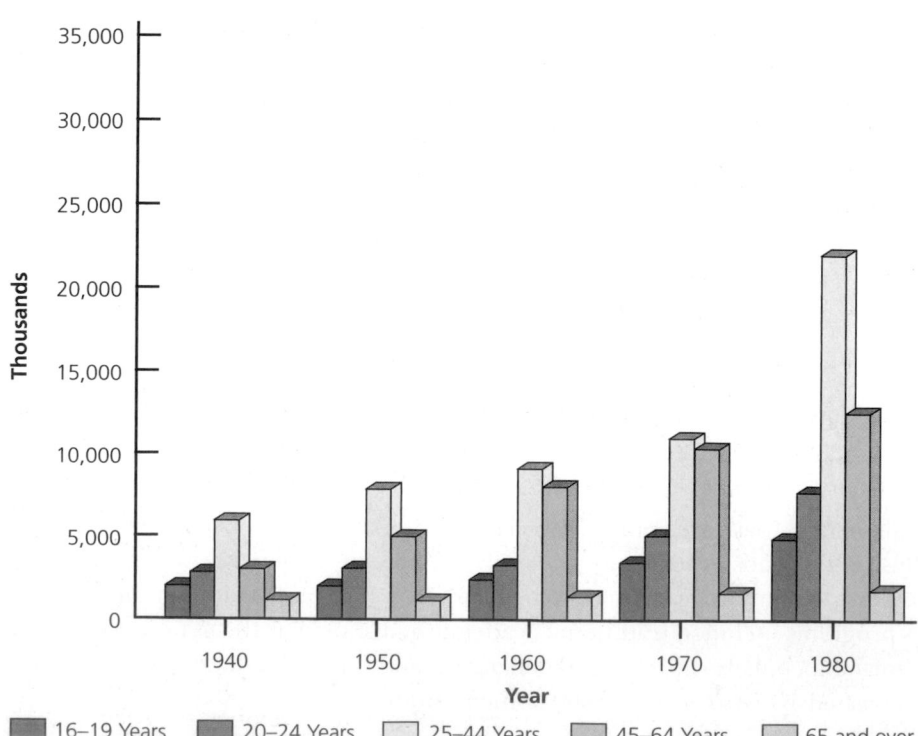

**Figure 29.2 Women in the Workforce, 1940–80**

U.S. Bureau of the Census.

■ 16–19 Years    ■ 20–24 Years    □ 25–44 Years    ■ 45–64 Years    ■ 65 and over since World War II had viewed homosexuality as a treatable mental illness, reclassified it as a normal sexual orientation. Meanwhile, a slow process of decriminalization of homosexual acts between consenting adults began. In 1975 the U.S. Civil Service Commission ended its ban on the employment of homosexuals.

## THE CHICANO REBELLION

To many Americans, the Chicano movement seemed to burst onto the scene in 1965, when the United Farm Workers (UFW), a union of mainly migrant workers, struck against grape growers of the San Joaquin Valley in California. By 1968, strike leaders Cesar Chavez and Dolores Huerta were heading a nationwide boycott of non-union-picked grapes and lettuce.

**Labor activist Cesar** Chavez spearheaded the organization of Chicano agricultural workers into the United Farm Workers (UFW), the first successful union of migrant workers. In 1965, a strike of grape pickers in the fields around Delano, California, and a nationwide boycott of table grapes brought Chavez and the UFW into the media spotlight. Like Martin Luther King Jr., he advocated nonviolent methods for achieving justice and equality.

While Chavez emerged as a national hero, many young Mexican Americans spearheaded an urban-based movement based on identity politics, which Chavez himself rejected. They adopted the slang term *Chicano*, in preference to Mexican American, to express a militant ethnic nationalism. Chicano militants demanded not only their full civil rights but also recognition of their distinctive culture and history.

High school students were at the forefront of this new movement. In March 1968, the Brown Berets, a group modeled on the Black Panthers, helped to plan the "blow out" (walkout) that sent nearly 15,000 Chicano teenagers into the streets of East Los Angeles. The high school students demanded educational reform, including courses on the history, literature, art, and language of Mexican Americans. After the police arrested the protesters, students in San Antonio and Denver expressed their solidarity by conducting their own blow outs, holding placards reading "Teachers, Sí, Bigots, No!" Meanwhile, college students demanded Chicano studies programs.

The larger Chicano movement found vivid expression in the performing and visual arts and in literature. *Teatro*, comprising film and drama, flourished as an exploration of the political dimensions of Mexican American society. One of the most popular and visible media was the mural, often inspired by art of Mexican masters such as Diego Rivera. One of the most important writers to capture the excitement of the Chicano movement was Oscar Zeta Acosta, whose *Revolt of the Cockroach*, published in 1973, renders into fiction some of the major events of the era.

## RED POWER

The phrase **"Red Power,"** attributed to Vine Deloria Jr., commonly expressed a pan-Indian identity. At the forefront of this movement was the **American Indian Movement (AIM)**. Founded in 1968, AIM represented mainly urban Indian communities. Like Black Panthers and Brown Berets, its young, militant leaders organized initially to monitor law enforcement practices. They soon built a network of urban centers, churches, and philanthropic organizations as well as the "powwow circuit" that publicized news of protest and educational activities across the country (see Map 29.4).

The movement's major catalyst was the occupation of the deserted federal prison on Alcatraz Island in San Francisco Bay. On November 20, 1969, a group of eighty-nine "Indians of All Tribes" claimed the island according to the terms of

**myhistorylab**

Exploring America: *The American Indian Movement*

**Red Power**  Term for pan-Indian identity.

**American Indian Movement (AIM)** Group of Native-American political activists who used confrontations with the federal government to publicize their case for Indian rights.

# MAP EXPLORATION

To explore an interactive version of this map, go to **http://www.prenhall.com/faraghertlc/map29.4**

CANADA

WASHINGTON

OREGON

MONTANA

IDAHO

NORTH DAKOTA

MINNESOTA

SOUTH DAKOTA

WISCONSIN

MICHIGAN

WYOMING

NEBRASKA

IOWA

NEVADA

UTAH

COLORADO

KANSAS

MISSOURI

ILLINOIS

INDIANA

OHIO

KENTUCKY

WEST VIRGINIA

VIRGINIA

VERMONT

MAINE

NEW HAMPSHIRE

MASSACHUSETTS

NEW YORK

RHODE ISLAND

CONNECTICUT

NEW JERSEY

DELAWARE

MARYLAND

PENNSYLVANIA

CALIFORNIA

ARIZONA

NEW MEXICO

OKLAHOMA

ARKANSAS

TENNESSEE

NORTH CAROLINA

SOUTH CAROLINA

GEORGIA

ALABAMA

MISSISSIPPI

TEXAS

LOUISIANA

FLORIDA

PACIFIC OCEAN

ATLANTIC OCEAN

MEXICO

Gulf of Mexico

Reservation

**MAP 29.4**

**Major Indian Reservations, 1976** Although sizable areas, designated Indian reservations represented only a small portion of territory occupied in earlier times.

WHAT WERE the major goals of the American Indian Movement when it was formed?

---

an 1868 Sioux treaty that gave Indians rights to unused federal property on Indian land. For the next nineteen months, around a hundred Indians, including about eighty UCLA students, occupied the island. Although the protestors ultimately failed to achieve their specific goals, which included a deed to the land and federal funding for a cultural center, they rallied the larger Indian community. With the occupation at Alcatraz, a participant testified, "we got back our worth, our pride, our dignity, our humanity."

Another series of dramatic events began in 1972, when AIM sponsored the **"Trail of Broken Treaties"** caravan. First they went to Washington, DC, where they staged a weeklong occupation of the Bureau of Indian Affairs. AIM insurgents then headed west, to the Pine Ridge Reservation, the site of the 1890 massacre at Wounded Knee, South Dakota. There in the spring of 1973 they demanded a restoration of treaty rights and began a siege that lasted ten weeks. Dozens of FBI

**Trail of Broken Treaties** 1972 event staged by the American Indian Movement (AIM) that culminated in a week-long occupation of the Bureau of Indian Affairs in Washington, D.C.

agents with shoot-to-kill orders poured in, leaving two Indians dead and an unknown number of casualties on both sides.

The Red Power movement culminated in the "Longest Walk," a five-month march in 1978 from San Francisco to Washington, DC. Again, activists emphasized the history of the forced removal of Indians from their homelands and the U.S. government's repeated violation of treaty rights. By this time, several tribes had won in court, by legislation or by administrative fiat, small parts of what had been taken from them. But despite these victories, many tribal lands continued to suffer from industrial and government waste-dumping and other commercial uses. On reservations and in urban areas with heavy Indian concentrations, alcohol abuse and ill health remained serious problems.

## THE ASIAN AMERICAN MOVEMENT

In 1968 groups of Chinese, Japanese, and Filipino students began to identify for the first time as Asian Americans. Students at San Francisco State University formed the Asian American Political Alliance (AAPA), while UC-Berkeley students mobilized to "express Asian American solidarity in a predominantly white society." Within a short time "Yellow Power" organizations spread throughout California and to the East Coast and Midwest.

These groups stood firmly against the Vietnam War, condemning it as a violation of the national sovereignty of the small Asian country. They also protested the racism directed against Southeast Asian peoples. In response, Yellow Power activists proclaimed their solidarity with their "Asian brothers and sisters" in Vietnam.

Throughout 1968 and 1969 Asian American college students boycotted classes and demanded the establishment of ethnic studies programs. By 1973, major universities introduced courses on Asian American studies, and a few set up interdisciplinary departments.

Looking to the example of the Black Panthers, Yellow Power activists also took their struggle into the community. Community activists organized a variety of campaigns. The Redress and Reparations Movement, begun by Sansei (third-generation Japanese Americans), for example, encouraged children to ask their parents about their wartime internment experiences and prompted older civil rights organizations, such as the Japanese American Citizens League, to raise the issue of reparations. Trade unionists organized new Asian workers, mainly in service industries and garment trades. Other campaigns reflected the growing diversity of the Asian population. Filipinos, the fastest-growing group, demonstrated against the U.S.-backed Philippine dictator Ferdinand Marcos. Students from South Korea similarly denounced the repressive government in their homeland. Samoans publicized the damage caused by nuclear testing in the Pacific Islands. Ultimately, however, in blurring intergroup differences, the Asian American movement failed to reach the growing immigrant populations, especially the numerous Southeast Asians fleeing their devastated homeland.

## THE NIXON PRESIDENCY

Richard M. Nixon inherited not only an increasingly unpopular war but also a nation riven by internal discord. Without specifying his plans, he promised a "just and honorable peace" in Southeast Asia and the restoration of law and order at home. Yet, once in office, Nixon puzzled both friends and foes. He ordered unprecedented illegal government action against private citizens while agreeing with Congress to enhance several welfare programs and improve environmental protection. He widened and intensified the war in

**HOW DID** Nixon win the White House in 1968?

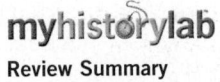
Review Summary

Vietnam, yet made stunning moves toward détente with the People's Republic of China. An architect of the Cold War in the 1950s, Nixon became the first president to foresee its end. Nixon worked hard in the White House, centralizing authority and reigning defiantly as an "Imperial President"—until he brought himself down.

## DOMESTIC POLICY

Nixon deeply desired to restore order in American society. "We live in a deeply troubled and profoundly unsettled time," he noted. "Drugs, crime, campus revolts, racial discord, draft resistance—on every hand we find old standards violated, old values discarded." Despite his hostility to liberalism, however, Nixon had some surprises for conservatives. Determined to win reelection in 1972, he supported new Social Security benefits and subsidized housing for the poor and oversaw the creation of the Environmental Protection Agency and the Occupational Safety and Health Administration. Most notable was his support, under the guidance of Democratic adviser Daniel P. Moynihan, for the Family Assistance Plan, which proposed a minimal income for the poor in place of welfare benefits. Conservatives judged the plan too generous while liberals found it inadequate. Moreover, the plan was expensive. Bipartisan opposition ultimately killed the bill.

Nixon also embraced a policy of fiscal liberalism, even accepting the idea of deficit spending. His ninety-day freeze on wages, rents, and prices, designed to halt the inflation caused by the massive spending on the Vietnam War, also closely resembled Democratic policies. Finally, Nixon's support of adjustments or quotas favoring minority contractors in construction projects—created an explosive precedent for "set-aside" programs later blamed on liberals.

Yet, for the most part, Nixon remained committed to the "Southern Strategy" that brought him into office. He lined up with conservatives on most civil rights issues and thus enlarged his southern Republican base. He slowed school desegregation and rejected the busing programs required to achieve racial balance. His nominees to the Supreme Court were far more conservative than those appointed by Eisenhower.

## NIXON'S WAR

Nixon promised to bring "peace with honor." Yet, despite this pledge, the Vietnam War raged for four more years before a peace settlement was reached (see Figure 29.3).

Much of the responsibility for prolonging the war rested with Henry A. Kissinger, Nixon's national security adviser. A forceful personality, Kissinger insisted that the United States could not retain its global leadership by appearing weak to either allies or enemies. After centralizing foreign policymaking in the White House, Kissinger and Nixon together overpowered those State Department members who had concluded that the majority of Americans no longer supported the war (see Figure 29.4).

In public Nixon followed a policy of "Vietnamization." On May 14, 1969, he announced that the time was approaching "when the South Vietnamese . . . will be able to take over some of the fighting." During the next several months, he ordered the withdrawal of 60,000

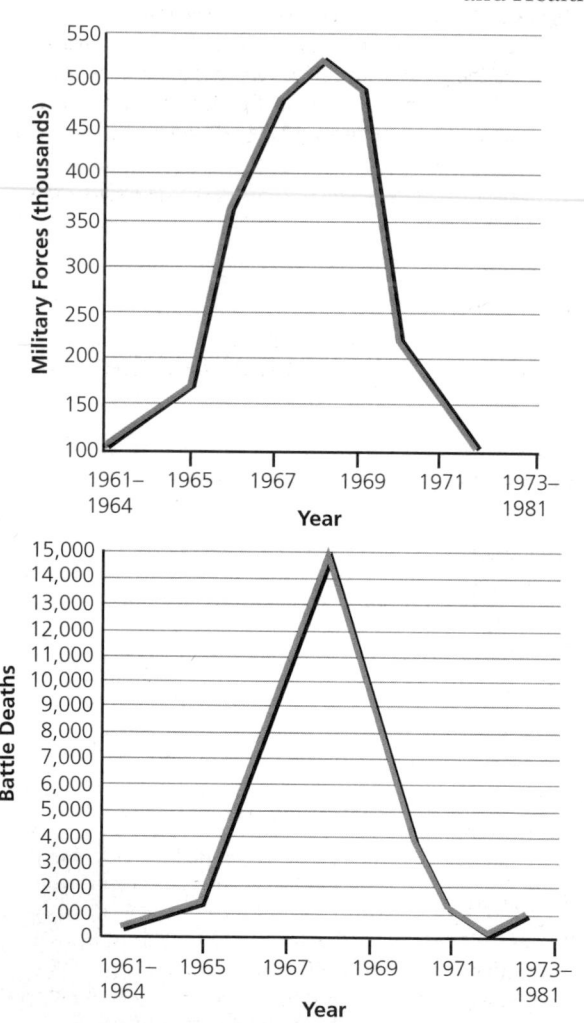

**Figure 29.3 U.S. Military Forces in Vietnam and Casualties, 1961–81**

The U.S. government estimated battle deaths between 1969 and 1973 for South Vietnamese troops at 107,504 and North Vietnamese and Vietcong at more than a half million. Although the United States suffered fewer deaths, the cost was enormous.

U.S. Department of Defense, *Selected Manpower Statistics*, annual and unpublished data; beginning 1981, National Archives and Records Service, "Combat Area Casualty File" (3-330-80-3).

U.S. troops. In private, Nixon mulled over the option of a "knockout blow" to the North Vietnamese.

On April 30, 1970, Nixon made one of the most controversial decisions of his presidency. Without seeking congressional approval, he ordered U.S. troops to invade the tiny nation of Cambodia. Nixon hoped in this way to end North Vietnamese infiltration into the South, but he also decided to live up to what he privately called his "wild man" or "mad bomber" reputation. The enemy would be unable to anticipate the location or severity of the next U.S. strike, Nixon reasoned, and would thus feel compelled to negotiate.

Nixon could not have predicted what followed the invasion of Cambodia. The largest series of demonstrations and police–student confrontations in the nation's history erupted. At Kent State University in Ohio, twenty-eight National Guardsmen shot into an unarmed crowd of students, killing four and wounding nine. Ten days later, on May 14, at Jackson State University, a black school in Mississippi, state troopers entered a campus dormitory and began shooting wildly, killing two students and wounding twelve others. Huge demonstrations took place on fifty campuses, and thirty-seven college and university presidents signed a letter calling on the president to end the war. A few weeks later the Senate adopted a bipartisan resolution outlawing the use of funds for U.S. military operations in Cambodia, starting July 1, 1970.

The president did not accept defeat easily. In February 1971 Nixon directed the South Vietnamese army to invade Laos and cut supply lines, but the demoralized invading force suffered a quick and humiliating defeat. Faced with enemy occupation of more and more territory during a major offensive in April 1972, Nixon ordered the mining of North Vietnamese harbors and directed B-52s to conduct massively destructive bombing missions in Cambodia and North Vietnam (see Seeing History).

Nixon also sent Kissinger to Paris for secret negotiations with delegates from North Vietnam. They agreed to a cease-fire specifying the withdrawal of all U.S. troops and the return of all U.S. prisoners of war. Knowing these terms ensured defeat, South Vietnam's president refused to sign the agreement. On Christmas Day 1972, hoping for a better negotiating position, Nixon ordered one final wave of bomb attacks on North Vietnam's cities. To halt the bombing, the North Vietnamese resumed negotiations. But the terms of the Paris Peace Agreement, signed by North Vietnam and the United States in January 1973, differed little from the settlement Nixon could have procured in 1969. U.S. troops began to withdraw in March 1973.

In April 1975 the North Vietnamese took over Saigon, and the Communist-led Democratic Republic of Vietnam soon united the small nation. The war was finally over. It had cost the United States 58,000 lives and $150 billion. The nation had not only failed to achieve its stated war goal but also had lost an important post in Southeast Asia. Equally important, the United States proved it could not sustain the policy of containment introduced by President Truman.

While Nixon was maneuvering to bring about "peace with honor," the chilling crimes of war had already begun to haunt Americans. In 1971 the army court-martialed a young lieutenant, William L. Calley Jr., for the murder of "at least" twenty-two Vietnamese civilians during a 1968 search-and-destroy mission subsequently known as the **My Lai Massacre**. Calley's platoon had destroyed a village and slaughtered more than 350 unarmed South Vietnamese, raping

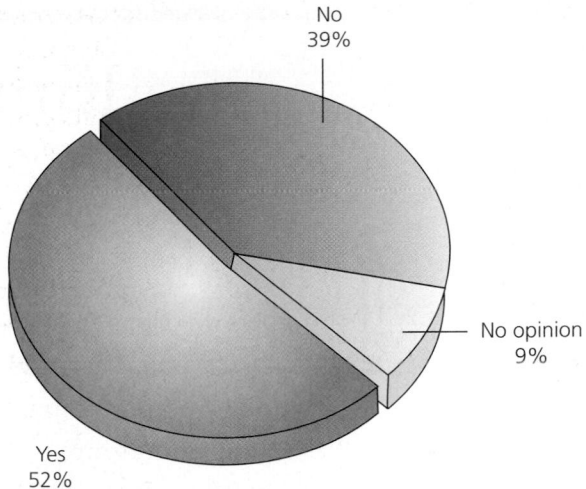

**Figure 29.4 Public Opinion on the War in Vietnam**
By 1969 Americans were sharply divided in their assessments of the progress of the war and peace negotiations. The American Institute of Public Opinion, founded in 1935 by George Gallup, charted a growing dissatisfaction with the war in Vietnam.

*The Gallup Poll: Public Opinion, 1935–74* (New York: Random House, 1974), p. 2189.

**28–11**
*Vietnamization* (1969)

## QUICK REVIEW

**The Nixon Doctrine**

◆ Nixon responded to antiwar protesters by reducing the role of U.S. ground forces in Vietnam.

◆ "Vietnamization": The withdrawal of U.S. troops as fast as possible without undermining the South Vietnamese government.

◆ The Nixon Doctrine substituted weapons and money for troops.

**My Lai Massacre**   Killing of twenty-two Vietnamese civilians by U.S. forces during a 1968 search-and-destroy mission.

# Kim Phuc, Fleeing a Napalm Attack near Trang Bang

In 1972, during the phase of the war termed "Vietnamization," South Vietnamese aircraft bombed the village of Trang Bang, about twenty-five miles from Saigon. They were attacking North Vietnamese and Vietcong fighters but mistakenly targeted a Buddhist pagoda. The incendiary bombs contained black, oily napalm that burned the villagers gathered there.

News photographer Nick Ut had been assigned to meet up with the South Vietnamese army at Trang Bang. "When we [the reporters] moved closer to the village we saw the first people running," he recalled in 1999. "I thought 'Oh my God' when I suddenly saw a woman with her left leg badly burned by napalm. Then came a woman carrying a baby, who died, then another woman carrying a small child with its skin coming off. When I took a picture of them I heard a child screaming and saw that young girl who had pulled off all her burning clothes. She yelled to her brother on her left. Just before the napalm was dropped soldiers [of the South Vietnamese Army] had yelled to the children to run but there wasn't enough time."

Ut, who took the severely burned girl to the hospital before delivering his film, won a Pulitzer Prize for the photograph. ■

**WHAT DOES** this photograph suggest about the role of the news media during the Vietnam war? In focusing on civilians, what does Nick Ut's photograph suggest about the course of the war?

and beating many of the women before killing them. "My Lai was not an isolated incident," one veteran attested, but "only a minor step beyond the standard official United States policy in Indochina." The platoon commander at My Lai, Calley was first sentenced to life imprisonment before receiving a reduced term of ten years. The secretary of the army paroled Calley after three years of house arrest in his apartment.

## PLAYING THE "CHINA CARD"

Apart from Vietnam, Nixon's foreign policy defied the expectations of liberals and conservatives alike. Playing the "China card" was the most dramatic of the president's moves. Early in his political career Nixon had avidly supported the archconservative China lobby. But as president he considered the People's Republic of China too important to be isolated by the West and too obviously hostile to the Soviet Union to be discounted as a potential ally.

"Ping-Pong diplomacy" began in April 1971, when the Chinese hosted a table tennis team from the United States. Henry Kissinger embarked on a secret mission a few months later. Finally, in February 1972, Richard and Pat Nixon flew to Beijing, where they were greeted by foreign minister Zhou Enlai and a band playing "The Star-Spangled Banner."

It was a momentous and surprising event, one that marked a new era in East-West diplomacy. The president's move successfully increased diplomatic pressure on the Soviet Union but simultaneously weakened the Nationalist Chinese government in Taiwan, which now slipped into virtual diplomatic obscurity.

Next the president went to Moscow to negotiate with Soviet leader Leonid Brezhnev, who was anxious about U.S. involvement with China and eager for economic assistance. Declaring, "There must be room in this world for two great nations with different systems to live together and work together," Nixon offered to sell $1 billion of grain to the Soviets. Winning the favor of American wheat farmers, this deal simultaneously relieved U.S. trade deficits and crop surpluses. Afterward, the Soviet leader became visibly more cautious about supporting revolutions in the third world. Nixon also completed negotiations of the **Strategic Arms Limitation Treaty** (SALT, known later as SALT I). A limited measure, SALT I represented the first success at strategic arms control since the start of the Cold War and a major public relations victory for the leaders of the two superpowers.

Nixon's last major diplomatic foray was far less effective. The president sent Kissinger on a two-year mission of "shuttle diplomacy" to mediate Israeli-Arab disputes, to ensure the continued flow of oil, and to increase lucrative U.S. arms sales to Arab countries. The Egyptians and Israelis agreed to a cease-fire in their October 1973 Yom Kippur War, but little progress toward peace in the area was achieved.

## FOREIGN POLICY AS CONSPIRACY

Nixon's conduct of foreign policy offered early clues into his political character. Although he had welcomed the publicity surrounding his historic moves toward détente with the Soviet Union and normalized relations with China, Nixon generally handled the nation's foreign affairs behind closed doors. But as opposition to the Vietnam War mounted in Congress, he began to face hard questions about this practice.

At the time, apart from the highly publicized tour to China, Nixon revealed little about his policy for other parts of the globe. Unknown to most Americans, he accelerated the delivery of arms supplies to foreign dictators, including the

**Strategic Arms Limitation Treaty**
Treaty signed in 1972 by the United States and the Soviet Union to slow the nuclear arms race.

**Richard Nixon bid** a final farewell to his White House staff as he left Washington, DC, on August 9, 1974. The first president to resign from office, Nixon had become so entangled in the Watergate scandal that his impeachment appeared certain. He was succeeded by Vice President Gerald Ford. After taking the oath of office later that day, President Ford remarked that the wounds of Watergate were "more painful and more poisonous than those of foreign wars."

shah of Iran, Ferdinand Marcos of the Philippines, and the white supremacist apartheid government in South Africa. His CIA assistants trained and aided SAVAK, the Iranian secret police force notorious for torturing political dissidents. They also stood behind the South African government in its effort to curtail the activities of the antiapartheid African National Congress. In Latin America, Nixon gave financial assistance and military aid to repressive regimes such as that of Anastasio Somoza of Nicaragua, notorious for its blatant corruption and repeated violations of human rights.

Still more controversial was Nixon's plan to overthrow the legally elected socialist government of Salvador Allende in Chile. With the assistance of nongovernment agencies, such as the AFL-CIO's American Institute for Free Labor Development, the CIA destabilized the regime by funding right-wing parties, launching demonstrations, and preparing the Chilean army for a coup. In September 1973, a military junta killed President Allende and captured, tortured, or murdered thousands of his supporters. Nixon and Kissinger warmly welcomed the new ruler, Augusto Pinochet, granting him financial assistance to restabilize the country.

## DIRTY TRICKS AND THE 1972 ELECTION

As Nixon approached the 1972 reelection campaign, he tightened his inner circle of White House staff who assisted him in withholding information from the public, discrediting critics, and engaging in assorted "dirty tricks." Staff members solicited illegal campaign contributions and laundered the money through Mexican bank accounts. They also formed a secret squad, "the plumbers," to halt the troublesome information leaks. This team, headed by former CIA agent E. Howard Hunt and former FBI agent G. Gordon Liddy, assisted in conspiracy at the highest levels of government.

The first person on the squad's "hit list" was Daniel Ellsberg, a former researcher with the Department of Defense, who in 1971 had turned over to the press secret documents outlining the history of U.S. involvement in Vietnam. The so-called **Pentagon Papers** exposed the role of presidents and military leaders in deceiving the public and Congress about the conduct of the United States in Southeast Asia. Nixon sought to bar publication by *The New York Times*, but the

**Pentagon Papers** Classified Defense Department documents on the history of the United States' involvement in Vietnam, prepared in 1968 and leaked to the press in 1971.

Supreme Court ruled in favor of the newspaper on the basis of the First Amendment. Frustrated in his attempt to suppress the report, Nixon directed the Department of Justice to prosecute Ellsberg on charges of conspiracy, espionage, and theft. Meanwhile, Hunt and Liddy, seeking to discredit Ellsberg, broke into the office of his former psychiatrist. They found nothing that would make their target less heroic in the eyes of an increasingly skeptical public, and by 1973 the charges against Ellsberg were dropped after the Nixon administration itself stood guilty of misconduct.

During the 1972 presidential campaign, the Committee to Re-Elect the President (CREEP) enjoyed a huge war chest and spent a good portion on dirty tricks designed to divide the Democrats and discredit them in the eyes of the voting public. In the short run, they tallied a monumental success. Nixon presented himself as the candidate of "middle Americans," the Great Silent Majority, and won reelection by a landslide. More important in the long run, the Republicans captured the once solidly Democratic South and the majority of blue-collar, Catholic, and urban voters. As the carrier of conservatism, Nixon achieved the grandest moment of his long and complex political career. Nevertheless, even with this huge mandate from voters, the most audacious plan of his reelection committee—wiretapping the Democratic National Committee headquarters—ultimately backfired.

## WATERGATE: NIXON'S DOWNFALL

On June 17, 1972, a security team had tripped up a group of intruders hired by CREEP to install listening devices in the Washington, DC, Watergate apartment and office complex where the Democrats were headquartered. The police arrested five men, who were later found guilty of conspiracy and burglary. Although Nixon disclaimed any knowledge of the plan, two *Washington Post* reporters, Bob Woodward and Carl Bernstein, followed a trail of evidence back to the nation's highest office.

Televised Senate hearings opened to public view more than a pattern of presidential wrongdoing: they showed an attempt to impede investigations of the **Watergate** case. Testifying before the committee, a former Nixon aide revealed evidence of secret tape recordings of conversations held in the Oval Office. After special prosecutor Archibald Cox refused to allow Nixon to claim executive privilege and withhold the tapes, the president ordered Cox fired. On June 24, 1974, the Supreme Court voted unanimously that Nixon had to release the tapes to a new special prosecutor, Leon Jaworski.

Although incomplete, the Watergate tapes proved damning. They documented Nixon's ravings against his enemies, including anti-Semitic and racist slurs, and his conniving efforts to harass private citizens through federal agencies. The tapes also proved that Nixon had not only known about plans to cover up the Watergate break-in but had in fact ordered it. The news media enjoyed a field day with the revelations of Nixon's role in a criminal conspiracy to obstruct justice. In July 1974, the House Judiciary Committee adopted three articles of impeachment, charging Nixon with obstructing justice, abusing the power of his office, and acting in contempt of Congress.

Charges of executive criminality had clouded the Nixon administration since his vice president left in disgrace. In 1972 Spiro Agnew admitted to accepting large kickbacks while serving as governor of Maryland. Pleading no contest to this and to charges of federal income tax evasion, Agnew resigned in October 1973. Gerald Ford, a moderate Republican representative from Michigan, replaced him and now stood in the wings while the president's drama unfolded.

 **30–1**
House Judiciary Committee, *Conclusion on Impeachment Resolution* (1974)

**Watergate** A complex scandal involving attempts to cover up illegal actions taken by administration officials and leading to the resignation of President Richard Nixon in 1974.

## CHRONOLOGY

**1964** President Lyndon Johnson calls for "an unconditional war on poverty" in his state of the union address

Gulf of Tonkin resolution

The Economic Opportunity Act establishes the Office of Economic Opportunity

Free speech movement gets under way at University of California at Berkeley

Johnson defeats conservative Barry Goldwater for president

**1965** President Johnson authorizes Operation Rolling Thunder, the bombing of North Vietnam

Teach-ins begin on college campuses

First major march on Washington for peace is organized

Watts uprising begins a wave of rebellions in black communities

**1966** J. William Fulbright publishes *The Arrogance of Power*

Black Panther Party is formed

National Organization for Women (NOW) is formed

**1967** Antiwar rally in New York City draws 300,000

Vietnam Veterans against the War is formed

Uprisings in Newark, Detroit, and other cities

Hippie "Summer of Love"

**1968** U.S. ground troop levels in Vietnam number 500,000

Tet Offensive in Vietnam, followed by international protests against U.S. policies

Martin Luther King Jr. is assassinated; riots break out in more than 100 cities

Vietnam peace talks begin in Paris

Robert Kennedy is assassinated

Democratic National Convention, held in Chicago, nominates Hubert Humphrey; "police riot" against protesters

Richard Nixon elected president

American Indian Movement (AIM) founded

**1969** Woodstock music festival marks the high tide of the counterculture

Stonewall Riot in Greenwich Village sparks the gay liberation movement

*Apollo 11* lands on the moon

**1970** U.S. incursion into Cambodia sparks campus demonstrations; students killed at Kent State and Jackson State universities

**1971** Lieutenant William Calley Jr. court-martialed for My Lai Massacre

*The New York Times* starts publishing the Pentagon Papers

**1972** Nixon visits China and Soviet Union

SALT I limits offensive intercontinental ballistic missiles

Intruders attempting to "bug" Democratic headquarters in the Watergate complex are arrested

Nixon is reelected in a landslide

Nixon orders Christmas Day bombing of North Vietnam

**1973** Paris Peace Agreement ends war in Vietnam

FBI seizes Indian occupants of Wounded Knee, South Dakota

Watergate burglars tried; congressional hearings on Watergate

CIA destabilizes elected Chilean government, which is overthrown

Vice President Spiro T. Agnew resigns

**1974** House Judiciary Committee adopts articles of impeachment against Nixon

Nixon resigns the presidency

A delegation from Congress, led by Senator Barry Goldwater, approached Nixon with the news that impeachment and conviction were certain. On August 8, 1974, in a speech underscoring his accomplishments and admitting only to "some errors in judgment," Nixon announced his intention to step down, becoming the first U.S. president to resign from office.

# CONCLUSION

The resignations of Richard Nixon and Spiro Agnew did little to relieve the feeling of national exhaustion that followed the Vietnam War. U.S. troops pulled out of Vietnam in 1973 and the war officially ended in 1975, but bitterness lingered over the unprecedented—and, for many, humiliating—defeat. Moreover, confidence in the government's highest office was severely shaken. The passage of the War Powers Act in 1973, written to compel any future president to seek congressional approval for armed intervention abroad and passed over Nixon's veto, dramatized both the widespread suspicion of an "Imperial Presidency" and a yearning for peace. But the positive dream of community that had inspired Johnson, King, and a generation of student activists could not be revived. No other vision took its place.

In 1968 seven prominent antiwar protesters had been brought to trial for allegedly conspiring to disrupt the Democratic National Convention in Chicago. Just a few years later, the majority of Americans had concluded that presidents Johnson and Nixon had conspired to do far worse. They had intentionally deceived the public about the nature and fortunes of the war. This moral failure signaled a collapse at the center of the American political system. Since Dwight Eisenhower left office warning of the potential danger embedded in the "military-industrial complex," no president had survived the presidency with his honor intact. Watergate, then, appeared to cap the politics of the Cold War, its revelations only reinforcing futility and cynicism. The United States was left psychologically at war with itself.

# REVIEW QUESTIONS

1. Discuss the events that led up to and contributed to U.S. involvement in Vietnam. How did U.S. involvement in the war affect domestic programs?

2. Discuss the reasons the protest movement against the Vietnam War started on college campuses. Describe how these movements were organized and how the opponents of the war differed from the supporters.

3. Discuss the programs sponsored by Johnson's plan for a Great Society. What was their impact on urban poverty in the late 1960s?

4. What was the impact of the assassinations of Martin Luther King Jr. and Robert Kennedy on the election of 1968? How were various communities affected?

5. How were the "politics of identity" movements different from earlier civil rights organizations? In what ways did the various movements resemble one another?

6. Why did Richard Nixon enjoy such a huge electoral victory in 1972? Discuss his foreign and domestic policies. What led to his sudden downfall?

## KEY TERMS

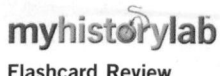
Flashcard Review

**American Indian Movement (AIM)** (p. 841)

**Black Panther Party** (p. 836)

**Black Power** (p. 836)

**Counterculture** (p. 827)

**Free speech movement** (p. 827)

**Gulf of Tonkin resolution** (p. 826)

**Medicare** (p. 831)

**My Lai Massacre** (p. 845)

**National Organization for Women (NOW)** (p. 838)

**Office of Economic Opportunity (OEO)** (p. 830)

**Pentagon Papers** (p. 848)

**Red Power** (p. 841)

**Strategic Arms Limitation Treaty** (p. 847)

**Students for a Democratic Society (SDS)** (p. 824)

**Trail of Broken Treaties** (p. 842)

**War on poverty** (p. 830)

**Watergate** (p. 849)

## RECOMMENDED READING

John A. Andrew III, *Lyndon Johnson and the Great Society* (1998). An assessment of the Great Society, with special emphasis on the two major issues of civil rights and poverty. Andrew discusses Johnson's aspirations and the obstacles that kept them out of reach.

Alexander Bloom, ed., *Long Time Gone: Sixties America Then and Now* (2001). Ten essays covering various aspects of the social and political movements of the 1960s. The authors draw out the meaning of the "sixties" for today and dispel commonplace myths by providing accurate information and a sound context for interpretation.

Winifred Breines, *The Trouble Between Us: An Uneasy History of White and Black Women in the Feminist Movement* (2006). Aims to explain the failure of feminists to create a racially integrated movement. The author deals equally with the experiences of both black and white women and uses a variety of sources, including oral histories, to document her case.

Robert Dallek, *Lyndon B. Johnson* (2005). A condensation of a two-volume study, Dallek's biography presents rich details of Johnson's life from his origins in Texas to his troubled years in the White House. The author does little to soften the image of Johnson and instead portrays him as both complex and flamboyant.

Jane F. Gerhard, *Desiring Revolution: Second-Wave Feminism and the Rewriting of American Sexual Thought, 1920–1982* (2001). Discusses the background of the feminist side of the sexual revolution with special attention to popular versions of Freud's theories. Gerhard discusses disagreements among feminists on the meaning and experience of sexual liberation.

Michael H. Hunt, *Lyndon Johnson's War: America's Cold War Crusade in Vietnam, 1945–1968* (1996). Tracks Johnson's decisions to wage all-out war in Vietnam. Hunt interprets Johnson's actions as consistent with the Cold War foreign policy that had prevailed since the Truman administration and its pledge to "contain" communism.

Maurice Isserman and Michael Kazin, *America Divided: The Civil War of the 1960s,* 3rd ed. (2007). A survey and astute analysis of the Vietnam War and its impact on domestic politics, with close scrutiny of the youth movements that rose in the late 1960s.

Rebecca E. Klatch, *A Generation Divided: The New Left, the New Right, and the 1960s* (1999). Compares and contrasts the respective roles of Students for a Democratic Society and the conservative Young Americans for Freedom on college campuses. Klatch, a sociologist, presents lengthy oral interviews with former student activists in both camps.

Joan Morrison and Robert K. Morrison, eds., *From Camelot to Kent State: The Sixties Experience in the Words of Those Who Lived It* (2001). A collection of fifty-nine oral histories with a range of people who lived through the 1960s. The volume includes stories of better-known activists, such as Eldridge Cleaver and Abbie Hoffman, as well as those who were soldiers in Vietnam or student activists. This edition also contains many photographs.

Laura Pulido, *Black, Brown, Yellow, and Left: Radical Activism in Los Angeles* (2006). A well-documented survey of activism in communities of color since the 1960s. Pulido examines the role of women in dealing within minority men within various organizations and movements.

Melvin Small, *AntiWarriors: The Vietnam War and the Battle for America's Hearts and Minds* (2002). A readable, succinct study of the groundswell of opposition to the war in Vietnam. Small covers many facets of the antiwar movement, ranging from hippies to Vietnam Veterans Against the War.

Anthony Summers, *The Arrogance of Power: The Secret World of Richard Nixon* (2000). A popular biography of Nixon's life from his early political career in California through his presidency. Summers drew on more than a thousand interviews, including those with Nixon's psychotherapist, to portray the former president's erratic behavior and mental instability during as well as before the disastrous Watergate affair.

For study resources for this chapter, go to **www.myhistorylab.com** and choose *Out of Many, Teaching and Learning Classroom Edition.* You will find a wealth of study and review material for this chapter, including pretests and posttests, customized study plan, key-term review flash cards, interactive map and document activities, and documents for analysis.

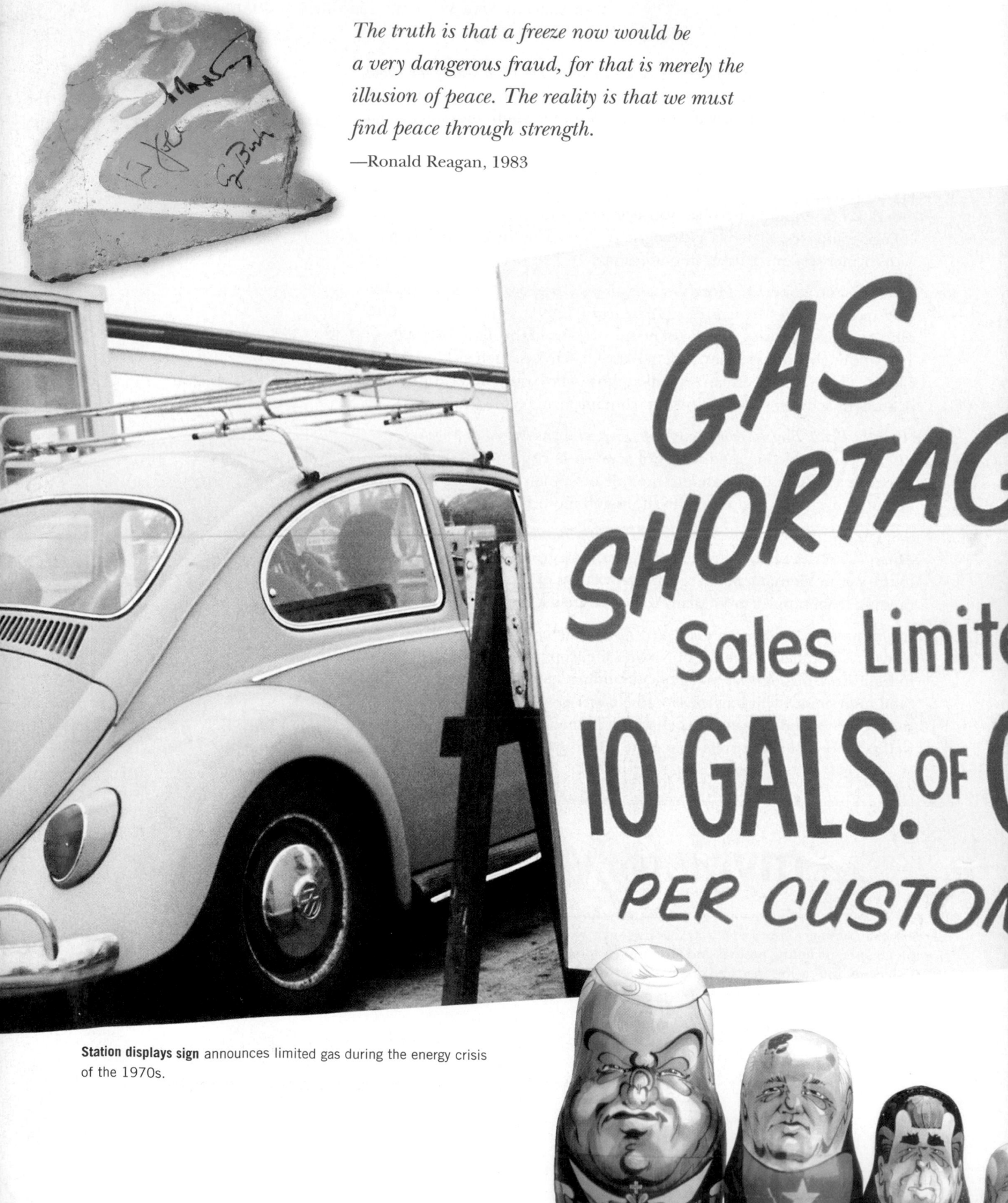

*The truth is that a freeze now would be a very dangerous fraud, for that is merely the illusion of peace. The reality is that we must find peace through strength.*

—Ronald Reagan, 1983

GAS SHORTAG

Sales Limite

10 GALS. OF C

PER CUSTOM

**Station displays sign** announces limited gas during the energy crisis of the 1970s.

# 30

# THE CONSERVATIVE ASCENDANCY
## 1974–1991

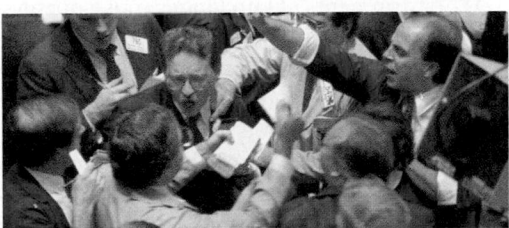

**WHAT EXPLAINS** the weakness of the U.S. economy in the 1970s?

**WHAT DID** Ford and Carter accomplish as presidents?

**WHAT EXPLAINS** the rise of the New Right in the 1980s?

**WHAT ECONOMIC** assumptions underlay "Reaganomics"?

**WHY DID** the gap between rich and poor grow in the 1980s?

**HOW DID** the Cold War end?

**WHAT FACTORS** led to U.S. involvement in the Persian Gulf War?

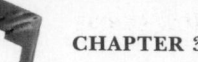

# AMERICAN COMMUNITIES
## Grassroots Conservatism in Orange County, California

IN 1962 BEE GATHRIGHT, A BROWNIE LEADER AND MOTHER OF THREE young girls, invited her neighbors to her suburban Garden Grove home to hear a political talk by a man from the nearby Knott's Berry Farm Freedom Center. "This is when I discovered that I was a conservative," she later recalled. She feared that "the Communists were going to bury us, were going to take over the world . . . . " She convinced her skeptical husband Neil, an aerospace engineer, to share her new conviction. They soon joined the California Republican Assembly, a volunteer organization committed to electing conservatives to office. In 1964 the Gathrights' home served as a local headquarters for the presidential campaign of conservative Arizona Senator Barry Goldwater.

In Orange County in the 1960s and 1970s thousands of "kitchen table" activists like the Gathrights began a transformation of American conservatism and American politics that culminated in the presidential election of Ronald Reagan in 1980. Most of them were middle-class men and women, including large numbers of professionals and small business owners. World War II and Cold War defense-related spending accelerated Orange County's growth, creating thousands of new manufacturing jobs. By 1960, more than 700,000 people lived in Orange County, an increase of nearly 400 percent since 1940, and the population doubled again to top 2 million in the 1980s.

While Barry Goldwater's 1964 campaign ignited great enthusiasm in Orange County, his national defeat forced conservatives to consider ways to shed the "extremism" label. In 1966 they successfully backed the gubernatorial campaign of Ronald Reagan, a former Hollywood actor and New Deal liberal who had evolved in the 1950s into a prominent conservative and Republican Party activist. As governor, Reagan sought to limit state support for welfare and other social services, while expanding state power to enforce law and order.

Reagan's success in California, as well as Richard Nixon's election as president in 1968, signaled an important new turn for American conservatives. They still championed anticommunism but no longer engaged in the loose talk about using nuclear weapons that had hurt Goldwater. They attacked "big government" but no longer spoke openly about repealing popular New Deal programs like Social Security. Instead, they focused on the "social issues" that increasingly troubled and mobilized Orange County's grassroots activists. Their concerns, largely defined by a "backlash" against the antiwar movement, counterculture, women's liberation, and urban uprisings, emphasized so-called family issues, in which opposition to sex education, obscenity, abortion rights, gay liberation, and the Equal Rights Amendment were all linked together. On the economic side, conservatives began to tap a deep well of resentment over rising property taxes and high inflation.

Two central themes of this new conservatism resonated with millions of Americans well beyond Orange County. One was the 1978 "revolt" of home owners that led to a sharp reduction in the property tax rate and soon spread to other states.

Orange County also helped form the second new force reshaping conservatism, "born-again" evangelical Christianity. Orange County's religious revival featured educated professionals and middle-class suburbanites who turned to Christianity for spirituality and as a way to assert order amid rapid cultural and social change. The political implications of the new evangelicalism soon became clear.

President Jimmy Carter, who took office in 1976, was a "born-again" Christian, and his successor, Ronald Reagan, raced to victory in 1980 with the strong backing of newly politicized Christian voters. For Bee Gathright, Reagan's victory vindicated her years of grassroots activism and set the nation on a conservative political course that led into the twenty-first century.

Orange County

---

**WHAT EXPLAINS** the weakness of the U.S. economy in the 1970s?

**Review Summary**

## THE OVEREXTENDED SOCIETY

Postwar prosperity had effectively kept conservatives at bay from the Eisenhower years through the 1960s. Then, in the 1970s, economic growth ground to a halt and additionally presented Americans with an unfamiliar combination of skyrocketing prices and rising unemployment. Meanwhile presidents Gerald Ford and Jimmy Carter promised little and, as far as many voters were concerned, delivered even less.

## A TROUBLED ECONOMY

The most vivid sign of the troubled economy, the energy crisis, seemed to appear suddenly in the fall of 1973, although it had been decades in the making. The United States, which used about 70 percent of all oil produced in the world, had a sufficient domestic supply until the mid-1950s. But rising demand began to outstrip national reserves, and by 1973 the nation was importing one-third of its crude oil, mainly from the Middle East. On October 17, members of the government-controlled **Organization of Petroleum Exporting Countries (OPEC)** announced an embargo on oil shipments to nations that had supported Israel in its war with Syria and Egypt, including the United States and its Western European allies (see Map 30.1).

President Nixon responded to the embargo by creating an "energy czar" and paving the way for the creation of the Department of Energy in 1977. He ordered a 10 percent reduction in air travel and appealed to Congress to lower speed limits on interstate highways to 55 miles per hour and to extend daylight-saving time into the winter months. But the impact of these measures was slight, and with the cost of gasoline, oil, and electricity up, many other prices also rose, from apartment rents and telephone bills to restaurant checks. Moreover, Americans became yet more dependent on Middle East oil supplies (see Figure 30.1).

Despite the drama of the oil crisis, the economic downturn had deeper roots in the failure of the United States to keep up with the rising industrial efficiency of other nations. U.S. automakers, determined to reduce costs, turned to "outsourcing"—that is, making cars and trucks from parts cheaply produced abroad and imported into the United States as semifinished materials. In high-tech electronics, the United States could scarcely compete against Japanese-made televisions, radios, tape players, cameras, and computers.

Between 1970 and 1982 the AFL-CIO lost nearly 30 percent of its membership. The only real union growth took place among public employees, including teachers, civil service workers, and health professionals—all of them dependent on sagging public budgets.

Typical of hard times, an increasing number of women sought jobs to support their families. By 1980 more than half of all married women with children in their care were working outside the home. Yet despite their numerical gains,

## IMAGE KEY

for pages 854–855

**a.** A piece of the fallen Berlin Wall.
**b.** Station displays sign announces limited gas during the energy crisis of the 1970s.
**c.** Nesting dolls of Communist or Russian leaders Boris Yeltsin, Mikhail Gorbechev, Leonid Brezhnev, Nikita Khruschev, Joseph Stalin, Vladimir Lenin, and Czar Nicholas II.
**d.** The black flying wing design of the stealth bomber resembles a bat.
**e.** Traders on the floor of the New York Stock Exchange on Monday, October 19, 1987. The Dow Jones Industrial Average plunged more than 500 points for the biggest one-day loss in history.
**f.** Abortion rights advocate Inga Coulter stands next to pro-life protester Elizabeth McGee during clashing demonstrations outside the Supreme Court building.
**g.** Three of the American hostages held in Iran arriving from Tehran at the Rhein-Main Airbase in Germany on 1/21/81.
**h.** An Hispanic female student raises her hand in class.
**i.** Mikhail Gorbachev and Ronald Reagan sign the INF treaty at the White House.

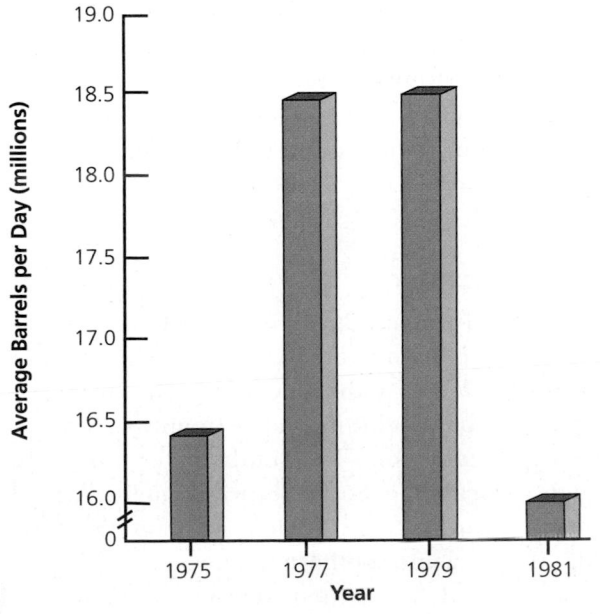

**Figure 30.1 Decline of U.S. Oil Consumption, 1975–81**
Boycotts causing shortages and high prices spurred the reduction in oil consumption. However, in the 1980s consumption once again began to rise to reach record highs.

Department of Energy, *Monthly Energy Review,* June 1982.

**Organization of Petroleum Exporting Countries (OPEC)** Cartel of oil-producing nations in Asia, Africa, and Latin America that gained substantial power over the world economy in the mid- to late-1970s by controlling the production and price of oil.

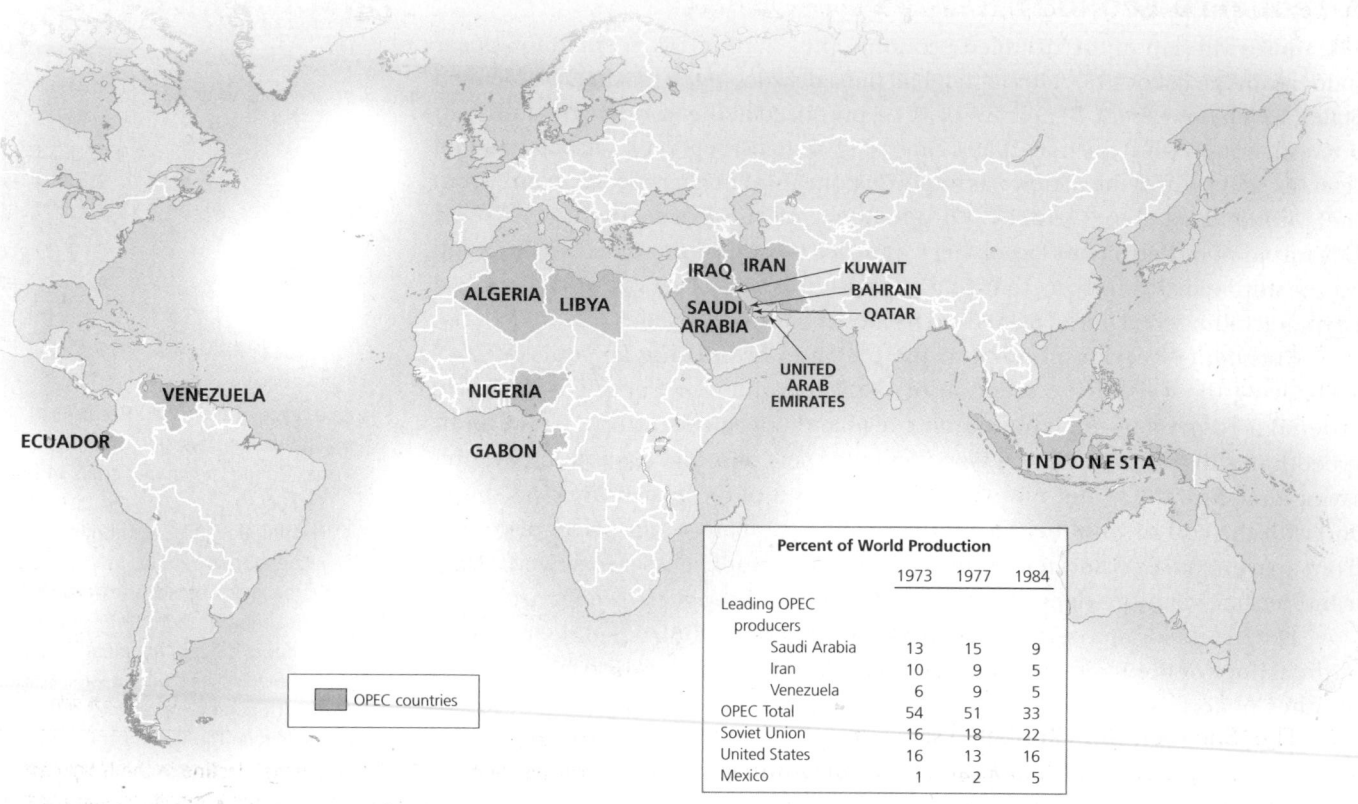

**MAP 30.1**
**World's Leading Oil Producers**

| Percent of World Production | | | |
|---|---|---|---|
| | 1973 | 1977 | 1984 |
| Leading OPEC producers | | | |
| Saudi Arabia | 13 | 15 | 9 |
| Iran | 10 | 9 | 5 |
| Venezuela | 6 | 9 | 5 |
| OPEC Total | 54 | 51 | 33 |
| Soviet Union | 16 | 18 | 22 |
| United States | 16 | 13 | 16 |
| Mexico | 1 | 2 | 5 |

WHY DID OPEC's share of world oil production drop between 1973 and 1984?

women lost ground relative to men. In 1955 women earned 64 percent of the average wages paid to men; in 1980 they earned only 59 percent. The growing service economy accounted for this dip: women clustered in occupations where the lowest wages prevailed.

African American women made some gains. Through Title VII of the Civil Rights Act, which outlawed workplace discrimination by sex or race, and the establishment of the Equal Employment Opportunity Commission to enforce it, they managed to climb the lower levels of the job ladder.

In contrast, Hispanic women, whose labor force participation leaped by 80 percent during the decade, were restricted to a very few occupations, mostly at or only slightly above the minimum wage.

## SUNBELT/SNOWBELT COMMUNITIES

The problems of the economy did not fall equally on all regions, and the distinctive pattern of economic growth and decline mirrored changes in the nation's political tenor. The bastion of prosperity as well as the bulwark of political conservatism was the **Sunbelt**, which extended from Florida to Orange County, California.

Much of the Sunbelt's growth depended on a huge outlay of federal funds, including defense spending and the allocation of Social Security benefits. Armed with retirement packages won decades earlier, huge "golden age" migrations created new communities in Florida, Arizona, and southern California. Immigrants from Latin America, the Caribbean, and Asia joined Americans fleeing the

**Sunbelt**  The states of the American South and Southwest.

depressed Northeast to boost the region's population (see Map 30.2).

The Sunbelt witnessed a dramatic turnaround in demographic and economic trends. Southern cities reversed the century-long trend of out-migration among African Americans. The Southwest and West changed yet more dramatically. California became the nation's most populous state; Texas moved to third, behind New York. Former farms and deserts were turned almost overnight into huge metropolitan areas ringed by new automobile-dependent suburbs. Phoenix grew from 664,000 in 1960 to 1,509,000 in 1980, Las Vegas from 127,000 to 463,000.

Much Sunbelt wealth tended to be temporary or sharply cyclical, producing a boom-and-bust economy. Income was also distributed unevenly. Older Hispanic populations made only modest gains, while recent Mexican immigrants and Indian peoples suffered from a combination of low wages and poor public services. The Sunbelt states directed their tax and federal dollars to strengthening police forces, building roads or sanitation systems for the expanding suburbs, and creating budget surpluses.

The "Snowbelt" (or "Rustbelt") states, longtime centers of voting strength for the Democratic Party, meanwhile suffered severe population losses accompanying the sharp decline of industry.

New York City offered a spectacular example of decline. A fiscal crisis in 1975 forced Democratic Mayor Abraham Beame to choose between wage freezes for public employees and devastating cuts and layoffs. Eventually, with the municipal government teetering on the brink of bankruptcy, he chose both. In response to cutbacks in mass transit and the deterioration of municipal services, a large sector of the middle class fled.

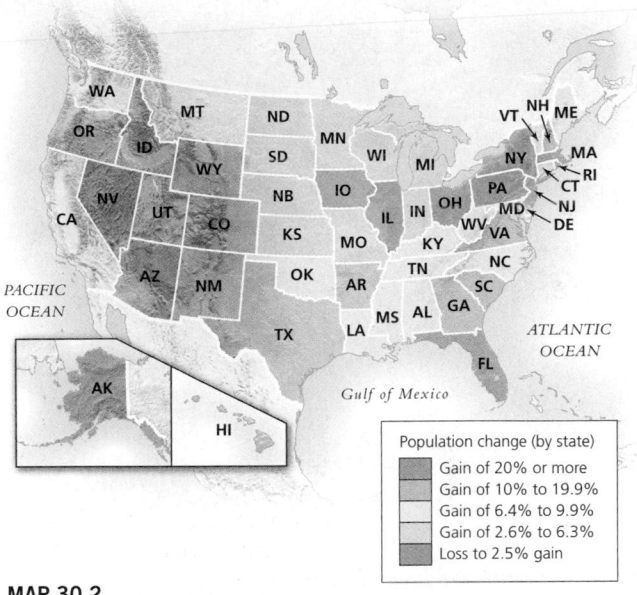

## MAP EXPLORATION

To explore an interactive version of this map, go to
**http://www.prenhall.com/faraghertlc/map30.2**

Population change (by state)
- Gain of 20% or more
- Gain of 10% to 19.9%
- Gain of 6.4% to 9.9%
- Gain of 2.6% to 6.3%
- Loss to 2.5% gain

**MAP 30.2**
**Population Shifts, 1970–80**   Industrial decline in the Northeast coincided with an economic boom in the Sunbelt, encouraging millions of Americans to head for warmer climates and better jobs.

HOW WERE the changes in population between 1970 and 1980 reflected in the American economy?

## THE ENDANGERED ENVIRONMENT

The environmental downside of the post–World War II economic boom was becoming painfully evident. Cutting across nearly all population groups and regions, concern for the environment reached into conservative areas as far as the Deep South with warnings of the dangers of toxic wastes, the destruction of wetlands, and the ruin of fishing industries. One of the most dramatic campaigns took place in Love Canal, near Buffalo, New York, following the discovery of high rates of cancer and birth defects in the community. Here toxic wastes dumped by the Hooker Chemical Laboratory had oozed into basements and backyards, and in 1978 homemaker Lois Gibbs organized her neighbors to draw attention to the grim situation.

The environmentalist movement gained strength. Congress responded to pressure by passing scores of bills designed to protect endangered species, reduce pollution caused by automobile emissions, limit and ban the use of some pesticides, and control strip-mining practices. The **Environmental Protection Agency (EPA)**, established in 1970, grew to become the federal government's largest regulatory agency.

Business-based groups fought back and sometimes found unexpected allies. City officials, both Democratic and Republican, generally avoided congressional mandates for reduction in air pollution by requesting lengthy extensions of deadlines

myhistorylab

**Exploring America:** *Rachel Carson*

**Environmental Protection Agency (EPA)**   Federal agency created in 1970 to oversee environmental monitoring and cleanup programs.

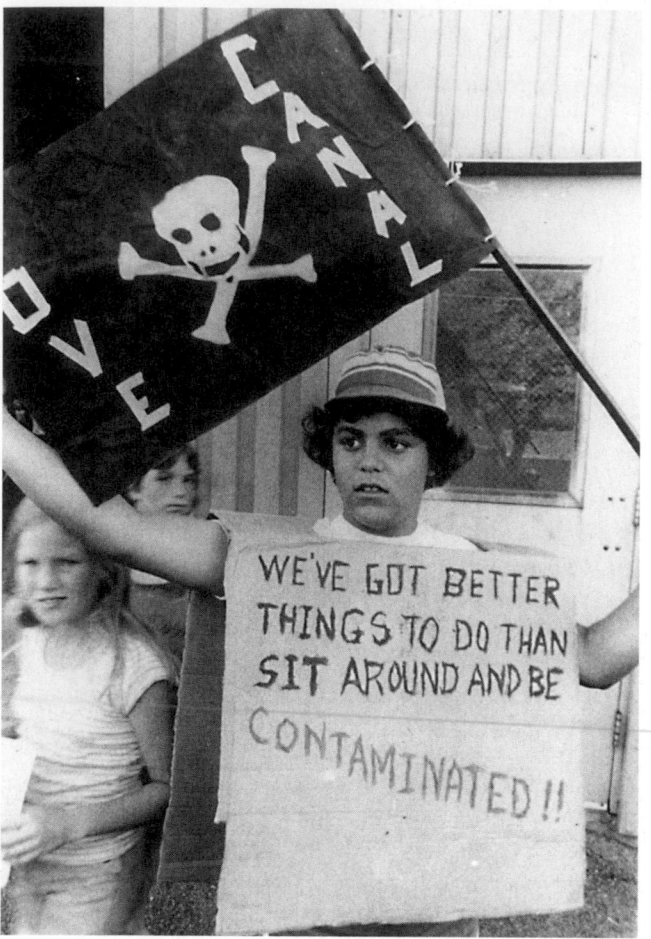

**The media attention** given to Love Canal residents, who reported high incidents of birth defects and rates of cancer, led to the passage of a new federal law in 1980 regulating toxic waste disposal. This photograph shows one of the endangered children demonstrating during a neighborhood meeting.

**QUICK REVIEW**

**The Election of 1976**

♦ Pardon of Nixon reinforced cynicism about Ford.

♦ Jimmy Carter, governor of Georgia, positioned himself as a political outsider.

♦ Carter's campaign focus on domestic issues won him 50 percent of the popular vote.

**Deregulation** Reduction or removal of government regulations and encouragement of direct competition in many important industries and economic sectors.

for compliance. Top labor officials such as George Meany, president of the AFL-CIO, denounced "tree hugger" environmentalists as enemies of economic growth, and United Auto Workers lobbyists joined automakers in resisting compulsory gas mileage and tighter emissions controls in new models. Again and again, efforts at more environmentally attuned policies on energy met defeat.

## "LEAN YEARS PRESIDENTS": FORD AND CARTER

Gerald R. Ford and Jimmy Carter presided over not only a depressed economy but also a nation of disillusioned citizens, many of them now wary of liberals and open to conservative appeals. The revelations of the Watergate break-in and Nixon's subsequent resignation as president had cast a pall over politics. Replacing Nixon in August 1974, Gerald Ford quickly pardoned Nixon for all the federal crimes he may have committed. At the time, the pardon reinforced public cynicism toward government and Ford in particular. The midterm elections held later that year added fifty-two Democrats to the House and four to the Senate (see Map 30.3). To many Americans, Ford seemed a pleasant person of merely modest ability.

Ford immediately annoyed the conservatives in his ranks by choosing New York Governor Nelson Rockefeller, a well-known liberal, as his vice president. He then annoyed Rockefeller by directing him to head his "Whip Inflation Now" campaign. Even First Lady Betty Ford alienated conservative Republicans by breaking ranks to champion gun control, the Equal Rights Amendment, and abortion rights.

Ford banked on his incumbency for the 1976 election, dumped Rockefeller and welcomed Senator Robert Dole of Kansas as his running mate, but only narrowly won renomination after holding off a challenge from Ronald Reagan. Democrats chose Jimmy Carter, a former navy officer and governor of Georgia, who presented himself as a political outsider.

A born-again Christian and successful southern politician, Carter was the first Democratic presidential candidate since the 1930s who declined to call himself a liberal, offering instead personal integrity as his chief qualification for the nation's highest office. On domestic issues, he campaigned as a moderate. Counting on support from both conservative and southern voters who would ordinarily vote Republican, he defended existing entitlement programs while opposing Senator Edward Kennedy's call for comprehensive health coverage. He won with just over 50 percent of the popular vote. Carter won more than 90 percent of the black vote, which provided his margin of victory in Pennsylvania, Ohio, and seven southern states. But apathy proved the next most important factor. A record 46.7 percent of eligible voters did not bother to cast ballots.

In office, Carter seemed to many observers enigmatic, even uninterested in the presidency, more conservative than liberal. His most successful innovation, **deregulation** of the airlines, brought lower fares for millions of passengers. But by freeing banks from congressional control, he inadvertently encouraged bad investments, outright fraud, and a round of disastrous bank failures. Inflation proved to be his worst enemy. Interest rates rose, driving mortgages out of reach for many would-be home buyers. Rents in many locations doubled, sales of automobiles and other consumer products slumped, and many small businesses went under. Tuition costs skyrocketed along with unemployment, and many young men and women who could neither afford to go to college nor find a job moved back home.

An outspoken fiscal conservative, Carter could not deliver on his promise to turn the economy around. By the time he left office in 1980, a majority of those polled agreed that "the people running the country don't really care what happens to you." He had managed to discredit the liberal tradition of the Democratic Party even while distancing himself from it, making his presidency the symbol of a larger political collapse.

# THE LIMITS OF GLOBAL POWER

In April 1975 the North Vietnamese struck Saigon and easily captured the city as the South Vietnamese army, now without U.S. assistance, fell apart. All fighting stopped within a few weeks, and Saigon was renamed Ho Chi Minh City. Vietnam was reunited under a government dominated by Communists. For many Americans, this outcome underscored the futility of U.S. involvement in the Vietnam War; for others, it suggested the limits of the global power of the United States.

## DÉTENTE

The military defeat in Vietnam forced U.S. foreign policy makers to reassess priorities. Both experienced a decline of power in world affairs. And both suffered from the already enormous and relentlessly escalating costs of their defense budgets.

Western European nations acted to nudge U.S. foreign policy away from its Cold War premises. In 1975, in Helsinki, Finland, representatives of thirty-five nations approved the national boundaries drawn in Eastern and Western Europe after World War II, and in return the Soviet Union agreed to enact a more liberal human rights policy, including the loosening of restrictions on the emigration of Soviet Jews. Recognizing that the Soviet Union no longer posed a military threat to their national sovereignty—if indeed it ever had—Western leaders also sought to strengthen economic relations between the two major blocs.

The Soviet Union joined the United States in moving toward détente. The signing of SALT I, the first Strategic Arms Limitation Treaty, during Nixon's administration, followed by the U.S. withdrawal from Vietnam, encouraged new negotiations on strategic arms control. In November 1974, Ford and Soviet leader Leonid Brezhnev met in Vladivostok to set the terms of SALT II, and President Carter secured the final agreement in 1979. However, the Senate refused to ratify the treaty when the Soviet Union invaded Afghanistan in December 1979.

# MAP EXPLORATION

To explore an interactive version of this map, go to
http://www.prenhall.com/faraghertlc/map30.3

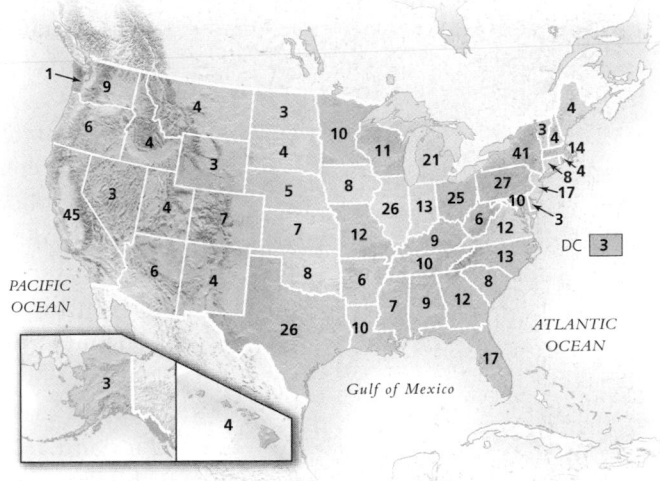

| | Electoral Vote (%) | Popular Vote (%) |
|---|---|---|
| **JIMMY CARTER** (Democrat) | 297 (55) | 40,828,929 (50.1) |
| **Gerald R. Ford** (Republican) | 240 (45) | 39,148,940 (47.9) |
| **Ronald Reagan** | 1 | — |
| **Other candidates** (McCarthy, Independent, Libertarian) | — | 1,575,459 (2.1) |

**MAP 30.3**

**The Election of 1976**   Incumbent Gerald Ford could not prevail over the disgrace brought to the Republican Party by Richard Nixon. The lingering pall of the Watergate scandal, especially Ford's pardon of Nixon, worked to the advantage of Jimmy Carter, who campaigned as an outsider to national politics. Although Carter and his running mate Walter Mondale won by only a narrow margin, the Democrats gained control of both the White House and Congress.

WHY DID Ford pardon Nixon? Did it cost him the election?

WHAT DID Ford and Carter accomplish as presidents?

**myhistorylab**
**Review Summary**

**Détente** (French for "easing of tension")   Used to describe the new U.S. relations with China and the Soviet Union in 1972.

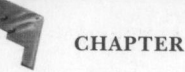

**Camp David Accords** Agreement signed by Israel and Egypt in 1978 that set the formal terms for peace in the Middle East.

## FOREIGN POLICY AND "MORAL PRINCIPLES"

Carter condemned policies that allowed the United States to support "right-wing monarchs and military dictators" in the name of anticommunism. In 1976 a powerful human rights lobby pressured Congress to pass a bill that required the secretary of state to report annually on the status of human rights in all countries receiving U.S. aid and to cut off assistance to any country with a record of "gross violations." The Carter Administration worked to punish or at least to censure repressive military regimes in Brazil, Argentina, and Chile. For the first time, leading U.S. diplomats spoke out against the South African apartheid regime. In line with this policy, Carter tried to reform operations at the CIA, particularly to halt intervention in the affairs of foreign governments.

Carter seemed within reach of a historic triumph in the Middle East. Early in his administration, Carter met privately with Israeli prime minister Menachem Begin to encourage conciliation with Egypt. When negotiations between the two countries stalled in 1978, Carter brought Begin together with Egyptian president Anwar el-Sadat for a thirteen-day retreat at Camp David, Maryland.

The **Camp David Accords**, signed in September 1978, set the formal terms for peace in the region. Egypt became the first Arab country to recognize Israel's right to exist, as the two nations established mutual diplomatic relations for the first time since the founding of Israel in 1948. In return, Egypt regained control of the Sinai Peninsula, including important oil fields and airfields.

But disappointment lay ahead. Carter staked his hopes for regional peace on the final achievement of statehood, or at least political autonomy, for Palestinians in a portion of their former lands now occupied by the Israelis. The accords specified that Israel would eventually return to its approximate borders of 1967. However, although Begin agreed to dismantle some Israeli settlements in the Sinai, the Israeli government continued to sponsor more and more Jewish settlements, expropriating Palestinian holdings. The final status of the Palestinians remained in limbo, as did that of Jerusalem. Meanwhile Sadat grew increasingly isolated within the Arab world. In 1981 he was assassinated by Egyptians allied with an Islamic Jihad organization.

**President Carter signs** the Middle East Peace Treaty with Egyptian President Anwar Sadat and Israeli Prime Minister Menachem Begin, in Washington, DC, March 1979. President Carter had invited both leaders to Camp David, the presidential retreat in Maryland, where for two weeks he mediated between them on territorial rights to the West Bank and Gaza Strip. Considered Carter's greatest achievement in foreign policy, the negotiations, known as the Camp David Peace Accords, resulted in not only the historic peace treaty but also the Nobel Peace Prize for Begin and Sadat.

Carter scored his biggest moral victory in foreign affairs by paving the way for Panama to assume the ownership, operation, and defense of the Panama Canal Zone. Carter pressured the Senate to ratify new treaties in 1978 that would turn the Panama Canal over to Panama by the year 2000.

## (MIS)HANDLING THE UNEXPECTED

Mired in problems inherited from his predecessors, Carter often found himself disoriented by contradictory advice. Secretary of State Cyrus Vance recommended well-planned negotiations to soothe Soviet–U.S. relations and resolve disagreements with Third World nations. Despite Carter's commitment to human rights, he put aside his principles to stabilize repressive regimes in nations considered vital to U.S. interests, such as South Korea and the Philippines.

In 1979 the overthrow of the brutal Nicaraguan dictatorship of Anastasio Somoza, longtime U.S. ally, left Carter without a successor to support. When the new Sandinista revolutionary government pleaded for help, Congress turned down Carter's request for $75 million in aid to Nicaragua. Meanwhile, in El Salvador, the Carter administration continued to back a repressive government.

The Soviet occupation of Afghanistan produced a major stalemate. In December 1979, 30,000 Soviet troops invaded their neighbor to put down a revolt by Islamic insurgents against the weakening Soviet-backed government. The invasion succeeded mainly in heating up the civil war, which the American press quickly labeled the "Russian Vietnam."

Noting that the Soviet occupation of Afghanistan posed "a grave threat to the free movement of Middle East oil," President Carter issued his own corollary to the Monroe Doctrine by affirming the right of the United States to use military force if necessary to protect its interests in the Persian Gulf. He backed up his increasingly hard-line policies by halting exports of grain and high technology to the Soviet Union, by supporting Afghan resistance against the Russians, and by canceling American participation in the 1980 Moscow Olympics. Carter also called for ever-larger increases in the military budget. The prospect of détente dried up.

## THE IRAN HOSTAGE CRISIS

On November 4, 1979, Iranian fundamentalists seized the U.S. embassy in Tehran and held 52 American employees hostage for 444 days. This event made President Carter's previous problems seem small by comparison.

In early 1979, a revolution led by the Islamic leader Ayatollah Ruhollah Khomeini had overthrown the U.S.-supported shah. After Carter had allowed the deposed ruler to enter the United States for medical treatment, a group of Khomeini's followers retaliated, storming the U.S. embassy and taking the American staff as hostages.

Cyrus Vance assured Carter that only negotiations could free Americans. Caught up in a reelection campaign and lobbied by Brzezinski for decisive action, Carter ordered U.S. military forces to stage a nighttime helicopter rescue mission. But a sandstorm caused some of the aircraft to crash and burn,

**29–9**
Jimmy Carter, The *"Malaise" Speech* (1979)

**Iranians demonstrate outside** the U.S. Embassy in Tehran, raising a poster with a caricature of President Carter. The Iran hostage crisis, which began November 8, 1979, when a mob of Iranians seized the U.S. embassy in Tehran, contributed to Carter's defeat at the polls the following year. Fifty-two embassy employees were held hostage for 444 days.

## QUICK REVIEW

**Hostages**

- November 4, 1979: Iranian fundamentalists seized U.S. embassy in Tehran.
- Fifty-two Americans held hostage for 444 days.
- Crisis doomed the Carter presidency.

**WHAT EXPLAINS** the rise of the New Right in the 1980s?

**myhistorylab**

Review Summary

## QUICK REVIEW

**The Conservative Critique**

- Free markets work better than government programs.
- Government intervention does more harm than good.
- Government assistance saps the initiative of the poor.

leaving eight Americans dead, their burned corpses displayed by the enraged Iranians. Short of an all-out attack, which surely would have resulted in the hostages' death, Carter had used up his options.

The political and economic fallout was heavy. Cyrus Vance resigned, the first secretary of state in sixty-five years to leave office over a political difference with the president. The price of oil rose by 60 percent. Carter had failed in the one area he had proclaimed central to the future of the United States: energy. He had also violated his own human rights policy, which was intended to be his distinctive mark on American foreign affairs.

# THE NEW RIGHT

The failures in U.S. foreign policy, accompanied by the faltering economy, played a large part in mobilizing what one writer termed "the politics of resentment."

## NEOCONSERVATISM

By the mid-1970s, a new variation of conservatism appeared on the political landscape: neoconservatism. The most prestigious leaders of this new movement had been liberal Democrats, some even socialists, in the preceding decades. The unsettling social movements of the 1960s had prompted them to turn against New Deal–style liberalism and the welfare state. "Neocons," as they were called, sought to repeal affirmative action programs and dismantle the antipoverty programs enacted during the Johnson administration. The heart of the neoconservatism was, however, foreign policy. Angered over the failure to pursue victory in Vietnam, neoconservatives called for a stronger national defense against communism.

Neoconservatives played an important role in building the institutional foundation for the rightward turn in American politics. Richly funded by corporate donors, they established think tanks to engage scholars and intellectuals in policy-shaping discussions. The surge rightward gained intellectual respectability for neoconservatives and prepared the way for broader popular support.

## THE RELIGIOUS RIGHT

Evangelical Protestants, more than 50 million Americans by the late 1970s, became the backbone of the new conservatism. The Religious Right typically endorsed neoconservative positions on foreign and domestic policy. As grassroots activists, they provided the political muscle that carried Bee Gathright's conservatism from the margins to the center of the Republican Party.

Finding huge audiences among the growing evangelical and Pentecostal congregations, Protestant ministers took to the airwaves. By the late 1970s more than 1,400 radio stations and 30 TV stations specialized in religious broadcasts that reached perhaps 20 million listeners weekly and became a major source of fundraising for conservative organizations and campaigns.

In 1979, the Reverend Jerry Falwell, a Bible Baptist, formed the Moral Majority following his U.S. tour to get evangelical Christians "saved, baptized, and registered" to vote. As a major political lobbying group, the Moral Majority, which claimed 2 to 3 million members, advocated tough laws against homosexuality and pornography and promoted a reduction of government services (especially welfare payments to single mothers) and increased spending for a stronger national defense. The Moral Majority also waged well-publicized campaigns against public school integration and especially the busing of schoolchildren.

## THE PRO-FAMILY MOVEMENT

Most of all, the New Right embraced what they termed "traditional family values": defeating the Equal Rights Amendment (ERA) stood at the top of their political agenda. Approved by Congress in March 1972, nearly fifty years after its introduction (see Chapter 22), the ERA stated: "Equality of rights under the law shall not be denied or abridged by the United States or by any State on account of sex." Endorsed by both the Democratic and Republican parties, the amendment appeared likely to be ratified by the individual states.

Cued by this groundswell of support in favor of the ERA, conservatives swung into action. Phyllis Schlafly, a self-described suburban housewife and popular lecturer, headed the STOP-ERA campaign. Under Schlafly's leadership, the New Right mounted large, expensive campaigns in each swing state and overwhelmed pro-ERA resources. Her supporters also built a strong, religious-based coalition, with southern Protestants, western Mormons, northeastern Catholics, and Orthodox Jews temporarily putting aside differences to join forces to defeat the amendment that they believed was "against God's plan."

Although thirty-five states had ratified the ERA by 1979, the amendment remained three votes short of passage. Despite a three-year extension, the ERA died in Congress in 1982, with 85 percent of the Democrats and only 30 percent of the Republicans voting in its favor.

Meanwhile, the anti-ERA campaign had grown into a comprehensive "pro-family" movement that placed abortion rights at the top of its political agenda. In 1973 the Supreme Court had ruled in *Roe* v. *Wade* that state laws decreeing abortion a crime during the first two trimesters of pregnancy constituted a violation of a woman's right to privacy. Opponents of *Roe* rallied for a constitutional amendment defining conception as the beginning of life and then argued that the "rights of the unborn" supersede a woman's right to control her own body.

Antiabortion groups also rallied against sex education programs in public schools. They picketed Planned Parenthood counseling centers, intimidating potential clients. A small minority turned to more extreme actions and bombed dozens of abortion clinics.

## THE 1980 ELECTION

Ultimately, his bid for renomination depended more on his incumbency than on his popularity. Democrats unenthusiastically endorsed Carter along with his running mate, Walter Mondale.

On the Republican side, former California governor Ronald Reagan had been building his campaign since his near nomination in 1976. Former CIA director and Texas oil executive George H. W. Bush, more moderate than Reagan, became the Republican candidate for vice president.

The Republicans cruised to victory. Carter won only 41.2 percent of the popular vote to Reagan's 50.9 percent. The Republicans won control of the Senate for the first time since 1952 and with the largest majority since 1928. White working people, the traditional supporters of the Democratic Party, had defected to the

**Christian televangelists Jim** and Tammy Bakker hosted the popular "PTL Club" and capitalized on their success to build the PTL Network and "Heritage USA," which grew to become one of the largest and best attended theme parks in the United States. This photograph, taken in 1986, shows the couple shortly before reports of financial irregularities and a sex scandal forced Jim Bakker to resign his PTL ministry. They divorced in 1992 following Jim Bakker's conviction on federal charges of fraud and racketeering.

**29–7**
*Roe* v. *Wade* (1973)

*Roe* v. *Wade*   U.S. Supreme Court decision (1973) that disallowed state laws prohibiting abortion during the first three months (trimester) of pregnancy and established guidelines for abortion in the second and third trimesters.

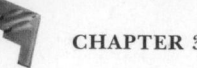

Republicans in large numbers, although both women and African Americans voted for Reagan in far fewer numbers. And barely half of the eligible voters had turned out, bringing Ronald Reagan into office with a slim mandate of 25 percent. However, Reagan began on a high note: the Iranians released the American hostages on January 20, 1981, the day he took the oath of office (see Seeing History).

**30–2**
Ronald Reagan, *First Inaugural Address* (1981)

**WHAT ECONOMIC** assumptions underlay "Reaganomics"?

**myhistorylab**
**Review Summary**

## MAP EXPLORATION
To explore an interactive version of this map, go to
**http://www.prenhall.com/faraghertlc/map30.4**

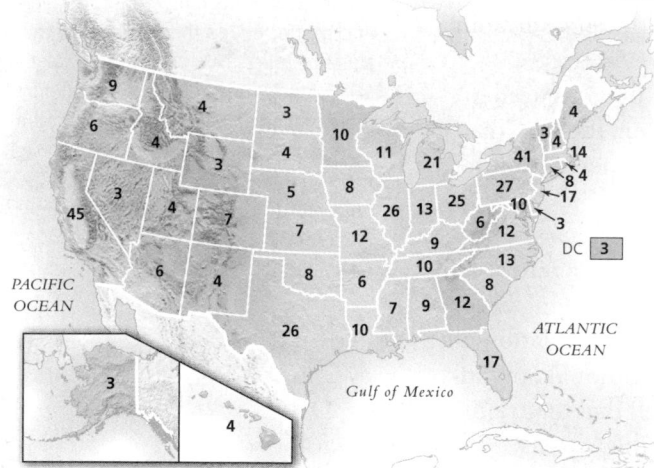

| | Electoral Vote (%) | Popular Vote (%) |
|---|---|---|
| **RONALD REAGAN** (Republican) | 489 (91) | 43,201,220 (50.9) |
| **Jimmy Carter** (Democrat) | 49 (9) | 34,913,332 (41.2) |
| **John B. Anderson** (Independent) | — | 5,581,379 (6.6) |
| **Other candidates** (Libertarian) | — | 921,299 (1.1) |

**MAP 30.4**
**The Election of 1980**  Ronald Reagan won a landslide victory over incumbent Jimmy Carter, who managed to carry only six states and the District of Columbia. Reagan attracted millions of traditionally Democratic voters to the Republican camp.

WHAT ATTRACTED many Democratic voters to Ronald Reagan?

# THE REAGAN REVOLUTION

No other twentieth-century president except Franklin D. Roosevelt left as deep a personal imprint on American politics as Ronald Reagan. Reagan and his allies proceeded to reshape the political and social landscape of the nation along conservative lines (see Map 30.4).

## THE GREAT COMMUNICATOR
By midcentury, Reagan had emerged as one of the most prominent conservative politicians in the nation. While serving as president of the Screen Actors Guild from 1947 to 1952, he distanced himself from other New Deal Democrats by leading the anti-Communist forces in Hollywood. In 1954 he hosted a new national television program, *General Electric Theater*. In this role he repeatedly celebrated the achievements of corporate America and emphasized the dangers of excessive liberalism and radical trade unions.

Reagan switched his party affiliation and became a successful fundraiser and popular speaker for the California Republican Party. He won the 1966 race for California governor, securing 72 percent of the Orange County vote. As governor, Reagan cut the state welfare rolls, reduced the number of state employees, and funneled a large share of state tax revenues back to local governments. He vigorously attacked student protesters and black militants, thereby tapping into the conservative backlash against the 1960s' activism.

When Reagan entered the White House in January 1981, his supporters interpreted his election as a popular mandate for the conservatism that had been growing since Nixon took office. The "Reagan Revolution," they confidently predicted, would usher in a new age in American political life.

## REAGANOMICS
Supply-side theory, dubbed "Reaganomics" by the media, dominated the Reagan administration's economic planning and helped redirect the American economy. Supply-side theorists urged a sharp break with the Keynesian policies that had prevailed since the New Deal era (see Chapter 24). During recessions, Keynesians traditionally favored moderate tax cuts and increases in government spending to stimulate the economy and reduce unemployment.

By contrast, supply-siders called for simultaneous tax cuts and reductions in public spending. This combination

# The Presidential Inauguration of Ronald Reagan

I n 1977, Jimmy Carter held a "people's inaugural." He took the oath of office wearing a plain business suit and walked with his wife Rosalynn along the parade route.

On January 21, 1981, Ronald Reagan became the nation's fortieth president wearing a formal black coat, striped pants, and black shoes and accompanied First Lady Nancy Reagan down the parade route in a limousine.

Everything about Reagan's inauguration reflected what Nancy Reagan described as her aspiration to put the White House "symbolically back up on a hill in people's minds, to have stature and loftiness." The Reagans hired a public relations expert to ensure that every event was telecast. All the inaugural balls, concerts, and receptions were planned to entertain and astound at-home audiences. Festivities at the Washington, DC, balls were also beamed through a $2 million satellite hookup to "mini-balls" held simultaneously across the nation.

Reagan's inauguration, touted by the press as the most expensive in U.S. history, showcased the theme the president-elect had chosen for his administration: "America—A New Beginning." Not the belt-tightening, "homespun ways" of the Carter presidency, noted one reporter, but an unabashed celebration of wealth would prevail. ■

**WHY DID** the newly elected President Reagan choose to celebrate wealth? What had happened in the United States between the mid-1970s and the beginning of the 1980s to make such a display of wealth and power acceptable to the public?

Seeing History

**Ronald Reagan, the** fortieth president of the United States, was known for his ability to articulate broad principles of government in a clear fashion. The most popular president since Dwight Eisenhower, he built a strong coalition of supporters from long-term Republicans, disillusioned Democrats, and evangelical Protestants.

would give private entrepreneurs and investors greater incentives to start businesses, take risks, invest capital, and thereby create new wealth and jobs. Whatever revenues were lost in lower tax rates would be offset by revenue from new economic growth. At the same time, spending cuts would keep the federal deficit under control and thereby keep interest rates down.

On the political level, supply-siders looked to reward the most loyal Republican constituencies: the affluent and the business community. At the same time, they hoped to reduce the flow of federal dollars to two core Democratic constituencies: the recipients and professional providers of health and welfare programs.

Reagan quickly won bipartisan approval for two key bills that culminated in the largest tax cut in the nation's history. The **Economic Recovery Tax Act of 1981** brought across-the-board class cuts for corporations and individuals. The new legislation also reduced the maximum tax on all income from 70 percent to 50 percent, lowered the maximum capital gains tax—the tax paid on profitable investments—from 28 percent to 20 percent, and eliminated the distinction between earned and unearned income. This last measure proved a boon to the smallest although richest fraction of the population that derives most of its income from rent, dividends, and interest instead of from wages.

With the help of conservative southern and western Democrats in the House, the administration also pushed through a comprehensive program of spending cuts, awkwardly known as the Omnibus Reconciliation Act of 1981. This bill mandated huge cuts affecting more than 200 social and cultural programs. The hardest-hit areas included education, the environment, health, housing, urban aid, food stamps, research on synthetic fuels, and the arts.

While reducing spending on domestic programs, the Reagan administration greatly increased the defense budget, a trend already under way during Carter's final two years as president. Overall, the military buildup indicated a significant shift in federal budget priorities.

Meanwhile, the Reagan administration created a chilly atmosphere for organized labor. In the summer of 1981, some 13,000 federal employees, all members of the Professional Air Traffic Controllers Organization (PATCO), went on strike. The president retaliated by firing all the strikers, and a crash program started by the Federal Aviation Administration permanently replaced them. Conservative appointees to the National Labor Relations Board and the federal courts toughened their antiunion position.

Deregulation also served as a key element in Reaganomics. The president's appointments to head the Environmental Protection Agency, the Occupational Safety and Health Administration, and the Consumer Product Safety Commission abolished or weakened hundreds of rules governing environmental protection, workplace safety, and consumer protection, all to increase the efficiency and productivity of business.

Following supply-side theory, large corporations, Wall Street stock brokerages, investment banking houses, and the savings and loan industry were all allowed to operate with a much freer hand than ever before. By the late 1980s, the unfortunate consequences of this freedom would become apparent in a series of unprecedented scandals in the nation's financial and banking industries.

## THE ELECTION OF 1984

Hoping to win back disgruntled voters, Democrats chose Carter's vice president, Walter Mondale, as their nominee. At the Democratic National Convention, Mondale named New York Representative Geraldine Ferraro as his running mate, a first for women in American politics.

Opinion polls showed Mondale for a time running even with Reagan, but the president's enormous personal popularity, along with the booming economy, overwhelmed the Democratic ticket.

In one of the biggest landslides in American history Reagan won 59 percent of the popular vote—nearly 75 percent in Orange County—and carried every state but Minnesota and the District of Columbia. A majority of blue-collar voters cast their ballots for the president, as did 54 percent of women, despite Ferraro's presence on the Democratic ticket. Even a quarter of all Democrats voted for Reagan.

## RECESSION, RECOVERY, AND FISCAL CRISIS

Reagan's supply-side policies produced a mixed record but a highly favorable outcome for the wealthiest Americans. In 1982 a severe recession, the worst since the 1930s, gripped the nation. The official unemployment rate reached nearly 11 percent, or more than 11.5 million people. Another 3 million were out of work so long they no longer actively looked for jobs and, therefore, were not counted in official statistics. But by 1983 the economy recovered and headed into a long period of growth and expansion. The administration took credit for the turnaround, hailing the supply-side policies that had drastically cut taxes and domestic spending. But critics pointed to other factors: the Federal Reserve Board's tight-money policies, an energy resource glut and a consequent sharp drop in energy prices, and the billions of dollars pumped into the economy for defense spending.

Few doubted, however, that the supply-side formula intensified a significant fiscal crisis. Although Reagan had promised to balance the federal budget, his policies had the opposite effect. The national debt tripled, growing from $914 billion in 1980 to over $2.7 trillion in 1989, more than the federal government had accumulated in its entire previous history.

During the Reagan presidency the fiscal crisis became a structural problem with profound and long-lasting implications for the American economy. Big deficits kept interest rates high, as the government drove up the cost of borrowing the money it needed to pay its own bills. Foreign investors, attracted by high interest rates on government securities, pushed up the value of the dollar in relation to foreign currencies. The overvalued dollar made it difficult for foreigners to buy American products, while making overseas goods cheaper to American consumers. Since World War I, the United States had been the world's leading creditor; in the mid-1980s it became its biggest debtor (see Figure 30.2).

On Wall Street, the bull market ended abruptly in the fall of 1987. After

**30–5**
T. Boone Pickens, *My Case for Reagan* (1984)

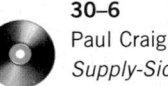

**30–6**
Paul Craig Roberts, *The Supply-Side Revolution* (1984)

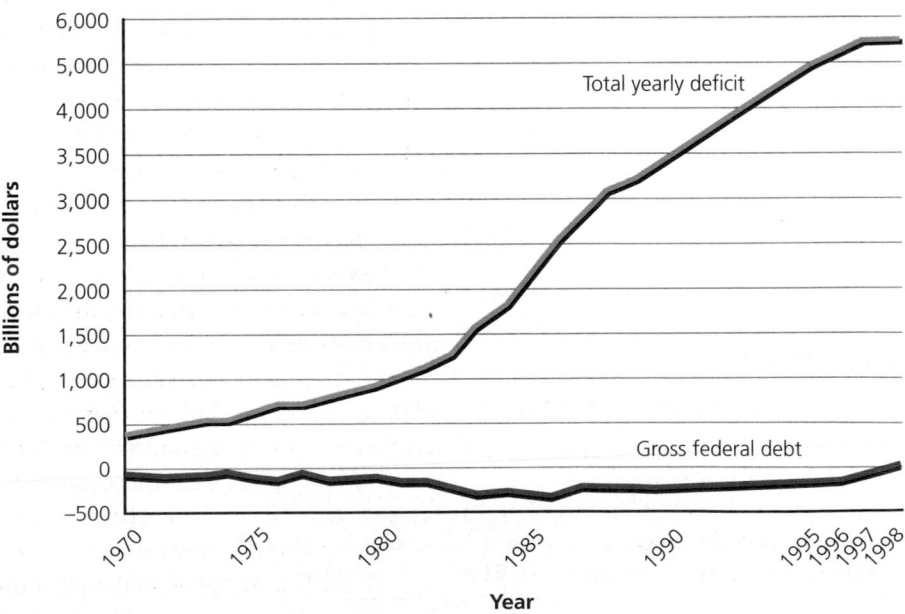

**Figure 30.2 Federal Budget Deficit and National Debt, 1970–98**
Tax cuts combined with huge increases in defense spending created a sharp increase in the budget deficit during the Republican administrations.

*Statistical abstract of the United States,* in Nash et al., *The American People,* 5th ed., p. 988.

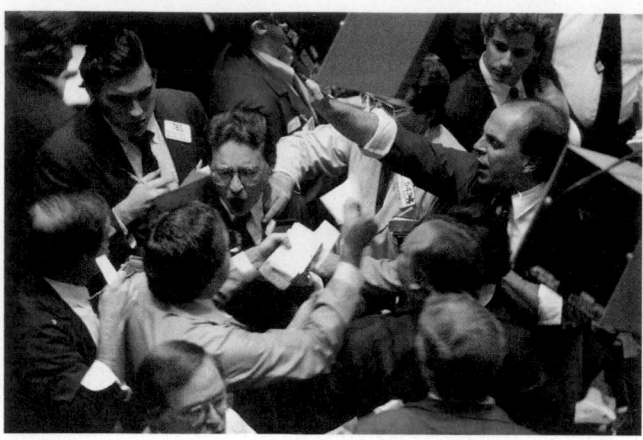

**After the Dow** Jones reached an all-time high at the end of August, stocks began to slide and then crashed. On October 19, 1987—"Black Monday"—traders at the New York Stock Exchange panicked, selling off stocks at such a rate that the market lost almost 23 percent of its value, marking the end of a five-year bull market. The market soon bounced back, and by September 1989 the Dow Jones had made up all its losses.

WHY DID the gap between rich and poor grow in the 1980s?

myhistorylab
**Review Summary**

myhistorylab
**Exploring America:** *Graving Inequality*

**29-6**
*Swann v. Charlotte-Mecklenburg Board of Education* (1971)

## TABLE 30.1

### Share of Total Net Worth of American Families

|  | 1983 | 1989 |
| --- | --- | --- |
| Richest 1 percent of families | 31% | 37% |
| Next richest 9 percent | 35 | 31 |
| Remaining 90 percent | 33 | 32 |

*The New York Times,* April 21, 1992, from Federal Reserve Survey of Consumer Finances.

reaching its new high, the Dow Jones average of thirty leading industrial stocks began to slide downward and then crashed. On October 19, the Dow lost almost 23 percent of its value. The panic on the trading floors recalled the pandemonium set off by the 1929 stock market crash.

## BEST OF TIMES, WORST OF TIMES

The celebration of wealth, moneymaking, and entrepreneurship dominated much of popular culture, politics, and intellectual life in the 1980s, establishing a pattern that would persist into the twenty-first century. Grimmer realities lay under the surface. Various data indicated that the nation was moving toward greater inequality, that the middle class was shrinking, and that poverty was on the rise. Analysts disagreed over the causes of these trends. Two of their most cherished beliefs—that life would improve for most people and their children, and that membership in the comfortable middle class was possible for all who worked for it—looked shaky by the end of the decade (see Table 30.1).

### A TWO-TIERED SOCIETY

During the 1960s, despite the diversion of federal funds to military spending during the Vietnam War, President Johnson's Great Society brought a higher living standard to many Americans. By the time Carter took office in 1977, the sinking economy undercut these advances. Reagan's supply-side policies rescued the economy but widened the gap between rich and poor.

Affluent Americans made huge gains at the same time that 5 percent of families earned 15.3 percent of the nation's total income; by 1992 their share had grown to 17.6 percent, an increase of 15 percent, with an average income of $156,000 a year. In 1980 the top 20 percent of families earned 41.6 percent of the nation's total; by 1992 their share had grown to 44.6 percent, an increase of about 7 percent, with an average income of $99,000 a year. In contrast, the bottom 40 percent of families had 16.7 percent of aggregate income in 1980; by 1992 their share had declined to 14.9 percent, a drop of nearly 2 percent, with an average income of about $16,500 a year.

The number and percentage of Americans in poverty grew at an alarming rate. The number of fully employed workers earning below poverty-level incomes increased by 50 percent.

The gains for African Americans achieved by the civil rights movement steadily eroded. In 1954, the year of the *Brown* v. *Board of Education* decision, black families earned about 53 percent of the income of white families. This figure rose to 60 percent in 1969 and peaked at 62 percent in 1975. By 1979, black family income had fallen back to 57 percent and continued to slide during the next decade.

The majority of African Americans, six out of ten, lived in central cities with high unemployment rates, and the bleak prospects took a toll especially on the young. A black child was twice as likely as a white child to die before reaching the first birthday and four times more likely to be killed between the ages of one and four. Among black teenagers, the unemployment rate topped 40 percent; the few jobs available to them were among the lowest paid in the economy. Meanwhile, the high school dropout rate skyrocketed, and the number of serious crimes, such as burglary, car theft, and murder, perpetrated by children between the ages of ten and seventeen increased at an alarming rate.

Moreover, opportunities for advancement into the middle class were dwindling. By 1980 fewer black students attended integrated schools than in 1954, except in the South, where about half the black students did. The turnabout resulted in part from increasing opposition by white parents to court-ordered school busing, which had served since *Brown* v. *Board of Education* as the principal means of achieving racial balance in urban school systems. During the 1980s the busing controversy nearly disappeared because federal judges hesitated to mandate such programs. But more important was the change in the racial composition of American cities. As a consequence of "white flight" to the suburbs, big-city school systems were serving mainly African American and Latino children, making the issue of integration moot (see Table 30.2, and 30.3).

New legal rulings closed off important routes to employment in the professions. A 1978 U.S. Supreme Court decision dealt a sharp blow to affirmative action. To ensure acceptance of a minimum number of minority students, the University of California at Davis Medical School had established a quota system under **affirmative action** guidelines. In 1973 and 1974 the school denied admission to Allan Bakke, a white student. Bakke sued the university for "reverse discrimination," claiming his academic record was better than that of the sixteen minority students who were admitted. The U.S. Supreme Court handed down a five-to-four decision on June 18, 1978, stating that the use of an "explicit racial classification" in situations where no earlier discrimination had been demonstrated violated the equal protection clause of the Fourteenth Amendment. The Court ordered the University of California to admit Bakke to its medical school. During the 1980s, therefore, affirmative action programs could operate only when "a legacy of unequal treatment" could be proved.

## THE FEMINIZATION OF POVERTY

While the gap between the rich and poor was growing to its widest point since 1945, the experience of poverty became the lot of primarily women and children. Throughout the era, women with young children continued to enter the labor force at a fast pace, but the majority found jobs that paid too little to support themselves and their children. It took the financial support of an adult male breadwinner to keep a family out of poverty.

The rising rate of divorce and desertion paralleled the increasing number of women and children in poverty. Most women usually lost ground following a divorce, which now affected nearly half of all new marriages. New no-fault divorce laws lowered or eradicated alimony, pushing even many middle-class women into poverty. Moreover, the majority of men defaulted on child-support payments within one year after separation. Whereas divorced men enjoyed a sizable increase in their standard of living, divorced women and their children suffered a formidable decline.

### TABLE 30.2
## Number of Poor, Rate of Poverty, and Poverty Line, 1979–92

|  | 1979 | 1992 |
|---|---|---|
| Millions of poor | 26.1 | 36.9 |
| Rate of poverty | 11.7% | 14.5% |
| Poverty line (family of four) | $7,412 | $14,335 |

U.S. Bureau of the Census, *Current Population Reports: Consumer Income,* Series P-60, Nos. 161 and 185, 1988, 1993. U.S. federal data compiled by Ed Royce, Rollins College.

**29–8**
Ione Malloy, *Southie Won't Go* (1975)

**Affirmative action**   A set of policies to open opportunities in business and education for members of minority groups and women by allowing race and sex to be factors included in decisions to hire, award contracts, or admit students to higher education programs.

### TABLE 30.3
## Median Family Income and Ratio to White, by Race and Hispanic Origin, 1980–92 (in 1992 Dollars)

| Year | All Races | White | Black | Hispanic |
|---|---|---|---|---|
| 1980 | $35,839 | $37,341 | $21,606 (58%) | $25,087 (67%) |
| 1985 | 36,164 | 38,011 | 21,887 (58%) | 25,596 (67%) |
| 1992 | 36,812 | 38,909 | 21,161 (54%) | 23,901 (61%) |

U.S. Bureau of the Census, *Current Population Reports,* Series P-60, No. 184, 1993. U.S. federal data compiled by Ed Royce, Rollins College.

**War on drugs** A paramilitary operation to halt drug trafficking in the United States.

**Acquired Immune Deficiency Syndrome (AIDS)** A complex of deadly pathologies resulting from infection with the human immunodeficiency virus (HIV).

A sharp rise in teenage pregnancy reinforced this trend. By the end of the decade, nearly one in four babies was born to unmarried mothers. By 1992, female-headed households, comprising 13.7 million people, accounted for 37 percent of the nation's poor. More than half of all black babies were now born to unmarried mothers. With few jobs for black men, especially for teenagers, the prospects for two-parent families were dim. But even in prosperous Orange County, by 1990 more than one in ten families was headed by a female householder with no husband present.

## EPIDEMICS: DRUGS, AIDS, HOMELESSNESS

Drug addiction and drug trafficking took on frightening new dimensions in the early 1980s. Even the urban poor could afford the new arrival, "crack," a cheap, smokable, and highly addictive form of cocaine. The crack trade spawned a new generation of young drug dealers who were willing to risk jail and death for enormous profits. In city after city, drug wars over turf took the lives of dealers and innocents, both caught in the escalating violence.

In 1982, the Reagan administration declared a highly publicized "**war on drugs**," a multibillion-dollar paramilitary operation to halt drug trafficking. Critics charged that the war on drugs focused on supply from abroad when it needed to look at demand here at home. They urged more federal money for drug education, treatment, and rehabilitation, dismissing as insufficient.

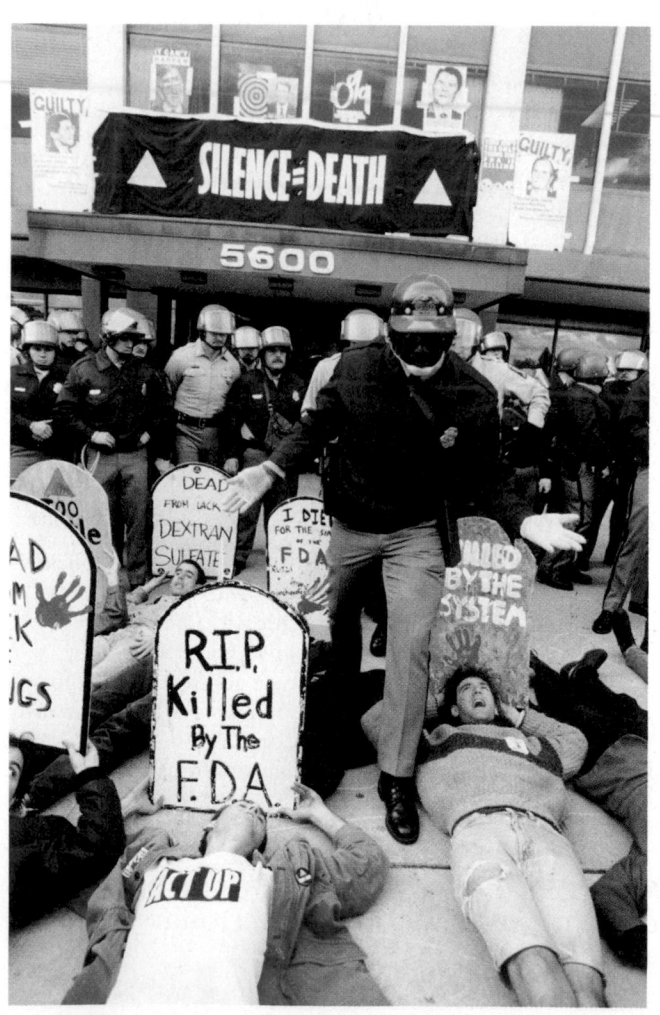

**In May 1987,** members of the Lesbian and Gay Community Services in downtown Manhattan organized ACT-UP. Protesting what they perceived to be the Reagan administration's mismanagement of the AIDS crisis, they used nonviolent direct action, which often took the form of dramatic acts of civil disobedience. ACT-UP grew to more than seventy chapters in the United States and around the world.

In 1981 doctors in Los Angeles, San Francisco, and New York began encountering a puzzling new medical phenomenon. Young homosexual men were dying suddenly from opportunistic infections such as pneumonia and cancer caused by a mysterious viral disease that damaged the body's immune system. Researchers at the Centers for Disease Control (CDC) in Atlanta called the new disease **Acquired Immune Deficiency Syndrome (AIDS)**. Because the majority of early victims were homosexual men who acquired AIDS through sexual contact, many Americans perceived AIDS as a disease of homosexuals. But other victims became infected through intravenous drug use, blood transfusions, heterosexual transmission, or birth to AIDS-carrying mothers.

AIDS provoked fear, anguish, and anger. It also brought an upsurge of organization and political involvement. In city after city, the gay community responded to the AIDS crisis with energy and determination. Most gay men changed their sexual habits, practicing "safe sex" to lessen the chances of infection. The Reagan administration, playing to antigay prejudices, largely ignored the epidemic.

Homelessness emerged as a chronic social problem during the 1980s. In the early 1980s, the Department of Housing and Urban Development placed the number of the nation's homeless at between 250,000 and 350,000. But advocates for the homeless estimated that the number was as high as 3 million.

Who were the homeless? Analysts agreed that at least a third were mental patients who had been discharged from psychiatric hospitals amid the deinstitutionalization trend of the 1970s. Many more were alcoholics and drug addicts unable to hold jobs. But the ranks of the homeless also included female-headed families, battered women, Vietnam veterans, AIDS victims, and elderly people with no place to go. Some critics pointed to the decline in decent housing for poor people and the deterioration of the nation's health care system as the major causes.

# TOWARD A NEW WORLD ORDER

Reagan revived Cold War patriotism and championed U.S. interventionism in the Third World, especially in the Caribbean and Central America. His infusion of funds into national security programs had enormous consequences for the domestic economy as well as for America's position as a global power. Yet along with hard-line exhortations against the Soviet Union and international terrorism, the Reagan administration also pursued a less ideological, more pragmatic approach in key foreign policy decisions. Most important, sweeping and unanticipated internal changes within the Soviet Union made the entire Cold War framework of international affairs largely irrelevant by the late 1980s.

## THE EVIL EMPIRE

In the early 1980s, the Reagan administration made vigorous anti-Communist rhetoric the centerpiece of its foreign policy. In a sharp turn from President Nixon's pursuit of détente and President Carter's focus on human rights, Reagan described the Soviet Union as "an evil empire . . . the focus of evil in the modern world."

Administration officials argued that during the 1970s the nation's military strength had fallen dangerously behind that of the Soviet Union. Critics disputed this assertion, pointing out that the Soviet advantage in intercontinental ballistic missiles (ICBMs) was offset by U.S. superiority in submarine-based forces and strategic aircraft. Polls showed that more than 70 percent of Americans favored not an escalation of the arms race but instead a nuclear freeze with the Soviet Union. Nonetheless, the administration proceeded with plans to enlarge America's nuclear strike force.

In 1983 President Reagan introduced an unsettling new element into superpower relations when he presented his **Strategic Defense Initiative (SDI)**, the plan for a space-based ballistic-missile defense system that journalists dubbed "Star Wars," after the popular Hollywood film series. As critics pointed out, this plan was unworkable, impossibly expensive, and likely to destabilize existing arms treaties. The Reagan administration pressed ahead, spending $17 billion in research before the president left office but without achieving any convincing results. The prospect of meaningful arms control dimmed in this atmosphere, and U.S.–Soviet relations deteriorated.

## THE REAGAN DOCTRINE AND CENTRAL AMERICA

Declaring the "Vietnam syndrome" over, the president confidently reasserted America's right to intervene anywhere in the world to "roll back" communism by supplying overt and covert aid to anti-Communist resistance movements. The so-called Reagan Doctrine assumed that all political instability in the Third World resulted not from indigenous factors such as poverty or corruption but from the pernicious influence of the Soviet Union. It found its most important expression in Central America, where the United States hoped to reestablish its historical control over the Caribbean basin (see Map 30.5).

**HOW DID** the Cold War end?

myhistorylab
Review Summary

**30–4**
Ronald Reagan, *Address to the National Association of Evangelicals* (1983)

**30–3**
Ronald Reagan, *Speech to the House of Commons* (1982)

**30–7**
Bill Chappell, *Speech to the American Security Council Foundation* (1985)

**Strategic Defense Initiative (SDI)**
President Reagan's program, announced in 1983, to defend the United States against nuclear missile attack with untested weapons systems and sophisticated technologies.

# MAP EXPLORATION

To explore an interactive version of this map, go to **http://www.prenhall.com/faraghertlc/map30.5**

Countries influenced by U.S.- Latin American activities

UNITED STATES

*ATLANTIC OCEAN*

*Gulf of Mexico*

Thousands of Cubans come
to U.S. Apr–Sept 1980

BAHAMAS

CUBA

Virgin Islands (U.S.)    Virgin Islands (Br.)

DOMINICAN REPUBLIC

HAITI

JAMAICA

Puerto Rico (U.S.)

ANTIGUA and BARBUDA

Guadeloupe

ST. CHRISTOPHER-NEVIS

DOMINICA

Pro–U.S. regime
elected Nov 1980

MEXICO    BELIZE

Staging area for Nicaraguan
anti-Sandinista rebels
aided by U.S.

GUATEMALA    HONDURAS

Sandinista rebels in
power July 1979

*Caribbean Sea*

Martinique

ST. LUCIA

Pro–Castro regime in power Mar 1979;
U.S. forces land Oct 1983;
Election held Dec 1984

BARBADOS

ST. VINCENT AND
THE GRENADINES

GRENADA

Continued guerrilla
activity against
rightist regimes

EL
SALVADOR    NICARAGUA

Panama Canal Treaties, 1978:
Canal Zone under Panamanian
control, 1979
Canal under Panamanian
control by 2000

TRINIDAD
AND TOBAGO

VENEZUELA

Civil war begins, 1979

*PACIFIC
OCEAN*

U.S. sends
military advisors
early 1981

COSTA RICA

PANAMA

GUYANA

COLOMBIA

BRAZIL

**MAP 30.5**

**The United States in Central America, 1978–90**   U.S. intervention in Central America reached a new level of intensity with the so-called Reagan Doctrine. The bulk of U.S. aid came in the form of military support for the government of El Salvador and the Contra rebels in Nicaragua.

HOW DID Reagan explain and justify U.S. policy in Central America?

---

In El Salvador, the Reagan administration continued to support the pro-American yet highly repressive regime, which received more U.S. economic assistance than any other Latin American country. By 1983 right-wing death squads had tortured and assassinated thousands of opposition leaders. The election in 1984 of centrist president José Napoleón Duarte failed to end the bloody civil war. Some 53,000 Salvadorans, more than one in every hundred, lost their lives in the conflict.

In Nicaragua, the Reagan administration accused the Sandinistas of shipping arms to antigovernment rebels in El Salvador. In December 1981, Reagan approved a CIA plan to arm and organize Nicaraguan exiles, known as **Contras**, to fight against the Sandinista government. As Reagan escalated this undeclared war, the aim became not merely the cutting of Nicaraguan aid to Salvadoran rebels but also the overthrow of the Sandinista regime itself.

**Contras**   Nicaraguan exiles armed and organized by the CIA to fight the Sandinista government of Nicaragua.

In 1984 the CIA secretly mined Nicaraguan harbors. When Nicaragua won a judgment against the United States in the World Court over this violation of its sovereignty, the Reagan administration refused to recognize the court's jurisdiction in the case and ignored the verdict. Predictably, the U.S. covert war pushed the Sandinistas closer to Cuba and the Soviet bloc. Meanwhile, American grassroots opposition to Contra aid grew more vocal and widespread.

In 1984 Congress sought to rein in the covert war by passing the Boland Amendment, introduced by Democratic Representative Edward Boland of Massachusetts. It forbade government agencies from supporting "directly or indirectly military or paramilitary operations" in Nicaragua. Denied funding by Congress, President Reagan turned to the National Security Council (NSC) to find a way to keep the Contra war going. Between 1984 and 1986, the NSC staff secretly assisted the Contras, raising $37 million in aid from foreign countries and private contributors, creating the largest mercenary army in hemispheric history. In 1987 the revelation of this unconstitutional scheme exploded before the public as part of the Iran-Contra affair, the most damaging political scandal of the Reagan years.

## The Middle East and the Iran-Contra Scandal

In 1987 the revelations of what became known as the Iran-Contra scandal laid bare the continuing contradictions and difficulties of the U.S. role in world affairs. The scandal also revealed how overzealous and secretive government officials subverted the Constitution and compromised presidential authority under the guise of patriotism.

Terrorist acts, including the seizing of Western hostages and the bombing of commercial airplanes and cruise ships, continued to redefine the politics of the Middle East. Many of these attacks were desperate attempts by small pro-Palestinian sects or Islamic extremists opposed to U.S. support of Israel. However, the Reagan administration insisted that behind international terrorism lay the sinister influence and money of the Soviet bloc, the Ayatollah Khomeini of Iran, and Libyan leader Muammar el-Qaddafi. In the spring of 1986 the president, eager to demonstrate his antiterrorist resolve, ordered the bombing of Tripoli in a failed effort to kill Qaddafi, whom he called "the mad dog of the Middle East."

As a fierce war between Iran and Iraq escalated, the administration tilted publicly toward Iraq to please the Arab states around the Persian Gulf. Iraq's dictator, Saddam Hussein, was treated as an ally and provided much sophisticated weaponry. But in 1986 Reagan's advisers changed course and began secret negotiations with the revolutionary Iranian government. They eventually offered to supply Iran with weapons for use against Iraq in exchange for help in securing the release of Americans who were being held hostage by radical Islamic groups in Lebanon (see Map 30.6).

Subsequent disclosures elevated the arms-for-hostages deal into a major scandal. Some of the money from the arms deal had been secretly diverted into covert aid for the Nicaraguan Contras. The American public soon learned the sordid details from investigative journalists and through televised congressional hearings held during the summer of 1987. Under the direction of National Security Advisers Robert McFarlane and later Admiral John Poindexter, the National

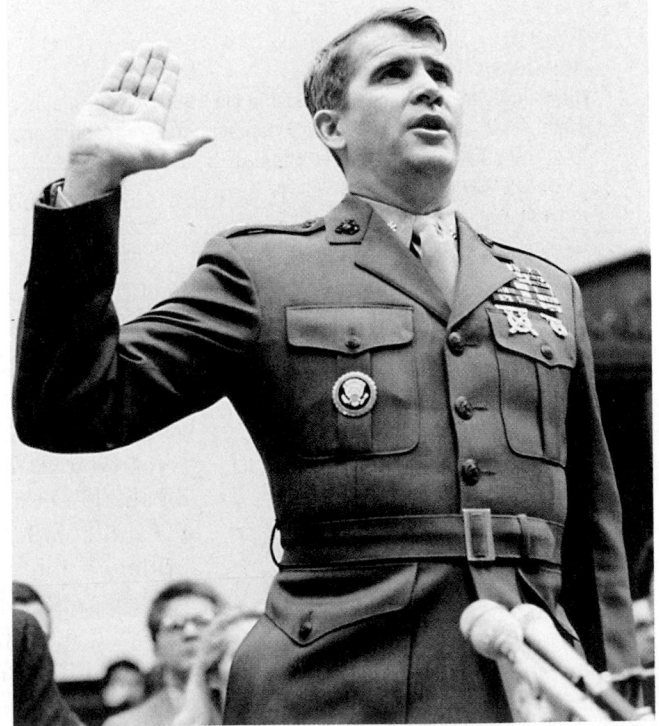

**Lt. Col. Oliver North,** who once described the scheme to sell arms to Iran to help the Contras as a "neat idea," is shown testifying in July 1987 before a joint Congressional committee formed to investigate the Iran-Contra affair.

# MAP EXPLORATION

To explore an interactive version of this map, go to **http://www.prenhall.com/faraghertlc/map30.6**

ALBANIA
ITALY
GREECE
SOVIET UNION
*Caspian Sea*
SOVIET UNION
*Soviet invasion, Dec 29, 1979*
TURKEY
*U.S. Marines in multinational peacekeeping force, 1982–84*
*Tigris R.*
*Mediterranean Sea*
*Euphrates R.*
SYRIA
U.S. bombs military targets Apr 14, 1986
Beirut
Damascus
LEBANON
*Golan Heights*
ISRAEL
IRAQ
Gaza Strip (Israeli occupied)
Jerusalem
Amman
West Bank (Israeli occupied)
Basra
Tehran
*Americans held hostage, Nov 4, 1979–Jan 20, 1981*
IRAN
AFGHANISTAN
Suez Canal
Cairo
Sinai Peninsula
JORDAN
Iran-Iraq War begins Sept 22, 1980
KUWAIT
Iraq attacks international shipping 1984
*Strait of Hormuz*
PAKISTAN
Final Israeli withdrawal, 1982
LIBYA
*Persian Gulf*
BAHRAIN
EGYPT
*Nile R.*
*Red Sea*
SAUDI ARABIA
QATAR
UNITED ARAB EMIRATES
OMAN
INDIA
CHAD
SUDAN
YEMEN
P.D.R. OF YEMEN
Major actions, Iran-Iraq war
Oil fields
Soviet invasion, Afghanistan
DJIBOUTI
SOMALIA
ETHIOPIA

*INDIAN OCEAN*

**MAP 30.6**

**The United States in the Middle East in the 1980s**    The volatile combination of ancient religious and ethnic rivalries, oil, and emerging Islamic fundamentalism made peace and stability elusive in the Middle East.

IN WHAT ways was the U.S. involved in the Middle East in the 1980s?

Security Council (NSC) had sold weapons and missiles to the Iranians, using Israel as a go-between. Millions of dollars from these sales were then given to the Contras in blatant and illegal disregard of the Boland Amendment.

In the televised congressional hearings, NSC staffer and Marine Lieutenant Colonel Oliver North emerged as the principal actor in what he euphemistically referred to as the "Enterprise." North defended his actions in the name of patriotism. Some Americans saw the dashing North as a hero; most were appalled by his and Poindexter's blithe admissions that they had lied to Congress, shredded evidence, and refused to keep the president fully informed in order to guarantee his "plausible deniability."

Ultimately, the Iran-Contra investigation raised more questions than it answered. The full role of CIA Director Casey, who died in 1987, particularly his relationships with North and the president, remained murky. The role of Vice President George H. W. Bush remained mysterious as well. Both North and Poindexter were convicted of felonies, but higher courts overturned their convictions on technical grounds. Reagan held fast to his plea of ignorance. When pressed on what had happened, he repeatedly claimed, "I'm still trying to find out."

# THE COLLAPSE OF COMMUNISM

Meanwhile, momentous political changes within the Soviet Union led ultimately to the end of the Cold War itself. In 1985 a reform-minded leader, Mikhail Gorbachev, took over as Soviet leader. Although a lifelong Communist, Gorbachev represented a new generation of disenchanted party members who wanted to end the Cold War.

Gorbachev and his advisers opened up political discussion and even encouraged critiques of the Soviet economy and political culture. The government released longtime dissidents from prison and took the first halting steps toward profit-based, private initiatives in the economy.

In Gorbachev's view, improving the economic performance of the Soviet system depended first on halting the arms race. Fully aware that the Soviet Union could not compete with Reagan's Star Wars program, Gorbachev took the lead in engaging with the United States. The historical ironies were stunning. Reagan had made militant anticommunism the centerpiece of his administration, but between 1985 and 1988 he had four separate summit meetings with the new Soviet leader. Culminating in a modest treaty allowing comprehensive, mutual, on-site inspections, the meetings also provided an important psychological breakthrough. At one of the summits a Soviet leader humorously announced, "We are going to do something terrible to you Americans—we are going to deprive you of an enemy."

Indeed, the reforms initiated by Gorbachev—and, more immediately, the failed Soviet war in Afghanistan—led to the dissolution of the Soviet Union and to the end of Communist rule throughout Eastern Europe. Beginning in June 1989, when Poland held its first free elections since the close of World War II in 1945, prodemocracy demonstrations forced out longtime Communist leaders in Hungary, Czechoslovakia, Bulgaria, and Romania. Most dramatic of all were the events in East Germany. The Berlin Wall, for thirty years the ultimate symbol of Cold War division, came down on November 9, 1989.

Political changes in the Soviet Union came more slowly, accompanied by such drastically reduced living standards that successful transition to a market economy and democratic political system was uncertain. In March 1989 the Soviet Union held its first open elections since 1917, and a new Congress of People's Deputies replaced the old Communist Party–dominated Supreme Soviet. In August 1991 party hard-liners made a final attempt to hold on to the old order and staged a coup, placing President Gorbachev under house arrest. The coup quickly failed, and meanwhile most of the fifteen republics had announced their withdrawal from the Soviet Union. On Christmas Day 1991 the weary and bitter president of the Soviet Union recognized the new Commonwealth of Independent States and resigned.

The Soviet Union's dissolution marked the end of the great superpower rivalry that had shaped American foreign policy and domestic politics for nearly a half century. Reagan's successor, President George H. W. Bush, proclaimed the end of the Cold War as an event of "biblical proportions."

## QUICK REVIEW

**The Fall of Gorbachev and the Soviet Union**

- August 1991: Old-line communists attempted a coup against Gorbachev.
- Coup failed and all fifteen Soviet republics declared their independence.
- Gorbachev lost control of the government and resign.

**In August 1961,** the border between East and West Berlin was closed, and the Berlin Wall was built to divide the city into two sections. After twenty-eight years, on November 9, 1989, the government in East Germany lifted travel restrictions. This photograph shows demonstrators defiantly tearing down the Berlin Wall, which for three decades had embodied the political divisions of the Cold War.

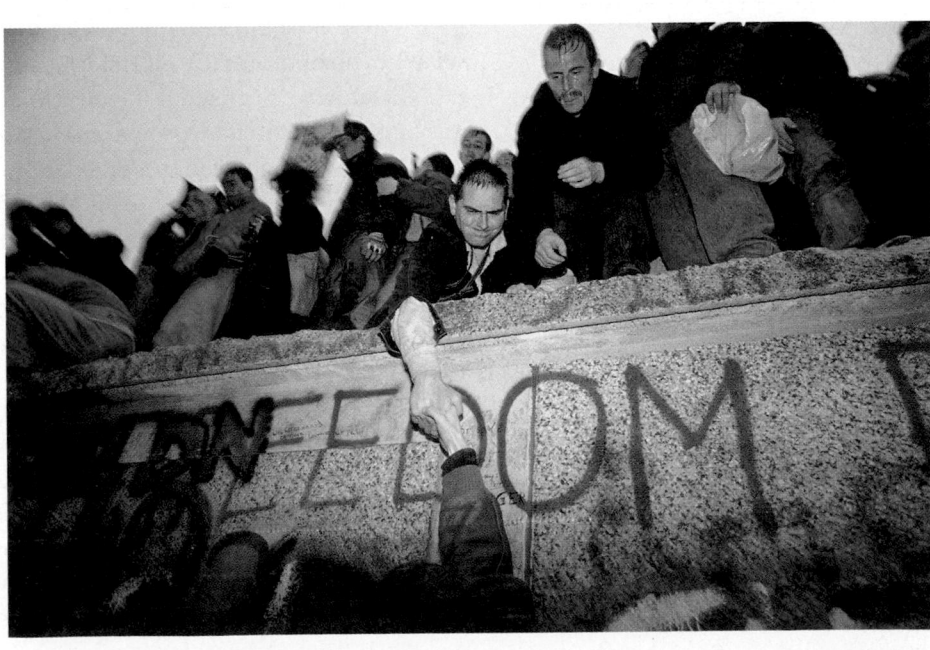

WHAT FACTORS led to U.S. involvement in the Persian Gulf War?

Review Summary

# "A KINDER, GENTLER NATION"

Hoping to ride on Reagan's coattails during his 1988 presidential campaign, George Herbert Walker Bush also made a clear-cut pledge to voters: "Read my lips: no new taxes." He won the general election handily over Massachusetts governor George Dukakis with forty out of fifty states and 56 percent of the popular vote and concluded that, with such widespread support, he could set his own agenda. President Bush began to distance himself from Reagan, promising in his inaugural address to deliver a "kinder, gentler nation."

## REAGAN'S SUCCESSOR: GEORGE H. W. BUSH

President Bush carried over several policies from the Reagan administration, such as the war on illegal drugs. In December 1989, President Bush sent U.S. troops to Panama on a mission to capture General Manuel Noriega, an international drug dealer who at one time had been on the CIA payroll. Thousands of Panamanians died before Noriega was taken into custody and brought to the United States to stand trial on drug trafficking and racketeering charges. During the Bush presidency, the federal budget for drug control tripled.

As a self-proclaimed "compassionate" Republican, President Bush endorsed the **Americans with Disabilities Act**, which had been introduced during the Reagan administration and now passed through Congress. The act penalized employers who discriminated against qualified workers with disabilities and required employers and local governments to provide access to their facilities. Against the opposition of many business leaders, President Bush signed the bill in July 1990. Showing less compassion, he vetoed a family-leave bill that would have provided up to six months of unpaid leave to workers with new children or with family emergencies.

## THE PERSIAN GULF WAR

President Bush soon saw that the end of the Cold War did not bring world peace but instead let loose a multitude of furies in the form of renewed nationalism, ethnic and religious conflict, and widening divisions between the world's rich and poor. Just as dramatically, as the old geopolitical order disappeared, ideological rivalry shifted to the Middle East and other areas in the world where Islamic militants had forcefully turned against the West.

On August 2, 1990, Iraqi troops swept into neighboring Kuwait and quickly seized control of its rich oil fields. The motives of Saddam Hussein, Iraq's military dictator, were mixed. Like most Iraqis, Hussein believed that oil-rich Kuwait was actually an ancient province of Iraq that had been illegally carved away by British imperial agents in the 1920s as part of the dismemberment of the Ottoman Empire. Control of Kuwait would give Saddam Hussein control of its huge oil reserves, as well as major Persian Gulf ports for his almost landlocked country. Just emerging from an exhausting and inconclusive eight-year war with Iran, Iraqis also bitterly resented Kuwait's production of oil beyond OPEC quotas, which had helped send the world price of oil plummeting from the highs of the 1970s and early 1980s.

The United States responded swiftly to news of the invasion. Its first concern was that Saddam Hussein might also attack Saudi Arabia. On August 15, President Bush ordered U.S. forces to Saudi Arabia and the Persian Gulf, calling the action Operation Desert Shield. The United States also led a broad coalition in the United Nations, including the Soviet Union, that condemned the Iraqi invasion of Kuwait and declared strict economic sanctions against Iraq if it did not withdraw. In early November, President Bush announced a change in policy to what he called

**Americans with Disabilities Act** An act that required employers to provide access to their facilities for qualified employees with disabilities.

"an offensive military option." In January 1991, Congress narrowly passed a joint resolution authorizing the president to use military force.

After a last-minute UN peace mission failed to break the deadlock, President Bush announced, on January 16, 1991, the start of **Operation Desert Storm**. U.S.-led air strikes began forty-two days of massive bombing of Iraqi positions in Kuwait, as well as Baghdad and other Iraqi cities. The ground war, which began on February 24, took only 100 hours to force Saddam Hussein's troops out of Kuwait.

The limits of military power to solve complex political and economic disputes became clear in the aftermath of victory. The **Persian Gulf War** failed to dislodge Saddam Hussein, who remained in power despite CIA attempts to overthrow him and repeated bombings of Iraqi military positions. Iraqi Kurds, who had supported the U.S. invasion in hopes it would topple Saddam, faced violent reprisals, including gassing and chemical weapons, from the Iraqi army. Trade sanctions did little to weaken his rule, although the economic boycott, which brought increasing hardship to the civilian population, eventually divided the Western powers, leaving the United States and Great Britain isolated in their sanctions against Iraq.

The repercussions of the Gulf War were long-lasting. The leading U.S. ally in the region, the oil-rich kingdom of Saudi Arabia, had served as the launching pad for the invasion of Iraq, and following the war the Saudis had allowed the continuing presence of U.S. troops and weapons. This occupation of Saudi territory, which included Islamic holy sites, intensified the hatred of Americans among many Muslims and prompted appeals for revenge.

Among those actively opposed to the U.S. role in the region was Saudi millionaire Osama bin Laden, just a few years earlier a close ally of the United States during the Soviet invasion of Afghanistan. He now turned squarely against his former arms suppliers and CIA contacts. Using his own funds and a vast tribal network, bin Laden built his shadowy Al Qaeda organization, training small groups in terror tactics to be used against Western interests, particularly to force U.S. troops out of the Middle East.

## THE ECONOMY AND THE ELECTION OF 1992

Politically, the Persian Gulf War marked the high point of Bush's popularity. His approval rating reached nearly 90 percent, higher than President Roosevelt's during World War II. Basking in his success, Bush proclaimed the United States the leader in the creation of a "new world order."

However, it was the economy rather than foreign affairs that fueled the 1992 presidential election campaign. Republicans took credit for forcing the fall of communism and reviving America's military strength. But they had also promised to cut government spending and balance the budget. Just as Bush was about to take office in 1989, many of the nation's savings and loan institutions, which had been deregulated by Reagan, collapsed. Then, on Friday, October 13, 1989, the stock market took its worst nosedive since 1987, signaling a major recession. With the national debt reaching $4 trillion, the paradoxes of the Reagan-Bush years became readily apparent.

As the 1992 campaign heated up, President Bush found himself facing a formidable opponent, William Jefferson Clinton. Personable, articulate, and highly intelligent, Bill Clinton won the Democratic nomination on the first ballot and chose Tennessee senator Albert Gore as his running mate. In the Democrats' campaign headquarters a sign humorously reminded the staff: "It's the economy, stupid." Candidate Clinton promised economic leadership.

**30–9**
George Bush, *Address to the Nation Announcing Allied Military Action in the Persian Gulf* (1991)

**Operation Desert Storm**   U.S. military campaign to force Iraqi forces out of Kuwait.

**Persian Gulf War**   War initiated by President Bush in response to Iraq's invasion of Kuwait.

## CHRONOLOGY

**1973**  *Roe* v. *Wade* legalizes abortion

Arab embargo sparks oil crisis in the United States

**1974**  Richard Nixon resigns presidency; Gerald Ford takes office

President Ford pardons Nixon and introduces anti-inflation program

**1975**  Unemployment rate reaches nearly 9 percent

South Vietnamese government falls to communists

Antibusing protests break out in Boston

**1976**  Percentage of African Americans attending college peaks at 9.3 percent and begins a decline

Democrat Jimmy Carter defeats incumbent Gerald Ford in presidential election

**1977**  President Carter announces human rights as major tenet in foreign policy

**1978**  *Bakke* v. *University of California* decision places new limits on affirmative action programs

Camp David meeting sets terms for Middle East peace

California passes Proposition 13, cutting taxes and government social programs

**1979**  Three Mile Island nuclear accident threatens a meltdown

Nicaraguan Revolution overthrows Anastasio Somoza

Iranian fundamentalists seize the U.S. embassy in Tehran and hold U.S. citizens hostage for 444 days

Soviets invade Afghanistan

**1980**  Inflation reaches 13.5 percent

Republican Ronald Reagan defeats incumbent Jimmy Carter in presidential election

**1981**  Reagan administration initiates major cuts in taxes and domestic spending

Military buildup accelerates

AIDS is recognized and named

**1982**  Economic recession grips the nation

**1983**  Reagan announces the Strategic Defense Initiative, labeled "Star Wars" by the media

241 marines killed in Beirut terrorist bombing

**1985**  Mikhail Gorbachev initiates reforms in the Soviet Union

**1986**  Iran-Contra hearings before Congress reveal arms-for-hostages deal and funds secretly and illegally diverted to Nicaraguan rebels

**1988**  Republican George H. W. Bush defeats Michael Dukakis in presidential election

Communist authority collapses in Eastern Europe

**1990**  Iraqi invasion of Kuwait leads to massive U.S. military presence in the Persian Gulf

**1991**  Operation Desert Storm forces Iraq out of Kuwait

Soviet Union dissolves into Commonwealth of Independent States

**1992**  Democrat Bill Clinton defeats incumbent George H. W. Bush and independent candidate Ross Perot in the presidential election

Clinton effectively adopted many of the conservative themes that proved so advantageous to Republicans over the past twelve years. He called for "responsibility" on the part of recipients of social programs and spoke of the importance of stable families, promised to be tough on crime and to reduce the bureaucracy, and stressed the need for encouraging private investment to create new jobs. Economic issues also fueled the independent campaign of Texas billionaire H. Ross Perot, who with his folksy East Texas twang argued that someone as successful in business as himself was better qualified to solve the nation's economic woes than Washington insiders.

At the polls in November, Clinton won 43 percent of the popular vote. He also carried thirty-two states. Although failing to carry a single state, Perot scored 19 percent of the popular vote. The newly elected Clinton interpreted Perot's relative success at the polls as a mandate to focus, as he put it, "like a laser beam on the economy."

## CONCLUSION

The success of conservatives to halt and in some cases actually reverse key trends in American politics, from Franklin Roosevelt's New Deal to Lyndon Johnson's Great Society, was made possible by the legacy of the Cold War and the trauma of defeat in Vietnam. But it also owed a great deal to a deepening anxiety about cultural changes and a growing pessimism about the ability of politicians to offer solutions, especially at the national level. Those community activists struggling to broaden the 1960s' protest movements into an updated, comprehensive reformism encompassing such issues as feminism, ecology, and affirmative action readily recognized that the liberal era had ended.

President Ronald Reagan, a charismatic figure who sometimes invented his own past and seemed to believe in it, offered remedies for a weary and nostalgic nation. By insisting that the rebellious 1960s had been a terrible mistake, lowering national self-confidence along with public morals and faith in the power of economic individualism, he successfully wedded the conservatism of Christian fundamentalists, many suburbanites, and Sunbelt voters with the more traditional conservatism of corporate leaders. In many respects, the Reagan administration actually continued and added ideological fervor to the downscaling of government services and upscaling of military spending already evident under President Jimmy Carter, while offering supporters the hope of a sweeping conservative revolution.

In the end, critics suggested, supporters of Ronald Reagan and Reaganism could not go back to the 1950s—just as the erstwhile rebels of the 1960s could not go back to their favorite era. Economically, conservatives achieved many of their goals, including widespread acceptance of sharper economic divisions within society and fewer restraints on corporations and investments. But socially and culturally, their grasp was much less secure.

## REVIEW QUESTIONS

1. Evaluate the significance of the major population shifts in the United States from the 1940s through the 1970s. What was their impact on local and national politics?

2. Discuss the connections between the energy crisis and the rise of the environmental movement.

3. Interpret the decline of liberalism and the rise of conservative political groups. How did these changes affect the outcome of presidential elections?

4. Was the Iran hostage crisis a turning point in American politics or only a thorn in Carter's reelection campaign? How did the Iran-Contra scandal affect the Republicans?

5. Describe the central philosophical assumptions behind Reaganomics. What were the key policies by which it was implemented? To what extent were these policies a break with previous economic approaches?

6. Evaluate Reagan's foreign policy. How did it differ from Carter's approach to foreign affairs?

7. Analyze the key structural factors underlying recent changes in American economic and cultural life. Do you see any political solutions for the growth of poverty and inequality?

## KEY TERMS

**myhistorylab**
Flashcard Review

**Acquired Immune Deficiency
    Syndrome (AIDS)** (p. 872)
**Affirmative action** (p. 871)
**Americans with Disabilities Act**
    (p. 878)
**Camp David Accords** (p. 862)
**Contras** (p. 874)
**Deregulation** (p. 860)
**Détente** (p. 861)
**Economic Recovery Tax Act of 1981**
    (p. 868)

**Environmental Protection Agency
    (EPA)** (p. 859)
**Operation Desert Storm** (p. 879)
**Organization of Petroleum Exporting
    Countries (OPEC)** (p. 857)
**Persian Gulf War** (p. 879)
*Roe* v. *Wade* (p. 865)
**Strategic Defense Initiative (SDI)**
    (p. 873)
**Sunbelt** (p. 858)
**War on drugs** (p. 872)

## RECOMMENDED READING

Lee Edwards, *The Conservative Revolution: The Movement That Remade America*
    (1999). Traces the rise of modern political conservatism from its origins
    in Cold War anticommunism. A longtime conservative activist and writer,
    Edwards credits much of Reagan's success in office to the presence of a
    strong, vital, and grassroots conservative movement.

David Farber, *Taken Hostage: The Iran Hostage Crisis and America's First Encounter
    with Radical Islam* (2004). Examines the events of November 1979, empha-
    sizing the larger context of a decade of uncertainty and anxiety. Farber
    also considers the meaning of Carter's hostage crisis for the larger war on
    terrorism at the turn of the century.

Frances FitzGerald, *Way Out There in the Blue: Reagan, Star Wars, and the End of the
    Cold War* (2000). A well-documented study of the conservative mood that
    made Star Wars both credible and popular among conservatives. FitzGer-
    ald provides a sweeping historical context for Star Wars with special atten-
    tion given to the impact of the Cold War on traditional isolationism.

John Karaagac, *Between Promise and Policy: Ronald Reagan and Conservative Re-
    formism* (2000). Assesses Reagan's major polities, such as increased fund-
    ing for federal government and regulatory reform, in light of his
    professed conservative ideals. Karaagac argues that Reagan wielded ideol-
    ogy as a political weapon to gain support for his programs while acting
    pragmatically and with a good deal of flexibility on particular issues.

Melani McAlister, *Epic Encounters: Culture, Media, and U.S. Interests in the Middle
    East, 1945–2000* (2001). A close reading of American popular culture, in-
    cluding films, television news broadcasts, museum exhibits, and fiction,
    representing relationships between the Middle East and the United States.
    McAlister considers the importance of the abundance of oil and the Islam-
    ic religion of the Middle East as factors shaping U.S. foreign policy.

Lisa McGirr, *Suburban Warriors: The Origins of the New American Right* (2001).
    Traces the resurgence of American conservatism by analyzing issues that
    galvanized grassroots middle-class activism in southern California in the
    1960s and 1970s.

Michael Schaller, *Right Turn: American Life in the Reagan-Bush Era, 1980–1992*
    (2007). A succinct overview of the rise of conservatism and its impact on

national and foreign policies, with ample attention paid to major developments in American society and culture during the era.

Bruce J. Schulman, *The Seventies: The Great Shift in American Culture, Society, and Politics* (2001). Examines the move away from the public-spirited universalism that characterized the New Deal and civil rights movement toward the sovereignty of the free market and celebration of private life. With a geopolitical twist that emphasizes the increasing importance of the Sunbelt, Schulman argues that the conservative 1980s actually began a decade earlier.

Judith Stein, *Running Steel, Running America: Race, Economic Policy, and the Decline of Liberalism* (1998). Discusses the impact of the decline of the U.S. steel industry on its large African American labor force. Stein analyzes trade policy, especially under Carter, that benefited foreign steel producers and led to the closing of American plants.

Robert A. Strong, *Working in the World: Jimmy Carter and the Making of American Foreign Policy* (2000). A collection of nine case studies of international affairs covering Carter's presidency. Strong's goal is not to provide new insight into the central crises of the era but to open a window to the range of presidential responsibilities in the diplomatic arena.

Andrew Szasz, *EcoPopulism: Toxic Waste and the Movement for Environmental Justice* (1994). A careful analysis of a turning point in federal regulation of toxic waste. Szasz shows how the prevention of pollution, previously considered a local issue, through strengthened state and federal regulations became a national issue and a springboard for the environmental movement.

J. Samuel Walker, *Three Mile Island: A Nuclear Crisis in Historical Perspective* (2004). Sponsored by the United States Nuclear Regulatory Commission, this book provides a detailed description of the "accident" at Three Mile Island and a broad historical context, including the growth of commercial nuclear power and the emergence of forces in opposition to this source of energy.

Winifred D. Wandersee, *On the Move: American Women in the 1970s* (1988). A highly readable overview of the changes that brought Americans women into political life but also kept them at the margins of power. This study includes a close description of the National Organization for Women as well as media personalities, such as Jane Fonda, who gave feminism a public face.

Natasha Zaretsky, *No Direction Home: The American Family and the Fear of National Decline, 1868–1980* (2007). Studies the fears Americans faced in the aftermath of the Vietnam War, a sense of imperiled national identity fatefully linked to images of a family similarly endangered.

*. . . the looks on the faces of the people*
*coming out of the city that day will haunt me forever . . .*
*everyone was the same color . . . dust white . . .*
*women crying . . . men crying . . . we must never forget*
*the men and women that died that day . . .*

—*John McNamara,* The September 11 Digital Archive, *April 13, 2002*

**The twisted ruins** of the World Trade Center in the aftermath of the
terrorist attacks of September 11, 2001.

# 31

# THE UNITED STATES IN A GLOBAL AGE

## 1992–2008

**WHAT CHANGES** in public policy did Bill Clinton promote during his presidency?

**WHAT FACTORS** contributed to the economic boom of the 1990s?

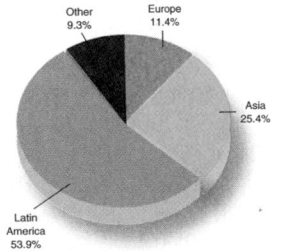

**WHAT WERE** the major divisions in American society at the end of the twentieth century?

**HOW DID** the threat of international terrorism transform the American political landscape in the first decade of the twenty-first century?

# AMERICAN COMMUNITIES
## Transnational Communities in San Diego and Tijuana

AS THE NEW MILLENNIUM BEGAN, NORMA OJEIDA CROSSED THE U.S.-Mexico border on a daily basis, leaving for work in the morning and returning home at night. She held a position at a high-powered research institute in Rosarito, a suburb of the booming city of Tijuana in Baja, California, Mexico, and made her home in suburban San Diego, in the border community of Chula Vista, where nearly half the population was Hispanic. The second largest city in San Diego County was known locally as "Chulajuana" because it was just as much a suburb of Tijuana as of San Diego. Ojeida therefore had plenty of company in making the daily journey across the busiest border crossing in North America. Thousands of other affluent, educated professionals made the same trip southward, while a steady stream of 40,000 Mexicans left Tijuana to work on the U.S. side of the border.

Many of these "fonterizos" or "borderlanders" enjoyed some of the best of both nations. Often fluent in both Spanish and English, they could choose between upward mobility in Mexico and a rewarding life in San Diego County. Their children, growing up bilingual, often crossed the border to attend school or to go on dates. This transnational lifestyle, Ojeida explained, gave the residents of this growing region "the luxury of living where you want, working where you want, having the identity you want," a luxury, however, that only a minority of residents on either side was fortunate enough to enjoy.

For better or worse, the fates of San Diego and Tijuana had become increasingly intertwined. In 1961, the Border Industrialization Program paved the way for a closer economic relationship between Tijuana and San Diego. The program fostered the creation of maquiladoras, assembly plants for such American-owned firms as Ford Motors and General Electric; in the 1990s, the adoption of the North American Free Trade Agreement (NAFTA) helped to secure these economic structures. By the end of the twentieth century Tijuana, the fourth largest city in Mexico and home to 1.5 million people, had become the only Mexican border city where the size of the middle class most nearly approached that of the impoverished population. Well-heeled shoppers from Tijuana were able to pour about $2.8 billion a year into the San Diego economy, $120 million from sales tax revenue alone.

San Diego and Tijuana, one of eight transnational metropolitan regions on the 2,000-mile U.S.-Mexico border, had come to share not only people but also problems that flout political boundaries. For example, unregulated growth on both sides of the border threatened ecological disaster, created bumper-to-bumper traffic on highways, and encouraged the kind of suburban sprawl that surrounded most large American cities. The Tijuana River, which flows into the San Diego Bay, by the 1990s was carrying 1.5 million gallons of untreated sewage per day. The virtually unregulated airborne pollution of the maquiladoras posed additional threats to the region. And the continuous cross-border traffic in goods and people caused substantial amounts of native vegetation to succumb to exotic weedy grasses.

By the end of the century, the Californian and Mexican governments began to catch up with problems festering for decades. A joint feasibility study was funded by the California legislature for the construction of an aqueduct to the Colorado River to bring more water into the region. Other plans included mass transit on the San Diego side and airport expansion on the Tijuana side to relieve congestion at San Diego's overtaxed international airport. The bright promise of the transnational San Diego/Tijuana community was held in check, however, by the dark shadows of world recession and environmental exhaustion that gathered in the first decade of the twenty-first century.

The governments of Mexico and the United States continued to explore scores of binational projects, while San Diego and Tijuana invested in a major border initiative to promote sustainable development and effective public health programs on both sides of the border. It seemed clear to everyone that the accelerating diffusion of information technologies, such as television, film, and the Internet, continued to create sources of community where none had previously existed. But the key word of the new era, "globalization," held together many contradictory tendencies. For one, international terrorism offered dramatic and unwelcome proof that no part of the world was far removed—or safe—from the conflicts of any other part.

San Diego
Tijuana

# THE PRESIDENCY OF BILL CLINTON

During his campaign, Bill Clinton promised to bring a new kind of Democratic leadership to the presidency. Since 1985, he had been active in the Democratic Leadership Council (DLC), a group of Democrats serving in Congress or as governors who feared for the fate of their party after the Reagan Republicans won forty-nine of fifty states during the 1984 election. Responding to the conservative challenge, they sought to distance the Democratic Party even further from the liberal tradition established by Franklin D. Roosevelt and revived by Lyndon Johnson in the 1960s. They sought to recapture the blue-collar and white southern defectors "by redefining and reclaiming the political center."

## A "NEW DEMOCRAT" IN THE WHITE HOUSE

Despite his awesome powers of persuasion, President Clinton got off to a rocky start. Clinton's biggest stumbling block during his first term was health care reform. Nearly 40 million Americans had no health insurance at all. Many simply could not afford it, and others were denied coverage by private insurers because of preexisting conditions ranging from cancer, cardiovascular disease, and diabetes to AIDS. For millions of others, health insurance was tied to the workplace and a loss or change of jobs threatened their coverage. National spending on health care skyrocketed from roughly $200 billion in 1980 to more than $800 billion in 1992, constituting about one-seventh of the entire domestic economy.

Shortly after taking office, in a controversial move, President Clinton appointed First Lady Hillary Rodham Clinton, an accomplished attorney, to head a task force charged with preparing a sweeping legislative overhaul of health care. The task force's effort to find a political middle ground ultimately produced an impossibly complicated compromise. Opposed by such powerful forces as the Chamber of Commerce, the National Association of Manufacturers, the Health Insurance Association of America, and most Republicans, the plan died in Congress in August, 1994, just as the midterm election campaign moved into its final phase.

In the 1994 midterm elections, Clinton's defeat on health care reform helped the Republicans gain control of both the House and Senate for the first time in forty years—a disaster of historic proportions for Clinton and the Democratic Party. Congress was now dominated by conservative Republicans led by the new House Speaker, Newt Gingrich of Georgia. With his scathing denunciations of big government and celebration of entrepreneurship, the formidable polemicist Gingrich challenged Clinton's leadership by presenting his own set of proposals labeled the **"Contract with America."** The House did indeed pass much of the "Contract," including a large tax cut, an increase in military spending, cutbacks in federal regulatory power in the environment and at the workplace, a tough anticrime bill, and a sharp reduction in federal welfare programs.

Meanwhile, Clinton undercut the Republicans by adapting many of their proposals to his own. He endorsed the goal of a balanced federal budget and declared, in his January 1996 State of the Union message, that "the era of big government is over." Clinton opposed his own party's efforts to block a Republican plan to dismantle the federal welfare system in place since the New Deal and instead backed new legislation—the **Welfare Reform Act**—that abolished the sixty-year-old Aid to Families with Dependent Children program (AFDC). After Congress passed the act in August 1996, Clinton held a public signing ceremony and declared "an end to welfare as we know it."

With such deft maneuvers, Clinton set the theme for his 1996 reelection campaign against Robert Dole of Kansas, the Republican majority leader of the

**WHAT CHANGES** in public policy did Bill Clinton promote during his presidency?

**Review Summary**

**30–12**
*Republican Contract with America* (1994)

## IMAGE KEY

for pages 884–885

a. The twisted ruins of the World Trade Center in the aftermath of the terrorist attacks of September 11, 2001.

b. A cell phone like those used by many in the stricken World Trade Center and aboard the four hijacked airliners to call for help or give their loved ones their last goodbyes.

c. Computer chips have come to symbolize the boom of the 1990s.

d. A paper voting card like those used in Florida in the contentious 2000 presidential election.

e. A gas mask used as protection from a chemical or biological attack.

f. German soldiers watch the collapse of the Berlin Wall amid a crowd of Berliners and photographers.

g. S.V. Marshall High School students join other Mississippi teens in building more than 125 new high-speed multimedia computers during a Computer Blitz Build at Jackson State University's E-center.

h. A pie chart shows the population shifts of the 1990s.

i. A soldier stops to watch the sunset during military exercises in Kuwait, November 18, 2002.

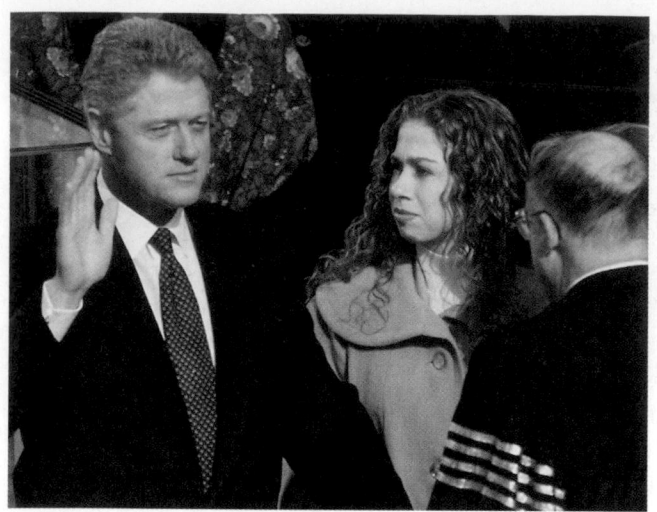

**Chief Justice William** Rehnquist administers the oath of office to President William Jefferson Clinton on January 20, 1993. Daughter Chelsea and wife Hillary Rodham Clinton stand by his side. In his Inaugural Address as the nation's 42nd president, Clinton invited his fellow citizens to "celebrate the mystery of the American renewal" and to help him "revitalize our democracy."

**Contract with America** Platform proposing a sweeping reduction in the role and activities of the federal government on which many Republican candidates ran for Congress in 1994.

**Welfare Reform Act** Act passed by Congress in 1996 that abolished the Aids to Families with Dependent Children (AFDC) welfare program.

**North American Free Trade Agreement (NAFTA)** Agreement reached in 1993 by Canada, Mexico, and the United States to substantially reduce barriers to trade.

**World Trade Organization (WTO)** International organization that sets standards and practices for global trade, and the focus of international protests over world economic policy in the late 1990s.

**Bosnia** A nation in southeast Europe that split off from Yugoslavia and became the site of bitter civil and religious war, requiring NATO and U.S. intervention in the 1990s.

Senate. By staking out the political center, the president won a resounding reelection victory in November 1996. But it was a victory without coattails: the Republicans retained control of both houses of Congress.

## THE "GLOBALIZATION" PRESIDENT

Following in the footsteps of his Democratic predecessor, Jimmy Carter, Clinton insisted that U.S. foreign policy reflect "the moral principles most Americans share." But even more central to his vision was the goal of enlarging "the world's free community of market democracies" under the leadership of the United States. The editors of *Foreign Affairs* dubbed Clinton the "globalization" president.

These two principles drove Clinton's policy toward the People's Republic of China (PRC). During the spring of 1989, Chinese government forces had brutally attacked prodemocracy demonstrators in Beijing's Tiananmen Square, resulting in the death of some 3,000 protestors and the wounding of 10,000 more. During the 1992 election campaign, Clinton criticized Bush for continuing "to coddle" China in light of such gross human rights violations. Then, after taking office, he modified his position and, looking for "hopeful seeds of change," recommended restoring Most Favored Nation (MFN) status with the PRC. Clinton acknowledged that serious human rights abuses continued, but he pointed out that China, the world's most populous nation, had the world's fastest growing economy—as well as a nuclear arsenal and veto in the Security Council of the UN.

During his first term, President Clinton pushed through Congress two major trade agreements to expand markets and encourage "free trade," both building on the earlier efforts of the Reagan and Bush administrations. Approved in November 1993, the **North American Free Trade Agreement (NAFTA)** eased the international flow of goods, services, and investments among the United States, Mexico, and Canada by eliminating tariffs and other trade barriers. The second trade agreement, which led to the establishment of the **World Trade Organization (WTO)** in 1995, continued the GATT policy of keeping tariffs low on thousands of goods throughout the world and phased out many import quotas imposed by the United States and other industrialized nations—except in agriculture, where the United States and Europe maintained quotas to the detriment of the developing peasant-based Third World economies. The WTO would also mediate commercial disputes among 117 nations.

On humanitarian grounds, Clinton's accomplishments fell far short of his lofty goals. During his first year in office, in October 1993, the United States took part in a UN mission to restore civil order in Somalia in East Africa. Eighteen ill-equipped American soldiers were killed in battle, while several thousand Somalian fighters and civilians died in the ill-fated attack. The president aborted the military mission and adopted a more cautious policy of intervention for humanitarian reasons.

In 1995, acting reluctantly, Clinton committed U.S. troops to a multinational effort in **Bosnia** where, following the collapse of communism and the dissolution of Yugoslavia, ethnic and religious rivalry among Serbs, Croats, and Muslims had erupted into a civil war. As reports of "ethnic cleansing"—forced removal and murder of Croats and Muslims by Bosnian Serbs—increased, and as the numbers of refugees grew, Clinton, with congressional support, joined NATO in bombing Serbian strongholds in Bosnia. After negotiating with Yugoslav president Slobodan Milosevic, on November 27 Clinton announced a peace accord that called for a federated, multiethnic state of Bosnia.

Clinton's worst foreign crisis erupted in the region of **Kosovo**, Yugoslavia, where intensifying clashes between Serbs and Albanians spread to neighboring Macedonia and to Albania itself. President Clinton once again tried to negotiate, but he failed to resolve the problems through diplomacy. After NATO authorized air strikes, he addressed Americans in March 1999, stating that U.S. armed forces had that day joined the attack on Serbian forces in Kosovo.

The so-called Clinton Doctrine, articulated in 1999 to justify the dispatch of U.S. troops to Yugoslavia, departed sharply from Cold War policies that sanctioned intervention primarily on the grounds of strategic interest and national security. In a later statement, Clinton insisted that "genocide is in and of itself a national interest where we should act." In 1998, he acknowledged that the United States, as part of the global community, must share the blame for failing to intervene in Rwanda in 1994, where a struggle for power led to genocide in the killing of up to 1 million Tutsis and moderate Hutu by Hutu extremists.

## PRESIDING OVER THE BOOM

By any number of measures, Bill Clinton presided over one of the strongest and longest economic booms in American history. With government spending down and economic growth increasing tax revenues, the largest federal budget deficit in American history (a quarter trillion dollars) became a surplus nearly as large by the time Clinton left office.

Perhaps the greatest boost to Clinton's second term as president came from the soaring stock market of the 1990s, with "tech stocks" leading the way. Throughout the decade, the market remained volatile, but profits were extraordinarily high. Equally remarkable was the involvement of ordinary citizens "in the market." By the end of the century, Americans had 60 percent of their investments and savings in stocks, more than double the proportion in 1982.

The downside of the economic boom was nearly invisible. Productivity had risen sharply since the 1970s while labor costs had actually declined, hoisting profits to new levels. But critics observed that while a corporate official had earned around twenty or thirty times the pay of a blue-collar worker at the same company a few decades earlier, corporate executive income was more than two hundred times greater than that of a blue-collar employee. In the blue-collar sector, industrial jobs continued to disappear as factories closed or companies moved production of textiles, auto parts, and even electronics across borders or overseas.

## HIGH CRIMES AND MISDEMEANORS

Questions of private and public morality dogged Bill Clinton's political career. During his second term as president, Clinton had to answer many questions about his moral conduct. Real estate deals involving both him and Hillary Rodham Clinton blew up into a scandal known as Whitewater. A former Arkansas state employee, Paula Jones, charged Clinton with sexual assault during his gubernatorial term. Attorney General Janet Reno, appointed an independent counsel, former judge Kenneth Starr, to investigate allegations. But in the summer of 1998, Starr delivered to the House Judiciary Committee a report focusing on an extramarital affair that the president conducted with a young White House intern, Monica Lewinsky. Starr's report outlined several potential impeachable offenses, including false testimony under oath, witness

**After the 1994** midterm election gave Republicans control of the House of Representatives for the first time in forty years, the new Speaker, Newt Gingrich of Georgia, presented a list of legislative initiatives to be completed within the first one hundred days of the new session. On April 7, 1995, he appeared at a rally on Capitol Hill to celebrate the success of the Republicans' "Contract with America."

**Kosovo** Province of Yugoslavia where the United States and NATO intervened militarily in 1999 to protect ethnic Albanians from expulsion.

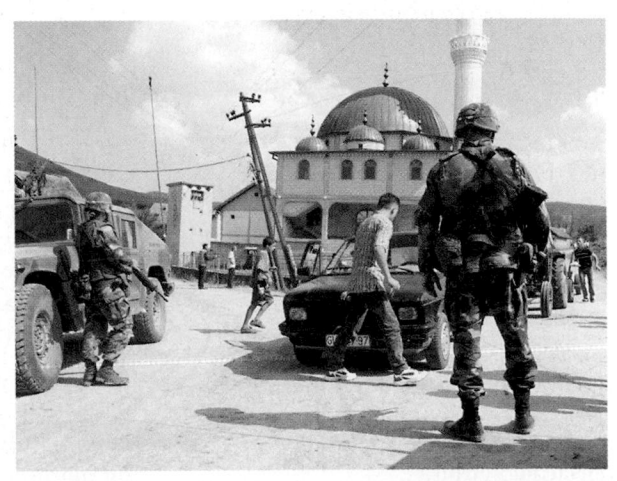

**U.S. Army Military** Police stop and search vehicles for weapons and explosives at this checkpoint near Vitina, Kosovo in Yugoslavia, 1999. They were part of the NATO led international force sent to attack Serbian forces in Kosovo.

tampering, and obstruction of justice, all allegedly committed by the president to keep his relationship with Lewinsky secret.

For only the third time in history, in October 1998, the House of Representatives voted to open an inquiry into possible grounds for impeachment. Republicans hoping to reap a wholesale victory from the scandal in the midterm elections were bitterly disappointed. Contrary to predictions, the president's party added seats, trimming the Republican majority in the 105th Congress. Newt Gingrich, under pressure from Republican colleagues angry about a campaign strategy that had narrowly focused on Clinton's impeachment problem, announced his resignation as Speaker of the House and from his seat in Congress.

In the aftermath of the 1998 midterm election, most politicians and analysts, and indeed most Americans, believed the impeachment inquiry to be at a dead end. But the House Judiciary Committee voted to bring four articles of impeachment—charging President Clinton with perjury, obstruction of justice, witness tampering, and abuse of power—to the full House. But unlike the bipartisan case the Judiciary Committee brought against Richard Nixon in 1974 (see Chapter 29), this time the votes were strictly along party lines. On February 12, 1999, the Senate trial concluded with the president's acquittal.

**30–13**
*Articles of Impeachment against William Jefferson Clinton* (1998)

**WHAT FACTORS** contributed to the economic boom of the 1990s?

**myhistorylab**
**Review Summary**

# CHANGING AMERICAN COMMUNITIES

During the Clinton administration, economists coined the phrase "the new economy" to underscore the increasing importance of globalization and corporate restructuring as well as the growing service sector, which included all those workers not directly involved in producing or processing a physical product: from highly paid lawyers, financial analysts, and software designers to poorly paid fast food employees.

## SILICON VALLEY

The real and symbolic capital of the new economy was a thirty-by-ten-mile strip of Santa Clara County, California. Dubbed **"Silicon Valley"** in 1971 after the material in semiconductor chips, the region flourished thanks to its unique combination of research facilities, investment capital, attractive environment, and a large pool of highly educated people. At first, military contracts predominated, but the consumer electronics revolution of the 1970s fueled an explosive new wave of growth. It became home to more than 1,700 high-tech firms that specialized in gathering, processing, or distributing information or in manufacturing information technology.

The prime example of the new economy, Silicon Valley was part of a global enterprise. Its firms were closely linked to the microelectronics industry of the greater Pacific Rim. The end of the Cold War and the accompanying decline in military spending in the United States forced high-tech firms in California into greater competition on the world market and especially against similar companies in Japan, Korea, China, and Malaysia. But many American companies protected themselves against such competition by owning and managing a large share of the plants in these countries.

By the end of Clinton's administration, the rate of growth showed signs of slowing, dramatized by the sharp plunge of technology stocks. In the aftermath of this burst of the so-called dot-com bubble in March 2000, entrepreneurs throughout the Pacific Rim found it more difficult to start successful new companies and to make the leap from a small, start-up company to a large corporation. By this time, scarcity in housing, traffic jams, and an inflated cost of living were already leading many companies and individuals to move out of the area.

**Silicon Valley** The region of California including San Jose and San Francisco that holds the nation's greatest concentration of electronics firms.

## AN ELECTRONIC CULTURE

The technological developments produced in Silicon Valley helped recon-figure cultural life in the United States and the world. The new technologies changed the way people worked, played, and conducted business and politics.

The twin arrivals of cable and the videocassette recorder (VCR) expanded and redefined the power of television. By the early 1990s pay cable services and VCRs had penetrated roughly two-thirds of American homes.

More than ever, television drove the key strategies and tactics defin-ing American political life. Politicians and their advisers focused intently on a candidate's television image. Fewer citizens voted or took an active role in campaigns, and most relied on television coverage to make their choices.

New digital technologies continued to reshape American culture into the early 2000s. Compact discs (CDs) and digital video discs (DVDs) emerged as the dominant media for popular music and movies, replacing tape-based technologies. Millions of Americans now used digital cameras to document their vacations and everyday lives. Digital telephones—"cell phones"—became a ubiquitous presence in the streets, malls, campuses, cars, and workplaces of American communities.

Perhaps no aspect of the electronic culture was more revolutionary than the creation of cyberspace, the conceptual region occupied by people linked through computers and communications networks. It began with ARPANET, the first computer network, which the Department of Defense developed in the early 1970s. Computer enthusiasts known as "hackers" created unexpected grassroots spinoffs from ARPANET, including electronic mail, computer conferencing, and computer bulletin board systems. In the mid-1980s, alongside the launch of Microsoft Word and Windows operating programs, the boom in cheap personal computers capable of linking individuals to the worldwide telecommunications net-work began a population explosion in cyberspace. By the beginning of the new cen-tury, the U.S. Census Bureau estimated that more than half of all households had at least one computer and more than 40 percent were connected to the **Internet**.

These new information technologies gave birth to a media community that tran-scended national boundaries. During the 1980s, exports from Hollywood to the rest of the world doubled in value. The number of hours of television watched throughout the world nearly tripled: MTV was broadcast to an estimated 250 million households. By the mid-1990s there were more television sets in China than in the United States.

## THE NEW IMMIGRANTS AND THEIR COMMUNITIES

The 2000 census showed that the nation's population during the 1990s grew by 32.7 million, a number greater than that of any other decade in U.S. history. In October 2006, the U.S. population hit 300 million.

At the turn of the twenty-first century, more than a third of the nation's pop-ulation growth came from the influx of new immigrants (see Figure 31.1). Nation-ally, the percentage of Americans born outside the United States was 11.2 percent, its highest point since 1930; in California the percentage of foreign born approached 26 percent.

The Immigration Act of 1965 had revolutionary consequences, some of them unintended (see Chapter 28). The act abolished the discriminatory national ori-gins quotas that had been in place since the 1920s. It also for the first time limited immigration from the Western Hemisphere, while giving preference to people from the nations of the Eastern Hemisphere who had specialized job skills and train-ing. This provision created the conditions for Asian immigrants to become the fastest-growing ethnic group in the United States. But in setting limits on Western

**Yi Li, a graduate** student from Taiwan, uses a computer terminal at the New York Public Library to gain access to the Internet. By the 1990s banks of person-al computers had become a familiar sight in American offices, businesses, schools, and libraries. Millions of Americans made connecting with the new world of cyberspace a part of their daily routines.

**31–7**
Lou Dobbs, *The Attack on the Middle Class* (2006)

### QUICK REVIEW

**Cable Television, VCRs, and the Internet**

◆ Cable television reflected the frag-mentation of American society and the increasing dependence on instant communication.

◆ Cable and VCRs expanded and redefined the power of television.

◆ The World Wide Web expanded dramatically in the 1990s.

**Internet** The system of interconnected computers and servers that allows the exchange of email, posting of Web sites, and other means of instant communication.

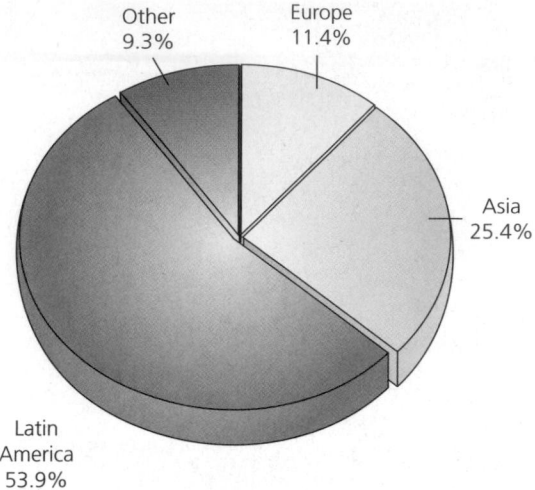

Other
9.3%

Europe
11.4%

Asia
25.4%

Latin
America
53.9%

**Figure 31.1 Continent of Birth for Immigrants, 1990–2000**
By 2000, the number of foreign-born residents and their children—56 million according to the Census Bureau—had reached the highest level in U.S. history.

**31–11**
*Illegal Immigration* (2007)

Hemisphere immigration, the 1965 act tempted many thousands of people from Latin America to enter the United States illegally.

By the mid-1980s, growing concern over "illegal aliens" had become a hotly debated political issue, particularly in the Southwest. The Immigration Reform and Control Act of 1986 marked a break with the past attempts to address this problem. Instead of mass deportation programs, the law strengthened the patrol along the border with Mexico and simultaneously offered an amnesty to all undocumented workers who had entered the country since 1982. Four years later, additional revisions of this act enlarged the quota of immigrants, once again giving priority to skilled and professional workers. In 2006 millions of immigrants—both legal and undocumented—took to the streets in American cities to demand amnesty for so-called illegals and calling for reforms that would allow a clear and legal path to citizenship. These protests marked a new attempt to flex the political muscle of immigrant communities and served notice that anti-immigrant forces would not go unchallenged in the political arena.

The 2000 census showed that Mexicans were the largest Hispanic group in the United States at 20.6 million, representing nearly 60 percent of the total Hispanic population. The boom of the U.S. economy in the 1990s provided a significant "pull" for these newcomers. But other factors encouraged many immigrants to make an often difficult and dangerous sojourn. First, a drop in worldwide oil prices followed by the deflation of the Mexican national currency dramatically lowered living standards in Mexico in the mid-1990s. NAFTA and the greater integration of the U.S. and Mexican economies brought new jobs but often with increasingly expensive living conditions. Tens and perhaps hundreds of thousands of Mexicans worked in the United States temporarily while planning a permanent move north—with or without legal documentation.

The cultural implications of immigration were far-reaching. Children born to the new immigrants of the 1980s and 1990s, despite increasing neighborhood segregation by race, played on the streets together, attended the same schools, and often married outside their racial group. In the 2000 census, 6.8 million Americans nationwide listed themselves as multiracial. Identities blurred as popular entertainment created new mixes of traditions and styles. Alternalatino (alternative Latin music—a mixture of salsa and merengue), Tjano, Reggae, and other music in fusion mixtures became as common to Manhattan or Los Angeles as to Mexico City or Rio.

Although smaller in number than Hispanics, Asians were the fastest-growing racial group in the United States. With a steady flow of professionals and workers skilled in technology into their communities, Chinese Americans maintained their status as the largest Asian ethnicity in the United States. However, other groups grew at faster rates, particularly Indo Americans (from the subcontinent of India), whose numbers doubled during the 1990s to become the third-largest Asian group. Meanwhile Japanese Americans, once the largest and most influential members of the pan-Asian community, declined.

The 2000 census also revealed sharp divisions among Americans. Although the poverty rate had dropped to 11.3 percent of the population, near the lowest level ever recorded, more than 31 million people still lived in poverty. Five years later, average incomes had dipped further, and nearly half of all Americans earned less than $30,000. Moreover, the new economy had done little to close the gap between the highest and lowest income earners. Women as a group made few gains, earning 73 cents to each dollar earned by men. And with African Americans and Latinos continuing to earn, on average, far less than non-Hispanic whites, race relations benefited little from the economic boom of the 1990s.

# A New Age of Anxiety

Despite the prosperity of the 1990s, many Americans experienced an uneasiness that resembled the anxiety of the mid-twentieth century, when the world seemed on the brink of nuclear destruction.

## THE RACIAL DIVIDE

In the spring of 1992 an upheaval in Los Angeles offered the starkest evidence that racial tensions had not eased. Outrage over police brutality ignited the worst riot of the century. A year earlier, Rodney King, a black motorist, had been pulled from his vehicle and severely beaten by four white police officers. When, despite the graphic evidence of an amateur videotape of the incident, a jury acquitted the officers of all but one of eleven counts of assault, South Central Los Angeles erupted, with crowds looting and burning businesses throughout the community and into Koreatown. More than fifty people were killed, and 500 buildings were destroyed before L.A. police and National Guard troops restored order.

The events in Los Angeles exposed the deep animosity among various groups—so much so that the observers referred to the event as a "multicultural riot." Almost 2,000 Korean businesses were destroyed, and Koreans angrily accused the police of making no effort to defend their stores. The division was sharpest, though, between whites and the minority populations.

The situation in Los Angeles was not unique. The 2000 census showed that segregation was on the rise, and not only in cities but also in their surrounding suburbs. Similarly, in the nation's schools, the gains from the civil rights era diminished and, in some communities, disappeared altogether. A 2001 report showed that, despite the increasing racial and ethnic diversity of the nation's youth, segregation was more pronounced in grades K–12.

The publicity generated by Rodney King's arrest fed several major controversies concerning the U.S. criminal justice system. Racial disparities were evident, with ethnic and racial minorities accounting for approximately two-thirds of state prison inmates. In 2007, the Bureau of Justice estimated that 32 percent of African American men would enter a state or federal prison during their lifetimes.

Various civil liberties groups reviewed these statistics and concluded that African Americans were not necessarily more prone to criminal activity but were far more likely to be stopped, searched, arrested, convicted, and given harsher penalties than white Americans. By 1999, "driving while black" had become a news item in all the major media, leading to the introduction of a bill into the U.S. Senate in 1999 to collect statistics on traffic stops.

## THE CULTURE WARS

At the 1992 Republican National Convention, the conservative Patrick Buchanan gave the opening speech. "There is a religious war going on in our country for the soul of America," he declared. "It is a cultural war, as critical to the kind of nation we will one day be as was the Cold War itself." Into the twenty-first century, politics focused on issues like reproductive rights and reproductive technology, homosexuality and gay rights, the curriculum in public schools, codes of speech and standards in the arts, gun control, and scientific developments such as cloning, genetic alteration, and fetal tissue research, and even the validity of Darwin's theory of evolution.

The growing racial and ethnic diversity of American society, as well as the expansion of rights for groups such as women and gays,

**WHAT WERE** the major divisions in American society at the end of the twentieth century?

**myhistorylab**
**Review Summary**

### QUICK REVIEW

**Los Angeles Riots**

◆ Spring 1992: Riots sparked by acquittal of officers in Rodney King case.

◆ Fifty-one people were killed and $850 million in damage was reported.

◆ Riots exposed ethnic and economic divisions in the city.

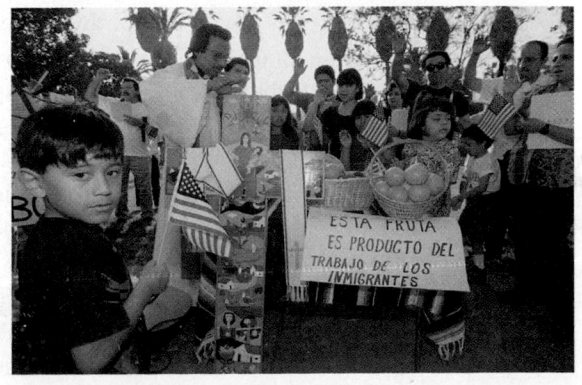

**The sign at** this 1996 vigil in Echo Park, Los Angeles, reads, "This fruit is the product of immigrants' labor." Members of the city's Latino community bless fruit baskets as they protest a state crackdown on illegal immigration and the increase of border patrol guards.

**31–3**
*Dissent Within the World
Episcopal Church over Gay
Rights* (2004)

had sparked a broad and controversial movement known as **"multiculturalism."**
Unlike earlier descriptions of America as a "melting pot," new metaphors such as
"salad bowl" or "mosaic" became popular expressions to call attention to the
unique attributes and achievements of formerly marginal groups and recent immigrants. On college campuses, multiculturalism marked the high point of the cur-
ricular reform that had been ongoing since the late 1960s and early 1970s, when
women's and ethnic studies programs were launched (see Chapter 29).

Reaching well beyond the academic world, the culture wars played out in
immigration policy. In 1994, a California ballot initiative, **Proposition 187**, called
for making all undocumented aliens ineligible for any social service, public schooling, and nonemergency medical care, and it required teachers and clinic doctors
to report illegal immigrants to the police. Passed by a three-to-two margin, the new
legislation was immediately challenged in the streets and in the courts. In 1998,
after several years of legal wrangling, a federal judge ruled that Proposition 187
unconstitutionally usurped federal authority over immigration policy. In June 2001,
the U.S. Supreme Court ruled that immigrants are entitled to the same protection
by the Constitution as that afforded to citizens.

Similar controversies surrounded gay rights, particularly around a push for
the legal recognition of civil unions and marriage for same-sex couples. In 2000,
Vermont became the first state to recognize civil unions, allowing same-sex couples to receive many, although not all, of the legal benefits of marriage. Several
other states passed versions of civil union or domestic partner laws. In 2004, Massachusetts became the first state in America to legally permit gay marriage. Meanwhile, seventeen states passed constitutional provisions defining marriage as a
union of one man and one woman, while twenty-five others enacted legislative
statutes with similar definitions. Gay marriage would continue as a powerful symbolic issue.

Nearly as volatile as a political issue was government financing of an area of
scientific research of growing importance since the birth of the first test-tube baby
in 1981—human embryonic stem cell research. Religious conservatives opposed
this research because it may involve the destruction of human embryos, usually
derived from the excess products of *in vitro* fertilization processes and scheduled
for disposal by fertility clinics. In 1995, in response to pressure from conservative
groups such as the National Right to Life Committee, Congress enacted legislation
banning the use of federal funds for research that involves the destruction of
human embryos. However, in his last year in office, Clinton loosened the ban and
thereby generated another round of controversy.

## THE FORCES OF FEAR

During the 1990s, anxiety about terrorism and random violence escalated. Within
their own borders, Americans were actually far safer from terrorist attacks than
the citizens of many other countries. Nevertheless, two events—the attack on the
World Trade Center in 1993 and the destruction of the federal building in Oklahoma City in 1995—alerted Americans to danger at home and to U.S. interests
abroad.

On February 26, 1993, a small group of Arab Islamist terrorists bombed
the World Trade Center in New York City, killing six people and injuring more
than a thousand others. Taken in retaliation for U.S. intervention in the Middle
East, the attack was the most destructive act of terrorism committed within the
United States to that time. It spurred the Antiterrorism and Effective Death
Penalty Act of 1996, which greatly expanded the budget and powers of federal
authorities to monitor likely terrorists. Despite increased surveillance, terrorists

**Multiculturalism** Movement that
emphasizes the unique attributes
and achievements of formerly
marginal groups and recent
immigrants.

**Proposition 187** California
legislation adopted by popular vote
in California in 1994, which cuts off
state-funded health and education
benefits to undocumented or illegal
immigrants.

struck another lethal blow. On August 7, 1998, car bombings of U.S. embassies in Kenya and Tanzania injured more
than 4,000 people and killed 220.

   The bombing of the Alfred P. Murrah Federal Building
in Oklahoma City raised an entirely different specter: terrorism by self-described patriotic Americans. Two years earlier, on February 28, 1993, agents of the FBI and the Federal
Bureau of Alcohol, Tobacco, and Firearms (ATF) had conducted a "search and arrest" operation against the Branch
Davidians that turned deadly. Their object was David Koresh,
the leader of the obscure religious sect who was suspected of
stockpiling illegal firearms and ammunition. After a round
of shots, which took the lives of four ATF agents and six
Branch Davidians, Koresh's heavily armed followers barricaded themselves in their compound in Waco, Texas. Fifty-
one days later, on April 19, government agents brought their
siege to a fiery end. Nine Davidians managed to escape the flames engulfing their
buildings, while seventy-six others, including twenty-one children, perished.

   Choosing April 19, 1995, the anniversary of the federal raid at Waco, as their
"Date of Doom," Timothy McVeigh and his accomplices took their revenge. Shortly
after 9:00 A.M., a bomb went off in the federal office building in Oklahoma City,
killing 168 people, including 19 children, and injuring more than 500 others. Picked
up within hours of the bombing on a misdemeanor traffic violation, McVeigh was later
indicted on eleven charges, including eight counts of first-degree murder. After a
trial in federal court and demonstrations both for and against the death penalty, he
was executed in June 2001.

   Medical clinics that provided abortion services to women became a prime target. Although the ratio of abortions to live pregnancies had been declining since
1979, antiabortion groups became more belligerent. Several medical providers
were murdered outside their clinics. In 1994, with the support of President Clinton, Congress enacted the Freedom of Access to Clinic Entrance Act, which provides protection to any abortion clinic requesting it. The number of violent
incidents declined from the peak of thirty-two bombings, arsons, or attempted
attacks in 1992 and twelve murders or attempted murders in 1994. After the turn
of the century, the attacks continued to diminish but did not stop.

The California ballot initiative Proposition
187 was designed to deny basic social
services, including health and education,
to undocumented immigrants. To express
their opposition to the legislation, as
many as 250,000 people took the
streets in downtown Los Angeles. This
photograph shows Grace Lee and a group
of fellow students demonstrating in the
Westwood section of the city shortly after
voters approved the bill known as "the
last gasp of White America in California"
on November 8, 1994.

# THE PRESIDENCY OF GEORGE W. BUSH AND THE WAR ON TERROR

The end of the Cold War had reconfigured global politics, ending the bilat-
eralism that had dominated international affairs since the end of World
War II. The United States alone held fast to its superpower status, but
this achievement did not necessarily make Americans more secure or safe. The old
enemy, Soviet communism, was succeeded by more fanatic, less predictable foes.
The September 11, 2001, attacks on the World Trade Center and other targets
proved to be a critical turning point for the Bush presidency as it looked to recon-
figure American foreign policy and domestic politics around the strategy of a "war
on terror." The Bush administration justified the American invasion of Iraq in
2003 largely as a necessary part of that strategy. The Iraq war defined the Bush presidency more than any other issue.

**HOW DID** the threat of
international terrorism transform the
American political landscape in the
first decade of the twenty-first
century?

myhistorylab
**Review Summary**

**Rescue workers carried** an injured man from the rubble of the U.S. Embassy in Nairobi, Kenya. A terrorist bomb killed more than 100 people and injured more than 1,600 on August 8, 1998.

## THE ELECTION OF 2000

After a relatively dull campaign season, the 2000 election played out as high drama. Voters went to the polls as usual on election day, watched as late-night television newscasters projected a victory for the Democratic candidate, Clinton's vice president Al Gore, and then woke up the next morning to learn that perhaps the winner was not the vice president but his Republican opponent, Governor George W. Bush of Texas, son of former president George H. W. Bush. It was clear that Gore and his running mate, Connecticut Senator Joseph Lieberman, had won the popular vote, although by the closest margin since John F. Kennedy defeated Richard Nixon in 1961. In doubt was the number of votes in the electoral college. At 2:15 A.M., the pollsters who had projected Gore as the winner changed their minds. The cliffhanger in Florida had finally ended with the state's decisive twenty-five electoral votes earmarked for the Republicans. By morning Gore had called Bush to concede. *The New York Times*, however, ran a guarded headline "Bush Appears to Defeat Gore." Only a few hundred votes in Florida gave Bush the edge, and in cases where the margin is so narrow Florida law mandates a machine recount in all sixty-seven counties. Gore soon retracted his concession (see Map 31.1).

The 2000 campaign played out as the first disputed presidential election since 1876, when Democrat Samuel J. Tilden, who won the popular vote, charged his Republican opponent, Rutherford B. Hayes, with fraudulent vote counting. A similar question of legitimacy hung over the 2000 election. After Florida completed its machine recount of votes, the Democrats requested a hand tally in selected counties where the ballots were in dispute. The Republicans responded by suing in the Miami district court to prohibit the manual recounting. Meanwhile Florida election officials, mainly Republicans, set November 14 as the date to certify the election results, thereby disallowing the returns on overseas ballots that might favor Al Gore. In turn, Democrats sued to extend the deadline. Eventually, appeals by both parties reached the Florida Supreme Court and finally the U.S. Supreme Court, which voted five to four along partisan lines to halt the counting. Time had run out, and on December 12 Gore conceded defeat, despite having received over 500,000 more votes than Bush. With less fanfare than usual, George W. Bush took the oath of office in January 2001.

## A GLOBAL COMMUNITY?

On policies concerning the environment, Bush acted quickly and aggressively to defer or to overturn several key programs established under Clinton. In July 2001, the Environmental Protection Agency announced a delay in asking states to draft plans to protect some 21,000 waterways severely impaired by agricultural runoff. Meanwhile, Bush's advisers reconsidered proposals that would have prohibited the development of nearly one-third of the national forests.

No issue was so important or so controversial as climate change, a challenge that most scientists and world leaders agreed required international solutions. Shortly after taking office, President George W. Bush announced his opposition to the terms of the Kyoto Protocol, leaving 178 other countries to agree to mandatory reductions in greenhouse gases without the participation of the United States. Bush instead created a task force to conduct additional studies on the impact of human activity on climate change. The Kyoto treaty took effect in early 2005, but with the United States on the sidelines, its greatest value may prove mostly symbolic.

The changing climate was only one issue tied to globalization, a term used to characterize the belief that worldwide processes were causing national economies, cultures, and borders to melt away. The big questions concerning globalization centered on political economy. Now that communism has collapsed, they asked, would a steady expansion of free trade among nations create the basis for a global community?

There were many answers to this question. Some observers argued that the interpenetration of markets and cultural patterns—the enormous sales of Hollywood movies in China, for example—set the stage for other exchanges. Others argued that the global economy depended less on "interpenetration" than "domination" of the marketplace by the industrialized nations. Whereas physical occupation of territory defined the form of colonialism that prevailed before World War II, a new "colonialism" had come into existence since the 1960s that relied on a few multinational corporations controlling distant economies throughout the world. About 90 percent of the multinational corporations that did business worldwide were headquartered in the industrialized nations of North America, Europe, and Japan. Known collectively as the Triad, the consortium of these nations, home to only 15 percent of the world's population, produced nearly 75 percent of the world's goods by the late 1990s.

What made the current trend toward globalization distinctive was, therefore, not the rate of growth but the absolute volume and character of the exchange. Revenues from multinational corporations grew phenomenally at the end of the twentieth century. Because the member nations of the Triad were homes to the world's largest multinational corporations, they also reaped the largest share of the wealth. A UN annual human development report offered statistics showing that the gap in wealth between the upper 20 percent and the world's poorest people at the end of the nineteenth century was 30 to 1; by 1990 it reached 60 to 1; and by the end of the twentieth century it had widened to 74 to 1.

While many political observers and scholars predicted that globalization would bring both free markets and democracy to more and more of the world's people, others became increasingly skeptical. In November 1999, thousands of protestors converged in Seattle, Washington, site of the annual meeting of the World Trade Organization (WTO), only to be pushed back by local police. In response, the WTO formulated new procedures for its meetings, secreting delegates behind walls and banning demonstrations from the area near future sites. Nevertheless, confrontations continued, the most dramatic occurring at a meeting of delegates from the eight leading industrial nations in Genoa, Italy, in 2001, which resulted in the death of one protestor.

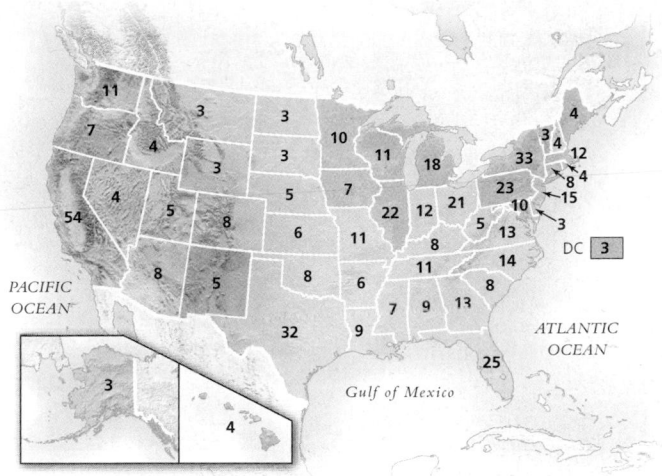

| | Electoral Vote (%) | Popular Vote (%) |
|---|---|---|
| GEORGE W. BUSH (Republican) | 271 (50.5) | 50,456,169 (48.0) |
| Al Gore (Democrat) | 266 (49.5) | 50,996,116 (48.0) |

**MAP 31.1**
**The Election of 2000**  The 2000 presidential election was the closest one in U.S. history and the first one to be decided by a decision of the Supreme Court.

WHY DID the framers of the Constitution create the electoral college? Does the election of 2000 support the argument for direct election of presidents?

**QUICK REVIEW**

**Election Controversy**
- Al Gore secured a majority of the popular vote.
- Both sides needed Florida's contested electoral votes to secure election.
- The U.S. Supreme Court voted 5–4 to end the recount in Florida, making George W. Bush the new president.

## TERRORIST ATTACK ON AMERICA

On September 11, 2001, hijackers, armed only with knives and box cutters, crashed two jetliners into New York's World Trade Center towers, while a third jetliner slammed into the Pentagon in Virginia. A fourth plane, diverted from its terrorist mission by courageous passengers, hurtled to the ground near Pittsburgh. In all, 246 people

More than 5,000 activists gathered in Seattle in November 1999 to demonstrate against the meeting of the World Trade Organization. The event, which was marked by a violent clash with police and the arrest of dozens of protestors, marked the beginning of a movement for global economic justice.

31–1
George Bush, *Address to the Nation* (2001)

perished in the four planes. At the sites of the attack, the damage was devastating. At the Pentagon, the death toll soon reached 184, including 59 people who had been on board the hijacked airliner. In New York City, the collapse of the twin towers, most likely caused by the intense fires propelled by the planes' jet fuel, killed 2,752 people, including hundreds of police and rescue workers who had run into the buildings to help. At the end of the day, the New York City Fire Department had lost 350 firefighters, nearly thirty times the number ever lost by the department in a single incident (see Seeing History).

While the media recalled Pearl Harbor, President Bush declared the deadly attacks an act of war and vowed to hunt down those responsible for the "evil, despicable acts of terror." Congress, with only one dissenting vote, granted him power to take whatever steps necessary. The Department of Justice began what it described as the largest and most intensive investigation ever conducted, and the president issued a blanket warning to all nations that harbor terrorists. Secretary of State Colin Powell stated clearly, "You're either with us or against us." For the first time ever, NATO invoked the mutual defense clause in its founding treaty, which in effect supported any U.S. military response.

Observers described Bush's response as the defining moment of his presidency, as it was for the lives of many Americans. Millions rushed to donate blood, and thousands traveled to New York to assist rescue efforts. Prayer vigils were held in churches, synagogues, mosques, public buildings, and parks, and flags were displayed on homes and cars. Millions of dollars were soon raised for the relief effort and to assist the families of those who perished.

The day following the highly coordinated terrorist attack, President Bush identified the Saudi Arabian Osama bin Laden as the prime suspect. Administration officials linked the airline hijackers, all presumed to be Islamic fundamentalists, to his Al Qaeda network, which apparently had dispatched them to train at American flight schools. Bin Laden and Al Qaeda had based their operations in Afghanistan, where they enjoyed the protection of a government run by the Taliban, a radical Islamist group. The Taliban said its aim was to set up the world's most pure Islamic state, banning what they viewed as the corrupt influences of Western culture. Although a communiqué from bin Laden denied involvement, U.S. intelligence sources insisted that only bin Laden had the resources to carry out such a sophisticated operation and sufficient motivation. In 1998, bin Laden had issued a decree that granted religious legitimacy to all efforts to expel the United States from the lands of Islam in the Middle East. His network of terrorist cells, which reportedly operated in sixty countries, had directed rage at what they believe to be the global arrogance of the United States—its accumulation of unprecedented wealth when poverty and hopelessness extended across the Middle East.

## RESHAPING U.S. FOREIGN POLICY

The September 11 terrorist attacks transformed the presidency of George W. Bush and prompted dramatic changes in the conduct and goals of American foreign policy. At a memorial service for victims, Bush issued an ominous warning: "Our responsibility to history is already clear: to answer these attacks and rid the world of evil." And he outlined a new vision that would guide his policies. "From this day forward," the president announced, "any nation that continues to harbor or support terrorists will be regarded by the United States as a hostile regime." The first theater of the campaign against terror would be Afghanistan. With the support of

# The 9/11 Attacks

The first plane hit at 8:48 a.m.; the second, at 9:03 a.m. Then, as millions of disbelieving television viewers watched, the 110-story Twin Towers collapsed. Already, many Americans were saying that they would forever remember where they were and what they were doing when they heard the news.

Journalists and ordinary Americans alike repeatedly invoked two twentieth-century catastrophes as parallels to 9/11: the Japanese attack at Pearl Harbor on December 7, 1941, and the assassination of John F. Kennedy on November 22, 1963. But neither disaster played out in real time over modern media.

The World Trade Center attack occurred virtually before the eyes of millions. Video cameras caught the image of the second plane hitting the South Tower, panic on the faces of those fleeing, smoke billowing from the towers, and their collapse. Reporters were soon pulling comments from traumatized survivors. The networks immediately preempted regular programming and allowed millions of horrified Americans to watch endless replays. Newscasters drew out the Pearl Harbor analogy as another "Day of Infamy." Within days, programmers edited the videotapes to enhance the drama—adding images of cell phones (to remind viewers of the final calls many of the victims made), overlaying

**WHAT ROLE** did the media play in shaping our understanding of the events of September 11, 2001? How does the ability of modern media to dramatize the horror and immediacy of such events enhance their "value" to terrorists launching attacks? In what ways did the 9/11 attacks facilitate the Bush administration's decision to go to war in Iraq?

images of the collapsing towers with an unfurling American flag, and piping in patriotic music. To enhance the emotional impact, they borrowed such cinematic techniques as slowing the pace and using jump cuts that fast-timed images of the burning towers with close-ups of anguished observers' faces.

Some seventy history-oriented institutions created an Internet site, 911history.net, to collect oral histories and artifacts. Said Diane Kresh of the Library of Congress, "The Internet has become for many the public commons, a place where they can come together and talk." But the searing pictures of the burning towers will likely remain the preeminent image for 9/11. ■

a United Nations Security Council resolution, the United States delivered an ulti-matum to the Taliban-dominated government of Afghanistan: hand over Osama bin Laden and other Al Qaeda leaders presumed to be responsible, and close all terrorist training camps immediately and unconditionally.

On October 7, after the Taliban had refused to comply, President Bush announced the beginning of Operation Enduring Freedom, a joint American–British military campaign aimed at capturing bin Laden and overthrowing the Taliban regime that had sheltered him. An aerial bombing campaign targeted Taliban and Al Qaeda forces, many of whom were Arab fighters from abroad. U.S. Special Forces launched a raid deep into the Taliban stronghold of Kandahar, in southeastern Afghanistan. By mid-November American and British forces, joined by a loose coalition of anti-Taliban Afhgans known as the Northern Alliance, cap-tured the capital city of Kabul.

Fierce fighting continued through December as U.S.-led coalition troops grew to a force of over 10,000. Intensive bombing routed the last remnants of Tal-iban and Al Qaeda forces from the mountain cave complex of Tora Bora. But bin Laden and much of the Al Qaeda leadership escaped into the tribal areas of Pak-istan to the south and east. Despite a massive manhunt and the aid of Pakistan's government, American forces proved unable to capture bin Laden.

A grand council, or *loya jirga*, of Afghan factions and tribal leaders established an interim Afghan government in Kabul under the leadership of Hamid Karzai. In the fall of 2004 Karzai became the first democratically elected president of Afghanistan. But his power was limited largely to Kabul, and old problems stubbornly persisted. Warlords dominated much of the country, the Taliban remained a force in much of the countryside, and the illegal opium trade flourished.

In his January 2002 State of the Union address President Bush expanded on his vision of a global war on terror. He argued that America now faced a grave and unprecedented danger not merely from Al Qaeda terrorists but also from nation-states seeking chemical, biological, or nuclear weapons of mass destruction. He denounced the regimes of North Korea, Iran, and Iraq as an "axis of evil, arming to threaten the peace of the world." The new focus on the threat of weapons of mass destruction formed a central part of a sweeping reformulation of American foreign policy. In the fall of 2002 the Bush administration released a new National Secu-rity Strategy Report that offered the most radical revision of American foreign pol-icy since the Truman administration in the early days of the Cold War (see Chapter 26). It argued that "the struggle against global terrorism is different from any other war in our history," requiring the United States to "deter and defend against the threat before it is unleashed," acting preemptively and alone if necessary.

The war on terror had a domestic front as well. The partisan bitterness of the 2000 election largely dissolved amid post–9/11 calls for national unity, mak-ing it easier for the Bush administration to push new legislation through Con-gress. Signed into law in the fall of 2001, the **USA Patriot Act** gave federal officials greater authority to track and intercept communications for law-enforcement and intelligence-gathering purposes, new powers to curb foreign money launder-ing, and broader discretion in tightening borders against suspected foreign ter-rorists. It created new crimes and penalties against suspected domestic and international terrorists. In the months after the 9/11 attacks, over a thousand Muslims, some of them U.S. citizens, were arrested and detained. Only a few of these suspects were actually charged with crimes related to terrorism. Congress passed the USA Patriot Act II in 2003, further expanding the ability of law-enforcement and intelligence-gathering authorities to perform surveillance and authorize secret arrests.

**USA Patriot Act**    Federal legislation adopted in 2001 in response to the terrorist attacks on September 11 to facilitate anti-terror actions by federal law enforcement and intelligence agencies.

The Bush administration also created a new cabinet-level **Department of Homeland Security (DHS)**, consolidating twenty-two different domestic agencies to coordinate the nation's defense against military threats. Its components included the Immigration and Naturalization Service, the U.S. Customs Service, the Secret Service, the Coast Guard, and the Federal Emergency Management Agency. Not surprisingly, combining so many huge federal bureaucracies into one effective whole proved quite difficult. Critics of the new department worried especially about the continued vulnerability of the nation's ports, rail system, chemical facilities, and nuclear plants to terrorist attacks.

Many questions remained unanswered about the events and circumstances surrounding the 9/11 attacks, particularly the multiple failures within the U.S. intelligence community. The Bush administration at first resisted efforts to mount a full-scale inquiry. But pressure from the families of 9/11 victims, as well as widespread calls for a bipartisan investigation, forced the administration to reverse its opposition, and in November 2002 Congress established the National Commission on Terrorist Attacks upon the United States. In July 2004 the commission issued its final report—which became an instant best seller—concluding that the government "failed to protect the American people" because it did not understand the "gravity of the threat."

The report was especially damning on the bureaucratic rivalry between the CIA and FBI, which made it difficult to act despite clear evidence that "Islamist terrorists mean to kill Americans in high numbers." It noted that as late as August 2001 National Security Adviser Condoleeza Rice had ignored urgent warnings of impending Al Qaeda attacks brought directly to her by Richard Clarke, the president's counterterrorism chief.

## INVASION OF IRAQ

The new pledge to confront threats to security before they reached American shores became known as the Bush Doctrine, and its first major test was Iraq. Planning for a U.S.-led invasion and the overthrow of Saddam Hussein had actually begun in the first weeks after the September 11 attacks. President Bush himself had come to believe that "regime change" was necessary, and several major figures in his administration focused their attention on making the case to the nation and the world. Vice President Dick Cheney, Secretary of Defense Donald Rumsfeld, and his deputy secretary, Paul Wolfowitz, had all worked for Bush's father, President George H. W. Bush, and they viewed removal of Saddam as the unfinished business of the Persian Gulf War of 1991. Along with National Security Adviser Condoleeza Rice and a more reluctant Secretary of State Colin Powell, these aides began to plan for war in early 2002.

Proponents of war made three central claims that they repeated in various public speeches, testimony before Congress, and finally at the United Nations. First, Saddam Hussein must be removed by force because he possessed biological and chemical weapons that posed an imminent threat, and he was making serious efforts to develop nuclear weapons. Second, they argued that Saddam's intelligence services had direct connections to the September 11 hijackers and had broader linkages with Al Qaeda operatives around the world. Third, toppling Saddam would make possible a democratic Iraq that could then stand as a beacon of political change throughout the Middle East and Muslim world.

Throughout late 2002 and early 2003, as American military planners prepared for battle, significant opposition to war emerged at home and abroad. In the United States, many intelligence analysts and veteran diplomats expressed serious doubts about Bush administration claims regarding Saddam's weapons capabilities. They charged that Vice President Cheney and Secretary Rumsfeld

**31–2**
*President Bush Addresses the Nation on the Iraq Invasion* (2003)

**Department of Homeland Security (DHS)** Cabinet-level department created by George Bush to manage U.S. security.

**President George W. Bush** announces the end of major combat operations in Iraq, May 1, 2003, speaking on the deck of the aircraft carrier USS *Abraham Lincoln*, anchored near San Diego. A banner proclaimed "Mission Accomplished," but American troops would continue to face stiff opposition and endure thousands of casualties battling Iraqi insurgents.

had manipulated Pentagon intelligence estimates, selectively emphasizing data based on ideology rather than dispassionate analysis. Others doubted Saddam's links to Al Qaeda and argued that war with Iraq was a distraction from the hunt for bin Laden. A growing number of Americans questioned the assumption that removing Saddam would make America safer, and many worried that an invasion would likely boost the recruitment efforts of Al Qaeda and other terrorist organizations. Antiwar groups pointed to the large amounts of weapons of mass destruction that had already been identified and destroyed by UN inspectors before they had left Iraq in 1998. Why not let these inspections resume as an alternative to invasion? Millions of citizens began organizing against the push for war via Internet organizations such as MoveOn.org and in vigils and gatherings in their local communities.

Growing opposition to war helped impel the Bush administration to seek international support. In November 2002 the UN Security Council unanimously passed Resolution 1441 calling upon Iraq to fully disarm, provide a detailed account of its weapons programs, and to accept the return of UN weapons inspectors. The U.S. Senate and House of Representatives both voted to authorize the use of military action against Iraq should Saddam Hussein refuse to comply with UN resolutions. But although Iraq released voluminous records about its weapons programs as UN inspectors resumed their work, the United States concluded in December that the documents were inadequate and that Iraq was in "material breach" of Resolution 1441.

In February 2003 Secretary of State Powell made a detailed argument for war before the Security Council. Meanwhile, the antiwar movement went global on February 15 as millions of demonstrators turned out in the streets of over 300 cities. This was the single largest expression of antiwar sentiment in history. At the UN, facing staunch opposition to war from France, Russia, and Germany, who argued for giving the UN inspection process more time, the United States withdrew its proposed resolution authorizing the use of force in Iraq (see Map 31.2).

Lacking UN approval, the Bush administration would invade Iraq with what it called a "coalition of the willing," with Great Britain as its major partner. On March 19 President Bush announced the beginning of war. Some 150,000 American troops based in Kuwait, along with a smaller British force, began a thrust toward Baghdad; and a "shock and awe" campaign of massive aerial bombing began on several major Iraqi cities. The American and British forces overwhelmed the regular Iraqi army fairly easily, suffering relatively light casualties. By early April they had secured Baghdad, Mosul, Basra, Kirkuk, and other major cities. On May 1, 2003, on the flight deck of the USS *Abraham Lincoln*, anchored off the San Diego coast, President Bush made a dramatic appearance before a cheering throng of American sailors and a live television audience. Standing beneath a large banner reading "Mission Accomplished," Bush announced the official end of combat operations. "In the battle of Iraq," the president declared, "the United States and our allies have prevailed."

But the purely military act of removing Saddam's regime from power proved far simpler than bringing peace and stability to Iraq. And rather than weaken terrorists, it instead strengthened a new generation of terror networks now drawn to do battle with American forces there. As the invasion turned into an occupation, the plight of ordinary Iraqis and American soldiers worsened quickly. In the summer of 2003 the Coalition Provisional Authority (CPA), led by Ambassador Paul Bremer, created the Governing Council to serve as an interim government for the new Iraq. But many parts of the country plunged into chaos amid widespread looting, killing, and near anarchy. Several decisions made by the CPA, including

**MAP 31.2**

**Invasion in Iraq**   On March 20, 2003, American and British troops poured into Iraq from bases in Kuwait, crossing the Iraqi border to the east near Safwan. The American Third Infantry Division used armored bulldozers to create wide gaps in the Iraqi defensive line.

WHAT WERE Bush's justifications for invading Iraq?

the disbanding of the Iraqi Army, contributed to the lawless climate. Millions of Iraqis found their electricity, water, and basic food supplies disrupted or unavailable.

As UN relief workers, journalists, and private American contractors poured into the country to help with reconstruction efforts, a violent campaign of suicide bombings, shootings, roadside ambushes, and kidnappings spread across Iraq. In December 2003 the capture of Saddam Hussein, who had gone into hiding, proved a symbolic victory at best.

A coordinated, heavily armed, and well-financed resistance to the American occupation gained strength in early 2004. It included elements of Saddam's Baath party, foreign Islamist fighters, disaffected Sunni Muslims, and criminal gangs. Desperate poverty, widespread unemployment, deep anger toward the American occupiers, and hundreds of thousands of alienated former soldiers provided a continual supply of fresh recruits. The CPA was both unprepared and overwhelmed as it tried to wrestle with problems no one had even thought about, much less planned for. Tensions between major religious groups fueled the insurgency, as Sunni Muslims feared the loss of their traditional power to the majority Shiites. Badly stretched American forces, which included a high percentage of National Guard and Army Reserve units, were forced back into combat.

**U.S. Marines and** Iraqi Special Forces conduct a security patrol in the war-torn city of Falluja, November 23, 2004. The brutal fighting there made it clear that defeating the Iraqi insurgency would be a tougher battle for American forces than the overthrow of Saddam Hussein's government.

Troubling new questions about the decision to invade and the conduct of the war emerged. In early 2004 David Kay, the Bush administration's former chief weapons inspector, told Congress that any stockpiles of chemical or biological weapons Saddam might have possessed in the early 1990s had been destroyed by UN inspections and Iraq's own actions. Nor was there any nuclear weapons program.

In the spring of 2004, graphic images and descriptions of Iraqi detainees abused and tortured by American guards in the Abu Ghraib prison were broadcast around the world, inciting international outrage and protest. In public President Bush expressed "a deep disgust that those prisoners were treated the way they were treated." But White House memos revealed that the president's legal counsel Alberto Gonzales had urged Bush to declare the war on terror and the treatment of Al Qaeda and Taliban prisoners exempt from the provisions of the Geneva Convention.

With American forces bogged down in the occupation and the resistance to it widening, American military commanders found themselves strapped for replacement troops. Tens of thousands of National Guard and Army Reserve soldiers were forced to stay in Iraq beyond their regular tour of duty, subject in effect to a "backdoor draft." By early 2005, over 1,500 Americans had been killed in Iraq and nearly 12,000 wounded, many of them severely. Estimates of Iraqi civilian casualties ranged as high as 100,000.

In July 2004 the Coalition Provisional Authority dissolved itself and formally transferred sovereignty to the interim Iraqi government. In January 2005 Iraq conducted its first national elections for an assembly charged with writing a new constitution by 2006. Amidst enormous media coverage, the Bush administration hailed the elections as a historic step toward democracy. Shiite Muslims, representing roughly 60 percent of the population, stood ready to replace the minority Sunni Muslims as the dominant political force. The Shiites themselves were divided into factions, including those with close ties to the Shiite rulers of neighboring Iran.

## THE ELECTION OF 2004

President Bush launched his reelection bid determined to make national security and the war on terror the centerpieces of his campaign. With Iraq dominating the news, Bush described himself as a "wartime president" and appealed to patriotism and national unity. This strategy allowed him to largely ignore domestic issues, where his political strength was less certain. Bush promoted a sweeping tax cut in 2001 as the best way to jump-start the economy and create new jobs. The Economic Growth and Tax Relief Reconciliation Act squeaked through Congress with bipartisan support. Yet a small percentage of wealthy Americans benefited disproportionately from the cuts, which also expanded budget deficits as the government took in less money. The historically unprecedented combination of fighting an expensive war abroad while lowering income and corporate taxes at home brought spiraling budget deficits that wiped out the surpluses of the Clinton years.

As the American dollar weakened against foreign currencies like the Euro and the Chinese *yuan*, a growing chorus of economists warned that high levels of American consumption and the superheated real estate markets in many U.S. cities made the economy increasingly vulnerable to the whims of foreign investors. If budget deficits continued to grow, foreign buyers of U.S. government securities might look elsewhere, with potentially devastating effects on the American economy.

Democrats, still smarting from the disputed 2000 election in which their nominee Al Gore had won the popular vote by over half a million, believed their chances for retaking the White House were strong. But the political aftermath of the September 11 attacks, the new focus on strengthening national security, and the invasion of Iraq forced attention away from the economic issues that had traditionally been their greatest source of voter appeal.

After winning in Iowa and New Hampshire, Senator John Kerry of Massachusetts quickly assumed the mantle of front-runner and captured the Democratic nomination. Kerry's life story helped him appeal to a broad cross section of the party. He had volunteered for naval combat duty in Vietnam, where he was wounded and highly decorated. When he returned home he became a leader in the Vietnam Veterans Against the War (VVAW) and in 1971 had made a memorable televised appearance before Congress criticizing U.S. policy. He had gone into state politics and won election to the Senate in 1984. His biography suggested he could bridge some of the deep Vietnam-era differences that still divided Americans. And his status as an authentic war hero would bolster Democrats' chances of appealing to voters' concerns about national security.

But after capturing the nomination, Kerry's campaign faltered. Perhaps most damningly, Kerry was unable to communicate a clear position on the Iraq war. Along with many other Democrats he had voted to authorize the use of force, but he criticized President Bush's conduct of the war. Yet even when asked, in the late summer of 2004, whether he would have voted differently if he knew that there was no Iraqi weapons of mass destruction threat and no Iraqi link with the September 11 attacks, he refused to change his view.

President George W. Bush won reelection with 51 percent of the popular vote to Kerry's 48 percent, a 3-million-vote margin. He garnered 279 electoral votes to Kerry's 252, as Ohio, with 20 electoral votes, proved the key state.

President Bush claimed his victory represented a victory for his Iraq war policy and promised to spend his hard-won "political capital" on the domestic front as well. In his State of the Union address delivered in February 2005, Bush defined his second-term agenda around two issues. On the foreign policy front, he hailed the recent Iraqi elections and promised to keep American forces there until Iraqis could provide their own security. Domestically, the president challenged Congress to "reinvent Social Security," as he called for a major overhaul of the New Deal–era social insurance program by emphasizing private investment accounts. Though not as close as the 2000 election, and without the disconnect between popular and electoral vote, few would dispute that the 2004 election revealed a nation that was as politically divided as any time since the Civil War.

## HURRICANE KATRINA

In his second term, President Bush discovered that the "political capital" he had invoked in celebrating his narrow reelection victory would soon evaporate. As the Iraq war dragged into its third year, the post–9/11 political consensus largely dissolved as victory proved elusive and increasingly difficult to define. On the domestic front, his administration also endured a heated and prolonged controversy sparked by its response to one of the most cataclysmic events of the new century—Hurricane Katrina.

Hurricane Katrina made three landfalls in Louisiana, blowing houses off their foundations and submerging others. In New Orleans, several parishes were destroyed, including the Lower Ninth Ward, the home to an African American population already steeped in poverty. Canal levees failed, and by August 31, 80 percent of New Orleans was under water. The National Guard moved in, and the U.S. Navy relocated ships to support the relief efforts. President Bush, who had been vacationing at his ranch in Crawford, Texas, did not rush to the area but instead four days after the hurricane hit flew over in *Air Force One* on his early return to the White House. He declared a public health emergency for the entire Gulf Coast but predicted that, despite the enormous devastation, New Orleans would eventually recover from the costliest disaster in U.S. history.

**A U.S. Coast** Guard helicopter rescues flood-stranded victims of Hurricane Katrina from their homes in New Orleans, September 2005. Images like this one received wide circulation in the news media, prompting criticism of the government's failures to offer more and swifter help to Katrina's victims.

**31–12**
*National Failure toward Veterans of the Iraq War* (2007)

**Federal Emergency Management Agency (FEMA)** Agency charged with providing assistance to communities hit by natural disasters.

Meanwhile, the rescue operations stalled amid bureaucratic mishaps. The American Red Cross, poised to set up a shelter in New Orleans, was told to wait while the National Guard handled the distribution of food and water. Conditions at the Superdome deteriorated to a point that newscasters described a reign of anarchy. Shortages of food, water, blankets, sanitary facilities, and medical supplies had put the lives of the 5,000 refugees at risk. Governor Blanco requested an additional 40,000 National Guard troops to quell the unrest, now spread across the city. Only slowly did the **Federal Emergency Management Agency (FEMA)** relocate staff to the area and, worse, actually hampered private relief efforts. For example, FEMA officials turned away six trailer trucks of water dispatched by Wal-Mart. Television crews captured scenes of people stranded on rooftops, waiting rescue while the waters continued to rise, and bodies floating in the streets.

President Bush appeared perplexed by the situation. He excused FEMA's inept response by claiming that the disaster caught everyone off guard, although the National Weather Service had warned that Katrina could bring "human suffering incredible by modern standards." Everyone knew that the levees would not withstand a surge of water that a Category 5 hurricane would surely cause. Only on the sixth day after the hurricane did Bush visit the Gulf area, although even then he did not approach the people dislocated by the storm. The press vilified President Bush, labeling his performance in the face of this disaster as "a national disgrace."

Much of the shame resulted from the way the unfolding of events underscored the race and class dimensions of the tragedy. The population of New Orleans, with a poverty rate of 23 percent, 76 percent higher than the national average, was nearly 68 percent African American, and more than a quarter of the black citizens of New Orleans lacked access to an automobile. When the mandatory evacuation order came, the majority of white residents drove away from the city, while many black residents had no choice but to board the special buses headed for the ill-equipped Superdome. When mainly black evacuees attempted to cross a bridge linking New Orleans with the suburb of Gretna, the white suburbanites turned them back at gunpoint.

More than 1,600 people had died in New Orleans alone, and nearly a million had fled the greater region. In 2007 the population of New Orleans still hovered around 250,000, down from the nearly 485,000 who had lived inside the city limits at the time of the 2000 U.S. census. By 2007 business activity—especially tourism in the French Quarter district—had begun to revive, and the city managed to hold its annual Mardi Gras celebration, long a magnet for visitors from around the world. But the long range effects of Katrina loomed over the city's future. The devastating mental health problems associated with the catastrophe—the abrupt loss of loved ones and homes, the break-up of families, the sense of hopelessness and depression—were difficult to quantify but continued to plague tens of thousands of people. Two years after Katrina struck, the future of New Orleans—its housing, its economic base, and the world of its working class African American population—remained unclear at best.

## DIVIDED GOVERNMENT, DIVIDED NATION

The Bush administration found itself on the defensive from attacks on its weak response to Hurricane Katrina. The president's plan to privatize Social Security also proved politically unpopular, as did rising gasoline prices. It also faced growing disillusionment with the Iraq War, the single issue that most clearly defined the Bush presidency. Thus, the 2006 elections loomed as a kind of referendum on the war itself.

## CHRONOLOGY

| | | | | |
|---|---|---|---|---|
| **1981** | MTV and CNN start broadcasting as cable channels | | **1995** | Bombing of Alfred P. Murrah Federal Building in Oklahoma City kills 168 people |
| **1986** | Immigration Reform and Control Act addresses concerns about replaced illegal aliens | | **1996** | Congress passes Welfare Reform Act |
| | | | | Congress enacts the Antiterrorism and Effective Death Penalty Act |
| **1987** | Allan Bloom publishes *The Closing of the American Mind* | | | President Bill Clinton is reelected |
| **1988** | George H. W. Bush is elected president | | **1997** | Kyoto Protocol endorsed by European Union but not United States |
| **1989** | Tiananmen Square demonstration in China | | **1998** | U.S. embassies in Kenya and Tanzania bombed by terrorists |
| **1990** | Iraqi invasion of Kuwait leads to massive U.S. military presence in the Persian Gulf | | | House of Representatives votes to impeach President Clinton, but vote fails in Senate |
| **1991** | Operation Desert Storm forces Iraq out of Kuwait | | **1999** | U.S. joins NATO forces in Kosovo |
| | Operation Rescue launched in Wichita, Kansas | | | Protesters disrupt meetings of the World Trade Organization in Seattle |
| **1992** | Rodney King verdict sparks rioting in Los Angeles | | **2000** | USS *Cole* bombed by terrorists |
| | Bill Clinton is elected president | | **2001** | George W. Bush becomes president after contested election |
| **1993** | Terrorist bombing of World Trade Center kills six people | | | Terrorists attack World Trade Center and Pentagon |
| | Federal agents conduct seige of Branch Davidian compound in Waco, Texas | | | U.S. begins military campaign in Afghanistan |
| | Clinton administration introduces comprehensive health care reform, but it fails to win passage in Congress | | | Homeland Security Department established |
| | | | | USA Patriot Act passed |
| | Congress approves the North American Free Trade Agreement (NAFTA) | | **2003** | Invasion of Iraq and occupation |
| | | | | USA Patriot Act II passed |
| **1994** | Republicans win control of Senate and House for first time in forty years | | **2004** | Release of *The 9/11 Commission Report* |
| | Congress approves the General Agreement on Tariffs and Trade (GATT) | | | Reelection of George W. Bush |
| | Congress passes the Comprehensive AIDS Revenue Emergency Act | | **2005** | Elections in Iraq |
| | Congress passes Defense of Marriage Act | | | Hurricane Katrina devastates New Orleans and the Gulf Coast |
| | California voters approve Proposition 187 | | | |

By the summer of 2007 the number of Americans killed in Iraq had climbed above 3,800. Over 27,000 more Americans had been wounded, with over half suffering such severe injuries as amputation and serious burns.

In Iraq itself the government of Prime Minister Nouri al-Maliki proved unable to provide basic security and services in Baghdad and many other areas of the country. The insurgency against the American occupation continued to spread, attracting elements of Al Qaeda, ex–Iraqi Army soldiers, foreign Islamic fighters, criminal gangs, and many Iraqi Sunnis fearful of the growing power of the Shiite majority. These groups were by no means united, as temporary alliances formed and dissolved depending on local conditions. The situation deteriorated further as heavily armed Shiite and Sunni militias escalated sectarian violence. Violent struggles between rival Shiite factions also destabilized Baghdad and contributed to a lawless atmosphere. Some 2 million Iraqis, including much of the nation's educated middle class and professionals,

**31–8**
Nancy Pelosi, *Inaugural Address* (2007)

fled the country to nearby nations such as Syria, Jordan, and Egypt. Another 2 million Iraqis, forced to leave their neighborhoods and towns, found themselves refugees within their own country. American forces and their Iraqi Army allies could not establish order amid what looked more and more like a civil war.

The 2006 midterm elections in the United States brought a return of the divided government that had characterized the Clinton years. But this time, the parties and players were reversed. Democrats took control of both the House (233–202) and the Senate (51–49) for the first time since 1992. Nancy Pelosi (D-CA) became the first female Speaker of the House. A large number of Democrats had originally supported the invasion of Iraq, but many had since changed their minds and now believed that a military "victory" was both impossible and an illusion. Congress tried to reassert itself in the foreign policy arena by putting limits on the president's requests for war funding. But Democrats enjoyed only a narrow majority in Congress and were unable to override President Bush's vetoes. Thus, as the war dragged into its fifth year—longer than the United States' involvement in World War II—the government and the nation remained deeply divided over Iraq.

# REVIEW QUESTIONS

1. How is the "new economy" different from the old economy? How has it reshaped American business and financial practices? Explain the relationship between the new economy and electronic media, such as the Internet and cable television.

2. Evaluate the presidency of Bill Clinton. Compare his domestic and foreign policies to those of the Republican presidents who preceded and followed him in office. What was the impact of the scandals that plagued his presidency?

3. Describe the major demographic trends revealed by the 2000 census. Identify the racial and ethnic groups with the greatest gains in population. How have various legislative acts since 1965 affected immigration to the United States? How have communities changed as a result of the influx of new immigrants?

4. The concept of globalization is highly controversial. Are borders between nations "melting away" as some scholars contend? How does this concept square with the description of the United States as the single superpower in the world? Does this concept apply primarily to economics, or is it useful for discussing issues related to culture, media, the environment, and population trends?

5. How has the "war on terror" differed from other wars in this century? How and why did the 9/11 attacks lead to fundamental changes in the conduct of U.S. foreign policy? What arguments for the American invasion of Iraq in 2003 do you find most and least persuasive?

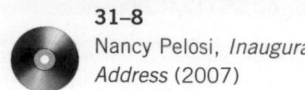

**Flashcard Review**

# KEY TERMS

**Bosnia** (p. 888)
**Contract with America** (p. 888)
**Department of Homeland Security (DHS)** (p. 901)
**Federal Emergency Management Agency (FEMA)** (p. 906)
**Internet** (p. 891)
**Kosovo** (p. 889)
**Multiculturalism** (p. 894)

**North American Free Trade Agreement (NAFTA)** (p. 888)
**Proposition 187** (p. 894)
**Silicon Valley** (p. 890)
**USA Patriot Act** (p. 900)
**Welfare Reform Act** (p. 888)
**World Trade Organization (WTO)** (p. 888)

# RECOMMENDED READING

William C. Berman, *From the Center to the Edge: The Politics and Policies of the Clinton Presidency* (2001). A highly readable assessment of Clinton's accomplishments as president. Although focusing on domestic issues, including the impact of Clinton's impeachment trial, Berman also considers major foreign policy developments in the context of globalization.

Douglas Brinkley, *The Great Deluge: Hurricane Katrina, New Orleans, and the Mississippi Gulf Coast* (2006). The first comprehensive narrative history of Hurricane Katrina, the government response, and the aftermath.

Richard Clarke, *Against All Enemies: Inside America's War on Terror* (2004). A critical look at the war on terror from a veteran diplomat and counterterrorism expert who argues that the invasion of Iraq will serve to strengthen Al Qaeda and allied groups.

Stephen Coll, *Ghost Wars: The Secret History of the CIA, Afghanistan, and Bin Laden from the Soviet Invasion to September 10, 2001* (2004). Deeply researched examination of the CIA's influence in Afghanistan and its support for Islamic fundamentalists resisting Soviet occupation.

Thomas Frank, *What's the Matter with Kansas? How Conservatives Won the Heart of America* (2004). A provocative look at how political conservatives have successfully recast themselves as the voice of populism and ordinary Americans over the last thirty years.

James Glanz and Eric Lipton, *City in the Sky: The Rise and Fall of the World Trade Center* (2003). A thorough investigation of the planning that gave birth to the two iconic towers in New York City and their destruction on September 11, 2001. Written by two journalists, this clear, detailed, and well-illustrated study poses hard questions about the collapse and recovery efforts.

National Commission on Terrorist Attacks upon the United States, *The 9/11 Commission Report* (2004). The best-selling final report of the independent bipartisan inquiry into the events surrounding the 9/11 attacks, including recommendations for reorganizing American intelligence to more effectively meet terrorist threats.

Todd S. Purdum, *A Time of Our Choosing: America's War in Iraq* (2004). An excellent narrative account of how the Bush administration made the decision to invade Iraq.

Thomas E. Ricks, *Fiasco: The American Military Adventure in Iraq* (2006). The first comprehensive and critical account of the American invasion of Iraq with a focus on lack of prewar planning for the occupation.

Sam Roberts, *Who We Are Now: The Changing Face of America in the Twenty-First Century* (2004). Using the 2000 census, Roberts focuses on the changes in American society that occurred between 1990 and 2000. He discusses population growth, the largest decadal increase in American history, as well as shifts in ethnic composition, family structure, and inequality.

Mary C. Waters and Reed Ueda, eds., *The New Americans: A Guide to Immigration since 1965* (2007). A team of interdisciplinary scholars provides an overview of the new immigrant populations since 1965.

Laurence Wright, *The Looming Tower: Al-Qaeda and the Road to 9/11* (2006). Pulitzer Prize–winning analysis of the origins, ideology, and operations of the group responsible for the 9/11 terrorist attacks.

**myhistorylab**
Where it's a good time to connect to the past!

For study resources for this chapter, go to **www.myhistorylab.com** and choose *Out of Many, Teaching and Learning Classroom Edition*. You will find a wealth of study and review material for this chapter, including pretests and posttests, customized study plan, key-term review flash cards, interactive map and document activities, and documents for analysis.

# The Threat of War to Democratic Institutions

s early as 1798 and the Alien and Sedition Act of the Adams adminis-tration, American governments have been willing to suppress civil liber-ties in the name of national defense. Adams was fearful of French immigrants who added to the voting power of Democratic Republicans and the poisoned pens of Democratic Republicans whose newspaper torn at his public reputation. In the Civil War Lincoln suspended the right of habeas corpus in Maryland and arrested members of Congress who were known secessionists.

**HOW HAS** the use of the Patriot Act and its later revisions in line with wartime actions of earlier American governments during wartime or times of perceived threat to the United States?

In the twentieth century, the events of the 18th and 19th century during war were paralleled during World War One, World War Two, the Cold War, and during the current War on Terror which began on Sep-tember 11, 2001. In World War II hysteria over the Japanese attack on Pearl Harbor combined with a long standing racism against Asians in West Coast states resulted in the imprisonment of approximately 120,000 Japanese Amer-icans, many native born citizens, under Roosevelt's Executive Order 9066. During the Cold War and the era of Joseph McCarthy Americans lost their jobs, faced government investigation of the most intrusive nature, and public dis-grace. Civil libertarians have criticized the Patriot Act of 2001 also called The Uniting and Strengthening America by Providing Appropriate Tools Required to Intercept and Obstruct Terrorism Act of 2001 (Public Law 107–56), as an inappropriate curtailment of constitutional rights and a dangerous expan-sion of executive police powers.■

---

## GEORGE W. BUSH, PRESIDENT'S STATEMENT ON H.R. 3199, THE "USA PATRIOT IMPROVEMENT AND REAUTHORIZATION ACT OF 2005," MARCH 9, 2006

TODAY, I have signed into law H.R. 3199, the "USA PATRIOT Improvement and Reauthorization Act of 2005," and then S. 2271, the "USA PATRIOT Act Additional Reau-thorizing Amendments Act of 2006." The bills will help us continue to fight terrorism effectively and to combat the use of the illegal drug methamphetamine that is ruining too many lives.

The executive branch shall construe the provisions of H.R. 3199 that call for furnishing information to enti-ties outside the executive branch, such as sections 106A and 119, in a manner consistent with the President's con-stitutional authority to supervise the unitary executive branch and to withhold information the disclosure of which could impair foreign relations, national security, the deliberative processes of the Executive, or the perfor-mance of the Executive's constitutional duties.

The executive branch shall construe section 756(e)(2) of H.R. 3199, which calls for an executive branch official to submit to the Congress recommendations for legislative action, in a manner consistent with the Presi-dent's constitutional authority to supervise the unitary executive branch and to recommend for the considera-tion of the Congress such measures as he judges necessary and expedient.■

# SEDITION ACT OF 1918, MAY 16, 1918 (REPEALED 1921)

SECTION 3. Whoever, when the United States is at war, shall willfully make or convey false reports or false statements with intent to interfere with the operation or success of the military or naval forces of the United States, or to promote the success of its enemies, or shall willfully make or convey false reports, or false statements, . . . or incite insubordination, disloyalty, mutiny, or refusal of duty, in the military or naval forces of the United States, or shall willfully obstruct . . . the recruiting or enlistment service of the United States, or . . . shall willfully utter, print, write, or publish any disloyal, profane, scurrilous, or abusive language about the form of government of the United States, or the Constitution of the United States, or the military or naval forces of the United States . . . or shall willfully display the flag of any foreign enemy, or shall willfully . . . urge, incite, or advocate any curtailment of production . . . or advocate, teach, defend, or suggest the doing of any of the acts or things in this section enumerated and whoever shall by word or act support or favor the cause of any country with which the United States is at war or by word or act oppose the cause of the United States therein, shall be punished by a fine of not more than $10,000 or imprisonment for not more than twenty years, or both. . . .■

Esther C. Brunauer, an employee of the State Department, testified before the Senate Subcommittee on Foreign Relations to defend herself against allegations made against her by Senator Joseph McCarthy.

# FRANKLIN D. ROOSEVELT, EXECUTIVE ORDER 9066, FEBRUARY 19, 1942

I HEREBY authorize and direct the Secretary of War, and the Military Commanders whom he may from time to time designate, whenever he or any designated Commander deems such action necessary or desirable, to prescribe military areas in such places and of such extent as he or the appropriate Military Commander may determine, from which any or all persons may be excluded, and with respect to which, the right of any person to enter, remain in, or leave shall be subject to whatever restrictions the Secretary of War or the appropriate Military Commander may impose in his discretion.■

The hysteria and fear following the Pearl Harbor attack resulted in the internment of 110,000 Japanese Americans in "War Relocation Centers" located in isolated areas of the West for the duration of the war. In 1944 the U.S. Supreme Court upheld this action by the government with the comment that it was a "pressing public necessity."

**Camp X-ray Detainees – Guantanamo Bay Detention Camp**
In his War on Terrorism President Bush deemed it necessary to intern approximately 775 enemy prisoners captured in Afghanistan and elsewhere in a military facility. Bush claimed these prisoners did not possess rights under the terms of the Geneva Conventions. The U.S. Supreme Court ruled against his position in 2006 and ordered the U.S. military to extend international rights granted under the Geneva Conventions to enemy combatants to these individuals.

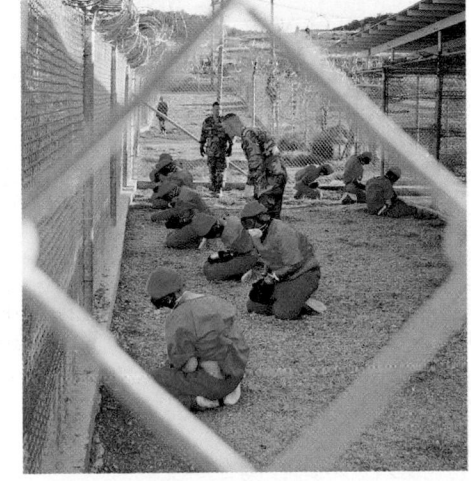

# THE DECLARATION OF INDEPENDENCE

When in the course of human events it becomes necessary for one people to dissolve the political bands which have connected them with another and to assume, among the powers of the earth, the separate and equal station to which the laws of nature and of nature's God entitle them, a decent respect to the opinions of mankind requires that they should declare the causes which impel them to the separation.

We hold these truths to be self-evident, that all men are created equal; that they are endowed by their Creator with certain unalienable rights; that among these are life, liberty, and the pursuit of happiness. That, to secure these rights, governments are instituted among men, deriving their just powers from the consent of the governed; that, whenever any form of government becomes destructive of these ends, it is the right of the people to alter or to abolish it, and to institute a new government, laying its foundation on such principles, and organizing its powers in such form, as to them shall seem most likely to effect their safety and happiness. Prudence, indeed, will dictate that governments long established should not be changed for light and transient causes; and, accordingly, all experience hath shown that mankind are more disposed to suffer, while evils are sufferable, than to right themselves by abolishing the forms to which they are accustomed. But when a long train of abuses and usurpations, pursuing invariably the same object, evinces a design to reduce them under absolute despotism, it is their right, it is their duty, to throw off such government and to provide new guards for their future security. Such has been the patient sufferance of these colonies, and such is now the necessity which constrains them to alter their former systems of government. The history of the present King of Great Britain is a history of repeated injuries and usurpations, all having, in direct object, the establishment of an absolute tyranny over these States. To prove this, let facts be submitted to a candid world:

He has refused his assent to laws the most wholesome and necessary for the public good.

He has forbidden his governors to pass laws of immediate and pressing importance, unless suspended in their operation till his assent should be obtained; and, when so suspended, he has utterly neglected to attend to them.

He has refused to pass other laws for the accommodation of large districts of people, unless those people would relinquish the right of representation in the legislature, a right inestimable to them and formidable to tyrants only.

He has called together legislative bodies at places unusual, uncomfortable, and distant from the depository of their public records, for the sole purpose of fatiguing them into compliance with his measures.

He has dissolved representative houses, repeatedly for opposing, with manly firmness, his invasions on the rights of the people.

He has refused, for a long time after such dissolutions, to cause others to be elected; whereby the legislative powers, incapable of annihilation, have returned to the people at large for their exercise; the state remaining, in the mean-time, exposed to all the danger of invasion from without and convulsions within.

He has endeavored to prevent the population of these States; for that purpose, obstructing the laws for naturalization of foreigners, refusing to pass others to encourage their migration hither, and raising the conditions of new appropriations of lands.

He has obstructed the administration of justice by refusing his assent to laws for establishing judiciary powers.

He has made judges dependent on his will alone for the tenure of their offices and the amount and payment of their salaries.

He has erected a multitude of new offices and sent hither swarms of officers to harass our people and eat out their substance.

He has kept among us, in time of peace, standing armies, without the consent of our legislatures.

He has affected to render the military independent of, and superior to, the civil power.

He has combined with others to subject us to a jurisdiction foreign to our Constitution and unacknowledged by our laws, giving his assent to their acts of pretended legislation—

For quartering large bodies of armed troops among us;

For protecting them by mock trial, from punishment for any murders which they should commit on the inhabitants of these States;

For cutting off our trade with all parts of the world;

For imposing taxes on us without our consent;

For depriving us, in many cases, of the benefit of trial by jury;

For transporting us beyond seas to be tried for pretended offences;

For abolishing the free system of English laws in a neighboring province, establishing therein an arbitrary government, and enlarging its boundaries, so as to render it at once an example and fit instrument for introducing the same absolute rule into these colonies;

For taking away our charters, abolishing our most valuable laws, and altering, fundamentally, the powers of our governments.

For suspending our own legislatures and declaring themselves invested with power to legislate for us in all cases whatsoever.

He has abdicated government here by declaring us out of his protection and waging war against us.

He has plundered our seas, ravaged our coasts, burnt our towns, and destroyed the lives of our people.

He is, at this time, transporting large armies of foreign mercenaries to complete the works of death, desolation, and tyranny already begun with circumstances of cruelty and perfidy scarcely paralleled in the most barbarous ages, and totally unworthy the head of a civilized nation.

He has constrained our fellow citizens, taken captive on the high seas, to bear arms against their country, to become the executioners of their friends and brethren, or to fall themselves by their hands.

He has excited domestic insurrections amongst us and has endeavored to bring on the inhabitants of our frontiers, the merciless Indian savages, whose known rule of warfare is an undistinguished destruction of all ages, sexes, and conditions.

In every stage of these oppressions, we have petitioned for redress in the most humble terms; our repeated petitions have been answered only by repeated injury. A prince whose character is thus marked by every act which may define a tyrant is unfit to be the ruler of a free people.

Nor have we been wanting in attention to our British brethren. We have warned them, from time to time, of attempts made by their legislature to extend an unwarrantable jurisdiction over us. We have reminded them of the circumstances of our emigration and settlement here. We have appealed to their native justice and magnanimity, and we have conjured them, by the ties of our common kindred, to disavow these usurpations, which would inevitably interrupt our connections and correspondence. They, too, have been deaf to the voice of justice and consanguinity.

We must, therefore, acquiesce in the necessity which denounces our separation, and hold them, as we hold the rest of mankind, enemies in war, in peace, friends.

We, therefore, the representatives of the United States of America, in general Congress assembled, appealing to the Supreme Judge of the world for the rectitude of our intentions, do, in the name and by the authority of the good people of these colonies, solemnly publish and declare, that these united colonies are, and of right ought to be, free and independent states: that they are absolved from all allegiance to the British Crown, and that all political connection between them and the state of Great Britain is, and ought to be, totally dissolved; and that, as free and independent states, they have full power to levy war, conclude peace, contract alliances, establish commerce, and to do all other acts and things which independent states may of right do. And, for the support of this declaration, with a firm reliance on the protection of Divine Providence, we mutually pledge to each other our lives, our fortunes, and our sacred honor.

# The Constitution of the United States of America

We the people of the United States, in order to form a more perfect union, establish justice, insure domestic tranquillity, provide for the common defense, promote the general welfare, and secure the blessings of liberty to ourselves and our posterity, do ordain and establish this Constitution for the United States of America.

## ARTICLE I

SECTION 1.   All legislative powers herein granted shall be vested in a Congress of the United States, which shall consist of a Senate and House of Representatives.

SECTION 2.   1. The House of Representatives shall be composed of members chosen every second year by the people of the several States, and the electors in each State shall have the qualifications requisite for electors of the most numerous branch of the State legislature.

2. No person shall be a representative who shall not have attained to the age of twenty-five years, and been seven years a citizen of the United States, and who shall not, when elected, be an inhabitant of that State in which he shall be chosen.

3. Representatives and direct taxes[1] shall be apportioned among the several States which may be included within this Union, according to their respective numbers, which shall be determined by adding to the whole number of free persons, including those bound to service for a term of years, and excluding Indians not taxed, three fifths of all other persons.[2] The actual enumeration shall be made within three years after the first meeting of the Congress of the United States, and within every subsequent term of ten years, in such manner as they shall by law direct. The num-

ber of representatives shall not exceed one for every thirty thousand, but each State shall have at least one representative; and until such enumeration shall be made, the State of New Hampshire shall be entitled to choose three, Massachusetts eight, Rhode Island and Providence Plantations one, Connecticut five, New York six, New Jersey four, Pennsylvania eight, Delaware one, Maryland six, Virginia ten, North Carolina five, South Carolina five, and Georgia three.

4. When vacancies happen in the representation from any State, the executive authority thereof shall issue writs of election to fill such vacancies.

5. The House of Representatives shall choose their speaker and other officers; and shall have the sole power of impeachment.

SECTION 3.   1. The Senate of the United States shall be composed of two senators from each State, chosen by the legislature thereof,[3] for six years; and each senator shall have one vote.

2. Immediately after they shall be assembled in consequence of the first election, they shall be divided as equally as may be into three classes. The seats of the senators of the first class shall be vacated at the expiration of the second year, of the second class at the expiration of the fourth year, and of the third class at the expiration of the sixth year, so that one third may be chosen every second year; and if vacancies happen by resignation, or otherwise, during the recess of the legislature of any State, the executive thereof may make temporary appointments until the next meeting of the legislature, which shall then fill such vacancies.[4]

3. No person shall be a senator who shall not have attained to the age of thirty years, and been nine years a cit-

---

[1]See the Sixteenth Amendment.
[2]See the Fourteenth Amendment.

[3]See the Seventeenth Amendment.
[4]See the Seventeenth Amendment.

izen of the United States, and who shall not, when elected, be an inhabitant of that State for which he shall be chosen.

4. The Vice President of the United States shall be President of the Senate, but shall have no vote, unless they be equally divided.

5. The Senate shall choose their other officers, and also a president pro tempore, in the absence of the Vice President, or when he shall exercise the office of the President of the United States.

6. The Senate shall have the sole power to try all impeachments. When sitting for that purpose, they shall be on oath or affirmation. When the President of the United States is tried, the chief justice shall preside: and no person shall be convicted without the concurrence of two thirds of the members present.

7. Judgment in cases of impeachment shall not extend further than to removal from office, and disqualification to hold and enjoy any office of honor, trust or profit under the United States: but the party convicted shall nevertheless be liable and subject to indictment, trial, judgment and punishment, according to law.

SECTION 4. 1. The times, places, and manner of holding elections for senators and representatives, shall be prescribed in each State by the legislature thereof; but the Congress may at any time by law make or alter such regulations, except as to the places of choosing senators.

2. The Congress shall assemble at least once in every year, and such meeting shall be on the first Monday in December, unless they shall by law appoint a different day.

SECTION 5. 1. Each House shall be the judge of the elections, returns and qualifications of its own members, and a majority of each shall constitute a quorum to do business; but a smaller number may adjourn from day to day, and may be authorized to compel the attendance of absent members, in such manner, and under such penalties as each House may provide.

2. Each House may determine the rules of its proceedings, punish its members for disorderly behavior, and, with the concurrence of two thirds, expel a member.

3. Each House shall keep a journal of its proceedings, and from time to time publish the same, excepting such parts as may in their judgment require secrecy; and the yeas and nays of the members of either House on any question shall, at the desire of one fifth of those present, be entered on the journal.

4. Neither House, during the session of Congress, shall, without the consent of the other, adjourn for more than three days, nor to any other place than that in which the two Houses shall be sitting.

SECTION 6. 1. The senators and representatives shall receive a compensation for their services, to be ascertained by law, and paid out of the Treasury of the United States. They shall in all cases, except treason, felony, and breach of the peace, be privileged from arrest during their attendance at the session of their respective Houses, and in going to and returning from the same; and for any speech or debate in either House, they shall not be questioned in any other place.

2. No senator or representative shall, during the time for which he was elected, be appointed to any civil office under the authority of the United States, which shall have been created, or the emoluments whereof shall have been increased, during such time; and no person holding any office under the United States shall be a member of either House during his continuance in office.

SECTION 7. 1. All bills for raising revenue shall originate in the House of Representatives; but the Senate may propose or concur with amendments as on other bills.

2. Every bill which shall have passed the House of Representatives and the Senate, shall, before it become a law, be presented to the President of the United States; If he approves he shall sign it, but if not he shall return it, with his objections, to that House in which it shall have originated, who shall enter the objections at large on their journal, and proceed to reconsider it. If after such reconsideration two thirds of that House shall agree to pass the bill, it shall be sent, together with the objections, to the other House, by which it shall likewise be reconsidered, and if approved by two thirds of that House, it shall become a law. But in all such cases the votes of both Houses shall be determined by yeas and nays, and the names of the persons voting for and against the bill shall be entered on the journal of each House respectively. If any bill shall not be returned by the President within ten days (Sundays excepted) after it shall have been presented to him, the same shall be a law, in like manner as if he had signed it, unless the Congress by their adjournment prevent its return, in which case it shall not be a law.

3. Every order, resolution, or vote to which the concurrence of the Senate and the House of Representatives may be necessary (except on a question of adjournment) shall be presented to the President of the United States; and before the same shall take effect, shall be approved by him, or being disapproved by him, shall be repassed by two thirds of the Senate and House of Representatives, according to the rules and limitations prescribed in the case of a bill.

SECTION 8. 1. The Congress shall have the power

1. To lay and collect taxes, duties, imposts, and excises, to pay the debts and provide for the common defense and general welfare of the United States; but all duties, imposts, and excises shall be uniform throughout the United States.

2. To borrow money on the credit of the United States;

3. To regulate commerce with foreign nations, and among the several States, and with the Indian tribes;

4. To establish a uniform rule of naturalization, and uniform laws on the subject of bankruptcies throughout the United States;

5. To coin money, regulate the value thereof, and of foreign coin, and fix the standard of weights and measures;

6. To provide for the punishment of counterfeiting the securities and current coin of the United States;

7. To establish post offices and post roads;

8. To promote the progress of science and useful arts, by securing for limited times to authors and inventors the exclusive right to their respective writings and discoveries;

9. To constitute tribunals inferior to the Supreme Court;

10. To define and punish piracies and felonies committed on the high seas, and offenses against the law of nations;

11. To declare war, grant letters of marque and reprisal, and make rules concerning captures on land and water;

12. To raise and support armies, but no appropriation of money to that use shall be for a longer term than two years;

13. To provide and maintain a navy;

14. To make rules for the government and regulation of the land and naval forces;

15. To provide for calling forth the militia to execute the laws of the Union, suppress insurrections and repel invasions;

16. To provide for organizing, arming, and disciplining the militia, and for governing such part of them as may be employed in the service of the United States, reserving to the States respectively, the appointment of the officers, and the authority of training the militia according to the discipline prescribed by Congress;

17. To exercise exclusive legislation in all cases whatsoever, over such district (not exceeding ten miles square) as may, by cession of particular States, and the acceptance of Congress, become the seat of the government of the United States, and to exercise like authority over all places purchased by the consent of the legislature of the State in which the same shall be, for the erection of forts, magazines, arsenals, dockyards, and other needful buildings; and

18. To make all laws which shall be necessary and proper for carrying into execution the foregoing powers, and all other powers vested by this Constitution in the government of the United States, or any department or officer thereof.

SECTION 9. 1. The migration or importation of such persons as any of the States now existing shall think proper to admit, shall not be prohibited by the Congress prior to the year one thousand eight hundred and eight, but a tax or duty may be imposed on such importation, not exceeding ten dollars for each person.

2. The privilege of the writ of habeas corpus shall not be suspended, unless when in cases of rebellion or invasion the public safety may require it.

3. No bill of attainder or ex post facto law shall be passed.

4. No capitation, or other direct, tax shall be laid, unless in proportion to the census or enumeration hereinbefore directed to be taken.[5]

5. No tax or duty shall be laid on articles exported from any State.

6. No preference shall be given by any regulation of commerce or revenue to the ports of one State over those of another: nor shall vessels bound to, or from, one State be obliged to enter, clear, or pay duties in another.

7. No money shall be drawn from the treasury, but in consequence of appropriations made by law; and a regular statement and account of the receipts and expenditures of all public money shall be published from time to time.

8. No title of nobility shall be granted by the United States: and no person holding any office of profit or trust under them, shall, without the consent of the Congress, accept of any present, emolument, office, or title, of any kind whatever, from any king, prince, or foreign State.

SECTION 10. 1. No State shall enter into any treaty, alliance, or confederation; grant letters of marque and reprisal; coin money; emit bills of credit; make any thing but gold and silver coin a tender in payment of debts; pass any bill of attainder, ex post facto law, or law impairing the obligation of contracts, or grant, any title of nobility.

2. No State shall, without the consent of the Congress, lay any imposts or duties on imports or exports, except what may be absolutely necessary for executing its inspection laws: and the net produce of all duties and imposts laid by any State on imports or exports, shall be for the use of the treasury of the United States; and all such laws shall be subject to the revision and control of the Congress.

3. No State shall, without the consent of the Congress, lay any duty of tonnage, keep troops, or ships of war in time of peace, enter into any agreement or compact with another State, or with a foreign power, or engage in war, unless actually invaded, or in such imminent danger as will not admit of delay.

# ARTICLE II

SECTION 1. 1. The executive power shall be vested in a President of the United States of America. He shall hold his office during the term of four years, and, together with the Vice President, chosen for the same term, be elected, as follows:

2. Each State shall appoint, in such manner as the legislature thereof may direct, a number of electors, equal to the whole number of senators and representatives to which the State may be entitled in the Congress: but no senator or representative, or person holding any office of trust or profit under the United States, shall be appointed an elector.

The electors shall meet in their respective States, and vote by ballot for two persons, of whom one at least shall not be an inhabitant of the same State with themselves. And they shall make a list of all the persons voted for, and of the number of votes for each; which list they shall sign and certify, and transmit sealed to the seat of the government of the United States, directed to the president of the Senate. The president of the Senate shall, in the presence of the Senate and House of Representatives, open all the certificates, and the votes shall then be counted. The person having the greatest number of votes shall be the President, if such number be a majority of the whole number of electors appointed; and if there be more than one who have such majority, and have an equal number of votes, then the House of Representatives shall immediately choose by ballot one of them for President; and if no person have a majority, then from the five highest on the list the said House shall in like manner choose the President. But in choosing the President, the votes shall be taken by

---

[5]See the Sixteenth Amendment.

States, the representation from each State having one vote; a quorum for this purpose shall consist of a member or members from two thirds of the States, and a majority of all the States shall be necessary to a choice. In every case after the choice of the President, the person having the greatest number of votes of the electors shall be the Vice President. But if there should remain two or more who have equal votes, the Senate shall choose from them by ballot the Vice President.[6]

3. The Congress may determine the time of choosing the electors, and the day on which they shall give their votes; which day shall be the same throughout the United States.

4. No person except a natural born citizen, or a citizen of the United States, at the time of the adoption of this Constitution, shall be eligible to the office of President; neither shall any person be eligible to the office who shall not have attained to the age of thirty-five years, and been fourteen years a resident within the United States.

5. In case of the removal of the President from office, or of his death, resignation, or inability to discharge the powers and duties of the said office, the same shall devolve on the Vice President, and the congress may by law provide for the case of removal, death, resignation or inability, both of the President and Vice President, declaring what officer shall then act as President, and such officer shall act accordingly until the disability be removed, or a President shall be elected.

6. The President shall, at stated times, receive for his services a compensation which shall neither be increased nor diminished during the period for which he shall have been elected, and he shall not receive within that period any other emolument from the United States, or any of them.

7. Before he enter on the execution of his office, he shall take the following oath or affirmation:—"I do solemnly swear (or affirm) that I will faithfully execute the office of President of the United States, and will to the best of my ability, preserve, protect and defend the Constitution of the United States."

SECTION 2.   1. The President shall be commander in chief of the army and navy of the United States, and of the militia of the several States, when called into the actual service of the United States; he may require the opinion in writing, of the principal officer in each of the executive departments, upon any subject relating to the duties of their respective offices, and he shall have power to grant reprieves and pardons for offenses against the United States, except in cases of impeachment.

2. He shall have power, by and with the advice and consent of the Senate, to make treaties, provided two thirds of the senators present concur; and he shall nominate, and by and with the advice and consent of the Senate, shall appoint ambassadors, other public ministers and consuls, judges of the Supreme Court, and all other officers of the United States, whose appointments are not herein otherwise provided for, and which shall be established by law; but the Congress may by law vest the appointment of such infe-

rior officers, as they think proper, in the President alone, in the courts of laws, or in the heads of departments.

3. The President shall have power to fill up all vacancies that may happen during the recess of the Senate, by granting commissions which shall expire at the end of their next session.

SECTION 3.   He shall from time to time give to the Congress information of the state of the Union, and recommend to their consideration such measures as he shall judge necessary and expedient; he may, on extraordinary occasions, convene both Houses, or either of them, and in case of disagreement between them with respect to the time of adjournment, he may adjourn them to such time as he shall think proper; he shall receive ambassadors and other public ministers; he shall take care that the laws be faithfully executed, and shall commission all the officers of the United States.

SECTION 4.   The President, Vice President, and all civil officers of the United States, shall be removed from office on impeachment for, and conviction of, treason, bribery, or other high crimes and misdemeanors.

# ARTICLE III

SECTION 1. The judicial power of the United States shall be vested in one Supreme Court, and in such inferior courts as the Congress may from time to time ordain and establish. The judges, both of the Supreme and inferior courts, shall hold their offices during good behavior, and shall, at stated times, receive for their services, a compensation, which shall not be diminished during their continuance in office.

SECTION 2.   1. The judicial power shall extend to all cases, in law and equity, arising under this Constitution, the laws of the United States, and treaties made, or which shall be made, under their authority;—to all cases of admiralty and maritime jurisdiction;—to controversies to which the United States shall be a party;[7]—to controversies between two or more States;—between a State and citizens of another State;—between citizens of different States;—between citizens of the same State claiming lands under grants of different States, and between a State, or the citizens thereof, and foreign States, citizens or subjects.

2. In all cases affecting ambassadors, other public ministers and consuls, and those in which a State shall be party, the Supreme Court shall have original jurisdiction. In all the other cases before mentioned, the Supreme Court shall have appellate jurisdiction, both as to law and fact, with such exceptions, and under such regulations as the Congress shall make.

3. The trial of all crimes, except in cases of impeachment, shall be by jury; and such trial shall be held in the State where the said crimes shall have been committed; but when not committed within any State, the trial shall be such place or places as the congress may by law have directed.

[6]Superseded by the Twelfth Amendment.

[7]See the Eleventh Amendment.

SECTION 3.   1. Treason against the United States shall consist only in levying war against them, or in adhering to their enemies, giving them aid and comfort. No person shall be convicted of treason unless on the testimony of two witnesses to the same overt act, or on confession in open court.

2. The Congress shall have power to declare the punishment of treason, but no attainder of treason shall work corruption of blood, or forfeiture except during the life of the person attained.

# ARTICLE IV

SECTION 1. Full faith and credit shall be given in each State to the public acts, records, and judicial proceedings of every other State. And the Congress may by general laws prescribe the manner in which such acts, records and proceedings shall be proved, and the effect thereof.

SECTION 2.   1. The citizens of each State shall be entitled to all privileges and immunities of citizens in the several States.[8]

2. A person charged in any State with treason, felony, or other crime, who shall flee from justice, and be found in another State, shall on demand of the executive authority of the State from which he fled, be delivered up to be removed to the State having jurisdiction of the crime.

3. No person held to service or labor in one State under the laws thereof, escaping into another, shall, in consequence of any law or regulation therein, be discharged from such service or labor, but shall be delivered up on claim of the party to whom such service or labor may be due.[9]

SECTION 3.   1. New States may be admitted by the Congress into this Union; but no new State shall be formed or erected within the jurisdiction of any other State, nor any State be formed by the junction of two or more States, or parts of States, without the consent of the legislatures of the States concerned as well as of the Congress.

2. The Congress shall have power to dispose of and make all needful rules and regulations respecting the territory or other property belonging to the United States; and nothing in this Constitution shall be so construed as to prejudice any claims of the United States, or of any particular State.

SECTION 4.   The United States shall guarantee to every State in this Union a republican form of government, and shall protect each of them against invasion; and on application of the legislature, or of the executive (when the legislature cannot be convened) against domestic violence.

# ARTICLE V

The Congress, whenever two thirds of both Houses shall deem it necessary, shall propose amendments to this Constitution, or, on the application of the legislatures of two thirds of the several States, shall call a convention for proposing amendments, which in either case shall be valid

to all intents and purposes, as part of this Constitution, when ratified by the legislatures of three fourths of the several States, or by conventions in three fourths thereof, as the one or the other mode of ratification may be proposed by the Congress; Provided that no amendment which may be made prior to the year one thousand eight hundred and eight shall in any manner affect the first and fourth clauses in the ninth section of the first article; and that no State, without its consent, shall be deprived of its equal suffrage in the Senate.

# ARTICLE VI

1. All debts contracted and engagements entered into, before the adoption of this Constitution, shall be as valid against the United States under this Constitution, as under the Confederation.[10]

2. This Constitution, and the laws of the United States which shall be made in pursuance thereof; and all treaties made, or which shall be made, under the authority of the United States, shall be the supreme law of the land; and the judges in every State shall be bound thereby, any thing in the Constitution or laws of any State to the contrary notwithstanding.

3. The senators and representatives before mentioned, and the members of the several State legislatures, and all executive and judicial officers, both of the United States and of the several States, shall be bound by oath or affirmation to support this Constitution; but no religious test shall ever be required as a qualification to any office or public trust under the United States.

# ARTICLE VII

The ratification of the conventions of nine States shall be sufficient for the establishment of this Constitution between the States so ratifying the same.

Done in Convention by the unanimous consent of the States present the seventeenth day of September in the year of our Lord one thousand seven hundred and eighty-seven, and of the independence of the United States of America the twelfth. In witness whereof we have hereunto subscribed our names.

[Signatories' names omitted]

*Articles in addition to, and amendment of, the Constitution of the United States of America, proposed by Congress, and ratified by the legislatures of the several States, pursuant to the fifth article of the original Constitution.*

### Amendment I
### [First ten amendments ratified December 15, 1791]

Congress shall make no law respecting an establishment of religion, or prohibiting the free exercise thereof; or abridging the freedom of speech, or of the press; or the right of the people peaceably to assemble, and to petition the government for a redress of grievances.

---

[8]See the Fourteenth Amendment, Sec. 1.

[9]See the Thirteenth Amendment.

[10]See the Fourteenth Amendment, Sec. 4.

### Amendment II

A well regulated militia, being necessary to the security of a free State, the right of the people to keep and bear arms, shall not be infringed.

### Amendment III

No soldier shall, in time of peace be quartered in any house, without the consent of the owner, nor in time of war, but in a manner to be prescribed by law.

### Amendment IV

The right of the people to be secure in their persons, houses, papers, and effects, against unreasonable searches and seizures, shall not be violated, and no warrants shall issue, but upon probable cause, supported by oath or affirmation, and particularly describing the place to be searched, and the persons or things to be seized.

### Amendment V

No person shall be held to answer for a capital or otherwise infamous crime, unless on a presentment or indictment of a grand jury, except in cases arising in the land or naval forces, or in the militia, when in actual service in time of war or public danger; nor shall any person be subject for the same offense to be twice put in jeopardy of life or limb; nor shall be compelled in any criminal case to be a witness against himself, nor be deprived of life, liberty, or property, without due process of law; nor shall private property be taken for public use, without just compensation.

### Amendment VI

In all criminal prosecutions, the accused shall enjoy the right to a speedy and public trial, by an impartial jury of the State and district wherein the crime shall have been committed, which district shall have been previously ascertained by law, and to be informed of the nature and cause of the accusation; to be confronted with the witnesses against him; to have compulsory process for obtaining witnesses in his favor, and to have the assistance of counsel for his defense.

### Amendment VII

In suits at common law, where the value in controversy shall exceed twenty dollars, the right of trial by jury shall be preserved, and no fact tried by a jury shall be otherwise reexamined in any court of the United States, than according to the rules of the common law.

### Amendment VIII

Excessive bail shall not be required, nor excessive fines imposed, nor cruel and unusual punishments inflicted.

### Amendment IX

The enumeration in the Constitution of certain rights shall not be construed to deny or disparage others retained by the people.

### Amendment X

The powers not delegated to the United States by the Constitution, nor prohibited by it to the States, are reserved to the States respectively, or to the people.

### Amendment XI [January 8, 1798]

The judicial power of the United States shall not be construed to extend to any suit in law or equity, commended or prosecuted against one of the United States by citizens of another State, or by citizens or subjects of any foreign State.

### Amendment XII [September 25, 1804]

The electors shall meet in their respective States, and vote by ballot for President and Vice President, one of whom, at least, shall not be an inhabitant of the same State with themselves; they shall name in their ballots the person voted for as President, and in distinct ballots, the person voted for as Vice President, and they shall make distinct lists of all persons voted for as President and of all persons voted for as Vice President, and of the number of votes for each, which lists they shall sign and certify, and transmit sealed to the seat of the government of the United States, directed to the President of the Senate;—The President of the Senate shall, in the presence of the Senate and House of Representatives, open all the certificates and the votes shall then be counted;—The person having the greatest number of votes for President, shall be the President, if such number be a majority of the whole number of electors appointed; and if no person have such majority, then from the persons having the highest numbers not exceeding three on the list of those voted for as President, the House of Representatives shall choose immediately, by ballot, the President. But in choosing the President, the votes shall be taken by States, the representation from each State having one vote; a quorum for this purpose shall consist of a member or members from two thirds of the States, and a majority of all the States shall be necessary to a choice. And if the House of Representatives shall not choose a President whenever the right of choice shall devolve upon them, before the fourth day of March next following, then the Vice President shall act as President, as in the case of the death or other constitutional disability of the President. The person having the greatest number of votes as Vice President shall be the Vice President, if such number be a majority of the whole number of electors appointed, and if no person have a majority, then from the two highest numbers on the list, the Senate shall choose the Vice President; a quorum for the purpose shall consist of two thirds of the whole number of Senators, and a majority of the whole number shall be necessary to a choice. But no person constitutionally ineligible to the office of President shall be eligible to that of Vice President of the United States.

### Amendment XIII [December 18, 1865]

SECTION 1. Neither slavery nor involuntary servitude, except as a punishment for crime whereof the party shall have been duly convicted, shall exist within the United States, or any place subject to their jurisdiction.

SECTION 2.    Congress shall have power to enforce this article by appropriate legislation.

## Amendment XIV [July 28, 1868]

SECTION 1.    All persons born or naturalized in the United States, and subject to the jurisdiction thereof, are citizens of the United States and of the State wherein they reside. No State shall make or enforce any law which shall abridge the privileges or immunities of citizens of the United States; nor shall any State deprive any person of life, liberty, or property, without due process of law; nor deny to any person within its jurisdiction the equal protection of the laws.

SECTION 2.    Representatives shall be apportioned among the several States according to their respective numbers, counting the whole number of persons in each State, excluding Indians not taxed. But when the right to vote at any election for the choice of electors for President and Vice President of the United States, representatives in Congress, the executive and judicial officers of a State, or the members of the legislature thereof, is denied to any of the male inhabitants of such State, being twenty-one years of age, and citizens of the United States, or in any way abridged, except for participating in rebellion, or other crime, the basis of representation there shall be reduced in the proportion which the number of such male citizens shall bear to the whole number of male citizens twenty-one years of age in such State.

SECTION 3.    No person shall be a senator or representative in Congress, or elector of President and Vice President, or hold any office, civil or military, under the United States, or under any State, who having previously taken an oath, as a member of Congress, or as an officer of the United States, or as a member of any State legislature, or as an executive or judicial officer of any State, to support the Constitution of the United States, shall have engaged in insurrection or rebellion against the same, or given aid or comfort to the enemies thereof. But Congress may by a vote of two thirds of each House, remove such disability.

SECTION 4.    The validity of the public debt of the United States, authorized by law, including debts incurred for payment of pensions and bounties for services in suppressing insurrection or rebellion; shall not be questioned. But neither the United States nor any State shall assume or pay any debt or obligation incurred in aid of insurrection or rebellion against the United States, or any claim for the loss or emancipation of any slave; but all such debts, obligations, and claims shall be held illegal and void.

SECTION 5.    The Congress shall have the power to enforce, by appropriate legislation, the provisions of this article.

## Amendment XV [March 30, 1870]

SECTION 1. The right of citizens of the United States to vote shall not be denied or abridged by the United States or by any State on account of race, color, or previous condition of servitude.

SECTION 2. The Congress shall have power to enforce this article by appropriate legislation.

## Amendment XVI [February 25, 1913]

The Congress shall have power to lay and collect taxes on incomes, from whatever source derived, without apportionment among the several States, and without regard to any census or enumeration.

## Amendment XVII [May 31, 1913]

The Senate of the United States shall be composed of two senators from each State, elected by the people thereof, for six years; and each senator shall have one vote. The electors in each State shall have the qualifications requisite for electors of the most numerous branch of the State legislature.

When vacancies happen in the representation of any State in the Senate, the executive authority of such State shall issue writs of election to fill such vacancies: Provided, That the legislature of any State may empower the executive thereof to make temporary appointments until the people fill the vacancies by election as the legislature may direct.

This amendment shall not be so construed as to affect the election or term of any senator chosen before it becomes valid as part of the Constitution.

## Amendment XVIII [11] [January 29, 1919]

After one year from the ratification of this article, the manufacture, sale, or transportation of intoxicating liquors within, the importation thereof into, or the exportation thereof from the United States and all territory subject to the jurisdiction thereof for beverage purposes is thereby prohibited.

The Congress and the several States shall have concurrent power to enforce this article by appropriate legislation.

This article shall be inoperative unless it shall have been ratified as an amendment to the Constitution by the legislatures of the several States, as provided in the constitution, within seven years from the date of the submission hereof to the States by Congress.

## Amendment XIX [August 26, 1920]

The right of citizens of the United States to vote shall not be denied or abridged by the United States or by any State on account of sex.

Congress shall have the power to enforce this article by appropriate legislation.

## Amendment XX [January 23, 1933]

SECTION 1.    The terms of the President and Vice President shall end at noon on the 20th day of January and the terms of Senators and Representatives at noon on the 3d day of January, of the years in which such terms would have ended if this article had not been ratified; and the terms of their successors shall then begin.

SECTION 2.    The Congress shall assemble at least once in every year, and such meeting shall begin at noon on the 3d day of January, unless they shall by law appoint a different day.

---

[11]Repealed by the Twenty-first Amendment.

SECTION 3. If, at the time fixed for the beginning of the term of President, the President-elect shall have died, the Vice President-elect shall become President. If a President shall not have been chosen before the time fixed for the beginning of his term, or if the President-elect shall have failed to qualify, then the Vice President-elect shall act as President until a President shall have qualified; and the Congress may by law provide for the case wherein neither a President-elect nor a Vice President-elect shall have qualified, declaring who shall then act as President, or the manner in which one who is to act shall be selected, and such person shall act accordingly until a President or Vice President shall have qualified.

SECTION 4. The Congress may by law provide for the case of the death of any of the persons from whom, the House of Representatives may choose a President whenever the right of choice shall have devolved upon them, and for the case of the death of any of the persons from whom the Senate may choose a Vice President whenever the right of choice shall have devolved upon them.

SECTION 5. Sections 1 and 2 shall take effect on the 15th day of October following the ratification of this article.

SECTION 6. This article shall be inoperative unless it shall have been ratified as an amendment to the Constitution by the legislatures of three-fourths of the several States within seven years from the date of its submission.

## Amendment XXI [December 5, 1933]

SECTION 1. The Eighteenth Article of amendment to the Constitution of the United States is hereby repealed.

SECTION 2. The transportation or importation into any State, Territory, or possession of the United States for delivery or use therein of intoxicating liquors in violation of the laws thereof, is hereby prohibited.

SECTION 3. This article shall be inoperative unless it shall have been ratified as an amendment to the Constitution by conventions in the several States, as provided in the Constitution, within seven years from the date of the submission thereof to the States by the Congress.

## Amendment XXII [March 1, 1951]

No person shall be elected to the office of the President more than twice, and no person who has held the office of President, or acted as President, for more than two years of a term to which some other person was elected President shall be elected to the office of the President more than once.

But this article shall not apply to any person holding the office of President when this article was proposed by the Congress, and shall not prevent any person who may be holding the office of President, or acting as President, during the term within which this article becomes operative from holding the office of President or acting as President during the remainder of such term.

This article shall be inoperative unless it shall have been ratified as an amendment to the Constitution by the legislatures of three-fourths of the several States within seven years from the date of its submission to the States by the Congress.

## Amendment XXIII [March 29, 1961]

SECTION 1. The District constituting the seat of Government of the United States shall appoint in such manner as the Congress may direct.

A number of electors of President and Vice President equal to the whole number of Senators and Representatives in Congress to which the District would be entitled if it were a State, but in no event more than the least populous State; they shall be in addition to those appointed by the States, but they shall be considered, for the purposes of the election of President and Vice President, to be electors appointed by a State; and they shall meet in the District and perform such duties as provided by the twelfth article of amendment.

SECTION 2. The Congress shall have power to enforce this article by appropriate legislation.

## Amendment XXIV [January 23, 1964]

SECTION 1. The right of citizens of the United States to vote in any primary or other election for President or Vice President, for electors for President or Vice President, or for Senator or Representative in Congress, shall not be denied or abridged by the United States or any State by reason of failure to pay any poll tax or other tax.

SECTION 2. The Congress shall have power to enforce this article by appropriate legislation.

## Amendment XXV [February 10, 1967]

SECTION 1. In case of the removal of the President from office or of his death or resignation, the Vice President shall become President.

SECTION 2. Whenever there is a vacancy in the office of the Vice President, the President shall nominate a Vice President who shall take office upon confirmation by a majority of both Houses of Congress.

SECTION 3. Whenever the President transmits to the President pro tempore of the Senate and the Speaker of the House of Representatives his written declaration that he is unable to discharge the powers and duties of his office, and until he transmits to them a written declaration to the contrary, such powers and duties shall be discharged by the Vice President as Acting President.

SECTION 4. Whenever the Vice President and a majority of either the principal officers of the executive departments or of such other body as Congress may by law provide, transmit to the President pro tempore of the Senate and the Speaker of the House of Representatives their written declaration that the President is unable to discharge the powers and duties of his office, the Vice President shall immediately assume the powers and duties of the office as Acting President.

Thereafter, when the President transmits to the President pro tempore of the Senate and the Speaker of the House of Representatives his written declaration that no inability exists, he shall resume the powers and duties of his office unless the Vice President and a majority of either the principal officers of the executive departments or of such other body as Congress may by law provide, transmit within four days to the President pro tempore of the Senate and the Speaker of the House of Representatives their written declaration that the President is unable to discharge the powers and duties of his office. Thereupon Congress shall decide the issue, assembling within forty-eight hours for that purpose if not in session. If the Congress, within twenty-one days after receipt of the latter written declaration, or, if Congress is not in session, within twenty-one days after Congress is required to assemble, determines by two-thirds vote of both Houses that the President is unable to discharge the powers and duties of his office, the Vice President shall continue to discharge the same as Acting President; otherwise, the President shall resume the powers and duties of his office.

### Amendment XXVI [June 30, 1971]

SECTION 1.    The right of citizens of the United States who are eighteen years of age or older to vote shall not be denied or abridged by the United States or by any State on account of age.

SECTION 2.    The Congress shall have power to enforce this article by appropriate legislation.

### Amendment XXVII[12] [May 7, 1992]

No law, varying the compensation for services of the Senators and Representatives, shall take effect until an election of Representatives shall have intervened.

---

[12]James Madison proposed this amendment in 1789 together with the ten amendments that were adopted as the Bill of Rights, but it failed to win ratification at the time. Congress, however, had set no deadline for its ratification, and over the years—particularly in the 1980s and 1990s—many states voted to add it to the Constitution. With the ratification of Michigan in 1992 it passed the threshold of 3/4ths of the states required for adoption, but because the process took more than 200 years, its validity remains in doubt.

# PRESIDENT AND VICE PRESIDENT

1. George Washington (1789)
   John Adams (1789)

2. John Adams (1797)
   Thomas Jefferson (1797)

3. Thomas Jefferson (1801)
   Aaron Burr (1801)
   George Clinton (1805)

4. James Madison (1809)
   George Clinton (1809)
   Elbridge Gerry (1813)

5. James Monroe (1817)
   Daniel D. Thompkins (1817)

6. John Quincy Adams (1825)
   John C. Calhoun (1825)

7. Andrew Jackson (1829)
   John C. Calhoun (1829)
   Martin Van Buren (1833)

8. Martin Van Buren (1837)
   Richard M. Johnson (1837)

9. William H. Harrison (1841)
   John Tyler (1841)

10. John Tyler (1841)

11. James K. Polk (1845)
    George M. Dallas (1845)

12. Zachary Taylor (1849)
    Millard Fillmore (1849)

13. Millard Fillmore (1850)

14. Franklin Pierce (1853)
    William R. King (1853)

15. James Buchanan (1857)
    John C. Breckinridge (1857)

16. Abraham Lincoln (1861)
    Hannibal Hamlin (1861)
    Andrew Johnson (1865)

17. Andrew Johnson (1865)

18. Ulysses S. Grant (1869)
    Schuyler Colfax (1869)
    Henry Wilson (1873)

19. Rutherford B. Hayes (1877)
    William A. Wheeler (1877)

20. James A. Garfield (1881)
    Chester A. Arthur (1881)

21. Chester A. Arthur (1881)

22. Grover Cleveland (1885)
    T. A. Hendricks (1885)

23. Benjamin Harrison (1889)
    Levi P. Morgan (1889)

24. Grover Cleveland (1893)
    Adlai E. Stevenson (1893)

25. William McKinley (1897)
    Garret A. Hobart (1897)
    Theodore Roosevelt (1901)

26. Theodore Roosevelt (1901)
    Charles Fairbanks (1905)

27. William H. Taft (1909)
    James S. Sherman (1909)

28. Woodrow Wilson (1913)
    Thomas R. Marshall (1913)

29. Warren G. Harding (1921)
    Calvin Coolidge (1921)

30. Calvin Coolidge (1923)
    Charles G. Dawes (1925)

31. Herbert C. Hoover (1929)
    Charles Curtis (1929)

32. Franklin D. Roosevelt (1933)
    John Nance Garner (1933)
    Henry A. Wallace (1941)
    Harry S. Truman (1945)

33. Harry S. Truman (1945)
    Alben W. Barkley (1949)

34. Dwight D. Eisenhower (1953)
    Richard M. Nixon (1953)

35. John F. Kennedy (1961)
    Lyndon B. Johnson (1961)

36. Lyndon B. Johnson (1963)
    Hubert H. Humphrey (1965)

37. Richard M. Nixon (1969)
    Spiro T. Agnew (1969)
    Gerald R. Ford (1973)

38. Gerald R. Ford (1974)
    Nelson A. Rockefeller (1974)

39. James E. Carter Jr. (1977)
    Walter F. Mondale (1977)

40. Ronald W. Reagan (1981)
    George H. Bush (1981)

41. George H. Bush (1989)
    James D. Quayle III (1989)

42. William J. Clinton (1993)
    Albert Gore (1993)

43. George W. Bush (2001)
    Richard Cheney (2001)

# PRESIDENTIAL ELECTIONS

| Year | Number of States | Candidates | Party | Popular Vote* | Electoral Vote[†] | Percentage of Popular Vote |
|------|------|------|------|------|------|------|
| 1789 | 11 | GEORGE WASHINGTON | No party designations | | 69 | |
| | | John Adams | | | 34 | |
| | | Other Candidates | | | 35 | |
| 1792 | 15 | GEORGE WASHINGTON | No party designations | | 132 | |
| | | John Adams | | | 77 | |
| | | George Clinton | | | 50 | |
| | | Other Candidates | | | 5 | |
| 1796 | 16 | JOHN ADAMS | Federalist | | 71 | |
| | | Thomas Jefferson | Democratic-Republican | | 68 | |
| | | Thomas Pinckney | Federalist | | 59 | |
| | | Aaron Burr | Democratic-Republican | | 30 | |
| | | Other Candidates | | | 48 | |
| 1800 | 16 | THOMAS JEFFERSON | Democratic-Republican | | 73 | |
| | | Aaron Burr | Democratic-Republican | | 73 | |
| | | John Adams | Federalist | | 65 | |
| | | Charles C. Pinckney | Federalist | | 64 | |
| | | John Jay | Federalist | | 1 | |
| 1804 | 17 | THOMAS JEFFERSON | Democratic-Republican | | 162 | |
| | | Charles C. Pinckney | Federalist | | 14 | |
| 1808 | 17 | JAMES MADISON | Democratic-Republican | | 122 | |
| | | Charles C. Pinckney | Federalist | | 47 | |
| | | George Clinton | Democratic-Republican | | 6 | |
| 1812 | 18 | JAMES MADISON | Democratic-Republican | | 128 | |
| | | DeWitt Clinton | Federalist | | 89 | |
| 1816 | 19 | JAMES MONROE | Democratic-Republican | | 183 | |
| | | Rufus King | Federalist | | 34 | |
| 1820 | 24 | JAMES MONROE | Democratic-Republican | | 231 | |
| | | John Quincy Adams | Independent-Republican | | 1 | |
| 1824 | 24 | JOHN QUINCY ADAMS | Democratic-Republican | 108,740 | 84 | 30.5 |
| | | Andrew Jackson | Democratic-Republican | 153,544 | 99 | 43.1 |
| | | William H. Crawford | Democratic-Republican | 46,618 | 41 | 13.1 |
| | | Henry Clay | Democratic-Republican | 47,136 | 37 | 13.2 |
| 1828 | 24 | ANDREW JACKSON | Democrat | 647,286 | 178 | 56.0 |
| | | John Quincy Adams | National Republican | 508,064 | 83 | 44.0 |
| 1832 | 24 | ANDREW JACKSON | Democrat | 687,502 | 219 | 55.0 |
| | | Henry Clay | National Republican | 530,189 | 49 | 42.4 |
| | | William Wirt | Anti-Masonic | 33,108 | 7 | 2.6 |
| | | John Floyd | National Republican | | 11 | |

* Percentage of popular vote given for any election year may not total 100 percent because candidates receiving less than 1 percent of the popular vote have been omitted.

[†] Prior to the passage of the Twelfth Amendment in 1904, the electoral college voted for two presidential candidates; the runner-up became Vice-President. Data from Historical Statistics of the United States, Colonial Times to 1957 (1961), pp. 682–683, and The World Almanac.

# PRESIDENTIAL ELECTIONS   (CONTINUED)

| Year | Number of States | Candidates | Party | Popular Vote | Electoral Vote | Percentage of Popular Vote |
|------|------|------------|-------|--------------|----------------|------------|
| 1836 | 26 | MARTIN VAN BUREN | Democrat | 765,483 | 170 | 50.9 |
|      |    | William H. Harrison | Whig |  | 73 |  |
|      |    | Hugh L. White | Whig |  | 26 |  |
|      |    | Daniel Webster | Whig | 739,795 | 14 | 49.1 |
|      |    | W. P. Mangum | Whig |  | 11 |  |
| 1840 | 26 | WILLIAM H. HARRISON | Whig | 1,274,624 | 234 | 53.1 |
|      |    | Martin Van Buren | Democrat | 1,127,781 | 60 | 46.9 |
| 1844 | 26 | JAMES K. POLK | Democrat | 1,338,464 | 170 | 49.6 |
|      |    | Henry Clay | Whig | 1,300,097 | 105 | 48.1 |
|      |    | James G. Birney | Liberty | 62,300 |  | 2.3 |
| 1848 | 30 | ZACHARY TAYLOR | Whig | 1,360,967 | 163 | 47.4 |
|      |    | Lewis Cass | Democrat | 1,222,342 | 127 | 42.5 |
|      |    | Martin Van Buren | Free Soil | 291,263 |  | 10.1 |
| 1852 | 31 | FRANKLIN PIERCE | Democrat | 1,601,117 | 254 | 50.9 |
|      |    | Winfield Scott | Whig | 1,385,453 | 42 | 44.1 |
|      |    | John P. Hale | Free Soil | 155,825 |  | 5.0 |
| 1856 | 31 | JAMES BUCHANAN | Democrat | 1,832,955 | 174 | 45.3 |
|      |    | John C. Frémont | Republican | 1,339,932 | 114 | 33.1 |
|      |    | Millard Fillmore | American ("Know Nothing") | 871,731 | 8 | 21.6 |
| 1860 | 33 | ABRAHAM LINCOLN | Republican | 1,865,593 | 180 | 39.8 |
|      |    | Stephen A. Douglas | Democrat | 1,382,713 | 12 | 29.5 |
|      |    | John C. Breckinridge | Democrat | 848,356 | 72 | 18.1 |
|      |    | John Bell | Constitutional Union | 592,906 | 39 | 12.6 |
| 1864 | 36 | ABRAHAM LINCOLN | Republican | 2,206,938 | 212 | 55.0 |
|      |    | George B. McClellan | Democrat | 1,803,787 | 21 | 45.0 |
| 1868 | 37 | ULYSSES S. GRANT | Republican | 3,013,421 | 214 | 52.7 |
|      |    | Horatio Seymour | Democrat | 2,706,829 | 80 | 47.3 |
| 1872 | 37 | ULYSSES S. GRANT | Republican | 3,596,745 | 286 | 55.6 |
|      |    | Horace Greeley | Democrat | 2,843,446 | * | 43.9 |
| 1876 | 38 | RUTHERFORD B. HAYES | Republican | 4,036,572 | 185 | 48.0 |
|      |    | Samuel J. Tilden | Democrat | 4,284,020 | 184 | 51.0 |
| 1880 | 38 | JAMES A. GARFIELD | Republican | 4,453,295 | 214 | 48.5 |
|      |    | Winfield S. Hancock | Democrat | 4,414,082 | 155 | 48.1 |
|      |    | James B. Weaver | Greenback-Labor | 308,578 |  | 3.4 |
| 1884 | 38 | GROVER CLEVELAND | Democrat | 4,879,507 | 219 | 48.5 |
|      |    | James G. Blaine | Republican | 4,850,293 | 182 | 48.2 |
|      |    | Benjamin F. Butler | Greenback-Labor | 175,370 |  | 1.8 |
|      |    | John P. St. John | Prohibition | 150,369 |  | 1.5 |
| 1888 | 38 | BENJAMIN HARRISON | Republican | 5,447,129 | 233 | 47.9 |
|      |    | Grover Cleveland | Democrat | 5,537,857 | 168 | 48.6 |
|      |    | Clinton B. Fisk | Prohibition | 249,506 |  | 2.2 |
|      |    | Anson J. Streeter | Union Labor | 146,935 |  | 1.3 |

*Because of the death of Greeley, Democratic electors scattered their votes.*

# PRESIDENTIAL ELECTIONS    (CONTINUED)

| Year | Number of States | Candidates | Party | Popular Vote | Electoral Vote | Percentage of Popular Vote |
|------|------|------|------|------|------|------|
| 1892 | 44 | GROVER CLEVELAND | Democrat | 5,555,426 | 277 | 46.1 |
| | | Benjamin Harrison | Republican | 5,182,690 | 145 | 43.0 |
| | | James B. Weaver | People's | 1,029,846 | 22 | 8.5 |
| | | John Bidwell | Prohibition | 264,133 | | 2.2 |
| 1896 | 45 | WILLIAM MCKINLEY | Republican | 7,102,246 | 271 | 51.1 |
| | | William J. Bryan | Democrat | 6,492,559 | 176 | 47.7 |
| 1900 | 45 | WILLIAM MCKINLEY | Republican | 7,218,491 | 292 | 51.7 |
| | | William J. Bryan | Democrat; Populist | 6,356,734 | 155 | 45.5 |
| | | John C. Woolley | Prohibition | 208,914 | | 1.5 |
| 1904 | 45 | THEODORE ROOSEVELT | Republican | 7,628,461 | 336 | 57.4 |
| | | Alton B. Parker | Democrat | 5,084,223 | 140 | 37.6 |
| | | Eugene V. Debs | Socialist | 402,283 | | 3.0 |
| | | Silas C. Swallow | Prohibition | 258,536 | | 1.9 |
| 1908 | 46 | WILLIAM H. TAFT | Republican | 7,675,320 | 321 | 51.6 |
| | | William J. Bryan | Democrat | 6,412,294 | 162 | 43.1 |
| | | Eugene V. Debs | Socialist | 420,793 | | 2.8 |
| | | Eugene W. Chafin | Prohibition | 253,840 | | 1.7 |
| 1912 | 48 | WOODROW WILSON | Democrat | 6,296,547 | 435 | 41.9 |
| | | Theodore Roosevelt | Progressive | 4,118,571 | 88 | 27.4 |
| | | William H. Taft | Republican | 3,486,720 | 8 | 23.2 |
| | | Eugene V. Debs | Socialist | 900,672 | | 6.0 |
| | | Eugene W. Chafin | Prohibition | 206,275 | | 1.4 |
| 1916 | 48 | WOODROW WILSON | Democrat | 9,127,695 | 277 | 49.4 |
| | | Charles E. Hughes | Republican | 8,533,507 | 254 | 46.2 |
| | | A. L. Benson | Socialist | 585,113 | | 3.2 |
| | | J. Frank Hanly | Prohibition | 220,506 | | 1.2 |
| 1920 | 48 | WARREN G. HARDING | Republican | 16,143,407 | 404 | 60.4 |
| | | James M. Cox | Democrat | 9,130,328 | 127 | 34.2 |
| | | Eugene V. Debs | Socialist | 919,799 | | 3.4 |
| | | P. P. Christensen | Farmer-Labor | 265,411 | | 1.0 |
| 1924 | 48 | CALVIN COOLIDGE | Republican | 15,718,211 | 382 | 54.0 |
| | | John W. Davis | Democrat | 8,385,283 | 136 | 28.8 |
| | | Robert M. La Follette | Progressive | 4,831,289 | 13 | 16.6 |
| 1928 | 48 | HERBERT C. HOOVER | Republican | 21,391,993 | 444 | 58.2 |
| | | Alfred E. Smith | Democrat | 15,016,169 | 87 | 40.9 |
| 1932 | 48 | FRANKLIN D. ROOSEVELT | Democrat | 22,809,638 | 472 | 57.4 |
| | | Herbert C. Hoover | Republican | 15,758,901 | 59 | 39.7 |
| | | Norman Thomas | Socialist | 881,951 | | 2.2 |
| 1936 | 48 | FRANKLIN D. ROOSEVELT | Democrat | 27,752,869 | 523 | 60.8 |
| | | Alfred M. Landon | Republican | 16,674,665 | 8 | 36.5 |
| | | William Lemke | Union | 882,479 | | 1.9 |
| 1940 | 48 | FRANKLIN D. ROOSEVELT | Democrat | 27,307,819 | 449 | 54.8 |
| | | Wendell L. Willkie | Republican | 22,321,018 | 82 | 44.8 |

# PRESIDENTIAL ELECTIONS (CONTINUED)

| Year | Number of States | Candidates | Party | Popular Vote | Electoral Vote | Percentage of Popular Vote |
|------|------|------------|-------|--------------|----------------|----------------------------|
| 1944 | 48 | FRANKLIN D. ROOSEVELT | Democrat | 25,606,585 | 432 | 53.5 |
|      |    | Thomas E. Dewey | Republican | 22,014,745 | 99 | 46.0 |
| 1948 | 48 | HARRY S. TRUMAN | Democrat | 24,105,812 | 303 | 49.5 |
|      |    | Thomas E. Dewey | Republican | 21,970,065 | 189 | 45.1 |
|      |    | J. Strom Thurmond | States' Rights | 1,169,063 | 39 | 2.4 |
|      |    | Henry A. Wallace | Progressive | 1,157,172 | | 2.4 |
| 1952 | 48 | DWIGHT D. EISENHOWER | Republican | 33,936,234 | 442 | 55.1 |
|      |    | Adlai E. Stevenson | Democrat | 27,314,992 | 89 | 44.4 |
| 1956 | 48 | DWIGHT D. EISENHOWER | Republican | 35,590,472 | 457* | 57.6 |
|      |    | Adlai E. Stevenson | Democrat | 26,022,752 | 73 | 42.1 |
| 1960 | 50 | JOHN F. KENNEDY | Democrat | 34,227,096 | 303† | 49.9 |
|      |    | Richard M. Nixon | Republican | 34,108,546 | 219 | 49.6 |
| 1964 | 50 | LYNDON B. JOHNSON | Democrat | 42,676,220 | 486 | 61.3 |
|      |    | Barry M. Goldwater | Republican | 26,860,314 | 52 | 38.5 |
| 1968 | 50 | RICHARD M. NIXON | Republican | 31,785,480 | 301 | 43.4 |
|      |    | Hubert H. Humphrey | Democrat | 31,275,165 | 191 | 42.7 |
|      |    | George C. Wallace | American Independent | 9,906,473 | 46 | 13.5 |
| 1972 | 50 | RICHARD M. NIXON‡ | Republican | 47,165,234 | 520 | 60.6 |
|      |    | George S. McGovern | Democrat | 29,168,110 | 17 | 37.5 |
| 1976 | 50 | JIMMY CARTER | Democrat | 40,828,929 | 297 | 50.1 |
|      |    | Gerald R. Ford | Republican | 39,148,940 | 240 | 47.9 |
|      |    | Eugene McCarthy | Independent | 739,256 | | |
| 1980 | 50 | RONALD REAGAN | Republican | 43,201,220 | 489 | 50.9 |
|      |    | Jimmy Carter | Democrat | 34,913,332 | 49 | 41.2 |
|      |    | John B. Anderson | Independent | 5,581,379 | | |
| 1984 | 50 | RONALD REAGAN | Republican | 53,428,357 | 525 | 59.0 |
|      |    | Walter F. Mondale | Democrat | 36,930,923 | 13 | 41.0 |
| 1988 | 50 | GEORGE BUSH | Republican | 48,901,046 | 426 | 53.4 |
|      |    | Michael Dukakis | Democrat | 41,809,030 | 111 | 45.6 |
| 1992 | 50 | BILL CLINTON | Democrat | 43,728,275 | 370 | 43.2 |
|      |    | George Bush | Republican | 38,167,416 | 168 | 37.7 |
|      |    | H. Ross Perot | United We Stand, America | 19,237,247 | | 19.0 |
| 1996 | 50 | BILL CLINTON | Democrat | 45,590,703 | 379 | 49.0 |
|      |    | Robert Dole | Republican | 37,816,307 | 159 | 41.0 |
|      |    | H. Ross Perot | Reform | 7,866,284 | | 8.0 |
| 2000 | 50 | GEORGE W. BUSH | Republican | 50,459,624 | 271 | 47.9 |
|      |    | Albert Gore, Jr. | Democrat | 51,003,328 | 266 | 49.4 |
|      |    | Ralph Nader | Green | 2,882,985 | 0 | 2.7 |
| 2004 | 50 | GEORGE W. BUSH | Republican | 59,117,523 | 286 | 51.1 |
|      |    | John Kerry | Democrat | 55,557,584 | 252 | 48.0 |
|      |    | Ralph Nader | Green | 405,623 | 0 | 0.3 |

*Walter B. Jones received 1 electoral vote.

†Harry F. Byrd received 15 electoral votes.

‡Resigned August 9, 1974: Vice President Gerald R. Ford became President.

# ADMISSION OF STATES INTO THE UNION

| State | Date of Admission | State | Date of Admission |
|---|---|---|---|
| 1. Delaware | December 7, 1787 | 26. Michigan | January 26, 1837 |
| 2. Pennsylvania | December 12, 1787 | 27. Florida | March 3, 1845 |
| 3. New Jersey | December 18, 1787 | 28. Texas | December 29, 1845 |
| 4. Georgia | January 2, 1788 | 29. Iowa | December 28, 1846 |
| 5. Connecticut | January 9, 1788 | 30. Wisconsin | May 29, 1848 |
| 6. Massachusetts | February 6, 1788 | 31. California | September 9, 1850 |
| 7. Maryland | April 28, 1788 | 32. Minnesota | May 11, 1858 |
| 8. South Carolina | May 23, 1788 | 33. Oregon | February 14, 1859 |
| 9. New Hampshire | June 21, 1788 | 34. Kansas | January 29, 1861 |
| 10. Virginia | June 25, 1788 | 35. West Virginia | June 20, 1863 |
| 11. New York | July 26, 1788 | 36. Nevada | October 31, 1864 |
| 12. North Carolina | November 21, 1789 | 37. Nebraska | March 1, 1867 |
| 13. Rhode Island | May 29, 1790 | 38. Colorado | August 1, 1876 |
| 14. Vermont | March 4, 1791 | 39. North Dakota | November 2, 1889 |
| 15. Kentucky | June 1, 1792 | 40. South Dakota | November 2, 1889 |
| 16. Tennessee | June 1, 1796 | 41. Montana | November 8, 1889 |
| 17. Ohio | March 1, 1803 | 42. Washington | November 11, 1889 |
| 18. Louisiana | April 30, 1812 | 43. Idaho | July 3, 1890 |
| 19. Indiana | December 11, 1816 | 44. Wyoming | July 10, 1890 |
| 20. Mississippi | December 10, 1817 | 45. Utah | January 4, 1896 |
| 21. Illinois | December 3, 1818 | 46. Oklahoma | November 16, 1907 |
| 22. Alabama | December 14, 1819 | 47. New Mexico | January 6, 1912 |
| 23. Maine | March 15, 1820 | 48. Arizona | February 14, 1912 |
| 24. Missouri | August 10, 1821 | 49. Alaska | January 3, 1959 |
| 25. Arkansas | June 15, 1836 | 50. Hawaii | August 21, 1959 |

# DEMOGRAPHICS OF THE UNITED STATES

## POPULATION GROWTH

| Year | Population | Percent Increase |
|------|-----------|------------------|
| 1630 | 4,600 | |
| 1640 | 26,600 | 478.3 |
| 1650 | 50,400 | 90.8 |
| 1660 | 75,100 | 49.0 |
| 1670 | 111,900 | 49.0 |
| 1680 | 151,500 | 35.4 |
| 1690 | 210,400 | 38.9 |
| 1700 | 250,900 | 19.2 |
| 1710 | 331,700 | 32.2 |
| 1720 | 466,200 | 40.5 |
| 1730 | 629,400 | 35.0 |
| 1740 | 905,600 | 43.9 |
| 1750 | 1,170,800 | 29.3 |
| 1760 | 1,593,600 | 36.1 |
| 1770 | 2,148,100 | 34.8 |
| 1780 | 2,780,400 | 29.4 |
| 1790 | 3,929,214 | 41.3 |
| 1800 | 5,308,483 | 35.1 |
| 1810 | 7,239,881 | 36.4 |
| 1820 | 9,638,453 | 33.1 |
| 1830 | 12,866,020 | 33.5 |
| 1840 | 17,069,453 | 32.7 |
| 1850 | 23,191,876 | 35.9 |
| 1860 | 31,443,321 | 35.6 |
| 1870 | 39,818,449 | 26.6 |
| 1880 | 50,155,783 | 26.0 |
| 1890 | 62,947,714 | 25.5 |
| 1900 | 75,994,575 | 20.7 |
| 1910 | 91,972,266 | 21.0 |
| 1920 | 105,710,620 | 14.9 |
| 1930 | 122,775,046 | 16.1 |
| 1940 | 131,669,275 | 7.2 |
| 1950 | 151,325,798 | 14.5 |
| 1960 | 179,323,175 | 18.5 |
| 1970 | 203,302,031 | 13.4 |
| 1980 | 226,542,199 | 11.4 |
| 1990 | 248,718,301 | 9.8 |
| 2000 | 281,421,906 | 13.1 |

Source: *Historical Statistics of the United States* (1975); *Statistical Abstract by the United States* (2001).
Note: Figures for 1630–1780 include British colonies within limits of present United States only; Native American population included only in 1930 and thereafter.

## WORK FORCE

| Year | Total Number Workers (1000s) | Farmers as % of Total | Women as % of Total | % Workers in Unions |
|------|------|------|------|------|
| 1810 | 2,330 | 84 | (NA) | (NA) |
| 1840 | 5,660 | 75 | (NA) | (NA) |
| 1860 | 11,110 | 53 | (NA) | (NA) |
| 1870 | 12,506 | 53 | 15 | (NA) |
| 1880 | 17,392 | 52 | 15 | (NA) |
| 1890 | 23,318 | 43 | 17 | (NA) |
| 1900 | 29,073 | 40 | 18 | 3 |
| 1910 | 38,167 | 31 | 21 | 6 |
| 1920 | 41,614 | 26 | 21 | 12 |
| 1930 | 48,830 | 22 | 22 | 7 |
| 1940 | 53,011 | 17 | 24 | 27 |
| 1950 | 59,643 | 12 | 28 | 25 |
| 1960 | 69,877 | 8 | 32 | 26 |
| 1970 | 82,049 | 4 | 37 | 25 |
| 1980 | 106,940 | 3 | 43 | 23 |
| 1990 | 125,840 | 3 | 45 | 16 |
| 2000 | 140,863 | 2 | 47 | 12 |

Source: *Historical Statistics of the United States* (1975); *Statistical Abstract of the United States* (2001).

## VITAL STATISTICS (IN THOUSANDS)

| Year | Births | Deaths | Marriages | Divorces |
|------|--------|--------|-----------|----------|
| 1800 | 55 | (NA) | (NA) | (NA) |
| 1810 | 54.3 | (NA) | (NA) | (NA) |
| 1820 | 55.2 | (NA) | (NA) | (NA) |
| 1830 | 51.4 | (NA) | (NA) | (NA) |
| 1840 | 51.8 | (NA) | (NA) | (NA) |
| 1850 | 43.3 | (NA) | (NA) | (NA) |
| 1860 | 44.3 | (NA) | (NA) | (NA) |
| 1870 | 38.3 | (NA) | 9.6 (1867) | 0.3 (1867) |
| 1880 | 39.8 | (NA) | 9.1 (1875) | 0.3 (1875) |
| 1890 | 31.5 | (NA) | 9.0 | 0.5 |
| 1900 | 32.3 | 17.2 | 9.3 | 0.7 |
| 1910 | 30.1 | 14.7 | 10.3 | 0.9 |
| 1920 | 27.7 | 13.0 | 12.0 | 1.6 |
| 1930 | 21.3 | 11.3 | 9.2 | 1.6 |
| 1940 | 19.4 | 10.8 | 12.1 | 2.0 |
| 1950 | 24.1 | 9.6 | 11.1 | 2.6 |
| 1960 | 23.7 | 9.5 | 8.5 | 2.2 |
| 1970 | 18.4 | 9.5 | 10.6 | 3.5 |
| 1980 | 15.9 | 8.8 | 10.6 | 5.2 |
| 1990 | 16.7 | 8.6 | 9.8 | 4.7 |
| 1997 | 14.6 | 8.6 | 8.9 | 4.3 |

Source: *Historical Statistics of the United States* (1975); *Statistical Abstract of the United States* (1999).

# RACIAL COMPOSITION OF THE POPULATION

(IN THOUSANDS)

| Year | White | Black | Indian | Hispanic | Asian/Pacific Islander |
|------|-------|-------|--------|----------|------------------------|
| 1790 | 3,172 | 757 | (NA) | (NA) | (NA) |
| 1800 | 4,306 | 1,002 | (NA) | (NA) | (NA) |
| 1820 | 7,867 | 1,772 | (NA) | (NA) | (NA) |
| 1840 | 14,196 | 2,874 | (NA) | (NA) | (NA) |
| 1860 | 26,923 | 4,442 | (NA) | (NA) | (NA) |
| 1880 | 43,403 | 6,581 | (NA) | (NA) | (NA) |
| 1900 | 66,809 | 8,834 | (NA) | (NA) | (NA) |
| 1910 | 81,732 | 9,828 | (NA) | (NA) | (NA) |
| 1920 | 94,821 | 10,463 | (NA) | (NA) | (NA) |
| 1930 | 110,287 | 11,891 | (NA) | (NA) | (NA) |
| 1940 | 118,215 | 12,866 | (NA) | (NA) | (NA) |
| 1950 | 134,942 | 15,042 | (NA) | (NA) | (NA) |
| 1960 | 158,832 | 18,872 | (NA) | (NA) | (NA) |
| 1970 | 178,098 | 22,581 | (NA) | (NA) | (NA) |
| 1980 | 194,713 | 26,683 | 1,420 | 14,609 | 3,729 |
| 1990 | 208,727 | 30,511 | 2,065 | 22,372 | 2,462 |
| 2000 | 211,461 | 34,658 | 2,476 | 35,306 | 10,642 |

Source: U.S. Bureau of the Census, U.S. *Census of Population: 1940,* vol. II, part 1, and vol. IV, part 1; *1950,* vol. II, part 1; *1960,* vol. I, part 1; *1970,* vol. I, part B; and *Current Population Reports,* P25-1095 and P25-1104; *Statistical Abstract of the United States* (2001).

# IMMIGRATION BY THE ORIGIN

(IN THOUSANDS)

| Period | Europe | Americas | Asia |
|--------|--------|----------|------|
| 1820–30 | 106 | 12 | — |
| 1831–40 | 496 | 33 | — |
| 1841–50 | 1,597 | 62 | — |
| 1851–60 | 2,453 | 75 | 42 |
| 1861–70 | 2,065 | 167 | 65 |
| 1871–80 | 2,272 | 404 | 70 |
| 1881–90 | 4,735 | 427 | 70 |
| 1891–1900 | 3,555 | 39 | 75 |
| 1901–10 | 8,065 | 362 | 324 |
| 1911–20 | 4,322 | 1,144 | 247 |
| 1921–30 | 2,463 | 1,517 | 112 |
| 1931–40 | 348 | 160 | 16 |
| 1941–50 | 621 | 355 | 32 |
| 1951–60 | 1,326 | 997 | 150 |
| 1961–70 | 1,123 | 1,716 | 590 |
| 1971–80 | 800 | 1,983 | 1,588 |
| 1981–90 | 762 | 3,616 | 2,738 |
| 1991–2000 | 1,100 | 3,800 | 2,200 |

Source: Historical Statistics of the United States (1975); *Statistical Abstract of the United States* (1991); Population Estimates Program, Population Division, U.S. Census Bureau, April 2001.

**Acquired Immune Deficiency Syndrome (AIDS)**  A complex of deadly pathologies resulting from infection with the human immunodeficiency virus (HIV).

**Act of Toleration**  Act passed in 1661 by King Charles II ordering a stop to religious persecution in Massachusetts.

**Affirmative action**  A set of policies to open opportunities in business and education for members of minority groups and women by allowing race and sex to be factors included in decisions to hire, award contracts, or admit students to higher education programs.

**Alamo**  Franciscan mission at San Antonio, Texas that was the site in 1836 of a siege and massacre of Texans by Mexican troops.

**Albany Conference**  A 1754 meeting, held in Albany, NY, between the British and leaders of the Iroquois Confederacy.

**Albany Movement**  Coalition formed in 1961 in Albany, a small city in southwest Georgia, of activists from SNCC, the NAACP, and other local groups.

**Alien Act**  Act passed by Congress in 1798 that authorized the president to imprison or deport suspected aliens during wartime.

**Alliance for Progress**  Program of economic aid to Latin America during the Kennedy administration.

**Allies**  In World War I, Britain, France, Russia, and other belligerent nations fighting against the Central Powers but not including the United States.

**Almanac**  A combination calendar, astrological guide, and sourcebook of medical advice and farming tips.

**American Colonization Society**  Organization founded in 1817 by antislavery reformers, that called for gradual emancipation and the removal of freed blacks to Africa.

**American Federation of Labor (AFL)**  Union formed in 1886 that organized skilled workers along craft lines and emphasized a few workplace issues rather than a broad social program.

**American Indian Movement (AIM)**  Group of Native-American political activists who used confrontations with the federal government to publicize their case for Indian rights.

**American Society for the Promotion of Temperance**  Largest reform organization of its time dedicated to ending the sale and consumption of alcoholic beverages.

**American System**  The program of government subsidies favored by Henry Clay and his followers to promote American economic growth and protect domestic manufacturers from foreign competition.

**Americans with Disabilities Act**  An act that required employers to provide access to their facilities for qualified employees with disabilities.

**Annapolis Convention**  Conference of state delegates at Annapolis, Maryland, that issued a call in September 1786 for a convention to meet at Philadelphia to consider fundamental changes.

**Anti-Federalists**  Opponents of the Constitution in the debate over its ratification.

**Archaic period**  The period roughly 10,000 to 2,500 years ago marked by the retreat of glaciers.

**Articles of Confederation**  Written document setting up the loose confederation of states that comprised the first national government of the United States.

**Athapascan**  A people that began to settle the forests in the northwestern area of North America around 5000 B.C.E.

**Atlantic Charter**  Statement of common principles and war aims developed by President Franklin Roosevelt and British Prime Minister Winston Churchill at a meeting in August 1941.

**Axis powers**  The opponents of the United States and its allies in World War II.

**Aztecs**  A warrior people who dominated the Valley of Mexico from 1100–1521.

**Bank War**  The political struggle between President Andrew Jackson and the supporters of the Second Bank of the United States.

**Battle of the Bulge**  German offensive in December 1944 that penetrated deep into Belgium (creating a "bulge"). Allied forces, while outnumbered, attacked from the north and south. By January, 1945, the German forces were destroyed or routed, but not without some 77,000 Allied casualities.

**Bay of Pigs**  Site in Cuba of an unsuccessful landing by fourteen hundred anti-Castro Cuban refugees in April 1961.

*Beatnik*  Term used to designate members of the Beats.

**Beats**  A group of writers from the 50s whose writings challenged American culture.

**Beaver Wars**  Series of bloody conflicts, occurring between 1640s and 1680s, during which the Iroquois fought the French for control of the fur trade in the east and the Great Lakes region.

**Beringia**  A subcontinent bridging Asia and North America, named after the Bering Straits.

**Berlin blockade**  Three-hundred-day Soviet blockade of land access to United States, British, and French occupation zones in Berlin, 1948–1949.

**Bill for Establishing Religious Freedom**  A bill authored by Thomas Jefferson establishing religious freedom in Virginia.

**Bill of Rights**  A written summary of inalienable rights and liberties.

**Black codes**  Laws passed by states and municipalities denying many rights of citizenship to free black people before the Civil War.

**Black Panther Party**  Political and social movement among black Americans, founded in Oakland, California, in 1966 and emphasizing black economic and political power.

**Black Power**  Philosophy emerging after 1965 that real economic and political gains for African Americans could come only through self-help, self-determination, and organizing for direct political influence.

**Bleeding Kansas**  Violence between pro- and antislavery forces in Kansas Territory after the passage of the Kansas-Nebraska Act in 1854.

*Blitzkrieg*  German war tactic in World War II ("lightning war") involving the concentration of air and armored firepower to punch and exploit holes in opposing defensive lines.

**Bohemian**  Artistic individual who lives with disregard for the conventional rules of behavior.

**Bolsheviks**   Members of the Communist movement in Russia that established the Soviet government after the 1917 Russian Revolution.

**Bonus Army**   Unemployed veterans of World War I gathering in Washington in 1932 demanding payment of service bonuses not due until 1945.

**Bosnia**   A nation in southeast Europe that split off from Yugoslavia and became the site of bitter civil and religious war, requiring NATO and U.S. intervention in the 1990s.

**Boston Massacre**   After months of increasing friction between townspeople and the British troops stationed in the city, on March 5, 1770, British troops fired on American civilians in Boston.

**Boston Tea Party**   Incident that occurred on December 16, 1773, in which Bostonians, disguised as Indians, destroyed £18,000 worth of tea belonging to the British East India Company in order to prevent payment of the duty on it.

**Brown v. Board of Education**   Supreme Court decision in 1954 that declared that "separate but equal" schools for children of different races violated the Constitution.

**Cahokia**   One of the largest urban centers created by Mississippian peoples, containing 30,000 residents in 1250.

**Californios**   Californians of Spanish descent.

**Calvinist theology of election**   Belief that salvation was the result of God's sovereign decree and that few people would receive God's grace.

**Caminetti Act**   1893 act giving the state the power to regulate the mines.

**Camp David Accords**   Agreement signed by Israel and Egypt in 1978 that set the formal terms for peace in the Middle East.

**Carpetbaggers**   Northern transplants to the South, many of whom were Union soldiers who stayed in the South after the war.

**Central Intelligence Agency (CIA)**   Agency established in 1947 that coordinates the gathering and evaluation of military and economic information on other nations.

**Central Powers**   Germany and its World War I allies in Austria, Italy, Turkey, and Bulgaria.

**Chinese Exclusion Act**   Act which suspended Chinese immigration, limited the civil rights of resident Chinese, and forbade their naturalization.

**Civil Rights Act of 1964**   Federal legislation that outlawed discrimination in public accommodations and employment on the basis of race, skin color, sex, religion, or national origin.

**Civil Rights Bill**   1866 act that gave full citizenship to African Americans.

**Clayton Antitrust Act**   Replaced the old Sherman Act of 1890 as the nation's basic antitrust law. It exempted unions from being construed as illegal combinations in restraint of trade, and it forbade federal courts from issuing injunctions against strikers.

**Coercive Acts**   Legislation passed by Parliament in 1774; included the Boston Port Act, the Massachusetts Government Act, the Administration of Justice Act, and the Quartering Act of 1774.

**Cold war**   The political and economic confrontation between the Soviet Union and the United States that dominated world affairs from 1946 to 1989.

**Committee on Public Information (CPI)**   Government agency during World War I that sought to shape public opinion in support of the war effort through newspapers, pamphlets, speeches, films, and other media.

**Compromise of 1850**   The four-step compromise which admitted California as a free state, allowed the residents of the New Mexico and Utah territories to decide the slavery issue for themselves, ended the slave trade in the District of Columbia, and passed a new fugitive slave law to enforce the constitutional provision stating that a slave escaping into a free state shall be delivered back to the owner.

**Compromise of 1877**   The Congressional settling of the 1876 election which installed Republican Rutherford B. Hayes in the White House and gave Democrats control of all state governments in the South.

**Confederate States of America**   Nation proclaimed in Montgomery, Alabama, in February 1861, after the seven states of the Lower South seceded from the United States.

**Congress of Industrial Organizations**   An alliance of industrial unions that spurred the 1930s organizational drive among the mass-production industries.

**Congress of Racial Equality (CORE)**   Civil rights group formed in 1942 and committed to nonviolent civil disobedience.

**Congressional Reconstruction**   Name given to the period 1867–1870 when the Republican-dominated Congress controlled Reconstruction-era policy.

**Conspicuous consumption**   Highly visible displays of wealth and consumption.

**Constitution**   The written document providing for a new central government of the United States.

**Constitutional Convention**   Convention of delegates from the colonies that first met to organize resistance to the Intolerable Acts.

**Constitutional Union Party**   National party formed in 1860, mainly by former Whigs, that emphasized allegiance to the Union and strict enforcement of all national legislation.

**Continental Army**   The regular or professional army authorized by the Second Continental Congress and commanded by General George Washington during the Revolutionary War.

**Contract with America**   Platform proposing a sweeping reduction in the role and activities of the federal government on which many Republican candidates ran for Congress in 1994.

**Contras**   Nicaraguan exiles armed and organized by the CIA to fight the Sandinista government of Nicaragua.

**Copperheads**   A term Republicans applied to Northern war dissenters and those suspected of aiding the Confederate cause during the Civil War.

**Council of Economic Advisers**   Board of three professional economists established in 1946 to advise the president on economic policy.

**Counterculture**   Various alternatives to mainstream values and behaviors that became popular in the 1960s, including experimentation with psychedelic drugs, communal living, a return to the land, Asian religions, and experimental art.

**Coureurs de bois**   French for "woods runner," an independent fur trader in New France.

**Covenant Chain**  An alliance between the Iroquois Confederacy and the colony of New York which sought to establish Iroquois dominance over all other tribes.

**Coxey's Army**  A protest march of unemployed workers, led by Populist businessman Jacob Coxey, demanding inflation and a public works program during the depression of the 1890s.

**Cuban missile crisis**  Crisis between the Soviet Union and the United States over the placement of Soviet nuclear missiles in Cuba.

**Culpeper's Rebellion**  The overthrow of the established government in the Albermarle region of North Carolina by backcountry men in 1677.

**Dawes Severalty Act**  An 1887 law terminating tribal ownership of land and allotting some parcels of land to individual Indians with the remainder opened for white settlement.

**Declaration of Sentiments**  The resolutions passed at the Seneca Falls Convention in 1848 calling for full female equality, including the right to vote.

**D-Day**  June 6, 1944, the day of the first paratroop drops and amphibious landings on the coast of Normandy, France, in the first stage of Operation Overlord during World War II.

**Declaratory Act**  Law passed in 1776 to accompany repeal of the Stamp Act that stated that Parliament had the authority to legislate for the colonies "in all cases whatsoever."

**Democrats**  Political party formed in the 1820s under the leadership of Andrew Jackson; favored states' rights and a limited role for the federal government.

**Denmark Vesey's conspiracy**  The most carefully devised slave revolt in which rebels planned to seize control of Charleston in 1822 and escape to freedom in Haiti, a free black republic, but they were betrayed by other slaves, and seventy-five conspirators were executed.

**Department of Homeland Security (DHS)**  Cabinet-level department created by George Bush to manage U.S. security.

**Deregulation**  Reduction or removal of government regulations and encouragement of direct competition in many important industries and economic sectors.

**Desert culture**  A way of life based on hunting small game and the foraging of plant foods.

**Détente**  (French for "easing of tension") Used to describe the new U.S. relations with China and the Soviet Union in 1972.

**Dixiecrat**  States' Rights Democrats.

**Doughboys**  Nickname for soldiers during the Civil War era who joined the army for money.

***Dred Scott* decision**  Supreme Court ruling, in a lawsuit brought by Dred Scott, a slave demanding his freedom based on his residence in a free state, that slaves could not be U.S. citizens and that Congress had no jurisdiction over slavery in the territories.

**Economic Recovery Tax Act of 1981**  A major revision of the federal income tax system.

**Edmunds Act**  1882 act that effectively disenfranchised those who believed in or practiced polygamy and threatened them with fines and imprisonment.

**Edmunds-Tucker Act**  1887 act which destroyed the temporal power of the Mormon Church by confiscating all assets over $50,000 and establishing a federal commission to oversee all elections in the Utah territory.

**Emancipation Proclamation**  Decree announced by President Abraham Lincoln in September 1862 and formally issued on January 1, 1863, freeing slaves in all Confederate states still in rebellion.

**Embargo Act**  Act passed by Congress in 1807 prohibiting American ships from leaving for any foreign port.

**Emergency Banking Act**  1933 act which gave the president broad discretionary powers over all banking transactions and foreign exchange.

**Empresarios**  Agents who received a land grant from the Spanish or Mexican government in return for organizing settlements.

**Enclave**  Self-contained community.

**Encomienda**  In the Spanish colonies, the grant to a Spanish settler of a certain number of Indian subjects, who would pay him tribute in goods and labor.

**Engagés**  Catholic immigrants to New France.

**Enlightenment**  Intellectual movement stressing the importance of reason and the existence of discoverable natural laws.

**Enumerated goods**  Items produced in the colonies and enumerated in acts of Parliament that could be legally shipped from the colony of origin only to specified locations.

**Environmental Protection Agency (EPA)**  Federal agency created in 1970 to oversee environmental monitoring and cleanup programs.

**Equal Pay Act of 1963**  Act that made it illegal for employers to pay men and women different wages for the same job.

**Era of Good Feelings**  The period from 1817 to 1823 in which the disappearance of the Federalists enabled the Republicans to govern in a spirit of seemingly nonpartisan harmony.

**Espionage Act**  Law whose vague prohibition against obstructing the nation's war effort was used to crush dissent and criticism during World War I.

**Executive Order 9835**  Signed by Harry Truman in 1947 to establish a loyalty program requiring federal employees to sign loyalty oaths and undergo security checks.

**Federal Emergency Management Agency (FEMA)**  Agency charged with providing assistance to communities hit by natural disasters.

**Federal Reserve Act**  The 1913 law that revised banking and currency by extending limited government regulation through the creation of the Federal Reserve System.

**Federal Trade Commission (FTC)**  Government agency established in 1914 to provide regulatory oversight of business activity.

**Federalists**  Supporters of the Constitution who favored its ratification.

**Female Moral Reform Society**  Antiprostitution group founded by evangelical women in New York in 1834.

**Field Order 15**  Order by General William T. Sherman in January 1865 to set aside abandoned land along the southern Atlantic coast for forty-acre grants to freedmen; rescinded by President Andrew Johnson later that year.

**Fifteenth Amendment**    Passed by Congress in 1869, guaranteed the right of American men to vote, regardless of race.

**Fireside chat**    Speeches broadcast nationally over the radio in which President Franklin D. Roosevelt explained complex issues and programs in plain language, as though his listeners were gathered around the fireside with him.

**First Continental Congress**    Meeting of delegates from most of the colonies held in 1774 in response to the Coercive Acts.

**First Reconstruction Act**    1877 act that divided the South into five military districts subject to martial law.

**Forest Efficiency**    Creation of a comfortable life through the development of a sophisticated knowledge of available resources.

**Forest Management Act**    1897 act which, along with the National Reclamation Act, set the federal government on the path of large-scale regulatory activities.

**Fourteen Points**    Goals outlined by Woodrow Wilson for war.

**Frame of Government**    William Penn's constitution for Pennsylvania which included a provision allowing for religious freedom.

**Free silver**    Philosophy that the government should expand the money supply by purchasing and coining all the silver offered to it.

**Free speech movement**    Student movement at the University of California, Berkeley, formed in 1964 to protest limitations on political activities on campus.

**Freedmen's Bureau**    Agency established by Congress in March 1865 to provide social, educational, and economic services, advice, and protection to former slaves and destitute whites; lasted seven years.

**Freedom Summer**    Voter registration effort in rural Mississippi organized by black and white civil rights workers in 1964.

**French and Indian War**    The last of the Anglo-French colonial wars (1754–1763) and the first in which fighting began in North America. The war ended with France's defeat. Also known as the **Seven Years' War**.

**Fugitive Slave Law**    Part of the Compromise of 1850 that required the authorities in the North to assist Southern slave catchers and return runaway slaves to their owners.

**Gang System**    The organization and supervision of slave field hands into working teams on Southern plantations.

**General Land Revision Act of 1891**    Act which gave the president the power to establish forest reserves to protect watersheds against the threats posed by lumbering, overgrazing, and forest fires.

**G.I. Bill**    Legislation in June 1944 that eased the return of veterans into American society by providing educational and employment benefits.

**Gilded Age**    Term applied to late nineteenth-century America that refers to the shallow display and worship of wealth characteristic of that period.

**Gospel of wealth**    Thesis that hard work and perseverance lead to wealth, implying that poverty is a character flaw.

**Grandfather clauses**    Rules that required potential voters to demonstrate that their grandfathers had been eligible to vote; used in some Southern states after 1890 to limit the black electorate.

**Grange**    The National Grange of the Patrons of Husbandry, a national organization of farm owners formed after the Civil War.

**Granger laws**    State laws enacted in the Midwest in the 1870s that regulated rates charged by railroads, grain elevator operators, and other middlemen.

**Great Awakening**    Tremendous religious revival in colonial America striking first in the Middle Colonies and New England in the 1740s and then spreading to the southern colonies.

**Great Compromise**    Plan proposed at the 1787 Constitutional Convention for creating a national bicameral legislature in which all states would be equally represented in the Senate and proportionally represented in the House.

**Great Depression**    The nation's worst economic crisis, extending through the 1930s, producing unprecedented bank failures, unemployment, and industrial and agricultural collapse.

**Great Migration**    The mass movement of African Americans from the rural South to the urban North, spurred especially by new job opportunities during World War I and the 1920s.

**Great Sioux War**    From 1865 to 1867 the Oglala Sioux warrior Red Cloud waged war against the U.S. Army, forcing the U.S. to abandon its forts built on land relinquished to the government by the Sioux.

**Great Society**    Theme of Lyndon Johnson's administration, focusing on poverty, education, and civil rights.

**Great Uprising of 1877**    Unsuccessful railroad strike to protest wage cuts and the use of federal troops against strikers; the first nationwide work stoppage in American history.

**Gulf of Tonkin resolution**    Request to Congress from President Lyndon Johnson in response to North Vietnamese torpedo boat attacks in which he sought authorization for "all necessary measures" to protect American forces and stop further aggression.

**Harlem Renaissance**    A new African American cultural awareness that flourished in literature, art, and music in the 1920s.

**Hepburn Act**    Act that strengthened the Interstate Commerce Commission (ICC) by authorizing it to set maximum railroad rates and inspect financial records.

**Hispanic-American Alliance**    Organization formed to protect and fight for the rights of Spanish Americans.

**Holocaust**    The systematic murder of millions of European Jews and others deemed undesirable by Nazi Germany.

**Homestead Act**    Law passed by Congress in May 1862 providing homesteads with 160 acres of free land in exchange for improving the land within five years of the grant.

**Homestead Act of 1862**    1862 act which granted a quarter section (160 acres) of the public domain free to any settler who lived on the land for at least five years and improved it.

**Horizontal combination**    The merger of competitors in the same industry.

**House Concurrent Resolution 108**    Resolution passed in 1953 that allowed Congress to pass legislation to terminate a specific tribe as a political entity.

**House of Burgesses**    The legislature of colonial Virginia. First organized in 1619, it was the first institution of representative government in the English colonies.

**House Un-American Activities Committee (HUAC)**  Originally intended to ferret out pro-Fascists, it later investigated "un-American propaganda" that attacked constitutional government.

**Huguenots**  French Protestant religious dissenters who planted the first French colonies in North America.

**Immigration Act**  1921 act setting a maximum of 357,000 new immigrants each year.

**Immigration and Nationality Act**  Act passed in 1965 that abolished national origin quotas and established overall hemisphere quotas.

**Imperialism**  The policy and practice of exploiting nations and peoples for the benefit of an imperial power either directly through military occupation and colonial rule or indirectly through economic domination of resources and markets.

**Indentured Servants**  Individuals who contracted to serve a master for a period of four to seven years in return for payment of the servant's passage to America.

**Indian Removal Act**  President Andrew Jackson's measure that allowed state officials to override federal protection of Native Americans.

**Indios**  Name first used by Christopher Columbus for the Taino people of the Caribbean.

**Industrial Revolution**  Revolution in the means and organization of production.

**Intercourse Act**  Passed in 1790, this law regulated trade and intercourse with the Indian tribes and declared public treaties between the U.S. and Indian nations the only means of obtaining Indian lands.

**International Monetary Fund (IMF)**  International organization established in 1945 to assist nations in maintaining stable currencies.

**Internet**  The system of interconnected computers and servers that allows the exchange of email, posting of Web sites, and other means of instant communication.

**Interstate Commerce Commission (ICC)**  The 1887 law that expanded federal power over business by prohibiting pooling and discriminatory rates by railroads and establishing the first federal regulatory agency, the Interstate Commerce Commission.

**Intolerable Acts**  American term for the Coercive Acts and the Quebec Act.

**Irreconcilables**  Group of U.S. senators adamantly opposed to ratification of the Treaty of Versailles after World War I.

**Island-hop**  The Pacific campaigns of 1944 that were the American naval versions of the Blitzkrieg.

**Jay's Treaty**  Treaty with Britain negotiated in 1794 in which the United States made major concessions to avert a war over the British seizure of American ships.

**Jim Crow laws**  Segregation laws that became widespread in the South during the 1890s.

**Judicial review**  A power implied in the Constitution that gives federal courts the right to review and determine the constitutionality of acts passed by Congress and state legislatures.

**Judiciary Act of 1789**  Act of Congress that implemented the judiciary clause of the Constitution by establishing the Supreme Court and a system of lower federal courts.

**Kansas-Nebraska Act**  Law passed in 1854 creating the Kansas and Nebraska Territories but leaving the question of slavery open to residents, thereby repealing the Missouri Compromise.

**King George's War**  The third Anglo-French war in North America (1744–1748), part of the European conflict known as the War of the Austrian Succession.

**King Philip's War**  Conflict in New England (1675–1676) between Wampanoags, Narragansetts, and other Indian peoples against English settlers; sparked by English encroachments on native lands.

**King William's War**  The first of a series of colonial struggles between England and France, these conflicts occur principally on the frontiers of northern New England and New York between 1689 and 1697.

**Knights of Labor**  Labor union founded in 1869 that included skilled and unskilled workers irrespective of race or gender.

**Know-Nothings**  Name given to the antiimmigrant party formed from the wreckage of the Whig Party and some disaffected Northern Democrats in 1854.

**Kosovo**  Province of Yugoslavia where the United States and NATO intervened militarily in 1999 to protect ethnic Albanians from expulsion.

**Ku Klux Klan**  Perhaps the most prominent of the vigilante groups that terrorized black people in the South during Reconstruction era, founded by the Confederate veterans in 1866.

**Land Ordinance of 1785**  Act passed by Congress under the Articles of Confederation that created the grid system of surveys by which all subsequent public land was made available for sale.

**Landrum-Griffin Act**  1959 act that widened government control over union affairs and further restricted union use of picketing and secondary boycotts during strikes.

**League of Nations**  International organization created by the Versailles Treaty after World War I to ensure world stability.

**League of Women Voters**  League formed in 1920 advocating for women's rights, among them the right for women to serve on juries and equal pay laws.

**Lecompton constitution**  Proslavery draft written in 1857 by Kansas territorial delegates elected under questionable circumstances; it was rejected by two governors, supported by President Buchanan, and decisively defeated by Congress.

**Legal Tender Act**  Act creating a national currency in February 1862.

**Lend-Lease Act**  An arrangement for the transfer of war supplies, including food, machinery, and services to nations whose defense was considered vital to the defense of the United States in Word War II.

**Liberal Republicans**  Disaffected Republicans that emphasized the doctrines of classical economics.

**Liberty Bonds**  Interest-bearing certificates sold by the U.S. government to finance the American World War I effort.

**Liberty Party**  The first antislavery political party, formed in 1840.

**Limited Nuclear Test-Ban Treaty**  Treaty, signed by the United States, Britain, and the Soviet Union, outlawing nuclear testing in the atmosphere, in outer space, and under water.

**Lincoln-Douglas debates**    Series of debates in the 1858 Illinois senatorial campaign during which Douglas and Lincoln staked out their differing opinions on the issue of slavery.

**Loyalists**    British colonists who opposed independence from Britain.

**Manhattan Project**    Scientific research project during World War II specifically devoted to developing the atomic bomb.

**Manifest Destiny**    Doctrine, first expressed in 1845, that the expansion of white Americans across the continent was inevitable and ordained by God.

**Manumission**    The freeing of a slave.

*Marbury* v. *Madison*    Supreme Court decision of 1803 that created the precedent of judicial review by ruling as unconstitutional part of the Judiciary Act of 1789.

**March on Washington**    Historic gathering of over 250,000 people in Washington D.C. in 1963 marching for jobs and freedom.

**Market revolution**    The outcome of three interrelated developments: rapid improvements in transportation, commercialization, and industrialization.

**Marshall Plan**    Secretary of State George C. Marshall's European Recovery Plan of June 5, 1947, committing the United States to help in the rebuilding of post–World War II Europe.

**Massachusetts Bay Company**    A group of wealthy Puritans who were granted a royal charter in 1629 to settle in Massachusetts Bay.

**Mayflower Compact**    The first document of self-government in North America.

**McCarthyism**    Anti-Communist attitudes and actions associated with Senator Joe McCarthy in the early 1950s, including smear tactics and innuendo.

**Medicare**    Basic medical insurance for the elderly, financed through the federal government; program created in 1965.

**Mercantilism**    Economic system whereby the government intervenes in the economy for the purpose of increasing national wealth.

**Mesoamerica**    The region stretching from central Mexico to Central America.

**Mexican-American War**    War fought between Mexico and the United States between 1846 and 1848 over control of territory in southwest North America.

**Middle Passage**    The voyage between West Africa and the New World slave colonies.

**Militarism**    The tendency to see military might as the most important and best tool for the expansion of a nation's power and prestige.

**Missouri Compromise**    Sectional compromise in Congress in 1820 that admitted Missouri to the Union as a slave state and Maine as a free state and prohibited slavery in the northern Louisiana Purchase territory.

**Monroe Doctrine**    Declaration by President James Monroe in 1823 that the Western Hemisphere was to be closed off to further European colonization and that the United States would not interfere in the internal affairs of European nations.

**Mormonism**    The doctrines based on the Book of Mormon, taught by Joseph Smith and the succeeding prophets and leaders of the Church.

**Morrill Act of 1862**    Act by which "land-grant" colleges acquired space for campuses in return for promising to institute agricultural programs. Also known as Morrill Land Grant Act.

**Morrill Land Grant Act**    Law passed by Congress in July 1862 awarding proceeds from the sale of public lands to the states for the establishment of agricultural and mechanical colleges.

**Morrill Tariff Act**    Act that raised tariffs to more than double their prewar rate.

**Muckraking**    Journalism exposing economic, social, and political evils, so named by Theodore Roosevelt for its "raking the muck" of American society.

**Multiculturalism**    Movement that emphasized the unique attributes and achievements of formerly marginal groups and recent immigrants.

**My Lai Massacre**    Killing of twenty-two Vietnamese civilians by U.S. forces during a 1968 search-and-destroy mission.

**Nat Turner's Revolt**    Uprising of slaves in Southampton County, Virginia, in the summer of 1831 led by Nat Turner that resulted in the death of fifty-five white people.

**National Aeronautics and Space Administration (NASA)**    Federal agency created in 1958 to manage American space flights and exploration.

**National American Woman Suffrage Association (NAWSA)**    The organization, formed in 1890, that coordinated the ultimately successful campaign to achieve women's right to vote.

**National Association for the Advancement of Colored People**    Interracial organization co-founded by W. E. B. Du Bois in 1910 dedicated to restoring African American political and social rights.

**National Bank Act**    Act prohibiting state banks from issuing their own notes and forcing them to apply for federal charters.

**National Industrial Recovery Act**    1933 act which was meant to be a systematic plan for economic recovery.

**National Labor Relations Act**    Act establishing Federal guarantee of right to organize trade unions and collective bargaining.

**National Organization for Women (NOW)**    Organization founded to campaign for the enforcement of laws related to women's issues.

**National Reclamation Act**    1902 act which added 1 million acres of irrigated land to the United States.

**National Security Council (NSC)**    The formal policymaking body for national defense and foreign relations, created in 1947 and consisting of the president, the secretary of defense, the secretary of state, and others appointed by the president.

**National Security Council Paper 68 (NSC-68)**    Policy statement that committed the United States to a military approach to the Cold War.

**Nation of Islam (NOI)**    Religious movement among black Americans that emphasizes self-sufficiency, self-help, and separation from white society.

**Nativism**    Favoring the interests and culture of native-born inhabitants over those of immigrants.

**Neutrality Act of 1939**    Permitted the sale of arms to Britain, France, and China.

**New Deal**   The economic and political policies of the Roosevelt administration in the 1930s.

**New Deal coalition**   Coalition that included traditional-minded white Southern Democrats, big-city political machines, industrial workers of all races, trade unionists, and many Depression-hit farmers.

**New Freedom**   Woodrow Wilson's 1912 program for limited government intervention in the economy to restore competition by curtailing the restrictive influences of trusts and protective tariffs, thereby providing opportunities for individual achievement.

**New Frontier**   John F. Kennedy's domestic and foreign policy initiatives, designed to reinvigorate sense of national purpose and energy.

**New Jersey Plan**   Proposal of the New Jersey delegation for a strengthened national government in which all states would have an equal representation in a unicameral legislature.

**New Lights**   People who experienced conversion during the revivals of the Great Awakening.

**Niagara movement**   African American group organized in 1905 to promote racial integration, civil and political rights, and equal access to economic opportunity.

**Nisei**   U.S. citizens born of immigrant Japanese parents.

**Nonimportation movement**   A tactical means of putting economic pressure on Britain by refusing to buy its exports to the colonies.

**North American Free Trade Agreement (NAFTA)**   Agreement reached in 1993 by Canada, Mexico, and the United States to substantially reduce barriers to trade.

**North Atlantic Treaty Organization (NATO)**   Organization of ten European countries, Canada, and the United States whom together formed a mutual defense pact in April 1949.

**Northwest Ordinance of 1787**   Legislation that prohibited slavery in the Northwest Territories and provided the model for the incorporation of future territories into the union as co-equal states.

**Nullification**   A constitutional doctrine holding that a state has a legal right to declare a national law null and void within its borders.

**Nullification Crisis**   Sectional crisis in the early 1830s in which a states' rights party in South Carolina attempted to nullify federal law.

**Office of Economic Opportunity (OEO)**   Federal agency that coordinated many programs of the War on Poverty between 1964 and 1975.

**Old Lights**   Religious faction that condemned emotional enthusiasm as part of the heresy of believing in a personal and direct relationship with God outside the order of the church.

**Omaha Act of 1882**   Act which allowed the establishment of individual title to tribal lands.

**Open Door**   American policy of seeking equal trade and investment opportunities in foreign nations or regions.

**Open shop**   Factory of business employing workers whether or not they are union members; in practice, such a business usually refuses to hire union members and follows antiunion policies.

**Operation Desert Storm**   U.S. military campaign to force Iraqi forces out of Kuwait.

**Operation Overlord**   United States and British invasion of France in June 1944 during World War II.

**Operation Torch**   The Allied invasion of Axis-held North Africa in 1942.

**Oregon Trail**   Overland trail of more than two thousand miles that carried American settlers from the Midwest to new settlements in Oregon, California, and Utah.

**Organization of Petroleum Exporting Countries (OPEC)**   Cartel of oil-producing nations in Asia, Africa, and Latin America that gained substantial power over the world economy in the mid- to late- 1970s by controlling the production and price of oil.

**Panic of 1857**   Banking crisis that caused a credit crunch in the North; it was less severe in the South, where high cotton prices spurred a quick recovery.

**Pan-Indian military resistance movement**   Movement calling for the political and cultural unification of Indian tribes in the late eighteenth and early nineteenth centuries.

**Patriots**   British colonists who favored independence from Britain.

**Pendleton Civil Service Reform Act**   A law of 1883 that reformed the spoils system by prohibiting government workers from making political contributions and creating the Civil Service Commission to oversee their appointment on the basis of merit rather than politics.

**Peninsular campaign**   Union offensive led by McClellan with the objective of capturing Richmond.

**Pentagon Papers**   Classified Defense Department documents on the history of the United States' involvement in Vietnam, prepared in 1968 and leaked to the press in 1971.

**Pequot War**   Conflict between English settlers and Pequot Indians over control of land and trade in eastern Connecticut.

**Persian Gulf War**   War initiated by President Bush in response to Iraq's invasion of Kuwait.

**Pilgrims**   Settlers of Plymouth Colony, who viewed themselves as spiritual wanderers.

**Plan of Union**   Plan put forward by Benjamin Franklin in 1754 calling for an intercolonial union to manage defense and Indian affairs. The plan was rejected by participants at the Albany Congress.

***Plessy* v. *Ferguson***   Supreme Court decision holding that Louisiana's railroad segregation law did not violate the Constitution as long as the railroads or the state provided equal accommodations.

**Popular sovereignty**   A solution to the slavery crisis suggested by Michigan senator Lewis Cass by which territorial residents, not Congress, would decide slavery's fate.

**Populism**   A mass movement of the 1890s formed on the basis of the Southern Farmers' Alliance and other reform organizations.

**Powhatan Confederacy**   A village of communities of the Chesapeake united under Chief Wahunsonacook, who was called King Powhatan by the colonists.

**Preparedness**   Military buildup in preparation for possible U.S. participation in World War I.

**Progressivism**   A national movement focused on a variety of reform initiatives, including ending corruption, a more business like approach to government, and legislative responses to industrial excess.

**Prohibition**    A ban on the production, sale, and consumption of liquor, achieved temporarily through state laws and the Eighteenth Amendment.

**Proposition 187**    California legislation adopted by popular vote in California in 1994, which cuts off state-funded health and education benefits to undocumented or illegal immigrants.

**Proprietary colony**    A colony created when the English monarch granted a huge tract of land to an individual or group of individuals, who became "lords proprietor."

**Protective association**    Organizations formed by mine owners in response to the formation of labor unions.

**Protestant Reformation**    Martin Luther's challenge to the Catholic Church, initiated in 1517, calling for a return to what he understood to be the purer practices and beliefs of the early church.

**Protestants**    All European supporters of religious reform under Charles V's Holy Roman Empire.

**Pueblo Revolt**    Rebellion in 1680 of Pueblo Indians in New Mexico against their Spanish overlords.

**Pure Food and Drug Act**    Act that established the Food and Drug Administration (FDA), which tested and approved drugs before they went on the market.

**Puritanism**    Movement to purify and reform the English Church.

**Puritans**    Individuals who believed that Queen Elizabeth's reforms of the Church of England had not gone far enough in improving the church. Puritans led the settlement of Massachusetts Bay Colony.

**Putting-out system**    Production of goods in private homes under the supervision of a merchant who "put out" the raw materials, paid a certain sum per finished piece, and sold the completed item to a distant market.

**Quakers**    Members of the Society of Friends, a radical religious group that arose in the mid-seventeenth century. Quakers rejected formal theology, focusing instead on the Holy Spirit that dwelt within them.

**Quartering Act**    Acts of Parliament requiring colonial legislatures to provide supplies and quarters for the troops stationed in America.

**Quasi-War**    Undeclared naval war of 1797 to 1800 between the United States and France.

**Quebec Act**    Law passed by Parliament in 1774 that provided an appointed government for Canada, enlarged the boundaries of Quebec, and confirmed the privileges of the Catholic Church.

**Queen Anne's War**    American phase (1702–1713) of Europe's War of the Spanish Succession.

**Radical Republicans**    A shifting group of Republican congressmen, usually a substantial minority, who favored the abolition of slavery from the beginning of the Civil War and later advocated harsh treatment of the defeated South.

**Rancherias**    Dispersed settlements of Indian farmers in the Southwest.

**Reconquista**    The long struggle (ending in 1492) during which Spanish Christians reconquered the Iberian peninsula from Muslim occupiers.

**Red Power**    Term for pan-Indian identity.

**Red Scare**    Post–World War I public hysteria over Bolshevik influence in the United States directed against labor activism, radical dissenters, and some ethnic groups.

**Referendum**    Submission of a law, proposed or already in effect, to a direct popular vote for approval or rejection.

**Renaissance**    The intellectual and artistic flowering in Europe during the fourteenth, fifteenth, and sixteenth centuries sparked by a revival of interest in classical antiquity.

**Republican Party**    Party that emerged in the 1850s in the aftermath of the bitter controversy over the Kansas-Nebraska Act, consisting of former Whigs, some Northern Democrats, and many Know-Nothings.

**Republicanism**    A complex, changing body of ideas, values, and assumptions that influenced American political behavior during the eighteenth and nineteenth centuries.

**Roe v. Wade**    U.S. Supreme Court decision (1973) that disallowed state laws prohibiting abortion during the first three months (trimester) of pregnancy and established guidelines for abortion in the second and third trimesters.

**Roosevelt Corollary**    President Theodore Roosevelt's policy asserting U.S. authority to intervene in the affairs of Latin American nations; an expansion of the Monroe Doctrine.

**Royal Proclamation of 1763**    Royal proclamation declaring the trans-Appalachian region to be "Indian Country."

**Rush-Bagot Treaty of 1817**    Treaty between the United States and Britain that effectively demilitarized the Great Lakes by sharply limiting the number of ships each power could station on them.

**Sabbatarianism**    Reform movement that aimed to prevent business on Sundays.

**Sand Creek Massacre**    The near annihilation in 1864 of Black Kettle's Cheyenne band by Colorado troops under Colonel John Chivington's orders to "kill and scalp all, big and little."

**Santa Fé Trail**    The 900-mile trail opened by American merchants for trading purposes following Mexico's liberalization of the formerly restrictive trading policies of Spain.

**Scalawags**    Southern whites, mainly small landowning farmers and well-off merchants and planters, who supported the Southern Republican party during Reconstruction.

**Second American Party System**    The basic pattern of American politics of two parties, each with appeal among voters of all social voters and in all sections of the country.

**Second Great Awakening**    Religious revival among black and white Southerners in the 1790s.

**Sedition Act**    An act passed by Congress in 1798 that provided fines for anyone convicted writing, publishing, or speaking out against the government or its officers.

**Segregation**    A system of racial control that separated the races, initially by custom but increasingly by law during and after Reconstruction.

**Selective Service Act**    The law establishing the military draft for World War I.

**Self-determination**    The right of a people or a nation to decide on its own political allegiance or form of government without external influence.

**Seneca Falls Convention**    The first convention for women's equality in legal rights, held in upstate New York in 1848.

**Separatists** Members of an offshoot branch of Puritanism. Separatists believed that the Church of England was too corrupt to be reformed and hence were convinced they must "separate" from it to save their souls.

**Seven Years' War** War fought in Europe, North America, and India between 1756 and 1753, pitting France and its allies against Great Britain and its allies.

**Shakers** The followers of Mother Ann Lee, who preached a religion of strict celibacy and communal living.

**Sharecropping** Labor system that evolved during and after Reconstruction whereby landowners furnished laborers with a house, farm animals, and tools and advanced credit in exchange for a share of the laborers' crop.

**Sheppard-Towner Act** The first federal social welfare law, passed in 1921, providing federal funds for infant and maternity care.

**Sherman Antitrust Act** The first federal antitrust measure, passed in 1890; sought to promote economic competition by prohibiting business combinations in restraint of trade or commerce.

**Sherman Silver Purchase Act** 1890 act which directed the Treasury to increase the amount of currency coined from silver mined in the West and also permitted the U.S. government to print paper currency backed by the silver.

**Silicon Valley** The region of California including San Jose and San Francisco that holds the nation's greatest concentration of electronics firms.

**Sixteenth Amendment** Authorized a federal income tax.

**Slaughterhouse cases** Group of cases resulting in one sweeping decision by the U.S. Supreme Court in 1873 that contradicted the intent of the Fourteenth Amendment by decreeing that most citizenship rights remained under state, not federal, control.

**Slave codes** A series of laws passed mainly in the Southern colonies in the late seventeenth and early eighteenth centuries to defend the status of slaves and codify the denial of basic civil rights to them.

**Social Darwinism** The application of Charles Darwin's theory of biological evolution to society, holding that the fittest and wealthiest survive, the weak and the poor perish, and government action is unable to alter this "natural" process.

**Social Security Act of 1935** Act establishing federal old-age pensions and unemployment insurance.

**Sons of Liberty** Secret organizations in the colonies formed to oppose the Stamp Act.

**Southern Christian Leadership Conference (SCLC)** Black civil rights organization founded in 1957 by Martin Luther King Jr., and other clergy.

**Southern Farmers' Alliance** The largest of several organizations that formed in the post-Reconstruction South to advance the interests of beleaguered small farmers.

**Southern Manifesto** A document signed by 101 members of Congress from Southern states in 1956 that argued that the Supreme Court's decision in *Brown* v. *Board of Education of Topeka* itself contradicted the Constitution.

**Specie Circular** Proclamation issued by President Andrew Jackson in 1836 stipulating that only gold or silver could be used as payment for public land.

**Stamp Act** Law passed by Parliament in 1765 to raise revenue in America by requiring taxed, stamped paper for legal documents, publications, and playing cards.

**States' Rights** Favoring the rights of individual states over rights claimed by the national government.

**Stono Rebellion** One of the largest and most violent slave uprisings during the Colonial Period that occurred in Stono, South Carolina.

**Strategic Arms Limitation Treaty** Treaty signed in 1972 by the United States and the Soviet Union to slow the nuclear arms race.

**Strategic Defense Initiative (SDI)** President Reagan's program, announced in 1983, to defend the United States against nuclear missile attack with untested weapons systems and sophisticated technologies.

**Student Nonviolent Coordinating Committee (SNCC)** Black civil rights organization founded in 1960 and drawing heavily on younger activists and college students.

**Students for a Democratic Society (SDS)** The leading student organization of the New Left of the early and mid-1960s.

**Suffrage** The right to vote in a political election.

**Sugar Act** Law passed in 1764 to raise revenue in the American colonies. It lowered the duty from 6 pence to 3 pence per gallon on foreign molasses imported into the colonies and increased the restrictions on colonial commerce.

**Sunbelt** The states of the American South and Southwest.

**Taft-Hartley Act** Federal legislation of 1947 that substantially limited the tools available to labor unions in labor-management disputes.

**Tammany Society** A fraternal organization of artisans begun in the 1780s that evolved into a key organization of the new mass politics in New York City.

**Tariff of 1816** A tax imposed by Congress on imported goods.

**Tea Act** Act of Parliament that permitted the East India Company to sell through agents in America without paying the duty customarily collected in Britain, thus reducing the retail price.

**Tejanos** Persons of Spanish or Mexican descent born in Texas.

**Temperance** Reform movement originating in the 1820s that sought to eliminate the consumption of alcohol.

**Temperance groups** Groups dedicated to reducing the sale and consumption of alcohol.

**Tenements** Four- to six-story residential dwellings, once common in New York, built on tiny lots without regard to providing ventilation or light.

**Tennessee Valley Authority (TVA)** Federal regional planning agency established to promote conservation, produce electric power, and encourage economic development in seven Southern states.

**Tenure of Office Act** Act stipulating that any officeholder appointed by the president with the Senate's advice and consent could not be removed until the Senate had approved a successor.

**Thirteenth Amendment** Constitutional amendment ratified in 1865 that freed all slaves throughout the United States.

**Tories** A derisive term applied to Loyalists in America who supported the king and Parliament just before and during the American Revolution.

**Townshend Revenue Acts**   Act of Parliament, passed in 1767, imposing duties on colonial tea, lead, paint, paper, and glass.

**Trail of Broken Treaties**   1972 event staged by the American Indian Movement (AIM) that culminated in a week-long occupation of the Bureau of Indian Affairs in Washington, D.C.

**Trail of Tears**   The forced march in 1838 of the Cherokee Indians from their homelands in Georgia to the Indian Territory in the West.

**Treaty of Fort Laramie**   The treaty acknowledging U.S. defeat in the Great Sioux War in 1868 and supposedly guaranteeing the Sioux perpetual land and hunting rights in South Dakota, Wyoming, and Montana.

**Treaty of Ghent**   Treaty signed in December 1814 between the United States and Britain that ended the War of 1812.

**Treaty of Greenville**   Treaty of 1795 in which Native Americans in the Old Northwest were forced to cede most of the present state of Ohio to the United States.

**Treaty of Paris**   The formal end to British hostilities against France and Spain in February 1763.

**Truman Doctrine**   President Harry Truman's statement in 1947 that the United States should assist other nations that were facing external pressure or internal revolution.

**Underwood-Simmons Act of 1913**   Reform law that lowered tariff rates and levied the first regular federal income tax.

**Union League**   Republican party organizations in Northern cities that became an important organizing device among freedmen in Southern cities after 1865.

**USA Patriot Act**   Federal legislation adopted in 2001 in response to the terrorist attacks on September 11 to facilitate anti-terror actions by federal law enforcement and intelligence agencies.

**Versailles Treaty**   The treaty ending World War I and creating the League of Nations.

**Vertical integration**   The consolidation of numerous production functions, from the extraction of the raw materials to the distribution and marketing of the finished products, under the direction of one firm.

**Virginia Company**   A group of London investors who sent ships to Chesapeake Bay in 1607.

**Virginia Plan**   Proposal calling for a national legislature in which the states would be represented according to population.

**Virtual representation**   The notion that parliamentary members represented the interests of the nation as a whole, not those of the particular district that elected them.

**Volstead Act**   The 1920 law defining the liquor forbidden under the Eighteenth Amendment and giving enforcement responsibilities to the Prohibition Bureau of the Department of the Treasury.

**Voting Rights Act**   Legislation in 1965 that overturned a variety of practices by which states systematically denied voter registration to minorities.

**War Democrats**   Those from the North and the border states who broke with the Democratic Party and supported the Abraham Lincoln's military policies during the Civil War.

**War Hawks**   Members of Congress, predominantly from the South and West, who aggressively pushed for a war against Britain after their election in 1810.

**War Industries Board (WIB)**   The federal agency that reorganized industry for maximum efficiency and productivity during World War I.

**War of 1812**   War fought between the United States and Britain from June 1812 to January 1815 largely over British restrictions on American shipping.

**War on Drugs**   A paramilitary operation to halt drug trafficking in the United States.

**War on Poverty**   Set of programs introduced by Lyndon Johnson between 1963 and 1966 designed to break the cycle of poverty by providing funds for job training, community development, nutrition, and supplementary education.

**War Powers Act**   Gave the U.S. president the power to reorganize the federal government and create new agencies; to establish programs censoring news, information, and abridging civil liberties; to seize foreign-owned property; and award government contracts without bidding.

**Watergate**   A complex scandal involving attempts to cover up illegal actions taken by administration officials and leading to the resignation of President Richard Nixon in 1974.

**Welfare capitalism**   A paternalistic system of labor relations emphasizing management responsibility for employee well-being.

**Welfare Reform Act**   Act passed by Congress in 1996 that abolished the Aids to Families with Dependent Children (AFDC) welfare program.

**Whigs**   The name used by advocates of colonial resistance to British measures during the 1760s and 1770s.

**Whiskey Rebellion**   Armed uprising in 1794 by farmers in western Pennsylvania who attempted to prevent the collection of the excise tax on whiskey.

**Wilmot Proviso**   The amendment offered by Pennsylvania Democrat David Wilmot in 1846 which stipulated that "as an express and fundamental condition to the acquisition of any territory from the Republic of Mexico ... neither slavery nor involuntary servitude shall ever exist in any part of said territory."

**Wobblies**   Popular name for the members of the Industrial Workers of the World (IWW).

**Woman's Christian Temperance Union (WCTU)**   Women's organization whose members visited schools to educate children about the evils of alcohol, addressed prisoners, and blanketed men's meetings with literature.

**Women's Educational and Industrial Union**   Boston organization offering classes to wage-earning women.

**World Trade Organization (WTO)**   International organization that sets standards and practices for global trade, and the focus of international protests over world economic policy in the late 1990s.

**XYZ Affair**   Diplomatic incident in 1798 in which Americans were outraged by the demand of the French for a bribe as a condition for negotiating with American diplomats.

**Yalta Conference**   Meeting of U.S. President Franklin Roosevelt, British Prime Minister Winston Churchill, and Soviet Premier Joseph Stalin held in February 1945 to plan the final stages of World War II and postwar arrangements.

**Yeoman**   Independent farmers of the South, most of whom lived on family-sized farms.

## Text, Tables, Maps and Figures

New Orleans; **Page 405:** D. Dave King/Dave King/Dorling Kindersley © Confederate Memorial Hall, New Orleans; E. Dave King/Dave King/Dorling Kindersley © Confederate Memorial Hall, New Orleans; F. The Granger Collection, New York; G. William Washington, "Stonewall Jackson Entering the City of Winchester, Virginia." Oil painting. Valentine Museum Library, Richmond, Virginia; H. © CORBIS; I. Getty Images Inc. - Hulton Archive Photos; J. The New-York Historical Society; **Page 407:** The Granger Collection, New York; **Page 410:** Corbis/Bettmann; **Page 413:** Library of Congress; **Page 414:** Courtesy of the Library of Congress. J. B. Elliott, Cincinnati, 1861; **Page 421:** Center of Military History, U.S. Army; **Page 426:** Culver Pictures, Inc.; **Page 427:** Courtesy of the Library of Congress.

**Chapter 17** Image Key: **Page 432:** A. Library of Congress/Courtesy of the Library of Congress; B. Library of Congress/Courtesy of the Library of Congress; D. © CORBIS; E. Musselman Library/Courtesy of Special Collections, Musselman Library, Gettysburg College, Gettysburg, PA; **Page 433:** F. Thomas C. Roche/Courtesy of the Library of Congress; G. The Granger Collection, New York; H. Library of Congress; I. The Picture Bank, Frank & Marie Therese Wood Print Collection; **Page 435:** The Granger Collection, New York; **Page 436:** Corbis/Bettmann; **Page 438:** Library of Congress; Courtesy of the Library of Congress; **Page 441:** Courtesy of Schlesinger Library, Radcliffe Institute, Harvard University; **Page 444:** The Granger Collection; **Page 445:** The Granger Collection, New York. **Page 447:** (bottom left) Library of Congress; (top right) Courtesy of the Library of Congress; **Page 449:** (left) From The Henry Clay Warmoth Papers #752, Southern Historical Collection,Wilson Library, University of North Carolina at Chapel Hill; (right) Rutherford B. Hayes Presidential Center; **Page 454:** The Denver Public Library, Western History Collection, Photographer J. B. Silvis, Call Number X-22221. **Page 456:** The Picture Bank, Frank & Marie Therese Wood Print Collection; **Page 462:** Collection of The New-York Historical Society, [negative and/or accession number]; **Page 463:** (top) John Vachon/Courtesy of the Library of Congress; (bottom) Dorothea Lange/Library of Congress.

**Chapter 18** Image Key: **Page 464:** A. Lynton Gardiner/Lynton Gardiner © Dorling Kindersley, Courtesy of The American Museum of Natural History; B. The Granger Collection, New York; C. Dave King/Dave King/Dorling Kindersley © Confederate Memorial Hall, New Orleans; **Page 465:** D. © Dorling Kindersley; E. © Judith Miller/Dorling Kindersley/Cowan's Historic Americana Auctions; F. Chinese mining laborers, Idaho, 76-119.2/A, Idaho State Historical Society; G. Library of Congress; H. Nebraska State Historical Society, Solomon D. Butcher Collection; I. Library of Congress; **Page 471:** National Anthropological Archives, Smithsonian Institution (3238E); **Page 474:** Jackson, William Henry. American (1843–1942) John, The Cook, baking slapjacks. 1874. Albumen print 9.7 × 8.8 cm. Museum purchase 74:0041:0212; **Page 479:** The Granger Collection; **Page 478:** Denver Public Library; **Page 481:** Nebraska State Historical Society, Solomon D. Butcher Collection; **Page 483:** Library of Congress; **Page 487:** Courtesy of the Library of Congress; **Page 490:** Granger/The Granger Collection.

**Chapter 19** Image Key: **Page 498:** A. © Rykoff Collection/CORBIS; B. Lewis W. Hine/George Eastman House; **Page 499:** C. © Schenectady Museum; Hall of Electrical/CORBIS; D. "The Two Philanthropists." Color lithograph by J. Keppler from "Puck," February 23, 1881, neg. #48872. Collection of The New-York Historical Society, New York City; E. The Granger Collection, New York; F. U.S. Department of the Interior, National Park Service, Edison National Historic Site; G. Mark Rykoff/© Rykoff Collection/CORBIS; **Page 503:** Andrew Leyerle © Dorling Kindersley. Courtesy of Marshall Field and Company; **Page 505:** Courtesy of the Library of Congress; **Page 506:** The Granger Collection, New York; **Page 507:** North Wind Picture Archives; **Page 508:** © Bettmann/CORBIS. **Page 510:** Cook Collection, Valentine Richmond History Center; **Page 514:** "The Bowery at Night," 1885. Watercolor. Museum of the City of New York; **Page 516:** Courtesy of the Library of

Congress; **Page 517:** The Granger Collection; **Page 520:** The Granger Collection, New York; **Page 521:** Courtesy of the Library of Congress.

**Chapter 20** Image Key: **Page 524:** A. Picture Research Consultants/Picture Research Consultants & Archives; B. Courtesy of the Library of Congress; C. ICHi-08428; Destruction of the battleship Maine in Havana harbor; in the Spanish-American war; Havana (Cuba) 1898 Feb. 15; Creator-Kurz & Allison/Chicago Historical Society; D. © Bettmann/CORBIS; E. © Bettmann/CORBIS; **Page 525:** F. © Bettmann/CORBIS; G. The Granger Collection, New York; H. Library of Congress; I. Courtesy of the Library of Congress; J. Culver Pictures; K. By permission of the Houghton Library, Harvard University; L. The Granger Collection, New York; **Page 524:** M. © Bettmann/CORBIS; **Page 525:** N. Courtesy of the Library of Congress; **Page 529:** The Granger Collection, New York; **Page 530:** Library of Congress; **Page 533:** The Granger Collection, New York; **Page 534:** Courtesy of the Library of Congress; **Page 535:** Courtesy of the Library of Congress; **Page 536:** North Wind Picture Archives; **Page 539:** The Granger Collection, New York; **Page 543:** Courtesy of the Divinity School, Yale University; **Page 545:** North Wind Picture Archives; **Page 548:** The Granger Collection; **Page 550:** Library of Congress; **Page 554:** The Granger Collection, New York; **Page 555:** Courtesy of the Library of Congress.

**Chapter 21** Image Key: **Page 556:** A. © Bettmann/CORBIS; B. Library of Congress; C. Corbis/Bettmann; **Page 557:** D. © Bettmann/CORBIS; E. Indiana Historical Society, A70; F. The original Paterson Pageant Program, on which this drawing appeared, is part of the collection of the American Labor Museum/Botto House National Landmark. The poster is a copy of the program cover; G. © Bettmann/CORBIS; H. The Granger Collection, New York; **Page 561:** The Jacob A. Riis Collection 157, Museum of the City of New York; **Page 563:** Wallace Kirkland/Time Life Pictures/Getty Images/Time Life Pictures; **Page 565:** Daniel J. Czitrom; **Page 571:** The Granger Collection, New York; **Page 574:** UPI/Corbis/Bettmann; **Page 577:** The original Paterson Pageant Program, on which this drawing appeared, is part of the collection of the American Labor Museum/Botto House National Landmark. The poster is a copy of the program cover. **Page 578:** CORBIS-NY; **Page 582:** The Granger Collection, New York. **Page 584:** Theodore Roosevelt Collection, Harvard College Library.

**Chapter 22** Image Key: **Page 590:** A. © Bettmann/CORBIS; B. Getty Images Inc. - Hulton Archive Photos; C. Bettmann/© Bettmann/CORBIS; **Page 591:** D. Richard Ward © Dorling Kindersley; E. The Granger Collection; F. Library of Congress; G. The Granger Collection, New York; H. National Archives and Records Administration; I. The Granger Collection, New York; **Page 594:** The Granger Collection; **Page 597:** The Granger Collection, New York; **Page 600:** Courtesy of the Library of Congress; **Page 602:** Getty Images Inc.-Hulton Archive Photos; **Page 603:** (bottom left) © CORBIS All Rights Reserved; (bottom right) Courtesy of the Library of Congress; (top center) Courtesy of the Library of Congress; **Page 607:** Russ Lappa/Prentice Hall School Division; **Page 609:** National Archives and Records Administration; **Page 612:** © Harris & Ewing, Inc./CORBIS All Rights Reserved; **Page 615:** © Stock Montage.

**Chapter 23** Image Key: **Page 622:** A. Getty Images Inc. - Hulton Archive Photos; B. Swim Ink/© Swim Ink/CORBIS; C. EyeWire Collection/Getty Images - Photodisc; **Page 623:** D. C Squared Studios/Getty Images, Inc. - Photodisc; E. Wisconsin Historical Society/WHi-5020; F. By permission of Campbell Soup Company; G. Courtesy W. A. Swift Photograph Collection, Archives and Special Collections, Ball State University; H. Courtesy W. A. Swift Photograph Collection, Archives and Special Collections, Ball State University; **Page 627:** A&P Food Stores LTD; **Page 628:** Brown Brothers; **Page 629:** Ford Motor Company; **Page 637:** (left) Picture Desk, Inc./Kobal Collection; (middle) Everett Collection; (right) Everett Collection; **Page 639:** National Baseball Hall of Fame Library, Cooperstown, N.Y.; **Page 640:** Corbis/Bettmann; **Page 641:** Corbis/Bettmann;

**Page 645:** Ball State University Libraries, Archives & Special Collections, W.A. Swift Photo Collection; **Page 649:** Goldbeck Collection, Harry Ransom Humanities Research Center, University of Texas at Austin. Photo by Summerville; **Page 658:** Library of Congress; **Page 659:** Courtesy of the Library of Congress.

**Chapter 24** Image Key: **Page 660:** A. © CORBIS; B. © David J. & Janice L. Frent Collection/CORBIS; C. Culver Pictures, Inc./SuperStock. D. © CORBIS; **Page 661:** E. Getty Images, Inc. - Photodisc; F. Brown Brothers; G. UPI/Corbis/Bettmann; H. The Granger Collection/Art © Estate Of Ben Shahn/Liscensed By Vaga, New York, NY; I. Isaac Soyer, "Employment Agency." Oil on canvas, 34 1/2″ × 45″. The Whitney Museum of American Art. **Page 664:** The Granger Collection; **Page 668:** Franklin D. Roosevelt Library; **Page 669:** ALBERT EINSTEIN and related rights TM/© of The Hebrew University of Jerusalem, used under license. Represented exclusively by Corbis Corporation; **Page 673:** Milton Brooks/AP Wide World Photos; **Page 676:** © CORBIS All Rights Reserved; **Page 682:** AP Wide World Photos; **Page 685:** (top left) Courtesy of the Library of Congress; (bottom left) Courtesy of the Library of Congress.

**Chapter 25** Image Key: **Page 692:** A. Andy Crawford/Andy Crawford/Dorling Kindersley © Imperial War Museum, London; B. © Minnesota Historical Society/CORBIS; C. Andy Crawford/Andy Crawford/Dorling Kindersley © Imperial War Museum, London; D. The Granger Collection, New York; E. Harry_Todd/Getty Images Inc. - Hulton Archive Photos; **Page 693:** F. © CORBIS; G. National Archives and Records Administration; H. AP Wide World Photos; I. National Archives and Records Administration; J. Robert Capa/© Bettmann/CORBIS; **Page 697:** Navy Visual News Service; **Page 698:** AP Wide World Photos; **Page 701:** Harry_Todd/Getty Images Inc.-Hulton Archive Photos; **Page 704:** National Archives and Records Administration; **Page 708:** National Archives and Records Administration; **Page 709:** Stilpx/NARA National/National Archives and Records Administration; **Page 713:** Fred Ramage/Getty Images Inc.-Hulton Archive Photos; **Page 714:** Courtesy of the Library of Congress.

**Chapter 26** Image Key: **Page 726:** A. Corbis/Bettmann; B. Walter Sanders/LIFE/Getty Images/Time Life Pictures; C. © CORBIS; **Page 727:** D. Getty Images Inc. - Hulton Archive Photos; E. Charles Fenno Jacobs/Charles Fenno Jacobs/Getty Images, Inc.; F. AP Wide World Photos; G. UPI/Bettman/© Bettmann/CORBIS; H. Corbis/Bettmann; I. National Archives and Records Administration; **Page 732:** UPI/Corbis/Bettmann; **Page 735:** Corbis/Bettmann; **Page 736:** AP Wide World Photos; **Page 738:** © Bettmann/CORBIS; **Page 740:** Michael Barson/Michael Barson; **Page 743:** Hank Walker/Getty Images/Time Life Pictures; **Page 745:** Michael Barson/Getty Imges Inc. - Hulton Archive Photos; **Page 747:** Harold M Lambert/Getty Images Inc. - Hulton Archive Photos; **Page 750:** CORBIS - NY; **Page 751:** AP Wide World Photos; **Page 756:** U.S. Air Force/AP Wide World Photos; **Page 757:** Bernard Hoffman/Stringer/© Time & Life Pictures/Getty Images.

**Chapter 27** Image Key: **Page 758:** A. © CORBIS; B. Getty Images Inc. - Hulton Archive Photos; C. Getty Images Inc. - Hulton Archive Photos; D. Dorling Kindersley/© Dorling Kindersley; **Page 759:** E. © CORBIS; F. Bernard Hoffman/Bernard Hoffman/Life Magazine/© 1950 TimePix; G. Robert Altman/Retna Ltd.; H. Springer/Bettmann/© Springer/Bettmann/CORBIS; I. Library of Congress; J. Ralph Crane/Getty Images/Time Life Pictures; **Page 761:** © Bettmann/CORBIS; **Page 763:** © Bettmann/CORBIS; **Page 767:** Bernard Hoffman/Bernard Hoffman/Life Magazine/© 1950 TimePix; **Page 772:** (left) Robert Altman/Retna Ltd. (right) Getty Images, Inc.; **Page 774:** PPP/Popperfoto/Getty Images/Retrofile; **Page 775:** Bettmann/Corbis/Bettmann; **Page 776:** (top

left) Globe Photos, Inc.; (bottom) Bettmann/Corbis/Bettmann; **Page 779:** Getty Images Inc.-Hulton Archive Photos; **Page 784:** (top left) AP Wide World Photos; (bottom left) Robert Jackson/Dallas Morning News; (bottom right) Getty Images, Inc.

**Chapter 28** Image Key: **Page 788:** A. Courtesy of the Library of Congress; B. Corbis/Bettmann; C. John F. Kennedy Library, National Archives, document MS 2003-036. **Page 789:** D. Courtesy of the Library of Congress; E. Dorling Kindersley/© Dorling Kindersley; F. AP Wide World Photos; G. Corbis/Bettmann; H. Corbis/Bettmann; **Page 792:** Frank Driggs Collection; **Page 793:** Corbis/Bettmann; **Page 796:** Ed Clark/Getty Images/Time Life Pictures; **Page 797:** (left) The Oakland Tribune; (right) Library of Congress; **Page 799:** News & Record Library/John G. Moebes; **Page 803:** Corbis/Bettmann; **Page 807:** Black Star; **Page 809:** Steve Schapiro/Black Star; **Page 810:** Library of Congress; **Page 813:** Benson Latin American Collection; **Page 816:** Michael Newman/PhotoEdit Inc; **Page 821:** (top) Library of Congress; (center) Library of Congress; (bottom) Courtesy of the Library of Congress.

**Chapter 29** Image Key: **Page 822:** A. © Royalty-Free/CORBIS; B. © Royalty-Free/CORBIS; C. John Paul Filo/© John Paul Filo/Hulton/Archive; D. Wayne State University Archives of Labor and Urban Affairs; **Page 823:** E. © Henry Diltz/CORBIS; F. Corbis/Bettmann; G. UPI/Corbis/Bettmann; H. Bernie Boston; I. Jeffrey Blankfort/Jeroboam; J. AP Wide World Photos; **Page 826:** Jim Pickerell/Black Star; **Page 827:** Peter Simon/Peter Simon; **Page 829:** AP Wide World Photos; **Page 830:** From "THE VIETNAM PHOTO BOOK" by Mark Jury. Copyright © 1971, 1986 by Mark Jury Preface copyright © 1986 by Bernard Edelman. Used by permission of Random House, Inc.; **Page 836:** Library of Congress; **Page 838:** Matt Herron/© 2001 Matt Herron c/o Mira.com; **Page 840:** AP Wide World Photos; **Page 841:** Paul Fusco/Magnum Photos, Inc.; **Page 846:** Nick Ut/AP Wide World Photos; **Page 848:** CORBIS-NY.

**Chapter 30** Image Key: **Page 850:** A. Telepress Syndicate Agency/Corbis/Bettmann; B. Owen Franken/Corbis/Bettmann; C. © Neil Beer/CORBIS; **Page 851:** D. © Dorling Kindersley; E. AP Wide World Photos; F. Joe Marquette/AP Wide World Photos; G. UPI/Corbis/Bettmann; H. Jose L. Pelaez/© Jose Luis Pelaez, Inc./CORBIS; I. Denis Paquin/© Bettmann/CORBIS; **Page 860:** AP Wide World Photos; **Page 862:** Corbis/Bettmann; **Page 863:** AP Wide World Photos; **Page 865:** AP Wide World Photos; **Page 867:** Dennis Brack/Black Star; **Page 868:** Wally McNamee/CORBIS-NY; **Page 870:** AP Wide World Photos; **Page 872:** AP Wide World Photos; **Page 875:** AP Wide World Photos; **Page 877:** Robert Maass/CORBIS-NY.

**Chapter 31** Image Key: **Page 884:** A. REUTERS/Pool/Beth Kaiser/Corbis/Reuters America LLC; B. Steve Gorton © Dorling Kindersley; C. Dorling Kindersley/© Dorling Kindersley; **Page 885:** D. Agence France Presse/Getty Images; E. Geoff Dann/Geoff Dann © Dorling Kindersley, Courtesy of the Imperial War Museum, London; F. AFP/Agence France Presse/Getty Images; G. Barbara Gauntt/Barbara Gauntt/The Clarion-Ledger; H. Dorling Kindersley Media Library; I. Stephen Crowley/Stephen Crowley/The New York Times; **Page 888:** Susan Walsh/AP Wide World Photos; **Page 889:** (top) AP Wide World Photos; (bottom) Getty Images, Inc.; **Page 891:** AP Wide World Photos; **Page 893:** AP Wide World Photos; **Page 895:** Chris Pizzello/AP Wide World Photos; **Page 896:** Agence France Presse/Getty Images; **Page 898:** AFP/Agence France Presse/Getty Images; **Page 899:** Getty Images, Inc.; **Page 902:** AP Wide World Photos; **Page 904:** Reuters/Landov LLC; **Page 906:** David J. Phillip/AP Wide World Photos; **Page 911:** (top) Harris and Ewing Photos/Harris and Ewing Photos Courtesy Harry S. Truman Library; (center) National Archives and Records Administration; (bottom) AP Wide World Photos.

# A

ABC television network, 774
Abenakis, the, 63–64
Abernathy, Ralph, 798
Abolition/abolitionists
  American Colonization Society, 343
  controversy over, 344
  debate on, 261
  and Emancipation Proclamation, 418
  first states, 177, 243
  free African Americans, 343
  and politics, 344–345
  as a Southern threat, 244
  white reformers, 343–344
Abortion, 315, 865
Abortion clinics, attacks on, 895
Abraham Lincoln Brigade, 686
Abu Ghrab prison, 904
Acadia, 94
Acadians, 193
Accommodation, racial, 579–580
Acculturation, 88, 221
Acoma, 17
Acosta, Joseph de, 3
Acquired Immune Deficiency Syndrome (AIDS), 872
Act of Toleration (1689), 109
Adams, Abigail, 159
Adams, John
  and American Revolution, 160
  Declaration of Independence, 149–150
  diplomacy of, 231–232
  election of 1796, 198
  election of 1800, 200
  First Continental Congress, 128, 144
  framing of the Constitution, 184
  judiciary under, 216
  presidency of, 198, 199–200
  Second Continental Congress, 145
  Treaty of Paris, 169
  as vice-president, 191
Adams, John Quincy
  abolitionism, 345
  election of 1824, 271, 272, 292
  election of 1828, 274
  Monroe Doctrine, 232
  in Monroe's cabinet, 230
  and Texas, 364
Adams-Onís Treaty of 1819, 231
  map of, 233
Adams, Samuel
  Boston Massacre, 140–141
  Boston radicals, 137–138
  First Continental Congress, 144
  ratification of Constitution, 187
Addams, Jane, 563, 565, 599, 602, 618
Adena culture, 11
Administration of Justice Act, 140, 144
*Adventures of Ozzie and Harriet* (television show), 774
Advertising
  department stores, 503
  radio funding with, 636
  on television, 774
  in the twenties, 638–639
*Affluent Society, The* (Galbraith), 766
Afghanistan, 861, 863, 898, 900
AFL. *See* American Federation of Labor (AFL)
AFL-CIO, 769, 848, 857
Africa. *See also* Country names in Africa
  effect of slave trade on, 81–82
  slave trade originating from, 77–79
African Americans. *See also* Civil rights movement; Free African Americans; Reconstruction; Segregation; Slavery; Slaves
  and American Revolution, 158, 176–178
  and baseball, 521, 641
  Black Power, 837–838
  colleges for, 519
  in the Communist Party, 686
  cowboys, 477, 479

culture of, 87–88, 250–251
at end of twentieth century, 893
fighting in World War II, 708–709
during the Great Depression, 681–682
Great Migration, 613, 614, 630
in Harlem, 650–651
and Hurricane Katrina, 906
images of, 447
impact of Marcus Garvey on, 651
in Knights of Labor, 508
labor by, 506, 510
language of, 88
leaders of, 820–821
living in urban areas, 512
lynching of, 541, 560, 615
musical influence from, 760, 771–772
musicians, 639–640
"New Negro," 651–652
New York city draft riots, 423, 424
Niagara movement, 580
post–World War I activism by, 614–615
progressive era, 577
race riots, 831–833
racial accommodation, 579–580
during Reagan years, 870–871
response to Emancipation Proclamation, 418
social gospel, 538
stereotypes of, 332
suffrage, 271, 441
in Vietnam War, 829
voting in 1868 election, 441
women, 581
women's liberation movement, 840
women, wages of, 858
and World War I, 602–603
during World War II, 700–701
World War II era activism by, 704–705
writers, 177–178
African Methodist Episcopal (AME) church, 336
African religion, 250
African slaves, creoles *vs.*, 86
African slave trade. *See* Slave trade
Agent Orange, 826
Age of the Common Man and Rise of Democracy, 292
Agnew, Spiro, 849
Agrarian ideal, 214, 243–244, 539
Agricultural Adjustment Administration (AAA), 669, 674
Agricultural colleges, 518
Agriculture. *See also* Commercial agriculture; Cotton; Farming
  federal spending on, 762
  and Mexican immigration, 648
Aguinaldo, Emilio, 549
AIDS (Acquired Immune Deficiency Syndrome), 872
Aid to Families with Dependent Children (AFDC), 887
Air defense, 763
Air pollution, 514, 859–860
Alabama
  Freedom Rides, 802–803
  southern secession and, 398
"Alabama Fever," 241
Alamo, the, 352, 363
Alaska, 209–210, 467
Albania, 889
Albany Conference of 1754, 129
Albany, Georgia, 804
Albany Movement, 804
Albany, New York, 51, 325
Albermarle region, 65
Albermarle Sound, 61
*Albright, Smith* v. (1944), 705
Albuquerque, New Mexico, 17
Alcatraz Island (San Francisco Bay), 841
Alcohol use
  temperance movement, 337, 338–339
  during the twenties, 642–643
Alcott, Louisa May, 342
"A Letter Concerning Tolerance" (Locke), 109

Aleut peoples, 209–210
Aleut Revolt of 1766, 209
Alfred P. Murrah Federal Building (Oklahoma City), 895
Algeria, 713
Algonquian peoples, 19–21
El Alianzo Hispano-Americano (Hispanic-American Alliance), 476–477
Alien Act (1798), 910
Alien Act (1918), 618
Ali, Muhammad, 838
All-American Canal, 678
Allende, Salvador, 848
Allen, Ethan, 147–148
Alliance for Progress, 780, 781
Allies (World War I), 598, 600, 616
Almanac, the, 119
Almy, William, 300, 307
Al Qaeda, 879, 898, 900, 901
Altgeld, John Peter, 537, 564
AMA. *See* American Medical Association (AMA)
Amalgamated Iron, Steel and Tin Workers, 536
Amendments to the Constitution
  Bill of Rights, 187–188
  Eighteenth Amendment, 611, 642
  Fifteenth, 441, 442, 452
  First, 187
  Fourteenth, 434, 439, 442, 452
  Nineteenth Amendment, 611
  Seventeenth, 566
  Sixteenth, 585
  text of, A-6–A-10
  Thirteenth, 418, 442
  Twelfth, 200
  Twenty-first, 643
  Twenty-fourth, 810
  Twenty-second, 737
American Anti-Slavery Society, 343
American Civil Liberties Union (ACLU), 618, 646
American Colonization Society, 343
American Equal Rights Association, 441–442
American Expeditionary Force (AEF), 592, 604
American Federation of Labor (AFL), 508–509
  Committee for Industrial Organization *vs.*, 673
  in the fifties, 769
  on immigration, 644
  Progressive era, 575–576
  and World War I, 608
American Heritage Foundation, 747
American Historical Association, 529
American Indian Movement (AIM), 839
American Institute for Free Labor Development, 848
American League against War and Fascism, 696
American Legion, 592
American Liberty League, 671
American Medical Association (AMA), 529, 648, 770–771
American Missionary Association (AMA), 444
American Party
  election of 1856, 392
  and nativism, 391, 392
  split in, 396
American Philosophical Society, 287
"American Primitive," 489–490
American Protective Association, 540, 643
American Protective League, 613
American Psychiatric Association (APA), 840–841
American Railway Union (ARU), 537
"American Renaissance," 381
American Revolution (1775–1781)
  African Americans, 176–178
  battles/fighting in, 147–148, 160–162, 164–165
  British surrender, 166, 167
  campaign for New York and New Jersey, 160–161
  casualties, 158
  chronology, 178
  committees of correspondence, 141–142
  debt from, 183
  Declaration of Independence, 149–150
  events leading to, 136–144
  financing, 169